D0081919

THE FAIRCHILD DICTIONARY OF RETAILING

FAIRCHILD REFERENCE

BELL LIBRARY TAMU-CC

Ref
HF
5429
.O788
2009

THE FAIRCHILD

Dictionary *of* Retailing

SECOND EDITION

Rona Ostrow

LEHMAN COLLEGE, CITY UNIVERSITY OF NEW YORK

FAIRCHILD BOOKS, INC.
NEW YORK

Dedicated to my granddaughter,
Wren Ostrow Walston

Director of Sales and Acquisitions: Dana Meltzer-Berkowitz

Executive Editor: Olga T. Kontzias

Senior Development Editor: Jennifer Crane

Development Editor: Joseph Miranda

Art Director: Adam B. Bohannon

Production Director: Ginger Hillman

Production Editors: Jessica Rozler, Andrew Fargnoli

Cover Design: Adam B. Bohannon

Developed by Focus Strategic Communications, Inc.

Project Manager: Adrianna Edwards

Development Editors: Debbie Sawczak, Adrianna Edwards

Copyeditor: Susan McNish

Page Layout: Susan Ramundo

Copyright © 2009 Fairchild Books, A Division of Condé Nast Publications.

All rights reserved. No part of this book covered by the copyright hereon may be reproduced or used in any form or by any means—graphic, electronic, or mechanical, including photocopying, recording, taping, or information storage and retrieval systems—without written permission of the publisher.

Library of Congress Catalog Card Number: 2007942718

ISBN: 978-1-56367-344-3

GST R 133004424

Printed in the United States of America

CH15
TP13

Contents

Preface

Retailing has changed dramatically in the near quarter-century since the last edition of this dictionary was published, yet much has remained the same. The computerization and automation of warehousing, distribution, and point-of-use data collection have greatly influenced the way in which retailers do business. Electronic commerce and e-tailing, in particular, have allowed retailers to reach customers regardless of location. Similarly, global marketing has opened up a world of both new resources and new potential customers. Yet retailing remains at heart the industry that involves the selling of goods and services to the ultimate consumer for his or her personal use.

The language of retailing continues to evolve to facilitate this underlying purpose, and its vocabulary has come to incorporate myriad new terms relating to these new developments. Consequently, the current volume is more a dictionary for retailers than a dictionary of retailing, which would be more limited. Many of the terms come from related disciplines such as marketing, advertising, computer science, marketing research, transportation and distribution, and consumer behavior. However, as these are terms retailers will encounter in the new retailing paradigm, they are terms that retailers and students of retailing need to know.

The lexicon of retailing has always been filled with inconsistencies and ambiguities, largely because of the complexity and diversity of the industry itself, but also because so much of the terminology derives from an aural vernacular rather than from an academic tradition. There is no single vocabulary of retailing, but rather a number of vocabularies, each derived from a particular segment of the industry. Where I could find no consensus on the meaning of a word, I have, on the basis of the most reliable authorities at my disposal, exercised my judgment and chosen the one I regarded as most accurate and timely. Where I have included more than one meaning for a word, I have done so because I have found it used in more than one way in several sources. Where the current lexicon includes alternative or variant terms or phrases for a concept, I have entered them, directing the reader to the one I believe is the most commonly used.

Words and phrases have been assembled from glossaries, textbooks, periodicals, newspapers, and electronic media. Each definition has been written to express the essential meaning of the word or phrase and, if appropriate, its significance for related aspects of the industry. Examples are included to clarify meanings. Particular attention has been given to distinguish terms that might be confused because of their formal similarity.

Included are terms and phrases relating to

- accounting in retailing
- computer applications in retailing and distribution
- corporate culture
- data processing in retailing
- demographics and psychographics
- direct marketing, including mail order and e-mail
- e-commerce and e-tailing
- global marketing and retailing
- government agencies relevant to retailing (particularly U.S. agencies)
- inventory management and control
- laws and regulations relating to retailing (particularly U.S. laws)
- marketing
- marketing research and consumer behavior
- personnel management
- retail advertising
- retail buying
- retail site location
- shopping centers and malls
- stores, including virtual stores on the Internet
- supermarketing
- visual merchandising and display
- warehousing and distribution for retail
- wholesaling

Unlike the earlier edition, this one does not include capsule biographies of historical retailing figures. Most capsule descriptions of associations related to retailing have also been omitted due to space constraints.

—RONA OSTROW
NEW YORK CITY, 2008

Acknowledgments

A number of individuals have assisted in the preparation of *The Fairchild Dictionary of Retailing*, Second Edition. I would like to thank each of them for the expertise they brought to the project.

Foremost among them is my former co-author, Sweetman R. Smith, with whom I worked on the 1985 edition. That work, along with our *Dictionary of Marketing*, provided the core vocabulary for the current volume. While he preferred not to join me in this new undertaking, his presence remains in many of those earlier definitions.

Particular thanks are due to Olga T. Kontzias, Joseph Miranda, and Jennifer Crane of Fairchild Publications for their various roles in enlisting me to undertake a new edition and in making sure the project was completed and published. Thanks also to Adrianna Edwards, Debbie Sawczak, and Susan McNish, the Focus Strategic Communications team; their dedication, professionalism, and editorial expertise whipped the Dictionary into shape in an astonishingly short period of time. Finally, heartfelt thanks to my family and to the librarians of the Leonard Lief Library of Lehman College, CUNY, for their unending patience and support.

How to Use This Dictionary

The Dictionary is arranged in a single alphabetical sequence using letter-by-letter alphabetization and ignoring spaces and hyphens. This mitigates any confusion about whether or not words are hyphenated, spelled as one word, or spelled as two separate words, usages that often vary from source to source.

All headwords are entered in bold type, with the singular form of the term preferred wherever the sense would not be lost by doing so. In entries with more than one sense, definitions are numbered; part of speech is indicated only where more than one applies, depending on the context in which the term is used. It appears after the definition number. See the entry **teleconference** for an example.

Many entries contain "See also" references to entries for related terms that the reader may need to understand or entries that may shed additional light on the entry at hand. Such cross-references may be embedded in the text of the definition itself, or follow the definition; in either case, they appear in SMALL CAPITAL LETTERS. Any term constituting a variant, alternative, or close synonym for some other more frequently used term is followed immediately by a cross-reference in small capital letters. For example, the entry word **temporary worker** is followed immediately by the cross-reference "See TEMP."

Many of the definitions also include synonymous terms and alternative spellings that may or may not be defined elsewhere in the Dictionary. These are indicated by *italicized letters*, generally following the phrase "Also called." Similarly appearing in italics are terms of the same family as the entry word, whose meaning is obvious from the definition in which they appear. For example, at the entry for **tally card**, the italicized terms *tally* and *tally envelope* are essential to the definition and are embedded in it.

Certain terms have been conflated for the sake of brevity. For example, the "retail method of inventory valuation" may also be called the "retail method of inventory." This state of affairs is reflected by a single entry, **retail method of inventory (valuation)**, with parentheses enclosing the optional element. Slashes have also been used to accommodate similar nomenclature for the same idea: for example, the entry **tying agreement/contract** uses a slash to indicate that "tying agreement" and "tying contract" are both current terms for the same concept. Finally, terms beginning with either "principle of" or "theory of" have been defined under the subject of the principle or theory. For example, the "theory of heterogeneity" is defined at the entry **heterogeneity**.

A number of slang and informal terms are entered because of their high frequency; it was also considered worthwhile to include the occasional rare or obsolete term that may be encountered in some contexts. Such terms carry an appropriate label in parentheses after the headword.

A

A&P mix See ADVERTISING AND PROMOTION (A&P) MIX.

abandonment In transportation, cargo damaged in transit on a public carrier and refused at its destination by the intended recipient.

abandonment stage The final stage in the life cycle of a product. The product may have been successful and saturated the market, or it may have failed to find a market at all. Either way, the producer no longer finds it profitable and discontinues its manufacture. See also PRODUCT LIFE CYCLE (PLC).

abate To reduce or decrease a money obligation.

ABC analysis A technique used to identify those items in a firm's inventory that provide it with the highest sales. The technique is used for planning and control purposes. Items are listed by sales volume and classified into three categories: (a) those that account for the largest percentage of sales and must be stocked at all times; (b) those that account for medium levels of sales; and (c) those that account for the lowest level of sales. Lower levels of stock may be maintained for the *b* and *c* categories.

above-market price/pricing See PRICING ABOVE THE MARKET.

above-the-market pricing See PRICING ABOVE THE MARKET.

absence of demand A demonstrated lack of interest in a product or service so that a considerable segment of the market either feels no need for the product or service or is unwilling to pay the price asked by the seller. See also NEGATIVE DEMAND.

absolute advantage A trade theory model used to demonstrate the favorable circumstances inherent in national specialization and subsequent trade. The theory holds that the position of a nation in international marketing is greatly enhanced if it is the sole producer of a product or can produce the product more cheaply and efficiently than any other nation. If, instead of producing all products within its own borders, the nation produces only those goods for which it has an advantage and trades with another country having the advantage in another product, both trading partners will benefit. See also COMPARATIVE ADVANTAGE and COMPETITIVE ADVANTAGE.

absolute cost advantage See ABSOLUTE ADVANTAGE.

absolute product failure The failure of a product to recoup in the marketplace the investment made in its development, production, and marketing.

absolute sale An agreement between a buyer and a seller in which both parties agree that there will be no conditions or restrictions affecting the sales transaction.

absolute threshold The point at which sensory stimuli first become discernible. This is important to marketers seeking to discover means of differentiating their product in the marketplace as well as those seeking to create effective advertising messages. The basic premise is that people do not consciously sense stimuli above or below certain limits. See also JUST NOTICEABLE DIFFERENCE (JND).

absorbed freight cost See FREIGHT ABSORPTION (PRICING).

absorption costing system A method for determining the cost of goods in which all manufacturing costs, variable and fixed, direct and indirect, that are incurred in the manufacturing process are attached to the product and are included in the cost of inventory. Absorption costing is required by generally accepted accounting principles (GAAP) as the basis of INVENTORY VALUATION for financial statements. Also called the *full costing system*. See also FREIGHT ABSORPTION (PRICING) and VARIABLE COSTING SYSTEM.

absorption of freight See FREIGHT ABSORPTION (PRICING).

abstract display setting In VISUAL MERCHANDISING, a type of display in which the merchandise is the dominant feature while the setting serves to reinforce the message, often subliminally. The abstract setting is predominantly a nonrepresentational arrangement of lines and shapes (i.e., panels, cubes, cylinders, triangles, arcs, and circles).

abstract mannequin The most stylized and decorative of the mannequin varieties. An abstract mannequin's proportions may be exaggerated, but the human form is still suggested. Abstract mannequins are quite versatile and are often used by small retail establishments unable to afford a wide variety of different mannequins.

abstract setting See ABSTRACT DISPLAY SETTING.

accelerated development stage The second stage in the RETAIL LIFE CYCLE. Once a store or concept catches on, it enters a period of rapid growth (accelerated development) in which other retailers imitate or adopt the store's concept and seek to attract the same target customers. The store itself may experience rapid growth in sales and popularity. As competitors enter the market by using the same or similar strategies, the market eventually approaches saturation, and growth slows.

accelerator principle/effect A theory that describes the expected effect, on the production sector, of an increase or decrease in derived demand (demand at the consumer level). For example, a relatively small decrease in demand for housing at the consumer level may be expected to have an increasingly profound effect at various levels of the production/distribution system. Building supply houses, manufacturers of plumbing fixtures and pipe, copper and iron producers, etc. will experience a substantial decrease in demand for their products. The small decrease in demand at the consumer level triggers larger decreases in demand at the production level. Also called *acceleration principle*. See also DEMAND.

accent In fashion merchandising, the particular point of emphasis used by the designer to give the style a point of view.

accent lighting See SECONDARY LIGHTING.

acceptable prices The range of prices between the CEILING PRICE and the FLOOR PRICE.

acceptance 1. A written promise to pay, as in a promissory note. 2. Favorable reception of a product by the consuming public. See also ACCEPTANCE STAGE.

acceptance sampling In QUALITY CONTROL, the use of statistical sampling to determine the quality of produced goods and materials. A representative number of items is checked from each lot, and the results are used to determine the acceptability of the entire lot.

acceptance stage In the PRODUCT LIFE CYCLE (PLC), the stage in which a particular style or product catches on due to the desire of other consumers to imitate the original users. Also called the *emulation* stage.

accepted fashion A style that has received favorable reception in the marketplace.

accepting See RECEIVING.

accessible site A location for a retail establishment that may easily be reached by customers and employees. The driving time and distance to the site are short and the store's parking area is easy to enter and leave.

accessorial service Additional service accorded to a shipper by a carrier, such as precooling, storage, or heating.

accessories 1. Items used to complete a fashion look, such as handbags, scarves, jewelry, hats, gloves, and shoes. 2. In general, any subordinate items that add to the usefulness or attractiveness of the principal item, such as camera lenses or automobile mud flaps. Also called *accessory items*. See also ACCESSORY EQUIPMENT, ALLIED PRODUCTS OR LINES, and COMPLEMENTARY PRODUCTS/GOODS.

accessorize To provide ACCESSORIES for a product.

accessory equipment Products, usually movable, having a lower cost and shorter life span than installed equipment and not incorporated into the finished manufactured product (e.g., tools and office equipment). Although accessory equipment is often charged to the capital budget, it may be treated as an expense item in some organizations. Also called *production accessories*.

accidental exporting See CASUAL EXPORTING.

accommodation area/desk See CUSTOMER SERVICE DESK.

accommodation items Merchandise stocked by a retailer to satisfy the special needs of a few customers.

accommodation services Facilities and services offered by a store to customers for their convenience. Accommodation services include restrooms, children's strollers, gift wrapping, etc. Also called *convenience services* and *customer convenience services*.

accordion insert An ad inserted in a magazine, folded accordion style.

accordion theory See RETAIL ACCORDION THEORY.

account 1. In ADVERTISING, a business relationship between an ADVERTISING AGENCY and a client. 2. The client of an ADVERTISING AGENCY. 3. In ACCOUNTING, any device or formal record for accumulating additions and subtractions relating to a single asset, liability, revenue, expense, etc. May be expressed in terms of money or other unit of measurement. 4. In MARKETING, a customer with whom the marketer does business.

account classification Any systematic method used by a vendor to evaluate retailers or other buyers according to existing and potential sales.

account executive In ADVERTISING, an executive who serves as a liaison between an advertiser and its ADVERTISING AGENCY and who coordinates all aspects of the agency's work on behalf of the client. The account executive oversees and directs the planning, research, copywriting, artwork, media selection, ad promotion, sales promotion, public relations, and accounting functions of the advertising agency.

accounting According to the American Institute of Certified Public Accountants (AICPA) Committee on Terminology, "the art of recording, classifying, and summarizing in a significant manner and in terms of money, transactions, and events that are, in part at least, of a financial character, and interpreting the results thereof."

accounting department   In a retail establishment, a nonmerchandising department responsible for keeping accounting records and preparing financial reports and statements.

accounting period   The period of time for which an operating statement is customarily prepared. The most common accounting period is one month, but periods of 4 weeks, 26 weeks, one year, etc., may be used.

account management department   The department or division in an advertising agency that provides the link between the client and the agency. Also called *account management division*. See also ADVERTISING AGENCY.

account opener   In retail stores, a premium or special promotional item offered to encourage the opening of new charge accounts. Frequently used by banks or other financial institutions to encourage depositors to open new accounts or add funds to an existing account.

accounts payable   1. Amounts owed to a firm's creditors, usually arising from the purchase of merchandise or materials and supplies. They would include, for example, the amount a retailer must pay a vendor for goods ordered and received.   2. In a retail establishment or similar firm, the nonmerchandising department responsible for making payments to the firm's creditors. Short for *accounts payable department*.

accounts receivable   1. Claims against a firm's debtors, usually arising from the sale of goods or services rendered, such as the amount of money a vendor must collect from a retailer for goods shipped or the amount a retailer must collect from charge account customers.   2. In a retail establishment or similar firm, the nonmerchandising department responsible for collecting money due to the firm. Short for *accounts receivable department*.

account supervisor   See ACCOUNT EXECUTIVE.

accrual basis of accounting   The method of accounting that recognizes revenues as goods sold (or delivered) and services rendered, regardless of when the cash is received. Expenses are reported in the period in which they occur, regardless of when the cash is paid out.

accumulating   Synonym for ASSEMBLING. Also called *accumulating bulk*.

accumulation   1. As used in ADVERTISING, a method for counting audience. Each person exposed to a particular advertisement is counted once within a specified time period.   2. The process of developing an inventory of products from the small lots of a number of small producers so that they may be shipped and sold in larger lots further along the marketing channel. Also called *accumulation process* and ASSEMBLING. See also SORTING PROCESS.

accurate response   The practice of determining the precision of forecasts and refocusing the merchandise plan to minimize the impact of inaccurate forecasts. The paramount consideration is understanding what forecasters can and cannot predict with assurance.

ACG   See ADDRESS CODING GUIDE (ACG).

achievement motivation theory   A theory establishing a relationship between personal characteristics, social background, and achievement. Individuals with a strong need for achievement tend to value tasks over relationships and prefer tasks over which they have control and responsibility. They also tend to seek tasks that are challenging and allow a demonstration of expertise, avoid the likelihood and consequences of failure, require feedback on achievement, need to be identified closely with the successful outcomes of their actions, and seek opportunities for promotion.

achievement need   One of the three basic motivations comprising the TRIO OF NEEDS. The achievement need is the drive for personal accomplishment. See also AFFILIATION NEED and POWER NEED.

achiever   See VALS SEGMENTATION.

acid test ratio   A financial ratio that indicates the ability of a firm to meet its current obligations, thus summarizing the firm's financial position at a given moment in time. A ratio of 1 to 1 is usually considered satisfactory. If the ratio is 2 or more to 1, a minimum risk is presumably indicated. Also known as the *quick ratio*, the *net quick ratio*, and the *liquidity ratio*.

A Classification of Residential Neighbourhoods (ACORN)   See ACORN.

ACORN   An abbreviation for *A Classification of Residential Neighbourhoods*, a directory classifying neighborhoods in the UK under 39 types. It is used by companies to provide target areas for selling particular products or services. See also GEOGRAPHICAL INFORMATION SYSTEMS (GIS).

acquired needs   See SECONDARY NEEDS.

acquisition   1. The purchase and takeover of one company by another, using either hostile or friendly methods. Acquisitions provide ways for retail organizations to grow, particularly once they have reached the saturation point in most markets with few opportunities for building new stores. Acquisitions also allow retail organizations to reorganize and the industry to consolidate. International retailers use acquisition to gain a foothold in a foreign country. Also called a *buyout* or a *takeover*.   2. The process of searching, evaluating, and choosing among alternative items for purchase by consumers.

acquisition budget   Funds to be used in obtaining customers through sales promotion activities and advertising. See also PROMOTIONAL BUDGETING and ADVERTISING AND PROMOTION (A&P) MIX.

acquisition cost   Any of the expenses associated with obtaining inventory through either manufacturing or buying the product. For the manufacturer, all the costs associated with beginning production are considered acquisition costs (raw materials, new plants or equipment, etc.). For retailers and wholesalers, acquisition costs are the expenses for keeping records and handling the paperwork for each order, thus influencing the REORDER POINT (ROP) and the ECONOMIC ORDER QUANTITY (EOQ).

acronym   A word formed from the first letters of the words in a name or phrase, sometimes evolving into a company name or the name by which the company is known. For example, "LIFO" is an acronym for "last in, first out." Similarly, "GEICO insurance" is more recognizable than "Government Employee Insurance Company." If it cannot be pronounced as a word, however, the initialism is not an acronym (e.g., IBM).

action item   An item with strong customer appeal and, consequently, strong sales.

action plan   The step-by-step detailed outline for implementing tactics (specific tasks with deadlines) that will achieve the strategies set forth in the overall MARKETING PLAN. The action plan sets forth exactly what should be done, the time frame for the completion of each activity or task, and the person or group of persons responsible for each activity or task. Action plans can and should be revisited and revised during implementation to keep the plan on track and to ensure that expectations are realistic in terms of both resources and personnel.

action program   In a MARKETING PLAN, the specific steps that are calculated to achieve the plan's objectives.

action tendency   See BEHAVIORAL COMPONENT.

active buyer   In DIRECT MARKETING, any customer whose last purchase was made within the past 12 months. Also called *active* and *active customer*.

active exporting   Activities of firms that vigorously seek export business.

active international Internet marketer   An Internet marketer actively developing an international buyer base and engaging in international Internet marketing activities. Compare PASSIVE INTERNATIONAL INTERNET MARKETER.

active member   In DIRECT MARKETING, particularly in such operations as book and record clubs, any member/subscriber who is currently fulfilling the original commitment or who has already fulfilled that commitment and has made additional purchases in the past 12 months. The member has either paid a fee (on a six-month, annual, or lifetime basis, etc.) for the right to receive information about and/or actually purchase items, or has committed to make a minimum number of purchases during a particular period of time by virtue of goods and/or services already received.

active subscriber   A customer who has committed to receiving regular delivery of magazines, books, stamps, or other goods and/or services for a period of time currently in effect.

activewear   Apparel designed to be worn for participation in sports and recreational activities. The category includes clothing specially designed for aerobic exercise, biking, skiing, gymnastics, riding, tennis, swimming, etc., but activewear is also worn as casual dress and for leisure activities. See also SPORTSWEAR.

activities, interests, and opinions (AIO) inventory   See AIO INVENTORY.

act of God   A legal concept referring to an act or event having purely natural causes, exclusive of human intervention. Examples include floods, hurricanes, tornadoes, etc. Often applied to legal cases involving property loss.

actual cost   The billed cost, as it appears on the seller's invoice, less any cash discount earned.

actual count   See PERIODIC ACTUAL COUNT.

actualizer   See VALS SEGMENTATION.

actuals   Merchandise available for purchase.

actual sales   Synonym for NET SALES.

actual self-concept   See SELF-IMAGE.

ad   See ADVERTISEMENT.

ADA   See AMERICANS WITH DISABILITIES ACT (ADA).

ADAC   See ATLANTA DECORATIVE ARTS CENTER (ADAC).

adaptation   1. The successful response of both individuals and organizations to changes in the surrounding environment, including both opportunities and threats.   2. A design that modifies or reinterprets the main stylistic features of the product that inspired it. In fashion design, the adaptation is often made to produce a less expensive version of the original item. Not a direct copy. See also BODY COPY.

adaptation policy   In global marketing, a basic strategy that may be used when entering foreign markets. The company makes some changes to its own marketing strategy to fit the requirements of the new market. It may choose to extend either product design or communications (i.e., ADVERTISING and promotional activities) while adapting the other, or it may adapt both. Two alternative strategies are the EXTENSION STRATEGY and the INVENTION STRATEGY.

adaptive behavior theory   A theory of evolutionary change in which firms most capable of adapting or adjusting to changing conditions in the marketplace are seen as having the best chance of survival. Also called *natural selection theory*.

adaptive-control model A method used by some firms to set the advertising budget and measure the sales effect of advertising expenditures. The model assumes that the advertising sales-response function changes through time due to changing competitive activity, advertising copy, product design, and economic climate. In order to be successful, the advertising budget should remain flexible and be reevaluated periodically to allow for the changing marketing environment.

adaptive corporate culture The culture of a firm characterized by the ability to adjust to a continually changing business environment. In both its policies and its practices, the firm welcomes change and seeks out new market opportunities. See also ORGANIZATIONAL CULTURE.

adaptive forecasting A method of forecasting sales in which a considerable amount of unit sales history has been compared to overall sales trends. For example, seasonal sales patterns may be compared to long-term sales trends.

adaptive product See EMULATIVE PRODUCT.

ad banner See BANNER AD.

added gravy (Slang) Synonym for ADD-ON SALES.

added selling A salesperson's attempt to sell additional products and/or services to a customer who has just made a purchase. Such sales are referred to as ADD-ON SALES.

added value See VALUE ADDED.

additional markdown A further decrease in an item's selling price beyond the original markdown. This may become necessary if the item fails to sell at the reduced price or to clear remaining inventories at the end of a selling season. The additional markdown, sometimes called a *second markdown*, is often stated as a percentage of the already marked down price. For example, an additional markdown of $10 on a $50 item already marked down to $40 is 25%.

additional markup An increase in the original retail price of goods due to errors in original pricing or to an increase in the market value of the goods. Additional markup is used to equate the retail prices of goods purchased at different costs to maintain a store's standard percentage markup. Additional markup may become an attractive strategy if demand for the item increases or supply dwindles. See also MARKUP CANCELLATION.

additional markup cancellation A decrease in the retail price of an item that offsets an ADDITIONAL MARKUP. Some cancellations correct an error in pricing and some end a pre-planned sale. The lowered price is not recorded as a markdown. Also known as a *revision of retail downward*.

additional markup percentage Additional markup calculated as a percentage of net sales in dollars. It may also be calculated as a percentage of the retail onto which the markup is added.

additions In DIRECT MARKETING, names of individuals or organizations newly added to a mailing list.

addition to retail percentage The total price change a product undergoes as a percentage of the original price.

add-ons Synonym for ADD-ON SALES.

add-on sales 1. In credit card sales, additional charge purchases made before all previous purchases have been paid in full. 2. In personal selling, additional purchases of related merchandise made at the suggestion of the salesperson. For example, the salesperson may suggest the purchase of batteries to a consumer who has purchased a battery-operated flashlight. Popularly referred to by the slang term *added gravy*.

add-on service A service provided by the Direct Marketing Service that allows customers to request that their names be added to specific mailing lists.

address See WEB ADDRESS.

address coding guide (ACG) A manual used by direct marketers to identify potential customers. The guide contains the actual or potential beginning and ending house numbers, block groups and/or district numbers, zip codes, and other geographic codes for all city delivery service streets in the United States.

address correction requested A message printed in the upper left-hand corner of the address portion of a piece of mail, authorizing the U.S. Postal Service to provide the known new address of a person no longer residing at the address appearing on the mailing. The Postal Service charges a fee to direct marketers requesting this service.

ADI See ASSORTMENT DIVERSITY INDEX (ADI).

adjacencies In television ADVERTISING, adjacencies are the time periods immediately before and immediately after a television program, generally used as a commercial break between programs.

adjacency The location of merchandise next to other, related merchandise for customer convenience and to stimulate sales of the related goods. For example, handbags are frequently sold next to shoes. Similarly, retailers often situate private label goods adjacent to branded products in the hope that customers lured to heavily advertised branded products will select the higher-margin private labels instead.

adjacent stockroom Space immediately off the selling area in which reserve quantities of merchandise are stored to replace items on the selling floor as they are sold. Adjacent stockrooms are located immediately next to the selling area for that item or class of items to promote convenient and efficient restocking. Also called a *forward stockroom*. See also STOCKROOM.

adjusted balance method A method used by retailers to calculate the portion of the balance in a charge account that will be assessed an interest charge. Under the adjusted balance method, charges are calculated after payments made during the billing period have been subtracted from the outstanding balance. Also called *adjusted balance procedure*. See also PREVIOUS BALANCE METHOD and AVERAGE DAILY BALANCE METHOD.

adjusted retail book value   In accounting, the book value is the original cost of merchandise less the amount of accumulated depreciation, depletion, or amortization. The adjusted retail book value is, therefore, an ending retail book value further corrected to reflect stock shortages and overage.

adjustment   1. The settlement of a customer's complaints to the satisfaction of both the customer and the store. This may entail the resolution of differences regarding price or a refund. Also called a *merchandise adjustment*. See also STORE SERVICES.   2. In retail charge accounts, the correction of such errors as overcharging, improper recordings, or incorrect dating.   3. A lowering of price, as in the case of damaged or soiled goods.

adjustment allowance   Compensation made to a customer to settle a claim or complaint.

adjustment department   The nonselling department or area of a store responsible for the resolution of customer complaints, especially when they have failed to be resolved on the selling floor.

administered channel   Synonym for ADMINISTERED VERTICAL MARKETING SYSTEM.

administered distribution system   Synonym for ADMINISTERED VERTICAL MARKETING SYSTEM.

administered marketing network   Synonym for ADMINISTERED VERTICAL MARKETING SYSTEM.

administered pricing   Prices set by the seller rather than by competitive market forces and designed to meet the seller's objectives, such as RETURN ON INVESTMENT (ROI). Prices may be set, or administered, by the manufacturer or other members of the supply chain. The seller may hold this set price steady over a period of time, but unless the firm sells directly to the ultimate consumer, other supply chain members may make the *administered price* difficult to hold. For example, wholesalers selling to discount outlets will tend to bring down the price set by the manufacturer. Most firms do administer prices; all firms engaged in MONOPOLISTIC COMPETITION do. Also called *business-controlled pricing*.

administered system   A manufacturer's control of one or more lines sold by the retailer, often involving special merchandising plans.

administered vertical marketing system   A system in which the supply chain members, while retaining much of their autonomy, are informally coordinated in their marketing activities by the dominant member of the supply chain or channel. Dominance is achieved through the exercise of political or economic power rather than through outright ownership. Also called *administered VMS*. See also VERTICAL MARKETING SYSTEM (VMS), CORPORATE VERTICAL MARKETING SYSTEM, and CONTRACTUAL VERTICAL MARKETING SYSTEM.

administration   1. The management and direction of a business organization, government body, or similar institution.   2. That section or department of an organization charged with overseeing and directing the day-to-day activities and planning functions of the organization. See also MANAGEMENT.

administrative offices   A term employed by the U.S. Census of Business to designate locations such as central, executive, and district offices engaged in administrative functions for the retail stores within a multiunit organization.

adnorm   In print media ADVERTISING, the average readership of a print publication over a two-year period. The average is used as a baseline figure.

adoption   See ADOPTION PROCESS.

adoption curve   A distribution curve that graphically represents the diffusion of an innovation as various groups adopt new products or fashion styles. The curve illustrates the number of adopters who have purchased a new product or service during each time period beginning with the launch date. It takes the shape of a normal statistical distribution in that a small number of people adopt the innovation when it first becomes available and this rate of adoption increases until 50 percent of the potential users have tried it. After this point has been reached, the number of individuals adopting the product within each time period decreases until there are no potential adopters who have not yet tried the innovation. Also called a *diffusion curve*. See also DIFFUSION PROCESS.

adoption curve cumulative   See ADOPTION CURVE.

adoption process   1. The stages of awareness, interest, evaluation, trial, and adoption that each consumer experiences in the course of becoming a regular purchaser of a product. Also known as the *buying decision-making process* and the *consumer decision process*.   2. The flow of fashion from one class or group to another as acceptance becomes more widespread. Also known as the *product adoption process* and the *purchase decision process*. See also DIFFUSION PROCESS.

adoption process segmentation variables   See ADOPTION PROCESS and SEGMENTATION VARIABLES.

ad specialties   See ADVERTISING SPECIALTIES.

ad valorem duty   A tax on imports calculated as a percentage of the value of the merchandise.

advance   1. A partial payment made before due, as in wages. 2. A *down payment* on the sale of a product.

advance bill A bill presented to a purchaser before goods are actually received or services performed. It may be requested by the purchaser in order to include a payment within a certain accounting period.

advance buying See ADVANCE ORDER.

advance dating The practice of setting a specific future date, after shipment and after the invoice date, when the terms of sale become applicable. It delays the beginning of the discount and payment periods. For example, under the terms "2/10, net 30 as of March 1," a 2% discount will be made for payment within 10 days and the net payment period will be calculated from March 1, regardless of the shipping and/or invoice dates. Full payment is due by March 31 (i.e., 30 days after the "as of" date). Advance dating is sometimes used to allow for transportation of merchandise and sometimes to encourage orders in advance of the normal buying season. Commonly used in the menswear industry. Also called *advanced dating, post dating, postdating,* or *seasonal dating.*

advanced dating See ADVANCE DATING.

advanced sales training Ongoing or continuing training for sales personnel, sometimes intended as a refresher course but more often providing more sophisticated and problem-oriented sales techniques. Advanced sales training is much more concerned with strategies and skills in consultative selling, system selling, and sales negotiation than is the initial sales force indoctrination training. See also SALES APPROACH and SALES TRAINING.

advanced shipping notice See ADVANCE SHIPPING NOTICE (ASN).

advanced training See ADVANCED SALES TRAINING.

advance order A sales order placed well ahead of the desired date of delivery. This practice generally enables a buyer to obtain a lower price for the goods by giving the manufacturer business during a slack period or in advance of the normal buying season.

advance premium An incentive, usually in the form of merchandise, given to convince a new or potential customer to begin using a home delivery service (such as newspaper, soda, or diaper delivery). The service firm anticipates that the cost of the incentive will be recouped in time as the service is used.

advance shipping notice (ASN) A supplier's electronic notification to a retailer that an order has been shipped. ASN is a key component of ELECTRONIC DATA INTERCHANGE (EDI) systems.

advantage 1. A circumstance favorable to success. 2. An organization's position of superiority over competitors or a country's position of superiority over competing countries engaged in international marketing. See also ABSOLUTE ADVANTAGE, COMPETITIVE ADVANTAGE, and COMPARATIVE ADVANTAGE.

advergaming An online promotion hybrid that uses custom-designed games (advergames) on a Web site to promote a brand.

advertise To announce or promote a product or service by means of a public communications medium (such as newspaper, magazine, television, radio, the Internet, billboards, etc.) in hopes of attracting customers, supporters, and/or users.

advertisement The paid, nonpersonal communication of a message intended to sell or promote a product, service, person, idea, or issue. The sponsor of the message is almost always identified. Media that carry advertisements include newspapers, magazines, television, radio, direct mail, e-mail, and the Internet, etc., and are carefully selected by the advertiser to reach a particular target market.

advertisement manager See ADVERTISING SALES MANAGER.

advertiser An individual, firm, or other organization that originates or sponsors an ADVERTISEMENT or ADVERTISING CAMPAIGN. The advertiser, whether the client of an ADVERTISING AGENCY or the producer of in-house advertising, may be a political candidate, a manufacturer, a retail organization, a wholesaler, an association, or a public service organization, etc.

advertising The use of public media (i.e., mass media) to communicate paid, nonpersonal messages to persuade, remind, or inform the target audience. There are, basically, only two types of advertising: (a) institutional advertising (sometimes called *public relations advertising, corporate advertising,* or *image advertising*) and (b) product or brand advertising. Both are a part of the promotion process, that, in turn, forms the marketing communication system. See also INSTITUTIONAL ADVERTISING, BRAND ADVERTISING, PROMOTIONAL ADVERTISING, MEDIA, TRYVERTISING, and PRODUCT ADVERTISING.

advertising agency An independent business organization equipped to provide all phases of ADVERTISING for its clients. The agency prepares and places advertisements, and may perform related research and promotional activities. In a full-line agency these services are paid primarily by commissions from the media that carry the advertising (a percentage of the dollar value of the media the agency purchases for a client). Most large advertising agencies have at least four departments: (a) research (collects data on customers), (b) creative (prepares and produces copy and art), (c) media (selects the communication vehicles for the ads and buys the time and/or space), and (d) account management (serves as the liaison between the client and the agency). Agencies often specialize in the type of goods they handle (such as consumer goods, industrial goods, international business, services, etc.). There are several types of advertising agencies, including the BOUTIQUE AGENCY (also known as *creative boutique*), which focuses on the creative and art aspects of the ADVERTISING CAMPAIGN, and the A LA CARTE AGENCY, which charges clients on a per-job basis for the specific services provided.

advertising allowance A monetary commitment made by a vendor to a retailer to share the advertising costs of a specified product, brand, or line. The allowance is generally a percentage of the retailer's purchases from the vendor and covers a percentage of the retailer's advertising cost. See also COOPERATIVE ADVERTISING.

advertising and promotion (A&P) mix   The manner in which funds are allocated to support a firm's advertising and sales promotion efforts. Specifically, the amount of money allocated to each of the various forms of advertising and promotion at the firm's disposal. See also PROMOTIONAL BUDGETING.

advertising and sales promotion director   See ADVERTISING MANAGER.

advertising appeal   The central theme, motif, or idea of an ADVERTISEMENT that tells the potential consumer what the advertised product or service offers and why it should be purchased. The appeal may be expressed in terms of sexual attractiveness, prestige, convenience, etc., with motivation to buy being the primary object.

advertising appropriation   The total amount of money allocated for an organization's ADVERTISING program during a specific time period. The appropriation may be based on a percentage of past or projected sales, calculated according to the cost of the task at hand, or a combination of the two. In retailing, the sum of money available for advertising is allocated both to the store as a whole and to separate departments. See also PROMOTIONAL BUDGETING.

advertising by nonprofit organizations   See NONCOMMERCIAL ADVERTISING.

advertising calendar   A retail firm's schedule identifying what items will be advertised when and where. The calendar is used by the promotion department to prepare ads or send merchandise samples and product information to the retailer's advertising agency.

advertising campaign   A planned ADVERTISING effort that extends over a period of time and is designed to promote a particular product or service. The advertising campaign involves setting objectives, determining an advertising budget, positioning the product, selecting the appropriate media, and measuring the campaign's effectiveness. Also called a *coordinated advertising campaign*.

advertising credit   The inclusion of the names of one or more retail stores in a vendor's advertisement to indicate sources for the advertised merchandise.

advertising department   The in-house department of a store or other business that handles all types of paid publicity, including copywriting, typography, and artwork. The advertising department may function in lieu of, or in conjunction with, an ADVERTISING AGENCY. In a retail organization, the advertising department is part of the PROMOTION DIVISION and is responsible for planning, creating, placing, and evaluating the effectiveness of ads. The head of the advertising depart-

ment is generally called the *director of advertising* or the *advertising director*.

advertising director   See ADVERTISING DEPARTMENT.

advertising display   In RADIO FREQUENCY IDENTIFICATION (RFID), custom ads shown to the customer in supermarket aisles. The ads are based on the customer's buying habits and demographic profile.

advertising goals   Those specific purposes that underlie an ADVERTISEMENT or ADVERTISING CAMPAIGN. Most advertising has as its goal the stimulation (within a particular time frame) of some specific and immediate activity on the part of the consumer. See also ADVERTISING OBJECTIVES.

advertising jingle   See JINGLE.

advertising links   See RECIPROCAL ADVERTISING LINKS.

advertising manager   In retail or other business organizations, the advertising manager is the employee responsible for supervising the development of advertising for the firm. He or she provides expertise in communication and promotion, the design of commercial messages, media, and publicity, and reviews and approves ads that are ready to be placed in the media. Known as the *communications manager* in some organizations. Distinct from the ADVERTISING SALES MANAGER, who is an employee of the media organization.

advertising measures   See ADVERTISING METRICS.

advertising media   All of the communication channels employed by advertisers to reach their audiences and convey their sales messages. Advertising media include print media (such as newspapers and magazines), broadcast media (radio and television), electronic media (such as the Internet, e-mail, Usenet newsgroups), outdoor media (such as billboards), transit (such as car cards and posters in stations), and point-of-purchase displays. See also ADVERTISING.

advertising medium   Singular form of ADVERTISING MEDIA.

advertising message   The creative component of an ADVERTISEMENT or ADVERTISING CAMPAIGN. The function of the MESSAGE is to carry out the advertising objectives of the product or service. The success of the message depends on its ability to engage the attention and interest of the largest possible audience and to motivate that audience to act in a particular way.

advertising metrics   Measures of the effectiveness of an individual ADVERTISEMENT or an ADVERTISING CAMPAIGN. Effectiveness is measured in terms of audience size and reach, brand building, audience contact with ads, and recall. See also WEB ADVERTISING METRICS.

advertising models   Computer-generated decision making tools used in ADVERTISING to determine budgets, schedule media, and generate sales and profit expectations.

advertising objectives The communication and sales objectives assigned to ADVERTISING, which flow from prior decisions regarding the product's target market, target position, and marketing mix. Advertising objectives may fall into the categories of informing, persuading, or reminding. Also called *promotion objectives* and/or *promotional objectives*. See also ADVERTISING GOALS.

advertising plan In retailing, a store's projection of its advertising usage during a specific period of time.

advertising platform The main issues or selling points an advertiser wishes to include in an ADVERTISING CAMPAIGN.

advertising recall A test of a consumer's ability to remember an ADVERTISEMENT and, consequently, a means of determining the ad's effectiveness. Recall tests may be aided or unaided. See also AIDED RECALL and UNAIDED RECALL.

advertising record sheet A method for testing the effectiveness of an ADVERTISEMENT or ADVERTISING CAMPAIGN by monitoring sales or orders for merchandise received as a result of the advertisement. Records may be kept on a daily, weekly, and/or monthly basis.

advertising research Studies designed to test and improve the effectiveness of ADVERTISING. Advertising research may focus on a particular advertisement or advertising campaign, or it may seek a better understanding of how advertising affects consumers or how consumers process and use the information they receive in advertising. Advertising research includes readership studies, recall and recognition studies, measurement of radio and television audiences, the analysis of coupon returns, etc. Pretesting is used to determine the appropriateness and effectiveness of the ad before it is run; focus groups of consumers are frequently used for this purpose. Posttesting is used to determine the impact of the ads following their appearance in the marketplace. See also FOCUS GROUP.

advertising response function See PROMOTION-ADVERTISING RESPONSE FUNCTION.

advertising sales manager The employee of a media organization (newspaper, magazine, television network, etc.) responsible for selling ADVERTISING SPACE or time to prospective advertisers. In the broadcast media, the advertising sales manager is more commonly called the *sales manager*. Distinct from the ADVERTISING MANAGER, who is an employee of the retail firm or other marketer.

advertising sales-response and decay model A model used to measure the response of sales to advertising in an effort to determine the most appropriate advertising budget. The model was developed by M.L. Vidale and H.B. Wolfe; it postulates that the change in the rate of sales at a particular time (t) is a function of four factors: the advertising budget; the sales-response constant (defined as the sales generated per advertising dollar when $S = 0$); the saturation level of sales; and the sales-decay constant (defined as the fraction of sales per time unit when $A = 0$). In essence, the model states that the rate of sales will be higher, the higher the advertising expenditure, the higher the untapped sales potential, and the lower the decay constant. The model may also be used to estimate the profit consequences of alternative advertising budget strategies. Also called simply a *decay mode*, the *decay rate*, the *sales-response model*, or the *sales-response and decay model*. See also ADVERTISING SALES-RESPONSE CURVE. Compare S-SHAPED CURVE MODEL.

advertising sales-response curve The graphic representation of the relationship between advertising expenditures on the horizontal axis and the results in sales on the vertical axis. The usual assumption is that sales will increase as advertising expenditures increase. However, as illustrated by the advertising response function, there may be a point at which additional advertising expenditures result in little or no additional sales. Compare S-SHAPED CURVE MODEL.

advertising schedule A buyer's timetable of the items to be advertised during a given time period.

advertising space The portion of the total page space in print media (newspapers, magazines, etc.) allocated to advertising as distinguished from news and/or editorial matter.

advertising specialties Items of little value (e.g., key rings, ash trays, pencils, ballpoint pens, matchbooks) that carry the name of the firm or product, its picture, logo, etc., and that are used as giveaways. The objective of such advertising is to generate goodwill and to keep the firm or product name in the mind of the recipient/customer. Also called *specialty advertising*.

advertising specialty distributor See SPECIALTY DISTRIBUTOR.

advertising target The particular segment of the population at which a promotional image is aimed. For example, marketers may gear their advertisements to appeal to Generation X or to baby boomers. Also called *target audience*. See also AUDIENCE.

advertising testing See ADVERTISING RESEARCH.

advertising theme The central concept, sales point, or product feature around which an ADVERTISING CAMPAIGN or individual advertisement is built. In general, the advertising theme will attempt to demonstrate the superiority of the product, service, retail establishment, etc. featured in the advertisement or advertising campaign.

advertising time Advertising placed in broadcast media, usually in the form of 30- or 60-second segments.

advertorial insert 1. A special section or insertion in print media (such as magazines and newspapers) that combines ADVERTISING with editorial content. For example, advertorial inserts frequently consist of several pages sponsored by the tourist board or economic development agency of a foreign country, inviting tourism and/or foreign investment. Retailers and their parent companies may use advertorial inserts to commemorate major anniversaries or significant events, such as mergers. Also called a *preprinted advertising insert,* a *preprinted insert,* a CIRCULAR, or simply an *insert.* 2. A Web site serving the same function as advertorial inserts in the print media, providing the mission and history of the company, information about the parent company and all subsidiaries, and highlighting chief personnel.

advice note A list of items sent to a customer prior to an invoice, detailing the items to be included in the shipment. The advice note may either precede or accompany the actual merchandise. The advice note identifies the nature and quantity of the goods included in the shipment, but does not include prices. Many e-tailers automatically e-mail an advice note to the online customer immediately upon receipt of the order; some follow through with a second advice note when the item has been shipped.

ADVISOR Project A five-year study conducted by Gary L. Lilien in the 1970s in which he examined and attempted to evaluate the methods by which industrial marketers set their advertising budgets. The study led to the building of several models for setting marketing and advertising budgets for industrial marketers.

advisory service An organization specializing in providing advice, counsel, or information rather than a tangible product. The proliferation of online diet-advice Web sites, most of which charge a membership fee or fee for service, qualify as advisory services as do debt consolidation service firms.

advocacy advertising ADVERTISING (i.e., paid, nonpersonal communications) whose objective is to support a particular belief or course of action on the part of its audience with regard to controversial subjects such as equal employment opportunities.

advocate channel A personal communication channel consisting of the company salespeople contacting buyers in the target market. Retail sales personnel, for example, may telephone known customers to notify them of sales and special promotions, new products, or new services. Salespersons may also contact these target groups to solicit opinions about the quality of service and availability of merchandise in the store.

AFDT See AIR FREIGHT DECISION TOOL (AFDT).

affect See AFFECTIVE COMPONENT.

affective component In attitude research, particularly in the tripartite view or structural approach, the individual's overall feelings of like or dislike toward a service, product, or similar object. It is the emotional component of attitude formation. See also ATTITUDE.

affiliated buying See COOPERATIVE BUYING.

affiliated cooperative/co-op See RETAIL COOPERATIVE/CO-OP.

affiliated retailer A retail member of a voluntary chain. Member stores buy all or most of their merchandise from the sponsoring wholesaler who, in turn, provides a variety of services to the members. Such associations are formed to maximize the economies of scale inherent in bulk purchases. See also VOLUNTARY CHAIN and RETAIL COOPERATIVE/CO-OP.

affiliated store 1. A store owned and operated as a unit of a VOLUNTARY CHAIN or FRANCHISE group. 2. A store controlled by another store but operated under a separate name, thus maintaining its own identity.

affiliated wholesaler A wholesale organization at the center of a VOLUNTARY CHAIN. The affiliated wholesaler sells merchandise to the member stores and provides certain management services such as accounting systems, display advice, standardized merchandise packages, central data processing, etc.

affiliation need One of the three basic motivations comprising the trio of needs. The affiliation need is the drive to belong to a particular group. See also TRIO OF NEEDS, ACHIEVEMENT NEED, and POWER NEED.

affiliative group Any reference group such as the family, church, school, etc., to which an individual actually belongs.

affinities Retail stores that tend to be located in close proximity to one another, generally to benefit from the TRAFFIC and customers generated by the surrounding stores.

affinity The attractiveness of a particular area as a retail site location, owing to the store's ability to blend in and cooperate with neighboring establishments.

affinity analysis The use of MARKET BASKET ANALYSIS to determine which products are most frequently purchased together (i.e., in the same market basket). This knowledge may inform decisions about SPACE ALLOCATION and PRODUCT PLACEMENT. For example, items frequently purchased together might generate additional sales if they were placed closer together on the selling floor.

affinity credit card A CREDIT CARD jointly sponsored by a lending organization (such as a bank) and another organization (such as a union, fraternal organization, sports franchise, airline, sports team, or retail store) in which the holder has a membership or other affiliation. The card generally bears the logo of the membership organization. Some retail stores have replaced or supplemented their store charge card with an affinity credit card. See also CO-BRANDED CARD.

affinity purchase Any of the items most often purchased with other items in the same MARKET BASKET. See also AFFINITY ANALYSIS.

affirmative action Activities undertaken by businesses to recruit and promote minorities, giving special benefits to disadvantaged and underrepresented groups to ensure equal opportunity. Beginning in the 1960s, all private companies doing business with the U.S. federal government were required to develop affirmative-action programs for hiring and promoting women and minorities.

affirmative consent   In e-tailing, affirmative consent is a recipient's express agreement to receive marketing communications from the e-tailer or other marketer. The CAN-SPAM ACT (2003) specifies that an e-tailer's request for such permission must be clear and conspicuous. Alternatively, the recipient may initiate a request to receive such communications. Affirmative consent also specifies that those who wish to rent their e-mail lists to third parties must provide clear and conspicuous notice of their intent to do so to recipients at the time of consent. Consent must be incorporated into the registration form rather than buried in the e-tailer's privacy policy. Also called *opt-in* or *permission*. See also IMPLIED CONSENT.

affirmative disclosure   A procedure adopted by the FEDERAL TRADE COMMISSION (FTC) in its attempt to regulate ADVERTISING. The procedure stipulates that if the information contained in an advertisement is deemed insufficient by the commission, it may require a company to disclose some of the limitations of its product or service within its subsequent advertising. This is done so that the consumer may judge the negative as well as the positive attributes of the product or service.

after-inventory clearance (sale)   A promotional event and sale designed to clear the store of all remaining merchandise after INVENTORY has been taken. Prices are often drastically reduced to help clear the store for the arrival of new shipments. Such a sale is often *storewide*. See also CLEARANCE SALE.

aftermarket   The aggregate demand for parts and service that follows the sale of a product such as an automobile or computer.

after spoiling date   A trend in consumer behavior in which affluent parents decide that their children are old enough not to be spoiled by their wealth. At that time, the parents feel comfortable donating money, assets, and/or luxury goods to their children. Retailers and other marketers may wish to focus on this stage in the children's lives, thus working with the affluent parents rather than against them. The term was coined by trendwatching.com at www.trendwatching.com.

agate   A unit of measuring newspaper ADVERTISING SPACE. It is ¹⁄₁₄ of an inch deep and one column wide. A space one inch deep contains 14 agate lines, regardless of the printed lines actually set up within that space, and is priced accordingly.

Age Discrimination in Employment Act (1968)   Federal legislation designed to prevent discrimination against older workers. It also extended the retirement age to 70.

agency shop   A workplace in which nonunion workers covered by agreements negotiated by the union are required to pay service fees to that union.

agent   1. An individual who represents another and is authorized to act on behalf of that other, particularly when negoti-ating business contracts or facilitating trade.   2. A shorthand form of AGENT INTERMEDIARY. See also MANUFACTURER'S AGENT and SELLING AGENT.   3. In e-commerce, a form of ROBOT, a program that performs an information-gathering or processing task in the background. For example, an agent may act as a SHOPPING BOT, searching the Internet for certain types of product information.

agent intermediary   A wholesaling middleman (sometimes called an *agent wholesaler* or simply an AGENT) who, acting as a go-between, performs a number of wholesaling functions without taking title to the goods and frequently without taking physical possession of the goods. The agent intermediary is highly specialized and has an extensive knowledge of the market. The agent intermediary's principal function is to facilitate the passing of title to goods from one party to another. Also called an *agent middleman*, an *agent middleperson*, a *functional middleman*, *functional middleperson*, or a *non-title-taking agent middleman*. Included under the term *agent intermediary* are SELLING AGENT, MANUFACTURER'S AGENT, BROKER, COMMISSION MERCHANT, and AUCTION HOUSE.

agent middleman/middleperson   See AGENT INTERMEDIARY.

agent wholesaler   Synonym for AGENT INTERMEDIARY.

aggregate (monetary) demand   The total planned expenditure (within an economy) by consumers, firms, government, and foreigners on goods and services produced within that economy. Indirect taxes and import components are deducted before calculating the aggregate monetary demand.

aggregation   A theory of MARKET SEGMENTATION that assumes that all consumers are essentially alike. Retailers subscribing to the theory rely, therefore, on mass distribution, mass advertising, and the appeal of low prices. They focus on the broadest possible spectrum of consumers and the common dimensions of the market. See also UNDIFFERENTIATED MARKETING and DEMAND AGGREGATOR.

aggregator   See DEMAND AGGREGATOR.

aggressive demarketing response to shortages   An approach to actual or anticipated shortages of the raw materials required for production. When companies feel they cannot produce enough goods to meet their customers' needs, they may take any or all of the following steps: raise price sharply; cut product quality and new product development; eliminate weaker customers; reduce customer services; allocate supplies to customers according to their ability to pay; cut marketing budgets for research, advertising, and sales calls; and drop low-profit items in their product lines. Aggressive DEMARKETING in this fashion, however, may have unwanted negative consequences, especially losing the goodwill of many customers.

aggressive pricing   A method of setting prices that focuses on the desire to undercut competitors' prices. Aggressive pricing methods include PENETRATION PRICING (setting a low price on a product when competition is high), EXPERIENCE

CURVE PRICING (reducing the price consistently for the duration of the product's stay on the selling floor), and *meeting competition* (matching or beating competitors' prices). Compare PASSIVE PRICING and NEUTRAL PRICING.

aging   1. In retailing, the length of time merchandise has been in stock.   2. For certain products such as tobacco, liquor, and cheese, part of the curing process.

aging accounts receivable   The process of classifying accounts receivable according to the period of time they have been outstanding. Used for determining the amount of uncollectible accounts receivable as of a given date. Also called *analysis of accounts*.

agree and counterattack technique   See YES, BUT TECHNIQUE.

agreeing and neutralizing technique   See YES, BUT TECHNIQUE.

agribusiness   The business function related to agriculture, including farming as well as the processing of food and other agricultural products (such as flowers), the manufacture of farm equipment, and the production of ancillary farm goods such as fertilizers.

agricultural co-op/cooperative   See PRODUCERS' COOPERATIVE/CO-OP.

AIDA model   AIDA is an acronym for attention, interest, desire, and action. The acronym represents the desirable qualities found in an ADVERTISING or personal selling message. An advertising or personal sales message should get attention, arouse interest, create desire, and precipitate action. The concept was first propounded by E.K. Strong in 1924.

aided recall   A method of testing a consumer's ability to remember an advertisement and, consequently, a means of determining the ad's effectiveness. Participants are asked to identify advertisements they have recently seen or heard and are given hints or clues in the form of lists of products, brands, or company names in an effort to stimulate the memory. Compare UNAIDED RECALL.

AIO inventory   In psychographic research, a method used to determine consumers' activities, interests, and opinions (AIO) by means of a lifestyle measurement survey.

air bubble packing   Packing materials made of plastic with air pockets for cushioning, used to protect fragile products during the shipping process and to minimize the shifting of the packed contents.

air curtain   In food retailing establishments, a stream of air used as a barrier to prevent the loss of heat or cold to the surrounding air. Air curtains are used over some refrigerated or freezer cases out on the selling floor as well as between back rooms used for storage.

airedale   (Slang) An aggressive, fast-talking, high-pressure salesperson.

air freight   The use of airplanes for transporting goods. Because air freight rates are generally more expensive than truck or rail freight rates, this mode of shipping is usually reserved for situations in which speed is essential and/or distant markets must be reached. It is a particularly effective means of shipping perishables (such as fresh fish or flowers) and high-value, low-bulk items (such as jewelry). The cost of air freight may also be justified when it leads to decreases in the inventory levels that must be maintained, the number of warehouses required, and packaging costs. See also AIR FREIGHT DECISION TOOL (AFDT).

air freight decision tool (AFDT)   A computer model designed to help shippers determine when to use air freight instead of truck or rail as the preferred mode of transportation.

air transportation   See AIR FREIGHT.

air waybill   A document giving evidence of an air shipping carrier's receipt of a shipment. It also serves as a contract between carrier and shipper. In other forms of shipping, this document is generally called a BILL OF LADING (B/L).

airport shop   A shop or stand located in an airport terminal. These specialty-store retailers cater to the many high-income leisure and business travelers who spend considerable time in airports because of flight delays and slack time between check-in and departure. Once home to souvenir shops and fast food vendors, airports are now attracting more upscale retailers.

airport-to-airport shipping   Transportation of merchandise from one airport to another by an air carrier.

airtruck   A coordinated mode of shipping goods that involves the combined use of air freight and truck freight. Its ease of use is made possible through CONTAINERIZATION.

airway bill of lading (AWB)   A written receipt given by an air freight carrier for goods accepted for transportation. See also BILL OF LADING (B/L).

aisle   A walkway or path between or along rows of seats (as in a theater), shelves, racks, or counters (as in a retail store). As TRAFFIC carriers, aisles are an important factor in defining the value of selling space. Space that is close to an aisle is more valuable than space remote from an aisle. Aisles are classified according to their size and the amount of customer traffic they carry. See also MAJOR AISLE and SECONDARY AISLE.

aisle advertising   An in-store DISPLAY located at the end of an aisle and designed to highlight a particular product or group of products. The location of the merchandise also makes the products more accessible to customers and, particularly if the products are on sale at a reduced price, more likely to become impulse purchases. Particularly in supermarket retailing, aisle advertising tends to use the same motif (graphics and copy) used in other promotional efforts for the product.

aisle interrupter   A sign, usually made of cardboard, that protrudes into an aisle and calls attention to a particular product or group of products. It is frequently found in grocery and drug stores. Compare WOBBLER and DANGLER.

aisle jumper   An overhead wire or other line stretched across an aisle in a store, from which signs, banners, flags, etc. may be hung.

aisle table   A table in a store aisle, generally between departments, used to feature special promotional values. It may be used for clearance items sold at a reduced price or new merchandise sold at a popular price.

à la carte agency   An ADVERTISING AGENCY that charges its clients on a per job basis for the specific services it provides them.

alert box   See BOX.

algorithm   A formula or set of steps for solving a problem. The rules of an algorithm are unambiguous and have clear stopping points. An algorithm may be expressed in any language, including natural languages (e.g., English) and programming languages (e.g., Fortran). Most computer programs consist of algorithms; programmers endeavor to devise elegant algorithms that require the fewest possible steps to achieve the program's goals.

alias   See HOST NAME.

alien corporation   A classification assigned by a state government to describe out-of-state corporations doing business within its borders.

all capital earnings rate   The financial ratio that results from adding the net income of the company to the minority share of after-tax income and the interest charges net of tax effects, and dividing the sum by the average total assets during the accounting period. The ratio is used to summarize the operations of the company for an accounting period (generally one year).

allied products or lines   Related types of merchandise in the same usage category. These items are often grouped together on the same selling floor or in the same section of the store for the convenience of customers and for increased sales through association and suggestion. See also COMPLEMENTARY PRODUCTS/GOODS and ACCESSORIES.

allocated expense   Any expenditure that benefits the entire store but is divided among departments on the basis of time, space, or capital requirements. For example, total store rent may be allocated to each department on the basis of the square footage it occupies.

allocating skills   The techniques used by marketing managers to budget time, money, and personnel for the firm's functions, policies, or programs. For example, an effective marketing manager must be able to decide how much money to spend on trade shows, how to distribute sales personnel to various geographic regions, etc. See also MONITORING SKILLS, ORGANIZING SKILLS, and INTERACTING SKILLS.

allocation   The process by which large, homogeneous inventories are broken down into smaller lots as the goods get closer to the final market. Allocation may involve several levels of MARKETING INTERMEDIARY, each handling increasingly smaller quantities. Retailers complete the process by selling individual items to the individual consumer. Allocation helps to alleviate the DISCREPANCY OF QUANTITY. Also called *break bulk, breaking bulk, bulk-breaking, sorting out,* and *dispersion.*

allocation analyst   The individual in a large retail organization responsible for analyzing sales trends, making crucial distribution decisions, and acting as a liaison between the distribution centers and buyers. Reports to the SENIOR ALLOCATION ANALYST.

allocation of space   See SPACE ALLOCATION.

allocation process   See ALLOCATION.

allocators   Allocators work as liaisons between the merchandising and distribution divisions of a retail organization by providing detailed distribution information. In a chain store or other multiple-unit organization, allocators ensure that each store has the appropriate assortment of merchandise, monitor stock levels in order to advise buyers about rates of sale, monitor local needs and competitors' activities, and communicate merchandise information to the individual stores. Allocators are often officially part of the distribution division, but they work closely with the buying team to ensure a smooth flow of merchandise. See also DISTRIBUTOR.

all-one-can-afford approach (to promotional budgeting)   See ALL-YOU-CAN-AFFORD APPROACH.

allowance   A reduction from list or invoice price made by the manufacturer, wholesaler, or retailer in return for the performance of certain services or activities on the part of the customer or to compensate the customer for some other reason. For example, ADVERTISING and promotional allowances compensate wholesalers and retailers for the expenses incurred in promoting a product locally. Cost allowances compensate the customer for such problems as goods delivered late or damaged. Trade-in allowances compensate the customer for old equipment turned in when new equipment is purchased. Also called a *reduced rate.* See also DISCOUNT, a similar form of price reduction.

allowance for bad debts   Monthly credit entries made as a contra to accounts receivable. Shows the estimated amount of accounts receivable that will not be collected. Also called *allowance for doubtful accounts* and *allowance for uncollectibles.*

allowance for depreciation   In accounting, an account showing the accumulated DEPRECIATION taken and used to establish the net valuation of the assets of the organization.

allowance for doubtful accounts   See ALLOWANCE FOR BAD DEBTS.

allowance for uncollectibles   See ALLOWANCE FOR BAD DEBTS.

allowance from vendor See RETURNS AND ALLOWANCES FROM SUPPLIERS.

allowance to customers See RETURNS AND ALLOWANCES TO CUSTOMERS.

all-purpose revolving account/credit Synonym for REVOLVING CREDIT.

all rail (AR) A shipping term indicating that the entire shipment is being sent by railroad.

all the traffic will bear See PROFIT MAXIMIZATION OBJECTIVE.

all-you-can-afford approach A method of developing a promotional budget in which all nonpromotional marketing expenses are budgeted first and remaining funds are allocated to promotional purposes. See also PROMOTIONAL BUDGETING.

alphanumeric In computer terminology, consisting of a combination of letters, numbers, and other special symbols that are machine-processable.

alteration cost/expense The expense involved in modifying garments to fit the needs of individual customers. Includes labor, supplies, and other expenses.

alteration room A nonselling department in which tailors and other workers modify garments to meet the needs of specific customers and make repairs to items damaged in stock.

alterations Modifications made in standard-sized garments to provide a better fit for an individual customer. Also called *clothing alterations.*

altruistic display 1. In VISUAL MERCHANDISING, a method of displaying items for charitable organizations and the like. For example, a food or other retailer may display materials promoting philanthropic donations such as food drives. Stores may devote floor or window space to promoting these causes despite the fact that the causes bear no direct relation to the store's own merchandise. 2. An in-store or store window display featuring a storewide selection of seasonal items without reference to a particular brand or product.

altruists In the *Roger Starch Worldwide* study, altruists are outer-focused individuals interested in social issues and causes. They tend to be well-educated females and represent 18 percent of the total adult consumer population.

ambiance The pervading mood or environment that characterizes a store. Ambiance is developed by tangible and intangible store design tools to create a store image and attract customers. It includes the choice of decor and color schemes, lighting, sound (such as background music), and aroma (such as fragrances in the air). Ambiance helps convey to the consumer whether a store is high-end or low-end, traditional or

cutting-edge. Ambiance plays a similar role in the design of an e-tailer's Web site. Also spelled *ambience.*

American FactFinder See CENSUS OF THE POPULATION.

American Housing Survey (AHS) A survey conducted by the U.S. Bureau of the Census for the Department of Housing and Urban Development (HUD). The AHS collects data on apartments, single-family homes, mobile homes, vacant housing units, household characteristics, income, housing and neighborhood quality, housing costs, equipment and fuels, size of the housing unit, and recent movers. The AHS is available online at www.census.gov. See also METROPOLITAN AREA (MA).

American Standard Code for Information Interchange (ASCII) See ASCII.

American Stock Exchange (AMEX) See STOCK EXCHANGE.

Americans with Disabilities Act (ADA) A law of Congress enacted on July 26, 1990, prohibiting discrimination and ensuring equal opportunity for persons with disabilities in employment, state and local government service, public accommodations, commercial facilities, and transportation. It also mandated the establishment of TDD/telephone relay services. ADA regulations have been amended over the years to elucidate the prohibition of discrimination on the basis of disability. Information about the ADA regulations as well as technical assistance materials may be found on the Web site of the U.S. Department of Justice at www.usdoj-gov.crt/ada.

American Universal Product Code See UNIVERSAL PRODUCT CODE (UPC).

AmericasMart–Atlanta A MARKET CENTER in Atlanta, Georgia, that includes the ATLANTA APPAREL MART, the ATLANTA GIFT MART, and the ATLANTA MERCHANDISE MART. The market center consists of three buildings totaling 4.2 million square feet of exhibit space. The buildings, connected via aerial walkways, house permanent showroom space, exhibit halls, and convention and meeting room space. Exhibited categories include apparel, gifts, home furnishings, and a wide variety of other consumer goods. The center maintains a Web site at www.AmericasMart.com.

AMEX (American Stock Exchange) See STOCK EXCHANGE.

amortization The writing off of the cost of an asset over a period of years.

AMS See ANALYTICAL MARKETING SYSTEM (AMS).

analog method A geographical information system (GIS) used in RETAIL SITE LOCATION to forecast sales by comparing potential sites to existing sites. As the word *analog* suggests, the method seeks to make an *analogy* between existing stores and the potential new site to determine the new site's feasibility. Marketing analysts first identify a store or sample group of stores similar to the proposed store in terms of store characteristics, target market, customer shopping patterns, demographic and psychographic customer characteristics, and the level of competition within the trading area. Next, the analysts plot customers' home addresses on a map to determine how many sales dollars the existing store or group of sample stores draws from each point. Taken in aggregate, the data show the source of the existing store's total sales volume. The level of market penetration or per capita sales achieved by the store or stores is used as the basis for forecasting sales at the new site. By indicating a percentage of those sales dollars (typically 70 percent), the analysis establishes the store's TRADING AREA. Several software packages are available for this type of analysis.

analysis of accounts   See AGING ACCOUNTS RECEIVABLE.

analysis of causal relationships   See CAUSAL RESEARCH.

analytical competence   The ability to pull together a vast array of information and data and to assemble relevant facts necessary for success in the global marketplace.

analytical CRM   Synonym for ELECTRONIC CUSTOMER RELATIONSHIP MANAGEMENT (E-CRM).

analytical marketing system (AMS)   One of four subsystems of a company's MARKETING INFORMATION SYSTEM (MIS), which consists of a statistical bank and a model bank for analyzing marketing data and solving marketing problems. The statistical bank is essentially a collection of statistical procedures or routines that may be used to extract meaningful information from data. The model bank is a collection of models used by marketers to make marketing decisions, and includes models for new product sales forecasting, site selection, sales-call planning, media mix, and marketing-mix budgeting. Also called *scientific marketing*. See also MARKETING SYSTEM.

analytical pricing   See MARGINAL ANALYSIS.

anchor   An underlying belief or rule of thumb by which consumers evaluate the information they receive from an advertisement or other communication. For example, consumers may believe that higher-priced items are inherently better. Such thinking serves as the basis for their decision making and purchasing behavior. See also ANCHOR STORE.

anchoring   In Faith Popcorn's lifestyle and social trend reports, a lifestyle choice in which the consumer is seeking greater spirituality. Such customers are considered a prime market for items such as angel paraphernalia, aromatherapy supplies, psychic seminars, and meditation tools.

anchorless mall   A shopping center containing small specialty stores but no large department stores. See also ANCHOR STORE.

anchor store   In a SHOPPING CENTER or mall, a large store that provides the attraction needed to draw large numbers of customers to the shopping center. Anchor stores are major tenants, generally occupying large corner or end sites; they are

often national or regional chain stores or large department stores. Also called a *generator store* or a *major tenant*.

ancillary customer service   Any customer service provided by a retailer for the convenience of the customer, though not related to sales. Ancillary customer services include the ACCOMMODATION SERVICES as well as credit, check cashing, restaurants, repairs, interior decoration, etc.

angel   (Slang) In retailing and in theater, a person who invests capital in a business venture while assuming no management role.

angled front window   A display window that is part of a recessed entrance to a store and provides additional display space. Large display windows make up one or both sides of the storefront, thus creating an aisle through which the customer walks to the door. The display windows may be on an angle or parallel to the back wall of the display space.

animated graphics   See ANIMATION.

animation   Streaming video, flash animation, video clips, and other forms of moving images that may be incorporated into Web sites.

anniversary sale/celebration   A storewide promotional event held to celebrate the anniversary of the store's founding. Anniversary sales are generally held in mid-autumn and mid-spring, regardless of the actual date of the store's founding, and serve to call attention to the store's longevity in the community. Also called *birthday sale*. See also INSTITUTIONAL EVENT.

annual marketing plan   See MARKETING PLAN.

annual merchandise plan   See MERCHANDISE PLAN.

annual report of merchandising statistics   A yearly compilation of merchandising statistics by department, which may be prepared by a RESIDENT BUYING OFFICE for its member stores. The report features comparative percentages for markdowns and gross margin (comparing the current year to the previous year), employee discounts for the current year, shortages, and cash discount percentages. The report also includes turnover and an aged inventory indicator, the percentage of inventory over six months old, as well as the par (i.e., the middle number of the best half of the statistics when ranked from worst to best) and median (i.e., the middle number when the statistics are ranked from worst to best) for each group of figures reported.

annuity   A series of payments, usually made at equally spaced intervals for a fixed or contingent time period.

anonymizer   See TAG ANONYMIZER.

ANSI ASC X12   See VOLUNTARY INTERINDUSTRY COMMERCE STANDARDS (VICS-EDI).

anticipation   A discount added to the cash discount for payment in advance of the cash discount date.

anticipation dating   An invoice dating agreement stipulating that an additional discount is added to the cash discount for payment in advance.

anticipation of demand   The efforts of retailers and other marketers to predict, develop, and introduce products and services that will be required by customers before there is any actual demand or before the selling season. Retailers and marketers do extensive consumer research on a regular basis in order to make the requisite predictions and preparations. For example, retailers will want to anticipate the swimsuit preferences of their customers before the summer season and the most desirable children's toys before the start of the holiday selling season.

antidumping   See DUMPING and ANTIDUMPING TARIFF.

antidumping tariff   A tax levied against imported goods that are being dumped (sold at prices below those in the home market) on the domestic market. See also DUMPING and COUNTERVAILING DUTY.

Antimerger Act (1950)   See CELLER-KEFAUVER ANTIMERGER ACT (1950).

antiquated   Out-of-date, obsolete, and no longer used. For example, in the age of the computer, both software and hardware become antiquated in a relatively short period of time due to rapid technological advances in the industry.

AOG   See ARRIVAL OF GOODS (AOG).

A-1 condition   Best or first-class condition.

apathetic shopper   An indifferent consumer who shops only out of necessity, wants to finish shopping as quickly as possible, and values convenience. Compare PERSONALIZING SHOPPER, ECONOMICAL SHOPPER, and ETHICAL SHOPPER.

apothecary   A pharmacy or pharmacist.

apparel   Clothing or garments. Includes all categories of clothing from intimate apparel to outerwear for men, women, teens, and children. Synonymous with *attire, clothes, clothing, costume, dress, garb, garment,* etc.

apparel contractor   An independent manufacturing firm that agrees to construct apparel for another apparel manufacturer or directly for a retailer. The contractor is engaged in sewing and sometimes cutting the garments. Also called, in industry slang, an *outside shop.*

apparel designer   An individual who creates original clothing and accessories for the fashion industry. Fashion or apparel designers create ideas for new styles of clothing and accessories. Some own their own businesses while others are employed by manufacturers. Also called *fashion designer.* See also COUTURIER (COUTURIÈRE).

apparel firm   A business involved in the manufacture and/or distribution of apparel. Apparel firms are frequently multi-functional and sometimes vertically integrated. The five essential components of the apparel firm are executive management, merchandising, marketing, operations, and finance.

apparel industry   The aggregate of manufacturers, jobbers, and contractors engaged in the manufacture of ready-to-wear clothing for men, women, and children. Also known as the *garment trade,* the *needle trades,* the *rag trade* (slang) and the *rag business* (slang).

apparel jobber   An agent in the apparel industry that sells closeouts and job lots to retailers or carries inventories of apparel immediately available for shipment to retailers. The JOBBER does not ordinarily sell merchandise directly to the consumer. See also WHOLESALER.

apparel price ranges   A continuum of price points used in the apparel industry. From highest- to lowest-priced, these ranges are designated DESIGNER LINE, BRIDGE LINE, BETTER LINE, MODERATE LINE, BUDGET LINE, and LOW-END MERCHANDISE.

Apparel Retail Model (ARM)   A computer simulation of the merchandising process. ARM performs rapid cost/benefit analyses of specific assortment situations and allows the user to plan a merchandise assortment, a pricing strategy, and a delivery strategy.

apparel sourcing   See SOURCING.

appeal   See ADVERTISING APPEAL.

applets   Small application programs written in Java script and embedded in Web pages. Applets allow for such added functionality as text scrolling, animated graphics, calculators, and other customized functions attractive to both e-tailers and online shoppers. Applets download quickly and require little bandwidth.

applied behavioral analysis   See BEHAVIORAL ENGINEERING.

applied research   The use of scientific methods to solve a problem. Applied research generally has practical applications and fulfills immediate needs. For example, apparel manufacturers use applied research methods to test sewn products to determine which is likely to fail first: the fabric or the stitched seam. Compare PURE RESEARCH.

appraiser   An individual or firm in the business of determining the monetary worth of a piece of property. For example, appraisers are employed in the jewelry business, the real estate business, and the collectibles business.

approach   Short for SALES APPROACH.

approval sale   Merchandise sent to a customer for inspection and acceptance without obligation to purchase. The customer is not billed until the expiration of a predetermined time period during which the merchandise may be returned without incurring a charge. While the merchandise is in this transitional state, it is said to be *on approval.*

apron   See INVOICE APRON.

AR   See ALL RAIL (AR) or AUTOMATIC REPLENISHMENT (AR).

A/R   See AS READY.

arbitrary allocation   See ARBITRARY APPROACH.

arbitrary approach   A method of allocating a firm's promotional budget in which the amount spent on promotion for a particular time period is the result of an executive decision rather than scientific analysis. Also know as *arbitrary allocation*. See also PROMOTIONAL BUDGETING.

arbitration   In negotiations, the process by which both parties to a dispute agree to submit the dispute to a third party for a binding decision. Compare MEDIATION. See also ARBITRATOR.

arbitrator   An individual empowered to decide a dispute or settle differences such as contract terms involving labor and management. Compare MEDIATOR. See also ARBITRATION.

arcade front window   A storefront consisting of a series of windows with backs and three sides of glass. The windows protrude forward from the entrance wall, which is set back from the street, and are usually under some kind of overhead cover. The shopper enters the store between the protruding display windows.

arcade shopping center   A planned shopping center with a walkway sheltering customers and weather-protecting storefronts. The walkway, or *colonnaded walk*, may be open, or glass-enclosed and air-conditioned. Sometimes referred to simply as an *arcade*.

arcade storefront   See ARCADE FRONT WINDOW.

arc of fashion   See FASHION LIFE CYCLE.

area   See SELLING AREA.

area sample   A stratified research sample selected on the basis of geography rather than demographics or other population characteristics. Geographic areas (such as city blocks) serve as the segments or primary units. See also AREA SAMPLING.

area sampling   In marketing and other social sciences research, a method of PROBABILITY SAMPLING in which a STRATIFIED (RANDOM) SAMPLE is selected on the basis of geography rather than by demographics or other population characteristics. Geographic areas (such as city blocks) serve as the segments or primary units. The researcher divides the population first by mutually exclusive geographic areas and then draws a sample of the groups to interview. This method of obtaining a random sample is most useful when population lists are unavailable. Also called *cluster sampling*.

ARM   See APPAREL RETAIL MODEL (ARM).

arm's length policy   A practice in transfer pricing in which the home or parent company charges foreign subsidiaries the same price it charges firms who are not part of the organization.

army/navy store   See SURPLUS STORE.

arrears   Money owed. An account is said to be *in arrears* when payment is overdue.

arrival of goods (AOG)   An invoice dating agreement stipulating that a cash discount is granted if payment is made within a specified number of days after the goods are received by the retailer. This method is used primarily to accommodate distant customers; the cash discount is based on when the goods are received rather than when the goods were shipped.

art   In ADVERTISING, the illustration appearing in an advertisement (e.g., photographs, drawings, charts, graphs) as well as the layout of the visual components of the ad. In an ADVERTISING AGENCY, art is the responsibility of the creative department.

articles of partnership   A legal document that covers all items agreed upon by the partners in a business, signed by each partner. See also PARTNER and PARTNERSHIP.

articulated artist's figure   In visual merchandising displays, a life-sized figure constituting a possible alternative to a traditional MANNEQUIN. It is modeled on the small wooden figures used by artists and designers, with movable joints that allow it to be posed in multiple positions, sitting or standing. Articulated artist's figures also have the advantage of being abstractions. As such, they are gender-, age-, and ethnicity-neutral. Articulated artist's figures may be fully or partially dressed (as in displays of accessories) without appearing to be underdressed.

artificial obsolescence   The replacement of a firm's own product by its new and updated version of that product. The changed or updated version renders the old version outmoded, a fact reflected in the old product's decline in MARKET SHARE. Manufacturers may prefer to lose the original product's market share to their own new products rather than to those of the competition.

artificial trading area   The geographic area specified by a retail store as the territory in which it will conduct its business. The TRADING AREA has clearly defined boundaries, regardless of the fact that some of the store's customers may come from outside the specified area.

artwork   See ART.

Asch phenomenon   A consumer purchasing phenomenon named after a study conducted by E.E. Asch (published in 1958) in which he demonstrated the influence of groups upon individual choice. He found that if individuals can determine the expectations of the group to which they belong, they tend to adhere to those expectations in making purchase decisions.

ASCII   Acronym for the *American Standard Code for Information Interchange*. ASCII is a code for representing characters (i.e., letters and other symbols) as numbers, with each character assigned a number from 0 to 127. Uppercase letters have separate ASCII codes from lowercase letters; for example, uppercase M is 77. Most computers use ASCII codes to represent text, making it possible to transfer data from one computer to another. Text files stored in ASCII format are sometimes called ASCII files.

ASCII files   See ASCII.

aseptic packaging   A container for perishable foods that allows the product to be packaged in an air-free environment and sealed with an airtight seal, extending the product's shelf life without refrigeration.

as is   Of merchandise, in less than perfect condition and offered to the customer as a final sale, without the customary return or adjustment privileges. These goods are generally shopworn, damaged, or irregular, and are sold at a reduced price. See also DAMAGE MARKDOWN.

asking/asked price   The price officially requested by a seller for a product offered for sale. It represents the value the seller places on the product.

ASN   See ADVANCE SHIPPING NOTICE (ASN).

aspirational group   Any group to which an individual would like to belong (such as a little leaguer wishing to become a professional baseball player). For retail marketing, the implication is that the desire to emulate the chosen group influences consumer buying decisions. The little leaguer will want to eat the "breakfast of champions," the medical student will aspire to a Mercedes, the secretary seeking promotion to a management position will "dress for success," etc. Sometimes called the *aspiratory group*. See also MEMBERSHIP GROUP, DISSOCIATIVE GROUP, and REFERENCE GROUP.

aspirational wants   Products and services that people believe will help them achieve higher status. Aspirational wants are closely tied to an individual's ideal self, the self a person hopes to eventually become. Luxury goods, for example, serve as aspirational wants for a large portion of the consumer population, as does home ownership. See also MOTIVE.

aspiratory group   Synonym for ASPIRATIONAL GROUP.

ASR   See AUTOMATED STORAGE AND RETRIEVAL (ASR).

as ready   A term used by manufacturers to indicate that merchandise ordered by a retailer will be shipped as it is completed at the factory. No firm delivery date is promised.

assembler   See ASSEMBLING.

assembling   The process of developing an inventory of homogeneous products, such as agricultural produce, from the small lots of a number of small producers so that they may be handled economically further along the supply chain. Goods so accumulated may be shipped and sold in larger lots and thus benefit from such factors as lower shipping rates (in carload or truckload quantities). Goods are brought to collection points by the individual small producers and collected by an agent intermediary known as an *assembler*. Assemblers seldom take title to the goods they handle. Also called *accumulating, accumulating bulk, assembly,* and *concentration*. See also MAKING BULK.

assembly   Synonym for ASSEMBLING.

assembly line   In manufacturing, the systematic arrangement of machines, tools, and workers to facilitate the sequential assembly of a product. Assembly lines are characteristically arranged so that each worker continuously repeats the same task in the overall sequence. Assembly line production became widespread in factories in the early twentieth century. Many of the tasks formerly performed by human assembly line workers are now performed by robots. Also called a *production line.*

asset   1. According to the Financial Accounting Standards Board, a "probable future economic benefit obtained or controlled by a particular entity as a result of a past transaction or event" (1985).   2. In retailing, any such benefit whether tangible, such as merchandise and buildings, or intangible, such as goodwill. Assets are classified according to their LIQUIDITY, or the likelihood of their conversion to cash. Frequently used in the plural (i.e., *assets*). See also FIXED ASSET, TANGIBLE ASSET, and QUICK ASSETS.

asset conversion   A means of internally financing a firm's projects by liquidating one form of asset to employ elsewhere within the firm or repay a liability. For example, a company may sell one of its buildings to raise cash for repaying creditors or for opening a new building at a more desirable location.

asset protection   Synonym for LOSS PREVENTION (LP).

assets   See ASSET.

asset turnover ratio   A financial ratio that serves as an indicator of the efficiency of a firm's investment in assets and a means of examining the company's operations over a period of time. It is calculated by dividing the company's net sales for the accounting period by its average total assets during the same period.

assigned mailing date   In DIRECT MARKETING, the date on which a list user must mail a particular purchased list by virtue of a prior agreement between the list owner and the user. The user may not mail that list on any other date except with the specific authorization of the list owner.

assignment   1. The transfer of a claim, right, property, etc. 2. The legal paper authorizing this transfer.

assignment of accounts receivable   The transfer of the legal ownership of ACCOUNTS RECEIVABLE through their sale.

assist In SOURCING, an item or service (e.g., rivets or buttons) supplied free of charge or at a reduced cost to a contractor.

assistant buyer A buyer-in-training position involving exposure to all phases of the buyer's responsibilities, including managing the department budget, selecting and promoting merchandise, reordering merchandise, following up on orders placed, analyzing stock and sales reports, supervising sales and stock personnel, interacting with shoppers, and summarizing information for the BUYER. In large retail organizations, buyers may have several assistant buyers.

assistant planner The individual in a large retail organization responsible for creating and implementing seasonal merchandising plans, assessing developmental needs, and training analysts and senior analysts in the development of distribution strategies. Reports to the PLANNER.

assistant store manager of merchandising Synonymous with STORE MERCHANDISE MANAGER.

associate buyer Reporting to the store's BUYER, an associate buyer is an executive in training for a buyer's position. The associate buyer learns to make buying decisions and identify strategies for buying trips. He or she also acquires experience in traveling to vendor sites and in developing negotiating skills.

associated buying office A resident buying office controlled and financed cooperatively by a group of noncompeting, independent stores. The associated buying office performs a buying function for the member stores in a central market, with each store contributing a prorated share of expenses. The associated buying office makes possible the exchange of information among member stores and provides increased buying power for each member store. Managers of foreign-based associated buying offices make numerous visits to the stores they represent to determine the needs of individual stores and provide a wide assortment of samples for inspection by the various buyers. Also called *cooperative office, cooperative buying office, cooperative resident buying office, cooperatively owned resident buying office,* or simply, *associated office.* See also COMPANY-OWNED BUYING OFFICE.

associated independent A member store in the cooperative ownership of a merchandise-buying organization. The store is, aside from this affiliation, self-managed, self-owned, and largely self-merchandised.

associated office See ASSOCIATED BUYING OFFICE.

association See TRADE ASSOCIATION.

association advertising A form of HORIZONTAL COOPERATIVE ADVERTISING performed by trade associations (such as the Florida Citrus Growers) to promote primary demand for a class of products (such as Florida oranges). Distinct from ASSOCIATION ADVERTISING FORMAT.

association advertising format A type of ADVERTISEMENT that conveys its message by establishing a relationship in the consumer's mind between an event, an activity, or an image and the product being promoted. For example, an ad using this format might seek to transfer the excitement generated by skydiving to a product such as beer by featuring a skydiver in an ad for beer. Distinct from ASSOCIATION ADVERTISING.

assorting The process of developing a heterogeneous inventory of products for the convenience of customers. This function is usually performed by wholesalers or retailers in order to supply an assortment of products such as hardware, drugs, grocery items, etc. The convenience factor may motivate sellers to stock related items not directly associated with their principal line of goods. For example, a lawn mower dealer may sell grass seed and other related gardening items. See also SORTING PROCESS and GRADING.

assorting process See ASSORTING.

assortment The range of choice within a particular classification of goods, such as style, color, size, and price. Within a particular store, an assortment includes all the goods within the store defined in terms of breadth and depth of stock. The same concept, used by producers or vendors, is often called a *mix* or a *product mix.* See also SORTING PROCESS and PRODUCT MIX.

assortment advertisement An ADVERTISEMENT that features a range of merchandise from within a retail department, product division, or several unrelated departments. The ads emphasize the breadth of merchandise available in the store. Unrelated merchandise from a single vendor may be coordinated as a VENDOR ADVERTISEMENT.

assortment breadth A measure or description of the number of different categories or classifications available in a store or department without reference to the quantity available of any one style. An assortment is said to be *broad* when a large variety of different items is available within a classification. Also called *merchandise mix* and *breadth of assortment.* See also PRODUCT WIDTH.

assortment consistency The extent to which the various components of the merchandise assortment relate to one another, with particular emphasis on how they all relate to one another in the customer's mind. Also called *merchandise line consistency.*

assortment deep See ASSORTMENT DEPTH.

assortment depth A measure or description of the quantity of each item available in the assortment of goods offered to the customer. An assortment containing an item in great quantities and many sizes is said to be *deep.* An assortment containing only small quantities of an item is said to be *shallow.* Also called *merchandise line depth* and *product mix depth.* See also PRODUCT DEPTH.

assortment display A technique of VISUAL MERCHANDISING in which a sampling of all or most of the merchandise available in the store or department is exhibited, identified, and priced.

An example would be a shoe store window. Also called a *variety display*.

assortment diversity   The relationship between ASSORTMENT VOLUME and ASSORTMENT VARIETY; a combination of the total number of units in the assortment (i.e., assortment volume) and the number of stock keeping units (SKUs) in the same assortment (assortment variety). Assortment diversity is an alternative to assortment width and assortment depth as a way of looking at the composition and dimensions of assortments. Assortment diversity allows the assortment to be described in and of itself in quantifiable (i.e., measurable) terms.

assortment diversity index (ADI)   A predictor of the impact of the VOLUME PER SKU FOR THE ASSORTMENT (VSA). Assortments are characterized as fitting into one of six categories: very diverse (VSA of 2 or less), diverse (VSA of 2.01–5), transition (VSA of 5.01–10), focused (VSA of 10.01–20), very focused (VSA of 20.01–50), and unaffected (VSA of 50.01–100 with no impact on financial outcomes). See also ASSORTMENT DIVERSITY.

assortment error   The difference in distribution of assortment factors (e.g., style, size, and color) between planned and actual demand. For example, the retailer may find that the store has run out of size 6 yellow dresses but has too many size 22 red dresses left. The error can be reduced by reevaluating customer demand after evaluating POS feedback. See also VOLUME ERROR.

assortment plan   A projection of the variety and quantity of merchandise to be carried in a department to meet customer demand. Amounts may be expressed in terms of dollars or units. Assortment plans may be developed either through the BASIC STOCK LIST or by use of the MODEL STOCK PLAN/LIST/METHOD. See UNIT PLANNING.

assortment planning   See UNIT PLANNING.

assortment variety   The number of stock keeping units (SKUs) in the assortment. See also STOCK KEEPING UNIT (SKU).

assortment volume   The total number of units in the assortment.

assortment width   See ASSORTMENT BREADTH.

assumptive close   A sales close that takes place without the customer's verbal agreement. If the customer fails to protest the salesperson's preparation of the order or wrapping of the merchandise, the salesperson takes it for granted that the sale has been made.

asymmetrical balance   In the layout of a selling floor or visual DISPLAY, the positioning of items on either side of a center line so that the two sides are not equally weighted optically. Other design principles are relied upon to give the appearance of unity. Also called *informal balance*. Compare SYMMETRICAL BALANCE.

asymmetric encryption   Synonym for PUBLIC-KEY ENCRYPTION.

at best   In global marketing, an instruction accompanying a buying or selling order that indicates that it should be carried out quickly at the best possible price. Synonym for *at-the-market*.

atelier   A studio or workshop used by a COUTURIER (COUTURIÈRE) in the creation of fashion goods.

Atlanta Apparel Mart   A regional MERCHANDISE MART located in Atlanta, Georgia, and built in 1957. Its opening established the wholesale trade industry in the Southeast United States. The mart expanded to the present AMERICASMART–ATLANTA facility.

Atlanta Decorative Arts Center (ADAC)   A MERCHANDISE MART located in Atlanta, Georgia, and opened in 1961. It is a major center of residential and contract furnishings. Scores of wholesalers' showrooms offer top-name lines of furniture, fabrics, kitchen and bath products, lighting, accessories, and floor and wall coverings to design professionals and their clients. The mart maintains a Web site at www.adacdesigncenter.com.

Atlanta Gift Mart   A merchandise mart for gifts and decorative accessories located in Atlanta, Georgia, and part of AMERICASMART–ATLANTA.

Atlanta Merchandise Mart   A MERCHANDISE MART located in Atlanta, Georgia, and built in 1961 as the first phase of the AMERICASMART–ATLANTA market center.

ATM   See AUTOMATIC TELLER MACHINE (ATM).

atmosphere   See AMBIANCE.

atmospherics   The environmental factors in a retail store consciously designed to create a certain mood in customers. These factors include the store's architecture, layout, color scheme, and other sensory stimuli. Closely related to AMBIANCE. See also WEB SITE ATMOSPHERICS.

atomistic competition   A condition of the MARKETPLACE in which there are so many competitors that no one seller can influence the price of the product or commodity they all produce. This condition exists in farm commodity production and in the women's ready-to-wear industry.

ATR   See AWARENESS-TRIAL-REPEAT (ATR).

attachment   A file accompanying an e-mail message. The file may be a text file, a binary file, or a formatted text file (such as an MS Word document).

at-the-market   See AT BEST.

at-the-market price   See MARKET PRICE.

at-the-market pricing   See PRICING AT THE MARKET.

attire   Synonym for APPAREL.

attitude   A person's knowledge and positive or negative evaluations about an object such as a product or service. Attitudes are learned, enduring, and made up of three components: knowledge, affect, and action tendency. *Knowledge*, the cognitive component of attitude, is usually expressed as a belief. For example, "I believe whole grain breads are nutritionally superior to white bread." The consumer's feeling toward the product is called *affect*, or the *affective component*. For example, "I prefer whole grain bread to white bread." The action tendency, or behavioral component, is the consumer's readiness to act on those beliefs and feelings. For example, "I will buy whole grain bread on my next shopping trip." The more favorable a consumer's attitude toward a product or service, the more likely the consumer is to use and purchase the product or service. Retailers and other marketers are interested in changing negative attitudes as well as reinforcing the positive attitudes of satisfied customers. The enduring aspect of attitude enables consumers to behave in a fairly consistent way toward similar objects without having to interpret and react to every object in a fresh way.

attitude scale   A measurement tool used to determine the intensity of a subject's feelings toward a product, service, or other object. Participants respond to a series of adjectives, phrases, or sentences about the product by checking whether they "strongly agree, agree, have no opinion, disagree, or strongly disagree" with each statement on a Likert-type scale. Researchers then tally the answers to get an indication of the strength of consumer opinions.

attitudes, interests, and opinions (AIO)   Inventory See AIO INVENTORY.

attribute   See ATTRIBUTE-BASED SHOPPING PRODUCT and PRODUCT ATTRIBUTE.

attribute-based shopping product   Any product or service about which consumers accumulate information about features, warranties, performance ratings, options, and competitive products before making their purchase decisions. See also PRODUCT ATTRIBUTE.

attribute mapping   In new product planning, a statistical means of analyzing a market in an effort to find openings for new products. Existing products are positioned on a chart called an *attribute space* with each position being determined by the products' characteristics. Open spaces indicate gaps into which new products may be introduced. Also known as *market position analysis*.

attribute space   See ATTRIBUTE MAPPING.

attrition   A reduction in the number of employees in an organization due to resignations, retirements, or deaths.

auction   A public sale in which goods are sold to the highest bidder. Traditionally, auctions have not been a big factor in balancing supply and demand or in consumer purchasing. They have been a factor in agriculture, other commodity markets, fine art, and antiques. However, with the advent of the ONLINE AUCTION millions of Internet users participate in bidding on a wide array of objects. At times, live auctions taking place in real time are broadcast on electronic auction sites such as e-Bay, with remote participants competing electronically with bidders at the auction house site. See also PRODUCT-SPECIFIC AUCTION and DUTCH AUCTION, a reversal of the normal process.

auction bot   An Internet tool that helps the user retrieve current information on items of interest on auction sites. Auction bots eliminate the need for users to browse multiple sites and help them keep track of the items on which they are currently bidding.

auction company   See AUCTION HOUSE.

auctioneer   A person involved in selling things at AUCTION.

auction fraud   An example of online fraud. It includes nondelivery of goods, misrepresentation of goods auctioned, fee stacking (adding hidden charges post sale), and various bidding misrepresentations (such as shilling and cross-bidding to drive up online auction prices, price fixing and signaling). The Internet Fraud Complaint Center (IFCC) handles consumer complaints about online auction fraud.

auction house   An AGENT INTERMEDIARY selling by the AUCTION method, commonly employed in the sale of agricultural products, such as fruit, tobacco, livestock, etc. Customers may examine the product before engaging in competitive bidding for its purchase. The auction company receives a commission from the seller of the merchandise based on the final sales price and does not take title to the goods. Also known as an *auction company*.

audience   1. The total number of individuals reached by an ADVERTISEMENT or other promotion, for example, the number of viewers seeing a particular television commercial or seeing a particular print advertisement in a magazine or newspaper. 2. The target group or population segment at which a promotional message is aimed, such as yuppies. Also called *target audience* and *advertising target*.

audience comp/composite/composition   See AUDIENCE PROFILE.

audience profile   The characteristics of the audience reached by an advertising medium (print or broadcast) or a particular station, newspaper, or magazine, etc. It includes both demographic and psychographic characteristics. Generally presented as a percentage figure that may be compared to the population as a whole. Also called *audience comp, audience composite, audience composition*, or *profile*.

audience share   The percentage of the total listening or viewing audience (i.e., those with their radios or televisions actually turned on) tuned to a particular program at a specific time. Also called *share* or *share of audience*.

audience study   Survey research aimed at learning who the audience is for an advertising medium and how that audience reacts to the advertising message.

audio/video server   See SERVER.

audit   1. An examination of accounting records and of the evidence in support of their correctness. Auditing procedures are also applied to a systematic examination of the retailer's MARKETING PLAN.   2. In SOURCING, a systematic examination of the quality and/or quantity capabilities of the contractor, according to preestablished guidelines.

audited net sales   The total amount of sales for a specific period of time, calculated after returns and allowances have been deducted and verified by the auditing department of a store. The sales are credited to the book inventory of each department.

audited sales   See AUDIT OF CASH SALES.

audit form   A report or letter prepared by an auditor, addressed to the management of the organization, expressing the auditor's opinion regarding the propriety of financial statements.

auditing   The process of examining the financial data of a retail firm or other business enterprise.

auditing department   A department in the control division of a retail organization responsible for proving the accuracy of transactions in the accounting records. The department also supervises the sales audit, the charge audit, and the COD audit. See also AUDIT.

audit (marketing)   See MARKETING AUDIT.

audit of cash sales   The reconciliation of sales recorded on the cash register with cash on hand, charge sales totals, and returns, noted for a given accounting period.

auditor   An accounting professional who conducts an independent examination of the accounting data presented by a retailer or other business enterprise. The auditor determines whether the firm's financial statements present the financial position, results of operations, and cash flows fairly in accordance with generally accepted accounting principles. If satisfied, the auditor issues an unqualified opinion (also called a *clean opinion*). If not, the auditor adds an explanatory paragraph to the audit reports specifying uncertainties, lack of consistency, and emphasis of a matter. If not satisfied that the requirements have been met, the auditor may elect to issue a qualified opinion, an adverse opinion, or a disclaimer of an opinion.

augmented product   The CORE PRODUCT together with its attendant benefits and services, particularly those benefits and services not expected by the consumer and that may exceed the consumer's expectations.

authority   The power or right to give orders or commands, take actions, make decisions, and to expect obedience. See also MARKET DIVISION OF AUTHORITY.

authority and responsibility   A management concept asserting that the employee assigned the responsibility for performing a task should also be given the authority to carry out the requirements of that task. According to this theory, decisions should be made by the lowest possible level of employee capable of making that decision, and the entire decision making process should be delegated to subordinates whenever possible. Authority and responsibility is designed to develop the abilities of subordinates and to free the store manager for overall supervision. When applied to department managers, any authority not specifically denied becomes the authority of the department manager under the supervision of the store manager. Also called the *theory of authority and responsibility* and the *principle of authority and responsibility*.

authorization line   The maximum amount of money that a customer may charge to a credit card without receiving specific authorization for the purchase by the company issuing the card. Similar to FLOOR LIMIT in which authorization comes from the credit department.

authorized dealer   A retailer who has, by agreement with a manufacturer, the rights to the distribution of a product or line of products. The arrangement is similar though not identical to the relationship in FRANCHISING.

authorized dealership   See AUTHORIZED DEALER and PRODUCT FRANCHISE.

authorizing   The process of approving credit sales transactions when the amount of the sale exceeds the FLOOR LIMIT or when identification of the purchaser and the account is required.

autocratic leader   See LEADERSHIP STYLE.

automated markdown   See AUTOMATIC MARKDOWN (PLAN).

automated retailing/selling   See AUTOMATIC VENDING.

automated storage and retrieval (ASR)   A warehousing system that combines computerized control of stock records with the mechanical handling of merchandise. ASR offers better inventory control, savings in the cost of labor, and better customer service. See also AUTOMATED WAREHOUSE and RANDOM STORAGE.

automated warehouse   A warehouse controlled by a central computer and utilizing sophisticated electronic materials handling systems. Automated warehouses have gradually replaced older, less efficient warehouses and tend to be single-storied structures to facilitate materials handling. They tend to have a lower incidence of injury, pilferage, and breakage. Inventory control is also improved by the automated systems. See also AUTOMATED STORAGE AND RETRIEVAL (ASR) and RANDOM STORAGE.

automatic (bargain) basement   A downstairs or basement store where prices are successively reduced contingent upon the length of time the merchandise has remained in stock. "Automatic basement" is an innovation developed by Filene's of Boston, Massachusetts. See also BARGAIN BASEMENT.

automatic buying procedures   See AUTOMATIC REORDER.

automatic cancellation date   The latest acceptable shipping date as specified by the buyer on the purchase order. If goods are not shipped by that date, the order is canceled.

automatic markdown (plan)   Price reductions contingent upon a predetermined time schedule. The longer the merchandise remains on the selling floor, the deeper the markdown. At each predetermined time interval (e.g., each week), the price is further reduced by a predetermined percentage.

automatic markup   The application of uniform markup percentages to all merchandise.

automatic merchandising   See AUTOMATIC VENDING.

automatic open-to-buy   A form of central merchandising for multiunit organizations in which money for merchandise is allotted in part to the central buyer and in part to the individual store manager according to a predetermined formula. Under this plan, the store manager is given some control over reordering fast-selling merchandise already in stock and merchandise of special interest to the store's customers. New merchandise and popularly priced merchandise is selected by the central buying staff.

automatic ordering   See AUTOMATIC REORDER.

automatic reorder   The practice of monitoring supplies of staple merchandise and replenishing them only when they have been reduced to a predetermined minimum. At that minimum point a reorder procedure is activated. Also called *automatic ordering*.

automatic reordering system   A COMPUTERIZED QUICK RESPONSE SYSTEM generally used for basic merchandise. Weekly orders are generated based on sales in relation to a MODEL STOCK PLAN/LIST/METHOD (based on past sales and current trends). The use of computerized automatic reordering systems fosters the strengthening of partnerships between retailers and vendors, the placing of more frequent orders in smaller quantities, the placing of orders closer to the selling season, and the replenishment of basic merchandise based on actual sales, forecasts, and trends. See also AUTOMATIC REORDER.

automatic replenishment (AR)   A standing ORDER to restock supplies on a regular basis by prearrangement between buyer and seller. In Internet marketing, participants can change, add, delete, or cancel their standing order on the Web site at any time.

automatic selling   See AUTOMATIC VENDING.

automatic stabilizers   Those aspects of government participation in the marketplace (through both expenditures and taxation) that serve to counteract trends in economic activity without necessitating policy changes. Unemployment benefits, for example, prevent incomes from falling as fast as they normally would in a recession, thus helping to stabilize the economy.

automatic teller machine (ATM)   An electronic machine located in a bank or other establishment (such as a retail store) that allows customers to access cash from their savings accounts, checking accounts, and lines of credit, transfer money between accounts, check their balances and available cash, and make deposits without having to work through a human teller. ATMs allow 24/7 access to funds, reduce the number of employees needed in retail banking establishments, and tie into the banks' computerized information systems. Some banks and ATM operators charge customers a fee for using the ATM.

automatic vending   A form of nonstore, nonpersonal retailing of goods and services through self-service machines. Merchandise most commonly sold by this method includes candy, soft drinks, and hot beverages. Services provided by automatic vending machines include telephone calls via pay phones and banking services via automatic teller machines (ATMs). Also called *automatic merchandising, automatic selling, automated selling, automatic retailing,* and *vending machine retailing.*

automation   Any system or method in which many of the procedures are automatically performed or controlled by computers, robots, and other self-operating machinery. For example, automation in the automobile industry is characterized by the use of industrial robots in modern automobile manufacturing plants. AUTOMATED STORAGE AND RETRIEVAL (ASR) is an illustration of how automation is used in warehousing.

Automobile Information Disclosure Act (1958)   Federal consumer legislation that prohibited automobile dealers from inflating the factory prices of new cars.

autonomous operation   The treatment of branch stores on an equal basis with the downtown or flagship store. As branch stores grow larger and develop more autonomy in operation, they are often given more control of their own business.

autoresponder   In electronic marketing, a text file returned automatically via E-MAIL when requested by sending an e-mail message to a designated address. That address is set up for the purpose of automatically responding with another e-mail message. For example, a customer may receive a list of local stores carrying the desired merchandise by sending an e-mail message to a site's autoresponder address. Autoresponders are also used for customer service, marketing, and promotions. Also called an *infobot, mailbot,* or *e-mail on demand.*

auxiliary dimensions of a product   Features of a product, other than the product itself, that add to the product's attractiveness, usefulness, and consumer appeal. For example, packaging, warranties, repair services, and brand names are all examples of auxiliary dimensions of a product. They may influence the consumer to select it over other products or other brands of the same product.

auxiliary force   See CONTINGENT FORCE.

available market   The available market for a product or service consists of all the potential customers who can afford the product or service, who have access to it, and who have exhibited an interest in using or owning it.

avant-garde   New, ahead-of-its time, cutting edge. Often used to describe apparel design and other artistic creations that are extreme, unorthodox, or experimental.

avatar   In e-tailing, an animated graphic form that portrays a person. The avatar may be used on the Web site to entertain the potential customer or to assist with shopping. Some avatars are able to interact with customers and provide a more personalized shopping experience. Avatars can be conceived as online shopping companions, best friends, and fashion advisers. They serve to put a "human face" on the URL and may be thought of as the ultimate branding device. Avatars are products of specialized computer programs and may be voice-activated. An avatar traditionally is the incarnation of a Hindu god as an embodiment or personification of a principle, attitude, or philosophy of life.

average collection period of receivables   The financial ratio that results from dividing the number of days in one year (365) by the RECEIVABLES TURNOVER.

average cost   The total cost of doing business divided by the quantity of goods produced or sold.

average cost pricing   See COST-PLUS PRICING.

average daily balance method   A method used by retailers to calculate that portion of the balance in a charge account that will be assessed interest charges. In the average daily balance method, the customer's balance for each day of the billing period is added up and then divided by the number of days in the billing period. The resulting figure is used as a basis for computing the interest. See also ADJUSTED BALANCE METHOD and PREVIOUS BALANCE METHOD.

average fixed cost   The total fixed cost divided by the quantity of goods produced. A fixed cost is one that remains constant regardless of changes in sales volume.

average gross sales   The dollar amount of all sales divided by the number of transactions that produced those sales. This ratio is designed to give the retailer an approximate picture of the normal dollar figure per sale.

average inventory   See AVERAGE RETAIL STOCK.

average markon   The markon obtained when the costs and the retail prices of several items are combined and divided by the cost price.

average monthly sales   Total sales for a period (six months or one year) divided by the number of months in the period (6 or 12). While actual sales will vary from month to month, this method will provide the retailer with the usual sales for each month in the period. This number may be used to calculate the basic stock at retail.

average retail   The average price at which an item of merchandise will be sold. Since purchases may be made that have two or more costs, the buyer may want to manipulate markups to achieve the desired markup percentage.

average retail stock   In the retail method of inventory, the sum of the retail inventories at the beginning of each year, season, month, or week. This is added to the ending inventory and then divided by the number of inventories used. The resulting number represents the midpoint between the highest and lowest inventory levels for a given period. For example, to obtain an average retail stock figure for a year, the 12 stock inventories at the beginning of each month of that year are added to the ending inventory and the total sum is divided by 13. The method may also be used to calculate shorter time periods. See also RETAIL METHOD OF INVENTORY (VALUATION).

average revenue (line)   The total revenue (income generated by sales, etc.) divided by the quantity of goods required to produce that revenue. The average revenue line is the demand curve facing the firm.

average stock   See AVERAGE RETAIL STOCK.

average variable cost   The total variable cost divided by the quantity of goods produced. A variable cost is one that changes as sales volume changes (e.g., delivery costs).

averaging markups   The process of adjusting the proportions of goods purchased at different markups to achieve the desired aggregate markup, either for an individual item of merchandise or for a certain period of time. The markups are then averaged to determine the typical or usual amount of the markup. This helps the retailer realize the planned markup necessary for a profitable operation by allowing for deviations from the planned seasonal markup.

avoiding competition   See STATUS QUO PRICING.

awareness   The initial stage in the consumer adoption process during which the buyer becomes aware of the product but has gathered little information about it.

awareness of needs   See NEED AWARENESS.

awareness-trial-repeat (ATR)   A three-step explanation of the consumer adoption process in which the consumer progresses from being uninformed about the product or service to becoming a regular user. The consumer first becomes aware of the product or service's assets and availability (awareness), makes an initial purchase and tries the item or service (trial), and finally purchases the item or service again (repeat).

AWB   See AIRWAY BILL OF LADING (AWB).

awning   A shelter of canvas or other material extending over a doorway, window, deck, etc., to provide protection from the sun and rain. As a part of a store's exterior design, awnings provide shelter for the shopper during inclement weather and help cut down on glare on a sunny day. Awnings add color and eye appeal to the storefront; they may also become part of a seasonal DISPLAY or be used to announce storewide promotions.

B

baby boom See BABY BOOMERS.

baby boomers People born between 1946 and 1964, representing approximately 27 percent of the U.S. population (i.e., 76 million people). By virtue of their sheer numbers, baby boomers dominated consumer behavior discussions for two decades. As this age group ages, market segments are changing. See also ECHO BOOMERS, PIG IN A PYTHON, and the ME GENERATION.

baby-bust years The years between 1965 and 1976, which constituted a slow period of population growth in the United States. Individuals born during this period are now known as GENERATION X. They are also sometimes referred to as the *Sesame Street Generation*, having grown up with stronger media influences than previously experienced.

backbone The Internet's major transmission lines, handling its major electronic traffic flows.

backdoor selling 1. Practice by a wholesale establishment of selling to consumers while representing itself as a supplier to retailers only. 2. A salesperson's tactic of deliberately avoiding the purchasing department while calling on people in the department most likely to need the product or service.

backend In e-tailing, the functional technology that supports content and design. It enables navigation, product and information searching, order processing and fulfillment, dynamic content, data gathering, and databases (running shopping baskets, service centers, and other customer-centered operations). The Web site's INTERFACE seamlessly connects the backend to the FRONT END (also known as UPFRONT). Distinguished from BACK-END.

back-end 1. The fulfillment of a customer's ORDER by delivering and servicing the order. 2. Actions taken by the consumer after the initial order has been received, such as payment, cancellation, and renewal or reorder. *Back-end analysis* is the process by which the retailer or other seller studies the actions of the consumers. Distinguished from BACKEND.

back-end analysis See BACK-END.

backend construction The collection and management of data by an e-tailer's Web site. Backend construction typically includes establishing a dynamic database of customers and their purchases and data warehouses, which can then be entered and manipulated. It also includes maintaining, updating, and ensuring the security and integrity of the Web site. All of this takes place behind the scenes where it is invisible to the Web site's visitors.

back haul Reshipping freight over the route it just completed. This may occur when shipping foods to a customer located between the warehouse and the plant. Also spelled *backhaul*.

back haul allowance A price reduction given to customers who pick up their own merchandise at the manufacturer's or distributor's warehouse, thus saving the seller the cost of delivery.

backing activities Those store activities that do not involve direct contact with the customer. They may be carried out by salespeople or by employees expressly hired to perform the tasks.

backlog An accumulation of unfilled orders.

back of the window The rear of a DISPLAY WINDOW. In the traditional display window, the back extends from floor to ceiling and is usually fully constructed. Some stores use removable panels instead so that they can easily convert from a closed-back window to an open-back window, or so that they can convert the display space into selling space.

back order An order or part of an order to be shipped at a later date. If an item is listed as *back ordered* on an e-tail site, it generally indicates that an item is currently out of stock and that a new shipment is expected. Vendors SHORT-SHIP orders when they run out of the styles, colors, or sizes ordered by the retailer. For retail buyers, it means that the vendor has been unable to fill the order in the past and will do so as soon as possible.

back-to-school sale A promotional event held in the late summer and early fall, targeted at children and teenagers and their families preparing for the new school year. Items featured include apparel and footwear as well as school supplies. When college students are targeted, linens and other furnishings for dorm rooms may also be included.

backup merchandise Synonym for RESERVE STOCK.

backup order Merchandise retained by a manufacturer and available to a buyer for quick shipment in the event of subsequent need.

backup stock Synonym for RESERVE STOCK.

backward channel A marketing channel running backward from the consumer to the intermediary, and on occasion back to the manufacturer or producer. The recycling of aluminum cans, the return of empty soft drink bottles, and the collection of waste materials are examples of backward channel activities. Also referred to as *reverse distribution*.

backward integration The purchase or control by a retail firm of its supplier companies. For example, a large retail organization may own its own manufacturing facilities and operate its own distribution system.

backward invention A product planning strategy in international marketing by which firms doing business in developing countries modify their products to make them more usable and appealing in the absence of certain technologies. For example, water pumps ordinarily powered by electricity may be modified so that they are compatible with local power sources.

backward market segmentation Subdivision of a population into groups of potential customers on the basis of common behavior (e.g., the use of particular products or services or the viewing of particular television programs). The underlying assumption is that group members sharing common behaviors will also share attitudes and beliefs and will react uniformly to marketing programs.

backwoods chic An apparel trend reflecting outdoor living and characterized by flannel shirts, vests, and hiking boots. The appeal of backwoods chic is its rejection of the traditional corporate image and dress code. However, in some corporate environments (particularly computer firms headquartered in the Pacific Northwest), backwoods chic has become the apparel style of choice.

bad check A check returned by the bank on which it was drawn because of insufficient funds or other deficiency.

bad debt An uncollectible and hence worthless receivable (i.e., amount due). The account is open, but has been written off as an expense of the accounting period. Bad debt is usually expressed as a percentage of the revenue on account for the period. Also called *bad pay*. See also BAD DEBT ACCOUNT.

bad debt account The account to which losses from uncollectible debts are periodically charged. At the end of each accounting period estimates are generally made of the amount of current period revenue that will prove to be uncollectible. Such estimates are based on the experiences of past years, the current economic climate, the age of the receivables, and similar factors. See also ALLOWANCE FOR BAD DEBTS.

bad faith The intent to deceive or defraud another, as in a fraudulent business transaction.

bad pay Synonym for BAD DEBT.

bad pay list/file A list of customers with poor credit history, which may or may not be shared with advertisers and others. Such customers are removed from the list of customers slated to receive mailings and other promotions.

bad risk A person or organization whose credit record indicates a tendency not to meet financial obligations.

baffle Any device used to direct, divert, or disseminate light.

bag 1. n. A pouchlike container or receptacle made of pliant material (such as paper or plastic), capable of being closed at the mouth. Retailers often use distinctive bags in a variety of sizes (including the SHOPPING BAG) that help to identify the store. 2. v. To put merchandise into a bag (usually paper or plastic), particularly at a supermarket checkout counter.

bagel A round plastic marker that fits on hanger rods (thanks to a hole in its middle) and separates clothing sorted by size.

bagger A supermarket employee who packs groceries into bags or boxes at the checkout counter. Also called a *box boy* or *box girl*. See also BAG.

bailment lease A retail installment contract in which the merchandise is technically rented to the customer and the rent is paid in installments. Upon completion of a predetermined number of payments and collection of a nominal final fee, title is given to the customer.

bait advertising See BAIT AND SWITCH.

bait and switch Promotion of a product at a very low price for the purpose of luring customers into the store. The retailer has no intention of selling the advertised product at the reduced price and attempts to switch the customer to a more expensive item or to a lesser-valued and less desirable product. Sometimes called *bait-and-switch advertising, bait-and-switch merchandising, bait-and-switch pricing, bait advertising, bait pricing, bait merchandising, switch selling*, and *trading away*. See also LOWBALL PRICE and NAILED DOWN.

bait merchandising Synonym for BAIT AND SWITCH.

bait pricing 1. Synonym for BAIT AND SWITCH. 2. See also LEADER PRICING.

balance 1. The difference between the sum of debit entries and the sum of credit entries in an account. The balance may be positive (revenue or credits exceed expenses) or negative (expenses or debits exceed credits). 2. In VISUAL MERCHANDISING, the placement of materials around an imaginary line down the middle of the DISPLAY that serves as an axis. *Symmetrical balance* involves positioning items on either side of the axis so that they are equally weighted optically. It is also called *formal balance*. *Asymmetrical balance*, also called *informal balance*, is the positioning of items on either side of the axis so that they are not equally weighted optically. They appear unified because they draw upon other design principles such as proportion or contrast to create OPTICAL WEIGHT.

balance-and-mix   The proper combination of items in each line of merchandise to satisfy customer needs and the correct selection of lines to ensure that merchandise is consistent with the store's image.

balanced assortment   An assortment of merchandise with sufficient breadth and depth to meet the demand of the target customers while maintaining a reasonable investment in inventory. May be used both by mass merchandisers and high-end retailers. Also called *model stock, balanced stock,* or *ideal stock*. The maintenance of the balanced assortment is known as *stock balance*.

balanced product portfolio   The mix of old and new products maintained by a manufacturer.

balanced selling   The sale of products in a vendor's line in proportion to the sales potential or actual profit associated with the product.

balanced stock   See BALANCED ASSORTMENT.

balanced tenancy   The relationship between the type and number of stores in a SHOPPING CENTER and the needs of the center's customers. Also called the *tenant mix*.

balance of payments   In international trade, the sum of all transactions between a country and its trading partners. Such transactions include merchandise trade, travel, income on investments, military expenditures, foreign aid, and the flow of capital funds.

balance of trade   The relationship between the value of a country's imports (both goods and services) and the value of its exports. The balance of trade is favorable when a country exports more than it imports. A TRADE DEFICIT exists when imports exceed exports, a TRADE SURPLUS when exports exceed imports. Also called *trade balance*.

balance sheet   A classified financial statement that shows the financial condition of the firm at a particular point in time (usually the end of a given ACCOUNTING PERIOD). It shows the total assets, liabilities, and the owner's equity at a given point in time (usually the last day of the accounting period). Also called a *proprietorship equation*, a *statement of financial position*, or a *statement of assets and liabilities*. Compare INCOME STATEMENT.

balance sheet account   See REAL ACCOUNT.

balance sheet close   A sales close sometimes employed in personal selling when the customer appears unable to decide about a purchase. The SALESPERSON presents a list of the advantages and disadvantages of delaying the decision or of moving quickly. If the advantages of moving quickly prevail, the customer may be convinced to complete the transaction.

ballooning   A manipulation of prices upward beyond the safe or real limits. As such, ballooning depresses demand and acts as a deterrent to the successful sale of products and services.

balloon note   A form of credit agreement in which the purchaser pays a series of small installments until, at the end of a specified period, the balance comes due as a single, larger "balloon" payment.

ballpark pricing   A technique used to set the price for an item by checking the prices of similar items and setting the price within this range. Such a price is said to be *in the ballpark* or *in ballpark range*.

banded pack   Related items held together by a tape or plastic film strip and sold at retail as a unit. For example, a can of shaving cream and a razor, or a tube of toothpaste and a toothbrush, sold together in this manner constitute banded packs. Also called a *factory pack*.

banded premium   See WITH-PACK PREMIUM.

bandwidth   1. A range within a band of frequencies or wavelengths. 2. In the Internet environment, transmission capacity, i.e., the amount of data that can be transmitted through a particular communication line or channel per unit of time. Bandwidth is usually expressed in terms of bits per second (bps) or bytes per second. See also BROADBAND and NARROWBAND.

bangtail   The perforated flap on an envelope which, when detached, serves as an order blank. Often included by stores and banks when they mail monthly charge card statements and accompanying inserts to customers.

Bank Check Fraud Task Force   An inter-industry organization formed in 1993 by the American Bankers' Association and the NATIONAL RETAIL FEDERATION (NRF) to develop solutions to check fraud crimes. The task force has developed a data-sharing program for closed accounts that prevents individuals from opening new accounts if they have outstanding checks due to retailers. Participating financial institutions report all checking accounts closed for cause to a central database called *ChexSystems,* which transmits closed account information to the *Store Check Authorization Network (SCAN)*.

bank credit card plan   A bank-issued credit card accepted in lieu of cash by participating merchants. The merchants pay a fee to the bank, which, in turn, bills the customer. The customer has the option of paying in full or in installments.

banker's acceptance   A time DRAFT or bill of exchange drawn on and accepted by a bank. It is essentially an order to pay a specified sum of money at a fixed future date. By accepting the draft, the bank assumes an unconditional obligation to pay the face value of the draft at maturity to a *bona fide* holder.

bank of windows   In larger stores, some specialty stores, and downtown department stores, a group of two to four windows with a physical divider (such as a doorway, a wide area of masonry known as a pier, or even a small shadow box) situated between them. The windows in the group (i.e., bank) may be separate entities, completely framed and delineated from each other by a heavy molding or pier. Compare RUN-ON WINDOW.

bankruptcy   The state or condition of being unable to pay one's debts. The debtor may be an individual or a corporate body, and the bankruptcy proceeding may be voluntary (initiated by the debtor) or involuntary (initiated by creditors).

banner   1. A large, eye-catching sign used in a store interior or as a decorative element for window and exterior displays. 2. Short for BANNER AD.

banner ad   Graphic, interactive, billboard-style messages on or linked to Web pages. They can be used as a directed path to a purchase by providing a direct link to the purchase page of the current site or to an altogether different site. The effectiveness (and advertising cost) of a banner ad is often measured in its CLICK RATE, the number of visitors to the site who actually connect to the live link. Banners may be placed anywhere on a Web page, on all four sides as well as in the middle with wraparound text. While on the screen, banner ads block content. Sometimes simply called a banner.

bantam store   A small store open long hours each day and usually seven days a week. Bantam stores sell groceries, dairy products, beverages, and other convenience goods. Some bantam stores also sell coffee and sandwiches for take-out. May also be called a *deli*, a *bodega*, or a *vest pocket supermarket*. See also CONVENIENCE STORE and SUPERETTE.

bar chart   A type of diagram used to present business data. It uses either vertical or horizontal bars to compare information in a simple but visually effective manner. See also PICTOGRAPH.

bar code   A configuration of alternating dark bars and light spaces (i.e., printed stripes), usually vertically arranged and found on most products. Information is encoded into these bars and spaces by varying their individual widths. Bar codes contain information about vendors, departments, classifications, style numbers, etc. Use of a bar code system requires an OPTICAL CODE READER, bar-coded labels, and a computer. In January 2005 U.S. bar code labels conformed to the European bar code for the first time. The global bar code standard became the EUROPEAN ARTICLE NUMBERING CODE, which contains 13 digits as opposed to the 12-digit bar code formerly used in the United States and Canada. The European system, adopted in 1977 and patterned after the American system, added a thirteenth digit to allow for the identification of additional products and to distinguish between countries in the European Community. See also UNIVERSAL PRODUCT CODE (UPC).

bar coding   The identification of a product by means of a UNIVERSAL PRODUCT CODE (UPC) printed on the product. The UPC's printed stripes, or bar codes, contain information about vendors, departments, classifications, style numbers, etc., which is captured at the point of service by scanning the UPC with an electronic device.

bargain   1. v. To negotiate an agreement while seeking an advantage, such as a price reduction. The act of negotiating such an agreement is called *bargaining* or *price negotiation*. 2. n. An item of merchandise bought at a low or advantageous price.

bargain basement   The lower level of a department store (i.e., the basement), devoted to selling merchandise that has been marked down in upstairs departments or lower-priced merchandise not represented in upstairs departments at all. The bargain basement appeals to customers most concerned with low prices. Also called a *downstairs store*. See also AUTOMATIC (BARGAIN) BASEMENT.

bargain counter   A long table or cabinet top in a store designated for the display and sale of discounted items. In even the most exclusive high-end department stores, bargain counters may convey an image of rummaging and disarray; this image helps to make the discounted merchandise even more attractive to bargain hunters.

bargain hunter/seeker   A customer who seeks out the lowest possible prices. A bargain hunter will generally exert considerable effort to compare prices, quality, and style so as to get the best buy. Bargain hunters enjoy saving money as a matter of principle and will not be influenced to purchase items they do not believe are worth the price.

bargain square   An arrangement of four tables in the form of a square upon which sale merchandise has been arranged.

bargain store   A retail establishment in which low price is the most important consideration. Bargain stores often deal in large job lots and DISTRESS MERCHANDISE. They often have large quantities of specific items, but narrow assortments. Some bargain stores set an upper price limit on all goods, frequently below one dollar, and are known as a 99 CENT STORE. See also DOLLAR STORE and JOB LOT.

barn   A large discount store in which low price is of primary importance, often housed in a huge barn-like building. The size of the establishment and the huge quantity of merchandise contribute to the bargain store or warehouse image. The name *barn* has characteristically been attached to women's apparel retailers, household furnishings stores, sporting goods stores, and shoe outlets.

barn-burner wizard   (Slang) A high-pressure salesperson who aggressively pushes to achieve sales goals.

barter   1. n. The direct exchange of goods or services between the parties involved in a commercial transaction without the use of money. Also called a SWAP.   2. n. In international marketing, a type of COUNTERTRADE. It consists of a direct exchange of goods between two parties, involves no currency, and is realized without the help of intermediaries.   3. n. In INTERNET marketing, an instance of DIRECT BARTER or NETWORK POOL BARTER. An online barter site or virtual online SWAP SHOP can be general, brand-specific, product-specific, or even experience-specific (e.g., individuals wishing to trade travel experiences).   4. v. To engage in any of these types of trade.

barter dollars   In online NETWORK POOL BARTER, trade credits or tokens credited to members' accounts and used to make purchases.

base exchange   A government-owned store on a U.S. military base, where military personnel and their families are able to purchase goods and general merchandise at reduced prices. See also POST EXCHANGE (PX) and GOVERNMENT-OWNED STORE.

basement store   Traditionally, a store literally located below ground in the basement of a department store and featuring low-cost bargain items. Today, this bargain area may be situated elsewhere in the store and may be called a BUDGET STORE instead. See also BARGAIN BASEMENT and AUTOMATIC (BARGAIN) BASEMENT.

base period   In economic and business research, a one-year (or, sometimes, multi-year) span used as a reference to which current data is compared. A base period corresponding to a particular year is called a *base year*.

base point pricing   See BASING POINT PRICING.

base price   See LIST PRICE.

base record   A file on an individual customer, maintained by a store or other establishment (such as a credit agency). The record contains the customer's name and address in addition to other critical information.

base year   See BASE PERIOD.

basic customer service   See PRIMARY CUSTOMER SERVICE.

basic goods   Synonym for BASIC STOCK.

basic inventory   The amount of stock carried at all times, needed to cover anticipated sales for a given period plus a margin to cover unanticipated developments.

basic item   An item of merchandise in continual demand and therefore kept in stock at all times by a retailer.

basic list price   See LIST PRICE.

basic low stock   The predetermined level in inventory below which an item is never allowed to fall.

basics   See BASIC STOCK.

basic stock   The assortment of merchandise, largely staples, which is maintained at all times. This merchandise has a highly predictable sales history with stable customer demand. Basic stock items are not associated with either seasonal or year-round demand. See also STAPLE.

basic stock at retail   The dollar amount of the average inventory minus the average monthly sales.

basic stock list   A list composed largely of staple items, used in developing an ASSORTMENT PLAN. For this reason it is more specific than the MODEL STOCK PLAN/LIST/METHOD, which is also used for developing assortment plans. Included on the basic stock list will be the name of the item, brand identification, physical description, cost and retail price, and other information that precisely identifies the merchandise. Also called a *basic stock plan*. Compare MODEL STOCK PLAN/LIST/METHOD.

basic stock method of inventory   A tool for planning basic monthly stocks of merchandise that allows the retailer to calculate the average inventory for the period. This technique assumes that the retailer will begin each month with a minimum amount of basic stock that remains constant regardless of the monthly sales to be achieved. The basic stock is first calculated as the average stock for the season minus the average monthly sales. The value of the beginning of month (BOM) stock is then calculated as sales plus the net dollar amount of sales divided by the STOCK TURNOVER (ST) minus the net dollar amount of sales divided by the number of months in the period.

basic stock plan   Synonym for BASIC STOCK LIST.

basic trading center   A city that serves as a center for SHOPPING GOODS purchases for a significant surrounding area as well as for its own population. The term is used by the Rand McNally Company.

basing point pricing   A PRICING STRATEGY in which the cost of goods has two components: (a) their cost at the point of production and (b) the cost of transporting them from a designated center (the basing point), which may be different from the point of manufacture. Basing point pricing allows the producer to charge all customers in the same geographical area identical transportation costs regardless of the actual distance the goods are shipped.

batch picking   A warehousing practice in which a sufficient quantity of a product is picked up to fulfill multiple orders in one pass. The batch of products is later sorted by customer and/or delivery address. See also WAREHOUSE.

battleground map   A map used by the retailer to indicate the geographic location of its own flagship and branch stores as well as those of competitors in the TRADING AREA.

battle of the brands   The competitive struggle at the retail level between national brands on the one hand and private brands on the other. In addition, generic or no-name products have joined the competition to split up the market. See also BRAND.

battle plan   A carefully developed and formulated strategy intended to produce a particular goal or development.

bazaar   1. A marketplace, particularly one found in the Middle East.   2. A special sale of miscellaneous items for the benefit of a charitable organization or other worthy cause.   3. A store in which many types of diverse goods are sold. Sometimes spelled *bazar*.

BBB   See BETTER BUSINESS BUREAU (BBB).

BBS   See BULLETIN BOARD SYSTEM (BBS).

BCG Growth Share Matrix   See BOSTON CONSULTING GROUP (BCG) MATRIX.

beacons   See WEB BEACONS.

beat last year's figures   To exceed the sales figures for the corresponding period a year ago.

beauty parlor/shop   See SALON.

bedding   A classification that includes mattresses, conventional innerspring bedding, waterbeds, foundations, convertibles, and flotation sleep products.

before-after test   In retail advertising, a measure of consumer response to a product both before and after the product has been advertised. When properly conducted, the before-after test objectively demonstrates the quantity of sales of the product that can be attributed to the advertisement.

beginning inventory   See BEGINNING OF MONTH (BOM) INVENTORY.

beginning inventory at cost   In the cost method of inventory, the cost of the inventory on hand at the start of the accounting period. This figure is derived from and equal to the ending inventory at cost of the previous accounting period. See also COST METHOD OF INVENTORY and ENDING INVENTORY AT COST.

beginning of month (BOM) inventory   The amount of stock required to begin the month. There must be adequate stock on hand to achieve planned sales. In merchandising plans, the BOM inventory, beginning inventory for a period (usually a month) must be the value of the ending inventory. It is calculated by subtracting the average monthly sales from the retail value of average monthly stock, and adding the result to the planned sales for the month. Also called *beginning inventory, beginning of month (BOM) stock,* and *first of month (FOM) inventory.*

beginning of month (BOM) stock   See BEGINNING OF MONTH (BOM) INVENTORY.

behavioral biometric   A measurable behavioral trait that is acquired over time (i.e., learned) and that may be used to recognize a person, particularly for security purposes. Behavioral biometrics are sometimes used by stores dealing with customer and employee theft.

behavioral component   In attitude research, one's readiness to act on one's beliefs and feelings. In retailing and marketing, the behavioral component of a customer's attitude will result in the purchase of the product (if the attitude toward the product is favorable) or the purchase of a competing or alternative product (if the attitude toward the product is unfavorable).

behavioral engineering   A part of learning theory holding that people behave in direct relation to what they believe will be the consequences of their acts. Behavioral engineering has been applied in limited forms to retailing and marketing, having more uses in personnel management. Also known as *behavioral technology, applied behavioral analysis,* and *Skinnerian psychology.*

behavioral technology   See BEHAVIORAL ENGINEERING.

behavioral theories of the firm   Theories expounded by various merchandising theorists that describe the business firm as a coalition of individuals who share common goals in relation to production, inventory, sales, market share, or profit. Such theories further maintain that (a) each firm is divided into interdependent, internal subcoalitions or constituencies corresponding to functional divisions of the firm; (b) constituencies negotiate resource exchanges inside and outside the firm; (c) specialization occurs within the constituencies to enhance the effectiveness of negotiation; (d) conflicting goals develop among the constituencies because of specialization; (e) negotiation is the primary means of resolving conflicts; (f) the most powerful internal constituencies manage the most critical resources; and (g) the most powerful external coalitions offer and control the most critical resources.

behavioral theory of the apparel firm (BTAF)   One of the BEHAVIORAL THEORIES OF THE FIRM developed specifically for the apparel industry, both at the retail and manufacturing levels, by Grace I. Kunz in 1995. BTAF assumes that (a) an apparel firm can consist of manufacturing and/or distribution functions in various combinations; (b) a firm is a coalition of individuals with some common goals; (c) the coalition is made up of subcoalitions or constituencies that conform to the functional areas of the firm; (d) five constituencies perform all the business functions necessary for the apparel firm's operation (executive, merchandising, marketing, operations, and finance); (e) the firm's overall goals are formed by the executive constituency; (f) the focus of the apparel firm is on satisfying the customer's needs within the limitations of the firm; and (g) the interrelationships among the five constituencies form the internal decision making matrix for the firm.

behaviorism   1. The school of psychology that deals only with observable behavior as distinct from consciousness, meaning, or intent.   2. In an advertising context, an application of the stimulus-response theory of learning in which a stimulus (in the form of an advertising message) is repeated often enough to produce the desired response (the purchase of the product or service).

behavioristic segmentation   A system of classifying potential customers on the basis of their knowledge of, attitude toward, use of, and/or response to products or product characteristics.

being alive   A lifestyle trend for health and fitness devotees. These consumers may be vegetarians or vegans and may participate in tai chi and yoga for exercise. They provide a strong market for vitamins, organic and/or health foods, herbal remedies and supplements, therapeutic furniture, exercise equipment, and self-help books and audio recordings. Also known as the *wellness trend*.

being space   A commercial living-room-like setting provided by a retailer to facilitate activities typically carried on in a small office or living room, such as watching a movie, reading a book, meeting with friends and colleagues, or doing one's paperwork. Being spaces (e.g., Starbucks, Barnes & Noble, Borders, Kinko's) charge customers for eating and drinking at their establishments while they are playing, listening, Web surfing, working, or meeting. The trend was identified and the term coined by trendwatching.com at www.trendwatching.com.

belief   A thought or understanding held by a person about a thing or an occurrence. In retailing and other marketing activities, it specifically refers to how a consumer feels or thinks about a product or service. Beliefs influence buying behavior. Altering consumer beliefs is one goal of advertising and promotion. However, it may be one of the more difficult goals to achieve as beliefs are often deeply held and tenaciously defended.

believer   See VALS SEGMENTATION.

bell cow   (Slang) A frequently purchased item whose selling price far exceeds its manufacturing cost. Synonymous with *blue chip*. See also CASH COW.

bellwether department   In a departmentalized store, a department that effectively presents the store's fashion image or in some other way establishes the nature of the store in the eyes of the customer.

belly-to-belly selling   A form of personal selling in which the SALESPERSON confronts the customer face to face. Synonymous with *nose-to-nose selling*.

below par   Below average. May be used to denote poor quality or low price (i.e., a discount).

below-the-market pricing   See PRICING BELOW THE MARKET.

benchmark   A standard measure used to evaluate performance comparatively. See also BENCHMARKING.

benchmarking   Using the activities and practices of the competition as a standard by which to measure the performance of one's own retail establishment. See also BENCHMARK.

benefit   A gain or advantage received by an individual. In retailing and marketing, this translates into aspects of the product or service that fulfills a customer's need. See also EMPLOYEE BENEFIT.

benefit approach   A SALES APPROACH in which the SALESPERSON attempts to focus the prospect's thoughts directly on the benefits (i.e., advantages) to be derived from the good or service being sold. The benefit should be concrete and specific, such as a monetary saving. Also called the *benefits/features approach*, *benefit strategy*, *features/benefits approach*, *need-satisfaction approach*, and *features approach*.

benefit-cost analysis   See COST-BENEFIT ANALYSIS.

benefit market segmentation   A technique that attempts to divide the consumer market into subgroups based on the benefits (i.e., fulfillment of needs) they seek from a product or class of products. For example, in the market for women's shoes, customers may seek comfort, high fashion, durability, practicality, versatility, etc. Market researchers have found that consumers usually want a combination of benefits, but stress one or more when making a purchase decision. Benefit market segmentation is also useful in uncovering opportunities for new products.

benefits approach   See BENEFIT APPROACH.

benefits concept   See BUNDLE OF BENEFITS CONCEPT.

benefit segmentation   See BENEFIT MARKET SEGMENTATION.

benefits/features approach   See BENEFIT APPROACH.

benefit strategy   See BENEFIT APPROACH.

benefit structure analysis   Synonym for CONJOINT MEASUREMENT/ANALYSIS.

best before (date)   A label or stamp on a food package indicating the date before which the supplier intended the food should be consumed. The term is similarly used to indicate the date by which the item will have outlived its SHELF LIFE. The term refers to the quality of the product, not its safety. While some deterioration of the product may occur after the specified date, the product is not necessarily unsafe to consume. Compare USE BY (DATE).

best buy   An item of high quality and, at the same time, competitively priced in relation to prices charged by competing retailers. A lower-than-normal markup may be taken to achieve a price advantage.

best guess   See GUESSTIMATE/GUESTIMATE.

best seller   An item that consistently sells rapidly through a season or calendar year at full price. Best sellers characteristically have high unit sales (typically 50 or more units), high dollar sales (typically in excess of $1,000), and a SELL-THROUGH of 30 percent or better. They have been in stock four weeks or less, and are readily available in stock in sufficient quantities to continue to sell well (typically at least 10 units are on hand). A best seller is sometimes described as EXPLOSIVE and sometimes referred to as a FAST MOVER, LIVE GOODS, or an ITEM. Also called a *key item* or a *runner*.

best seller report   A management report common to many retail organizations that reflects the status of sales, inventory, and profitability for specified periods of time. The report highlights those items that have high unit sales. See also BEST SELLER and DAILY BEST SELLER REPORT.

best selling price lines   Those lines of merchandise, though relatively few in number, that produce a large proportion of a store's sales.

best time available (BTA)   In radio advertising, a scheduling format that typically offers lower rates than the total audience plan. Like a RUN OF TIME SCHEDULE (ROS) plan, the BTA plan may run at any time between 5:00 a.m. and 1:00 a.m. with no guaranteed distribution by day part.

Better Business Bureau (BBB)   A voluntary, nonprofit organization dedicated to promoting ethical business practices in Canada and the United States. Members are business executives working through over 150 local bureaus in the United States. BBB reports provide information on over two million organizations, including businesses and charities. In recent years the BBB has expanded its efforts to include e-commerce. The national BBB maintains a Web presence at www.bbb.org and, specifically for e-commerce, at www.bbbonline.org. Also referred to as the *three Bs*. Formally called the *Council of Better Business Bureaus*.

better line   In the apparel industry, a better line is a broadly distributed line of apparel that appears at less prestigious department store conglomerates. A store's better line falls between its BRIDGE LINE and its MODERATE LINE. See also APPAREL PRICE RANGES.

better offer complaint   A customer's assertion that a competitor is offering the same merchandise or service for a better price. If the customer has already purchased the item or service, some retailers honor this complaint with a store credit or refund. There is, however, no legal requirement to do so.

bias   See INTERVIEWER BIAS.

bid   1. An offer to buy, as in a public auction.   2. An offer to perform a service or supply goods at a price the vendor considers competitive and acceptable to the buyer. Bidding may be at the invitation of the buyer of the goods or services. Bidding may also be competitive, with several potential vendors making their best offer to the buyer, who then selects from among the various proposals. The vendor's participation in this process is known as *bidding* or *competitive bidding*, and the buyer's participation is known as *bid buying*. The bid submitted may also be called a COMPETITIVE BID/BIDDING. See also SEALED BID and OPEN BID.

bid buying   See BID.

bidding   See BID.

bidding war   In the acquisition of companies by other companies, a bidding war is a series of counteroffers by two or more parties interested in acquiring the same company through a purchase of its stock. Bidding wars may drive stock far above the value of the company being acquired.

bid pricing   The setting of a price for goods and services by a supplier in such a way as to include all the costs incurred and allow for a predetermined profit.

bid search engine   A search engine that allows Web site owners to pay for priority placement at the top of the search list. Web site owners compete for such placement by bidding against each other. The amount paid to the search engine is based on U.S. dollars per click.

big and tall men's   A menswear clothing category describing apparel falling outside the size range generally found in most apparel stores. These hard-to-find sizes may be carried in a separate department in a large retail store or in a specialty store catering to this NICHE MARKET.

big box retailer/store   A discount store typically housed in a huge, utilitarian, boxlike building. Also called a *big-box store* or a *box retailer*. See also DISCOUNT STORE and BOX STORE.

big-early, little-late method   A method of developing media advertising schedules in which the beginning of the campaign is regarded as the most significant and therefore allocated the largest amount of money. Subsequent expenditures for advertising diminish over time. See also PROMOTIONAL BUDGETING.

big pencil   (Slang) A term applied to a BUYER who represents a large store and can write large orders.

big-ticket item   Any item of merchandise that carries a high price tag. For example, refrigerators, garden tractors, furniture, computers, and automobiles are all considered big-ticket items. Consumers often comparison-shop, seek out product information, and consult knowledgeable acquaintances before purchasing these items. Big-ticket items are consequently considered SHOPPING GOODS by retailers.

big-ticket selling   Synonym for MEGASELLING.

bill   1. n. A statement detailing money owed for goods or services provided. Also called INVOICE or STATEMENT.   2. v. To send such a statement to the customer or client.

billboard   An outdoor sign containing an advertising message. Billboards are frequently situated at high-traffic sites, such as bridge and tunnel entrance routes, for maximum exposure. A billboard is one form of OUTDOOR ADVERTISING. See also THRILLBOARD.

billed cost   The actual price of goods as it appears on the seller's invoice. The billed cost reflects deductions made for trade discounts.

bill enclosure   Advertising matter included in the envelope containing a customer's charge account statement. Also called *statement insert*, a *statement stuffer*, a *stuffer*, or an *envelope stuffer*.

billing   The process by which the seller submits invoices (i.e., bills) to the customer. See also DATING OF INVOICES.

billing invoice   Synonym for INVOICE.

billing record   Synonym for PURCHASE JOURNAL.

bill-me order   See CREDIT ORDER.

bill of exchange   In domestic transactions, a DRAFT.

bill of lading (B/L)   A document issued by a carrier acknowledging receipt of a shipment. The bill indicates the name of the CONSIGNOR (i.e., vendor) and CONSIGNEE (i.e., recipient), describes merchandise, and states shipping charges. Also called a *waybill*. Each bill of lading is considered a contract between the shipper and the carrier. See also AIRWAY BILL OF LADING (AWB) and CLEAN BILL OF LADING.

bill of sale   A written agreement in law that transfers one person's or firm's right to goods to another person or firm.

bill to–ship to   Designating an instruction that merchandise is to be shipped to one name and address but billed to a different name and address. For example, if a consumer orders a gift online and wishes to ship it directly to the gift recipient, the "bill to" and "ship to" destinations will be different. The consumer will be billed; the gift recipient will receive the merchandise. Many online retailers provide bill to–ship to forms on their Web sites to allow for shipping directly to a third party.

bin   A display fixture that is essentially a cube or container open at the top. Tilted bins may be used for bulk items like candy in a grocery store or nuts and bolts in a hardware store. While the terms *bin* and CUBE are often used interchangeably, a cube is actually a container that is open on its sides. Cubes are used in fashion stores as wall treatments or as stand-alone floor fixtures.

binary digit   See BIT.

binary large object   See BLOB.

binary term   See BYTE.

biogenic need   Any of the basic physiological requirements common to all consumers, regardless of income, social class, education, etc. These include food, drink, shelter, sex, sleep, etc. Also called *primary need, innate need, physiological motive,* and *physiological need.* Compare PSYCHOGENIC NEED.

biostatistics   In retail, an individual's biometric (i.e., body) measurements.

bird dog   (Slang) An individual paid to obtain business for a high-power salesperson.

birdyback   (Slang) A coordinated transportation arrangement using both air and ground modes of transportation. For example, goods may be shipped partly by airplane and partly by truck.

birthday sale   See ANNIVERSARY SALE/CELEBRATION.

birth family   Synonym for FAMILY OF ORIENTATION.

bit   Short for *binary digit*, the smallest unit of information in a computer. The term was first used in 1946 by John Tukey, a leading statistician and adviser to five presidents. A single bit takes on only one of two values: 0 or 1. More meaningful information is obtained by combining bits into larger units. For example, a BYTE is composed of eight consecutive bits.

bits per second (bps)   A measure of the speed at which data is transmitted over the Internet. Dial-up modems typically transmit data at 28,800–57,600 bits per second. A DIGITAL SUBSCRIBER LINE (DSL) can transmit data at 6.1 megabits (millions of bits) per second. See also BANDWIDTH.

B/L   See BILL OF LADING (B/L).

black   See IN THE BLACK.

black book   See BUYER'S BLACK BOOK.

black box   1. Among marketing researchers, the consumer's mind, so called to suggest that what goes on inside it is largely hidden from the researcher's view.   2. The workings of computer technology, similarly considered as being largely hidden from the user's view.

Black Friday   The day after Thanksgiving, one of the major U.S. shopping days and the day many consumers begin their Christmas shopping. Traditionally, retailers looked to Black Friday as the day when they went from being unprofitable (i.e., IN THE RED), to being profitable (i.e., IN THE BLACK). Today, retailers are somewhat less focused on any particular day in the holiday season. See also CYBER MONDAY.

blacklist   A secret list circulated among employers to keep union organizers from getting jobs. See also BLACKLISTED.

blacklisted   Added to a list of persons who are under suspicion and who, consequently, are not to be hired, served, etc. See also RETURN FRAUD.

black market   1. Trade in products, commodities, currencies, etc. that is in violation of the law. Laws violated by black market operations include tax laws, exchange rate regulations, price ceilings, rationing, etc. Compare GRAY MARKET.   2. A place where such activities take place.

blank-check buying   A standing order placed by a retailer with a vendor.

blanket brand   See FAMILY BRAND.

blanket order A preseason order placed with a vendor, to be delivered in a number of future shipments covering all or part of a season. Quantities and styles may be specified, but detailed instructions regarding color, size, shipping dates, finish, etc., are generally omitted. The buyer places a requisition against these orders as the merchandise is needed. Also called a *yearly order*.

blanket pricing agreement An agreement that sets the price for merchandise ordered through a BLANKET ORDER. When the order is placed, the seller agrees to make shipments as requested at the contract price throughout the contract's duration.

blind check The inspection of received merchandise by an individual who does not have a copy of the shipper's invoice to compare to the actual goods on hand. The checker is thus not influenced by expectations of the shipment's contents. Compare DIRECT CHECK.

blind item pricing See BLIND ITEMS.

blind items Merchandise unique to a particular store and of more than routine interest. These items are difficult to price because the retailer generally has no other store with which to compare. Consequently, blind items tend to carry a higher markup. Also called *blind goods* or *blind products*.

blind selling (Slang) The sale of merchandise without allowing the customer to examine the item prior to purchase. In retail stores, this occurs when merchandise is prepackaged, with only a floor sample available for customer viewing. Customers are generally unable to determine the condition or completeness of the individual item they have purchased while still in the store.

blister pack A cardboard backing with a clear plastic bubble specially shaped to cover the product while keeping it visible. Many over-the-counter pharmaceutical products are sold in blister packs to prevent tampering. Blister packs thus serve the dual functions of protection and display.

BLOB Short for binary large object, a BLOB is a collection of binary data stored as a single entity in a DATABASE MANAGEMENT SYSTEM (DBMS). BLOBs usually encode multimedia objects such as images, videos, and sound.

blog A Web page made up of short, frequently updated posts that are arranged chronologically. Blogs can be useful in the workplace by providing teams of employees with a mechanism to communicate over an INTRANET. Blogs help keep everyone in the loop, promote cohesiveness and group culture, and provide a project or department with an informal voice. Software programs such as *Blogger* automate the communication process by providing a template for easy and customized blogs without requiring any code, special server software, or scripts. Also called a *weblog*.

blouse form See BUST FORM.

BLS See BUREAU OF LABOR STATISTICS (BLS).

blue chip Synonym for BELL COW.

blue-collar worker See SOCIAL CLASS.

bluefingers (Slang) In retailing, friends who spend considerable time shopping together. Because of shared interests and attitudes, these friends purchase similar styles and items in a particular price range. Also called *jebble*. See also PERSONAL INFLUENCE.

blue laws State and local laws prohibiting retail stores from operating on Sundays. Although this practice is usually defended on religious grounds, its effect is to reduce time competition, especially between large and small retailers. While blue laws have been contested as an infringement of individual and free enterprise rights, they remain in effect in a number of communities, largely because of small retailers' insistence that they cannot afford to remain open on Sundays in order to compete with larger stores. Many other communities, however, have discontinued enforcing blue laws or have struck them from the books, resulting in some retailers remaining open seven days per week. See also SUNDAY OPENING.

board Synonym for INTERNET DISCUSSION GROUP.

board of directors A group of people, elected by the shareholders of a CORPORATION, who have the ultimate authority in guiding the affairs of the corporation.

bodega Synonym for BANTAM STORE, used primarily in Spanish-speaking areas. *Der.* Spanish

body copy In the apparel trades, an imitation of an original design, usually made to sell at a lower price. A body copy is an attempt to replicate the original as closely as possible while reducing the costs involved in production. Sometimes simply referred to as a COPY. See also ADAPTATION.

body fashions Synonym for *foundations* or *foundation garments*. See INTIMATE APPAREL.

body trunk A male form that starts just above the waistline and ends just below the knees or, alternatively, at mid-thigh. Body trunks may be made of vacuum-formed vinyl or molded rubber-mâché and are used in visual marketing to display shorts, underwear, swimwear, etc. Also called a *trunk form*.

bogey (Slang) In retailing, a standard of performance beyond which a bonus is given.

BOGO See BUY-ONE-GET-ONE (BOGO).

boiler room (Slang) In telemarketing, the facility from which telemarketers make their solicitations.

BOM (inventory) See BEGINNING OF MONTH (BOM) INVENTORY.

bona fide sale A transaction in which the seller acts in good faith regarding the terms of the sale.

bond   See IN BOND.

bonded bin   See CUSTOMS BONDED WAREHOUSE.

bonded shed   See CUSTOMS BONDED WAREHOUSE.

bonded warehouse   A form of PUBLIC WAREHOUSE that stores imported goods or other goods on which a tax must be paid prior to the release of the products for sale (such as cigarettes and alcoholic beverages). See also CUSTOMS BONDED WAREHOUSE.

bonded yard   See CUSTOMS BONDED WAREHOUSE.

bonus   Money paid to employees in addition to regular salary and commissions, in recognition of special services performed or for some other reason (such as longevity, holidays, etc.)

bonus goods   Merchandise given by a manufacturer to a retailer without extra charge in return for the retailer's agreement to purchase a minimum number of units.

bonus pack   A promotional package offering the customer more than the regular quantity of the item for the regular price, such as a larger-than-average tube of toothpaste or jar of instant coffee sold for the same price as the regular size.

bonus plan   An arrangement by which CONTINUITY retailers and other marketers offer customers an extra item in exchange for multiple purchases. For example, book and music clubs may offer a free book or CD to customers making a predetermined number of purchases at the regular price. In retail stores, serving pieces may be offered free or at a reduced price when sets of dishes are purchased on a continuity basis. When mail order, Internet selling, or telemarketing is involved, shipping and handling is charged for the free item as it is for the purchased items.

booking   At the manufacturing level, order taking for the purposes of planning the production and delivery of goods.

book inventory   A system of perpetual inventory maintained by adding the value of incoming goods to the value of previous inventory and then subtracting the value of sales, markdowns, and discounts. Also called *book method of inventory*.

bookkeeping   The recording of financial data, especially purchases and sales, in such a way as to ensure the orderly functioning of an enterprise.

bookmark   A Web address (i.e., the UNIFORM RESOURCE LOCATOR) stored on the user's BROWSER in a listing of favorite sites readily available for future linking. The ease of BOOKMARKING encourages users to revisit the site. Bookmarks are sometimes called *favorites*.

bookmarking   The process of storing a UNIFORM RESOURCE LOCATOR (URL) on one's browser in order to return to it in the future. This is generally accomplished with a simple click of the mouse button.

book method of inventory   See BOOK INVENTORY.

book of original entry   In retail accounting, journals, cashbooks, register tapes, etc., used for the purpose of recording transactions and hence as a source of posting to ledgers.

book price   See LIST PRICE.

book value   In retail accounting, the original cost of the merchandise less the amount of accumulated depreciation, depletion, or amortization.

book value per share of common stock   The financial ratio that results when the total stockholders' equity less the preferred stockholders' equity is divided by the number of common stock shares outstanding. It is an indication of a company's financial position at a given point in time.

boomerang   A technique used by salespersons to overcome shoppers' objections. Through this technique, the SALESPERSON turns the shopper's stated reasons for not buying the item around and presents them as the precise reasons for making the purchase. Also called the *conversion process* and *positive conversion*.

booster   1. (Slang) A SHOPLIFTER. 2. Short for PROFIT BOOSTER.

booster box   Taken from the slang term BOOSTER (i.e., SHOPLIFTER), a booster box is a boxlike package with a spring-held side panel through which stolen merchandise may be passed and concealed.

bootlegger   One who sells illegal merchandise such as untaxed alcohol.

borax   (Slang) Cheap, undistinguished, or shoddy merchandise whose chief appeal is low price. The term comes from the premiums for cheap furniture offered at one time by a manufacturer of borax soap.

border tax adjustment   A return of tax paid on merchandise prior to export. Taxes returned may include sales, value-added, or other indirect taxes paid on merchandise. Since such taxes are aimed at the domestic customer, foreign travelers or exporters frequently receive refunds of these taxes when the goods leave the country.

borrow   1. To receive something from another for temporary use. The understanding is that the item will eventually be returned to its original owner. 2. To take or adopt an idea, design, or style as one's own. In this sense, borrowing may be used as a euphemism for stealing or PIRACY.

Boston Box   See BOSTON CONSULTING GROUP (BCG) MATRIX.

Boston Consulting Group (BCG) Matrix   A method for evaluating a company's product offerings and marketing opportunities developed by the Boston Consulting Group. It consists of a matrix (also called the *Boston Box*) made up of four compartments or boxes representing different combinations of the two variables, growth and market share. Products are classified as stars, cash cows, question marks, or dogs and assigned to one of the four compartments. Appropriate strategies may then be developed for the company's entire product portfolio. Also called the *business portfolio matrix* and the *growth/share matrix*.

bot   In the Internet environment, short for ROBOT, a program that runs automatically. See also SHOPPING BOT, CHATBOT, and AUCTION BOT.

bottom line   1. In accounting, the last line of a financial statement, expressing profit or loss.   2. Net profit or loss.   3. In more general use, the deciding or crucial factor, or the result or outcome.

bottom-up approach to promotional budgeting   Any of several PROMOTIONAL BUDGETING methods that consider a firm's goals and objectives and assign a portion of the budget to meet those objectives. Rather than using a TOP-DOWN APPROACH TO PROMOTIONAL BUDGETING, planners link appropriations to objectives and the strategies to accomplish them, taking into consideration both financial and communication objectives. The goal is to budget in such a way that the promotional mix strategies can be activated to accomplish the expressed objectives. These types of budgets work well in an INTEGRATED MARKETING COMMUNICATIONS (IMC) environment. The bottom-up approach includes *objective-task approach*, *payout planning*, and *quantitative mathematical models*. See also BUILD-UP APPROACH.

bottom-up fashion   See UPWARD FLOW THEORY.

bottom-up plan   A merchandise plan centered at the department level and involving those who work most closely with the actual merchandise. The sum total of the plans of the various departments feeds into the organizational sales objective. Most organizations combine top-down and bottom-up planning, recognizing that planning requires input at every level. Compare TOP-DOWN PLAN and INTERACTIVE PLAN.

bottom-up theory   See UPWARD FLOW THEORY.

bounce-back coupon   A coupon that is good for the same product as the one to which it is attached. Bounce-back coupons generate repeat sales.

boundaryless organization   An organizational structure in which the dividing lines between retailers and wholesalers are dissolved. Retailers and their suppliers collaborate, leading to agility in responding to shifts in customer demand, speed in bringing goods to market, and rapidity in bringing data to bear on marketing strategies, merchandising programs, and store operations. Overall costs are contained and productivity increases as the result of this form of cooperation.

boutique   A small specialty store or area within a larger store. Emphasis is on merchandise selected for a specific target customer, presented in an attractive and unified manner and accompanied by individualized attention on the part of the sales staff. Also called a *specialty shop* or a *store-within-a-store*.

boutique agency   An ADVERTISING AGENCY that specializes in writing and designing advertising material and thus focuses on the creative and artistic aspects of the advertising campaign. Unlike larger, full service agencies, boutique agencies charge on a per-job basis. Also known as a *creative boutique*.

boutique merchandising   See BOUTIQUE STORE LAYOUT.

boutique store layout   A form of store organization in which related merchandise from a number of departments is brought together in one shop to meet special customer demand. See also BOUTIQUE.

box   1. In graphical user interfaces used in Web page design, an enclosed area resembling a window on the screen. Unlike windows, boxes cannot generally be moved or resized. There are many different types of boxes. For example, a *dialog box* is a box that requests some type of information from the user (e.g., name, billing address, shipping address, credit card information). An *alert box* may suddenly appear on the screen to give the user additional (often crucial) information. A *zoom box* (also called a *grow box*) enables the user to make a window larger or smaller.   2. n. A stiff container, case, or receptacle, often with a lid or cover, usually made of cardboard.   3. n. The quantity of merchandise in a box (e.g., a box of tangerines).   3. v. To pack or put into a box, especially in supermarkets and other food stores.   4. See BIG BOX RETAILER/STORE.

box boy/girl   See BAGGER.

boxer form   See INNERWEAR FORM.

box retailer   See BIG BOX RETAILER/STORE.

box store   A no-frills, warehouse-type store that often displays merchandise on or in its shipping carton. See also BIG BOX RETAILER/STORE and WAREHOUSE STORE.

boycott   1. In international relations, a means of coercion in which one or more nations refuse to deal with another; in domestic economics, a refusal on the part of certain groups (for example, labor unions) to buy particular domestic or imported products as a means of bringing economic pressure to bear on government or private industry.   2. In labor relations, union activity in which members and sympathizers refuse to buy or handle the products of a target company. Millions of union members form an enormous bloc of purchasing power, which may be able to pressure management into making concessions. *Der.* From the name of a British agent (Captain Charles Boycott) in nineteenth-century Ireland. See also SECONDARY BOYCOTT.

boys' sizes   Apparel sizes 8–20, designed for male children. Boys' sizes include the designations *slim*, *regular*, and *husky* in each size. Sizes are determined by height, weight, circumference of chest, and circumference of waist.

BPI   See BUYING POWER INDEX (BPI).

BPS   See BITS PER SECOND (BPS).

bra form   In visual merchandising, a headless, armless female form that ends just below a defined bustline, with or without shoulders. The forms are used to display bras.

brainstorming   In MARKETING RESEARCH (MR), a research method, developed by Alex Osborn in the 1930s, that uses participants to generate ideas about issues or problems. Participants are encouraged to share opinions and generate creative responses. The same technique is now used online. Participants are selected and invited to join a brainstorming session similarly to the way focus group participants are selected. A password admits participants to a private, firewall-protected Web site where a trained facilitator begins a discussion thread to focus ideas and postings. Participants use self-selected nicknames (pseudonyms). Contributions are visible to all participants and they are encouraged to build upon previous ideas. Also called *ideation* or *idea generation*.

brain wave measurement   In ADVERTISING RESEARCH, one of the techniques used to establish a PHYSIOLOGICAL PROFILE of a participant. It involves taking electroencephalographic (EEG) measures from the skull to determine electrical frequencies in the brain in response to advertisements.

branch   A geographically detached unit of a firm that is still an integral part of the business. Branches of companies frequently restrict their activities to the selling function. See also MANUFACTURER'S BRANCH OFFICE and BRANCH STORE.

branch house/office   See MANUFACTURER'S BRANCH OFFICE.

branch store   In department or other large store organizations, a branch store is a smaller retail unit owned and operated by the parent store and generally located in the suburbs or in metropolitan area shopping centers. Sometimes called a *satellite store*. The main store of such an organization is known as the FLAGSHIP STORE/DIVISION. A department store organization consisting of a flagship store and two or more branch stores is considered a MULTIUNIT DEPARTMENT STORE. See also REPLACEMENT BRANCH.

branch store manager   The executive responsible for the operation of a retailer's BRANCH STORE.

brand   A particular product or line of products offered for sale by a single producer or manufacturer and made easily distinguishable from other similar products by a unique identifying name, symbol, design, or other element. For many companies, the brand name is the company name. A brand identifies ownership and provides tangible and intangible associations with successful products of the same company. As such, a brand conveys a promise, feeling, or set of expectations. A brand also positions a product in the marketplace by distinguishing it from its competitors. Products carrying such a brand are known as *branded merchandise* and/or *brand name merchandise*. See also RELATED PACKAGING.

brand acceptance   The process by which consumers learn about and eventually use a particular brand of products. Brand acceptance is often divided into five levels: BRAND REJECTION, BRAND NONRECOGNITION, BRAND RECOGNITION, BRAND PREFERENCE, and BRAND INSISTENCE. See also ACCEPTANCE STAGE.

brand advertising   Advertising (i.e., a paid, non-personal communication) whose objective is the stimulation of demand for a specific brand or line of products. Brand advertising may seek either a direct or an indirect response on the part of the consumer. See also DIRECT ADVERTISING and INDIRECT ADVERTISING.

brand awareness   Consumer cognizance of a BRAND. Brand awareness is built through online and offline promotions, advertising, direct marketing, sales promotions, positive word-of-mouth, and e-mail marketing. On the Internet, brand awareness is also built by listing brands in search engines. Some online marketers use VIRAL MARKETING to build brand awareness by spreading positive BUZZ about the brand. Sometimes called *brand consciousness*. See also AWARENESS.

brand building   See BRANDING.

brand buyer   A consumer who expresses a consistent preference for one brand over any other. See also BRAND LOYALTY.

brand category   A general classification of products and services. Competing items and services that are similar in nature are defined within the same brand category.

brand champion   In global marketing, a manager, senior manager, or product development group responsible for building and managing a global brand, often in a certain country.

brand character   See BRAND PERSONALITY.

brand choice   The act of selecting a particular brand of merchandise or services from the variety of available brands with similar purpose or content. For example, a consumer may choose Avis or Hertz when renting an automobile.

brand competition   A situation in the MARKETPLACE in which producers offering similar items are competing against each other for MARKET SHARE (e.g., Coca-Cola versus Pepsi-Cola).

brand competitor   An organization that competes with others to satisfy consumer demands for a specific product.

brand consciousness   See BRAND AWARENESS.

brand development   A measure of the penetration of a brand's sales, traditionally per thousand population. See also BRAND DEVELOPMENT INDEX.

brand development index   The percentage of a brand's sales in an area (based on population in that area) as compared to its sales throughout the United States (based on the total U.S. population).

brand differentiation   The identification of similarities and (especially) differences between one's own brand and those of the competition, appraising their relative importance to specific market segments, and establishing these differences in the mind of the consumer. Brand differences of importance to consumers result, through appropriate advertising, in BRAND LOYALTY and/or BRAND INSISTENCE. Sometimes called, simply, DIFFERENTIATION. See also PRODUCT DIFFERENTIATION.

brand dilution   Diminishing the value of a brand name through overexposure on too many Web sites (for e-tailing) or in too many markets (for traditional retailing). Luxury goods are particularly vulnerable to losing BRAND EQUITY through overexposure.

brand-driven purchase   A consumer choice based primarily on brand preference. Purchases are brand-driven when clear distinctions differentiate brands. When such distinctions do not exist, customers make their choices based on other factors such as price or color. For example, fragrance purchases are brand-driven because of each brand's distinctive scent. The purchase of designer merchandise is also brand-driven. Customers who consistently purchase the same brand are called BRAND LOYAL.

branded brand   A marketing trend in which certain focused and well-respected brands, often associated with quality, trendiness, and/or sophistication, enrich other, more all-encompassing brands. For example, airlines may serve branded pizza (e.g., Pizzeria Uno), branded coffee (e.g., Starbucks), or even McDonald's "friendly skies meals." Hotel rooms may provide branded toiletries for their guests and branded ice creams may appear on the menus of even upscale restaurants. Similarly, large department stores and discounters may replace or supplement their own food services with branded food services such as Starbucks and McDonald's. The trend was identified and the term coined by trendwatching.com at www.trendwatching.com.

branded concept shop   A store-within-store format featuring internationally known brand merchandise in a small specialty area within the confines of a department store. The strategy combines specialty store retailing and branded merchandise. Ready-to-wear designer apparel, brand-name linens and bedding, and lifestyle merchandise are the categories frequently sold in branded concept shops. Most department stores welcome branded concept shops as a method of increasing sales, creating higher margins, and increasing focus. See also CONCEPT SHOP.

branded merchandise   See BRAND.

brand equity   The level of consumer recognition of a brand, label, or store in the marketplace.

brand extension strategy   A marketing strategy in which a firm uses one of its established brand names on a modified product or an entirely new product so that the new product entering the marketplace is supported by the existing, well-recognized brand name. Also called *extension of brands*. See also LINE EXTENSION, MULTIPLE EXTENSIONS, and FRANCHISE EXTENSION.

brand familiarity   The customer's ability to recognize and accept a particular brand of products.

brand franchise   An agreement between a wholesaler or retailer and the manufacturer of brand name merchandise. A brand franchise gives the wholesaler or retailer the exclusive right to sell the brand manufacturer's item in a carefully defined location. This allows the wholesaler or retailer to sell the item in a noncompetitive market and to set prices as the traffic will bear.

brand image   The perception of a product formed in the mind of the consumer as the result of the symbols and meanings associated with a particular brand. Advertising is often employed to create a brand image. For example, automobile advertising on television commonly sells a lifestyle (e.g., glamour or outdoor adventure) rather than a mode of transportation. See also STORE IMAGE and PRODUCT IMAGE.

branding   The assignment of a brand name to a product or service. Branding is a means of achieving product differentiation in the marketplace. It is the process of developing, building, and maintaining a name in the marketplace. Brand building requires careful planning and knowledge of the product or company to be branded, knowledge of the target market, understanding of how the brand will benefit the target market, knowledge of the competition, and the careful monitoring of brand perceptions. See also BRAND.

brand insistence   An extreme instance of BRAND LOYALTY in which the customer will accept no substitute for the desired product. A brand-insistent consumer is known as a HARD-CORE LOYAL; as a group, such customers form the CORE MARKET. A consumer who shares loyalty between two or three brands is said to be a SOFT-CORE LOYAL, and a consumer who shifts from favoring one brand to another is called a SHIFTING LOYAL. The least brand-insistent consumer, one with no loyalty to any brand, is known as a BRAND SWITCHER. See also BRAND ACCEPTANCE.

brand label   A tag on a product that indicates the brand name, the manufacturer, and other information fulfilling legal requirements depending on the nature of the product.

brand leader   An item considered the best in its field and marketed with that assumption in mind.

brand-line representative   In cosmetics retailing, a trained salesperson who advises customers on the proper use of the line of cosmetics being sold at that counter.

brand loyal   A customer who consistently purchases the same brand.

brand loyalty   The consistent preference, on the part of the consumer, for one brand over any other, or for one set of brands over others competing in the same category.

brand management Those business activities concerned with the development of new brands, their introduction into the marketplace, and their management through the PRODUCT LIFE CYCLE (PLC). See also BRAND MANAGER.

brand manager An executive responsible for the planning and development of a particular brand. The brand manager oversees the development of a competitive strategy, coordinates all aspects of planning, and directs the advertising and promotional efforts of the brand. In essence, the brand manager is the MARKETING MANAGER for the brand.

brand manager system A middle-management system employed by firms marketing a relatively large number of distinct brands. Each brand has a manager who is totally involved in the development and marketing of the brand from its conception through to its commercialization. Such a system is meant to ensure that each brand receives adequate attention. When managers are assigned to individual products rather than brands, a similar system is known as a PRODUCT MANAGER SYSTEM.

brand mark The part of a brand that consists of signs, colors, symbols, and designs (i.e., nonverbal elements) closely identified with the product. Brand marks (e.g., the red tab on the back pocket of Levi's jeans or the apple on Macintosh computers) may also be a part of the firm's TRADEMARK.

brand marketing A strategy in which each of a firm's products is marketed independently, generally under the direction of a BRAND MANAGER. See also PRODUCT LINE MARKETING.

brand name The part of a BRAND that consists of actual letters or words (i.e., the part that can actually be vocalized) in the name of the product or service. The brand name is distinct from the other identifying signs, symbols, and designs incorporated into the overall design. See also BRAND MARK and TRADEMARK.

brand name bias In MARKETING RESEARCH (MR), a tendency on the part of persons being questioned about product use to name a widely advertised BRAND despite the fact that they may never have purchased it. This is generally the result of the respondent forgetting the name of the actual brand purchased and being reluctant to admit it.

brand name merchandise See BRAND.

brand name preemption See PREEMPTION OF A BRAND NAME.

brand nonrecognition Customers' inability to recognize a BRAND, though they may recognize the product. This generally occurs when the brand name is not part of the marketing strategy geared to the ultimate consumer, even when it is used by distributors and other marketing intermediaries. Products with brand nonrecognition problems include novelties, school supplies, and other inexpensive goods commonly found in discount stores. See also BRAND ACCEPTANCE.

brand personality Those characteristics of a brand that are comparable to human personality traits (e.g., likableness, dependability, cuteness), allowing the customer to empathize and identify with the product or store. A brand's personality is seen to depend more on what people think about it that on what it is or what it does. Distinct from BRAND IMAGE. Sometimes known as *brand character*.

brand position A product's NICHE in the marketplace. Refers to the product's relationship to competing brands and is generally measured in terms of how the consumer perceives the various attributes of the brand. Brand position depends on consumer attitudes.

brand positioning Efforts aimed at establishing a brand in a particular NICHE or segment of the marketplace. Advertising and other promotional activities are geared to attracting a particular target market. See also POSITIONING, MARKET POSITIONING, and REPOSITIONING.

brand preference In the process of BRAND ACCEPTANCE, brand preference is a middle stage in which the consumer will choose a particular brand over its competitors because of previous favorable experience with the brand. However, should the product prove to be unavailable, the consumer is willing to accept a substitute.

brand recognition A stage in BRAND ACCEPTANCE in which consumers remember having heard about or seen a product, even if they have not yet tried it. Such recognition is a company's first objective for a newly introduced product. The effectiveness of advertising and other publicity programs geared to familiarizing the consuming public with such a new product or brand may be tested by a RECOGNITION SURVEY/ TEST.

brand rejection In the process of BRAND ACCEPTANCE, the customer's refusal to buy a particular brand of goods because of its poor image or because of previous bad experiences with the brand. Remedies for brand rejection include changing the brand's current image, changing the product, and changing the target market segment. Also called, simply, *rejection*.

brand repositioning See REPOSITIONING.

brand share The portion or share of the market that one brand commands, expressed as a fraction of the total market. See also MARKET SHARE.

brandstanding In advertising and promotion, brandstanding is the tying together of a brand with an event, idea, or issue. The tactic employed generally involves the linking of a brand name (without regard to its particular attributes) to a highly publicized event or other activity. For example, marathon runners frequently wear numbers that also carry the name of the sponsor of the race.

brand strategy Plans and tactics relating to the use of brand names, the establishment of the brand in the marketplace, and the advertising and promotion of the brand to build recognition and improve BRAND SHARE.

brand switcher The least brand-insistent consumer, one with no loyalty to any particular brand. The brand switcher looks for the brand that is readily available, on sale, or novel. Consumers often maintain brand loyalty for certain items while displaying a willingness to accept substitutes for others. Brand switchers motivated by low price and premiums are said to be DEAL-PRONE. This is particularly true in the area of staple products such as tuna or toilet tissue (where there is little distinguishable difference between brands); consumers will often select the brand on sale that particular day. Brand switchers motivated by the desire to try something different are said to be VARIETY-PRONE. This trait shows up in the snack food industry, for example, where consumers may opt for a new cookie or other taste treat just for the sake of change. Also called, simply, a *switcher*. See also BRAND LOYALTY, BRAND INSISTENCE, and VARIETY-SEEKING BEHAVIOR.

brand-switching model A representation of consumer behavior used by managers to understand brand loyalty and the likelihood that a consumer will switch from one brand to another.

breach of warranty The failure of a manufacturer to honor the WARRANTY issued with a product (i.e., refusal to back up claims concerning the proper performance of the product).

bread-and-butter assortment/goods Merchandise that, because of consistent customer demand, is never allowed to go out of stock. Also called a *checklist*, a *staple stock list*, *never-outs*, and a *never-out list*. Bread and butter goods are also called *never-out goods*.

breadth of assortment See ASSORTMENT BREADTH.

breadth of merchandise offerings See ASSORTMENT BREADTH.

break bulk Synonym for ALLOCATION.

break-bulk center A central distribution point where large shipments of goods (such as CARLOAD [CL] and/or TRUCKLOAD [TL] quantities) are broken down into smaller quantities and shipped to customers closer to the final market. See also ALLOCATION and WAREHOUSE.

break-down approach A method used to allocate a firm's advertising budget. In the break-down approach, the firm begins with a predetermined total advertising budget, which is then allocated to particular lines of merchandise offered by the firm. The person or department in charge of promotions makes the allocations. Sometimes called the *break-down method*. Compare BUILD-UP APPROACH. See also TOP-DOWN APPROACH TO PROMOTIONAL BUDGETING.

break-even Short for BREAK-EVEN POINT.

break-even analysis A mathematical analysis in which the fixed and variable costs of production are compared to projected revenue in an effort to reveal the break-even point (i.e., the point at which expenses and revenues are balanced). The

analysis, also known as a *break-even model* and *traditional break-even analysis*, is frequently presented in the form of a BREAK-EVEN CHART. See also FLEXIBLE BREAK-EVEN ANALYSIS, MODIFIED BREAK-EVEN ANALYSIS, and PROFIT TARGET ANALYSIS.

break-even chart A graphic representation of fixed and variable costs juxtaposed to total revenue in such a manner that the firm's BREAK-EVEN POINT is revealed.

break-even model See BREAK-EVEN ANALYSIS.

break-even point The point at which an enterprise is showing neither a profit nor a loss; the point at which sales equal the cost of doing business. Also called, simply, the *break-even*. Also spelled *breakeven point*. The break-even point may be expressed in terms of units or sales dollars. See also PAYBACK.

breaking bulk Synonym for ALLOCATION.

breakthrough opportunity A marketing opportunity that enables an innovative firm to establish a new marketing strategy, develop and market a new product, or create a new marketing mix. The new strategy will be difficult for others to readily imitate and will, therefore, remain profitable for an extended period of time. The breakthrough opportunity gives the firm, in effect, a temporary monopoly and an edge over competitors. It also helps the firm capture a large portion of the market share, serving to discourage imitators from entering the market. The advantage will remain until competitors decide to meet the innovator in head-on competition.

bribe A payment made to an individual, company, or government agency in order to secure special privileges and/or advantages. These advantages may include contracts, favorable pricing, legal oversights, etc. The global economy has raised new issues regarding the ethical and legal issues surrounding bribery. Bribes are expected in some countries, where they may be overlooked even if they are illegal, and rarely used in others. Cultural values, choice of trading partners, presence of laws, punishment for violating those laws, the size of the bribe, and the ethical orientations of participants are some of the factors that affect the issue of bribery. See also COMMERCIAL BRIBERY.

bribery The attempt to influence business decision making by offering gifts or favors to the person charged with making the decision. The globalization of commerce has reopened the issue of commercial bribery, since expectations and practices vary widely from country to country. Some countries consider bribery illegal and unethical. In other countries, bribery is the norm. Most countries outlaw the bribing of their own government officials; the United States also bans the bribing of foreign officials. Nevertheless, many bribery scandals in international marketing involve government contracts and government employees. See also BRIBE.

bricks-and-clicks Of a business, marketing its products both online (clicks) and offline (bricks) using a dual- or multi-distribution channel strategy. See also CLICKS-ONLY, BRICKS-AND-

MORTAR, MULTICHANNEL RETAILING, DUAL DISTRIBUTION, and WEB STOREFRONT.

bricks-and-mortar   Of a business, marketing their products only offline in traditional stores and/or offices. Also called a STORE RETAILER. See also BRICKS-AND-CLICKS and OFFLINE.

bridal registry   The service or bureau in a retail store in which a bride and groom may register their choice of china and silver patterns and other gift preferences. The retailer records each purchase, so that gifts will not be duplicated. Bridal registries are also available online, usually on a store's own home page.

bridge jewelry department   A department handling merchandise that falls between COSTUME JEWELRY on the one hand and FINE JEWELRY on the other in terms of price and prestige or value. Bridge jewelry includes jewelry made from silver, gold, less expensive stones, and jewelry designed by artists using a variety of materials.

bridge line   In the apparel industry, a line of lower-priced designer creations with limited distribution through prestigious stores. The bridge line falls between the BETTER LINE and the DESIGNER LINE in terms of price and exclusivity. Bridge line apparel is at the upper end of the apparel price line, but is made with fewer details and less expensive fabrics than designer clothing. Also referred to as a *diffusion line*. See also APPAREL PRICE RANGES.

brief (and boxer) form   See INNERWEAR FORM.

broad   See ASSORTMENT BREADTH.

broadband   In the Internet environment, a very large BANDWIDTH with very high data transmission speed, generally ranging from 256 kbps (kilobits per second) to 6 MHz (Megahertz) wide. Both DIGITAL SUBSCRIBER LINE (DSL) services and cable TV are broadband services. Compare NARROWBAND.

broadcast advertising   See ADVERTISING and COMMERCIAL.

broadcasting   1. In e-commerce, the act of simultaneously sending the same E-MAIL message to everyone on the network. Broadcasting is also supported by some fax systems. Compare with MULTICASTING.   2. The act of transmitting speech, music, visual images, etc., by radio or television.

broadcast media   See MEDIA.

broadside   An advertising piece printed on a large single sheet and sometimes folded for mailing. Also called *broadsheet*.

brochure   In merchandising, a booklet printed on quality paper and featuring copy on the manufacturer's products or services, etc. Also called a *pamphlet* or a *leaflet*. See also PROMOTIONAL KIT.

broken assortments   Residual or remaining items within a group or set of related or coordinated merchandise. Such items become candidates for clearance markdowns. For example, in apparel, coordinated separates are generally marked down when so few pieces remain that it is no longer possible to coordinate an ensemble in any one size or color. Such broken assortments are said to be *piecy*. See also ODDS AND ENDS.

broken case-lot selling   The practice on the part of wholesalers of selling less than full case lots of merchandise in an effort to accommodate retailers who wish to buy smaller amounts.

broken sized lots   An assortment from which some sizes are missing.

broker   A nonmerchant marketing INTERMEDIARY who brings buyers and sellers of a product together, often directly and face-to-face. Generally a broker does not take title to merchandise and does not have physical possession of the goods. Most commonly operating in the grocery business, brokers also include real estate brokers, travel agents, and financial services brokers (who transact stock and bond exchanges). Brokers are increasingly vulnerable to the duplication of their services by Internet sites. Also called a *sales broker* or a *merchandise agent*. See also COMMISSION HOUSE.

broker's delivery order   Instructions issued by a CUSTOM HOUSE BROKER to an inland carrier to move, from the dock at the PORT OF ENTRY (POE) to a specified location, cargo that has been cleared through U.S. CUSTOMS SERVICE.

brood hen and chick organization   A form of store organization in which the FLAGSHIP STORE/DIVISION (usually the main, downtown store) exercises close control over activities in each BRANCH STORE. For example, buyers in the flagship store have considerable responsibility for merchandising the corresponding departments in the branches.

brown goods   Radios, television sets, and other consumer electronics, which traditionally have a brown exterior; small appliances as opposed to large ones. Compare WHITE GOODS (def. 1).

browse   See BROWSER and/or WINDOW SHOPPING.

browser   1. A piece of software allowing the user to view and retrieve Web pages. Browsers make the Web more user-friendly by making it searchable. See also KIOSK BROWSER.   2. A shopper who peruses merchandise in a leisurely and casual way. A nonbuying browser may just be killing time with no intention of making a purchase. However, some browsers enjoy shopping and spending money. Disinterested browsers have a detached attitude recognizable by sales staff.

browsing   See BROWSER or WINDOW SHOPPING.

BTA   See BEST TIME AVAILABLE (BTA).

BTAF   See BEHAVIORAL THEORY OF THE APPAREL FIRM (BTAF).

B2B   Business-to-business marketing transactions where businesses sell products and services to other businesses, online or offline. For example, the vendors and channel members that manufacture and supply the merchandise sold by retailers are operating in a B2B environment. B2B transactions do not directly involve the ultimate consumer. See also TRADE ADVERTISING.

B2B2C model Business-to-business-to-consumer. In the online environment, businesses may allow consumers to place orders online through one central Web site, but the purchased product is delivered offline by local affiliates. In this way the parent company avoids antagonizing the local affiliates since it does not in any way detract from their business.

B2B Web exchange A Web site that enables many businesses to buy and sell to one another, allowing them to realize transaction cost savings and greater efficiencies. Small businesses often pool their orders (a process called *demand aggregation*) to increase their buying clout. A Web exchange also allows businesses to find cheaper suppliers, better manage their supply chains, and reduce inventory holding costs through tighter inventory control. B2B Web exchanges are gradually replacing proprietary ELECTRONIC DATA INTERCHANGE (EDI) networks. See also WEB EXCHANGE.

B2C Business-to-consumer marketing exchanges where businesses sell directly to the consumer, either online or offline.

B2P The sale of products and services to the government and to public sector enterprises, both online and offline.

bubble wrap Plastic packaging material containing numerous small air pockets to cushion and protect the shipped merchandise.

buddy list A collection of screen names in an INSTANT MESSAGING (IM) program. The term is used in AOL Instant Messenger and Yahoo! Messenger, whereas the term *contact list* is used in MSN Messenger and ICQ. The buddy list is displayed in a window; double-clicking on any name will open an Instant Message session and allow the initiator to communicate with other people in real time.

budget A forecasting tool that structures a firm's short-range future plans on the basis of estimated revenues and expenditures expressed in numerical terms. Budgets are often established for a fiscal year and are important components of the planning process. See also PROMOTIONAL BUDGETING.

budget-book sale An INSTALLMENT PLAN/CONTRACT/ BUYING whereby the customer contracts for a specific amount to be paid on a regular basis with a small carrying charge. A book with coupons is provided for periodic payments. For example, if the payments are to be made monthly, the customer sends a coupon with the required dollar amount to the store each month. The payment plan is designed to allow individuals and families to purchase goods without violating the family budget. Rarely used in retailing since the advent of charge accounts and credit cards.

budget-conscious A consumer who is concerned with subsisting or living within an itemized allotment of funds. Budget-conscious consumers shop carefully, seek sales and bargains, and resist IMPULSE BUYING.

budgeting The process by which money is allocated to cover projected expenses. See also BUDGET.

budget line In the continuum of APPAREL PRICE RANGES, budget lines include apparel carried in value-oriented stores such as full line discounters. Budget lines are the least expensive and least prestigious apparel lines. Also called *mass-market line.*

budget store The section of a department store in which low-priced merchandise is carried. Often used as a euphemism for BASEMENT STORE.

buffer In computer use, a temporary storage area, usually in *RAM* (random access memory), that acts as a holding area. A buffer enables the *CPU* (central processing unit) to manipulate data before transferring it to a disk or other permanent storage device.

buffer inventory/stock See RESERVE STOCK.

bugs See WEB BEACONS.

building equipment See EQUIPMENT.

building lot See LOT.

building method See OBJECTIVE-TASK METHOD OF PROMOTIONAL BUDGETING.

build-up approach A method used to allocate a firm's advertising budget. In the build-up approach, the firm begins by ascertaining the advertising needs of each line of goods as determined by the person in charge of each line. Any necessary adjustments are made by the individual or group in charge of promotions, and the amounts for all lines are added together to determine the total budget. The firm does not begin with a predetermined total budget as in the BREAK-DOWN APPROACH. Sometimes called the *build-up method.* A sophisticated form of the build-up approach may be seen in the OBJECTIVE-TASK METHOD OF PROMOTIONAL BUDGETING. See also BOTTOM-UP APPROACH TO PROMOTIONAL BUDGETING.

build-up display In VISUAL MERCHANDISING, a display that carries the viewer's eye from grouping to grouping through a combination of steps, such as a series of forms of different sizes arranged in a straight line but leading the eye upward to one point.

build-up method of space allocation A method of planning space requirements for departments in retail stores. The method takes into consideration such factors as sales volume, stock quantities on display and in reserve, etc.

built-in sale A retail store sale held each year and generally involving the same classifications of merchandise. A January White Sale is a built-in sale.

bulk breaking   See ALLOCATION.

bulk checking   In receiving, the process of comparing arriving merchandise to invoices without actually opening the cartons to verify contents.

bulk delivery   See BULK MERCHANDISE DELIVERY.

bulk discount   A price reduction for a large quantity of multiple purchases. Synonymous with *volume discount*.

bulk e-mail   The same e-mail message sent to dozens, hundreds, or thousands of people simultaneously. Bulk e-mail may be used legitimately and effectively to announce a sale to preferred customers, alert customers to the availability of a new product, contact past purchasers of a product about enhancements (or defects), or inform customers about a change in the firm's contact information. Sometimes considered merely a polite term for SPAM.

bulk freight   See BULK GOODS.

bulk goods   1. Products such as coal, grain, or gravel that are sold and delivered in loose or unpackaged form.   2. Any large shipment of one item.

bulk mail   Second-, third-, and fourth-class mail, including parcel post, ordinary papers, and circulars used by retailers to reach a large cross-section of potential customers. Sometimes disparagingly referred to as *junk mail*.

bulk marking   The practice of marking prices on large lots of merchandise in their original shipping containers. Individual pieces are marked with their retail price at a later time in a *deferred marking* or *delayed marking* process.

bulk merchandise delivery   In retail, the delivery of large items beyond the capability of parcel delivery services, often necessitating more than one person.

bulk warehouse   A storage facility handling liquids stored in tanks and dry products stored in similar large containers.

bulletin board system (BBS)   An electronic message center. Often operated on a nonprofit basis, most bulletin boards serve specific interest groups and concentrate on a single theme. In short, electronic bulletin boards act as a virtual version of a physical bulletin board. Compare ONLINE SERVICE.

bumpback   In a SHOPPING CENTER or mall, the location of a smaller (usually temporary) tenant in the front portion of the space vacated by a large retailer. Bumpbacks use only the square footage in the portion of the site that faces out to the mall. This is done so that the mall appears to be full and to create a semblance of continuity when a large tenant moves out.

bundled pricing   The practice of offering a basic product, options, and customer service together as a package for one total price. Also called *bundling*. Compare UNBUNDLING PRICE/PRICING.

bundle of benefits concept   A theory that customers purchase not only the goods offered by a firm but also the advantages and capabilities those goods are expected to provide. The real value of the merchandise, therefore, resides in what the goods can do for the consumer and not in the goods themselves. For example, if the consumer needs equipment to shop online, pay bills, prepare income tax returns, do research, communicate with friends and acquaintances, etc., the consumer will purchase a personal computer for home use and expect the computer to provide those benefits. The product and its capabilities, therefore, are considered as a complete package. The same argument may be made for the industrial customer. See also PRODUCT LAYERS.

bundle of services concept   A theory in support of leasing rather than purchasing industrial equipment. The theory takes into account the comparative costs of leasing and buying, including the service and maintenance costs inherent in purchased equipment. According to the bundle of services concept, leased equipment is more cost-effective. Also called the *services concept*.

bundling   See BUNDLED PRICING.

burden   Synonym for OVERHEAD.

Bureau of Labor Statistics (BLS)   The principal fact-finding agency for the U.S. Federal Government in the field of labor economics and statistics. An independent national statistical agency, the BLS collects, processes, analyzes, and disseminates essential statistical data and serves as a statistical resource to the U.S. Department of Labor. These statistical reports include data on labor force, payroll, employment and wages, unemployment, compensation and working conditions, safety and health statistics, etc. Of particular interest to retailers and other marketers are the reports on prices and living conditions. These include the CONSUMER PRICE INDEX (CPI), the PRODUCER PRICE INDEX (PPI), IMPORT/EXPORT PRICE INDEX, and the CONSUMER EXPENDITURE SURVEY. The Bureau maintains a Web site at www.bls.gov.

busheling   The tailoring and altering of men's garments after purchase and fitting.

business analysis   In new product development, a business analysis is an attempt to estimate the profitability of a new product before large amounts of money have been spent on its development. This analysis can be assisted by computer programs that assimilate information about the proposed product, its potential market, consumer reactions, and other factors, and then recommend whether or not to go ahead with the product. Some companies, however, prefer to base their decisions on past experience and human judgment.

business associated site   A potential location for a store that will allow it to be near other stores, helping to generate traffic. See also BUSINESS ASSOCIATED STORES.

business associated stores   Stores aligned with one another because of their physical proximity. Such proximity helps each of the stores build TRAFFIC.

business communities Networks of businesses whose members help one another or facilitate B2B activities in the online environment.

business-controlled pricing See ADMINISTERED PRICING.

business cycle The fluctuations in business conditions that occur with some regularity over a period of time. The fluctuations are generally identified as *prosperity, recession, depression,* and *recovery.* During the prosperity stage, income and employment are high. During a recession, income, employment, and production begin to decline. If left uncorrected, the recession may become a depression, a period when business activities, employment, and incomes decline rapidly. The recovery that generally follows a depression once again shows an increase in production and employment. See also CYCLICAL VARIATION.

business district See NEIGHBORHOOD BUSINESS DISTRICT.

business domain The market sector targeted by a firm as its business environment. It may be defined in terms of a line of products, a particular group of customers, or some other combination of market factors.

business ethics Socially accepted rules of behavior that govern the relationship between business goals and practices and the good of society. Includes such issues as conflict of interest, company secrets, insider trading, interlocking directorates, corporate social responsibility, affirmative action, the sale of customer mailing (or e-mail) lists, relations with government agencies and officials, truth in advertising, the use of sweatshop labor, and maintaining honest business dealings with customers and employees.

business-industrial market See INDUSTRIAL MARKET.

business market See INDUSTRIAL MARKET.

business portfolio analysis A system used to analyze and evaluate product performance in order to develop future strategies. Portfolio analysis examines the comparative strengths and weaknesses of a product line. One such analysis system is the BOSTON CONSULTING GROUP (BCG) MATRIX. Another, more complicated system, is the *General Electric/ McKinsey & Co. Nine-Cell Matrix.* Also called *portfolio analysis* and *portfolio management.*

business portfolio matrix See BOSTON CONSULTING GROUP (BCG) MATRIX.

business-to-business See B2B.

business-to-business channel A CHANNEL OF DISTRIBUTION used when a manufacturer or vendor is selling to businesses instead of to consumers. In international business-to-business marketing, an EXPORT AGENT, an IMPORT INTERMEDIARY, or the manufacturer itself often contacts business customers directly without the use of further intermediaries.

business-to-business (B2B) exchanges Web-based businesses that facilitate purchasing and the development of partnerships between supply chain members.

bust form An armless, headless female form that ends just below the waistline and is used in visual merchandising to display women's blouses and sweaters. Bust forms may be made of vacuum-formed vinyl or molded rubber-mâché. Also known as a *blouse form* or *sweater form.*

buy at best Unlimited bidding at higher and higher prices until the required quantity has been purchased.

buyback A practice in international marketing regarded as a form of COUNTERTRADE. A product or service buyback agreement involves the sale of a product or service which, in turn, produces other products or services. For example, the sale of industrial production facilities leads to the production of goods. The seller generally agrees to accept some of the output of the production facility as partial compensation. Also called a *cooperation agreement.*

buyback agreement A provision in a sales contract stating that, if necessary, the seller will repurchase the items within a specified time period, usually for the original selling price. Also called a *product buyback agreement.* Compare BUYBACK.

buyclasses The three types (or classes) of industrial buying: the STRAIGHT REBUY, the MODIFIED REBUY, and NEW TASK BUYING/PURCHASING. Also spelled *buy classes.*

buyer 1. A line merchandising executive responsible for selecting and purchasing merchandise for a store or group of stores and selling it at a profit. Among the buyer's duties are selecting appropriate merchandise for the store or stores, supervising the assistant buyers and salespeople, planning advertising and displays, controlling and pricing stock, and budgeting. A buyer may work for a small independent retailer, a department store with branches, a chain organization with multiple units, a catalog operation, an Internet-based company, or a home shopping outlet. Buyers travel extensively to vendors' showrooms and central markets. Depending on the organization, buyers may also play a role in product development (for *private label* merchandise), communication with merchandise departments in member stores (in larger organizations), and department management. Also called a *retail buyer.* See also RESIDENT BUYER, PRODUCT DEVELOPER, ASSOCIATE BUYER, and REBUYER.   2. A synonym for CUSTOMER.

buyer behavior See CONSUMER BEHAVIOR.

buyer beware See CAVEAT EMPTOR.

buyer for export In international marketing, a MARKETING INTERMEDIARY who buys goods outright in the domestic market and then sells them overseas.

buyer power In the B2B environment, the influence large buyers have over supplier firms. Most importantly, large buyers can demand lower prices from suppliers in exchange for their volume business.

buyer's black book   The retail buyer's unit control book. Before the advent of computerization, the traditional black book included notes on fashion trends and hot numbers, sketchy dollar plans, and reminders about the reliability of vendors. The black book system was used as a system of MERCHANDISE PLANNING and LINE DEVELOPMENT. See also BUYER and STOCK BOOK.

buyer-seller dyad   In personal selling, the relationship between a SALESPERSON and a customer that strongly emphasizes personal, individual attention on the part of the salesperson.

buyer's market   An economic situation in which supplies of merchandise exceed demand. Such conditions favor the retail BUYER rather than the manufacturer, because they tend to lead to lower prices. Similarly, oversupply conditions favor the ultimate consumer rather than the retailer. As retailers compete to move their merchandise, they tend to lower their selling prices and consumers benefit from the lowered price. Also called a *loose market*.

buyer's order   The form used by a retail buyer to purchase merchandise from a vendor.

buyers over   A market situation in which there are more buyers than sellers. Demand exceeds supply.

buyer's remorse   Doubt, anxiety, or mixed feelings suffered by a customer immediately following a decision to purchase. See also COGNITIVE DISSONANCE.

buyer's surplus   The difference between what a buyer actually pays for an item and the highest price the buyer would have been willing to pay for the item, if necessary.

buying   1. In retailing, the process of purchasing goods at the wholesale level for resale at the retail level.   2. A synonym for PURCHASING (i.e., the acquisition of goods and services by the payment of money or its equivalent). See also INDUSTRIAL PURCHASING.

buying allowance   A reduction in price on specific goods offered by a producer or manufacturer to a purchaser as an incentive to buy.

buying behavior   See CONSUMER BEHAVIOR.

buying by committee   See COMMITTEE BUYING.

buying by description   The purchase of merchandise from a verbal and/or visual presentation. The customer usually has confidence in the business under consideration, since the physical item is not available for examination. Descriptive material should be clear and thorough, anticipating the customer's potential questions. Much of catalog and Internet selling is based on this premise.

buying by inspection   The purchase of merchandise when the actual items to be purchased have been examined.

buying by sample   The purchase of merchandise following the examination of a representative sample or portion of the item.

buying by specification   See SPECIFICATION BUYING.

buying calendar   A retail buyer's plan of merchandising activities for a period (often six months) including promotions and other seasonal events.

buying checklist   A list of matters to be considered before a retail BUYER makes a final commitment to purchase goods from a vendor.

buying close to the vest   The practice of buying a little at a time in an attempt to keep money outlays to a minimum. Also called *hand-to-mouth buying*.

buying club   Synonym for BUYING GROUP.

buying committee   In large retail organizations, especially those handling large numbers of staple products, a committee that assists individual buyers in making decisions regarding specific merchandise. See also COMMITTEE BUYING.

buying criteria   The requirements or specifications of a firm evaluating suppliers of a product or service. Criteria may include price, quality, delivery terms, availability, etc.

buying decision-making process   Synonym for ADOPTION PROCESS.

buying direct   The purchase of goods from the manufacturer, bypassing any intermediaries. See also DIRECT SELLING.

buying error   The failure to purchase appropriate goods for the store's customers. When the inappropriate goods do not move, a MARKDOWN (MD) is generally required to alleviate the situation.

buying function   All the activities undertaken by a BUYER for a store or larger retail organization. Includes selecting appropriate merchandise, planning advertising and displays, controlling and pricing stock, and budgeting. The buying function may also include product development (for private label merchandise), communication with merchandise departments in member stores (in larger organizations), and department management. See also BUYING.

buying group   A group of non-competing stores organized for the purpose of buying merchandise. Buying groups allow smaller stores to benefit from the discounts applied to volume purchases and hence compete more easily with larger retail organizations. Also called *buying club*.

buying hours   Specific store hours during which buyers will see sales representatives. See also ROAD BUYING.

buying incentive   A premium consisting of additional items, a discount, or a gift available to customers should they purchase an item or service. For example, cosmetics departments frequently offer GIFT-WITH-PURCHASE (GWP) buying incentives, either free or at a reduced price.

buying influence   See MULTIPLE BUYING INFLUENCE.

buying influential   An individual whose opinion is considered when purchasing decisions are being made by consumers. A buying influential may be a celebrity, a journalist, a designer, or even a friend or family member.

buying intent   A salesperson's evaluation of a customer's purpose. The salesperson tries to evaluate whether or not the customer is serious about making a purchase.

buying-into-trends   A form of retail buying in which an attempt is made to anticipate developing directions and styles in fashion. Buyers hope to identify such trends early enough so that goods may be ordered in time to take maximum advantage of them.

buying judgment   The retail buyer's ability to select the right merchandise for the store's customers.

buying line   A term used to designate buying and selling as the fundamental activities of a retailer. Consequently, in retailing, an employee involved in merchandising and/or store operations is considered to be filling a buying line. Also called *store line*. Compare STAFF FUNCTION, which refers to support functions not directly involved in buying and selling (e.g., a store's legal and human resources departments).

buying loader   A gift or bonus from a manufacturer or vendor to a retailer. The intent of the gift is to encourage the retailer to carry the manufacturer's goods. The gift may take the form of a discount or premium, etc.

buying motive   See MOTIVE and PRIMARY (BUYING) MOTIVE.

buying office   See RESIDENT BUYING OFFICE.

buying off the rack/peg   The purchase of ready-to-wear apparel without adjustments or alterations.

buying on consignment   See CONSIGNMENT BUYING.

buying on memorandum   See MEMORANDUM BUYING.

buying on time   Synonym for INSTALLMENT PLAN/CONTRACT/BUYING. See also ON TIME.

buying pattern   The form in which consumer demand is expressed; particularly when repeated, identifiable trends can be discerned.

buying period   The combined time of the *review period* (the time it takes to determine whether the order should be placed) and the *delivery period* (the elapsed time until the ordered merchandise arrives at the store).

buying plan   A description of the types and quantities of merchandise a buyer plans to purchase for a department over a specific period of time. Typically, the buying plan is prepared in advance of a BUYING TRIP. It includes purchases by classifications, price lines, styles, sizes, and colors. Buying plans are made to meet the needs of each branch of a large department store organization or for individual departments of a smaller business. Also called the *stock plan*. See also MERCHANDISE PLAN and SALES PLAN.

buying power   1. A retailer's capacity to purchase large quantities of merchandise, thereby commanding a favorable price from vendors. See also PURCHASING LEVERAGE. 2. The amount of money an individual or family has available for purchases after taxes. See also PERSONAL INCOME (PI) and DISCRETIONARY BUYING POWER.

Buying Power Index (BPI)   A measurement developed by *Sales & Marketing Management (S&MM)*, combining three elements (population, effective buying income, and retail sales) into one index that expresses a market's capacity to buy. The index, calculated as a percentage of the total U.S./Canada market potential, is used to forecast the demand for new stores and evaluate the performance of existing stores in a geographic area. See also EFFECTIVE BUYING INCOME (EBI).

buying process   Synonym for ADOPTION PROCESS.

buying quota   In a retail buyer's buying plan, the planned monetary expenditure for merchandise. In general, buyers try to stay within the limits of their quotas.

buying role   Any behavior pattern on the part of the customer enacted in the process of purchasing merchandise. This may include research and information-gathering, comparison shopping, negotiating prices, arranging for a demonstration, decision making, and other consumer behaviors depending on the particular product. See also CONSUMER BEHAVIOR and ADOPTION PROCESS.

buying to specifications   See SPECIFICATION BUYING and SPECIFICATIONS.

buying trip   The retail buyer's planned visit to the market for the purpose of selecting and writing orders for new merchandise. Buyers frequently travel to national and regional markets such as the Garment Center in New York City or the Chicago Apparel Mart, where they visit vendor showrooms. They also attend expos. An increasing number of buyers travel internationally to obtain lower wholesale prices, goods that are unavailable in the domestic markets, prestigious fashion collections, etc. Also called a *market trip* or a *market visit*.

buying with return privileges   The purchase of merchandise from a vendor with the understanding that certain items may be returned for credit if they remain unsold. This helps to mitigate some of the RISK involved in purchasing novel items still untested in the marketplace.

buy national   A protectionist appeal to restrict imports from other nations.

buy-one-get-one (BOGO)   A type of premium in which the customer receives a free item at the time the identical item is purchased. Also called *buy one, get one free*.

buyout   See ACQUISITION.

buzz   (Slang) Gossip; the latest inside information. Frequently used in the Internet community and in the celebrity gossip media. See also WORD-OF-MOUTH (WOM) COMMUNICATION.

buzz marketing   See BUZZ and WORD-OF-MOUTH (WOM) COMMUNICATION.

byte   Short for *binary term*, a unit of electronic data storage capable of holding a single character. On most modern computers, a byte is equal to 8 bits. Large amounts of memory are measured in *kilobytes* (1,024 bytes), *megabytes* (1,048,576 bytes) and *gigabytes* (1,073,741,824 bytes). See also BIT.

by the case   See CASE.

CA   See CERTIFICATE AUTHORITY (CA).

cable modem   A device that allows high-speed access to the Internet via a cable TV network. When a cable modem is attached to a computer, a splitter separates the coaxial cable line serving the cable modem from the line servicing the cable TV sets in the consumer's home.

cable system   An obsolete system of handling sales transactions by means of a container running along a wire from the selling department to the cashier's desk or credit authorizer.

cable television ordering system   A system that allows cable television viewers to select and order merchandise viewed at home on their television sets.

cachet   Superior status and prestige, particularly as perceived by the customer. For example, upscale stores and product lines may be said to have "a certain cachet." See also PRESTIGE LINE and PRICE-QUALITY ASSOCIATION.

CAD   See CASH AGAINST DOCUMENTS.

CAF   see COST AND FREIGHT (CAF).

cafeteria   1. A self-service restaurant in which moderately priced food is displayed on counters.   2. A comparable restaurant for employees of a store or other business, where food is served approximately at cost.

cafeteria benefit plan   An employee benefit plan in which the employer offers each participating employee a number of options such as disability insurance, medical coverage, tax deferred annuities, dental plans, etc. Individual employees choose from this "menu" those benefits they find most desirable. See also SMORGASBORD PLAN.

California Market Center (CMC)   Formerly known as the *California Mart,* the CMC serves wholesale buyers, distributors, manufacturers, and independent sales representatives in the fashion and textile industries. The center is located in downtown Los Angeles, California, and maintains a Web site at www.californiamarketcenter.com.

California Mart   Former name of the CALIFORNIA MARKET CENTER (CMC).

callback   A technique of persistence used by a sales representative to induce a potential customer to buy. It is used on the second and subsequent sales visits. See also USER CALL.

call bird   A method used in stores to increase traffic by lowering prices on items not usually stocked in quantity. The items are displayed in the retailer's store windows or advertisements to lure customers to the store.

call credit   A sum deducted from a customer's account when merchandise is picked up by the store's delivery system and returned to the store. The sum is equal to the selling price of the item.

call frequency   The number of times a sales representative contacts a customer or potential customer during a given year.

call pattern   See SALES CALL PATTERN.

call planning   A planning method used in telephone sales. The plan includes defining the goal of the call and devising a selling strategy.

call report   A salesperson's formal log, presented to a supervisor, of visits made to prospects and customers (i.e., accounts) in a specific market during a given period of time. The report indicates the date and time of each meeting and the topics under discussion. Also called a *conference report* and a *contact report.*

call slip   Synonym for WANT SLIP.

call station   An area in a retail establishment where pickup and delivery service is available.

call system   A method of rotating sales staff on a regular basis to allow each an equal opportunity to meet and wait on customers. The method is particularly germane at retail establishments in which compensation of salespersons is based at least in part on the amount of business they complete (e.g., COMMISSION).

call tag   A form notifying a delivery driver to pick up an article or parcel at a customer's address and return it to the store.

CAM   See COMMON AREA MAINTENANCE (CAM).

camera-ready (CR)   Of advertising and other copy, prepared to go to the printer. No additional changes are made to camera-ready paste-ups. See also MECHANICAL.

campaign   Short for ADVERTISING CAMPAIGN.

campaign plan   A series of consecutive mailings, used in direct mail advertising, to arouse interest in a coming event, such as the opening of a new store. Also called a *teaser plan* or a *teaser campaign*.

campus-area network (CAN)   See COMPUTER NETWORK.

CAN (campus-area network)   See COMPUTER NETWORK.

canalization   A sales technique that builds on a customer's fears and associations to bring about a dramatic change in behavior.

cancel   A customer's request to stop service (such as a magazine subscription) or to revoke an order for merchandise.

cancellation   1. A retraction of an order for merchandise sent from the buyer to the vendor or from the customer to the retailer.   2. Surplus merchandise sold by retailers to discount houses, often in broken lots.

cancellation notice   A form notifying a vendor that a buyer will not accept merchandise ordered but not yet received.

cancellation of markdown   See MARKDOWN CANCELLATION.

cancellation shoes   Slightly damaged or out-of-style shoes sold at reduced prices.

C&F   See COST AND FREIGHT (CAF).

canned presentation   A standardized sales talk memorized by members of the SALES FORCE and delivered to customers verbatim, often in telephone sales where supervisors make sure that individual sales personnel do not deviate from the scripted presentation. The steps typical of canned presentations are: greet the customer; determine the customer's wants and needs; explain product features and benefits; suggest additional merchandise; and close the sale. Also called a *canned approach*, *canned sales approach*, *canned sales presentation*, or *canned sales talk*.

cannibalism   See CANNIBALIZATION.

cannibalization   1. A condition in which a new product is introduced into the marketplace and sells at the expense of another product in the company's line (i.e., it eats into the market share and profitability of the other product).   2. A situation in which a chain retail organization opens new stores that detract from the sales of their existing stores by being too close to them either geographically or in terms of product lines offered and customers targeted. Also called *cannibalism* and *cannibalizing a market*. Cannibalization is the opposite of ENHANCEMENT. See also CHANNEL CANNIBALIZATION.

cannibalizing a market   See CANNIBALIZATION.

canonical name   See HOST NAME.

Can-Spam Act (2004)   Federal anti-SPAM legislation signed into law in December 2003 and in effect as of January 1, 2004. The law uses a process of AFFIRMATIVE CONSENT so that recipients receive messages only after having expressly agreed to do so, either in response to a clear and conspicuous request for permission from the e-tailer or at the recipient's own initiative. The law lays the groundwork for a national *do not e-mail list* modeled after the FTC's *do not call list*.

canvasser   A salesperson who attempts to solicit orders for goods by going from house to house or by telephoning prospects. Distinguished from a PEDDLER in that a canvasser does not carry any stock for immediate sale but only takes orders for future delivery.

canvassing   A door-to-door or telephone sales technique that involves the taking of orders for goods to be delivered at a future date. Also called *territory screening*. See also CANVASSER.

capability survey   The inspection of a prospective vendor's entire operation to determine its ability to produce goods of the quality and quantity desired.

capacity   The productive potential of a manufacturing firm, measured in terms of the amount of a product that can be produced per unit of time.

capacity fixture   A store FIXTURE (i.e., a store furnishing unit) designed to hold large quantities of merchandise. It is most often used to show just one style of a product bought in depth (e.g., several dozen sequined cardigan sweaters in assorted sizes from S to XXL). Because capacity fixtures are the largest floor fixtures in the store, they are usually positioned in the rear of a department or store layout.

capacity to buy   See MARKET POTENTIAL.

capital   1. The owner's equity in a business (i.e., the difference between assets and liabilities).   2. The total assets of a company, including the funds that support a business as well as the tools (e.g., machines, vehicles, and buildings) to produce goods and services.   3. The funding required to start or help start a business.

capital account   In accounting, the formal record showing the amount of investments in a business by noncreditors, together with undistributed earnings.

capital budget   A plan for proposed expenditures for acquiring long-term assets (such as new stores, plants, and equipment) and the means of financing these acquisitions. It lists future investment projects and includes a justification for each. The process of developing such a plan is *capital budgeting*.

capital consumption allowance   See DEPRECIATION.

capital equipment   See CAPITAL GOODS.

capital expenditures   Money paid out for tangible fixed assets such as land, buildings, equipment, fixtures, furniture, etc. One characteristic of capital expenditures is that their benefits often accrue in the future.

capital gain Profit resulting from the sale of capital investments such as stocks, real estate, etc.

capital goods Material property (sometimes called *capital-investment goods*, *capital items*, or *capital equipment*) in the form of installations (such as buildings and large machinery) and accessory equipment used in production operations (such as materials handling and office equipment). Capital goods are generally expensive, require infrequent replacement due to wear or obsolescence, and do not become a part of the product being manufactured. See also EXPENSE ITEMS/GOODS.

capital-intensive Of an industry or other undertaking, requiring a large investment in equipment, machinery, and automated devices while using relatively little labor. Also called *cost-intensive*. See also LABOR-INTENSIVE.

capital investment Money expended to acquire something of permanent value to a business (e.g., new facilities or equipment, machinery replacements, improvements required by law, land, acquisitions, or patent rights). Capital investments are considered in the capital budgeting process.

capital-investment goods See CAPITAL GOODS.

capitalism An ECONOMIC SYSTEM in which all or most of the means of production and distribution are privately owned and operated for profit, and in which competition determines the interaction of price, supply, and demand.

capital items See CAPITAL GOODS.

capitalize 1. To supply with capital. 2. To authorize a certain amount of stocks and bonds in a corporation's charter. 3. (with *on*) To turn to one's advantage.

capital stock The shares of a corporation, including all classes of common and preferred stock.

capital stock authorized The amount of stock (i.e., the number of shares) that a corporation may issue as defined in its certificate of incorporation.

capital surplus account Money reinvested in the company for growth purposes.

capital turnover A financial ratio used to measure the number of times the cost of the average inventory investment is converted into sales during a given period. It is equal to the dollar sales at retail during a specified period divided by the average inventory dollar value at cost.

captive jobber See MANUFACTURER'S BRANCH OFFICE.

captive market The potential customers of retail or service establishments located in hotels, airports, and other isolated locations where alternative or competitive businesses are relatively inaccessible.

captive product pricing A PRICING STRATEGY used by manufacturers of products that require supplies, accessories, or ancillary equipment for operation. The principal product is moderately priced while the supplies and accessories are given substantial markups. For example, ink-jet printers are relatively inexpensive and sometimes even included free with the purchase of a computer. The ink-jet cartridges, on the other hand, are relatively expensive and require frequent replacement.

captive warehouse See PRIVATE WAREHOUSE.

captive wholesaler See MANUFACTURER'S BRANCH OFFICE.

carbon-copy concept/theory In personal selling, a theory that new salespersons are best trained by memorizing the techniques of an exemplary experienced salesperson.

car card An advertisement in the form of a card or poster in a public transit vehicle such as a bus, subway, or train. See also OUTDOOR ADVERTISING.

career apparel 1. Apparel suitable for the executive man or woman (i.e., business suits). 2. Distinctive clothing and accessories manufactured to the specifications of an employer so that its employees will be dressed uniformly for a given position (i.e., uniforms).

care label A tag attached to an item of merchandise that specifies proper maintenance. In apparel, for example, this represents washing, ironing, and/or dry cleaning instructions. The label is sewn into the garment and shows the care instructions as well as the plant identification code. The label may also contain the product code, fiber content, size, country of origin, and other information. See also CARE LABELING RULE (1971).

Care Labeling Rule (1971) Federal legislation stipulating that all apparel selling for over $3.00 must carry labels with washing or dry-cleaning instruction. See also CARE LABEL.

cargo Freight carried by ship, airline, truck, etc.

carload (CL) A quantity of merchandise that fills a freight car or qualifies as a full car in railroad shipping rates. Also called a *carload lot (CL)*.

carload freight rate (CL) A reduced shipping rate allowed to large shipments of merchandise due to the economies of a large shipment over a partial shipment. Also called the *carload rate* and the *full car rate*. See also LESS-THAN-CARLOAD LOT (LCL) and POOL CAR SHIPMENT/SERVICE.

carload lot (CL) See CARLOAD (CL).

carload rate Synonym for CARLOAD FREIGHT RATE (CL).

car lot wholesaler A marketing intermediary who accepts shipments in CARLOAD (CL) lots and later divides them into smaller lots for sale to jobbers and chain store buyers. See also WHOLESALER.

carriage trade   The wealthy patrons of a store or other business who are accorded special services. The term derives from the private carriages in which these patrons formerly arrived.

carrier   1. A commercial transportation firm, such as an airline express company, trucking firm, or steamship line, engaged in the transportation of merchandise from vendor to store.   2. A cylindrical container used in old-fashioned pneumatic tube systems to transport cash, sales slips, and other records from the selling floor to the cashier and back again.

carrying charge   Interest or other service charge paid on the balance owed on a charge account or installment buying plan.

carrying cost   An expense incurred in the storing of inventory from the time of purchase until the time of sale or use. Carrying costs include inventory devaluation during storage, storage charges, and interest charges on funds tied up in inventory.

carryout   A purchase taken from the store by the customer and, therefore, not requiring delivery. Also spelled *carry-out*. Synonymous with *take with transaction* and *take transaction*.

carryover   The time elapsed between a customer's receipt of a catalog or advertisement and the sale. Carryover time is longer with catalogs than with item advertising done by stores. Also spelled *carry-over*.

carryover effect   Any consequence of marketing expenditures, such as for ADVERTISING or new package design, on future sales. When a time period has elapsed between the expenditure and its visible result, the result is known as a DELAYED RESPONSE EFFECT.

carryover merchandise   Unsold goods remaining from a previous season, held for future sale.

cart   Short for SHOPPING CART.

cartage   The fee paid to a carrier for transporting cargo from a pickup point to a destination. Also called *drayage*.

cartel   In international marketing, an agreement between independent businesses or between governments that produce and market similar products (e.g., petroleum). Cartels exist mainly to restrict competition in the marketplace and frequently engage in such activities as price setting, production quota allocations, assignment of markets, and, at times, the distribution of profits.

carton tag   In apparel manufacture, a coded label attached to a carton of finished garments, identifying the contents.

cart-top computing   In RADIO FREQUENCY IDENTIFICATION (RFID), a touch-screen located on the handle of a shopping cart. The computer reads the shopper's ID card, suggests items for purchase based on previous visits, and directs the customer to the shelves where the recommended items are located.

case   A container used for goods sold at wholesale rates (e.g., a case of canned tuna or a case of soda). Buying items *by the case*, even in a retail store, usually implies buying in bulk and paying lower than retail prices.

case allowance   A price reduction given by a wholesaler or manufacturer to a retailer when items are bought by the case. In general, the larger the number of cases purchased, the greater the price reduction.

case goods   Furniture, often made of wood and usually unupholstered, such as chests of drawers, dressers, bookcases, tables, etc.

case method of teaching   Teaching based on an actual problem faced by an actual business. Students are required to gather additional information and form an opinion concerning the action that should be taken.

case-pack/case-packed goods   Prepacked merchandise with a standard assortment of sizes, colors, and styles, shipped from the vendor to the retailer. See also PREPACK.

case product   Synonym for GENERIC PRODUCT.

case wraparound   A sales promotion DISPLAY created to be placed around the case of merchandise on the sales floor.

cash acknowledgment   A notice sent to a buyer confirming receipt of a cash order. The cash acknowledgment may also include new information about merchandise and prices, substitutions for out-of-stock items, and delivery delays.

cash against documents   Payment made for merchandise on the basis of documents indicating shipment.

cash-and-carry   A purchase arrangement in which customers must pay cash and take the merchandise with them when leaving the store (i.e., no delivery service is available).

cash-and-carry store   A retail establishment that sells merchandise for cash only and does not make deliveries.

cash-and-carry wholesaler   A distributor, serving a WAREHOUSING function, who sells quantities of goods at wholesale prices to retailers who pay cash and take away the merchandise. The cash-and-carry wholesaler makes no deliveries and offers no credit or sales assistance, but does offer goods at lower prices than full service wholesalers. See also WHOLESALER.

cash basis   An accounting method in which sales revenues are recorded only when the money from sales is actually received, and expenses only when they are paid. Service businesses (e.g., laundries and restaurants) and professionals (e.g., doctors, dentists, and lawyers) often operate on a cash basis.

cash before delivery (CBD)   Synonymous with CASH IN ADVANCE (CIA). See also CASH DATING.

cash budget   A forecast of expected cash receipts and disbursements for a specified period of time, designed to preclude possible cash-flow problems. By projecting buying and selling patterns for several successive future time periods, the cash budget calculates the firm's cash requirements and indicates its possible need to borrow additional funds.

cash buyer A customer who pays by cash, check, or money order when placing the order.

cash cancellation The revoking of a cash order, requiring a return of the merchandise to the seller and a refund to the buyer of money paid. Such cancellations occur because of customer dissatisfaction with the merchandise or service.

cash card A discount card given to customers by retailers, guaranteeing a discount for cash payment rather than CREDIT CARD payment.

cash cow (Slang) In a large business enterprise, a product that enjoys high earnings but often has low growth potential. Because these products generate large amounts of cash, their excess earnings are often "milked" (i.e., used to the fullest extent possible) to support other divisions of the enterprise or weaker selling products. See also BELL COW.

cash dating A payment arrangement with no provision for discount or payment periods. Suppliers ship CASH ON DELIVERY (COD) to new retailers with no established credit or to retailers with poor credit history. CASH IN ADVANCE (CIA), CASH WITH ORDER (CWO), and CASH BEFORE DELIVERY (CBD) are other forms of cash dating. See also SIGHT DRAFT/BILL OF LADING (SD/BL).

cash discount A reduction from the invoice price, granted to a buyer for prompt payment. For example, if the terms of the bill are 2/10, net 30, the buyer may deduct 2 percent from the billed amount if the invoice is paid within 10 days. Otherwise, the full amount is due in 30 days. Cash discounts are computed by multiplying the discount rate by the cost of the goods as billed on the invoice, and subtracting the result from the billed cost to determine the balance due. Sometimes referred to as a *cash discount on purchases, purchase discount,* or *settlement discount.* See also DATING OF INVOICES.

cash flow The movement of money both into the business (i.e., receipts and revenue) and out of the business (i.e., disbursements) for a given period of time.

cash flow analysis An examination of the timing of cash receipts and disbursements to identify periods of time in which working capital may be either inadequate or excessive. It expresses future income and expenditures in a dollar amount and predicts cash flow based on anticipated sales volume. A cash flow analysis may be prepared on a weekly or monthly basis for semiannual or annual projections, and involves the following steps: establishing the period; estimating sales; estimating anticipated cash inflows from the estimated sales; analyzing the expected cash outflow; comparing the estimated inflow with the estimated outflow to determine the net cash gain or loss for the period; and providing an estimated cash balance. The primary use of a cash flow analysis is to help plan the firm's needs for short-term CAPITAL to maintain the business.

cash flow statement An itemized list of cash receipts and disbursements over a particular period of time.

cashier A store employee whose job it is to collect and record customers' payments. The cashier works at the CASH REGISTER or POINT-OF-SALE TERMINAL (POST), rings up the customer's purchases, accepts payment (cash, check, credit card, etc.), makes change, and sometimes wraps the merchandise. See also RELIEF CASHIER.

cashier method A self-service method of organizing selling departments. Customers make their own selections and take them to a cashier for payment and wrapping.

cashier-wrapper A store employee whose job it is to wrap all merchandise at a given point and receive payment for that merchandise.

cash in advance (CIA) A term of sale used interchangeably with *cash before delivery (CBD).* The seller requires payment before goods are transferred to the purchaser. No credit is extended and no risk is assumed by the seller. See also CASH DATING.

cash incentive Any promotional method used to encourage customers to pay for their orders at the time of ordering. Cash incentives frequently take the form of small gifts or supplemental items, always less costly than the costs associated with billing customers at a future date and waiting for payment.

cashing out A lifestyle trend among individuals (mostly women) who opt out of corporate life or who have strong entrepreneurial drives. Such individuals tend to open their own businesses, often at home, and may be particularly interested in purchasing home office equipment, furniture, and services. This trend may be related to COCOONING.

cash king margin (CKM) An operating measure calculated by finding the difference between operating cash flow and capital expenditures and dividing it by sales. CKM indicates the company's cash-generating power.

cash on delivery (COD) A term of sale requiring payment for goods in cash upon their receipt by the purchaser. Synonymous with *collect on delivery (COD)* and *collection on delivery (COD).* See also CASH DATING.

cash order An order for merchandise accompanied by the required payment. Used interchangeably with CASH WITH ORDER (CWO).

cash rebate See REBATE.

cash receipts report A form used by salespeople to record money received from cash sales of merchandise at the close of each business day.

cash refund See REFUND.

cash refund offer   Synonym for REBATE.

cash register   Sometimes referred to as a *sales register* or simply a *register*, the cash register is used by cashiers and salespeople to record transactions, make change, perform arithmetical operations, calculate tax, tabulate sales by department, etc. A cash register may or may not be connected to a central computer as is a POINT-OF-SALE-TERMINAL (POST).

cash register bank   An assortment of change prepared at the end of the day by the SALESPERSON operating the register or a CASHIER for use at the start of the next business day. Sometimes called a *cash register fund*, a *reserve bank*, or (in Canada and the United Kingdom) a *float*.

cash register fund   Synonym for CASH REGISTER BANK.

cash register tape redemption plan   See TAPE PLAN.

cash sale   A transaction in which the customer pays money for merchandise at the time of purchase.

cash-send   A CASH SALE in which the customer elects to have the merchandise delivered.

cash-take   A CASH SALE in which the customer elects to take the purchase away at the time of the sale.

cash terms   An agreement to pay cash for purchased goods, usually within a specified period of time. See also CASH DATING.

cash with order (CWO)   A term of sale requiring that a payment sufficient to cover the cost of the merchandise and delivery accompany the customer's order. Used interchangeably with *cash order*. See also CASH DATING and CASH ORDER.

casual exporting   Activities of firms that engage in some export business but do not actively seek it. Also known as *accidental exporting*.

Casual Fridays   See DRESSDOWN TREND.

catalog   A promotional book, pamphlet, or electronic database in which merchandise is presented to prospective purchasers. Catalogs commonly provide a picture of the item being offered for sale together with descriptive copy and such essential information as price, shipping charges, delivery time, etc. Some retailers maintain a CATALOG SHOWROOM or store, either as a freestanding unit or as a department in the retail store's own facility. Many retailers now make all or part of their catalog available on their Web sites. Often called a *mail order catalog*. See also VENDOR CATALOG and MAGALOG.

catalog appliance showroom   A retail outlet that displays sample appliances for customers' inspection alongside catalog listing prices. Orders are filled from an adjoining stockroom, and prices are generally below list price.

catalog buyer   A customer who makes a purchase from a catalog.

catalog buying   The practice, frequently employed by chain store managers, of selecting and ordering merchandise from catalogs provided by a buying office. Many vendors, particularly those whose merchandise remains fairly stable, offer catalogs to prospective accounts. Products such as lighting fixtures, cabinetry, eating utensils, and dinnerware are often sold by catalog. Food retailers frequently utilize catalog buying to order merchandise such as canned goods and cleaning products. Distinct from CATALOG RETAILING, in which the ultimate consumer shops and buys at retail from printed catalogs provided by retailers.

catalog house   A wholesale merchant whose business is based primarily on orders deriving from catalogs and mail order solicitation aimed at retailers. Catalog houses now supply a very small percentage of the merchandise sold by stores. Also known as a *mail order wholesaler*. See also WHOLESALER.

catalog merchandising   Promotion of items for sale in a catalog.

catalog plan   See PRICE AGREEMENT PLAN.

catalog retailer   See CATALOG RETAILING.

catalog retailer coupon   See RETAILER (SPONSORED) COUPON.

catalog retailing   A form of selling in which the retailer provides the consumer with a merchandise catalog by either mailing it to the consumer's home or by making it available in a facility maintained by the retailer for that purpose. The consumer may submit an order by mail (usually using an attached order form), by telephone, or on the retailer's Web page (where there is often a special section for ordering by catalog number). The consumer may also fill out an order form at the retailer's CATALOG SHOWROOM. Merchandise ordered is delivered to the consumer by mail or parcel service. Full line general merchandise catalogs, once the hallmark of catalog retailing, have largely been replaced by smaller specialty catalogs. In addition, many catalog retailers have successfully made the transition to E-TAILING.

catalog sales   See CATALOG RETAILING.

catalog showroom   A warehouse showroom where catalog retailing and in-store retailing are brought together. Merchandise is presented in catalogs that the customer consults before placing an order with a clerk. Very little stock is on display and the barebones atmosphere is not designed for the comfort of the customer. Merchandise is brought in from the warehouse and the customer pays for it. Catalog showroom merchants concentrate on a wide selection of fast-moving, nationally advertised namebrand products, which they offer at prices below regular retail. Also known as a *catalog store* or a *retail catalog showroom*.

catalog showroom merchandising   See CATALOG SHOWROOM.

catalog showroom retailer   See CATALOG SHOWROOM.

catalog store   Synonym for CATALOG SHOWROOM.

catalogue   Alternative spelling of CATALOG.

catalog wholesaler See CATALOG HOUSE.

catchment area The geographic area served by a store or social service agency (e.g., a hospital) in which the majority of its clients or customers may be found.

category Synonym for CLASSIFICATION.

category killer A retailer, particularly a specialty superstore with discount overtones, that focuses on limited merchandise classifications and great breadth and depth of assortment. A category killer dominates its retail category in terms of both profitability and growth of market share. Consequently, it "kills" the category of business for more generalized retail stores whose assortments are shallow by comparison. Certain bookstores (e.g., Barnes & Noble and Borders), do-it-yourself (DYI) stores (e.g., Home Depot and Lowe's), toy stores (e.g., Toys 'R' Us), music stores (e.g., Virgin Records), and sporting goods retailers (e.g., Oshman's and The Sports Authority) are considered category killers in their particular areas of specialization. An unusually large category killer is often called a MEGASTORE or a SUPERSTORE. Synonymous with *specialized superstore*, *cult merchant*, and *specialty discounter*.

category week A special event that features a particular category of merchandise (e.g., lingerie). The event may be store-specific (i.e., at one store), or it may be sponsored by a producer or trade association and involve several competing retailers. During the week, in-store events are held at participating stores to increase the sales of the category. Events may include fashion shows, celebrity appearances, musical performances, etc. See also VENDOR WEEK.

causal relationships See CAUSAL RESEARCH.

causal research MARKETING RESEARCH (MR) that focuses on relationships of cause and effect in the MARKETPLACE. For example, causal researchers may study the effect of advertising on the rate at which products sell. Such studies are also known as the *analysis of causal relationships*.

cause marketing The application of marketing principles to political, social, educational, charitable, cultural, and religious causes in an effort to change people's attitudes and, ultimately, their behavior. Not to be confused with CAUSE-RELATED MARKETING.

cause-related marketing Marketing efforts (e.g., corporate sponsorship of the Olympic Games) in which a particular brand or product is linked to a particular cause or special event. The primary objective of cause-related marketing is the generation of revenue, although it may also result in increased GOODWILL. Not to be confused with CAUSE MARKETING.

caution/caution fee An admission or entrance payment required by HAUTE COUTURE houses from commercial customers during showings. Intended to deter copying, the fee may usually be applied to purchases, and is consequently called a MINIMUM.

caveat emptor A Latin term meaning *let the buyer beware*. As a policy of sellers, it implies that purchases are made at the cus-

tomer's own risk, the seller assuming no responsibility and offering no GUARANTEE or return privilege.

caveat subscriptor Synonym for CAVEAT VENDITOR/VENDOR, more commonly used in real estate and mortgage transactions.

caveat venditor/vendor A Latin term meaning *let the seller beware*. As a legal principle, it implies that the seller is responsible for the quality and quantity of the goods sold. Also called *caveat subscriptor*.

CBD See CASH BEFORE DELIVERY (CBD) or CENTRAL BUSINESS DISTRICT (CBD).

CBP See U.S. CUSTOMS SERVICE.

CBSA See CORE-BASED STATISTICAL AREA (CBSA).

CDM See CONSUMER DEMAND MANAGEMENT (CDM).

cease and desist order An order, often emanating from a court or administrative agency, prohibiting the continuance of a particular activity on the part of some individual or corporate entity. For example, the FEDERAL TRADE COMMISSION (FTC) may order a company to cease and desist from a particular marketing practice that has been judged deceptive.

ceiling grid A design element used in a store's window display. Made of a network or grating of metal wire, pipes, or wood lattices, ceiling grids allow the window dresser to attach things into a dense ceiling so that they may hang down into the display. See also WINDOW DISPLAY.

ceiling price 1. A maximum price at which goods may be sold as established by law. 2. The highest price buyers can or are willing to pay for a product. Also called the *price ceiling*. 3. The price set by direct competitors for identical products.

celebrity advertising See CELEBRITY MARKETING.

celebrity appearance A store promotion that features a well-known individual from inside or outside the fashion industry brought in to promote a new product or designer line. Celebrity appearances are often cooperative events with designers, retailers, and publishers participating. Cosmetics makers often celebrate new fragrances with the designer or celebrity spokesperson appearing at the in-store product launch. During slower sales periods, malls may invite television stars to make guest appearances and sign autographs, etc.

celebrity marketing A form of PERSON MARKETING in which the promotion of entertainers, sports figures, etc., is undertaken by managers, publicity directors, or agencies such as the William Morris Agency. In celebrity marketing, the goals of the marketing campaign are to create, maintain, or alter attitudes toward a particular celebrity or group of celebrities through media appearances, press coverage, and other publicity. See also POLITICAL CANDIDATE MARKETING. Not to be confused with CELEBRITY TESTIMONIAL.

celebrity testimonial A type of promotion in which big-name personalities are used to praise or recommend a particular product, service, idea, or institution. For example, retired professional athletes may be used to solicit contributions to a charity or to promote prosocial behavior such as not driving while intoxicated. Not to be confused with CELEBRITY MARKETING. See also TESTIMONIAL.

Celler-Kefauver Antimerger Act (1950) An amendment to the CLAYTON ACT (1914) that prohibits the acquisition of any part of the assets of a competing company, as well as its stock, if such an acquisition would substantially lessen competition or tend to create a monopoly. Sometimes referred to as the *Antimerger Act (1950)*.

cell phone A mobile telephone that is small, handheld, and wireless. Cell phones are increasingly ubiquitous; those with WIRELESS ACCESS PROTOCOL (WAP) can connect to the INTERNET, enabling potential customers to shop whenever they like and from wherever they happen to be. Short for *cellular phone*. Also called a *mobile cellular phone*.

CEM See CUSTOMER ELIMINATION MANAGEMENT (CEM).

census In MARKETING RESEARCH (MR), as in other social science research, a census is a complete canvass of every member of a POPULATION (or universe) under study, as opposed to SAMPLING. Also known as a *population survey*.

Census of Business See ECONOMIC CENSUS.

Census of Housing A report on housing availability and costs in the United States, made available by the U.S. Census Bureau in print and online at www.census.gov.

Census of the Population An official count of the population. In the United States, a census of the population is taken every ten years. It provides aggregated information about the age, gender, education, household income, presence of children in the household, etc., of people residing in a particular geographical area (from block level and census tract to city, county, and state, etc.). Retailers use census information in RETAIL SITE LOCATION and other merchandising activities involving an understanding of current or potential customers. The U.S. Bureau of the Census maintains a web presence at www.census.gov. In addition, the Census Bureau makes much of this data available online at the *American FactFinder* Web site at www.factfinder.census.gov. See also ECONOMIC CENSUS.

centers of influence method In sales prospecting, a salesperson's efforts to develop a list of prospects (i.e., potential customers) by asking influential and professional people for the names of potential customers.

center store In supermarket design, the middle area (or center), in which staples and similar products are often sold.

central business district (CBD) 1. The area of a city or town that contains a high concentration of retail businesses, offices, theaters, etc. CBDs are characterized by high traffic flow and often consist of one or more complete census tracts. Also called an *urban core*. 2. In a broader sense, a city's original retailing center (i.e., what is commonly referred to as downtown.) See also DOWNTOWN BUSINESS/SHOPPING DISTRICT.

central buyer A BUYER responsible for the selection and purchase of merchandise for a group of similar departments or merchandise classifications in chain stores or branches of a department store. See also CENTRAL BUYING.

central buying In large retail organizations, the concentration of the authority and responsibility for merchandise selection and purchase (for a chain of stores or branch stores of a department store) in the hands on the headquarters staff rather than in the individual units. The central buying function is generally located in the FLAGSHIP STORE/DIVISION. Also known as *consolidated buying* or *centralized buying*.

central buying office A buying office servicing a chain store operation and having the ultimate responsibility for selecting and buying the merchandise to be sold in the various stores.

central county Under the standards published in 2000, a county with at least 50 percent of its population, or at least five thousand people, residing in urban areas whose population is ten thousand or more. Additional outlying counties are included in the CBSA if they meet specified requirements of commuting to or from the central counties. Counties or equivalent entities form the geographic building blocks for metropolitan and micropolitan statistical areas throughout the United States and Puerto Rico.

centralization See CENTRALIZED ORGANIZATION.

centralized adjustment system A separate office or department in a retail store, staffed by trained personnel, in which all customer complaints, adjustments, or refunds are handled. This is an alternative to having these functions carried out in the individual selling departments.

centralized buying See CENTRAL BUYING.

centralized organization 1. An organizational structure in some multistore operations in which control of the decision-making processes remains with the central or parent organization, (e.g., with headquarters or the flagship store). 2. Similarly, in multinational marketing, an organizational structure in which control remains with the parent company in its home country. 3. Any organizational structure in which most of the authority and responsibility is concentrated at the top. Such an organization tends to be hierarchical, with only a narrow span of management at each level, and is consequently sometimes referred to as a *tall organization*.

centralized purchasing A system in which one department or unit of an organization is authorized to order, procure, and store all supplies, equipment, etc. required for carrying out the organization's business. These are then distributed to the other departments as requested.

centralized sales organization An organization in which the sales function is concentrated at the highest levels of management.

central market   A geographical area containing a large concentration of suppliers either in a MERCHANDISE MART (such as the Chicago Merchandise Mart) or simply clustered in the same general section of a city (such as the GARMENT CENTER in New York City). Also called a *trade mart*.

central merchandise plan   A form of BUYING found in multiunit organizations in which all buying functions are in the hands of a central authority that chooses the merchandise, sets prices, and supervises distribution to the various stores. See also CENTRAL BUYING.

central place   A cluster of retail establishments serving as a source of goods and services for an area larger than itself.

central place theory   A theory of geographical location for retailers developed by Walter Christaller in 1933 and translated into English in 1938. Christaller defined the CENTRAL PLACE as the location that required the least amount of travel and provided the greatest accessibility to the surrounding community. Subsequently modified by Lösch (1954), Berry and Garrison (1958), Beckmann (1958), and others, the theory provides much of the conceptual basis for the geography of RETAIL SITE LOCATION.

central warehousing and requisition (plan)   See WAREHOUSE AND REQUISITION PLAN.

central wrap   An area or department in which a store's wrapping and packaging services are localized, regardless of the selling department from which they were selected. Compare CLERK WRAP and DEPARTMENT WRAP. Also called *central wrapping department* and *regional wrap*.

cents-off coupon   A certificate entitling the customer to a reduced purchase price for the item being promoted. The product and the amount of the cash saving are specified in the certificate, which is generally redeemable at the point of purchase. Some supermarkets and other food retailers double the value of redeemed cents-off coupons (especially manufacturers' cents-off coupons) as a special promotion. With the advent of computerized checkout systems, some supermarkets and other food retailers offer clipless coupons requiring no certificate, while others generate cents-off coupons for future purchases directly from the register. Some cents-off coupons have stated expiration dates, while others are open-ended.

cents-off deal/offer   A form of price promotion, common in the grocery business, in which particular consumer products are marked down and prominently labeled to indicate the number of cents by which the price is reduced from the regular retail price.

CEO   See CHIEF EXECUTIVE OFFICER (CEO).

certificate   1. A document attesting to the status or qualifications of the holder.   2. A document attesting the truth of any claim, such as the origin, saleable condition, authenticity, etc., of an item. Certificates may also be digital. See CERTIFICATE AUTHORITY (CA).

certificate authority (CA)   A third-party organization or company that issues digital certificates used to create digital signatures and public-private key pairs. The CA guarantees that the individual granted the unique certificate is who he or she claims to be. The three most common methods of certification are based on X.509 Certificates and Certification Authorities PGP and SKIP.

certificate of authenticity   A document attesting to the fact that an item is genuine or real and that its origin is supported by unquestionable evidence. Such certificates help to establish the value of items such as original art, antiques, and autographed celebrity memorabilia.

certificate of inspection   A document attesting to the fact that the packed merchandise (e.g., perishable goods, apparel, home electronics) was in good condition immediately prior to shipment.

certificate of insurance   Written documentation that a shipment has been adequately insured against risks; part of the COMMERCIAL SET required in international merchandising.

certificate of manufacture   A document addressed to an importer and signed by an exporter, attesting to the fact that goods ordered by the importer have been finished and are ready for shipment. This document is used in conjunction with a LETTER OF CREDIT (L/C), enabling the exporter to receive payment from the importer's bank.

certificate of origin   A document attesting to the point of origin of a shipment. The document declares that goods purchased from a foreign country have actually been produced in that country and not in another. Under many trade accords, traders are required to submit duly completed certificates of origin to their international counterparts to claim full or partial exemption from customs duties.

certification   The administrative process that checks all necessary records and attests to the validity or authenticity of a product (e.g., celebrity autographs, Norwegian fox fur, etc.) or individual (e.g., a board-certified radiologist).

certification mark   1. A label, seal, or tag placed upon a product, testifying to its quality, worth, or origin.   2. A word or symbol used to designate a product or service as having special authenticity, quality, safety, etc. For example, the mark of the Underwriters Laboratories (UL) is a common certification mark indicating that a product meets certain safety standards. Similarly, the GOOD HOUSEKEEPING SEAL (OF APPROVAL) indicates that products have met the magazine's quality standards.

certified public accountant (CPA)   An accountant who has satisfied the licensing requirements of his or her jurisdiction with regard to age, education, residence, morality, and experience to be registered as a public accountant and who has passed a uniform examination administered by the American Institute of Certified Public Accountants.

CFPR   See COLLABORATIVE PLANNING, FORECASTING, AND REPLENISHMENT (CPFR).

CG   See ADDRESS CODING GUIDE (ACG).

chain   See CHAIN STORE and CHAIN STORE SYSTEM (CSS).

chain buying office   See CORPORATE BUYING OFFICE.

chain department store   See DEPARTMENT STORE.

chain discount   A series of discounts given by a merchandise RESOURCE to the retail buyer. The chain discount is based on an earlier discount for the same items. For example, an item may be discounted 40 percent, 5 percent, and 5 percent. Each discount is computed on the amount that remains after the preceding discount has been taken. In this case, the result is the equivalent of a single discount or 45.85 percent from the list price of the item. Extra trade discounts are given to secure the business of a particular retail store or to stimulate a greater volume of business. Also called a *discount chain*, *series discount*, and *series trade discount*. Compare SINGLE DISCOUNT EQUIVALENT. See also OFF-FACTOR and ON-FACTOR.

chain markup pricing   A form of DEMAND-BASED PRICING in which the final selling price is determined, markups for each channel member are examined, and the maximum acceptable cost to each channel member is computed.

chain of command principle   A management concept in which a traceable line of authority and responsibility runs from the highest to the lowest positions within an organization.

chain of stores   See CHAIN STORE SYSTEM (CSS).

chain organization   Synonym for CHAIN STORE SYSTEM (CSS).

chain-owned buying office   See CORPORATE BUYING OFFICE.

chain prospecting   A method used by salespersons to gather new leads by obtaining additional names from current prospects. When the current prospect is a satisfied customer, the leads are called *referral leads*. Also called the *endless chain method*.

chain ratio method   One of several methods used to determine the size of the potential market. The chain ratio method is focused on the number of prospective customers rather than the dollars to be earned. Retailers and other marketers use the chain ratio method to fine-tune a broad estimate of the market. They begin with a universe of all possible buyers (e.g., population of the United States) and proceed to use percentages systematically to break down the number of potential customers in a logical manner, considering the characteristics of increasingly smaller and more focused groups (e.g., U.S. female homemakers). The chain ratio method is an example of a DECOMPOSE AND BUILD-UP METHOD for estimating market size.

chain store   Two or more stores, usually in different locations, being operated by the same organization and usually owned by that organization. Larger chains (with 12 or more stores) are called CHAIN STORE SYSTEMS (CSS). Chain stores are classified as *local* (operating stores within a narrow geographic area, usually defined as a city and its outlying areas), *regional* (operating stores within a particular region of the country, such as Southwest or Northeast), or *national* (operating stores in virtually every region of the country). Also known as a *retail chain* and a *multiple retailer*.

Chain Store Law   A popular name for the ROBINSON-PATMAN ACT (1936).

chain store system (CSS)   A group of stores (usually a dozen or more) commonly owned and centrally merchandised and managed. The term is applied to large MASS MERCHANDISING organizations (such as JCPenney and Sears), FRANCHISE chains (such as Burger King and McDonald's), and SPECIALTY CHAINS (such as Gap and Bed Bath & Beyond), and is not limited to any particular line or classification of merchandise, nor to any particular price point. Chain stores that have typically located in shopping centers and malls in the past have recently shown interest in town centers (i.e., downtowns). Also known as a *retail chain*. See also VOLUNTARY CHAIN.

chain store warehouse   An establishment operated by a CHAIN STORE SYSTEM (CSS) for the assembly and distribution of goods and the performance of other WAREHOUSE functions for the stores of the multiunit organization.

channel   See CHANNEL OF DISTRIBUTION.

channel agreement   In producer-to-buyer distribution channels, a contract between a producer and a retailer. For example, some producers market their own products online and through other direct selling channels (e.g., catalogs) and may also reach agreements with traditional retailers for the in-store sale of their products. Some products may be sold both by the producer's Web site and the Web site of the retailer. Channel agreements are fairly volatile; they are regularly formed and just as regularly broken.

channel alignment   In a CHANNEL OF DISTRIBUTION, the structure adopted by the chosen channel members to achieve a unified distribution strategy.

channel cannibalization   The loss of sales (i.e., market share) in an existing channel when a new channel is introduced to sell the same product or products. For example, a manufacturer may introduce a new channel by creating a Web presence and using it to sell merchandise directly to the ultimate consumer. This new channel may eat into sales at the retail level. Consequently, some manufacturers use their Web sites to redirect potential customers to their dealers or retail distributors rather than to sell directly to the customers. This helps to avoid cannibalizing their dealer and distributor networks.

channel captain   The organization (usually a manufacturer or a wholesaler, but sometimes a retailer) that dominates and controls a CHANNEL OF DISTRIBUTION, almost always by virtue of economic power. The channel captain assumes leadership within the channel, often setting the distribution policy, and can influence the behavior of other members of the distribution channel. Also called *channel leader*.

channel change A switch, on the part of a marketer, to alternative methods of distribution as a result of conflict in the CHANNEL OF DISTRIBUTION (or when a new sales focus or increased marketing activity is required). Marketers are often reluctant to change channels, because doing so impacts virtually every area in the company. However, when the dealer, retailer, or independent agent has different objectives from the marketer's and therefore does not implement the marketing program as envisioned by the marketer, change may be necessary.

channel conflict Dissonance between two or more members at different levels of a CHANNEL OF DISTRIBUTION. Channel conflict is commonly found when one member of the channel (e.g., a dominant manufacturer) attempts to control the entire distribution system. VERTICAL CHANNEL CONFLICT is conflict between channel members at different levels in the distribution chain (e.g., between a wholesaler and a retailer). HORIZONTAL CHANNEL CONFLICT is dissonance between two or more members of a CHANNEL OF DISTRIBUTION who are operating at the same level (not to be confused with normal competition). For example, one retailer may feel that another retailer is gaining unfair advantage by intimidating a supplier on whom both depend. See also INTERTYPE CHANNEL CONFLICT.

channel control Synonym for CHANNEL POWER.

channel cooperation Positive interaction between all members of a CHANNEL OF DISTRIBUTION, resulting in increased sales and profits for all participants. In general, it is up to the CHANNEL CAPTAIN to win the voluntary cooperation of other CHANNEL MEMBERS, often by providing advertising materials, training a marketing intermediary's sales force, giving financial advice to a channel member, etc. In retailing, retail channel captains assist manufacturers by providing information on consumer preferences and buying patterns. If the channel captain is unsuccessful in fostering voluntary cooperation, it may attempt to coerce its channel members by such methods as an EXCLUSIVE DEALING AGREEMENT/CONTRACT, a TYING AGREEMENT/CONTRACT, FULL LINE FORCING, RECIPROCITY, RESALE PRICE MAINTENANCE (RPM), DISCRIMINATORY PRICING, or REFUSAL-TO-SELL. However, many of these methods are, if not illegal, closely monitored and limited by government regulations.

channel fit In product marketing, the degree to which a new product is suitable for an existing CHANNEL OF DISTRIBUTION. A product is said to have a good channel fit when it is simply added to an existing line and can be sold through the same wholesalers and retailers that handle the company's other products. Sometimes called, simply, FIT.

channel flow Any form of movement (of product, title, credit, information, etc.) connecting the various members of a CHANNEL OF DISTRIBUTION (manufacturers/producers, distributors, retailers, customers, etc.). Channel flows include *physical flow* (the actual movement of products or delivery of services toward the customer), *title or ownership flow* (the transfer of title to goods from one channel member to another), *financial or payment flow* (the granting of credit downward in the channel and the movement of payment upward), and the *communication or information flow* (the transfer of product information downward, personal selling efforts, and various promotional and advertising campaigns). Also called *transactional flow*.

channel integration See VERTICAL INTEGRATION.

channel interdependency A relationship among members of a CHANNEL OF DISTRIBUTION in which the activities of one may, to a considerable degree, influence the activities of others.

channel intermediaries Agents and brokers working in the CHANNEL OF DISTRIBUTION to bring manufacturers/producers and buyers/retailers together. Agents have legal authority to act in the name of another. The sales force of a manufacturer's agent may handle similar products for different manufacturers and sell them in different territories. Brokers bring the buyer and seller together to negotiate a sale. Channel intermediaries, particularly brokers, are vulnerable to Internet sites that can duplicate their services. See also BROKER, MARKETING INTERMEDIARY, and MIDDLEMAN.

channel leader Synonym for CHANNEL CAPTAIN.

channel length The various levels of wholesaling intermediaries and retailers, etc. taken as a whole (i.e., the number of intermediaries involved in bringing a product from the manufacturer to the consumer). Consumer goods often go through a four-link (or sometimes five-link) channel employing both wholesale and retail intermediaries on their way from producer to consumer. Industrial goods generally go through fewer channels, as they are often sold directly by the producer to the industrial customer. The length of the channel is affected by the product market characteristics, company characteristics, and the economic environment.

channel member Any firm participating in the distribution process that brings goods from the producer or manufacturer to the ultimate consumer or to the industrial buyer. Channel members contribute value-added service at each transfer point in the channel through their specialized knowledge, skills, experience, and contacts.

channel number The number of different marketing channels employed by a marketer. The number of different channels varies if the company is selling to entirely different markets or to different market segments. For example, a cosmetics manufacturer such as Revlon sells its high-priced line directly to department stores, but its low-priced products are sold through intermediaries to drugstores. The number of channels also depends on geographic regions and the size of retail firms buying the manufacturer's products.

channel of distribution The route along which goods and services travel from producer/manufacturer through marketing intermediaries (such as wholesalers, distributors, and retailers) to the final user. Channels of distribution provide DOWNSTREAM VALUE by bringing finished products to end users. This flow may involve the physical movement of the product or simply the transfer of title to it. Also known as a *distribution channel*, a *distribution chain*, a *distribution pipeline*, a *supply chain*, a *marketing channel*, a *market channel*, and a *trade channel*.

channel power   The capacity to make other members of a CHANNEL OF DISTRIBUTION conform to one's wishes. The member who exerts this power is called the CHANNEL CAPTAIN or *channel leader.*

channel strategy   The planned distribution of a product through selected channels to achieve a particular marketing goal. For example, a product may be sold directly to the consumer, through a wholesaler, through an agent, etc.

channel structure   The form a channel takes, including CHANNEL LENGTH, arrangement, composition (i.e., types of marketing intermediaries), and size. Channel structure is largely determined by company attributes, product type, customer characteristics and expectations, competitors in the marketplace, custom, and the overall marketing environment. In the e-tailing arena, the channel structure may include virtual intermediaries whose only function is to provide a platform where buyers and sellers can interact directly (e.g., eBay).

channel surfing   See SURFING.

channel system   See CONVENTIONAL CHANNEL.

channel vision   A firm's view of how marketing functions should be allocated among the members of the CHANNEL OF DISTRIBUTION to which it belongs, and its recognition of places in the channel where there are opportunities for improvement.

channel width   The number of different outlets or individual firms employed at each level of the CHANNEL OF DISTRIBUTION. Channel width is on a continuum from intensive to exclusive. It is considered intensive when the manufacturer/producer sells through almost any available wholesale or retail outlet, and exclusive when the manufacturer/producer sells through only one wholesaler or retailer in a given area. Channel width is considered selective when more than one but fewer than all the firms that might carry a product are used. Prestige items, such as automobiles, appliances, etc., use exclusive or selective distribution. See also INTENSIVE DISTRIBUTION, SELECTIVE DISTRIBUTION, and EXCLUSIVE DISTRIBUTION.

Chapter 11   A section of the 1978 amendments to the Federal Bankruptcy Law that freezes a debtor's indebtedness to lending institutions, suppliers, and bondholders. The debtor organization retains its assets for use in a PLAN OF REORGANIZATION (POR) designed to help the debtor regain profitability. See also BANKRUPTCY.

character merchandise   A subtype of licensed product involving a contractual relationship between the holder of the rights to a cartoon character, motion picture, television show, or other popular icon (particularly those appealing to children) and a manufacturer to produce items under that name or brand. A royalty fee, usually computed as a percentage of sales, is paid to the designer or owner of the rights to the character. For example, children's clothing bearing the images of various Muppets from *The Muppet Show* and *Sesame Street* were quite popular in the 1980s. Similarly, any Disney release generates an extensive line of toys, clothing, school supplies, and other paraphernalia bearing a Disney image and logo.

charge   The act of making a purchase for credit without making an immediate payment. Payment is generally made following billing. See also CHARGE ACCOUNT and CREDIT CARD.

charge account   A consumer credit arrangement whereby a store customer is allowed to buy goods or services and pay for them within a specified period (sometimes as much as 90 days, but usually approximately 30 days) without incurring interest or service charges. Also called an *open account,* an *open charge account,* a *regular account,* a *regular charge account,* or a *thirty-day charge.* See also REVOLVING CREDIT and INSTALLMENT PLAN/CONTRACT/BUYING.

charge account credit   A short-term extension of credit by a store to a customer, on the assumption that the customer will be able to meet payment obligations out of current income. The customer is generally allowed 30 days (sometimes up to 90 days) before the bill becomes due, during which time no interest or carrying charges are incurred. Also called *noninstallment credit.*

charge account plan   See CHARGE ACCOUNT CREDIT.

charge-a-plate   Copyrighted name, no longer in use, of the small card identifying a charge account customer and used to imprint the sales check in a charge sale. See also CHARGE PLATE.

charge audit   A check on the accuracy of charge transactions to insure the correspondence between the respective records of the accounts receivable department, salespersons, and selling departments.

charge-authorizing phone   A telephone located in the selling department, or at the point of sale, linking the salesperson to the credit files section and used exclusively to verify the customer's ability to make a charge purchase. See also CHARGE PHONE SYSTEM.

chargeback   A retailer's invoice for claims against a vendor. Such claims may result from damaged merchandise, cooperative advertising costs, adjustments, and the recovery of transportation charges for improperly routed merchandise. Also called a *retrieval request.* Sometimes spelled *charge-back.*

charge buyer   A customer who makes a purchase on credit, to be billed at a later time. Also called *credit buyer.*

charge card   Current term used for the small plastic card identifying a charge account customer by name, number, and signature. Differs from a CREDIT CARD in that its use is limited to the issuing store or other business. While some retailers continue to use the card to imprint sales checks, most electronic checkout systems simply read the information into the computerized checkout system and a receipt is generated from the register. The card entitles the holder to purchase goods or services either up to a prescribed limit or, in some cases, without limit provided that payment in full is made at regular intervals (usually monthly). Some charge cards are issued by retailers while others are issued by banks. Also called a *store card* or a *retail credit card.*

charge customer   A customer who has credit privileges, usually in the form of a CHARGE ACCOUNT.

charge phone system The process by which a salesperson may have certain orders approved and authorized by telephone. See also CHARGE-AUTHORIZING PHONE.

charge plate Term formerly used for the small card identifying a charge account customer by name, number, and signature and used to imprint sales checks. The original name was CHARGE-A-PLATE. The terms CHARGE CARD and CREDIT CARD are currently used instead.

charges See COSTS.

charge sale A retail transaction in which the amount of the purchase is added to a customer's account, payable at the end of the month or on a revolving basis.

charge-send sale/transaction A transaction in which the amount of the sale is charged to the customer's account and the merchandise is delivered to the customer. See also PREAUTHORIZATION.

charges forward An arrangement under which the customer pays for shipped goods only after they have been received or when the customer has been billed by the vendor.

charge-take sale A transaction in which the amount of the sale is charged to the customer's account and the customer takes the merchandise away.

charging what the traffic can bear Synonym for PROFIT MAXIMIZATION OBJECTIVE.

charity show A FASHION SHOW produced by one or more retailers to raise money and awareness for national, local, or fundraising charities. In addition to selling merchandise, the retailer is promoting GOODWILL and building a strong community image. Celebrities, designers, and models often lend their support to these events.

Charlotte Merchandise Mart A privately owned merchandise mart located in Charlotte, North Carolina. The mart maintains a Web site at www.charlottemerchmart.com.

chart of accounts A classified and systematic listing of all accounts maintained by a business, including names and numbers. Computer applications are often used to generate the listing as a database for easy sorting, manipulation, and searching.

chat Real-time, synchronous communication between two remote INTERNET users via computer. Users send text to each other's computers by typing on their respective keyboards. Their interaction is called a *chat session*. Most networks and online services offer chat capability. See also INTERNET RELAY CHAT (IRC), INSTANT MESSAGING (IM), CHAT ANALYSIS, and BUDDY LIST.

chat analysis In MARKETING RESEARCH (MR), the study of discussions in online chat groups that are active 24 hours a day every day of the year and address a myriad of topics. Conversations are analyzed without participants' knowledge, a type of research that has serious privacy and ethical implications. See also CHAT.

chatbot A ROBOT in general use in the Internet environment, simulating human conversation through artificial intelligence. A chatbot may communicate with a human being or with another chatbot. Chatbots may be used in e-commerce customer service, call centers, and Internet gaming, and are limited to conversations regarding a specific purpose. Sometimes spelled *chat bot*. Also called a *chatterbot*.

chat room A virtual room online where a CHAT session takes place. Its technical name is INTERNET RELAY CHAT (IRC) channel.

chat server See SERVER.

chat session See CHAT.

chattel mortgage An agreement between a borrower and a lender that while the movable property purchased through the loan belongs to the borrower, the lender has a legal right to the property if payments are not made as specified in the loan agreement.

chatterbot Synonym for CHATBOT.

cheap jack (Slang) An individual who sells merchandise rapidly and inexpensively, often by unorthodox methods such as selling out of an unoccupied store.

checker 1. A CASHIER who rings up a customer's purchases and takes payment, particularly in a supermarket. 2. A store employee who compares the goods received to the vendor's invoices. See also CHECKING.

checking The process by which a retail employee (i.e., a CHECKER) or an employee of a retail DISTRIBUTION CENTER (DC) examines a shipment from a vendor to be sure that the correct merchandise, in correct quantities and satisfactory quality, has been received. The process includes matching the purchase order to the invoice, opening shipping containers, sorting merchandise, and examining the quality and quantity of the goods received. Also called *order checking*. See also EVALUATION OF MERCHANDISE.

checklist 1. In RETAIL SITE LOCATION studies, a rudimentary form of geographical information system (GIS). Market analysts or their client retailers compile a list of desirable criteria and compare the list to the attributes of potential sites for the new store. Criteria vary, depending on the needs and interests of the retailer, but they often include such factors as traffic counts, proximity to highways, and demographic characteristics of potential shoppers in the TRADING AREA. 2. See BREAD-AND-BUTTER ASSORTMENT/GOODS.

checkout 1. (Slang) A fast-selling item. 2. Short for CHECKOUT COUNTER. Sometimes spelled *check-out*.

checkout counter The table or station where customers bring self-selected merchandise to pay the cashier and to have the merchandise wrapped. Sometimes spelled *check-out counter*. Also called a *checkout stand* or a *check-out stand*.

checkout pass In RADIO FREQUENCY IDENTIFICATION (RFID), the instant scanning of all items in the customer's shopping cart and the debiting of the customer's bank account for the total amount due. Sometimes spelled *check-out pass*.

checkout stand Synonym for CHECKOUT COUNTER.

check question In personal sales, a carefully phrased question designed to determine whether the customer is making progress toward a buying decision.

cherry picker A piece of warehouse equipment used to obtain merchandise from elevated locations. It consists of an elevator tower mounted on a truck. Cherry pickers are frequently found in a WAREHOUSE STORE.

cherry picking 1. The selection by a BUYER of only a few items from each vendor's line, without purchasing a complete line or classification of merchandise from any one resource. Also called *hi-spotting*. 2. The selection and purchase by a CUSTOMER of only a store's specials (which are often loss leaders). See also LOSS LEADER.

ChexSystems See BANKCHECK FRAUD TASK FORCE.

chic Elegant, stylish, sophisticated, smart. *Der.* French.

Chicago Board of Trade See COMMODITY EXCHANGE.

Chicago Board Options Exchange See COMMODITY EXCHANGE.

Chicago Mercantile Exchange See COMMODITY EXCHANGE.

Chicago Merchandise Mart See MERCHANDISE MART.

chief executive officer (CEO) 1. The manager in a large retail organization who occupies the top position in the hierarchy. The CEO may also have the title President or Chairman/woman of the Board, but it is the designation as CEO that makes the CEO first among equals, regardless of the number of other top executives. 2. In a CORPORATION, the officer appointed by the board of directors to carry out its policies and supervise the activities of the corporation. See also TANDEM MANAGEMENT.

chief marketing officer (CMO) In large business organizations, a management-level executive responsible for promoting the marketing perspective within the firm and for developing the firm's STRATEGIC MARKETING PLAN.

Child Protection Act (1966) Federal consumer legislation banning the sale of hazardous toys and other items intended for use by children. Amended by the CHILD PROTECTION AND TOY SAFETY ACT (1969).

Child Protection and Toy Safety Act (1969) A Federal consumer law designed to provide protection from dangerous children's toys, especially those posing electrical or thermal hazards. Updated and amended the CHILD PROTECTION ACT (1966).

childrenswear Clothing designed and sized especially for children.

child-resistant packaging See POISON PREVENTION PACKAGING ACT (PPPA) (1970).

china eggs (Slang) Individuals who appear at first to be good prospects but fail to make a purchase.

Chinese marketing A form of faulty reasoning (based largely on wishful thinking) in which a market is viewed as containing an unrealistically large number of potential customers. The underlying assumption is that the bigger the target market, the better. The term comes from a book published in the 1930s by Carl Crow, entitled *Four Hundred Million Customers*, in which the author claimed that the Great Depression could be ended if the United States could simply sell some product to each of the then 400 million Chinese.

Chinese walls An expression referring to the imaginary barriers between a store's departments. Salespeople, in an effort to avoid infringing on one another's territory, are often reluctant to cross these invisible lines between departments. See also CROSS-SELLING.

chiseler (Slang) 1. A CUSTOMER who attempts to take advantage of (i.e., cheat or swindle) retailers in the hopes of getting a lower price. 2. A BUYER who attempts to force down a vendor's price.

choice criteria Those critical attributes considered by a purchaser when evaluating merchandise for sale. Among the criteria commonly used are convenience of retail outlet, price, quality, etc.

chronological résumé See RÉSUMÉ.

chubettes Formerly, a larger size category in girls' clothing, allowing for pre-teen chubbiness, undefined waistlines, etc.

CI See COMPETITIVE INTELLIGENCE (CI).

CIA See CASH IN ADVANCE (CIA).

CIF See COST, INSURANCE, AND FREIGHT (CIF).

CIF pricing The inclusion in the seller's price of cost, insurance, and freight charges incurred in getting the shipment to a specified foreign port.

Cigarette Labeling and Protection Act (1967) Federal legislation intended to protect consumers from the hazards of cigarette smoking. Requires that cigarette packaging and advertising bear specific health warnings.

circ Short for CIRCULATION or CIRCULAR.

circular Advertising in the form of printed booklets, often included with newspapers, mailed to consumers, or delivered door-to-door. See also FLYER and ADVERTORIAL INSERT.

circulation In the print media, the number of copies of a single issue of a magazine or newspaper assumed to have reached a reader, whether by sale or by free distribution. The figure is always lower than the actual number printed. Advertising charges in print media are tied to circulation. See also PASS-ALONG CIRCULATION, PRIMARY CIRCULATION, and WASTE CIRCULATION.

circulation (pass-along) See PASS-ALONG CIRCULATION.

circulation (primary) See PRIMARY CIRCULATION.

circulation (waste) See WASTE CIRCULATION.

city size segmentation See MARKET SEGMENTATION BY CITY SIZE.

Civil Rights Act (1964) A piece of U.S. legislation outlawing discrimination by employers and/or unions on the basis of race, color, sex, or national origin. Exceptions are made, however, for jobs with special requirements and for enterprises employing fewer than 15 people.

CKM See CASH KING MARGIN (CKM).

CL See CARLOAD (CL).

claim 1. Charges for damages incurred while goods were in the possession of a carrier. More formally termed a *claim against a carrier*. 2. A retailer's request or demand for repayment or credit from a vendor for incomplete, late, or damaged shipments, etc.

claim against a carrier See CLAIM.

claims-paid complaint A consumer's assertion that payment for the billed service or merchandise has already been made, despite the retailer's assertions to the contrary.

class See SOCIAL CLASS or CLASSIFICATION.

class-action suit A lawsuit filed on behalf of many affected individuals.

classical functionalism A strategy in which the eight classical marketing functions are viewed as discrete tasks (i.e., they are not integrated into a comprehensive marketing program). These eight functions are buying, selling, transporting, storing, standardizing and grading, financing, risk bearing, and collecting and disseminating marketing information.

classic merchandise Styles that have remained popular for an extended period of time, not subject to fluctuations in fashion. These items are often considered fashion basics or investment purchases and have a long fashion cycle. Apparel classics may return to high fashion at intervals. Revived classic fashions retain the basic line of the original style, but are sometimes slightly updated. Classic merchandise is also referred to as TRADITIONAL MERCHANDISE. See also FASHION LIFE CYCLE.

classification 1. The process of breaking down merchandise into groups of items similar in nature or end use without regard for style, size, color, price, etc. These *classes* of merchandise are developed in direct response to the needs expressed by customers and, as they are fundamental merchandising units, change little from year to year even though the actual merchandise within each classification will be in a constant state of flux. Classifications provide a basic statistical structure to facilitate merchandise control. 2. Any of the categories so determined, particularly categories of merchandise. A classification is, therefore, a general type of merchandise that is housed within an individual department (e.g., sportswear, evening wear, lingerie, etc.). 3. A subdivision of a general line of merchandise that may be determined by price, size, material, color, or similar factors. For example, furs may be broken down into fun furs, expensive furs, and fur accessories. Also called a *category*, a *product category*, a *product classification*, a *merchandise category*, or a *merchandise classification*.

classification control A method of dollar inventory control that divides the stock of a department into several homogeneous classifications so that the dollar value of each is smaller than that of the total department. See also DOLLAR INVENTORY CONTROL and CLASSIFICATION MERCHANDISING.

classification dominance An assortment of merchandise so broad that it is nearly exhaustive (i.e., nearly every possible item is included), giving the customer the widest possible range of choices. Sometimes called a *dominant assortment*.

classification merchandising In retailing, the practice of planning the ASSORTMENT BREADTH on the basis of related types of classifications of merchandise. Data reporting is then controlled by these classifications. The theory behind this practice is that small, homogeneous classes of merchandise are preferable for purposes of control. See also CLASSIFICATION CONTROL.

Classification of Residential Neighbourhoods (ACORN) See ACORN.

classified ads/advertising In newspapers and magazines, classified advertising refers to those ads placed in special columns arranged by type of product or service. The format and typefaces used in these columns are generally fairly uniform. Classified ads may include homes or apartments for sale or rent, customer-to-customer sales of new and used household merchandise, used cars, pets available for adoption, business opportunities, announcements of garage sales or flea markets, personal ads seeking relationships, and help wanted ads. Many newspaper Web sites now run online classified ads. Some classified ads are featured on large sites or portals while others are run on Web sites dedicated to C2C, B2B, and/or B2C ads. See also DISPLAY ADVERTISING and YELLOW PAGES.

class rate The standard rate (i.e., calculated charge), established by government regulation, for shipping various commodities. These rates were originally established to guarantee fair prices to all users of both common and contract carriers and to avoid the abuses of railroad shipping prevalent in the nineteenth century. Class rates are established for shipping certain categories of goods between two geographical points, with distance and weight determining the rate. In general, the greater the distance and the greater the weight, the lower the rate (i.e., cost per pound or cost per ton). The COMMODITY RATE or the EXCEPTION RATE may be used as substitutes for the class rate where appropriate and where allowable by law.

Clayton Act (1914) Federal legislation intended to delineate and define acts considered unlawful restraints of trade. The Clayton Act outlawed discrimination in prices, exclusive and tying contracts, intercorporate stockholding, and interlocking directorates where their effect would be to substantially lessen competition and create a monopoly. The Clayton Act amended and clarified the SHERMAN ANTITRUST ACT (1890) and was itself amended by the CELLER-KEFAUVER ACT (1950). See also the ROBINSON-PATMAN ACT (1936).

Clayton Antitrust Act See CLAYTON ACT (1914).

clean bill of lading A BILL OF LADING (B/L) accepted by a carrier for goods received in appropriate condition (i.e., with no damages or missing items). Compare OVER, SHORT, AND DAMAGED (OS&D).

clear In retailing, to reduce inventory generally to make room for a new season. See also CLEARANCE SALE.

clearance advertisement In RETAIL PRODUCT ADVERTISING, an ad or set of ads used to promote the sale of end-of-the-month or end-of-the-season stock. The intent is to clear older merchandise from the retailer's shelves to make room for the next season's inventory. Clearance ads are also used during slow sales periods. See also CLEARANCE SALE.

clearance markdown A reduction in retail price for the purpose of stimulating sales of slow-moving merchandise. Unlike the promotional markdown, the clearance markdown is a defensive strategy calculated to reduce losses. Clearance markdowns may be taken on goods that sell more slowly than anticipated (i.e., SLOW SELLERS) and on goods that failed to move because of unseasonable weather; they may also be necessitated by a poor assortment, poor presentation, or late delivery. Clearance markdowns tend to induce the sale of even the slowest-selling merchandise. Despite their negative impact on gross margin, they are an important strategy in a buyer's effort to maintain clean assortments and to free up inventory dollars and fixtures for new merchandise. Compare PROMOTIONAL MARKDOWN.

clearance price A price that has been reduced due to a decline in value of the goods both to the merchant and to the customer. The lowered price is intended to rid the store of remaining inventory, and the MARKDOWN (MD) is never reversed.

clearance sale A special offering of goods at lowered prices to clear the store or department of slow-moving, shopworn, and other unsold seasonal items. Such a sale generally occurs at the end of a season to make room for new merchandise. See also HOUSE CLEARANCE and AFTER-INVENTORY CLEARANCE (SALE).

clearing a shipment In importing, a CUSTOMS process used to validate duty rates and, for goods subject to quota restrictions, to ensure sufficient quota is available.

clerk A store employee who sells merchandise to customers, assures the neat display of stock, and rings up sales. Also referred to as a SALESPERSON and, in some retail stores, *sales associate.*

clerking activities Retail store activities involving direct customer contact.

clerk wrap In retail sales, a system in which the salesperson who waits on the customer also wraps the purchases and arranges for the shipment of sent merchandise. A unit or department arranged according to this system is known as a *clerk wrap department.* The practice provides fast service to the customer, helps promote goodwill, and maintains the communication between the salesperson and the customer. As such, it may also result in additional sales. Also called *salesperson wrap.* Compare CENTRAL WRAP and DEPARTMENT WRAP.

CL freight rate See CARLOAD FREIGHT RATE (CL).

click On the Internet, the act of pressing one's mouse button to view a Web site or section thereof, make a selection, or activate a link. Of interest to e-marketers who advertise on others' Web sites. Also called a *mouse click.* See CLICK THROUGH.

click rate The percentage of times an Internet advertisement is clicked (activated by the visitor) divided by the number of times it is presented. For example, if an ad is placed before visitors 500 times and 10 visitors click on it to link to the advertiser's site, the click rate is 10/500 or 2 percent. The click rate is a measure of the effectiveness of a BANNER AD on an Internet Web site and a determining factor in setting advertising costs. Also called *click through rate.*

clicks-only (Storefront) A business, marketing its products solely online on the Internet, World Wide Web, and/or intranets and extranets. See also WEB STOREFRONT, BRICKS-AND-CLICKS, and BRICKS-AND-MORTAR.

clicks through See CLICK THROUGH.

clickstream 1. An early measure of the effectiveness of banner ads. The method used hits, pages, visits, users, and identified users. Resultant numbers tended to be exaggerated. 2. Electronic tracks or *digital footprints* left as a visitor moves from Web page to Web page and from Web site to Web site. E-tailers and other e-marketers use the visitor's clickstream in conjunction with COOKIES and WEB BEACONS (or *bugs*) to monitor traffic on their Web sites.

click through The active response of a Web site visitor to an advertisement appearing on that Web site. The visitor activates and connects by clicking the mouse on the ad and connecting via the live hypertext link to the advertiser's own site. Click through does not reflect whether or not a purchase was made by the visitor. It merely records that the visitor to the site actively responded to the ad and viewed the linked page. See also CLICK RATE.

click through rate (CTR) See CLICK RATE.

ClickZ Stats A source for Internet marketing data that summarizes online facts, Internet research, trends, and analyses of demographic and marketing data from dozens of online sources. Both U.S. and international statistics are available. Information relating to E-COMMERCE is included in the retailing section. Wireless and hardware information is also included. Formerly called *CyberAtlas*. Available online at www.clickz.com/stats.

client 1. An individual or group utilizing the services of a lawyer, accountant, architect, advertising agency, social worker, or other professional (similar to a CUSTOMER in a retail environment). 2. A computer application that runs on a personal computer or workstation and relies on a SERVER to perform some operations.

client departmentalization Synonym for CUSTOMER DEPARTMENTALIZATION.

clientele Synonym for customers, thought of collectively.

client public Those individuals who are the direct recipients of the services and products provided by nonprofit organizations.

clipless coupon A reduction in price given within a store for advertised sales. The customer does not need to clip a coupon from the store's circular or newspaper advertisement. Instead, the advertised discount is given at the register, particularly when used in conjunction with a membership card, and generally when a particular item is purchased. This has become a popular practice in supermarkets, although similar arrangements are sometimes offered by department stores to their credit card customers.

clipping bureau An agency or service that provides files of news stories, advertisements, etc., to clients on a subscription basis. Originally, clipping bureaus cut out competitors' print advertisements, enabling their clients to monitor advertising spending. Today's Internet-based clipping bureaus monitor what is being said about a client in the online and offline media such as newspapers, magazines, television and radio talk shows and newscasts, as well as Usenet groups, Web sites, and chat rooms. Coverage includes news, information, and even rumors. The goal is to collect and log mentions of the client's product, service, or organization. Clients are often publicists. Also known as a *clipping service*.

clipping service Synonym for CLIPPING BUREAU.

cloning (Slang) A method used to train sales staff (or wait staff in a restaurant) in which the trainee follows and emulates an experienced salesperson, trying to learn and reproduce that person's attitudes, vocabulary, and methods of dealing with various situations.

close See CLOSING.

closed assortment A set or collection of items of which all components needed by the consumer are included and available. Compare OPEN ASSORTMENT.

closed-back window A typical DISPLAY WINDOW comprising a wall, sides, and a large plate-glass window facing the pedestrian or street traffic. The configuration forms an enclosed, self-contained display area eliminating any distracting background. Also called an *enclosed window*.

closed bid See SEALED BID.

closed display Merchandise exhibited under counter glass or in a case.

closed-door discount house A retailer selling goods only to consumers who, by virtue of place of employment, membership in a union, or other affiliation, are regarded as "members." Closed-door discount houses charge prices as much as 40 percent below those found in department stores and depend on high volume and low overhead to make a profit. They carry nationally branded, high-quality merchandise for which there is strong consumer demand. Also known as a *membership club*, a *closed-door membership store*, a *members-only outlet*, and a *wholesale club*. Compare OPEN-END DISCOUNT STORE.

closed-door membership store Synonym for CLOSED-DOOR DISCOUNT HOUSE.

closed loop layout An arrangement of fixtures and aisles that encourages the customer to move around the outer periphery of a store. By so doing, a closed loop layout exposes shoppers to a great deal of merchandise. Shoppers follow a perimeter traffic aisle with departments on the right and left of the circular, square, rectangular or oval "racetrack." Also known as a *loop layout* and a *racetrack layout*.

closed loop system A computerized method of inventory control in which merchandise data is recorded at the point of sale for use in ordering and reordering. The item is removed from the inventory memory bank at the time of sale.

closed sales territory A geographically defined area in which a manufacturer allows only one marketing intermediary to handle certain merchandise. Also called *closed territory*. See also EXCLUSIVE DISTRIBUTION and SALES TERRITORY.

closed-sell fixture A FLOOR FIXTURE restricting customer access to merchandise by requiring the assistance of a salesperson for making selections. Easily damaged or highly pilferable big-ticket items, such as fine jewelry or printer cartridges, are housed in closed-sell fixtures. Compare OPEN-SELL FIXTURE.

closed shop A workplace in which union membership is a condition of employment.

closed stock Merchandise (e.g., china, glassware, and flatware) sold only in sets with no guarantee of future availability for additional purchases or replacements. Compare OPEN STOCK.

closed territory See CLOSED SALES TERRITORY.

closed window See CLOSED-BACK WINDOW.

closely held corporation A corporation whose stock is not available to the general public. Closely held corporations withhold their stock from public sale and finance any expansion out of their own earnings or borrow from other sources. A corporation whose shares are owned by fewer than 500 people or that has less than $1 million in assets is not required to disclose its finances to the general public unless its stock is traded on a national exchange. A closely held corporation's executives, who control the majority of the stock, are thus assured of complete control over their operations and are protected from being bought out by people who might dismantle the company. Hallmark is an example of a corporation that opted to remain private. Also known as a *private corporation*.

closeout An offering of selected discontinued goods by the vendor to the retailer at reduced prices. This merchandise has been discontinued because of slow sales, a broken assortment, overstock, the need to make space for a new season, etc. The savings are often passed along to the consumer as a closeout sale, used to generate increased store traffic. See also CLOSEOUT SALE and PROMOTIONAL MERCHANDISE POLICY.

closeout sale A store event designed to increase traffic by offering discontinued merchandise, broken assortments, overstocks, etc., to the customer at reduced prices. The retailer, having obtained the merchandise at reduced prices from the vendor, passes the savings along to the customer. See also CLEARANCE SALE and AFTER-INVENTORY CLEARANCE (SALE).

closeout store A type of DISCOUNT STORE established as a clearance center through which a retailer can eliminate slow-selling or end-of-season merchandise from its regular-price stores. Closeout stores occasionally include manufacturers' closeouts that were never part of the sponsoring retailer's inventory. Two examples of closeout stores sponsored by department stores are Nordstrom Rack and Off 5th .

closer A master SALESPERSON responsible for bringing the sales process to a conclusion (i.e., CLOSING the sale). Also known as a *turnover man* or *T.O. man*.

close rate The number of actual sales made by a salesperson divided by the number of calls made to potential customers. This is one factor used in the evaluation of salespersons.

closing The step in the sales process when the SALESPERSON must ask the customer to conclude the purchase. Closing techniques include asking for the order, recapitulating the points of the agreement, offering to help write up the order, or indicating what the buyer will lose if the order is not placed immediately. Alternatively, the salesperson may offer some incentive to the buyer, such as a special price or an extra quantity of the goods in question at no extra charge in order to finalize and close the deal. Also called a *sales closing*.

closing book inventory See CLOSING INVENTORY AT BOOK.

closing clue A verbal comment or body language movement indicating that the potential customer is about to place an order. The astute SALESPERSON watches for telltale signs that the customer is on the verge of closing a deal.

closing entry The final record of an accounting item in a temporary account, which may be transferred to the appropriate REAL ACCOUNT.

closing inventory The value of the goods on hand at the end of an accounting period, either at cost or at retail value. Also called *inventory at end of period*.

closing inventory at book The inventory remaining at the end of an accounting period, determined by subtracting the total of retail reductions from the total merchandise handled.

closing physical inventory The dollar value of stock remaining at the close of the accounting period as determined by an actual count of the stock.

closing technique Any method employed by a SALESPERSON to finalize a sale.

closing the books The process by which the balances of the income and expense accounts are transferred into the profit and loss account, preparatory to the completion of the balance sheet and operating statement.

closing the sale See CLOSING.

closure See CLOSING.

clothes/clothing Synonym for APPAREL.

clothing alterations See ALTERATIONS.

clouter (Slang) A SHOPLIFTER who, making no attempt to conceal the activity, simply grabs merchandise in a store and runs. The clouter relies on the element of surprise to provide sufficient time for an escape.

club packs Products sold in large, institutional-size packages.

club plan selling A retail distribution technique in which the selling organization merchandises only to members. Member consumers are awarded prizes for bringing in new members, who join by making purchases. Membership usually requires registration and the payment of a fee. Selling usually takes place at a WAREHOUSE CLUB location, though online purchases are also available to members. *Sam's Club* and *Costco* are examples of contemporary businesses utilizing the club plan. Also called *club scheme*.

club scheme See CLUB PLAN SELLING and LOYALTY CARD.

clucking hens (Slang) New, unusual, or pressing problems that demand the full and immediate attention of the store's senior management.

cluster 1. A group of customers in a particular geographic area, assumed to share basic demographic and psychographic

attributes and behaviors. See also GEOGRAPHICAL INFORMA-
TION SYSTEMS (GIS) and MARKET SEGMENTATION. 2. A form
of shopping center often consisting of a number of smaller
stores built around a single department store.

cluster analysis A method used to group customers in a
particular geographic area according to their demographic and
psychographic attributes and behaviors. The results are used by
retailers to determine the appropriate location for new stores,
to select appropriate retail tenants for a mall or shopping
center, and other similar RETAIL SITE LOCATION decisions.

clustered demand A demand pattern in which identified
consumer needs can be separated into two or more segments
or clusters.

clustering techniques Methods used in the analysis of MAR-
KETING RESEARCH (MR) data to find usable patterns. Patterns
may be established for such factors as demographic data, customer attitudes, psychographic data, and purchasing behavior.
Using a computer, researchers attempt to identify homogeneous groups of people and then analyze the data in search of
new or improved marketing strategies to appeal to them. See
also CLUSTER ANALYSIS.

cluster of benefits See TOTAL PRODUCT CONCEPT.

cluster sample See AREA SAMPLE.

cluster sampling See AREA SAMPLING.

clutter 1. In advertising, the crowding together of advertising
messages in the print and electronic media, resulting in a loss
of effectiveness. Advertisers may avoid clutter by buying more
time or reserving more space in the media used. They may also
pay a premium for positioning their advertisement in such a
way as to avoid clutter. For example, in magazine advertising,
the inside front cover is considered a less cluttered position for
an ad. Advertisers may also select those media that minimize
clutter, refuse to accept PIGGYBACK ads, or otherwise regulate
the amount of advertising. 2. In Web advertising, the glut of
online ads, e-mail messages, and sales promotions on Web sites
and pages, making it difficult for marketers' messages to be
received. It proliferates mainly because it is profitable to site
owners. *E-mail clutter* is growing as more commercial e-mail is
sent to growing numbers of receivers and as messages are
changing from text-only to high-bandwidth streaming media
(audio and video).

CMC See CALIFORNIA MARKET CENTER (CMC).

CMO see CHIEF MARKETING OFFICER (CMO).

CMQ/CMPQ In SOURCING contracts, an initialism standing
for cut, make, pack, and quota.

CMSA See CONSOLIDATED METROPOLITAN STATISTICAL AREA
(CMSA).

CMT See CUT, MAKE, TRIM (CMT) SOURCING.

coat form A headless, usually armless male form for displaying apparel. The coat form starts at the neck and ends
around the hips. Coat forms are used to present suits, jackets,
and sweaters. Also called a *suit form*.

co-branded card A dual purpose credit card that combines
the features of a store credit card and a bank card. The issuer
(i.e., the financial institution) and a retailer or service
provider both have their logo on the card. Some retail stores
and service organizations have replaced or supplemented
their store charge card with a co-branded card. See also
AFFINITY CREDIT CARD.

co-branding The practice by which two separate retailers
(brands) form a partnership for the purpose of reaching customers more efficiently and increasing sales for both parties.
The location of Starbucks cafés in Barnes & Noble bookstores
is an example of co-branding.

cocooning The lifestyle trend in which consumers prefer to
stay at home engaged in such activities as entertaining or exer-
cising. Such consumers may choose to home-educate their
children and may focus on activities such as gardening,
cooking, and homemaking. They may also work from home.
Cocooning stimulates the sale of furniture, exercise equipment,
consumer electronics, gourmet cookware, and casual glassware
and dinnerware. Cocooning consumers may also change their
shopping habits because of fear of crime in traditional shopping areas. As such, they may be excellent targets for catalog
and Internet marketing. Cocooning is also called *nesting*.

COD See CASH ON DELIVERY (COD).

COD audit A systematic inspection of accounting records
pertaining to CASH ON DELIVERY (COD) transactions. The procedure involves proving that all COD merchandise has reached
the delivery department or common carrier and that all merchandise entrusted to the deliverer has been accounted for in
case of returned merchandise.

code number A number identifying the source of a sale. For
example, CENTS-OFF COUPONS include code numbers indicating
where customers obtained them (e.g., which newspaper ad carried the coupon). Mail order catalogs contain similar code
numbers, usually found in a box on the last page of the catalog.

coding A method of identifying merchandise numerically or
alphabetically on price tickets in a way that cannot be detected
by the average customer.

coding process See ENCODING.

COD sale See CASH ON DELIVERY (COD).

coefficient of elasticity A measure of the relative response of
one variable to changes in another variable, represented as a
number. It is used to show the relationship between supply and
demand by quantifying price elasticity of demand, price elasticity of supply, income elasticity of demand, and cross elasticity of demand. See also ELASTICITY OF DEMAND. It is

calculated by dividing the percentage change in variable B by the percentage change in variable A.

coefficient of income sensitivity   A comparison between a product's percentage variation in sales over a number of years and a 1 percent change in personal disposable income, used to forecast the effect of a 1 percent change in available discretionary funds on a product's sales.

coefficient of multiple correlation   A measure of the amount of correlation among multiple variables. See also MULTIPLE CORRELATION.

coercive reciprocity   See RECIPROCITY.

Coffee, Sugar, and Cocoa Exchange   See COMMODITY EXCHANGE.

COG   see CUSTOMER-OWNED GOODS (COG).

cognition   1. The process of knowing or becoming aware of something in one's environment. 2. Something known, believed, or perceived. See also COGNITIVE PROCESSES.

cognitive component   In attitude research, particularly in the TRIPARTITE VIEW or structural approach, the cognitive component is the knowledge and beliefs a consumer has about a product or service, including evaluative beliefs. It is the intellectual component of attitude. Also called *knowledge*.

cognitive consonance   The opposite of COGNITIVE DISSONANCE; the feeling of satisfaction experienced by a customer on or immediately after deciding to purchase.

cognitive dissonance   Doubt and anxiety suffered by a customer on or immediately after deciding to purchase. This dissonance (anxiety or mixed feelings) is the result of a conflict between two or more of the purchaser's cognitions (beliefs or perceptions) regarding the purchased product. This *postpurchase doubt* is also called *buyer's remorse*.

cognitive judgment   See COGNITIVE PROCESSES.

cognitive processes   Mental activities, such as learning and judging, that involve thought and reasoning. Retailers and marketers strive to understand consumers' cognitive processes in order to sell more effectively to those consumers.

cohort   In the study of DEMOGRAPHICS, a group of persons sharing a statistical or demographic characteristic. *Cohorts* (plural) are the various age groups that make up the total population. See also MARKET SEGMENTATION.

coin-operated phone/telephone   See PAY PHONE.

COLA   See COST-OF-LIVING ADJUSTMENT (COLA).

cold calling   Door-to-door or telephone solicitation of orders for merchandise without the benefit of leads or prior appointments. Also called *cold canvassing*.

cold canvassing   Synonym for COLD CALLING.

cold list   In door-to-door or telephone sales, a list of the names of potential customers (i.e., prospects) who have not yet been contacted in any way about the product or service being sold.

cold mail promotion   A mail order merchandising campaign sent out to prospects who are not yet listed customers.

Colgate Doctrine (1919)   A Supreme Court decision that a seller can unilaterally decide the terms under which goods will be sold and can, therefore, refuse to sell to those who do not meet those terms. Intended to curtail the activities of known price-cutting retailers such as discount houses and catalog retailers, its effects have been mitigated over the years by subsequent decisions. Nevertheless, the basic thrust of the Colgate Doctrine was incorporated into the ROBINSON-PATMAN ACT (1936). See also REFUSAL-TO-DEAL.

COLI   See COST-OF-LIVING INDEX (COLI).

Collaborative Planning, Forecasting, and Replenishment (CPFR)   An industry-wide initiative that uses technology, supply chain efficiencies, and strategic partnerships to significantly improve the rate at which retailers can stock their selling floors. In some cases, use of CPFR has reduced the time it takes to get products from domestic manufacturers onto the selling floor from 30 days to 24 hours.

collateral   In a SECURED LOAN, a tangible asset (such as a home or car) that may be seized by the lender should the borrower fail to repay the loan. In business, such tangible assets often include accounts receivable, inventories, and other property.

collection   In fashion buying and merchandising, the accumulated styles and designs of an apparel designer or manufacturer, completed for a particular season and presented to buyers and the press.

collection agent   A representative whose job it is to attempt to collect delinquent accounts for a fee or a percentage of the dollar amount collected.

collection letter   A written or printed request to a debtor for payment of a delinquent account. Initial letters are generally polite, but the language of each subsequent letter becomes stronger.

collection on delivery (COD)   Synonym for CASH ON DELIVERY (COD).

collection period   A ratio comparing the average period of time it takes to collect accounts receivable to the number of days it takes to obtain that volume of sales. It is used as an indication of the size of customers' accounts.

collection shop   A boutique housed within a department store, or a stand-alone specialty shop, featuring top-of-the-line, fashion-forward, exclusive merchandise by internationally renowned designers. Both the existence and the mystique of collection shops are driven primarily by European designers turned retailers, but American designer-retailers also fit this category and have opened successful collection shops in foreign markets.

collection system The established procedure used by retailers to encourage customers to pay debts, especially delinquent accounts. The procedure includes several levels of increasing intensity, such as impersonal routine billing, impersonal appeals, personalized appeals, and drastic legal action. Vendors employ similar procedures to collect from delinquent retail accounts.

collect on delivery (COD) Synonym for CASH ON DELIVERY (COD).

college board A group of college students working with a retail store in a volunteer advisory capacity, especially with regard to new products and styles. See also TEEN BOARD and FASHION BOARD.

collusion The coming together of two or more parties in a secret understanding or agreement to the detriment of one or more other parties. When this is done to fix prices, it is called *price collusion*. RESTRAINT OF TRADE agreements commonly involve collusion.

collusive pricing Synonym for HORIZONTAL PRICE FIXING.

colonnaded walk See ARCADE SHOPPING CENTER.

colorable imitation A form of deception in which a mark or symbol resembling a registered TRADEMARK is used to confuse the customer. Intended to make the customer think the merchandise is a known branded product.

colorfast See FAST-COLOR.

color theme A recurring idea, based on color, used in a retail store to create a feeling about merchandise presented to customers. Trends relating to color offer endless suggestions for themes (e.g., green for St. Patrick's Day and the beginning of spring). The color theme may be extended to many departments in the retail store beyond apparel and home furnishings. See also THEME.

colorways The assorted colors or groups of colors a manufacturer has chosen for its line of fashion products, such as jewel-toned solids, pastel floral prints, or earth-toned plaids.

column A decorative, freestanding pillar out in the open of a retail floor and unattached. Compare PIER, a thickening or extension of the constructed wall to which it is attached.

COM (customer owned merchandise) See CUSTOMER-OWNED GOODS (COG).

COM (customer's own merchandise) See CUSTOMER-OWNED GOODS (COG).

combination advertising See COMBINATION RETAIL ADVERTISING.

combination drug store See COMBO STORE.

combination house A MARKETING INTERMEDIARY serving the wholesale, retail, and institutional markets.

combination offer A form of consumer fraud involving the sale of a product at a low price tied to the purchase of a continuing service. The sale of food freezers tied to the purchase of frozen foods is a notorious example, as the food is frequently of inferior quality.

combination pricing An approach to pricing in which aspects of cost-based pricing, demand-based pricing, and competitive-oriented pricing methods are integrated.

combination retail advertising A method of advertising in which both institutional and promotional approaches are blended together in the same advertisement. For example, a store may blend its own prestige characteristics with a merchandise ad in order to distinguish it from similar or identical merchandise sold in competing stores.

combination sale An item of merchandise paired with a premium so that both are sold together at one price. A combination sale lowers the cost of promotion per dollar of revenue. Sometimes referred to as a *combo promotion*.

combinations in restraint of trade See RESTRAINT OF TRADE.

combination store See SUPERCENTER.

combination supermarket Synonym for COMBO STORE.

combined target market approach A method of subdividing the population of potential customers in which two or more distinct market segments are combined into one larger target market. A single MARKETING STRATEGY is then used to appeal to the larger group. Firms adopting this method do so to increase the size of their target markets and so to gain certain economies of scale, minimize their risks, or allocate limited resources economically. They try to extend or modify their basic offering to appeal to these combined groups of customers, relying heavily on promotion to convince each subsegment that the product will satisfy its particular needs.

combiner A retailer or other marketer that merges two or more distinct market segments into one larger target market in order to achieve certain economies of scale. See also COMBINED TARGET MARKET APPROACH.

combo promotion See COMBINATION SALE.

combo store 1. An outgrowth of the supermarket having a significantly larger share of floor space devoted to higher-margin general merchandise. Although retaining many aspects of the SUPERMARKET, the combo store is in fact an incipient full line DISCOUNT STORE. Also called a *combination supermarket*.

2. An outgrowth of the large DRUG STORE in which general merchandise is combined with drugs and health and beauty care products. Also called a *combination drug store*. Sometimes called a *combination store*, although that term is usually reserved for a much larger SUPERCENTER.

COMEX   See COMMODITY EXCHANGE.

command headline   A heading in an advertisement that strongly encourages a reader to use or purchase a product or service. The encouragement is presented in the form of a command or imperative sentence, as in "Drink Pepsi!" or "Buy American!"

commerce server   In e-commerce, the Web software that runs some of the major functions of an online storefront. These functions include product display, online ordering, and inventory management. Commerce server software is used in conjunction with online payment systems to process payments. See also SERVER.

commercial   1. adj. Relating to trade, commerce, stores, office buildings, and other business activities and properties.   2. n. A paid ADVERTISEMENT appearing in the broadcast media of radio and television. Commercials are filmed or taped and copies are distributed to subscribing networks for airing. See also SPONSOR and STORYBOARD.

commercial advertising   ADVERTISING directed toward the profit-making sector. Compare NONPROFIT ADVERTISING.

commercial bank   A profit-making business that accepts deposits and uses these funds to make loans. Traditionally, commercial banks offer savings and checking in addition to their loan services. There are two types of commercial bank: *national banks,* chartered by the federal government, and *state banks,* chartered by state governments. Commercial banks are an important source of capital for businesses, particularly for short-term financing.

commercial bribery   See BRIBERY.

commercial buyer of farm products   A WHOLESALER engaged primarily in buying farm products on a commission basis for others in the supply chain.

commercial e-mail   Advertising and marketing promotional messages sent by E-MAIL to businesses and/or consumers with or without their permission. Like all sales promotions, they are designed to create an immediate inducement to purchase. Commercial e-mail is a form of DIRECT MARKETING and an interactive method for making an offer and initiating a transaction. As the result of the CAN-SPAM ACT (2004) and AFFIRMATIVE CONSENT, consumers may OPT-IN or OPT-OUT of commercial e-mail, which many consider SPAM.

commercialization   The final stage in new product development, in which a manufacturer is committed to the production of a new product.

commercial marketing   The application of marketing strategies, concepts, and techniques to profit-making endeavors (as distinct from their use in the nonprofit sector).

commercial name   Synonym for TRADE NAME.

commercial palace   (Obsolete) An early department store, particularly one conceived along the lines of an Italian palace or PALAZZO.

commercial paper   A loan in the form of a short-term note issued to a borrower by a company and backed by the company's good name. The borrower promises to pay back a stated amount of money within a stated number of days (legally, from 3 to 270 days).

commercial set   In international marketing, a set of four major negotiable documents that stand for and take the place of the goods themselves when financing a cargo sales transaction: the INVOICE, the BILL OF LADING (B/L), the CERTIFICATE OF INSURANCE, and the DRAFT.

commercial traveler   Synonym for TRAVELING SALESPERSON.

commissary store   1. A store operated by the military (and commonly staffed by civilian employees) for the benefit of military personnel and their dependents.   2. A store operated by a large employer for the benefit of its employees. Commissary stores generally sell food products and other supplies for prices substantially below those on the open market. Also known as a *company store* or an *industrial store.*

commission   A method of compensating salespersons, brokers, or agents in which all or part of their compensation is based on a percentage of the dollar amount of their sales. Sometimes termed *commission on sales.* STRAIGHT COMMISSION means that all of one's compensation is based on a percentage of sales. SALARY PLUS COMMISSION means that this percentage is added to a fixed base pay.

commission agent   A marketing intermediary who receives shipped goods, mainly perishables, to sell for a PRINCIPAL. See also COMMISSION HOUSE.

commissionaire   A foreign-based buying agency, under foreign management, acting as a store's representative abroad. The commissionaire is remunerated by a percentage of the store's purchases and assists in bringing the buyer into contact with vendors, handling foreign exchange rates, and arranging shipping from foreign ports. The term *commissioner* is sometimes used instead. Compare PURCHASING AGENT (def. 2).

commission buying office   A RESIDENT BUYING OFFICE that receives its compensation from manufacturers as a percentage of orders placed with retailers. It generally deals with small retailers and provides few or no services other than the procurement of goods. The commission buying office may represent many manufacturers and gives the retailer the advantage of choosing from a large assortment of merchandise without paying a fee. Sometimes called simply a *commission office*. Also known as a *merchandise-broker office*.

commission department　A store department in which the salespeople are compensated primarily through the payment of a COMMISSION on sales.

commissioner　Alternative form of COMMISSIONAIRE.

commission house　A MARKETING INTERMEDIARY supplying large retailers, especially in the food trade and most often in the central market. It generally exercises physical control over the goods handled and negotiates their sale. Although still subject to the instructions of the PRINCIPAL, a commission house enjoys broad powers as to prices, methods, and terms of sale, and may also arrange delivery, extend credit, make collections, etc., for the principal. See also BROKER.

commission man　Synonym for COMMISSION MERCHANT.

commission merchant　A MARKETING INTERMEDIARY who has physical control over the goods being sold but does not take title to them. Commission merchants most commonly represent the sellers of such agricultural products as grain, livestock, and produce, which are usually accepted on consignment, and often do so on a one-time rather than a continuing, contractual basis. The commission merchant has the authority to negotiate prices and terms of sale on behalf of the PRINCIPAL and may arrange delivery, extend credit, make collections, etc. In this respect the commission merchant has more freedom than the BROKER. See also EXPORT COMMISSION HOUSE/MERCHANT.

commission office　See COMMISSION BUYING OFFICE.

commission on sales　Synonymous with COMMISSION.

commission rebating　The payment of rebates to advertising agencies by the owners of the media. The size of an agency's rebate is based on the value of the orders it has placed in a given medium. The rebate forms part of the income earned by the advertising agency and is separate from the fee paid by its clients, the advertisers.

commission with draw　A method of compensation for salespeople in which payments are based on a percentage of sales (i.e., the commission) but in which regular payments are made from an account set aside for that purpose (i.e., the draw).

commitment　An order for merchandise that the store's BUYER has obligated the store to accept but that has not yet been authorized by the MERCHANDISE MANAGER.

committee buying　Purchasing activities collectively performed by a group of buyers on behalf of a multiunit committee. See also BUYING COMMITTEE.

commodity　Generally, an agricultural or mineral product, specifically one used as a raw material in producing other goods. Examples are wheat, cattle, eggs, cotton, gold, silver, hides, coffee, lumber, pork bellies, petroleum, etc. Occasionally the term may be applied to manufactured goods, but never to services. At a COMMODITY EXCHANGE, traders buy and sell contracts for delivery of a set amount of these raw materials at a given time.

commodity approach to marketing　An approach to the study of marketing in which the movement of goods from producer to consumer is viewed as the key to understanding the marketing process. The focus of attention, therefore, is on the CHANNEL OF DISTRIBUTION.

commodity exchange　A nonprofit organization, functioning much like a STOCK EXCHANGE, that provides members with a place to trade commodities on a commission basis. The exchange does not engage in buying or selling, but does make and enforce rules governing such transactions and may adjust disputes among member traders. Members buy a seat on the exchange, which entitles them to trade with other members. Products do not actually change hands at the commodity exchange; instead, traders buy and sell contracts to deliver a specified quantity of goods at a future time. Commodity exchanges tend to specialize in particular types of products and raw materials. For example, the *Chicago Board of Trade* handles corn, soybeans, wheat, oats, plywood, gold, silver, and financial futures while the *Chicago Mercantile Exchange* handles cattle, hogs, pork bellies, lumber, potatoes, Treasury bills, gold, and foreign currencies. Other commodity exchanges in the United States include the *Chicago Board Options Exchange*; the *New York Futures Exchange*; the *New York Mercantile Exchange*; the *Commodity Exchange (COMEX)*; the *New York Cotton Exchange*; the *Minneapolis Grain Exchange*; the *Kansas City Board of Trade*; the *MidAmerica Commodity Exchange*; and the *Coffee, Sugar, and Cocoa Exchange*. Also called an *organized market*.

Commodity Exchange, The (COMEX)　See COMMODITY EXCHANGE.

commodity products　1. Those products of basic industry which, although they may carry brand names, are not clearly distinguishable from one another in the public eye (e.g., bearings, steel, electronic components, etc.). 2. In food retailing, those staple products that are in continuous demand but are not clearly distinguishable from one another in the public eye. Consequently, these items (including bread, milk, sugar, eggs, etc.) are marketed primarily on the basis of price.

commodity rate　An allowable, government-regulated deviation from the CLASS RATE charged by shippers to their customers. The reduced commodity rate (i.e., calculated charge) may be awarded to the customer for regular use or for the quantity shipped. See also EXCEPTION RATE.

commodity warehouse　A WAREHOUSE that stores commodity goods such as cotton, wool, tobacco, and agricultural products.

common area maintenance (CAM)　In a shopping center, the upkeep of common areas such as walkways, parking lots, etc., the cost of which is divided among the tenants. Charges for general mall upkeep, housekeeping, snow removal, window washing, and outside refurbishing are assessed on retailers by the center's developer on the basis of square footage leased. See also TRIPLE NET.

common carrier   A transportation firm (rail, truck, barge, etc.) engaged in shipping merchandise. Common carriers operate on regular schedules over established routes, charge published standard rates, and are available to all shippers. All are subject to one or more forms of government regulation. Compare CONTRACT CARRIER and PRIVATE CARRIER.

common cost   See INDIRECT COST.

common-law copyright   See COPYRIGHT.

common market   A group of countries that have agreed to have no internal tariffs, a common external tariff, and laws coordinated to facilitate exchange. Common markets encourage the free flow of labor and capital among member nations. There is usually an attempt to coordinate tax codes, social welfare systems, and other legislation influencing resource allocation. Exchange rates among member nations are often fixed or permitted to fluctuate only within a narrow range. The European Union (EU) and the Central American Common Market (CACM) are examples of common markets. See also CUSTOMS UNION.

communication   The exchange of ideas, information, or messages by any effective means. Communication may be seen as a process. As such, it involves the transmission of information, ideas, emotions, skills, etc., through the use of words, pictures, figures, graphs, and other symbols. See also COMMUNICATION PROCESS.

communication adaptation   A marketing strategy employed in international trade, in which a company exporting products identical to those manufactured for the domestic market changes the advertising accompanying them so as to gear the new messages to the other culture.

communication channel   Any medium available for the transmission of mass or interpersonal messages. Communication channels include everything from print media (books, newspapers, magazines, newsletters, etc.) to broadcast media (radio and television), telephones, telegraphs, and electronic media (Internet communications). The Internet may be considered a multimedia communication channel that enables users to make telephone calls, listen to the radio, watch television, participate in video conferences, fax messages, and send and receive e-mail. See also MEDIA and ADVERTISING MEDIA.

communication expense   Any expenditure for telephone equipment and service, telegrams, mailings to consumers, Internet connections, etc., used to contact consumers or vendors.

communication flow   See CHANNEL FLOW.

communication or information flow   See CHANNEL FLOW.

communication overload   Confusion in the mind of the consumer or other individual, resulting from an excess of information furnished by a salesperson or advertisement.

communication process   A process consisting of five components: a source or sender; an encoding process; transmission; a decoding process; and the reception of the message at its destination.

Communications Act (1934)   See FEDERAL COMMUNICATIONS COMMISSION (FCC).

communications manager   Synonym for ADVERTISING MANAGER.

communicator   Synonym for SENDER.

communism   An economic system in which all productive resources are owned and operated by the government, there is no private property, and resource allocation is centrally planned. See also ECONOMIC SYSTEM.

community center   Synonym for COMMUNITY SHOPPING CENTER.

community market   See PUBLIC MARKET.

community relations   The interaction between a retailer and the surrounding TRADING AREA, generally cultivated to generate good feeling toward the store. For example, a retailer may support the local Little League team, buying uniforms for it that bear the store's name and/or logo. See also PUBLIC RELATIONS.

community room   A room made available by a retailer or shopping center for meetings of civic and other organizations in its trading area as part of a COMMUNITY RELATIONS program.

community shopping center   A medium-sized shopping center generally anchored by two or more anchors (a variety store, supermarket, discount store, and/or a junior department store). The anchor stores are complemented by as many as 50 smaller retail stores and related businesses. The center sells both convenience and shopping merchandise. Most community shopping centers have a gross leasable area of between 100,000 and 350,000 square feet and require a surrounding POPULATION of from 40,000 to 150,000 people to operate profitably. The TRADING AREA will not usually extend beyond the community in which the center is located. The radius of attraction extends to approximately 10 to 15 minutes of drive time (or three to six miles). Also called a *community center*.

community show   A FASHION SHOW produced by one or more retailers to raise money and awareness for a local charity or community organization (e.g., the Girl Scouts or the local volunteer fire department). In addition to selling merchandise, the retailer is promoting GOODWILL and building a strong community image. Celebrities, designers, and models often lend their support to these events.

companion goods   See RELATED MERCHANDISE.

company analysis A self-analysis of a firm planning to engage in Web marketing. The company analysis considers the unique benefits and value the company can offer its target market by Web marketing, how the company expects to benefit from it, and the company's readiness for it. For example, an office supply Web site adds *convenience value* to its target market by selling office supplies online that are delivered directly to the customer's home or office. The company itself may benefit by attracting new customers, penetrating an existing market, or entering a new market. Readiness is examined from management, cost, and human resource perspectives.

company brand A BRAND that is associated with the name of a company. In Internet marketing, many of the early cyberbrands were company brands, such as AOL, Yahoo!, and Amazon; they were aggressively marketed through the advertising media to call attention to their name and to their business.

company demand The total amount of goods or services a particular firm might reasonably be expected to sell in the marketplace over a specified time period and to a particular market segment. See also MARKET SHARE.

company image Synonym for MISSION IDENTITY.

company induction A planned, formal orientation program to inform the new employee about the firm. The information imparted includes details about the firm's history, development, organization, policies, and regulations as well as facts about the operation of the company (e.g., the number and location of stores, warehouses, and manufacturing facilities, if any). Also included in the typical induction are the terms of employment, disciplinary policies and procedures, company benefits, and advancement opportunities. The orientation is often accompanied by an EMPLOYEE ORIENTATION BOOKLET. See also EMPLOYEE ORIENTATION, JOB INDUCTION, and STORE INDUCTION.

company man Synonym for ORGANIZATION MAN/WOMAN.

company marketing environment See MARKETING ENVIRONMENT.

company marketing opportunity A NICHE in a market perceived by a company as having sales potential. Also called, simply, a *marketing opportunity.*

company-owned buying office A RESIDENT BUYING OFFICE owned by a store or larger retail organization (e.g., a group of noncompeting stores). Large department and specialty stores generally use this type of service. Variations of the company-owned buying office include the PRIVATE BUYING OFFICE, the ASSOCIATED BUYING OFFICE, the CORPORATE BUYING OFFICE, and the SYNDICATED BUYING OFFICE. Also called a *company-owned office* and a *store-owned buying office.* Includes the *store-owned foreign buying office.*

company planning Synonym for STRATEGIC PLANNING.

company sales potential See SALES POTENTIAL.

company store Synonym for both COMMISSARY STORE and FACTORY OUTLET.

company warehouse See PRIVATE WAREHOUSE.

company woman See ORGANIZATION MAN/WOMAN.

comparative advantage A theory of international marketing and world trade in which a country is said to have especially favorable circumstances when it can produce certain goods (or, for that matter, all goods) more cheaply than another country. In terms of actual trade, however, it is to each individual country's advantage to specialize in the production of those goods that it produces most advantageously (i.e., in which it has a relative advantage, and not in the production of all goods). It is not necessary for a country to have an ABSOLUTE ADVANTAGE in order to engage profitably in international trade. See also COMPETITIVE ADVANTAGE.

comparative advertising A form of competitive advertising in which specific brands are named and compared in terms of their specific characteristics and attributes. In retailing, this may take the form of naming specific stores in the trading area and comparing them in terms of prices, services, and policies. Also known as *comparison advertising* and *competitive sell.*

comparative balance sheet Two or more balance sheets for the same company for different times, displayed side by side to facilitate the observation of similarities or differences, growth or decline. See also BALANCE SHEET.

comparative cost advantage In international business, one country's COMPARATIVE ADVANTAGE (i.e., the ability to manufacture a given product better than other nations) based on lower production costs.

comparative marketing In international marketing and world trade, the study of the differences and similarities between various national systems regarding supply and demand as well as distribution.

comparative message An instance of COMPARATIVE ADVERTISING.

comparative price 1. A promotional price appearing in an advertisement or display showing the current price as well as a higher previous price, a suggested retail price, a competitor's price, or an estimated price. The old price is characteristically slashed out for dramatic effect. 2. In auctions, both online and offline, the price of identical or comparable products recently sold at auction. The comparative price helps determine the OPENING BID PRICE.

compare-a-price Little-used informal term for UNIT PRICING.

comparison advertising Synonym for COMPARATIVE ADVERTISING.

comparison department The department of a retail store responsible for checking similarities or differences in prices, styles, quality, service, etc., between the store and its competitors. An employee of this department is known as a COMPARISON SHOPPER.

comparison shopper   An employee of a retail store, or of an outside consulting firm engaged by a store, responsible for shopping other stores to examine the merchandise assortments, prices, and promotion policies of other retailers in the area and reporting on their activities. See also SERVICE SHOPPER.

comparison shopping   1. The practice of visiting other retailers to observe the merchandising activities of the competition. This may be accomplished by the store's own employees (see COMPARISON SHOPPER) or by an outside comparison shopping firm hired for this purpose.   2. The review of the marketing strategies of several competing firms by an industrial purchasing executive. The purchasing executive reviews new products offered, competitors' pricing concepts, and promotional initiatives before selecting a vendor from whom to purchase goods for the firm.   3. Consumer activities in which the consumer expends the time and energy necessary to get the best product at the best price before actually making a purchase. The consumer shops multiple stores, mail order catalogs, Web sites, television retailers, etc., before making an actual purchase. See also SHOPPING.

comparison shopping bureau   An outmoded synonym for COMPARISON DEPARTMENT.

compatibility of product assortments   A measure of how poorly or how well a store's merchandise lines complement each other and correspond to the needs and wants of the store's customers.

compensating balance   In the case of an UNSECURED LOAN, the minimum amount of money a borrower must keep in the issuing bank while the loan is outstanding.

compensation   Payment for services, especially salary and commission.

compensation arrangement   Synonym for COMPENSATION TRANSACTION.

compensation cafeteria   A type of compensation plan often offered to top-level managers in which they are allowed to select from a variety of possible combinations of salary, bonuses, fringe benefits, stock options, insurance, deferred bonuses, deferred retirement benefits, etc.

compensation deal   In international marketing, a form of COUNTERTRADE in which payments are made partly in the form of currency and partly in the form of goods.

compensation transaction   In global marketing, a COUNTERTRADE transaction in which the value of an export delivery is at least partially offset by an import transaction, or vice versa. Compensation transactions are typical in the case of large government purchases, such as for defense projects, when a country wants to obtain some additional exports in exchange for the awarding of a contract. Winners of major government contracts are sometimes required to take part of their payment in the commodities of the awarding government. Categories of compensation transactions include FULL COMPENSATION, PARTIAL COMPENSATION, TRIANGULAR COMPENSATION, the OFFSET DEAL, and the COOPERATION AGREEMENT or BUYBACK.

competing against all comers   An aggressive store policy indicating a willingness to meet all competition on quality, quantity, price line, and services.

competing stores   See DIRECTLY COMPETING STORES.

competition   1. In marketing and retailing, a form of business activity in which two or more parties are engaged in rivalry for customer acceptance and MARKET SHARE.   2. One's competitors or rivals in the MARKETPLACE. See also RESTRAINT OF TRADE.

competition-based pricing   See COMPETITIVE-ORIENTED PRICING.

competitive advantage   A position of superiority one firm may establish over its competitors in the marketplace. The FOUR PS OF MARKETING (product, place, promotion, and price) are all possible avenues to a firm's finding itself in a favorable marketing situation. Also called a *competitive edge*. See also COMPARATIVE ADVANTAGE, COMPETITIVE MARKETING, and ABSOLUTE ADVANTAGE.

competitive advertising   Advertising that features specific brands rather than broad product categories and is intended to motivate the consumer to buy the particular product. Also called *selective advertising*.

competitive bid/bidding   An offer to provide a product or service at a particular price to a buyer who has solicited offers from several vendors or service providers. In government purchasing, for example, several bids are commonly required and solicited from possible vendors. The vendor who can provide the specified good or service at the lowest price generally wins the contract. A competitive bid may be a SEALED BID (in which competitors do not know what other firms are bidding) or an OPEN BID (in which all participants know each other's offers). A vendor's participation in this process is known as *bidding* or *competitive bidding*.

competitive edge   Synonym for COMPETITIVE ADVANTAGE.

competitive environment   To any company in the marketplace, the sum total of other firms marketing products similar to or substitutable for the company's own. For example, to a marketer of sugar, the competitive environment would include all other companies marketing sugar as well as those marketing artificial sweeteners.

competitive intelligence (CI)   A systematic process of gathering and analyzing information about one's competitors in order to find new opportunities, avoid threats, and remain competitive. Direct competitors regularly keep track of the MARKETPLACE as well as each other. The Internet facilitates the process, as much of the needed data may be gleaned from a competitor's own Web site. CI can be done in-house by a firm's CI unit or by professionals hired specially for the job. See also MARKETING INTELLIGENCE.

competitive marketing A marketing orientation in which attention is paid to the competition as well as to consumers. Companies seek a COMPETITIVE ADVANTAGE by offering the lowest possible price for a product or by offering a unique benefit that justifies an equal or higher price. Compare PRODUCTION-ORIENTED MARKETING, SALES-ORIENTED MARKETING, and the MARKETING CONCEPT.

competitive monopoly Synonym for DIFFERENTIATED OLIGOPOLY.

competitive-oriented pricing The policy of some retailers to base their prices on those of competing stores rather than on demand or cost considerations. Also called *competition-based pricing*.

competitive parity An approach to PROMOTIONAL BUDGETING based on the promotional expenditures of one's competitors. Also known as *defensive budgeting* and *defensive spending* on the grounds that spending at least as much on advertising as one's closest competitors do is one good form of defense against them. The practice of setting the promotional budget by imitating one's competitors is known as the *competitive parity technique*.

competitive position The position of a product that has achieved a noticeable percentage share of the market in comparison to similar products. At this point, the product is considered a viable competitor for MARKET SHARE.

competitive price The price determined by market forces when there are a number of independent buyers and sellers in the marketplace. Since no one firm is sufficiently powerful to set or manipulate the price at which goods are bought or sold, the competitive price is ultimately reached through bargaining between buyers and sellers.

competitive screen In global marketing, one of the barriers or hurdles that must be overcome by a firm seeking to do business with a foreign government. During this stage of negotiations, the firm must bid against other firms seeking the contract and display an ability to be flexible as situations evolve and change. The firm's reputation, its past experience in developing countries, and its cultural sensitivity are all taken into account. See also ELIGIBILITY SCREEN, PROCEDURAL SCREEN, LINKAGE SCREEN, and INFLUENCE SCREEN.

competitive segmentation analysis (CSA) A procedure used by retailers to help select the target market for their establishments. It includes five steps: identifying the potential market segment; identifying the competition; analyzing the competition; analyzing the environment; and selecting the target market.

competitive sell Synonym for COMPARATIVE ADVERTISING.

competitive stage See MATURITY STAGE.

competitive variables The activities of rival establishments that may influence a retailer's own sales. Such activities include, but are not limited to, the competitor's advertising policies, pricing policies, e-tailing presence, and store location.

competitor 1. Any person, team, or company that strives to outdo another. 2. In retailing, any other store that has targeted the same or similar target market and/or does business in the same trading area. 3. In marketing, a rival firm that produces a similar product or provides a similar service. Rival firms compete for MARKET SHARE. 4. In Internet marketing, a business whose online presence is in the middle of the pack. The competitor waits for solid evidence of success or failure before adding any innovations to the online effort. See also FAST FOLLOWER, INNOVATOR, and CONSERVATIVE.

compiled database Computer-accessible data collected by others and purchased by a firm seeking to expand customer reach. Compiled databases often use multiple data sources (e.g., public records, private data sources, and overlays of customer response data) and are regularly updated. They may also provide predictive scores for customer response rates based on data mining or survey data. A compiled database is a possible alternative or supplement to a company's own IN-HOUSE DATABASE built from the company's own data and customer records.

complaint department Synonym for ADJUSTMENT DEPARTMENT.

complaint management The practice of providing quality customer service by accepting and quickly responding to customer complaints. Complaint management involves understanding how best to provide customer services and how to resolve customer problems as they arise.

complementary demand See JOINT DEMAND.

complementary products/goods Merchandise purchased as a supplement or accessory to the basic product, such as computer software for computers or shoelaces for shoes. For consumer convenience and to generate additional sales, complementary products are often sold in the same section of the store as the primary product. See also ALLIED PRODUCTS OR LINES and ACCESSORIES.

complementary stores In a shopping center or other shopping area, those stores whose products stimulate each other's sales. For example, the sale of a new outfit in an apparel store may stimulate the sale of a pair of shoes in a nearby shoe store.

complement of (cumulative) markup percentage The difference between the total retail price (100%) and the percentage of markup at retail (e.g., 40%). The result is usually the cost of the goods. For example, if an item is sold at retail for $10.00 (100%) and the markup is 40%, the complement of markup percentage is 60%. Multiplying the retail price by the complement of markup percentage will give the cost of the goods. $10.00 × .60 = $6.00.

completed cancel   A consumer who fulfills all commitments to the seller (i.e., who has received the goods and made all payments) before canceling the order.

complete order   An order that has been shipped in its entirety by the vendor and received by the retailer. Also called a *filled order.*

complete segmentation   A view of the population of potential customers in which each one is treated as an individual rather than as part of an aggregation because each is seen as identifiably distinct from all others. See also CUSTOM MARKETING.

complete standardization   See STANDARDIZATION.

completion date   A date on a purchase order that specifies the last day on which a manufacturer may deliver goods to a retailer without the threat of cancellation. While goods on the same order may arrive separately and on different dates, the total order must be fulfilled by the completion date.

compliance department/bureau   An administrative department of a store responsible for seeing to it that applicable government regulations are properly observed, particularly with regard to merchandising and personnel practices. Also known as a *compliance office* or *compliance division.*

compliance division/office   See COMPLIANCE DEPARTMENT/ BUREAU.

compliment approach   See PRAISE APPROACH.

component materials   Unfinished goods (such as raw materials, farm commodities, ores, fiber, lumber, cement, etc.) that are incorporated into finished manufactured products. Compare COMPONENT PART. See also MATERIALS AND PARTS.

component part   A manufactured product that is incorporated as a constituent of a finished whole. For example, an automobile engine is a component part of an automobile. Compare COMPONENT MATERIALS. See also MATERIALS AND PARTS.

component percentage   A ratio that expresses an INCOME STATEMENT COMPONENT (i.e., gross margin, expenses, or net income) as a percentage of net sales. Component percentages may be used to evaluate performance between two time periods (i.e., time series comparison).

composition   In VISUAL MERCHANDISING, the organization or grouping of different parts or elements of a DISPLAY in order to achieve a unified whole. It includes the arrangement of lines, forms, shapes, and colors into an aesthetically pleasing whole that directs the viewer's eye to the various elements of the setting and relays a particular message.

comprehensive income   According to the Financial Accounting Standards Board (1985), the "change in equity (net assets) of an entity during a period from transactions and other events and circumstances from nonowner sources. It includes all changes in equity during a period except those resulting from investments by owners and distributions to owners."

comptroller   Alternative spelling of CONTROLLER.

computer crime   Synonym for CYBERCRIME.

computerized checkout   See POINT-OF-SALE TERMINAL (POST).

computerized quick response system   The implementation of computer technology to automate the reordering process. Computerized quick response ensures that BASIC STOCK will be reordered on a regular basis, thus avoiding a STOCKOUT for items in regular demand. It also frees the buyer to concentrate on other buying activities, allows the retailer to operate on a just-in-time (rather than a just-in-case) basis, and forms strong partnerships between retailers and vendors. See also AUTOMATIC REORDERING SYSTEM.

computerized retail system   A system using computers to collect and analyze retail information. See also POINT-OF-SALE TERMINAL (POST).

computerized shopping   See ELECTRONIC RETAILING and E-TAILING.

computer modem   See MODEM.

computer monitor   See MONITOR.

computer mouse   See MOUSE.

computer network   A group of two or more computer systems linked together. There are many types of computer networks, including *local-area networks (LANs)*, in which the computers are geographically close together (i.e., in the same building); *wide-area networks (WANs)*, in which the computers are farther apart and connected by telephone lines or radio waves; *campus-area networks (CANs)*, in which the computers are within a limited geographical area such as a campus or military base; *metropolitan-area networks (MANs)*, for a town or city; and *home-area networks (HANs)*, networks contained within users' own homes to connect a variety of digital devices.

computer user   See USER.

computer virus   See VIRUS.

con artist/man   See CONMANSHIP.

conation   The mental processes having to do with purposive behavior, including desiring, resolving, and striving. See also CONATIVE COMPONENT.

conative component   In attitude research, particularly in the TRIPARTITE VIEW or structural approach, the conative component is the readiness of an individual to purchase a particular product or service or take some other action. It is the active component of attitude.

concealed damage/loss See CONCEALED LOSS AND DAMAGE CLAIMS.

concealed discount A discount given by a VENDOR to a retailer, applied uniformly to all items on a purchase order whether or not individual items are price-fixed.

concealed loss and damage claims A claim made against a carrier for loss or damage to merchandise while the merchandise was in the carrier's possession (i.e., in transit). At the time of delivery, the loss or damage was not apparent either because the shipping container was not opened or because the merchandise was reshipped from a distribution point for delivery to an ultimate consignee without having been inspected.

concentrated marketing 1. In retailing, a strategy by which the most appropriate segments of the population at large may be reached by a retail organization. All efforts are devoted to reaching those segments rather than the market at large. 2. More generally, a marketing strategy in which a firm's resources are devoted to capturing a large share of a narrow market segment. The targeted segment may not be the largest segment, but it will have the greatest potential for successful sales because of some other factor (such as ethnicity, age, educational level, or presence of children in the household). See also MARKET SEGMENTATION.

concentration Synonym for ASSEMBLING.

concentration approach Synonym for CONCENTRATED MARKETING.

concentric circles method See RING ANALYSIS.

concentric diversification A retailer's strategy for expansion by means of acquiring another retailer carrying similar product lines but appealing to and attracting a different set of customers. For example, a staid and established department store may acquire a specialty apparel retailer in hopes of appealing to younger, more FASHION-FORWARD customers.

concept shop A specially designated area in a retail store used to display and sell highly specialized merchandise or merchandise with high brand recognition. As such, it is a store-within-a-store format. Concept shops allow retailers to expand without the high overhead of chain store expansion. Instead of opening new stores, the retailer expands by placing its merchandise in established venues such as large department stores and airports. A BRANDED CONCEPT SHOP features internationally known megabrand merchandise.

concept statement A statement of a firm's marketing orientation in terms of its focus on the PRODUCT CONCEPT, PRODUCTION CONCEPT, MARKETING CONCEPT, or SELLING CONCEPT. Each of these concepts represents a different focus and a different understanding of what customers most want in a product. For example, a manufacturer may choose to focus on product improvement, efficient production, fulfilling the needs of the customer, or an aggressive sales campaign.

concept testing An early stage in the product development process, intended to determine consumer reaction to new product concepts before large amounts of money are committed to their production. To test their understanding of the idea behind a proposed product, potential customers are typically shown pictures of proposed products and asked to react to them.

concession 1. An independently owned and operated department within a retail store, in-store shop, or mall site. A concession is owned and operated by a manufacturer or distributor and is similar to a LEASED DEPARTMENT owned and operated by an outside retailer. Concessions cross all product and service lines. The manufacturer or distributor pays rent directly to the retailer for square footage in the store and sometimes also pays a percentage of sales or profits. Customers generally do not realize that the concession is independent of the host store. The owner/operator of the concession is known as a *concessionaire*. 2. A right granted to an outside company to sell its products or services. For example, a food company may have a concession at a lakeside beach. 3. A deviation from regular terms or previous conditions, as in a contract.

concessionaire See CONCESSION.

conclusive research Research studies, often based on such methods as surveys, observation, simulation, and experimentation, that generate large quantities of reliable data. Retailers and other marketers often employ conclusive research in an effort to solve specific problems and employ the results as a basis for decision making.

condition 1. A clause in a contract that suspends, rescinds, or modifies the principal obligation as set forth in the contract. The fulfillment of the contract is said to be *on condition* of the satisfaction of a number of prerequisites or variables. 2. The physical state of merchandise received by a retailer from a vendor or sold by the retailer to the ultimate consumer. For example, old or damaged merchandise may be sold in AS IS condition. Similarly, used items such as automobiles, books, or sound recordings are often described in terms of their condition, as in *a-one*, *mint*, *excellent*, *very good*, *good*, or *acceptable* condition. Merchandise received in poor condition from a vendor may serve as grounds for a CHARGEBACK.

conditional sale See CONDITIONAL SALES CONTRACT.

conditional sales contract A retail installment contract that requires the buyer to pay monthly installment payments to the retailer or other creditor. The retailer retains title of ownership until all payments have been made, so that merchandise may be repossessed whenever the buyer fails to meet the terms of the contract. If the repossessed item is resold, the resale price is credited to the customer's balance, but the customer remains liable for the remainder of the balance due.

conditions of sale In RETAIL PRODUCT ADVERTISING, the terms under which the advertised merchandise is being sold. For example, merchandise may be sold at regular price, special price, or clearance price; or it may be sold exclusively by Internet, telephone, or mail order.

conference 1. A meeting held within an organization or within a larger grouping such as a trade association. Members of a professional association often meet annually at a specified location over a period of several days. Within a store or other business, a conference may involve all the department heads, who meet to share their insights about the company's operations and to plan for the future. The TELECONFERENCE, WEB CONFERENCE, and VIDEOCONFERENCE are technological substitutes for in-person conferences. 2. An online area on a BULLETIN BOARD SYSTEM (BBS) or ONLINE SERVICE in which participants can discuss a topic of common interest. Synonym for FORUM.

conference carriers An organization of ocean carriers that fixes rates and sailing times.

conference report Synonym for CALL REPORT.

confidence artist/man See CONMANSHIP.

confidence game See CONMANSHIP.

confidence interval In QUANTITATIVE RESEARCH based on RANDOM SAMPLING, a confidence interval is the range on either side of an estimate most likely to contain the actual value with a stated percentage of certainty. The size of the sample determines the percentage of certainty. If a sample of 100 were taken in a random sampling for a new brand of tooth whitener and it was found that 10 percent of the sample preferred the new tooth whitener over existing brands, then it may be stated with 95 percent certainty that between 4 and 16 percent of the population actually prefers the new tooth whitener.

confined label See PRIVATE BRAND.

confined merchandise/goods In retailing, merchandise sold by a producer or distributor to a limited number of stores so that, in effect, each retailer has exclusive resale rights in its own trading area. Also called *confinement, exclusivity,* and *exclusive merchandise.* See also EXCLUSIVE DISTRIBUTION.

confinement See CONFINED MERCHANDISE/GOODS.

confirmation of an order See CONFIRMED ORDER.

confirmed order The order form, usually signed by the retail buyer and the merchandise manager, that makes an order official and binding upon the store. From the vendor's standpoint, confirmation of an order acknowledges receipt of the order and its legal acceptance.

confiscation 1. In international business, the seizure or expropriation of foreign-owned property by a government without provision for reimbursement of the owners. See also EXPROPRIATION, NATIONALIZATION, and DOMESTICATION. 2. The seizure of private property by a government, often as a penalty.

confusion of items The intermingling of the items of two or more owners so that they are difficult or even impossible to separate.

con game See CONMANSHIP.

conglomerate A large business organization made up of a number of independently operated subsidiaries and operating divisions, often engaged in different enterprises, under a unified ownership. The operating divisions in a conglomerate remain autonomous, though the conglomerate may perform certain centralized functions for them such as merchandise distribution and inventory management. A conglomerate is often referred to as a PARENT COMPANY, but there are differences in the amount of control exerted by each over the subsidiaries. See also MERCHANDISING CONGLOMERATE.

conglomerate diversification A retail business's strategy for expansion whereby newly acquired retail stores or companies have no direct relationship to the conglomerate itself. This allows the parent company to enter an entirely new line of business. For example, a retail conglomerate primarily engaged in selling toys may acquire a store or chain of stores engaged in selling children's apparel. Compare CONCENTRIC DIVERSIFICATION.

conglomerate integration Synonym for CONGLOMERATE MERGER.

conglomerate market competition The sale of the identical item by different dealers and distributors, thus multiplying the channels of distribution.

conglomerate merger The combining of two or more organizations in unrelated industries into a single organization (i.e., a MERGER). For example, a merger between a cosmetics manufacturer and a children's clothing manufacturer would constitute a conglomerate merger. The two firms may be on different levels of the CHANNEL OF DISTRIBUTION, such as an apparel manufacturer and a retail store, or a car rental agency and a food manufacturer. The companies involved undertake the merger in order to provide diversity of operations for each other, augment the company's growth, and protect their profits from economic fluctuations by diversifying RISK.

conglomerchant (Rare) Synonym for MERCHANDISING CONGLOMERATE.

congruent innovation The development of products that, because they are so slightly changed, are virtually identical to their antecedents. The old and new products frequently differ only in terms of higher or lower quality or in that the new product incorporates a relatively insignificant new feature. Congruent innovation almost never disrupts existing consumptive patterns.

congruent production diversification Additional items or lines of items added to a store's product mix based on management decisions. Synonymous with PRODUCTION-ORIENTED DIVERSIFICATION.

conjoint measurement/analysis A measurement tool used in product planning in which product attributes are analyzed in an effort to determine which are most attractive to potential customers. Also called *benefit structure analysis* and *trade-off analysis*.

conmanship (Slang) The ability to persuade customers to buy something that will not provide the promised benefits or to delude them into parting with their money for nothing at all. The act of tricking customers in this way is known as a *con game* (from *confidence game*) since the scam depends on gaining the confidence of the target (or *mark*). The practitioner of conmanship is known as a *con man* (or *confidence man*) or *con artist*, since either gender may be involved.

conscious level of need awareness See NEED AWARENESS.

conscious parallel action The deliberate setting of identical prices by competing organizations. The practice is considered illegal in the United States, as evidenced by a number of antitrust cases. See also PRICE FIXING.

consensus A judgmental technique for forecasting business results based on the combined opinions of groups of individuals. See also JUDGMENTAL TECHNIQUES.

conservative In online marketing, a business that maintains a minimal Internet presence, allowing competitors to take the lead while focusing on other aspects of the business. See also FAST FOLLOWER and COMPETITOR.

consideration Something of value (money or other variables) that induces a party to enter into a contract or other agreement with another party.

consign To order, by means of a BILL OF LADING (B/L), a carrier to deliver merchandise from a given starting point to a given destination. The vendor (i.e., shipper) who initiates the shipment is known as the CONSIGNOR. The ultimate recipient of the goods is known as the CONSIGNEE.

consigned goods See CONSIGNMENT.

consignee 1. In shipping, the ultimate party to whom goods are shipped and delivered (i.e., consigned). 2. When goods are sold on CONSIGNMENT, the party (i.e., a reseller or agent) to whom the merchandise is sent for sale. The consignee may return anything that is not sold. See also WITHDRAWAL.

consignee mark An identifying symbol placed on a package before it is exported, generally consisting of a square, triangle, diamond, circle, cross, etc., combined with letters and/or numbers.

consignment Merchandise shipped by a producer to a retailer (or wholesaler) with the understanding that the producer retains title to the goods until they are sold. Consignment arrangements are not common, but are sometimes used to sell big-ticket items with a slow or unpredictable rate of sale, such as works of art, to minimize the retailer's RISK. Goods are returned to the vendor if not sold within a specified time period. The title to consignment goods passes from the vendor to the consumer but never to the retailer. Goods acquired in this manner (i.e., *consigned goods*) are said to be *on consign-*

ment. Compare MEMORANDUM BUYING and RETURN PRIVILEGE. See also CONSIGNMENT BUYING.

consignment buying An agreement under which the retailer takes possession of merchandise while title remains with the manufacturer or vendor. Unsold merchandise may be returned to the vendor after a specified time has elapsed. Some high-end retailers use consignment buying to introduce products by new designers or vendors into their stores. Some low-end retailers sell used clothing and household furnishings *on consignment*, dividing the proceeds according to a predetermined percentage with the customer who brought the item into the store. Also called *consignment purchase* and *consignment sale*.

consignment note A document given when merchandise is sent that provides details of the item, the name and address of the sender, and the recipient to whom the merchandise has been sent. The recipient signs it upon arrival, providing proof of delivery.

consignment purchase/sale See CONSIGNMENT BUYING.

consignment terms See CONSIGNMENT.

consignor In shipping, the company shipping the merchandise.

consistency The degree to which items in an assortment of merchandise are compatible with each other and with other merchandise in the store. See also ASSORTMENT CONSISTENCY.

consistency of product mix A firm's product mix has three attributes: width, depth, and consistency. A firm's lines are said to be consistent when they share certain common characteristics such as similar end use, shared channels of distribution, common production facilities, etc.

consolidated buying See CENTRAL BUYING.

consolidated delivery system A delivery service operated by a private organization whose purpose is to deliver packages for retailers. United Parcel Service is such a system in the United States.

consolidated metropolitan statistical area (CMSA) Formerly, a group of closely related primary metropolitan statistical areas forming a cluster, such as Dade and Broward counties in Florida. The adoption of the concept of the CORE-BASED STATISTICAL AREA (CBSA) changed the way in which the U.S. Office of Management and Business (OMB) refers to statistical areas, and this term is no longer used.

consolidator A person or organization that brings together merchandise from a number of sources into one order for shipment. See also ASSEMBLING.

consolidator model (of EBPP) See ELECTRONIC BILL PRESENTMENT AND PAYMENT (EBPP).

consortium 1. In international marketing, a partnership arrangement similar to the JOINT VENTURE, with the exception that it typically involves a large number of participants and functions in a market in which it was not previously involved. A consortium helps to bring together financing and spread RISK among more participants.   2. In any form of purchasing, a group of individuals or firms who join together to reap the benefits of ECONOMIES OF SCALE. In this sense, a consortium functions like a COOPERATIVE in helping members achieve the lowest possible price for goods and services they buy as a group. The plural form of consortium is *consortia*.

conspicuous consumption   The spending of money for consumer goods in a manner easily seen by others. Goods are purchased for the purposes of enhancing one's status and expressing one's wealth. See also VEBLEN GOODS.

conspiracy in restraint of trade   See RESTRAINT OF TRADE.

constant cost   See FIXED COSTS (FC).

constant dollars   A dollar amount modified so that the effects of inflation have been removed. A base year is selected and all subsequent calculations and comparisons are relative to the dollar value in that year. All the resultant dollar values are then constant and comparable. Constant dollars are used in time series analysis, other statistical series, and economics.

constrained decision making   Limitations imposed on the discretionary decision making abilities of a business, especially as a result of a FRANCHISE agreement. See also FRANCHISING.

consular invoice   A special form (usually available at foreign consulates located in the exporting country) whose main purpose is to provide information to local CUSTOMS officials about the goods being imported into the foreign country. After the exporter has filled out the form it must generally be sworn to at the foreign consulate at the U.S. port of shipment.

consultant   An individual who, for a fee, provides services, expertise, and experience to an organization to help analyze problems and suggest solutions.

consultative selling   A form of face-to-face DIRECT SELLING that takes place in the customer's home or office. Consultative selling is characterized by specialists whose expertise is valued by the customer. Consultants who work for home furnishings, shop-at-home apparel, kitchen tool, and cosmetics companies frequently use this method.

consumer   A member of a broad class of persons who buy, use, and dispose of products and services for themselves, their families, and their friends. The consumer is the person buying goods or services for his or her own use or for use in the home. In retailing, the term is commonly taken to mean the store's customers. Also called the *ultimate consumer,* the *end user* or the *final consumer*. Frequently used interchangeably with CUSTOMER. See also GLOBAL CONSUMERS.

consumer advertising   ADVERTISING whose target is the ultimate consumer and whose purpose is to induce individuals to purchase specific goods and services.

consumer advocate   One who speaks for or represents the interests of the consuming public, particularly with respect to social, economic, and ecological matters.

consumer analysis   Synonym for CONSUMER RESEARCH.

consumer behavior   The actions of consumers in the MARKETPLACE and the underlying motives for those actions. Retailers and other marketers expect that by understanding what causes consumers to buy particular goods and services they will be able to determine which products are needed in the marketplace, which are obsolete, and how best to present those goods to the consumer. Also called *purchase behavior*. See also CONSUMER RESEARCH, SPENDING PATTERNS, and MOTIVE.

consumer behavior research   Synonym for CONSUMER RESEARCH.

Consumer Bill of Rights (1962)   Principles stated by President Kennedy in 1962 outlining the rights consumers should expect from the MARKETPLACE and providing the framework for much subsequent consumer legislation. As stated by President Kennedy, the consumer is entitled to be safe from injury; to be correctly informed about products; to have a proper forum in which to be heard when problems and complaints arise; to have a choice in the selection of goods and/or services; and to have a voice in the decision making process through which goods and/or services become available in the marketplace. Also known as *rights of consumers*. See also CONSUMERISM.

consumer buying   Shopping at the level of the ultimate consumer (i.e., the individual in search of goods and services).

consumer community   In ONLINE marketing to consumers, a consumer community is a group of individuals with a common purpose or interest who interact online to share information, support, and concern. Consumer communities are sometimes maintained on business Web sites. Members of such sites are encouraged to engage in such activities as reviewing the business's products, sharing recipes and tips, and making recommendations to other consumers.

consumer confidence   A measure used to gauge consumers' feelings about the reliability and trustworthiness of the nation's economy as well as about their own economic security. It is frequently used as a key predictor of consumers' willingness to purchase. The Conference Board, through the Consumer Research Center (CRC), compiles and publishes a monthly *Consumer Confidence Index* based on a survey of a representative sample of 5,000 U.S. households. Consumer confidence is compared to a base year of 1985 (i.e., 1985 = 100). Published as the *Consumer Confidence Survey*, the monthly report details consumer attitudes and buying intentions. Data are available by age, income, and region.

Consumer Confidence Index   See CONSUMER CONFIDENCE.

Consumer Confidence Survey   See CONSUMER CONFIDENCE.

consumer contest See CONTEST.

consumer convenience goods See CONVENIENCE GOODS/ITEMS/PRODUCTS.

consumer cooperative A retail operation owned by its customers and usually incorporated on the basis of one vote for each customer/member. Merchandise is commonly sold below the prevailing market price, and profits are divided among the customer-members in proportion to their patronage of the store. For a small membership fee, cooperators own shares (or stakes), receive lower prices, and participate in PROFIT SHARING. Also known as a *consumers' cooperative, cooperative retailer, cooperative store,* and *purchasing cooperative.*

consumer credit The ability of individual consumers to obtain money, goods, or revenues on the strength of their promise to pay at some specified time in the future, generally in installments.

Consumer Credit Protection Act (1968) A U.S. statute, passed in 1969 and amended in 1970, requiring finance companies, banks, retailers, and other grantors of consumer credit to reveal to the consumer the true cost of credit, both in terms of annual percentage rates and dollar amounts. This federal legislation was designed to allow consumers to compare competing sources of credit. The 1970 amendment protects the holder of credit cards from liability if the cards are fraudulently used. Commonly referred to as the *Truth-in-Lending Act (1968).*

consumer culture A culture in which MASS CONSUMPTION and production both fuel the economy and shape perceptions, values, desires, and construction of personal identity.

consumer deal Synonym for RETAIL DEAL.

consumer decision process Synonym for ADOPTION PROCESS.

consumer demand The level of desire for goods exhibited by consumers in the marketplace coupled with their ability to purchase these goods.

consumer demand management (CDM) Computer applications used to identify and manage opportunities for manufacturers to increase their sales to the retail trade by demonstrating to retailers how they can deliver total category and total store impact.

consumer demographic profile A composite description of a group of consumers based on demographic characteristics such as age, gender, location, income, race, educational level, and occupation. See also MARKET SEGMENTATION and DEMOGRAPHICS.

consumer demographics The vital statistics of the consuming population (or customer group), including age, gender, birth and death rates, location, income, race, educational level, and size of the group. The most-studied demographic variables tend to be those that are relatively easy to identify, collect, measure, and analyze. See also DEMOGRAPHICS and MARKET SEGMENTATION.

consumer diary In ADVERTISING RESEARCH, a booklet in which each member of a representative sample of consumers records what he or she is actually viewing on television and/or listening to on radio for one week. The consumers are also asked to provide information about their age, gender, occupation, etc. Use of the consumer diary is intended to give advertisers insight into the makeup of the broadcast media audience.

consumer durables Consumer goods having a relatively long period of usefulness (sometimes arbitrarily set at three years). These tend to be relatively expensive items such as major appliances (e.g., washing machines, refrigerators, power lawn mowers), television sets, automobiles, etc.

consumer education Formal efforts on the part of schools, professional societies, government agencies, and nonprofit organizations to teach consumers the skills, attitudes, knowledge, and understanding needed to allocate their resources wisely in the MARKETPLACE. Consumer education includes both the rights and the responsibilities of consumers and often focuses on such issues as the environment and globalization. The underlying philosophy behind consumer education is that articulate and demanding individuals are less likely to be duped.

consumer efficiency A theory of retail institutional change according to which consumers' cost-saving efforts (with regard to price, transportation, time, and physical effort) influence the development of new retail organizations. For example, the growth of shopping centers may be attributed to consumers' desire for time-efficient shopping.

consumer electronics According to the 2002 NORTH AMERICAN INDUSTRY CLASSIFICATION SYSTEM (NAICS), the classification known as consumer electronics generally includes household-type electrical appliances, room air-conditioners, clothes dryers, and/or household audio and video equipment. It includes such items as answering machines, electric blankets, electric cooking equipment, household dishwashers, electric clothes dryers, hair dryers, fans, electric housewares, heaters, electric razors, smoke detectors, television sets, toasters, electric toothbrushes, vacuum cleaners, video cameras, and water heaters—all designed for personal or home use by the ultimate consumer.

Consumer Expenditure Survey A publication of the BUREAU OF LABOR STATISTICS (BLS) comprising data on the buying habits of American consumers by socioeconomic characteristics.

consumer goods Goods produced for the retail customer (i.e., the ultimate consumer) that require no further processing. They may fall into one of four categories: CONVENIENCE GOODS (gum, magazines, etc.); IMPULSE GOODS; SHOPPING GOODS (clothing, cars, etc.); and SPECIALTY GOODS (gourmet foods, etc.) Also called *end-use products.*

Consumer Goods Pricing Act (1975)   Federal legislation that halted all interstate usage of RESALE PRICE MAINTENANCE (RPM) agreements. The legislation ended many of the so-called *fair trade agreements* used by manufacturers to control the prices at which their products would be sold at subsequent stages of distribution.

consumer inducement   Synonym for PREMIUM.

consumer information   Information supplied to the consumer by a business, government agency, independent consumer group (e.g., Consumers Union, publishers of *Consumer Reports*), media source (e.g., magazine, newspaper, radio, television, or Internet source), family and/or friends, including such data as the cost, quality, and availability of products in the MARKETPLACE.

consumer insight   An in-depth understanding of what consumers need and want, their product preferences and perceptions, past market behaviors, and possible future actions. Retailers and other marketers rely on consumer MARKETING RESEARCH (MR) to provide such insight.

Consumer Internet Barometer   A quarterly survey, created and published by the Consumer Research Center (CRC) of the Conference Board, that purports to reveal what U.S. consumers think, feel, and do relating to the Internet.

consumerism   The organized demand that businesses increase their concern for the public in both the manufacture and the sale of merchandise. See also CONSUMER BILL OF RIGHTS (1962).

consumerist   Synonym for CONSUMER ADVOCATE.

consumer jury   In retail advertising, a group of consumers who represent potential buyers of a product or service. They are given a test in which they view a number of advertisements and rank them by preference.

consumer laws/legislation   Legislation enacted on the local, state, or national level to protect consumers from unscrupulous business practices. On the federal level in the United States, these laws include the KEFAUVER-HARRIS DRUG AMENDMENTS TO THE FOOD AND DRUG ACT (1962), the WHOLESOME MEAT ACT (1967), the CHILD PROTECTION AND TOY SAFETY ACT (1969), the HAZARDOUS SUBSTANCES LABELING ACT (1960), the FAIR PACKAGING AND LABELING ACT (1966), the CONSUMER CREDIT PROTECTION ACT (1968), the CONSUMER PRODUCT SAFETY ACT (1972), the EQUAL CREDIT OPPORTUNITY ACT (ECOA) (1975), and the NUTRITION LABELING AND EDUCATION ACT (1990), among many others.

consumer list   In sales, a series of names of prospective and current customers who may be contacted in the future.

consumer market   All those persons who purchase goods and services for their own use or for the use of those in their household (i.e., they do not resell the purchased product nor use it in some other business enterprise).

consumer marketing research   See MARKETING RESEARCH (MR).

consumer motivation   The driving force in an individual that impels action in the marketplace. It may be positive or negative depending on how one perceives one's needs and goals.

consumer obsolescence   The rejection of presently owned goods by consumers in favor of something new, despite the continuing utility of the original goods.

consumer orientation   A marketing philosophy stating that the authority for business operations is vested in the consumer. Satisfaction of the consumer's desires thus becomes the prime objective of the marketer. Compare PRODUCT ORIENTATION and PRODUCTION CONCEPT.

consumer panel   In MARKETING RESEARCH (MR), a group of individuals brought together for the purpose of determining consumer preferences with regard to products or ideas. The panel members are interviewed collectively and their expressed opinions are tabulated for use in new product development and similar activities. Compare FOCUS GROUP.

consumer-perceived risk   A consumer's perception or intuition of the possible effects, mostly negative, of an incorrect purchase decision. Includes functional risk, physical risk, financial risk, social risk, and psychological risk. Also called *perceived risk*.

consumer premium   See PREMIUM.

Consumer Price Index (CPI)   A measure of the changes, over time, in the retail prices of a representative market basket of goods and services purchased for day-to-day living by urban consumers. A composite of 1982–1984 prices serves as the index or reference base, with current prices expressed in relation to that base. Change is measured in relation to the base year figure. Thus, if 1982–1984 = 100, an index of 110 in a subsequent year means there has been a 10% increase in price since the reference period. The items making up the market basket are of constant quality and quantity. The CPI is not a true cost-of-living index (which would measure such variables as the total amount families spend to live, how price fluctuations affect the standard of living, or the relative difference in the cost of living between two or more geographic areas). See also COST-OF-LIVING INDEX (COLI) and DEPARTMENT STORE INVENTORY PRICE INDEX.

consumer products   Synonym for CONSUMER GOODS.

Consumer Product Safety Act (CPSA) (1972)   Federal legislation establishing the CONSUMER PRODUCT SAFETY COMMISSION (CPSC). The act stipulates that manufacturers must notify the CPSC within 24 hours of discovering that they have produced and sold a product representing a substantial hazard to consumers. A recall procedure must be instituted by the manufacturer to correct the defect.

Consumer Product Safety Commission (CPSC)   A government agency serving as a watchdog to protect the consumer from risk of serious injury or death from over 15,000 types of consumer products. The commission originated with the passage of the CONSUMER PRODUCT SAFETY ACT (CPSA) (1972); it maintains a Web site at www.cpsc.gov.

Consumer Product Safety Commission Improvements Act (1976)   An amendment to the CONSUMER PRODUCT SAFETY ACT (CPSA) (1972) intended to improve the effectiveness of the Commission by providing standards, enforceability, litigation procedures, and funding.

consumer profile   A description of the demographic and psychographic characteristics of a customer for a particular item or service. See also TARGET MARKET.

consumer promotion   A SALES PROMOTION aimed at the ultimate consumer. It may include free samples, coupons, premiums, trading stamps, fashion shows, and other product demonstrations. E-mail and conventional mail are often used to alert customers to the promotion.

Consumer Protection Act (1968)   See CONSUMER CREDIT PROTECTION ACT (1968).

consumer protection legislation   Synonym for CONSUMER LAWS/LEGISLATION.

consumer research   The study of the ultimate consumer to determine the factors that influence purchase decisions involving time, money, and effort. Consumer behavior comes under the related studies of demography, sociology, anthropology, and psychology. Retailers and other marketers look to consumer research to help them identify their target markets and determine how to market their goods and/or services most efficiently. See also MARKETING RESEARCH (MR).

consumer rights   See CONSUMER BILL OF RIGHTS (1962).

consumer risk   See CONSUMER-PERCEIVED RISK.

consumer-sale disclosure statement   A form presented by a dealer to a customer making a purchase on an installment plan. The form specifies essential details on finance charges relative to the purchase. This disclosure is required under the CONSUMER CREDIT PROTECTION ACT (1968).

consumers' cooperative   See CONSUMER COOPERATIVE.

consumer's decision process   The perceived stages in a consumer's decision whether or not to purchase a product. Includes stimulus, problem awareness, the search for information, evaluation of alternatives, purchase, and post-purchase behavior. The process is influenced by the demographic and psychographic profile of the individual consumer. See also SORTING THEORY.

consumer show/fashion show   A FASHION SHOW produced by a retailer to sell ideas and merchandise to the ultimate consumer. Consumer shows may feature seasonal, storewide, departmental, designer, private label, or manufacturer's brand merchandise. Manufacturers may cooperatively produce the show or contribute elements for the show in which their merchandise is featured. Consumer shows are popular magazine tie-in events.

consumer's income expectations   Monetary income that a consumer anticipates receiving sometime in the future that influences present buying behavior. It particularly affects the purchase of big-ticket items such as automobiles and major appliances. Also called *expected income* or, simply, *income expectation.*

consumers' liquid assets   The amount of cash, and other assets readily convertible into cash, available to consumers for purchases. Liquid assets influence consumer buying behavior decisions, particularly for big-ticket items such as major appliances, furniture, etc. See also PERSONAL INCOME (PI).

consumer socialization   The process by which consumers form attitudes and opinions in the context of the society around them and develop the skills necessary to become consumers within that society. The process is an ongoing one, beginning in childhood and continuing throughout life. Also called, simply, *socialization.*

consumer sovereignty   A concept in marketing in which the consumer is seen as the final arbiter in the marketplace, having the power to decide which products will succeed and which will fail.

consumer's surplus   See CONSUMER SURPLUS.

consumer stimulant   Any promotion or incentive employed to attract the consumer and to stimulate demand. Consumer stimulants may take the form of free samples and premiums offered at retail, contests and sweepstakes, and other promotional activities. See also PREMIUM and PROMOTIONS AND SALES.

consumer surplus   The difference, as perceived by a consumer, between the value of a purchase and the price paid for it. A consumer surplus exists if consumers perceive they are getting more than their money's worth and if they would even be willing to pay a somewhat higher price for the same product or service.

consumer variables   DEMOGRAPHICS as they influence the sale of a product or service. Consumer variables include the ways consumers may differ from each other (i.e., age, gender, education, income, race, occupation, etc.).

consumption patterns   The patterns in which consumers use or do not use a product (e.g., frequency of purchase, place of purchase, etc.). Consumption patterns are commonly employed as a basis for MARKET SEGMENTATION.

contact list   Synonym for BUDDY LIST.

contact report   Synonym for CALL REPORT.

container   Any receptacle capable of closure, used for packaging or shipping purposes.

containerization The consolidation of a number of smaller packages into a larger standardized container that can be sealed at its point of origin and shipped unopened to its destination. Containerized freight is subject to less damage and pilferage than loose cargo and easier to handle. The standardized containers can be easily stacked and moved from cargo ships to trucks or trains, facilitating the relatively seamless transportation of goods from distant overseas locations to local destinations. See also FISHYBACK.

containerized freight See CONTAINERIZATION.

container premium Packaging for goods that is reusable for another purpose (e.g., a decorative canister), serving as an added inducement for the consumer to purchase the product.

containership A ship outfitted with large numbers of cargo holders shaped like tractor-trailer beds and designed to hold standardized containers. Containerships carry containerized retail products to and from major ports where they are easily loaded onto other modes of cargo transportation.

contemporary styling A women's apparel classification distinguished by sophisticated, updated, and fashion-conscious style. The classification was originally intended for the age group that had outgrown junior sizes but was still interested in fashion and reluctant to adopt a matronly style of dress. The existence of this classification is an acknowledgment of the aging of the BABY BOOMERS.

contender See CONTENDER STRATEGY.

contender strategy A strategy for smaller, local firms competing with powerful multinationals. The local firm upgrades its capabilities to take on the multinational companies by expanding its resources to invest in the necessary RESEARCH AND DEVELOPMENT (R&D) expenditures and larger-scale production capabilities that their industries can demand. This strategy may involve going public to raise more money through a public stock offering. Contenders may also seek out niches that are underserved by their multinational competitors. Other strategies for local firms competing against multinationals are the DEFENDER STRATEGY, the EXTENDER STRATEGY, and the DODGER STRATEGY.

content See WEB SITE CONTENT.

content audit A process used to monitor a company's Web site and Web pages on a regular basis to identify outdated or incorrect information (i.e., content). After review, outdated content is removed and/or replaced. See also MARKETING AUDIT.

content label A tag or label affixed in conformity to the requirements of the U.S. federal acts regarding wool, fur, or textile fiber products. These acts are intended to protect the consumer from the misbranding, mislabeling, and false advertising of furs and other textile products.

content management In the development of retail Web sites, an organized system for identifying needed content, procuring it, determining when and how it should be changed, and implementing the changes. Site owners and Web administrators often turn to automated processes or outsourcing to handle content management as sites grow, evolve, and age. See also WEB SITE CONTENT.

content motivation theory Any explanation of consumer buying behavior focusing on factors within the consumer that start, arouse, energize, or stop the buying behavior.

content pricing Charging a fee for access to information contained on a Web site. While many sites offer their content for free, hoping to generate revenue from on-site paid advertising, others charge a fee. For example, some Web sites offer limited free public content, then charge by subscription or per unit of access for private, premium content. Other Web sites limit access on a members-only basis.

content sites Web sites offering content through online newspapers and magazines, television and radio sites, games sites, and other entertainment storefronts.

contest A sales promotion device in which participants compete for prizes by submitting an entry that requires a degree of skill or judgment to prepare (e.g., a statement or a jingle). Unlike games and sweepstakes, a contest eliminates the element of pure chance. Also called a *consumer contest*. See also SALES CONTEST. Compare GAME and SWEEPSTAKES.

contingency leadership Synonym for SITUATIONAL MANAGEMENT.

contingency pricing A payment plan in which a service organization does not receive payment for services performed until the customer's satisfaction can be assured.

contingent force Collective name for the store employees who move from department to department as needed to replace absent workers, cover breaks, or cover particularly heavy sales traffic. An individual employee assigned to the contingent force is known as a *contingent*. Contingents are generally on the store's regular payroll and may be either part- or full-time employees. Also called a *flying squad* and an *auxiliary force*.

contingent liability A potential legal obligation to pay a sum of money in return for a past or present benefit.

continuity 1. The retail sale of a series of related items over a long period of time (e.g., glassware, dishes, flatware, encyclopedias, etc.) as a promotional device to bring the customer into the store for several consecutive weeks. In general, the first item is specially priced, with subsequent items sold at a somewhat higher price. See also CONTINUITY PREMIUM. 2. In advertising, the steady flow of advertising messages over a period of time. Continuity is like a schedule or plan in that it provides some control over the spacing and frequency of ads; the pattern could mean that ads appear every day, every week, or every month. Especially well suited for continuity advertising scheduling are products that consumers purchase on a regular basis without regard for seasonality (e.g., BASIC STOCK items). Compare PULSING and FLIGHTING, two other methods of scheduling advertising.

continuity premium   The sale of sets of merchandise for coupons. The items are offered one at a time or one for a certain number of coupons, thus ensuring multiple purchases of the advertised product with which the coupons are distributed. Trading stamps are another form of continuity premium, popular in the mid-twentieth century. See also TRADING STAMPS and CONTINUITY.

continuity series   In direct marketing, a multipart product, such as a set of books, shipped one part at a time to the customer.

continuity strategy   See CONTINUITY.

continuous demand   A need and/or desire for goods or services that remains stable for a long period of time. For example, the demand for staple items such as bread and milk may be described as continuous.

continuous innovation   An ongoing process by which new products are developed and introduced into the marketplace. Rather than representing a major new departure, these new products commonly were already in production and have been slightly altered or improved.

continuum of online innovation   The spectrum of options open to an e-tailer in terms of novelty in developing an online presence. An e-tailer can choose to be at the forefront of the latest technology, follow what others have already done successfully, or attempt a moderate degree of novelty. Positions on the spectrum of innovation include the *innovator*, the *fast follower*, the *competitor*, or the *conservative*.

contra account   In accounting, an account that accumulates subtractions from another account so as to establish the net valuation of the other account. For example, an accumulated depreciation account would be a contra account for machinery. Also called a *valuation account*.

contraband   Merchandise whose import or export is forbidden by law, but that is sometimes smuggled and unlawfully sold.

contract   A legally enforceable agreement between two or more parties, generally set forth in writing. The legality of any contract depends on the following factors: a lawful promise; competent parties; an offer and its acceptance; agreement. The contract must be in writing if it involves a certain amount of money (as determined by the individual state) or is of more than one year's duration. See also EXPRESS CONTRACT, PURCHASE CONTRACT, and IMPLIED CONTRACT.

contract account   Any credit arrangement that requires customers to pay for goods or services in periodic installments as stipulated in a CONTRACT. See also INSTALLMENT PLAN/CONTRACT/BUYING.

contract buying   See SPECIFICATION BUYING.

contract buying office   See SALARIED (BUYING) OFFICE.

contract carrier   A transportation company that ships goods for one or more clients on the basis of a legal or business agreement (i.e., a CONTRACT). The contract carrier negotiates individual agreements with each shipper or small group of shippers. Also called *contract hauler*. Compare COMMON CARRIER and PRIVATE CARRIER.

contract dating   An agreement that determines when a cash discount can be taken and when an invoice is due to be paid in full. The terms of the contract may be CASH ON DELIVERY (COD) or any of the other agreements defined in this section.

contract department   A unit in a department store that arranges for the sale of large quantities of goods at special prices to institutions and other large buyers.

contract farming   A contractual arrangement between farmers and marketing intermediaries or manufacturers in which the farmer receives supplies and/or working capital and the manufacturer or marketing intermediary agrees to purchase the farmer's crop, sometimes at a guaranteed price.

contract hauler   Synonym for CONTRACT CARRIER.

contract manufacturing   1. In international marketing, a form of JOINT VENTURE in which a foreign company contracts with local manufacturers in the host country to produce a product.   2. A business arrangement, common in the apparel industry, under which one manufacturer (a SUBCONTRACTOR) produces goods for another manufacturer.

contract office   See SALARIED (BUYING) OFFICE.

contractor   An individual or firm that agrees to do work for another at a certain price, generally governed by a signed contract. See also APPAREL CONTRACTOR.

contractor evaluation   The process of determining a potential contractor's ability to meet standards of quality, cost, delivery reliability, and financial stability.

contract price   The sale price negotiated between a U.S. exporter and the foreign buyer, payable in the United States, for the export of U.S. goods and services. This price may include such charges as freight and marine insurance. However, it excludes any charges payable for non-U.S. goods and services (unless otherwise permitted), certain engineering services, import duties, charges for local costs, and any other charges not legally payable in the United States.

contract purchasing   A form of purchasing defined in a contract for orders and deliveries covering a specific period of time (e.g., one year).

contract-type buying office   See SALARIED (BUYING) OFFICE.

contractual channel system   See CONTRACTUAL VERTICAL MARKETING SYSTEM.

contractual vertical marketing system   A VERTICAL MARKETING SYSTEM (VMS) in which the units are independently owned, coming together by means of contractual agreements to obtain the economies and efficiencies of VERTICAL INTEGRATION. Also called *contractual VMS* and *contractual channel system*.

contractual VMS   See CONTRACTUAL VERTICAL MARKETING SYSTEM.

contract warehouse   A storage facility that combines public and private warehousing services. It is like a PUBLIC WAREHOUSE in that it serves a variety of customers. It differs from a public warehouse, however, in that the arrangements are long-term rather than on a monthly basis. The contracts may also include special warehouse services such as packaging or assembly. The contract warehouse provides the stability of a PRIVATE WAREHOUSE, therefore, through long-term leases and special services. Contract warehouses are independently owned and operated.

contract wholesaler   A WHOLESALER servicing a RETAIL COOPERATIVE/CO-OP.

contracyclical pricing   A PRICING STRATEGY that runs counter to the usual economic cycle in that the firm increases production and reduces prices during periods of prosperity (because of the high level of DEMAND), and reduces production and increases prices during an economic downturn (because of reduced demand).

contrast   In VISUAL MERCHANDISING, the composition of elements in order to show a sharp difference between them. Different forms, lines, or colors are juxtaposed in a DISPLAY composition in order to intensify each element's properties. For example, a white gown may be displayed against a black background.

contribution   1. In MARKETING COST ANALYSIS and BREAK-EVEN ANALYSIS, the sum of money generated by sales after variable costs have been subtracted.   2. The amount of money a unit or department in a firm provides toward discharging the firm's overall fixed costs. Also called *unit contribution*.

contribution expense plan   See CONTRIBUTION PLAN.

contribution-margin approach to cost analysis   In MARKETING COST ANALYSIS, an accounting method in which only direct expenses are charged to each marketing unit within a firm. The term CONTRIBUTION refers to the amount of money provided by the unit and applied to the firm's overall fixed expenses. MARGIN is the amount of money that constitutes profit from that unit (i.e., gross sales less variable costs). This method of analysis is particularly useful when a number of alternative courses of action are being compared, since only the COSTS relating directly to the particular alternatives under consideration are used, while other costs are ignored. The system focuses on variable costs, which can be allocated more readily than some fixed costs, especially those fixed costs that do not change over short periods of time and which, therefore, can be omitted from the analysis. See also FULL-COST APPROACH TO COST ANALYSIS.

contribution margin plan   Synonym for CONTRIBUTION PLAN.

contribution plan   A method of allocating expenses to departments in a retail store. Departments are assigned only those expenses that are controllable and can be charged directly to the department, while indirect expenses are not allocated. Also called *expense allocation, contribution expense plan,* and *contribution margin plan.*

contribution plan of expense allocation   See CONTRIBUTION PLAN.

contribution pricing   A PRICING STRATEGY in which, under special conditions (e.g., the promise of a very large order), a firm sets the price of the product lower than that which would cover the full cost of production. Contribution pricing covers the variable costs associated with the production of the specific product and makes a contribution toward meeting the firm's overall fixed costs, even though prices at this level may not contribute to the firm's overall profits.

contributor   In developing new products for global markets, a local subsidiary or foreign affiliate with competence in a distinct area who adapts some products for smaller but nonetheless important markets. Compare STRATEGIC LEADER and IMPLEMENTER, two other models of the subsidiary's relationship to the parent.

control   1. In marketing, that aspect of management concerned with monitoring the firm's performance in the MARKETPLACE, with particular attention given to determining whether or not the basic objectives of the firm are being achieved. The firm implements measures to compare actual marketing performance and outcomes to projected performance and outcomes. In Web marketing, some controls run continuously, particularly those tracking site traffic and sales. Also called *marketing control.*   2. In retailing, any system or device for checking reports, dates, or information as well as the conscious manipulation of such factors as volume, initial markup, turnover, etc. to achieve a particular net profit.

control account   A record of financial data summarizing entries and balances that appear in a subsidiary ledger. For example, ACCOUNTS RECEIVABLE is a control account summarizing the accounts of each customer regarding their outstanding balances. Also known as a *controlling account.*

control ad   In a PORTFOLIO TEST, an ad that has already been evaluated extensively over a period of time and that provides a basis for comparing the effectiveness of the TEST AD.

control audit   An examination and evaluation of the results of a MARKETING PLAN. A control audit is designed to help identify and correct any deviations from the plan and to monitor the plan's progress.

control division A functional division of a retail store responsible for maintaining accounting records, credit management, inventory management, financial analysis, merchandise budgeting, etc. Usually headed by a controller or treasurer, it is also known as a *controller's division* or a *finance and control division*.

control interval The time frame over which performance measures are taken. Depending on the standard or goal being measured, the interval may be hourly, daily, weekly, monthly, quarterly, seasonally, or annually. Some controls encompass multiple time intervals; for example, sales are often controlled by week, month, season, and year.

controllable cost An amount paid for goods and services that is incurred and regulated by the organizational unit and may, therefore, vary. A controllable cost may be raised or lowered according to management expectations and/or strategy.

controllable expense See DIRECT EXPENSE.

controllable factor In marketing, any of those business decisions over which the firm has significant discretion. The choice of product, choice of target customer, how the product is to be distributed, selling price, overall marketing objectives, etc., are all controllable factors. In retailing, this concept is often referred to as a CONTROLLABLE VARIABLE. Also called a *marketing controllable*.

controllable variable Any aspect of business operations that can be modified, altered, or improved by the retailer. Controllable variables include store location, product and service offerings, store image, promotion, pricing, and operations costs. In marketing, this concept is sometimes referred to as a CONTROLLABLE FACTOR.

controlled brand A BRAND of merchandise owned by its manufacturer and restricted to a limited number of distributors. These distributors are generally selected because they are not large enough to support a private brand of their own and/or they are not in direct competition with one another.

controlled circulation The free distribution of a business publication to a list of industrial or trade recipients determined by the publisher to be good prospects for the publication's advertisers.

controlled label See PRIVATE BRAND.

controller A store executive whose primary responsibilities include all of the store's fiscal and accounting operations. The controller administers the store's finances, credits, collections, and accounting records. Controllers in other types of organizations perform similar functions for those organizations. Also spelled *comptroller*.

controller's division Synonym for CONTROL DIVISION.

control level The organizational level (i.e., category, department, store, division, district, or region) at which controls are imposed and measured. The frequency of measurement (i.e., the CONTROL INTERVAL) may vary according to the level at which the measure is taken. For example, a store manager may monitor a store's sales by category daily while the district manager monitors total store sales daily and the regional manager monitors total store sales weekly.

controlling account Synonym for CONTROL ACCOUNT.

control standard Any of a business firm's measurable objectives and goals, particularly regarding monetary and physical performance, serving as a reference point or benchmark to evaluate performance. In a retail store, this often amounts to a *monetary standard* or goal for each department, such as the quota that a particular sales department must attain during a particular selling period. Standards are often based on prior performance (e.g., last year's sales during the same period). A retail store will also have certain *physical standards* (i.e., exterior and interior design, window displays, and signage), all of which will readily identify the store, particularly when it is part of a chain or franchise operation. Finally, a retail store will typically establish a number of *intangible standards* such as quality service, good performance, or store loyalty. These are more difficult to measure. Once control standards are established and communicated to store personnel, performance measures are implemented to determine whether or not the standards have been met. See also PERFORMANCE MEASURE.

control system A method used to measure the performance of the retail store and inform top management as to whether established goals and standards are being achieved. A control system also provides management with a basis for making changes to correct problems as they are identified. Good control systems call attention to deviations from the plan, suggest a means of solving problems that may arise, are accurate and timely, are understood by the members of the organization, and are economical to carry out.

convenience food store Synonym for CONVENIENCE STORE.

convenience goods/items/products Those items generally purchased by the customer in small quantities with a minimum of SHOPPING and at the most accessible retail outlet. Daily necessities such as food, toiletries, and small hardware items qualify as convenience goods. Staples, emergency, and/or impulse products are all convenience goods as well. Although usually branded merchandise, substitutes are seen as acceptable and even interchangeable. Also called *consumer convenience goods*, *convenience items*, and *convenience products*. See also CONSUMER GOODS.

convenience sample A form of NONPROBABILITY SAMPLE in which the researcher interviews those members of the POPULATION most readily available. For example, "man-in-the-street" interviews are a form of convenience sample.

convenience sampling In marketing and other social science research, the practice of selecting a group of participants simply because they are available. Some research firms maintain large pools of willing, prescreened participants.

convenience services   See ACCOMMODATION SERVICES.

convenience store   A grocery store, generally small, carrying a limited line of high-demand daily necessities (e.g., gasoline, fast foods, soft drinks, dairy products, beer, cigarettes, newspapers and magazines, grocery items, snacks, nonfood items, etc.), is open for extended hours, and charges prices generally higher than those found in a supermarket. Convenience stores appeal to the customer seeking to avoid the time and effort involved in shopping at a larger store or who is shopping during off-hours. According to the National Association of Convenience Stores (NACS), convenience stores are usually open seven days per week for longer hours than conventional supermarkets and generally stock 1,500–3,000 items. Convenience stores also tend to be conveniently located and readily accessible. For example, many gas stations now include convenience stores on their premises. Also called a *drive-in market, a midget market,* or a *convenience food store.* See also DEPOT STORE, BANTAM STORE, and EXPRESS STORE.

convenience value   See COMPANY ANALYSIS.

convention   1. A meeting or formal conference to discuss matters of common concern. Trade and professional organizations commonly hold annual conventions. Political parties in the United States hold their conventions during an election year to nominate candidates and adopt platforms.   2. A standard way of structuring certain types of information, particularly as used on the Internet (i.e., accepted usage).

conventional channel   A loosely organized CHANNEL OF DISTRIBUTION whose members are largely autonomous. Most consumer goods follow a conventional channel from manufacturer to wholesaler to retailer to ultimate consumer. Also called a *traditional channel system.* Compare VERTICAL MARKETING SYSTEM (VMS).

conventional department store   See DEPARTMENT STORE.

conventional retail method of inventory   See RETAIL METHOD OF INVENTORY (VALUATION).

conventional supermarket   See SUPERMARKET.

conversion process   See BOOMERANG.

conversion rate   In e-marketing, the number of visitors to a Web site who become subscribers or buyers.

converter   In the textile industry, a firm or merchant who purchases cloth in the greige (i.e., grey cloth, woven but unfinished) from mills, contracts to have it bleached, dyed, printed, etc., and sells the finished goods.

cookie   A small data file placed on a user's browser by a Web site's server. Cookies store direct data, provided by the user or recorded automatically without the user's knowledge, as well as indirect data, including CLICKSTREAM records of where the user went on the site, how much time was spent at each click, and the user's computer information. *Der.* UNIX term, *magic cookies,* "tokens that are attached to a user or program and change depending on the areas entered by the user of program."

cooling-off laws   Local laws allowing customers a period of time (usually three days) in which to reconsider a purchase and, if they so choose, to cancel the commitment. These laws have been passed to protect consumers from deceptive or high-pressure tactics employed by telephone and door-to-door salespeople.

cooling-off period   A period allowed by COOLING-OFF LAWS for a customer to reconsider a purchase.

cool medium   As defined by Marshall McLuhan, in 1964, a communications medium that requires a higher degree of user participation in order to engage meaningfully with it. Face-to-face speech, television, and the telephone are considered cool media. The World Wide Web is considered, for the most part, a cool medium. Compare HOT MEDIUM.

co-op   Short for COOPERATIVE as well as for COOPERATIVE EDUCATION.

co-op advertising   Short for COOPERATIVE ADVERTISING.

cooperation agreement   In global marketing, a COMPENSATION TRANSACTION or COUNTERTRADE agreement extending over a long period of time. Cooperation agreements usually involve related goods, such as payment for new textile machines in the form of the output produced by these machines. Also called a BUYBACK.

cooperative   A term applied to a wide range of organizations, including apartment houses, credit unions, mutual insurance companies, electric power distributors, and marketing enterprises, that are jointly owned by their members and were established to take advantage of the economic power inherent in large size. In marketing, cooperatives include such organizations as the *consumer cooperative* (usually a retail outlet owned by shareholding customers), the *producers' cooperative* (an association of the producers of certain commodities such as citrus fruit), and the *supply cooperative* (which sells goods to members at less than open-market prices). Members of cooperatives, who usually own shares in the organization, may be individuals or companies. Cooperatives are distinguished from profit-making ventures in that they render economic services to their members or shareholders on a nonprofit basis. Cooperatives pay periodic patronage dividends or rebates to members based on the volume of expenditures by members and the availability of surplus funds. Members are limited to one vote each, regardless of the amount of stock owned. In addition, cooperatives tend to eliminate at least one MARKETING INTERMEDIARY in the distribution channel by making purchases a step closer to the producer/manufacturer level.

cooperative advertising   A strategy in which advertising costs are shared by seller and reseller (commonly manufacturer and retailer). Ads are run at the local level by the retailer and part of the cost is reimbursed by the manufacturer upon receipt of verification that the ads were actually run. This arrangement, because it involves more than one level of the market, is called VERTICAL COOPERATIVE ADVERTISING; when the cooperative effort is at one level of the market (as in the case of two or more retailers sharing advertising costs) it is called HORIZONTAL COOPERATIVE ADVERTISING. Also known as *vertical advertising, dealer-cooperative advertising, co-op advertising,* and *manufacturer's cooperative advertising.* See also VENDOR CO-OP and PROMOTIONAL ALLOWANCE.

cooperative buying The consolidation of orders by a number of stores, generally to take advantage of quantity discounts. The cooperating stores may be independent or members of a consolidated group. The term includes group, committee, and central buying as well as buying by clubs, cooperative wholesalers, wholesaler-retailer cooperative groups, and manufacturers' cooperative retail groups. Also know as *affiliated buying.*

cooperative buying office See ASSOCIATED BUYING OFFICE.

cooperative chain See RETAIL COOPERATIVE/CO-OP.

cooperative delivery Joint ownership and management of a delivery system by several retailers, all of whom are served by the delivery system.

cooperative display fund The allotment of money provided by a vendor, and generally matched by a retailer, for the development, construction, and installation of VISUAL MERCHANDISING materials and devices to promote the vendor's products. See also COOPERATIVE ADVERTISING.

cooperative education A structured educational program at the college level that integrates formal study with paid, productive work experience in a field related to a student's academic or career goals. Both formal study and work experience are requirements for graduation.

cooperative group See RETAIL COOPERATIVE/CO-OP.

cooperative international marketing organization A group of several domestic manufacturers who have come together to market their goods abroad. The cooperative organization is partly under the administrative control of its member firms. This type of international MARKETING INTERMEDIARY is used frequently by producers of primary products such as fruits, nuts, grains, etc. Compare INDIRECT EXPORT.

cooperative links See RECIPROCAL ADVERTISING LINKS.

cooperatively owned resident buying office See ASSOCIATED BUYING OFFICE.

cooperative marketing Any combination of independent manufacturers, wholesalers, and retailers working collectively to buy and/or sell goods and services.

cooperative money Formal form of CO-OP MONEY.

cooperative office See ASSOCIATED BUYING OFFICE.

cooperative promotion CO-OP PROMOTION.

cooperative resident buying office See ASSOCIATED BUYING OFFICE.

cooperative retailer/retailing See CONSUMER COOPERATIVE.

cooperative store See CONSUMER COOPERATIVE.

cooperative wholesaler A wholesale operation at the heart of a RETAIL COOPERATIVE/CO-OP.

co-op links See RECIPROCAL ADVERTISING LINKS.

co-op money The amount of money a vendor contributes to the retailer for the promotion of the vendor's goods. Also called *vendor money, promotional money,* or *paid money.* See also CO-OP PROMOTION, VENDOR CO-OP, and COOPERATIVE ADVERTISING.

co-op promotion A campaign to publicize and advertise a product or products in which the retailer joins forces with the manufacturer or vendor. The cost of the campaign is usually shared, and the vendor offers the retailer a PROMOTIONAL DISCOUNT to encourage participation. Also called *cooperative promotion.* See also CO-OP MONEY and COOPERATIVE ADVERTISING.

coordinated advertising campaign See ADVERTISING CAMPAIGN and PRODUCT LINE MARKETING.

coordinates Apparel separates such as skirts, sweaters, blouses, jackets, and slacks designed to mix and match harmoniously with regard to color and fabric content.

coordination Synonym for INTEGRATION.

copy 1. In advertising, the wording of an advertisement including both the text and the headline. The words may be written (as in print and electronic advertising) or spoken (as in broadcast advertising commercials). 2. In the apparel trades, an imitation of an original design, usually made to sell at a lower price. Synonymous with BODY COPY. See also ADAPTATION.

copyist In the apparel trades, an individual hired to make replicas of designs. The copyist translates expensive items into lower-priced items by using less expensive materials and manufacturing processes.

copy research See MESSAGE RESEARCH.

copyright A grant of property rights to a writer or artist that protects creative work from unauthorized sale, reproduction, display, performance, etc. In the United States, copyright protection is granted under the terms of the Federal COPYRIGHT ACT (1976). According to the U.S. Copyright Office, "Copyright is a form of protection provided by the laws of the United States (Title 17, US Code) to the authors of 'original works of authorship,'" including literary, dramatic, musical, artistic, and certain other intellectual works. This protection is available to both published and unpublished works. Any work created on or after January 1, 1978, is protected for the lifetime of the creator plus 50 years. The DIGITAL MILLENNIUM COPYRIGHT ACT (1998) (Public Law 105-304) amends Title 17 to include digital products. *Common-law copyright* protects a work before it is published. U.S. copyright information is available from the Copyright Office Web site at www.copyright.gov.

Copyright Act (1976)   Federal legislation revising U.S. copyright laws. The act extends the length of copyright protection to the duration of the creator's life plus 50 years. The act also sets standards for fair use and reproduction of copyrighted material and a new system of compulsory licensing for cable television and jukeboxes. U.S. copyright information is available from the Copyright Office Web site at www.copyright.gov. See also COPYRIGHT.

copyright infringement   The violation of copyright laws, particularly by the illegal copying of protected intellectual property. The Internet has escalated copyright infringement issues by making it relatively easy to copy and reproduce online materials. FILE-SHARING of music, for example, remains controversial. The Napster case of 1999–2000 is an example of how file-sharing can raise copyright infringement issues. The free copying of intellectual property, including but not limited to music, has an effect on the marketing and sales of the copied product.

copy strategy statement   A description of the objectives, content, support, and tone of the advertising a firm desires for its product. The statement may be directed to either an in-house advertising department or to an advertising agency. In the copy strategy statement, the advertiser also sets out the style, tone, words, and format selected for the ADVERTISING MESSAGE. Since this is done prior to the preparation of the ADVERTISING CAMPAIGN, it serves to give direction to the advertising specialists.

copy testing   See MESSAGE RESEARCH.

copy thrust   In advertising and promotion, copy thrust refers to the message to be communicated by the written COPY and the accompanying illustrations. It flows directly from the objectives of the promotion, whether intended to inform customers of a sale or to persuade them that the product is worthwhile. See also ADVERTISING OBJECTIVES.

core-based statistical area (CBSA)   Metropolitan and micropolitan statistical areas, collectively. In general, a metropolitan or micropolitan statistical area is that of a core area containing a substantial population nucleus, together with adjacent communities having a high degree of economic and social integration with that core. The standards established in 2000 provide that each CBSA must contain at least one urban area with a population of 10,000 or more. See also RETAIL SITE LOCATION and TRADING AREA.

core market   Those brand-insistent customers who will accept no substitute for the desired product. A brand-insistent consumer is known as a HARD-CORE LOYAL. As a group, such customers form the core market. See also BRAND INSISTENCE.

core product   1. Those aspects of a product that are so basic as to be definitive. The core product includes functional elements, design, benefits offered, needs satisfied, and patent protection. See also SUPPORT, PACKAGING, and PRODUCT POTENTIAL; all four are components in the creation of a complete product. 2. The main benefit or purpose for which a consumer purchases a product. 3. Also used as a synonym for GENERIC PRODUCT.

core services   The basic services that a store or other company should provide to its customers in order to remain competitive. They are the services customers have come to expect from the retailer. Consequently, these services are often considered essential.

corner front window   A DISPLAY WINDOW located so that it faces two perpendicular streets. As a result, it can be viewed from either street and can attract passersby coming from either direction.

corporate advertising   See INSTITUTIONAL ADVERTISING.

Corporate Branding, LLC   See E-BRANDING INDEX.

Corporate Brand Power   See E-BRANDING INDEX.

corporate buying office   A RESIDENT BUYING OFFICE owned and operated by a department store ownership group or by a chain store organization. Buyers perform many of the functions of an ASSOCIATED BUYING OFFICE, but their recommendations carry considerably more weight as member stores share a common ownership. However, unlike a CENTRAL BUYING OFFICE, the corporate buying office does not have the responsibility for actually selecting and buying merchandise for individual stores in a chain operation. A corporate buying office may also be known as a *chain-owned buying office* or *chain buying office*. See also SYNDICATED BUYING OFFICE.

corporate casual   See DRESSDOWN TREND.

corporate chain   A CHAIN STORE organization having 25 or more stores with identical or similar formats under central ownership. Most corporate chains are centrally managed and the BUYING function is performed centrally. Shares in the company are traded in the stock market. A corporate chain may follow any of four formats including the *unified format* (the majority of the stores are owned and operated under the name of the parent company, e.g., Sears, JCPenney, and Kmart), the *segmented format* (composed of acquired or newly created stores not all of which adopt the name of the parent company, e.g., Gap/Banana Republic), the *manufacturer-based format* (manufacturers that have evolved into retailers and operate chains of factory outlet stores or other specialty divisions, e.g., Liz Claiborne's acquisition of Mexx), and the *holding company format* (huge conglomerates composed of many individual companies doing business under a variety of names). Many holding companies operate in the multinational arena and may conduct manufacturing, service, and/or retail business in their home countries as well as abroad.

corporate controller The head of the FINANCIAL CONTROL DIVISION of a retail organization. Often called the VICE PRESIDENT (VP) OF FINANCE.

corporate culture Synonym for ORGANIZATIONAL CULTURE.

corporate distribution system Synonym for VERTICAL INTEGRATION.

corporate image The customer's perception of a company. Corporate image is the revealed personality of the organization, and is often carefully orchestrated.

corporate image advertising See INSTITUTIONAL ADVERTISING.

corporate licensing The use of a firm's name to enhance the salability of a product. See also LICENSING.

corporate mission statement See MISSION STATEMENT.

corporate social responsibility See SOCIAL RESPONSIBILITY.

corporate system Synonym for CORPORATE VERTICAL MARKETING SYSTEM.

corporate vertical marketing system A system in which a large CORPORATION controls two or more levels of a CHANNEL OF DISTRIBUTION. For example, a manufacturer may own the distribution facilities for its product as well as the retail outlets through which it is sold. Also called *corporate system*. See also VERTICAL INTEGRATION and VERTICAL MARKETING SYSTEM (VMS).

corporation An association of individuals united for some common purpose and allowed by law to use a common name and change its members without the dissolution of the association. Corporations are created by individual state governments, which grant a charter or articles of incorporation to the association. Thus a corporation is a legally chartered enterprise with most of the legal rights of a person, including the right to conduct a business, to own and sell property, to borrow money, and to sue or be sued. A corporation has five important characteristics: it is an artificial person with specific legal standing; it has an unlimited life span; it is empowered by the state to carry on a specific line of business; it is owned by SHAREHOLDERS (i.e., *stockholders*); and its shareholders are usually liable for damages only to the extent of their holdings. See also PUBLICLY HELD COMPANY and MULTINATIONAL CORPORATION.

corrective advertising An ADVERTISING MESSAGE designed to disclaim previous statements. Corrective advertising is sometimes ordered by the FEDERAL TRADE COMMISSION (FTC) when an advertisement is deemed to be unfair and/or deceptive. Compare AFFIRMATIVE DISCLOSURE.

correlation Any statistical relationship between two or more variables. A correlation may be a *positive correlation* (in which case the statistical relationship shows that an increase or decrease in one variable is associated with another variable's change in the same direction) or a *negative correlation* (in which case a change in one variable is associated with another variable's change in the opposite direction). See also CORRELATION ANALYSIS.

correlation analysis In MARKET FACTOR ANALYSIS, a procedure that makes it possible to translate the behavior of variables in the MARKETING ENVIRONMENT into estimates of future sales. Correlation analysis involves the sophisticated manipulation of MARKET FACTOR statistics in an effort to project potential sales for a product or service. See also DIRECT DERIVATION.

corset form See INNERWEAR FORM.

cosign A signature of a responsible second party added to a document to attest the reliability of the original signer. When this is required on a loan or other credit transaction, the cosigner is liable in the event of a default.

cosmetic Any preparation intended to be applied to the face, skin, hair, etc. for improving the appearance of the user. It may remove, cover up, or correct blemishes. The category does not include soap. Often used in the plural (i.e., *cosmetics*).

cost See COSTS.

cost accounting A branch of managerial accounting that involves classifying, summarizing, recording, reporting, and allocating current or predicted costs.

cost allowance A reduction in invoice price made by a manufacturer or supplier to compensate the buyer for an incorrect shipment, goods damaged in transit, delay in delivery, or a similar problem with the order.

cost analysis See MARKETING COST ANALYSIS.

cost and freight (CAF) A shipping term indicating that the seller will cover the freight charges to the destination but not the insurance or other charges. The freight charges are actually included in the price the seller quotes to the buyer.

cost-based pricing See COST-PLUS PRICING.

cost-benefit analysis A technique used for sorting out alternatives in order to find the one that will produce the smallest cost-benefit ratio (i.e., the alternative that will provide the greatest benefit for the lowest expenditure). The benefit need not be expressed in terms of profit. Cost-benefit analysis is frequently used in planning government expenditures. Also called *crossover analysis*, *cost-utility analysis*, *cost effectiveness analysis* and *benefit-cost analysis*.

cost-benefit constraint In financial accounting, any of the considerations governing the decision as to what financial information should be reported. Such considerations include cost-benefit relationships, materiality, industry practices, and conservatism, and serve to ensure that the information provided is useful and necessary to the full disclosure financial report.

cost-benefit ratio/relationship   See COST-BENEFIT ANALYSIS.

cost center   Synonym for EXPENSE CENTER.

cost code   The system of symbols used to indicate the cost of merchandise on price tickets while concealing that information from the customer. For example, the code may consist of letters from an easily remembered word or expression with 10 nonrepeating letters corresponding to numerals. See also MARKING AND TICKETING.

cost complement   The average relationship that exists between the cost and the retail value of the goods handled during an accounting period, expressed as a ratio. The dollar value of the inventory at cost is divided by the dollar value of the inventory at retail. Also called *cost multiplier*.

cost complement percent   The COST COMPLEMENT expressed as a percentage. Also called *cost percent*.

cost department   Within a retail store: 1. An operation, such as a restaurant, barbershop, fur storage vault, or beauty salon, that maintains no inventory at retail and so operates on the COST METHOD OF ACCOUNTING rather than the RETAIL METHOD OF ACCOUNTING for determining profits and losses. 2. A manufacturing or processing department operating on the COST METHOD OF ACCOUNTING.

cost-effectiveness analysis   Synonym for COST-BENEFIT ANALYSIS.

cost, insurance, and freight (CIF)   In the import/export trade, an arrangement under which the seller of the goods (i.e., the exporter) pays the cost of transporting them to their foreign shipping point (dock, railroad platform, etc.), pays the charges incurred in loading the goods on the conveyance/vehicle employed, and finally, pays all insurance and transportation costs to the destination of the goods. These costs are included in the price the seller quotes to the buyer. The buyer pays landing costs and all charges incurred in unloading, as well as any duties or taxes levied by the importing country. See also CIF PRICING.

cost-intensive   Synonym for CAPITAL-INTENSIVE.

cost inventory   The actual price paid or market value of inventory on hand at any time. The lower of the two figures is always used. Consequently, cost inventory represents the present depreciated worth rather than the original price paid.

cost ledger   The accounting record that shows, for each job in the workroom or alteration department of a retail store, debits for the material, labor, and overhead involved as well as the credits for the amount of revenue realized.

cost method of accounting   An accounting system in which all percentages relate to the cost of the goods to the merchant. For example, if an article is purchased for $2.00 and sold for $4.00, the margin is $2.00, which is 100% of the cost price. Compare RETAIL METHOD OF ACCOUNTING.

cost method of inventory   A technique for determining the cost of inventory on hand based on the price of the goods. The actual cost of the goods is marked on each price ticket in code. Inventory is taken by actual physical count and recorded at cost prices, with an allowance made for depreciation. This method is used primarily in small stores and for high-priced items. It differs from the retail method of inventory in that markdowns are taken into consideration when making the calculation. For example, consider two items purchased for $5.00 apiece (for a total of $10.00) and for which the original sales price was set at $10.00 each (for a total of $20.00). One item was subsequently marked down to $2.00. Assuming no sales for the period, if markdowns are considered, the COST-TO-RETAIL RATIO would be calculated by dividing $10.00 (the combined cost of the two items) by $12.00 (the new combined selling price after the markdown) = 83.3%. The ending inventory at cost would then be $12.00 x .833 (i.e., 83.3%) = $10.00. This method may be used to calculate the cost of goods sold and the gross margin of the store. Also referred to as the *cost method of inventory valuation* and the *cost method of inventory valuation and control*. Compare RETAIL METHOD OF INVENTORY (VALUATION), which does not consider markdowns in the cost-to-retail ratio.

cost method of inventory valuation (and control)   See COST METHOD OF INVENTORY.

cost multiplier   Synonym for COST COMPLEMENT.

cost of capital   The price a company must pay to raise money, expressed as the average rate of interest it pays on its combination of debt and equity. The cost of capital generally depends on the RISK associated with the company, the prevailing interest rates, and management's selection of funding sources.

cost of credit   The dollar amount expended for the privilege of borrowing money, such as interest, or purchasing merchandise using a credit card. The cost of credit may be calculated by subtracting the actual cost of the purchased product plus sales tax from the total amount of all payments.

cost of delivered purchases   Synonym for COST OF GOODS PURCHASED.

cost of goods handled   The total cost of merchandise in inventory plus the cost of new purchases. It represents the cost of merchandise available for sale during the accounting period.

cost of goods purchased   The net price paid to the vendor for merchandise, plus the price paid for transportation and delivery. In calculating the *net cost of delivered purchases*, cash discounts are subtracted from the above amount. In calculating the *net cost of purchases*, cash discounts are subtracted from the original invoice price, without consideration of transportation and delivery fees. Also called *net cost*, *net cost of delivered purchases*, *net cost of purchases*, and *cost of purchases*.

cost of goods sold   1. In retailing, the price paid for any merchandise required to obtain the sales of the accounting period (i.e., the expense of buying merchandise). It generally includes all charges (i.e., invoice costs) for goods on hand, goods on order, freight-in charges, and workroom and alteration costs. The cost of goods sold may be calculated either before or after cash discounts have been deducted (or alteration and workroom costs added). The cost of goods sold may also be determined by subtracting the closing inventory cost from the operating inventory plus purchases at cost. Also called *merchandise cost, total merchandise cost,* and *total cost of goods sold.* 2. For the manufacturer, the expense of producing the firm's goods, including expenses for labor, raw materials, and factory operations. These costs are added to the value of the inventory of finished goods on hand at the beginning of the year. The value of the inventory (i.e., finished goods not sold) at the end of the year is then subtracted.

cost-of-goods-sold budget   A forecasting tool used to determine the price paid for merchandise required to obtain the sales of the period. It is based on estimates of the cost of materials used in the manufacture or acquisition of the goods.

cost of living   The average of the retail prices of all goods and services required for a reasonable living standard. When labor contracts and other agreements (e.g., Social Security) use this figure for across-the-board increases, it is called a COST-OF-LIVING ADJUSTMENT (COLA).

cost-of-living adjustment (COLA)   A clause in a union or other contract (e.g., the U.S. Social Security Administration) designed to ensure that workers' and/or other recipients' income will keep pace with inflation. During the terms of the contract, workers' wages are automatically increased in proportion to inflation. In the United States, this practice was first adopted in 1950 as part of the United Auto Workers' and General Motors Corporation's collective bargaining agreement.

cost-of-living index (COLI)   A measure of living cost differences among urban areas, produced by ACCRA. Originally titled the *Inter-City Cost of Living Indicators Project,* the ACCRA cost-of-living index has been published quarterly since 1968. ACCRA maintains a Web site at www.coli.org. See also CONSUMER PRICE INDEX (CPI).

cost of purchases   Synonym for COST OF GOODS PURCHASED.

cost of sales   Synonym for COST OF GOODS SOLD.

cost-oriented audit   An examination and evaluation of the results of a MARKETING PLAN from the point of view of costs and cost-effectiveness.

cost-oriented pricing   A method of determining the price at which goods will be sold on the basis of their cost to the retailer plus any retail expenses incurred and a margin of profit.

cost percent   See COST COMPLEMENT PERCENT.

cost per click (CPC)   The amount of money an advertiser pays a Web site or e-mail newsletter for every click on (i.e., visit to) the ad from the Web site. The seller of the space for the ad gets paid only if the ad performs.

cost-performance criterion   In industrial purchasing, a measurement used to select and purchase machinery, intermediate goods, and raw materials for use in the manufacturing process. In order to maximize profit, the performance of the product is compared to its cost. Selection is made on the basis of best performance per expenditure.

cost per inquiry   The average cost of a mailing or advertising campaign for each inquiry received as a result. The total cost of the mailing or advertising campaign is divided by the total number of inquiries.

cost per order   A measurement of the average costs incurred in selling each order of merchandise. The total cost of all goods sold is divided by the number of orders received.

cost per point (CPP)   See COST PER RATINGS POINT (CPRP).

cost per ratings point (CPRP)   A way of determining charges for television advertising. The result of this method is that advertising on a program that reaches a larger audience will cost more than on one with a smaller audience. To calculate the CPRP, the cost of commercial time is divided by the program rating. Also called *cost per point (CPP).*

cost per sale   A measurement of the average costs incurred in making each sale of merchandise. The total cost of all goods sold is divided by the number of sales that were made.

cost per thousand (CPM)   1. In advertising, the expenditure involved in reaching 1,000 people in a medium's audience. This is a standardized ratio that converts the total cost of advertising space to the more meaningful cost of reaching 1,000 people with the ad. Cost per thousand is especially useful for comparing media that reach similar audiences.   2. In Internet advertising, the cost of 1,000 ad impressions. CPMs vary according to the value of the host site. *Der.* Latin, "cost per mille."

cost per thousand per commercial minute of advertising (CPM/PCM)   See CPM PCM.

cost-plus pricing   A method of determining the selling price of merchandise based on the cost of manufacture (to the producer) or the cost of acquisition (to the distributor or retailer), with a standard markup added to the cost figure. Current demand and the competitive situation in the marketplace are not factored into this PRICING STRATEGY. Also called *average cost pricing* and *cost-based pricing.*

cost price   The dollar amount at which goods are billed to a store exclusive of any cash discounts.

cost pricing   See FULL-COST APPROACH TO PRICING.

cost-push inflation   Inflation (i.e., a general rise in prices) caused by increases in the costs of production (e.g., wages or energy).

cost-recovery fee   A sum of money charged a customer by a retail store to cover the cost of certain sales-supporting services (i.e., delivery of merchandise, alterations, installment credit accounts, bridal consultants, etc.).

cost-recovery method of accounting An accounting method in which no profit is recognized until cash payments by the buyer exceed the seller's cost of the merchandise sold.

costs 1. While the terms *costs* and *expenses* are occasionally used interchangeably, strictly speaking costs are those expenditures made for materials such as raw materials (for manufacturers) and stock (for retailers). 2. In retailing, any money expended to bring merchandise into the store, including the wholesale price of the merchandise, freight charges, etc. Also called *retailing cost*. 3. The prices a vendor charges a retailer for goods. 4. The amount spent on producing or manufacturing a commodity (e.g., raw materials). Costs are generally limited to money, but may be understood in a broader context to include time and effort, etc. Distinguished from EXPENSES, which are expenditures for the process of doing business that arise in generating revenues as delineated on the firm's INCOME STATEMENT.

cost-sharing agreement An agreement entered into by two or more parties to divide a joint cost between them. For example, horizontal and vertical COOPERATIVE ADVERTISING agreements are both cost-sharing agreements, as is COOPERATIVE DELIVERY.

cost-to-cost method of accounting A method of accounting used to recognize revenue before the delivery of merchandise or services has been completed. The method uses *percentage-of-completion* criteria to evaluate progress toward the fulfillment of the contract. The percentage of completion is measured by comparing costs incurred to date with the most recent estimate of the total costs to complete the contract.

cost-to-retail ratio The cost of goods available divided by the sum of the original retail price of these goods plus the net markups. In the *retail method of inventory*, markdowns are excluded from the calculations; in the *cost method of inventory*, they are included. See also COST METHOD OF INVENTORY and RETAIL METHOD OF INVENTORY (VALUATION).

costume 1. Style of dress characteristic of a particular nationality, group, or historical period. 2. Garments meant to be worn together with coordinated accessories, as an outfit or ENSEMBLE. 3. Garments worn to disguise one's true identity, as at a fancy dress ball, Halloween party, etc. 4. Theatrical attire worn on stage. 5. Native or ethnic attire worn for festivals, holidays, rites and rituals, etc. 6. Synonym for APPAREL.

costume jewelry Jewelry fabricated from relatively inexpensive materials such as glass, plastic, ceramics, or wood, or set with imitation gems. The introduction of costume jewelry is credited to French couturière Gabrielle Chanel, who showed imitation pearls, emeralds, and rubies for daytime wear in the 1920s. Also called *fashion jewelry* and *junk jewelry*.

costumer A freestanding FIXTURE unit on a floor, ledge, or counter. It has a hanger set into the top of an adjustable upright, which is set into a weighted base. The unit usually has a skirt bar that makes it possible to display a pair of pants or skirt under a blouse, shirt, or jacket. See also VALET FIXTURE and DRAPER.

cotenancy requirements In the contracts of retailers in shopping centers and malls, stipulations regarding the center's other tenants. For example, an upscale retailer may require the presence of other prestigious stores to ensure that the mall's customers will be sufficiently upscale to meet its own demographic, psychographic, and lifestyle profiles.

count and estimate reorder system A method of determining the quantity of stock to be reordered based on physical inventory by actual count and the retailer's experience in calculating the approximate additional stock needed. See also PHYSICAL INVENTORY.

count and recount A method of calculating the results of a sale. The merchandise is counted, the sale is run, and then the merchandise is counted again.

count certificate A shipping document confirming the quantity of merchandise. Count is taken at either the time of shipment or the time of delivery, or both.

counter A long table or cabinet top used for the display and sale of goods in a store or for the serving and preparation of food in a restaurant. Counters are used as points-of-purchase, where sales are actually made. The typical store counter is out on the floor and free-standing. Counters combine the storage capacities of a cabinet, the selling surface of a table, and the display potential of a shadow box. The counter fixture allows the merchandise to be displayed conveniently for customer selection and invites the potential customer to touch, try, and eventually purchase the merchandise. Also called a SHOWCASE. See also DISPLAY CASE.

counteradvertising Advertising whose aim is to counteract the effect of other advertising. For example, antismoking advertising to controvert cigarette advertising.

counter card A sign or poster placed on a COUNTER to promote an article for sale at that location.

counterfeit product Any product carrying a trademark, brand name, logo, or distinctive design that has been illegally copied and is, consequently, a forgery. Vendors of such products characteristically try to sell their illegal copies as the originals, usually at lower prices, to cash in on the brand equity of the original. This illegal practice is known as *counterfeiting* (also called *industrial counterfeiting*) and its practitioners are called *counterfeiters*. Counterfeiting of trademark-protected products flourishes in countries where legal protection of such trademarks is weak. In recent years, it has been enabled by advanced computer applications. See also PIRACY and UNFAIR TRADE PRACTICES.

counterfeiters See COUNTERFEIT PRODUCT.

counterfeiting The process of creating a COUNTERFEIT PRODUCT.

counter fixture   See COUNTER.

counter-googling   The use of data created by the popular INTERNET search engine, GOOGLE, to identify customers. Counter-googling allows retailers and other marketers to gather personal details about their customers thus allowing them to personalize their services and offerings. The strategy is seen as a response to GOOGLING, in which potential customers check out stores, restaurants, hotels, etc., before deciding to visit. The trend was identified and the term coined by trendwatching.com at www.trendwatching.com.

countermarketing   Efforts aimed at eliminating entirely the demand for a product, service, or idea. Countermarketing is generally carried out by parties who find the product in question undesirable or unwholesome. The efforts of the U.S. federal government and the American Cancer Society to discourage cigarette smoking are an example of countermarketing. Also known as *unselling*.

countermand   To revoke or cancel an order, particularly one that has not yet been carried out.

counterparry   In global marketing, a defense against competitive attack in one country by counterattacking in another country. For example, when Fuji captured a large share of the U.S. film market, Kodak counterparried by aggressively marketing film in Japan.

counterpurchase   In international marketing, a form of COUNTERTRADE in which the trading parties negotiate two contracts. Under the terms of the first contract, the seller receives cash from the buyer. Under the terms of the second contract, the seller agrees to buy goods from the original seller at a monetary value equal to that in the first contract. The original seller, in return for cash payment, agrees to become a buyer at some future time (generally within six to twelve months).

counter sample   In apparel SOURCING, a copy of the prototype garment made by the contractor.

countersegmentation   A strategy in which the number of market segments targeted by a company is reduced, generally through the elimination of products that have been serving narrow segments of the population.

countersign   On a document already signed by one party, another signature attesting the reliability and authenticity of the first.

countertop sign   A sign placed on top of a COUNTER in a store's interior to highlight the merchandise displayed.

countertrade   International business in which some payments are made in the form of goods rather than currency, generally because the customer is unable to arrange hard-currency financing. The supplier must then turn the goods offered into hard currency. Countertrade includes four types of transactions: BARTER, COMPENSATION DEAL, COUNTERPURCHASE, and BUYBACK.

countervailing duty   A tariff levied on imported goods that have been granted an export subsidy or bounty by the government of the exporting country. The countervailing duty is meant to offset any advantage the subsidized exporter would gain over domestic producers in the import market. See also DUMPING and ANTIDUMPING TARIFF.

counterval   An alternative festival that latches on to an existing, well-known festival in order to gain the attention of the media, key buyers, elite customers, and visitors unable to gain access to the main festival. For example, an alternative fashion festival featuring new designers on the Lower East Side during Fashion Week in New York city would be considered a counterval. The trend was identified and the term coined by trendwatching.com at www.trendwatching.com.

country club billing   A form of credit billing in which the store sends a copy of each sales ticket along with the monthly billing statement to the customer.

country of origin   1. In global marketing, the country with which a firm is associated, typically its home country. For example, IBM is associated with the United States and SONY is associated with Japan. The reputation of some countries appears to enhance the credibility of companies in product groups for which the country is well known, such as wines and perfumes for France and consumer electronics for Japan. The positive or negative effect of country of origin affects consumers' perceptions and is often product-specific.   2. The country in which a product was produced or grown. See also COUNTRY OF ORIGIN LABEL. Distinguished from POINT OF ORIGIN.

country of origin label   A tag affixed to a product indicating the country in which it was produced or grown.

country store   Synonym for GENERAL STORE.

coupling   Joint efforts between stores (or between stores and individuals) to innovate on new merchandise. Coupling may be upstream (between stores and vendors), downstream (between stores and customers), or sideways (with competing stores).

coupon   A certificate, card, voucher, or other printed offer distributed to customers and redeemable for specified goods or services at a reduced price or free. Used as a sales promotion technique, coupons may come from a manufacturer or vendor (in which case the coupon is redeemable at a wide variety of retailers) or from a retailer (in which case they may be used only in that store). A coupon may be attached to a product and be redeemed for a cash discount. Coupons serve to reduce the perceived RISK to the consumer, encouraging the consumer to try a new product or to repurchase a product once a sample has been tried. Coupons are used to introduce new products, to promote multiple purchases, to encourage the purchase of larger sizes or the trial purchase of smaller sizes, to quickly increase the sales volume of a particular line, to introduce new product features, etc. Coupons may be mailed to customers, placed in a package of another item, published in an advertisement, or made available online at sites featuring electronic coupons, etc. Also called a *discount coupon* and a *redemption coupon*.

coupon account   An arrangement by which the customer purchases coupons for cash and exchanges them for goods in the store.

coupon credit plan   An account in which the customer is given coupons that may be used in the store as cash. Payment for the coupons is made over a period of time, thus eliminating the need for a monthly billing. The customer encloses a coupon with payment on the monthly due date.

couponing   The use of a COUPON to offer consumers a special, but temporary, price reduction on merchandise without changing the regular market price of the item. Consequently, customers who do not have a coupon continue to pay full retail price. Couponing is also now available on the Internet at sites featuring electronic coupons.

courtesy bias   A phenomenon that may occur in MARKETING RESEARCH (MR) when respondents attempt to guess the answer the interviewer wants to hear and reply accordingly. This pattern of response tends to skew the research results since the respondents, in an attempt to be courteous and helpful, try to please the interviewer rather than express their true views. This is potentially problematic when doing cross-cultural or international marketing research (MR), as the rules for courteous behavior as well as the desire to please the researcher vary from culture to culture.

courtesy counter   That area of a store, particularly a supermarket, in which such services as verifying or cashing checks, accepting returned goods, etc., are performed. See also STORE SERVICES.

courtesy day   A day set aside by a store so that its credit customers may avail themselves of reduced-price merchandise prior to the public sale.

courtesy period   Synonym for GRACE PERIOD.

couture   Apparel that is both expensive and exclusive (i.e., produced in limited quantities), often made by designers of wide reputation. *The couture,* however, has traditionally referred to what may more properly be regarded as an institution, the French design houses belonging to the Chambre Syndicale de la Couture Parisienne. See also HAUTE COUTURE. *Der.* French, "dressmaking."

couturier (couturière)   A designer of women's high-fashion apparel, especially one in the business of making and selling the clothing. Used particularly to refer to French high-fashion designers. *Couturière* is the feminine form of the word. *Der.* French, "dressmaker".

covenant not to compete   An agreement that restrains or prevents a person or business from performing a lawful profession, trade, or business. While the practice may be seen as

RESTRAINT OF TRADE, there are a number of exceptions that are allowable in some states. For example, some states will allow an agreement to refrain from carrying on a similar business within a given geographic area for a specified period of time. Covenants not to compete with an employer upon termination are also enforceable in many states in the United States. Considerations such as customer relations, customer lists, and business trade secrets are taken into account.

coverage   1. In advertising, the potential audience that may receive the message through a media outlet (e.g., the total readership of a magazine). Compare REACH, which reports the actual audience. Reach is always smaller than coverage. 2. Synonym for RESERVE STOCK.

CPA   See CERTIFIED PUBLIC ACCOUNTANT (CPA).

CPC   See COST PER CLICK (CPC).

CPFR   See COLLABORATIVE PLANNING, FORECASTING, AND REPLENISHMENT (CPFR).

CPI   See CONSUMER PRICE INDEX (CPI).

CPM   See COST PER THOUSAND (CPM) and/or CRITICAL PATH METHOD (CPM).

CPM/PCM   The cost per thousand (CPM) per commercial minute (PCM) of advertising.

CPP   See COST PER RATINGS POINT (CPRP).

CPRP   See COST PER RATINGS POINT (CPRP).

CPSA   See CONSUMER PRODUCT SAFETY ACT (CPSA) (1972).

CPSC   See CONSUMER PRODUCT SAFETY COMMISSION (CPSC).

CR   See CAMERA-READY (CR).

Cr.   In accounting, a standard abbreviation for CREDIT.

cracker   An Internet vandal, whether an individual or a group, who attacks Web sites to breach their security defenses, change prices and content, steal credit card numbers or data, do damage, and boast about their vandalism. Crackers infiltrate corporate sites and penetrate protected source code. They are characterized by criminal intent and are particularly active against online banking software, Web registration forms, and other sources of consumer data. Compare HACKER.

craft union   See LABOR UNION and TRADE UNION.

craze   A current fad or fashion characterized by enthusiastic customer response.

creaming   Synonym for SKIMMING.

creaming a list   Selecting only key prospects from a list, focusing on those who are most likely to purchase an item or service. The selection is based on a variety of selection criteria, depending on the product.

creative boutique   Synonym for BOUTIQUE AGENCY.

creative demarketing   See DEMARKETING.

creative department   See ADVERTISING AGENCY and CREATIVE SERVICES DIVISION.

creative packaging   Packaging designed to be informative, attractive, and appealing as well as protective.

creatives   The smallest group in the *Roger Starch Worldwide* study, representing only 10 percent of the global adult population. However, they are the highest consumers of media, including books, magazines, and newspapers. Creatives value knowledge and technology, own PCs, and surf the Web.

creative selling   A SALES APPROACH involving a thorough knowledge of both the product and the ascertained needs of the customer. The product or service is demonstrated, explained, and persuasively presented to the customer in such a way as to satisfy the customer's needs and wants. Considered a high-level sales technique, creative selling is the opposite of routine order-taking.

creative services director   See CREATIVE SERVICES DIVISION.

creative services division   The division of an ADVERTISING AGENCY responsible for the creation and execution of the advertisements. The creative services division is managed by the *creative services director,* who sets the creative philosophy for the firm and is directly involved in the creation of ads for the agency's most important clients. See also FULL SERVICE (ADVERTISING) AGENCY and ADVERTISING AGENCY.

credit   1. In marketing, the capacity of an individual or organization to buy and sell under a variety of arrangements other than CASH-AND-CARRY. An essential component in the concept of credit is faith or trust (i.e., the notion that the person who promises to pay in a given period of time will, in fact, do so). 2. In accounting, an entry on the right side of an account. All assets and expense accounts are decreased on the credit side. The equality of debits and credits provides the basis for the double-entry system of recording transactions (sometimes referred to as double-entry bookkeeping). Commonly abbreviated *Cr.* See also DEBIT. 3. See CREDIT LINE (DEF 1).

credit balance   The amount of credit remaining in a charge or other credit account that may still be used by the borrower or charge customer before exceeding the CREDIT LIMIT.

credit bureau   An agency that acts as a clearinghouse by collecting and maintaining credit information about individuals or firms and providing that information to members or subscribers.

credit bureau score   See FICO SCORE.

credit buyer   Synonym for CHARGE BUYER.

credit cancellation   The cancellation of an unpaid credit order. Also called *kill* and *kill bad pay.*

credit card   A card establishing the ability of the issuee to charge goods and services at all participating restaurants, stores, airlines, hotels, gas stations, etc. While a CHARGE CARD is limited to the issuing store or other business, a credit card is issued by a bank or other financial institution and may be used to pay for products and services from any participating business. Most Internet purchases are made with credit cards, and e-tailers have established secure sites to verify and protect customer information. Also called, informally, *plastic money.*

credit card bulletin   A publication of a credit card company listing the numbers of cards that should not be honored by retailers or other merchants.

credit card order   An order for merchandise placed by including one's credit card number. The purchase price is charged to the credit card and the customer pays the credit card issuer. Both catalog retailing and e-tailing rely heavily on credit cards to facilitate remote transactions.

credit crunch   A severe tightening of credit available in an economy, reducing its availability to businesses and consumers. Credit crunches are typically created by government efforts to curb inflation.

credit interchange   A network of information sources that may be contacted by merchants seeking credit information about potential customers. A credit interchange may include other merchants, trade associations, or a CREDIT BUREAU.

credit limit   The maximum amount a customer may have outstanding on a charge card or other credit account.

credit line   1. In a newspaper, motion picture, etc., an acknowledgment, by name, of a person who has done work or given assistance. Often called a *credit.* 2. A synonym for LINE OF CREDIT. 3. In an ad run by a vendor, a listing of stores in which its merchandise may be purchased.

creditor   A person or business that lends money and extends credit, or to whom money is owed. A seldom-used synonym is *debtee.* Used synonymously with LENDER.

credit order   An order placed without payment. The customer is billed at a later date and under separate cover. Also called *bill-me order.*

credit rating   An evaluation of the financial standing of an individual or business as a business risk. Credit ratings are based on past records of debt repayment, financial status, employment history, etc. See also FICO SCORE.

credit record analysis   See STORE CREDIT RECORD ANALYSIS.

credit report/score   See FICO SCORE.

credit slip A certificate issued by a store, redeemable for merchandise of a specified dollar value. Credit slips are often issued to customers in lieu of cash refunds for merchandise returned to the store. Also called *due bill, store credit, play money, merchandise certificate, credit voucher, store money, voucher,* or *scrip coupon.*

credit suspension The act of withholding credit, merchandise, and services from individuals with unpaid credit accounts. The names of delinquent credit customers are placed on an inactive status list but they continue to receive bills.

credit terms The obligations and conditions the store sets down in granting consumer credit, including interest rate, method of computation of interest, frequency of billing and payment, etc. Also called *terms of credit.* See also TERMS OF SALE.

credit union A COOPERATIVE financial institution, chartered by a state or by the federal government, that serves the members of a homogeneous group such as the employees of a firm, the members of a union, etc. Credit unions resemble savings and loan institutions in the services they provide to their members (i.e., savings accounts, checking accounts, credit cards, and consumer loans). Because of their tax-exempt status and low overhead, they can generally provide credit on favorable terms.

credit voucher See CREDIT SLIP.

creeping inflation Modest increases in the general price level at a rate of 4% to 9% annually.

crescendo method See SNOWBALLING METHOD.

cribtimonial A consumer trend in which customers increasingly seek to emulate the home lifestyles, including the domestic luxury goods and amenities, of celebrities. The trend has gained impetus from celebrity reality television programs that show the homes of celebrities. As the trend becomes increasingly commercial, the programs will be used for PRODUCT PLACEMENT of luxury goods and products. The trend was identified and the term coined by trendwatching.com at www.trendwatching.com. See also LIFESTYLE.

crisscross directory A reverse telephone directory arranged by street addresses and providing the names and telephone numbers of residents. Useful for retailers and telephone marketers trying to delineate a trading area or identify their target customer. A number of crisscross directories are currently available on the Web. Also called *cross-reference book* and *cross-reference directory.*

critical mass The minimum effort, participation, etc., necessary to achieve an impact. In global marketing, it is one of the principles governing the decision to enter market groupings larger than an individual country. It may be worthwhile for the marketer, already expending the energy and resources necessary to enter the global marketplace, to choose a group of proximate countries so as to take advantage of the potential added

sales volume, the ease of distribution due to geographic proximity, and the similarity of barriers to entry. The other principle used to determine the cost-effectiveness of entering larger international markets is ECONOMIES OF SCALE.

critical path method (CPM) An analytical process that breaks large projects down into component parts and analyzes the time needed to complete each part. The sequence of individual operations leading to the completion of the whole project is called the *critical path.* The critical path method provides managers with an estimate of the least possible amount of time required for completion of the total project, thus enabling them to estimate the time required for production. Similar to PROGRAM EVALUATION AND REVIEW TECHNIQUE (PERT).

CRM See CUSTOMER RELATIONSHIP MANAGEMENT (CRM).

cross-bidding In online auctions, a fraudulent practice by which groups of SHILL BIDDERS (i.e., individuals who pose as legitimate bidders in order to decoy others into participating) work together to drive up online auction prices.

cross-border pricing Price transparency that occurs on the INTERNET. Prices posted on Web sites are visible to all Web users worldwide, exposing price discrepancies that were not obvious before the Internet. This makes it easier to compare prices for the same products in different national or regional markets. One's ability to purchase merchandise from a state or country other than one's own may result in a downward pressure on regional prices and reduce the differences.

cross-branding A form of brand promotion calculated to enhance an existing product by drawing on the brand strength of one or more of its ingredients or constituent parts. For example, advertising for a personal computer may include reference to its well-known and respected processor in an effort to trade on the processor's brand equity.

cross-classification matrix A device, usually in the form of a grid, employed to isolate specific subdivisions in a market for purposes of segmentation. See also MARKET SEGMENTATION.

cross-country subsidization In global competition, the use of profits from a firm's operations in one country to subsidize its competitive activities in another country.

cross-couponing See CROSS-RUFF COUPON.

cross-docking In physical distribution, the use of the distribution center as a trucking terminal. FLOOR-READY MERCHANDISE (FRM) arrives in a truck in one bay and goes out in another truck in another bay with virtually no processing in between. Cross-docking is designed to move goods faster by eliminating unnecessary stops in physical distribution systems. It allows a vendor to ship all pieces of a coordinated apparel group simultaneously rather than in small increments, cutting distribution costs and time. Vendors are expected to pack goods by STOCK KEEPING UNIT (SKU) according to company specifications.

cross-elasticity   The relation between the change in PRICE of one product and a change in DEMAND for another product. Cross elasticity may be positive (i.e., the increase in price for product A may generate increased demand for product B, which may now be a cheaper alternative), or it may be negative (i.e., the increase in price for product A may reduce demand for product B because demand for product B is dependent on sales of product A). Also known as *price cross elasticity* and *demand cross elasticity*.

cross-licensing   The use of two licensed properties (e.g., a necktie depicting Bugs Bunny wearing a New York Giants sweatshirt). See also LICENSING.

cross-merchandising   1. The practice of allocating the same merchandise to two or more areas of the store. For example, chocolates may be displayed in several locations.   2. The practice of displaying complementary items facing each other, with the expectation that customers will buy the complementary product along with their original purchase.

crossover analysis   Synonym for COST-BENEFIT ANALYSIS.

cross-promotion   1. In E-TAILING, the use of other media (e.g., newspapers, billboards, television, and radio) to encourage use of a store's Web site.   2. Synonym for TIE-IN PROMOTION.

cross-reference book/directory   Synonym for CRISSCROSS DIRECTORY.

cross-ruff coupon   A coupon enclosed with or attached to merchandise and offering a price reduction toward the purchase of another item, usually by the same manufacturer. Some supermarket register tapes also provide cross-ruff coupons, sometimes good for the same or related product, but sometimes good for a competing product in the same category. The practice is also known as *cross-couponing*.

cross-selling   A store policy enabling salespersons to sell merchandise in one another's departments. Also called *interselling*. See also CHINESE WALLS.

cruisewear   Apparel designed for winter vacations in warm, sunny climates and voyages at sea (i.e., cruises). Also called *resort wear* or *resort apparel*. Primarily sold during the FIFTH SEASON, when it would be otherwise difficult to find swimsuits, shorts, etc. in the stores.

CSA   See COMPETITIVE SEGMENTATION ANALYSIS (CSA).

CSS   See CHAIN STORE SYSTEM (CSS).

C to C   See C2C.

C2C   Consumer-to-consumer sales transactions where consumers sell products and services directly to other consumers, online or offline. For example, consumers selling merchandise at a garage sale or flea market or by means of online auctions are operating in a C2C environment. C2C transactions do not directly involve any marketing intermediaries.

CTR (click through rate)   See CLICK RATE.

cube   A container forming part of one of several types of DISPLAY fixtures designed for nonhanging goods such as flat, packaged, and folded merchandise. The cube is typically made of glass and used to present folded goods such as shirts and sweaters. While the terms BIN and cube are often used interchangeably, a cube is actually a container that is open on its sides. Cubes are used in fashion stores as wall treatments or as stand-alone floor fixtures.

cue   In psychology, and hence in consumer research, a minor stimulus that guides behavior, often without the awareness of the individual. A cue helps determine when, where, and how the consumer responds to products and services in the environment. The advertisements seen or heard by the consumer, the consumer's exposure to the product or service, and the attitudes of other people toward that product or service are all cues that influence the consumer's decision to buy.

cull   Merchandise rejected as not being up to standard or otherwise imperfect.

cult merchant   Synonymous with CATEGORY KILLER.

culturalization   In e-tailing, the practice of adapting a Web site to conform to cultural standards and preferences in targeted international markets See also ONLINE CULTURE.

culturally centric Web site   A Web site biased toward a particular culture. This is particularly applicable to culturally U.S.-centric Web sites owing to the predominance of U.S. sites on the Web. See also ONLINE CULTURE.

culturally local Web site   A Web site that targets local users with specific cultural nuances. See also ONLINE CULTURE.

culturally neutral Web site   A Web site that tries to avoid cultural nuances and attempts to appeal across cultures to cultural universals. See also ONLINE CULTURE.

culturally U.S.-centric Web site   See CULTURALLY CENTRIC WEB SITE.

culture   From a marketing standpoint, the combined patterns of marketplace behavior that characterize a group of people and distinguish it from other groups. Culture includes the group's extrinsic factors (such as language, rituals, food, espoused values, laws, institutions, art, the socialization of new members, and technology) as well as its intrinsic factors (such as underlying beliefs, assumptions, norms, and ideologies). Cultures are emotionally charged and taken for granted; they provide members with meaning and a way of interpreting new developments in light of past realities. See also ORGANIZATIONAL CULTURE and ONLINE CULTURE.

cume   The total number of homes or individuals reached during a given period of time by one of the broadcast MEDIA. The term stands for the *cumulative reach over time*. Also called *cumulative reach*. See also REACH.

cumulative adoption curve   See ADOPTION CURVE.

cumulative audience   See REACH.

cumulative (initial) markon   When expressed in dollars, cumulative markon is the difference between the cost price of merchandise and the highest retail price at which it is offered for sale. The concept is generally applied to classifications, departments, or the entire store rather than to individual items, yielding an average figure useful in setting PRICE POLICY.

cumulative markon percent   The difference between cost price of merchandise and the highest retail price at which it is offered for sale, expressed as a percentage rather than in dollars. Cumulative markon is applied to merchandise in aggregates (i.e., entire classifications or a complete department) rather than on individual items.

cumulative markup   The difference between the total cost of merchandise and the total original retail value of that merchandise for a specified period of time. Included in the total are all additional markups for the period. Sometimes called *cumulative markon*.

cumulative quantity discount   A discount from a VENDOR or WHOLESALER based on all the purchases made during a specified period. Also called a *deferred discount* and a *patronage discount*.

cumulative reach (over time)   See CUME.

curated consumption   A consumer trend in response to the sometimes overwhelming number of choices available in the MARKETPLACE. Consumers allow "curators" or "editors" (i.e., experts) to preselect for them what to buy, experience, wear, read, eat, drink, etc. As arbiters of style and taste, the curators make use of unprecedented access to broadcasting and publishing channels to reach their audience, from their own blogs to niche TV channels (e.g., those of Oprah Winfrey and Martha Stewart). Curated consumption has led to the morphing of magazines into catalogues and eclectic stores, as well as the proliferation of "Top 10" lists and other popularized listings of recommendations. The trend was identified and the term coined by trendwatching.com at www.trendwatching.com.

curiosity approach   A SALES APPROACH in which the SALESPERSON presents the prospect with an unexpected question or gadget to arouse the prospect's immediate interest and curiosity.

current asset   Cash or some other ASSET that is readily convertible to cash and expected to be so converted within the normal operating cycle of the firm. For example, merchandise, accounts receivable, and marketable securities are all current assets.

current gross margin   See OPERATING MARGIN.

current liability   A debt or other obligation that must be paid within a short time, generally within the fiscal year.

current margin   See OPERATING MARGIN.

current ratio   The sum of a firm's current assets divided by the sum of its current liabilities. The current ratio is a measure of the firm's ability to meet its financial obligations.

Curtis Amendment   See MEAT INSPECTION ACT (1906).

curved (floor) plan   A store layout used in boutiques, salons, and other high-end stores. The curved floor plan creates an inviting environment for customers. Curved walls or counters encourage TRAFFIC FLOW and enhance eye appeal.

CU-SeeMe   An Internet service that provides videoconferencing opportunities whereby users send and receive sound and pictures on their computers. The service may be used for MARKETING RESEARCH (MR).

cushion   Synonym for RESERVE STOCK.

custodial warehouser   See FIELD WAREHOUSER.

customary price   A price that has become traditional or customary because it has not changed in a long time. Inflation has made customary prices virtually impossible to maintain, but in the past such items as postcards, soft drinks, and candy bars had such stable prices that the consuming public came to expect them to remain constant. Sometimes referred to as a *custom price*.

customer   Any person who buys merchandise from a store, Web site, or other marketer. The customer of a retail establishment is the ultimate CONSUMER. The store itself, however, is the customer of all the vendors with whom it does business. Also called *clientele*, denoting customers collectively, and *patron*. Frequently used interchangeably with CONSUMER.

customer acceptance trend   See PRODUCT LIFE CYCLE (PLC).

customer base   See TARGET MARKET.

customer-centric   Of a form of retailing in which marketing, merchandising, and store operations work together to create compelling promotions as part of a local market strategy. Information technology and CUSTOMER RELATIONSHIP MANAGEMENT (CRM) work together to personalize the shopping experience, while merchandising operations and the supply chain work together to find a cost-effective way to implement an effective and viable target customer strategy. The goal is to retain and reactivate customers by making shopping pleasant and convenient.

customer convenience services   See ACCOMMODATION SERVICES.

customer demand   The amount and dollar value of merchandise purchased by customers in a specified period of time.

customer departmentalization   The grouping of employees within an organization so as to concentrate on customers, particularly the major segments of the company's market. Employees are grouped according to the types of customers with whom they deal. For example, in an advertising department, an employee might specialize in selling space to a particular industry, such as the airline industry. Also called *departmentalization by customer, departmentalization by client,* or *client departmentalization.*

customer division of authority Synonym for MARKET DIVISION OF AUTHORITY.

customer elimination management (CEM) A spoof on CUSTOMER RELATIONSHIP MANAGEMENT (CRM). The term is applied primarily to the practice of OUTSOURCING the customer service function. The point of the spoof is that both telephone and electronic customer services, if not handled properly, can alienate customers and subvert the firm's goals of providing excellent service.

customer franchise A loyal following of customers for a product or service. Customer loyalty of this type leads to repeat sales.

customer information profile 1. The use of both in-store and out-of-store resources to gather as much data as possible about the store's customers and their spending habits. In-store information sources include past and current sales, returned goods and adjustments, credit and loyalty program data, and internal research. Out-of-store information sources include the competition, vendors, resident buying offices, trade shows, consumer publications, trade publications, consulting firms, external research, and testing laboratories. Keeping close track of customer purchasing habits allows retailers to modify their unit plans and change their formats to keep pace with changing demographics. 2. In e-tailing, similar data on customer buying habits, gathered in order to develop appropriate market offers. Online marketers seek to discover where, how, why, and when target customers go online, and what they do once they are there. E-marketers must also understand and track the adoption of new Internet-based technologies and access alternatives as they appear (e.g., wireless access). Also called *customer insight.*

customer insight Synonym for CUSTOMER INFORMATION PROFILE.

customer interchange The extent to which the customers of one store are also the customers of nearby stores. See also TRADING AREA.

customer interview The process of questioning residents of an area via mailed questionnaires, personal interviews, telephone inquires, etc. to determine the store's TRADING AREA.

customer loyalty The faithfulness or allegiance of a customer to a particular store, brand, or product. See also LOYALTY PROGRAM/SCHEME.

customer loyalty card See LOYALTY CARD.

customer loyalty program/scheme See LOYALTY PROGRAM/SCHEME.

customer-made The phenomenon of corporations creating goods, services, and experiences in close cooperation with consumers, tapping into their intellectual capital and in exchange giving them a direct say in what actually gets produced, designed, serviced, or processed. Much of the customer participation is via the INTERNET. In the development of a new airplane, Boeing used customer input in the form of message boards and extensive discussions about what customers like and don't like about air travel today. The trend was identified and the term coined by trendwatching.com at www.trendwatching.com.

customer market focus Synonym for MARKETING CONCEPT.

customer need Any customer service requirement of a business-to-business or business-to-ultimate-consumer relationship. Customer needs include responsiveness, promptness, knowledgeable people, accuracy, and accessibility.

customer orientation See MARKETING CONCEPT.

customer-owned goods (COG) Merchandise that belongs to the customer and is so marked when brought into the store for servicing, repair, engraving, etc. See also OWNED GOODS SERVICE.

customer-owned merchandise (COM) See CUSTOMER-OWNED GOODS (COG).

customer profile The demographic and psychographic characteristics of a firm's customers, particularly those who comprise the target market, and the purchasing patterns they display. Generally presented as a percentage of the population as a whole. DEMOGRAPHICS include the vital statistics of a population, including the size of the group, the age, gender, birth and death rates, location, income, occupation, race, education, etc. PSYCHOGRAPHICS include such variables as personality, lifestyle, attitudes, and self-concept. Sometimes called, simply, a *profile.*

customer profiling The practice of developing a CUSTOMER PROFILE.

customer relations Synonym for CUSTOMER RELATIONSHIP MANAGEMENT (CRM).

customer relationship management (CRM) The planning and implementation of strategies designed to serve the customer in an efficient and satisfying manner. All aspects of interaction a company has with its customers are included, whether sales or service. With the advent of electronic commerce, the CRM relationship is increasingly managed electronically. Online companies are seeking ways to personalize online experiences (a process known as *mass customization*) through such tools as help-desk software, e-mail organizers, and Web development applications. CRM is also called *customer resource management (CRM).* See also ELECTRONIC CUSTOMER RELATIONSHIP MANAGEMENT (E-CRM) and DYNAMIC WEB PAGE.

customer resource management (CRM)   Synonym for CUS-TOMER RELATIONSHIP MANAGEMENT (CRM).

customer returns   See RETURNS AND ALLOWANCES TO CUSTOMERS.

customer sampling   See SAMPLING.

customer satisfaction   A measure of the degree to which a customer's expectations are being met (i.e., a comparison of expectations to perceptions). SERVQUAL is an instrument developed to measure customer satisfaction with level of service.

customer service   1. Any activity performed by a vendor for a client (such as a retailer) to facilitate the buying process and establish a good relationship. Customer service has become a key competitive strategy for both manufacturers and retailers. 2. Any activity performed by retail stores for their customers. See also STORE SERVICES, CUSTOMER RELATIONSHIP MANAGEMENT (CRM), PREMIER CUSTOMER SERVICE, and PERSONAL SELLING SERVICE.

customer service department   The department of a retail establishment responsible for providing personnel and services such as elevator operators, telephone and order taking operations, parking space, etc.

customer service desk   A service area or counter in a department store where customers may check parcels, have packages wrapped, buy stamps, have parking permits validated, make adjustments for returned merchandise, etc. Also called, simply, a *service desk*.

customer service level   In physical distribution, a measure of a firm's ability to deliver quickly and dependably what the customer wants. A higher service level may be desirable in highly competitive environments, such as pure competition or oligopoly, where it may allow the firm to increase its MARKET SHARE without changing its products, prices, or promotions. An increase in the customer service level may increase total costs, however, since it may require additional distribution points, warehousing facilities, and inventory costs.

customer services   Any and all activities performed by a retailer for its customers' convenience and not directly related to the sale of a specific product within the store. For example, gift wrapping, credit, and delivery. Vendors similarly provide customer services to their retail clients. See also ACCOMMODATION SERVICES.

customer service standards   In the distribution of goods, the quality of service that a firm's customers can expect to receive. These standards include the receipt of goods in undamaged condition, speedy and reliable delivery, availability of items ordered, and accuracy in filling orders. In general, most companies try to meet or exceed the standards set by their competitors.

customer share   The relative portion of revenue produced by a customer and projected over that customer's purchasing life-time. Higher-spending customers visit the site more often, spend more at each visit, communicate more frequently with the enterprise, and have lasting loyalty. Consequently, such customers may be said to have a higher CUSTOMER VALUE or customer share.

customer's own goods (COG)   Synonym for CUSTOMER-OWNED GOODS (COG).

customer's own merchandise (COM)   Synonym for CUSTOMER-OWNED GOODS (COG).

customer value   According to the *Pareto Principle*, or EIGHTY-TWENTY (80-20) PRINCIPLE, approximately 80 percent of a firm's revenues are contributed by approximately 20 percent of its customers. Consequently, some customers contribute more to the BOTTOM LINE than do others and are said to have higher customer value. Retailers and e-tailers respond to the higher-value, high-margin, preferred customer segments by providing them with special prices and other benefits.

customer-vendor relationship   See VENDOR RELATIONSHIP.

custom house broker   An individual or firm specializing in the expeditious clearance of imported goods through the U.S. CUSTOMS SERVICE. Custom house brokers are licensed by the Treasury Department and are employed by importers who do not have representation at the port of entry of their goods. Custom house brokers prepare and file customs entries, arrange payment of duties due, take steps to release goods from Customs, and represent clients in Customs matters. Sometimes known as a *customs broker,* a *customs house broker,* and a *foreign freight forwarder.*

customization   The act of modifying and specifically tailoring a product or service to suit the customer's preferences and past purchasing behaviors, or the degree to which this is done. Firms may customize their products on more than one level. For example, a computer manufacturer/marketer may offer MASS CUSTOMIZATION for consumers purchasing individual PCs and *true customization* (i.e., meeting the customer's exact specifications) for high-volume businesses ordering large numbers of computers.

customized marketing   A marketing program in which each individual customer is treated as a separate segment. The marketing mix is tailored to the individual customer's specific requirements. This approach is used in industrial markets and for many consumer services such as interior design, home repairs, and custom tailoring. See also DIFFERENTIATED MARKETING, UNDIFFERENTIATED MARKETING, CUSTOMIZATION, and MARKET SEGMENTATION.

custom-made   1. Of apparel, made by a tailor or couture house for an individual customer. The correct size is achieved either by fitting the garment on a dress form adjusted to the customer's measurements or by a series of personal fittings. See also TAILOR-MADE and MADE-TO-MEASURE. 2. Of any product, made per an individual customer's specifications. See also CUSTOMIZATION.

custom marketing   A form of marketing in which the target customers are completely segmented, i.e., each customer is so distinct from all others that he or she must be treated as an individual. A unique marketing mix is developed for each customer. See also COMPLETE SEGMENTATION.

custom marketing research firm   A MARKETING RESEARCH FIRM/COMPANY hired to perform specific research assignments. The resulting reports become the property of the client.

custom price   See CUSTOMARY PRICE.

customs   1. Duties (i.e., taxes) imposed by law on imported (and sometimes exported) goods.   2. A government department or agency responsible for collecting these duties.   3. The section of a port of entry into a country (airport, station, dock, etc.) where baggage is checked for contraband and for goods subject to an import duty. See also U.S. CUSTOMS SERVICE.

Customs bonded warehouse   A building or other secured area in which dutiable goods may be stored, manipulated, or subjected to manufacturing processes without payment of CUSTOMS DUTY. Upon entry of goods into the warehouse, the importer and warehouse owner incur liability under a bond. This liability is generally cancelled when the goods are exported, withdrawn for supply to a vessel or aircraft engaged in international traffic, destroyed under Customs supervision, or withdrawn for consumption within the United States after payment of the appropriate duty. Eleven types or classes of Customs bonded warehouses are authorized under Customs regulations. They are: (a) premises owned or leased by the government and used for the storage of merchandise that is undergoing Customs examination, is under seizure, or is pending final release for Customs custody; (b) an *importers' private bonded warehouse* used exclusively for the storage of merchandise belonging or consigned to the proprietor of the warehouse; (c) a *public bonded warehouse* used exclusively for the storage of imported merchandise; (d) a *bonded yard* or *bonded shed* used for the storage of heavy and bulky imported merchandise; (e) a *bonded bin* or part of a building or elevator to be used for the storage of grain; (f) warehouses for the manufacture in bond, solely for exportation, of articles made wholly or partly of imported materials or of materials subject to internal revenue tax; (g) warehouses for smelting and refining imported metal-bearing materials for exportation or domestic consumption; (h) bonded warehouses for the cleaning, sorting, repacking, or otherwise changing the condition of, but not the manufacturing of, imported merchandise, under Customs supervision and at the expense of the proprietor; (i) bonded warehouses known as DUTY-FREE stores, used for selling conditionally duty-free merchandise for use outside the Customs territory; (j) bonded warehouses for international travel merchandise, goods sold conditionally duty-free aboard aircraft and not at a duty-free store; and (k) bonded warehouses established for the storage of GENERAL ORDER (GO) MERCHANDISE (i.e., any merchandise not claimed or entered for 15 days after arrival in the United States). An advantage of using a Customs bonded warehouse is that no duty is collected until the merchandise is withdrawn for consumption. Duties owed on articles that have been manipulated are determined at the time of withdrawal from the Customs bonded warehouse.

customs broker   Synonym for CUSTOM HOUSE BROKER.

customs duty   The actual amount of an import tax (i.e., TARIFF), which varies with the product and its country of origin. Customs duties are designed to protect domestic businesses against foreign competition by raising the price of imports to a level comparable to similar domestic merchandise. Customs duties are frequently used as a weapon in foreign policy (i.e., the products of friendly nations are often taxed at a lower rate than those of hostile countries).

custom selling   A shop-at-home service whereby a salesperson calls on a customer at home and measures, designs, or partially designs merchandise specifically for that customer. For example, draperies and slipcovers are often sold this way. See also SHOP-AT-HOME RETAILING.

customs house broker   See CUSTOM HOUSE BROKER.

Customs Service   See U.S. CUSTOMS SERVICE and CUSTOMS.

customs union   An association of countries that have agreed to reduce or eliminate the trade barriers existing between them and who have, in addition, agreed to levy a TARIFF on goods imported from countries outside the union. Individual countries relinquish the right to set independent trade agreements outside the group. A supranational policymaking committee makes all external tariff decisions. See also COMMON MARKET.

cut carton   A method of supermarket selling in which goods are displayed in their opened original shipping containers (i.e., cartons) rather than unpacked and placed on shelves. Some supermarkets mix this display method with traditional shelved merchandise, often to indicate the special low price of the goods so displayed. Also called *cut-case display.*

cut-case display   See CUT CARTON.

cut, make, trim (CMT) sourcing   A form of apparel SOURCING in which the supplier is responsible for product development, including designs, patterns, product specifications, and the sourcing of materials. The primary contribution of the contractor is sewing. Compare FULL PRODUCT SOURCING (FPS).

cutout figure   A two-dimensional silhouette figure made of wood or heavy cardboard, true to human proportions, and used as a display form. Clothes are pinned or draped over it for a frontal or elevated display of the merchandise.

cutout form   An abstract, almost cubist display form used to show clothing and related merchandise. Photographs of life-sized frontal views of men or women are sometimes pasted to the form to give it a semblance of reality. The arms may be removable to facilitate dressing.

CWO   See CASH WITH ORDER (CWO).

CyberAtlas   Former name of CLICKZ STATS.

cyberboomer   A member of the first generation to grow up with electronic media, virtual reality, and the Internet. They are the youngest members of GENERATION Y. Also called *technotots*.

cyberbrand   A BRAND that exists only on the World Wide Web. Early cyberbrands were created online from scratch. Since they represented CLICKS-ONLY enterprises, these brands could not build on existing brand recognition. Most early cyberbrands were company brands for such early online companies as America Online (AOL), Yahoo!, Netscape, eBay, and Amazon.com. See also E-BRANDING INDEX.

cybercrime   Crimes that are committed online, on the INTERNET and other computer networks. The U.S. Department of Justice categorizes computer crime as attacking the computers of others (e.g., spreading viruses); using the computer as a weapon (i.e., using a computer to commit traditional crimes such as fraud or illegal gambling); and using the computer as an accessory to store illegal or stolen information. Includes copyright infringement, computer fraud, child pornography, and hacking. Also called *computer crime*.

cyberethics   Responsible online social behavior. See also NETIQUETTE.

cyber group   An online FOCUS GROUP, also called an *e-group*, *virtual group*, or *focus chat*, using chat room technology. Such online focus groups are winning wide acceptance by marketing researchers because they reach a more widespread market than traditional focus groups, provide greater access to groups that are harder to reach, ensure anonymity, enable more equitable participation by each individual group member, provide greater cost-effectiveness than traditional focus groups, and facilitate the faster reporting of results.

Cyber Monday   The Monday following Thanksgiving, believed to be the biggest E-TAILING day of the retail year. Customers who visit the stores on BLACK FRIDAY may use that Monday to check the INTERNET for bargains and special offers.

cybershopping   Shopping on the INTERNET. Cybershopping potentially offers the customer more choices and greater convenience than traditional shopping.

cyberspace   The realm of electronic communication, particularly virtual reality and the INTERNET.

cyberterrorism   The commission of terrorist acts designed to disrupt the INTERNET, its networks, and/or linked computers. It serves to spread fear, cause economic chaos, corrupt or steal information, or otherwise compromise the system.

cyberterrorist   See CYBERTERRORISM.

cycle billing   A procedure by which customers receive monthly invoices on a rotating alphabetical basis throughout the month rather than all at the first of the month.

cycle time   See LEAD TIME.

cyclical demand   The demand for products and services that is responsive to changes in the country's economic cycles or otherwise occurs in a regular, repeating pattern. For example, the demand for new homes follows a cycle related to the economy and, in particular, to interest rates available for mortgages.

cyclical variation   Change that occurs in a regularly repeating process over a number of years, such as the BUSINESS CYCLE.

DAGMAR An advertising planning and control tool developed in the 1960s by Russell H. Colley for determining the effectiveness of advertising. The method lists 52 possible advertising goals that may be considered with respect to a single advertisement, a year's campaign, or for a company's entire advertising philosophy. DAGMAR outlines criteria by which each of the 52 goals, pertaining to sales, image, attitude, or awareness, may be measured.

daily best seller report A management report listing the merchandise selling in the largest quantities on a day-by-day basis. Once a time-consuming and tedious process, the daily best seller report is now generated by computerized inventory management systems that compile the DATA into reliable real-time reports. The report allows store managers to monitor best sellers and sales associates' productivity. Also called a *best seller report*.

daily lubricant Any product or service that caters to the consumer's need for simplicity and eases daily life (i.e., makes life go more smoothly). The trend is seen as a response to the complexity of modern life and the ready availability of an avalanche of products and services. Daily lubricants include storage devices, time-saving devices, simplicity magazines, and household services (e.g., concierge services). The trend was identified and the term coined by trendwatching.com at www.trendwatching.com.

Dallas Market Center A market center located in Dallas, Texas, the Dallas Market Center is a six-building complex of 6.9 million square feet housing more than 2,400 showrooms. Included in the Dallas Market Center are the International Menswear Mart, the International Apparel Mart, Market Hall, and the Trade Market and World Trade Center.

damage claims See CONCEALED LOSS AND DAMAGE CLAIMS.

damage markdown A price reduction on goods damaged after delivery from a vendor. Some retailers sell damaged goods to customers AS IS. For example, a $100 dress with broken buttons may be reduced to $75 and sold to a customer willing to spend a few dollars and a little time sewing on a new set of buttons.

damages Merchandise offered for sale in a broken, battered, dirty, or otherwise poor (i.e., damaged) condition, generally at greatly reduced prices.

dangler A sign suspended from a shelf. Danglers are popular in grocery and drug stores. Compare WOBBLER and AISLE INTERRUPTER.

data 1. Concrete information such as statistics or measurements, particularly when used as a basis for reasoning and decision making. 2. In computer technology, anything that can be processed by a computer, including text, numbers, sounds, images, or other elements typically translated into binary digital machine-readable form. See also DATABASE (DB) and MARKETING DATA.

data bank (Obsolete) Synonym for DATABASE (DB).

database (DB) A collection of factual information and other DATA organized for quick retrieval, particularly on a computer. Computer software quickly finds and retrieves selected pieces of data for analysis and application. The information extracted is used in planning and in the decision making process. Traditional databases are organized by fields (i.e., a single piece of information in a designated category, such as customer name or customer zip code), records (i.e., a complete set of fields, such as all the information about an individual customer), and files (i.e., a collection of records, such as the complete information about all customers).

database management system (DBMS) A collection of software programs that store, modify, process, and extract data from databases. The DBMS gives the retailer or other marketer easy access to data in databases as well as the tools for converting that data into useful information. The information from a DBMS can be presented in a variety of formats, including graphic, and the user characteristically receives the output in the form of a report. See also MARKETING DATABASE.

database marketing A system in which marketing activities are based on data (typically stored in a computer) gathered through MARKETING RESEARCH (MR) projects and kept available for further analysis and use. Large files of names, addresses, and demographic and psychographic information are scanned by computers to identify those target customers most likely to respond to promotions. Database marketing is frequently used in DIRECT MAIL and TELEMARKETING. Synonymous with *one-on-one marketing* and *relationship marketing*. See also GEOGRAPHICAL INFORMATION SYSTEMS (GIS).

database server   See SERVER.

data cleansing   The act of finding, removing, and/or correcting data that is incorrect, out-of-date, redundant, incomplete, or incorrectly formatted in a database. Software applications are used for this purpose, eliminating virtually all human error. Also called *data scrubbing*.

data-knowledge-action continuum   The process by which potential data is converted to usable knowledge. Retailers analyze the multitude of data confronting them and capitalize on the opportunities this information affords. Such analysis provides a deeper understanding of customers and their needs, enabling retailers to execute programs in merchandising, marketing, stores, and the supply chain that ensure that the right products will be in the right places at the right time.

data link control (DLC)   The computer address that uniquely identifies a node on a NETWORK. All network addresses must ultimately be translated to DLC address, although not all network protocols use the DLC address the same way. ETHERNET used it exclusively. Other network protocols, such as TCIP/IP, use a logical address to identify nodes, which is then translated to the DLC.

data marketing   Synonym for DATABASE MARKETING.

data mining   Machine-driven use of software to look for hidden patterns and relationships in databases and data warehouses. The software systematically sifts through the database looking for statistically significant patterns, correlations, and predictive relationships, particularly those that were previously unrecognized. Data mining can prove or disprove an educated guess about marketing relationships and has an advantage over earlier systems of data collection and analysis in that it can ask more sophisticated questions of the data and make predictions based on the answers. Data mining functions both as a descriptive and as a predictive tool and is utilized by marketers trying to distill useful consumer data from Web sites. Also called *machine learning* or *knowledge discovery*. See also DATA WAREHOUSE.

data packet   A small independent digital unit tagged with a unique identification number. E-MAIL messages are broken into data packets for routing along network transmission lines. Many different routers (computers) select the best paths for each packet to travel. When they arrive at their destination, the data packets are reassembled into the original e-mail message.

data reduction   The process of transforming large amounts of data (such as retailing and marketing data) into useful, condensed, usable information.

data scrubbing   Synonym for DATA CLEANSING.

data warehouse   1. An electronic storage place for huge amounts of data housed in databases. Data warehouses are used for online and offline strategic marketing. Selected areas in a data warehouse are frequently opened to the company's suppliers, partners, and customers.   2. A system that allows the extraction and management of large quantities of data. See also DATA MINING.

data warehousing   The process of collecting, arranging, and storing data for use in strategic marketing. See DATA WAREHOUSE.

date for value determination   The date on which imported goods were exported from the country of origin. The date is used to determine the value of the goods when setting duties.

date of invoice (DOI)   1. The date on which an invoice was issued.   2. A dating arrangement under which the discount period begins with the date of the invoice. The cash discount period runs a specified number of days from the date of the invoice. Also called the *net credit period*.

dating   See DATING OF INVOICES.

dating of invoices   A means of indicating the period allowed for the payment of an invoice. For example, NET THIRTY is a typical dating arrangement meaning that full payment of the invoice is due within 30 days of the DATE OF INVOICE (DOI) (i.e., the date the invoice was issued). During the specified time period (e.g., 30 days), specified DISCOUNTS may be taken by a reseller customer (typically a retailer). At the end of the time period, the total dollar amount on the invoice becomes due. See also CASH DISCOUNT and NET PAYMENT PERIOD. Sometimes called *dating*.

dating period   The length of time allowed between shipment (or, sometimes, delivery) and payment. For example, in an agreement reading 2/10 net 30, the payment must be made 30 days from the date of the invoice (DOI). A 2 percent discount is afforded to buyers who pay within 10 days. See also DATING OF INVOICES.

datum   (Rare) Singular form of DATA.

day part   In radio advertising, any of the segments into which radio time is divided for the purpose of setting differential advertising rates.

days of average inventory on hand   The financial ratio that results from dividing the number of days in a year (i.e., 365) by the stock turnover during that year. The ratio is used as a means of examining the company's performance during the accounting period.

days of supply   The number of days an INVENTORY will last if sold at the current rate of sale. See also WEEKS OF SUPPLY METHOD.

days per outstanding   The ratio of ACCOUNTS RECEIVABLE to CREDIT sales per day.

days' supply   Synonym for DAYS OF SUPPLY.

DB   See DATABASE (DB).

DBMS   See DATABASE MANAGEMENT SYSTEM (DBMS).

DC   See DISTRIBUTION CENTER (DC).

dead area   Space in a store where displays normally cannot be set up due to physical obstructions, such as corners, stairs, etc., that adversely affect the retailing function. Also called *dead corner*.

deadbeat   1. A person who tries to avoid paying for things or avoids financial responsibilities.   2. In retailing, a customer who fails to pay a monthly revolving charge account. Such customers may be dropped from future promotions. Also called a *delinquent*.

dead stock   Merchandise that has remained unsold for an extended period of time. See also STICKER.

deal   A temporary special offering of merchandise (or services) either in the form of a price reduction (e.g., CENTS-OFF DEAL/OFFER) or as multiple units at a special price. When this takes place on the retail level, it is often termed a RETAIL DEAL. When it takes place earlier in the channel of distribution, it is often termed a *trade deal*.

dealer   An individual or firm that sells merchandise without altering it. The term is most frequently applied to retailers (e.g., automobile dealer) but is sometimes used synonymously with WHOLESALER, VENDOR, or DISTRIBUTOR.

dealer aid   Promotional material provided by a manufacturer to a dealer or other retailer. See also SELLING AID and DEALER DISPLAY.

dealer brand   A private BRAND that carries the name of the dealer while the actual manufacturer of the product or group of products remains anonymous. See also PRIVATE BRAND.

dealer cooperative advertising   See COOPERATIVE ADVERTISING.

dealer display   In retail stores, promotional posters, placards, signs, etc. provided by manufacturers or distributors and often displayed at POINT-OF-SALE (POS). Actual merchandise is sometimes incorporated into the display. Also called *free display material*. See also DEALER AID and PROMOTIONAL KIT.

dealer helps   Nonpersonal services provided by the manufacturer or wholesaler, such as readying merchandise for resale through packaging, labeling, pricing, ticketing, etc. Also called *vendor helps*.

dealer imprint   The name and address of a local retailer, added to an advertising piece by a manufacturer to indicate where merchandise may be purchased. Also known as a *hooker*.

dealer listing   1. In a print (i.e., newspaper or magazine) or broadcast (particularly television) advertisement, the list of local retailers from whom specific advertised products may be purchased.   2. A similar list used by some online marketers on their Web pages, directing visitors to participating stores and dealerships in addition to, or rather than, marketing directly to the online ultimate consumer. Also called *dealer listing ad* and *manufacturers' dealer listing ad*.

dealer listing ad   Synonym for *dealer listing*.

dealer loader   1. A gift from a manufacturer to a marketing intermediary to encourage the placement of an ORDER.   2. A POINT-OF-PURCHASE (POP) fixture provided to a store by the manufacturer or vendor. The dealer loader is usually placed next to a cash register or checkout counter to display items. Synonymous with *loader* and *display loader*.

dealer-service salesperson   A MANUFACTURER'S SALESPERSON employed by a manufacturer to call regularly on established customers. See also MISSIONARY (SALESPERSON) and DETAILER.

dealership   An authorized sales agency, often a franchise, for an exclusive territory. See also FRANCHISING and LEASED DEALERSHIP.

dealer tie-in   See TIE-IN AGREEMENT.

deal pack   An item of merchandise to which is attached a free item at no additional cost as a special promotion.

deal prone   Of brand switchers, motivated by low price and premiums. This is particularly true in the area of staples such as tuna or toilet tissue, where there is little distinguishable difference between brands and consumers will often select the brand on sale that particular day. See also BRAND SWITCHER.

debit   An accounting term for an entry on the left side of an account. All assets and expense accounts are decreased on the debit side. The equality of debits and credits provides the basis for the double-entry system of recording transactions (sometimes referred to as double-entry bookkeeping). Commonly abbreviated *Dr*. See also CREDIT.

debit bank card   Synonym for DEBIT CARD.

debit card   A plastic card (resembling a standard plastic CREDIT CARD) encoded electronically to allow purchase transactions to be paid by deducting money directly from the customer's bank account at the point-of-purchase. The store's point-of-sale terminals are tied electronically to the bank's computer. See also SMART CARD.

debit transfer system   A purchase arrangement in which the amount of the purchase is immediately charged against the buyer's account. No delayed billing is permitted without an interest charge.

debt   Funds for operating a business, obtained through borrowing and having to be repaid (generally with interest) out of earnings. Most businesses are financed with a mixture of debt and EQUITY.

debtee   (Rare) Synonym for CREDITOR.

debt-equity ratio   See DEBT-TO-EQUITY RATIO.

debtor   An individual, company, or nation under financial obligation to repay borrowed money.

debt-to-equity ratio   A company's total liabilities divided by its total equities, representing the company's financial position at a given point in time. It indicates the extent to which a business is financed by DEBT (which must be repaid with interest out of earnings) as opposed to invested capital (EQUITY).

debt-to-total assets ratio   The financial ratio that results when a company's total liabilities are divided by its total assets, demonstrating the company's ability to carry long-term DEBT. The rule of thumb is that the amount of debt should not exceed 50 percent of the value of the company's total assets. See also ASSET.

decal/decalcomania   A piece of transparent film bearing an advertisement that may be affixed to a glass door or window. Also called *transparency*, or *transfer*.

decay curve   In product development, a graphic representation of the survival rate of new product ideas. As each item is subjected to screening and analysis, development, and testing, more and more products are dropped from further consideration until only a small percentage remain at the commercialization stage. Also called a *product decay curve*. See also DECLINE STAGE.

decay model/rate   See ADVERTISING SALES-RESPONSE AND DECAY MODEL.

deceit   Fraudulent behavior in business intended to mislead another (generally, the customer).

decentralization   See DECENTRALIZED ORGANIZATION.

decentralized adjustment system   A system in which customers' complaints are handled at the department level by salespeople, managers, buyers, etc.

decentralized organization   An organizational structure in which authority, decision making, and responsibility have been distributed to the greatest possible number of members, departments, or employees at the lowest possible level of the organizational hierarchy. An example of decentralized organization is the DEPARTMENT STORE OWNERSHIP GROUP in which member stores (usually once-independent department stores) are centrally owned and controlled in terms of broad policy making but operate and merchandise autonomously. The process of creating an organization so structured is known as *decentralization*. A decentralized organization is also referred to as a *flat organization*, because its hierarchy has relatively few levels.

deceptive advertising   Advertising calculated to deceive, defraud, or otherwise trick the consumer.

deceptive packaging   The packaging of products offered for sale in a manner calculated to deceive the purchaser. For example, large boxes only partially filled with merchandise may be considered an instance of deceptive packaging.

deceptive practice   Business practices calculated to deceive, defraud, or otherwise trick the consumer. Most deceptive practices fall into one of two categories: deceptive advertising and promotion, and fraudulent and confusing selling practices.

deceptive pricing   PRICING tactics calculated to deceive, defraud, confuse, or otherwise trick the purchaser. Included are all misrepresentations of credit terms as well as the use of fraudulent reference (or list) prices and other deceptive markdown practices.

deceptive promotion   A promotional practice calculated to deceive, defraud, or otherwise mislead the consumer, as, for example, by misrepresenting price or performance.

decision making unit (DMU)   In purchasing, the person or persons responsible for determining what is to be purchased for the firm and from whom.

decision process   Synonym for ADOPTION PROCESS.

decision support system (DSS)   A type of management support system based on interactive computerized information retrieval and in use since the 1960s. DSS helps decision makers answer questions, solve problems, and support or refute conclusions. In more recent times, DSS has been somewhat replaced by the EXECUTIVE SUPPORT SYSTEM (ESS) and ONLINE ANALYTICAL PROCESSING (OLAP). The term, however, remains a useful and inclusive term for many types of information systems that support decision making. See also MARKETING INFORMATION SYSTEM (MIS), MANAGEMENT INFORMATION SYSTEM (MIS), ENTERPRISE-WIDE DECISION SUPPORT SYSTEM (DSS), and DESKTOP DECISION SUPPORT SYSTEM (DSS).

decision tree   In marketing planning, a method of graphically depicting a series of alternative courses of action in the shape of a tree, with each branch of the tree representing a possible decision along with its projected outcome. Decision trees aid managers in visualizing an array of alternatives.

decked parking   See PARKING.

declared value   The value of merchandise as stated by the owner when the goods are delivered to a carrier.

decline stage   The next-to-last stage in the PRODUCT LIFE CYCLE (PLC), when sales are in decline and profits more difficult to achieve. It precedes the ABANDONMENT STAGE. See also RETAIL LIFE CYCLE.

declining distinctiveness   See PERISHABLE DISTINCTIVENESS.

decoder   An electronic device that transforms input signals into letters, images, etc., comprehensible to the recipient.

decoding   The translation of a message from the form in which it was transmitted into a form comprehensible to the recipient.

decompose and build-up method   Any of a series of methods used to determine the size of the potential market for goods and services. Such methods are based on breaking down the larger market size problem into its component parts (i.e., the number of buyers in the market, the average quantity purchased per buyer per year, and the price per unit) and then multiplying them together to arrive at the final result.

decorative prop   See PROP.

decorative stone   A natural GEMSTONE that is much less rare and costly than a PRECIOUS STONE or a SEMIPRECIOUS STONE.

dedicated hosting   See WEB HOSTING.

deep   See ASSORTMENT DEPTH.

deep discount   See DEEP DISCOUNTING.

deep discount drugstore   A drugstore in which the main attraction is low price. Deep discount drugstores appeal to that segment of the consuming public that makes its buying decisions strictly on the basis of low cost. In these stores almost nothing is sold at regular retail prices and selection is often limited to merchandise on which the store operator was able to secure a deal.

deep discounter   A DISCOUNT STORE that operates on much lower markups and gross margin than conventional or other discount retailers.

deep discounting   An off-price retailing practice in which merchandise is purchased by the retailer on a DEAL basis from the manufacturer (price reductions may be as high as 20 percent). The store then passes the savings on to the customer by selling at 25 to 40 percent off suggested retail prices. This results in gross margins in the 15 to 20 percent range. Deep discounting is most commonly found among drug chains.

deep stock (of key items)   Fast-selling merchandise maintained in large quantities and many sizes and colors.

deep Web   Invisible Web sites inaccessible to most search engines and the general public. Many of these sites are on an INTRANET or EXTRANET. Some deep Web sites use technology that search engines cannot penetrate, while others are blocked because a subscription or registration is required to access protected pages.

defender strategy   A strategy for smaller, local firms competing with powerful multinationals. The local firm leverages local assets (such as knowledge of local tastes and customs as well as good relationships with local distributors and suppliers) in market segments where multinational firms may be weak. For example, local restaurants featuring regional cuisines may compete with multinational fast-food chains by focusing on and adapting the local product. See also EXTENDER STRATEGY, CONTENDER STRATEGY, and DODGER STRATEGY.

defensive budgeting/spending   See COMPETITIVE PARITY.

defensive pricing   A strategy in which a company prices its products so as to protect (or defend) its own established products or MARKET SHARE. For example, a new product may be introduced at a price higher than another of the firm's existing products so as not to cannibalize its market share. See also CANNIBALIZATION.

deferred billing   A billing system under which the payment due date is moved forward a specified period of time to provide an added incentive to purchase. See also DATING OF INVOICES.

deferred discount   See CUMULATIVE QUANTITY DISCOUNT.

deferred marking   See BULK MARKING.

deferred payment sale   1. A purchase made on an installment plan. See INSTALLMENT PLAN/CONTRACT/BUYING and LAYAWAY.   2. A sale that allows customers to extend payments beyond the customary credit period. For example, some furniture retailers promise that no payment need be made for a year after purchase. See also PROMOTIONS AND SALES.

Delaney Act (1958)   Popular name for the Federal FOOD ADDITIVES AMENDMENT (1958).

delay card   A postcard sent to a customer to explain a delay in the shipment of ordered merchandise. May include the expected date of delivery.

delayed dating   See FORWARD DATING.

delayed marking   See BULK MARKING.

delayed-quotation bidding   A PRICING strategy, employed in the industrial market, in which the final price of the product or service is not set until the item is either complete or delivered. Delayed-quotation bidding is most commonly employed in large projects involving extensive development time.

delayed response effect   Any consequence of marketing expenditures, such as advertising or new package design, that becomes visible only after a period of time has elapsed.

deli   Synonym for BANTAM STORE.

delicatessen buying   A form of merchandise buying in which many lines are sampled, but none is bought in depth.

delinquent   Synonym for DEADBEAT.

deliverability   The extent to which merchandise can be provided or serviced by an organization as promised.

delivered at frontier   In global retailing, an agreement specifying that the seller (i.e., exporter) must deliver the goods to the buyer (i.e., importer) at the border of the importing country by a specified time. The buyer then takes responsibility for complying with import formalities and CUSTOMS DUTY payments required to cross the border with the merchandise.

delivered cost   The price at which goods are delivered to the store by the vendor. Includes transportation charges as well as the cost of the goods themselves.

delivered duty exempt In global retailing, an agreement by which the seller (i.e., the exporter) takes on the responsibility for the cost of the goods, insurance against loss, freight charges to get the goods to the named port of destination, and any duties, surcharges, or taxes levied on the items by the importing nation.

delivered price A price quotation, at the wholesale or retail level, that includes the cost of delivery.

delivered sale See FREE ON BOARD (FOB) DESTINATION.

delivery The transportation of goods from the retailer to the ultimate consumer. Also called *package delivery* or *parcel delivery*. The four major types of delivery systems used by retailers are the STORE-OWNED DELIVERY SERVICE, the INDEPENDENT DELIVERY SERVICE, PARCEL POST (PP), and EXPRESS DELIVERY SERVICE. See also SHIPPING.

delivery date 1. The date on which a retail buyer wants an order to be delivered to the store by the vendor. 2. The date on which a customer is promised delivery of purchased merchandise.

delivery expense Expenditures for providing delivery service, including preparation, wrapping, packing, trucking, parcel post, delivery service charges, the cost of picking up returns, etc.

delivery period The elapsed time between the placing of an order and receipt of the merchandise. This is equally applicable both to orders placed by the consumer and to orders placed by retail buyers. See also BUYING PERIOD.

deluxe goods/items Expensive, stylish, trendsetting, top-of-the-line merchandise.

Delphi Method/Technique A method of eliciting information and judgments from expert participants to facilitate problem solving, planning, decision making, and arriving at business forecasts. A group of knowledgeable individuals is polled under the assumption that their reactions will be predictive of the broader population. These experts record their individual judgments, compare the results, and repeat the cycle until a consensus is reached. At each new estimate, a company analyst reviews and revises the results. Also known as the *jury of executive opinion technique*.

demalling The breaking up of aging enclosed malls into open-concept shopping centers characterized by clusters of stores.

demand In the market, a readiness on the part of purchasers to buy a product or service. The concept of demand has two components. On the one hand, purchasers must have a need or desire for the product or service offered for sale and, on the other hand, they must be willing and able to pay the price asked by the seller. Also called *market demand* and the *principle of demand*. The condition in which buyers can actually fulfill their needs is known as *effective demand*. See also SUPPLY and POINT OF EQUILIBRIUM.

demand aggregation technology See DEMAND AGGREGATOR.

demand aggregator A MARKETING INTERMEDIARY who brings buyers together to form a group and organizes a reverse auction for the goods they want to purchase. Technology (i.e., *demand aggregation technology*) is employed to help the group gain price discounts by driving prices down through bulk purchases.

demand analysis An examination of the factors governing the sale and use of a product or service. Such factors include economic conditions, price, scarcity, and buying habits. Demand analysis is concerned with explaining changes in the demand curve and the relationship between price levels and demand in the marketplace.

demand-backward pricing A method of setting prices that starts with what is considered an acceptable final (i.e., retail) price and works backward to what a producer can actually charge. Starting with this acceptable final price (the *demand-backward price*), the producer determines how much may be spent on producing the item by subtracting the margins typically expected by channel members and the average or planned marketing expenses. Demand-backward pricing, to be effective, requires demand estimates, since the quantity demanded will affect production costs. The producer must also determine whether quality will play a significant role in demand or if improved quality may be sacrificed to reduce the costs of production. Also known as *demand-minus pricing* or *market-minus pricing*.

demand-based pricing A pricing technique that employs sophisticated market analysis and an understanding of the range of prices acceptable to the consumer to set the price of an item. See also DEMAND-ORIENTED PRICING.

demand collection A method by which buyers name their own price for a good or service (such as an airline ticket or hotel room) in an anonymous online auction. Customers lock in their bid for a particular product and guarantee it with their credit card. Consumers cannot generally pick brands, sellers, or product features (such as flight time), although they may be given a range of preferences before placing their bid. Buyers learn the details of their purchase (e.g., the name of the airline or hotel) only after the deal is closed. Also called *name your own price*.

demand creation See SALES PROMOTION.

demand cross-elasticity See CROSS-ELASTICITY.

demand curve A table or graph depicting the relationship between a series of prices for a product and the demand for the product in the marketplace. Also known as a *demand schedule*.

demand deposit In banking, a sum of money kept in a bank account (particularly a checking account) to which the depositor has access at all times. The bank will release the requested amount on demand (i.e., whenever the depositor writes a check).

demand elasticity See ELASTICITY OF DEMAND.

demand expansibility   Market demand that can be stimulated through advertising alone. If demand for a product is expansible, an increase in advertising expenditures will result in an increase in sales, even though the price of the product remains the same.

demand inelasticity   See INELASTICITY OF DEMAND.

demand merchandise   Goods for which the customer is specifically shopping.

demand-minus pricing   See DEMAND-BACKWARD PRICING.

demand-oriented pricing   A strategy used in setting retail prices based on the level of consumer DEMAND for the product. When this PRICING STRATEGY is used, merchandise for which there is strong demand will carry a higher price than merchandise for which there is relatively weak demand. See also DEMAND-BASED PRICING and DEMAND PRICE.

demand pattern   Any discernible trend in consumer demand for particular goods and services.

demand price   A price derived from and tied to the level of demand for the product or service on the part of the customers. Merchandise for which there is strong demand will carry a higher price than merchandise for which there is relatively weak demand. See also DEMAND-ORIENTED PRICING.

demand-pull inflation   Inflation (i.e., a general rise in prices) caused by excessive demand for goods and services relative to supply.

demand-pull innovation   Change in a product or service caused or stimulated by the needs, wants, or desires of customers.

demand reestimation   The recalculation of sales forecasts based on POINT-OF-SALE (POS) data.

demand rigidity   See RIGIDITY OF DEMAND.

demand schedule   See DEMAND CURVE.

demand sensitivity   The speed at which merchandise moves in a retail store. See also STOCK TURNOVER (ST).

demand state   See UNWHOLESOME DEMAND STATE.

demand stimulation   See SALES PROMOTION.

demarketing   A marketing strategy calculated to reduce rather than increase demand for a product or service. Demarketing efforts are usually confined to periods of product shortage. Sometimes called *creative demarketing*. See also AGGRESSIVE DEMARKETING RESPONSE TO SHORTAGES.

demo   Short for demonstration. See SALES DEMONSTRATION.

democratic leader   See LEADERSHIP STYLE.

demographic bases for segmentation   See DEMOGRAPHIC SEGMENTATION.

demographics   The vital statistics of a population, including the size of the group and the age, gender, birth and death rates, location, income, occupation, race, educational level, and earnings of its members. When applied to a group of consumers or customers, it is often referred to as CONSUMER DEMOGRAPHICS. See also MARKET SEGMENTATION.

demographic segmentation   A method of market segmentation based on geographic location (such as world or national region, population density, city size, etc.) or shared socioeconomic characteristics (such as age, gender, religion, education, income, etc.). See also DEMOGRAPHICS.

demonstration   See SALES DEMONSTRATION.

demonstration advertising   A form of advertising in which the attributes of a product are actually displayed and its competitive benefits are emphasized. For example, demonstration advertising may be used to show the relative strength of wet paper towels.

demonstration cube   A rug-upholstered, laminate-covered, or wood-finished block found on the selling floor. Demonstration cubes may be used individually or grouped or clustered in a variety of configurations. They may be used as mannequin platforms, display surfaces, or demonstration platforms for presentations made by sales personnel.

demonstration model   An item of merchandise (usually in a hard goods category) put out on the selling floor so that customers can see how it works. The customer actually purchases a fresh item from the stockroom. See also FLOOR MODEL.

demonstrator   A person employed by either a retail store or a manufacturer to promote a product by showing how it works or simply encouraging customers to buy it. When provided by the manufacturer or middleman, a demonstrator is considered a SELLING AID. In housewares and cosmetics especially, vendors often provide their client stores with demonstrators who show and explain the product to the store's salespeople, pointing out product advantages, suggesting selling techniques, and relating pertinent merchandise facts that will help sell the product. Demonstrators may also show customers how to use a particular product to its best advantage. Demonstrators are usually used in departments where brand reputation is important. Their work helps reduce the department's selling costs, since trained demonstrators are responsible for increasing department sales.

demurrage   In transportation and shipping, a fee payable to the owner of a vessel or truck for failure to unload in the time allowed or for otherwise detaining the departure of the vessel.

denial-of-service (DOS) attack   A form of CYBERTERRORISM that occurs when vandals block legitimate Internet users from accessing a Web site by overloading it with traffic designed to tie up or crash its server or servers. Unsuspecting computers connected to the Internet can be taken over specifically to launch DOS attacks. When launched against a commercial Web site, a DOS attack can result in the loss of millions of dollars of business.

Denver Merchandise Mart   The Rocky Mountain region's premier wholesale MERCHANDISE MART located in Denver, Colorado. Showrooms feature women's, children's, and men's apparel and accessories, gifts, resort merchandise, souvenirs, decorative accessories, gourmet, home furnishings, and western apparel. The mart maintains a Web site at www.denvermart.com.

denying method   See DIRECT DENIAL METHOD.

department   A major subdivision in a store, either selling or nonselling, having a specialized function. See also MERCHANDISE DEPARTMENT.

departmental advertisement   In RETAIL PRODUCT ADVERTISING, an advertisement that presents merchandise from a specific department. The artwork used in the ad may coordinate the merchandise into a single image, or the items may be presented in graphically separate segments of a larger layout. A variation of a departmental ad places several single-item products from one department as ads on one page. See also SINGLE-ITEM ADVERTISEMENT.

departmental (dollar) control   See DEPARTMENTAL INVENTORY CONTROL.

departmental inventory control   Retail dollar inventory control applied at the individual department level. Sales records, customer returns, returns to vendors, markups and markdowns, physical inventory counts, and rate of stock turnover are compared with those of other store departments and with the profit objectives of the store. The practice helps store management to determine strengths and weaknesses in each department and develop measures that will improve individual department operations. Sometimes called, simply, *departmental control* or *departmental dollar control*. See also DOLLAR INVENTORY CONTROL.

departmentalization   The grouping of people within an organization according to one of the following criteria: function, product, process, client, or territory. In retailing, this is most obviously epitomized in the department store. Stores may be departmentalized by FUNCTIONAL DEPARTMENTALIZATION, PRODUCT LINE DEPARTMENTALIZATION, GEOGRAPHICAL DEPARTMENTALIZATION, or some combination of the three.

departmentalization by client   See CUSTOMER DEPARTMENTALIZATION.

departmentalization by customer   See CUSTOMER DEPARTMENTALIZATION.

departmentalization by function   See FUNCTIONAL DEPARTMENTALIZATION.

departmentalization by process   See PROCESS DEPARTMENTALIZATION.

departmentalization by product   See PRODUCT-LINE DEPARTMENTALIZATION.

departmentalization by territory   See TERRITORY DEPARTMENTALIZATION.

departmentalize   To divide the activities of a store into separate units having closely related merchandise (selling departments) or similar duties (nonselling departments). Sometimes called *departmentize*.

departmentalized specialty store   A store in which related merchandise is organized into units much like a DEPARTMENT STORE, but whose range of categories is more limited. Also called a *specialty department store* or a *departmentized specialty store*.

departmental pricing   The ability of the BUYER to manipulate the MARKUP PERCENTAGE on individual items within a department in order to meet management's overall profitability expectations for the department. For example, a buyer who is told that the department is expected to produce a markup of 50% is not generally forced to fit every item into that slot. The 50% markup is an average and the buyer may go above or below it on individual items. The buyer essentially averages the various markups within the department to arrive at the expected department markup percentage.

Department and Specialty Store Financial Operating Results (FOR)   See FINANCIAL OPERATING RESULTS OF DEPARTMENT AND SPECIALTY STORES (FOR).

Department and Specialty Store Merchandising and Operating Results (MOR)   See MERCHANDISING AND OPERATING RESULTS OF DEPARTMENT AND SPECIALTY STORES (MOR).

departmentize   (Rare) Synonym for DEPARTMENTALIZE.

departmentized specialty store   (Rare) Synonym for DEPARTMENTALIZED SPECIALTY STORE.

department manager   The individual responsible for running a particular selling area in a store. In some stores, the department manager may be involved in both the buying and selling of merchandise. In other, more centralized organizations, the department manager is primarily responsible for presentation of merchandise, supervision of personnel, and customer service. In larger stores with hierarchical organizations, the department manager usually reports to a store MERCHANDISE MANAGER and is responsible for an area defined by a department or division. This position usually includes both merchandising and operational responsibilities. In some organizations, this position is called a SALES MANAGER.

department operating statement (DOS)   A monthly report detailing a store department's sales, inventory, markdowns, expenses, etc.

department/specialty store   A limited line department store that usually focuses on up-market soft lines. Department/specialty stores are considered FASHION-FORWARD in their apparel merchandising. They operate on high gross margins and carry branded merchandise in stores large enough to be anchors in shopping centers. Examples of department/specialty stores include Lord & Taylor, Saks Fifth Avenue, and Neiman Marcus.

department store A large-scale retail establishment that sells a wide variety of goods, including both soft lines (e.g., apparel and household textile products) and hard lines (e.g., nontextile products such as furniture and consumer electronics), and, with some exceptions, provides its customers with extensive services. The department store takes its name from the sections (i.e., departments) within the store in which related kinds of merchandise are grouped for purposes of promotion, service, and control. It is characterized by considerable breadth in terms of categories of merchandise and the diversity of shoppers whose needs it seeks to satisfy. The origin of many department stores can be traced to the major cities of the nineteenth century. Most were large emporiums with hundreds of categories of merchandise including toys, sporting goods, and major appliances. Elaborate store buildings attracted the public with their sheer size, luxurious appointments, and technological innovations. Although the *traditional (or conventional) department store* with its downtown FLAGSHIP STORE and its emphasis on fashion and service (exemplified by such stores as Macy's and Marshall Field's) is the most clearly recognized form of department store, there are other retail organizations that fall into this category. Included are the DEPARTMENTALIZED SPECIALTY STORE, with its narrower assortment of goods concentrated at the high end in terms of price and fashion (e.g., Lord & Taylor and Neiman Marcus), and the *chain department stores* (e.g., the great mass merchandisers, Sears and JCPenney), which have taken on many of the aspects of the traditional department store even though the profit base is the entire store rather than the individual department. The *discount department stores* (e.g., Kmart and Wal-Mart), characterized by low margins and self-service, sell merchandise in such great varieties that they may also be regarded as department stores. The DEPARTMENT STORE OWNERSHIP GROUP rounds out the category (e.g., Federated Department Stores and May Department Stores Company). These organizations, generally unknown to the public, pull together a number of department stores and their branches into a single, centrally managed (but individually merchandised) retailing group. See also PROMOTIONAL DEPARTMENT STORE, FULL-LINE DEPARTMENT STORE, and JUNIOR DEPARTMENT STORE.

department store chain/group See DEPARTMENT STORE OWNERSHIP GROUP.

Department Store Inventory Price Index A monthly publication of the BUREAU OF LABOR STATISTICS (BLS) that reports price inflation for various categories of merchandise. Now available online at the BLS Web site, www.bls.gov/data, the *Index* is part of the CONSUMER PRICE INDEX (CPI). It provides data from 1941 to the present and compares monthly and annual price indices for total store as well as for soft, durable, and miscellaneous goods. Tabular and graphic representations are available.

department store ownership group A retailing organization whose member stores (usually once-independent department stores) are centrally owned and controlled in terms of broad policy making, but operate and merchandise autonomously. The individual stores retain their names and the general public is seldom aware of their affiliation with the group. Often called, simply, an *ownership group* or a *store ownership group*.

Department Store Price Index See DEPARTMENT STORE INVENTORY PRICE INDEX.

department wrap An area in each selling department of a store in which the customer's purchases may be wrapped. Compare CENTRAL WRAP and CLERK WRAP.

deposit plan See LAYAWAY.

depot store A small store stocking staple items, whose convenient location is a prime attraction to customers. See also CONVENIENCE STORE.

depreciated value The worth of an asset or product after it has been in use for a time, which is less than its value when new. For example, new cars depreciate in value from the moment they leave the dealership.

depreciation The reduction in the value of property (such as a building) due to wear and tear or the passage of time. Depreciation may be clearly observable, as in the rusting away of machinery, or it may be less easily detectable, as in the eroded value of fashion goods held too long in inventory. Accountants use depreciation to spread the cost of a tangible asset systematically over its estimated useful lifetime.

depreciation rate The rapidity with which a fixed asset loses its usefulness or value, expressed as a percentage of its cost.

depression See BUSINESS CYCLE.

depth interview A technique in MOTIVATION RESEARCH (MR) that uses an informal open discussion to uncover unconscious motives and to delve beneath the superficial answers of the participants. Also called an *in-depth interview*.

depth (of assortment) See ASSORTMENT DEPTH.

deregulation The systematic discontinuance of laws and regulations that once controlled business activities. For example, the deregulation of the airline industry allowed airlines to compete on the basis of rates and charges (i.e., ticket prices), whereas they had previously been forced to compete on the basis of peripheral services to customers (e.g., meals). Similarly, the *Motor Carrier Act (1980)* deregulated the trucking industry so that private carriers were permitted to solicit back haul merchandise for the first time in nearly 50 years.

derived demand Market demand for one product that can be traced to the demand for another product. Most derived demand is, finally, traceable to consumer demand.

description buying   In industrial buying, the practice of purchasing a product on the basis of a verbal (i.e., written or oral) description of the product without first inspecting it. Description buying is facilitated by guarantees of quality in the form of grading, branding, and buying by specification. For example, accepted government standards of grading produce allow these goods to be sold without further inspection or sampling by wholesalers or retailers.

descriptive billing   A CHARGE ACCOUNT statement sent to the charge customer on which each credit transaction is listed. The statement shows the name of the department selling each item and the price of each item. Individual sales checks are not returned to the customer.

descriptive label   A tag that explains the important characteristics or benefits of a product. Descriptive matter includes the identification of the product and its manufacturer, its trademark, instructions for use, content, size, etc.

descriptive research   MARKETING RESEARCH (MR) calculated to yield information about a particular problem (e.g., how consumers behave under specific marketplace conditions or how one can identify the users of a given product).

design   The arrangement of the visual elements of an object, including such considerations as color, texture, material, shape, etc. The design itself is a combination of details and other features (e.g., in apparel, design refers to the total concept of the garment including fabric, color, silhouette, detailing, and trim). A particular design is often referred to as a NUMBER or a STYLE NUMBER. In retailing, many lines of merchandise (such as clothing, housewares, home furnishings, fabrics, china, glassware, etc.) have significant design aspects. Also called *product design*. See also STORE LAYOUT AND DESIGN.

designated market area (DMA)   A term coined by Nielsen Media Research to describe a group of U.S. counties covered by a specific television station. There are 210 such areas in the United States. The size of a DMA is determined by the number of television households contained within that area, and the percentage of the area's population in relation to the total population of the United States. These figures are used by Nielsen to determine ratings for specific television shows and television stations.

designation   Any of a number of categories by which merchandise in a retail store may be classified or divided. Item (e.g., shirts) and vendor (e.g., Tommy Hilfiger) are the most common. Other designations include price range (e.g., moderate), size range (e.g., junior), end use (e.g., sportswear), lifestyle (e.g., active), selling season (e.g., holiday), composition/fabrication (e.g., silk), and target customer (e.g., female). See also MULTIPLE DESIGNATIONS.

design division   In an apparel manufacturing firm, the department or division responsible for designing and producing at least four collections or lines of garments each year. After garments are created, the design department produces samples or prototypes that are used by the sales and/or promo-tion divisions to sell products to retail buyers and make the media aware of the new lines of merchandise. A nonapparel manufacturing firm may call this activity NEW PRODUCT DEVELOPMENT.

design elements   Color, texture, proportion, direction, size, shape, line, sequence, and tension, and how these are used in VISUAL MERCHANDISING to create a particular shopping environment.

designer   A person who makes original sketches and patterns for apparel, scenery, automobiles, packaging, and a wide variety of other products. An APPAREL DESIGNER (i.e., a fashion designer) creates ideas for new styles of clothing and accessories. An *industrial designer* creates new ideas for consumer products and industrial applications. Some designers own their own businesses, while others are employed by manufacturers. See also COUTURIER (COUTURIÈRE).

designer brand   The use of a DESIGNER name as a brand name. Also called a *signature brand*. See also DESIGNER MERCHANDISE.

designer institutional advertising   INSTITUTIONAL ADVERTISING produced by a designer to stress the designer's reputation for innovation, quality, or social commitment. Also called *designer's institutional advertising*.

designer line   The exclusive creation of a well-known fashion designer. Distribution is limited and sometimes restricted to the designer's own boutiques. A designer line represents the top of the price/quality hierarchy. See also DESIGNER BRAND.

designer merchandise   Products actually created by a designer, or carrying the approval of the designer whose name appears on the product, usually under a licensing arrangement. See also DESIGNER BRAND and ORIGINAL.

designer ready-to-wear   Seemingly an oxymoron, designer ready-to-wear is apparel that is mass-produced in standard sizes, yet bears the approval and the logo of an apparel designer. Usually such garments are produced under a licensing agreement. See also READY-TO-WEAR (RTW) and DESIGNER BRAND.

designer's advertisement   A consumer advertisement placed by a designer to presell its brands to the target customer at the national and international market levels. Ads placed in national and international fashion magazines, for example, increase consumer awareness of lines of designer merchandise.

designer's institutional advertising   See DESIGNER INSTITUTIONAL ADVERTISING.

design principles   Unity, harmony, repetition, balance, rhythm (movement), contrast, emphasis, and, sometimes, surprise, and how these are used in VISUAL MERCHANDISING to create a particular shopping environment.

desk jobber   See DROP SHIPPER.

desktop decision support system (DSS) Any DECISION SUPPORT SYSTEM (DSS) designed to be used on an individual PC or from a server. Desktop DSS may be used to support a number of decision making situations, including the structuring of complex problems, development of priorities and ranking of alternatives, measurement of the consistency of judgments, allocation of resources, and cost/benefit analysis. Typically, problem-related information is organized in a hierarchical model consisting of a goal, possible scenarios, criteria, and alternatives.

destination center A SHOPPING CENTER so attractive that customers will go out of their way and possibly travel many miles in order to shop there. An OUTLET CENTER is one type of destination center.

destination service In a SUPERSTORE, any service area able to lure customers to the store. Pharmacies, banks, florists, and quick-processing photo labs are often considered destination services.

destination shopping Shopping in which customers go out of their way, if necessary, to purchase a particular brand of SPECIALTY GOODS or shop at a particular retailer.

destination store A store that has drawing power because it offers unique merchandise or strong brand identification. Customers will go out of their way to shop at a destination store and will not accept substitutes. Destination stores make attractive shopping center tenants because of their ability to lure customers.

detailer 1. An individual, usually a salesperson, who sets up vendor displays in retail stores and maintains inventory of the product. As such, the term is sometimes used as a synonym for MISSIONARY (SALESPERSON). 2. A MANUFACTURER'S SALESPERSON whose job it is to visit professionals such as physicians, hospital administrators, etc., to introduce new products. The activities of a detailer are known as *detailing.*

detailing See DETAILER.

detail person 1. A salesperson who visits a manufacturer's customers and is responsible for most of the service details in current and future sales. 2. A salesperson who offers customers current product information and other selling assistance. Sometimes used as a synonym for MISSIONARY (SALESPERSON).

detention time The period of time beyond agreed limits that railroad cars and trucks are delayed at unloading facilities. The consignee may be billed by the carrier for excessive detention time.

determining dimensions Customer needs and preferences that affect the purchase of a specific product type or specific brand in the marketplace. Such factors as a product's value as a status symbol, color of the product, demographic characteristics of the customer, behavioral needs, attitudes, the degree of a customer's urgency for satisfaction of those needs, and brand name are examples of determining dimensions. See also MOTIVE and QUALIFYING DIMENSIONS.

devaluation A reduction, undertaken by a national government, of the value of a nation's currency (i.e., EXCHANGE RATE) relative to other currencies or to gold. Devaluations may become necessary due to bank failures, stock market crashes, unrestricted foreign investments, poor financial management, and panic. A devaluation may also be undertaken to bring a nation's currency more into line with other currencies in an effort to facilitate international trade by making exported goods more affordable to foreign consumers. Theoretically, this action stimulates exports and discourages consumers in the devaluing country from buying imports, thereby reducing a TRADE DEFICIT. See also REVALUATION.

developing countries/nations Countries moving out of third world or emerging nation status. Usually such countries are in transition from an agricultural economy to an industrial economy. A developing country is also called a *less-developed nation (LDN),* although less frequently now than previously.

development See NEW PRODUCT DEVELOPMENT.

development package In apparel SOURCING, a set of deliverables consisting of the sketch and fabric descriptions (or prototype and swatches) along with sample size specifications and size range. This package forms the basis of the COUNTER SAMPLE and costing for the garment.

devouts According to the *Roger Starch Worldwide* study, the 22 percent of adults worldwide who value faith, duty, obedience, and respect for elders above all. They are concentrated in Africa, Asia, and the Middle East. Of the six groups, devouts are the least involved with the media and the least likely to want Western brands.

diagonal (floor) plan A store layout that is optimal for small self-service stores. Aisles are placed at 45-degree angles to the side walls. The cashier is usually near the front, with sight lines to all areas of the store. Drug, video, and record stores sometimes use the diagonal plan since it maximizes the visibility of many small items on display.

dialog box See BOX.

diary study/method A form of consumer research using a sample group of a store's customers, each of whom records all purchases for a period of time. A researcher analyzes these lists to determine the type of merchandise the store should carry. See also USAGE RATE SEGMENTATION.

diaspora management The growing practice, by home governments, of using the business and cultural skills of their nonresident citizens to the best advantage of the home country. The governments maintain links with emigrants, particularly those doing business with the home country and traveling back and forth between the old country and the new, and encourage them to invest in the home country. See also

HOME TROTTING. The trend was identified and the term coined by trendwatching.com at www.trendwatching.com.

differential advantage The advantage one firm has over its competitors because of its wide range of experience, greater resources, higher level of competence, superior reputation, familiarity to the consuming public, and other unique characteristics.

differential pricing A form of DEMAND-ORIENTED PRICING commonly applied to markets that can be divided into segments—some in which demand for the product or service is elastic and some in which demand is inelastic. Marketers attempt to sell at a high price in market segments having INELASTIC DEMAND and at a lower price in segments having ELASTIC DEMAND. See also DEMAND and MARKET SEGMENTATION.

differentiated marketing A marketing strategy in which a manufacturer produces a number of related products, each targeting a narrow segment of the total market, rather than attempting to market a single product for all customers. Each market segment is offered a different MARKETING MIX. Also called *multiple market segmentation, the multiple target market approach,* or the *multiple market approach.* See also UNDIFFERENTIATED MARKETING, CUSTOMIZED MARKETING, and MARKET SEGMENTATION.

differentiated oligopoly A condition in the marketplace characterized by the presence of a relatively small number of competing firms who are selling similar but not identical products. One or two producers are large enough to set prices industry-wide. The automobile industry is an example of a differentiated oligopoly. Also called a *competitive monopoly.*

differentiated product A product or service marketed on the basis of what makes it different, unique, superior, and/or preferable to the competitors' products. Promotional materials emphasize these differences. Compare UNDIFFERENTIATED PRODUCT.

differentiation 1. In organizational structure, the structuring of jobs in such a way as to allow specialization of functions for maximum efficiency. The larger the organization, the greater the opportunity for differentiation. In large companies, the marketing task may be differentiated into such specialized units as commercial research, advertising and promotion, application development, sales, and customer service. 2. A method used by manufacturers to create an identity in a particular market. The manufacturer introduces different varieties of the same basic merchandise under the same name into a particular item category, thereby covering the range of items available in that category. 3. A strategy used to position a brand or product so as to distinguish it from its competition and create a unique image for it. Also called *segmentation strategy.* See also BRAND DIFFERENTIATION and PRODUCT DIFFERENTIATION.

differentiation strategy See DIFFERENTIATION (def. 3).

diffused demand A demand pattern in which consumer needs are so diverse as to make the identification of clear market segments difficult, if not impossible.

diffusion See DIFFUSION PROCESS.

diffusion curve See ADOPTION CURVE.

diffusion line In the French fashion industry, a synonym for BRIDGE LINE.

diffusion of innovation See DIFFUSION PROCESS.

diffusion process The process by which information about a new product or service is spread and the product is adopted in successive stages by members of a target market. Diffusion may be divided into stages of awareness, interest, evaluation, trial, and adoption. Consumers vary in their willingness to accept new goods and services and may be classified as innovators (the first group of customers to buy a product), early adopters, the early majority, the late majority, laggards, and, finally, non-adopters (those who do not buy the product at all). Also called *innovation diffusion, diffusion of innovation,* and *product diffusion.* See also ADOPTION PROCESS.

digital cash In e-commerce, a system that allows a Web site visitor to pay for goods or services by transmitting a unique number from one computer to another. Digital cash is anonymous and reusable, which differentiates it from credit card Web purchases. A participating bank issues cash numbers or other unique identifiers that carry a given value; to obtain a certificate, the user must have an account at the bank. When the user purchases digital cash certificates, the money is withdrawn from the account. The user transfers the certificate to the vendor to pay for a product or service and the vendor deposits the cash number in any participating bank or retransmits it to another vendor. If necessary, the vendor can check the validity of a cash number by contacting the issuing bank.

digital certificate In e-commerce, an attachment to an electronic message, used for purposes of security (for example, when sending a credit card number to pay for a purchase). The digital certificate verifies the identity of the user and provides the recipient with the means to encode a reply. The process utilizes PUBLIC KEY ENCRYPTION to facilitate the exchange of data. Digital certificates are issued by a CERTIFICATE AUTHORITY (CA). The most widely used standard for digital certificates is X.509.

digital denial In some views, the negative response of the music and film industries to the digital revolution, with its massive shifts in consumer behavior and related new business models. According to this view, the industries failed to acknowledge new trends that required a new business model. The response pitted consumers who yearned for certain products and services against corporations that went out of their way to ignore them, overcharge them, or sue them. Compare DIGITAL EMBRACE.

digital divide The gap between INTERNET users and consumers and those enterprises that are not ONLINE. Economic, educational, and other demographic factors may constitute reasons for the presumed existence of this gap. For example, digital divides may exist between the richer and the poorer countries, between richer and poorer residents of the same country or region, between the more educated and the less educated, between urban and rural residents, and between various ethnic groups. The implication for online marketers and e-tailers is that not all potential customers are equally reachable by online means.

digital embrace   In some views, the positive response of certain industries to the digital revolution. Rather than sue consumers or deny them products and services, firms embracing digitization responded instead with new, innovative products, improved services, and novel business models that included mutually satisfactory pricing strategies. The trend was identified and the term coined by trendwatching.com at www.trendwatching.com. Compare DIGITAL DENIAL.

digital footprints   Synonym for CLICKSTREAM.

Digital Millennium Copyright Act (1998)   Public Law 105-304, the an amendment to Title 17 of the U.S. COPYRIGHT ACT (1976) designed to strengthen copyright protection over digital products and the right of transmission. The act also ratifies U.S. membership in the World Intellectual Property Organization (WIPO).

digital products   Products that are purchased ONLINE and delivered electronically, directly to the recipient's computer. Software, online games, music, information, tickets, etc., may all be digital products. Also called *digitals* or *electronic products.*

digitals   See DIGITAL PRODUCTS.

digital signature   An online encrypted certificate that verifies authenticity with the same authority as a traditional signature on a paper document. Digital signatures are intended to be authenticated, unforgeable, and uncopyable. This has been addressed by the *Electronic Signatures in Global and National Commerce Act (ESIGN)*, which became effective October 1, 2000.

digital subscriber line (DSL)   In ONLINE communications, a home or office line that can transmit 6.1 megabits per second and is, therefore, faster than a dial-up modem.

digital superhighway   A term for the INTERNET popularized in the United States by the Clinton administration. It was conceived as a communication and information tool to be used by governments, schools, businesses, and citizens as well as a means for the federal government to achieve significant savings in purchasing (E-PROCUREMENT). Also known as the *information superhighway.*

digital wallet   In E-COMMERCE, a piece of encryption software that holds a customer's payment information. A digital wallet can hold payment information, a DIGITAL CERTIFICATE to identify the user, and shipping information to speed transactions, all of which is encrypted against piracy. Most digital wallets reside on the customer's PC, but some versions provide a *thin wallet* that resides on the credit card issuer's server.

dime store   Synonym for VARIETY STORE. Also called *five and ten* or *five and dime store.*

diminishing demand   See LAW OF DEMAND.

diminishing marginal utility   See DIMINISHING UTILITY.

diminishing returns   In retailing, a situation in which the cost of attracting additional customers outweighs the revenues derived from the new customers. Also called the *law of diminishing returns.* See also THRESHOLD EXPENDITURE LEVEL and DIMINISHING RETURNS MODEL.

diminishing returns model   A visual representation of how increased spending on advertising affects sales. The model is based on the belief that the more a firm spends on advertising, the more it will sell, up to a certain point. At that point, the benefits of spending more on advertising will be seen to fall off. This is believed to be due to the fact that the customers most likely to purchase the advertised goods or services have already responded to the initial, earliest promotional messages. Compare to the S-SHAPED CURVE MODEL. See also DIMINISHING RETURNS and PROMOTIONAL BUDGETING.

diminishing utility   The principle that the satisfaction one experiences from possessing a product (i.e., the product's UTILITY) decreases as the number of units increases. That is, the more one has of something, the less pleasure each added unit produces in the consumer. Also called the *law of diminishing utility,* the *law of diminishing marginal utility,* or the *principle of diminishing utility.*

direct-action advertising   See DIRECT ADVERTISING.

direct advertising   Advertising (i.e., paid, nonpersonal communication) designed to stimulate the demand for a specific product or service. Direct advertising, a form of PRODUCT ADVERTISING, seeks an immediate response on the part of the customer. Also called *direct-action advertising.* Compare INDIRECT ADVERTISING.

direct authorization   Credit approval obtained from the credit department before merchandise is released to the customer, either as a take transaction or as a delivery.

direct barter   A type of online BARTER in which items are traded one for one, from one individual to another. Compare NETWORK POOL BARTER.

direct buying   At the retail level, the practice of buying directly from the manufacturers rather than from a JOBBER.

direct channel (of distribution)   A CHANNEL OF DISTRIBUTION in which the manufacturer uses no marketing intermediaries but sells directly to the ultimate consumer. This arrangement is also known as a *zero-level channel,* a *direct distribution channel,* and/or a *direct-to-user channel* See also DIRECT SELLING.

direct check   The inspection of received merchandise by an individual who compares the goods on hand to the seller's invoice. The goal of the direct check is to determine whether the quantity of merchandise billed tallies with the quantity of merchandise received. Also called a *direct merchandise check*. Compare BLIND CHECK.

direct close A way of concluding a sale, used when the SALESPERSON has received positive buying signals from the customer. Without resorting to any form of persuasive manipulation, the salesperson simply asks the customer for a favorable purchase decision.

direct competition In retailing, head-to-head competition between two or more stores, generally offering potential customers similar or identical products or services.

direct competitor A store or other business competing head-to-head with another store or business, generally offering potential customers similar or identical products and/or services. See also DIRECTLY COMPETING STORES.

direct cost Any cost involved in doing business that can be directly ascribed to a particular product or organizational unit. Commonly, materials and supplies, wages, and overhead are regarded as direct costs; they vary with the volume of production.

direct costing system Synonym for VARIABLE COSTING SYSTEM.

direct delivery Synonym for DROP SHIPMENT.

direct denial method A SALES APPROACH in which the SALESPERSON, to overcome the customer's resistance to purchasing the product or service, presents reasons why the consumer is incorrect. Also known as the *denying method*.

direct derivation In MARKET FACTOR ANALYSIS, a procedure for translating the behavior of variables in the marketing environment into estimates of future sales. It involves the relatively nontechnical examination of statistics in an effort to project the market potential for a product or service. See also CORRELATION ANALYSIS.

direct distribution Synonym for DIRECT SELLING.

direct distribution channel See DIRECT CHANNEL (OF DISTRIBUTION).

direct expense In a store, any expenditure that can be allocated to a specific department or store and is the result of the operation of that department or store. Direct expenses cease to exist when the unit of business is eliminated. For example, a store's rent is a direct expense that no longer exists once the store is closed. Compare INDIRECT EXPENSE.

direct export/exporting A method of exporting goods in which the domestic firm handles its own exporting, directly to customers or through marketing intermediaries located in foreign markets. No domestic intermediaries are involved. Direct export, which gives the marketer a greater degree of control over its channels of distribution, may be achieved through the use of a domestic-based export department or division within the firm, an overseas sales branch or sub-sidiary, traveling export sales representatives, or foreign-based distributors or agents.

direct inventory 1. In a retail business or other commercial firm, all merchandise purchased for resale. Compare INDIRECT INVENTORY. 2. In an industrial concern, all raw materials, finished goods, and work in various stages of completion.

direct investment The act of investing in long-term ownership of foreign-based manufacturing facilities rather than entering into competition with local foreign manufacturers. This form of DIRECT EXPORT/EXPORTING provides the company with cost economies such as cheaper labor and/or raw materials, government investment incentives, and freight savings. Direct investment also provides the investing company with a better image in the host country, closer ties to the government of the host country, better relationships with suppliers and distributors, and better control over its investment than may be possible with other forms of direct export.

directly competing stores Stores in a shopping center, mall, or other shopping area that offer essentially the same merchandise to potential customers and target the same customer base. Compare INDIRECTLY COMPETING STORES.

direct mail The use of the postal service to arouse the interest of consumers in a product or service or upcoming event. Direct mail may be regarded as a form of ADVERTISING (in contrast to MAIL ORDER RETAILING, which is a method of doing business) and may be employed to prospect for new customers or to maintain contact with existing ones. Sales letters, postcards, circulars, letters, CDs, diskettes, and catalogs are frequently used in direct mail activities. E-MAIL may be used to perform the identical functions. An individual mailing flyer or brochure is called a *direct mail piece* or a *direct mailing*. Also called *direct mail retailing*. See also MAILER.

direct mail advertising See DIRECT MAIL.

direct mailing See DIRECT MAIL.

direct mail piece See DIRECT MAIL.

direct mail retailing See DIRECT MAIL.

direct mail shipper See DROP SHIPPER.

direct manufacturer's outlet See MANUFACTURER'S OUTLET.

direct marketing Marketing via direct mail, telephone retailing, mail order retailing, catalog retailing, mail order ads and inserts (preprints) in magazines, DOOR-TO-DOOR RETAILING, and such electronic media as the INTERNET (e.g., COMMERCIAL E-MAIL) and two-way cable television. Direct marketing efforts are direct communications to a consumer or business customer and are calculated to elicit a direct response on the part of potential customers in the form of an order (direct order), a request for further information (lead generation), or a visit to a store or other place of business for the purchase of specific products or services (traffic generation).

Direct marketing advertising pieces convey a sense of immediacy to the consumer. Many bricks-and-mortar retailers use direct marketing techniques to reach their customers. Direct marketing practices vary from country to country. In the United States, for example, direct marketing is dominated by specialty catalogs, in France by general merchandise catalogs. Direct marketing is also popular in Japan. In Russia and India, however, direct marketing is often viewed with suspicion and the infrastructure may be insufficient to generate enough business to make direct marketing worthwhile. Compare DIRECT SELLING.

direct marketing agency A service agency furnishing research, database management, creative assistance, direct mail, media services, and production capabilities to its client firms. Direct marketing agencies help client firms identify new customers and develop loyalty among existing customers. They also help client firms develop a direct response program and arrange for media placement. These agencies may by paid on a fee-for-service basis or by commission.

direct marketing channel A CHANNEL OF DISTRIBUTION in which the manufacturer sells directly to the ultimate consumer (e.g., catalog sales and/or Internet sales). Compare LIMITED MARKETING CHANNEL and EXTENDED MARKETING CHANNEL. See also DIRECT MARKETING.

direct merchandise check Synonym for DIRECT CHECK.

direct model (of EBPP) See ELECTRONIC BILL PRESENTMENT AND PAYMENT (EBPP).

direct order See DIRECT MARKETING.

director of advertising See ADVERTISING DEPARTMENT.

director of creative services See CREATIVE SERVICES DIVISION.

director of fashion See FASHION DIRECTOR.

director of marketing Synonym for MARKETING MANAGER.

director of public relations See PUBLIC RELATIONS DIRECTOR.

director of research See RESEARCH DEPARTMENT.

director of stores In department and specialty stores with far-flung branches, the executive (usually one with a strong merchandising background) who is responsible for the total look and character of the branches. Also called the *stores director*.

director of visual merchandising See VISUAL MERCHANDISING DEPARTMENT.

direct premium Free merchandise given to the customer with the purchase of specified other products. The direct premium is attached to or placed inside the promoted items and available to the consumer immediately upon purchase. See also GIFT-WITH-PURCHASE (GWP).

direct product profitability (DPP) A detailed financial picture of an item's profitability that takes into account all allowances and EXPENSES related to the sale of an item as well as the item's gross margin. See also ALLOWANCE and GROSS MARGIN.

direct promotion See PERSONAL SELLING.

direct purchase See DIRECT SELLING.

direct response An advertising technique that solicits an immediate action on the part of the recipient. The action may be an order for merchandise, a visit to the store, or any other activity that may develop business.

direct response advertising In RETAIL PRODUCT ADVERTISING, advertisements run by retail firms offering merchandise through nonstore sales. This is an alternative to bringing the customer physically into the store. Products may be identical or similar to those offered in the store or they may be items available only by placing a mail, Internet, or telephone order.

direct response broadcast media All direct response advertising communications conducted through local, national, or cable radio and television channels. The two major direct response television outlets are the Home Shopping Network and the INFOMERCIAL. See also INTERACTIVE TELEVISION (ITV).

direct response driver consumer A class of consumers targeted by billboard advertisers and consisting of drivers, particularly drivers with cell phones. The expectation is that such drivers may, on seeing a billboard or hearing a radio commercial while driving, use the cell phone to respond directly to the advertising. See also OUT-OF-HOME DIRECT RESPONSE MEDIA.

direct response electronic media ONLINE services and the INTERNET as used for advertising purposes, specifically to solicit a DIRECT RESPONSE (i.e., immediate action) on the part of the recipient. Also called *direct response interactive media* and *direct response online media*.

direct response interactive media Synonym for DIRECT RESPONSE ELECTRONIC MEDIA.

direct response marketing See DIRECT MARKETING and DIRECT RESPONSE.

direct response media Print, broadcast, electronic, outdoor, mail, telephone, out-of-home and other media used in DIRECT MARKETING. Direct response media encourage the message recipient to respond directly to the advertiser in order to initiate a purchase or other transaction.

direct response online marketing All DIRECT RESPONSE advertising communications conducted over the computer, using an interactive electronic computer network over telephone or cable lines and displayed on a user's computer screen. Direct marketers can advertise their products and services on the INTERNET using e-mail communications, place a direct response ad online, or set up an electronic storefront on a Web site. E-MAIL can be used by a firm to inform subscribers about merchandise, news topics, chat sessions, or service special offers.

direct response online media   Synonym for DIRECT RESPONSE ELECTRONIC MEDIA.

direct response print media   Promotional pieces, delivered to the consumer, encouraging the recipient to respond directly to the manufacturer or retailer by telephone, by return mail, or by visiting a store location or Web site. Examples are direct mail, brochures displayed in stores or distributed by store personnel, package inserts, sales promotion premiums such as matchbooks, Yellow Pages advertisements and listings, newspaper advertising inserts, and direct response advertising space in newspapers and magazines.

direct response retailing   See DIRECT RESPONSE and MAIL ORDER RETAILING.

direct retailing   See DIRECT SELLING and TELEVISION SHOPPING CHANNEL.

direct-sales results test   A test designed to measure the effectiveness of advertising or other promotional activities by calculating the increase in revenue achieved by each dollar expended for advertising and promotion. See also PROMOTIONAL BUDGETING.

direct sell   A type of advertising message that focuses on a single unique product benefit and hammers it home to the target audience through constant repetition. This approach is often used in conjunction with product demonstrations, such as those illustrating the superior absorbency of certain paper towels. Not to be confused with DIRECT SELLING. Compare IMAGE SELL, the opposite of direct sell.

direct seller   1. A firm that sells directly to the consumer, such as Mary Kay and Avon, thus bypassing a retail distributor. 2. A personal salesperson working either within a retail store or through a direct selling channel. Direct sellers in the cosmetics industry and related fields refer to themselves as *image consultants* and are trained to help individuals create a more positive self-image through skin care, health, fitness, beauty, cosmetics, apparel, color, wardrobe, etc.

direct selling   1. At the industrial level, selling from the producer or manufacturer to the final user without recourse to wholesalers, retailers, or any other intermediary. This arrangement is also known as a *zero-level channel, direct purchase,* or a *direct-to-user channel.*   2. At the retail level, such activities as telephone sales, door-to-door selling, or in-home parties, reflecting a personal form of selling that involves meeting with the customer face-to-face. Typically, a salesperson contacts a customer directly in a convenient location such as the customer's home or workplace, demonstrates the product's features, takes an order, and delivers the merchandise to the customer. Also called *direct retailing, home retailing,* and *door-to-door selling.* Compare DIRECT MARKETING. See also DOOR-TO-DOOR RETAILING.

direct shipment   Synonym for DROP SHIPMENT.

direct store delivery   Synonym for DROP SHIPMENT.

direct-to-consumer advertising   A form of DIRECT MARKETING that bypasses the traditional intermediary and aims advertising campaigns directly at the ultimate consumer. For example, pharmaceutical companies previously advertising to doctors and other medical professionals now aim their advertisements directly at the consumer in broadcast, print, and other media. This trend has developed as the result of the relaxation of FOOD AND DRUG ADMINISTRATION (FDA) rules limiting the advertisement of prescription drugs on television.

direct-to-the-home selling   Synonym for DOOR-TO-DOOR RETAILING.

direct-to-user channel   See DIRECT SELLING.

disaggregated market   A market in which the customers are all so distinct from one another that no aggregates (i.e., groupings) may be formed. Such markets are said to be completely segmented. See also AGGREGATION and MARKET SEGMENTATION.

disclaimer   A disavowal of liability (i.e., legal responsibility). In E-TAILING, where some Web sites carry disclaimers, marketers face the additional complication of differing international standards and definitions of legal responsibility.

discontinued goods   Merchandise that will not be included in future assortments. Discontinued goods may include a whole category, a product line, or a single style, pattern, or color. For example, a manufacturer or a retailer may discontinue unpopular colors in an assortment of bath towels. Discontinued goods are good candidates for clearance markdowns. See also CLEARANCE MARKDOWN.

discontinuous innovation   The development of products that are so new and innovative that they have no clearly discernible antecedents. An entirely new market must be developed for these products.

discount   A reduction in PRICE from the list or regular price given to the store by suppliers or manufacturers, or by the store to its customers. Discounts available to the retail buyer take one of four forms: quantity discounts, seasonal discounts, trade discounts, and cash discounts. Since these discounts can have a dramatic impact on a retailer's profitability over time, retailers with cash flow problems frequently borrow money in order to pay the invoice on time and benefit from the discount. See also PRICE CUTTING.

discount chain   See CHAIN DISCOUNT.

discount consolidator   In E-TAILING, an online marketer that purchases the first-quality excess inventory of brand name product manufacturers and sells it directly to online consumers at greatly reduced prices. Brand name manufacturers sell excess inventory to consolidators to avoid having sale items on their own sites at the same time that they are selling regular priced merchandise.

discount coupon   Synonym for COUPON.

discount department store   A retail establishment that seeks, like the DEPARTMENT STORE, to meet the needs of all family members and provide one-stop shopping for its customers. However, the discount department store also seeks to appeal to consumers who value savings over service. Consequently, discounters offer an extensive selection in a modest setting with few salespeople and minimal service. Emphasis is on selling nationally advertised brands at low prices. Discount department stores tend to focus on the fastest-moving merchandise and encourage self-selection by the customer. Wal-Mart, Kmart, and Target are examples of discount department stores. See also DISCOUNT STORE.

discounted cash flow   Synonym for NET PRESENT VALUE.

discounter   Synonym for DISCOUNT STORE.

discount house   Synonym for DISCOUNT STORE.

discounting   See DISCOUNT MERCHANDISING.

discount loading   See LOADING OF CASH DISCOUNT.

discount merchandising   Retailing at less than the manufacturer's list price while providing few customer services. Also called, simply, *discounting*.

discount retailer   Synonym for DISCOUNT STORE.

discount retailing   The selling of merchandise to consumers at less than regular prices. In contrast to OFF-PRICE RETAILING (where the retailer buys merchandise at cut-rate prices and passes the savings along to customers), the discounter pays the same price for merchandise as everyone else and sells it for less than traditional retailers. See also DISCOUNT STORE.

discount sale   A price reduction allowed to employees and members of other special groups such as the clergy and senior citizens. Also called *sales discount*. See also DISCOUNT.

discount store   A retail establishment that operates on a low MARGIN in order to offer merchandise at prices below the recognized market level. Low wholesale prices and low operating costs are the key to the discount store's ability to keep prices low. Discounters purchase large quantities of first-quality goods or buy manufacturers' closeouts, end-of-season merchandise, and overruns. The discount store emphasizes a no-frills, self-service shopping environment and generally charges for additional customer services if offering them at all. Customers may pay for their merchandise at a centrally located checkout area or FRONT END. Typically volume-oriented, the discount store is distinguished primarily by its emphasis on price. Its success depends on high volume and low overhead. Types of discounters include the FULL LINE DISCOUNT STORE, the CATEGORY KILLER, the OFF-PRICE DISCOUNT STORE, the CLOSEOUT STORE, MANUFACTURER'S OUTLET, the WAREHOUSE CLUB, and the SUPERCENTER. Also called, simply, a *discounter* or an *underselling store*. See also PRICE CUTTING and SUPERSTORE.

discrepancy of assortment   The difference between the lines made by the producer and the assortment wanted by the consumer. Wholesalers and retailers compensate for this discrepancy by putting together an appropriate product mix for their customers.

discrepancy of quantity   The difference between the number of goods it is economical for a producer to make and the quantity normally wanted by the consumer. Wholesalers and retailers in the CHANNEL OF DISTRIBUTION compensate for this discrepancy by regrouping the goods into increasingly smaller quantities through ALLOCATION.

discrepancy of size   See SIZE DISCREPANCY.

discrepancy of variety   The difference between the number of different types of goods that the customer would like to have available and the number of types of goods actually carried by a given store.

discretionary adaptations   In global marketing, changes made in a product that are optional and depend on the judgment of the marketer, who initiates them in order to meet the standards or preferences of different national markets. See also MANDATORY ADAPTATIONS.

discretionary buying power   The amount of money an individual or family has available for purchases after taxes and other obligations. The consumer has a certain amount of choice (i.e., discretion) in how this money will be spent. Sometimes called *discretionary spending power*. See also DISCRETIONARY INCOME and BUYING POWER.

discretionary expenditure   A purchase made by a consumer with money left over after taxes, necessities, and financial obligations have been met. Also called a *personal expenditure*. Compare to NONDISCRETIONARY EXPENDITURE. See also DISCRETIONARY BUYING POWER and DISCRETIONARY INCOME.

discretionary income   The portion of an individual's earnings that remains after taxes have been paid, contracted payments made, and the necessities of life purchased. The individual has a certain amount of choice (i.e., discretion) as to how the balance will be spent. Retailers are particularly interested in discretionary income, since it allows for the purchase of nonessential goods; any such expenditure is called a DISCRETIONARY EXPENDITURE. Also called *discretionary personal income*. See also DISPOSABLE INCOME.

discretionary spending power   Synonym for DISCRETIONARY BUYING POWER.

discriminatory pricing   The sale of goods or services at different prices to different customers. Pricing is discriminatory when it is calculated to give one party an unfair advantage over another. Discriminatory pricing is illegal under the provisions of the ROBINSON-PATMAN ACT (1936) when it reduces competition in interstate commerce.

discussion group   See INTERNET DISCUSSION GROUP.

diseconomies of scale   Cost increases and other operating disadvantages arising out of large-scale operations. For example, a business may grow so large that size in itself attracts the notice of government regulators. Compare ECONOMIES OF SCALE, its opposite.

disguised retail audit   An audit carried on without the knowledge of the store's employees.

disincentive   In retailing, anything that discourages or deters the customer from making a purchase. For example, poor service can act as a disincentive for shopping at a particular store for at least some of the store's potential customers.

disinflation   An economic condition in which the rate of price increases moderates. Disinflation may result from a variety of causes, both internal and external to a particular economy. For example, a combination of forces affecting the United States in the 1980s (i.e., a weakening of OPEC, deregulation, a decline in the power of labor unions, and restrictions on the amount of money put into general circulation) had the combined effect of bringing about a period of disinflation.

disintermediation   A reduction in the number of marketing intermediaries (or the total elimination of intermediaries) in the CHANNEL OF DISTRIBUTION so as to reduce costs, increase efficiency, and better serve customer needs. Disintermediation is practiced by many online merchants; consumers, in turn, use disintermediation when they access financial services, make travel arrangements, or order merchandise directly online. See also REINTERMEDIATION, its opposite.

disk/diskette   A popular storage medium for electronic data, consisting of a thin, portable, plastic plate coated with magnetic materials. Also called a *floppy disk*.

disk space   The amount of memory available on a DISK/DISKETTE for storing electronic data.

dispatcher   The agent or employee responsible for routing and sending merchandise to its destination.

dispersion   See ALLOCATION.

display   The impersonal, visual presentation of goods or ideas. Display is frequently employed in the retail trade in store windows and interiors to facilitate customer examination and selection of merchandise. A display may be one of the following types: the one-item display, the line-of-goods display, the related merchandise display, and the variety or assortment display. Also called a *retail display*. See also VISUAL MERCHANDISING.

display advertising   In newspapers, advertisements featuring illustrations, photography, headlines, and other visual components as well as copy (i.e., words). Display ads are purchased by amounts specified on a RATE CARD that lists the costs based on space, production (mechanical and copy) requirements, deadlines, preferred position, circulation, etc.

display allowance   See RETAIL DISPLAY ALLOWANCE.

display card   A poster or sign of any size or shape used as a window or interior display. Display cards often provide information about special offers, prices, and merchandise. They may even be reproductions of actual print advertisements.

display case   1. A suitcase-like carrying case used by traveling and door-to-door salespersons to display their merchandise to potential customers.   2. A type of COUNTER used in a store's interior display, typically having a glass or transparent plastic top and at least three transparent sides. It enables customer viewing of the items displayed for sale while protecting them from tampering. See also MUSEUM CASE.

display fixture   A store furnishing unit used to show goods not available for customer selection. The customer may, however, view the displayed sample. A salesperson must be summoned to obtain the goods from a higher shelf, a storage area, or a stockroom. See also FIXTURE.

display form   See FORM.

display loader   Synonym for DEALER LOADER.

display merchandising   See VISUAL MERCHANDISING.

display until (date)   Synonym for SELL BY (DATE).

display window   An opening in the façade of a storefront, fitted with panes of glass, that may be used to show merchandise for sale in the store. Display windows are constructed as "rooms," with three side walls, a window wall, a floor, and a ceiling. See also WINDOW DISPLAY.

displaying   The process of making merchandise available for purchase by the customer. It includes moving merchandise to the sales floor for presentation or to the stockroom for storage. See also DISPLAY.

disposable goods   Items of merchandise that are expendable and intended to be used once and then discarded. Disposable goods include paper items such as cups, towels, and tissues as well as some plastic items such as flatware. Many disposable items may also be purchased online. Also called simply *disposables*.

disposable income   Earnings that remain after taxes and other mandatory payments (such as health care and retirement fund contributions) have been deducted; roughly equivalent to *take-home pay*. Also called *disposable personal income (DPI)* and *personal disposable income*. Compare DISCRETIONARY INCOME. See also PERSONAL CONSUMPTION EXPENDITURE.

disposable personal income (DPI)   See DISPOSABLE INCOME.

dissatisfier   Any characteristic of a product that is not pleasing to the consumer. According to Frederick Herzberg's well-known theory of customer motivation, consumers seek to minimize the number of dissatisfiers when selecting an item for purchase. Contrast with SATISFIER, any characteristic of a product that is intrinsically pleasing to the customer. See also TWO-FACTOR THEORY OF MOTIVATION.

dissection Synonym for CLASSIFICATION.

dissociative group A reference group from which an individual makes an effort to separate or distance himself or herself (e.g., a particular social class, ethnic group, or professional affiliation). See also MEMBERSHIP GROUP, REFERENCE GROUP, and ASPIRATIONAL GROUP.

dissonance See COGNITIVE DISSONANCE.

dissonance reduction Post-purchase behavior on the part of the consumer who, fearing that a purchase was not a good idea after all, seeks reassurance and, perhaps, further information about the product to assuage feelings of doubt. Marketers may anticipate the need for dissonance reduction by following up purchases with thank-you letters and/or additional information. See also COGNITIVE DISSONANCE and RISK.

distinctiveness stage In the FASHION LIFE CYCLE, the introductory stage in which some consumers seek and are willing to pay for new and innovative products, different from those accepted by the majority. See also FASHION LIFE CYCLE.

distress merchandise Goods at either the wholesale or retail level that have been drastically marked down to facilitate quick sale, generally as the result of some financial exigency. See also PROMOTIONAL MERCHANDISE POLICY.

distribution 1. The process of receiving, sorting, storing, allocating, picking, and shipping merchandise. In a broad sense, distribution includes those activities involved in physically transferring goods from the point at which they are produced to the point of their consumption. Functions in the distribution process include transportation, warehousing, wholesaling, and retailing. Distribution may best be understood as the part of the marketing process following production (i.e., those activities taking place after there is a physical product). A retail DISTRIBUTION CENTER (DC) performs the distribution function when it allocates shipments to stores. See also DISTRIBUTOR. 2. Sometimes, at the manufacturing level, includes selling and advertising functions as well as order processing, customer service, and delivery. 3. At retail, the activities involved in transferring goods within a retail organization, from DISTRIBUTION CENTER (DC) to stores, from department to department, and from stockroom to selling floor. See also PHYSICAL DISTRIBUTION (PD) and CHANNEL OF DISTRIBUTION. 4. More generally, marketing. Hence the term DISTRIBUTIVE EDUCATION.

distribution-based alliance In GLOBAL MARKETING, a relationship between firms that falls short of a full-scale merger and is centered on distribution. A company seeking to position its products in a foreign country forms a global alliance with a foreign company, resulting in the formation of a new company equally owned by the two firms. The product knowledge of the first company combined with the distribution network of the second forms a powerful force in the global market. Distribution alliances are also part of international express mail. See also TECHNOLOGY-BASED ALLIANCE, PRODUCTION-BASED ALLIANCE, and STRATEGIC ALLIANCE.

distribution center (DC) A central distribution point, used by most multiunit retailers, where goods are processed and then distributed to the individual stores. Distribution centers perform critical inventory management functions, expedite processing, and work closely with retail buyers. The major functions of the DC are RECEIVING, CHECKING, MARKING AND TICKETING, PUTAWAY, PICKING, DISTRIBUTION, SHIPPING, VENDOR RETURN, and TRAFFIC. Also called a *retail distribution center*. See also MANUFACTURER'S BRANCH OFFICE.

distribution center delivery A method of PHYSICAL DISTRIBUTION in which merchandise shipped from the vendor to the retailer is first received in distribution centers (where it is sorted and allocated) and then shipped to individual stores. Receiving merchandise at a DISTRIBUTION CENTER (DC) permits the retailer to adjust the allocation of merchandise to individual stores based on sales that occur between the preparation of an order and its receipt. See also DROP SHIPMENT.

distribution chain Synonym for CHANNEL OF DISTRIBUTION.

distribution channel Synonym for CHANNEL OF DISTRIBUTION.

distribution cost analysis An analysis of the COSTS incurred, both direct and indirect, in selling a company's products. Such a study is calculated to reveal which salespeople are most productive and which products are most profitable, as well as to gather other data useful for managing the marketing effort.

distribution density The amount of exposure or coverage desired for a product, particularly the number of sales outlets necessary to provide adequate coverage of the entire market.

distribution intensity A measure of the exposure a product actually receives at wholesale or retail. The more outlets, the more intense the distribution.

distribution intensity response function See PLACE-DISTRIBUTION INTENSITY RESPONSE FUNCTION.

distribution intermediary Synonym for MARKETING INTERMEDIARY.

distribution logistics The physical flow of products through the CHANNEL OF DISTRIBUTION.

distribution model A statistical model used by management to select and assess the pros and cons of alternative channels of distribution. The use of a distribution model can also help determine store and warehouse locations and plan the logistics of inventory.

distribution pipeline Synonym for CHANNEL OF DISTRIBUTION.

distribution planning The systematic planning effort calculated to facilitate the storage and transfer of goods as they move from producer to consumer. Distribution planning includes transportation, inventory management, and customer transactions.

distribution standards In customer service, standards of performance with respect to response time, delivery time, accuracy in filling orders, depth of inventory, etc.

distributions to owners According to the Financial Accounting Standards Board (1985), "decreases in net assets of a particular enterprise resulting from transferring assets, rendering services, or incurring liabilities by the enterprise to owners. Distributions to owners decrease ownership interests (or equity) in an enterprise."

distribution strategy The decision to market goods through a particular CHANNEL OF DISTRIBUTION in order to achieve the most economic or cost-effective result.

distribution streamlining The elimination of some channel members for the sake of expediency. For example, goods purchased directly from a producer by a retailer receive less handling and, consequently, spend less time in the distribution pipeline than goods distributed through a wholesaler. The issue is particularly critical in the case of perishable goods, such as food, or goods with a short selling cycle, such as fashion apparel.

distribution structure The totality of all the channels of distribution existing in an industry. See also CHANNEL OF DISTRIBUTION.

distribution system responsiveness In PHYSICAL DISTRIBUTION (PD), the degree to which a system can react to a change in demand. A system is judged responsive if it can increase the flow of products quickly when demand increases.

distribution warehouse Synonym for BREAK-BULK CENTER.

distributive education Training, primarily at the secondary and junior college level, for careers in retailing, wholesaling, and allied trades.

distributor 1. A BUYER specialization frequently found at the corporate merchandising level, where buying may be split into four specialized functions: buying, planning, distribution, and product development. The distributor allocates arriving shipments of merchandise to individual stores based on each store's capacity, current sales trends, and inventory levels. Distributors correct stock imbalances in stores and are a critical link between stores and the corporate merchandising division. See also DISTRIBUTION and ALLOCATORS. 2. A broad, generic term often used synonymously with WHOLESALER and, more specifically, with GENERAL MERCHANDISE WHOLESALER. 3. In some segments of manufacturing, an exclusive sales representative. See also DEALER.

distributor brand A private BRAND that carries the name of the distributor while the actual manufacturer of the product or group of products remains anonymous. See also PRIVATE BRAND.

distributor without a yard See DROP SHIPPER.

district manager In a large retail organization, the individual responsible for a group of stores located within a defined geo-graphic area. The district manager often reports to a REGIONAL MANAGER. See also MULTISTORE RETAILER.

district office See MANUFACTURER'S BRANCH OFFICE.

diversification 1. In retailing, the practice of acquiring or developing stores that are not related to a company's core business in order to gain or reacquire a competitive edge. For example, a department store group may add a specialty chain. Some large-format retailers diversify by opening scaled-down versions of their predominant format in areas too small to support the full-scale store. 2. An organizational growth strategy that involves entering a line of business different from one's current business. This may take a number of forms. A firm may introduce new products into existing markets, existing products into new markets, or new products into new markets. Some diversification is accomplished through mergers and acquisitions. The object of diversification is almost always expansion, with a concurrent increase in profit. It also insulates the company against environmental changes that may affect its existing businesses. Also called *market diversification, product-market diversification,* and *product diversification.* See also HORIZONTAL DIVERSIFICATION, PRODUCT MIX DIVERSIFICATION, and DIVESTITURE, the opposite of diversification. 3. The inclusion of underrepresented groups in an organization's workforce. In particular, retailers may seek to hire employees who more closely reflect their customer base.

diversionary pricing A deceptive retailing practice in which a below-market price on a small number of items is widely promoted to create the impression that all merchandise is comparably priced.

diversion in transit A practice in rail transportation of goods in which their final destination is determined after they have left the shipping point. As long as the route involves no backtracking, the shipper receives the regular CARLOAD FREIGHT RATE (CL) from the railroad. This practice allows producers of goods, especially perishables, to move those goods in the general direction of their markets before a final destination is known.

diverter A third-party WHOLESALER that sells branded products to retail outlets against the wishes of producers. The diverter's activities may serve to diminish the brand's image by making the merchandise available in discount establishments at lower prices.

divest-and-exit strategy Efforts designed to minimize losses by eliminating a product or service line through sale or discontinuation. The strategy may be employed when the item or service fails to meet sales expectations or when overall market growth slows. Also called a *divest strategy.*

divestiture The selling of a business, such as a retail store, by one company to another. Large companies usually sell off parts of their business for economic reasons (i.e., to gain capital or to concentrate on other areas of business), but occasionally on the insistence of the government. Particular targets for divestiture include companies that are underperformers (i.e., unprofitable units or divisions) and companies that are out of character with the parent organization's other holdings. Like DIVERSIFICATION, its opposite, divestiture is a tool retailers use to gain or reacquire a competitive edge.

divest strategy   Synonym for DIVEST-AND-EXIT STRATEGY.

divider   See WALL DIVIDER.

division   In a large store, an administrative unit handling a particular group of retail functions. There are commonly four divisions: merchandising, control, operations, and publicity. Also called a *store division.*

divisional merchandise manager (DMM)   The retail executive responsible for MERCHANDISING activities or for a related group of selling departments or merchandise divisions. The DMM monitors the sales, inventories, and assortments of the departments within the division to ensure consistency with the organization's merchandising and profit objectives. Divisional merchandise managers characteristically report to the GENERAL MERCHANDISE MANAGER (GMM) or the VICE PRESIDENT (VP) OF MERCHANDISING. See also MERCHANDISE MANAGER.

divisional organization   A form of business organization in which employees are grouped according to their organizational output. People with diverse skills and resources are grouped into self-contained teams in order to produce a single product or provide a service to a single client. Decisions are made at the divisional level rather than by the company president. Divisional organization is an alternative to the LINE-AND-STAFF ORGANIZATION model.

divisional sales manager   Synonymous with STORE MERCHANDISE MANAGER.

DIY   See DO-IT-YOURSELF (DIY).

DLC   See DATA LINK CONTROL (DLC).

DMM   See DIVISIONAL MERCHANDISE MANAGER (DMM).

DMU   See DECISION MAKING UNIT (DMU).

DNC   See DO-NOT-CALL (DNC) LISTS.

DNS   See DOMAIN NAME SERVER (DNS) and DOMAIN NAME SYSTEM (DNS).

dock   An area, generally on the side or in back of a store or warehouse, where merchandise is unloaded from trucks or freight cars and moved into the receiving department. Also called a *loading dock* or a *receiving dock.*

dock warrant   Authorization to store imported items in a warehouse until delivery is required. Such warehouses are owned by the dock authority or by a public warehouser.

dodger   See DODGER STRATEGY or FLYER.

dodger strategy   A strategy for smaller, local firms competing with powerful multinationals. A local firm can avoid (i.e., dodge) competition by finding a way to cooperate with its more powerful competitors. For example, the local firm may become a contract manufacturer or a local distributor for the multinational firm. Some dodgers simply sell out to the multinational firm that wishes to acquire them. See also DEFENDER STRATEGY, EXTENDER STRATEGY, and CONTENDER STRATEGY.

dog   (Slang) An unprofitable business unit or product viewed as having little future potential.

DOI   See DATE OF INVOICE (DOI).

do-it-yourself (DIY)   A category of retail businesses that sell home improvement merchandise. Such merchandise is most frequently sold in a full line discount store, a small, privately owned hardware store, online, or at a huge CATEGORY KILLER.

dollar channel   The category comprising all dollar stores.

dollar control   See DOLLAR INVENTORY CONTROL.

dollar format   Synonym for DOLLAR STORE.

dollar inventory control   An inventory information system in which planning is based on the number of dollars invested in goods rather than on the number of units in stock. Sometimes called, simply, *dollar control.*

dollar margin method of pricing   A retail price setting method in which merchandise classifications are assigned a markup percentage on the basis of estimated volume without regard to the profitability of the individual items. For example, a store may mark up an item by a lesser amount if it anticipates very heavy demand, increasing the gross margin significantly.

dollar markdown   The amount of markdown expressed in terms of dollars. For example, if the original retail price of an item is $5 and it is reduced by $1, $1 is the dollar markdown. The new price is $4.

dollar markup   The difference between the cost price of merchandise and its retail price, expressed in dollars. See also MARKUP.

dollar merchandise/merchandising plan   See DOLLAR PLAN.

dollar open-to-buy   The OPEN-TO-BUY (OTB) expressed in terms of dollars. It is traditionally determined by calculating the difference between planned sales and the combination of inventory already owned and merchandise on order. The purpose of dollar open-to-buy is to prevent overinvestment in merchandise.

dollar plan   The SALES PLAN expressed in terms of dollars. Dollar plans are traditionally calculated to show an improvement for the coming accounting period. For example, the dollar plan may set goals of improved sales, increased turnover, improved profit margins, or reduced markdowns.

Dollars allocated to departments or merchandise categories determine the amount of merchandise that can be made available for sale. Also called *dollar merchandise plan* and/or *dollar merchandising plan.*

dollar program   A program launched by a conventional supermarket or discount store designed to compete with dollar stores. See also DOLLAR SECTION.

dollar sales   Sales for the accounting period expressed in dollars rather than in numbers of units sold. Compare UNIT SALES.

dollar section   In a conventional discount store or supermarket, an area used to compete with dollar stores, featuring private label merchandise as well as items typically sold in a DOLLAR STORE.

dollar shopper   Synonym for DOLLAR STORE SHOPPER.

dollars returned   Synonym for NET PROFIT.

dollar store   A BARGAIN STORE offering damaged or irregular goods or manufacturers' closeouts at prices that are about half regular retail. Typical dollar store categories include candy, paper products, detergents, stationery and school supplies, wrapping materials and bags, snacks, household cleaners, laundry supplies, pet food, and batteries & flashlights. Also called a *dollar format.* See also 99 CENT STORE.

dollar store shopper   A customer who shops in a DOLLAR STORE on a regular basis. The classification has seen penetration growth across all income groups, although trip frequency increases as the income level decreases. Dollar store shoppers include the WALK-IN SHOPPER (who lacks transportation); the older shopper (in the 55+ age group); the TREASURE HUNT SHOPPER (who, regardless of income level, is entertained by the experience of looking for bargains); and the QUICK TRIP SHOPPER (who spends less than $25). Also called a *dollar shopper.*

domain   Short for TOP-LEVEL DOMAIN (TLD).

domain name   The middle part of the URL identifying a particular Web site. In its original role, a domain name is a shared name for a group of machines connected to the Internet. While each machine on the Internet has a unique identifying number called an IP ADDRESS, domain names for those machines are easier to remember than long numbers. The domain name ends with a TOP-LEVEL DOMAIN (TLD) which may be .com, .edu, .gov, .net, .info, etc. The SECOND-LEVEL DOMAIN is most important for e-tailers, as it identifies the company to the user. For example, www.fairchildpub.com is the domain name of the publisher of this dictionary. The names and their corresponding numbers, each of which must be registered, are stored on an Internet server called a DOMAIN NAME SERVER (DNS). Most domain name contracts run from one to ten years.

domain-name broker   A speculator who reserves unneeded domain names in hopes of selling them to a high bidder at a later date.

domain name contract   See DOMAIN NAME.

domain name server (DNS)   An Internet server that stores the registered domain names and corresponding IP ADDRESS numbers of companies, government agencies, educational institutions, and other organizations with a presence on the INTERNET.

domain name system (DNS)   A hierarchical order for top and secondary level domains. See also DOMAIN NAME.

domestic   Of goods, manufactured in one's own country as opposed to a foreign country. Not to be confused with DOMESTICS.

domestication   The limiting of certain economic activities to local citizens. This may result in a situation in which foreign businesses are forced by the government of the host country to give up control of their operations. The final step in the domestication process is the outright ownership of the corporation's property by nationals of the host country. See also NATIONALIZATION, EXPROPRIATION, and CONFISCATION.

domestic-based export agent   An independent international MARKETING INTERMEDIARY used in INDIRECT EXPORT. The domestic-based export agent negotiates foreign purchases for the domestic manufacturer and receives compensation in the form of a commission. A TRADING COMPANY is one form of domestic-based export agent.

domestic-based export department/division   In DIRECT EXPORT/EXPORTING, the part of a domestic firm whose activities are directed toward selling goods abroad. This is a self-contained unit of the producer and does not involve the use of an independent international MARKETING INTERMEDIARY. The department may eventually evolve into a division or subsidiary of the producer. Also called a *domestic-based export division.*

domestic-based export merchant   An independent international MARKETING INTERMEDIARY used in INDIRECT EXPORT. The domestic-based export merchant (i.e., based in the same country as the manufacturer) buys the manufacturer's product and sells it abroad.

domestic-based export subsidiary   See DOMESTIC-BASED EXPORT DEPARTMENT/DIVISION.

domestic marketing   Marketing aimed exclusively at the firm's home country. The domestic marketer deals with only one competitive environment and one set of national consumers.

domestic-only orientation   A marketing strategy that focuses on domestic business only and excludes all foreign business, both import and export.

domestic retailer   A retail company that does business only in its home country. The domestic retailer deals with only one competitive environment and one set of national consumers. Compare INTERNATIONAL RETAILER and GLOBAL RETAILER.

domestics Merchandise for the home, including sheets, pillows, towels, blankets, bedspreads, and other textile products. Not to be confused with DOMESTIC.

dominance In VISUAL MERCHANDISING, the element or object that, by its color, size, or position in the composition, attracts the eye first and possibly directs the viewer to other parts of the DISPLAY. Such an element is said to be the *dominant element*.

dominant assortment See CLASSIFICATION DOMINANCE.

dominant element See DOMINANCE.

dominant store The store commanding the largest share of the available business in a retail TRADING AREA.

do-not-call (DNC) lists Lists maintained by various states as well as the federal government to prevent consumers from receiving unwanted direct marketing communications. Consumers place their names on a list indicating that they do not want to be called by telemarketers. The federal list is maintained by the FEDERAL TRADE COMMISSION (FTC). Such a list may also be called a *do-not-call (DNC) registry*.

do-not-call (DNC) registry See DO-NOT-CALL (DNC) LISTS.

do not e-mail list See CAN-SPAM ACT (2004).

do not ship before/after date See SHIPPING DATE.

don't want (Slang) A COD package refused by the customer at the time of delivery.

doors (Slang) In the cosmetic industry, the stores in which a company's product line is offered for sale.

door-to-door retailing Selling directly to ultimate consumers in their own homes, in their offices, or at home sales parties, a sales method originally started in the United States with the Fuller Brush Company. Also called *door-to-door selling* and *direct-to-the-home selling*. See also DIRECT SELLING and SPECIALTY SELLING.

door-to-door salesperson A sales representative who visits homes in an attempt to make direct sales. Also called a *house-to-house salesperson*.

door-to-door selling Synonym for DOOR-TO-DOOR RETAILING.

dormant account A charge account not in active use by the charge customer. Also called an *inactive account*.

DOS See DEPARTMENT OPERATING STATEMENT (DOS).

DOS attacks See DENIAL-OF-SERVICE (DOS) ATTACKS.

dot-com A business with an online component. The popular term is derived from the .com in the URL of a business, indicating the commercial nature of the site.

double opt-in A form of permission given by a visitor to a marketer's Web site, indicating consent to be added to the marketer's e-mail distribution list. Two types of opt-in are involved. The first is standard OPT-IN. The second is a confirmation opt-in to ensure that the visitor is the same person who gave the original permission. It also serves as a reminder and avoids the misperception of spam when the e-mail arrives.

double search Marketplace activity characterized by consumers looking for products they need and producers looking for customers.

double top (Slang) A situation that occurs when a price reaches its high point twice, only to fall back. The likelihood is that the price will continue to fall.

down-aging A lifestyle category characterized by the search for eternal youthfulness. Consumers in this category tend to be BABY BOOMERS. They value retro clothing, furniture, and music, and provide a substantial market for such products as anti-aging cosmetics, hair-replacement products, moisturizers, hair dyes, and dermatological services.

download 1. The process of receiving data from a large computer (such as a server or a mainframe) and transmitting it to a different, usually smaller, computer (such as a personal computer). 2. To carry out this process. Compare UPLOAD.

download status test See UPLOAD/DOWNLOAD STATUS TEST.

down payment Synonym for ADVANCE.

downsizing The act of laying off employees in an attempt to become more profitable.

downstairs store Synonym for BARGAIN BASEMENT.

downstream value Value added to a product moving through the CHANNEL OF DISTRIBUTION from the producer/manufacturer to end users. CHANNEL MEMBERS contribute value-added services at each transfer point in the channel through their specialized knowledge, skills, experience, and contacts.

downtown business/shopping district The central business district (or the center city section) where a large number of stores still operate. Often it is the older, commercial part of the city and sometimes contains the flagship store of a retail chain along with numerous specialty stores. Also called an *urban core*. See also CENTRAL BUSINESS DISTRICT (CBD).

downtown store See FLAGSHIP STORE DIVISION.

downward flow theory A theory of fashion adoption that posits that the more affluent socioeconomic classes are the first to adopt new fashions and that the less affluent middle and lower classes adopt fashion innovations in imitation of the more affluent fashion leaders. This view was clearly set forth by the sociologist Georg Simmel in a 1904 paper entitled "Fashion." Also called *trickle-down theory* and *vertical fashion trend*.

DPI (disposable personal income)   See DISPOSABLE PERSONAL INCOME (DPI).

DPP   See DIRECT PRODUCT PROFITABILITY (DPP).

Dr.   In accounting, a commonly used abbreviation for DEBIT.

draft   A written order from a creditor to a debtor to pay an amount of money to a third party (a payee). In domestic transactions, a draft is synonymous with *bill of exchange.*

dramatic approach   A SALES APPROACH in which the salesperson presents an eye-opening demonstration of how the product or service works. Often the prospect is involved in the demonstration.

draper   A shaped hanger set atop a vertical rod that is supported by a base. The draper is a simple, uncomplicated alternative to the mannequin for displaying apparel. In recent years drapers have become increasingly sophisticated and widely used, available in wood, metal, plastic, and assorted combinations of the three. Drapers are selected to further a particular look or lifestyle.

draw   The ability of an activity, such as a store promotion, to attract customers.

drawing account   An account from which employees working on commission are permitted to withdraw money at regular intervals as an advance against future commissions. See also GUARANTEED DRAW.

drayage   Synonym for CARTAGE.

dress   1. General term for a one-piece garment composed of a top and a skirt. In Western history, dresses are worn primarily by women.   2. Synonym for APPAREL.   3. To put apparel on oneself, a mannequin, or another person.

dress code   A set of rules, either formal or informal, delineating what is regarded by management as appropriate attire for store employees. Also called *dress regulations.*

dressdown trend   A fashion movement toward the wearing of more casual attire in the workplace. The trend, which began with "Casual Fridays," was prevalent in the 1990s. Dressing down quickly spread to the rest of the workweek in many workplace environments. This style is also known as *corporate casual.*

dress form   An armless version of the three-quarter form.

dressmaker   See DRESSMAKING.

dressmaking   The work of making clothing for individual private customers, as opposed to READY-TO-WEAR (RTW). The person who performs this work, usually a woman, is also called a *dressmaker* or a *seamstress.* See also TAILOR.

dress regulations   Synonym for DRESS CODE.

drill-down   In accessing an Internet site, the act of moving from the front page through successive pages on the site to the page where the task (e.g., a purchase) is completed. Since excessive drill-down can drive off prospective customers who become bored or frustrated, e-tailers test their sites with this in mind. Testing and analysis can identify appropriate click-reduction strategies.

drip-dry fabrics   See DURABLE PRESS.

drive   In psychology (and hence in consumer research), a strong stimulus from within a person that necessitates action. For example, an individual may have a drive to succeed in a professional career. When such a drive is directed toward a particular object that will help realize (and hence reduce) the drive, it becomes a MOTIVE. Thus, the same individual may attend college and select a particular major in order to achieve success: the drive to succeed has now become the individual's motive to attend college. Marketers investigate the drives that motivate customers in order to determine how their products may be used to help realize these drives and how best to promote their products to the customer. Thus, in the same example, an apparel manufacturer may emphasize "dressing for success" as a way of marketing clothing to the success-driven consumer.

drive aisle   In a big box store or superstore, any of the main aisles that lead and direct shoppers. Visual displays of the merchandise located in the section are often located on the drive aisles.

drive-in market   Synonym for CONVENIENCE STORE.

drive stimulus   A sales promotion conducted throughout an advertising campaign, encouraging retailers or other prospective customers to purchase the advertised product or service.

drive time   The time of day when most people are going to and from work, generally 7 a.m. to 8:30 a.m. and 4:30 p.m. to 6:00 p.m. In radio advertising, higher rates are charged for these hours, as peak audiences can be expected to be reached while commuting. See also PRIME TIME.

drop shipment   1. Merchandise delivered by a vendor to individual branch stores rather than to a central WAREHOUSE or other intermediate location. Also called *direct shipment, direct shipment delivery,* and *store door delivery.*   2. Ordered merchandise delivered by a vendor to a consumer instead of to the store where the consumer placed the order. Often shortened to *drop.*

drop shipment wholesaler   See DROP SHIPPER.

drop shipper   A WHOLESALER who, although taking title to the goods being sold, never actually possesses them. The drop shipper, also called a *desk jobber, direct-mail shipper, parlor shipper,* or *distributor without a yard,* receives orders from retailers, sees that the goods are shipped directly from the manufacturer to the retailer, extends credit, and bills the buyer. See also JOBBER.

druggist   Synonym for PHARMACIST.

Drug Listing Act (1972)   U.S. federal legislation giving the FOOD AND DRUG ADMINISTRATION (FDA) access to information on drug manufacturers so as to protect consumers. The act amended the FOOD, DRUG, AND COSMETIC ACT (1938) by requiring firms that engage in the manufacture, preparation, propagation, compounding, or processing of drugs to register their establishments and to list all their commercially marketed drug products with the FDA.

drug store   Traditionally, a drug store (also called a PHARMACY) is a retail store where drugs and medicines are prepared and dispensed according to a physician's written prescription. Over the years, however, drug stores have increasingly expanded their product mix to include over-the-counter (OTC) drugs, health and beauty aids, and related items and several major *drug store chains* have taken over the bulk of the drug store business. In addition, some department stores, proprietary stores, and supermarkets have added pharmacy departments in which licensed pharmacists fulfill the traditional functions of their profession. Also spelled *drugstore*. See also DRUG STORE CHAIN and PROPRIETARY STORE.

drug store chain   Large regional or national chain stores fulfilling all the requirements of a traditional DRUG STORE (i.e., filling prescriptions for drugs) while adding over-the-counter (OTC) drugs, health and beauty aids, and related items such as packaged food, film and developing services, pet and baby needs, paper goods, sewing needs, seasonal items, greeting cards, and magazines.

drug testing   See EMPLOYEE DRUG TESTING.

drumming   (Slang) The practice, on the part of SOFT GOODS salespersons, of calling on retailers at their stores or meeting with them at buying centers.

dry goods   Older term for SOFT GOODS.

DSL (connection)   See DIGITAL SUBSCRIBER LINE (DSL).

DSS   See DECISION SUPPORT SYSTEM (DSS).

dual adaptation   A strategy employed in international marketing in which the product offered for export is different from the domestic product. The product is also promoted differently in the foreign market. See also ADAPTATION POLICY.

dual billing and posting   The accounting practice of posting a customer's purchases to ledger independently from the preparation of a bill for the customer.

dual channels of distribution   Synonym for DUAL DISTRIBUTION.

dual-country marketing   Synonym for EXPORT MARKETING.

dual distribution   The use of more than one CHANNEL OF DISTRIBUTION to reach customers at different levels of the marketplace. For example, a manufacturer may sell to large retailers directly, but to smaller retailers through a wholesaler. The manufacturer may also sell through its own retail outlets while at the same time selling through other retailers or on the INTERNET. CHANNEL CONFLICT and CHANNEL CANNIBALIZATION may arise when more than one channel is used to reach the same MARKET SEGMENT. Also called *dual channels of distribution, multiple channel, multiple distribution,* and *multichannel marketing system.* See also MULTICHANNEL RETAILING, VERTICAL INTEGRATION, and DUAL MARKETING.

dual marketing   The practice of selling the same or similar products to both individual consumers and industrial or institutional customers. For example, automobile manufacturers sell cars to individuals through franchised dealers (i.e., retailers) while at the same time selling fleets of cars to automobile rental firms. See also DUAL DISTRIBUTION.

dual merchandising   The practice of selling another firm's products along with one's own.

dual offer   A SALES PROMOTION technique in which customers are offered a choice of two alternative special offers. The offer is designed to enhance the perceived value of the items.

dual pricing   The practice of including both the unit price and the price per package on an item of merchandise. For example, a quart of blueberries may display both a price per pound and a price for the package in hand. See also UNIT PRICING.

dual target market   In nonprofit marketing, the market in which nonbusiness organizations are seen as functioning, consisting of two distinct groups: on the one hand such organizations have to address the sources of their funds (e.g., donors, government agencies, organized charities, etc.) and on the other hand they must provide for their clients and other recipients of their services.

dud   (Slang) A slow-selling item of merchandise.

due bill   See CREDIT SLIP.

due diligence   The in-depth evaluation of financial and other considerations preparatory to a merger or acquisition. Attention must also be paid to locations, leasing arrangements, the competition, etc.

dummy invoice   A statement prepared by the retailer as a temporary replacement for a missing vendor's invoice when the shipped goods are to be received, marked, and put into inventory.

dump bin/display   An enclosed space or container in which merchandise is piled without any formal arrangement, generally to project a bargain image. Unlike a jumble display, the dump bin generally contains only one type of merchandise. A table may be used instead of a bin, in which case the display may be called a *dump display*.

dumping   Price discrimination in international trade resulting in the sale of like goods at different prices in the home market and in one or more foreign markets. Dumping occurs when goods are sold in a foreign market at a price that does not cover production costs or that is below the price charged in the home market. For example, a producer might sell a product in a foreign market at a predatory price level and make up the difference through profits on sales at a higher price in the home market. Dumping is a strategy sometimes employed by exporting firms to capture a foreign market and is viewed as a threat by domestic producers of the same or substitutable products. Most governments have adopted regulations against dumping, as recognized under provisions of the World Trade Organization (WTO). Sometimes called *unloading*. See also ANTIDUMPING TARIFF and NONDUMPING CERTIFICATE.

dun   To persistently demand payment of a delinquent account.

dunnage   Loose material, often lumber, packed around cargo on trucks, railroad cars, ships, etc., to protect it from damage in transit.

duplicated media audience   Those individuals exposed to an advertising message more than once. Marketers and advertisers are interested in knowing the number of individuals and households that have been exposed to their advertising for the first time. Duplicates, therefore, are eliminated whenever possible. See also REACH.

durability   The ability of an item to withstand frequent and sustained use.

durable goods/merchandise   Tangible capital or consumer goods having a relatively long useful life (sometimes arbitrarily set at three years).

durable press   A special finish for garments that enhances shape retention and wrinkle resistance during use and after laundering. Some of the first fabrics that did not require ironing were called *drip-dry fabrics*. Also called *wash and wear*.

durables   See DURABLE GOODS/MERCHANDISE.

during-the-period trend analysis   The retailer's systematic review of the merchandise plan during the current selling period (e.g., every four weeks), with subsequent modifications made as needed. The during-the-period trend analysis helps retailers identify fast and slow sellers and is also used to plan the corresponding selling period in the following year. See also TREND ANALYSIS and END-OF-PERIOD TREND ANALYSIS.

Dutch auction   An auction sale in which the price of the item is continually lowered until a bidder responds favorably and bids. See also AUCTION and ONLINE AUCTION.

duty   Short for CUSTOMS DUTY.

duty classification   Part of the process used to apply taxes and duties to imported goods.

duty-free   Items of merchandise brought into the country that are not affected by customs duty and are, therefore, sold at a lower price. *Duty-free shops*, limited to shoppers about to leave the country, are found in international airports. See also CUSTOMS BONDED WAREHOUSE.

duty-free shop   See DUTY-FREE.

dyad   See BUYER-SELLER DYAD.

dye lot   Large quantities of yarn, dyed together in the same vat, and generally assigned a d*ye lot number* to ensure a perfect match. Also called a LOT.

dye lot number   See DYE LOT.

dynamically continuous innovation   The development of products that are either completely new or substantially altered versions of existing products. Innovation of this type is generally attributable to changes in the lifestyles and expectations of consumers, and may bring with it considerable disruption in consumption patterns.

dynamic database   See DYNAMIC WEB PAGE.

dynamic pricing   1. In Internet marketing, price changes made online, in real time, based on demand and product inventory level. The price changes can be made as visitors shop the site and may be triggered by changing levels of inventory. 2. In BRICKS-AND-MORTAR stores, the use of RADIO FREQUENCY IDENTIFICATION (RFID) to update prices of items each night in response to real-time fluctuations of supply and demand.

dynamic Web page   A Web page providing personalized content that changes with each visitor and reflects that customer's reason for visiting the site. *Dynamic databases,* used with such sites, are the source of the personalized content.

EAP See EMPLOYEE ASSISTANCE PROGRAM (EAP).

early acceptors See INNOVATORS.

early adopters In the adoption and diffusion process, those consumers who are generally among the first to purchase a new product. Early adopters are not quite innovators, but anxious to keep up with the latest trends and fashions. Also called *fast followers* and *fashion specialists.*

early followers See EARLY MAJORITY.

early majority In the adoption and diffusion process, those consumers in the mass market who have relatively high social status and are receptive to innovation. The early majority adopts new products and services at an above-average rate, but after the innovators and early adopters. Also know as *early followers.*

early markdown A reduction in the selling price of goods, taken early in the season while demand is still relatively strong.

Early Write A program used by some vendors to check the accuracy of sales forecasts. A select group of customers (i.e., retail buyers representing about 20 percent of sales) is invited to place orders a month earlier than everyone else, and these orders are used to reevaluate the accuracy of the firm's sales forecasts and the salability of products and styles. Early Write participants receive, in exchange for their cooperation, earlier shipments than other retail buyers.

earmuff problem A situation in which the salesperson becomes so involved in monopolizing a customer's interest that incoming communications from the customer are missed. See also SALES APPROACH.

earnings Money made by a business enterprise. The term may denote either INCOME or PROFIT.

earnings per share A measure of how much profit a company earns for each share of stock outstanding. As such it is an indicator of the company's ability to grow and pay dividends. Earnings per share is the financial ratio that results from dividing the company's net income during the accounting period by the average number of shares of common stock outstanding during the same period.

earnings per share of common stock The financial ratio derived by subtracting the preferred stock dividends from the company's net income and dividing the difference by the average number of common shares outstanding during the accounting period.

EAS See ELECTRONIC ARTICLE SURVEILLANCE (EAS).

easel An adjustable folding frame or tripod (such as those used by artists to hold paintings) used in VISUAL MERCHANDISING. Small easels may be used to hold a price card or message. Larger easels are designed specifically to hold a shirt and tie. An artist's easel may also be used; these are capable of holding a fully accessorized outfit.

easement agreement An agreement that allows limited use of land owned by someone else. For example, an easement agreement may limit parking to certain areas or specify infrastructure improvements. For example, a local government may have an easement agreement with store owners that gives utility workers access to sewers and electric lines on their property.

EBI See EFFECTIVE BUYING INCOME (EBI).

EBPP See ELECTRONIC BILL PRESENTMENT AND PAYMENT (EBPP).

e-Branding Index A branding benchmark, consisting solely of Internet companies, to measure the effectiveness of the branding efforts of those companies. The success and strength of a cyberbrand is determined by measuring its familiarity to decision makers (vice-presidents or higher) in the top 20 percent of U.S. companies. The e-Branding Index, introduced in 2000, is a composite of the *Corporate Brand Power* scores of top clicks-only companies and a product of *Corporate Branding, LLC.*

e-business See E-COMMERCE.

e-cash card Short for ELECTRONIC CASH CARD.

eccentric shopper An individual who shops compulsively, but never buys. Eccentric shoppers visit retail stores regularly and often become known to the sales associates. The sales associates eventually learn that the eccentric shopper is not likely to make a purchase.

echo boomers   Children of the BABY BOOMERS who represent a new peak in the demographic curve. Echo boomers, born in the late 1970s and early 1980s, began reaching adulthood in the 1990s and represent a major market for goods and services. They are known for their desire to be team players (as opposed to individual achievers) and their interest in building systems rather than tearing them down (as did their parents, the BABY BOOMERS). Echo boomers were the first generation to grow up with home computers and are therefore extremely computer savvy. They are also characterized by having been brought up in programmed or scheduled group activities such as day care centers and after-school activities. All of these factors continue to shape the way echo boomers think, act, and shop. Also called *millennials*. See also GENERATION Y.

ECML   See ELECTRONIC COMMERCE MODELING LANGUAGE (ECML).

ECOA   See EQUAL CREDIT OPPORTUNITY ACT (ECOA) (1975).

e-commerce   Business activities conducted online on the INTERNET, WORLD WIDE WEB (WWW), and other networked electronic systems. Also known as *e-business*, *Web commerce*, *electronic commerce*, and E-TAILING. See also M-COMMERCE.

econometric analysis   In causal research, the attempt to project sales or other activities by constructing a mathematical model of economic factors and simulating a future outcome. The model uses two or more regression or similar analyses to simulate future events on the basis of past relationships. See also ECONOMETRICS.

econometrics   The study of economic measures, utilizing mathematical and statistical models to solve problems, verify existing theories, and develop new theories in economics. See also ECONOMETRIC ANALYSIS.

economical shopper   A consumer who is particularly sensitive to price, quality, and merchandise assortment and shops for the best values available. Compare PERSONALIZING SHOPPER, APATHETIC SHOPPER, and ETHICAL SHOPPER.

Economic and Monetary Union (EMU)   The system set up by the Maastricht Treaty (1992) to facilitate the adoption and use of the EURO for participating members of the EUROPEAN UNION (EU).

economic approach to pricing   An overall economic strategy in which price levels are viewed as being determined by the interaction between SUPPLY AND DEMAND in the MARKETPLACE.

economic base   The industry or industries that serve as the source of income for the residents of a store's TRADING AREA.

economic base analysis   A study of the economic health and growth potential of a TRADING AREA by examining the industry or industries on which local residents depend for their income.

Economic Census   In the United States, a report on economic activity prepared every five years by the Census Bureau. It provides economic and business data from the local level to the overall national level, collected by means of questionnaires sent out to millions of businesses nationwide. The material is analyzed and made available in print and on the INTERNET in a variety of formats based on industry or geographic region. The U.S. Census Bureau maintains a Web site at www.census.gov.

economic climate   The combined effects of economic forces such as the profit motive, scarcity and opportunity costs, competition, supply and demand, circular flow, and the multiplier effect, which reasonably predict the economic life of a society and either encourage or discourage business.

economic community   Any organization of nations formed to remove barriers to trade among their members and establish uniform barriers to trade with nonmember nations. Also called a *free trade association*.

economic concept of rent   A principle used to determine the maximum allowable rent expenditure by a retailer. It involves a formula subtracting all other projected operating expenses (i.e., nonrent) and a planned profit figure from projected sales. Also called *economic rent*.

economic emulation stage   The third stage in the FASHION LIFE CYCLE, in which many consumers desire the fashion in question and manufacturers mass-produce the product at low cost. This continues until the market passes through the growth and maturity stages and rapidly moves into decline. Also called the *regression stage*.

economic environment   The interaction of all phases of the economy in which a retailer or other marketer conducts business. Such factors as national income, economic growth, recession, inflation, and economic depression must be taken into account by retailers and marketers, since they affect the success or failure of a firm's marketing strategy. For example, during a period of recession (i.e., rapid business decline), customers curtail their purchases or stop buying a product completely. This will cause the marketing strategy to fail no matter how well-planned it may be. Similarly, the shortage of certain natural resources will affect the manner in which the marketer conducts business; for example, an energy crisis will cause consumers to seek out and purchase more fuel-efficient automobiles or use their automobiles less for trips to shopping malls and other retail establishments. The availability of the natural resources or raw materials needed in the manufacture of a product will also affect the marketer. During World War II, for example, when available silk was needed to produce parachutes, hosiery manufacturers were forced to switch to nylon for women's stockings. See also TECHNOLOGICAL ENVIRONMENT.

economic forces   Conditions in a society that affect business. Free enterprise is affected by such factors as the profit motive, scarcity and opportunity costs, competition, and supply and demand.

economic forecasting   The process of predicting the effects, on specific industries, of certain changes in the national and international business climate. For example, changes in the GROSS NATIONAL PRODUCT (GNP) are said to affect changes in

U.S. automobile sales: when the GNP increases (indicating prosperity), auto sales rise accordingly. Commonly used predictors or indicators are the GNP, the unemployment rate, the increase (or decrease) in average weekly hours worked, the increase (or decrease) in the employment cost per person-hour, gross private domestic investment, corporate profits, housing starts, interest rates, disposable personal income, consumer price indexes, retail sales, etc. These indicators are compiled and published in the United States both by the government and by outside organizations such as banks, brokerage houses, and universities. Economic forecasting may be used to predict impending changes in the demand for both consumer and industrial goods. See also FORECASTING, SALES FORECASTING, TREND EXTENSION, and FASHION FORECASTING.

economic infrastructure See INFRASTRUCTURE.

economic life The period of time over which the benefits of an ASSET are expected to be received. For example, the economic life of a piece of machinery used in the production of consumer goods may be five years (i.e., until the machinery must be replaced).

economic lot technique A method used to determine the optimum amount of an item that should be made or sold at one time in order to minimize the total costs involved.

economic man theory A view of consumer behavior postulating price as the primary motivating factor for consumer purchase decisions. The theory maintains that people compare choices in terms of cost and value received in an attempt to maximize their satisfaction. See also MOTIVE.

economic needs Those customer needs concerned with making the best use of limited resources (from the customer's own point of view). These needs include convenience of product use, efficiency of product operation or use, dependability of the product, reliability of service, durability, improvement of earnings, improvement of productivity of property, and economy of purchase or use. Economic needs govern how and why customers select certain product features over others. See also MOTIVE.

economic order quantity (EOQ) The optimum size of an order, calculated to minimize carrying and procurement costs, especially the cost of frequent re-ordering, while maintaining sufficient quantities to meet the average level of demand. An EOQ model is the technique used to balance the costs of holding inventory against the cost involved in placing orders. Also called *economic ordering quantity* and *optimal lot size*.

economic order quantity model See ECONOMIC ORDER QUANTITY (EOQ).

economic rent See ECONOMIC CONCEPT OF RENT.

economics The study of the production, distribution, and consumption of the goods and services that constitute a society's wealth.

economic system The manner in which an economy is organized to utilize scarce resources to produce goods and services and distribute them for consumption. The economic system of any given society will reflect that society's goals and the nature of its political institutions. Nevertheless, all economic systems must develop some method of deciding what and how much is to be produced and distributed as well as by whom, when, and to whom. In planned economic systems, such as SOCIALISM and COMMUNISM, government planners make these decisions. In a MARKET-DIRECTED ECONOMIC SYSTEM such as CAPITALISM, the individual choices of producers and consumers make these decisions for the economy as a whole. In a pure market-directed economy, also known as a FREE MARKET ECONOMY, consumers determine a society's production by their choices in the marketplace without government intervention of any kind.

economies of scale 1. In retailing, lowered costs per unit resulting from an increase in the number of units purchased. Savings may also result from an increase in the size of the operation itself. 2. In manufacturing, cost reductions and other operating advantages accruing from efficient, large-scale production. Such economies are generally reflected in lower unit prices. Lower costs per unit increase profitability. Compare DISECONOMIES OF SCALE, its opposite.

economies of scope In manufacturing, cost reductions and other operating advantages accruing from the use of the same equipment and distribution channels for a variety of products.

economy 1. Thrifty management in the expenditure or consumption of money. 2. The management of the resources of a community or country, etc., particularly regarding budgetary and productivity issues. See also ECONOMIC SYSTEM.

economy pack Several units of the same product, wrapped together and sold at a lower price than if each were sold separately, to provide a saving to the consumer. For example, an economy pack of toilet tissue may include six rolls packaged together in a clear plastic wrapper. The economy pack most often comes directly from the producer, but marketing intermediaries sometimes repackage merchandise to create an economy pack.

economy size A large quantity of a product, such as laundry detergent, sold in a single package to provide the consumer with lower per unit (e.g., per ounce) costs. Also called *jumbo economy size*.

economy size factory pack See BANDED PACK.

ecopsychology See SIMPLIFIED LIFESTYLE.

eco-retailing The sale of environment-friendly products at retail.

e-coupon See ELECTRONIC COUPON.

ECR See POINT-OF-SALE TERMINAL (POST).

e-CRM   See ELECTRONIC CUSTOMER RELATIONSHIP MANAGEMENT (E-CRM).

edge city   See MINIMETROPOLIS.

edge of downtown site   A store location in an unplanned cluster of business-associated stores situated at the outer perimeter of the DOWNTOWN BUSINESS/SHOPPING DISTRICT.

EDI   See ELECTRONIC DATA INTERCHANGE (EDI).

editing   In the analysis of data for MARKETING RESEARCH (MR), the process of checking the collected information for omissions, errors, irrelevancies, outriders, etc., before coding it.

editorial calendar   The monthly plan for the editorial content of a (fashion) magazine. It is of great interest to potential advertisers in the planning of their ad campaigns.

editorial credit   A listing, as a service for readers, of retail sources for merchandise featured in a magazine or newspaper. In addition to stores, editorial credit may include the names of designers and suppliers of items featured in the publicity.

EDLP   See EVERYDAY LOW PRICING (EDLP).

EDM   See ELECTRONIC DIRECT MARKETING (EDM).

EDP   See ELECTRONIC DATA PROCESSING (EDP).

EEOC   See EQUAL EMPLOYMENT OPPORTUNITY COMMISSION (EEOC).

effective buying income (EBI)   A measurement developed by *Sales & Marketing Management (S&MM)* magazine that is roughly the equivalent of DISPOSABLE INCOME calculated for residents of a geographic area. EBI represents wages, salaries and other income (such as rent) less federal, state, and local taxes and other deductions such as insurance premiums, pension contributions, etc. Totaled for the population of an area, it is a measurement of market potential and is viewed as most effective when employed in making generalizations about a market's capacity to buy. See also BUYING POWER INDEX (BPI).

effective demand   The condition in which buyers can actually fulfill their needs. See also DEMAND.

effective rate of protection   A measure of the impact of trade protection, equal to the annual percentage of domestic prices of items that can be attributed to tariffs. The tariffs raise the cost of imported merchandise to consumers in order to dissuade them from buying.

effort scale   In consumer behavior research, an attempt to represent graphically the amount of time and effort consumers are prepared to expend in SHOPPING for a particular product.

EFT   See ELECTRONIC FUNDS TRANSFER (EFT).

ego-bolstering drive   In consumer motivation research, a psychological buying MOTIVE characterized by the need to enhance one's personality, prestige, and self-image while avoiding ridicule. See also PSYCHOLOGICAL (BUYING) MOTIVE.

ego-involved product/item   Merchandise to which consumers attach emotional or psychological significance. For example, the kind of automobile one drives may be seen as a way to enhance one's self-image.

egoistic need   The need to enhance one's own self-esteem or sense of personal worth, equivalent to the fourth level in MASLOW'S HIERARCHY (OF NEEDS).

egonomics   A lifestyle trend in which consumers seek escape from what they perceive to be a sterile, high-tech era by indulging in products that encourage individuality and personal expression. Tattoo parlors and eclectic choices of apparel and home furnishings reflect this trend.

e-group   Synonym for CYBER GROUP.

eight hundred number (800 number)   A *toll-free telephone number* created to facilitate shopping by telephone. The company pays for the service so that customers need not make long-distance calls to order a product or service.

eighty-twenty (80–20) principle   1. A rule of thumb stating that approximately 80% of a firm's business is generated by approximately 20% of its customers.   2. Also used to imply that approximately 80% of a store's business is generated by 20% of its merchandise. Also called the *Pareto Principle*.

EKB model   See ENGEL-KOLLAT-BLACKWELL (EKB) MODEL.

elastic demand   See ELASTICITY OF DEMAND.

elasticity   The adaptability of a market and its ability to respond to a change in price. Elasticity is calculated as the percent change in the quantity demanded divided by the percent change in price. See also ELASTICITY OF DEMAND and ELASTICITY OF SUPPLY.

elasticity method   A system in which the firm's advertising appropriation is based on SUPPLY AND DEMAND curves. The ratio of the average cost of any additional expenditure is compared with the average return in the form of increased profit, indicating the point beyond which additional advertising is uneconomic.

elasticity of demand   A concept that relates quantities of goods sold to changes in price. Normally, demand for goods will vary inversely with price, other factors remaining constant. For example, if a 1% decrease in price produces an increase in demand of less than 1%, demand is said to be inelastic. Conversely, if a 1% decrease in price produces an increase in demand of more than 1%, then demand is said to be elastic. If a 1% decrease in price produces an increase in demand of exactly 1%, a condition of unitary elasticity is said to exist. Also called *price elasticity of demand* or *price-demand elasticity*. See also COEFFICIENT OF ELASTICITY and PRICE SENSITIVITY. Compare INELASTICITY OF DEMAND.

elasticity of expectations   The ratio of a future expected percent change in price to a recent percent change in price.

elasticity of supply   The relationship between the supply of goods and their market price. As the price of goods increases, producers are inclined to respond by producing more, thus increasing the supply in the marketplace. If, on the other hand, supply does not respond to an increase in price, it is regarded as inelastic. Also called *elastic supply* and/or *price elasticity of supply*.

elastic supply   See ELASTICITY OF SUPPLY.

electrodermal response   Synonym for GALVANIC SKIN RESPONSE (GSR).

electronic article surveillance (EAS)   A method used by retailers to combat shoplifting. Plastic-enclosed electronic tags are affixed to merchandise and must be removed or deactivated with special devices by a salesperson after purchase. If the tag is not removed, sensors near the store's exit trigger an alarm. The sensors may be hidden in vases, pedestals, or even in mannequins. See also RADIO FREQUENCY IDENTIFICATION (RFID).

electronic banking   The use of AUTOMATIC TELLER MACHINES (ATMS) and the instant processing of retail purchases through a variety of technologies including ELECTRONIC FUNDS TRANSFER (EFT) and the DEBIT CARD.

electronic banking network   Synonym for ELECTRONIC FUNDS TRANSFER SYSTEM.

electronic bill presentment and payment (EBPP)   The process by which companies bill customers and receive payments electronically over the INTERNET. There are two EBPP models currently in use. In the *direct model*, the merchant delivers the bill to customers by means of its own Web site or a third party's site. In the *consolidator model*, bills from multiple merchants are delivered to a single Web site and presented in aggregate to the customer for viewing and payment.

electronic box   A form of INTERACTIVE TELEVISION (ITV) in which the system stores information at the television set and allows viewers to choose programs from a box in their home. The system operates in much the same way as a VCR.

electronic cash card   A SMART CARD that can load and hold cash values in any currency via an ATM or the telephone. Also called an *e-cash card*.

electronic cash register (ECR)   See POINT-OF-SALE TERMINAL (POST).

electronic catalog   Pictures of merchandise shown on a television monitor or computer screen on a preset basis. The monitors can be scattered about the store, placed in public buildings, or displayed in shopping malls. Catalogs may even be broadcast on the consumer's own television set. Some electronic catalogs, such as those sometimes used in a BRIDAL REGISTRY, are interactive, permitting viewers to select merchandise electronically. Others, however, remain noninteractive, requiring the use of another means to respond, such as calling in on a telephone. E-tailers generally maintain interactive electronic catalogs on their Web sites, allowing Internet users to browse their merchandise by category, brand, size range, etc. Some e-tailers who also produce a print CATALOG provide an area on their Web page in which the customer can enter the catalog item number and go directly to the desired item. Online electronic catalogs often allow the customer to add items to an electronic shopping cart as they are selected. When the customer is finished shopping, the merchandise may be paid for instantaneously by credit card.

electronic commerce   See E-COMMERCE.

electronic commerce modeling language (ECML)   A universal, open standard for the exchange of payment and order information between a customer's DIGITAL WALLET and merchant Web sites.

electronic coupon   Electronic coupons, introduced to the online environment in 1995, are distributed to consumers in several ways, including coupon sites established specifically for that purpose. The coupons are otherwise used identically to the way conventional coupons are used. The Internet is a cost-effective means of getting coupons into the hands of customers. However, the practice has the potential to result in counterfeiting, misuse, and fraud. Collecting e-mail addresses at site registrations provides marketers with lists of current users who can be targeted with site-specific mailings, so that companies can send shoppers the coupons and promotions they are likely to use. Like conventional coupons, electronic coupons may be issued for products available at a range of stores or for use restricted to particular stores. Some e-tailers use coupons for online purchases only, to encourage the use of their Web sites. Other e-tailers distribute coupons through PDAs and other wireless devices. Also called an *e-coupon* and an *Internet coupon*.

electronic customer relationship management (e-CRM)   The customizing and personalizing of a Web site's content for individual visitors. It is a broad strategy that uses a Web-analytical approach to operationalize customer data gleaned primarily from the Web. E-CRM is a five-stage process of identifying customers, segmenting them by their needs and interests, interacting with them effectively, customizing the marketing offer made to them, and continually updating information about them to make the process even more targeted and effective. It is based on the belief that all customers need not be treated identically. Its goal is to anticipate, understand, and respond to current and potential customer needs. Also called *analytical CRM*. See also CUSTOMER RELATIONSHIP MANAGEMENT (CRM) and DYNAMIC WEB PAGE.

electronic data exchange   Synonym for ELECTRONIC DATA INTERCHANGE (EDI).

electronic data interchange (EDI)   1. The transfer of data between companies using networks such as the INTERNET. EDI transactions on the Internet are increasingly important as a way for companies to buy, sell, and trade information.   2. An early EDI network used by pre-Internet companies to speed supply chain transactions. Pre-Internet EDI was able to process applications, inquiries, acknowledgments, purchasing, and other transactions electronically, but was far less flexible and efficient than the Internet. Pre-Internet EDI systems were often proprietary and hence incompatible with any firms not part of the system. They were also limited in their capacity, not interactive, and asynchronous; potentially lengthy delays between a call and a response were commonplace. However, EDI did provide retailers with several positive outcomes, including improved in-stock position, better inventory management, shortened lead time, greater efficiency, and increased profitability. The move to Internet-based systems has made the EDI even more efficient and responsive. The computer language supporting inventory control and business-to-business functions is moving rapidly from EDI to EXTENSIBLE MARKUP LANGUAGE (XML). See also VOLUNTARY INTERINDUSTRY COMMERCE STANDARD (VICS EDI).

electronic data processing (EDP) The use of computers and other automated equipment to process, classify, interpret, and report information. May be used by retailers in billing, bookkeeping, and in the preparation of reports.

electronic detection device An electronic tag attached to merchandise that, if not properly removed at the point of sale, will trigger an alarm as the customer leaves the store. See also ELECTRONIC ARTICLE SURVEILLANCE (EAS).

electronic direct marketing (EDM) An interactive system, such as two-way cable television, in which the concept of DIRECT MARKETING is combined with the electronic media (i.e., television, radio, telephone, and the Internet). For example, the customer can see items displayed on Home Shopping Network (HSN) and place an order using either the telephone or the HSN home page on the Web. EDM is calculated to elicit a direct response on the part of potential customers. See also TELEMARKETING and ELECTRONIC RETAILING.

electronic funds transfer (EFT) In retailing, the use of automated electronic equipment (such as computer terminals) to move money directly from the customer's account to the retailer's, either at the point-of-sale or in the payment of the customer's charge account invoice. EFT may also be used to speedily obtain credit authorization, verify checks, approve credit card transactions, etc.

electronic funds transfer system A computerized banking network that brings branch banking to the customer in the retail store and allows money to be transferred from the customer's account to the retailer's automatically. Electronic funds transfer systems process financial transactions, exchanges, and/or information. Also called an *electronic banking network*.

electronic kiosk A small display unit in a store or other location, using a computer to generate sales or provide extended customer services. Electronic kiosks require little space and can be located wherever people are in transit, shopping, or seeking services—even at odd hours when the store is closed. Some are used for selling such products as CDs and flowers without human intervention. Information kiosks give customers highlights of the store or local area, directions to local destinations, and, sometimes, Internet access. Some innovative electronic kiosks enable customers to create their own greeting cards,

enlarge their own photographs, make prints from digital photographs, access home improvement suggestions, or find the department in the store in which the product they seek is located. Internet electronic kiosks are also called *public access Internet terminals* and, simply, *kiosks*. See also KIOSK BROWSER.

electronic mail See E-MAIL.

electronic marketing The gathering of consumer purchase data by computers for use in marketing, retailing, and sales promotion activities. Supermarkets and other retail stores issue computer-readable loyalty cards to consumers, offer discounts for loyalty card users, and use the data they collect at the POINT-OF-PURCHASE (POP) to record product purchases.

electronic media See MEDIA.

electronic point-of-sale systems See POINT-OF-SALE TERMINAL (POST).

electronic products See DIGITAL PRODUCTS.

electronic retailing An early umbrella term used to describe a range of computerized retailing operations (now mostly subsumed under the E-TAILING or Internet marketing categories), all of which refer to the use of electronically transmitted information to facilitate consumer shopping without the need to enter a store. Electronic retailing is a form of DIRECT MARKETING in which telephone lines connected to home computers, television sets equipped with special decoders, and interactive cable television may be employed to transmit information to the consumer. The potential buyer views a menu combining text and graphics and including all merchandise offered for sale. If the consumer decides to purchase an item, a number is entered on a keyboard (or, in some systems, a telephone call is made to a central location) and the item is ordered. Electronic retailing also includes systems that employ transactional discs (either in the store or placed in remote locations) equipped with video-disc players or other electronic equipment on which the customer may view a merchandise menu. Sales are commonly executed through the use of a keyboard or by an in-store clerk. Although some systems bypass the traditional retailer completely (e.g., when the manufacturer sells directly to the consumer), electronic retailing is generally viewed as an adjunct to in-store shopping rather than a replacement for it. While some of the early experiments with electronic retailing devices never fulfilled their expectations, e-tailing and the HOME SHOPPING NETWORK (HSN) represent important and successful developments in the retail environment. Also called *e-retailing*. See also TELEVISION SHOPPING CHANNEL.

electronic shopping See ELECTRONIC RETAILING.

Electronic Signatures in Global and National Commerce Act (ESIGN) See DIGITAL SIGNATURE.

electronic wallet Synonym for DIGITAL WALLET.

elements of design Synonym for DESIGN ELEMENTS.

elevated window   A DISPLAY WINDOW that is higher (up to three feet above street level) and often shorter and shallower than a typical display window. Windows of this type require novel solutions, particularly in the selection of an appropriate MANNEQUIN.

elevator sign   A sign attached to the wall in a store elevator as a permanent sign or placed as a freestanding unit near an elevator. These signs are generally directional, used to help customers find their way through the store.

elevator-type window   A DISPLAY WINDOW whose floor is an elevator platform that can be lowered to the basement level where the display is prepared and set. When the window display is ready, it is raised to the desired level where it is viewable by passersby. The Lord & Taylor FLAGSHIP STORE/DIVISION in New York City is an example of a store with elevator-type windows.

eligibility screen   In global marketing, one of the barriers or hurdles that must be overcome by a firm seeking to do business with a foreign government. During this stage of negotiations, the firm must overcome the foreign government's desire to weed out firms that are not serious or are too small to handle the contract. The government may require a large fee to be submitted along with the application. See also PROCEDURAL SCREEN, LINKAGE SCREEN, COMPETITIVE SCREEN, and INFLUENCE SCREEN.

e-mail   Short for electronic mail, the transmission of messages (both notes entered via the keyboard and files stored on disk) over communication networks. Many e-mail systems have gateways to other computer systems, enabling users to send e-mail anywhere in the world. Sending a message to many users at once is called BROADCASTING or, more selectively, MULTICASTING. Sent messages are stored in the recipient's MAILBOX until read, after which the message may be saved or deleted. All online services and Internet service providers (ISPs) offer e-mail and most also support gateways. Also spelled *email*. See also GATEWAY, NETWORK, ONLINE SERVICE, DATA PACKET, and INTERNET SERVICE PROVIDER (ISP).

e-mail account   A service arrangement between an individual or organization and an INTERNET SERVICE PROVIDER (ISP) that provides the user with E-MAIL, sometimes (but not always) for a fee. E-mail accounts are often included without charge to subscribers to INTERNET services.

e-mail address   A name that identifies an electronic post office box on a NETWORK where E-MAIL can be sent. On the INTERNET, all e-mail addresses have the form username@domain name. Every user on the Internet has a unique e-mail address. See also DOMAIN NAME.

e-mail client   A computer application that enables one to send, organize, and receive E-MAIL. The e-mail client runs on a personal computer or workstation. Mail is sent from many clients to a central SERVER, which reroutes the e-mail to its intended destination.

e-mail clutter   See CLUTTER.

e-mail discussion list   An e-mail based list that may be used by individual subscribers for learning, making contacts, and discussing issues of mutual interest. The lists cover a wide range of topics. They may be used by e-tailers, retailers, and other marketers to learn more about their industry and to promote one's business. In essence, an e-mail discussion list is a redistribution tool through which an e-mail message is sent to one address and then automatically forwarded to all the people who subscribe to that address. This is done either post-by-post (i.e., individual messages are forwarded one at a time) or by digest (i.e., a compilation of the discussion is forwarded at regular intervals). Also called a LISTSERV.

e-mail list   See E-MAIL DISCUSSION LIST and LISTSERV.

e-mail newsletter   A collection of articles, commentary, special offers, tips, quotes, and other pieces of information delivered to subscribers via E-MAIL. Since recipients make the first contact by subscribing, and since the content is useful, recipients are less likely to ignore the e-mail newsletter than they would regular e-mail or pop-up ads. Also called an *e-newsletter*.

e-mail on demand   Synonym for AUTORESPONDER.

e-mail spoofing   The practice, illegal in many jurisdictions, of forging an e-mail HEADER to make it appear as if the message came from somewhere or someone other than the actual source.

e-market/e-marketer   See E-MARKETING.

e-marketing   Marketing in the electronic environment, primarily on the Internet, World Wide Web, intranets, and extranets. Also called *online marketing*.

embargo   The most stringent form of trade restriction or quota under which all trade is banned with a particular country or specific products are barred from entering that country. An embargo is sometimes used politically as a sanction against an offending country (e.g., the U.S. ban on Cuban cigars), but is most often intended to protect domestic industries or invoked for health and safety reasons. Also called *trade embargo*.

embourgeoisement   The theory that industrial workers adopt middle-class standards, lifestyles, and purchasing patterns as their earnings increase. *Der*. French.

EMC   See EXPORT MANAGEMENT COMPANY (EMC).

emergency items/goods/products   1. Merchandise that consumers do not purchase until it is actually needed (e.g., new tires for one's car).   2. Merchandise that is required by the consumer in response to an unusual situation (e.g., plywood sheets to shore up one's home against an impending hurricane).   3. Merchandise purchased in noncrisis situations as a precaution against future emergencies (e.g., a personal survival kit or a hand-cranked emergency radio).

emoticon   In Internet messages (including e-mail), the so-called *smiley face* or any of its variations, used to display and convey emotions such as happy, sad, just joking, angry, etc. Emoticons are an attempt to convey emotional content information sometimes lacking (and easily misunderstood) in electronic communications.

emotional approach See IMAGINATIVE APPROACH.

emotional buying motive/trigger Any factor contributing to a customer's impulse to buy certain merchandise that is rooted in the customer's self-image and personal feelings rather than in logical thought. Purchases may be triggered by any drive or emotion, such as self-assertion, acquisitiveness, or curiosity. See also its opposite, RATIONAL BUYING MOTIVE.

empathy The ability to put oneself in another's place. In retailing and marketing, this allows the perceptive seller to anticipate a customer's reaction to appeals and campaigns.

empirical credit system A method for determining the credit-worthiness of applicants. Based on creditors' experience with borrowers, it awards points to particular traits describing the applicant (e.g., previous credit history, whether the applicant owns or rents a dwelling, length of employment, salary, etc.) See also STORE CREDIT.

empirical method of trading area delineation A system used to determine the size and boundaries of a retailer's TRADING AREA based on observation and experimentation.

employee A person hired by a company or another person to work for wages (salary and/or commission). See also PERSONNEL.

employee assistance program (EAP) A program provided by some private employers and government agencies, intended to help employees with problems that affect their workplace performance. The EAP offers counseling to identify the employee's problems and, when appropriate, makes a referral to an outside organization, facility, or program that can assist the employee. EAPs are frequently available for employees who have alcohol and/or drug problems or experience emotional difficulties. EAP is also used to help employees deal with a workplace trauma such as a shooting or bombing. The goal of an EAP is to restore the employee to full productivity. Also called *employee counseling program, employee rehabilitation program,* or *employee counseling and support services.*

employee benefit Any of the nonwage forms of employee compensation, including paid sick leave, holidays and vacations; group medical, dental and life insurance; retirement programs; etc. Sometimes called a *fringe benefit* or, simply, *benefit.*

employee benefits handbook A booklet containing the full range of benefits a firm offers its employees, generally given to a new employee during the induction and/or orientation period. The handbook may be bound, but is sometimes in a looseleaf format to allow changes and updates. See also EMPLOYEE HANDBOOK.

employee counseling and support services See EMPLOYEE ASSISTANCE PROGRAM (EAP).

employee development A program designed to upgrade employee skills through training. Employee development is intended to improve employees' performance at their present jobs or to qualify them for advancement within the organization.

employee discount A reduction in retail price granted to a store's own employees (and sometimes their dependents) when purchasing goods at the store.

employee discount percent/percentage In any given month, the portion of net sales derived from employee discounts, expressed as a percentage.

employee drug testing The testing of one's employees for substance abuse. Drug testing may be carried out before employment, as a condition of employment, or while the employee is employed.

employee evaluation See PERFORMANCE APPRAISAL and PERFORMANCE REVIEW.

employee handbook A manual of facts and instructions provided to the employees of a business. The handbook may include the history and philosophy of the firm, regulations, policies, procedures, benefits, dress code, etc. Employee handbooks are often used in the orientation of new employees.

employee indoctrination/induction See EMPLOYEE ORIENTATION.

employee indoctrination/induction booklet See EMPLOYEE ORIENTATION BOOKLET.

employee orientation A period in which all new employees are familiarized with the policies, history, and operations of the business as well as the responsibilities of their particular jobs. The employees are also introduced to employee benefits and opportunities for advancement during the orientation period. An EMPLOYEE ORIENTATION BOOKLET is provided by some firms. Employee orientation is intended to give new employees insight into the company, an understanding of what is expected of them, and information about what they may expect in return. Also called *employee indoctrination, employee induction,* or *new employee indoctrination.* See also JOB INDUCTION, STORE INDUCTION, SPONSOR METHOD, and COMPANY INDUCTION.

employee orientation booklet A printed pamphlet or manual distributed to new store employees, typically including details about the store's history, development, organization, and policies as well as general information about the store's operations and facilities. Employment policies and practices are often spelled out. The orientation booklet, which is often distributed at a COMPANY INDUCTION, is intended to give new employees insight into the company, delineate what is expected of them, and what they may expect in return. Also called *employee indoctrination booklet, employee induction booklet,* or *new employee induction booklet.*

employee-owned business A business in which the employees have purchased the firm from management and continue to run the firm. The sale of the firm to the employees is sometimes selected as an alternative to shutting down the company permanently. Employee owners are motivated by having a stake in their own success.

employee pilferage   See PILFERAGE.

employee rehabilitation program   See EMPLOYEE ASSISTANCE PROGRAM (EAP).

Employee Retirement Income Security Act (ERISA) (1974)   Federal legislation that sets pension plan requirements for employers and their employees. ERISA established a federal agency to insure the assets of pension plans, thus guaranteeing that (with some exceptions and limitations), retirement benefits will be paid no matter what happens to the company or the plan. It also sets standards for managing pension funds and requires public disclosure of a plan's operations.

employee services   Provisions made for the well-being and satisfaction of a store's employees (e.g., parking facilities, cafeterias, clubs, and credit unions).

employee stock ownership plan/program (ESOP)   A trust fund created by a corporate employer that enables employees to acquire stock in the corporation. In essence, this program enables employees to become owners or part owners of the company in which they work. The employer is allowed to contribute up to 25 percent of its payroll to the trust and receives tax benefits in return. The assets of the trust must be used for the benefit of the employees. Assets are usually in the form of common stock in the CORPORATION. Also called *employee stock ownership trust*.

employer   A person or company that hires others to work for wages (salary and/or commission).

emporium   (Obsolete) A major retailer, a large store selling a wide variety of merchandise, a chief commercial center, or an early department store.

empty nest I   The category made up of two-income families with no children remaining at home. These empty nesters may be considering retirement and have substantial income. They enjoy travel, join golf clubs, indulge their grandchildren, and purchase future retirement homes. Responsibility for the care of elderly parents, however, may change their financial situation.

empty nest II   The category comprising couples likely to be retired, or at least of retirement age. Some will still be in the workforce full- or part-time. The income level at this stage ranges from fixed to ample. Health care products and basic necessities are the dominant categories for those on fixed incomes. However, more affluent empty nesters may spend their money on travel, leisure activities, and restaurant meals.

EMU   See ECONOMIC AND MONETARY UNION (EMU).

emulation stage   See ACCEPTANCE STAGE.

emulative product   A new product, offered by a competitor, designed to rival and thereby compete with an existing product.

enclosed display   A display used in a store's interior, made up of a fully glassed-in platform large enough to contain a mannequin or two. An enclosed display is used to show merchandise in a protected area and is generally located at the entrance to a department, lining an aisle, or as part of a PERIMETER WALL.

enclosed mall/shopping center   An indoor, roofed SHOPPING CENTER in which all stores face an internal central promenade (i.e., a pedestrian walkway) and which is air-conditioned on a year-round basis.

enclosed window   See CLOSED-BACK WINDOW.

encoder   See ENCODING.

encoding   In communications, the process of putting plain language into an easily transmitted symbolic form. The individual who performs this function is known as an *encoder*.

encryption   In computer operations and E-COMMERCE, the translation of data into a secret code (*encryption code*) to achieve data security (i.e., to prevent HACKERS from committing crimes such as fraud, identity theft, and unauthorized accessing of personal information). Users require a secret key or password to decipher an encrypted file. Unencrypted data is called *plain text*; encrypted data is referred to as *cipher text*. There are two main types of encryption: *asymmetric encryption* (also called PUBLIC-KEY ENCRYPTION) and SYMMETRIC ENCRYPTION.

end-aisle display   Used most frequently in discount stores and supermarkets, end-aisle displays are POINT-OF-PURCHASE (POP) displays located at the end of a row of shelving. Like other point-of-purchase displays, they are designed to attract the customer's attention and increase sales of the featured items. Also called *endcap*, *end display*, and *end of aisle*. See also AISLE TABLE.

endcap   Also spelled *end-cap*. See END-AISLE DISPLAY.

end display   See END-AISLE DISPLAY.

ending inventory   Synonym for END OF MONTH (EOM) INVENTORY/STOCK.

ending inventory at cost   In the cost method of inventory, the cost of inventory on hand at the end of the accounting period. The ending inventory at cost becomes the beginning inventory at cost for the next accounting period. See also COST METHOD OF INVENTORY and BEGINNING INVENTORY AT COST.

endless chain method   Synonym for CHAIN PROSPECTING.

end of aisle   See END-AISLE DISPLAY.

end of month (EOM)   See END OF MONTH (EOM) DATING or END OF MONTH (EOM) INVENTORY.

end of month (EOM) dating   In the dating of invoices, an agreement indicating that cash discounts and net credit periods begin at the end of the month in which the goods were shipped. These terms are generally stipulated in an *end of month notation*. For example, if the terms of an August 15 invoice are 2/10 net 30 EOM, the discount period begins August 31 (i.e., the end of the month) and a 2% discount may be deducted until September 10 (i.e., 10 days after the end of the month). Full payment is due September 30. Invoices dated on the 25th of the month or later are often treated as if dated on the first day of the following month. For example, if an August 25 invoice is dated 2/10 net 30 EOM, a 2% discount may be deducted through October 10, since the invoice will be treated as though dated September 1. Full payment is due by October 30. This gives the retailer approximately six weeks to generate cash from the sale of the merchandise and still take advantage of the discount. Also called *end of month terms*.

end of month (EOM) inventory/stock   The dollar value or unit count of merchandise on hand at the end of a given month. Also called *EOM inventory* and *ending inventory*.

end of month (EOM) notation   See END OF MONTH (EOM) DATING.

end of month, receipt of goods (EOM-ROG) dating   An invoice agreement specifying that the length of time allowed for payment is to be calculated from the end of the month in which shipment was made. The cash discount period begins upon the retailer's receipt of the goods.

end of month terms   See END OF MONTH (EOM) DATING.

end-of-period trend analysis   See TREND ANALYSIS and DURING-THE-PERIOD TREND ANALYSIS.

end run   A form of COMPETITION in which a store develops a new, indirect, and evasive way of securing sales that allows it to avoid direct collision with an established competitor.

end sizes   The extreme ends of a size ASSORTMENT, including both the smallest and the largest. Also called *fringe sizes*.

end-use application segmentation   In INDUSTRIAL MARKETING, the subdivision of a market on the basis of how the product is to be used by its purchaser.

end-use products   Synonym for CONSUMER GOODS.

end user   Synonym for CONSUMER, particularly in reference to computer applications.

energy management   The development and implementation of energy conservation policies and procedures by a store or other business.

e-newsletter   See E-MAIL NEWSLETTER.

Engel-Kollat-Blackwell (EKB) model   A model of buyer behavior in which the individual's psychological makeup (personality, emotions, attitudes, etc.) is believed to affect mental processes and, consequently, behavior in the marketplace.

Engel's Laws   A widely held nineteenth-century theory of spending behavior developed by Ernst Engel, a German statistician. Engel postulated that as a family's income increases, the family spends a smaller percentage of that income on food, about the same percentage of that income on housing and household operations, and a larger percentage of that income on other (less essential) items. This theory was a precursor to MASLOW'S HIERARCHY (OF NEEDS). See also MOTIVE.

engrossing   The practice of purchasing and withholding large quantities of merchandise, speculating that the goods can be sold at a higher price in the future. The goal is to control and monopolize the market and maximize profits.

enhancement   A condition in which a new product introduced into the marketplace increases the sales of one or more other products in the company's line. Opposite of CANNIBALIZATION.

ensemble   1. A COSTUME consisting of matching, complementary, or harmonious items of APPAREL that create a coordinated look.   2. More than one item of clothing designed and coordinated to be worn together, such as a matching dress and coat.

ensemble display   The arrangement of matching or harmonious merchandise in a visual presentation to help customers coordinate items and to promote increased sales of component parts. See also TWO-WAY FIXTURE/DISPLAY and FOUR-WAY FIXTURE/DISPLAY/RACK.

enterprise   A group or similar entity, such as a business, government, hospital, university, or other organization, that produces, supplies, purchases, or services products. Some enterprises supply products designed for use by other enterprises rather than by individual persons. Electronic marketplaces bring together the suppliers of these enterprise products with the purchasing agents of the enterprises that require them. The World Wide Web, corporate and supplier Web sites, extranets, corporate intranets, and one-to-one supplier ELECTRONIC DATA INTERCHANGES (EDI) are used for this purpose. See also ENTERPRISE PRODUCT.

enterprise buyer   An owner or employee making purchases for a business, government agency, hospital, organization, or other ENTERPRISE in a marketplace.

enterprise product   Any product used to make other products, run the operations of an ENTERPRISE, or to resell products. Enterprise products are classified by how they solve problems and include the following categories: raw materials and parts (inputs in the production process); equipment and supplies (products to run the business or organization, including both capital equipment and expendable supplies); finished goods (for resale to the ultimate consumer); DIGITAL PRODUCTS (purchased online and delivered electronically, such as DIGITAL CASH); and services (including repair services and information, such as competitive market intelligence).

enterprise resource planning (ERP) A business management system that integrates all facets of the business. ERP includes planning, manufacturing, sales, and marketing. Software applications are available to help business managers implement ERP for inventory control, order tracking, customer service, finance, and human resources.

enterprise-wide decision support system A large DECISION SUPPORT SYSTEM (DSS) with a very large data warehouse that allows decision makers to find out almost anything about their companies in a matter of moments. Decision makers can zero in on pertinent information, manipulate it in a number of ways, and graph and chart corporate and EXTERNAL DATA. Such systems can range from fairly simple systems to a complex, data-intensive, and analytically sophisticated EXECUTIVE SUPPORT SYSTEM (ESS). Some enterprise-wide decision support systems use computerized analytical tools such as statistical packages and DATA MINING. The most sophisticated systems provide access to a series of decision-oriented databases, predefined models and charts, and alerts linked to events or variables in the corporate DATA WAREHOUSE.

entertainment value See COMPANY ANALYSIS.

entrance See POINT OF ENTRANCE.

entrapment study A technique sometimes used in MARKETING RESEARCH (MR), in which the purpose of the study is not revealed to the respondent.

entrepôt A commercial center that receives and redistributes goods and is free of import duty or maintains bonded warehouses. London, Amsterdam, and Rotterdam's Europort are examples.

entrepreneur An individual who organizes, launches, and directs a new commercial undertaking such as a business, product, or production process. Entrepreneurs organize land, labor, and capital in new ways in order to produce goods and services more efficiently. They also accept the RISK involved in starting something new. Compare INTRAPRENEUR.

entry point See POINT OF ENTRANCE.

envelope stuffer Synonym for BILL ENCLOSURE.

environment The economic, technological, regulatory, political, social, cultural, and competitive situation in which a retail store or other business operates. A firm's environment must be taken into account in business planning and forecasting. In retailing, also called the *retail environment*.

environmental analysis An assessment of such factors as the economy, technology, and competition that can affect a company in the marketplace. In the global marketplace, the environmental analysis includes knowledge of foreign environments.

environmental competence Knowledge about the dynamics of the world economy, major national markets, and political, social, and cultural environments needed for success in the global marketplace.

environmental display setting A realistic visual presentation of merchandise designed as a simulated room with three sides. The display is used to show an assortment of related items in a setting that illustrates how and where they might eventually be used. For example, a bedroom setting, shown with the bed fully made up, matching curtains, area rug, bedroom furniture, and easy chair may be used to display bed linens. The merchandise is displayed under conditions resembling the customer's own home. Environmental selling not only helps the customer visualize the overall effect but also generates additional sales of coordinated merchandise. Also called *environmental selling* and *environmental setting display*.

environmental dynamics The interaction of legal, political, economic, and social influences that surround a firm and affect its MARKETING ENVIRONMENT. See also MARKETING ENVIRONMENT and MARKETING DYNAMICS.

environmental forecasting The study of environmental factors by retailers and other marketers in order to predict future events.

environmental opportunity A part of the business environment in which there is an unmet need for products or services. An astute firm can fill the void by providing the product or service.

environmental review In global marketing, a detailed study focusing on the economic, physical, sociocultural, regulatory, and political environments. See also ENVIRONMENTAL SCAN.

environmental scan The process by which an organization monitors its external environment (including competitors) for opportunities, problems, and trends. See also ENVIRONMENTAL REVIEW.

environmental selling See ENVIRONMENTAL DISPLAY SETTING.

environmental setting display See ENVIRONMENTAL DISPLAY SETTING.

environmental variable Any factor such as the weather, the national economy, legislation, fuel shortages, and unemployment that, while external and not directly related to retailing functions, may have a significant effect on a retailer's sales.

EOM Short for END OF MONTH (EOM).

EOM dating See END OF MONTH (EOM) DATING.

EOM inventory See END OF MONTH (EOM) INVENTORY/STOCK.

EOM-ROG dating See END OF MONTH (EOM), RECEIPT OF GOODS (EOM-ROG) DATING.

EOM stock See END OF MONTH (EOM) INVENTORY.

EOM terms   See END OF MONTH (EOM) DATING.

EOQ   See ECONOMIC ORDER QUANTITY (EOQ).

e-panel   Synonym for ONLINE PANEL.

e-procurement   Business-to-business buying online. Designed to reduce paperwork, speed transaction times, and streamline purchasing procedures. Also called *online automated supply procurement.*

Equal Credit Opportunity Act (ECOA) (1975)   A U.S. federal law prohibiting the denial of credit to any applicant on the basis of age, gender, marital status, national origin, and childbearing intentions. The act went into effect in stages between 1975 and 1977. It further stipulates that creditors must provide each unsuccessful applicant with reasons for denial of credit, that married persons may request separate accounts, and that alimony and child support payments must be considered as income.

Equal Employment Opportunity Commission (EEOC)   A U.S. federal regulatory agency established to enforce the employment sections of civil rights legislation and all subsequent amendments. The EEOC requires that retailers and other employers hire and promote employees without discrimination due to gender, age, color, race, religion, or national origin. The agency also oversees the AFFIRMATIVE ACTION programs required of all companies doing business with the federal government and enforces Title VII of the Federal CIVIL RIGHTS ACT (1964).

Equal Pay Act (1963)   An amendment to the FAIR LABOR STANDARDS ACT (FLSA) (1938) that outlaws discrimination in rates of pay on the basis of gender. All employees covered by the Fair Labor Standards Act are also protected by the Equal Pay Act.

equal store concept   Synonym for EQUAL STORE OPERATION/ORGANIZATION.

equal store operation/organization   The organization of a retail business in which all branch stores are treated on the same basis as the flagship store and in which there is complete separation between the centralized buying function and the selling responsibilities. Also called *equal store organization* and *sister-store concept.*

equation price   A price reached in the marketplace through a series of adjustments by competing stores. Supply and demand become equal at that price.

equilibrium point   In SUPPLY AND DEMAND, the point at which the quantity and price that sellers are willing to offer for a product or service equals the price that buyers are willing to pay for it and the quantity they are willing to purchase. Graphically, the equilibrium point may be represented as the point at which the SUPPLY CURVE and the DEMAND CURVE intersect. The price of a particular product or service so determined is known as the *equilibrium price.*

equipment   1. In a store, the heating and cooling, plumbing, and lighting systems as well as elevators, cleaning machinery, etc. 2. In the realm of ENTERPRISE PRODUCTS, the products needed to run the business or organization, from machinery (to manufacture the products) to office supplies such as printer cartridges.

equity   Funds for operating the business, obtained by selling shares of ownership in the company (generally to stockholders and other investors). Equity does not have to be repaid, but it entitles the stockholder or other investor to a piece of the company and a share of future profits. Most businesses are financed with a mixture of DEBT and equity. Also called *owner's equity, shareholders' equity,* and *shareowners' equity.*

equity joint venture   A type of JOINT VENTURE in which the partners share the risk. State-approved joint ventures in the People's Republic of China are frequently equity joint ventures.

equity ratio   The financial ratio that results from dividing the total stockholders' equity in a company by the total equities or assets. It is an indication of the company's financial position at a given point in time. Also called the *worth-debt ratio.*

equity theory   An explanation of employee motivation according to which employees must see a relationship between the amount of work they perform (i.e., input) and the rewards they obtain (i.e., outcome).

e-retailing   See ELECTRONIC RETAILING.

ERISA   See EMPLOYEE RETIREMENT INCOME SECURITY ACT (ERISA) (1974).

ERP   See ENTERPRISE RESOURCE PLANNING (ERP).

erratic demand   A situation that exists when the need and/or desire for goods or services is unstable and unpredictable over a protracted period. See also SEASONAL DEMAND.

erratic fluctuations   Short-term, unexpected, and unpredictable changes in the business ENVIRONMENT that sometimes make retail planning difficult.

escalator clause   In PRICING, a stipulation in an agreement between a seller and a buyer that permits the seller (i.e., a producer or manufacturer) to increase prices above those quoted based on a specified formula, such as the COST-OF-LIVING INDEX (COLI).

escalator sign   A sign placed as a freestanding unit near an escalator landing or along the walls on either side of the escalator. These signs are generally directional, used to help customers find their way through the store.

escort shopper   A salesperson who accompanies individual shoppers throughout the store to assist them in making purchase decisions. See also STORE SERVICES.

escrow   Funds belonging to a first party held in abeyance by a third party with instructions to turn them over to a second party upon fulfillment of previously negotiated conditions.

ESIGN (Electronic Signatures in Global and National Commerce Act)   See DIGITAL SIGNATURE.

ESOP   See EMPLOYEE STOCK OWNERSHIP PLAN/PROGRAM (ESOP).

ESS   See EXECUTIVE SUPPORT SYSTEM (ESS).

essential customer service   See PRIMARY CUSTOMER SERVICE.

established trend   A pattern of increased demand for specific merchandise by style, color, material content, price line, etc., as indicated by customer preferences reflected in sales or by consumer research.

establishment   1. In business, a store, factory, or other place of business under the ownership of a single management, usually located in one geographic area.   2. *The establishment*, those in power and the system under which such power is exercised, maintained, and extended. The term is frequently used to refer to big business and the government.

esteem need   See MASLOW'S HIERARCHY (OF NEEDS).

estimated liability   The projected costs to be incurred for uncertain, variable things such as repairs under warranty.

étagère   A tall furniture unit with open shelves. It may be used in a store as a display fixture as well as in a home as a piece of furniture.

e-tail   See E-TAILER and E-TAILING.

e-tailer   A retail business that sells its products and services online via the INTERNET. An e-tailer may be CLICKS-ONLY (selling merchandise exclusively over the Internet) or BRICKS-AND-CLICKS (combining traditional in-store retailing with sales over the Internet). Also known as an *Internet retailer* or an *online storefront*. See also ONLINE SHOPPING.

e-tailer coupon   See RETAILER (SPONSORED) COUPON.

e-tailing   The practice of selling merchandise over the Internet directly to the ultimate consumer. Sometimes combined with traditional storefront retailing (called BRICKS-AND-CLICKS), sometimes exclusively an online operation (CLICKS-ONLY). Frequently successfully combined with CATALOG RETAILING. Also known as *Internet retailing*. See also M-COMMERCE.

Ethernet   A LOCAL-AREA NETWORK (LAN) architecture developed by Xerox Corporation in conjunction with DEC in 1976. Newer and faster versions of Ethernet are now available. See also DATA LINK CONTROL (DLC).

ethical advertising   Advertising that meets industry standards of fairness, honesty, and equitable content, consciously and consistently.

ethical drug   Synonym for PRESCRIPTION DRUG.

ethical pricing   Pricing policy in which the seller consciously holds back from charging all that the traffic will bear so as not to overcharge the customer.

ethical shopper   1. A customer who feels obligated to patronize small stores or other local establishments to help them stay in business. The ethical shopper is willing to sacrifice the potential price and assortment benefits available in larger stores or chains in order to do so.   2. A shopper who cares about social issues such as the working conditions in the producing country, the assurance of a fair price to the producer, the environmental effects of a product, etc., and who allows these considerations to affect purchasing decisions even if it means higher price or less convenience. Compare PERSONALIZING SHOPPER, ECONOMICAL SHOPPER, and APATHETIC SHOPPER.

ethics   See BUSINESS ETHICS.

ethnic buying habits   The ways in which various ethnic groups conduct their shopping and buying activities. Retailing, marketing, and advertising strategies are often targeted to fulfill the needs of a particular ethnic group. See also ETHNIC SEGMENTATION.

ethnicity   1. An individual's identification with a particular group on the basis of race, country of origin, language, etc.   2. A synonym for ETHNIC MARKET. See also ETHNIC SEGMENTATION.

ethnic market   A group of customers defined by race, country of origin, language, or other ethnic distinction. See also ETHNIC SEGMENTATION.

ethnic segmentation   The practice of targeting retailing, marketing, and advertising strategies to meet the needs of particular ethnic groups. The goal is to attract group members as customers by providing the goods and services they seek. In some instances, entire malls are geared to a particular ethnic group, featuring stores and restaurants that cater to their needs and preferences.

ethnocenter   A retail establishment, such as a bookstore, that appeals to and focuses on customers of a specific ethnicity. The ethnocenter tends to serve as a magnet and central meeting place for the ethnic group and may provide special programming and events in addition to targeted merchandise.

ethnocentric   Seeing everything from the point of view of one's own culture, as though it were the universal standard. See also ENTHNOCENTRISM and GEOCENTRIC.

ethnocentrism   The belief that one's own cultural values are, or should be, the norm or reference point for others. See also GEOCENTRISM and REGIOCENTRISM.

euro   The common currency of the EUROPEAN UNION (EU), which has replaced the national currencies of most member nations. The *European Central Bank (ECB)* regulates the euro and administers currency policy for the EU.

Eurobrand   See PANREGIONAL BRAND.

European Article Numbering Code   The 13-digit BAR CODE used in Europe and most places other than the United States (which has used a 12-digit bar code). When Europe established its code in 1977, it was patterned after the American UNIVERSAL PRODUCT CODE (UPC). However, the Europeans realized they needed a thirteenth number to identify more products and to identify countries. In January 2005 the United States and Canada adopted the 13-digit bar code as well in order to facilitate global marketing.

evaluation of employees   See PERFORMANCE APPRAISAL and PERFORMANCE REVIEW.

evaluation of merchandise   The inspection and sampling of purchases made by a retailer to determine quality and assortment. See also CHECKING.

evaluation rating system   In human resources management, a method of appraising employees periodically and systematically through the use of a classified point system. See also PERFORMANCE APPRAISAL and PERFORMANCE REVIEW.

evaluative criteria   In consumer behavior, those aspects of a product or service that a consumer considers during the process of weighing alternative courses of action.

even-cent pricing   See EVEN-LINE PRICING.

even-ending prices   See EVEN-LINE PRICING.

even exchange   A transaction in which the customer returns an item of merchandise and obtains another item with the same selling price rather than a cash refund. See also STORE CREDIT.

evening gown   See FORMAL ATTIRE.

even-line pricing   A method of ascribing whole number selling prices to merchandise to give the impression of high-end retailing. For example, a retailer using even-line pricing would charge $100 for an item rather than $99.95. Also called *even-cent pricing* or *even pricing*, See also ODD-LINE PRICING.

even prices/pricing   See EVEN-LINE PRICING.

event   Any nonpersonal communication (such as a news conference, grand opening, etc.) designed to communicate particular messages to target audiences. See also NONPERSONAL COMMUNICATION CHANNEL.

Eveolution   A LIFESTYLE trend that focuses on the growing power, and purchasing power, of women in the workplace. The trend tends to favor convenience items that simplify housework, such as cleaning wipes and prepared foods, as well as luxury items that appeal to working women who can afford them.

everyday low pricing (EDLP)   A value-oriented PRICING STRATEGY in which continuous promotion pricing is used without the support of advertised events. EDLP facilitates inventory management since product demand is more stable when not driven by occasional sales. The *everyday low price* may be either a retailer's lowest promotional price or a price between the highest regular price and the lowest promotional price. Lowered gross margins are offset by savings in advertising and the labor expenses associated with floor moves and retagging merchandise. For shoppers, EDLP is an advantage for customers too busy to seek out sales. EDLP is fundamental to the WAREHOUSE CLUB concept.

evoked set   In CONSUMER RESEARCH, the specific brands a consumer will actually consider when shopping within a product category. Customers commonly do not consider every possible choice or alternative when making buying decisions. Evoked sets are relatively small compared to the total number of choices in the marketplace. See also SPAN OF RECALL, INERT SET, and INEPT SET.

ex   The point from which merchandise is shipped, not necessarily its point of origin; for example, ex warehouse, ex dock, ex Elizabeth, etc. Shipping is free of charge to the purchaser until the merchandise is removed from the specified shipping place.

exact interest   Interest calculated on a 365-day-a-year basis, as opposed to ORDINARY INTEREST calculated on a 360-day basis.

exception rate   A freight rate (i.e., calculated charge) charged by shippers to their customers. The exception rate is a deviation from the CLASS RATE allowed under special circumstances, though still subject to government regulation. It may be either higher or lower than the class rate and applies to both contract and common carriers. In general, lower exception rates may be charged to encourage competition or otherwise aid the shipping industry. Higher rates are allowed for special services, such as express or overnight delivery. See also COMMODITY RATE.

exception report/reporting   A statement or account of sales showing only major deviations from the normal pattern as established by the store's buyer in the SALES REPORT. Minor deviations are omitted. For example, an exception report may include only deviations that are 10% over or 10% under plan. Even good deviations (e.g., 10% over planned sales) are reported in an exception report. The reasoning behind this is that, since inventory allocations are based on planned sales, a store that is significantly ahead of plan runs the risk of being UNDERINVENTORIED.

exchange   1. n. In retailing, a substitution for returned merchandise instead of a refund. See also EVEN EXCHANGE.   2. n. The practice, or an instance, of swapping, purchasing, or selling between two or more parties (e.g., an exchange of information). See also TRANSACTION and SWAP.   3. v. To engage in any of these kinds of transactions.   4. v. A place where trade is carried on in SECURITIES, commodities, etc. See also COMMODITY EXCHANGE and STOCK EXCHANGE.

exchange desk   An area within a store in which customers may return merchandise for a replacement, credit, or refund, depending on the store's exchange policy.

exchange functions   The buying and selling activities in the marketing process that result in the transfer of title to goods or services. Exchange is regarded as one of the basic marketing functions.

exchange manager   An online business that acts as a manager for others' online exchanges rather than selling directly from a Web storefront of its own. For example, eBay is an exchange manager that facilitates auctions for consumers, businesses, and other enterprises. See also ONLINE AUCTION.

exchange rate   The price of one country's currency expressed in terms of another country's currency. Expressed as a ratio, the exchange rate makes it possible to compare domestic and foreign prices. Most major currencies are *freely floating* (i.e., their exchange rates are determined by the market forces of supply and demand). See also FOREIGN EXCHANGE.

excise   A tax levied on the manufacture, sale, or consumption of a commodity. Excise taxes are intended to help control potentially harmful practices or to help pay for government services used only by certain people or businesses. For example, the United States imposes excise taxes on gasoline, tobacco products, liquor, firearms, tires, automobiles, sugar, fishing tackle, air travel, and telephone calls. Also called a *sin tax*. See also FEDERAL EXCISE TAX (FET).

exclusionary international Internet marketing strategy   In E-MARKETING, a strategy that focuses solely on selling to the domestic market, excluding and ignoring international customers. Small and mid-size marketers may find internationalization beyond their capacities and needs. Compare INCLUSIONARY INTERNATIONAL INTERNET MARKETING STRATEGY.

exclusive   Synonym for CONFINED MERCHANDISE/GOODS.

exclusive agency method of distribution   Synonym for EXCLUSIVE DISTRIBUTION.

exclusive agency selling   Synonym for EXCLUSIVE DISTRIBUTION.

exclusive dealing agreement/contract   A form of EXCLUSIVE DISTRIBUTION in which the marketing intermediary or retailer, in exchange for having an exclusive distributorship granted by a manufacturer or supplier, is prohibited from carrying competing lines.

exclusive distinctiveness   See PERISHABLE DISTINCTIVENESS.

exclusive distribution   A form of DISTRIBUTION in which a product or service is offered for sale to only one distributor or retailer in a particular SALES TERRITORY. Exclusive distribution is considered a SELLING AID (i.e., a special service offered by the vendor to client stores). Also known as the *exclusive agency method of distribution, exclusive outlet selling, exclusive selling,* and an *exclusive territory.* Compare OPEN DISTRIBUTION, INTENSIVE DISTRIBUTION, and SELECTIVE DISTRIBUTION. See also CONFINED MERCHANDISE/GOODS and CLOSED SALES TERRITORY.

exclusive line   A line of products created exclusively for a retailer with a brand or designer name. For example, in addition to its own apparel line Benetton produces a less expensive line of apparel called Benetton USA exclusively for distribution at Sears. Should not be confused with a *private label*. See also PRIVATE BRAND.

exclusive merchandise   Synonym for CONFINED MERCHANDISE/GOODS.

exclusive outlet selling   Synonym for EXCLUSIVE DISTRIBUTION.

exclusive selling/territory   See EXCLUSIVE DISTRIBUTION.

exclusivity   See CONFINED MERCHANDISE/GOODS.

ex dock (named port of importation)   A term of sale under which the quoted price includes the cost of the goods and all costs necessary to bring them to the named port, including duty, if any. Shipping charges begin when the merchandise is shipped from the port to the purchaser.

executive   Any person whose function is to administer or manage the affairs of a business or other organization. In retailing, the term refers primarily to managers and assistant managers of divisions and departments.

executive development manager   The store executive responsible for identifying, employing, and training potential new managers.

executive leadership   The ability to direct and guide the work of individuals and departments, provide direction, motivation, and impetus, and cause others to follow.

executive panel survey   A technique used in MARKETING RESEARCH (MR) to estimate demand for a product. The individuals surveyed are all involved in some aspect of the marketing process, such as executives with experience in marketing similar or related products.

executive search firm   See HEADHUNTER.

executive support system (ESS)   An interactive computerized decision making system of the 1980s that used sophisticated graphics, communications, and data storage methods to provide executives with easy online access to current information about the status of their companies. The most current and sophisticated DSS systems, such as ENTERPRISE-WIDE DECISION SUPPORT SYSTEM (DSS), are based on the ESS model.

executive trainee   An employee who works in various divisions or departments while being trained on the job for an executive position.

exed out   See XED OUT.

exempt carrier   A transportation company (using rail, highway, river, etc.) that, when moving specified products, has been granted an exemption from certain regulations by the localities in which it operates. For example, a barge line may be exempt from all local laws except those governing safety when it is transporting a commodity like wheat.

exempt commodity Merchandise shipped in interstate commerce to which published rates do not apply.

exempt employee An employee, usually in a managerial or executive position, not covered by the provisions of the FAIR LABOR STANDARDS ACT (FLSA) (1938). For example, exempt employees do not qualify for extra pay for overtime.

exhibit See IN-STORE EXHIBIT.

exhibit approach A SALES APPROACH in which the SALESPERSON hands the item to be sold to the PROSPECT for inspection. The prospect is then asked for an opinion of the product. Also called the *product approach* or *product-or-exhibit approach.*

exhibit booth A temporary display of merchandise and/or information set up by vendors at a TRADE SHOW. Booths are often grouped together by product category or price level.

expectation The benefit or feeling of satisfaction the customer hopes to derive from the purchase of a product or service.

expectation impact The change in DEMAND caused by anticipated changes in price. For example, rising prices can increase the demand for merchandise as customers rush to secure the item before the price rises even further. Conversely, buyers may put off purchasing a product or service in a falling price situation, anticipating that the price will continue to fall.

expectation-value theory A theory of consumer motivation maintaining that consumers' choices are based on value (i.e., utility) and costs or other risks involved.

expected (customer) service Any product-related customer service assumed by customers to be available at a store. For example, delivery of major appliances, free alteration of men's clothing, dressing rooms in apparel departments, etc. Also called, simply, *expected service.*

expected income See CONSUMER'S INCOME EXPECTATIONS.

expected net profit See EXPECTED PROFIT CONCEPT.

expected price The level at which the customer anticipates a product or service to be priced (i.e., what the customer thinks a product or service is worth).

expected profit concept A strategy employed by firms engaged in competitive bidding. The profit that might be expected to accrue from each bid price is calculated in the knowledge that the probability of an acceptable bid decreases as projected profit increases. See also COMPETITIVE BID/BIDDING.

expected service See EXPECTED (CUSTOMER) SERVICE.

expected value A concept used in selecting alternative courses of action. The expected value of an alternative is an average of all the conceivable consequences of that alternative, with each consequence being assigned a probability percentage. When applied to the marketing of new products, the expected value concept facilitates the sorting out of the many probabilities existing in the marketplace.

expediting payment In global marketing, a small sum paid to civil servants abroad (particularly in developing countries) so that they will do their jobs. Despite the fact that the U.S. FOREIGN CORRUPT PRACTICES ACT (FCPA) (1977) forbids U.S. citizens to bribe high-ranking foreign government employees and politicians, expediting payments are allowed.

expenditure Anything that is paid out or spent. In business, this usually refers to money, but it may also refer to time, energy, etc. Also called an *outlay.*

expenditure multiplier The increase in store expenses that results from additional store sales. See also EXPENSES.

expense See EXPENSES.

expense account A listing of work-related expenses by an employee, to be reimbursed by the employer. The expense account may include reimbursement for travel costs, business luncheons and dinners, client entertainment, etc.

expense allocation See CONTRIBUTION PLAN.

expense budget A statement outlining the projected operating expenditures for a given period (usually, in retailing, a season).

expense center Any area of a store (e.g., a department) to which particular, controllable costs may be assigned and which becomes responsible for those costs. Compare PROFIT CENTER.

expense center accounting An accounting method that groups expenses according to their necessity in performing a particular store service.

expense control The analysis and classification of expenses in an attempt to determine the most profitable spending to generate optimum business and/or profits.

expense items/goods Any short-lived products or services that may be charged off as they are used, usually in the year of purchase. See also CAPITAL GOODS and SUPPLIES.

expense management A procedure used to determine whether the spending needs of the store have been properly allocated.

expense manager The store executive charged with analyzing and checking up on expenses.

expense plan/planning Part of the overall planning process designed to make informed forecasts of expenses and costs so that proper controls can be established to meet them. Expense planning thus safeguards the store's profit objective. The process consists of making a series of dollar estimates of the various expenses a retail business will incur in a specified budget period. Top store management and buyers are responsible for estimating future expenses and preparing the expense plan or budget. Remedial action may be taken where and when required. See also PLANNED EXPENSES.

expenses The expenditures incurred in the course of running a business, doing one's work, etc. In retailing, this involves all money paid out to get the merchandise out of the store and into the hands of the customers. Expenses include such items as wages, rent, utilities, delivery, alterations, repairs, and promotions. The term excludes the cost of the goods themselves. Distinguished from COSTS, that is, expenditures for the materials needed for production (in manufacturing) or for stock (in retailing).

experience card See EXPERIENCE STORE.

experience curve 1. A graphic representation of a marketing reality: those firms having the largest share of the market will have an advantage over their smaller competitors because of their learning advantage, greater specialization, economies of scale, etc. 2. The predictable decline of all costs associated with a product as the total number of units produced increases. This is due to a number of factors, including lowered costs per unit with increased volume; economies of scale in production, distribution, and promotion; and the increased production and marketing expertise of employees. The experience curve gives companies an incentive to price their products relatively low initially in order to build volume. See also EXPERIENCE CURVE PRICING.

experience curve pricing A strategy used in pricing manufactured goods in which the selling price is calculated on the basis of projected costs at the time of production rather than on costs prevailing during the planning stages.

experience items Merchandise for which the consumer tries to ascertain the validity of claims for the product before making a purchase. Consumers may utilize such aids as word-of-mouth, published reviews in specialty magazines and *Consumer Reports*, and the online consumer recommendations, reviews, and ratings available on many e-tail Web sites. See also SEARCH GOODS.

experiencer See VALS SEGMENTATION.

experience store A retail or (more commonly) e-tail establishment in which a variety of experiences (e.g., trapeze lessons, a professional photography session, or hypnosis sessions) are sold. Customers may purchase their own experiences, or they may purchase gift cards (i.e., experience cards) to be redeemed for an experience of the recipient's choice, depending on the card's value.

experiment In MARKETING RESEARCH (MR) and other social science research, a primary data-gathering technique that manipulates variables in such a way as to make cause and effect relationships apparent. The research tries to find out how one set of conditions will affect another by setting up a situation in which all factors may be carefully measured. Experiments often provide a basis for small-scale trial runs before the firm totally commits itself to a course of action. This method of empirical research is called *experimental method* or *experimental research*.

experimental gaming A research method utilizing a simulated environment to observe behavior.

experimental method/research See EXPERIMENT.

experimentation See EXPERIMENT.

expert channel A PERSONAL COMMUNICATION CHANNEL consisting of independent experts making statements to target customers.

expiration date In food retailing, the last date on which perishable merchandise may be sold. For packaged goods, the date is generally stamped or printed directly onto the package. When the product has been prepared and wrapped in-store, the expiration date generally appears on the store-generated label that also indicates weight and price.

expire file A list of the store's inactive customers, used primarily for promotional activities, to lure inactive customers back to the store. Retailers purge the names and addresses of these former customers after a few years because they are no longer considered useful.

explicit cost Any expenditure, such as wages, utilities, supplies, etc., that is clearly stated and readily observable. Explicit costs appear on the account record as costs and are charged against the operation of the business. Compare IMPLICIT COST.

exploration stage The initial stage of NEW PRODUCT DEVELOPMENT, during which ideas for new products are either searched out or internally generated by a firm.

explosive A very successful item (i.e., a BEST SELLER).

exponential growth/diffusion The slow initial growth in store sales of a new item that continues to improve as the product becomes better known and accepted. As the market becomes saturated and additional sales come increasingly from repeat or replacement purchases, this growth in sales slows down, levels off, and eventually declines. See also PRODUCT LIFE CYCLE (PLC).

exponential smoothing In time-series analysis, the practice of making predictions on the basis of a weighted average of experiences. Experiences are weighted according to their occurrence in time, with the most recent given more weight than the others. For example, if a store's sale of skirts for the four previous months had been 600, 500, 700 and 750 units respectively, the forecast for the coming month would be above 750.

export   1. v. To send or transport goods to another country or countries especially for the purpose of sales. The industry is generally referred to as *exporting*. See also EXPORT MARKETING. 2. n. An item sent to another country or countries. Collectively, such merchandise is referred to as *exports*.

export agent   In DIRECT EXPORT, a foreign company that sells the goods on behalf of the exporting company. The agent may have either exclusive or general rights to represent the exporter in that country. An export agent is similar to an EXPORT MANAGEMENT COMPANY (EMC), except that it tends to provide more limited services and focuses on a single country or part of the world. Export agents focus on the sale and handling of goods, freeing the manufacturer from all the documentation and shipping tasks usually handled by a firm's own EXPORT MANAGER. The main disadvantage of using an export agent is the agent's limited market coverage. Also called a *foreign-based agent* and a *foreign-based export agent*.

export broker   An AGENT INTERMEDIARY involved in international trade, performing the functions of a BROKER for domestic firms exporting their goods to foreign markets. The export broker brings buyers and sellers together and provides information to each of them, connecting the needs of the buyers to the available goods of the suppliers. See also DOMESTIC-BASED EXPORT MERCHANT and IMPORT BROKER.

export commission house/merchant   A COMMISSION MERCHANT involved in international trade and selling domestic goods in a foreign market. The export commission house handles goods shipped to it by sellers, completes the sales, and sends the money to each seller. The export commission house is reimbursed for its services by means of a commission paid by the seller.

export consortium   A cooperative effort of firms, including competitors in the domestic market, that pool their resources for the purpose of exporting to foreign markets. The cooperating companies unite to share the logistical and promotion costs of entering foreign markets. The pooling of resources is also called *export cooperation*.

export cooperation   See EXPORT CONSORTIUM.

export department   A full complement of in-house specialists in international trade who primarily perform a sales function. They respond to inquiries, manage exhibits at international trade shows, and handle export documentation, shipping, insurance, and financial matters. The export department may use the services of an EXPORT AGENT, an EXPORT MANAGEMENT COMPANY (EMC), or an IMPORT INTERMEDIARY to assist in the process. The alternative to an in-house export department is the INTERNATIONAL SPECIALIST, an outside firm or organization specializing in the same functions.

export distributor   See FOREIGN-BASED EXPORT DISTRIBUTOR.

export duty   See EXPORT TARIFF.

exporter   See FOREIGN EXPORTER.

Export-Import Bank of the United States   A U.S. government agency designed to help U.S. companies compete abroad. One way it does so is by granting inexpensive financing to overseas buyers of American-made goods. Such financing is particularly important in making sales to a LESS-DEVELOPED NATION (LDN) with a heavy debt burden. The bank also offers *mixed credit*, a combination of subsidies and low-cost financing to buyers in several countries that purchase U.S. products. These practices enable U.S. industries to compete with overseas companies whose governments provide subsidies regularly.

exporting   See EXPORT and EXPORT MARKETING.

export license   A government document that permits the licensee to export specific, designated merchandise to specified destinations.

export management company (EMC)   An independent international marketing intermediary that manages a company's export activities in indirect exporting and is paid a set fee under a contractual agreement. The EMC handles all aspects of export operations, including marketing research, patent protection, channel credit, shipping and logistics, and the actual marketing of products in a foreign market. An EMC can act as either a merchant (i.e., taking title to the goods) or an agent (i.e., not taking title to the goods). The manufacturer gains by using an EMC in that little or no investment is required to enter the international marketplace, no in-house personnel are required, and the EMC offers an established network of sales offices as well as international marketing and distribution knowledge. However, the manufacturer gives up direct control of the international sales and marketing effort. Compare EXPORT AGENT. See also INDIRECT EXPORT.

export manager   An employee of an exporting firm responsible for handling all the documentation and shipping tasks involved in bringing goods to market in a foreign marketplace.

export marketing   Marketing activities that enable a firm to sell its products outside its home country or domestic base of operations through physically shipping the goods from one country to another. Export marketers select the appropriate markets or countries, determine the product modifications needed to meet the requirements of these markets, and develop export channels through which the company can market its products abroad. Since the movement of goods across national borders is a major part of export marketing, knowledge of shipping and export documentation plays an important role in the process. Commonly called *exporting*.

export price escalation   The effect of the COSTS of exporting on the end-user price of an exported product, sometimes raising it substantially above its domestic price so that the exporting firm's products have difficulty competing in the foreign market. These costs include profit and cost factors (such as transportation costs, tariffs, taxes, local production costs, and channel costs), market factors (such as income level, buyer power, and competition), and environmental factors (such as exchange rate fluctuations, inflation rates, price controls, and dumping regulations). To counter export price escalation, a company may elect to accept its price disadvantage and position its goods as luxury items, reengineer its products to be less costly, or grant a discount to bring the end-user prices more in line with those charged for the domestic product.

export sales representative In DIRECT EXPORT, a domestic-based salesperson sent abroad at intervals to find foreign customers for the producer. Also called a *traveling export sales representative*.

export tariff A tax on a country's exports, generally levied by nations that are heavy exporters of raw materials. Export duties are designed to protect and encourage domestic industries or simply to raise revenue. The taxes are imposed on goods moving across an economic or political boundary. Constitutionally prohibited by the United States, export tariffs exist in some other countries but are not as prevalent as the IMPORT TARIFF.

Export Trading Companies Act (1982) U.S. legislation that helped to ease the antitrust rules limiting joint activities in the United States for firms engaged in international business. The act allows companies and banks to form export trading companies to market products abroad. See also the WEBB-POMERENE EXPORT TRADE ACT (1918).

exposure The degree to which an advertising message is actually perceived by members of the target audience. For an ad to be exposed it must be more than simply seen; it must be noticed to an extent that there is some measurable impact. See also IDEAL MARKET EXPOSURE and ADVERTISING RESEARCH.

exposure area The area in a store that is actually visible to customers. More specifically, areas of shelving on which products are exposed to view by customers.

express company Synonym for EXPRESS DELIVERY SERVICE.

express contract A CONTRACT (i.e., an exchange of promises enforceable by law) derived from the words, either oral or written, of the parties involved. See also IMPLIED CONTRACT.

express delivery service A private company (such as FedEx) that provides essentially the same services as PARCEL POST (PP) without the restrictions on weight, size, and perishability of the parcels handled. In this respect it fills the gaps left by parcel post services. Express delivery services often offer quick (even one-day) delivery. The U.S. Postal Service has met the challenge of competing with express delivery services by introducing Express Mail and Priority Mail services. See also DELIVERY.

expressed warranty 1. A statement that specifies the conditions under which a manufacturer is responsible for a product's performance, expressed orally or (usually) in writing. 2. In retailing, a seller's statement concerning the quality, benefit, or value to a consumer of his or her goods, expressed orally or (usually) in writing. The consumer has the right to expect the seller to back up these statements. See also IMPLIED WARRANTY and WARRANTY.

express mail industry See EXPRESS DELIVERY SERVICE.

express store A CONVENIENCE STORE with many of the items found in a large supermarket, but with a limited assortment.

expropriation The formal (i.e., legal) seizure of foreign-owned property by a government, with or without some provision for reimbursing the owners. See also CONFISCATION, DOMESTICATION, and NATIONALIZATION.

extended family In many cultures, the group of relatives that includes members outside the NUCLEAR FAMILY, such as grandparents, in-laws, aunts, uncles, cousins, etc.

extended marketing channel A CHANNEL OF DISTRIBUTION (i.e., *marketing channel*) in which wholesalers obtain products from manufacturers and sell them to retailers or to jobbers who, in turn, sell them to retailers. Compare LIMITED MARKETING CHANNEL and DIRECT MARKETING CHANNEL.

extended product An item of merchandise plus all accompanying services such as warranty and repairs.

extended terms Additional time given to pay a bill or other debt. Extended terms must be agreed to by both the lender and the borrower. Also called an *extension*.

extender See EXTENDER STRATEGY.

extender strategy A strategy for smaller, local firms competing with powerful multinationals. Extenders focus on expanding into foreign markets similar to their own, using successful practices developed in their home market. See also DEFENDER STRATEGY, CONTENDER STRATEGY, and DODGER STRATEGY.

extensible market A market that can be expanded, either through an increase in per capita consumption or by attracting more first-time customers.

extensible markup language (XML) An electronic message format that integrates forms of hardware and software and allows data sharing by many users. It is becoming widely used in computerized inventory control and business-to-business functions, where it is replacing ELECTRONIC DATA INTERCHANGE (EDI).

extension Synonym for EXTENDED TERMS.

extension of brands See BRAND EXTENSION STRATEGY.

extension strategy One of three basic strategies for introducing a product into a foreign market. In the extension strategy, the marketer simply adopts the same approach as in the home market. Both the product design and the communications (i.e., advertising and promotional activities) may remain the same, or one of the factors can be extended while the other is adapted to meet the needs of the new market. The alternative strategies are the ADAPTATION POLICY and the INVENTION STRATEGY.

extensive distribution Wide distribution, required for those consumer goods for which consumers make little or no shopping effort (i.e., CONVENIENCE GOODS/ITEMS/PRODUCTS). Such merchandise benefits from being available in a large number of convenient, easily accessible outlets. Compare INTENSIVE DISTRIBUTION.

extensive market opportunities Opportunities in the marketplace for new growth that involves a company in activities not previously part of its marketing effort. For example, a company may develop an entirely new product line to appeal to customers of its existing products.

extensive problem solving In consumer behavior, the effort made to understand one's own needs and how to satisfy them. This is particularly applicable when a need is completely new to the individual consumer. For example, a woman approaching middle age may notice that her skin is drier than it was previously and may seek moisturizers in the marketplace. Selecting from the myriad moisturizing products with various formulations requires extensive problem solving. She may do research, pay close attention to advertising, consult friends, family members, cosmeticians, or doctors, and carefully examine product labels before actually selecting the product that seems most likely to meet her needs. She may even try several different products before making a final selection. See also LIMITED PROBLEM SOLVING.

exterior visibility The extent to which a storefront, marquee, or window display may be seen by a passing pedestrian or vehicular passenger. See also DISPLAY and DISPLAY WINDOW.

external audit A review of a store's records, reports, financial statements, etc. to verify their accuracy and conformity with the organization's policies. The external audit is conducted by a certified public accountant or other auditor who is not an employee of the firm being audited.

external coalitions All the external groups related to a retailer, such as the communities in which the firm is located, competitors, customers, employees' families, shareholders, and suppliers. Such groups influence a retailer's forecasting activities and merchandise plans.

external credit Consumer credit at the retail level financed by a bank or other lending institution rather than by the retailer. See also CREDIT CARD.

external data Data obtained from outside sources (i.e., sources other than the firm itself), such as government agencies, trade associations, trade periodicals, etc. Retailers are particularly interested in data on broad economic and social trends. Compare INTERNAL DATA.

external environment See MARKETING ENVIRONMENT.

external factors Factors outside the firm itself, such as the businesses and people that interact most closely and directly with it and contribute to its external ENVIRONMENT. These include suppliers, marketing intermediaries, buyers, competi-

tors, and stakeholders. External factors are economic, technological, societal, cultural, natural, governmental, and legal.

external marketing Internet marketing that targets the ultimate consumer. Compare INTERNAL MARKETING.

external marketing environment See MARKETING ENVIRONMENT.

external promotion In retailing, communication with potential customers with the goal of bringing them into the store. Broadcast, print, and electronic media may be used. Compare INTERNAL PROMOTION. See also PROMOTIONAL TOOLS and PROMOTOOLS.

external site A store location along a highway between major cities, depending upon intercity automobile traffic for its clientele.

external theft Theft (i.e., shoplifting) committed by customers. Shoplifting creates shortages, as the shoplifted items cause the book value to exceed the physical value when a physical inventory is taken.

external traffic management The control and direction of merchandise between the vendor or other supplier and the receiving division of the store.

extinction pricing See PREDATORY PRICING.

extra dating A deferred payment agreement that allows the purchaser a specified number of days before the ordinary dating of the bill begins. During this time the bill may be paid and the discount earned. For example, if the terms of an August 15 invoice are 2/10, 60X or 2/10, 60 ex., the purchaser has 60 extra days before ordinary dating begins (i.e., October 15). A 2% discount may be deducted until October 25 (i.e., 10 days after October 15). Full payment is due November 15 (i.e., 30 days after October 15). Vendors use extra dating to convince retailers to accept early shipments of merchandise and to test merchandise in certain stores as predictors of a season's selling trends.

extra-expense insurance Business insurance that covers the added expense associated with operating in temporary facilities after an event such as a fire or flood.

extraneous items Items such as charges for gift wrap, etc., that appear on sales checks but must be excluded when sales are audited in order to arrive at a true net sales figure.

extranet A private, proprietary network that links several INTRANETS and users. Extranets allow approved visitors (e.g., B2B customers) access to a company's intranet or to a specifically constructed multicompany Web site, protected from unauthorized users by means of a firewall.

extranet pricing The practice of posting prices on an EXTRANET where they are continuously updated and accessible 24/7. An extranet selectively allows approved visitors access to a company's intranet or a specifically constructed multicompany Web site protected from unauthorized users by means of a firewall. Suppliers post price changes to their extranet Web pages, and visitors use internal search engines to locate current price information. Extranet pricing is dynamic and accessible.

extras   Part-time sales help used on an irregular basis as needed.

extreme market segmentation   A theory according to which the uniqueness of each consumer makes standardized products unacceptable. Compare FRAGMENTATION.

extreme value store   A general merchandise discounter that sells basic household and food items as well as health and beauty aids. Smaller than full line discount stores, extreme value stores cater to low- and fixed-income consumers in locations not often served by larger format discounters. Family Dollar and Dollar General are two of the largest extreme value chains.

extrinsic cue   Any attribute of a product or service, external to its actual physical characteristics, that arouses positive or negative feelings in the customer. For example, country of origin may serve as an external cue. Compare INTRINSIC CUE.

exurbia   A geographic area beyond the suburbs but with access to major cities. The term *exurbia* was coined in 1955 by A.C. Spectorsky. Exurbia is largely inhabited by persons in the upper income brackets and has become the preferred site of many major corporations (such as IBM) and their employees' families.

ex warehouse   A term of sale under which shipping from the manufacturer to the WAREHOUSE is free of charge to the customer. Shipping charges begin when the merchandise is removed from the warehouse and sent on to the purchaser.

ex works   A term of sale under which the seller of goods is responsible only for making them available at the factory (i.e., the works). The buyer is responsible for loading the goods and transporting them to their final destination.

eyeball control   The visual examination of stock levels at periodic intervals to determine replenishment needs. Eyeball control assumes that a MODEL STOCK concept exists in the mind of the observer. The method relies on observation rather than record keeping. Also called *visible inventory control*, *visual inventory control*, *visual system of stock control*, and *visual control*.

eyeballs   (Slang) The number of visitors (i.e., sets of eyeballs) that see an ad on the Web.

eye-blink test   In ADVERTISING RESEARCH, the recording of the eye-blink rate of respondents by hidden cameras in order to reveal the extent of emotional tension experienced while viewing a television commercial. Also called *eye tracking*. See also EYE CAMERA.

eye camera   In ADVERTISING RESEARCH, a device that uses infrared light sensors to track eye movements as a subject reads an advertisement. The beam allows researchers to determine the exact point at which the subject focuses. The reading provides data on which elements of the ad attract attention, how long the viewer focuses on them, and the order in which the components are being viewed. One of the PHYSIOLOGICAL PROFILE techniques. See also EYE-BLINK TEST.

eye candy   In Web page design, any graphic or automated feature meant to please and attract the potential customer.

eye flow movement test   In ADVERTISING RESEARCH, a test using eye-movement cameras to determine the length of time the viewer's eyes rest on each focal point of an advertisement.

eye-level merchandising   An in-store DISPLAY technique in which products are placed within approximately 18 inches of eye level. The method uses the zone of vision to determine where to situate displayed items. See also VISUAL MERCHANDISING.

eye tracking   See EYE-BLINK TEST.

fabricating material   A component product, such as pig iron, cement, or flour, that has been processed past the raw material stage before being incorporated into a finished product. Unlike a FABRICATING PART, fabricating materials usually change form as they are further processed.

fabricating part   A manufactured component, such as an automobile battery or coat buttons, that becomes part of a larger finished product. Despite the fact that fabricating parts are incorporated into another product, they do not change form. Also called, simply, *parts*. Compare FABRICATING MATERIAL.

fabrication type   The kind of product a manufacturer wishes to make. In the overseas sourcing of the manufacturing process, for example, the manufacturer must ascertain the availability of the required materials in the host country and the capability of the contractor to produce the kind of product the manufacturer has in mind. This is one of several factors informing the decision to manufacture one's products abroad.

fabric booking confirmation   In SOURCING, a letter of intent that reserves a particular fabric for use by a specified retail merchant when the same fabric is required for use by several contractors (e.g., for coordinates).

fabric forward   An international trade agreement for apparel, stipulating that the fabric (as well as the garment) must be manufactured in one of the countries party to the agreement in order to qualify for free trade. The United States and Canada, for example, have such an agreement; in order to qualify for free trade, apparel must be made from fabric manufactured in the United States or Canada (and not from imported fabrics).

fabric testing   A series of laboratory tests used on fabrics to ensure that quality standards have been met and to identify the fabric's characteristics (e.g., shrinkage, tear strength, fading, water absorption) so that appropriate care instructions can be provided.

fabric theme   A recurring idea or motif based on the popular fabric of a given season, such as denim, tweed, or cashmere. A fabric theme may be created in one department or by a specific designer; it may also be extended to a number of departments.

façade   Synonym for STOREFRONT.

faced out   Of merchandise on the selling floor, placed so that customers can see the product head-on. See also FACE-OUT DISPLAY.

face-out display   A fixture, used in display, on which apparel or other merchandise is hung so that the merchandise faces the customer.

face-to-face selling   See PERSONAL SELLING.

facilitating agency   In marketing, businesses that provide services essential to the marketing process without either taking title to the product or engaging directly in the buying or selling function. These organizations (e.g., financial institutions, transportation companies, exchanges, marketing research firms, insurance companies, etc.) provide assistance to channel members but, unlike wholesalers and retailers, they are not actually a part of the CHANNEL OF DISTRIBUTION. Also called a *facilitator*.

facilitating function   Any activity that assists marketers in the performance of the universal marketing functions. Includes standardization, grading, risk-taking, financing, and the gathering of market information. See also MARKETING FUNCTIONS and TRANSACTIONAL (MARKETING) FUNCTION.

facilitator   Synonym for FACILITATING AGENCY.

facing   1. A unit of measurement for a retail shelf, indicating the number of times an item fits across the front of it. For example, three facings would mean that three of the same item may be displayed side by side.   2. In apparel manufacture, a piece of fabric attached to the edge of a garment (e.g., at the neckline) in order to finish that edge.

facing text matter   In a periodical, the positioning of an advertisement opposite editorial matter, particularly an article relating to the product being advertised. This is considered a highly desirable placement. For example, an advertisement for low-carb yogurt would be well placed facing an article on the benefits of a low-carb diet.

factor   A financial institution that facilitates the flow of money between buyers and sellers by buying accounts receivable from sellers (such as manufacturers and wholesalers) at discount. The factor, which assumes the risk and responsibilities of collection, is paid by commission and makes a profit by collecting the outstanding debts. This process, known as *factoring*, provides the seller with ready cash and is frequently found in the apparel manufacturing industry. This type of transaction gives the manufacturer the cash necessary to operate while the garments are being made and shipped. Sometimes the factor will also take over the billing and financial management of the manufacturing firm.

factor endowment   The presence, in a given country, of resources such as labor, land, natural resources, capital, etc., that give it a COMPARATIVE ADVANTAGE (i.e., the ability to produce goods inexpensively).

factoring   See FACTOR.

factor method   A method used to forecast sales by establishing a relationship between the company's sales and some other variable (i.e., factor). The past sales of the company (or of the entire industry) are multiplied by one or more of the variables to produce the sales forecast. Several variables may be used together for greater accuracy.

factor's lien   The right of a FACTOR to retain the merchandise consigned as reimbursement for all advances previously made to the consignor.

factory   A manufacturing plant where goods are produced.

factory outlet   Originally, a manufacturer-owned retail store located at the factory site, through which unwanted inventory (i.e., overruns, seconds, discontinued items, closeouts, irregulars, etc.) could be unloaded at greatly reduced prices without offering competition to the traditional retailers. These stores now commonly sell in-season, first-quality merchandise of one or more manufacturers and are often located in factory outlet malls far from the factory. As such, they compete directly with traditional retailers. Some, however, sell the manufacturer's SECOND-LINE MERCHANDISE. Previously known as a *mill store* or a *company store*, a factory outlet is now also known as an *outlet store*. See also FACTORY OUTLET MALL and RETAIL OUTLET.

factory outlet mall   A SHOPPING CENTER that focuses on quality name brand items offered at lower than usual prices. The stores are factory outlet stores owned and operated by manufacturers, clustered in the mall rather than located near the factory as they were previously. The factory outlet mall tends to feature pared-down décor, facilities, and prices. As amenities are added, the prices tend to approach regular retail. See also OUTLET CENTER.

factory pack   See BANDED PACK.

factory-positioned warehouse   A facility located near the place of manufacture in which goods may be stored. A factory-positioned warehouse may be used to store raw materials and fabricating parts to be used in production, or to store finished goods awaiting shipment.

fact sheet   An informational document, included in a package of sales materials, that provides information about the product and the manufacturer.

factual approach   A SALES APPROACH in which the SALESPERSON turns an interesting fact connected with the product or service into an enticing opening sentence. The salesperson appeals to the prospect's logic and appreciation of the product's benefits. Also called the *reason-why approach*.

factual survey   A SURVEY technique used in MARKETING RESEARCH (MR) in which consumers are asked to report actual facts about their own shopping habits and preferences (e.g., brand of a product used, stores patronized).

fad   A style or product that is accepted quickly by large numbers of consumers but whose popularity is short-lived. A fad may be a manner of behavior or a product. When the fad is a product, it may also be called a *fad item* or a *fad product*. Also called a *miniature fashion* or a *minor fashion*. See also FLASH IN THE PAN, IT-ROULATION, IT-GAP, IT-STATUS, and IT-THING.

FAD   See FREQUENCY OF ADDITIONAL DELIVERIES (FAD).

Fair Credit Billing Act (FCBA) (1975)   U.S. federal legislation that spells out customers' rights in disputes over billing errors (e.g., unauthorized charges, charges listing the wrong date or amount, mathematical errors, failure to post payments and other credits). The customer must file any complaint over billing by contacting the retailer or other creditor within 60 days, and the complaint must be acknowledged by the retailer or other creditor within 30 days after receipt. A final solution to the problem should be made in 90 days. The FCBA also provides that every applicant for credit be informed of customers' rights when applying for credit and periodically informed as to where inquiries and complaints are to be made. The FEDERAL TRADE COMMISSION (FTC) provides information about the FCBA on its Web site at www.ftc.gov.

Fair Credit Reporting Act (FCRA) (1970)   U.S. federal legislation that permits any credit applicant rejected for credit on the basis of adverse information supplied by a credit bureau to be notified of the reasons for such a rejection. The applicant may examine the credit file and have it corrected. Adverse credit information may not be used if it is more than seven years old, and information that is only three months old must be verified before it is used. The FEDERAL TRADE COMMISSION (FTC) provides information about the FCRA on its Web site at www.ftc.gov.

Fair Debt Collection Practices Act (1978)   U.S. federal legislation prohibiting the use of abusive, deceptive, and unfair debt collection practices. The act, amended and updated in 1996, is essentially a list of specific practices that retailers, other creditors, and collection agencies may no longer use. The FEDERAL TRADE COMMISSION (FTC) provides information about the Fair Debt Collection Practices Act on its Web site at www.ftc.gov.

Fair Labor Standards Act (FLSA) (1938)   An act setting the minimum wage rate and the maximum number of hours that may be worked. It also makes provisions for overtime pay and governs equal pay, child labor, and working conditions for covered employees. Retail stores were exempt prior to 1964, and smaller retailers still are. Executives and administrative personnel are generally exempt. The U.S. Department of Labor provides information about FLSA on its Web site at www.dol.gov. See also EQUAL PAY ACT (1963).

fair market value (FMV)   The price at which an imported item would sell, under similar circumstances of sale, if it were sold in the country of origin.

Fair Packaging and Labeling Act (1966)   Federal legislation enabling the FEDERAL TRADE COMMISSION (FTC) and the FOOD AND DRUG ADMINISTRATION (FDA) to take action against the use of false or misleading matter on labels, the omission of ingredients, the omission of net quantity and size of serving information on food products, and the use of misleading shapes and sizes in packaging. Every label must carry the product name, as well as the name and address of the manufacturer or distributor, and must conspicuously show the net quantity. Both the FTC and the FDA provide information about the act on their respective Web pages: www.ftc.gov and www.fda.gov. Also known as the *Truth-in-Packaging Act.*

fair price hypothesis   A theory of retail price strategy stating that customers react to prices by making mental reference to what they believe is a fair price. According to this theory, buying decisions are less influenced by price comparisons to other similar products than they are by comparisons to this mental reference.

fair trade   Synonym for RESALE PRICE MAINTENANCE (RPM).

fair trade acts/laws   U.S. state laws that obligated retailers to maintain specified prices on select goods. In recent years, fair trade pricing has been withdrawn by many retailers and manufacturers. The practice was enabled on the federal level by the MILLER-TYDINGS ACT (1937), but the act was later ruled unconstitutional by the U.S. Supreme Court. The MCGUIRE-KEOGH FAIR TRADE ENABLING ACT (1952), no longer in effect, attempted to exempt from antitrust laws any interstate contract fixing retail prices in states where intrastate contracts are allowed. The CONSUMER GOODS PRICING ACT (1975) is U.S. federal legislation prohibiting the use of resale price maintenance laws in interstate commerce; it resulted in the near elimination of fair trade arrangements. See also RESALE PRICE MAINTENANCE (RPM), the MILLER-TYDINGS ACT (1937), and the SHERMAN ANTITRUST ACT (1890).

fair trade price   Under RESALE PRICE MAINTENANCE (RPM) agreements (now largely defunct), the fair trade price was the retail price of a branded item, fixed by the manufacturer, below which the retailer was prohibited by law from selling the product. See also FAIR TRADE ACTS/LAWS.

falling demand   See FALTERING DEMAND.

falling price game   A type of forward auction in which prices begin at full retail and fall at regular, preset intervals once or twice daily. Buyers place a bid at any incremental price point. Bids are tallied and winners notified after the close of the sale.

faltering demand   That point in the PRODUCT LIFE CYCLE (PLC) when demand for a product or service begins to wane (i.e., when purchasers have less need and/or desire for the product). Also called *falling demand.*

Family and Medical Leave Act (FMLA) (1996)   U.S. federal legislation granting workers 12 weeks unpaid leave to deal with personal or family health needs.

family brand   A line of products offered for sale by a single producer, all of which carry the company's brand name, logo, or similar identifying design. Also known as *family packaging, house mark, umbrella brand, umbrella mark,* and *blanket brand.*

family life cycle (FLC)   Those stages through which a family passes from formation to dissolution, including single persons, young married couples, couples with children, couples without children at home (the so-called empty nest), and finally single persons again (i.e., solitary survivors). FLC is a factor in MARKET SEGMENTATION since the expenditures of families are affected by these stages of development. The presence of young children, for example, will influence the type of merchandise a family is likely to want and need. Five stages are usually described. Murphy and Staples (1979), however, identify 13 life cycle stages in their "Modernized Family Life Cycle" (*Journal of Consumer Research*, June 1979, pp. 161–17). Their categories reflect the prevalence of divorce in our society as well as the presence of children in the household.

family life cycle segmentation   Subdivision of the population of potential customers based on marital status and the presence (or absence) of children in the family. Purchasing power and spending habits differ at each stage of the FAMILY LIFE CYCLE (FLC) according to the number of dependent children.

family of orientation   The family into which an individual is born. Also called one's *birth family.*

family of procreation   A family created by the marriage of two individuals.

family packaging   See FAMILY BRAND.

fantasy adventure   A lifestyle category whose members seek new thrills and experiences as an escape from stress or boredom. This trend favors the marketing of exotic vacations, intercultural foods, and recreational challenges such as rock climbing and extreme sports. Virtual reality games and computer gaming also appeal to customers in this category.

fantasy display setting   A visual presentation of merchandise in an imaginative, unrealistic, but creative and eye-catching setting.

FAQs   See FREQUENTLY ASKED QUESTIONS (FAQS).

Farmer's Exemption   See MEAT INSPECTION ACT (1906).

farmers' market An assemblage of farm stands, usually in an urban area. Farmers' markets allow farmers to sell fresh PRODUCE and related items directly to the customer in the town square or similar venue, once or several times each week. See also FARM STAND.

farm products Raw materials produced by farmers (such as cotton, hogs, eggs, and milk). These are unprocessed goods that are moved to the next step in the production process with as little handling as possible. They become part of the physical good when they are processed in the form of textiles, frozen or canned foods, etc. Compare PRODUCE, fresh fruits and vegetables sold at retail.

farm stand A stall or booth where fresh-picked PRODUCE is displayed for sale. Flowers are frequently sold as well as homemade cakes, pies, honey, cheese, etc. Farm stands are frequently located on the road closest to the farm itself. Also called a *fruit stand*, *vegetable stand*, or *produce stand*, but these can also be found in towns and cities and are not necessarily located on or adjacent to a farm.

FAS See FREE ALONGSIDE SHIP (FAS).

FASA See FEDERAL ACQUISITION STREAMLINING ACT (FASA) (1994).

fascia A horizontal band, board, or panel at least four feet wide. In stores, it is often found six to seven feet above the ground (i.e., above the bins, shelves, or clothing rods attached to a wall or partition). A fascia can be used to conceal lights and as a background for merchandise displays.

fashion Collectively, those styles (clothing, automobiles, etc.) that are currently most popular. Styles said to be "in fashion" are widely accepted by consumers at one or more levels of the market. Since styles constantly change in response to consumer demand for novelty, it may be said that fashion is, in fact, change (i.e., that fashion is not a state so much as it is an ongoing process). See also STYLE.

Fashion Accessories Market An area in New York City in which are found a large number of accessory product manufacturers showrooms. The area is actually part of the FASHION CENTER.

fashion adoption process The mechanism by which fashions are diffused throughout a population. There are three basic theories of fashion adoption: the downward flow (or trickle-down) theory in which adoption and diffusion are seen as flowing from higher socioeconomic classes downward to the lower classes; the horizontal flow (or mass market) theory in which fashions are believed to move from group to group in the same social class (i.e., opinion leaders within the large middle class have as much influence on fashion adoption as do leading members of the upper classes); and the upward flow theory in which generally younger people (and sometimes young people of relatively low socioeconomic levels) are seen as influencing fashions, as they quickly adopt new styles that will later be diffused up the class structure.

fashion-advanced Synonym for FASHION-FORWARD.

fashion appeal The intangible quality in a design that makes it attractive to the consumer.

fashion/basic continuum In apparel merchandising, the full range of products from the most basic (i.e., those with no demand for styling changes during a full 52-week merchandising cycle) to the fashion product that experiences weekly demands for styling changes (i.e., high-fashion or fad items). These are the two extremes. The majority of goods fall somewhere in between. Compare SEASONAL/STAPLE CONTINUUM.

fashion board A group of consumers, often high school or college students, used by stores to test consumer acceptance of new products and styles. See also COLLEGE BOARD and TEEN BOARD.

fashion calendar 1. A schedule or plan for the current year that indicates the market weeks during which the designers' or manufacturers' new lines may be seen by buyers. 2. A retail store schedule listing all fashion promotions for the store (e.g., fashion shows, advertising, and special promotion). Also called a *retail fashion theme calendar*.

fashion center See FASHION/SPECIALTY CENTER.

Fashion Center The area immediately west and east of Seventh Avenue in New York City (running from 35th to about 41st Street) in which much of the women's ready-to-wear industry is located. The area, considered the most important MARKET for womenswear, contains myriad showrooms of womenswear manufacturers. The FASHION ACCESSORIES MARKET is located in the same general vicinity. Also known as the *Garment District*. Formerly known as the GARMENT CENTER.

fashion clinic In a store, a seminar organized by the FASHION DIRECTOR and reporting on such aspects of fashion as color, fabric, silhouette, etc. It is presented either for the benefit of store personnel (from top management down to salespeople) or for customers, and may or may not include a FASHION SHOW.

fashion consultant A person or firm that gives professional fashion advice to groups, businesses, or individuals.

fashion coordination The perpetual monitoring and analysis of fashion trends to ensure that merchandise sold in the various apparel departments of a retail store is harmonious in style, quality, and appeal.

fashion coordinator At the retail level, an employee responsible for organizing in-store fashion promotions, doing trend research for various fashion departments, etc. Fashion coordinators usually do not have direct merchandising responsibilities. In large retail organizations, the fashion coordinator often works under the FASHION DIRECTOR.

fashion cycle See FASHION LIFE CYCLE.

fashion department   In a retail organization, the part of the PROMOTION DIVISION involved in developing the company's fashion image. Fashion department staff interpret general trends to meet the needs of the store's target customer, then provide appropriate information and training to salespeople. Fashion shows and special events are also designed by the fashion department staff. The head of the fashion department is generally called the FASHION DIRECTOR.

fashion designer   Synonym for APPAREL DESIGNER.

fashion director   The person whose primary responsibility is to promote the store's fashion merchandise. Much of the fashion director's energy is used in researching trends, developing plans for the next season, and communicating this information to store personnel and customers. In particular, the fashion director provides the store's buyers with the latest information on current fashion trends. See also FASHION DEPARTMENT.

fashion emulator   Synonym for FASHION FOLLOWER.

fashion fakes   The low end of the FASHION JEWELRY business.

fashion follower   A consumer who adopts a new fashion after the fashion leaders. Also called a *fashion emulator*. See also ADOPTION PROCESS.

fashion forecasting   The practice of predicting fashion trends in fabric, color, style, etc., for apparel and accessories. The prediction, usually in the form of a report, is known as a *fashion forecast*. See also FORECASTING, ECONOMIC FORECASTING, TREND EXTENSION, and SALES FORECASTING.

fashion-forward   Of designers, retailers, consumers, and merchandise, representing the newest, most fashionable styles. Also called *fashion-advanced*.

fashion goods   Distinctive items of merchandise that possess a great deal of current customer appeal and experience demand for change in styling. Fashion goods are characterized by a short product life span and unpredictable levels of sales (both of which make them financially riskier than BASIC STOCK), as well as the importance of style and color and the need for broad assortments to create a favorable store image. Purchase of fashion goods by consumers is often on impulse (or at least as the result of subjective buying decisions). The term is often applied to the newest, currently popular apparel for which there is great demand. See also PERISHABILITY.

fashion image   The impression held by the public, and fostered by the retail store, of a retailer's fashion expertise, leadership, and place within the fashion cycle.

fashion industry   The sum total of the businesses involved in the design, production, distribution, merchandising, and sale of fashionable goods (i.e., apparel, accessories, shoes, etc.) both domestically and internationally.

Fashion Industry Modernization Center (FIMC)   A centralized apparel training and technology center located at 193 Centre Street in New York City. The FIMC gives garment workers and managers the opportunity to meet the ever-changing needs of the apparel industry. It houses modern production equipment used for demonstrations to contractors and manufacturers as well as for the hands-on skills training of garment workers. The GARMENT INDUSTRY DEVELOPMENT CORPORATION (GDIC) holds evening classes for garment workers at the facility. The FIMC also provides services to management in the form of technology demonstrations, management training seminars, a computer laboratory, and business consulting services.

fashion influential   An individual whose advice is sought by friends and associates regarding apparel styles and trends and whose adoption of a new style promotes its acceptance by a peer group. See also OPINION LEADER and PERSONAL INFLUENCE.

fashion innovator   A person who tends to be in the vanguard of accepting and adopting a new style. See also INNOVATOR.

fashionista   A very fashionable person (usually a woman) who is knowledgeable about the ins and outs of fashion and design and an avid follower of high fashion. The term is especially used to refer to such a person who is working in the FASHION INDUSTRY.

fashion jewelry   High-quality, expensive COSTUME JEWELRY. The term was coined in the 1980s and includes such items as pave collars, flashy brooches, lapel pins, necklaces, earrings, and hat pins made of imitation gems. Identical imitation of precious stone jewelry is called *paste*.

fashion leader   An individual who is among the first to adopt a new fashion. See also ADOPTION PROCESS.

fashion life cycle   A theory, somewhat akin to that of the PRODUCT LIFE CYCLE (PLC), in which styles are seen to appear and rise in popularity, flourish, peak, and finally decline and disappear. The cycle may be seen as having three stages: introduction, acceptance, and regression. Alternatively, it may be seen as having six stages: rise/origination, acceptance or rejection, popularity, mass production, decline in popularity, and abandonment. The cycle is considered complete when a new style appears and the process begins again. Also referred to as the *arc of fashion, retail fashion cycle,* or *fashion cycle*.

Fashion Market of San Francisco (FMSF)   A manufacturer's representative trade show located in the SoMa district of San Francisco and offering the latest trends in fashion and accessories five times a year. FMSF maintains a Web site at www.fashionsanfrancisco.com.

fashion merchandise   Synonym for FASHION GOODS.

fashion merchandising   The planning, advertising, promotion, and selling of apparel and other fashion-related merchandise to meet the needs of prospective customers as to price, quantity, quality, and style.

fashion merchandising policy   The general, long-range merchandising strategy of a store, including fashion aims, quality standards, price ranges, and competition.

fashion model   See MODEL.

fashion obsolescence   See PLANNED STYLE OBSOLESCENCE.

fashion piracy   The practice, fairly common in the apparel industry, of copying another manufacturer's fashion design, usually at a cheaper price point. The resulting product is known as a KNOCKOFF.

fashion plate   1. Originally, a picture (i.e., printed from an engraved plate, of the kind used to illustrate and advertise fashions in nineteenth-century women's magazines) showing a current style of attire and accessories.   2. A person consistently dressed according to the latest fashions.

fashion press   The reporters and photographers who cover the news on fashion for trade and consumer magazines, newspapers, broadcast media, etc.

fashion product   See FASHION GOODS.

fashion promotion   The use of newspaper and magazine advertising, window and interior displays, publicity, fashion shows, broadcast media, etc., to promote the sale of fashion merchandise in a retail store. E-MAIL and other INTERNET advertising may also be used to bring customers into the store or to encourage them to order the fashions online.

fashion research   MARKETING RESEARCH (MR) as applied to the fashion industry. Fashion research may involve consumer surveys and the study of an item's past performance in order to forecast the demand for various types of fashion merchandise.

Fashion Row   A shopping district in New York City (along Sixth Avenue between 14th and 23rd Streets) that was home to many of the earliest department stores beginning in the 1880s. Most of the early department stores in this area were built in the PALAZZO DESIGN. Many of the original buildings are still standing, although the original stores relocated during the early twentieth century and many have since gone out of business. After many years of neglect, during which the buildings were used as warehouses, etc., the district is once again a thriving commercial area featuring many national and regional chain stores.

fashion season   Any of the four seasons (i.e., spring, summer, fall, and winter) used to denote and name apparel collections. The collections correspond to the seasons in which consumers are most likely to wear those items. For example, a designer will come out with a fall collection (i.e., clothing suitable to be worn in the autumn) well in advance of the fall season in which it is meant to be worn. The so-called FIFTH SEASON is often included in discussions of the fashion seasons. Also called, simply, a *season*.

fashion sense   An ability to detect those products and styles that will capture the public's aesthetic attention and develop into respectable sellers.

fashion shopping   The activity of a customer seeking high fashion merchandise in upscale apparel stores. Fashion shopping is often compared to RECREATIONAL SHOPPING and VALUE SHOPPING.

fashion show   The formal presentation of a group of new apparel styles, either by a manufacturer or designer to buyers and the press, or by retailers to consumers. It is often held in advance or at the beginning of a new FASHION SEASON to introduce the season's clothes and uses live models to display the apparel on a runway or stage. The fashion show may also be a benefit performance for charity. The first American fashion show using live models was staged by *Vogue* magazine editor Edna Woolman Chase in November 1914. Current trends in fashion shows include the use of TV, videotapes, film, and the Internet. Also called a *showing* or a *style show*. See also MODEL, PRODUCTION SHOW, RUNWAY SHOW, and INFORMAL FASHION SHOW.

fashion show planning calendar   A tool used by the fashion and sales staffs of a retail store that lists locations, themes, dates, and times for the planned fashion shows. The tool allows staff to plan and perform the various steps in fashion show production.

fashion show production agency   A firm that provides the services necessary to present a FASHION SHOW. Organizations or retail stores may utilize these services when they determine that it is not beneficial to maintain an in-house staff to fulfill these functions. Services may include selecting and supervising models; reserving the show location; setting up the stage; hiring the lighting, music, and backstage personnel; and hiring the caterers. Services are usually paid on a contractual basis.

fashion specialist   In the fashion adoption process, an individual who follows the lead of the FASHION INNOVATOR group, but is not quite an innovator herself/himself. See also EARLY ADOPTERS.

fashion/specialty center   An anchorless shopping center that focuses on a lifestyle cluster, unique merchandise, or specific price level. Suitable for high-traffic locations in urban or suburban areas, fashion/specialty centers target customers with refined fashion tastes or particular lifestyles, vacationers seeking unique local merchandise, etc. The typical tenant of a fashion/specialty center is the high-end SPECIALTY STORE.

fashion statement   A particular style or look selected by an individual as a comment about his or her own identity and relationship to the larger society. A fashion statement usually refers to a style of dress that says something about the individual, but may extend to choices of hairstyle and body art as well.

fashion stylist   The individual responsible for the presentation of merchandise in the store under the direction of the FASHION DIRECTOR or a FASHION COORDINATOR. Often a fashion stylist will pull together a variety of garments and accessories for a FASHION SHOW or for the DISPLAY department. The fashion stylist also performs other tasks in which creative judgment is necessary.

fashion theme   A central motif around which the merchandise assortment in fashion departments may be coordinated.

For example, a popular movie that makes a major fashion statement (e.g., *Dr. Zhivago*) may serve as a fashion theme.

fashion theme calendar   A guide that indicates fashion trends and creative interpretations of basic categories. In a fashion theme calendar, the basic categories take on new and creative interpretations reflecting fashion trends and the themes and motifs used in promotional activities. This is generally tied closely to VISUAL MERCHANDISING plans. See also VISUAL MERCHANDISING CALENDAR.

fashion trend   1. A developing vogue or style moving from limited to popular acceptance.   2. The general or prevailing direction in which apparel styles seem to be moving. Fashion trends may be influenced by a variety of societal factors including political events, films, celebrities, dramas, sports events (such as the Olympic Games), etc. See also TREND.

fashion victim   An individual who, in an attempt to keep up with fashion trends, succeeds only in wearing tasteless, unbecoming, and inappropriate fashions. The fashion victim slavishly follows the trends without regard for what is becoming or appropriate and sacrifices individuality to trendiness.

fashion watch   A woman's wristwatch that serves as a decorative accessory as well as a functional timepiece.

FAS pricing   See FREE ALONGSIDE SHIP (FAS) PRICING.

fast-color   Dyed fabric that will not fade when subjected to sunlight or run when washed. Fabrics so dyed are also called *colorfast*.

fast follower   1. In Internet marketing, an online business that monitors and adopts competitors' good ideas for its own Web site, thereby avoiding some risks and expensive mistakes by letting others make them first. See also INNOVATOR, COMPETITOR, and CONSERVATIVE.   2. See EARLY ADOPTERS.

fast food outlet/restaurant   A food retailer featuring a limited menu of prepared food, a takeout capability, a rapid turnover of customers, and self-service counters. Also called *quick service restaurant (QSR)*.

fast freight service   In physical distribution, the use of special, fast trains for the shipment of perishable goods, goods in urgent demand, or high-value items.

fast mover/seller   A high-demand item that sells rapidly. Sometimes described as EXPLOSIVE. See also BEST SELLER.

fast-selling stock report   A record or statement charting the rate of sale of high-demand, fast-selling items as a safeguard against stock shortages. See also BEST SELLER REPORT.

fat budget   (Slang) Ample OPEN-TO-BUY (OTB) provided to the retail BUYER by the merchandise manager.

fat budget item   An item of merchandise approved by the retail buyer in the hope that the item will substantially increase store or department sales.

favorite   See BOOKMARK.

FC   See FIXED COSTS (FC).

FCBA   See FAIR CREDIT BILLING ACT (FCBA) (1975).

FCC   See FEDERAL COMMUNICATIONS COMMISSION (FCC).

FCN treaties   See FRIENDSHIP, COMMERCE, AND NAVIGATION (FCN) TREATIES.

FCPA   See FOREIGN CORRUPT PRACTICES ACT (FCPA) (1977).

FCRA   See FAIR CREDIT REPORTING ACT (FCRA) (1970).

FDA   See FOOD AND DRUG ADMINISTRATION (FDA).

feature   1. A characteristic of a product or service. For example, a favorite feature of a cell phone is its convenience.   2. The component of an item or service that yields a benefit. For example, the best-used feature of a new refrigerator may be its ice-dispensing unit.   3. A product specially highlighted in a sales promotion. For example, cheese may be one of the features in the supermarket's weekly circular. Also called *featured item*.   4. To highlight a particular item or group of items in a display or promotion. For example, a store may feature outdoor furniture in its July DISPLAY WINDOW.

featured item   See FEATURE.

feature fixture   In apparel retailing, a store furnishing unit used to display small quantities of TREND MERCHANDISE, TEST MERCHANDISE, and COORDINATES and SEPARATES that are being presented as coordinated outfits. Feature fixtures highlight the newest and most exciting items in stock and are intended to build multiple sales. Shoppers look to feature fixtures for guidance in fashion. Conventional feature fixtures include the TWO-WAY FIXTURE/DISPLAY and the FOUR-WAY FIXTURE/DISPLAY/RACK. See also FIXTURE.

feature improvement   The addition of new components or characteristics to a product to improve its versatility or convenience of use. For example, a speaker phone feature may be added to a cell phone. See also PRODUCT IMPROVEMENT.

features approach   See BENEFIT APPROACH.

features/benefits approach   See BENEFIT APPROACH.

Federal Acquisition Streamlining Act (FASA) (1994)   An act signed into law by President Clinton on October 13, 1994, mandating that the federal government use E-PROCUREMENT to reduce paperwork, speed transaction times, and streamline purchasing procedures.

Federal Communications Commission (FCC)   The U.S. federal agency responsible for administering the Communications Act of 1934 and subsequent related legislation regarding the licensing of television and radio broadcasters. The FCC exercises control over the practices of broadcasters in an effort to ensure that they operate for the public interest, convenience, and necessity. The FCC has the authority to issue, renew, and withdraw broadcast station licenses as well as the authority to monitor advertising on these stations. Keeping pace with the evolution of communication technology, the FCC now also has authority over telephone, telegraph, private radio, cellular telephone, pagers, cable TV, international communications, and satellite communications. Along with several other agencies seeking to regulate the Internet, the FCC is involved with online commercialization.

Federal Excise Tax (FET) A tax or duty levied by the U.S. federal government on the manufacture, sale, or consumption of various commodities within the country (e.g., liquor and tobacco) or on the license necessary to engage in certain businesses, trades, or occupations. See also EXCISE.

Federal Insurance Contributions Act (FICA) (1935) The law that instituted Social Security in the United States. The act determines Social Security taxes and benefits for all participants. FICA was removed from the Social Security Act in 1939 and incorporated into the Internal Revenue Code. Also called the *Social Security Law*.

Federal Mediation and Conciliation Service (FMCS) An independent agency of the U.S. federal government created in 1947 as part of the LABOR-MANAGEMENT RELATIONS ACT (1947). The FMCS works to prevent and/or minimize the impact of labor-management disputes on the free flow of commerce by providing mediation, conciliation, and voluntary arbitration services. It maintains a Web site at www.fmcs.gov.

Federal Trade Commission (FTC) A regulatory agency of the U.S. government charged with policing anti-monopoly laws. In the 1970s, the FTC emerged as a protector of consumer rights by regulating children's advertising, cigarette package labeling, the funeral industry, etc. It now maintains the federal do-not-call (DNC) registry. The FTC has a Web site at www.ftc.gov. See also FEDERAL TRADE COMMISSION ACT (FTCA) (1914).

Federal Trade Commission Act (FTCA) (1914) U.S. federal legislation establishing the FEDERAL TRADE COMMISSION (FTC) and empowering it to enforce the SHERMAN ANTITRUST ACT (1890), the CLAYTON ACT (1914), and subsequent related legislation. The FTCA makes it illegal for anyone to commit an unfair or deceptive act of commerce or to engage in deceptive business practices. See also the WHEELER-LEA ACT (1938), which amended the Federal Trade Commission Act.

Federal Trade Commission Act (1980) An act limiting the power of the FEDERAL TRADE COMMISSION (FTC) to set and enforce trade regulation. It amended the FTCA of 1914.

feedback 1. The process by which supervisors or employers evaluate their employees and inform them as to how their performance compares with the employer's expectations. The goal of feedback is to reinforce appropriate behavior and discourage unproductive behavior. 2. In marketing, advertising, and promotion, customer comments and actions associated with the marketing communication that may be used to refine the message or change the channel or product.

feed reader Software designed to display an RSS FEED in a format that is readable, understandable, and usable to humans. Also called a *news reader*.

fenestration The placement of windows in a building or other structure. Fenestration is an important consideration when planning a window display. See also WINDOW DISPLAY.

fertility rate The birth rate expressed as the number of children per woman. It is an important consideration for retailers and others engaged in MARKET SEGMENTATION, as it indicates the demand for a wide array of products including maternity clothes, disposable diapers, baby strollers, toys, etc.

festival center See FESTIVAL MARKETPLACE.

festival marketplace A shopping center composed of specialty stores, pushcart peddlers, and food merchants that is often a tourist attraction within a city's cultural and entertainment center. The centers are sometimes the result of creative reuse of abandoned warehouses or factories. Examples of some well-known festival marketplaces are New York's South Street Seaport, Boston's Faneuil Hall/Quincy Market, Baltimore's Harborplace, New Orleans' Riverwalk, and San Francisco's Ghirardelli Square. Socializing and dining are often as important as shopping in the festival marketplace. Also called a *festival center, urban specialty center, theme shopping center,* or *theme center*.

FET See FEDERAL EXCISE TAX (FET).

FICA See FEDERAL INSURANCE CONTRIBUTIONS ACT (FICA) (1935).

FICO score A credit score developed by Fair, Isaac & Co. to determine the likelihood that credit users will pay their bills. A *credit score* condenses a borrower's credit history into a single number, calculated by using scoring models and mathematical tables to assign points for different pieces of information. Factors contributing to the score include late payments, the amount of time credit has been established, the amount of credit used versus the amount of credit available, length of time at present residence, employment history, and negative credit information such as bankruptcies. In the United States, three bureaus calculate FICO scores, and each method is slightly different. Some lenders use one of the three scores, while other lenders may use whichever is the middle score.

fidelity bond An insurance contract protecting a business against losses resulting from any dishonest acts of employees (e.g., embezzlement, forgery, larceny, and theft) involving money, merchandise, or property. A *fidelity bonding program* serves as an insurance policy and is sometimes used by state governments, at no cost to the employer or the employee, to encourage employers to hire ex-offenders.

field 1. In retailing, the geographic location where goods and services are sold. 2. In sales or marketing research, the external environment into which the salesperson or researcher ventures. 3. In DATABASE (DB) design, a single piece of information in a designated category, such as customer name or customer zip code. A complete set of fields constitutes a record.

field sales manager   A lower level sales manager, generally at the district or regional level, to whom the FIELD SALESPEOPLE report.

field salespeople   Salespeople who make direct, face-to-face calls on potential buyers. Compare IN-HOUSE SALESPEOPLE, who respond to customers who call or come to the company on their own initiative.

field warehouser   A specialized PUBLIC WAREHOUSE organization that provides cash for goods on hand. The field warehouser holds some of a manufacturer's finished goods as its own property. In exchange, it issues a WAREHOUSE RECEIPT to the manufacturer. The warehouse receipts may be used as COLLATERAL to borrow money. This is a particularly valuable service to manufacturers whose goods are not yet sold. The manufacturer's own warehouse is used to avoid the expense of transporting the goods, and the seller retains title to the goods. Control of the goods, however, passes to the field warehouser. Also known as a *custodial warehouser*.

FIFO   Acronym for FIRST IN, FIRST OUT (FIFO).

fifth season   A slack, midwinter period when sales must be encouraged by clearance sales, white sales, etc. Also characterized by some demand for CRUISEWEAR and resort apparel. See also SEASON.

fighting brand   An individual brand used to meet the competition at a lower price point while the status of the company's other, higher-quality, better-known, and more expensive brand is protected. See also INDIVIDUAL BRAND.

figure-eight layout   An arrangement of fixtures and aisles in a store that forms a figure-eight or chain-link pattern to allow for greater flexibility in organizing the store's physical space. Also called a *link traffic pattern layout*.

file   1. On a computer, any collection of data of one kind, stored under one title and manipulated by a particular application. A file may be a text document, a digital image, a digital audio recording, an executable program, etc.   2. Specifically, in DATABASE (DB) design, a collection of records of one kind, such as complete information about all customers. A file is made up of multiple records, which are in turn made up of fields. Each field contains one piece of information.   3. A collection of papers, records, etc., on one subject, arranged in a convenient order (e.g., alphabetically, numerically, chronologically).   4. The cabinet or container used to house papers, letters, records, invoices, order forms, etc.

file server   See SERVER.

file-sharing   Made famous by the *Napster Case* (2001), file-sharing is peer-to-peer (P2P) computing that allows users to share files they have downloaded with others over the Internet. Napster, for example, allowed music lovers to download free

Napster file-sharing software and then copy MP3 music files to their computer hard drives. The private use of downloaded music is legal, but sharing music with others is considered piracy if the music is copyright-protected.

file transfer protocol (FTP)   An INTERNET service that allows a user to store files on a site where they can be accessed and retrieved by other authorized users.

filled order   See COMPLETE ORDER.

fill-in item/order   See FILL-INS.

fill-ins   Merchandise purchased late in the buying season, when inventories have been depleted, in order to bring stocks up to proper levels. Fast-moving items are particularly likely to require fill-in orders.

fill rate   The percentage of times a manufacturer or vendor is able to ship all goods ordered. A fill rate lower than 100% results in sales lost at retail.

FIMC   See FASHION INDUSTRY MODERNIZATION CENTER (FIMC).

fin   A panel used in a DISPLAY WINDOW to form side walls, much like a *flat* or *teaser* in stage design. Fins limit the view of what is on the sides and direct the viewer's sight line to the center of the DISPLAY.

final consumer   Synonym for CONSUMER.

final consumer's decision process   The procedure by which a consumer collects and analyzes information and makes choices among available alternatives. The process consists of six stages: STIMULUS, PROBLEM AWARENESS, INFORMATION SEARCH, EVALUATION OF ALTERNATIVES, PURCHASE, and POSTPURCHASE BEHAVIOR. Demographics, social factors, and psychological factors are likely to affect this decision making process.

final markup   See MAINTAINED MARKUP.

final price   See FINAL SELLING PRICE.

final sale   The completion of a purchase that cannot be returned or exchanged. Sales receipts are generally marked "final sale" to reflect this policy.

final sales   The total of net sales to consumers, governments, and foreigners. Final sales exclude sales made to producers, except sales of durable parts and machinery.

final selling price   The price received when an item is actually sold (i.e., the price actually received for the merchandise). This may differ from the initial or retail price, which is the first price placed on merchandise for resale (i.e., the price the retailer hopes to realize).

finance and control division   Synonym for CONTROL DIVISION.

finance and credit A SELLING AID provided by many vendors to their client stores. The vendor allows the retail buyer to work on an open account basis, with 30 days allowed from the date of the invoice until payment. Often a DISCOUNT is allowed if the bill is paid in a shorter period of time. See also DATING OF INVOICES.

finance company A business firm that specializes in lending money to consumers, purchasing accounts receivable, and extending credit to businesses in the form of short-term loans. Also called a *personal finance company.*

financial audit The formal and systematic examination of the performance of a company in terms of dollars. Financial audits utilize generally accepted accounting procedures and standards.

financial control division 1. In retailing, the division responsible for administering the budget and handling all the financial functions (e.g., payroll, accounts receivable, accounts payable, and inventory control). Auditing is used to check and verify that information is accurate. In a large retail establishment, the head of this division is the vice president of finance or corporate controller. 2. In an apparel manufacturing firm, a division having similar responsibilities to the financial control division of a retail firm. However, the apparel manufacturer must also deal with the FACTOR (i.e., a finance company that buys a manufacturer's accounts receivable). This type of transaction gives the manufacturer cash necessary to operate while the garments are being made and shipped. Sometimes the factor will also take over the billing and financial management of the manufacturing firm. May also be called the *financial division.* The head of this division is the VICE PRESIDENT (VP) OF FINANCE or CORPORATE CONTROLLER.

financial division See FINANCIAL CONTROL DIVISION.

financial flow See CHANNEL FLOW.

financial objectives The profit and return on investment sought by a company in the current year as expressed in the MARKETING PLAN. See also MARKETING OBJECTIVES.

Financial Operating Results of Department and Specialty Stores (FOR) An annual statistical study formerly published by the NATIONAL RETAIL FEDERATION (NRF) and earlier by the NATIONAL RETAIL MERCHANTS ASSOCIATION (NRMA). The FOR was based on the financial statements and operating results submitted by participating member stores, and included tables of performance (in which individual store identities were not disclosed) for purposes of comparison. FOR ceased publication in 1996–1997 and was replaced, at least in part, by RETAIL HORIZONS.

financial ratios The series of ratios (i.e., proportional relationships) used to measure a company's productivity, solvency, liquidity, and other items on the company's BALANCE SHEET. The ratios indicate trends in these financial areas and provide a means of comparing companies within an industry. The finan-

cial ratios are grouped into two types: those that summarize an aspect of the business operation for a period of time (generally one year); and those that summarize an aspect of the company's financial position at a given moment in time (i.e., a snapshot).

financial risk The CONSUMER-PERCEIVED RISK that a product may not be worth its purchase price.

financial statements The balance sheet, income statement, statement of retained earnings, statement of changes in financial position, statement of changes in owner's equity with notes, and the profit and loss statement. Taken together, they reflect the financial position of the company at the end of the accounting period and any changes in financial position that have occurred during that period. Organizations use financial statements to spot problems and opportunities. Managers and outsiders use them to evaluate a company's performance in relation to the economy as a whole and to the company's competitors in the industry.

financing The raising of needed money, credit, or capital to launch or maintain a business operation. See also FINANCING FUNCTION.

financing function A FACILITATING FUNCTION by which funding is provided to manufacture, transport, sell, buy, and store products. See also FINANCING and SALES FINANCE COMPANY.

findings FABRICATING PARTS used in the manufacture of apparel (e.g., buttons, zippers, and thread).

fine A dollar penalty levied on a store for deceptive promotions and other illegal practices.

fine jewelry Superior quality JEWELRY made of precious metals and often set with precious or semiprecious stones.

finished goods Manufactured products ready for sale to wholesalers, retailers, or consumers.

finished goods inventory The items a manufacturer has made for sale to customers.

fire sale Goods for sale at reduced prices as the result of fire or water damage. The term has come to be applied to any sale held under alleged emergency conditions, indicating that merchandise must be moved quickly. Some jurisdictions have enacted laws regulating the use of the term to protect the public from false advertising.

firewall 1. In the ONLINE environment, a combination of hardware and software used to stop unauthorized access to an intranet via the INTERNET. 2. In E-TAILING, hardware used to check and maintain transaction sites to protect stored customer data from hackers and crackers, site defacement, denial of service attacks, viruses and worms, theft of data with credit card information, etc. Most ISP hosts offer firewall protection on their servers.

firm   1. A business entity or enterprise, often in the form of a partnership or incorporated association of two or more persons.   2. Of a price or value, not subject to fluctuation or bargaining. For example, a retailer may quote a firm price to a customer, indicating that it is not negotiable. See also FIRM ORDER and FIRM PRICE.

firm bidding   A policy stipulating that bids (e.g., for a contract) are final and that changes cannot be accepted under any circumstances.

firm market   A condition of stable prices. Such a market is more predictable for all channel members than one in which prices are fluctuating.

firm order   An order that is final and cannot be canceled or modified. The order may be either written or oral, but is binding.

firm price   1. A price that is not subject to change. If the manufacturer or marketing intermediary delivers the goods on time and in the specified quantity, the retailer is obligated to pay the stated price.   2. Any retail price not subject to bargaining or negotiation on the part of the consumer.

first cost   The wholesale price for goods in a foreign market, exclusive of shipping and customs.

first in, first out (FIFO)   A method of INVENTORY VALUATION that assumes that merchandise acquired first was sold (or otherwise disposed of) first. What remains, therefore, represents more recent merchandise costs. Compare LAST IN, FIRST OUT (LIFO).

first in, still here (FISH)   A method of INVENTORY VALUATION that assumes that merchandise acquired first has remained in stock. Firms experiencing this situation may find themselves buried in inventory while profits decline.

first markup   Synonym for MARKON.

first mover   A dot-com business that went online in the first wave of Internet commercialization.

first of month (FOM) inventory   See BEGINNING OF MONTH (BOM) INVENTORY.

first price   See ORIGINAL RETAIL.

first quality   Of goods, having no flaws, defects, or imperfections.

first-time buyer   A customer who is making an initial purchase of a particular item or service. First-time buyers are considered good prospects for additional, follow-up sales. Consequently, they are often recipients of promotional materials.

fiscal year   Any period of 12 consecutive months selected by a business and used as an accounting period for annual reports.

fish   (Slang) In INTERNET chat rooms, an individual who spends too much time ONLINE. Der. acronym for *first in, still here.*

FISH   See FIRST IN, STILL HERE (FISH).

fishyback   (Slang) A coordinated transportation arrangement in which truck trailers are loaded directly onto ships. This use of CONTAINERIZATION helps eliminate costly and time-consuming unloading and reloading of the goods being shipped.

fit   1. Short form of CHANNEL FIT.   2. The extent to which a garment is the right size or shape for the wearer.   3. Short for PROMOTIONAL FIT.

fit model   A live model whose body dimensions correspond to the manufacturer's sample size. Designers use the fit model to assess the fit, styling, and overall look of a new garment.

fitting room   A place in an apparel store or department where customers can try on clothing before making a final selection and purchase. In a self-service store, merchandise is typically counted in and out of the fitting room by an employee of the store. The customer returns the merchandise to the racks. In a limited service setting, the merchandise is counted in and out of the fitting room but some assistance may be available from sales personnel. A sales associate returns unselected merchandise to the racks. In a full service environment, the fitting room is larger, allowing the sales associate to assist the customer with dressing. The sales associate is available to provide additional merchandise and gather and return unwanted merchandise to inventory. Finally, in a premier service environment, spacious fitting rooms may be equipped with telephones as well as food and beverage service. Sales associates gather merchandise, assist customers, and return unwanted merchandise to inventory.

five-and-dime store   Synonym for VARIETY STORE. Also called *five and ten* or *dime store.*

five and ten   Synonym for VARIETY STORE. Also called *dime store* or *five-and-dime store.*

five P playbook   The five Ps of marketing: product, price, place, people, and promotion. See also FOUR PS OF THE MARKETING MIX.

five Ps of marketing   See FIVE P PLAYBOOK and FOUR PS OF THE MARKETING MIX.

five-star living   A trend in consumer LIFESTYLE preferences that is leading five-star hotels to join forces with real estate developers. The hotels offer guest services to owners of luxury residential properties located next to or even on top of their hotels. Such services may include use of the spa, bellboys, restaurant reservations, and 24/7 room service (i.e., products and services that fit the DAILY LUBRICANT category). The trend was identified at www.trendwatching.com.

fixed asset   An ASSET such as a building, machinery, land, or natural resource, intended to be used in carrying on the business rather than sold.

fixed base budgeting   A method of determining the store's budget by allowing an estimated amount of disbursement for each of the store's expenses. At the end of the period, the actual expenditure is placed alongside the estimate, and variations are shown in dollar amounts and/or percentages. See also PRODUCTIVITY-BASED BUDGET.

fixed charges   See FIXED COSTS (FC).

fixed cost contribution   The portion of a selling price deriving from costs that remain constant in spite of changes in output. These are the costs left over after variable costs (i.e., those that fluctuate in direct proportion to changes in output) have been accounted for. See also SELLING PRICE.

fixed costs (FC)   Those operating costs that do not fluctuate in direct relation to production levels or sales volume. Fixed costs vary over a period of time but are relatively independent of short-term changes in output. Included are rent, property taxes, plant and equipment depreciation, interest on bonds, etc. Also called *fixed expenses, fixed charges, standby cost,* or *period costs.* See also OVERHEAD.

fixed expenses   See FIXED COSTS (FC).

fixed fee (buying) office   See SALARIED BUYING OFFICE.

fixed-order period model   A method used to determine the number of items to be ordered and re-ordered at specified time intervals up to a predetermined maximum. In this model it is the time period between orders that is fixed, while the order quantity varies according to need. Also called a *fixed period system.* Compare FIXED-ORDER QUANTITY MODEL. See also ORDER.

fixed-order quantity model   A method used to determine the standard (i.e., fixed) number of items to be ordered when the inventory reaches a predetermined low level. In this model it is the order quantity that is fixed, while the time period between orders varies as inventories decrease. Also called fixed quantity system. Compare FIXED-ORDER PERIOD MODEL. See also ORDER.

fixed period system   Synonym for FIXED-ORDER PERIOD MODEL.

fixed price (policy)   See ONE-PRICE POLICY.

fixed quantity system   Synonym for FIXED-ORDER QUANTITY MODEL.

fixed rate   Synonym for FLAT RATE.

fixed routing   In personal selling, the practice of calling on customers on a regular basis.

fixed-sum-per-unit approach   A method of computing a promotional budget by allocating a set amount of money for each unit produced or sold. See also PROMOTIONAL BUDGETING.

fixture   A table, counter, rack, etc. used by a store to stock and display its merchandise. Also called *store fixture* and *selling equipment.* See also entries for specific types of fixtures, DISPLAY FIXTURE, FIXTURING, VENDOR FIXTURE, and FORM.

fixture topper   A sign placed on top of various fixtures, such as round racks, T-stands, and four-way fixtures. Fixture toppers promote a particular category of merchandise, brand, or theme.

fixturing   The selection and arrangement of store fixtures, such as racks and counters, for the purposes of display and customer convenience (especially in the case of self-service stores). Fixtures and visuals are sometimes provided to the retail store by the vendor, particularly in supermarkets and other food stores. The fixture is known as a VENDOR FIXTURE, a *vendor-provided fixture,* or *a vendor-supplied fixture.* These fixtures frequently contain vendor identification. See also STORE LAYOUT AND DESIGN.

flag   1. A large, eye-catching sign that may be used inside the store or in window and exterior displays.   2. See NAMEPLATE.

flagging an account   The temporary suspension of a charge account in an attempt to keep it under control. The account may eventually become a REFER ACCOUNT, requiring approval from the credit office for future charges.

flagship store/division   The main store of a large retailing firm having a number of branches. The flagship store is usually the original downtown store and often houses the executive, merchandising, information technology, financial, and promotional personnel responsible for the centralized operation of the entire enterprise. A department store organization consisting of a flagship store and two or more branch stores is considered a MULTIUNIT DEPARTMENT STORE. Also called the *downtown store, parent store, main store,* or the *flagship division.* See also BRANCH STORE.

flame   In Internet marketing, the direct and usually angry E-MAIL response of the recipient to SPAM, a POP-UP AD, or other offensive electronic message. Also called *flame mail.* Sending such messages is called *flaming.*

Flammable Fabrics Acts (1953, 1967, DF)   U.S. federal legislation, passed in 1953 and amended in 1967, prohibiting the manufacture or sale of fabrics or apparel that are dangerously flammable according to frequently revised standards. The 1967 act also expanded textile legislation to include the Department of Commerce Flammability Standards for additional products (e.g., carpets, mattresses, and children's sleepwear). The act is enforced by the CONSUMER PRODUCTS SAFETY COMMISSION (CPSC).

flanker product/brand   1. A new product related to an already established companion product and bearing the same BRAND NAME. For example, a new hair conditioner bearing the same name as an established shampoo would be an appropriate flanker product. The introduction of flanker products may be used to help boost the sales of the mature product.   2. A new product introduced by a company that already markets an existing product in the same category. The flanker may be of a different shape or size, but it is basically the same product.

flanking   The process of bringing to market new products related to established products. See FLANKER PRODUCT/BRAND.

flash in the pan   (Slang) An item that is popular and successful for a short time, but not expected to generate enduring interest. See also FAD.

flash (sales) report   An unaudited report showing gross sales by department. The flash report is prepared from sales checks and register tapes during the day or at the close of each business day.

flat   1. Not subject to modification or change; fixed (e.g., a flat rate with no additional charges).   2. Lifeless, dull, lacking vitality or interest. Lack of consumer interest in a product may be termed flat.   3. Of sales of a product, consistent, even, without any discernable increase or decrease.   4. A panel used in a DISPLAY WINDOW to form side walls; synonym for FIN.

flat organization   Synonym for DECENTRALIZED ORGANIZATION.

flat rate   A fixed charge per unit, not subject to modification or change (e.g., 10 cents per pound, 60 cents per mile, $5 per hour). Similar to a fixed price or a one-price policy, but used in different situations (e.g., when multiple units or quantities are purchased at the same time). See also ONE-PRICE POLICY.

flat-rate Internet access pricing   An agreement between an INTERNET SERVICE PROVIDER (ISP) and an Internet user in which the user pays a flat monthly fee for Internet access irrespective of time actually spent online. The widespread adoption of flat-rate Internet access pricing greatly accelerated the adoption of Internet use in the United States and led to its commercialization. Compare METERED INTERNET ACCESS.

flat sales   Sales of a product that remain fairly constant, usually at a low level.

FLC   See FAMILY LIFE CYCLE (FLC).

flea market   Originally an outdoor bazaar in which vendors offered cheap, secondhand goods for sale to the public. Now flea markets may also be held indoors, and goods sold may be new (though still inexpensive compared to prices paid in stores). Flea markets may be held continuously or occasionally in such locations as barns, buildings, and parking lots.

Flesch formula   See READABILITY TEST.

flexible approach to pricing   A price setting policy that takes many variables into account. Full costs are computed to set a minimum price at which the goods may be sold. The merchant uses this as a starting point, with variable markups that can be adjusted to meet changes in consumer demand, competition, etc. Also called *flexible markup pricing*.

flexible break-even analysis   A form of business analysis used to project the performance of a product in the market-place at various price points. BREAK-EVEN ANALYSIS reveals the number of units of a product that must be sold for total revenue to equal total product cost (i.e., the BREAK-EVEN POINT). Flexible break-even analysis allows the market researcher to estimate the expected sales volume at a number of different prices.

flexible charge account   Synonym for REVOLVING CREDIT.

flexible manufacturing   A manufacturing system in which computer-controlled machines easily adapt to different versions of similar operations. The manufacturer can change from one product design to another with only a few signals from the computer, rather than a complete refitting of the machinery as required in HARD MANUFACTURING. Also called *soft manufacturing*.

flexible manufacturing system (FMS)   Faster, smaller, more adaptable production units used in the apparel industry in place of traditional production factories.

flexible markup pricing   See FLEXIBLE APPROACH TO PRICING.

flexible price policy   See FLEXIBLE APPROACH TO PRICING.

flexible pricing   1. A variable pricing policy that allows for bargaining between buyer and seller as well as for the adjustment of prices to conform to peaks and slumps in the normal business cycle. Flexible prices are commonly found in the industrial market but occur at the retail level in the used car and appliance markets. See also VARIABLE PRICE POLICY.   2. See FLEXIBLE APPROACH TO PRICING.

flier   Alternative spelling of FLYER.

flighting   An irregular advertising schedule marked by periods with moderate to heavy exposure followed by a hiatus or lapse. This may be accompanied by substantial advertising expenditures followed by periods with limited expenses. Seasonal items (e.g., skis and ski apparel) benefit from a flighting scheduling pattern for promotion. Advertising and advertising expenditures resume after the lapse in time for the new season. Compare CONTINUITY and PULSING, two other methods of scheduling advertising.

float   1. The period of time between the crediting of a check to a depositor's bank account and the debiting of the same check to the drawer's bank account. Also called *float time*.   2. See CASH REGISTER BANK.

floatation   A method of interior packaging designed to protect a packed item from shock and vibration. The merchandise is wrapped in a cushioning substance thick enough so that the wrapped shape of the item conforms to the dimensions of the shipping container. Also spelled *flotation*.

floating display   A portable visual presentation of merchandise that is moved to various locations in a store or between branch stores.

floodlight   A high-intensity artificial light that shines in a broad beam so as to give a uniform illumination over a large area (i.e., it floods the area with light). Floodlights are incandescent bulbs, usually in a frosted glass enclosure, and are less concentrated than spotlights because of their wider beam. Floodlights may be used in parking lots, storefronts, and display windows, etc. See also INCANDESCENT LIGHT.

floor   A tier or LEVEL in a multilevel store or other building (e.g., main floor, fifth floor). See also SELLING FLOOR.

floor allowance   A price reduction given to a retail customer on the selling floor, either in the selling department itself or at the point of sale, when purchasing a soiled or otherwise defective article of merchandise.

floor audit   The use of the selling floor cash register to obtain total cash and credit sales for each salesperson, department, and type of sale. Also called *register audit*.

floor care   The maintenance of carpeting, wooden, or other floor surfaces in the store, using electrical or manual means.

floor fixture   A freestanding unit used to present goods on the selling floor where the traffic is. Floor fixtures are classified according to customer accessibility. The major types are round racks, T-stands, and quad racks (i.e., four-way face-outs). See also CLOSED-SELL FIXTURE and OPEN-SELL FIXTURE.

floor limit   The pre-established maximum credit purchase a customer may make without obtaining authorization from the credit department. Similar to the AUTHORIZATION LINE in which permission comes from the credit card issuing company. The process of approval is called AUTHORIZING.

floor model   A product (such as a computer, refrigerator, stove, vacuum cleaner, television, or other item in the hard goods categories) put out on the selling floor for examination by customers and sometimes for the purpose of demonstration. What the customer actually buys, in most cases, is fresh stock from the stockroom. Floor models are frequently sold "as is" for a reduced price when the merchandise is about to be discontinued. See also DEMONSTRATION MODEL.

floor plan   A scale drawing of the layout of rooms and facilities on a floor of a store or other building.

floor plan financing   A form of financing commonly used by retailers when purchasing big-ticket items such as appliances, automobiles, electronics, boats, etc. The retailer borrows money from a lending institution and pays the vendor (a manufacturer or distributor) for the goods at the time of receipt. Proceeds from sales are used to repay the lender. Also called *floor planning*.

floor planning   Short for FLOOR PLAN FINANCING.

floor price   In marketing, the minimum price, which normally cannot be further reduced (due to economic, political, or trade reasons). It is the lowest price that a business can afford or is willing to accept. Also called a *price floor*.

floor pyramid   A POINT-OF-PURCHASE (POP) advertising display where products for sale are piled in the shape of a step pyramid, wide at the base and narrowing toward the top. Also called a *pyramid format display* or a *pyramid display*.

floor-ready merchandise (FRM)   Merchandise that is packaged, cased, folded, hung on selling-floor hangers and/or ticketed by the vendor in such a way that it is ready for the selling floor upon receipt by the retailer. FRM is arranged through a negotiated agreement between the retailer and the vendor and may also involve SOURCE TAGGING of goods with antitheft or price tags. It is designed to increase efficiency, reduce redundancy, and accelerate the process of getting merchandise to the selling floor. FRM assortments are packed according to the specific replenishment needs of individual stores. Compare CASE PACK/CASE-PACKED GOODS. See also CROSS-DOCKING and VENDOR PREMARKING/PRETICKETING.

floor stand   A rack for goods in a POINT-OF-PURCHASE (POP) advertising display. See also FLOOR FIXTURE.

floor stock   Backup merchandise that is actually on the selling floor and accessible to customers instead of behind the scenes in a stockroom. See also FORWARD STOCK and SHELF STOCK.

floor value factor   A ratio that relates productivity to the location of the selling department in the store. The distance from the store entrance to the back of the store is divided by the distance from the store entrance to the department. See also STORE LAYOUT AND DESIGN.

floorwalker   A retail store employee who moves about the store through various selling departments and assists customers in ways not handled by sales personnel.

floppy disk   Synonym for DISK/DISKETTE.

floridasation   A European consumer trend, in the southernmost areas of the continent, emulating the state of Florida in the United States. Such areas as southern Spain and Portugal are becoming retirement communities or destinations for wealthy baby boomers seeking warmer climates. In addition to the real estate development potential, floridasation will lead to the need for insurance and tax specialists, health care centers, inexpensive airline flights, car dealers, decorators, language and art teachers, childcare centers, gardeners, cleaners, security systems, easy online access systems, etc. The trend was identified at www.trendwatching.com.

flotation   Alternative spelling of FLOATATION.

flow   See CHANNEL FLOW.

flow aesthetics   See WEB SITE FLOW AESTHETICS.

flow-through concept   A concept in warehousing in which priority is given to the rapid movement of the warehoused goods. Flow-through is most generally applied to distribution centers in an effort to meet customer demand quickly.

FLSA   See FAIR LABOR STANDARDS ACT (FLSA) (1938).

fluctuating demand   In industrial marketing, the volatile demand for industrial goods and services, particularly for new plants and equipment. This demand is generally regarded as less stable than the demand for consumer goods and services. See also ACCELERATOR PRINCIPLE/EFFECT.

fluorescent lighting   Lighting by tubular electric discharge lamps in which light is produced by the fluorescence (i.e., the emission of visible light) of phosphors coating the inside of the tube. Some retail stores are illuminated by rows of fluorescent lighting fixtures that span the length or width of the store. Fluorescent lighting may also be used in showcases or hidden beneath shelves of merchandise on display.

flyer   A form of direct media advertising. Single sheets of advertising material are printed and handed to passersby, distributed in the store, delivered to the homes of potential customers, or placed on the windshields of parked cars. Some flyers consist of several sheets or a folded folio sheet, like a small booklet or newspaper supplement. A flyer is often called a *handbill, circular, throwaway,* or *giveaway. Dodger* is an old-fashioned term used for the same item. Alternatively spelled *flier.* See also PROMOTIONAL KIT.

flying   A window display technique, particularly used with apparel, that avoids the use of a three-dimensional display form such as a MANNEQUIN. Garments seem to be in movement, soaring through a DISPLAY WINDOW and controlled by invisible wires, pins, and tissue-paper padding. The technique is frequently used in conjunction with elevated windows. See also ELEVATED WINDOW.

flying squad   See CONTINGENT FORCE.

FMCS   See FEDERAL MEDIATION AND CONCILIATION SERVICE (FMCS).

FMLA   See FAMILY AND MEDICAL LEAVE ACT (FMLA) (1996).

FMS   See FLEXIBLE MANUFACTURING SYSTEM (FMS).

FMSF   See FASHION MARKET OF SAN FRANCISCO (FMSF).

FMV   See FAIR MARKET VALUE (FMV).

FOB   See FREE ON BOARD (FOB).

FOB factory/plant   See FREE ON BOARD (FOB) FACTORY.

FOB origin pricing   See FREE ON BOARD (FOB) FACTORY.

FOB plant—freight absorbed   See FREIGHT ABSORPTION (PRICING).

FOB pricing   See FREE ON BOARD (FOB) PRICING.

FOB shipping point   See FREE ON BOARD (FOB) FACTORY.

focal point   Any point in the retail setting where emphasis has been placed to attract the shopper, such as a mannequin or form on a platform with an unusual prop and special lighting.

focus chat   Synonym for CYBER GROUP.

focused factory   A manufacturing facility that deals with only one narrow set of products for a particular market.

focused market unit   A market-oriented division that services potential customers regardless of their location.

focus group   In ADVERTISING RESEARCH, a small group of consumers invited to participate in a spontaneous discussion intended to reveal the participants' real feelings about products, services, or an advertising campaign. The sessions are led by professional advertising or marketing research personnel and are generally taped or filmed so that the researchers can more carefully study participants' responses. A session involving this type of research is known as a *focus group interview.* An online focus group is called alternatively a CYBER GROUP, *e-group, virtual group,* or *focus chat.* Compare CONSUMER PANEL and INTERVIEW.

fold-over statement   A bill to a charge customer that comes pre-folded so that the name and address of the store or other creditor will appear in the transparent window when the bill is properly inserted into the enveloped provided.

follow-the-leader pricing   A pricing situation in which a MARKET LEADER sets a price and everyone else more or less follows it. Some stores make it a matter of policy to more or less copy the price determinations made by specific competitors. See also PARITY PRICE.

follow-up interview   See INTERVIEW.

follow-up letter   A sales communication sent to someone who has made an inquiry about a product or service. The letter invites the potential customer to make a purchase. This form of communication is generally reserved for expensive merchandise.

FOM   See BEGINNING OF MONTH (BOM) INVENTORY.

Food Additives Amendment (1958)   An amendment to the FOOD, DRUG, AND COSMETIC ACT (1938) requiring that food additives be limited to those that do not cause cancer in humans or animals. Popularly known as the *Delaney Act.*

Food and Drug Act (1906)   U.S. federal legislation prohibiting the manufacture, sale, or transportation of adulterated or fraudulently labeled foods and drugs in interstate commerce. The act was replaced by the FOOD, DRUG, AND COSMETIC ACT (1938), amended by the FOOD ADDITIVES AMENDMENT (1958), and the KEFAUVER-HARRIS DRUG AMENDMENTS TO THE FOOD AND DRUG ACT (1962). Also called the *Pure Food and Drug Act (1906).*

Food and Drug Administration (FDA)   The U.S. federal agency responsible for monitoring the purity of foods, food additives, and drugs in interstate commerce. The FDA maintains a testing program to ensure this, and enforces penalties against misbranding, adulteration, and related offenses. The FDA was created by the FOOD AND DRUG ACT (1906). The agency maintains a Web site for the benefit of consumers and industry at www.fda.gov.

food broker   A MARKETING INTERMEDIARY who sells grocery products to all kinds of food outlets in a given territory at a great savings in cost to the many sellers the broker represents.

Food, Drug, and Cosmetic Act (1938)   Federal legislation that expanded the responsibility of the FOOD AND DRUG ADMINISTRATION (FDA) to include cosmetics and therapeutic devices.

Food Safety and Inspection Service (FSIS)   The public health agency in the U.S. Department of Agriculture responsible for ensuring that the commercial supply of meat, poultry, and egg products is safe, wholesome, and correctly labeled and packaged. FSIS maintains a Web site at www.fsis.usda.gov.

football item   (Slang) Merchandise used to attract customers to a retail store as the retailer raises and lowers its price from day to day.

foot form   See SHOE AND FOOT FORM.

footwear   Shoes, boots, slippers, etc., that constitute the outermost covering for the foot. See also SHOE.

FOR   See FINANCIAL OPERATING RESULTS OF DEPARTMENT AND SPECIALTY STORES (FOR).

forced distribution   Advertisements and other promotional activities that encourage consumers to ask for (and even demand) merchandise not handled by some retailers. The object of the campaign is to compel retailers to order the requested product or products. Also known as the PULL DISTRIBUTION STRATEGY. See also the PUSH DISTRIBUTION STRATEGY.

forced sale   The sale of a product below MARKET PRICE, usually to enable the merchant to liquidate merchandise so as to meet the demands of creditors. A forced sale may also be conducted under court order as a public auction of assets. See also GOING-OUT-OF-BUSINESS SALE (GOB).

forced saving   The withholding of a portion of a consumer's income so that it cannot be spent on present consumption. Such savings go into pension funds or other financial instruments for the consumer's future benefit.

forcing method   In personal selling, the use of a stimulus designed to motivate the consumer to the immediate purchase of the item. The salesperson tries to convey a sense of urgency, as with a limited-time offer. The technique is usually short-lived in its effects, and customers may balk at the idea of being pressured. See also SALES APPROACH.

ford   See FORD ITEM.

ford item   (Slang) A popular, mass-produced item or style of apparel that sells in great quantities and may be widely copied at a variety of price levels (i.e., like the original Ford automobiles).

forecast   A prediction of future sales potential or customer acceptance of a new style or product. Also called a *market forecast* or a *projection*. See also FORECASTING and SEASONAL FORECAST.

forecast-based merchandise plan   The generation of an initial pre-season MERCHANDISE PLAN based on various trends, demographics, the store's customer profiles, econometrics, etc. FORECASTING also helps to generate in-season plans. See also SALES PLAN.

forecasting   The practice of predicting future demand and trends in the MARKETPLACE over a given period of time, often using both subjective and statistical methods. Estimates are based on previous experience and expectations of environmental conditions in the selling place. Forecasting may be long-range, short-range, or rolling (which integrates the two), and is used to help plan sales and the related needs of business. Also called *market forecasting* and *projecting*. See also SALES FORECASTING, ECONOMIC FORECASTING, TREND EXTENSION, SEASONAL FORECAST, and FASHION FORECASTING.

forecasting model   A model for predicting the sale of goods or services, market share, and other related variables. See also FORECASTING.

forecasting service   A fee-based subscription service that studies prevailing socioeconomic and market conditions to predict trends in advance of a selling season. For example, the Color Association of the United States (CAUS) and Intercolor are color-forecasting services used by fiber, textile, and apparel manufacturers as well as by retailers with private label merchandise. See also REPORTING SERVICE.

foreign-based (export) agent   Synonym for EXPORT AGENT.

foreign-based export distributor   In DIRECT EXPORT/EXPORTING, a company located in the host country that buys and owns goods from the exporter. See also EXPORT AGENT.

foreign buying office   A RESIDENT BUYING OFFICE situated abroad to facilitate buying merchandise from foreign vendors. See also ASSOCIATED BUYING OFFICE, COMMISSIONAIRE, and COMPANY-OWNED BUYING OFFICE.

Foreign Corrupt Practices Act (FCPA) (1977)   U.S. federal legislation that forbids U.S. citizens to bribe high-ranking foreign government employees and politicians, or to pay money to agents or other individuals who pass money on to government employees. Any bribery within their organizations must be reported. An EXPEDITING PAYMENT to civil servants is, however, allowed.

foreign direct investment   A corporation's purchase of production facilities and equipment outside its own country. See also MULTINATIONAL CORPORATION (MNC).

foreign exchange   The trading of one country's currency for another at a market-determined rate. Foreign exchange transactions are handled in an over-the-counter market, largely by phone or e-mail. Private and commercial customers as well as banks, brokers, and central banks conduct millions of transactions worldwide daily. See also EXCHANGE RATE.

foreign exporter   A MIDDLEMAN organization that exports goods from a particular country. Foreign exporters often locate in major market centers such as New York City, where buyers may come to their showrooms and see samples of the various lines they represent. Foreign exporters facilitate foreign buying since they are in a better position to understand market conditions and deal with shipping and supply problems. They may also communicate frequently with their foreign buying sources. Also called a *selling house* or, simply, an *exporter*.

foreign freight forwarder   Synonym for CUSTOM HOUSE BROKER.

foreign licensing   A form of JOINT VENTURE in which a domestic manufacturer seeks entry into a foreign market by granting a licensee in the foreign market permission to use a manufacturing process, trademark, trade secret, etc. in exchange for a royalty or fee. The partnership thus formed allows the domestic manufacturer to enter the host country market with minimal risk, since the licensee is providing the means of production. The licensee, on the other hand, gains access to a well-known product or product line. Also called *international franchising*. See also LICENSING.

foreign-market channel member   Any firm located in an overseas host country and employed in the distribution of a manufacturer's products to overseas markets. A foreign-market channel member may be an IMPORT INTERMEDIARY, a local WHOLESALER or AGENT, a RETAILER, or a business-to-business channel. See also HOME-MARKET CHANNEL MEMBER.

foreign national pricing   The local price structure in another country.

foreign sales agent (FSA)   An individual or firm that assists the foreign representative of a domestic supplier by seeking sales opportunities abroad.

foreign subsidiary   An operation in the host country that is fully owned by a foreign parent firm. See also SUBSIDIARY and WHOLLY OWNED SUBSIDIARY.

foreign trade zone (FTZ)   A city (often a seaport) designated by a country to receive foreign goods, store, and further process them. Merchandise entering a foreign trade zone may be stored, destroyed, displayed, sampled, re-exported and salvaged. Such zones facilitate international trade in that exporters can ship from the zone (where large quantities of goods are stored) to other countries without being subject to the host country's trade restrictions. The zone is, in fact, an enclave free of these regulations. Also known as a *free trade zone (FTZ)* or *free port*.

foreign valuation   The value of imported goods expressed in terms of the currency of the country of origin for purposes of

levying a duty. For example, U.S. goods shipped to France would be valued in U.S. dollars.

forfeit   A penalty that entails giving up expected benefits (such as payments), particularly for having committed a crime, broken a rule, or violated a contract.

form   A three-dimensional representation of a part of the human anatomy, used to display apparel and similar merchandise. As such, a form may substitute for a MANNEQUIN in visual merchandising. See also DISPLAY.

formal attire   Clothing worn by men and women on ceremonious (i.e., formal) occasions. The category is also called *formalwear*. A woman's dress designed for formal occasions is usually called a *formal, gown, formal gown, evening gown,* or *ball gown*. A man's formal attire usually consists of a *tuxedo*.

formal balance   See SYMMETRICAL BALANCE.

formal gown   See FORMAL ATTIRE.

formal runway show   See RUNWAY SHOW.

formalwear   Synonym for FORMAL ATTIRE.

form competition   A situation in the marketplace in which products that perform the same function but are structured differently are competing against each other for MARKET SHARE.

former purchaser   A customer who has not made any purchases for an extended period of time, usually one year. In general, former purchasers represent potential future sales since they have previously demonstrated an ability to buy merchandise.

formula for periodic replenishment of staple merchandise/stock   See PERIODIC REPLENISHMENT OF STAPLE MERCHANDISE/STOCK.

formula pricing   A PRICING STRATEGY in which the final price is established through the use of a predetermined rule or principle (i.e., formula). For example, prices may be set at three times cost without consideration of any other variables or competitive conditions in the marketplace.

form utility   The usefulness (or consumer satisfaction) arising from the physical transformation that raw materials undergo in processing or manufacture. Form utility may be regarded as the economic UTILITY derived from the actual physical product, particularly when the goods are available in the desired size, color, technical specification, and appearance.

for sale   Of merchandise, available for purchase. Sometimes used as a synonym for ON SALE. See also SALE.

fortnight   A storewide promotional program featuring the merchandise of a particular country, usually for a two-week period (i.e., a fortnight). These are often annual events and include tie-ins with the community. The first fortnight was organized by Stanley Marcus of Neiman Marcus, Dallas, in the fall of 1957. France was the featured country. See also IMPORT FAIR.

forum An online discussion group provided by an ONLINE SERVICE or a BULLETIN BOARD SYSTEM (BBS). Participants with common interests use forums to exchange open messages. Sometimes called a *newsgroup* (particularly on the INTERNET) or *conference*. Essentially synonymous with INTERNET DISCUSSION GROUP.

forward auction See ONLINE AUCTION.

forward buying The making of purchases far in advance of requirements.

forward dating In the dating of invoices, a tactic to encourage present purchases by moving the billing date ahead to a future time. Same as *delayed dating*. See also ADVANCE DATING.

forwarder Short for FREIGHT FORWARDER.

forward integration A marketing system in which a producer or manufacturer owns or controls the CHANNEL OF DISTRIBUTION (up to, and sometimes including, retail outlets) through which its products pass on their way to the ultimate consumer.

forward invention In international marketing, the development of new products for foreign markets. When an entirely new approach for introducing products into a foreign market is required or desired, a company may adopt an INVENTION STRATEGY.

forward market segmentation See MARKET SEGMENTATION.

forward order An agreement between a retailer and a vendor in which the retailer orders goods in advance of need. The merchandise is to be delivered at a predetermined, mutually accepted future date, thus allowing lead time for the retailer.

forward price In international business, a price quoted in terms of future (rather than current) exchange rates because of the likelihood of fluctuation in the rate. The forward price quotes the number of dollars (or other currency) to be paid for a foreign currency bought or sold 30, 90, or 180 days from the day of quoting. See also SPOT PRICE and UNCOVERED POSITION.

forward stock Backup merchandise stored on the selling floor of a department rather than in a stockroom. Unlike FLOOR STOCK, forward stock may be concealed from the customers in an ADJACENT STOCKROOM. See also SHELF STOCK.

forward stockroom Synonym for ADJACENT STOCKROOM.

foul-weather pricing A PRICING STRATEGY in which a company charges so little for its product that it is sold at no profit or, in extreme cases, production costs are not even met. This strategy is employed as a short-term effort to keep a company in business during times of economic crisis.

foundation garments See INTIMATE APPAREL.

four Cs of credit evaluation The four factors considered when determining whether clients are eligible for credit: credit (i.e., payment history and paying habits), cash flow, collateral, and character.

four Cs of diamonds The four criteria by which diamonds are classified and subsequently priced: cut, color, clarity, and carat weight.

four Cs of marketing Fundamental marketing concepts on which all else is based: customer solution (i.e., a product that satisfies a customer's need), customer cost (i.e., a price the customer finds reasonable and affordable), convenience, and communication.

four Cs of vending According to the National Automatic Merchandising Association (NAMA), the four products traditionally representing 80 percent of vending machine sales: cigarettes, candy, coffee, and cold drinks.

four-five-four calendar (4-5-4 calendar) See RETAIL CALENDAR.

four-function plan See MAZUR PLAN.

four Os The basic characteristics of a market: objects (what is purchased); objectives (why the product or service is purchased); organization; and operations. See also SIX OS.

four Ps of marketing See FOUR PS OF THE MARKETING MIX.

four Ps of the marketing mix The four principal variables that must be considered by marketers: PRODUCT (i.e., the right product matched to the right market); PLACE (i.e., reaching the market through adequate distribution channels); PROMOTION (i.e., informing the target market of the product); and PRICE (i.e., setting a competitive price). Also known as the *four Ps of marketing*, the *promotional quadrangle*, and the *marketing mix variables*. See also MARKETING MIX ANALYSIS and FIVE P PLAYBOOK.

four-way Short for FOUR-WAY FIXTURE/DISPLAY/RACK.

four-way fixture/display/rack A four-armed FEATURE FIXTURE, often made of chrome. Goods are hung so that their most visually appealing side faces the customer. Four-way fixtures are frequently used to feature small quantities of trend merchandise, test merchandise, and COORDINATES and separates that are being presented as coordinated outfits. Also called a *costumer* or a *four-way display*. See also ENSEMBLE DISPLAY and SUPERQUAD.

FPS See FULL-PRODUCT SOURCING (FPS).

fragmentation Such fine subdivision of the population of potential customers that a target group is no longer discernible. Compare EXTREME MARKET SEGMENTATION.

frame of reference The manner in which individuals perceive their external environments, particularly as understood from a sociological and/or psychological perspective. The customer's frame of reference helps to determine consumer behavior in the marketplace. See also REFERENCE GROUP.

frames Independently functioning sections into which a Web page is divided. HTML frames allow Web page designers to present online documents in multiple views, so that certain information can remain visible while other views are scrolled or replaced. For example, one frame might display a static banner, a second a navigation menu, and the third the main document that can be scrolled through or replaced by navigating in the second frame.

franchise 1. A contractual agreement between a manufacturer, wholesaler, or service organization (*franchiser*) and a retail outlet (*franchisee*), under which the franchiser provides its name, product line, services, and marketing and management expertise in exchange for an initial payment and an ongoing share of the profits. The franchisee, while essentially an independent retailer, agrees to adopt a common store front and management procedures and to purchase products from the franchising company. The most commonly known franchises are in the fast food industry, but there are many in the consumer goods business as well. Though most often an independent operator, the franchisee may also be another retailer. See also DEALERSHIP, LEASED DEALERSHIP, and TURNKEY OPERATION. 2. The privilege, often exclusive, of marketing a manufacturer's products or providing a service within a specified territory. The franchise is granted to a dealer by a manufacturer or other company. Also called a *territorial franchise*. See FRANCHISING for types of franchises.

franchise cooperative A voluntary association of entrepreneur-retailers who form a franchise organization by setting up a wholesale operative or chain for their mutual benefit. The Medicine Shoppe pharmacies and TruServ (i.e., True Value Hardware Stores) exemplify franchise cooperatives. Such cooperatives generally arise when small, independent retailers band together to be able to compete with large chain operations.

franchised dealer A retail dealer who carries a supplier's products under the terms of a franchise agreement.

franchise department See LEASED DEPARTMENT.

franchisee See FRANCHISE.

franchise extension A new product that capitalizes on a firm's market strength, its relationships with customers, and the success of the firm's other products. See also LINE EXTENSION and BRAND EXTENSION STRATEGY.

franchise-lease agreement See LEASED DEPARTMENT.

franchiser See FRANCHISE.

franchise store An independently owned store that sells branded items produced by a franchise holder. The store pays the franchiser a percentage of sales for the use of the name.

franchise wholesaler A full service MERCHANT WHOLESALER affiliated with a number of retailers. The retailers agree to use a standardized storefront, business format, name, and purchase system. See also FRANCHISE.

franchising A VERTICAL MARKETING SYSTEM (VMS) in which a manufacturer or service organization confers upon an individual or firm the privilege of marketing a product or service. Franchising is thus seen as a system of doing business in which the franchiser and the franchisee enter into a contractual relationship involving clearly established rights and responsibilities. Franchise organizations take four basic forms: those that are part of a limited distribution system for particular products (e.g., automobile dealerships and gasoline stations); wholesaler-sponsored retail outlets (e.g., certain drug stores and automobile parts stores); wholesaler licensing systems (e.g., soft drink bottlers and beer distributors); and retail outlets that carry the trade name of a nationally known organization and commonly provide a service (e.g., fast food restaurants, car rental agencies, and gyms). Franchising is also a means for a retailer to enter a foreign market.

franchisor Alternative spelling of *franchiser*. See FRANCHISE.

fraud The intentional misrepresentation of the truth in order to deceive another person.

fraudulent purchase 1. An order written by a retail buyer to a vendor that is paid for by the store but never delivered. 2. Stolen merchandise returned to a store for credit or refund.

free-after-rebate discount model A failed model for discounting merchandise purchased on the INTERNET. Up to 100% of the purchase price of merchandise was rebated to the buyer; customers were expected to pay for their purchases, take delivery, and apply for the rebate. Too many customers took advantage of the offer for it to be profitable or even sustainable.

free alongside (FAS) See FREE ALONGSIDE SHIP (FAS).

free alongside ship (FAS) A shipping agreement under which the seller pays transportation charges to the ship's side. The expense of loading the goods onto the vessel, the shipping charges, and all concomitant risks are the buyer's responsibility. See also FREE ALONGSIDE SHIP (FAS) PRICING.

free alongside ship (FAS) pricing A billing term indicating that the seller's price includes the cost of getting the goods to a position alongside the ship being used to transport the goods (i.e., to the dock). The price does not include the actual cost of shipping the goods to the buyer.

free carrier Similar to FREE ON BOARD (FOB) except that the seller's obligations are fulfilled when the merchandise is delivered into the custody of the carrier at the named point.

free competition See PURE COMPETITION.

free deal See FREE GOODS OFFER.

free display material   See DEALER DISPLAY.

free enterprise   Under the economic system known as CAPITALISM, the right of private citizens to own businesses and the self-regulation of the market on the sole basis of SUPPLY AND DEMAND, with little or no government intervention.

free examination offer   See TRIAL OFFER.

free-flow floor layout/pattern   See FREE-FLOW LAYOUT.

free-flow layout   The physical arrangement of a store's fixtures using a series of circular, octagonal, oval, or U-shaped patterns to create an atmosphere of informality, considerable open space, and the ability of the shopper to choose many different directions and browse freely. The critical factor is providing enough room between fixtures to allow traffic to flow smoothly. Department stores often use a combination of grid and free-flow layouts. Also called a *free-flow floor pattern, free-flow pattern, free-flow pattern layout, free-flow traffic, free-form layout, free-form pattern,* or *free-form floor plan.*

free-flow pattern (layout)   See FREE-FLOW LAYOUT.

free-flow traffic   See FREE-FLOW LAYOUT.

free foods offer   See FREE SAMPLE.

free-form floor plan   See FREE-FLOW LAYOUT.

free-form layout/pattern   See FREE-FLOW LAYOUT.

free-form retail organization   Synonym for MERCHANDISING CONGLOMERATE.

free gift   See GIFT-WITH-PURCHASE (GWP).

free gift in exchange for proof-of-purchase   See MAIL-IN PREMIUM.

free gift with proof of purchase   See MAIL-IN PREMIUM.

free goods offer   Additional merchandise included with a retailer's order at no additional charge. The free goods are given by the vendor in lieu of a special discount and in appreciation for the size of the order. Free goods are treated as price concessions by the FEDERAL TRADE COMMISSION (FTC). Also called *free merchandise offer.*

freely floating   See EXCHANGE RATE.

freely offered   (Rare) Of merchandise, offered for sale to all customers on essentially the same basis in the course of doing business. In a sense it is the most fundamental of retailing concepts.

free market economy/system   A pure market-directed ECONOMIC SYSTEM in which consumers determine the society's production solely by their choices in the MARKETPLACE, without government intervention of any kind. The manner in which people spend their money determines which products will be produced and what these products will cost. See also SUPPLY AND DEMAND.

free mat   Prepared advertising copy made available to the retailer, who has only to fill in the name and location of the store. The copy is supplied by the vendor.

free merchandise offer   Synonym for FREE GOODS OFFER.

free on board (FOB)   A shipping agreement under which the buyer of goods pays the freight charges from the point of origin (i.e., the FREE ON BOARD [FOB] POINT). Also called *freight on board (FOB).*

free on board (FOB) destination   A shipping agreement under which the seller of the goods pays the freight charges to the buyer's destination and retains title to the merchandise until the destination has been reached.

free on board (FOB) destination, charges reversed   A shipping agreement under which the seller retains title to the goods until they have reached their destination. The buyer is later billed for the freight charges incurred in the shipment.

free on board (FOB) destination, freight prepaid   A shipping agreement under which title to the goods passes from the seller to the buyer at the point of shipment and freight charges are paid by the seller.

free on board (FOB) factory   A shipping agreement in which the buyer pays all freight charges from the factory to the destination. The buyer takes title to the goods at the point of shipment. Also called *free on board (FOB) origin pricing.*

free on board (FOB) origin pricing   Synonym for FREE ON BOARD (FOB) FACTORY.

free on board (FOB) plant   See FREE ON BOARD (FOB) FACTORY.

free on board (FOB) plant—freight allowed   See FREIGHT ABSORPTION (PRICING).

free on board (FOB) point   In shipping agreements, the POINT OF ORIGIN (e.g., the factory, the port of entry).

free on board (FOB) pricing   A geographic pricing policy, incorporated into some shipping agreements, in which buyers pay transportation costs from the point at which they take title to the product.

free on board (FOB) shipping point   A shipping agreement under which the seller of the goods pays crating and freight charges to the point where the merchandise is to be shipped (a port, depot, etc.). The buyer takes title to the goods at this point and assumes freight charges to the ultimate destination (e.g., the buyer's store or warehouse). See also POINT OF ORIGIN.

free on rail   A shipping agreement under which the buyer pays transportation costs once the goods are loaded on a train.

The shipper's price to the buyer includes all costs involved in getting the merchandise to the train depot and loading it on the freight train.

free on truck   A shipping agreement under which the buyer pays transportation costs once the goods are loaded on a truck. The shipper's price to the buyer includes all costs involved in getting the merchandise to the truck and loading it on the truck.

free port   Synonym for FOREIGN TRADE ZONE (FTZ).

free sample   A trial size of a product given to customers free of charge to get them to try the product. The strategy is frequently employed in supermarkets (e.g., a customer is offered a taste of a new food product, in which case it is also called a *free foods offer*) and in the cosmetics industry (e.g., small trial sizes of products are given to customers who purchase cosmetics in department stores). Also called *trial size, sample size,* or *sample package.* See also TRIAL OFFER.

free send-away premium   See MAIL-IN PREMIUM.

freestanding location   A store site that is not physically connected to other stores in the vicinity. The store may be large with its own parking facilities (as in highway retailing), or it may be a neighborhood retailer such as a small corner grocery store. Also called a *freestanding store.*

freestanding neighborhood store   See NEIGHBORHOOD STORE.

freestanding store   See FREESTANDING LOCATION.

free trade   The conduct of international business without boundaries or taxation. The European Union (EU) is an example of free trade in which the borders of member nations are open to the flow of goods and services and all tariffs have been eliminated.

free trade agreement (FTA)   In international trade, an accord to lower or eliminate tariffs on imported merchandise. A free trade agreement is intended to promote the free flow of goods and services between nations subscribing to the agreement.

free-trade area   An agreement between nations to drop trade barriers among themselves while retaining independent trade relations with countries outside the group. Such areas do not generally permit labor and capital to flow freely across national borders. Each country retains autonomy over its money supply so that exchange rates can fluctuate relative to both member and nonmember countries.

free trade association   Synonym for ECONOMIC COMMUNITY.

free trade zone (FTZ)   Synonym for FOREIGN TRADE ZONE (FTZ).

free trial offer   See TRIAL OFFER.

freight   Merchandise, goods, products, or commodities shipped by train, plane, truck, or ship. The term does not include baggage, express mail, or regular mail.

freight absorption (pricing)   A pricing policy in which the seller of goods assumes some or all of the cost of shipping the products to their destination in an effort to maintain a competitive selling price in the local marketplace. Also called *freight equalization, freight-absorption pricing,* and *free on board (FOB) plant—freight allowed.* See also UNSYSTEMATIC FREIGHT EQUALIZATION.

freight allowance   A reduction in transportation costs to the retailer, paid in part by the manufacturer or other supplier when shipping merchandise to a store. Considered a means of equalizing transportation costs for distant retailers, the allowance may be based on the cost of the merchandise, its weight, or the quantity ordered.

freight allowed pricing   An agreement in which a store pays the transportation charges on goods it receives from a vendor, but is permitted to charge back all or part of that cost to the vendor. The allowance may be based on the cost of the merchandise, the weight of the merchandise, or the quantity of the merchandise ordered. Also called, simply, *freight allowed.* See also FREIGHT ALLOWANCE.

freight audit   The systematic examination of freight charges for their accuracy. A fee is charged based on a percentage of the overcharges detected. The person responsible for conducting a freight audit is known as a *freight auditor.*

freight equalization   See FREIGHT ABSORPTION (PRICING).

freight forwarder   1. An independent middleman organization that consolidates less-than-carload shipments from several manufacturers, distributors, or other shippers for transportation to one location. The freight forwarder groups these shipments into truckload, railroad, or container shipment lots and ships them by rail and/or truck. The freight forwarder also picks up and delivers merchandise, handles claims, and acts as a traffic department for shippers. The cost for this service, which saves both the retailer and the supplier considerable freight costs, is generally paid by the buyer of the goods (i.e., the retailer). Freight forwarding allows channel members to take advantage of the lower rates offered by common carriers. Also called a *package consolidating agency* and a *packing house.* 2. A person or firm acting as an agent in the shipping of exports and imports and in the clearing of merchandise through customs.

freight-in   Shipping charges on goods purchased (i.e., coming in to the store). Also called *freight inward.*

freight inward   Synonym for FREIGHT-IN.

freight on board (FOB)   Synonym for FREE ON BOARD (FOB).

freight outward   Shipping charges on goods leaving the factory, warehouse, or other distribution point (i.e., going out to the customer).

freight paid to   The destination point to which the seller agrees to forward the goods, assuming all expenses and risks to that point.

freight pool   A cooperative shipping arrangement involving a group of manufacturers who frequently ship in less-than-carload lots. Participants reduce their respective shipping costs by combining their small shipments into one *carload lot.*

frequency   In advertising, the number of times an audience is exposed to a message during the period of the advertising campaign. This applies to Internet promotions as well as to the print and broadcast media. Frequency increases the chance that the target audience will be reached.

frequency of additional deliveries (FAD)   The number of additional deliveries required in a selling period for MERCHANDISE REPLENISHMENT.

frequently asked questions (FAQs)   Computer site pages listing anticipated user queries and their corresponding answers. Sometimes these lists are derived from actual inquiries. FAQs cut down on the number of times a visitor must contact the site administrator by e-mail or phone and reduce the number of personal replies site administrators must make to identical questions.

freshness date   A date used by the American brewing industry on bottles and cans of beer to indicate either the date the beer was bottled or the date by which the beer should be consumed. See also SHELF LIFE.

friendly suitor   See FRIENDLY TAKEOVER.

friendly takeover   An acquisition or merger in which the organization being acquired or taken over is happy about this fact and welcomes the ability of the acquiring organization to finance their poorly capitalized or fiscally troubled company. The acquiring company is known as a *friendly suitor.* Compare HOSTILE TAKEOVER.

friend-of-a-friend promotion   The offering of incentives (e.g., gifts) to established customers who refer names of people who might be interested in the product or service. For example, a gym may offer a free month's membership to a member who brings in a friend once the friend becomes a member. Compare MEMBER-GET-MEMBER PROMOTION.

friendship, commerce, and navigation treaties (FCN)   International agreements that cover a wide range of commercial matters such as marketing practices in the trading partner's country, agreements on duties and other taxes, foreign exchange, travel, and communications.

fringe area   See FRINGE TRADING AREA.

fringe assortment   Merchandise generating only marginal customer interest and therefore having a slow rate of turnover.

fringe benefit   See EMPLOYEE BENEFIT.

fringe market   The segment of the consumer market that finds a store or product acceptable for occasional purchases, though not as the preferred source or regular brand. For

example, a regular customer of a large supermarket may shop in a small neighborhood grocery store for an occasional container of milk.

fringe sizes   Synonym for END SIZES.

fringe stock   Any category of merchandise that generates only a small percentage of a store's sales. See also FRINGE ASSORTMENT.

fringe trading area   The area outside a store's PRIMARY TRADING AREA and SECONDARY TRADING AREA. The fringe trading area provides 5 to 25 percent of the store's customers but they are widely dispersed. Also called a *tertiary trading area, a fringe area,* or a *fringe trade area.*

FRM   See FLOOR-READY MERCHANDISE (FRM).

front   In retailing, the SELLING AREA of the store where customers shop.

front end   1. In the design and construction of Web pages, synonymous with UPFRONT. The front end is what the visitor to the Web site sees and experiences. A Web site's INTERFACE seamlessly links the front end to the BACKEND, where most of the activities of the transaction actually take place.   2. The area in a store, particularly a discount store or a food store, where self-selected merchandise is checked, paid for, and bagged or boxed. See also FRONT-END CHECKOUT.

front-end checkout   A store layout that provides checkstands and registers at or near the store's entrance rather than throughout the store. See also CHECKOUT COUNTER.

front page   Synonym for HOME PAGE.

fruit stand   See FARM STAND.

FSA   See FOREIGN SALES AGENT (FSA).

FSIS   See FOOD SAFETY AND INSPECTION SERVICE (FSIS).

FTA   See FREE TRADE AGREEMENT (FTA).

FTC   See FEDERAL TRADE COMMISSION (FTC).

FTCA   See FEDERAL TRADE COMMISSION ACT (FTCA) (1914).

FTP   See FILE TRANSFER PROTOCOL (FTP).

FTZ   See FOREIGN TRADE ZONE (FTZ).

fulfilled   See VALS SEGMENTATION.

fulfillment   Any and all activities needed to deliver purchased products to the buyer (i.e., everything the seller must do after the order is placed to make sure the merchandise reaches the customer).

fulfillment system   Processes devised for receiving, servicing, and tracking orders. Ideally, fulfillment systems are designed to fill orders rapidly, maintain customer files, send invoices, record payments, react to customer complaints and other inquiries, and produce purchase and payment data for use in future marketing.

full car rate   Synonym for CARLOAD FREIGHT RATE (CL).

full compensation   In global marketing, a COMPENSATION TRANSACTION resembling barter in that a 100% mutual transfer of goods takes place. Deliveries are made and paid for separately, and the exporting firm commits itself to purchasing products or services at an amount equal to that specified in the export contract. An option exists to sell the commitment to a third party, who may take over the commitment from the exporter for a fee. Compare PARTIAL COMPENSATION.

full cost approach to cost analysis   A method of MARKETING COST ANALYSIS in which all functional costs, including fixed and common costs, are allocated in some way to products, customers, or other similar categories. This allows analysts and marketing managers to find the profitability of various customers, products, etc. by subtracting costs from sales. See also CONTRIBUTION-MARGIN APPROACH TO COST ANALYSIS and MARKETING COST ANALYSIS.

full cost approach to pricing   A method of determining retail prices in which the price of each product sold in the store covers all the costs of bringing the particular item to the selling floor. Every selling cost is taken into account, including rent, utilities, salaries, delivery costs, and returns. Added to these considerations are the cost of the merchandise itself and a percentage high enough to provide a reasonable profit. Also called *cost pricing* and *full cost pricing*.

full costing system   Synonym for ABSORPTION COSTING SYSTEM.

full cost pricing   See FULL COST APPROACH TO PRICING.

full demand   A condition in the marketplace in which purchasers want and are willing to pay for all the products being produced.

full disclosure   The practice of making available to the consumer all relevant data about a product or a service so that an informed purchase decision can be made. For products, this information is provided on the label and advertisements. Full disclosure is one of a number of consumer protections against deceptive business practices.

full figure fashions   Synonym for PLUS SIZES.

full function wholesaler   See FULL SERVICE WHOLESALER.

full line   Stock in a given classification of merchandise, made available to the customer in every variation of size, material, and color that can reasonably be expected at a given price. Includes staples, style merchandise, novelties, and outsizes.

full line department store   A DEPARTMENT STORE that offers both SOFT GOODS (e.g., apparel and household textile products)

and HARD GOODS (nontextile products such as furniture and consumer electronics).

full line discounter   A retailer that sells a wide selection of merchandise at prices lower than the conventional prices of other retailers. Merchandise generally includes apparel, home accessories, consumer electronics, housewares, health and beauty products, and toys. Automotive and hardware products are sometimes added to the mix. The brand name goods sold by full line discounters are generally lower-priced brands not offered by department stores. Like department stores, however, full line discounters complement their brand offering with private-label merchandise, especially in the apparel categories. Some full line discounters have upscaled their image by offering higher-priced brands and emulating the ambiance of department and specialty stores. Examples of full line discounters are Wal-Mart, Kmart, and Target. Also called a *full line discount house*, a *full line discount store*, or a *general merchandise discounter*.

full line discount house/store   See FULL LINE DISCOUNTER.

full line forcing   A trade practice in which a manufacturer requires wholesalers and retailers to buy the entire line of merchandise (including the less saleable items) if they are to sell any of the manufacturer's products.

full line pricing   A PRICING STRATEGY that considers the relationship among the prices of different products in a line. An effort is made to present buyers with a logical pricing system. For example, General Motors prices its automobiles in a predictable manner from the least expensive Chevrolet to the most expensive Cadillac. Also called *product line pricing* and *interdependent product pricing*.

full line store/retailer   A retail store that carries all the merchandise expected for that type of store. For example, a full line department store carries both SOFT GOODS (e.g., apparel and household-textile products) and HARD GOODS (i.e., nontextile products such as furniture and consumer electronics).

full line strategy   A marketing strategy in which sellers offer a wide variety of products for sale in an effort to broaden their customer base. See also PRODUCT LINE STRATEGY and LIMITED LINE STRATEGY.

full line wholesaler   See GENERAL LINE WHOLESALER.

full mark/markup   A keystone markup of 100% over cost price. Sometimes called, simply, *full mark*. See also KEYSTONE MARKUP.

full nest I   The category comprising families of one or two incomes in which the youngest child is under six years old. Such families have moderate discretionary income and their expenditures are child- and family-oriented. Toys, games, family travel, and household necessities dominate their purchases.

full nest II   The category made up of families (usually with two incomes) in which the youngest child is over six years old.

This group has slightly more *discretionary income* than full nest I, but the needs of growing children still dominate their expenditures. Items such as clothing and electronic goods gradually replace toys as major purchases. Saving for college may be a major interest.

full nest III The category comprising families (usually with two incomes) who are very future-oriented and may be starting to plan for retirement. The children of full nest III families are mostly living independently, but the youngest child may still live at home. At this point in their lives, families may be redecorating their homes, and travel and dinners out are priorities. Educational expenditures may be a major part of the family budget, particularly for those in second or third marriages.

full product sourcing (FPS) A form of apparel SOURCING in which the contractor provides everything required to make the garment. The contractor purchases materials, develops samples, makes garments, and ships the goods to the sourcing company. Under FPS no fabrics or findings are owned by the sourcing company; these are sourced and purchased by the contractor. Compare CUT, MAKE, TRIM (CMT) SOURCING.

full service See FULL SERVICE STORE.

full service (advertising) agency An ADVERTISING AGENCY that offers a full range of marketing, communications, and promotion services. This type of agency is involved in planning, creating, and producing advertising; selecting and buying media time or space; and evaluating advertising effectiveness. The *creative services division* is the heart of a full service agency; it is responsible for the creation and execution of the advertisements.

full service merchandiser A vendor who provides promotional assistance, accounting systems, training programs, and other services to the retailer in addition to merchandise. The retailer, in turn, agrees to purchase a substantial amount of merchandise from the vendor.

full service store A retail store that is adequately staffed with sales and support personnel so as to provide a full range of services to the customer. These services include individual sales assistance, credit, delivery, gift wrapping, installation, repair, alterations, etc. See also LIMITED SERVICE STORE and SELF-SERVICE.

full service wholesaler A marketing intermediary (i.e., WHOLESALER) who, in addition to taking title to the goods that will later be resold, often takes physical possession of them. Full service wholesalers usually operate warehouses and provide their customers with delivery services, credit, and assistance in the form of accounting, inventory, and marketing information. Also called a *full function wholesaler, functional wholesaler, wholesale merchant, wholesaler merchant,* or *regular wholesaler.*

full-time employee/worker A worker in a store or other business who is employed year-round and works a full workweek (generally 35 to 40 hours per week). Also called *full-timer.*

full-timer Synonym for FULL-TIME EMPLOYEE/WORKER.

full warranty See WARRANTY and MAGNUSON-MOSS WARRANTY ACT (1975).

fully integrated global marketing mix See GLOBAL MARKETING MIX STRATEGY.

functional account In retail and marketing accounting, an account that indicates the purpose for which the expenditure was made. In retailing, such accounts include administrative, occupancy, publicity, buying, and selling expenses. In marketing, such accounts may include marketing research, sales and sales promotional activities, order processing, shipping, warehousing, bookkeeping, etc. Sometimes referred to as a *marketing function account.* Accountants use the term *functional expense classification* to describe the same method of accounting. See also FUNCTIONAL EXPENSE CLASSIFICATION.

functional approach to marketing An approach to the study of marketing in which such activities (i.e., functions) as sales, distribution, advertising, etc., are viewed as key to understanding the marketing process. The investigator studies how each of these functions works and from these findings generalizes about the larger marketing picture.

functional classification A system of dividing jobs and responsibilities among specialized functional areas such as sales promotion, buying, and store operations.

functional competence Thorough background in all areas of marketing necessary for success in the global marketplace.

functional costing The practice of classifying costs by allocating them to the various functions performed (e.g., warehousing, delivery, billing). See also FUNCTIONAL ACCOUNT.

functional departmentalization The grouping of sets of similar activities involving similar expertise into departments in a store or other business. Employees are assigned to departmental groups according to what they do. Such specialization encourages workers to become more efficient and develop expertise. In retailing, departments usually handle publicity (i.e., advertising and promotion), merchandising (i.e., acquiring, displaying, and selling the store's goods), general services (i.e., store security, customer service, etc.), and finance. Also called *departmentalization by function.* See also PROCESS DEPARTMENTALIZATION.

functional discount See TRADE DISCOUNT.

functional expense classification A system of identifying the purpose of an expenditure by assigning it to a particular retail activity (i.e., function). The five functions to which expenses may be ascribed are administration, occupancy, publicity, buying, and selling.

functional manager A manager who is responsible for a specialized area or department of the business, such as retailing. See also FUNCTIONAL DEPARTMENTALIZATION.

functional middleman/middleperson Synonym for AGENT INTERMEDIARY.

functional need Any need of the consumer that is met by the practical application and use of a product or service without referring to style, image, etc. For example, an adhesive bandage meets the functional need of covering a cut. See also FUNCTIONAL SATISFACTION.

functional obsolescence See PLANNED PRODUCT OBSOLESCENCE.

functional organization A form of business organization in which specialists have direct authority in their area of expertise. For example, a company may have a word-processing pool supervised by an expert in office automation rather than a word processor assigned to each department head. An alternative to LINE ORGANIZATION. See also LINE-AND-STAFF ORGANIZATION and DIVISIONAL ORGANIZATION.

functional product group The arrangement and DISPLAY of merchandise according to use.

functional prop See PROP.

functional résumé See RÉSUMÉ.

functional risk The CONSUMER-PERCEIVED RISK that a product, if purchased, may not perform as it is supposed to.

functional satisfaction Consumer satisfaction received from a product's ability to fill its intended function, without regard to style or image. For example, consumers derive satisfaction from an adhesive bandage that sticks and stays in place, protects cuts and other wounds from becoming infected, and is easy to remove when it is no longer needed. See also FUNCTIONAL NEED.

functional wholesaler See FULL SERVICE WHOLESALER.

functions of marketing See MARKETING FUNCTIONS.

functions of physical supply Those activities related to the distribution, transportation, and warehousing of merchandise.

fundamental research Synonym for PURE RESEARCH.

fun seekers The youngest group of global consumers in the *Roger Starch Worldwide* study, prizing values such as pleasure, excitement, adventure, and physical attractiveness. They represent 15 percent of the population and are avid users of electronic media.

Fur Labeling Act See FUR PRODUCTS LABELING ACT (1951).

furnishings 1. The things in a store not regarded as equipment or fixtures (e.g., carpeting, furniture, office appointments). 2. In menswear, ties, shirts, socks, underwear, sleepwear, robes, and accessories.

fur products labeling See FUR PRODUCTS LABELING ACT (1951).

Fur Products Labeling Act (1951) U.S. federal legislation protecting the public against the false labeling and advertising of furs. The act requires that furs be honestly labeled as to the name of the fur, the country of origin, and processing (i.e., sheared, dyed, etc.). A label authority tag must also be attached to each fur garment, indicating support of U.S. Fair Labor Standards. Sometimes called the *Fur Labeling Act*.

future dating A sales agreement that sets the beginning of the discount and NET PAYMENT PERIOD for some time in the future rather than the time the goods are shipped. For example, the terms 2/10 net 30 as of November 1, for goods shipped in August, indicates that the discount and net periods begin on November 1. See also ADVANCE DATING.

G

GAFF/GAFFO A set of abbreviations used to designate a store's category, including G for general merchandise, A for apparel and accessories, F for furniture and/or home furnishings, and O for "other."

gain According to the Financial Accounting Standards Board (1985), any increase in equity (i.e., net assets) "from peripheral or incidental transaction of an entity and from all other transactions and other events and circumstances affecting the entity during a period except those that result from revenues or investments by owners."

gallery exhibit A form of INSTITUTIONAL EVENT that includes the presentation of fashion items in an artistic setting at a gallery.

galvanic skin response (GSR) In ADVERTISING RESEARCH, a measure used to build a PHYSIOLOGICAL PROFILE of a participant. It is a measure of the skin's resistance to or conductance of a small amount of current passed between two electrodes. Researchers assume that an increase in GSR indicates arousal of interest in the advertisement. Also known as *electrodermal response*.

game A sales promotion device in which the participant competes for prizes by engaging in an activity that depends on chance and requires no skill. For example, winning numbers may be revealed on a rub-off card. Some games have a continuity element (i.e., they have been set up so as to encourage the participant to enter more than once). Also called a *game of chance*. Compare CONTEST and SWEEPSTAKES.

gap table Synonym for TIER TABLE (FIXTURE).

garage 1. A building or indoor area for parking or storing automobiles and other vehicles. Also called a *parking garage* or a *parking deck*. See also PARKING and VALIDATE. 2. A service establishment for repairing and maintaining cars and other motor vehicles.

garage influential An amateur critic, reviewer, commentator, blogger, etc., who uses the resources of the WORLD WIDE WEB (WWW) to share content in the form of reviews and opinions with the INTERNET community. The resulting trend indicates that traditional professional reviewers no longer hold the monopoly on telling consumers what to buy, read, experience, eat, watch, play with, or listen to. The trend was identified and the term coined by trendwatching.com at www.trendwatching.com.

garb Synonym for APPAREL.

garbage in, garbage out (GIGO) A computer axiom meaning that if bad, corrupt, or invalid data is entered into a computer system, the output will be similarly bad, corrupt, or invalid.

garden center A retail establishment typically selling plants, trees, seeds, bulbs, gardening tools and equipment, garden hoses, soil, fertilizer, mulch, decorative stones, and related items. Also called a *lawn and garden center*, a *lawn and gardening center*, or a *gardening center*.

garment Synonym for APPAREL.

Garment Center Traditional name for that area to the immediate west and east of Seventh Avenue in New York City (running from 35th to about 41st Street) in which much of the women's READY-TO-WEAR (RTW) industry is located. Although now officially called the FASHION CENTER, the old name is still used extensively. Also known as the *Garment District*. See also SEVENTH AVENUE (SA).

Garment District See GARMENT CENTER.

Garment Industry Development Corporation (GIDC) A nonprofit consortium of labor, industry, and government dedicated to strengthening New York's apparel industry and retaining jobs in fashion. GIDC represents the interests of workers, manufacturers, contractors, private label manufacturers, and international buyers. Based in New York City, the GIDC maintains a Web site at www.gidc.org. See also FASHION INDUSTRY MODERNIZATION CENTER (FIMC).

garment purchase agreement (GPA) In SOURCING, a legal contract used to purchase a specified quantity of apparel goods at a certain price and within specified dates. The GPA also states terms and conditions pertaining to the sale. The GPA is usually accompanied by a TECHNICAL PACKAGE.

garment trade Synonym for APPAREL INDUSTRY.

garnishee To withhold the wages or property belonging to a debtor.

gatekeeper An individual within an organization who controls the flow of information within the organization. In industrial purchasing, persons wishing to sell to the organization must find a way to get their message past the gatekeeper (often the firm's purchasing agent). See also INFLUENCER.

gateway 1. In the INTERNET environment, a NODE on a NETWORK that serves as an entrance to another network. In firms, the gateway is the computer that routes traffic from a workstation to the outside network serving the Web pages. In homes, the gateway is the INTERNET SERVICE PROVIDER (ISP) that connects the user to the Internet. 2. A land-based computer system that switches data and voice signals between satellites and networks. 3. An earlier term for ROUTER.

gateway ad An advertisement sold on the WORLD WIDE WEB (WWW); it appears on the page that links the user's computer to the Web.

GATT See GENERAL AGREEMENT ON TARIFFS AND TRADE (GATT) (1947).

gazebo A DISPLAY fixture, similar to an open latticework pavilion or garden house, that acts as a FOCAL POINT in a department. Merchandise is often arranged in and around a gazebo in such a way as to facilitate customer access.

GDP See GROSS DOMESTIC PRODUCT (GDP).

GDSN See GLOBAL DATA SYNCHRONIZATION NETWORK (GDSN).

gemstone A mineral found in nature that is suitable for use in jewelry because of its beauty, clarity, rarity, etc. While some stones are far more valuable than others, there is less tendency today than formerly to divide them into precious and semiprecious categories. See also PRECIOUS STONE, SEMIPRECIOUS STONE, and DECORATIVE STONE.

general advertising Synonym for NATIONAL ADVERTISING.

general auction An AUCTION, online or offline, in which a wide variety of merchandise is put up to bid. This distinguishes the general auction from the PRODUCT-SPECIFIC AUCTION. See also ONLINE AUCTION.

General Agreement on Tariffs and Trade (GATT) (1947) A multilateral trade treaty in force as of January 1, 1948, with 23 signatories. GATT sets down reciprocal rights and obligations for member countries, having as its principal goal the reduction of tariffs and the removal of trade barriers between these countries. The principles of a world economy embodied in the articles of GATT are RECIPROCITY, NONDISCRIMINATION, and TRANSPARENCY. GATT and its subsequent revisions have succeeded in lowering tariffs and reducing quota barriers on many goods worldwide and have opened doors to foreign markets. Headquartered in Geneva, Switzerland, GATT was replaced, in its final act, by the WORLD TRADE ORGANIZATION (WTO) in 1996.

general credit contract A retail installment contract that gives no right of REPOSSESSION to the merchant or other creditor. However, the merchant may sue the buyer if the terms of the contract have not been met. Some merchants use wage assignments to secure the credit. In these cases, a default permits the retailer to GARNISHEE the wages of the debtor.

General Electric/McKinsey & Co. Nine-Cell Matrix See BUSINESS PORTFOLIO ANALYSIS.

General Electric Strategic Planning Approach A company-wide approach to marketing planning that takes a number of factors (i.e., market growth, competition, market share, profitability, margins, technology, etc.) into account in order to set corporate strategies and objectives.

general expenses One of the two subclassifications of operating expenses (the other being SELLING EXPENSES), including office salaries, rent, utilities, supplies, insurance, taxes, professional services (e.g., accounting and legal fees), depreciation, etc. In essence, they are the operating expenses incurred in the overall administration of the business.

generalizable See SAMPLING PRINCIPLE.

general ledger The accounting record book in which are entered, in summary form, all the transactions of the business. It is a collection of all the asset, liability, owners' equity, revenue, and expense accounts of the firm. See also LEDGER and SUBSIDIARY LEDGER.

general lighting See PRIMARY LIGHTING.

general line distributor/house See GENERAL LINE WHOLESALER.

general line retailer A retail store that carries a wide range of products, such as a FULL LINE DISCOUNTER.

general line wholesaler A merchant wholesaler who carries a complete supply of one type (i.e., line) of merchandise (e.g., groceries). Also called a *full line wholesaler, general line house, general line distributor,* or *single line wholesaler.*

general manager Synonym for STORE MANAGER.

general merchandise chain (Obsolete) A chain department store such as Sears or JCPenney. See also DEPARTMENT STORE.

general merchandise discounter Synonym for FULL LINE DISCOUNTER.

general merchandise distributor See INDUSTRIAL DISTRIBUTOR.

general merchandise manager (GMM) The retail executive responsible for the store's total MERCHANDISING operation, who supervises the divisional merchandise managers (DMMs) and interprets and executes the policies of the store. The GMM, typically at the vice-president or senior-management level, manages a group of related merchandise divisions and participates in major policymaking. The GMM also acts as a liaison executive between the merchandise divisions and all other major store divisions.

general merchandise retailer/store A retail establishment carrying a wide variety of merchandise in some depth. Department, discount, and variety stores as well as some mail order houses may be regarded as general merchandise stores.

general merchandise warehouse A form of PUBLIC WAREHOUSE that may store any type of manufactured goods.

general merchandise wholesaler A full service WHOLESALER that maintains a broad inventory of a number of unrelated products (such as nonperishable groceries, plumbing supplies, hardware, soft goods, etc.). Although they sometimes sell to manufacturers, general merchandise wholesalers are mainly suppliers for smaller stores and noncommercial organizations. See also DISTRIBUTOR.

general order (GO) merchandise Any merchandise not claimed or entered from Customs within 15 days after arrival in the United States. See also CUSTOMS BONDED WAREHOUSE.

general partner See PARTNER.

general partnership See PARTNERSHIP.

general product manager The executive who supervises a number of product managers and is responsible for coordinating their plans and programs for submission to the firm's MARKETING MANAGER. See also PRODUCT MANAGER.

general sales manager The sales executive responsible for coordinating the store's (or the division's) sales force. The general sales manager also develops strategies and methods to fulfill the store's sales plan.

general sales tax A tax, on most items sold at retail, levied at the time of purchase. In many states, purchases of food and medicine are excluded from this tax.

general-specific-general theory See RETAIL ACCORDION THEORY.

general store A small, undepartmentalized version of the GENERAL MERCHANDISE RETAILER, commonly found in rural areas and selling food, clothing, farm implements, garden supplies, hardware, and other highly utilitarian items. Also called a *country store*.

general trading area The geographical area from which most of the store's customers will be drawn.

Generation C The cohort of consumers involved in generating the avalanche of content (the C stands for content) on the WORLD WIDE WEB (WWW). The trend is driven by the creative urges of consumers and by the manufacturers of content-creating tools that make it easier to unleash that creativity. Instead of passively watching, listening, and playing online, consumers increasingly participate in pushing trends and developing products. The trend was identified and the term coined by trendwatching.com at www.trendwatching.com.

Generation X The relatively small group of individuals born in the United States during the *baby-bust years* of 1965–1976. Also called the *Sesame Street Generation*, they are the children of early BABY BOOMERS and are the first generation to grow up with heavy media influence from early childhood on.

Generation Y The generation born between 1977 and 1994. The youngest members of this demographic segment are also known as *techno-tots* or *cyberboomers*. They are the first generation to grow up with a majority of working mothers and have attended preschool in record numbers. Their experiences encompass everything from the INTERNET and prosperity to academic pressure and high divorce rates. Now young adults and teenagers, they have already had an effect on the retail market. Also called *millennials*. See also CYBERBOOMER.

generative business The portion of a store's business that is generated through its own efforts (such as promotions, high-quality merchandise, competitive prices).

generator store Synonym for ANCHOR STORE.

generic brand In common usage, an unbranded product. The term is something of a misnomer inasmuch as a BRAND is a product made distinguishable from other similar products by a unique identifying name, and generics lack just such a name. *Generics*, as they are often called, are unadvertised, plain-label grocery or pharmacy items that often sell for 30 to 40 percent less than advertised brands. Also called *unbranded merchandise*. See also GENERIC PRODUCT.

generic competition A condition in the marketplace in which items in totally separate categories, but performing the identical function, compete against each other for MARKET SHARE.

generic competitor An organization that competes with others to satisfy consumer needs within a general category of products and/or services.

generic demand See PRIMARY DEMAND.

generic goods Synonym for GENERIC PRODUCT.

generic management system standard In GLOBAL MARKETING, a management performance standard adopted by participating countries and coordinated by the International Standards Organization (ISO).

generic market A MARKET, viewed broadly and from the customer's perspective, in which vendors offer products that, while different physically or conceptually, can substitute for each other because they satisfy the same customer need. For example, there are several different items that will satisfy a customer's need for status. Vendors in the generic status market aim to satisfy the need for status rather than focus on the differences between the individual products that will satisfy it. Quite different products may therefore compete with each other; for example, luxury cars compete with cruises, furs, jewelry, and other status goods. Each of these products will confer the desired status, and so may be viewed by the customer as substitutes for each other. Compare PRODUCT MARKET.

generic merchandise Synonym for GENERIC PRODUCT. See also GENERIC BRAND.

generic name A product's common, non-proprietary name as distinct from its brand name. *Generics* are common in the pharmaceutical industry where drugs are sold under their common chemical name as well as under their BRAND NAME. See also GENERIC PRODUCT.

generic portal See PORTAL.

generic product 1. A product sold under a common name rather than a brand name. Generic products are merchandised in a no-frills manner, given little or no advertising support, and are sold at a lower price than branded items. Also called *case product, no-frills merchandise, unbranded product, unbranded merchandise,* or *no-frills product.* See also GENERIC BRAND and GENERIC NAME. 2. In a broader sense, not the item itself but a concept of the item, which includes the buyer's expectations of it (i.e., the benefits the consumer sees the product embodying). See also BUNDLE OF BENEFITS CONCEPT.

generic product advertising Advertising that features a product type without identifying a brand name or company. This type of advertising is undertaken to stimulate primary demand for a class of products and may be sponsored by an industry council or similar organization (for example, advertisements promoting milk consumption sponsored by the National Dairy Council). See also PRIMARY DEMAND.

generics See GENERIC NAME and GENERIC PRODUCT.

gentlemen's pricing A form of pricing generally found in professional services. For example, a physician may charge a flat $3,000 for performing an operation, making no effort to actually cost out the price in terms of hours worked, skill level employed, etc. See also PROFESSIONAL PRICING.

geocentric Of a worldview, global in its scope; not using a particular culture or geographic region as its frame of reference. See also GEOCENTRISM, ETHNOCENTRISM and REGIOCENTRISM.

geocentrism A form of organization, found in some multinational marketing firms, in which the marketing effort focuses on the whole world rather than on any particular nation or region. No single national market is preferred over others or taken as a norm for others. Employees, including management personnel, are hired from diverse backgrounds

and nationalities. As a worldview, geocentrism takes the entire world as its frame of reference and sees it as a locus for ideas, opportunities, and decision making. See also ETHNOCENTRISM, its opposite.

geodemographics Computer-based methods used to identify consumers in specific geographic locations. Neighborhood classification techniques are used to blend demographics, psychographics, and geography to identify specific customer groups whose location is then pinpointed to the level of a specific address. *Cluster-Plus* and *Prizm* are two software tools used in geodemographics. See also LIFESTYLE SEGMENTATION.

geodemographic segmentation Subdivision of the population of potential customers according to demographic variables (e.g., income and age) and identified by a geographic variable (e.g., zip code). The base data are obtained from the census data. The process relies on two basic assumptions: people who live in the same neighborhood are likely to share similar buying habits; and neighborhoods can be categorized in terms of their population (i.e., two or more neighborhoods with similar populations can be placed in the same category).

geodemography A method used by retailers to link households with geographic locations to identify regional and local lifestyles that impact directly on consumer attitudes, behaviors, and buying patterns. See also CORE-BASED STATISTICAL AREA (CBSA), TRADING AREA, and GEODEMOGRAPHICS.

geographical departmentalization A method of business organization in which activities are departmentalized on a territorial or geographical basis. The department or specialty store will use geographical departmentalization if it has expanded into several cities or regions.

geographical information systems (GIS) Computer programs that allow retailers to analyze and map potential sites for new stores on the basis of interrelated demographic, psychographic, and geographic data. Market analysts access information from a variety of databases and other business information sources and superimpose them on a map. GIS may also be used to help chains determine the degree to which the trading areas of their various stores overlap. Also called *geographic information systems (GIS).* See also MARKET SEGMENTATION, TRADING AREA, and RETAIL SITE LOCATION.

geographical (market) segmentation See GEOGRAPHIC SEGMENTATION.

geographic division of authority In marketing management, a form of organization in which line authority is organized along geographic lines (i.e., management is set up on a regional basis), often in an effort to promote better supervision.

geographic information system (GIS) See GEOGRAPHICAL INFORMATION SYSTEMS (GIS).

geographic segmentation Subdivision of the population of potential customers based on geographic location. The target market may be subdivided by a range of *geographic segmenta-*

tion factors such as world region (e.g., continent, developing countries, East, Middle East, Far East, West), national region (East, Midwest, Far West, Sunbelt, etc.), population density (urban, suburban, rural), and city size. Also called *geographic market segmentation* and *market segmentation by geographical bases*.

Gephart Amendment See OMNIBUS TRADE AND COMPETITIVENESS ACT (1988).

GIF See GRAPHICS INTERCHANGE FORMAT (GIF).

Giffen good Any product with a positive price elasticity of demand. When price goes up, the quantity demanded also goes up, and vice versa. This is the opposite of most products, for which price elasticity of demand is negative (i.e., price and demand pull in opposite directions; as the price goes up, the quantity demanded goes down and vice versa). In order to be a true Giffen good, price must be the only thing that changes to induce a change in demand. There are three necessary preconditions for this situation to arise. The product in question must be an INFERIOR GOOD; there must be a lack of close substitutes; and the good must take up a substantial percentage of the buyer's income. Giffen goods are named after Sir Robert Giffen, who is considered the author of this idea. The existence of Giffen goods is often referred to as the *Giffen Paradox*. Compare NORMAL GOOD.

Giffen Paradox See GIFFEN GOOD.

gift card 1. The modern equivalent of a GIFT CERTIFICATE consisting of a plastic card (resembling a credit card or debit card) electronically encoded with a specified amount of money selected by the customer. The recipient of the gift uses the card to make purchases, the amount of each purchase being electronically deducted from the total. Some retailers limit the length of time the gift card remains valid (e.g., one year) or devalue it after a specified period of time. Several states and municipalities are fighting these practices. See also EXPERIENCE STORE. 2. An enclosure included with a purchase intended as a gift. The gift card generally carries a message (e.g., "Happy Birthday") and the name of the gift giver.

gift certificate A document, often resembling a bank check, purchasable in any dollar amount and given as a gift. The gift certificate may be used in lieu of cash and is redeemable in merchandise at the store of purchase. Many retailers now issue a GIFT CARD instead.

gift close A salesperson's closing method in which the prospect is tempted with an added incentive to buy the product or service immediately. Such incentives generally include services rather than actual gifts. For example, free or same-day shipping may be offered in a gift close.

gift-giving approach See PREMIUM APPROACH.

gift receipt A copy of the sales receipt that may be enclosed with a gift to facilitate returns or exchanges by the recipient. The gift receipt does not include the price of the merchandise.

The purchaser (i.e., the gift giver) is issued another receipt that does contain the price of the goods.

gift transaction A sales transaction in which the merchandise is to be a gift intended for a recipient other than the purchaser. Instructions for removal of price tags and wrapping are included on the sales check.

gift-with-purchase (GWP) A special gift or bonus package offered to customers with the purchase of a certain dollar amount of other merchandise. Cosmetic companies use this type of premium extensively. Similar to PURCHASE-WITH-PURCHASE (PWP) except that there is no additional charge for the gift.

gift wrapping/wrap The provision, at the customer's request, of decorative boxes and wrapping paper for merchandise purchased in the store or on the Web site. Some stores have special gift wrapping departments, although smaller stores may combine this function with CLERK WRAP. Some Web sites have special online forms that customers may use to request gift wrapping, sometimes with the enclosure of an electronically generated GIFT CARD. Two kinds of gift wrapping services may be provided: regular gift wrapping, provided free of charge, in boxes and paper bearing the store name and/or logo; and special gift wrapping, provided for a fee, consisting of artistically wrapped packages in decorative paper, ribbons, etc.

gigabyte See BYTE.

GIGO See GARBAGE IN, GARBAGE OUT (GIGO).

girls' sizes The apparel size ranges from 4 to 6X and from 7 to 16 for female children.

GIS See GEOGRAPHICAL INFORMATION SYSTEMS (GIS).

giveaway 1. A free item given out by a store to help generate TRAFFIC. Also called TRAFFIC-BUILDING MERCHANDISE. 2. Synonym for FLYER.

giveaway site A Web site where Internet users can win cash or merchandise without making a purchase or buying a lotto ticket. E-tailers and other marketers use the opportunity to compile e-mail lists and customer data.

GLA See GROSS LEASABLE AREA (GLA).

global advertising Advertising done on an international basis. The advertiser must decide whether to use a global or a local approach to presenting internationally marketed products. In the global approach, the advertisements remain consistent regardless of the country in which the ad will appear. In the local approach, the ads are tailored to particular national or regional markets. See also GLOBAL MARKETING MIX STRATEGY.

global advertising strategy See GLOBAL MARKETING MIX STRATEGY.

global brand A recognizable BRAND identity adopted by a manufacturer or retailer with merchandise in international distribution. The goal of global branding is to establish a name known and preferred by customers throughout the world. A global brand is sometimes defined as one with sales of at least 20 percent outside the firm's domestic market. Other definitions of global brand stipulate that the brand's positioning, advertising strategy, personality, look, and feel are virtually the same in all countries. Firms that develop global brands with these characteristics are said to follow a *global brand strategy*.

global commerce   See GLOBAL MARKETING.

global competition   See GLOBALIZATION OF COMPETITION.

global consumers   Six groups characterized by particular sets of values, identified in the 1990s by *Roger Starch Worldwide*, a research group based in New York City. The study identified the characteristics of consumer groups based on underlying belief systems that cross national lines. An understanding of these consumer groups and their value systems is important for global marketers hoping to make inroads into overseas markets.

global corporation   A MULTINATIONAL CORPORATION (MNC) that (with few modifications) sells the same merchandise in the same way throughout the world, transcending national boundaries and contributing to the erosion of differences in national or regional taste.

Global Data Synchronization Network (GDSN)   A global, Internet-based initiative that enables companies around the world to exchange accurate, up-to-date, standards-compliant supply chain information. The GDSN allows trading partners who choose certified data pools to exchange trade information with any other company, regardless of where they operate geographically. Improving information accuracy reduces costs and improves efficiency and performance. UCCNET, a subsidiary of the UNIFORM CODE COUNCIL (UCC) serves as a participating data pool in GDSN.

global economy   An evolving situation in which the world is becoming increasingly economically integrated. This trend, resulting from such factors as multinational corporations and joint ventures, includes the blurring of lines between exports and imports.

globalization   The extension of one's business to other parts of the globe, making it worldwide.

globalization of competition   Competition between international firms that must learn to compete effectively against other firms from many different countries. Global marketers compete not only with other international firms but also with local competition in foreign markets.

globally coordinated moves   In global competition, the mounting of a coordinated assault in which competitive moves are made in different countries. For example, a firm may introduce a new product in all major national markets simultaneously. Such a move is intended to prevent global competitors from learning from one market and responding in another.

global marketing   In INTERNATIONAL MARKETING, the creation of a single marketing strategy for a product, service, or company over the entire global market, while maintaining some flexibility to adapt to local market requirements where necessary. Global marketing does not rely on tailoring a MARKETING STRATEGY perfectly to any individual market, but seeks instead to offer an undifferentiated marketing mix to markets perceived as homogeneous worldwide. Coca-Cola is considered an example of a global product. Also called *global commerce*. Compare INTERNATIONAL MARKETING and MULTINATIONAL MARKETING.

global marketing mix strategy   A GLOBAL MARKETING STRATEGY in which a firm pursues global integration along all or several MARKETING MIX elements (e.g., pricing, distribution, communications, product). If all elements are involved, it is known as a *fully integrated global marketing strategy*. If some but not all aspects of the marketing mix are included, it is known as a *partially integrated global marketing strategy*. Two common partially integrated global marketing strategies are the *global product strategy* (in which the company has largely integrated its product offering so that it is at least partially standardized) and the *global advertising strategy* (in which similar, if not identical, advertising themes are used worldwide). Compare MULTIDOMESTIC (MARKETING) STRATEGY.

global marketing strategy   A MARKETING STRATEGY predicated on the fact that consumers worldwide are becoming more and more alike, particularly with the advent of inexpensive and convenient transportation and communications. Consequently, a single strategy is applied worldwide and strategies specific to individual countries are abandoned. See also GLOBAL PRODUCT CATEGORY STRATEGY, GLOBAL SEGMENT STRATEGY, and GLOBAL MARKETING MIX STRATEGY. Compare MULTIDOMESTIC (MARKETING) STRATEGY.

global marketplace   The international world of business, trade, and economics. See also MARKETPLACE.

global perspective   The worldview of a company employing a GLOBAL MARKETING STRATEGY. The perspective is based on the perceived homogenization of customers worldwide and the resulting increase in possible standardization of the MARKETING STRATEGY.

global product   Ideally, a standardized product that does not have to be modified to sell in foreign markets. Since there are relatively few opportunities to completely standardize products for the GLOBAL MARKETPLACE, marketers may develop a global product that is partially standardized. The design retains some flexibility, however, so that the end product can be tailored to meet the needs of individual markets. Coca-Cola is generally considered the perfect global product.

global product category strategy   A GLOBAL MARKETING STRATEGY in which firms compete in the same product category country after country. However, marketers employing this strategy may target different segments in each category or tailor their product, advertising, and branding according to local market requirements.

global product strategy   See GLOBAL MARKETING MIX STRATEGY.

global quota   An explicit limit set by a country on the value or quantity of merchandise that may be imported or exported through its borders during a given period. See also QUOTA.

global retailer   A retail firm that does business in its home country and in more than one other TRADING BLOC (i.e., major geographic trading area such as Europe, North America, or the Pacific Rim). Wal-Mart, for example, is a U.S.-based retailer that also does business in the Pacific Rim, North and South America, and Europe.

global segment strategy   A GLOBAL MARKETING STRATEGY based on targeting the same consumer or industrial market segments in many countries. A firm's understanding of a particular customer base may thus be leveraged around the world.

global sourcing   The use of worldwide resources by retailers interested in finding the best products for their stores at the most advantageous prices. Through importing, retailers are able to offer well-designed products that their competitors are less likely to have. Retailers are also able to achieve higher markups on imports because they usually cost less to produce offshore. See also SOURCING.

global theme   An approach to advertising in the GLOBAL MARKETPLACE. In this approach the same advertising theme is used around the world but is varied slightly with each local execution. See also MODULARIZED APPROACH.

glocal strategy   In Internet marketing, a LOCALIZED INTERNET MARKETING STRATEGY applied globally. This is achieved by adapting Web sites to the local cultures of key target markets while still maintaining some standardization globally.

glocalization   The use of a combination of global branding practices and localized marketing. The recently coined term is attributed to Hans Hijlkema, founder of the European Marketing Confederation.

glossy   A photographic print having a shiny, reflective surface finish. Glossies are often used for reproduction purposes in advertising.

glut   An oversupply in the MARKETPLACE. Gluts generally cause prices to drop, as supply greatly exceeds demand. The term is most often applied to a COMMODITY.

GMM   See GENERAL MERCHANDISE MANAGER (GMM).

GMROI   See GROSS MARGIN RETURN ON INVESTMENT (GMROI).

GNI   See GROSS NATIONAL INCOME (GNI).

GNP   See GROSS NATIONAL PRODUCT (GNP).

GO   See GENERAL ORDER (GO) MERCHANDISE.

goal   The mission or purpose of an organization; what the organization wishes to achieve. While the term is often used interchangeably with OBJECTIVE, goals are the broad, long-range targets of the organization while objectives are the specific, short-range targets it sets along the way. Often used in the plural as *goals*. See also MISSION STATEMENT, ADVERTISING GOALS, and OBJECTIVE.

goals down-plans up planning   A form of planning in which managers at the top of the organizational hierarchy set corporate goals and then communicate them downward to the various operating units within the organization. These units develop plans for the achievement of the goals and communicate these plans upward for management's approval.

GOB   See GOING-OUT-OF-BUSINESS SALE (GOB).

Goffman Model   A view of consumer behavior based on the sociology of Erving Goffman in which consumers are seen as role-players and the goods for which they are shopping are seen as props in a play. Customers are thus viewed as players in a drama of their own making.

going-out-of-business sale (GOB)   A special sale designed to liquidate all merchandise in a retail store because it is closing its doors and ending operations. The LIQUIDATION, or conversion of assets into cash, is generally done at the insistence of creditors who are demanding payment. GOBs are regulated at the state and local levels. Many states require that a business operate for a minimum time period, such as a year, before conducting a GOB sale. State laws also require that the sale be validated by a planned cessation of business. The sale inventory should not be mixed with lower-quality goods at higher than normal markup that appear to be part of the regular inventory. States ensure adherence to these guidelines by requiring a complete list of inventory on hand at the point at which a going-out-of-business notice is filed. Also called a *liquidation sale*. See also FORCED SALE.

going-rate pricing   A "collective wisdom" approach to PRICING STRATEGY in which a firm bases the prices of its products less on what it costs to make them and more on what their competitors are charging or on what the firm believes its customers may be willing to pay. Also called *imitative pricing*.

golden parachute   In takeovers and acquisitions, the guarantee of a sizeable payment to top executives whose companies are taken over by other firms. See also ACQUISITION.

Golden Rule   A cash-only sales policy.

gondola   A movable, bin-type DISPLAY fixture, often two-sided, having shelves at the top and storage space at the bottom. Its primary function is to display merchandise (often promotional) and provide room for backup stock.

Good Housekeeping Seal (of Approval)   A certification of product quality awarded by *Good Housekeeping Magazine* by way of the Good Housekeeping Institute since 1909. The certification guarantees that if a product bearing the seal proves to be defective within two years of purchase, Good House-keeping will replace the product or refund the purchase price. The Good Housekeeping Seal Web site, located at www.goodhousekeepingseal.com, includes a list of products bearing the Seal. See also CERTIFICATION MARK.

goods A store's articles of trade (i.e., merchandise). Also called *physical goods*.

goods in free circulation Merchandise not subject to customs regulations.

goods-producing business Any business, such as a MANU-FACTURER, that produces tangible products, as distinguished from businesses in the SERVICE INDUSTRIES.

goods-services continuum A means of visualizing the distribution between goods and services as a spectrum with pure goods at one end (e.g., a bottle of shampoo) and a pure service at the other (e.g., a haircut). One moves along the continuum from the tangible to the intangible.

good-till-canceled order (GTC) An order to buy or sell that remains in effect until it is either executed or canceled. See also OPEN ORDER.

goodwill The intangible favor with which a store or other business is viewed by its customers. Goodwill is based on the reputation and performance of that business and is distinct from the tangible assets of the business even though it has a dollar value. Sometimes spelled *good will*.

Google A popular search engine on the WORLD WIDE WEB (WWW) whose stated mission is to organize the world's information and make it universally accessible and useful. It has become so predominant in the search engine category that *Googling* has become a generic term for searching the Web. See also GOOGLING and COUNTER-GOOGLING.

Googling 1. The practice of looking up information about something on the INTERNET via the popular search engine, GOOGLE. 2. Generically, the use of any search engine to search the WORLD WIDE WEB (WWW).

gouge (Slang) 1. n. The achievement of an excessive profit by overcharging or defrauding one's customers. 2. n. An instance of extortion or swindling. See also PRICE GOUGING. 3. v. To overcharge.

gourmet shop An independent store, or an area in a larger store, that specializes in fancy groceries and other food products such as pasta, baked goods, candy, delicatessen, and imported epicurean delicacies.

government market The government as a customer. Most governments are large purchasers, though the size of government purchases depends on the economic or political orientation of the country. In free-market economies, the government plays a lesser role than in other markets. The amount purchased by a government is also a function of state-owned oper-ations: the fewer of these there are, the more government must buy from private businesses. Government buying processes tend to be highly bureaucratic and, in the United States at least, involve getting onto the bidding lists of the various agencies. The government market will often prefer local suppliers, if available, and set requirements for those local suppliers (such as hiring policies, etc.). Developed countries have established deterrents to influence-peddling and other corrupt practices, but standards and expectations vary from country to country. The government market is a part of the larger INDUSTRIAL MARKET. See also INSTITUTIONAL MARKET and PRODUCER MARKET.

government-owned store A retail establishment owned and operated by a local, state, or federal government. Government-owned stores cover a broad spectrum of store types and locations. For example, military families may shop at a BASE EXCHANGE or POST EXCHANGE (PX), government-owned stores where food and general merchandise can be purchased at reduced prices. The U.S. Postal Service, a quasi-governmental agency, owns Postmark America, a retail store at the Mall of America in Bloomington, Minnesota. Post office outlets throughout the United States carry a variety of retail products including stamps, packaging supplies, stationery, commemorative apparel, memorabilia, and gifts. In several states, such as New Hampshire, liquor stores are state-owned and all proceeds go into state coffers. In Singapore, some general merchandise and food stores are government-owned, and in China, the government is a partner in every business venture proposed by foreigners, including retail stores.

gown See FORMAL ATTIRE.

GPA See GARMENT PURCHASE AGREEMENT (GPA).

grace period An extended period of time, beyond the nominal terms of sale, during which customers may make credit purchases without first paying their accounts or arranging to do so. Also called a *courtesy period*.

grade label A tag or legend on a product indicating its quality classification, generally in the form of a letter or number symbol (e.g., Grade A eggs).

grading The process by which goods (e.g., eggs) are compared in terms of quality, size, or some other factor. The standards for grading are set by governmental agencies, by the industry itself, or by an independent testing bureau. See also GRADE LABEL, SORTING, STANDARDIZE, STANDARDIZATION, and ASSORTING.

graduated lease A rental agreement in which rent is increased in prespecified stages over a period of time. The rent increases are not related to gross sales or any other measure of the retailer's performance, but the initially lower rents do give the retailer an opportunity to become established and develop a customer base.

graphical user interface (GUI) A program interface that takes advantage of a computer's graphic capabilities to make the program easier to use and to free the user from learning complex command languages. Graphical user interfaces characteristically include a pointer (often in the shape of an arrow), a pointing device (e.g., a mouse or a trackball), icons (small pictures that represent commands, files, windows, etc.), a desktop (the area on the display screen where icons are grouped), windows, and menus.

graphic eye candy   (Slang) Attractive, high-impact graphics displayed on a Web site. The graphics may or may not be animated.

graphics   1. Artwork in the form of prints, drawings, photography, paintings, lettering, engraving, etching, lithography, etc. 2. In retail stores, images or signage concerned with department identification and merchandise presentation. Oversized photographs, blowups, or light box art are most often used. See also LIFESTYLE GRAPHIC. 3. In advertising, artwork that illustrates text in the print media or that is used in television advertisements. 4. In Web site design, images or artistic lettering, often with animation, designed to catch attention and illustrate the products being sold on the site. *Randomized graphics* are a useful method for displaying an array of images without cluttering a page: the images appear in a box and change at regular intervals to give the site a fresh appearance in a montage-like display.

graphics interchange format (GIF)   A bitmapped graphics file used on the Web and other systems. GIF supports color and various resolutions and includes data compression. However, because it is limited to 256 colors, it is more effective for scanned images such as illustrations than for color photos.

grass-roots method   A sales forecasting method that relies on input from salespersons in the field who report knowledge they have gained working with customers.

gravanity   A consumer trend represented by the obsession of ordinary citizens with leaving something behind in print, audio, or imagery, preferably in the public domain. It has given rise to an entire industry catering to this obsession, with entrepreneurs willing to name or rename their goods and services on behalf of eager consumers. For example, museums may sell sponsorships of the smallest works of art, theaters may offer named seats, real estate developers may auction off the rights to have one's name among those adorning apartment buildings and lobbies, and pizzas may be named after ordinary consumers who reveal their favorite toppings to the world. The trend was identified and the term coined at www.trendwatching.com. *Der.* graffiti + vanity.

gravity models   Calculations used to identify the power of a given center to draw customers from the surrounding geographic area. Several types of pertinent data can be combined in order to measure customer tendencies. Gravity models are based on the assumption that two cities draw customers from the surrounding towns in direct proportion to the square footage, attraction, and number of retailers in those cities. The distance between the cities is also factored into the calculation. The geographic point at which the influence of one city exceeds

that of the other can be calculated. The underlying premises are that the larger the city, the greater the pull, and that the greater the distance, the less the pull. See also REILLY'S LAW OF RETAIL GRAVITATION.

gravy   (Slang) Synonym for PLUS BUSINESS.

gray-collar worker   See SOCIAL CLASS.

gray goods   Synonym for GREIGE GOODS.

gray market   The import and sale of consumer and industrial products outside a manufacturer's authorized distribution channels. Unlike the BLACK MARKET, which is the venue of illegal trade, the gray market is generally supplied by distributors or retailers who redirect goods from their regular marketing channels to alternative outlets in a manner within the limits of the law. Goods sold at relatively low prices in one country are purchased by individual buyers or independent entrepreneurs and re-exported to countries in which the goods will bring a higher price. Gray market goods are sometimes called *parallel imports*.

greenmail   A strategy used to avoid the takeover of one's company by another. The greenmail strategy involves buying up a large block of a company's stock in order to push up stock prices and offering to repurchase that stock at an inflated price. See also ACQUISITION.

Green River ordinance   Any law passed by a local government to restrict door-to-door selling. The name is derived from Green River, Wyoming, one of the first places to pass such an ordinance.

greige goods   Unfinished fabric as it comes from the loom before being sent to converters for bleaching, dyeing, printing, or the application of special finishes. Also called *gray goods*.

grey-collar worker   See SOCIAL CLASS.

grey goods   See GREIGE GOODS.

grid   See MARKET GRID.

grid card   In radio advertising, a rate card that provides potential advertisers with multiple advertising rates. The rates for each time period vary, week to week, depending on available air time. In this system, an advertiser wishing to book time on very short notice may pay a higher rate than an advertiser willing to wait. Compare SINGLE-PRICE CARD.

grid floor layout/plan   See GRID LAYOUT.

grid layout   A rigid, geometric spatial arrangement of fixtures and aisles in a store. The grid layout is based on rectangles, squares, and other right-angle patterns. There may also be one primary aisle and several secondary aisles, depending on the total square footage of the store. The grid layout creates natural sight lines leading to focal points at the ends of aisles. Often found in CATEGORY KILLERS, SUPERMARKETS, SUPER-

STORES, and DISCOUNTERS, grid layouts allow retailers to maximize SQUARE FOOTAGE and maintain low margins by displaying merchandise efficiently and inexpensively. Also called a *grid floor plan*, *rectangular layout*, or *gridiron pattern* (due to its resemblance to a football field).

gridiron pattern   See GRID LAYOUT.

gridwall system   A wall system of metal wire that accepts brackets and display accessories with fittings specially designed for the purpose. Gridwall wire panels are fabricated in a variety of gridlike patterns permanently fastened to store walls. Compare PEGWALL SYSTEM and SLATWALL SYSTEM.

grievance   In employee relations, a complaint brought by an employee against an employer and handled formally through fixed procedures.

grocer   See GROCERY.

grocery   A store that sells general food products and certain nonedible articles for household use such as laundry and cleaning products. The proprietor (i.e., owner or operator) of the store is called a *grocer*. A grocery is also called a *grocery store*.

gross   In merchandising, 12 dozen.

gross amount   The total amount of anything before deductions. The gross amount minus deductions equals the net amount. Also called *gross response*. See also GROSS PROFIT.

gross cost of goods handled/sold   See COST OF GOODS HANDLED.

gross cost of merchandise handled/sold   See COST OF GOODS HANDLED.

gross domestic product (GDP)   The total value of all goods and services produced by a country during a specified period of time. In the United States, consumer spending contributes two-thirds of the national GDP.

gross floor space   The total store area, including selling and nonselling (i.e., behind-the-scenes) departments.

gross leasable area (GLA)   A standard unit of measure used by the shopping center industry. GLA is the total floor area designed for tenant occupancy and exclusive use, including basements, mezzanines, and upper floors. It is measured from the center line of joint partitions and from outside wall faces. GLA is that area on which tenants pay rent. It excludes common areas such as walkways, shopping center management offices, and parking area.

gross margin   The difference between the total cost of goods and their final selling price. Gross margin may be expressed as net sales less the cost of goods sold. Since markdowns, shortages, and discounts have been deducted in computing gross margin, the figure is not the same as maintained markup. Gross margin is often used synonymously with the term GROSS PROFIT. The former term is more usually found in retailing and the latter in manufacturing usage. Also called the *profit margin* and the *gross margin of profit*.

gross margin per dollar of (cost) inventory   See GROSS MARGIN RETURN ON INVESTMENT (GMROI).

gross margin pricing   A system for determining prices based on wholesale costs rather than on the full cost. Retailers using this method simply add a percentage of the wholesale cost or a percentage of the retail price to the wholesale cost to arrive at a price.

gross margin return on inventory (GMROI)   See GROSS MARGIN RETURN ON INVESTMENT (GMROI).

gross margin return on investment (GMROI)   A concept that relates a store's gross margin to the cost of the merchandise inventory needed to generate the profit. Although GMROI is not, in the strictest sense of the word, a measure of return on investment, it is an attempt to measure the return on one of a retailer's most significant investments, the inventory. The concept of gross margin return on inventory investment may best be regarded as a standard used in effective merchandise management. GMROI (pronounced jim-roy) can be calculated as gross margin divided by the average inventory at cost, or as gross margin as a percent of turnover divided by 100% less markup percent. The result is identical for either calculation, but the second method shows the relationship of the components and demonstrates how future results may be improved. Also called *gross margin per dollar of cost inventory*, *gross margin return on inventory investment*, or *gross margin return per dollar of inventory (GMROI)*.

gross margin return per dollar of inventory (GMROI)   See GROSS MARGIN RETURN ON INVESTMENT (GMROI).

gross markdown   The original reduction in price made on goods, before any markdown cancellations. See also NET MARKDOWN and MARKDOWN CANCELLATION.

gross national income (GNI)   An indicator of total consumer potential in an economy, reflecting the generation of wealth in a country. The GNI per capita expresses this value per person, an indicator of market size.

gross national product (GNP)   The total value (at current market prices) of all final goods and services produced by a nation over a specified period of time (commonly one year). Prosperity is usually expressed in terms of gross national product (GNP), so that a rise in GNP is a sign of economic growth. When GNP is compared for two or more years, a pattern or trend may appear in the national economy. GNP may also be used to compare two or more economies, especially when expressed as the PER CAPITA GROSS NATIONAL PRODUCT.

gross profit   Total receipts less the cost of goods sold, but before selling and other operating expenses and income taxes have been deducted. Gross profit is often used synonymously with GROSS MARGIN, but gross profit is more commonly used in the manufacturing sector, gross margin more commonly in retailing. See also PERCENTAGE OF GROSS PROFIT.

gross profit on merchandise investment   The total profit realized on the amount invested in the average inventory of an item or line, expressed as a percentage.

gross profit per square foot of selling space   The total profits realized from the sales of an item, classification, or department compared to the amount of selling space devoted to that item, classification, or department. The calculation is used to guard against the allocation of too much or too little space to particular lines, depending on their contribution to the overall profit or MARGIN. Also called *profit per square foot of selling space.*

gross rating points (GRPs)   In media planning and measurement, the sum of all ratings delivered by a commercial schedule. The ratings are the PROGRAM RATINGS established by independent research services such as Nielsen Media Research. See also TARGET RATING POINTS (TRPS).

gross response   Synonym for GROSS AMOUNT.

gross revenue/sales   Sales REVENUE before deductions have been made for returns and allowances, but after sales and excise taxes have been deducted. See also SALES.

gross weight   The full weight of a package, including goods and the packaging in which they are contained. Compare TARE (WEIGHT), which is the weight of the packaging alone.

groupage   A service that consolidates small shipments into containers for shipping.

group buying   A form of buying in which a number of non-competing stores consolidate orders for goods (usually staple merchandise), store fixtures, and services to meet minimum order requirements and secure a lower price through VOLUME PURCHASING.

group concept   In the planning of a line of merchandise, a concept existing within the LINE CONCEPT. Group concepts are factors such as style features, repetition of color or fabric, coordinated printed designs, etc., that give unanimity to merchandise groups, enabling manufacturers and retailers to sell them together.

group discount   A reduction in price for the purchase of large quantities of a product or service by a number of individuals acting together (e.g., group discounts on air fares or theater tickets).

group plan   Synonym for PARTY-PLAN SELLING.

group purchase plan   A selling situation in which the retailer offers purchase incentives to a group. An identity card is frequently issued to participants to show membership in the group.

group purchasing   See GROUP BUYING.

group selling   A sales presentation directed at two or more potential customers simultaneously.

grow box   See BOX.

growth/share matrix   See BOSTON CONSULTING GROUP (BCG) MATRIX.

growth stage   That stage of the PRODUCT LIFE CYCLE (PLC) during which demand for the product picks up momentum and competitive products are introduced into the marketplace. During the growth stage, production increases and profits rise until COMPETITION begins to drive down the prices. Also called the *market growth stage.*

growth strategy   A plan to expand a firm's customer base either by targeting the customers of the competition or by targeting people who have never before used the firm's product.

GSR   See GALVANIC SKIN RESPONSE (GSR).

GTC   See GOOD-TILL-CANCELED ORDER (GTC).

guarantee   1. A written or implied statement by the seller of merchandise in which assurances are made concerning the proper performance of the product. The statement also stipulates the corrective measures that will be taken should the merchandise not perform satisfactorily (e.g., a MONEY-BACK GUARANTEE on an appliance). The guarantee may come from either the manufacturer or the retailer. Compare WARRANTY. See also PRODUCT RELIABILITY.   2. The second party in a GUARANTY (i.e., the party whose performance or product must fulfill the terms of the contract or similar agreement).

guarantee against price decline   Synonym for PRICE GUARANTEE.

guaranteed audience plan   See TOTAL AUDIENCE PLAN.

guaranteed draw   A means of compensating salespersons who are wholly or partially paid on a commission basis. Salespersons are allowed to withdraw a specified amount of guaranteed commission in advance. If the salesperson's sales quota is not met in the allotted time, the salesperson need not return the withdrawn funds. See also DRAWING ACCOUNT.

guarantor   See GUARANTY.

guaranty   A warrant, pledge, or formal assurance given as a security that an individual's promised obligations will be fulfilled. Three parties (i.e., individuals or firms) are generally involved. The first party (the *guarantor*) agrees to see that the performance of the second party (the GUARANTEE) is fulfilled according to the terms of the contract or other agreement. The third party is the CREDITOR, the party to benefit by the performance. Compare WARRANTY and GUARANTEE.

guaranty against price decline   Synonym for PRICE GUARANTY.

guerilla marketing   In Internet marketing, any strategy used to maximize limited financial resources. Guerilla marketers use time, energy, and imagination more than money to bring their products and services to market. Online tactics of guerilla marketers include newsletters, e-mail lists, newsgroup postings, multiple press releases, dynamic Web sites, submitting information to search engines, posting product reviews, and listing the product or service in appropriate places on the Web. See also VIRAL MARKETING.

guerilla warfare   In retailing, a form of competition used by smaller firms when competing with larger organizations. The small firm identifies a well-defined small market of its own and defends it vigorously. The remaining portion of the market is conceded to the larger competitor.

guesstimate/guestimate   An informal term for an estimate arrived at by guessing, without any substantial basis in facts or statistics. A best guess.

guesting   In the INTERNET environment, visiting a Web site or newsgroup without actually subscribing as a user.

GUI   See GRAPHICAL USER INTERFACE (GUI).

GWP   See GIFT-WITH-PURCHASE (GWP).

HABA   Acronym for HEALTH AND BEAUTY AIDS (HABA).

haberdashery   A retail store (or department in a larger store) that sells men's apparel furnishings and accessories.

habitual purchasing   A customer's repeat purchases of the same items and/or services, not out of BRAND LOYALTY but simply out of indifference to features that may distinguish them from competing products.

hacker   An INTERNET vandal (an individual or a group) who uses programmable systems to solve programming problems. Hackers are generally more driven by their interest in solving programming problems than by a desire to engage in illegal acts. Indeed, tame hackers are often hired by companies to test their Internet security. Compare CRACKER, one who is driven primarily by the desire to vandalize Web sites to steal or change data.

haggle   To bargain over a price or other matters affecting trade. Also called *higgle*.

half sizes   Women's apparel designed for a mature figure, providing extra room in the waist and hips. Half sizes are usually designated 10½ to 24½. Often used interchangeably with PLUS SIZES.

halo effect   The transfer of consumer trust and loyalty from one of a manufacturer's products to another. The halo effect is more likely to occur when both products share a BRAND NAME. See also BRAND LOYALTY.

HAN (home-area network)   See COMPUTER NETWORK.

handbill   Synonym for FLYER.

handheld computer   See PERSONAL DIGITAL ASSISTANT (PDA) and POCKET PC (PPC).

handheld (wireless) device   See PERSONAL DIGITAL ASSISTANT (PDA) and POCKET PC (PPC).

handling allowance   1. A reduction in price given by the manufacturer to a wholesaler, distributor, or retailer to cover special treatment of the manufacturer's goods.   2. A price reduction given to a retailer by a manufacturer as an incentive for participating in a particular promotional program that demands extra effort on the retailer's part.

hand marking   The labeling or tagging of merchandise by hand. Price and other information is written out in pencil, pen, or other writing instrument.

handset   See PERSONAL DIGITAL ASSISTANT (PDA).

hand-to-mouth buying   Retail buying in small quantities to meet immediate needs. The process minimizes the initial outlay the retailer must make for merchandise and favors a JUST-IN-TIME (JIT) rather than a JUST-IN-CASE philosophy of order-placing. Also called *buying close to the vest*.

hanger   A shoulder-shaped frame with a hook at the top, usually made of wire, wood, or plastic. Used as an alternative to the mannequin for draping and hanging a garment as well as for stocking apparel on a garment rack. Padded or dimensionalized hangers are available to ensure that the garment drapes better.

hanger appeal   The degree to which apparel attracts customers while still on the hanger. This attraction is meant to entice the customer to try on the garment and possibly purchase it.

hanging sign   A sign hung from the ceiling. Some hanging signs are permanent and identify a department or provide directions. Others are temporary signs signifying a special theme or event.

hard-core loyal   A brand insistent consumer; one who will accept no substitute for the desired product. See also BRAND INSISTENCE.

hard-core market   That segment of the consumer population composed of particularly brand-loyal buyers. See also BRAND LOYALTY and BRAND INSISTENCE.

hard goods   1. In global marketing, salable merchandise. See also TRIANGULAR COMPENSATION.   2. Nontextile products such as furniture, major appliances, toys, housewares, and consumer electronics. Also called *hardlines* or *hard lines*.

189

hardlines/hard lines   Synonym for HARD GOODS.

hard manufacturing   The use of specialized production equipment to manufacture goods. Such equipment is not readily converted to new uses, as it is in FLEXIBLE MANUFACTURING. See also REPETITIVE MANUFACTURING.

hard offer   A promotion that requests payment at the time an order is placed. The customer may opt to review the merchandise first and then pay for it or return the items if so desired. The right of the purchaser to return unwanted items for a refund (or prior to payment) will be honored by most retailers, regardless of the stated terms of the hard offer.

hard sell   Vigorous personal selling generally directed at the reluctant customer. Also called *high-pressure selling*.

hardship point   In direct selling, the location of a prospective customer in an area that is difficult to reach or in an isolated part of the community.

hard-to-wrap   Of merchandise, difficult to prepare for shipment because of its shape, fragility, perishability, etc., and therefore requiring special handling.

hardware   1. Tools, locks, hinges, etc., usually made of metal and generally sold in a *hardware store*, a FULL LINE DISCOUNTER, or a CATEGORY KILLER. However, supermarkets, convenience stores, and other retail formats often carry a few hardware items.   2. The physical components of a computer system, in contrast to the operating system and other programs that run it.

hardware store   See HARDWARE.

harmonization   In international trade, policies that bring tax rates across several countries into equilibrium so as to create an integrated economy and facilitate trade.

harvesting   See MILKING.

hatbox show   An INFORMAL FASHION SHOW held in a small space and put on with a limited budget (as though carrying everything in a hatbox). A single person acts as MODEL and commentator, changing outfits behind a screen while at the same time maintaining the commentary. See also FASHION SHOW.

haute couture   Clothing in original designs from a French fashion house produced in limited quantities for the fashion-conscious innovator. See also COUTURE, HAUTE COUTURE SHOW, and ORIGINAL. *Der.* French, high fashion.

haute couture show   An international FASHION SHOW in which fashion designers and design houses reveal their latest styles and trends. Paris and Milan are among the most significant international cities for haute couture fashion. Spring haute couture shows begin in January and include the most famous design houses. Fashion shows in London and Tokyo traditionally follow before the trends are presented on New York runways. The cycle repeats itself in July, with showings of the fall haute couture fashions. See also HAUTE COUTURE and PRÊT-À-PORTER SHOW.

Hazardous Substances Labeling Act (1960)   U.S. federal legislation requiring manufacturers to place warning labels on all items containing dangerous household chemicals. Also known as the *Federal Hazardous Substances Labeling Act (1960)*.

HBA   See HEALTH AND BEAUTY AIDS (HABA).

header   1. In many computer applications, a unit of information that precedes a data object.   2. In a network transmission, a header is part of the data packet and contains transparent information about the file or transmission. In the case of an E-MAIL, this would include the sender's e-mail address, the date of transmission, and the recipient's e-mail address. If there are many recipients, such as in BROADCASTING or MULTICASTING, the e-mail addresses of all addressees are listed.

headhunter   (Slang) An individual or business (i.e., an *executive search firm*) hired to find executive and/or managerial personnel for a company, often from competing firms.

headless mannequin   A figure consisting of a full-sized realistic body with arms and legs but no head. The pose is often quite natural, but without a head the mannequin has no face, hence no personality and no attitude. Headless mannequins work well in windows and interior spaces where height is a problem.

headline   In print advertising, the heading at the top of the ad, usually in bold type, intended to attract the attention and interest of the reader. An effective headline attracts attention, arouses interest, and leads the reader to read the entire advertisement.

head of stock   The individual in a retail store who is charged with keeping stock on the selling floor in good order, maintaining merchandise in reserve, and monitoring inventory levels. The head of stock generally reports to the DEPARTMENT MANAGER or to the department's BUYER.

head-on positioning   A MARKET POSITIONING strategy in which two nearly identical products compete with each other directly.

health and beauty aids (HABA)   Products such as deodorants, soaps, shaving preparations, shampoos, facial treatments, bath preparations, toothpastes, cosmetics, mouthwashes, etc.

heartland   Any central, vital area of a country considered essential to the survival of the whole. In marketing and retailing, this translates into the PRIMARY MARKET AREA.

heating, ventilation, and air conditioning (HVAC)   See HVAC.

heavy buyers   Synonym for HEAVY HALF.

heavy half   That segment of the marketplace that accounts for half or more of total sales. Also called *heavy buyers, heavy users,* and *heavy-half users.*

heavy market   A declining market situation that occurs when there are more sellers than buyers in the MARKETPLACE. This situation generally results in falling prices.

heavy users   Synonym for HEAVY HALF.

hedging   In COMMODITY marketing, a buying and selling practice in the futures market calculated to protect the purchaser against unfavorable price changes. Some commodities are purchased at current market prices and some are purchased on the commodity futures market at a speculative price for delivery at a later time. The hedge lies in the purchaser's expectation that a change in one of those prices will be accompanied by a compensatory change in the other price. Instead of accepting whatever market rate exists in the future, a company can opt to contract for future delivery at a set price, regardless of the market price at that time. This practice is also used in the trading of foreign currencies.

hedonic goods/items   Consumer goods whose attractiveness lies principally in that they give the purchaser pleasure.

heterogeneity   A theory asserting that the consumer market is composed of diverse, dissimilar elements. The concept of MARKET SEGMENTATION is based on this theory. Also referred to as the *theory of heterogeneity* or the *principle of heterogeneity*.

heterogeneous shopping goods/items   SHOPPING GOODS perceived by the customer as different in quality and suitability. For example, clothing and home furnishings are considered heterogeneous shopping goods, since style and quality play a significant role in the customer's decision to buy them. Price is of lesser significance. Compare HOMOGENEOUS SHOPPING GOODS/ITEMS.

heterogeneous staples   Staples (i.e., items kept in stock at all times because of constant demand) that are not identical but are closely related to one another. Compare HOMOGENEOUS STAPLES. See also STAPLE and HETEROGENEOUS SHOPPING GOODS/ITEMS.

heuristic ideation technique (HIT)   An invention of Edward M. Tauber of the Carnation Company, who called the technique "a systematic procedure for new product search." Words that describe existing products are separated and reassembled in new combinations to generate ideas for new products. The term *heuristic* is employed to suggest that the technique involves a process of discovery.

HH   See HOUSEHOLD (HH).

HID   See HIGH-INTENSITY DISCHARGE (HID) LIGHTING.

hidden buyer   In purchasing, a person other than the purchasing agent who, having the power and knowledge to specify the characteristics of a product, is the real buyer. Technicians, managers, and others within an organization may have the capacity to exert such influence.

hidden cost   Any of the costs of doing business that cannot be recorded by an accountant and so do not show up on a firm's balance sheet or income statement. These include, for example, the losses resulting from the cancellation of orders and from customers' failure to reorder.

hidden service sector   Services that are to some extent concealed because they are provided by firms that are also, or primarily, manufacturers. For example, manufacturers of photocopiers also provide supplies and maintenance service.

hierarchy of (behavior) effects   Those stages (beginning with unawareness and ending with purchase of the product) through which consumers pass when responding to a firm's promotional efforts. In order, they are: unawareness, awareness, knowledge, liking, preference, conviction, and purchase.

hierarchy of needs   See MASLOW'S HIERARCHY (OF NEEDS).

higgle   Synonym for HAGGLE.

high-end   In terms of the price range at retail, falling into the category of the highest-priced merchandise in the store. See also UPSCALE.

high fashion   In the United States, high-priced, innovative apparel from well-known designers or design houses and targeting fashion-conscious, trendy individuals. *Der.* direct translation from French HAUTE COUTURE.

high-intensity discharge (HID) lighting   An energy-efficient lamp increasingly used for overall store lighting. HIDs are relatively small in size and provide shadows and highlights similar to incandescent lighting. Illumination is produced when an electric current passes through any of several assorted gases. The most common types include the *mercury vapor lamp*, the *metal halide lamp*, and the *sodium vapor lamp*.

highlight shop   See TREND SHOP.

high-pressure selling   See HARD SELL.

high-risk decision   A decision with relatively substantial chances of resulting in a loss.

high street   In the United Kingdom, a busy retail thoroughfare.

high-trust society   A culture with a history of voluntary associations (civic, religious, business, etc.) that extend beyond the family. People in such cultures need not be blood relations to be trusted, making this type of society fertile ground for the formation of large, publicly owned corporations. Family businesses feel secure raising money outside the family and stockholders can trust their investments to the hands of professional managers. Compare LOW-TRUST SOCIETY.

highway site   A freestanding store location isolated from other businesses and located on a highway or major artery.

hire purchase   An installment buying agreement in which title does not pass to the buyer until the final payment has been made.

hi-spotting   Synonym for CHERRY PICKING.

HIT   See HEURISTIC IDEATION TECHNIQUE (HIT).

hit list   A salesperson's list of prospective customers to pursue. Both weak and strong prospects are included, with the stronger ones receiving the greatest attention. See also PROSPECTING and PROSPECT LIST.

hits   In Internet advertising, the number of files served from a Web page. When a visitor requests a Web page and it is served, the hits are the number of ads (e.g., banner ads) in the page. This is no longer considered a reliable metric for Internet advertising, as it fails to identify any contact between the ad and the visitor and makes no attempt to track what happens after the viewing. See also PAGE IMPRESSION.

hits per day   The number of connections made per day to the Web server to receive HTML files, graphics files, or any other files on a given Web site. This is not necessarily a good measure of the number of visitors to the Web site, because some Web surfers surf with graphics turned off. PAGE IMPRESSIONS, the number of HTML files that have been downloaded from one's Web site, is considered a better measure of the number of visitors.

HNO   See HUMAN NATURE ORIENTATION (HNO).

HNO-negative/HNO-positive societies   See HUMAN NATURE ORIENTATION (HNO).

hoarding   The planned effort by persons or nations to accumulate items beyond normal need, sometimes in anticipation of a price hike or shortage.

Hofstede Measures of Culture   A four-dimensional framework developed by Geert Hofstede by which to measure several key attributes of culture. The insights derived from Hofstede's framework are of great interest to international marketers. The four dimensions are power distance (the extent to which the distance between leaders and followers is coupled with deference), individualism/collectivism (the good of the individual versus the good of the group), masculinity/femininity (assertive vs. supportive and nurturing traits), and uncertainty avoidance (ability to cope with ambiguity, innovate, and "roll with the punches"). The framework helps marketers understand the differences in cultures and allows them to plan accordingly when entering the GLOBAL MARKETING arena.

Holder in Due Course Act (1976)   A U.S. federal credit law designed to protect the right of consumers to raise claims and defenses against misconduct by sellers, including breach of contract, misrepresentation, and fraud. All third-party contract holders, such as finance companies, are now subject to all claims and defenses that the customer would otherwise have claimed against the retailer.

holding company   A company that owns most, if not all, of another company's stock but does not actively participate in the management of that other company (known as a sub-sidiary). See also RETAIL HOLDING COMPANY. Compare PARENT (COMPANY/ORGANIZATION).

holding company format corporate chain   See CORPORATE CHAIN.

holding cost   See INVENTORY CARRYING COSTS.

hold slip   A form used to identify merchandise that a customer desires to purchase later. The merchandise may be held for the customer at the register or other service point and there may be a limit (e.g., 24 hours) on the length of time the item remains off the selling floor.

home and hearth   In retailing, DOMESTICS and HOUSEWARES.

home-area network (HAN)   See COMPUTER NETWORK.

home center   A store, or a department within a store, specializing in hardware, lumber, tools, and a variety of other building materials for the home improvement customer. This segment of the market is frequently referred to as DO-IT-YOURSELF (DIY).

home country orientation   A marketing orientation in which a firm gives domestic business top priority, making little or no effort to develop markets overseas. When overseas business is conducted, management and decision making are centered in the home country rather than in the overseas host country. Compare HOST COUNTRY ORIENTATION.

home furnishings   Furniture, decorative accessories, drapery, and upholstery fabrics. The center of home furnishings in the United States is High Point, North Carolina, home of the semi-annual International Home Furnishings Market.

home-market channel member   Any firm located in a manufacturer's home country that is employed in the distribution of the manufacturer's products to overseas markets. Home-market channel members may include an EXPORT MANAGEMENT COMPANY (EMC) or an EXPORT AGENT. Some companies export their own goods directly through DIRECT EXPORT or use the INTERNET to give foreign clients easier access to the goods. See also FOREIGN-MARKET CHANNEL MEMBER.

home page   The first screen image that a user views when entering a WEB SITE. It may be considered the cyberspace equivalent of a store window. E-tailers use the home page to convey their retail image graphically and attractively. The goal is to encourage potential customers to enter and peruse the site. Sometimes spelled *homepage*.

home retailing/selling   See DIRECT SELLING and DOOR-TO-DOOR RETAILING.

home sale   A sales event in which all home furnishings and related items are sold at a reduced price. Often held in the summer.

Homescan MegaPanel   A project of ACNielsen to expand the study of consumer behavior and make it available to retailers and other businesses. The expansion studies consumer behavior in channels and individual retailers across 52 markets, providing manufacturers and retailers with more complete insights into consumer and shopping behavior.

home shopping network   Several television shopping networks that originated in the 1980s. Hosts, designers, and celebrities converse while promoting various items of merchandise. The industry is dominated by two of these home shopping networks, QVC and Home Shopping Network (HSN). See also ELECTRONIC RETAILING and TELEVISION SHOPPING CHANNEL.

home trotting   A demographic trend in which large numbers of immigrants travel back and forth between their old and new homelands, opening up many opportunities for travel and telecommunications industries. See also DIASPORA MANAGEMENT and IMMI-MERCE. The trend was identified at www.trendwatching.com.

homogeneous demand   A demand pattern in which consumers have relatively uniform, steady needs and desires for a product or service.

homogeneous shopping goods/items   SHOPPING GOODS perceived by the customer as being basically the same, so that the customer is willing to substitute one brand for another and seeks only the lowest price. Because a slight price cut can significantly increase sales volume, price competition tends to be keen in this category. Compare HETEROGENEOUS SHOPPING GOODS/ITEMS.

homogeneous staples   Staples (i.e., items kept in stock at all times because of constant demand) that are so much alike as to be indistinguishable from one another even though they may have been produced by different companies. Compare HETEROGENEOUS STAPLES. See also STAPLE and HOMOGENEOUS SHOPPING GOODS/ITEMS.

homosexual partners   A category of consumers comprising same-sex couples who may function as traditional married or cohabiting couples and may have children in the household. Their expenditures and interests are similar or identical to other couples in the same cycle and social class.

honor system   The practice, on certain Web sites, of asking visitors to donate small sums of money to their continued operation. The underlying premise is that a visitor gaining value from the site should want it to survive. Such sites include a *paybox icon* for this purpose.

hook   (Slang) In retailing, a free offer given along with the purchase of a product. See also GIFT-WITH-PURCHASE (GWP).

hooker   (Slang) Synonym for DEALER IMPRINT.

horizontal advertising   See HORIZONTAL COOPERATIVE ADVERTISING.

horizontal channel conflict   Dissonance (not to be confused with normal competition) between two or more members of a CHANNEL OF DISTRIBUTION who are operating at the same level. For example, one retailer may feel that another is gaining unfair advantage by intimidating a supplier on which both depend. Compare VERTICAL CHANNEL CONFLICT. See also CHANNEL CONFLICT.

horizontal channel integration   Synonym for HORIZONTAL INTEGRATION.

horizontal competition   1. In retailing, competition between stores of the same type, such as discount stores.   2. Competition between members of a CHANNEL OF DISTRIBUTION at the same level of the channel. Not to be confused with CHANNEL CONFLICT.

horizontal cooperative advertising   A COOPERATIVE ADVERTISING strategy with two or more firms at the same level of the CHANNEL OF DISTRIBUTION (e.g., two or more retailers) sharing the advertising costs. Compare VERTICAL COOPERATIVE ADVERTISING.

horizontal cooperative promotion   Promotional efforts sponsored by two or more members of a CHANNEL OF DISTRIBUTION who are operating at the same level. For example, a number of manufacturers may cooperatively sponsor events in support of U.S. participation in the Olympic Games.

horizontal diversification   An effort to increase sales (primarily to current customers) by introducing products unrelated to the firm's existing line. For example, a producer of apparel may diversify by adding a line of perfumes targeted to the same market. See also DIVERSIFICATION.

horizontal fashion trend   See HORIZONTAL FLOW THEORY.

horizontal flow theory   A theory of adoption that posits that the adoption of fashion and other innovations in the marketplace moves from group to group within the same social class. This theory holds that opinion leaders within the large middle class have as much influence on fashion adoption as do leading members of the upper classes. Also known as the *trickle-across theory* and the *mass market theory.*

horizontal industrial market   A broad market for industrial goods that includes a number of industries. Products sold in horizontal markets have a relatively wide range of potential customers. See also INDUSTRIAL MARKET.

horizontal integration   The ownership, achieved by acquisition or internal expansion, of additional business units at the same CHANNEL OF DISTRIBUTION level. Retail organizations often expand through horizontal integration, either adding units or buying up other retail organizations. Also called *horizontal channel integration*. See also ACQUISITION, HORIZONTAL MERGER, and MERGER.

horizontal merger   A MERGER involving the combination of competing companies that perform the same function; for example, a merger between two department stores.

horizontal portal   See PORTAL.

horizontal price fixing   A RESALE PRICE MAINTENANCE (RPM) agreement between firms at the same level of the market (e.g., a collusive agreement between two or more manufacturers of the same product to fix prices at an artificially high level). Generally, the objective of horizontal price fixing is higher profits or the restriction of competition, or both. See also PRICE FIXING.

horizontal sales   The practice of selling additional products and services to existing customers of one or more products in a firm's line.

horizontal sales company   A company whose sales force is arranged along the lines of geographic location, form of merchandise being sold, type of customer, or specific selling activities.

horizontal saturation   See SATURATED AREA and INDEX OF (RETAIL) SATURATION (IRS).

hosiery   A classification including socks, knee-highs, stockings, and pantyhose.

hosiery form   See STOCKING (LEG) FORM.

host   1. The computer on which one's Web site resides, functioning as the beginning and end point of data transfers on the INTERNET. An Internet host has a unique Internet address (i.e., IP ADDRESS) and a unique DOMAIN NAME or HOST NAME. 2. A *Web hosting company*, that is, an independent business that hosts the Web sites of multiple companies. Also called a *host site*. See also WEB HOSTING.

host country   In global marketing, the country into which a global marketer wishes to extend its operations (i.e., the foreign country).

host country orientation   An overseas marketing orientation in which a firm's overseas subsidiaries are often managed by local people and are thus more responsive to the needs of the local consumer. Compare HOME COUNTRY ORIENTATION.

hostile takeover   A situation in which an outside individual or firm buys enough stock in a corporation to take control against the wishes of the board of directors and corporate officers (i.e., the existing management). If the *raider* succeeds in taking over the company, the existing managers are generally dismissed.

hosting   See WEB HOSTING.

hosting company   See HOST (def. 2).

host name   The unique name by which a HOST (def. 1) is known on a network. It identifies the host in e-mail, Usenet news, and other forms of electronic communication and is translated into an Internet address. It consists of a local part and a domain name; for example, the host name alpha.lehman.cuny.edu has *alpha* as its local part and *lehman.cuny.edu* as its domain name. It is possible for one computer to have more than one host name, of which one is designated as its *canonical name* while each of the others is an *alias*. See also WEB HOSTING.

host site   Synonym for HOST (def. 2).

hot item   Any article in a merchandise assortment that sells out quickly, is usually reordered, and contributes most to the profit margin of a department. See also BEST SELLER, FAST MOVER/SELLER, REORDER NUMBER, and FAD.

hot link   1. n. A LINK between two software applications so that changes in one effect changes in the other. For example, documents, databases, and spreadsheets may be linked in a desktop publishing system.   2. v. To create such a link between two applications.

hot medium   A communications medium giving the viewer or listener a message that is well-filled with data. As defined by Marshall McLuhan (*Understanding Media*,1964), a hot medium, such as film, print, or radio, extends one of the five senses in high definition; the viewer is provided with a wealth of information. A COOL MEDIUM, on the other hand, provides a meager amount of information and requires the viewer or listener to fill in the remainder. See also MEDIA and ADVERTISING MEDIA.

house ad   In INTERNET advertising, a house ad is self-promotion on one's own WEB SITE. Such ads promote the site or a product sold on the site.

house agency   An ADVERTISING AGENCY owned or controlled by a single firm and commonly providing service only to that firm.

house auction   See ONLINE AUCTION.

house brand   A private BRAND that carries the name of the retailer while the actual manufacturer of the product or group of products remains anonymous. Often used for food items, such as coffee carrying the brand name of the supermarket in which it is sold. See also PRIVATE BRAND.

house charge   A purchase made by an employee on the employee's store account.

house clearance   An Internet promotion in which first-quality, branded products are sold at large discounts on the Web site of the original e-tailer. Similar to a clearance sale at a traditional retailer. See also CLEARANCE SALE.

household (HH)   According to the U.S. Bureau of the Census, AMERICAN HOUSING SURVEY (AHS), "all people who occupy a particular housing unit as their usual residence, or who live there at the time of the [census] interview and have no usual residence elsewhere. The usual residence is the place where the person lives and sleeps most of the time. This place is not necessarily the same as a legal residence, voting residence, or domicile. Households include not only occupants related to the householder but also any lodgers, roomers, boarders, partners, wards, foster children, and resident employees who share the living quarters of the householder. It includes people temporarily away for reasons such as visiting, traveling in connection with their jobs, attending school, in general hospitals, and in other temporary locations. By definition, the count of households is the same as the count of occupied housing units." The AHS is available online at www.census.gov.

housekeeping In a retail store, the work of STOCK KEEPING (ensuring that stock on the floor and in reserve is kept neat, clean and accessible) as well as the physical maintenance of the store (e.g., collecting trash, sweeping floors, changing light bulbs).

house list 1. A MAILING LIST of existing customers and those who have made inquiries about the store's products or service, used internally by the retailer for mailing out promotional materials. 2. In E-TAILING, a similar list of the customers and visitors who have already interacted with the business on its Web site.

house mark See FAMILY BRAND.

house organ A publication produced by an organization for the purposes of informing employees of policies, events, etc. It is distributed internally within the business or other organization.

house-to-house retailing Synonym for DOOR-TO-DOOR RETAILING.

house-to-house salesperson Synonym for DOOR-TO-DOOR SALESPERSON.

house-to-house sampling The distribution of a product sample to homes in a market as a way of introducing people to the merchandise. The strategy is used to stimulate word-of-mouth promotion.

housewares Articles of household equipment such as kitchen utensils and glassware. See also DOMESTICS.

Howard-Sheth (H-S) Theory A theory of buyer behavior in which consumer buying is treated as rational and systematic. The Howard-Sheth Theory attempts to describe the processes occurring in an individual between the receipt of a stimulus (i.e., advertising message) and the initiation of some form of buying response.

H-S Theory See HOWARD-SHETH (H-S) THEORY.

HTML See HYPERTEXT MARKUP LANGUAGE (HTML).

HTML e-mail/mail E-MAIL that is formatted using HYPERTEXT MARKUP LANGUAGE (HTML) as opposed to plain text, so that graphics and links appear in the body of the e-mail. In order to see the format and images correctly, both the sender and the recipient must have an e-mail program that supports HTML e-mail. Also called *HTML mail.*

HTTP See HYPERTEXT TRANSFER PROTOCOL (HTTP).

hub See RETAIL HUB.

huckster 1. An aggressive peddler, promoter, or petty retailer who will attempt to sell anything as long as it is profitable. 2. Anyone in the advertising industry. A slightly pejorative term. 3. A hawker of small items such as fruits and vegetables.

Huff's Model A theory of consumer shopping behavior propounded by David L. Huff in which the distance from a shopping center is seen as directly affecting the probability of consumers shopping there.

human nature orientation (HNO) A description of societal differences proposed by Jean-Claude Usunier. A society may be HNO-positive (i.e., it operates under the basic assumption that people can be trusted to obey the rules) or HNO-negative (i.e., it operates under the basic assumption that people cannot be trusted to obey the rules). Power distance also plays a role in how such societies perceive their citizens and how citizens perceive their government. In an HNO-positive society with low power distance, for example, rules tend to be pragmatic and most people respect and obey them.

human resources division The division or department of a store or other organization that is responsible for the hiring and training of employees. Human resources departments may also be involved in the administration of payroll and benefits as well as in the evaluation of employees. Formerly called the *personnel department* or *personnel division.* The executive responsible for the management of this division is the VICE PRESIDENT (VP) OF HUMAN RESOURCES or the HUMAN RESOURCES MANAGER.

human resources manager The executive charged with hiring, training, and assisting in the evaluation of employees. The human resources manager may also be responsible for projecting personnel needs, establishing personnel policies, developing job descriptions, controlling turnover, developing a personnel manual, administering wage and price policies, maintaining employee relations, establishing a company medical program, and interpreting and complying with laws, ordinances, and rules affecting labor. Also called a *personnel manager* or a *personnel director.* See also HUMAN RESOURCES DIVISION.

humorous sell An ADVERTISING MESSAGE or SALES APPROACH that jokes about the product being sold. This technique was very much in vogue in the late 1960s and early 1970s. As a selling technique, it is convincing, subtle, and indirect. Also called the *soft sell.*

husky See BOYS' SIZES.

HVAC Heating, ventilation, and air conditioning.

hybrid center A shopping area of mixed composition, combining the qualities of two or more basic center configurations with contemporary twists.

hygienia   A worldwide trend among mature consumers who are interested in and knowledgeable about the various hygiene factors associated with each and every good, service, and experience available in the marketplace. Such consumers base their knowledge on many years of self-training in consumption as well as on information currently available to them on the WORLD WIDE WEB (WWW) and from other media sources. Such consumers demand progressively better quality at progressively lower prices. Price comparison Web sites and blogs add to the consumers' information base. The trend was identified and the term coined by trendwatching.com at www.trendwatching.com. See also GLOBAL CONSUMERS.

hyper   In France, a HYPERMARKET; an informal shortening of *hypermarché*.

hyperinflation   Rapid, uncontrolled inflation such as that affecting Germany from 1920 to 1923. Hyperinflation is marked by prices changing so rapidly that they cannot be trusted from day to day, or even hour to hour. In such an economic climate, the national currency becomes virtually worthless.

hyperlink   Synonym for HYPERTEXT LINK.

hypermarché   In France, a HYPERMARKET.

hypermarket   A European retailing development (called a *hypermarché* in France) that brings food and general merchandise together in a warehouse atmosphere. These stores include elements of the traditional discount operation as well as those of the supermarket and may be as large as 200,000 square feet. The products carried by a hypermarket are almost always high-volume sellers, as the operation depends on moving large quantities of goods to turn a profit. Typically, 70 percent of the store is devoted to general merchandise and 30 percent to food products. A hypermarket goes beyond the size and scope of the SUPERSTORE by offering extended services (such as insurance and travel agencies, ticket kiosks, etc.); RETAILTAINMENT (provided by store employees, especially demonstrators); a unique merchandise mix (fewer products than conventional supermarkets, but in greater quantities). See also SUPERCENTER.

hypertasking   A trend in consumer behavior in which consumers are seen as carrying their MULTITASKING activities out of the workplace and into their everyday lives. Such consumers seem to enjoy their ability to do everything at the same time. They regularly combine a number of activities, such as surfing the Web and listening to the radio or watching television. Hypertaskers may also combine such activities as meeting friends for dinner or coffee with checking their e-mail, talking on a cell phone, or looking up data. The trend has implications for advertisers who want to capture the hypertaskers' attention and for marketers who need to adapt products and services to more versatile, on-the-go customers. The trend was identified and the term coined by trendwatching.com at www.trendwatching.com.

hypertext   Text in the formatting language used for creating Web pages. See also HYPERTEXT MARKUP LANGUAGE (HTML).

hypertext link   A connection from a word, image, or object to another area on a Web page, another page in a Web site, or a different Web site. The highlighted word is the most common link, although images and animated graphics are often linked. When a user clicks on a hypertext link, the browser initiates delivery of the linked item, page, or site. The hypertext link is created by means of a tag in HYPERTEXT MARKUP LANGUAGE (HTML). Also called a *hyperlink* or, simply, a *link*.

Hypertext Markup Language (HTML)   The language used to create documents for the WORLD WIDE WEB (WWW). HTML defines the structure and layout of a Web document by using a variety of *tags* and attributes. Hundreds of tags are used to format the information on a Web page and to specify HYPERTEXT LINKS.

Hypertext Transfer Protocol (HTTP)   The standard Internet PROTOCOL (i.e., the specification that describes how computers talk to each other on a network) for the exchange of information on the WORLD WIDE WEB (WWW). It defines a UNIFORM RESOURCE LOCATOR (URL) by telling the SERVER what to send to the CLIENT. HTTP enables Web authors to code hyperlinks into documents. Information is retrieved without any input from the user beyond clicking on a link. The abbreviation also appears in lower case, *http*, especially in Internet addresses.

hypodermic needle model   A largely discredited theory of mass communication holding that the mass media have a direct, immediate, and powerful effect on the people receiving their messages. The people (i.e., the audience) are seen as helpless victims whose attitudes and behaviors are influenced by the mass media messages much as if they had been injected with a hypodermic needle. The theory was superseded first by the TWO-STEP FLOW MODEL and later by the MULTISTEP FLOW MODEL.

hypothesis   A theory or proposition tentatively accepted to explain certain facts or relationships, make predictions about the future, and provide a basis for further investigation (in which case it is often referred to as a *working hypothesis*). Researchers develop hypotheses from observation and intuition, then go on to test each hypothesis scientifically.

I-am-here-to-help-you approach A SALES APPROACH that involves a direct, enthusiastic offer to help in increasing profit or productivity, etc., (for industrial clients) or household efficiency, personal money management, etc. (for the ultimate consumer).

ICC (integrated circuit card) See SMART CARD.

iceberg principle In the evaluation of marketing performance, the principle that much valuable information is inadequately represented in summary data. Such summary data is, in fact, the tip of the iceberg. Only detailed figures will reveal the submerged information.

icon A small image on a computer desktop or Web browser that one clicks to activate a program or link.

idea approach A SALES APPROACH in which the SALESPERSON offers a helpful new idea to interest the prospect. For example, when approaching an industrial customer, the salesperson should suggest an idea illustrating how the product or service will increase the prospect's profits, productivity, etc.

idea generation See BRAINSTORMING.

ideal customer See TARGET MARKET.

ideal market exposure Sufficient EXPOSURE of a product to potential customers to meet customer needs without exceeding them. Exceeding customer needs by providing additional exposure of the product is seen as adding unnecessarily to the total market cost of the product.

ideal other The way an individual would most like to be perceived by others. See also OTHERS-SELF-CONCEPT/OTHERS-SELF-IMAGE.

ideal points The combination of attributes that consumers would most like products to possess.

ideal self The person an individual would like to be; the end to which the individual is striving. See also SELF-IMAGE.

ideal self-concept/self-image Synonyms for IDEAL SELF.

ideal stock See BALANCED ASSORTMENT.

idea marketing The application of marketing principles to promote ideas, issues, causes, etc. (i.e., rather than commercial products or services). Idea marketing may be employed by profit and nonprofit organizations.

ideation See BRAINSTORMING.

illegal goods/merchandise Stolen property, certain drugs, firearms under certain circumstances, and other items unlawfully sold.

illustration In print advertising, the artwork or graphic portion of the ad. The illustration is intended to attract attention to the whole advertisement and develop the reader's interest in the product.

ILs See INTERNET LEADERS (ILS).

IM See INSTANT MESSAGING (IM).

image See SELF-IMAGE, BRAND IMAGE, PRODUCT IMAGE, and STORE IMAGE.

image advertising See INSTITUTIONAL ADVERTISING.

image builder pricing A retailing practice in which one product in a line is offered at a substantially higher price than other products in the line. The goal is to enhance the line's image in the mind of the consumer. For example, the Corvette helps stimulate sales for all the models in the Chevrolet line.

image building Advertising and other promotional efforts intended to influence customers' perceptions of a retail store or other firm. For example, a store may engage in activities that enhance its reputation for being socially responsible. See also INSTITUTIONAL ADVERTISING.

image consultant A DIRECT SELLER in the cosmetics industry and related fields.

image marketing The application of marketing principles to enhance the image of a person or organization (i.e., the alteration of the public's perception of the person or organization).

image sell   An approach in advertising that focuses on creating and conveying a particular image for the product or service being advertised. For example, the use of popular retired athletes in beer commercials is meant to convey an image of masculinity and success. The opposite of DIRECT SELL. See also ASSOCIATION ADVERTISING FORMAT.

imaginative approach   In advertising copy, a focus on the possibilities for self-fulfillment and life-enrichment to be derived from the product or service. For example, buying the toothpaste will lead to getting the fancy sports car. Also called the *emotional approach*, it is calculated to take advantage of the customer's emotional buying motive. See also EMOTIONAL BUYING MOTIVE/TRIGGER.

IMC   See INTEGRATED MARKETING COMMUNICATIONS (IMC).

imitative combiner   A firm that uses the combined target market approach to market its goods to an already-established combination of submarkets. The imitative combiner seeks to offer an improved marketing mix to the target market established by the INNOVATIVE COMBINER. The products so developed tend to resemble or even duplicate the innovator's product. See also COMBINED TARGET MARKET APPROACH and IMITATIVE SEGMENTER.

imitative pricing   See GOING RATE PRICING.

imitative segmenter   A segmenter that tries to offer an improved MARKETING MIX to meet the needs of a target market already identified by an innovative segmenter. The products so developed tend to resemble or even duplicate the innovator's product. See also INNOVATIVE SEGMENTER and IMITATIVE COMBINER.

immediate dating   See CASH DATING.

immi-merce   A consumer trend linked to the travel of large numbers of immigrants back and forth between their ancestral homes and their adopted countries. The commercial implications include an increasing flow of money from selling and buying goods in or from the immigrants' countries of origin. E-COMMERCE has in many ways facilitated this flow by enabling immigrants to order goods and services online for their families in the home country. Retailers abroad may also be contacted online to provide goods to nonresident citizens living abroad. The trend was identified and the term coined by trendwatching.com at www.trendwatching.com. See also HOME TROTTING.

impact analysis   In channel development, a study of the results a change of channel (or set of channels) will have on an operation. Such a change can impact sales methods, product requirements, support requirements, and business infrastructure. It can also affect other members of the CHANNEL OF DISTRIBUTION. The study (i.e., analysis) seeks to aid implementation planning by anticipating possible results.

impact pricing   See PENETRATION PRICING.

imperfect competition   See MONOPOLISTIC COMPETITION.

imperfects   Synonym for SECONDS.

implementation   The process of activating or operationalizing the marketing plan. Resources (people and money), technology, and materials are brought together to execute plan tactics and achieve marketing strategies, objectives, and goals.

implementer   A small local subsidiary of an international company located in a less strategic market. It is expected only to carry out (i.e., implement) the overall marketing strategy of the parent firm without making a major contribution either technologically or strategically. Compare STRATEGIC LEADER and CONTRIBUTOR, two other models of the subsidiary's relationship to the parent.

implicit cost   Any expenditure in a business that is less obvious and accountable than an explicit cost, but may affect the overall profitability of the business. Implicit costs may include the owner's salary (even if the actual money is not paid out) or the rental value of the building (even if owned by the business, since it is not being rented out to others). Compare EXPLICIT COST.

implied consent   In the CAN-SPAM ACT (2004), a clause enabling companies to send e-mail to people if a business transaction has taken place between the sender and the recipient within the previous three years and if the recipient has not made use of a clear and conspicuous opportunity to opt out of receiving the company's messages.

implied contract   A CONTRACT (i.e., an exchange of promises enforceable by law) that is not verbally explicit but derived from the actions or conduct of the parties involved. See also EXPRESS CONTRACT.

implied warranty   An unwritten assurance given by the manufacturer of a product that, in the event the product does not function properly, it will be replaced or repaired. The assumption is that, written or not, a promise is implied whenever goods are offered for sale. See also EXPRESSED WARRANTY, MAGNUSON-MOSS WARRANTY ACT (1975), and WARRANTY.

import   1. v. To bring or transport goods into a country especially for the purpose of sales.   2. n. Any item brought into a country. See also IMPORT GOODS and GLOBAL SOURCING.

import agent   In international trade, a MANUFACTURER'S AGENT involved with the importation of foreign goods. The import agent sells similar products for several noncompeting foreign manufacturers in the host market and receives a commission on what is sold.

importance-performance analysis   A MARKETING RESEARCH (MR) tool employed to identify strengths and weaknesses in a company's products as they are perceived by customers or potential customers. The results are plotted on a two-dimensional grid in an effort to give the MARKETING MANAGER an indication of how the firm's products are regarded in the marketplace.

import broker In international trade, an AGENT INTERMEDIARY who brings buyers and sellers together for the purpose of selling foreign goods in a domestic market. Import brokers provide the domestic buyers of imported goods with information about the availability of such goods. They also provide potential importers with information about the needs of domestic buyers. See also EXPORT BROKER.

import commission house A COMMISSION MERCHANT involved in the sale of foreign goods in a domestic market. The import commission house handles goods shipped to it by foreign sellers, completes the sales, and sends the money to the seller. The import commission house is reimbursed for its services by means of a COMMISSION paid by the seller.

importers' private bonded warehouse See CUSTOMS BONDED WAREHOUSE.

Import/Export Price Index A monthly report of the BUREAU OF LABOR STATISTICS (BLS) featuring changes in the prices of imported and exported nonmilitary goods traded between the United States and the rest of the world.

import fair A store promotion in which the imported goods of a particular country or region are featured. See also FORTNIGHT.

import goods Merchandise manufactured in one country and offered for sale in another. See also IMPORT.

import intermediary In international marketing, a firm that identifies consumer needs in its own local market and searches the world market to satisfy those needs. Import intermediaries purchase goods in their own name and act independently of manufacturers. These independent CHANNEL MEMBERS use their own marketing strategies and keep in close contact with the markets they serve. For the exporter, this channel partner is an important conduit to wholesalers and retailers in the host country.

import quota A protective ruling establishing fixed limits on the quantity of specific products that can be imported. These quotas are frequently negotiated between countries that are trading partners.

import snobbery The tendency for people to believe that better products come from other countries.

import tariff A special tax levied against goods imported into a country. Most tariffs are protective; they make foreign goods more expensive, giving domestic producers an advantage. There are two forms of tariff: *revenue tariffs* (which raise money) and *protective tariffs* (which are meant to protect domestic producers or manufacturers by raising the price of the imported goods to a competitive level). The imposition of tariffs is sometimes used as a tactic in trade disputes. The actual amount of the tax is referred to as the *duty* or CUSTOMS DUTY. See also NONTARIFF (TRADE) BARRIER and EXPORT TARIFF.

import wholesaler See PRIVATE IMPORT WHOLESALER.

import window A related merchandise window display in which all the items are from the same foreign country.

impression Short for PAGE IMPRESSION.

impulse buying Consumer purchases made without prior planning, generally on the basis of the immediate appeal of the merchandise and its proximity to the POINT-OF-PURCHASE (POP). See also POINT-OF-IMPULSE (POI).

impulse goods/items/merchandise/products Items purchased by the consumer on the spur of the moment, with virtually no planning or forethought. Candy and tabloids are displayed at many supermarket checkout lines so that consumers will add them to their shopping carts while waiting in line to pay for their groceries. Impulse goods are not necessarily low-end products. In-store virtual merchandising encourages impulse purchases. See also CONSUMER GOODS and POINT-OF-IMPULSE (POI).

impulse purchasing/shopping Synonyms for IMPULSE BUYING.

IMU See INTERACTIVE MARKETING UNIT (IMU).

inactive account Synonym for DORMANT ACCOUNT.

in arrears See ARREARS.

in bond Of merchandise, being held in a store's warehouse until the selling season begins, having been shipped by a producer several months in advance.

inbox The portion of an E-MAIL program interface in which the subscriber receives messages from other e-mailers.

incandescent light Lighting used in retail stores, sometimes in combination with fluorescent light, to create their primary lighting. Incandescent lights are used for warmth, emphasis, and highlighting, as well as to illuminate merchandise directly. Both the SPOTLIGHT and the FLOODLIGHT are forms of incandescent lighting. See also STORE LIGHTING PLAN.

incentive 1. A promotion, such as a CENTS-OFF COUPON, product sample, SWEEPSTAKES, or other short-term inducement to move the customer to make an immediate purchase. 2. In sales, a prize or gift used to motivate the sales force to increase their productivity.

incentive buying The practice by which the retail BUYER places orders early in the season, stimulated by the discounts offered by manufacturers for the early orders.

incentive pay Money above straight salary, paid to salespeople as a reward for high levels of sales.

inclusionary international Internet marketing strategy In E-MARKETING, the practice of marketing to international as well as domestic online customers. The E-TAILER or other marketer attempts to target, reach, interact, and trade with some or all international buyers. International offline marketers are likely to be international online marketers. Compare EXCLUSIONARY INTERNATIONAL INTERNET MARKETING STRATEGY.

income   1. The total money receipts of an organization or individual.   2. In certain accounting usages, receipts less expenses and losses. See also NET PROFIT and PERSONAL INCOME (PI).

income expectation   See CONSUMER'S INCOME EXPECTATIONS.

income producing services   Services, such as insurance sales, equipment rentals, beauty salons, fur storage, jewelry and watch repair, gift wrapping, etc., provided in retail stores and paid for by the customer. Consequently, these services generate additional income for the store.

income segmentation   The division of a population on the basis of the earnings of each segment. The segments are usually expressed as incremental ranges. For example, one segment may include households with annual incomes of $80,000 to $99,000 while another would include those who earn $100,000 to $119,000.

income statement   An accounting statement of net profit based on the firm's revenues less expenses and losses for a specific period of time, usually one year. It summarizes all revenues (or sales), the amounts that have been or are about to be received from customers for goods or services delivered to them, and all expenses (i.e., costs that have arisen in generating revenues). The expenses are subtracted from the revenues to show the actual profit or loss of the company. Also called *profit and loss statement, operating statement,* or *statement of operations.* See also INCOME STATEMENT COMPONENT. Compare BALANCE SHEET.

income statement component   There are five components of retail income statements: net revenue, cost-of-goods sold, gross margin, expenses, and net profit. See also COMPONENT PERCENTAGE and INCOME STATEMENT.

inconsistent merchandise assortment   Lines of merchandise offered for sale together which do not relate to one another in terms of customer end use. Inconsistent merchandise assortments generally lack logic and, except in the case of small general merchandise stores, reflect poor planning.

incorporate   To form a legal CORPORATION.

incorporation   The act of forming a legal CORPORATION.

incremental pricing agreement   A pricing schedule in which the price per unit decreases as the number of units purchased increases.

incremental revenue   The increase or decrease in revenue resulting from the addition or subtraction of a unit of sales or from an advance or decline in price.

incremental technique   A strategy used in budgeting for promotional purposes in which the current budget is based on previous expenditures and on the firm's expectations of future business. Depending on the planner's feelings, money is either added to or subtracted from the previous year's promotional budget to determine the current budget. See also PROMOTIONAL BUDGETING.

indebted   Obligated to repay money owed to a creditor.

indebtedness   The extent to which an individual or firm owes money to creditors.

independent   In retailing, a store that does not belong to a chain or parent company. It may, however, be a member of a VOLUNTARY CHAIN. Typically, an independent is owned and operated by an individual, a family, or a partnership, and is either a GENERAL MERCHANDISE RETAILER/STORE or a LIMITED LINE STORE. Groups of independents may join together to buy through an associated buying office to reap the benefits of large-scale buying afforded to chains and other large retailers. Also called a *small store, independent retailer,* or *independent store.* Compare POWER RETAILER. See also ASSOCIATED BUYING OFFICE.

independent buying office   A privately owned and operated resident buying office often used by store buyers as consultants. Two variations of the independent office are the SALARIED (BUYING) OFFICE and the COMMISSION BUYING OFFICE.

independent delivery service   A company organized solely for the purpose of providing delivery service to other companies on a contractual basis. The independent delivery service picks up parcels from the retailer, sorts and warehouses them, and delivers them to the customer, assuming responsibility for lost merchandise. The service may also make CASH ON DELIVERY (COD) deliveries and pick up customer returns. The retailer is charged on the basis of size, weight, and the number of items to be delivered, often passing these charges along to the customers. Also called *independently owned delivery service.* See also DELIVERY.

independent display   A visual presentation of merchandise that does not relate to adjoining display windows in terms of either content or theme.

independent distributor   See DIRECT EXPORT/EXPORTING.

independent retailer/store   Synonym for INDEPENDENT.

independent stylist   See STYLIST.

independent wholesaler   See MERCHANT WHOLESALER.

independently owned delivery service   Synonym for INDEPENDENT DELIVERY SERVICE.

in-depth interview   Synonym for DEPTH INTERVIEW.

index   A number or formula expressing a ratio or a relationship. See also INDEX NUMBER and INDEXING.

indexation See INDEXING.

indexing A strategy employed to mitigate the effects of inflation by tying increases in wages, taxes, interest rates, etc., to changes in a price index. As prices advance and retreat, other aspects of the economy are brought into line. For example, Social Security payments may be tied to fluctuations in the CONSUMER PRICE INDEX (CPI).

index number A percentage representing the amount of fluctuation between a base figure (e.g., a price or cost) at one period and the corresponding current figure. Index numbers allow for comparisons between time periods and are used to study changes over time. See also INDEXING and CONSUMER PRICE INDEX (CPI).

index of (retail) saturation (IRS) A measure of the number of stores a retail area can accommodate. Three factors are taken into account: the total dollars expended on specific goods and services, the number of existing retail stores, and the size of the population. Also called the *index of saturation (IS)*. See also TRADING AREA and RETAIL SITE LOCATION.

index of sales activity A relative measure of a store's sales record within a given market.

indirect action advertising See INDIRECT ADVERTISING.

indirect advertising Advertising (i.e., paid, nonpersonal communications) designed to stimulate demand for a specific product or service. Indirect advertising seeks a response at some time in the future rather than immediate action. See also DIRECT ADVERTISING and PRODUCT ADVERTISING.

indirect channel of distribution The movement of products from manufacturer through independent marketing intermediaries (i.e., middlemen) to the ultimate consumer or industrial user. The employment of marketing intermediaries in the CHANNEL OF DISTRIBUTION gives the producer somewhat less control over distribution and less contact with customers.

indirect compensation A nonmonetary reward given to employees in addition to their salary or wages. Indirect compensation may take the form of paid vacations, paid insurance, free parking, retirement plans, etc. Compare PERK.

indirect competition A form of business activity in which potential customers for a firm's product satisfy their needs by buying a totally different product or by buying nothing at all. For example, a labor-saving device may go unpurchased when cheap labor is readily available. The competition between these two alternatives may not be directly recognizable, but each provides a different solution to fulfill the same need. See also INDIRECTLY COMPETING STORES.

indirect cost Any cost involved in doing business that cannot be directly related and assigned to a particular product or service or organizational unit. Included in this category are the cost of heat and light, administrative expenses, building depreciation, etc. Also known as *common cost*.

indirect expense In a store, any expenditure not attributable to the operation of a particular department. Indirect expenses are storewide, such as heating, lighting, security, administrative expenses, etc. Compare DIRECT EXPENSE.

indirect export A method of exporting goods that involves the use of independent international marketing intermediaries to enter the foreign market. These marketing intermediaries include the domestic-based export merchant, the domestic-based EXPORT AGENT, cooperative international marketing organizations, and the EXPORT MANAGEMENT COMPANY (EMC). Markets are contacted through an intermediary located in the home country. A major advantage of using a domestic intermediary lies in its knowledge of foreign market conditions. A firm interested in indirect export may use any of these intermediaries to reach the foreign market. Compare DIRECT EXPORT/EXPORTING, in which markets are reached directly or through an intermediary located in the foreign market.

indirect exposure Influence on a consumer who has not seen an advertisement for a product or service by another individual who has.

indirect interview A technique used in MARKETING RESEARCH (MR) to gather information through a spontaneous group discussion or other indirect methods. A FOCUS GROUP is one such method.

indirect inventory All supplies used to carry on the business and not purchased for resale. They are usually considered deferred assets. Compare DIRECT INVENTORY.

indirectly competing stores Stores in a shopping center, mall, or downtown area offering the same type of merchandise but with a different selection of prices and brands. Compare DIRECTLY COMPETING STORES.

indirect promotion The more impersonal rather than personal methods of bringing a product or service to the attention of one's market. For example, advertising, branding, and packaging are all forms of indirect promotion. Compare PERSONAL SELLING.

indirect purchasing The use of an outside market specialist or resident buyer by an OFF-PRICE DISCOUNT STORE, (or off-pricer), to cover the markets in their absence. The outside agencies help the store's buyer get a better handle on market conditions, since a daily examination of the wholesale marketplace is vital to the success of the off-pricer. Some companies that specialize in off-price purchasing are either in business solely to cater to this retail segment or have separate divisions that deal exclusively with discounted goods. They represent their clients in both domestic and foreign venues. In addition, indirect purchasing is used to alleviate vendors' overstocks by quickly moving and disposing of merchandise to off-pricers.

indirect retail outlet An independent retailer that purchases factory outlet merchandise through a wholesaler. The retailer has no direct relationship to the manufacturer or the factory.

individual brand   A particular product offered for sale by its producer under a unique brand name not carried by any of the manufacturer's other products. Examples of individual brands include Kleenex, Xerox, and Tide. See also FIGHTING BRAND.

individual branding   See MULTIPLE BRANDING.

individual buying office   See PRIVATE BUYING OFFICE.

individualism—collectivism   See HOFSTEDE MEASURES OF CULTURE.

individual offering   In a firm's product mix, a single product in the line.

individual proprietorship   Synonym for SOLE PROPRIETORSHIP.

individual resident buying office   See PRIVATE BUYING OFFICE.

indoctrination   See EMPLOYEE ORIENTATION and SALES FORCE INDOCTRINATION.

indoctrination booklet/pamphlet   See EMPLOYEE ORIENTATION BOOKLET.

induced consumption   Additional consumer purchase of goods and services stimulated by new capital formation in the economy. See also INDUCED INVESTMENT.

induced investment   New capital formation in the economy driven by an increase in consumer buying. See also INDUCED CONSUMPTION.

induction   See EMPLOYEE ORIENTATION.

induction booklet/pamphlet   See EMPLOYEE ORIENTATION BOOKLET.

inductive statistics   Synonym for INFERENTIAL STATISTICS.

industrial advertising   Advertising by producers of industrial goods or by providers of business services, directed to purchasing agents or other industrial buyers.

industrial buying   See INDUSTRIAL PURCHASING.

industrial consumer   See INDUSTRIAL MARKET.

industrial counterfeiting   See COUNTERFEITING.

industrial designer   See DESIGNER.

industrial distribution   The sale of goods to producers and manufacturers rather than to retailers. See also INDUSTRIAL DISTRIBUTOR.

industrial distributor   A WHOLESALER of goods to producers and manufacturers rather than to retailers. Industrial distributors may provide their customers with a wide range of services, including calls by salespersons, the extension of credit, the stocking of large assortments, delivery, etc. Depending on where it operates in the industry, an industrial distributor may be called a *mill supply house, supply house, industrial supply house,* or *general merchandise distributor.*

industrial espionage   Corporate intelligence gathering to keep tabs on what the competition is doing (e.g., their sales plans, corporate strategies, plant capacity, technology used, principal suppliers and customers, new products under development). Industrial espionage may be performed illegally, but there are many legal means to gain the information. For example, much information can be gained by interviewing applicants for positions who currently work for the competitor. For publicly held corporations, a good deal of financial and product information is publicly disclosed by law and available through both print and online resources.

industrial goods   Products whose end use is at the manufacturing level (i.e., that will be used to make other products). Included are raw materials, machinery, tools, components, and supplies necessary in the manufacturing process. Also called *industrial products, organizational products, processing materials,* or *producer goods.*

industrialized countries   Countries that have attained full production capabilities and have well-developed infrastructures and technologies.

industrial market   All those organizations involved in production, manufacturing, providing services, wholesaling, and retailing, together with the many levels of government and a wide variety of institutions (i.e., all potential customers with the exception of ultimate consumers, individuals buying goods for themselves or their immediate families). Most products purchased in the industrial market are used to produce a commodity, manufacture a product, deliver a service, or facilitate the day-to-day operation of the organization. Also known as the *business market* or the *industrial consumer.* See also HORIZONTAL INDUSTRIAL MARKET.

industrial marketing   Those activities intended to promote the sale of goods or services at the organizational level of the marketplace (i.e., at the production, manufacturing, wholesaling, institutional, governmental, or retailing levels) rather than to ultimate consumers.

industrial products   Synonym for INDUSTRIAL GOODS.

industrial purchasing   The buying of goods and services at the business, industrial, or institutional level. Most industrial purchasing is carried out by professionals skilled in negotiating prices and buying in large quantities. Also known as *procurement.* See also BUYING and ORGANIZATIONAL MARKET.

industrial store   Synonym for COMMISSARY STORE.

industrial supply house   See INDUSTRIAL DISTRIBUTOR.

industrial union   A LABOR UNION representing both skilled and unskilled workers from all phases of a particular industry.

industrial user See INDUSTRIAL MARKET.

industry forecasting The practice of predicting sales expectations for a class of products (e.g., shampoos) rather than for a particular product (e.g., Finesse shampoo). Industry forecasting is based on the amount of industry-wide marketing activity as well as the prevailing social and legal climate of the marketing area. The goal of industry forecasting is to predict the share of income that consumers are willing to spend on a product rather than save or spend elsewhere.

industry standards Data representing the aggregate performance of similar business units, compiled by a trade association or other organization external to the individual store. The performance of all similar stores can be used as a standard or benchmark to measure the performance of an individual store. The DEPARTMENT AND SPECIALTY STORE MERCHANDISING AND OPERATING RESULTS (MOR) and the DEPARTMENT AND SPECIALTY STORE FINANCIAL OPERATING RESULTS (FOR) served for many years as the industry standards for the members of the NATIONAL RETAIL FEDERATION (NRF). They have since been replaced, at least in part, by another NRF publication, RETAIL HORIZONS. See also INTERNAL STANDARDS.

inelastic demand See INELASTICITY OF DEMAND.

inelasticity of demand The relative insensitivity of a product's sales volume to changes in price. A product that has *inelastic demand* does not motivate its marketer to cut the price, since sales revenue per unit of product decreases more rapidly than unit sales increase. This is a relative concept, however. For example, a small change in the price of gas heat will not significantly affect the market for natural gas, and the demand may be said to be *inelastic*. A major decrease in the price of natural gas, however, may cause consumers to switch to gas heat, use more of it, and thus increase demand. In the second case, demand for gas may be said to be *elastic*. Demand for expensive products, particularly those that are not immediate necessities and can be put off for a later date (e.g., the purchase of a new car), is relatively *inelastic*; for such purchases, demand is relatively insensitive to price. Also called *inelastic demand*, *price-inelastic demand*, *price inelasticity*, or, simply, *inelasticity*.

inept set In consumer behavior research, all those specific brands that, for one reason or another, the buyer excludes from consideration when shopping a product category. See also EVOKED SET and INERT SET.

inert set In consumer behavior research, all those specific brands to which the buyer exhibits indifference when shopping a product category. See also EVOKED SET and INEPT SET.

infants' sizes The range of juvenile apparel specially designed and sized for babies from newborns up to toddlers. The sizes are generally given in terms of months (i.e., 0 to 12 months).

inferential statistics Statistical tools used in MARKETING RESEARCH (MR) to project the findings from a sample onto a larger population, under the assumption that the sample is representative of that larger population. Probability theory and inferential statistics (also called *inductive statistics*) may be used to reduce random error.

inferior good An item of poor quality for which demand decreases as income increases. A commonly used example is intercity bus service. Those with more money will fly or take the train. Compare GIFFEN GOOD.

inflatable form A life-sized balloon that simulates parts of the human anatomy (e.g., the lower half of the body when used to show jeans and pants).

inflation An economic condition characterized by rising prices, so that a set dollar amount buys less than it did previously. Inflation may be fed by a situation in which the demand for goods and services exceeds the supply, thus raising prices (demand-pull inflation). For example, when governments borrow large sums of money to bolster the economy, the total amount of money circulating tends to increase. With more money available to purchase the same quantity of goods and services, demand increases relative to supply, causing inflation. However, inflation may also be caused by increases in the costs of production (e.g., wages) even without any excess demand (cost-push inflation). The increase in the cost of production is known as the *wage-price spiral*. When doing business in countries with extremely high inflation, global marketers may price their goods and services in a reasonably stable currency, such as the U.S. dollar, and translate prices into local currencies daily.

inflation rate The amount of increase in prices and cost of living (i.e., INFLATION), often expressed as a percentage change. Inflation rates have traditionally fluctuated over time and have differed from country to country.

influencer In industrial purchasing, an individual who does not make the final buying decision but has input during preliminary discussions regarding the transaction, generally on the strength of some technical expertise. See also GATEKEEPER.

influence screen In global marketing, one of the barriers or hurdles that must be overcome by a firm seeking to do business with a foreign government. That is, the firm must identify the ultimate decision makers and their agendas and be sure it meets their needs. See also ELIGIBILITY SCREEN, PROCEDURAL SCREEN, LINKAGE SCREEN, and COMPETITIVE SCREEN.

influential See OPINION LEADER.

infobot Synonym for AUTORESPONDER.

infomercial A program-length advertisement, often resembling a standard 30-minute TV show. Infomercials were introduced to the television medium in the 1980s and generally appear in a TV program guide as *paid programming*. They have proven effective in the marketing of fitness programs, speed-reading courses, weight loss programs, hair removal systems, cooking products, and courses on moneymaking opportunities. With its longer format, the infomercial can be more detailed, informative, and imaginative than a standard television commercial and often has the look of an objective, unbiased TV report. Consumers are encouraged to call a toll-free number or log on to a Web site to place an order during or immediately following the show.

informal balance See ASYMMETRICAL BALANCE and BALANCE.

informal buying group See POOLED BUYING/PURCHASING.

informal fashion show A FASHION SHOW in which merchandise is presented on models in a casual environment. Lighting, music, staging, and other special elements are not used; instead, a model walks through a sales floor, manufacturer's showroom, or restaurant, showing the merchandise and answering questions about the product. Models may carry signs or distribute business cards, coupons, or handouts. Types of informal fashion shows include TEAROOM MODELING, TRUNK SHOW, and HATBOX SHOW.

informal organization In an organization, the structure that exists outside the structure represented on the organization chart. It is a network of informal, personal relationships that often exerts significant influence on decision making within any business.

information flow See CHANNEL FLOW.

information interview An informal meeting between an executive and a person seeking information on an industry or company and the career opportunities it offers.

information-need-product (INP) A traditional, step-by-step method of selling in which the SALESPERSON presents information about a product, establishes the fact that the customer has a need for such a product, and proceeds to show how the product will fulfill the customer's need.

information product Any product (such as competitive marketing intelligence, a research report, an economic forecast, or a trend analysis) that is essentially a compilation of data about a company or an industry. Such information products are often available for purchase from vendors who specialize in intelligence gathering. Information products are increasingly available online for a fee.

information search In marketing, an activity by which consumers gather product information and weigh the alternatives. The search may be carried out internally as the consumer recollects relevant information gathered in the past, or it may be carried out externally through the examination of advertising or editorial content, discussions with friends or salespeople, or consultation of consumer rating guides (such as *Consumer Reports*) in print or on the INTERNET.

information superhighway Synonym for DIGITAL SUPERHIGHWAY.

information technology (IT) The use of computers to process and analyze information. In retailing, IT is an umbrella term that includes the computer-based DECISION SUPPORT SYSTEM (DSS). Retailers use IT to review past performance, analyze alternatives, plan inventories, and facilitate interaction between retailers and vendors. See also EXECUTIVE SUPPORT SYSTEM (ESS), ONLINE ANALYTICAL PROCESSING (OLAP), MARKETING INFORMATION SYSTEM (MIS), ENTERPRISE-WIDE DECISION SUPPORT SYSTEM (DSS), and DESKTOP DECISION SUPPORT SYSTEM (DSS).

information utility Consumer satisfaction derived primarily from advertising and promotion efforts on the part of a marketer. For example, billboards along a highway have information utility when they inform the motorist of available services.

information Web site A marketing Web site that provides information about products and services without any interaction or selling. See also TRANSACTION WEB SITE and INTERACTIVE WEB SITE.

informative advertising A form of advertising that figures heavily in the pioneering stage of new product development and other situations in which the aim is to build primary demand. Informative advertising serves to tell customers about a new product, suggest new uses for a product, inform the market of a price change, explain how the product works, describe available services, correct false impressions, reduce consumers' fears, build a company's image, etc. See also PRIMARY DEMAND.

informative institutional advertising See INSTITUTIONAL ADVERTISING.

informative label An attachment to a product or its packaging that provides important facts about the product. Such a label may, for example, advise consumers about the care, use, or preparation of the merchandise.

infrastructure 1. A term used in international marketing to refer to a country's essential facilities and services, such as its transportation and communications systems or its banking and financial system; in other words, those facilities that make marketing activities in the country possible. 2. The physical equipment, software, and protocols that make up the INTERNET.

infringement 1. In patent law, the manufacture of a machine that achieves the same results by the same action as a patented machine; a *patent infringement*. 2. In merchandising, the reproduction of a registered trademark and its use on merchandise to mislead the public into believing the items are the product of the true owner of the trademark; a *trademark infringement*.

in-home selling/retailing Sales made through a visit to the customer's home, at which time samples may be displayed, colors coordinated, space measured, products demonstrated, etc.

in-house database A collection of information about a business's own customers. It includes records for buyers who have already made purchases, buyers who have not purchased recently, and prospects. In Internet marketing, such prospects include those who have visited the Web site but have not yet purchased. The use of in-house databases is based on the belief that past purchasing behavior is a good predictor of future purchasing behavior. An alternative or supplement to the in-house database is the COMPILED DATABASE, consisting of data collected by another.

in-house salespeople   Salespeople who respond to consumers who call or come to the company on their own initiative. Compare FIELD SALESPEOPLE.

in-house video   The use of closed-circuit TV by buyers at some major retailers to communicate the highlights of new merchandise headed for the selling floor. The buyer shows each item and discusses its selling features. New fabrics, new colors, and new silhouettes are potential topics for such broadcasts within the store organization. Department managers and sales associates are the targets of these communications.

initial contact   The first interaction between the salesperson and a customer in the store. See also SALES APPROACH.

initial delivery   Part or all of the original order shipped to an individual store at the beginning of the selling period, calculated as a percentage of total INVENTORY. The initial delivery usually consists of the styles and sizes that the manufacturer put into production first.

initial indoctrination of sales force   See SALES FORCE INDOCTRINATION.

initial interview   See INTERVIEW.

initial markon   See MARKON and INITIAL MARKUP.

initial markup   The difference, expressed in dollars, between the cost price of merchandise and its first retail price. When expressed as a percentage, it is computed by dividing the difference between the cost price and the first retail price by the retail price. In both cases, markdown and stock shortages are not counted in the computation. Initial markup is sometimes referred to as *original markup*, *initial markon*, *original markon*, *planned markup*, *starting markup*, or MARKON.

initial markup percent/percentage   The difference between the cost of merchandise and the price at which it sells, converted to a percentage figure and expressed on a departmental or store-wide basis.

initial order   A request by a retailer to a vendor, manufacturer, or marketing intermediary to receive merchandise not previously stocked.

initial price   See INITIAL RETAIL PRICE.

initial public offering (IPO)   In the evolution of a company from private to public, the first offering of stock on a public stock exchange. The money used from the sale of shares is used as capital to expand the organization.

initial purchase   The first purchase of an item from a store by a customer.

initial retail price   The cost of merchandise plus the amount of INITIAL MARKUP. Also called the *initial price*.

injunction   A court order directing someone to do or refrain from doing something. In the early days of unionism, management used this weapon freely, seeking injunctions to order striking workers back to work on the grounds that the strikers were interfering with business. Today, injunctions are legal only in certain labor cases, such as workers subject to the LABOR-MANAGEMENT RELATIONS ACT (LMRA) (1947) (i.e., the Taft-Hartley Act).

innate need   See BIOGENIC NEED.

inner-directed   Guided primarily by goals and ideals stemming from one's own value system rather than by the opinions of others. Inner-directed people are often considered nonconformists by their peers. Compare OTHER-DIRECTED.

inner envelope   In direct mail, the envelope enclosed with promotional materials for the customer's use (e.g., for payment or ordering). Compare OUTER ENVELOPE.

inner fashions   See INTIMATE APPAREL.

innerwear   See INTIMATE APPAREL.

innerwear form   A mannequin alternative used to display briefs and boxers, panties, corsets, lingerie, swimwear, and bras. Innerwear forms are available in a variety of sizes and skin tones, fabrications and finishes, for both genders and all ages. Also called a *lingerie form*.

innocent reciprocity   See RECIPROCITY.

innovation   In the product development process, a change or addition to a firm's product line that will generally be perceived as new by consumers. Innovations fall into two categories: a *minor innovation* is a product already existing in the marketplace but not previously produced by the firm, while a *major innovation* is a product never produced before by any firm.

innovation diffusion   See DIFFUSION PROCESS.

innovation stage   The first stage in the RETAIL LIFE CYCLE, that is, the evolution of a retail store. In the innovation stage, the store (or other retail format) is new and must be introduced to customers in the hope that it will attract a following. Its goal is to differentiate itself from other retailers, develop its own unique strategies, and establish its own clientele. See also ACCELERATED DEVELOPMENT STAGE, MATURITY STAGE, and DECLINE STAGE.

innovative combiner   A marketing firm using the combined target market approach to identify a new combination of submarkets. Innovative combiners are often followed into the marketplace by a number of imitators; compare IMITATIVE

COMBINER. See also COMBINED TARGET MARKET APPROACH and INNOVATIVE SEGMENTER.

innovative maturity A stage near the end of the PRODUCT LIFE CYCLE (PLC) in which the product is either repositioned or modified to extend its lifespan. Tactics employed include finding new uses for the product, encouraging more frequent use by current customers, and attracting new customers by expanding the market for the product.

innovativeness The degree to which an individual or firm is able to accept and embrace what is new and different. The innovative retail firm, for example, is flexible and adapts readily to change with new ideas and/or new products and services.

innovative segmenter A segmenter that seeks out new sub-markets, identifies unsatisfied needs, and attempts to develop a MARKETING MIX to reach the new segment. Innovative segmenters are often followed into the MARKETPLACE by a number of imitators (i.e., imitative segmenters) seeking to utilize the newly identified market segment for their own products. See also IMITATIVE SEGMENTER and INNOVATIVE COMBINER.

innovator 1. In INTERNET marketing, an online business whose online presence is larger, more expensive, and has more of the latest features than its competitors.   2. In the diffusion or adoption process, a member of the group of consumers who are first to accept and adopt a new product, service or idea. Innovators tend to be young, high in social and economic status, and willing to take considerable risk in adopting new trends and fashions. Also known as *early acceptor*. See also FASHION INNOVATOR. Compare FAST FOLLOWER, COMPETITOR, and CONSERVATIVE.

INP See INFORMATION-NEED-PRODUCT (INP).

in-pack premium A free gift or other item of value placed inside the package of the item being promoted by the manufacturer, such as the toy inside each box of Cracker Jack.

inplacement In retailing, the practice of reassigning and shifting employees around the store.

input-output model A technique employed to measure and forecast fluctuations in supply and demand in the industrial market. The model is based on a relationship between industries in which the output of one is purchased by others in the marketplace. These goods and services become, in turn, their input.

inquiry conversion In sales, the process of turning a request for information or an expression of interest in a product or service into a sale. See also SALES APPROACH.

insert See ADVERTORIAL INSERT.

inside buying organization A method of organizing a retail store's BUYING operation so that the buying function is performed by the store's own employees. Distinct from an arrangement whereby merchandise is purchased through a RESIDENT BUYING OFFICE.

inside order-taker See ORDER TAKER.

inside salespeople Salespeople, usually involved in wholesaling, who take calls from customers in an office. See also ORDER TAKER.

insolvency A condition in which a business is unable to pay its debts, generally as a result of liabilities exceeding assets.

inspection The act of viewing or examining fully, officially, and formally. For example, a public company's balance sheet is open for inspection. Similarly, a food plant may undergo an inspection by a federal agency for compliance with health codes and cleanliness standards.

inspection buying In INDUSTRIAL PURCHASING, the practice of purchasing a product only after every item has been carefully examined. This method is used primarily for products that are not standardized and require inspection. For example, one-of-a-kind products such as cars and buildings must be inspected.

insperience A trend in which consumers invite brands offering experiences previously exclusive to the public or semi-public domains to set up shop within their own homes. For example, consumers may choose to set up, in their spare rooms, exercise equipment owned and operated by a local or nationally branded gym. Insperiences are as much about extending outside world experiences as replacing them. The same consumers, for example, may elect, on occasion, to visit the real gym. The trend was identified and the term coined by trendwatching.com at www.trendwatching.com.

installations See INSTALLED EQUIPMENT.

installed equipment Capital equipment that is generally fixed, long-lasting, and expensive, such as the plant machinery used to manufacture a firm's products. Installed equipment does not become a part of the finished product and is thus distinct from materials and components used in manufacture. Also referred to as *major equipment* and *installations*.

installment The partial payment of a debt or credit purchase. Payments are made at regular intervals (e.g., monthly) over a specified period of time, usually according to a contract. Also spelled *instalment*.

installment plan/contract/buying A consumer credit arrangement between store and customer, generally implemented for the purchase of expensive durable goods. Unlike revolving credit, the installment plan usually involves a formal contract secured by an ADVANCE (i.e., down payment). The customer agrees to pay the balance at periodic intervals, each installment including interest and service charges. Under this plan the store retains title to the merchandise until it is fully paid for, leaving the way open for repossession if necessary. Also called *buying on time, installment credit,* or *time payment*. See also INSTALMENT.

instalment   Alternative spelling of INSTALLMENT.

instant coupon   A MANUFACTURER COUPON placed on the outside of a package, generally in a supermarket or other food retail establishment. The instant coupon is designed to encourage the consumer to purchase the item immediately. The coupon is *instant* in that it is valid for the current purchase; the customer does not have to wait for a repurchase in order to use it. Some instant coupons are made available through dispensers placed alongside the item on the supermarket shelf.

instant message   See INSTANT MESSAGING (IM).

instant messaging (IM)   The act of communicating in real time with two or more people over a network such as the INTERNET. Instant messaging requires the use of a client program that hooks up an instant messaging service. Most services offer an indication of whether people on one's list of contacts (one's BUDDY LIST or *contact list*) are currently online and available to CHAT.

institutional advertising   Paid, nonpersonal communications intended to enhance the prestige, image, and reputation of a firm or institution rather than to promote a specific product or induce an immediate response on the part of the target audience. Institutional advertising has as its principal purpose the promotion of GOODWILL toward the organization by informing the public of the role the organization plays in the community and representing it as responsible and civic-minded regarding such issues as energy conservation, environmental quality, etc. This form of advertising, geared to enhancing the firm's reputation, is more closely associated with long-term objectives. Sometimes called *corporate advertising, public relations advertising, image advertising, informative institutional advertising, a reminder promotion,* or *corporate image advertising.* See also RETAIL INSTITUTIONAL ADVERTISING, and IMAGE BUILDING. Distinguished from PUBLIC SERVICE ADVERTISING.

institutional approach to marketing   An effort to understand marketing systems by studying the various types of organizations involved in the marketing process (i.e., manufacturers and producers, wholesalers, retailers, etc.).

institutional display   A visual presentation of an idea rather than an item or product. For example, since an institutional display seeks to present the store as a worthwhile member of the community, it may feature a charity drive or commemorate the passing of a hero without including any store merchandise.

institutional event   A special event designed to draw attention to the company. Institutional events may be produced to enhance the company image, exhibit good corporate citizenship, improve customer relations, contribute to the community's economic development, or promote a charitable cause.

institutional investor   An organization that owns many shares of stock. Examples of institutional investors include banks, mutual funds, pension funds, insurance companies, college endowment funds, and foundations. See also CORPORATION.

institutional market   The portion of the market that consists of a wide variety of organizations, many of them nonprofit, including schools, churches, hospitals, etc. The institutional market is a part of the larger INDUSTRIAL MARKET. See also PRODUCER MARKET and GOVERNMENT MARKET.

institutional sales   Sales of merchandise to such organizations as schools, hospitals, prisons, etc. See also INSTITUTIONAL MARKET.

institutional store   Synonym for NONPROMOTIONAL STORE.

institutions in marketing   See MARKETING INSTITUTIONS.

in stock   Of merchandise, on hand and available for sale or shipment. See also INVENTORY.

in-store demonstration   A SALES DEMONSTRATION that takes place within the retail store and is designed to increase store sales.

in-store exhibit   A special event involving the presentation of fashion items in a retail setting. In-store exhibits are used to entice regular and new customers into a store. The customers attend the event and view merchandise offered by the firm.

in-store lighting   See STORE LIGHTING PLAN.

in-store show   A FASHION SHOW presented for the benefit of store employees to inform them of new and exciting trends for the upcoming season, coordinated with the advertising and visual display departments to create a storewide theme. The in-store show stimulates enthusiasm and contributes to *suggestion selling.* Informed sales associates can influence customers by sharing their expertise. See also SUGGESTION SELLING.

in-stream ad   Advertising sold on the WORLD WIDE WEB (WWW) that is run within the streamed content of the WEBCAST. See also WEBCAST AD.

instrumented store   A retail outlet in which information gathered and analyzed by computers has determined the layout and shelf space. Inventory control, ordering, and related functions are similarly determined, usually through POINT-OF-PURCHASE (POP) scanning.

intangibility of services   The notion that most services have no physical properties and have no existence until they are performed. See also STORE SERVICES.

intangible resources   A firm's strength in the form of its reputation in the marketplace, the relationship it maintains with customers, the quality level of its products or services, etc.

intangible standard   See CONTROL STANDARD.

integrated circuit card (ICC)   See SMART CARD.

integrated marketing   A strategy in which all of a company's coordinated marketing efforts are handled by a single organization, generally a large advertising agency (sometimes called a superagency). These agencies are equipped to provide services such as direct mail, coupons, and other promotions, publicity releases, and public relations activities as well as traditional advertising. For example, Walt Disney used integrated marketing (which he called *synergy*) in the 1950s and 1960s to drive the Disney company forward.

integrated marketing communications (IMC) According to the American Association of Advertising Agencies (AAAA), "a concept of marketing communications planning that recognizes the added value of a comprehensive plan that evaluates the strategic roles of a variety of communication disciplines—for example, general advertising, direct response, sales promotion and public relations—and combines these disciplines to provide clarity, consistency, and maximum communications impact." IMC requires a big-picture approach, including coordination of the various communications, marketing, and promotion functions. True integration occurs when all aspects of the product, from product development, package design, and brand name creation to price and type of sales venue, are coordinated. IMC attempts to project a consistent impression of the product in the marketplace. See also PROMOTIONAL BUDGETING.

integrated, one-brand name strategy A strategy employed by many BRICKS-AND-CLICKS organizations in which the same brand name is used online and offline. The strategy invests Web sites with immediately identifiable name brands on which to build a Web presence. Some bricks-and-clicks with well-established, highly regarded offline brand names rely on them to build online Web site awareness. Other bricks-and-clicks separate online and offline branding. See also MIXED BRAND NAME STRATEGY.

integrated retailing A strategy in which a retail organization has consolidated its activities to include such functions as production, wholesaling, distribution and transportation, etc. See also VERTICAL INTEGRATION.

integration In business organizations, particularly large, complex firms, the attempt to coordinate all the firm's functions into a cohesive whole working toward the same goal. This effort is particularly important when timing and consistency are issues, as they are in marketing firms. Some larger organizations employ *integrators* whose primary function is to coordinate demand and supply, packaging programs, and customer service functions. Integrators are expected to maintain the balance between production and sales, long-term and short-term goals, and similar counterpoising influences while resolving interdepartmental conflicts. Also called *coordination* or *organizational integration*. See also HORIZONTAL INTEGRATION and VERTICAL INTEGRATION.

integrative market opportunities Opportunities for new growth in the marketplace that generally involve new production or different levels of distribution. See also BACKWARD INTEGRATION, FORWARD INTEGRATION, VERTICAL INTEGRATION, and HORIZONTAL INTEGRATION.

integrator See INTEGRATION.

intelligence A system for collecting and transforming data and knowledge for use in making marketing decisions. The intelligence process in business is a continuous cycle of defining one's goals, identifying data sources (gathering and organizing the data), analyzing and evaluating the data (preparing a report), and disseminating the results and recommendations. Feedback, evaluating the intelligence process itself, completes the loop. See also COMPETITIVE INTELLIGENCE (CI) and MARKETING INTELLIGENCE.

intensity of distribution A measure of the number of wholesale and retail outlets through which a manufacturer's products are available. Intensity increases with the number of outlets (wholesale and retail). See also INTENSIVE DISTRIBUTION.

intensive distribution A marketing strategy in which goods are placed in the maximum number of retail outlets by the manufacturer or distributor, giving the product the widest possible exposure to the public. Also known as *mass distribution* and *extensive distribution*. Compare OPEN DISTRIBUTION, EXCLUSIVE DISTRIBUTION, and SELECTIVE DISTRIBUTION. See also INTENSITY OF DISTRIBUTION.

intensive market opportunity A favorable condition or situation in the marketplace that may be further developed through more aggressive marketing activities. For example, a company may increase sales by persuading existing customers to buy more of the firm's product, by persuading customers of competing products to switch to one's own brand, by improving distribution through such means as VERTICAL INTEGRATION, etc. Also called *market intensification*.

interacting skills The techniques used by marketing managers to influence others to implement the firm's marketing strategy. These skills include motivating employees of the firm as well as others on whom the firm relies (e.g., marketing research firms, advertising agencies, dealers, wholesalers, agents). For example, managing conflict within a channel of distribution is one area in which the marketing manager must utilize interacting skills. See also ALLOCATING SKILLS, MONITORING SKILLS, and ORGANIZING SKILLS.

interaction In sales, the relationship or interplay that develops between the salesperson and the customer. See also SALES APPROACH.

interactive business relations In online marketing, actively selling directly to buyers from a Web storefront. This is accomplished through two-way online communication with customers and other activities designed to solicit business directly from a target market. Compare PASSIVE BUSINESS RELATIONS.

interactive marketing unit (IMU) A voluntary guideline and standard issued by the Interactive Advertising Bureau (IAB) for ad formats used by Web publishers. The intent of the guideline is to standardize the size of online ads.

interactive plan A merchandise plan that combines a TOP-DOWN PLAN and a BOTTOM-UP PLAN. Interactive planning is a teamwork approach with input from all the firm's constituencies, enabled by information technology systems that make it possible for everyone in the firm to have access to the appropriate data and reports.

interactive retailing Any retailing system that utilizes immediate two-way communication between buyer and seller. See also ELECTRONIC CATALOG, ELECTRONIC RETAILING, E-TAILING, INTERACTIVE TELEVISION (ITV), and VIDEO DATACASTING.

interactive television (ITV) A trend in DIRECT RESPONSE MEDIA in which the viewer uses the television and attached apparatus to affect events on the screen. Specifically, the user helps to define the amount or type of information he or she wants to receive, utilizing a computer, a touch screen, or the push of a button to enter requests. ITV thus involves direct two-way communication between the sponsor and the viewer of the message. Online retailing is expected to utilize interactive television in the future.

interactive Web site A marketing Web site where customers communicate interactively with the marketer but cannot carry out actual purchases. Compare TRANSACTION WEB SITE and INFORMATION WEB SITE.

interactivity utility Consumer satisfaction derived from the interaction of buyers and sellers on the INTERNET in real time, regardless of their geographical location.

intercepting site A retail site location between two crucial areas: the area where people live and the area to which people are drawn to shop.

Inter-City Cost of Living Indicators Project Former name of the COST-OF-LIVING INDEX (COLI).

interdepartmental merchandise See TRANSFERS.

interdependent product pricing See PRODUCT LINE PRICING.

interest 1. A service charge paid by borrowers of money or users of credit. 2. A return on money invested or saved in a savings account, certificate of deposit, retirement account, etc. 3. The characteristic of a product, line of products, advertisement, visual display, etc., that attracts the attention and/or curiosity of the customer and makes the merchandise desirable.

interface In the design and construction of Web pages for e-tailing, the seamless and invisible link where UPFRONT and BACKEND interact.

interindustry competition Competitive activity in the MARKETPLACE between large industries, particularly those manufacturing complementary products. For example, competition between the textile and the apparel industries.

interior display The presentation of merchandise within the store in such a way that the customer is encouraged to try the product. Interior displays are intended to stimulate unplanned purchases and to enhance the atmosphere of the store.

intermediary In retailing and marketing, any person or firm playing a role in the CHANNEL OF DISTRIBUTION between the producer of the goods and the ultimate consumer of the goods. See also MARKETING INTERMEDIARY.

intermediate customer Any buyer between the producer of the basic raw materials used to make a product and the ultimate consumer of the product. Manufacturers, wholesalers, retailers, and other marketing intermediaries are all intermediate customers.

intermediate markdown A reduction in retail price made before the current, and usually final, reduction is advertised. The current retail price may have been reached in stages by means of several intermediate markdowns.

intermediate market The entire spectrum of wholesalers and retailers that buy goods from others and resell them. See also MARKETING INTERMEDIARY.

intermodal transportation/services In transportation, such coordinated services as PIGGYBACK and FISHYBACK that combine two or more modes of transportation owned by one company (e.g., truck trailers on railroad flatcars). Intermodal transportation plays a vital role in importing and exporting. The combined modes allow retailers to reap the economic advantages of rail and the door-to-door efficiencies of truck.

intern A student in a formal training program that includes on-the-job learning by working closely with professionals in the field. Internships may be paid or unpaid. In either case, college (or, occasionally, high school) credit is usually earned because the internship is treated as a learning experience.

internal audit A review of a store's records, reports, financial statements, etc. to verify their accuracy and conformity to the organization's policies. The internal audit is conducted by employees of the store rather than by an outside firm as in an external audit.

internal buyout The acquisition of an organization by its employees. For example, 348 Macy's executives acquired Macy's from its shareholders in 1986. See also LEVERAGED BUYOUT.

internal credit Consumer credit financed by the retailer.

internal data Marketing information derived from a firm's own in-house records. Included are such accounting records as profit and loss statements, financial ratios, sales revenues, costs, inventory data, etc. Compare EXTERNAL DATA. Also known as *operating data*.

internal environment See MARKETING ENVIRONMENT.

internal inventory transfer In plant operations, the movement of semifinished goods through the manufacturing process. Also called, simply, *inventory transfer*.

internal marketing   1. Management strategies for employee development, particularly for those employees involved in selling. The intent of internal marketing is to improve the organization's relations with its customers.   2. A term used to describe Internet marketing targeted to dealers and employees. See also EXTERNAL MARKETING.

internal marketing environment   See MARKETING ENVIRONMENT.

internal presentation   See LINE PRESENTATION.

internal promotion   The communication of ideas and information to customers inside the store. Promotional tools include signs, posters, sound and video systems, electronic kiosks, and displays. For example, announcements to shoppers over the store's public address system call attention to special sale items. Compare EXTERNAL PROMOTION. See also PROMOTIONAL TOOLS.

internal standards   Performance indicators based on data obtained from within an organization. For example, last July's performance in better sportswear may be compared to this July's performance in the same classification. See also INDUSTRY STANDARDS.

international brand   See MANUFACTURER'S BRAND.

international department   That part of a firm charged with the conduct of foreign operations.

international franchising   Synonym for FOREIGN LICENSING.

International Home Furnishing Center (IHFC)   The largest wholesale home furnishings show in the U.S., and perhaps the world. Located in High Point, North Carolina, the center is home to over 850 of the world's leading home furnishings manufacturers. In addition to furniture, a wide variety of decorative accessories, lighting, wall décor, and rugs are available for sale. IHFC maintains a Web site at www.ihfc.com.

International Home Furnishings Market (IHFM)   A semiannual market held in High Point, North Carolina for the home furnishings industry. Retail buyers of home furnishings attend the market to buy for their establishments and learn about the most recent trends in the classification. See also INTERNATIONAL HOME FURNISHINGS CENTER (IHFC).

international Internet market   An INTERNET market outside the marketer's home country. It may consist of consumers, enterprises, or both. The marketing mix is adjusted to meet the needs of the target market.

international Internet marketing   Marketing in an electronically mediated environment that utilizes the Internet, the World Wide Web, intranets, and/or extranets to make and receive offers from more than just the marketer's home market.

international marketing   The practice of selling goods and services outside one's home country. There are two basic forms of international marketing: operations carried on in the home country that produce goods to be exported and marketed in a foreign country; and operations in foreign countries that produce goods in those countries for sale there. Some foreign operations are wholly-owned subsidiaries of the parent company, while others may be joint or licensed ventures or contract manufacturing operations. Compare GLOBAL MARKETING and MULTINATIONAL MARKETING.

International Menswear Mart   A component of the Dallas Market Center in Dallas, Texas, a MERCHANDISE MART that houses more than 3,000 lines of men's and boy's apparel and accessories.

international retailer   A retail company that operates both in its home country and abroad. Compare DOMESTIC RETAILER and GLOBAL RETAILER.

International Retail Federation (IRF)   The global division of the NATIONAL RETAIL FEDERATION (NRF). Membership includes all retail formats and channels of distribution related to retailing. Headquartered in Washington, D.C., the IRF may be contacted through the NRF Web site at www.nrf.com.

international retailing   Retail activities taking place beyond the borders of a company's home country. See also INTERNATIONAL RETAILER and GLOBAL RETAILER.

international specialist   An expert in international trade (often acting as a consultant) who primarily performs a sales function. The international specialist responds to inquiries, manages exhibits at international trade shows, and handles export documentation, shipping, insurance, and financial matters. He or she may also maintain contact with embassies, export financing agencies, and various departments of commerce, and may use the services of an EXPORT AGENT, an EXPORT MANAGEMENT COMPANY (EMC), or an IMPORT INTERMEDIARY to assist in the process. The alternative to an international specialist is an in-house EXPORT DEPARTMENT, a department within the organization specializing in handling the same functions.

International Standard Book Number (ISBN)   A unique machine-readable number that identifies a book. The use of the ISBN has revolutionized the book trade, and 159 countries and territories are officially ISBN members. The administration of the ISBN system is carried out on three levels: international, group, and publisher. ISBN maintains a home page at www.isbn.org.

International Standard Serial Number (ISSN)   An eight-digit number that identifies periodical publications, including electronic serials. ISSN is managed by a worldwide network of 77 national centers, coordinated by an International Centre based in Paris and backed by UNESCO and the French Government. The ISSN is used by libraries, subscription agents, researchers, information scientists, and newsagents and other retail magazine vendors (through its barcode version). The ISSN maintains a home page at www.issn.org.

international trade The importing and exporting of goods and services between countries. Also called *world trade*.

international transfer price The price paid by the importing or buying unit of a firm to the exporting unit of the same firm. See also TRANSFER PRICE.

Internet The world's largest matrix of interconnected distributed computer networks. All computers operating on the Internet conform to TCP/IP protocols, communication standards that allow for seamless communication and data transmission across great distances in real time between different operating systems. The Internet, which began as a means of scholarly and academic communication, began to be commercialized in 1993. The process has skyrocketed since then, changing the very nature of the Internet itself. The Internet is used by retailers to advertise and market their products as well as to sell them directly to the customer. Also known by the shortened term, *Net*.

Internet access price The price that consumers and some business enterprises pay to an INTERNET SERVICE PROVIDER (ISP) to connect to the service and the INTERNET. Originally, pricing was per hour online. In recent years, most ISPs charge users a flat monthly rate.

Internet adoption Acceptance and use of the Internet by consumers and enterprises. Like the adoption process for other products and services, Internet use has innovators, early adopters, early majority, late majority, laggards, and nonadopters. The Internet adoption curve follows essentially the same normal distribution as the adoption curve for other products.

Internet advertising Any form of promotion, whether commercial or noncommercial, used on the Internet, intranets, or extranets. This includes such things as banner ads, advergames, sponsorships, interstitials and other rich media ads, pop-ups, pop-unders, classified ads, Yellow Pages, and in-stream and gateway Webcast ads. Like other forms of advertising, Internet ads are paid for by an identified sponsor and designed to build awareness, drive traffic, make a sale, remind, position and reposition products, and entertain. Hypertext links directly deliver potential customers to the advertiser's site if the customers click through.

Internet chat services See INTERNET RELAY CHAT (IRC).

Internet coupon See ELECTRONIC COUPON.

Internet discussion group An online open public forum whose participants share common interests. With few exceptions, discussion groups are accessible to anyone, without permission or special authorization, through a standard Web browser or newsreader software. Discussion groups can spread news very quickly. The predominant type of Internet discussion group is the USENET NEWSGROUP. Also called a *message board*, *forum*, *board*, or *discussion*.

Internet e-mail list Synonym for E-MAIL DISCUSSION LIST.

Internet Fraud Complaint Center An agency of the U.S. federal government charged with handling consumer complaints of Internet fraud. The agency maintains a Web site at www.ic3.com.

Internet gateway See GATEWAY.

Internet leaders (ILs) A group of countries, including the United States, Canada, nations in Western Europe, Japan, Australia, New Zealand, Taiwan, South Korea, and Israel, that contribute innovations fueling Internet commercialization. Compare LEAST-INTERNET-READY AREAS (LIRAS) and INTERNET-READY AREAS (IRAS).

Internet marketing See E-MARKETING.

Internet marketing research MARKETING RESEARCH (MR) conducted on or about the Internet or any of its sectors. Marketing researchers use the Internet to administer surveys and to conduct focus groups, interviews, experiments, and observations as well as to collect secondary research. Online operational data tools track individual online behaviors and mine vast databases for relationships, thus refining and extending marketing research capabilities.

Internet protocol See PROTOCOL.

Internet protocol name The first part of a UNIFORM RESOURCE LOCATOR (URL), specifying the code for deciphering messages (i.e., the protocol) used in that particular Internet service. For example, the WORLD WIDE WEB uses HYPERTEXT TRANSFER PROTOCOL (HTTP), usually seen on the Web as http. A colon and a double slash are used as separators, so the Internet protocol name always appears within a URL as http://.

Internet readiness (IR) The degree to which a country, region, or other area is prepared to make Internet access and activities widely available, use information and communication technologies effectively, and participate in Internet-related commercial and public sector activities. IR also serves as an indicator of Internet marketing receptiveness and competitiveness.

Internet-ready areas (IRAs) Countries or regions in which the population is generally aware of the Internet. Such countries have communication and information infrastructures, although not always equally distributed, and are Internet-ready, although not universally so. IRAs stand to benefit from Internet commercialization and are prime Internet marketing targets. As such, they are poised between INTERNET LEADERS (ILS) and LEAST-INTERNET-READY AREAS (LIRAS).

Internet Relay Chat (IRC) A CHAT system developed by Jarkko Oikarinen in Finland in the late 1980s. IRC enables people connected anywhere on the Internet to join in live discussions. Unlike older chat systems, IRC is not limited to just two participants. Use requires an IRC client (i.e., a program that runs on the user's computer and sends and receives messages to and from an IRC server) and Internet access. The IRC server ensures that all messages are broadcast to everyone participating in a discussion. Many discussions may go on simultaneously and each one is assigned a unique channel. IRC can also be used for voice communications. Marketing focus groups are sometimes conducted in the virtual environment of an IRC.

Internet retailer   Synonym for E-TAILER.

Internet retailing   Synonym for E-TAILING.

Internet sales promotion   Temporary inducements or incentives to stimulate demand, increase storefront traffic and sales, and encourage distribution channel members to distribute, stock, or purchase a product. Sales promotions are found on about 93 percent of commercial Web sites. For example, a Web site may run a contest or sweepstakes or offer downloadable discount coupons for purchases made at offline retailers. They may also provide games, free product samples, or memberships in product clubs. In an effort to encourage online purchases and reduce offline call center costs, print catalogs increasingly include dollars-off coupons for purchases made from the company's Web site.

Internet service provider (ISP)   A business that provides Internet access to users (both consumers and business enterprises). ISPs vary in size from small, local businesses with low-speed Internet access to huge international companies (part of the backbone) with high-speed access. Low-transmission-capacity ISPs do not connect directly to the Internet, providing instead access to a larger service provider that connects to the backbone. National ISPs with high transmission capacity connect directly to the backbone. These larger ISPs often offer several types of high-speed access in addition to low-speed dial-up service. Many ISPs also provide E-MAIL service to their customers. See also STAND-ALONE INTERNET SERVICE PROVIDER (ISP).

Internet surfer   See SURFER.

Internet surfing   See SURFING THE NET/WEB.

Internet Tax Freedom Act (ITFA) (1998)   U.S. federal legislation, enacted in 1998 and extended in 2001, that limits the collection of taxes based on Internet sales. The original legislation called for a three-year moratorium (October 1, 1998, to October 21, 2001) on state and local taxes on Internet access, unless such tax was generally imposed and enforced before October 1, 1998. The moratorium also applied to multiple or discriminatory taxes on e-commerce.

interpretive survey   A method used in MARKETING RESEARCH (MR) that seeks to explain the personal feelings, motives, and attitudes of consumers. Respondents are asked to explain why they use certain products. See also SURVEY.

interselling   Synonym for CROSS-SELLING.

Interstate Commerce Act (1887)   A U.S. federal regulation that created the first independent regulatory body in the United States, the *Interstate Commerce Commission*. The Commission regulates interstate shipping rates and establishes standards for interstate commerce. See also TARIFF.

Interstate Commerce Commission   See INTERSTATE COMMERCE ACT (1887).

interstitial   In online Internet advertising, a rich media ad that resembles a television commercial. Interstitials are flashy, intrusive ads using audio, animation, and video and lasting five to thirty seconds. They play between Web pages, much like print ads in magazines. While the ad is running, screen content is blocked and access to the desired site is delayed. See also SUPERSTITIAL.

intertype channel conflict   A form of distribution CHANNEL CONFLICT that occurs when intermediaries of different types (e.g., specialty stores and department stores) attempt to interfere with and impede each other's operations.

intertype competition   A situation in which stores of different types sell the same merchandise. For example, magazines may be found in pharmacies, supermarkets, newsstands, bookstores, and variety stores.

interurbia   A strip of seemingly continuous urban-suburban population centers. For example, the East Coast of the United States may be considered an interurbia joining the cities of Washington, D.C., Baltimore, Philadelphia, New York, and Boston and including the suburban areas surrounding each city.

interview   1. In MARKETING RESEARCH (MR), a method of gathering data in which a questionnaire is administered to a respondent. Interviews may be conducted one-to-one or with a group, and may be carried out face-to-face, by telephone or mail, or by a respondent filling out a questionnaire on the spot. A one-to-one interview is also called a *personal interview*. A group interview is called a FOCUS GROUP.   2. A face-to-face meeting between a job applicant and a potential employer. The *initial interview* for staff personnel is usually conducted at the time the application is filled out. Its purpose is to obtain additional information about the applicant, verify information on the application, eliminate applicants who do not seem to qualify for the jobs available, and inform the applicant about the company. A *follow-up interview* is offered to a candidate who is under serious consideration for employment. Some companies subject the applicant to a *stress interview*, a screening tool in which a panel of interviewers fire questions requiring quick, thoughtful answers and evidence of problem-solving ability by the candidate.

interviewer bias   In MARKETING RESEARCH (MR), as in social science research generally, distortion in the results of an interview due to the intentional or unintentional intervention of the interviewer. For example, factors such as the gender or age of the interviewer may affect the way the interview is conducted or the interviewer's interpretation of the data elicited.

in the black   Of a store or other enterprise, profitable. The term dates from the days when accounting records were kept by hand in ledgers and black ink was used to show a profit. See also IN THE RED and BLACK FRIDAY.

in the pipeline Of a manufacturer's inventory, purchased by wholesalers and retailers but not as yet purchased by consumers. The merchandise is en route or in the channel along which it must pass on its way to the ultimate consumer.

in the red Of a store or other enterprise, unprofitable. The term dates from the days when accounting records were kept by hand in ledgers and red ink was used to show a loss. See also IN THE BLACK and BLACK FRIDAY, the day on which retailers traditionally hoped to move from being *in the red* to being *in the black.*

intimate apparel Women's apparel in three basic categories: *foundations* (bras, girdles, corsets, etc.), *lingerie* (daywear and sleepwear) and *loungewear* (robes, housecoats, and other casual apparel for at-home entertaining). Foundations are also called *body fashions, inner fashions,* and *innerwear.* Daywear includes slips, panties, etc. Sleepwear includes nightgowns, pajamas, etc.

intimates In the *Roger Starch Worldwide* study, the 15 percent of worldwide adult consumers who focus on personal relationships close to home (such as spouses, family, colleagues, and friends). Intimates are frequently found in Britain, Hungary, the Netherlands, and the United States. They are heavy users of media, particularly those that can be shared with others such as television, movies, and radio. What they have heard or seen in the media often forms the basis of their conversations with their family, friends, and colleagues.

intrabrand competition Competition between resellers, or between resellers and the direct sales force, for sales of products of the same brand. Manufacturers who sell their merchandise online may similarly find themselves in this type of competition with their retail outlets or distributors.

intranet A private, proprietary computer network that operates like the Internet, using TCP/IP protocols, but is closed to outside users and typically restricted to employees.

in transit Of merchandise, having left its point of origin but not yet arrived at its destination.

in-transit mixing A practice in rail shipping in which shippers are allowed to unload carload lots of goods at a warehouse, mix the goods into new carload lots, reload the cars, and ship to their destination without incurring additional charges for stopover privileges.

intrapreneur An ENTREPRENEUR within an existing organization. Intrapreneurs use corporate resources to pursue their own product line under the corporate umbrella, taking hands-on responsibility for INNOVATION within the organization.

intrastore transfer The purchase of goods from one selling department for use by another selling department in the same store. See also TRANSFERS.

intratype competition Retail competition between stores of the same type and using the same selling concepts (e.g., head-to-head competition between two specialty stores).

intrinsic cue Any characteristic of a product or service (particularly a physical characteristic) that arouses feelings in the customer, either positive (preferred) or negative. Compare EXTRINSIC CUE.

introduction (of a product) See INTRODUCTORY STAGE.

introductory approach A SALES APPROACH featuring a letter of introduction, business card, or testimonial from someone known to the prospect, presented by the SALESPERSON as a means of gaining the prospect's trust and attention.

introductory offer A free gift, premium, or discount given to encourage potential customers to try a new product or service. Introductory offers may also be used to reintroduce an old product or service that has been altered or improved.

introductory price A price that is cut temporarily during an INTRODUCTORY OFFER and raised again at the end of the introductory period. The set time period of the price cut distinguishes introductory price dealing from PENETRATION PRICING. Some competitors meet introductory price cuts in order to maintain customer loyalty to their products. Others prefer to ignore such dealing, especially if the introductory offer is neither too long nor too successful The process of setting prices this way is called *introductory pricing, introductory technique,* or *introductory price dealing.*

introductory stage The beginning (or pioneering) stage in the PRODUCT LIFE CYCLE (PLC), during which the marketing effort is directed toward introducing the product (rather than the specific brand) to the consuming public. Many products fail at this stage because they never capture the interest of the consumer. Also called *market introduction,* the *pioneering stage,* or the *primary stage.*

introductory technique See INTRODUCTORY PRICE.

invention strategy One of three basic strategies for introducing a product into a foreign market. In the invention strategy, the marketer adopts a totally new approach in the new market. For example, the product may be redesigned to a lower level of complexity. The alternative strategies are the EXTENSION STRATEGY and the ADAPTATION POLICY.

inventory 1. The assets of a business other than those commonly referred to as plant and equipment. Inventory includes raw materials, semifinished goods or works in progress, and finished goods to be either used internally or offered for sale. Also called *merchandise inventory.* 2. A detailed, often descriptive list of goods held in stock for future sale. Inventory may be expressed in terms of the number of units available or the dollar value of the merchandise. 3. Any of a number of processes and methods used to count and keep track of the amount of stock available for sale.

inventory and profitability (IP) A method of evaluating retail performance developed by Ting-Sheng Lin (1996) and composed of five measures: percent of inventory jobbed off (i.e., leftover merchandise sent off to a diverter or wholesaler);

percent gross margin; percent adjusted gross margin; GROSS MARGIN RETURN ON INVESTMENT (GMROI), and average inventory. The measure demonstrates that reduced inventory is the major reason for the improved performance in inventory and profitability (IP). See also REVENUE AND SERVICE (RS) and OVERALL PERFORMANCE (OP).

inventory at end of period   See CLOSING INVENTORY.

inventory audit   See STOCK COUNT.

inventory carrying cost   Any of the costs of doing business directly related to goods held in inventory (i.e., held in stock), including warehousing, deterioration and obsolescence, theft, and insurance charges. Also called an *inventory holding cost* or, simply, a *holding cost.*

inventory change   The amount of increase or decrease in the stock available in a store or department during a specified period.

inventory control   Synonym for STOCK CONTROL.

inventory count   See STOCK COUNT.

inventory cutoff   Synonym for INVOICE CUTOFF.

inventory echeloning   In LOGISTICS management, the practice of basing the number of inventory locations for an item on sales. In general, this means that high-volume goods will be stocked at a greater number of distribution centers within the marketing territory (including some in outlying areas), while low-volume goods will be stocked at fewer locations (perhaps even at a single, central location).

inventory holding cost   See INVENTORY CARRYING COST.

inventory management   Those activities calculated to ensure that the proper stock levels are maintained at all times. Included in the inventory management function is the responsibility for the smooth flow of goods from producer to consumer (i.e., LOGISTICS). Other functions include the estimation of such factors as customer demand, production capacity, lead times, etc. Inventory management is a commonly available feature of merchandising technology systems.

inventory overage   Synonym for STOCK OVERAGE.

inventory policy   The relationship between the quantity of stock on order and the quantity available, as preset and determined by the individual retailer. The inventory policy spells out what the ratio (or relationship) should be.

inventory position (and sales) report   A management report common to many chain retail organizations that reflects the status of sales, inventory, and profitability for specified periods of time. A typical inventory position and sales report for a retail chain will include the BOM inventory, receipts, interstore transfers, markdowns, sales, and EOM for each store and for the chain, as well as each store's percentage of the chain's BOM, receipts, sales, and EOM.

inventory profit   Profits accrued on goods held in inventory during a period when the value of the goods has increased. Such profits are above and beyond original expectations.

inventory risk   The MARKETING RISK undertaken by any firm that carries an inventory (i.e., the danger that changes in SUPPLY AND DEMAND will result in some of the inventory not being sold or that insufficient inventory will prevent the firm from being able to fill orders).

inventory shortage   Synonym for STOCK SHORTAGE.

inventory shrinkage   Synonym for STOCK SHORTAGE. See also INVISIBLE SHRINKAGE and VISIBLE SHRINKAGE.

inventory stock shortage   Synonym for STOCK SHORTAGE.

inventory stock turn rate   See STOCK TURNOVER (ST).

inventory transfer   Synonym for INTERNAL INVENTORY TRANSFER.

inventory turnover   Synonym for STOCK TURNOVER (ST).

inventory valuation   Any process used to determine the monetary value of stock on hand. Also called *valuation of inventory*. See also FIRST IN, FIRST OUT (FIFO), FIRST IN, STILL HERE (FISH), and LAST IN, FIRST OUT (LIFO).

investment opportunity chart   A tool used for strategic planning, consisting of a grid or matrix representing opportunities available to a firm in the marketplace.

investments by owners   According to The Financial Accounting Standards Board (1985), "increases in net assets of a particular enterprise resulting from transfers to it from other entities of something of value to obtain or increase ownership interests (or equity) in it. Assets are most commonly received as investments by owners, but that which is received may also include services or satisfaction or conversion of liabilities of the enterprise."

invisible shrinkage   Stock shortages due to shoplifting, employee theft, clerical error, etc., that remain undiscovered until a physical inventory is performed. See also SHRINKAGE and VISIBLE SHRINKAGE.

invisible supply   Additional merchandise in the hands of marketing intermediaries and manufacturers that may be made available to the retailer as needed. Compare VISIBLE SUPPLY.

invoice   A BILL or STATEMENT, usually itemized, that is enclosed with a shipment of merchandise or mailed later by the seller. Information generally includes quantities shipped, prices of goods, terms of sale, discount, applicable taxes, method of shipment, and other particulars, including the total amount of payment due the seller. Online invoices may appear in printable form on the Web site or may be e-mailed to the customer. Also called *purchase invoice* or *billing invoice*. See also RETAILING THE INVOICE and DATING OF INVOICES.

invoice apron An attachment to an INVOICE form, prepared by either the shipper of goods or by the receiving party, on which relevant notations may be made. For example, on the receiving end, an apron may be prepared on which quantities received are noted so that the goods may be passed through to the selling floor before the vendor's invoice arrives by mail. Sometimes simply referred to as an *apron*. Also called a *rider* or *receiving apron*.

invoice cutoff A specified date after which invoiced merchandise will not be added in to the physical count for the current accounting period but will be carried over instead into the next period. Also called *inventory cutoff*.

involuntary bankruptcy See BANKRUPTCY.

involuntary response See PHYSIOLOGICAL PROFILE.

involvement The emotional importance a customer attaches to a particular item of merchandise. A high-involvement item is one that has significant emotional importance to the consumer.

inward freight Charges accrued by moving merchandise from a vendor to the store.

IP See INVENTORY AND PROFITABILITY (IP).

IP address The unique identifying number of every computer on the Internet. Since this is generally a long number and difficult to remember, most computers are also assigned a corresponding DOMAIN NAME. See also HOST.

IPO See INITIAL PUBLIC OFFERING (IPO).

IR See INTERNET READINESS (IR)

IRAs See INTERNET-READY AREAS (IRAS).

IRC See INTERNET RELAY CHAT (IRC).

IRF See INTERNATIONAL RETAIL FEDERATION (IRF).

irregular An item that contains some imperfection not apparent to the naked eye. An irregular is less imperfect than a SECOND. Irregulars are also called IRs.

irregular demand Variations in the demand for products or services that cannot be directly attributed to seasonal changes or fluctuations in the local or national economy.

IRs See IRREGULAR.

IRS See INDEX OF (RETAIL) SATURATION (IRS).

IS (index of saturation) See INDEX OF (RETAIL) SATURATION (IRS).

ISBN See INTERNATIONAL STANDARD BOOK NUMBER (ISBN).

island A freestanding store display having space all the way around it.

island display A featured display area found in newer mall stores at the entry to the store. The area is visible from all sides, well-lit, and clearly identified by a raised platform, a change of flooring materials, or an area rug. The island display is used to present a story based on color trend, style, an event, or a storewide promotion. Also called a *merchandise island* and a *platform display*, although platforms are generally less permanent than islands in the store's layout.

island window A DISPLAY WINDOW having glass on all four sides, allowing the merchandise presentation to be viewed from any angle and from any direction. Also known as a *lobby window*.

isolated site/location A retail location in which the store has no nearby retail neighbors who could assist in building traffic.

isolated store A freestanding store building having no other retail outlets in the immediate vicinity.

ISSN See INTERNATIONAL STANDARD SERIAL NUMBER (ISSN).

IT See INFORMATION TECHNOLOGY (IT).

item 1. A specific article of merchandise. 2. A BEST SELLER.

item merchandising The planning involved in selling those specific articles of merchandise that, as best sellers, account for a significant portion of sales.

item price removal The practice of marking prices only on store shelves or aisle signs and not on individual articles of merchandise. The practice is common in supermarkets where bar codes are used at the register to tally prices. See also BAR CODE.

item pricing A method of setting prices that allows for deviations from the standard markon percentage. The retailer considers such factors as whether an item is a fast or slow mover, personal experience, the amount of risk involved, etc., to raise or lower the selling price.

ITFA See INTERNET TAX FREEDOM ACT (ITFA) (1998).

it-gap The commercial trend to focus on those items, countries, etc., that are not currently considered "in" or chic. This focus leads to a strategy of developing a new trend and building a new craze. The trend was identified and the term coined by trendwatching.com at www.trendwatching.com. See also IT-ROULATION, IT-ISM, IT-STATUS, and IT-THING.

it-ism Consumer obsession with the latest "in" thing, whether it be apparel, makeup, restaurants, neighborhoods, etc. The trend was identified and the term coined by trendwatching.com at www.trendwatching.com. See also IT-ROULATION, IT-GAP, IT-STATUS, and IT-THING.

it-roulation   The principle that every well-known color, cuisine, decade, city, country, or anything else commercially exploitable will get its turn in the limelight, over and over again. The principle was identified and the term coined by trendwatching.com at www.trendwatching.com. See also IT-ISM, IT-GAP, IT-STATUS, and IT-THING.

it-status   The position enjoyed by whatever is currently "in" or chic. The trend was identified and the term coined by trendwatching.com at www.trendwatching.com. See also IT-ROULATION, IT-GAP, IT-ISM, and IT-THING.

it-thing   The current hot trend or fad. The trend was identified and the term coined by trendwatching.com at www.trendwatching.com. See also FAD, IT-ROULATION, IT-GAP, IT-STATUS, and IT-ISM.

ITV   See INTERACTIVE TELEVISION (ITV).

jam auction/pitch (Slang) A store that sells inexpensive jewelry, souvenirs, and the like.

Japanese management See THEORY Z.

Java trap A particularly vicious type of pop-up ad designed to hijack a user's INTERNET session. Java traps sometimes spawn multiple windows, with the closure of each window by the user activating code that spawns another window, sometimes indefinitely. Also called a *spam cascade* or *pop-up hell.* Usually the only way to stop this is to close the BROWSER.

jebbles (Slang) Synonym for BLUEFINGERS.

jewelry Articles of personal adornment made of either precious or nonprecious materials. Included are necklaces, rings, earrings, pins, chains, etc.

jingle A short song with catchy words, often light or humorous, forming part of an advertisement. Advertisers intend the jingle to remain in the consumers' consciousness and influence their buying decisions.

jingle casting An advertising trend in which corporations, organizations, or political parties entice consumers to download and use commercial tunes for use in their cell phones or other handheld devices. The trend was identified and the term coined by trendwatching.com at www.trendwatching.com.

JIT purchasing/system See JUST-IN-TIME (JIT).

JND See JUST NOTICEABLE DIFFERENCE (JND).

job 1. In merchandising, to purchase or sell assorted merchandise in quantity but not in selected categories. Such merchandise may be leftovers, overstock, discontinued styles, etc. See also JOBBER and JOB LOT. 2. A piece of work or a task done as part of one's occupation or for an agreed price. 3. A position of employment.

job analysis A general review of a job's requirements, the tasks involved, and the training and education required of the jobholder. The job analysis is based on research, including observation, questionnaires, and personal interviews. The data gathered is used to generate a meaningful JOB DESCRIPTION.

jobber 1. A MARKETING INTERMEDIARY who buys from a manufacturer and sells to a wholesaler. 2. A MARKETING INTERMEDIARY who handles merchandise in odd or job lots. Some jobbers take possession of the title to the goods, which they resell to another jobber, a retailer, or directly to the consumer. Others have a buying agreement with the manufacturer to drop-ship the merchandise on orders obtained by the jobber. See also JOB LOT and JOB OFF. 3. Synonym for PIECEWORKER.

job description A systematic written summary of the requirements of a particular job, including the duties involved as well as the skills needed. It also identifies the immediate supervisor. Job descriptions are used in the hiring, promotion, and evaluation of employees, and alert the employees to performance expectations and requirements for promotion. See also JOB SPECIFICATION and PRIMARY JOB ASSIGNMENT.

job enrichment The addition of challenges, opportunities, and nonmonetary rewards to a position in a firm in order to improve an employee's efficiency and self-satisfaction. Job enrichment recognizes the employee's needs for recognition, self-esteem, and fair treatment. Job enrichment programs also encourage employees to demonstrate initiative and go the extra step to increase company profits or promote cost savings.

job evaluation A process in which jobs are compared with one another in an attempt to determine their relative rank, generally on the basis of job content. For *employee evaluation* see PERFORMANCE APPRAISAL and PERFORMANCE REVIEW.

job induction The informal orientation of a new employee, emphasizing the responsibilities of the job and the role the employee will play in the department. The job induction is usually performed by the department manager or other direct supervisor of the new employee and includes expectations, hours, schedule, pay rate, pay schedule, etc. See also EMPLOYEE ORIENTATION, STORE INDUCTION, and COMPANY INDUCTION.

job lot A broken lot, unbalanced assortment, or discontinued merchandise, reduced in price for quick sale. Some retailers specialize in job lot merchandising and deal only with incomplete assortments of goods. Also called *odd lot.*

job off   The practice of selling and shipping leftover merchandise to a diverter or wholesaler. The retailer may elect to use this method to reduce inventory and improve productivity. See also INVENTORY AND PROFITABILITY (IP) and JOBBER.

job security   Protection of workers against layoffs, whether temporary due to economic slowdowns or permanent due to closure of plants or an increase in subcontracting. Job security for members is frequently a bargaining demand of labor unions.

job shop   A business that produces work on a special order basis. Generally the job moves through the shop (e.g., metal stamping or forging, printing) in one batch, which is completed and sent to the customer.

job specification   A profile, derived from the information provided in a JOB DESCRIPTION, of the personal qualifications necessary for the successful performance of a job. The job specification indicates the education, experience, and personal attributes (e.g., leadership, collegiality, service orientation, attention to detail) needed for each position in a firm.

job ticket   A tag affixed to an order, giving details of the work to be done as well as the individual or firm for whom the job is being done. For example, in advertising agencies the job ticket gives the date, name of agency, name of client, and the instructions to be carried out. Similar job tickets are used in repair shops.

joint costs   In product line PRICING, those costs that are shared in the process of manufacturing or producing all the products in the line, as in, for example, the case of a line of household detergents that all share a common production process.

joint decision making   The process in which two or more consumers (e.g., in the case of married or cohabiting couples) have input into purchases.

joint demand   The demand for industrial products so closely related to each other that a change in the demand for one directly affects demand for the other. Also called *complementary demand.*

joint ownership venture   A form of JOINT VENTURE in which foreign and domestic investors join to create a local business. Each firm shares in the ownership and control of the new firm. Some foreign governments require joint ownership as a condition for entry into their markets.

joint promotion   A marketing effort, generally widely advertised, whose cost is shared by the two participating companies. Joint promotions are used in the case of undifferentiated products or services (e.g., airline tickets, soap, hosiery, hotel lodgings), whether to introduce new ones or revitalize those already established.

joint venture   1. A business partnership in which two or more companies combine forces to work on a project.   2. In international marketing, a partnership arrangement in which a domestic company shares the ownership and control of production and marketing facilities with at least one foreign partner (i.e., the LOCAL PARTNER). Some production facilities are established in the host country, a fact that distinguishes a joint venture from exporting. A joint venture also differs from a DIRECT INVESTMENT in that a partnership is established with a citizen of the host country. In some countries, a joint venture may be the only logical form of business because of local restrictions on direct investment. There are several types of joint venture, including LICENSING, CONTRACT MANUFACTURING, MANAGEMENT CONTRACTING, and the WHOLLY-OWNED SUBSIDIARY. See also REGIONAL COOPERATION GROUP.

journal   See SALES JOURNAL.

judgment forecasting   The use of good sense, discernment, and experience to predict sales.

judgmental approach (to promotional budgeting)   See TOP-DOWN APPROACH TO PROMOTIONAL BUDGETING.

judgmental techniques   Forecasting techniques based on the opinions of individuals or groups of individuals. When based on the combined opinions of a group of individuals, such as customers or salespersons, the judgmental technique is said to be a CONSENSUS. When the group is a panel of experts, the DELPHI METHOD/TECHNIQUE is often used.

judgment sample   A form of NONPROBABILITY SAMPLE in which researchers select subjects whom they deem to be good prospects for accurate information. This form of sample selection relies on the predisposition and, hence, the bias of the researcher. In some cases, such as in award nominations, the judgment sample is desirable, since it uses experts who are thought to be especially qualified in the area of interest.

jumble display/basket   Merchandise of various types dumped together in a bin or on a table without any formal arrangement. The merchandise so displayed is generally on sale at a reduced price. The jumble enhances the notion that the customer is getting a bargain. Also called a *jumble basket*, particularly when the display is in a bin or basket. Compare DUMP BIN/DISPLAY.

jumbo   A product or other item sold in a very large package.

jumbo economy size   See ECONOMY SIZE.

junior   See JUNIOR SIZES.

junior department store   A store that carries a relatively wide variety of merchandise in a departmentalized form of organization but is not as large as the traditional DEPARTMENT STORE. Prices are often moderate and major appliances and furniture are usually not included in the merchandise offering. In many respects the junior department store is a large SPECIALTY STORE.

junior petite sizes   Women's garments cut proportionately for small adult women 5' to 5'1" tall. The sizes usually run from 3JP to 13JP.

junior sizes   Women's garments cut for a well-proportioned adult figure, about 5'4" to 5'5" tall and short-waisted. Junior sizes usually run from 5 to 15. Also called *juniors*.

junk bond   A type of financing often used in a leveraged buyout. The assets of the organization are used as collateral to borrow from lending institutions, and high-yield, high-risk bonds are issued. The interest payments on these large debts puts an increased burden on the retailer and has resulted in a significant number of retail bankruptcies.

junk e-mail   The online equivalent of JUNK MAIL. See also SPAM and UNSOLICITED COMMERCIAL E-MAIL (UCE).

junk jewelry   Synonym for COSTUME JEWELRY. Also called *fashion jewelry*.

junk mail   Unsolicited promotional mail. Vast quantities of advertising circulars and catalogs, etc., are sent by retailers to consumers in the form of BULK MAIL. The electronic equivalent of junk mail is JUNK E-MAIL.

jury   See CONSUMER JURY.

jury of executive opinion technique   Synonym for DELPHI METHOD/TECHNIQUE.

just-in-case   The keeping of inventory on hand, either in manufacturing or retailing, in hopes that it will eventually be needed. The practice tends to increase carrying costs. Compare JUST-IN-TIME (JIT).

just-in-time (JIT)   1. In manufacturing, a control system in which inventory carrying costs are minimized by keeping just enough supplies and parts on hand at the point of production to maintain uninterrupted production. Materials are scheduled to arrive just when needed (i.e., just in time to be used). See also KANBAN.   2. In retailing, the delivery of additional merchandise to a store just when needed (i.e., just in time to replace diminished stock). Carrying costs are minimized by keeping just enough merchandise in stock to meet current needs and relying on frequent shipment of goods. Accurate forecasting is crucial to the success of the JIT method. Upgraded supply chain management systems, increasingly sensitive to retailers' needs, allow for these reduced inventory levels and provide quick response time on the part of suppliers. See also MASSED RESERVES, MATERIALS MANAGEMENT, and MATERIAL REQUIREMENTS PLANNING (MRP).

just noticeable difference (JND)   A formula developed by Ernst Weber to measure how large a change must occur to be noticed in human perception. The change, or just noticeable difference, is not an absolute quantity but rather an amount relative to the intensity of the original stimulus. According to Weber's formula, the stronger the initial stimulus, the greater the secondary stimulus must be if it is to be recognized as different. The formula is used by marketers trying to determine how much of a difference must be built into a product to distinguish it from its competitors. It is also used in setting prices, the theory being that the more expensive an item is originally, the larger the price drop required before it is seen as a bargain by consumers. Also called *Weber's Law*. See also SUBLIMINAL PERCEPTION, PERCEPTION, and THRESHOLD OF PERCEPTION.

K

kanban A system that controls inventory carrying costs by allowing a manufacturer to maintain just enough parts or other goods to meet current demand. New parts or goods are ordered so that they arrive just as they are needed. *Der.* Japanese, "visible record," "card," or "sign." See also JUST-IN-TIME (JIT) and QUICK RESPONSE (QR).

KBI See KEY BUYING INFLUENCE (KBI).

KD See KNOCKDOWN (KD).

keep it simple, stupid (KISS) An admonition to avoid over-complicating the marketing message. In online marketing, it serves as a maxim to avoid designing Web sites that are too wordy, too complicated, and hence likely only to frustrate and annoy the customer.

keep-out pricing See PREEMPTIVE PRICING.

Kefauver-Harris Drug Amendments to the Food and Drug Act (1962) U.S. federal legislation requiring the manufacturer to test both the safety and the effectiveness of drug products before marketing them to consumers. The legislation also required that the generic name of the drug appear on the label of the product.

key account marketing Synonym for NATIONAL ACCOUNT MARKETING.

key buying influence (KBI) The person in a store or other business organization who is responsible for making buying decisions regarding specific merchandise or services.

key item Synonym for BEST SELLER.

key resource A VENDOR whose past dealings with a retailer have been excellent and from whom the retailer has consistently bought a substantial portion of its merchandise. Also called a *key vendor, preferred vendor, preferred resource, primary supplier, prime resource, prime vendor,* and *principal resource.* See also PREFERRED VENDOR LIST and PRIOR SOURCE.

key selling price The price that is nearly dead center between the prices a store's customers regard as low and those they regard as high. When a bell curve is drawn to represent a store's price range, the key selling price will be at the top of the curve.

keystone markup A 100% markup over cost price. The retail price is reached by doubling the cost price. For example, if a dress costs the buyer $75, the original selling price is $150. This is the same as a 50% markup at retail. Also called the *keystone method* and *keystoning.* See also FULL MARK/MARKUP and KEYSTONE PLUS MARKUP.

keystone plus markup A markup in which the cost has been doubled and a few extra dollars added to arrive at the retail price. Many department stores work on keystone plus, as do many off-pricers. See also KEYSTONE MARKUP.

keystoning See KEYSTONE MARKUP.

key vendor See KEY RESOURCE.

kickback In vendor-vendee relations, a monetary payment to the retail buyer by the vendor as a recompense for the buyer's patronage. Kickbacks are generally considered unethical and illegal in the United States.

kickback marketing Any one of several online marketing methods (e.g., affiliate marketing programs, cost-per-action, revenue sharing agreements, bounty systems) whereby Web sites and media sites form alliances to refer customers back and forth to each other, thereby sharing in the revenues.

kill/kill bad pay (Slang) Synonym for CREDIT CANCELLATION.

kilobytes See BYTE.

Kimball ticket/tag A print-punch merchandise tag, manufactured by the Kimball Co., on which information (vendor's name, size, style, season, color, price, etc.) is represented in both human-readable form and in machine-readable code in the form of punched holes. Largely replaced by the UNIVERSAL PRODUCT CODE (UPC).

king size A size larger or longer than the standard size.

kinked demand curve A form of DEMAND CURVE commonly found in oligopolistic markets. With few members operating in an industry, any price increase by one member results in a reduction in sales revenue as customers buy from competitors. Any price cut invites the competition to retaliate in kind. The kink in the demand curve occurs at the point above which demand is *elastic* and below which it is *inelastic*.

kiosk   1. A small structure or building used as a newsstand, refreshment stand, information booth, etc.   2. A columnlike structure on which notices and advertisements are posted.   3. An interactive computer terminal available for public access to the Internet or to site-specific information (such as a store's bridal registry). See also ELECTRONIC KIOSK.

kiosk browser   A secure and customizable Web browser for public use in places such as schools, libraries, retail stores, and Internet cafés. The kiosk browser allows the administrator to configure restricted access to Web sites, limit or disallow file downloads, customize the toolbar with company logos, etc. Some kiosk browsers also allow the administrator to deny access to the desktop of a public computer and to include an integrated e-mail client. For Internet cafés and other pay-per-use terminals, a kiosk browser may also include a time logger that will automatically limit the amount of time users can spend online, determined by the amount they have prepaid to use the system. See also ELECTRONIC KIOSK.

KISS   See KEEP IT SIMPLE, STUPID (KISS).

kit   Short for PROMOTIONAL KIT.

knee-high form   See STOCKING (LEG) FORM.

knitwear   Apparel made either by hand knitting or a knitting machine. The classification includes underwear, nightwear, knit shirts, fleece goods, sportswear, activewear, and other apparel types made of yarn.

knockdown (KD)   Of furniture, delivered to the customer in a disassembled state. Sometimes referred to as lifestyle furniture, knockdowns generally appeal to younger people of moderate means. Knockdown merchandise enables both the manufacturer and the retailer to reduce freight, storage, and handling costs and to pass these savings on to the customer. IKEA has made a worldwide franchise business based on the knockdown concept.

knocked-down (KD)   Synonym for KNOCKDOWN (KD).

knocked-down price   In retailing, a seller's asking price that has been lowered for the purpose of making the sale.

knocker   (Slang) A door-to-door salesperson.

knockoff   In the apparel industry, a product copied from another manufacturer or designer and usually sold at a cheaper price point. Also spelled *knock-off*. The practice of copying is known as FASHION PIRACY. See also COUNTERFEITING and STYLE PIRACY.

knowledge   See COGNITIVE COMPONENT.

knowledge development   The interpretation and accumulation of data so that it can be put to good use by the firm. Marketing data is collected from and about markets, segments, competitors, suppliers, partners, consumers, and other areas of interest. See also DATA MINING.

knowledge discovery   Synonym for DATA MINING.

known loss   A shortage of merchandise discovered before or at the time of the delivery of a shipment. Compare INVISIBLE SHRINKAGE and VISIBLE SHRINKAGE.

label authority tag An attachment to a fur garment indicating the manufacturer's support of U.S. fair labor standards. See also FUR PRODUCTS LABELING ACT (1951) and FAIR LABOR STANDARDS ACT (FLSA) (1938).

labels and labeling A label is a cover, wrapper, or tag, often made of paper, affixed to a product. Labels are commonly regarded as an integral part of the product package and contain a variety of descriptive matter including identification of the product and its manufacturer, its trademark, instructions for its use, its contents, size, etc. See also PACKAGING.

labor-intensive Of an industry or other undertaking, making greater use of human labor than of machinery and automation, resulting in relatively high labor costs. The construction and garment industries are examples of labor-intensive industries.

Labor-Management Relations Act (LMRA) (1947) Federal legislation popularly known as the *Taft-Hartley Act*. The LMRA was enacted to modify the NATIONAL LABOR RELATIONS ACT (1935). The LMRA dealt with the procedures for national emergency strikes, listed unfair labor union practices, declared closed shops illegal, enlarged the NATIONAL LABOR RELATIONS BOARD (NLRB) to five members, and established the FEDERAL MEDIATION AND CONCILIATION SERVICE (FMCS) to mediate labor disputes.

Labor-Management Reporting and Disclosure Act (1959) U.S. federal legislation (commonly called the *Landrum-Griffin Act*) enacted to counteract union mismanagement and corruption. It provides union members with a *Bill of Rights*, requires the Secretary of Labor to enforce reporting, and defines criminal acts by unions to be monitored by the U.S. Department of Justice.

labor union An organization of workers formed to protect and advance their interests, particularly when these interests conflict with those of management. A *craft union* or TRADE UNION is a labor union made up of skilled artisans belonging to a single profession or practicing a single craft. An INDUSTRIAL UNION represents both skilled and unskilled workers from all phases of a particular industry.

Ladies Mile A commercial shopping district located in New York City (along Broadway between 14th and 23rd Streets) that was home to many of the earliest department stores beginning in the 1880s. Most of the early department stores in this area were built in the PALAZZO DESIGN. Many of the original buildings are still standing, although the original stores relocated during the early twentieth century and many have since gone out of business.

laggard In the diffusion or adoption process, a member of the last group of consumers to buy a product or service or to adopt a new idea. They are frequently older, tradition-bound individuals of low economic and social status. Sometimes called *lagger*.

lagger See LAGGARD.

laissez-faire 1. A theory according to which government intervention in private economic affairs is discouraged. A laissez-faire attitude is regarded as an encouragement to the FREE ENTERPRISE system. 2. A management style in which the leader essentially takes the role of consultant, providing encouragement for employees' ideas and offering insight or opinions when asked. This approach encourages group members to express themselves creatively. See also LEADERSHIP STYLE.

LAMS See LIST ACQUISITION AND MANAGEMENT SOFTWARE (LAMS).

LAN See LOCAL-AREA NETWORK (LAN).

landed cost The cost of a product including the cost of loading, transporting, and unloading at destination. Essentially, the landed cost is the cost of the goods up to the time they are delivered to the buyer's distribution center (i.e., the actual cost of the goods to the buyer).

landlord See LESSOR.

Landrum-Griffin Act (1959) Popular name for the LABOR-MANAGEMENT REPORTING AND DISCLOSURE ACT (1959).

Lanham Trademark Act (1947) U.S. federal legislation governing trademarks and other symbols used to identify merchandise sold in interstate commerce. As amended, it allows a manufacturer to protect its BRAND or TRADEMARK in the

United States by having it recorded on a government register in the U.S. Patent Office. The act also provides for the legal right to register any distinctive mark. Also known as the *Trademark Act (1947)* and the *Lanham Act (1947)*. See also TRADE DRESS.

large sizes A size category generally synonymous with BIG AND TALL MEN'S (for menswear) and PLUS SIZES (for womenswear.)

laser mouse See MOUSE.

last in, first out (LIFO) A method of INVENTORY VALUATION that assumes that merchandise most recently acquired is sold or otherwise disposed of first. What remains, therefore, at the end of the inventory period, is a composite of the oldest merchandise costs. Compare with FIRST IN, FIRST OUT (FIFO).

late delivery The arrival of seasonal and trend-sensitive goods after their selling season, a possible cause of slow-selling merchandise that may result in a MARKDOWN (MD).

late majority In the diffusion or adoption process, those consumers who are slow to purchase new products and services. Members of this group are likely to have below-average incomes and relatively little social prestige. Late majority consumers are relatively unresponsive to innovation.

late night only (LNO) Of a retail employee, working only when the store is open at night.

latent defect A fault or imperfection in a product that is not visible to the naked eye nor discernible by inspection at the time of shipping.

latent demand A condition in the marketplace in which consumers have a desire for a product or service but the desire is unmet, commonly because the product or service is as yet undeveloped.

launch To introduce and begin the sale of a new product or service or to begin a new advertising and/or promotional campaign. See also WEB SITE LAUNCH and PRODUCT LAUNCH.

lawn and garden/gardening center Synonym for GARDEN CENTER.

law of demand A principle of marketing (and economics) stating that as the price of a product is raised, the demand for the product will diminish. Conversely, as the price of a product is lowered, the demand for the product will increase. In short, consumers purchase more goods at a low price than at a high price. Also known as the *law of diminishing demand*. See also LAW OF SUPPLY.

law of diminishing demand See LAW OF DEMAND.

law of diminishing (marginal) utility See DIMINISHING UTILITY.

law of diminishing returns See DIMINISHING RETURNS and DIMINISHING RETURNS MODEL.

law of retail gravitation See REILLY'S LAW OF RETAIL GRAVITATION.

law of substitution See SUBSTITUTION LAW.

law of supply A principle of marketing (and economics) stating that sellers will supply more of a product at higher prices and less at lower prices.

law of supply and demand See SUPPLY AND DEMAND.

law of the vital few Synonym for the EIGHTY-TWENTY (80-20) PRINCIPLE.

law of threes A principle enjoining retailers to limit choices in each line of a merchandise assortment to good, better, and best. This avoids confusing the customer.

lawyer 1. (Slang) In retailing, a friend, shopping with another customer in a store, who advises the other customer on whether or not to purchase an item. Such advice frequently results in the customer not buying the item. 2. A person whose profession is to represent clients in a court of law or to represent them in legal matters.

layaway A retail purchase arrangement in which the store sets aside a customer's merchandise (on which the customer may or may not have made a deposit, depending on store policy) until the customer has fully paid for it. If the purchase is not completed by a specified date, the deposit may or may not be refunded, depending on store policy. This practice is sometimes called a *deposit plan* or a *layaway plan*. See also WILL CALL.

lay-down technique In the VISUAL MERCHANDISING of apparel, any of a variety of methods that may be used to place a garment in a display, whether in a window, on a ledge, in a case, pinned onto boards, or against a wall or column. It includes the folding, pleating, and placement of garments next to each other and next to coordinating accessories. Also called *lay-down* and *lay down display*. See also DISPLAY.

layette 1. Garments and accessories for a newborn baby (e.g., receiving blankets, undergarments, stretchies, footed pajamas, bonnets, baby bath towels and washcloths, crib linens, crib toys). 2. The department in a retail store that specializes in such garments and accessories (often a subdepartment of the children's apparel department).

layout 1. In print advertising, the arrangement of the advertisement, particularly with the goals of developing interest, creating desire, and securing action on the part of the reader. 2. See STORE LAYOUT AND DESIGN.

L/C See LETTER OF CREDIT (L/C).

LCL See LESS-THAN-CARLOAD LOT (LCL).

LCL freight rate See LESS-THAN-CARLOAD (LCL) FREIGHT RATE.

LDN   See DEVELOPING COUNTRIES/NATIONS.

lead   In sales, a possible new customer who may be recommended by another customer, another salesperson, or discovered in a listing (by industry, geographic location, etc.). A lead may be either a person or an organization, but the salesperson has not yet determined whether the lead is really interested in the product or service. Once this has been determined, the lead becomes a PROSPECT. Also called a *sales lead*.

leader   Short for LOSS LEADER. See also LEADER PRICING, PRICE LEADER, and MARKET LEADER.

leader brand   A particular product, usually well-known, that is priced below regular retail to attract customers to the store. See also LEADER PRICING.

leader merchandising   See LEADER PRICING.

leader pricing   The practice of pricing a certain number of items at less than regular price to speed stock turnover and to increase sales of items not specially marked down. These items are called loss leaders (or, simply, leaders) and the retailer uses them to increase customer traffic flow and create the general impression of storewide low prices. The price assigned is called a *leader price*. Also called *bait pricing, leader merchandising,* and *loss leader pricing*. See also VARIABLE LEADER PRICING and LOSS LEADER.

leadership style   The manner in which authority is used by a manager to lead others. A leader may be *autocratic* (i.e., the manager centralizes authority and does not involve others in decision making), *democratic* (i.e., the manager delegates authority and involves employees in decision making), or LAISSEZ-FAIRE (i.e., the manager leads by taking the role of consultant, leaving the actual decision making up to employees).

lead generation   The process by which a salesperson identifies and accumulates the contact information for potential customers to approach via sales calls or personal visits. Salespersons generate leads by asking known customers for the names of other potential customers, joining associations and networking, speaking before professional or community groups, etc. See also CHAIN PROSPECTING.

lead-in   1. The portion of a television or radio broadcast that precedes a commercial.   2. The part of a sales interaction that permits a SALESPERSON to move toward summing up or closing with a customer.

leading series   A TIME SERIES that changes in the same direction as the series under study but consistently precedes that change. The leading series is watched particularly closely as an indicator of future trends. See also TIME SERIES ANALYSIS.

lead market   Countries that lead the world in research, particularly scientific and technological research, and are also the home markets of major global competitors. In addition to technological development, the concept covers development in design, production processes, patterns in consumer demand, and methods of marketing. Lead market status is dynamic and continually changing.

lead time   1. In physical distribution, the elapsed time between the placement of an order and the arrival of the goods on the selling floor. Includes the transit times between manufacturer, distribution center, and retailer. Also known as *cycle time, order cycle time*, and *order lead time*. See also ORDER CYCLE.   2. In advertising, the elapsed time between the placement of an advertisement and its appearance in the media.

leaflet   See BROCHURE.

lean practice   In supply chain management, any method of doing business that leads to cost reductions, timing efficiencies, and increased inventory turns. Also called *supply chain lean practice*.

learning advantage   See LEARNING CURVE.

learning curve   In manufacturing, a graphic representation of the fact that as production increases, unit costs decrease. When a great many items are manufactured, each individual item will be cheaper because the manufacturer has learned to reduce expenses and increase efficiency. See also LEARNING CURVE PRICING.

learning curve pricing   A PRICING STRATEGY in which a manufacturer reduces the price of a product as production increases and becomes more cost-efficient.

lease   A contract or agreement for the use of equipment or the occupation of real property for a limited term at a predetermined cost to the LESSEE. Leases take many forms but, in general, it may be said that a lease agreement is a means of financing the use of equipment or property without the need for outright ownership on the part of the lessee. Ownership of leased equipment or property remains with the LESSOR. See also LEASING AND RENTING.

leaseback   A real estate transaction in which the owner of a property (such as a retail store) sells it to another (i.e., an investor or developer) but remains as a tenant of the new owner. The lease may include an option to buy. The strategy keeps the retailer's funds free, often for further expansion activity. Also called a *sale and leaseback* or a *sell-and-lease agreement*.

leased dealership   A retail establishment leased to an operator, with the operator buying supplies from the leasing company. For example, service stations are frequently leased to individuals by oil companies. See also DEALERSHIP and FRANCHISE.

leased department   A department or area within a store operated by an outside retail organization (although often not so identified to the customer). Generally the host store supplies the space and essential services such as lighting, security, etc., in return for a flat fee or a percentage of the leased department's sales. The agreement underlying this arrangement is known as a *franchise-lease agreement*. Shoes, jewelry repair, photo services, beauty shops, florists, and eye care centers are examples of leased departments frequently found in department, discount, or specialty stores; discount stores sometimes use the term *licensed department* instead. Leased departments are often chains themselves. Also called a *franchise department*. See also CONCESSION, a similar concept involving manufacturers or distributors rather than outside retailers. Compare OWNED DEPARTMENT.

lease department   See LEASED DEPARTMENT.

leasee   See LESSEE.

leaser   See LESSOR.

leasing and renting   The process by which the owner of a piece of property (such as a retail store or a car) allows another party to use it in exchange for regular payments. Under certain conditions, leasing provides tax advantages for both LESSOR and LESSEE. Leasing may also be a viable alternative for a company whose poor credit rating makes it difficult to obtain the loans necessary to buy. Leasing has become a popular way of obtaining an automobile, particularly for employees of a business organization; increasingly, the "company car" may be a leased vehicle. Renting and leasing are used synonymously, with renting being the preferred term for residences and leasing being the preferred term for commercial properties. In either case, the payments made are known as *rent* and the agreement between the two parties is known as a LEASE.

least-Internet-ready areas (LIRAs)   Those countries or regions of the world that represent the least likely target markets for most Internet marketers because the communication and information infrastructures necessary for Internet access are not readily available. Compare INTERNET LEADERS (ILS) and INTERNET-READY AREAS (IRAS).

leave behind   Synonym for LEAVE PIECE.

leave paper   See LEAVING PAPER.

leave piece   Informative, usually printed material that the salesperson uses and leaves with a PROSPECT. This piece usually includes the name and telephone number of the salesperson so that the prospect, upon making a decision, will contact the salesperson. Increasingly, salespersons are experimenting with leaving material in other than print formats, such as DVDs or CD-ROMs.

leaving paper   (Slang) An ORDER for merchandise, written by a buyer and left with the VENDOR.

ledge fixture   A store FIXTURE used in VISUAL MERCHANDISING that is larger and more imposing than a counter fixture. Most are placed where the customer cannot reach or touch them. A COSTUMER, VALET FIXTURE, or other display FORM may be placed on top of the ledge to display apparel and other merchandise.

ledger   The book (or computer file) containing the accounts of a business. Each account usually has a separate page. A GENERAL LEDGER is a collection of all the asset, liability, owners' equity, revenue, and expense accounts. A SUBSIDIARY LEDGER contains the details related to a given general ledger. See also NATURAL CLASSIFICATION OF EXPENSES.

ledger expenses   See NATURAL CLASSIFICATION OF EXPENSES.

leg form   See STOCKING (LEG) FORM.

legitimization   With reference to the introduction of new products into the marketplace, the process by which early purchasers of the product or service serve as examples for consumers who may be somewhat less innovative.

leisure living   A lifestyle characterized by shorter working hours and more time for recreation. The advent of leisure living in the United States has encouraged retailers to lengthen the business day by two or more night openings per week. Some stores are open seven days per week, while food and drug stores may stay open 24 hours per day. The merchandise assortment also reflects the increasing influence of leisure living (e.g., athletic apparel and shoes).

lemon law   In the United States, a state law designed to protect consumers against the purchase of defective automobiles and other consumer products. While the laws and remedies vary somewhat from state to state, their common theme is that a manufacturer must provide a refund or replacement for a defective new vehicle that is not repaired within a reasonable number of attempts. A number of Web sites provide information for consumers on the various state lemon laws, including: www.lemonlawamerica.com, www.nationallemonlawcenter.com, and the Better Business Bureau's site at www.bbb.org/lemonlaw.

lender   One who grants the use of something on condition that it or its equivalent will be returned. In business, it is most often money that is lent. In that sense, lender is a synonym for CREDITOR.

less-developed nation (LDN)   See DEVELOPING COUNTRIES/NATIONS.

lessee   In LEASING AND RENTING arrangements, the individual or firm that pays rent for the use of another's (i.e., the lessor's) property. Sometimes called a *leasee*.

lessor   In LEASING AND RENTING arrangements, the property owner, whether an individual or a business enterprise, that grants the lease and collects the rent from the lessee. Also called a *landlord* or a *leaser*.

less-than-carload (LCL) freight rate   The shipping rate paid when a freight shipment does not fill a rail freight car. It is almost always higher that the CARLOAD FREIGHT RATE (CL) charged for full car shipments. See also LESS-THAN-CARLOAD LOT (LCL) and TRANSLOADING.

less-than-carload lot (LCL)   A freight shipment that does not fill a rail freight car and does not, therefore, qualify for the full-car rate. A CONSOLIDATOR can remedy this situation by bringing together merchandise from a number of sources into one order for shipment. See also ASSEMBLING, CARLOAD FREIGHT RATE (CL), and TRANSLOADING.

less-than-truckload lot (LTL)   Goods in amounts that do not make a full truckload and hence do not qualify for full-load rates. A CONSOLIDATOR can remedy this situation by bringing together merchandise from a number of sources into one order for shipment. See also ASSEMBLING.

letter of credit (L/C)   A written document from a bank, obtained by a buyer of goods as evidence of the buyer's credit standing. The letter of credit is presented to the seller of the goods by the buyer, whereupon the seller delivers the goods and collects the money from the bank. The bank, in turn, collects from the buyer. The letter of credit is useful in international trade where the buyer has been unable to establish a LINE OF CREDIT with vendors abroad. A letter of credit may or may not be irrevocable or transferable.

letter of indemnity   A letter guaranteeing that contractual provisions will be met. If they are not, financial reparations will be made. The principle behind a letter of indemnity is the guarantee that losses will not be suffered should certain provisions of a contract not be met.

let the buyer beware   See CAVEAT EMPTOR.

let the seller beware   See CAVEAT VENDITOR/VENDOR.

level   A FLOOR or tier of a SHOPPING CENTER, parking garage, or other building (e.g., Level 1 or Upper Level).

level expenditure method   A method of developing media advertising schedules in which each segment of the campaign is treated equally. See also PROMOTIONAL BUDGETING.

level of saturation   The degree to which a TRADING AREA has enough stores to provide goods and services for the population without having so many that they all cannot make a fair profit. See also INDEX OF (RETAIL) SATURATION (IRS) and SATURATED AREA.

leverage   See PURCHASING LEVERAGE.

leveraged buyout   Acquisition of an organization financed by debt, in which the yet-to-be-owned assets of the acquired firm are used as collateral by the acquiring company. This is considered a risky and controversial practice. See also JUNK BOND.

liability   An obligation to pay a sum of money or to perform a service on whose value a dollar amount may be placed. In short, liabilities are debts owned by an organization. Liabilities are classified according to the time in which they are to be paid. A *long-term liability* is due in one year or longer; payment on a *short-term liability* is due within one year. In retailing, short-term liabilities include payables to suppliers and short-term debts to lending institutions for money borrowed to balance cash flow. A retailer's long-term liabilities include mortgages on land and buildings and long-term financing for extensive expansion and renovation projects. See also PRODUCT LIABILITY.

liability insurance   Insurance that covers a company's losses arising from injury or death to an individual, or damage to the property of others, due to something the company does.

liberal return policy   A retailer's practice of accepting goods returned for refund or exchange with a minimum of difficulty to the customer.

license   1. Formal, contractual permission from a government or other authority to do something such as carry on a particular business or profession.   2. A certificate giving proof of such permission. See also LICENSING.

licensed department   Synonym, often used by discount stores, for LEASED DEPARTMENT.

licensed merchandise/product   A product designed and sold through identification with a celebrity or fictional character or with a corporate name, logo, or slogan. For an extra cost, buyers have an instant and proven brand name to draw customers into their stores. Cartoon and storybook characters are the most popular among children. Names of sports stars and teams have also been very popular on licensed products. While licensed products run the gamut from trinkets to expensive collectibles, apparel products dominate the list. Licensed products are also viable in the bed and bath categories. See also LICENSING.

licensee   The person or organization granted a license by a LICENSOR. See also LICENSING.

license plate analysis   The observation and recording of license plate numbers of the cars parked in the parking lot of a store or shopping center. When the license plates are correlated to addresses, this procedure may be used to determine the store's TRADING AREA.

licensing   1. An agreement between the creator of a product or line of products and a manufacturer in which the creator (LICENSOR) gives the manufacturer (LICENSEE) permission to use his/her name in the marketing of a product in return for a royalty, usually computed as a percentage of sales. Also called *corporate licensing* and *product licensing*. See also LICENSED MERCHANDISE/PRODUCT.   2. In global marketing, a form of JOINT VENTURE. See also FOREIGN LICENSING.

licensor   The person or organization that grants a license to a LICENSEE. See also LICENSING.

lie detector   See POLYGRAPH.

lien   A legal claim upon goods for the satisfaction of a debt or duty. See also SELLER'S LIEN.

life cycle A series of developmental stages undergone by an organism, family, product, business, etc. See also FAMILY LIFE CYCLE (FLC), PRODUCT LIFE CYCLE (PLC), or RETAIL LIFE CYCLE.

life span of merchandise See PRODUCT LIFE CYCLE (PLC).

lifestyle A distinctive mode of living centered on certain activities, interests, opinions, and demographic characteristics, especially as these characteristics distinguish one segment of a population from another. In this view, one's lifestyle is seen as the sum of one's interactions with one's environment, that is, the way one lives, works, plays, and spends money. Lifestyle studies are a component of the broader behavioral concept of PSYCHOGRAPHICS. Also spelled *life-style*. See also LIFESTYLE SEGMENTATION.

lifestyle analysis See LIFESTYLE SEGMENTATION.

lifestyle center An outdoor shopping center encompassing several small retail strips and freestanding anchor stores in an appealing environment serving an upscale clientele (such as young, affluent families). Lifestyle centers are designed for easy access, convenience, and the ultimate in ambiance. Tenants sometimes include service and entertainment businesses in addition to high-end retailers.

lifestyle graphic A graphic used in a retail store as a selling tool. Lifestyle graphics show, for example, how an outfit goes together or how and where a product can be used. A lifestyle graphic encourages the customer to envision herself or himself in the picture. It can take the form of a photographic background panel and may be used in conjunction with other forms of DISPLAY. See also GRAPHICS.

lifestyle marketing See LIFESTYLE SEGMENTATION.

lifestyle merchandising A form of retail merchandising in which the store is continuously altering the merchandise mix to what the customer wants and will buy. Lifestyle merchandising recognizes that people are conscious of value, novelty, and quality and that the customer's lifestyle, demographics, value system, and buying habits all play a role in buying behavior. See also LIFESTYLE SEGMENTATION.

lifestyle segmentation The division of a market into subgroups based on the activities and interests of the members of each group. Also called *lifestyle analysis* or *lifestyle marketing*. See also VALS SEGMENTATION and PSYCHOGRAPHICS.

lifestyle theme A recurring idea based on lifestyle choices and used throughout a store or department. For example, the physical fitness trend may be used as a theme for athletic shoes, apparel, workout equipment, athletic shoes, etc. Lifestyle themes are sometimes accompanied by seminars and special events in the store. See also THEME.

LIFO Acronym for LAST IN, FIRST OUT (LIFO).

lighting plan See STORE LIGHTING PLAN.

light pen A device used in the optical scanning of machine-readable symbols. The light pen focuses a beam of light on bar-coded surfaces and senses reflections from them as its tip (usually made of ruby or sapphire) is moved along the surface. The light pen is wired to a decoder that provides computer-compatible output. Also called a *wand*. See also OPTICAL CODE READER (OCR).

limited distribution Synonym for SELECTIVE DISTRIBUTION.

limited function wholesaler See LIMITED SERVICE WHOLESALER.

limited line grocery store A store falling into a category between the SUPERMARKET and the CONVENIENCE STORE and specializing in nonperishable staples sold at discount prices.

limited line store A retail outlet similar to the specialty store in that it carries a limited number of product lines but has considerable depth in the lines it carries. Limited line stores are often known by the name of the product they sell (e.g., lingerie store, accessory store). A SINGLE LINE STORE is a type of limited line store that carries even fewer product lines, sometimes only a single product line (e.g., shoe store, furrier, flower shop).

limited line strategy A marketing strategy in which the number of products in a line is intentionally restricted so that all attention can be focused on producing and marketing a small number of items. See also PRODUCT LINE STRATEGY and FULL LINE STRATEGY.

limited line wholesaler See SPECIALTY MERCHANDISE WHOLESALER.

limited marketing channel A CHANNEL OF DISTRIBUTION in which merchandise is routed from the manufacturer directly to the retailer, who sells it to the consumer. See also DIRECT MARKETING CHANNEL and EXTENDED MARKETING CHANNEL.

limited order An order to purchase merchandise in which the buyer has set restrictions with respect to price. The order is contingent on the specified price being met. See also TIME ORDER.

limited problem solving In consumer behavior, the effort taken to understand one's needs and how best to satisfy them at a particular point in time, particularly when many possible solutions are available and possible. See also EXTENSIVE PROBLEM SOLVING.

limited service See LIMITED SERVICE STORE.

limited service store A retail outlet where some of the traditional store services may be lacking or, if provided, performed for an additional fee. Limited service stores combine some of the features of the self-service store and the full service store. They often require customers to self-select merchandise, although there may be greeters at the door to direct customers to appropriate areas. Visual merchandising techniques may be used to help customers find and choose appropriate merchandise. Labels and hang tags are the primary source of product information. Credit card services and liberal exchange policies are usually available. Delivery, alterations, and gift wrapping, if available, are usually not free. Most superstores and discount stores, many department stores, and some specialty stores provide some combination of limited customer service.

limited service wholesaler   A wholesaling marketing intermediary that, like its full service counterpart, takes title to the goods it resells, but that provides fewer services so as to reduce costs. Also known as a *limited function wholesaler*. Included under this rubric are the DROP SHIPPER, TRUCK WHOLESALER, CASH-AND-CARRY WHOLESALER, RACK JOBBER, CATALOG HOUSE, and PRODUCERS' COOPERATIVE/CO-OP.

line   1. In retailing, a group of closely related products. In a retail store, the various lines of merchandise make up what is known as variety, which is in turn a component of the merchandise assortment.   2. In manufacturing, a group of related products manufactured by the same company. See also PRODUCT LINE.

line-and-staff organization   A form of business organization dividing employees into those who are in the direct line of command (from the top level of the hierarchy to the bottom) and those who provide support (i.e., staff) services to line managers at various levels but report directly to top management. See also LINE ORGANIZATION, FUNCTIONAL ORGANIZATION, and DIVISIONAL ORGANIZATION.

linear programming   A mathematical technique employed in determining the allocation of resources to reach a particular objective (e.g., the maximization of profits), especially when there are a number of variables to consider. The term *linear* is derived from the straightline algebraic formulas used in expressing the problem.

linear system   A marketing system directly linked to a plant. If the merchandise fails to sell, it piles up at the plant.

line authority   See LINE ORGANIZATION.

line concept   The look and appeal that contribute to the identity and salability of a LINE. Elements of the line concept include the LINE DIRECTION and the GROUP CONCEPT.

line consistency   A property of lines of products that are closely related to one another in terms of end use and production requirements, or that are distributed through the same channels.

line development   The sum of the activities involved in determining the line of products to be sold and in translating a LINE PLAN into real merchandise. The first phase of line development is formulation of the LINE CONCEPT, followed either by the selection of finished goods at wholesale markets to fill the LINE PLAN, by in-house PRODUCT DEVELOPMENT, or by a combination of the two. Initial orders are placed for the desired merchandise and may represent 30% to 100% of the total

inventory required. Reorders are placed according to agreements with vendors, components of which include order processing, shipping, receiving, and distribution. The *line development timeline* (i.e., the scheduling of the steps required to develop the line and bring it to retail) is determined by the date when the merchandise must appear on the retail sales floor.

line development timeline   See LINE DEVELOPMENT.

line direction   In developing a LINE of products, particularly apparel products, the interpretation of trends in color, styling, and fabrication for the firm's target customers.

line executive   Synonym for LINE MANAGER.

line extension   A new product added to an existing line. For example, a new fragrance added to an existing line of perfumes would benefit from the positive image the consumer has of the entire line. A line extension may also be a new variation on a basic product. For example, a tartar-control toothpaste may be an extension of an existing toothpaste line. Also called a *product line extension*. See also BRAND EXTENSION STRATEGY.

line filling   The practice of developing items to fill gaps in the market that have been overlooked by competitors or that have emerged as consumers' tastes and needs shift.

line-for-line copy   In apparel, an exact copy of an original design, often of foreign origin. Some copies are made with the permission of the designer, others are simply appropriated. Advanced computer applications have made line-for-line copying easier and have led to an increase in counterfeiting and piracy. See also COUNTERFEIT PRODUCT.

line function   Any position in a firm that performs activities fundamental to the organization. In retailing, merchandising (i.e., buying and selling merchandise) and store operations are considered line functions. Also called BUYING LINE or *store line*. Compare STAFF FUNCTION.

line graph   A type of diagram used in presenting business data, consisting of a line connecting points along the intersection of a horizontal and a vertical axis. Line graphs are often used to show trends, such as an increase in profits over time.

line haul   The process of moving goods over long distances between cities and towns by truck. Large trucks, usually tractor-trailers, are used to deliver large quantities of cargo to major distribution centers. See also SHORT HAUL.

line management   See LINE MANAGER.

line manager   An executive in a firm having a LINE ORGANIZATION (i.e., a direct line of responsibility and control from top to bottom). The line manager has direct responsibility for certain operations representing the primary mission of the organization. In retailing, members of the line management team have responsibilities directly related to retail functions, such as operations, finance, information technology, and merchandising. Also called a *line executive.* Compare STAFF MANAGER.

linen sale   See WHITE SALE.

linens   Textile products used in the home, such as sheets, pillowcases, blankets, towels, etc.

line of authority   See MARKET DIVISION OF AUTHORITY.

line of business   The type or category of business in which a firm or an individual is involved. For example, a department store's line of business is retailing.

line of credit   An established sum of money that a borrower, such as a retailer, is allowed to have outstanding from a lending institution at any one time. The borrower may use available funds up to the specified amount over a period of time without additional approval from the lender. Also called a *credit line.*

line-of-goods display   A visual presentation and promotion that shows only one type of merchandise (e.g., all blouses, all skirts, all pots and pans), although they may be in a variety of designs or colors.

line of products   See PRODUCT LINE.

line organization   A form of organization in which each person reports to only one supervisor and has responsibility for a particular task. The simplest and most traditional of the chain-of-command organizational systems, the line organization establishes a clear line of authority flowing from the top downward to subordinates. Each employee knows who is responsible to whom and the ultimate authority is easily identified. See also LINE-AND-STAFF ORGANIZATION, DIVISIONAL ORGANIZATION, and FUNCTIONAL ORGANIZATION.

line plan   A strategy for product development based on and integrated with the overall business and marketing plan of the firm as well as on information provided by the operations and finance constituents.

line planning   A dynamic process that continues throughout the merchandising cycle and is used to determine the LINE or lines of merchandise offered for sale. The primary elements of the line planning process are synthesis of current issues (e.g., the positioning of new competitors with similar merchandise classifications as well as economic, social, and cultural influences on trends and potential sales); evaluation of past seasons or periods (i.e., a detailed analysis of the same selling period last year as well as an examination of the current selling period for any relevant trends; studies of customer spending patterns in relation to merchandise classifications; identification of hot selling merchandise groups and styles; and influences of pricing); classification analysis (i.e., establishing priorities for weeks of sale, price points, size ranges, and size standards); and the development of the merchandise budget (i.e., the identification of planned dollar investment by category or classification and open-to-buy) and assortment plans (which may include model stocks, basic stocks, and automated replenish-

ment). The result of line planning is the LINE PLAN, based on and integrated with the overall business and marketing plan. Implicit in this is the LINE CONCEPT. See also TOP-DOWN PLAN and BOTTOM-UP PLAN.

line presentation   The exhibition or introduction of a line of products at any of several stages. *Internal presentation* generally takes place within a firm at the point of evaluating the LINE PLAN or when evaluating designs for adoption during the product development process. *Wholesale presentation* takes place when products are offered for sale to retail buyers in showrooms, at seasonal markets, or by sales representatives calling on retail buyers in their stores. *Retail presentation* involves many different types of retail stores as well as catalog, television, and online selling. Strategies associated with line presentation include pricing; visual display using fixtures, light, and space; providing product information via labels, tickets, and signage; serving customers; and managing inventory.

line stretching   The practice of adding higher- or lower-priced items at either end of the current PRODUCT LINE to extend the appeal of the product to new economic groups.

line structure   The extension of a LINE of products by its manufacturer beyond the range currently produced. For example, the extension may involve products at higher and/or lower prices, or products at different levels of quality. See also PRODUCT LINE.

lingerie   See INTIMATE APPAREL.

lingerie form   See INNERWEAR FORM.

link   1. v. In computer applications, to paste a copy of an object into a document in such a way that it retains its connection with the original object. Updates to the original object can be updated in the duplicate.   2. n. In communications, a line over which data is transmitted.   3. n. Short for HYPERTEXT LINK.

linkage screen   In global marketing, one of the barriers or hurdles that must be overcome by a firm seeking to do business with a foreign government. During this stage of negotiations, the firm must seek to address and implement the various government requirements related to assisting local businesses (i.e., linking to those local businesses). This can include finding local suppliers to outsource a portion of the contract, finding a LOCAL PARTNER with whom to establish a JOINT VENTURE, etc. See also ELIGIBILITY SCREEN, PROCEDURAL SCREEN, COMPETITIVE SCREEN, and INFLUENCE SCREEN.

linking phrase   In sales, the words that connect a feature with a benefit in a smooth, logical fashion.

link traffic pattern layout   See FIGURE-EIGHT LAYOUT.

liquid assets/wealth   Cash that is readily available for use should the need arise. Liquid assets include unencumbered money in checking and savings accounts, stocks, bonds, other securities that are readily marketable, etc. Also called *liquid wealth.* Compare NONLIQUID ASSETS/WEALTH.

liquidation   The conversion of assets into cash, generally done at the insistence of creditors who are demanding payment. This may be accomplished through a *liquidation sale.* See also GOING-OUT-OF-BUSINESS SALE (GOB).

liquidity   The extent to which a firm has assets sufficient to meet obligations, often used to describe the firm's capacity to raise cash. In retail accounting, a firm's assets are classified by their liquidity, or the likelihood of their conversion to cash. Liquidity is an advantage a corporation has over other firms. Investments in publicly held corporations can easily be converted into cash through trade on the open market, enabling the corporation to raise far larger sums than can be raised by unincorporated businesses.

liquidity ratio   Synonym for ACID TEST RATIO.

LIRAs   See LEAST-INTERNET-READY AREAS (LIRAS)

list   Short for LIST PRICE.

List Acquisition and Management Software (LAMS)   Software available through the Direct Marketing Association (DMA) to help telemarketers manage state DO-NOT-CALL (DNC) lists and comply with state do-not-call laws.

list price   1. The manufacturer's price to the distributor or retailer as represented on a list or in a catalog.   2. More often, the retail price suggested (and sometimes advertised) by the manufacturer before any discounts or other price reductions are made. Also call *base price, basic list price, manufacturer's list price, manufacturer's suggested list price,* and *book price.* See also MANUFACTURER'S SUGGESTED RETAIL PRICE (MSRP).

listserv   An interactive mailing list on the Internet comprising people who share common interests and who subscribe to the list voluntarily. Discussions may be moderated or unmoderated. Also spelled *list serve.* See also MODERATOR and E-MAIL DISCUSSION LIST.

live goods   (Slang) High-demand items displayed for sale. See also FAST MOVER, a KEY ITEM, BEST SELLER, and ITEM.

LMRA   See LABOR-MANAGEMENT RELATIONS ACT (LMRA) (1947).

LNO   See LATE NIGHT ONLY (LNO).

loader   Short for DEALER LOADER.

loading   1. As practiced by manufacturers, the sale to wholesalers and retailers of more goods than they really need. Loading places the marketing intermediary in an overstocked inventory position.   2. The practice of adding monetary charges to an installment agreement to cover selling and administrative overhead, interest, risk, etc.   3. See LOADING OF CASH DISCOUNT.

loading dock   Synonym for DOCK.

loading of cash discount   A practice in which the vendor's invoice amount is intentionally increased (i.e., loaded) to compensate for a lower-than-expected cash discount. The increased amount is charged to the department buying the merchandise, creating the illusion on paper that the goods cost more than they really did. The object of this practice is to induce retail buyers to gain the largest discount possible to avoid the penalty of increased invoice prices and gain a higher markup on the merchandise. Also called *discount loading* and *loading the invoice.*

loading the invoice   See LOADING OF CASH DISCOUNT.

loan slip   A receipt given to a buyer in a selling department when merchandise is borrowed for use in window displays, advertising photography, etc. Also called a *merchandise loan slip.* See also MERCHANDISE LOAN BOOK.

lobby window   See ISLAND WINDOW.

local advertising   Advertising sponsored by local businesses who provide products or services in a particular vicinity (i.e., their immediate TRADING AREA). When conducted by stores, local advertising is frequently called RETAIL ADVERTISING, despite the fact that some retailers are national advertisers. Local advertising is targeted to customers who live in the immediate vicinity of the store and is often geared to generating an immediate response (i.e., getting the customer into the store). Local advertising may appear in area newspapers, in the local broadcast media, in flyers, circulars, outdoor advertising, and penny savers.

local-area network (LAN)   A COMPUTER NETWORK that spans a relatively small area, such as a single building or a group of buildings. A system of LANs connected over a larger distance via telephone lines and radio waves is called a WIDE-AREA NETWORK (WAN).

local borrowing   In global marketing, a method of minimizing risks to assets by financing local operations from indigenous banks (i.e., in the host country) and maintaining a high level of local accounts payable. Local borrowing also minimizes the negative effect of adverse political action on the local economy, as host governments are generally reluctant to cause problems for their local financial institutions.

local brand   Goods marketed in a particular, limited geographical region. Bread, beer, and dairy products are sometimes sold under local brand names.

local-content requirements   In the global marketing of products, the requirement by the host country that at least some part of the manufacturing be done in the host country. Such restrictions are often applied to encourage the use of local suppliers. Local-content requirements also appear in regional agreements such as NAFTA and Mercosur to ensure that products granted exemption from tariffs are primarily produced in the region.

local cost   For imported merchandise, any expense incurred for goods or services purchased from suppliers in the buyer's home country and necessary for completing the foreign exporters' contract with the buyer.

local firm   In global marketing, a marketer that competes almost exclusively in its home country, with little or no marketing outside its home region. Local firms can successfully compete with larger, more affluent global firms if they position themselves appropriately to resist incursions by the global marketer. A number of strategies can be employed by local firms facing competition from global firms. These include the DEFENDER STRATEGY, THE EXTENDER STRATEGY, THE CONTENDER STRATEGY, and the DODGER STRATEGY.

local government   In global marketing, the government of the HOST COUNTRY.

local industry association   In global marketing, the professional organization representing a particular trade or industry in the host country. When local businesses feel threatened by the incursions of global marketers, they may turn to their industry association to bring pressure to bear on the local government to stop or impede the plans of the global marketer.

localized Internet marketing strategy   In Internet marketing, the accommodation of Web pages and e-mail to local needs and cultural differences. See also GLOCAL STRATEGY.

local manufacturing   In global marketing, the practice of manufacturing products in the host country. This is frequently employed in order to gain market entry.

local market   See PRIMARY MARKET.

local partner   In a JOINT VENTURE, the partner located in the host country.

local sales force   See LOCAL SELLING.

local selling   In global marketing, the practice of maintaining a local sales force in the countries where the global firm does business. Having a sales force of local nationals helps the global firm bridge the cultural gap with clients. The local sales force can be expected to understand local customs, allowing the global marketer to gain additional acceptance in the host market.

local wholesaler   A wholesale business that operates within a small vicinity, usually within a radius of less than one hundred miles from the wholesaler's own operation. Compare NATIONAL WHOLESALER and SECTIONAL WHOLESALER.

location habit   A buyer's preconceived notion of the type of marketing establishment to be used as a source of supply for certain goods.

locked-up distribution channel   In international marketing, a CHANNEL OF DISTRIBUTION that is not easily accessible to an incoming foreign firm. A channel is considered locked up when the newcomer cannot easily convince any channel member to participate, often because channel members cannot break longstanding relationships with competitors. This may create difficulties for manufacturers who cannot gain access to retail or wholesale outlets in the host country.

lockout   A management activity in which union members are prevented from entering a struck business in order to force union acceptance of management's contract proposal.

log file analysis   A software program that collects information from Web visitors' browsers and facilitates a country-of-origin analysis. Such analyses help e-tailers determine whether or not to internationalize their operations.

logistical (marketing) function   Any of the MARKETING FUNCTIONS that involves the transportation and physical distribution of goods and services. Logistical marketing functions include storage, assorting, assembling, and related tasks.

logistics   A marketing support activity primarily concerned with the flow of goods, that is, the acquisition of supplies and materials, the distribution of finished products or the delivery of services, and the maintenance of clear channels of communication between producer and customer. See also PHYSICAL DISTRIBUTION (PD).

logistics costs   An umbrella term for the costs associated with the transportation and physical distribution of goods and services. Logistics costs include: transportation expenses, storage costs, the cost of breaking bulk shipments into smaller lot sizes, and the cost for customs paperwork (in the case of international marketing).

logo   One or more letters worked into a distinctive typographic or calligraphic design. Logos are often in the form of initials (representing the name of a brand or company), but the name is sometimes written out in full. The use of a TRADEMARK or corporate logo can also enhance brand recognition by contributing to the standardization of corporate advertising campaigns in the international marketplace. Also known as a *logotype*, a *signature cut*, or a *sig cut*. See also TRADE STYLE and TRADEMARK.

logotype   Old-fashioned synonym for LOGO.

long-range plan   A plan developed for up to several years (generally a three-to-five year period or longer) and involving the long-term goals of the organization. A long-range plan is often expressed in a statement of purpose. Developed by top management, it has a significant impact on an organization and includes strategies for expansion, market position, and major capital expenditures. Also called a *long-term plan*. Compare SHORT-RANGE PLAN. See also PLANNING and STRATEGIC PLANNING.

long-range planning   See LONG-RANGE PLAN and STRATEGIC PLANNING.

long-run planning capacity   The rate of ordering and reordering activity needed to meet a store's average sales demand over time. The period under consideration must be long enough to include seasonal and cyclical fluctuations.

long-term liability   See LIABILITY.

long-term loan   A loan, secured or unsecured, repaid over a period of five years or more.

long-term plan   Synonym for LONG-RANGE PLAN.

long-term planning   Synonym for STRATEGIC PLANNING.

long-term sales   The sales of goods and services on terms of five or more years. The term may be applied to a subscription or to a sales transaction paid in installments.

long-term transaction   In the BALANCE OF PAYMENTS between a country and any of its trading partners, a transaction that matures in more than a year. Compare SHORT-TERM TRANSACTION.

long-term trend   Synonym for SECULAR TREND.

looking-glass self   The way an individual thinks he or she is seen by others. See also SELF-IMAGE, of which this is a part.

loop (floor) layout   See CLOSED LOOP LAYOUT.

loose goods   Merchandise, such as produce, not enclosed in a package or other container. Since the items are not prepackaged, customers can select them individually. Compare PACKAGE GOODS.

loose market   Synonym for BUYER'S MARKET.

loss   According to the Financial Accounting Standards Board (1985), any "decrease in equity (i.e., net assets) from peripheral or incidental transactions on an entity and from all other transactions and other events and circumstances affecting the entity during a period except those that result from expenses or distributions to owners." Often used in the plural (i.e., *losses*). See also TOTAL LOSS.

loss claims   See CONCEALED LOSS AND DAMAGE CLAIMS.

losses   See LOSS.

loss leader   An item sold at retail prices so low that they do not yield a profit. The object is to increase customer TRAFFIC. Compare MERCHANDISING LEADER. See also LEADER PRICING and PRICE LEADER.

loss leader pricing   See LEADER PRICING.

loss prevention (LP)   The reduction of loss from shoplifting, employee theft, paperwork errors, and poor safety procedures. Also known as *asset protection* and SECURITY.

lot   1. A piece of land forming part of a district, city, or other community (e.g., a *building lot* on which a store may be con-

structed). See also RETAIL SITE LOCATION.   2. A piece of land having a specified use (e.g., a *parking lot*). See also PARKING. 3. Short for DYE LOT.   4. A number of things taken together, as in a shipment (e.g., a LESS-THAN-TRUCKLOAD LOT [LTL]).

loungewear   See INTIMATE APPAREL.

love needs   See MASLOW'S HIERARCHY (OF NEEDS).

lowball   1. To deliberately give an estimate at a lower price than what one intends to charge.   2. To give a false estimate for goods or services, including when bidding for a contract. See also LOWBALL PRICE.

lowball price   The promotion of a product at a very low price calculated to lead a customer into a store. Upon arrival at the store, the customer is informed by the salesperson that management will not allow the sale of the product at the promised price. The salesperson then attempts to pressure the customer into buying a more expensive item. See also BAIT AND SWITCH and LOWBALL.

low-cost merchandising   See LOW-END MERCHANDISING.

low-end merchandise   Inexpensive, low quality goods.

low-end merchandising   A retailing strategy in which stores are located in low-rent areas and in which the merchandise is presented with few amenities. Goods are often displayed on dump tables or in cartons and bins and little sales help is available. Low-end merchandisers depend largely on low prices to attract customers and to generate the high volume necessary to make a profit. These stores are sometimes called *low-margin/high-turnover stores*. Also called *low-cost merchandising* and *low-end strategy*.

lower class   See SOCIAL CLASS.

lower cost or market approach to inventory valuation   See RETAIL METHOD OF INVENTORY (VALUATION).

lower lower class   See SOCIAL CLASS.

lower middle class   See SOCIAL CLASS.

lower of cost or market approach   See RETAIL METHOD OF INVENTORY (VALUATION).

lower upper class   See SOCIAL CLASS.

low-involvement goods/merchandise   Regularly purchased merchandise that is low in cost and familiar to the customer. Low-involvement goods, such as pencils and disposable ballpoint pens, require little thought and planning on the part of the customer. Customers are usually indifferent to particular brands, as the purchase has few if any personal consequences.

low-margin/high-turnover store   Synonym for LOW-END MERCHANDISING.

low-margin retailing An umbrella term encompassing discount stores and MASS MERCHANDISING. See also DISCOUNT STORE.

low-pressure selling A strategy, generally used by a relatively new SALESPERSON, in which the potential buyer is led to make the purchase by skillful questioning and apparent hesitation and reluctance on the part of the salesperson. The salesperson gives the customer the impression that he or she has been in full control of the situation throughout.

low-risk decision A decision with little or no chance of resulting in a loss.

low-trust society A culture in which trust is extended only to immediate family members. Such cultures emphasize nuclear family relationships to the exclusion of all others. Compare HIGH-TRUST SOCIETY.

loyalty card A computer-readable card used in a LOYALTY PROGRAM/SCHEME and in ELECTRONIC MARKETING to track customer purchases. Retailers, particularly supermarkets, offer discounts for loyalty card users and use the data they collect to plan inventory and promotions. Also called a *supermarket loyalty card* or a *customer loyalty card*.

loyalty program/scheme An individualized mass-marketing strategy of tracking customer purchases to anticipate their future needs. The concept involves identifying customers at POINT-OF-PURCHASE (POP) by their credit cards, frequent-shopper cards, gift registries, participation in contests, etc., and maintaining a database of their brand and style preferences. Loyalty programs reward shoppers with perks, such as advance notice of promotional events, free gift wrapping, and discounts. By tracking customer purchases, loyalty programs can identify customers who are sensitive to price or prefer particular brands. Loyalty programs are facilitated by sophisticated database systems that track such items as department, category of merchandise, style number, and brand of purchase as well as customer demographic and psychographic characteristics. Some consumer advocacy groups see the ability to track customer purchases through loyalty programs as an invasion of privacy. See also LOYALTY CARD and PREFERRED CUSTOMER.

LP See LOSS PREVENTION (LP).

LTL See LESS-THAN-TRUCKLOAD LOT (LTL).

Luddites Originally, English workers who protested and tried to forestall industrialization in early nineteenth-century England (1811–1812). The protests spread to the United States, where they were squelched in 1813. In modern times, the term *Luddite*, or *neo-Luddite*, is used of an individual who fears the INTERNET and maintains that its use is detrimental to society.

luxuries Comforts and amenities of life beyond what is needed for normal or standard living. See also OPTIONAL CONSUMPTION.

luxury goods Top-of-the-line merchandise in terms of price and quality. See also SUPERIOR GOODS.

MA (Metropolitan Area)   See METROPOLITAN AREA (MA).

machine learning   Synonym for DATA MINING.

macroenvironment   See MARKETING ENVIRONMENT.

macroindicator (of market size)   Any of a number of indicators of market potential, size, and growth generally used in the first stage of the selection process for target countries (i.e., foreign markets) in which a company wishes to do business. This data is readily available and can be used to eliminate quickly those countries with little or no potential demand for the company's products or services. Included are geographic data (e.g., size of the country, climatic conditions, topography), demographic characteristics (e.g., total population, population growth rate, age distribution of the population, population density), and economic characteristics (e.g., total gross national product, per capita gross national product, per capita income, income growth rate, personal or household disposable income, and income distribution). Compare MICROINDICATOR.

macromarketing   The marketing system as seen in its broadest context (i.e., how the marketing system affects the social system in which it functions, both nationally and internationally). For example, the proliferation of communications and information technology may be seen within the context of economic inequities, gender discrimination, and carbon dioxide pollution across nations. Also spelled *macro-marketing*. See also MICRO-MACRO DILEMMA and MICROMARKETING.

macromarketing environment   See MARKETING ENVIRONMENT.

macrosales model   A way of illustrating the sales process by representing sales as one variable (in either dollars or units) and examining it in relation to other pertinent variables.

macrosegmentation   A strategy employed in industrial marketing in which the market potential for products or services is established by examining broad segmentation variables of businesses, such as the data provided by the ECONOMIC CENSUS.

macrovariable   In INTERNATIONAL MARKETING, any of the variables that help to describe a country's total market in terms of economic, social, geographic, and political information. The variables included by the marketer reflect the potential market size and the likelihood of its acceptance of the marketer's product or similar products. The use of macrovariables helps to screen out the less desirable countries.

MADA (money, authority, desire, access)   See MONEY, AUTHORITY, DESIRE, ACCESS (MADA).

made-to-measure   Custom-made (e.g., of apparel, cut and fitted to a particular individual; of slip covers, made for a particular piece of furniture). See also MADE-TO-ORDER CLOTHING, CUSTOM-MADE and TAILOR-MADE.

made-to-order   See MADE-TO-ORDER CLOTHING and MAKE-TO-ORDER.

made-to-order clothing   Apparel made specifically to fit the measurements of a customer, particularly through the use of computers. Sales associates input the customer's measurements on the touch-screen of a personal computer to create what amounts to a digital blueprint. The blueprint is then transmitted electronically to a factory, where a robotic tailor is instructed to cut a bolt of fabric precisely to the customer's measurements. This technology has been used successfully in Levi's jeans and is particularly beneficial for customers with unusual body shapes. See also MADE-TO-MEASURE, CUSTOM-MADE, and TAILOR-MADE.

made to specification   Made according to a detailed description of requirements, dimensions, materials, etc. See also SPECIFICATION BUYING and SPECIFICATIONS.

Madison Avenue   The advertising industry, named after a street in New York City where advertising firms were traditionally located. See also ADVERTISING and ADVERTISING AGENCY.

magalog   A combination magazine and CATALOG published by a retailer and distributed in stores or by direct mail. Magalogs combine product pitch with editorial content. See also CATALOG RETAILING.

magazine   A periodical publication that typically contains essays, stories, poems, editorial content, and often illustrations. Magazines, which may be general-interest or targeted to a specific readership, are an important medium for advertising.

magazine promotional tie-in   A team effort involving magazines, retailers, and other media (e.g., billboards), intended to boost magazine sales. Magazine publishers strive to improve the circulation and advertising revenues by participating in a variety of tie-in promotions, often in conjunction with retail stores. They may promote a particular designer, a particular fashion trend or theme, or a particular event in their magazines and link it to the retail store or stores where the merchandise may be found. See also TIE-IN PROMOTION.

magic cookie   In the computer operating system known as UNIX, a token attached to a user or program that changes depending on the areas entered by the user of the program. The term has come over to e-commerce simply as COOKIE.

magic price   A marked down price at which almost any merchandise will sell, regardless of condition, simply on the basis of the low price.

Magnuson-Moss Warranty Act (1975)   A U.S. federal consumer protection law requiring manufacturers and sellers of consumer goods to provide consumers with detailed information about warranty coverage. In addition, it affects both the rights of consumers and the obligations of warrantors under written warranties. The law is administered by the FEDERAL TRADE COMMISSION (FTC). See also WARRANTY, EXPRESSED WARRANTY, and IMPLIED WARRANTY. The FTC provides detailed information about the Magnuson-Moss Warranty Act (1975) on its Web site at www.ftc.gov.

mail bomb   In the E-MAIL environment, an automated mass mailing back to the sender that can choke the sender's e-mail with rapid-fire return junk mail. Also spelled *mailbomb*.

mailbot   See AUTORESPONDER.

mailbox   In E-MAIL applications, the area in memory or on a storage device where e-mail is placed. Each user in an e-mail system has a private mailbox. When the user receives e-mail, the mail system automatically puts it in the mailbox where it may be scanned, read, saved, printed, and/or deleted by the recipient.

mailer   A DIRECT MAIL advertising piece.

mailing list   A list of customers or potential customers, used in mailing out promotional materials. A mailing list may be a HOUSE LIST derived from a store's own customers and those who have inquired about the business. Alternatively, it may be a compiled mailing list purchased from list brokers. A number of e-mail companies specialize in providing addresses for people or firms that fit the list purchaser's specifications. Lists may also be compiled from membership lists, directories, and similar sources.

mail-in premium   A gift given as a special promotion by a manufacturer or store in exchange for proof that the promoted goods have been purchased. The PROOF-OF-PURCHASE is mailed to the manufacturer or store. Generally, mail-in premiums require more than one proof (such as three box tops or

five UPC codes from the package). A mail-in premium encourages multiple purchases and brand loyalty. Also called a *free send-away premium* and a *free gift in exchange for proof-of-purchase.*

mail interview   See INTERVIEW.

mail order   1. An order for goods received or shipped through the mail.   2. The industry that conducts its business by mail. See also MAIL ORDER HOUSE/FIRM and MAIL ORDER RETAILING.

Mail Order Action Line   A service offered by the Direct Marketing Association (DMA) to help consumers resolve difficulties with mail order purchases.

mail order catalog   See CATALOG.

mail order house/firm   A nonstore retailing organization whose business is generated through merchandise catalogs. Customers select goods from the company's catalog and mail or telephone their orders, which are subsequently filled by mail or other delivery service. The merchandise is shipped directly to the customer. Many mail order houses now also display all or part of their catalogs on their Web sites and allow customers to place their orders electronically. Also called a *mail order retailer* or a *mail order firm*. See also CATALOG.

Mail Order Preference   See MAIL PREFERENCE SERVICE.

mail order retailer   Synonym for MAIL ORDER HOUSE/FIRM.

mail order retailing   A form of selling in which personal contact and store operations have been eliminated. The retailer contacts potential customers through the use of direct mail, catalogs, television, radio, magazines, newspapers, e-mail, etc. Merchandise is described in words and pictures, customers order by telephone, fax, mail, or Internet, and orders are filled by the seller through the mail or via parcel delivery services. E-TAILING functions similarly by using electronic methods to reach customers and, for the most part (except for electronic products that can be downloaded), uses the same methods of order fulfillment and delivery.

mail order wholesaler   See CATALOG HOUSE and MAIL ORDER WHOLESALING.

mail order wholesaling   A form of WHOLESALING in which personal selling has been eliminated. Mail order wholesalers (also known as catalog houses) send catalogs to retail firms and/or other wholesalers along with instructions on how to order goods. Mail order wholesalers often handle the merchandise of several small manufacturers who cannot afford to produce their own catalogs but desire market exposure for their products. Many mail order wholesalers are found in the stationery and printing field. See also CATALOG HOUSE.

Mail Preference Service   A service offered by the Direct Marketing Association (DMA) for consumers who wish to receive more or less advertising mail. Also called *Mail Order Preference.*

mail survey A survey conducted through the mail. Survey question forms are mailed to participants, who return the completed forms in the mail as well. See also QUESTIONNAIRE.

main aisle See MAJOR AISLE.

main floor retailing The ground floor merchandising activities in a traditional department store. The main floor often includes the cosmetics department, handbags and other accessories, men's furnishings, jewelry, and misses' sportswear and separates.

main store Synonym for FLAGSHIP STORE/DIVISION.

mainstream Widely accepted. See also TRADITIONAL MERCHANDISE.

maintained markon (percentage) See MAINTAINED MARKUP (MMU).

maintained markup (MMU) The difference between the cost of the merchandise (including its transportation) and the selling price of that merchandise. It may also be expressed as the difference between net sales and the cost of goods sold. The maintained markup figure (expressed as a percentage of net sales) does not reflect deduction for cash discounts and workroom costs. It represents the actual markup achieved for the selling period and indicates how well merchandise sustains markup. Also called *maintained markon*. Compare GROSS MARGIN. MMU may be calculated either as the difference between cost price and final retail price, or the difference between total markups (initial and additional markups) and markdowns.

maintained markup percentage See MAINTAINED MARKUP (MMU).

maintained price See RESALE PRICE MAINTENANCE (RPM).

maintenance costs CHANNEL OF DISTRIBUTION costs that include the costs of the company's salespeople, sales managers, and travel expenses.

maintenance increase recoupment A provision written into leases whereby the owner may increase the lessee's rent if taxes, heating fuel, and other operating costs increase in price beyond a specified level.

maintenance marketing The form of marketing appropriate to a MARKETPLACE in a full-demand condition. Monitoring the market for changes in customer demand is of primary importance, the goal being to keep (i.e., maintain) strong demand for the product or service.

maintenance, repair and operating (MOR) items See SUPPLIES.

maintenance supplies See SUPPLIES.

MAJAPs See MAJOR APPLIANCES (MAJAPS).

major account marketing Synonym for NATIONAL ACCOUNT MARKETING.

major aisle A wide aisle that connects a store's extremes. Discounters sometimes refer to a major aisle as a *power aisle*, since they carry the bulk of the customer TRAFFIC. Contrasting colors or floor compositions of wood, marble, carpeting, or tile are often used to define major aisles. Also called a *main aisle*. Compare SECONDARY AISLE.

major appliances (MAJAPs) A category of merchandise that includes kitchen appliances such as ranges, refrigerators, and freezers as well as washing machines, dryers, and other large pieces of household equipment. Also referred to as *MAJAPs* and *hard lines*. See also HARD GOODS and WHITE GOODS.

major equipment Synonym for INSTALLED EQUIPMENT.

major innovation See INNOVATION.

majority fallacy An erroneous belief that the largest segments of a market are always the most profitable. Because the largest segments attract strong competition, they may, in fact, be less profitable than smaller segments in which there are fewer competitors.

major showroom building A building that houses a number of showrooms for a particular merchandise category or group of related categories. For example, in New York City, 1411 and 1407 Broadway are major showroom buildings for moderate-to-better dresses and sportswear; many resources in that category have their showrooms there. This concentration of vendors in close proximity to each other facilitates buying. See also SHOWROOM and MARKET.

major tenant Synonym for ANCHOR STORE.

make-bulk See MAKING BULK.

make-bulk center A central distribution point where small shipments of goods are consolidated into larger ones and then shipped to their ultimate destinations. See also ASSEMBLING and MAKING BULK.

make good 1. To fulfill an obligation, promise, deal, or debt. 2. To reimburse or otherwise compensate a dissatisfied customer.

maker 1. The MANUFACTURER of an item. 2. In VALS SEGMENTATION, a consumer who purchases value-oriented basic merchandise, listens to the radio, and is not interested in luxury goods.

make the cash See MAKING THE CASH.

make-to-order The practice of producing products after receiving purchase orders for them. From the manufacturer's perspective, the goal of make-to-order is to have zero inventory on hand at both the beginning and the end of the selling period. Fashion and seasonal goods are often produced in this way, while orders for basic and staple goods are traditionally filled from STOCK ON HAND (SOH).

make to specification See MADE TO SPECIFICATION and SPECIFICATION BUYING.

making bulk The process of putting together large shipments from multiple, smaller shipments to take advantage of large-volume discounts from carriers. See also ASSEMBLING.

making the cash (Slang) The practice of balancing the books at the end of the day. Funds on hand (i.e., receipts and payments) are compared to the record of sales and payments of obligations.

making the plan A possible outcome of the day-to-day comparison of sales with those of a year ago. If the current figures exceed those of last year, the buyer is said to be making the plan.

mall According to the International Council of Shopping Centers (ICSC), a climate-controlled structure in which retail stores are architecturally connected. The pedestrian walkways have been enclosed and provided with heating and air conditioning. The entrances to individual stores face inward toward the enclosed pedestrian walkway. A mall is usually surrounded by extensive on-site parking areas. Also called a *shopping mall* and/or a *shopping plaza*.

malling The expansion of the shopping center movement. Compare DEMALLING.

mall intercept interview In MARKETING RESEARCH (MR), a method of gathering data in which a researcher randomly chooses people walking around the mall.

MAN (metropolitan-area network) See COMPUTER NETWORK.

managed obsolescence See PLANNED PRODUCT OBSOLESCENCE.

management 1. Those activities involved in running a business or other enterprise, including planning, organizing, coordinating, implementing, directing, and monitoring the program of the organization. The term *management* is often treated as a synonym for *administration*, but management connotes less of the day-to-day activities and more of the overall planning and direction functions. 2. The individual or group of individuals responsible for directing an organization.

management and finance division In an ADVERTISING AGENCY, the division that handles commercial operations similar to the responsibilities of the operations, finance, and control divisions of a retail store. The division deals with business affairs such as managing the office, billing clients, making payments to the various media, and controlling personnel issues. The division is also involved in generating new business by soliciting new clients.

management by objectives (MBO) A management style that focuses on the goals and objectives of the organization and the contribution made by each individual toward attaining them. Formulated by management consultant and author Peter Drucker in the 1950s, MBO involves managers at all levels in the setting of goals, the implementation of the plan, and the review and appraisal of the results. An MBO program has four phases: (a) the clear communication of the overall objectives of the organization to everyone in the program; (b) the development of goals and objectives by middle managers and supervisory managers; (c) periodic meetings between middle managers and other participants to discuss each participant's performance in relation to the goals; (d) periodic meetings of all participants to evaluate whether long-range objectives are being met. The cycle is then refined and repeated. See also GOAL and OBJECTIVE.

management contracting A form of JOINT VENTURE in which a domestic firm provides management expertise to a foreign company. The foreign company provides the capital investment.

management information system (MIS) A system of organizing, storing, manipulating, and supplying data so that it may be used effectively to support management decision making. While the system may be computerized so as to process information more efficiently, a complete management information system involves people and procedures as well as computers. The management information system collects quantitative data as well as opinions and predictions, and organizes them for efficient storage and retrieval. Managers at each level of the organization utilize the information relevant to their own responsibilities. When used by marketers to plan the firm's MARKETING STRATEGY, the process is known as a MARKETING INFORMATION SYSTEM (MIS). See also DECISION SUPPORT SYSTEM (DSS).

managerial approach to marketing An approach to the study of marketing in which managerial functions (planning, the development of strategies, supervision, etc.) are viewed as the key to understanding the marketing process.

managerial competence The ability to implement programs and organize effectively on a global scale, necessary for success in the GLOBAL MARKETPLACE.

managerial marketing Marketing as it is conducted in large organizations. Managerial marketing involves formal planning, establishing objectives, developing strategies for their achievement, and other highly rationalized courses of action designed to reach the firm's marketing goals.

mandatory adaptations In global marketing, those changes to a product that are required in order to meet the standards or preferences of different national markets. For example, consumer electronics must be adapted to work with different voltages. Similarly, adaptations may be necessitated by the laws and regulations of the importing country. Compare DISCRETIONARY ADAPTATIONS.

manifest A statement itemizing the contents, value, point of origin, destination, etc., of cargo that is shipped by ship, plane, truck, or railroad.

manikin Alternative spelling of MANNEQUIN.

mannequin   1. In French usage, a human model who wears and models clothing in a fashion show.   2. In American usage, a lifelike human figure used to display clothing on the selling floor or in store windows. Sometimes referred to as a *silent salesperson*, the mannequin is an important part of conveying the store's fashion image and suggesting to customers how the items may be worn. Mannequins may also be used to represent human beings in displays of nonapparel products by creating a scene suggesting how other products may be used.

mannequin modeling   A form of INFORMAL FASHION SHOW in which the model acts as a live mannequin in a store window or on a display platform. Live models strike poses similar to those of stationary mannequins. Also called a *mannequin show*. See also FASHION SHOW.

mannequin show   See MANNEQUIN MODELING.

manufacture   To make or produce by hand or machinery, especially on a large, commercial scale.

manufactured parts and materials   See MATERIALS AND PARTS.

manufacturer   An organization that, through the use of materials, machinery, and labor, produces finished products. In retailing, a manufacturer may also be referred to as a VENDOR, *supplier*, or *resource*. See also MANUFACTURING, GOODS-PRODUCING BUSINESS, and PRODUCER.

manufacturer-based format corporate chain   See CORPORATE CHAIN.

manufacturer coupon   A coupon emanating from a manufacturer or vendor, redeemable at a wide variety of retailers. Manufacturer coupons may be used as a sales promotion technique for both new and established products, and do not rely on the retailer's cooperation. Manufacturer coupons allow the price-sensitive shopper to purchase a product at a reduced cost, while not decreasing the cost to all consumers. Also called *manufacturer's coupon* or *vendor coupon*.

manufacturer institutional advertising   INSTITUTIONAL ADVERTISING produced by a manufacturer to stress its reputation for design innovation, product quality, or social commitment rather than a particular product or line (e.g., Estée Lauder's Pink Ribbon campaign for Breast Cancer Awareness month).

manufacturer-owned chain   A CHAIN STORE SYSTEM (CSS) that sells (sometimes exclusively) those products made by the company that owns the chain. Many shoe stores, for example, are manufacturer-owned chains. See also MANUFACTURER-SPONSORED SPECIALTY STORE.

manufacturer's advertisement   A consumer advertisement placed by a manufacturer to presell its brands to the target customer at the national and international market levels.

manufacturer's agent   An AGENT INTERMEDIARY who repre-sents a producer or manufacturer in what is usually an exclusive territory. The manufacturer's agent may sell the products of a number of noncompeting clients simultaneously and may also carry an inventory of the products sold. Manufacturer's agents have limited control over prices and terms of sale and act as salespersons calling on industrial customers and retailers. Also called a *sole agent*. See also MANUFACTURER'S REPRESENTATIVE, PREMIUM REPRESENTATIVE, SELLING AGENT, and SERVICE PROVIDER'S AGENT.

manufacturer's branch office   A WHOLESALING establishment from which a producer or manufacturer conducts sales activities and which includes WAREHOUSING or other storage facilities. Sometimes known as a *branch office, captive jobber, captive wholesaler, manufacturer's branch house, manufacturer's sales branch*, or *district office*. See also DISTRIBUTION CENTER (DC) and MANUFACTURER'S SALES OFFICE.

manufacturer's brand   Nationally advertised goods offered for sale by their producer or maker. Manufacturer's brands often carry a distinctive and widely recognized BRAND NAME or TRADEMARK. Also called a *national brand*, although it may actually be an *international brand*.

manufacturer's cooperative advertising   See COOPERATIVE ADVERTISING.

manufacturer's coupon   See MANUFACTURER COUPON.

manufacturer's dealer listing ad   Synonym for DEALER LISTING.

manufacturer/service provider wholesaling   See MANUFACTURER WHOLESALING and SERVICE PROVIDER WHOLESALING.

manufacturer's institutional advertising   See MANUFACTURER INSTITUTIONAL ADVERTISING.

manufacturer's marking/ticketing   See VENDOR PREMARKING/PRETICKETING.

manufacturer's outlet   A type of DISCOUNT STORE originally conceived as a no-frills, break-even operation for unloading a producer's overruns and irregulars. Some manufacturers' outlets have evolved into profitable operations offering first-quality merchandise. The outlets allow the manufacturers to operate at full capacity and sell the additional merchandise, not ordered by retailers, in their own retail outlets at reduced prices. Manufacturers that operate outlet stores, however, run the risk of CHANNEL CONFLICT by competing with the conventional retail stores they supply. Also called a *direct manufacturer's outlet*.

manufacturer's overstock   See OVERSTOCK.

manufacturer-sponsored specialty store   An example of FORWARD INTEGRATION in which manufacturers vertically integrate for increased channel control and for the fiscal advantages associated with performing multiple channel functions. The manufacturer sells its product lines directly to consumers through *signature stores* that facilitate contact between manufacturers and consumers and permit manufacturers to retain control over the presentation and sale of their product lines. Some manufacturers also use signature stores as laboratories to test new items. See also MANUFACTURER-OWNED CHAIN and VERTICAL INTEGRATION.

manufacturer's premarking/preticketing See VENDOR PREMARKING/PRETICKETING.

manufacturer's representative An independent businessperson who works in a specific territory selling related but noncompeting products to more than one account. See also MANUFACTURER'S AGENT.

manufacturer's sales branch See MANUFACTURER'S BRANCH OFFICE.

manufacturer's sales office An establishment owned and operated by a producer or manufacturer and employing a permanent staff of salespeople. Manufacturers' sales offices carry no inventory and thus operate like drop shippers in that they have no warehouse from which goods can be shipped to the customer. Also called, simply, a *sales office*. Compare MANUFACTURER'S BRANCH OFFICE.

manufacturer's sales representative Synonym for MANUFACTURER'S AGENT.

manufacturer's salesperson A salesperson employed by a MANUFACTURER to sell products at all levels of the market (i.e., to industrial buyers, wholesalers, and retailers) except the ultimate consumer. Included are the DEALER-SERVICE SALESPERSON (who calls regularly on established customers), the MISSIONARY (SALESPERSON) (who arranges displays, demonstrates products, etc.), and the DETAILER (who visits professionals such as physicians, hospital administrators, etc.) to introduce new products.

manufacturer's store A retail outlet operated by the MANUFACTURER of a product (e.g., automobile tires) for the purpose of selling the product and providing services (e.g., installation) to the customer. Also known as a *producer outlet*. See also FACTORY OUTLET, MANUFACTURER-OWNED CHAIN, and MANUFACTURER'S OUTLET.

manufacturer's (suggested) list price See LIST PRICE.

manufacturer's suggested price See MANUFACTURER'S SUGGESTED RETAIL PRICE (MSRP) and LIST PRICE.

manufacturer's suggested retail price (MSRP) The price of merchandise at retail recommended by the manufacturer to the retailer. The policy of following this recommendation is known as *manufacturer's suggested retail pricing*. Also called the *recommended retail price, suggested resale price, suggested retail price,* and the *suggested price*. See also RESALE PRICE MAINTENANCE (RPM).

manufacturer's ticketing See VENDOR PREMARKING/PRETICKETING.

manufacturer wholesaler A MANUFACTURER that assumes the duties commonly performed by a WHOLESALER or other MARKETING INTERMEDIARY within the CHANNEL OF DISTRIBUTION. See also MANUFACTURER WHOLESALING.

manufacturer wholesaling A practice in which a MANUFACTURER assumes the duties commonly performed by a WHOLESALER or other MARKETING INTERMEDIARY within the CHANNEL OF DISTRIBUTION. Manufacturer wholesaling may be carried out through either the sales office or the branch offices. See also MANUFACTURER WHOLESALER.

manufacturing The process by which raw materials are converted into completed products by a mechanical, electrical, or chemical process. See also MANUFACTURER and PRODUCTION.

manufacturing-driven firm A company whose major emphasis is on manufacturing requirements rather than marketing considerations.

manufacturing resource planning (MRP II) In manufacturing, a companywide computer system that coordinates data from all departments in order to maintain minimum but sufficient inventories and a smooth production process. MRP II supports management with information for decision making. Managers in every department are provided with easy access to data from other departments, making it easier for the entire firm to generate and adhere to the organization's overall plans, forecasts, and schedules. See also MATERIALS MANAGEMENT, JUST-IN-TIME (JIT), and MATERIAL REQUIREMENTS PLANNING (MRP).

MAP See MINIMUM ADVERTISED PRICE (MAP).

margin 1. The difference between the cost of merchandise to the reseller and net sales achieved by that reseller. 2. The point at which the return from economic activity minimally covers the cost of production. Below this point production is unprofitable.

marginal analysis 1. In MARKETING COST ANALYSIS, a method of ascertaining the point at which marginal cost and marginal revenue equal one another. Prices set on the basis of this analysis are believed to maximize profits for the organization. Sometimes referred to as *analytical pricing*. 2. A method employed in the development of a firm's sales force. In this case salespeople are added to the sales force until the profits generated by the last person hired equal the costs generated by that person's hiring.

marginal buyer A customer in the MARKETPLACE who refuses to buy a product if the price is increased. Compare MARGINAL CUSTOMER and MARGINAL SELLER.

marginal cost The amount of money expended to produce one additional unit of a product or service.

marginal cost pricing In manufacturing, a price setting model stipulating that the price of merchandise should be equal to the cost of producing the final (i.e., marginal) unit of merchandise.

marginal customer   A customer judged to be on the border-line between providing a large enough profit to be continued as a worthwhile customer and a profit so small as to be considered for dropping. Compare MARGINAL BUYER.

marginal efficiency of capital   The PROFIT generated by the last dollar a firm has invested.

marginal product   The additional product resulting from increasing a factor of production by one additional unit.

marginal profit   The extra profit made on the last unit sold. Marginal profit may be calculated by subtracting the *marginal cost* from the MARGINAL REVENUE. For example, if the marginal revenue (i.e., the amount of money accrued from the sale of one additional unit of a product or service) is $10, and the marginal cost (i.e., the amount of money expended to produce that one additional unit of the product or service) is $9, the marginal profit is $1. On the other hand, if the marginal cost is higher than the marginal revenue, it may not be profitable to produce the extra unit of the product or service. For example, if the marginal cost is $11 and the marginal revenue is $10, the producer will lose $1 in producing the extra unit. See also MARGINAL COST.

marginal revenue   The amount of money accrued from the sale of one additional unit of a product or service. See also MARGINAL PROFIT and MARGINAL COST.

marginal seller   A seller in the marketplace who refuses to sell a product or service if the price is lowered. Compare MARGINAL BUYER.

marginal utility   The satisfaction a customer receives from the acquisition and use of one additional unit of a product or service.

margin of profit   A retailer's OPERATING INCOME divided by SALES. Income taxes are usually excluded and depreciation is usually included in calculating the operating expenses.

margin of safety   1. In retailing, the amount by which SALES exceed the BREAK-EVEN POINT. This provides a cushion against a drop in sales or other unforeseeable event. See also BREAK-EVEN ANALYSIS.   2. The income remaining after the payment of fixed charges. See also FIXED COSTS (FC).

margin requirement   A limit set by the U.S. Federal Reserve on the amount of money that stockbrokers and banks may lend customers for the purpose of buying stocks.

mark   1. n. Synonym for TRADEMARK.   2. v. To affix prices and other identifying information to merchandise. See also MARKING AND TICKETING.   3. n. The target of a *con game*. See also CONMANSHIP.

MARK   A research project of the Center for Retailing Education (CRER) at the University of Florida. The project is designed to help retail store buyers make optimal MARKDOWN (MD) and related INVENTORY decisions with respect to items of fashion merchandise. The PC-based model is particularly useful to the BUYER who must procure a quantity of the item in advance of the season and then has the opportunity to reprice the merchandise one or more times during the season. The buyer can sell an item at either the *initial retail price* or at one of a few *off-price* levels allowed by store policy. See also REPRICING.

markdown (MD)   A reduction from an original or previous retail price, generally either as a result of reduced demand for the item in question (i.e., a *clearance markdown*) or to increase store traffic (i.e., a *promotional markdown*). A markdown is often expressed as a percentage of the retail price on which it is taken; typical markdown percentages vary by merchandise category and type of store. Markdowns can be taken for a variety of reasons, including special promotion, stimulation of customer traffic; clearance of out-of-season, obsolete, and slow-selling merchandise; and clearance of damaged goods that vendors will not take back. Markdowns may also be necessitated by errors in buying, pricing, or selling.

markdown allowance   Compensation paid by the vendor to the retailer for markdowns, often based on the difference between a guaranteed gross margin and the actual gross margin with an allowance against future purchases. A strategy through which a retailer negotiates more favorable wholesale prices. Also called *markdown money* and *markdown dollars*. See also MARKDOWN (MD).

markdown cancellation   The act of restoring a price to its pre-markdown level, resulting in a price increase on merchandise that had been previously marked down (i.e., reduced). These upward changes often come at the end of a sale or promotion when merchandise is returned to the former retail price. An additional markup may also be added at the point of the markdown cancellation to establish the next price a customer will see. Markdown cancellations are much less common than they used to be because many large stores electronically program temporary markdowns into the cash register. This means of recording the markdown when an item is being sold is called a *point-of-sale (POS) markdown*. The markdown cancellation is equal to the difference between the higher retail price and the markdown price. For example, After a one-day sale at which blouses were being sold for $43, a buyer marked up the remaining 12 pieces to the original retail price of $50. The markdown cancellation is $7, which, when multiplied by 12 pieces, yields a total of $84.

markdown control   A system for analyzing reductions in retail price (i.e., markdowns) to determine their cause and, if they are excessive, to take corrective action.

markdown dollars   See MARKDOWN ALLOWANCE.

markdown insurance   A relatively new SELLING AID offered as a service by some vendors to their client stores. It is a form of risk-bearing used particularly in women's fashion apparel. Store buyers request that manufacturers guarantee them against markdowns, which are usually necessary late in the season, by reimbursing them for half the amount of the markdowns they find necessary. Many vendors are resisting this request, arguing that such a guarantee leads to poor planning and sloppy buying practices.

markdown money   See MARKDOWN ALLOWANCE.

markdown percentage   A MARKDOWN (MD) expressed as a percentage of the retail price on which the markdown is taken. For example, if the original price is $5 and the markdown price is $4, the dollar markdown is $1. The markdown percentage is the dollar markdown divided by the markdown price, multiplied by 100, or $1/$4 = .25 × 100 = 25%. Also called an *off-retail markdown percentage, percentage markdown, markdown percent, percent markdown,* and *off-retail percentage.* See also PERCENT MARKDOWN.

markdown ratio   In retailing, a measure of the operating efficiency of a department or firm. The dollar value of all markdowns and allowances is divided by net sales.

markdown threshold   In fashion merchandising, the point at which a style has fallen far enough (say, two weeks) behind the originally estimated rate of sale that it is certain not to sell out during its fashion life. The object is to spot slow movers early, mark them down quickly, and hope to sell out the style at the *marked-down price.*

markdown timing   The scheduling of planned price reductions so as to minimize lost profits.

marked-down price   The price that results from a MARKDOWN (MD). The new price is lower than the original retail selling price.

market   1. n. The physical place where goods and services are bought and sold (e.g., a farmers' market where growers sell their produce to the public).   2. n. The physical place where a substantial number of suppliers have established their businesses in an effort to make themselves readily available to retail buyers (e.g., the GARMENT CENTER in New York City where hundreds of apparel manufacturers maintain showrooms). 3. n. The aggregate demand for certain products or services; that is, all the actual or potential customers who have the means to purchase the product or service and who actually have access to it should they make a decision to buy.   4. n. The retail TRADING AREA of a store (i.e., a geographical entity containing potential customers).   5. n. A meeting place (mart, convention center, etc.) where representatives of manufacturers present their lines for the inspection of retail buyers. See also MARKETPLACE.   6. v. To deal commercially in goods and/or services. See also MARKETING.   7. v. To shop.

marketable   Of a product or service, able to be sold, especially readily. For example, an experienced retail buyer has many marketable skills.

marketable securities   See SECURITIES.

market aggregation   Synonym for UNDIFFERENTIATED MARKETING.

market analysis   The collection and evaluation of data on the potential markets for a firm's products or services to determine which market segments may offer opportunities for profitable entry or expansion. Market analysis encompasses much of what is regarded as MARKETING RESEARCH (MR), with an emphasis on demographic, geographic, and socioeconomic MARKET SEGMENTATION. Market analysis is a component of a company's MARKETING PLAN and, in the online environment, the WEB MARKETING PLAN.

market anticipation   Efforts made, generally on the basis of MARKETING RESEARCH (MR), to guess how customers will behave in the MARKETPLACE at some time in the future.

market appeal/attractiveness   The attractiveness of a market (to a retailer or other marketer) based on its size or annual rate of growth. The appeal is influenced by economic and technological forces, competitive variables, and environmental considerations.

market audit   See MARKETING AUDIT.

market-based pricing   See PRICING AT THE MARKET.

market basket   The items a customer actually purchases on a visit to a store. See also MARKET BASKET ANALYSIS.

market basket analysis   A method used to help determine how customers are buying. Retailers examine which products are in the customers' MARKET BASKET (i.e., what they've actually purchased) and associate each item with a product category. The percentage that each category represents is calculated. For example, if there are 10 items in a market basket and 5 are cosmetic products, 50 percent of the market basket is represented by the cosmetics category. The percentages allow the retailer to assign customers to *purchase profiles* (e.g., a beauty-conscious customer might be one with more than 25 percent of items in the beauty product category). The analysis captures the key reason that the customer was actually in the store. Retailers use this type of analysis to categorize shopping experiences and analyze customers' collective behavior while shopping. Once specific customer purchase profiles are identified, the information is provided to decision makers (e.g., the BUYER) so that they may act on it. A *gross margin* figure is calculated for each profile, which can then be used to base decisions about key areas of the business (e.g., where to spend advertising dollars). Market basket analysis may also be used in SPACE ALLOCATION and PRODUCT PLACEMENT decisions. The analysis is used to determine which items are most frequently purchased with other items in the same market basket (i.e., an AFFINITY PURCHASE). By using AFFINITY ANALYSIS in this way, a store can become more customer-driven.

market basket pricing   A PRICING STRATEGY, most commonly found in supermarkets, in which some items (generally those about which the consumer is most PRICE-CONSCIOUS) are priced low to create the impression of a bargain. Other, less familiar items are then given a higher MARKUP to compensate. Also spelled *marketbasket pricing.*

market build-up method   A FORECASTING technique in which information from a number of market segments is gathered, separately analyzed, and then added together to form a more or less complete picture of the MARKETING ENVIRONMENT for the purpose of forecasting sales.

market calendar   An itemized listing of the dates and locations of trade shows and markets. See also MARKET WEEK.

market center   A cluster of merchandise marts. For example, the DALLAS MARKET CENTER is a six-building complex of 6.9 million square feet housing more than 2,400 showrooms. Included in the Dallas Market Center is the International Menswear Mart, the International Apparel Mart, Market Hall, and the Trade Market and World Trade Center. See also CALIFORNIA MARKET CENTER (CMC).

market channel   Synonym for CHANNEL OF DISTRIBUTION.

marketcide   Self-inflicted and avoidable harm done to a retailer or other business through its own practices and policies. Also informally called *shooting oneself in the foot*.

market cleavage   Synonym for MARKET SEGMENTATION.

market concentration   1. A form of MARKET SEGMENTATION in which all of a firm's marketing efforts are concentrated on one segment of the consuming population.   2. That part of a product's sales volume (or that part of an entire industry's production) accounted for by a relatively small number of large companies. Such concentration may be expressed in terms of dollar volume, number of units sold, employment level, etc.

market delineation   The process of determining who the customers for a product will be and of identifying their characteristics for marketing purposes. See also MARKET SEGMENTATION.

market demand   Synonym for DEMAND.

market development   A strategy in which a firm develops new markets for its products or finds alternative uses for its products. The objective of market development is to increase sales.

market development manager   Synonym for MARKETING PLANNING MANAGER.

market-directed economic system   An ECONOMIC SYSTEM, such as CAPITALISM, in which the individual decisions of producers and consumers make the decisions for the economy as a whole.

market diversification   See DIVERSIFICATION.

market division of authority   In MARKETING MANAGEMENT, a form of organization in which the LINE ORGANIZATION is set up to correspond to the structure of the MARKETPLACE or to the way a firm's customers are segmented. This practice is prevalent in firms that market their products to two or more industries or distribute their products through two or more channels. Compare PRODUCT DIVISION OF AUTHORITY.

market economy   An ECONOMIC SYSTEM in which, at least theoretically, FREE ENTERPRISE is the operating principle. The forces of SUPPLY AND DEMAND are given free rein to determine the allocation of resources, and goals are achieved by the action of the free market with a minimum of government intervention.

marketer   Any firm or individual engaged in the supply of goods, services, or ideas in the MARKETPLACE. Marketers facilitate the exchange of goods and services as these move from production to the industrial user or the ultimate consumer. All organizations and individuals engaged in business may be regarded as marketers in that they are all, in one way or another, selling something to somebody. In addition, many nonbusiness organizations engage in what must be regarded as marketing activities and thus must be classified as marketers.

market expansion promotion   An effort calculated to attract new customers through the introduction of new products or through the fresh presentation of established merchandise.

market factor   Any variable in the MARKETING ENVIRONMENT that may affect demand for a product or service. For example, the number of teenagers in an area will affect the sale of MP3 recording and playback devices.

market factor analysis   Critical examination of variables in the MARKETING ENVIRONMENT. When such variables (i.e., market factors) can be correlated with sales trends, the resulting analysis may be used to forecast future sales. See also DIRECT DERIVATION and CORRELATION ANALYSIS.

market factor index   The expression, in relation to a base number, of a number of market factors taken together and analyzed. Such an INDEX is used in the projection of future sales trends. Also called the *market index*. See also MARKET FACTOR and MARKET FACTOR ANALYSIS.

market fit   In the marketing of products and services, the degree to which a new product or service is suited to a company's present market; that is, the degree to which the new product or service is likely to appeal to the company's existing customers.

market forecast   See FORECAST.

market forecasting   See FORECASTING.

market functions   Synonym for MARKETING FUNCTIONS.

market grid   A device employed in MARKET SEGMENTATION studies in which a total market is subdivided in an effort to target potential customers more precisely. The information is frequently presented in the form of a grid. Also called the *market matrix*, the *marketing matrix*, and the *marketing grid*. See also BOSTON CONSULTING GROUP (BCG) MATRIX.

market growth   See GROWTH STAGE.

market growth rate The annual expansion or contraction of a market, either at present or as forecast, most often expressed as a percentage.

market growth stage See GROWTH STAGE.

market index Synonym for MARKET FACTOR INDEX.

market information function A FACILITATING FUNCTION that includes the collection, analysis, and distribution of the information needed by marketers in the performance of universal MARKETING FUNCTIONS.

marketing 1. According to the American Marketing Association, "the process of planning and executing the conception, pricing, promotion, and distribution of ideas, goods, and services to create exchanges that satisfy individual and organizational objectives." Broadly construed, therefore, marketing is part of an economic process concerned with the supply of and demand for goods, services, and ideas in the society at large. It includes those activities that facilitate the exchange of goods and services as they move from production to the industrial user or ultimate consumer. 2. At the narrower level of the organization (both profit and nonprofit), preproduction activities such as planning and development (which may also include MARKETING RESEARCH [MR]), pricing, promotion, distribution, and follow-up services. When conducted scientifically and systematically, either definition may be called *marketing science.*

marketing against the competitor A strategy in which a firm focuses its marketing efforts on the strengths and weaknesses of its competitors rather than on the wants and needs of its customers. For example, when Pepsi-Cola determined that Coca-Cola was weakest in marketing to younger consumers, Pepsi focused its advertising attack on this vulnerable area.

marketing-as-usual approach to shortages An approach to actual or anticipated shortages of the raw materials required for production. When companies feel they cannot produce enough goods to meet customer demand, they may assume that such shortages are temporary and continue to produce the same quantities of their products and sell to the same customers. The firm adopting this approach continues to spend the same amount on advertising, sales force, MARKETING RESEARCH (MR), etc., as it did prior to the shortage. Minor changes may be made in the advertising message and prices may rise somewhat to cover cost increases, but other marketing factors remain unchanged. This approach is designed to maintain the firm's profit margin as well as the goodwill of its customers.

marketing audit A systematic, comprehensive evaluation of a firm's marketing philosophy, objectives, and strategy with a view toward implementing corrective action if deemed appropriate. The audit may be applied to ongoing marketing programs (a control audit) in an effort to determine their effectiveness, or to completed programs (a review audit) in an effort to evaluate their results.

marketing budget A financial plan, often based on projected or past sales, for the allocation of money to cover marketing costs over a future period. The marketing budget includes projected costs for administration and materials, marketing research, advertising and sales promotion, and other marketing functions. In many respects it is a projected income statement for the particular marketing functions included.

marketing channel Synonym for CHANNEL OF DISTRIBUTION.

marketing climate Synonym for MARKETING ENVIRONMENT.

marketing communication All those messages transmitted from sender to receiver that involve the buyer-seller relationship. In addition to formal promotional messages, such as ADVERTISING, informal nonsystematic avenues of communication such as WORD-OF-MOUTH (WOM) COMMUNICATION are also included. Frequently used in the plural (i.e., *marketing communications*). See also PROMOTIONAL MIX.

marketing communications mix Synonym for PROMOTIONAL MIX.

marketing company era A stage in the evolution of marketing (from the mid-1960s to the present) during which marketing departments took on dominant roles in many manufacturing organizations. See also MARKETING DEPARTMENT ERA.

marketing concept A MARKETING MANAGEMENT orientation in which the satisfaction of the customers' wants and needs is regarded as the primary goal of the organization, although these wants and needs may not yet be apparent to (and thus not expressed by) the consumer. In essence, the marketing concept recognizes the importance of the consumer in the buying process. Profits are generated by determining what the customer wants or may want in the future and then making it, rather than by making a product and then finding a way to create demand. Firms subscribing to the marketing concept rely heavily on MARKETING RESEARCH (MR) to ascertain consumer needs and to create a MARKETING MIX designed to satisfy those needs. A firm adopting a marketing concept is said to be *customer-oriented.* Also known as *customer orientation, marketing philosophy, market orientation,* and *customer market focus.* See also PRODUCT CONCEPT, PRODUCTION CONCEPT, and SELLING CONCEPT.

marketing control See CONTROL.

marketing controllable Synonym for CONTROLLABLE FACTOR.

marketing cooperative/co-op See PRODUCERS' COOPERATIVE/CO-OP.

marketing cost analysis An analysis of a firm's marketing operations in terms of the cost of activities such as selling, advertising, transportation, storage, delivery, etc. An effort is then made to correlate these tools to the profitability of various products, customer groups, territories, etc. The objective of the analysis is to determine the efficiency of the firm's marketing efforts. See also CONTRIBUTION-MARGIN APPROACH TO COST ANALYSIS and FULL COST APPROACH TO COST ANALYSIS.

marketing data   Information collected from and about markets, market segments, competitors, suppliers, partners, consumers, etc., particularly when stored electronically in a DATABASE (DB). In addition to demographic information and lifestyle preferences, the data collected by e-tailers and other online marketers about their customers includes transaction history, behavioral factors (e.g., time spent on a Web page, pages visited, links, and clickstreams), and technical information (e.g., browser used, computer operating system, and screen size).

marketing database   MARKETING DATA collected and stored electronically in an organized set of structured records. A marketing database may be used for many marketing purposes, including but not limited to the following: creating customer contact and inventory lists and directories; identifying receptive target customers for special offers; matching customers and products for UPSELL and CROSS-SELLING; tailoring marketing messages and offers; adjusting distribution schedules; and predicting purchase probability. Knowledge derived from successful database management can significantly change the way MARKETING is conducted, affecting MARKETING STRATEGY and day-to-day tactics. See also DATABASE MANAGEMENT SYSTEM (DBMS).

marketing decision support systems   See DECISION SUPPORT SYSTEM (DSS) and MARKETING INFORMATION SYSTEM (MIS).

marketing department era   A stage in the evolution of marketing during which the marketing department of a firm, although still subordinate to production and sales, is beginning to influence the development of the company marketing program. See also MARKETING COMPANY ERA.

marketing director   The individual responsible for overseeing all MARKETING activities within the store or larger retail organization.

marketing dyad   The buyer (i.e., customer) and seller (i.e., marketer) interacting in pursuit of an exchange of goods or services.

marketing dynamics   Changes in a firm's MARKETING MIX determined by changes in the external environment. Most marketing dynamics are controllable by organizations, in contrast to ENVIRONMENTAL DYNAMICS, which are largely out of the firm's control.

marketing environment   The complex of legal, political, economic, and social influences that surrounds a firm and affects its marketing activities. A firm may be seen as having two distinct marketing environments: an internal or *microenvironment,* over which the firm has a degree of control, and an external or *macroenvironment,* which is largely beyond the firm's control. Also called the *marketing climate.* See also PUBLIC POLICY ENVIRONMENT.

marketing ethics   Those standards, values, moral principles, etc., that govern the marketer's behavior in the MARKETPLACE.

marketing function account   Synonym for FUNCTIONAL ACCOUNT.

marketing functions   The activities that form the basis for marketing. They include product and planning development, financing, pricing, promotion (including advertising and personal selling), transportation, storage, distribution, etc. MARKETING RESEARCH (MR), which is sometimes regarded as a support function, may also be included. Marketing functions are also known as *functions of marketing, marketing variables, universal functions of marketing, universal marketing functions, marketing instruments,* and *market functions.* See also TRANSACTIONAL (MARKETING) FUNCTION and FACILITATING FUNCTION.

marketing grid   Synonym for MARKET GRID.

marketing information and decision program (MIDP)   See MARKETING INFORMATION SYSTEM (MIS).

marketing information system (MIS)   A complex of persons, procedures, and equipment (i.e., computers) acting in concert to collect information relevant to marketing decision making. It is more broadly based than MARKETING RESEARCH (MR) in that the system gathers data internally from within the firm as well as externally in the marketing environment. It also provides for evaluation of the collected data to determine its usefulness to the executives responsible for planning the firm's MARKETING STRATEGY. Also called a *marketing information and decision program (MIDP).* See also MANAGEMENT INFORMATION SYSTEM (MIS) and DECISION SUPPORT SYSTEM (DSS).

marketing institutions   The organizations that make up the marketing system. Marketing institutions include manufacturers and producers, middlemen (wholesalers, retailers, etc.), and a wide variety of facilitating organizations such as trucking firms, railroads, warehouse facilities, advertising agencies, etc.

marketing instruments   Synonym for MARKETING FUNCTIONS.

marketing intelligence   A process for collecting data, particularly about competitors' marketing tactics, and transforming it into information useful for making marketing decisions. Marketing intelligence is used to adjust market offers and the process of making them. A growing number of intelligence activities are Web-based, focusing on competitors' online market offers. See also COMPETITIVE INTELLIGENCE (CI) and MARKETING INTELLIGENCE SYSTEM.

marketing intelligence system   The network of outside information sources through which marketing executives collect data useful in making marketing decisions. See also MARKETING INTELLIGENCE.

marketing intermediary   Any of the wholesalers, retailers, and marketing specialists (e.g., transportation firms) that play a facilitating role between manufacturers or service providers and their customers. Also called a *distribution intermediary, middleperson, mercantile customer,* or (more commonly) MIDDLEMAN.

marketing management The process of planning, implementing, and directing a firm's marketing efforts with the intention of satisfying the customer and turning a profit. Among the many functions included in the marketing management process are strategy development and SALES FORECASTING, ADVERTISING and sales promotion, analysis of market opportunities, and the establishment of the proper MARKETING MIX. See also MARKETING MANAGER.

marketing manager The executive responsible for the firm's product planning and the development of the MARKETING STRATEGY. The marketing manager directs MARKETING RESEARCH (MR) activities, formulates goals for the sales force, develops a sales promotion and advertising strategy, sets pricing policy, establishes budgets for particular lines, and engages in other marketing activities aimed at maximizing the firm's position in the MARKETPLACE. The marketing manager may also be known as the *vice president of marketing* or the *director of marketing.* See also BRAND MANAGER and PRODUCT MANAGER.

marketing manager organization system A way of organizing a company for product management in which a number of areas (including product planning, advertising, and sales promotion) report to a single manager.

marketing matrix Synonym for MARKET GRID.

marketing middleman See MARKETING INTERMEDIARY, MIDDLEMAN, and WHOLESALING MIDDLEMAN.

marketing mix Marketing variables, such as product and product planning, pricing, promotion, and place (or distribution channel selection), blended together to form a MARKETING STRATEGY designed to satisfy the firm's customers. See also FOUR PS OF THE MARKETING MIX.

marketing mix analysis The collection and evaluation of data relating to the MARKETING MIX. The study shows how poorly or how well the marketing mix variables (i.e., the FOUR PS OF THE MARKETING MIX) are being used to make offers that target markets find attractive. Specific objectives, stated in the analysis in measurable terms as performance outcomes, provide details of how the marketing goals will be achieved. Such outcomes may include sales objectives, traffic objectives, customer service objectives, cost reduction objectives, and personnel reduction objectives.

marketing mix variables Synonym for the FOUR PS OF THE MARKETING MIX.

marketing myopia A short-sighted, narrow view of marketing that prevents some marketers from seeing the larger picture and the total MARKETING ENVIRONMENT. The metaphor, borrowing the medical term for nearsightedness, was first used by Theodore Levitt in 1975.

marketing objectives That part of a MARKETING PLAN that defines its goals regarding sales volume, market share, and profit. Effective marketing objectives are clear, measurable, stated in order of their importance, and realistically attainable while remaining challenging. See also MARKETING PLAN and FINANCIAL OBJECTIVES.

marketing opportunity analysis A study of the MARKETING ENVIRONMENT made in an effort to ascertain where changes might occur and when problems might develop. Marketing opportunity analysis is commonly employed in MARKETING PLANNING and strategy development, particularly with respect to the activities of competitors.

marketing organization An arrangement of formal and informal relationships forming a system through which marketing personnel execute a firm's MARKETING PLAN.

marketing orientation Synonym for MARKETING CONCEPT.

marketing performers The complex of organizations involved in the total marketing process. Marketing performers include manufacturers, service providers, wholesalers, retailers, marketing specialists, and customers (both organizational/institutional customers and ultimate consumers).

marketing philosophy Synonym for MARKETING CONCEPT.

marketing plan The formal written document that puts into action the decisions reached during the MARKETING PLANNING process. It specifies how MARKETING MIX strategies and tactics will be implemented to satisfy customer needs and meet business goals, typically over a one-year period; consequently, it is frequently referred to as an *annual marketing plan.* See also STRATEGIC MARKETING PLAN, OPERATIONAL MARKETING PLAN, and WEB MARKETING PLAN.

marketing planning A systematic process used to assess a firm's marketing objectives and sales targets. Activities included in marketing planning are MARKETING RESEARCH (MR), SALES FORECASTING, and MARKET PLANNING. The actual formulation of a MARKETING PLAN may be secondary to the strategic thinking carried on at the management level and leading ultimately to a consensus within the organization. Thus, while marketing planning anticipates future market developments, it also gives management the opportunity to evaluate long-term strategies along with the tactics necessary to execute the resulting plan.

marketing planning manager In organizations serving a number of markets, the executive who coordinates the MARKETING RESEARCH (MR) efforts and supervises a number of marketing managers. The marketing planning manager is essentially a strategic planner. Sometimes known as a *market development manager.*

marketing positioning Synonym for MARKET POSITIONING.

marketing program The overall plan maintained by a firm, blending all its strategic plans. The marketing program is the responsibility of the entire firm, not just one division. When the various plans are quite different, there is little concern for how they all fit together. When they are similar, however, the same sales force may have to carry out several plans. Consideration is always given to the way each plan competes for the firm's limited financial resources. See also STRATEGIC PLANNING.

marketing research (MR)   According to the American Marketing Association, "the function that links the consumer, customer, and public to the marketer through information— information used to identify and define marketing opportunities and problems; generate, refine, and evaluate marketing actions; monitor marketing performance; and improve understanding of marketing as a process. Marketing research specifies the information required to address these issues, designs the method for collecting information, manages and implements the data collection process, analyzes the results, and communicates the findings and their implications." Sometimes called *market research*. See also RETAIL MARKETING RESEARCH.

marketing research firm/company   An outside firm contracted to provide MARKETING RESEARCH (MR) to a company. There are three main types of marketing research firms: the SYNDICATED SERVICE RESEARCH FIRM, which gathers consumer and trade information on a regular basis and sells the data to clients for a fee (e.g., the reports on television audiences prepared by the ACNielsen Co.); the CUSTOM MARKETING RESEARCH FIRM, which is hired to perform specific research assignments and whose reports become the property of the client; and the SPECIALTY LINE MARKETING RESEARCH FIRM, which provides specialized research services (e.g., field interviewing services) to other marketing research firms and to the marketing research departments of clients. Sometimes called a *market research firm*.

marketing risk   The possibility that business may be lost due to changes in SUPPLY AND DEMAND as well as to natural hazards.

marketing science   See MARKETING, ANALYTICAL MARKETING SYSTEM (AMS), and MARKETING INFORMATION SYSTEM (MIS).

marketing segmentation   See MARKET SEGMENTATION.

marketing subsidiary   See DIRECT EXPORT/EXPORTING.

marketing strategy   The logical plan through which a firm intends to reach its marketing objectives. Included in the plan are the processes of identifying opportunities, targeting customers, adjusting the MARKETING MIX, and allocating resources. Also called a *market strategy*. See also GLOBAL MARKETING STRATEGY.

marketing survey   See SURVEY.

marketing system   Marketing viewed as a group of interdependent units that form a whole entity (i.e., a system). These include producers of goods and services, a number of mar-

keting intermediaries (i.e., wholesalers, distributors, retailers, shipping organizations, advertising agencies, etc.), and, finally, customers. The primary objective of the marketing system is the expeditious allocation of resources so as to efficiently meet the demands of the MARKETPLACE. See also ANALYTICAL MARKETING SYSTEM (AMS).

marketing variables   Synonym for MARKETING FUNCTIONS.

market intensification   See INTENSIVE MARKET OPPORTUNITY.

market introduction   See INTRODUCTORY STAGE.

market leader   The store that controls the largest MARKET SHARE of merchandise or services.

market liberalization   The encouragement of competition where prior monopolies or strict entry controls previously existed (e.g., in developing countries or the transitioning economies of the former Soviet Bloc). Production licensing is often relinquished and import controls relaxed. Host governments may also encourage multinational corporations to invest in their markets.

market matrix   Synonym for MARKET GRID.

market maturity   See MATURITY STAGE.

market measurement study   Research conducted to determine MARKET POTENTIAL, that is, to measure the combined realized and unrealized buying capacity that exists in a market or segment of a market.

market minimum   The rate of sales that would be achieved for a product or service without any demand-stimulating expenditures such as advertising or promotion.

market-minus pricing   The practice of setting prices lower than the market price, generally as the result of the merchandise being less attractive to the customer than predicted. The resulting price is known as a *market-minus price*. See also DEMAND-BACKWARD PRICING.

market news   Specific information about conditions in the marketplace bearing immediately on the conduct of business. For example, news of a crop failure quickly affects commodity traders.

market niche   A narrow market segment in which a company can successfully compete with a new or existing product or service. See also NICHE, NICHE MARKETING, and MARKET SEGMENTATION.

market opportunity   Short for COMPANY MARKETING OPPORTUNITY.

market orientation   A MARKETING MANAGEMENT focus in which the satisfaction of the customers' wants and needs is regarded as the primary goal of the organization. See also MARKETING CONCEPT.

market-oriented pricing   A method of setting retail prices in which the price at which the item or similar items is selling in the marketplace (i.e., what competitors are charging for the same item) is used as a standard rather than the cost of the merchandise.

market penetration   The extent to which a company has entered a particular market or the degree to which it seeks to expand its share of that market.

market penetration pricing   A MARKETING STRATEGY in which goods are priced low enough to have immediate wide appeal in the marketplace. The object of market penetration pricing is to quickly capture a significant MARKET SHARE.

market period   In the marketing process, that period from the time a product is manufactured (or a commodity is produced) until the time it is sold. During this period COSTS are fixed and the amount of product does not vary. PRICE will be determined by current DEMAND.

marketplace   1. In its broadest sense, the MARKETING ENVIRONMENT (i.e., the world of business, trade, and economics). See also GLOBAL MARKETPLACE. For a more restricted definition see MARKET.   2. An open area in a town where a market is held. Also spelled *market place*.

market plan   See MARKETING PLAN.

market planning   The process by which a firm identifies its customers and determines their needs. Market planning is a part of the MARKETING PLANNING effort together with such activities as SALES FORECASTING, SALES PLANNING, and PROMOTIONAL BUDGETING. Included in market planning are such factors as product development, quality control, packaging, shipping, pricing, advertising, sales force management, and customer service. See also PLANNING.

market-plus price   The price put on merchandise that is distinctive and highly desirable, often above the MARKET PRICE because demand is high. See also PRICING ABOVE THE MARKET.

market position analysis   Synonym for ATTRIBUTE MAPPING.

market-positioned warehouse   A facility in which goods may be stored. The market-positioned warehouse may be owned by a manufacturer, distributor, or retailer. It is used to consolidate shipments and position products near the ultimate consumer (i.e., the market).

market positioning   Efforts aimed at establishing a product or service in a particular NICHE or segment of the MARKETPLACE. Market positioning strategy usually includes those promotional activities that differentiate the product from competitors' products and vividly establish the product's image in the minds of potential customers. Also known as *positioning*, *product positioning*, *marketing positioning*, or *target positioning*. See also BRAND POSITIONING, SERVICE POSITIONING, and REPOSITIONING.

market potential   A calculation representing the total realized and unrealized *capacity to buy* existing in a market or segment of a market. The calculation includes all the goods or services offered by all the sellers competing in the particular market over a specific period of time and is used as an indication of opportunity for growth and expansion in a market, since at least some of this potential may be as yet latent and unrealized. Research undertaken to determine the market potential is called a *market measurement study*. See also SALES POTENTIAL and MARKET SHARE.

market price   A price determined by the unrestricted forces of SUPPLY AND DEMAND in the MARKETPLACE, over which the seller has little or no control. Prices for farm products are almost always set this way. In retailing, this generally turns out to be the price consumers are willing to pay for a product in the free market and therefore becomes the price charged for that item by all stores in a particular location. *Market pricing* is the policy of adopting the market price. Also called *at-the-market price*.

market representative   Synonym for RESIDENT BUYER. Sometimes called, simply, *market rep* or a *market specialist*.

market research   See MARKETING RESEARCH (MR).

market research company/firm   See MARKETING RESEARCH FIRM/COMPANY.

market saturation   See SATURATED AREA.

market segment   A subdivision of a population (commonly ultimate consumers). The members of the market segment share similar identifiable characteristics (e.g., age, wealth, style, educational level, marital status, gender, sexual orientation). A firm may develop different marketing programs for each segment of its target market. See also SOCIAL CLASS.

market segmentation   The division of a population (frequently ultimate consumers or potential customers) into smaller parts, or segments, having similar characteristics. Market segmentation uses such attributes as race, nationality, age, education, psychological traits, lifestyle characteristics, etc. The underlying assumption is that population groups that share certain attributes will react uniformly to marketing efforts. Market segmentation is used by retailers and other marketers to identify NICHE markets. Also called *market cleavage*. Compare WHOLE MARKET APPROACH/METHOD. See also DIFFERENTIATED MARKETING and POSITIONED RETAILING.

market segmentation by city size   The subdivision of the population of potential customers based on the size of the city in which they live. This is an important factor in determining whether or not a given location can support a store.

market segmentation by degree of urbanization   The subdivision of the population of potential customers based on whether they live in urban, suburban, or rural areas. See also URBANIZATION.

market segmentation by demographics The subdivision of the population of potential customers based on such factors as income, age, education, stage in the family life cycle, class, gender, occupation, race, and religion. See also DEMOGRAPHICS.

market segmentation by family life cycle The subdivision of the population of potential customers based on where they fall in the FAMILY LIFE CYCLE (FLC). Five stages are usually described: single or married head of household, under 40, with no children; married head of household, under 40, with young children and/or older children; married head of household, under 40 with older children and no young children; married head of household, over 40, no children present under 20; and head of household living alone, over 40, with no children in the household. Also called *segmentation by family life cycle.*

market segmentation by geographical bases See GEOGRAPHIC SEGMENTATION.

market segmentation by population density The subdivision of the population of potential customers by the number of people per square mile who reside in a particular geographical area. Market segmentation by population density helps to determine the types of goods to be sold by the retailer as well as the potential customer support the store may receive. Also called *population density segmentation* and *population segmentation.* See also TRADING AREA.

market segmentation by psychographics PSYCHOGRAPHIC SEGMENTATION.

market segmentation by size of city See MARKET SEGMENTATION BY CITY SIZE.

market share That part of a total market controlled by one firm. It is expressed as the firm's sales, or the sales of a particular product or line of products, in relation to total industry sales and is commonly computed as a percentage. Also known as *brand share, company share, sales penetration,* or *share of the market.* See also RELATIVE MARKET SHARE, MARKET POTENTIAL, and SALES POTENTIAL.

market share analysis A technique for evaluating a firm's sales that takes into account the activities of a firm's competitors and views the company as a participant in the general MARKETPLACE. Market share analysis is a more precise measure of performance than SALES VOLUME ANALYSIS.

market share objective/goal A benchmark representing that portion of a market a company wishes to capture.

market similarity A criterion used by international marketers in deciding which markets to enter. Marketers seek to expand to foreign markets most like their own, based on the belief that their success is more easily transferable to markets most like the one in which they already compete. See also PSYCHIC DISTANCE.

market skimming (pricing) See SKIMMING.

market specialist Synonym for RESIDENT BUYER.

market strategy Synonym for MARKETING STRATEGY.

market stretching A strategy employed in marketing products that have reached the maturity stage in their life cycle. Sales are maintained or expanded through such means as technical improvement and more effective MARKETING RESEARCH (MR). See also MATURITY STAGE.

market target See TARGET MARKET and MARKET TARGETING.

market targeting Those strategic decision making activities that precede both the selection of a target market and the market positioning of a product. Market targeting enables the organization to focus its resources on the achievement of specific goals by choosing between targeting the total market and limiting marketing efforts to one or more specific segments. Also called *target marketing.* See also TARGET MARKET.

market testing Synonym for TEST MARKETING.

market trip Synonym for BUYING TRIP.

market value The prevailing price at which a product can be expected to sell in a given market.

market visit Synonym for BUYING TRIP.

market week An event at which manufacturers introduce their new lines of merchandise and retail buyers shop the various lines. The events are scheduled seasonal showings of merchandise by manufacturers in the market centers. While different industries show their wares at different times, these events share a common goal: to give buyers the opportunity to see new merchandise. Market weeks may last less than a week or, as in the New York apparel industry, considerably longer. In most cases, market week showings are held in manufacturers' showrooms four to five times per year. Sometimes hotel suites are used and, in the case of the designer fashion market, more elaborate arrangements are made (e.g., fashion shows). See also MARKET CALENDAR.

marking See MARKING AND TICKETING.

marking and ticketing The affixing of prices (and sometimes other information, such as department identification, date received, cost price, etc.) to merchandise before it is placed on the selling floor or just before it is shelved. The prices may be affixed through the use of tickets, price tags, or labels. The identifying information is used in stocking, controlling, and selling the merchandise. See also RETAILING THE INVOICE and LABELS AND LABELING.

markon 1. A term often used synonymously with MARKUP, although certain distinctions can be made between the two. Markon is generally represented as *the target markup, first markup,* or INITIAL MARKUP. It is the difference between the billed cost of merchandise and its original or first retail price, and is expressed as a percentage of the cost price. When freight charges are known, they are added to the billed cost when calculating markon.   2. The total amount added to the cost of all merchandise in a department, rather than the amount added to individual items. For a department, a markon planned on a seasonal and/or annual basis can be expressed either in dollars or as a percentage. When calculated for individual items, it is more commonly called markup.   3. In manufacturing as opposed to retailing, the amount (expressed as a percentage) of markup necessary to achieve a desired profit that covers expenses, reduction, and profits. Also called INITIAL MARKUP or *markup on cost*. It is computed by dividing the difference between the retail price and the cost price by the cost price. MARKUP, on the other hand, is computed by dividing the same difference by the retail price.

markon goal   The desired results of the markon applied to each line of merchandise in the store. These results include: covering expenses; covering transportation costs of merchandise coming into the store; providing for net profit; and inspiring appropriate turnover.

markup   The difference between cost price of merchandise and its retail price, expressed in dollars or as a percentage of either cost price or retail price. Markup is sometimes used synonymously with MARKON, but there are certain distinctions between the two. While markon is computed by dividing the difference between retail and cost price by the cost price, markup is computed by dividing the same difference by the retail price. Also, markup is most commonly used to refer to the amount added to cost price for individual items, while markon more often refers to the total amount added to the cost of all the merchandise in a department. Finally, *markon* is a term more frequently found at the manufacturing level and markup at the merchandising or retail level of the CHANNEL OF DISTRIBUTION. Markup is also called a *percentage cost markup* or a *markup on retail*.

markup cancellation   A reduction in the price of an item after it has been subject to additional markup. Markup cancellation never, by definition, exceeds the amount of additional markup applied to an item. See also ADDITIONAL MARKUP.

markup on cost   Synonym for MARKON.

markup on retail   Synonym for MARKUP.

markup percent/percentage   MARKUP (i.e., a price increase) computed as a percentage of cost price rather than (as is usually the case) of retail price.

markup table   A chart showing markup percentages on both cost price and retail price.

marquee   A canopy or other rooflike construction built over the entrance to a store or other structure to shelter people as well as to provide a place to display the store's name and logo.

mart   Short for MERCHANDISE MART.

masculinity/femininity   See HOFSTEDE MEASURES OF CULTURE.

masking   The process of turning a large DISPLAY WINDOW area into a small SHADOW BOX window. Masking may be achieved by painting the surrounding plate glass with opaque paint or by partially covering the plate glass with panels set against the glass inside the window. A small constructed box can then be set into the opening that remains.

Maslow's Hierarchy (of Needs)   A theory developed by Abraham H. Maslow dividing needs that motivate human behavior into five hierarchical levels. According to Maslow, it is only when one need level is at least partially satisfied that the need at the next level arises. The first two levels of the hierarchy are the need for basic necessities of life such as food, clothing, and shelter and the need for physical safety. Both of these are primarily physical in nature and are called *physiological needs* and *safety needs*. The upper three levels, on the other hand, are psychological. These are the social needs (the need for love, affection, and belonging), esteem needs (the need to enhance one's sense of personal worth), and self-actualization needs (the need to become fully developed as a human being). Maslow's Hierarchy provides retailers and other marketers with a key to the design and marketing of products. Certain goods and services can be successfully marketed only in societies that have met their members' physical needs, leaving individuals free to concentrate on psychological needs. Marketing to subsistence farmers using advertising messages geared to enhance one's sense of self-esteem, for example, would be pointless. Sometimes called *Maslow's Hierarchy of Needs*, the *needs/wants hierarchy*, or the *hierarchy of needs*. See also MOTIVE.

mass class   A relatively new class of consumers that reflects the ongoing democratization of luxury. The availability of quality consumer goods and services at ever-decreasing prices has led to mass consumption in which hundreds of millions of global consumers seek goods and services of the best quality and value. This new class represents new markets, new consumers, and new competition for retailers and other marketers. The trend was identified and the term coined by trendwatching.com at www.trendwatching.com.

massclusivity   A trend that reflects the consumer's desire for special treatment in mass situations. This "exclusivity for the masses" includes special in-store coffee lounges or luxurious fitting rooms for members only, as well as similar members-only lounges at airports. The trend was identified and the term coined by trendwatching.com at www.trendwatching.com.

mass communications media   See MEDIA.

mass consumption   A condition in an economy that is a prerequisite for the success of MASS MARKETING. The economy must have a population with enough wealth to purchase the products being marketed, the means to deliver these products to the purchasers, and the desire to buy.

mass customization   1. The process by which consumers customize a semiproduced product within preset limits. This involves customers in the manufacturing process as they provide input about final product design. The process has been used online with products as diverse as cosmetics and computers. Compare MASS MARKETING STRATEGY.   2. The process by which e-tailers and other e-marketers try to personalize the online shopping experience for their customers. See also CUSTOMER RELATIONSHIP MANAGEMENT (CRM).

mass customized products   Semicompleted products to which customers are allowed to make their own adjustments using options and limits set by the manufacturer. See also MASS CUSTOMIZATION.

mass display   A large display of merchandise that is already also on the shelf in the appropriate selling area. The mass display, intended to boost sales of the displayed merchandise, is positioned in a prominent place in the store where the majority of store traffic will walk past it.

mass distribution   Synonym for INTENSIVE DISTRIBUTION.

massed promotion   See MASS PROMOTION.

massed reserves   The reduction of inventories at the retail level while inventories carried by wholesalers are increased. The intent is to lower the total stock carried in the retail store. See also JUST-IN-TIME (JIT).

mass fashion   Styles that have very broad appeal, relatively moderate price, and a high degree of fashion acceptance, particularly among lower social or economic classes. Also called *volume fashion.*

mass market   A broad segment of the market (i.e., a large group of customers) that overlaps and combines many other segments. The mass market does not include everyone, however; each organization selling to the mass market targets a large and widely dispersed but clearly defined group of consumers. Since mass market products are often described as typical or mainstream, people who are average (in terms of size, educational level, income, etc.) are considered mass market customers. Compare NICHE MARKET. See also MASS MARKETING.

mass market customer   See MASS MARKET.

mass marketing   A marketing strategy that targets a large percentage of the relevant population as potential customers for a particular product or service. The size of the market depends on the nature of the product sold and the goals of the company. The insistence on selling many units of a product and making money on volume, rather than selling fewer units and making money on the MARGIN between cost and selling price, was quite revolutionary at first but is a basic principle of mass marketing. The strategy depends for its success on the belief that a product will have a broad appeal. Beginning in the 1880s, visionary mass marketers enabled millions of Americans to purchase previously undreamed-of products and services; early pioneers in mass marketing include George Eastman (Kodak Brownie camera), Henry J. Heinz (pickles, relishes, and beans in cans or jars), and Henry Ford (Model T automobile). In order for mass marketing to succeed, however, the capacity for MASS CONSUMPTION must be present (i.e., the economy must have a population with enough wealth to purchase the products being marketed, the means to deliver these products to the purchasers, and the desire to buy). Compare NICHE MARKETING. See also MASS MARKET.

mass marketing strategy   A marketing strategy that assumes a homogeneous market composed of undifferentiated buyers who will accept standardized products, have the same general preferences as to price and place, and can be reached by the same types of advertising and promotion. Compare MASS CUSTOMIZATION.

mass market line   Synonym for BUDGET LINE.

mass market theory   See HORIZONTAL FLOW THEORY.

mass merchandise   Consumer goods with broad appeal that sell to large numbers of customers at relatively low prices. Compare NICHE PRODUCT.

mass merchandiser   A large-format chain store with broad geographic coverage. Mass merchandisers carry large assortments of general merchandise and are characterized by volume buying, competitive pricing, aggressive expansion, and forward-thinking managements. Large discount stores with broad distribution networks are also referred to as mass merchandisers.

mass merchandising   The retailing, on a very large scale, of goods (largely staples) at prices lower than those commonly found in department and specialty stores. Mass merchandising is characterized by an emphasis on products whose market is not highly segmented; customers who are willing to sacrifice sales assistance and store services in return for lower prices; high volume and a rapid stock turnover rate; and a very highly competitive marketplace. Also called *mass selling.* Compare MICROMERCHANDISING.

mass production   The manufacture of large quantities of the same item of merchandise by workers using machines for production. Mass production, which developed during the Industrial Revolution, has cut prices, made products available to more people, and contributed significantly to the high standard of living in countries where it has been implemented.

mass promotion   Sales promotion activities concentrated at a particular time (e.g., up to and during the Christmas season). Also called *massed promotion.*

mass selling   See MASS MERCHANDISING.

master franchise   In global retailing, an ownership arrangement in which one company buys the rights to sales in a large region of a country, setting up large numbers of individual stores.

master of the youniverse   A consumer trend in which consumers are seen as empowered and better informed than ever before. Such consumers prefer to be in charge, or at least have the illusion of being in charge, of their own destinies. The ONLINE environment has given consumers much of this control in entirely new ways. The trend was identified and the term coined by trendwatching.com at www.trendwatching.com.

masthead   See NAMEPLATE.

matching concept   In accounting, the pairing of costs and revenue in an effort to relate expenses to the income they helped to produce. The process is used to determine a firm's net income for a given period, usually one year.

material requirements planning (MRP)   In manufacturing, a method of inventory control used to get the correct materials to the production site on time and without unnecessary stockpiling. A computer is used to determine when materials are needed, when they should be ordered, and when they should be delivered so that they will not cost too much to store. See also JUST-IN-TIME (JIT) and MATERIALS MANAGEMENT.

materials and parts   Components incorporated into finished manufactured products, generally belonging to one of two classes: COMPONENT MATERIALS (including such raw materials as farm commodities, ores, fiber, and such products as lumber and cement); and component parts (such as electric motors, engine parts, glass windows, etc.) See also COMPONENT PART.

materials handling   The movement of goods within and between physical distribution facilities. Materials handling includes all the activities associated with moving goods within a plant, in and out of warehouses, and to shipping points. It includes moving, packing, storing, and inventorying goods. See also WAREHOUSING.

materials management   In manufacturing, logistic activities concerned with the movement of production materials from their place of origin to the site of manufacture and the movement of semifinished products within the manufacturing facility. See also MATERIAL REQUIREMENTS PLANNING (MRP), JUST-IN-TIME (JIT), and MANUFACTURING RESOURCE PLANNING (MRP II).

maternity clothes   Apparel designed to be worn by pregnant women. The category includes a full range of women's apparel such as dresses, pants, blouses, undergarments, tops, skirts, etc. Maternity dresses, for example, follow the prevalent style trends but are made with more fullness in the front. Similarly, maternity pants are constructed with either a cut-out section at top center front or a section of stretch fabric inserted over the abdomen.

mathematical models   See QUANTITATIVE MATHEMATICAL MODELS OF PROMOTIONAL BUDGETING.

matrix   See MARKET GRID.

matrix buying   See VENDOR MATRIX.

matrix organization   A type of business organization in which the FUNCTIONAL MANAGER is responsible for activities requiring special expertise (e.g., ADVERTISING) for all products, while the PRODUCT MANAGER (the executive responsible for the planning and development of a particular product or product line) or the BRAND MANAGER (an executive responsible for the planning and development of a particular brand) is responsible for marketing the products, brands, or product lines. These roles may sometimes overlap and even conflict.

matured goods   Those physical goods that cannot, by nature, be hurried into their desired shape, look, or state, and thus require a certain amount of patience from consumers. Such products may require customers to wait for days, weeks, months, or even years to fulfill the original purchase goal. Examples include stone-washed, ragged looking jeans and full-grown roof-terrace gardens. When the maturing is done in-house, the seller often charges a premium price. The trend was identified and the term coined by trendwatching.com at www.trendwatching.com.

mature market   See MATURITY STAGE and RETAIL LIFE CYCLE.

mature retail company   1. A large, well-developed retail organization that has the financial ability and the managerial expertise to consider global expansion.   2. An older, well-developed retail organization that has neared the saturation point in its market. As competitors enter the market using the same or similar strategies, growth slows and the store enters the *maturity stage.* See also RETAIL LIFE CYCLE.

maturialism   A consumer trend in which adult consumers, fed up with teen culture dominating everyday life, are pursuing premium, high-quality, or professional-grade goods and services. The trend was identified and the term coined by trendwatching.com at www.trendwatching.com.

maturity stage   1. The stage in the PRODUCT LIFE CYCLE (PLC) in which demand levels off and profits begin to decline. At this stage, levels of competition have increased to the point where a shakeout is taking place in the market. Also known as *competitive stage, mature market,* or *market maturity.* See also MARKET STRETCHING. 2. See MATURE RETAIL COMPANY and RETAIL LIFE CYCLE.

maximizing profit   A method used to calculate a firm's optimum output so that the marginal cost is just less than equal to the marginal revenue. Total cost and total revenue may also be used to calculate the optimum output. Also called the *rule for maximizing profit.* See also PROFIT MAXIMIZATION.

maximum distribution   In a retail audit, the number of outlets that have stocked a particular item since a previous retail audit. See also RETAIL AUDIT.

Mazur Plan   A theory of retail departmentalization in which activities in large stores are divided into four functional groups: merchandising, operations, publicity, and accounting and control. This organization plan was first propounded by Paul Mazur in 1927 and has since been altered in many stores to include a fifth function, personnel management. Some retail organizations have added a sixth function, research and marketing. Also called *four-function plan.*

MBO   See MANAGEMENT BY OBJECTIVES (MBO).

m-commerce   Business conducted on the WORLD WIDE WEB (WWW) using wireless devices such as cell phones or handheld personal digital assistants. See also E-COMMERCE and E-TAILING.

McGuire Act   See MILLER TYDINGS ACT (1937).

McGuire-Keogh Fair Trade Enabling Act (1952)   U.S. federal legislation, no longer in effect, exempting from all antitrust laws any interstate contract fixing retail prices in states where intrastate contracts are allowed. This exemption was confined to products in open competition. The act permitted the imposition of the NONSIGNER'S CLAUSE. See also FAIR TRADE ACTS/LAWS.

MD   See MARKDOWN (MD).

measures of productivity   See PRODUCTIVITY MEASURES.

Meat Inspection Act (1906)   Early consumer legislation providing for the enforcement of sanitary regulation in the meatpacking industry. The act was updated by the WHOLESOME MEAT ACT (1967) (requiring states to have inspection programs equal to that of the federal government), the *Texas Meat and Poultry Act (1969),* and the *Talmadge-Aiken Agreement* (relating to plants staffed by state employees but federally inspected). The *Curtis Amendment* exempts the custom slaughter of farm animals for farmers and game animals for hunters. The *Farmer's Exemption* excludes meat to be used by the farmer for his own use, for his family, and for his non-paying guests. The Federal Meat Inspection Act is administered by the FOOD SAFETY AND INSPECTION SERVICE (FSIS).

mechanical   In advertising, the final format of an ad, also known as a *paste-up.* The mechanical is prepared after all the decisions regarding layout, copy, use of logos, and artwork have been made and the roughs have been tested. It shows the format of the art, copy, and logo in its presentation layout, with the copy text converted into the desired typeface. The mechanical is considered CAMERA-READY (CR). No additional changes are made to camera-ready mechanicals.

media   1. In computer use, objects such as hard and floppy disks, CD-ROMs, etc., on which data can be stored.   2. In computer networks, cables linking workstations.   3. The forms and technologies used to communicate information (e.g., sound, pictures, and videos).   4. Specifically, in a marketing context, all the means used to convey marketing information, traditionally including television and radio (*broadcast media*), newspapers and magazines (*print media*), direct mail material, and displays such as billboards and posters. The media are also channels of communication for news, entertainment, and other messages. Internet and computer-related media are often referred to as *new media* or *electronic media.* See also ADVERTISING MEDIA and POSITION MEDIA.

media advertising   See ADVERTISING and MEDIA.

media buyer   The executive in charge of placing advertising who must weigh the pros and cons of each medium in relation to the store's advertising budget. See also PROMOTIONAL BUDGETING.

media buying service   An organization of media specialists that buys blocks of advertising time and space on behalf of a group of businesses. Media buying services thus wield a considerable amount of power and leverage. The use of a media buying service may make media buying more cost-effective for retailers.

media coverage   Synonym for REACH.

media department   See ADVERTISING AGENCY.

media division   The part of an ADVERTISING AGENCY that analyzes, selects, and contracts for space or time in the media in order to deliver the client's message.

media mix   The specific configuration of MEDIA chosen by an ADVERTISER for an ADVERTISING CAMPAIGN.

media organization   A provider of information and entertainment to subscribers, viewers, and readers (e.g., a newspaper, television network, or magazine). Media organizations are major participants in the advertising and promotion process by providing the mechanism for communication and distribution of advertising messages to large audiences. See also MEDIA and MEDIA REPRESENTATIVE.

media representative   An individual who sells space in a newspaper, magazine, or out-of-home media (such as a billboard), time on television or radio, or space on the Internet to carry the advertiser's broadcast message to the consumer. See also MEDIA and MEDIA ORGANIZATION.

media research   ADVERTISING RESEARCH that attempts to determine the size of advertising outlets and their ability to attract target audiences. Specific advertising media are evaluated by a number of targeted media measurement organizations.

mediation   The process of acting as an intermediary to help settle a dispute between parties. For example, a labor union and a company may use mediation to help settle contract disputes. Similarly, human resources managers may employ mediation to settle employee grievances. Mediation is not binding. Compare ARBITRATION. See also MEDIATOR.

mediator   In labor or contractual negotiations or in human resources grievance proceedings, an impartial evaluator hired to listen to both sides of a conflict and suggest solutions. Mediators are generally well-respected community leaders. Mediated decisions, however, are not binding. Compare ARBITRATOR. See also MEDIATION.

meeting competition   See PRICING AT THE MARKET.

megabrand   An internationally recognized BRAND, sold globally. A megabrand arises from the addition of related products to an existing line of branded products or the development of a new product line with the same brand identity (i.e., a BRAND EXTENSION STRATEGY). It encompasses several related merchandise categories (for example, dresses, accessories, shoes, and sportswear).

megabyte   See BYTE.

megamall   A MALL of well over one million square feet, drawing from a TRADING AREA of over 100 miles and, in some cases, several states or provinces. A megamall houses 400–800 stores, service businesses, restaurants, and entertainment facilities. Extensive acreage and tremendous draw is required to support a megamall. Examples of megamalls include the Mall of America in Bloomington, Minnesota, Palisades Center in West Nyack, New York, and the West Edmonton Mall in Alberta, Canada. See also VALUE MEGAMALL.

megamarketing   According to Philip Kotler of the Kellogg Graduate School of Management, Northwestern University, "the strategically coordinated application of economic, psychological, political, and public relations skills to gain the cooperation of a number of parties in order to enter and/or operate in a given market." Kotler thus added power and public relations to the FOUR PS OF THE MARKETING MIX.

MegaPanel   See HOMESCAN MEGAPANEL.

megaselling   The selling of large quantities of merchandise for considerable sums of money. Also called *big-ticket selling*.

megastore   An unusually large CATEGORY KILLER or specialty store. Also called a SUPERSTORE.

Me Generation   A consumer lifestyle that focuses on being good to oneself. Members of the so-called Me Generation are often seen as shallow, self-involved, and selfish. In the United States, the term is generally applied to adults who came of age in the 1980s. In the business arena, the period was characterized by hostile takeovers, leveraged buyouts, and megamergers. On the consumer front, the 1980s were characterized by binge buying, credit overextension, and the slogan, "shop till you drop." See also BABY BOOMERS.

member-get-member promotion   A sales promotion method used to bring in new customers by giving an incentive to current customers who make referrals. Compare FRIEND-OF-A-FRIEND PROMOTION.

membership club   Synonym for CLOSED-DOOR DISCOUNT HOUSE.

membership group   A REFERENCE GROUP to which an individual actually belongs and with which he or she interacts and identifies. The group may be primary (e.g., family, neighbors, friends, co-workers) or it may be secondary (e.g., voluntary associations, clubs, athletic teams, trade unions, religious organizations). See also REFERENCE GROUP, DISSOCIATIVE GROUP, PRIMARY GROUP, and ASPIRATIONAL GROUP.

membership warehouse club   Synonym for WAREHOUSE CLUB.

members-only outlet   Synonym for CLOSED-DOOR DISCOUNT HOUSE.

memorandum buying   An arrangement between a vendor and a retailer in which the retailer buys merchandise from the vendor and, while taking title to the goods, retains the right to return to the vendor merchandise unsold over a specified period of time. The retailer may also have the right to pay for the goods as they are sold, rather than on receipt, for an indefinite period of time. Also called *round trip*, *buying on memorandum*, and *on memorandum buying*. The term is used in conjunction with CONSIGNMENT sales as well as sales with a RETURN PRIVILEGE. See also SELLING AID .

memorandum sale   The sale in a retail store of *consigned goods*. Title to the goods remains with the vendor for a stated period. At the end of the period, unsold items are eligible for return to the vendor and only the sold goods are billed to the merchant. See also CONSIGNMENT.

men's   See MENSWEAR.

men's furnishings   See MENSWEAR.

men's wear   Alternative spelling of MENSWEAR.

menswear   1. Apparel and accessories for men. Also called *men's furnishings*. Also spelled *men's wear*.   2. A type of cloth (especially wool) used to make men's and women's tailored apparel.

menu   A list of functions or submenus in a computer application or links to other pages on a Web site. A menu may take the form of a *pulldown, rollover, pop-up,* or other format. On a Web site, a menu functions as a categorized SITE MAP and helps the user access desired information. In an application, menus provide convenient access to various operations such as saving or opening a file, quitting the program, or manipulating data. A *pulldown menu* is the type commonly used in menu bars located near the top of the window or screen, and usually lists operations. A *pop-up menu* is more likely to be used for setting a value; it may appear anywhere in a window.

mercantile credit   Credit at the trade level (i.e., credit extended by manufacturers or wholesalers to other channel members such as retailers). Such credit avoids the need for COD shipments or for limiting business to a CASH-AND-CARRY basis.

mercantile customer   See MARKETING INTERMEDIARY.

mercerization   A finishing process in which caustic soda is applied to cotton yarn, fabric, or thread. Mercerization increases the luster, strength, and dyeability of the fabric. The process is named for its originator, John Mercer, who introduced the process in England in 1844.

merchandise   1. n. Usually, manufactured goods for sale. The term is sometimes applied to commodities as well.   2. v. To buy and sell, carry on trade, or promote one's goods (e.g., to merchandise a line).

merchandise acceptance curve   Synonym for PRODUCT LIFE CYCLE (PLC).

merchandise adjustment   Synonym for ADJUSTMENT.

merchandise agent   Synonym for BROKER.

merchandise allowance   See RETURNS AND ALLOWANCES TO CUSTOMERS.

merchandise assortment   See ASSORTMENT.

merchandise-broker office   See COMMISSION BUYING OFFICE.

merchandise budget   A management financial plan in which an attempt is made to anticipate merchandise needs over a specific period of time (in retailing, often one season). The plan is expressed in dollars rather than units and may cover a single department or the entire store.

merchandise buying   See BUYING.

merchandise category   See CLASSIFICATION.

merchandise certificate   See CREDIT SLIP.

merchandise charge   Extraneous COSTS (e.g., shipping, insurance, demurrage) added to the cost of goods prior to calculating the MARKON.

merchandise checking   See CHECKING.

merchandise classification   See CLASSIFICATION.

merchandise control   The maintenance of a stock of merchandise that is adjusted to the needs of existing and prospective customers. Merchandise control takes two forms, *dollar control* and *unit control*, with each providing accurate information to management as to whether plans are being realized and to what extent changes might be in order. The type of *merchandise control system* that a retail store uses depends on the type and size of the business, kind and amount of data required, methods employed by the store's competition, and the store's own business objectives. See also DOLLAR INVENTORY CONTROL and UNIT INVENTORY CONTROL.

merchandise cost   Synonym for COST OF GOODS SOLD.

merchandise coverage   The amount of MERCHANDISE that must be kept in INVENTORY to meet basic customer DEMAND.

merchandise deal   A type of promotional service offered by a vendor to client stores. Extra goods are given free by the vendor if the store's buyer orders in quantity or performs a promotional service. For example, a buyer for stationery may be offered two dozen pencils free with an order of ten dozen boxes of writing paper.

merchandise deliverer   See TRUCK WHOLESALER.

merchandise department   A grouping of related merchandise for which separate expense and merchandising records are kept in order to determine the profitability of this grouping. The use of merchandise departments is not merely a physical segregation, but also an accounting separation. See also DEPARTMENT.

merchandise dissection   See CLASSIFICATION.

merchandise distributor   See TRUCK WHOLESALER.

merchandise division   See MERCHANDISING DIVISION.

merchandise-driven event   See MERCHANDISE EVENT.

merchandise-driven pricing   Any PRICING STRATEGY used by a retailer that puts merchandise policies at the center of pricing decisions. VALUE PRICING and PRICE LINING (METHOD) are two examples of merchandise-driven pricing techniques.

merchandise event   Any planned promotion or sales event designed to directly influence the sale of goods. Merchandise events are designed to sell large quantities of products in a short time while reaching specifically targeted market segments, enhancing customer relations, or promoting a charitable cause. Also called a *merchandise-driven event*.

merchandise-feature advertising   ADVERTISING in which the emphasis is on the current availability of merchandise being offered at regular prices. This stands in contrast to PRICE-FEATURE ADVERTISING in which reduced prices are the focus of the ADVERTISEMENT.

merchandise handled   A measure of the amount of merchandise moved in a given period. It is computed by adding the purchases for the period to the INVENTORY (i.e., stock on hand) at the beginning of the period. Merchandise handled may be calculated at either cost price or retail price.

merchandise inventory   Products held by marketing intermediaries with the intent of resale to customers. See also STOCK and INVENTORY.

merchandise island   See ISLAND DISPLAY.

merchandise life cycle   Synonym for PRODUCT LIFE CYCLE (PLC). Also called *merchandising life cycle*.

merchandise line consistency   See ASSORTMENT CONSISTENCY.

merchandise line depth   See ASSORTMENT DEPTH.

merchandise line width   See ASSORTMENT BREADTH.

merchandise loan   An item temporarily transferred to another department for use in a DISPLAY or for some other purpose. See also MERCHANDISE LOAN BOOK and LOAN SLIP.

merchandise loan book   A book in which merchandise loaned to other departments (e.g., for use in a DISPLAY), is recorded. This record-keeping is important for purposes of INVENTORY. See also LOAN SLIP.

merchandise loan slip   See LOAN SLIP.

merchandise management   An activity closely related to MERCHANDISING and primarily concerned with inventory balance and composition. However, buying, pricing, and selling are also important components. See also ASSORTMENT and MERCHANDISE MANAGER.

merchandise manager   The executive responsible, under the DIVISIONAL MERCHANDISE MANAGER (DMM), for all of the MERCHANDISING activities of one or more selling departments or divisions. In some organizations, the position is synonymous with that of divisional merchandise manager. Also called a *store merchandise manager*.

merchandise mart   1. A facility in which exhibition space is rented on a permanent basis to manufacturers and wholesalers so that they may display their products to potential customers (usually distributors and retailers, not the general public). Merchandise marts are often devoted to a particular line of products such as apparel or furniture and are designed to be one-stop shopping venues for retail buyers. Examples of merchandise marts include Chicago's Merchandise Mart, the Atlanta Apparel Mart, the International Menswear Mart, and the International Apparel Mart.   2. The name of the oldest merchandise mart in the United States. Chicago's Merchandise Mart was built by Marshall Field & Co. in 1930. Sixty percent of the building's area is devoted to wholesale showrooms. The Merchandise Mart also hosts major trade shows, conferences, seminars, and special events, and maintains a Web site at www.merchandisemart.com.

merchandise mix   See ASSORTMENT BREADTH.

merchandise orientation   In RETAIL PRODUCT ADVERTISING, advertisements that involve a definitive classification of merchandise. The classifications give a clear picture of the intention of the advertisement. Merchandise orientation in retail product advertising includes the SINGLE ITEM ADVERTISEMENT, the ASSORTMENT ADVERTISEMENT, the RELATED ITEMS ADVERTISEMENT, the VENDOR ADVERTISEMENT, the THEME ADVERTISEMENT, the DEPARTMENTAL ADVERTISEMENT, and the VOLUME ADVERTISEMENT.

merchandise overage   See STOCK OVERAGE.

merchandise plan   A projection, in dollars, of the sales goals of the store or department over a specified period (usually six months). The merchandise plan enables the retail buyer to determine how much money can be used to purchase goods and helps top management judge the effectiveness of prior merchandising decisions. Merchandise plans may be developed through either top-down or bottom-up planning. The plan normally conforms to two distinct selling seasons: spring-summer (February–July) and fall-winter (August–January). This allows the store the opportunity for clearance sales at the end of the summer and Christmas seasons before making plans for additional purchases. Most merchandise plans contain some combination of the following components: initial markup for the period; planned net sales; planned beginning of month inventory; planned end of month inventory; planned reductions, planned purchases at retail; and planned purchases at cost. With the exception of planned purchases at cost, all amounts on the merchandise plan are entered as retail values. Frequently called the *six-month merchandise plan* or the *six-month merchandising plan*. See also PLAN PURCHASE, SALES PLAN, BUYING PLAN, and FORECAST-BASED MERCHANDISE PLAN.

merchandise planning   The development of a strategy at the management level that will determine what merchandise to stock. Involved are considerations of consumer demand, budget limitations, and the formulation of a precise MERCHANDISE PLAN.

merchandiser   1. A DISPLAY unit that holds items to be sold on the floor of the store. See also FIXTURE.   2. A synonym for MERCHANT.

merchandise replenishment   The process of planning and placing reorders. Merchandise replenishment also includes handling, shipping, receiving, distributing (if necessary), and displaying the merchandise. See also MULTIPLE DELIVERY STRATEGY, QUICK RESPONSE (QR) REPLENISHMENT SYSTEM, and MERCHANDISE REPLENISHMENT MODEL.

merchandise replenishment model   A model of replenishment for manufacturing firms (particularly apparel manufacturers) selling to retailers and other marketing intermediaries. The model centers on the interaction of QUICK RESPONSE (QR), merchandising, operations, marketing, finance, and executive management to satisfy target customers' (e.g., stores') needs for merchandise within the limitations of the firm. See also MERCHANDISE REPLENISHMENT, MULTIPLE DELIVERY STRATEGY, and QUICK RESPONSE (QR) REPLENISHMENT SYSTEM.

merchandise replenishment system   A process or procedure used by retailers to determine what merchandise is available to buy at any particular point in time. The system is based on the underlying belief that complete assortments prevent stockouts and thus increase sales. Merchandise replenishment systems rely on a QUICK RESPONSE (QR) REPLENISHMENT SYSTEM and a MULTIPLE DELIVERY STRATEGY to fulfill orders for merchandise and to handle, ship, receive, distribute, and display that merchandise.

merchandise replenishment technology   Operating procedures that use information technology to automate manual activities, eliminate redundancies in operating procedures, reassign tasks for maximum supply chain efficiency, and reduce or eliminate control steps in operating procedures. The use of technology is intended to speed and improve the transmission of customer preferences back to all members of the supply chain. For both manufacturers and retailers, it is designed to expedite the process of converting raw materials into finished products and of getting them to the shelves. See also QUICK RESPONSE (QR) REPLENISHMENT SYSTEM and MERCHANDISE REPLENISHMENT SYSTEM.

merchandise resource   Synonym for VENDOR.

merchandise scrambling   See SCRAMBLED MERCHANDISE and SCRAMBLED MERCHANDISING.

merchandise shortage   See STOCK SHORTAGE.

merchandise source   Synonym for VENDOR.

merchandise space   In a store, all areas in which merchandise is stored (i.e., stockroom, behind counters, etc.).

merchandise transfer   The movement of merchandise within the retail organization from one accounting area to another. This movement is not recorded as a sale.

merchandise turnover   Synonym for STOCK TURNOVER (ST).

merchandise vending machine operator   Synonym for VENDING MACHINE OPERATOR.

merchandising   According to the American Marketing Association, "the planning involved in marketing the right merchandise at the right place at the right time in the right quantities at the right price." More specifically, merchandising is the buying and selling of appropriate goods coupled with the accurate targeting of consumers for the ultimate purpose of making a profit. It includes all activities connected with the buying and selling of merchandise, including display, promotion, pricing, and buying. See also MERCHANDISE MANAGEMENT and RETAIL MERCHANDISING.

merchandising accounting   See ACCOUNTING.

merchandising allowance   A reduction in the wholesale price of goods to compensate retailers for expenses incurred in promoting the goods. See also PROMOTIONAL ALLOWANCE.

Merchandising and Operating Results of Department and Specialty Stores (MOR)   An annual statistical study published until 1998 by the NATIONAL RETAIL FEDERATION (NRF), containing detailed information on the performance of the retail industry. Data was provided voluntarily by members of the NRF (and earlier, by the NRMA) and presented by store type and size, then by department and merchandise classification. Individual store results were not identified, only averages for all stores in a particular store category. The performance of all similar stores was used as a standard or benchmark against which to measure the performance of an individual store. The MOR constituted a listing of INDUSTRY STANDARDS for main-

tained markup, markdowns, shortage, gross margin, and turnover, compiled by merchandise category and sales volume. The MOR and FOR have ceased publication, but have been replaced at least in part by RETAIL HORIZONS.

merchandising conglomerate   A CORPORATION or CONGLOMERATE composed of a number of diversified retailing organizations under unified management. Stores may be of various types, including department, specialty, and discount stores. Sometimes referred to as a *conglomerchant* or a *retail conglomerate*.

merchandising control   See CONTROL STANDARD.

merchandising division   In large retail store organization, one of the functional areas responsible for planning, locating, buying, and selling merchandise, supervision of sales people, etc. It is considered the most essential division of the organization. Sometimes called the *merchandise division*. Its head is the VICE PRESIDENT (VP) OF MERCHANDISING or the GENERAL MERCHANDISE MANAGER (GMM).

merchandising group   Several members of a retail cooperative chain that join forces under a common name to facilitate their advertising and promotion efforts. See also RETAIL COOPERATIVE/CO-OP.

merchandising leader   A store that promotes several items at attractive prices for the purpose of building store TRAFFIC.

merchandising life cycle   Synonym for PRODUCT LIFE CYCLE (PLC).

merchandising salesperson   Synonym for MISSIONARY (SALESPERSON).

merchandising service   Assistance provided by one of the communications media for the placing of copy, advertising, commercials, layouts, etc. This service is often provided without charge to advertisers.

merchant   A MARKETING INTERMEDIARY who takes title to the goods bought and sold and who, in turn, resells them. Most merchants are wholesalers or retailers and are variously known as traders, distributors, dealers, storekeepers, merchandisers, shopkeepers, etc.

merchant intermediary   Synonym for WHOLESALING MIDDLEMAN.

merchantism   The theory, practice, and ethical credo of merchants. Merchantism includes the responsibility of merchants to customers, appropriate customer service, merchandise awareness, and knowledge of the goods.

merchant middleman/middleperson   See MIDDLEMAN and WHOLESALING MIDDLEMAN.

merchant review   On the Web, customer evaluations of the products and services they've purchased and their experiences in dealing with particular e-tailers. Consumers self-select to provide their written opinions, ranging from simple yes or no responses to extended written summaries of product use and merchant reliability. Also called, simply, a *review*.

merchant wholesaler An independently owned WHOLE-SALER that takes title to merchandise and then resells it to retailers or industrial or institutional users. Some merchant wholesalers provide a wide variety of services to their customers (e.g., storage, delivery, and marketing support). A RACK JOBBER is a form of merchant wholesaler. Also called an *independent wholesaler*.

mercury vapor lamp See HIGH-INTENSITY DISCHARGE (HID) LIGHTING.

merger The combination of two or more companies in which the old companies cease to exist and a new enterprise is created. In a merger, the two companies pool their interests. A HORIZONTAL MERGER involves the combination of competing companies performing the same function, such as two department stores. A VERTICAL MERGER involves companies in different phases of the same business, such as a manufacturer of children's toys and a retailer of children's toys. The aim of a vertical merger is often to guarantee access to supplies or markets. A CONGLOMERATE MERGER is one in which a corporation acquires strings of unrelated businesses in an effort to augment growth and diversify risk.

merit goods Items whose consumption the government determines or heavily influences through legislation and public policy. Individuals are not considered qualified to make the choices for themselves. These include such items as education, automobile safety equipment, etc.

MESBIC See MINORITY ENTERPRISE SMALL BUSINESS INVESTMENT COMPANY (MESBIC).

message Words (written or oral) and other symbols that constitute an intelligible communication. In marketing, messages are used to promote products and are frequently transmitted through the MEDIA (i.e., radio, television, newspapers, magazines, etc.). Messages are decoded by the receiver and either acted on immediately or stored in the receiver's memory for later use. Also called a *promotional message* or a *promo*. See also ADVERTISING MESSAGE.

message board Synonym for INTERNET DISCUSSION GROUP.

message research ADVERTISING RESEARCH evaluating the effectiveness of the creative message in advertising, from copy and ingenuity to the visual impact of the advertisement. Also called *copy research* or *copy testing*.

metal halide lamp See HIGH-INTENSITY DISCHARGE (HID) LIGHTING.

metamarket A Web site cluster of activities and vendors that consumers perceive to be related and complementary. Metamarkets provide advice and links for users seeking their serv-

ices. For example, the WeddingChannel.com is a site where visitors can find everything they might want for a wedding. See also METAMARKET INTERMEDIARY.

municipal market See PUBLIC MARKET.

metamarket intermediary A Web site that offers advice and links for users seeking a particular service or category of services, including links to related and complementary vendors. For example, WeddingChannel.com provides links to retailers offering bridal registry services, travel services, gowns, and everything associated with getting married. Metamarket intermediaries are virtual one-stop shops for all things relating to the topic of the site. Also called a *metamediary*. See also METAMARKET.

metamediary Synonym for METAMARKET INTERMEDIARY.

metaresearch SECONDARY RESEARCH comparing the results of large numbers of other studies.

metatag Two or more lines of code in HYPERTEXT MARKUP LANGUAGE (HTML) describing Web page contents. Information in a metatag is used by search engines to index a page so someone searching for that information can find it. The most important metatags for search engine indexing are keywords (the words or phrases that best describe page content) and description (a one- or two-sentence description of the page).

metered Internet access An arrangement between an INTERNET SERVICE PROVIDER (ISP) and an Internet user in which the user pays access charges calculated per minute online. See also FLAT RATE INTERNET ACCESS PRICING.

metroarea See METROMARKET.

metromarket The area from which a retail store draws most of its customers. The term most frequently refers to the inner city and its suburbs. Also called a *metroarea*.

metropolitan area (MA) Formerly, a collective U.S. Census term for METROPOLITAN STATISTICAL AREAS (MSAS), CONSOLIDATED METROPOLITAN STATISTICAL AREAS (CMSAS), and PRIMARY STATISTICAL AREAS (PMSAS). In 2000 it was replaced by the umbrella term CORE-BASED STATISTICAL AREA (CBSA).

metropolitan-area network (MAN) See COMPUTER NETWORK.

metropolitan division Under the 2000 Office of Management and Budget (OMB) standards, a smaller grouping within a METROPOLITAN STATISTICAL AREA (MSA) meeting specified criteria, (i.e., containing a single core with a population of 2.5 million or more). Titles of metropolitan divisions are typically based on principal city names, but in certain cases they consist of county names.

metropolitan statistical area (MSA) Under the standards established in 2000, a freestanding metropolitan area similar to the old standard metropolitan statistical area (SMSA), containing an urbanized area of at least 50,000 inhabitants. As of

June 6, 2000, there are 362 metropolitan statistical areas (MSAs) in the United States and 8 in Puerto Rico. The title of each metropolitan or micropolitan statistical area consists of the names of up to three of its principal cities and the name of each state into which the metropolitan or micropolitan statistical area extends.

MFA   See MULTIFIBER ARRANGEMENT (MFA).

MFN   See MOST FAVORED NATION (MFN) STATUS.

microanalytic sales model   A way of representing the sales process on the micro level by identifying all sales as the number of purchasers within the market, the percentage who purchase from the company, and the average rate of buying. See also MICROBEHAVIORAL SALES MODEL and MICROCOMPONENT SALES MODEL.

microbehavioral sales model   An analysis of the sales process on the micro level in which the individual customer's knowledge, attitudes, actions toward products, and environmental variables are carefully studied and used to predict the probability of a purchase. See also MICROANALYTIC SALES MODEL and MICROCOMPONENT SALES MODEL.

microcomponent sales model   An analysis of sales on the micro level in which each sale is separated into its smallest component variables. These variables may include sales by item, sales by customer, or sales by individual salesperson. The data are studied to identify performance and trends. See also MICROBEHAVIORAL SALES MODEL and MICROANALYTIC SALES MODEL.

microcomputer   The smallest and least expensive category of computer. Also known as a PERSONAL COMPUTER (PC).

microenvironment   See MARKETING ENVIRONMENT.

microindicator (of market size)   Any of a number of variables usually indicating potential market size for a company's product, particularly in a foreign market, on the basis of current consumption of that product or similar products. Microindicators include the number of radios, televisions, cinema seats, scientists and engineers, hospital beds, physicians, hotel beds, telephones, tourist arrivals, passenger cars, civil airline passengers, and farms present in the country's economy. Other indicators include the consumption of alcohol, coffee, gasoline, and electricity; the production of steel and rice; and the amount of land under cultivation. For example, the number of television sets can indicate the potential market for new television sets. Also *called microindicator of market size*. Compare MACROINDICATOR (OF MARKET SIZE).

micro-macro dilemma   In economics, the realization that what is beneficial for some producers and consumers may not necessarily benefit society as a whole. See also MICROMARKETING and MACROMARKETING.

micromarketing environment   See MARKETING ENVIRONMENT.

micromarketing   MARKETING as seen from its narrow perspective (i.e., at the level of individual sellers and buyers). See also MICRO-MACRO DILEMMA and MACROMARKETING.

micromarketing environment   See MARKETING ENVIRONMENT.

micromerchandising   The practice of creating and manufacturing product lines or items targeted to a specific market. Micromerchandising is a technique retailers use to counter mass merchandised assortments. They do so by tailoring an individual store's product mix to the local market based on the store's database of customer purchase history and knowledge of local tastes and demographics. Micromerchandising allows retailers to tailor products to specific interest groups in different parts of the country, personalize assortments, and increase sales. It is intended to improve SELL-THROUGH and TURNOVER as well as build customer loyalty. See also MARKET SEGMENTATION. Compare MASS MERCHANDISING.

micropayment   An online virtual cash system that allows consumers to make extremely small payments (e.g., $5 or fewer). Content providers may use the micropayment system to charge visitors for accessing such site features as games, maps, photo sharing, etc., particularly from wireless devices (such as cell phones).

micropolitan statistical area   Under the standards adopted in 2000, an area having at least one urban cluster of at least 10,000 but less than 50,000 population. As of June 6, 2000, there are 560 micropolitan statistical areas in the United States and 5 in Puerto Rico. The title of each metropolitan or micropolitan statistical area consists of the names of up to three of its principal cities and the name of each state into which the metropolitan or micropolitan statistical area extends.

microsegmentation   A market segmentation strategy employed by industrial marketing firms in which the market potential for products or services is established by gathering detailed information about the characteristics of potential customers, often through the personal experience of salespeople.

Microsoft Network (MSN)   One of the leading U.S. online service providers, a competitor of America Online (AOL). MSN may be accessed at www.msn.com.

MidAmerica Commodity Exchange   See COMMODITY EXCHANGE.

middle class   See SOCIAL CLASS.

middleman   An individual or firm acting as a MARKETING INTERMEDIARY between producers and manufacturers on the one hand and the end user on the other. The individual or firm may be a WHOLESALING MIDDLEMAN (e.g., WHOLESALER, AGENT, AGENT INTERMEDIARY, or BROKER) or a RETAILER. Middlemen perform a number of functions facilitating the transfer of goods in the CHANNEL OF DISTRIBUTION. Also called a *merchant middleman* and a *marketing middleman*.

middleman brand   See PRIVATE BRAND.

middle of month (MOM) dating In the dating of invoices, an agreement indicating that cash discount and net credit periods begin in the middle of the month. For example, all invoices dated through the 15th of the month are due by the 25th of the month if the terms include a 10-day discount period. The discount is available from the 15th of the month through the 25th.

midget market Synonym for CONVENIENCE STORE. See also BANTAM STORE.

MIDP (marketing information and decision program) See MARKETING INFORMATION SYSTEM (MIS).

Midwest Stock Exchange See STOCK EXCHANGE.

milking A strategy in which a company prices an established product above the level that would ordinarily be justified by production costs and competitive conditions in the marketplace. Companies employing this strategy are cashing in on consumer BRAND LOYALTY in an effort to increase short-term profits. Also called *harvesting*.

millennials Synonym for GENERATION Y or ECHO BOOMERS.

Miller-Tydings Act (1937) U.S. federal enabling legislation that permitted states to enact *fair trade* or RESALE PRICE MAINTENANCE (RPM) laws. The intent of the act was to insulate small, independent retailers from price competition with large chains that paid lower wholesale prices because of quantity discounts. The act was declared unconstitutional by the U.S. Supreme Court in 1951. See also RESALE PRICE MAINTENANCE (RPM).

milling in transit Synonym for TRANSIT PRIVILEGES.

mill store Older term for FACTORY OUTLET.

mill supply house See INDUSTRIAL DISTRIBUTOR.

MIME An encoding scheme for e-mail attachments. See also ATTACHMENT.

miniature fashion Synonym for FAD.

minimarket test A method of testing the market for a NEW PRODUCT in a very small, controlled way. The product is placed in a small number of outlets, but not sold and only minimally promoted. Minimarket testing ascertains interest in the new product and is preliminary to a larger promotional campaign.

mini-metropolis A planned suburban community in a high-growth, densely populated area. Also called *edge cities*, mini-metropolises have sprung up along interstate highways within the shadows of major urban cores.

minimovies Very short movielike ads filmed specifically for showing on the INTERNET. See also WEBCAST AD.

minimum 1. The lowest amount possible, allowable, or permissible. For example, a supermarket may provide free delivery for a certain minimum dollar amount of merchandise. 2. The admission charge for fashion showings; it may subsequently be applied to purchases. See also CAUTION/CAUTION FEE.

minimum advertised price (MAP) The lowest price at which a retailer will be permitted by a manufacturer or producer to sell the goods featured in COOPERATIVE ADVERTISING. Producers structure their cooperative advertisement agreements to make retailers that sell below the MAP ineligible for cooperative advertising dollars.

minimum markup law Local legislation passed in some states to protect the small retailer from being undersold by larger retail organizations. Minimum markup laws provide that all goods must be marked up a predetermined minimum percentage, except in the case of legitimate clearance sale merchandise. Also called a *sales below cost law*. See also UNFAIR TRADE PRACTICES ACTS.

minimum order The smallest possible order a resource will allow a buyer to place. This is used by buyers whose strategy is to buy in small quantities only those goods they can sell within a short period of time. Minimum orders are costly for manufacturers to handle and some vendors charge extra in order to discourage the practice. The strategy has been known to cause friction between vendors and buyers.

minimum order requirement A dollar or unit amount that defines the smallest order a VENDOR is willing to accept from a retail BUYER.

minimum stock The lowest level of merchandise in inventory that can be reached before a STOCKOUT is likely.

minimum total transactions The use of the fewest intermediaries possible in the CHANNEL OF DISTRIBUTION in order to keep prices low and speed merchandise to the ultimate consumer. Also called the *principle of minimum total transactions*.

Minimum Wage Law See FAIR LABOR STANDARDS ACT (FLSA) (1938).

mining See DATA MINING.

minipreneur A trend in which consumers actively participate in the marketplace instead of merely being passive members of it. These consumers-turned-entrepreneurs include small and micro businesses, freelancers, side-businesses, weekend entrepreneurs, Web-driven entrepreneurs, part-timers, free agents, cottage businesses, seniorpreneurs, co-creators, mompreneurs, eBay traders, etc. Many of these small businesses are INTERNET and home-based. The trend was identified and the term coined by trendwatching.com at www.trendwatching.com.

ministry of trade A government office that assists businesses with importing and exporting.

miniwarehouse mall A SHOPPING CENTER housed in a large warehouse. The warehouse provides space to a variety of sellers, including both retailers and wholesalers.

Minneapolis Grain Exchange See COMMODITY EXCHANGE.

minor fashion Synonym for FAD.

minor innovation See INNOVATION.

minority enterprise small business investment company (MESBIC) A federally licensed, shareholder-owned investment company that provides equity capital to minority-owned small businesses. Acting through the SMALL BUSINESS ADMINISTRATION (SBA), these companies borrow money at reduced rates to put into new ventures. A MESBIC is similar in operation to a VENTURE CAPITALIST firm, although tending to make smaller investments and willing to consider less glamorous businesses. See also SMALL BUSINESS INVESTMENT COMPANY (SBIC).

mint In original, unused condition, as newly made. The term is frequently used in auctions, both online and offline.

mirror principle An approach to sales based on the principle that customers will respond in the same way they are treated. Distinguished from MIRROR RESPONSE TECHNIQUE.

mirror response technique A sales technique in which the SALESPERSON responds to the customer's objections to a product or service by repeating what the customer is understood to have said. The method is intended to help the prospective customer reconsider the stated objection. Also called the *repeating technique.* Distinguished from MIRROR PRINCIPLE.

MIS See MARKETING INFORMATION SYSTEM (MIS) or MANAGEMENT INFORMATION SYSTEM (MIS).

misdirected (marketing) effort A marketing program or campaign based on incomplete, inconclusive, incorrect, or misleading DATA. A misdirected marketing effort is often the result of management's inability to calculate marketing costs accurately. See also MISMARKETING.

mismarketing A failed marketing effort generally resulting from faulty information and poor decision making. See also MISDIRECTED (MARKETING) EFFORT.

misredemption Error or fraud occurring in the redemption of manufacturer coupons.

misses (sizes) Size ranges in women's apparel in even numbers from 4 or 6 through 16 or 18. Also called *missy.*

mission The overall purpose of an organization. See also MISSION STATEMENT.

missionary (salesperson) A manufacturer's representative who assists the customers of the manufacturing firm (usually wholesalers and retailers) by demonstrating the manufacturer's products, arranging displays, planning advertising programs and other promotions, etc. The missionary salesperson does not usually engage directly in selling activities. Also called, simply, a *missionary, merchandising salesperson, detail person,* or *detailer.*

mission identity A company as perceived by its customers in terms of its goals. Sometimes referred to as *company image,* mission identity is more accurately the sense of purpose that keeps a firm on track.

mission statement A detailed articulation of the goals and objectives of an organization, calculated to give its members a sense of direction and channel their energies in that direction. The mission statement succinctly describes the business and states its reasons for existence. A mission statement is implemented through goals (i.e., the broad, long-range targets of the organization) and objectives (the specific, short-range targets of the organization). Also called a *corporate mission statement, statement of purpose,* or *organizational mission statement.* See also GOAL and OBJECTIVE.

missy (sizes) Synonym for MISSES (SIZES).

mix See PRODUCT MIX.

mixed brand method/strategy 1. A branding strategy in which a manufacturer produces a number of similar items under different brand names. 2. A branding strategy in which a retailer or other marketing intermediary sells items under a dealer or generic name as well as under the manufacturer's name.

mixed brand name strategy A branding strategy used by some BRICKS-AND-CLICKS enterprises that separates the brand names used by the parent company from those of the individual products or brands and provides each with a separate Web presence.

mixed credit See EXPORT-IMPORT BANK OF THE UNITED STATES.

mixed merchandising See SCRAMBLED MERCHANDISING.

mixed product A combination or blending of different products or services; for example, an oil change (a good and a service), an upgrade to a computer operating system offered on a software vendor's site (a digital product and a service), video training lessons that accompany an exercise machine (a service and a good), a restaurant dinner (a good and a service).

mixed use (shopping) center (MXD) A retail, office, parking, and hotel complex that may also include a convention center and/or a high-rise condominium or apartment complex. MXDs were often constructed as part of revitalization projects designed to salvage a downtown CENTRAL BUSINESS DISTRICT (CBD). Some mixed-use centers started as regional centers and grew by adding services and facilities. Some MXDs are located in renovated public buildings while others are part of totally planned communities. Theme/festival centers are sometimes considered mixed-use centers. See also FESTIVAL MARKETPLACE.

MLM See MULTILEVEL MARKETING (MLM).

m-marketing The marketing of goods and services to consumers through their WIRELESS devices (such as wireless handsets, cell phones, and PDAs). Also called *mobile marketing.* See also MOBILE AD.

MMIS See MULTINATIONAL MARKETING INFORMATION SYSTEM (MMIS).

MMU See MAINTAINED MARKUP (MMU).

MNC See MULTINATIONAL CORPORATION (MNC).

mobile ad An advertisement designed for use with wireless access devices such as PDAs or mobile Internet sets. Since these devices have smaller screens and slower downloads than computers, advertising has to be modified in size and content to accommodate the screen and download time. Also called *mobile advertising.* See also M-MARKETING.

mobile cellular phone See CELL PHONE.

mobile franchise A FRANCHISING arrangement in which the franchisee dispenses merchandise from a vehicle that is taken from place to place. In all other respects the mobile franchise resembles a conventional FRANCHISE.

mobile marketing See M-MARKETING.

mode Synonym for FASHION. *Der.* French.

model 1. A sample, usually handmade, serving as the prototype for a manufactured product. 2. A person who wears clothes for the purpose of displaying them. Models are used in fashion shows and apparel showrooms as well as in magazine layouts, advertising photographs, etc. Also called (as applicable) a *fashion model, showroom model, runway model, photographer's model,* etc. See also FASHION SHOW. 3. A conceptual representation of some complex reality, attempting to explain how that reality functions.

modeling 1. The changes in human behavior, on the part of either individuals or groups, that result from the influence of leadership. 2. The practice of displaying apparel on live persons at fashion shows, in showrooms, etc. See also MODEL and FASHION SHOW.

model stock The desired assortment of stock, broken down according to predictable factors such as classification, price, material, color, and size, based on consumer demand. See also BALANCED ASSORTMENT and MODEL STOCK PLAN/LIST/METHOD.

model stock plan/list/method A method for developing the ASSORTMENT PLAN. The model stock plan, although it may include some staples, is largely composed of shopping and specialty merchandise. It is therefore less specific than the BASIC STOCK LIST, despite the fact that it includes certain information such as classification, cost price, color, size, retail selling price, etc. The inclusion of fashion and seasonal merchandise in the model stock plan adds to it an element of unpredictability. See also MODEL STOCK.

modem A device that modulates an analog carrier signal (i.e., a sound) to encode digital information. It also demodulates the carrier signal to decode the transmitted information. Modems thus enable computer users to connect to other computers and to the INTERNET over telephone lines. Also called a *computer modem.*

moderate line In the apparel industry, a group of closely related products (i.e., a LINE) falling between a store's BETTER LINE and BUDGET LINE. Moderate lines are broadly distributed and may appear at less prestigious retailers. See also APPAREL PRICE RANGES.

moderator 1. In INTERNET communication, a person who presides over a LISTSERV or E-MAIL DISCUSSION LIST. 2. A person who presides over an event or meeting.

modification 1. An adjustment made to an existing product's style, color, or model. 2. A product improvement. 3. A BRAND change.

modified break-even analysis A form of BREAK-EVEN ANALYSIS in which the demand for a product is analyzed at various levels in an effort to determine the price-quantity mix that will maximize profits. Such analysis recognizes that profit does not necessarily increase as quantity sold increases, since increased sales are frequently the result of lowered prices. See also FLEXIBLE BREAK-EVEN ANALYSIS and PROFIT TARGET ANALYSIS.

modified rebuy An industrial buying situation in which some adjustments have been made in the specifications or price of the product to be ordered, making the process somewhat more complex than the STRAIGHT REBUY. See also NEW TASK BUYING/PURCHASING.

modified standardization See STANDARDIZATION.

modified uniform pricing In global marketing, a practice of adjusting prices to different international markets by monitoring price levels in each country and avoiding large gaps. See also UNIFORM PRICING STRATEGY.

modular fixture Synonym for MODULE.

modularity The process of developing standard components (i.e., modules) that can be connected to other standard modules to increase the variety of products. New products are designed using combinations of components from various modules. The MODULARIZED APPROACH (def. 2) has become especially important in the automobile industry and is a factor in the development of products for the global marketplace.

modularized approach 1. An advertising strategy used in the global marketplace. In this approach a company may select some features of the advertising campaign as standard for all its advertisements, while localizing other features. See also GLOBAL THEME. 2. In the development of products, particularly for the global marketplace, the use of standard components (i.e., modules) that can be connected to other standard modules to increase the variety of products. See also MODULARITY.

module 1. A separable component, often used in VISUAL MERCHANDISING, that is interchangeable with others for assembly into units of differing size or function. Modules are adaptable, movable, easy to rearrange, and inexpensive to produce. Modules used in retail display are most frequently constructed of wood, with the same frame being adapted to hold shelves or hang-rods as required. Also called a *modular fixture*. 2. A standardized component part that can be used in manufacturing. Various modules are recombined to form new products or variations on existing products.

MOM   See MIDDLE OF MONTH (MOM) DATING.

mom-and-pop store/outlet   A small, independent store typically run by a husband and wife. Such stores are usually modest family businesses catering to a local clientele. See also BANTAM STORE, CONVENIENCE STORE, and SUPERETTE.

monetary standard   See CONTROL STANDARD.

monetary union   The highest form of international economic integration, in which national currencies are replaced by a common currency regulated by a central bank. The European Union (EU) is an example of a monetary union.

money and merchandise allowances   See ALLOWANCE and PUSH MONEY (PM).

money, authority, desire, access (MADA)   A method of predicting sales and measuring market potential commonly known by its acronym, MADA. Attributes are assigned to various populations to quantify the consumer's financial ability to buy a product (i.e., money), the power to make the buying decision (i.e., authority), the interest in making a purchase (i.e., desire), and the actual ability to obtain it (i.e., access).

money-back guarantee   A written statement or the implication, by the seller of merchandise, that the customer's money will be refunded should the merchandise not perform satisfactorily. The GUARANTEE may come from either the manufacturer or the retailer. Compare WARRANTY.

money income   PERSONAL INCOME (PI) in the form of cash, checks, or electronic funds transfers, coming from wages, salary, interest, rents, etc. Money income is calculated before deductions are made for income tax and Social Security Tax (FICA).

money refund offer   See REBATE.

monitor   1. v. To oversee, regulate, or keep track of something (e.g., a Web page or a store's performance data). 2. n. In broadcast communications and computer applications, a display screen (e.g., a *television monitor* or a *computer monitor*).

monitoring procedures   See MONITORING SKILLS.

monitoring results   The process of comparing the actual performance of a store, business, or product against planned performance for a specified period. Also called *results monitoring*.

monitoring skills   The techniques used by marketing managers to develop and manage a system of controls and provide

feedback on the results of marketing activities. These controls may be annual marketing plan controls, profitability controls, or strategic controls. Also called *monitoring procedures*. See also ALLOCATING SKILLS, ORGANIZING SKILLS, and INTERACTING SKILLS.

monopolist   See MONOPOLY and MONOPOLISTIC COMPETITION.

monopolistically competitive market structure   See MONOPOLISTIC COMPETITION.

monopolistic competition   The condition that obtains in the MARKETPLACE when a relatively large number of competing firms sell similar or identical products that are nevertheless perceived by the consumer as having recognizable differences. Each firm strives for some COMPETITIVE ADVANTAGE (such as a more favorable location than its competition) and thus carves out its own small monopoly. Much of the competition under these market conditions is the result of consumers' belief that they can differentiate between the various products being offered. Also known as *imperfect competition*.

monopolistic market structure   Synonym for PURE MONOPOLY.

monopoly   A business organization operating in a competition-free environment. Also called a *monopolist*. See also MONOPOLISTIC COMPETITION.

monopsonist   A buyer operating in a market in which there are no other buyers. See also MONOPSONY.

monopsony   A market condition in which there is only one buyer. See also MONOPSONIST. Compare MONOPOLY.

montage format   A form of advertising found in the print media and on television and Web pages in which a number of pictures or images are juxtaposed to create a unified overall impression.

monthly sales index   A measure of variations in monthly sales volume using the number 100 to represent sales for an average month. Changes are reflected as deviation from 100. The higher the number above 100, the more positive the change.

monthly sales report   A management report, common to many retail organizations, that reflects the status of sales, inventory, and profitability for a specified period (i.e., a month).

MOR   See MERCHANDISING AND OPERATING RESULTS OF DEPARTMENT AND SPECIALTY STORES (MOR).

most favored nation (MFN) status   In an international trade agreement, a status accorded to all members of the group guaranteeing that none of them receives less favorable treatment than any other. See also PREFERRED TRADING PARTNER (PTP) and NONDISCRIMINATION.

motivation   See MOTIVE.

motivational need   See MOTIVE.

motivational research   See MOTIVATION RESEARCH (MR).

motivation analysis   Synonym for MOTIVATION RESEARCH (MR).

motivation research (MR)   An aspect of MARKETING RESEARCH (MR) in which the principles of behavioral science are applied to marketing problems in an attempt to explain why consumers behave as they do in the MARKETPLACE. Motivation research is primarily concerned with people's feelings and attitudes and how they affect the individual's buying behavior. Also called *motivational research* and *motivation analysis*. See also CONSUMER BEHAVIOR.

motive   The inner state (or drive) that activates people toward satisfying a need or goal. Motives may be rational (i.e., aroused by appeals to reason) or emotional (i.e., aroused by appeals to feelings). Sigmund Freud, Abraham Maslow, and Frederick Herzberg formulated theories of human motivation that continue to have significant implications for marketers interested in analyzing consumer behavior. In brief, Freud's theory assumes that motivation is largely unconscious. Market researchers sharing this view seek to uncover customers' hidden reasons for choosing a particular product or service over others. For example, consumers may be said to avoid eating prunes because of an unconscious association between wrinkliness and old age. Maslow's theory states that human needs are arranged in a hierarchy, from the most pressing to the least pressing, and that only when needs are met on the most pressing levels will consumers be motivated to satisfy less pressing needs. Thus only when hunger, thirst, and the need for shelter are satisfied will the consumer be motivated to attend to his need for security, love, esteem, and self-actualization. Herzberg developed a TWO-FACTOR THEORY OF MOTIVATION postulating that consumers seek to maximize *satisfiers* (i.e., characteristics of a product that are intrinsically satisfying) and minimize *dissatisfiers* (i.e., characteristics of a product that are not pleasing). According to this theory of motivation, marketers must be aware of the dissatisfiers that may keep their products from selling. Also called *motivation* and a *motivational need*. See also MOTIVATION RESEARCH (MR).

motor carrier   Any organization that transports domestic goods from suppliers to retailers on trucks. Motor carriers provide door-to-door service by picking up shipments from suppliers and delivering them directly to a retailer's DISTRIBUTION CENTER (DC). Motor carriers are also used to supplement other forms of transportation that do not offer door-to-door service (e.g., railroads and air transportation). Also called a *trucker*.

mouse   A handheld pointing device for computers. A mouse consists of a small object fitted with one or more buttons and shaped to fit naturally under the hand. The underside of the mouse contains a device that detects the mouse's motion in relation to the flat surface on which it sits. This motion is translated into the motion of the cursor on the display. The device is called a mouse primarily because the cord on early models resembled a mouse's tail, and also because the quick motion of the pointer on the screen can be mouselike. Variations include the *optical mouse* and the *laser mouse*. Also called a *computer mouse*.

mouse click   Synonym for CLICK.

mousetrap   A variation of the POP-UP AD that fills an entire Internet browser screen with an ad or Web page while removing any menu bars or other on-screen icons by which the user can close the window.

moving average   In TIME SERIES ANALYSIS, the basis on which predictions are made, calculated by averaging outcomes over two or more recent time periods. The moving average for UNIT SALES, for example, assumes that the unit sales figures for the next period will be the average of the unit sales figures for a given number of previous time periods. Thus, if a firm's candy sales were 6,000, 5,000, 7,000, and 7,500 pieces respectively, the four-month moving average would be the sum of the sales (25,500) divided by 4, or 6,375 pieces.

MR   See MARKET REPRESENTATIVE (MR), MARKETING RESEARCH (MR), or MOTIVATION RESEARCH (MR).

MRO   See SUPPLIES.

MRP   See MATERIAL REQUIREMENTS PLANNING (MRP).

MRP II   See MANUFACTURING RESOURCE PLANNING (MRP II).

MS   See MULTIDIMENSIONAL SCALING (MS).

MSA (metropolitan statistical area)   See METROPOLITAN STATISTICAL AREA (MSA).

MSRP   See MANUFACTURER'S SUGGESTED RETAIL PRICE (MSRP).

multibrand strategy   See MULTIPLE BRANDING.

multicasting   The act of simultaneously sending an E-MAIL message to a select list of recipients. Compare BROADCASTING.

multichannel marketing system   See DUAL DISTRIBUTION.

multichannel retailing   The practice of trading through two or more methods of distribution concurrently, giving consumers more than one way to purchase the same product (e.g., through catalog sales, online, and in retail stores). Multichannel retailing has become increasingly prevalent with the advent of the INTERNET, as many retailers sell their goods both in stores and online. Also called a *multiple-channel system* and *multiple distribution*. See also BRICKS-AND-CLICKS and DUAL DISTRIBUTION.

multidimensional scaling (MS)   A MARKETING RESEARCH (MR) technique in which the perceptions and attitudes of respondents are geometrically represented. The information presented in this manner is subsequently analyzed in an effort to aid managers in solving marketing problems (e.g., determining how consumers perceive a particular BRAND or PRODUCT).

multidomestic An organization that runs many different businesses in a number of countries. See also MULTINATIONAL CORPORATION (MNC).

multidomestic (marketing) strategy A MARKETING STRATEGY (i.e., the logical plan through which a firm intends to reach its marketing objectives) in which a MULTINATIONAL CORPORATION competes by applying many different strategies, each tailored to a particular local market. Compare GLOBAL MARKETING MIX STRATEGY and GLOBAL MARKETING STRATEGY.

Multifiber Arrangement (MFA) A set of special rules under the GENERAL AGREEMENT ON TARIFFS AND TRADE (GATT) (1947) to control international trade in textiles and apparel. The MFA expired January 1, 2005.

multilevel marketing (MLM) A method of selling products directly, independently, and usually out of the home, without the medium of a retail outlet. Multilevel marketing firms are set up in a pyramid-style hierarchy in which salespeople pay commission on sales they generate to the leader (i.e., an independent contractor) who has recruited them. Recruits, in turn, recruit their own acquaintances. Amway and Mary Kay Cosmetics are examples of companies that are organized in this manner. Many direct selling companies are also considered multilevel marketing companies. Also known as *network marketing*.

multinational Short for MULTINATIONAL CORPORATION (MNC).

multinational corporation (MNC) A firm that conducts a significant proportion of its business in two or more countries and almost always has a direct investment in the countries in which it operates. Consequently, MNCs operate in each of the countries as though they were local companies. Multinational corporations typically perform their functions in a global context. Sometimes referred to as *world business* or a *transnational company*. Also called a *multinational* or a *multinational company*. See also GLOBAL CORPORATION and MULTINATIONAL MARKETING.

multinational marketing Marketing efforts in more than one country, sometimes including the operation of production and distribution facilities and the employment of local labor and management personnel. Multinational marketers compete by attempting to appear local in each country in which they operate. They do so by applying many different marketing strategies, each one tailored to a particular local market. Compare INTERNATIONAL MARKETING and GLOBAL MARKETING. See also MULTINATIONAL CORPORATION (MNC).

multinational marketing information system (MMIS) A system that organizes and analyzes data from within the MULTINATIONAL CORPORATION (MNC) and from its various marketing environments and then presents the organization's managers with the information they need to make marketing decisions. The overall system generally has a separate subsystem for each country in which the corporation operations.

multipack A container holding two or more separately packaged items, such as six or eight separately wrapped or boxed bars of soap wrapped together in plastic wrap and sold as a single unit. Sometimes spelled *multipak*. Compare MULTIPLE PACKAGING.

multiple approach to pricing See MULTIPLE PRICING.

multiple brand entries Several brand names used by a manufacturer for essentially the same product. The goal of this strategy is to open up new market segments. See also EMULATIVE PRODUCT.

multiple branding A marketing strategy in which a firm gives each item in a line of products a separate BRAND NAME. For example, a large cereal manufacturer may market several dry breakfast foods under different brand names as part of an effort to reach various segments of the market and to dominate supermarket shelf space. Sometimes called *individual branding* to emphasize the separateness of the different brand names.

multiple buying influence In industrial buying, the sharing of a purchase decision among several people, sometimes including top management. The influences that go into the purchase decision may include the users (workers and/or supervisors), influencers (engineering, research and development personnel, etc.), purchasing agents (buyers), deciders (individuals in the organization, such as purchasing agents or top management, who have the authority to select and approve the supplier), and gatekeepers (people who control the flow of information within the organization).

multiple-channel distribution A vendor's sale of a product or line of products to retail stores at different levels of the market (e.g., upscale vs. value-oriented retailers). Upscale stores often discontinue brands when their producers are distributing them through less prestigious stores.

multiple-channel system See MULTICHANNEL RETAILING and DUAL DISTRIBUTION.

multiple correlation In statistical analysis, the comparison of the effect of several independent variables on a single dependent variable. Each independent variable is carefully weighted to determine its effect. See also COEFFICIENT OF MULTIPLE CORRELATION.

multiple delivery strategy A means of MERCHANDISE REPLENISHMENT that employs an initial delivery followed by a series of reorders to accommodate customer needs and preferences and to adjust for MERCHANDISE PLANNING errors. See also QUICK RESPONSE (QR) REPLENISHMENT SYSTEM.

multiple designations The combination of a number of designations to classify or divide merchandise in a retail store. Item (e.g., shirts) and vendor (e.g., Tommy Hilfiger) are the most common designations. Others include price range (e.g., moderate), size range (e.g., junior), end use (e.g., sportswear), lifestyle (e.g., active), selling season (e.g., holiday), production composition/fabrication (e.g., silk), and target customer (e.g., female). Several of these designations (i.e., multiple designations) may be combined to create a single business-unit identity such as Misses better sportswear.

multiple distribution See MULTICHANNEL RETAILING and DUAL DISTRIBUTION.

multiple extensions Extension of a BRAND to a large number of related products added to an existing line of branded products. Multiple extensions result in a megabrand, a brand that encompasses several related merchandise categories such as dresses, accessories, shoes, and sportswear. See also MEGABRAND and BRAND EXTENSION STRATEGY.

multiple-line representative A salesperson carrying the lines of several manufacturers.

multiple market approach/segmentation Synonym for DIFFERENTIATED MARKETING.

multiple packaging The inclusion of more than one item in a single container (e.g., a six-pack of cola). Other items commonly packaged this way include underwear, cans of beer, packages of chewing gum, etc. Also called *multiple unit packaging*. Compare MULTIPACK.

multiple pricing 1. The practice of offering more than one unit at a given price (e.g., three for $1), creating the impression that the goods are being sold at a bargain price and also increasing the number of items sold per transaction. Also called *multiple unit pricing* and the *multiple approach to pricing*. 2. The practice, frequently found in supermarkets, of inadvertently marking an item with two or more prices.

multiple regression See REGRESSION ANALYSIS.

multiple retailer Synonym for CHAIN STORE.

multiple sales A successful strategy motivating the customer to buy more than one item at a time.

multiple source purchasing Buying goods from more than one vendor.

multiple target market approach A marketing strategy in which a manufacturer produces a number of related products, each with a narrow segment of the total market as its target. The manufacturer attempts to build sales by addressing various segments of the market individually rather than by marketing a single product for all customers. Each market segment is offered a different MARKETING MIX. See also DIFFERENTIATED MARKETING.

multiple-unit establishment Synonym for MULTIUNIT OPERATION.

multiple unit packaging See MULTIPLE PACKAGING.

multiple unit pricing See MULTIPLE PRICING.

multiprice store A store in which the merchandise is not price-marked. Salespeople vary prices quoted on the basis of what they believe the customer may be able and willing to pay. Bargaining is allowed and even expected. Also spelled *multi-price store*. See also PRICE and PRICING.

multistage pricing A planning strategy in which a broad price policy is developed by integrating a series of individual pricing decisions into a coherent price framework for the firm. A number of steps are taken in sequence, beginning with the selection of a TARGET MARKET and ending with the formulation of a specific PRICE.

multistep flow model A theory of mass communication complementing the HYPODERMIC NEEDLE MODEL and the TWO-STEP FLOW MODEL. The theory maintains that there are a variety of ways in which messages can flow from the mass media to the audience. In some cases, mass media may have a direct effect on the audience (as in the hypodermic needle model). In other cases, mass media messages may flow to opinion leaders and then to the general public (as in the two-step flow model). In yet other cases, however, as explained by the multistep flow model, messages may flow through a series of opinion leaders and involve more than two steps. The model also takes into account the diversified sources of information available to opinion leaders as well as the selective processes used by the audience to filter the messages they receive.

multistore retailer A retail organization with a geographically defined organizational hierarchy that links the stores to the corporate office. A DISTRICT MANAGER is responsible for a group of stores located within a defined geographic area. A REGIONAL MANAGER supervises a group of district managers and reports to a corporate level person, such as a vice-president or director of stores.

multitasking A trend in which consumers work on and accomplish several activities simultaneously, particularly in the workplace. The widespread use of computers in the workplace has largely given rise to this phenomenon, as workers become increasingly able to work on several projects at the same time. This has implications for advertisers who seek to gain their attention and for marketers who may need to adapt or modify their products to meet the needs of this consumer group. See also HYPERTASKING.

multitier pricing The practice of charging different prices for different levels of service or product types offered on a Web site. Content Web sites often use multitier pricing. For example, content in the entry or public level may be free. However, content on the next level (e.g., the full text of the article or news story) is by subscription or a per-unit price. Newspaper sites use subscriptions to control access.

multiunit department store A department store organization consisting of a FLAGSHIP STORE/DIVISION and two or more branch stores. Compare MULTIUNIT OPERATION. See also BRANCH STORE.

multiunit operation   A retail organization in which the various branches are of relatively equal importance and in which there is no main or FLAGSHIP STORE/DIVISION. All units are managed by a centrally located administrative group. Also called a *multiple-unit establishment*. Compare MULTIUNIT DEPARTMENT STORE.

multivariable segmentation   The use of more than one factor (e.g., age, race) to subdivide the population of potential customers.

municipal market   See PUBLIC MARKET.

museum case   A DISPLAY CASE that can also serve as a counter or demonstration area as part of a store's interior display. A museum case is similar to those found in museums and consists of a column or pedestal with a five-sided glass case on top. It is often taller than a counter, allowing the merchandise to be raised up closer to the viewer's eye level. Small platforms or risers can be used to enhance the presentation and help delineate assorted items displayed in the same case.

museum exhibit   A form of INSTITUTIONAL EVENT that involves the presentation of fashion items in an interpretive setting at a museum.

musical performance   A form of INSTITUTIONAL EVENT in which entertainment presentations are hosted by a retailer or manufacturer.

must-win market   A market that is considered crucial to global market leadership. Dominance in such a market can determine the overall success of a global company.

mutual delivery system   A parcel DELIVERY service formed by a number of retailers. The service picks up, sorts, and delivers customer purchases for each member store. Each member store shares in its ownership and in the expenses the service generates.

MXD   See MIXED USE (SHOPPING) CENTER (MXD).

myopia   See MARKETING MYOPIA.

mystery approach/technique   A SALES APPROACH in which the SALESPERSON uses an intriguing, dangling statement to attract the prospect's curiosity and attention.

NAFTA See NORTH AMERICAN FREE TRADE ASSOCIATION (NAFTA).

nailed down Of merchandise, often furniture or appliances, on display in the store and advertised as for sale, but that the merchant has no intention of selling at the price advertised or marked. This practice is often the first stage of a BAIT AND SWITCH strategy.

nameplate 1. A piece of metal, wood, or plastic on which the name of a person, company, etc. is printed or engraved. May be used as a synonym for SIGNATURE PLATE. 2. In newspaper publishing, the name of the newspaper printed on its front page. Also called a *masthead* or a *flag*.

name your own price See DEMAND COLLECTION.

NAMSB WorldSource An international exposition open to manufacturers from all countries, enabling them to develop customers for menswear, womenswear, childrenswear, accessories, textiles, and leather. Headquartered at the National Association of Men's Sportswear Buyers (NAMSB) in New York City, the exposition maintains a Web site at www.namsbworldsource.com.

Napster Case (2001) See FILE-SHARING.

narrowband In the Internet environment, a very small BANDWIDTH, usually capable of transmitting text only. Compare BROADBAND.

NASDAQ See STOCK EXCHANGE.

national account marketing A marketing strategy in which a firm's largest and most important national customers are given special attention in recognition of the volume of business they generate. These clients are frequently served by a specially dedicated sales force responsible for finding and maintaining such accounts. Also called *key account marketing* and *major account marketing*.

national advertising Advertising sponsored on a national or regional basis, generally by manufacturers or producers and promoting consumer products or retail stores that are widely available throughout the country. The goal of national adver-

tising is to encourage brand awareness and ultimately sales. The ads are placed in the major media. Local retail stores where customers can purchase the advertised product are sometimes included, in which case it is a form of COOPERATIVE ADVERTISING. Also known as *general advertising*.

national bank See COMMERCIAL BANK.

national brand See MANUFACTURER'S BRAND.

national department store (Obsolete) A chain department store such as Sears or JC Penney. See also DEPARTMENT STORE.

nationalization The seizure or purchase of a private company or other property, sometimes a foreign one that has already undergone DOMESTICATION, by a government so that it is wholly owned and operated by that government. See also EXPROPRIATION AND CONFISCATION.

National Labor Relations Act (1935) U.S. federal legislation, commonly known as the *Wagner Act*, giving employees the right to form labor unions and bargain collectively for their wages and other working conditions. See also the LABOR-MANAGEMENT RELATIONS ACT (LMRA) (1947) and the LABOR-MANAGEMENT REPORTING AND DISCLOSURE ACT (1959), which help clarify the issues and procedures mentioned here.

National Labor Relations Board (NLRB) The U.S. federal agency that conducts elections to determine whether employees want representation and that investigates and remedies unfair labor practices by employers and unions. The agency maintains a Web presence at www.nlrb.gov.

nationally advertised brand See MANUFACTURER'S BRAND.

National Retail Federation (NRF) The world's largest retail trade association, headquartered in Washington, D.C. The NRF is an international umbrella organization with membership in all retail formats and channels of distribution. It includes department, specialty, discount, catalog, Internet, and independent stores as well as industry trading partners of retail goods and services. International members operate stores in more than 50 countries worldwide. The NRF represents 32 national and 50 STATE RETAIL ASSOCIATIONS (SRAS) in the United States as well as 24 international associations representing retailers in other countries. It was formed in 1990 by the merger of the *American Retail Federation (ARF)* and the *National Retail Merchants Association (NRMA);* it absorbed the *Apparel Retailers of America* in 1995.

National Retail Merchants Association (NRMA) See NATIONAL RETAIL FEDERATION (NRF).

National Sizing Survey A fully automated anthropomorphic survey undertaken to determine accurate apparel sizes. First undertaken in the United Kingdom, the survey in the United States was completed in 2004. Also known as TC^2, which is actually the name of the three-dimensional body scanner used for it, the *SizeUSA* study began in 2002 to scan over 10,000 men and women in 13 cities across the United States. Some brands have already capitalized on the resulting data and have made adjustments in which a statistically greater number of consumers will be able to purchase from among graded sizes. Manufacturers who use the data may identify their garments with the "Fit By SizeUSA" logo to help customers identify these garments and expect a better fit. The survey maintains Web sites at www.sizeusa.com and www.tc2.com.

national wholesaler A wholesale operation whose activities can reach all or most of the country. Compare LOCAL WHOLESALER and SECTIONAL WHOLESALER.

natural 1. n. An item of merchandise that generates considerable customer interest. 2. adj. Having undergone little or no processing and containing no chemical additives (as in natural food). 3. adj. Made of fibers that exist in nature (i.e., nonsynthetic).

natural account See NATURAL CLASSIFICATION OF EXPENSES.

natural brand See PRODUCER-CONTROLLED BRAND.

natural business year A 12-month period, usually selected to end when inventory or business activity is at a low point.

natural classification of expenses An accounting practice in which expenses are grouped into classes based on the kinds of expenditure involved (e.g., rent, salaries, supplies, raw materials, taxes, interest) rather than on the function of the expenditure (e.g., the costs of operating a particular department). Also known as a *natural account, ledger expenses,* and *object-of-expenditure cost.*

natural monopoly A condition in the marketplace in which there is only one seller because this is the best way to serve the public. Public utilities are examples of natural monopolies in which prices are regulated by a public agency.

natural products RAW MATERIALS that occur in nature, such as fish, game, lumber, metals, minerals, and coal.

natural resources Raw materials, often called *wasting assets,* characterized by the complete consumption of the asset and its replacement only by an act of nature. These include petroleum, minerals, and timber. Unlike plant and equipment (fixed costs), natural resources are consumed physically over the period of use and do not maintain their physical characteristics once used.

natural selection theory See ADAPTIVE BEHAVIOR THEORY.

natural trading area The geographic area containing the customers who patronize a firm. Natural trading areas seldom have clearly defined boundaries; customers simply thin out as distance increases.

navigation 1. In Web page design, the links and design elements that enable a visitor to move easily from page to page. 2. The act of moving from page to page on the Internet.

near pack premium A manufacturer's promotion that offers a completely different product free with one purchase of the product being promoted. The premium is displayed near the basic product but in a display of its own.

NECTA See NEW ENGLAND CITY AND TOWN AREA (NECTA).

need awareness The degree to which consumers may be cognizant of their needs and willing to discuss them with others. Three degrees or levels of need awareness are generally described: *conscious, preconscious,* and *unconscious.* At the conscious level of need awareness, consumers are not only aware of their needs, but are also willing and able to discuss them with others. At the preconscious level, consumers may be aware of their needs but are reluctant or unable to discuss them with others, largely because of a lack of understanding of what is actually motivating their needs. At the unconscious level, consumers are not aware of the forces that are driving them. See also NEEDS.

needle trades A familiar term for the APPAREL INDUSTRY.

needs The basic motivations that cause individual consumers to make purchase decisions or take other actions. Needs may be physiological, such as the need for food, warmth, and shelter, or psychological and concerned with an individual's self-image and relationships with others. See also MASLOW'S HIERARCHY (OF NEEDS) and NEED AWARENESS.

need-satisfaction approach See BENEFIT APPROACH.

needs/wants hierarchy See MASLOW'S HIERARCHY (OF NEEDS).

negative authorization The use of lists of poor credit risks as a tool in granting credit. If a name does not appear on the delinquent list, the credit sale is approved.

negative correlation See CORRELATION.

negative demand A condition in the marketplace in which a major segment of the market dislikes the merchandise so much that it will avoid the item. See also ABSENCE OF DEMAND.

negative option plan A form of direct marketing in which the customer (who may or may not be member of a club) is shipped a preannounced product at regular intervals unless the seller is advised not to ship before a predetermined date. The Book-of-the-Month Club was a typical negative option plan as are several other book and record clubs. All such arrangements are regulated by the FEDERAL TRADE COMMISSION (FTC) through the *Code of Federal Regulations* (16 *CFR* 425).

negotiated buying An alternative to competitive bidding. The buyer and seller work out a mutually satisfactory arrangement codified in a NEGOTIATED CONTRACT. Negotiated buying is most likely to be the process of choice when there is a sole supplier of the desired goods or no competition in the marketplace.

negotiated contract An agreement (i.e., a contract) to buy goods or services in which the buyer and seller arrange specific and mutually satisfactory terms. Negotiated contracts are frequently employed instead of competitive bidding when there is a sole supplier and thus no competition in the marketplace. See also NEGOTIATED BUYING.

negotiated contract buying See NEGOTIATED BUYING and NEGOTIATED CONTRACT.

negotiated price A price reached by bargaining or haggling between buyer and seller. The negotiation opens with a proposed price, then participants counter back and forth until a mutually satisfactory price seals the sale. The practice is called *negotiated pricing* or *negotiated price policy*. Compare ONE-PRICE POLICY. See also VARIABLE PRICE POLICY.

negotiation process In retail buying, the procedure by which the vendor and the retail buyer bargain and, eventually, settle on a price, terms, delivery dates, etc. Also called, simply, *negotiation*.

neighborhood business district A cluster of several stores located in a section of a large town or city and serving the needs of that section of the city. The stores within the neighborhood business district are relatively small, and sales are derived almost entirely from customers who live or work near the store. These stores may include a bakery, a drug store, a grocery or small supermarket, etc. Also called a *neighborhood cluster*.

neighborhood center See NEIGHBORHOOD SHOPPING CENTER.

neighborhood cluster See NEIGHBORHOOD BUSINESS DISTRICT.

neighborhood shopping center A small SHOPPING CENTER, often arranged on the strip plan, which serves its surrounding community (i.e., typically persons living within three miles of the center or five minutes of drive time). Neighborhood centers are frequently anchored by a supermarket or variety store and may include service retailers (beauty shops, etc.) and stores selling convenience goods (drug stores, etc.). They typically serve 5,000 to 40,000 people and are found in predominantly residential areas. Sometimes called *neighborhood center*. See also STRIP SHOPPING CENTER.

neighborhood shopping district See NEIGHBORHOOD BUSINESS DISTRICT.

neighborhood site See NEIGHBORHOOD STORE.

neighborhood store A freestanding retail outlet serving the needs of a small section of a town or city. Also called a *neighborhood site*.

Nielsen reports Commercial reports that provide information on market share, sales, and trends useful to retail planners. Prepared by the ACNielsen Company, a national research organization, the reports are based on customer surveys to develop valuable information for the industry.

nested Fitting together for easy storage, one within the other. A set of bowls may be nested.

nesting See COCOONING.

net 1. In BILLING, a term of sale indicating that full payment for the goods contained in the invoice is due immediately. See also 1/10 NET 30 (ONE TEN NET 30) and DATING OF INVOICES. 2. That which remains after deductions, such as expenses or tare weight (as opposed to gross expenses or gross weight). 3. A short, popular term for the INTERNET, usually spelled Net.

net alteration and workroom cost The difference between what it costs to provide alteration and workroom services and what the customer pays for them.

net back A sales arrangement in which such costs as freight expenses, agent's commissions, etc., are deducted from the selling price in order to expedite the transfer of the merchandise from the factory to its point of sale.

net cash flow For a given accounting period, the amount of cash consumed or produced by an activity or product, including all revenue and expenses except noncash items such as depreciation. For example, if the cash received from customers is $85,000 and expenses are salaries ($46,000) and utilities ($8,000), the equation for net cash flow would be $85,000 − $54,000 = $31,000.

NetCheque A process developed at the University of Southern California's Information Sciences Institute allowing registered users to write checks to other registered users through e-mail or other network protocols. When the check is deposited, funds are transferred from the issuer's account to the receiver's account. All information is kept on a dedicated server responsible for keeping accounts for customers, approving payments, and making the necessary changes in client accounts. NetCheque uses SYMMETRIC ENCRYPTION.

net cost Synonym for COST OF GOODS PURCHASED.

net cost of (delivered) purchases See COST OF GOODS PURCHASED.

net cost of goods sold See COST OF GOODS SOLD.

net cost of purchases   See COST OF GOODS PURCHASED.

net credit period   See DATE OF INVOICE (DOI).

nethood   A trend in which local communities (i.e., neighborhoods) and even individual apartment buildings are starting to set up their own INTERNET and INTRANET sites, dubbed nethoods. These sites are used to promote qualities the neighborhoods have to offer prospective and current inhabitants as well as to provide communal interaction and localized services. The trend was identified and the term coined by trendwatching.com at www.trendwatching.com. *Der. net* (short for *Internet*) + *neighborhood.*

net income   See NET PROFIT.

netiquette   Basic unwritten rules of Internet etiquette (i.e., the dos and don'ts). Netiquette applies to e-mail as well as to other text-based Internet services and even to the text of the e-tailer's Web site. Basic rules include keeping the message short, not typing in all capital letters, avoiding EMOTICONS (i.e., *smileys*), and using Net-savvy abbreviations. *Der. Net* (short for *Internet*) + *etiquette.*

netizen   (Slang) A user of the INTERNET. The term connotes civic responsibility and participation. *Der. Net* (short for *Internet*) + *citizen.*

net lease   An agreement under which a lessee must assume such expenses as heating, maintenance, insurance, etc., as well as basic rent charges.

net loss   A situation that exists when expenses exceed revenues (i.e., more money is flowing out of the business than coming in). Compare NET PROFIT.

net markdown   The price reduction on merchandise in stock due to a lowering of the value of the merchandise. Net markdown is calculated as the difference between the GROSS MARKDOWN and the MARKDOWN CANCELLATION.

net markup   The increase over cost price at which an item is sold after markup cancellations have been made.

net-net   A retail buying strategy in which all advertising allowances and terms of payment are eliminated from the cost of the merchandise (especially in the case of branded merchandise) so that a competitive edge may be gained over other stores.

net operating income   Synonym for NET PROFIT.

net operating profit   Synonym for NET PROFIT.

net payment date   In the DATING OF INVOICES, the final date on which the full amount of the invoice must be paid. Commonly, this is 30 days after the date of invoice (DOI). In that case, the terms of the agreement would be stated as 2/10 net 30. A 2% discount may be deducted from an invoice paid within 10 days of the DOI, but otherwise the full payment is due by the thirtieth day.

net payment period   In the DATING OF INVOICES, the time between the cash discount date and the specified net payment date. For example, if the terms of the agreement are 2/10 net 30, a 2% discount may be deducted from an invoice paid within 10 days of the DATE OF INVOICE (DOI). The net payment period for the full amount extends from the eleventh day to the thirtieth day after the date of invoice (DOI).

net period   Synonym for NET PAYMENT PERIOD.

Net presence   A site on the Internet. For retailers and other marketers, this may mean an informative site (giving, for example, the company's history and financial information for the purposes of investors, or product information accompanied by retail listings for customers) or an actual online store where visitors may make purchases.

net present value   In accounting, a means of taking into account the value of money to be expended in an investment project. Net present value, or as it is sometimes called, *discounted cash flow,* expresses in terms of current value the outlays and inflows that will occur in the future as the project is developed. Also called *present value.*

net price   The price paid to the vendor for merchandise, not including transportation and delivery costs. See also COST OF GOODS PURCHASED.

net profit   Gross (i.e., total) margin (or, in manufacturing terminology, gross profit) less operating expenses such as payroll, advertising, insurance, cost of operating the store, etc. In short, net profit is the excess of all the revenues of the business over all costs and expenses incurred to obtain that income during the accounting period. Synonymous with *operating profit, dollars returned, net operating profit, net operating income, net revenue,* and *net income.* Compare NET LOSS. See also INCOME and PROJECTED NET PROFIT.

net profit plan/method   A method of allocating EXPENSES in large retail organizations in which each department is treated as a separate entity and charged with both direct and indirect expenses.

net purchases   The invoice cost of merchandise purchased plus the transportation charges for the items, minus the sum of returns, allowances, and cash discounts taken.

net quick ratio   See ACID TEST RATIO.

net realizable value   The selling price of an item of merchandise less reasonable selling costs associated with the sale of that item.

net revenue   Synonym for NET PROFIT.

net sales   Gross (i.e., total) sales minus the sum of allowances, discounts, and returns. Also called *actual sales.*

net sales to inventory level ratio   The ratio that results when the annual net sales figure is divided by merchandise inventory as it appears on the balance sheet. Not a measure of actual physical turnover, it is used instead to compare the STOCK-TO-SALES RATIO (SSR) of one store with that of another or of the industry as a whole.

net space yield   An approach to determining the profitability of specific products in a store. Handling costs and space costs are computed along with the cost of the merchandise to produce a GROSS MARGIN figure for each product. These gross margin figures may then be compared to determine which products yield the greatest profit.

net terms   A term of sale in which no provision is made for a cash discount.

net thirty   A typical arrangement for the payment of invoices, indicating that full payment of the invoice is due within 30 days of the DATE OF INVOICE (DOI). See also DATING OF INVOICES.

net weight   The weight of the goods contained in a package. The TARE (WEIGHT) is subtracted from the gross weight to determine the net weight.

network   Two or more computers connected together so that they can share resources. Two or more networks linked together constitute an INTERNET. See also COMPUTER NETWORK.

Network Advertising Initiative (NAI)   An association of Internet companies dealing with privacy issues associated with tools such as Web beacons. NAI also offers consumers opt-outs from COOKIES and WEB BEACONS placed by its member companies. NAI maintains a Web site at www.networkadvertising.org.

networking   1. In the job search process, the cultivation of a group of acquaintances who help build business contacts, potentially resulting in career opportunities.   2. The linking together of a number of computers so that they can share resources.

network marketing   Synonym for MULTILEVEL MARKETING (MLM).

network news transport protocol (NNTP)   A protocol for the distribution, inquiry, retrieval, and posting of news articles using a reliable stream-based transmission of news among the ARPA-Internet community. NNTP is designed so that news articles are stored in a central database, allowing subscribers to select only those items they wish to read. NNTP facilitates USENET communication.

network pool barter   An online form of BARTER in which members do not trade directly with each other but make purchases using barter dollars (trade credits or tokens) credited to their accounts. Most online barter sites offer free memberships, though some have small transaction fees for products traded.

net workroom cost   The total cost of operating a workroom, including payroll and supplies.

network server   See SERVER.

net worth   In terms of an owner's EQUITY in a store or other business, the difference between total assets and total liabilities.

neural computing   Synonym for NEURAL NETWORK.

neural network   A statistical technique providing a close approximation to a solution to a particular problem. As used in retailing, a computerized neural network allows retailers to track forecasts and compare them to what is actually taking place. For example, neural networks can help retailers determine the optimal mix of markdowns and advertising to maximize gross profit. In direct marketing, neural networks can be used to cluster the various characteristics of a market segment.

neutral pricing   A pricing method based on adding enough to the cost of products to cover overhead and profit. Products are priced without reference to the competition's prices. COST-PLUS PRICING, that is, the adding of a fixed margin to the cost of products to arrive at a price, is a neutral pricing approach that is used by many small independent retailers and some specialty stores. Compare PASSIVE PRICING and AGGRESSIVE PRICING.

never-out goods/list   BREAD-AND-BUTTER ASSORTMENT/GOODS.

never-outs   See BREAD-AND-BUTTER ASSORTMENT/GOODS.

newbie   In the computer environment, a new INTERNET user, characteristically considered to be helpless, Web-illiterate, nervous, and reluctant to use a credit card to purchase goods and services ONLINE. Compare OLDBIES.

new customer gift   A small, free gift given to new customers as a premium the first time they patronize the retailer.

new employee indoctrination   See EMPLOYEE ORIENTATION.

new employee indoctrination booklet   See EMPLOYEE ORIENTATION BOOKLET.

New England city and town area (NECTA)   Under the standards adopted in 2000, any of a number of geographic areas defined using cities and towns in the six New England states. These NECTAs are identified as either metropolitan or micropolitan, based, respectively, on the presence of either an urbanized area of 50,000 or more population or an urban cluster of at least 10,000 but less than 50,000 population. If the specified criteria are met, a NECTA containing a single core with a population of at least 2.5 million may be subdivided to form smaller groupings of cities and towns, referred to as New England city and town area divisions.

New England city and town area division   Any of the smaller groupings of cities and towns that result from subdividing a NECTA containing a single core with a population of at least 2.5 million. Comparable to a METROPOLITAN DIVISION.

newly married   The category of consumers made up of recently married couples, usually with two wage earners, an orientation toward the future, and good *discretionary income*. Their priorities are setting up a new household with new furniture, appliances, and carpeting. Many couples save for starter homes, while others are good targets for luxury goods and travel.

New Mart   A MERCHANDISE MART located in downtown Los Angeles, California. It focuses on contemporary and young designer fashions from New York, California, and Europe.

new media   See MEDIA.

new product   To customers, a product perceived as significantly different from other available products; for manufacturers, distributors, and retailers, a product never before produced or sold. New products range from the truly unique and innovative to those that are merely modifications or copies of existing merchandise. See also NEW PRODUCT DEVELOPMENT and PRODUCT LIFE CYCLE (PLC).

new product committee   Synonym for PRODUCT PLANNING COMMITTEE. See also VENTURE TEAM.

new product development   The process by which an idea for a NEW PRODUCT is carried through a series of developmental stages to final commercialization. New product development is largely concerned with determining customers' needs, the technical development of a product to meet those needs, and the introduction of the new product into the marketplace. Sometimes called, simply, PRODUCT DEVELOPMENT. See also PRODUCT LIFE CYCLE (PLC).

new product planning   See NEW PRODUCT DEVELOPMENT and PRODUCT PLANNING.

new product planning process   The stages through which a product passes in the developmental process. Included are idea generation and screening, analysis and evaluation, product development and production, branding, test marketing and positioning, and, finally, full-scale marketing and production. To be effective, the new product planning process must be sensitive to the needs of the marketplace. See also PRODUCT PLANNING and PRODUCT SCREENING.

new product screening checklist   A form used in the systematic evaluation of ideas for new products. Such factors as marketability and growth potential are included for consideration by the PRODUCT PLANNING COMMITTEE.

news approach/technique   A SALES APPROACH in which the SALESPERSON uses newspaper stories or trade journal articles as a lead-in to the presentation. The approach capitalizes on recent news events (such as a series of fires to sell fire insurance or an increase in burglaries to sell burglar alarms) to bring the message home to the prospect.

newsgroup   An online discussion group on USENET or an area on a BULLETIN BOARD SYSTEM (BBS) or ONLINE SERVICE in which participants can discuss a topic of common interest online. Synonym for FORUM. See also POSTING.

news reader   See FEED READER.

news release   Synonym for PRESS RELEASE.

news technique   See NEWS APPROACH/TECHNIQUE.

new task buying/purchasing   A form of industrial buying in which the purchasing officer must buy a new product or service. New task buying requires greater attention to detail than rebuying and often involves more than one person. See also STRAIGHT REBUY and MODIFIED REBUY.

new unsought goods/items   Products offering new ideas and applications of which the consumer is not at all aware. The marketing of such goods requires informative promotion so that potential customers will accept and seek out the product. Also called *new unsought items.* See also UNSOUGHT GOODS/PRODUCTS.

New York Cotton Exchange   See COMMODITY EXCHANGE.

New York Futures Exchange   See COMMODITY EXCHANGE.

New York Gift Mart   A dedicated gift, home décor, and tabletop building on the site of the former Ohrbach's in New York City. The New York Gift Mart's extensive marketing plan includes direct mail, e-mail, a high-tech, interactive Web site, and trade advertising.

New York Mercantile Exchange   See COMMODITY EXCHANGE.

New York Stock Exchange (NYSE)   See STOCK EXCHANGE.

niche   In retailing and other marketing endeavors, a distinct segment of the market. See also TARGET MARKET, BRAND POSITION, NOUVEAU NICHE, and MARKET NICHE.

niche market   A small and relatively homogeneous subgroup of consumers with needs and characteristics that differ from those of the mass market. For example, big-and-tall men's stores meet the clothing needs of the niche market consisting of men who are larger than the standard sizes found in most retail stores. Niche market members seek out specialty retailers who meet their special needs and interests, since these are not adequately met by mass marketers. As a result they tend to be loyal to the retailers who do respond to their needs. Compare MASS MARKET. See also TARGET MARKET and NOUVEAU NICHE.

niche marketing   A marketing strategy in which a manufacturer or supplier identifies a narrow market segment in which the company can successfully compete with a new or existing product or service. Products and services may be created specifically to fill these perceived niches. Compare MASS MARKETING. See also TARGET MARKET and NOUVEAU NICHE.

niche portal   See PORTAL.

niche product   A product or service created specifically to fill perceived unfulfilled needs in particular segments of the market. Compare MASS MERCHANDISE. See also NICHE MARKET and NICHE MARKETING.

99 cent store A BARGAIN STORE that sells all or most of its merchandise at a uniform price of 99 cents.

99 lives A lifestyle pursued by individuals who seek instant gratification. These consumers tend to multitask both on the job and in their personal lives and are therefore overstressed. They tend to purchase items that free up even a small amount of time. Prepared foods, cell phones, PDAs, and shopping services attract them. Consumers in this category may find Internet and catalog shopping particularly attractive.

nixie (Slang) A piece of mail returned by the Post Office as undeliverable.

NLEA See NUTRITION LABELING AND EDUCATION ACT (NLEA) (1990).

NLRB See NATIONAL LABOR RELATIONS BOARD (NLRB).

NNTP See NETWORK NEWS TRANSPORT PROTOCOL (NNTP).

no-back window See OPEN-BACK WINDOW.

node An individual computer in a NETWORK.

no demand A condition in the marketplace in which there is no need or desire on the part of consumers for a product or service offered for sale.

no-frills chic Low-cost goods and services that add design, third-party high-quality elements, or exceptional customer service to create top-quality experiences at low prices (e.g., JetBlue and Song airlines and Target's "design within reach"). The trend was identified and the term coined by trend-watching.com at www.trendwatching.com.

no-frills merchandise/product Synonym for GENERIC PRODUCT.

noise In a communications system, interference (such as static or distortion) occurring during the transmission of a message, reducing its effectiveness.

nominal account Any of the temporary accounts representing the income and expenses for a particular accounting period and closed at the end of the accounting period. Revenue, expense, and dividend accounts are considered temporary, nominal accounts. They appear on the INCOME STATEMENT rather than the balance sheet and are periodically closed; real accounts are not. Also called an *operating account*. Compare REAL ACCOUNT.

nonadopter In the diffusion or adoption process, one of those consumers who do not buy the new product at all. Also spelled *non-adopter*.

no-name brand See GENERIC BRAND.

nonbusiness marketing Synonym for NONPROFIT MARKETING.

nonbusiness organization Somewhat imprecisely, any of a wide variety of nonprofit or not-for-profit organizations. These include schools, cultural institutions, charities, fraternal organizations, health care delivery organizations, etc. Many nonbusiness organizations (e.g., universities and colleges, religious groups, and charities) maintain Web sites. Also called a *nonprofit organization (NPO)* and a *not-for-profit organization*.

noncabled point-of-sale WIRELESS capabilities that permit stores to move cash registers wherever they are needed. These registers may be existing terminals (modified to run on a wireless network) or handheld wireless devices. Also called *wireless point-of-sale*. See also POINT-OF-PURCHASE (POP).

noncommercial advertising Advertising (i.e., paid nonpersonal communications) by nonprofit organizations to promote public interests (such as automobile safety or equal rights), encourage contributions to charities or other philanthropic causes (such as the American Red Cross), or promote political causes.

noncompeting retailers Stores that do not compete with each other, although they carry similar merchandise, because they operate in different markets.

noncumulative quantity discount A reduction in price, usually granted by a vendor on a one-time basis (i.e., noncumulative), based on the size of an order. Such discounts are usually made by sellers to encourage large orders.

noncyclical rich Individuals so fabulously wealthy that their fortunes are immune to economic changes such as recessions, presenting opportunities for retailers and other marketers to sell them luxury goods with huge margins. Marketing to such individuals may involve acknowledging their purchasing power and ignoring any talk of discounts or savings. The phenomenon was identified and the term coined by trendwatching.com at www.trendwatching.com.

nondiscretionary expenditure Any purchase or payment made by consumers for such necessities as shelter, food, and clothing (i.e., the consumer has little or no choice about making the expenditure). Compare DISCRETIONARY EXPENDITURE. See also PERSONAL INCOME (PI).

nondiscrimination One of the cornerstone principles of international trade agreements such as the GENERAL AGREEMENT ON TARIFFS AND TRADE (GATT) (1947). Nondiscrimination means that one country should not give one member or group of members preferential treatment over other members of the group. This principle is embodied in the MOST FAVORED NATION (MFN) STATUS. See also RECIPROCITY and TRANSPARENCY, the other two underlying principles of GATT.

nondisguised retail audit An audit carried on with the knowledge of the employees of the store.

nondisguised survey In MARKETING RESEARCH (MR), a method of gathering information in which respondents are told the real purpose of the QUESTIONNAIRE.

nondumping certificate In international trade, a seller's document indicating that the goods described are being sold at a price no lower than they would be sold in the country of origin. See also DUMPING and ANTIDUMPING TARIFF.

nondurable goods See NONDURABLES.

nondurables Merchandise (e.g., shampoo, toothpaste, and cat litter) that has to be replaced on a regular basis. Many nondurables may now be purchased online, with some e-tailers providing for prescheduled periodic replacements shipped automatically to the customer. Also called *nondurable goods*.

nongoods services 1. A form of retailing in which the firm offers a service rather than a tangible product. Usually an individual performs some function for the customer (e.g., a personal shopper, babysitter, doorman) in return for a fee. 2. A category of consumer service in which no tangible product is offered for sale or rental (e.g., hairdressing, medical care).

noninstallment credit See CHARGE ACCOUNT CREDIT.

nonliquid assets/wealth Valuable property such as real estate or jewelry that may be difficult to turn into cash on short notice. Compare LIQUID ASSETS/WEALTH.

nonmarking The practice of offering goods for sale in a store without marking the price on each item.

nonmerchandise services Synonym for STORE SERVICES.

nonmerchant marketing intermediary Synonym for NONMERCHANT MIDDLEMAN.

nonmerchant middleman A category of MARKETING INTERMEDIARY that includes a BROKER, a COMMISSION MERCHANT, a SELLING AGENT, a MANUFACTURER'S AGENT, and an AUCTION HOUSE. Nonmerchant middlemen do not generally take title to the goods in which they deal, but they do facilitate the transfer of the goods from the seller to the buyer. Also called *nonmerchant marketing intermediary*.

nonoperating expense Any expenditure resulting from transactions incidental to a company's main line of business (i.e., outside daily operations). In a retail store these are expenses not directly connected with the buying and selling of merchandise (e.g., interest expenses and losses from the sale of buildings, machinery, equipment). Compare OPERATING EXPENSE.

nonoperating revenue Any REVENUE not directly related to the sale of products and/or services. For example, interest, dividends, and rents are considered nonoperating revenue. Compare OPERATING REVENUE, which is derived from the sale of goods and/or services in the ordinary operation of the store.

nonpackaged staple See STAPLE.

nonperpetual inventory An inventory control system in which a physical count must be made to determine how much stock is on hand. Compare PERPETUAL INVENTORY (CONTROL).

nonpersonal communication channels Any medium that carries messages without personal contact or feedback. Nonpersonal communication channels include mass media (e.g., DIRECT MAIL), ATMOSPHERICS (i.e., environmental factors designed to stimulate sales and/or establish a particular image), or an EVENT (e.g., a grand opening). See also PERSONAL COMMUNICATION CHANNEL, MEDIA, and ADVERTISING MEDIA.

nonpersonally identifiable information (NP-II) Information about a visitor to a Web site that does not reveal the visitor's identity. It does, however, reveal such information as the user's COOKIE number, the time and date when a page was viewed, and a description of the page at the moment when the WEB BEACON revealing this information was placed.

nonpersonal promotion aid Any of the services provided by a vendor to a retailer that directly influences the buying behavior of the consumer. Nonpersonal promotion aids include DEALER HELPS and *consumer inducements*. Compare PERSONAL PROMOTIONAL AID. See also DEALER AID and SELLING AID.

nonpersonal retailing A form of selling in which the customer does not visit a store and in which there is no face-to-face contact between seller and buyer. Nonpersonal retailing includes CATALOG RETAILING, MAIL ORDER RETAILING, AUTOMATIC VENDING, and E-TAILING.

nonpersonal selling A method of communicating with customers indirectly. Information about a store is communicated through nonpersonal selling devices such as advertising, sales promotion, publicity, word of mouth, and packaging. Many types of nonpersonal selling devices are used by store buyers in various combinations.

nonprice competition Competitive activity between stores that have comparable prices. The stores may offer different services, project different images, or otherwise attempt to distinguish themselves from their competitors through variables other than price. Compare PRICE COMPETITION.

nonprobability sample In marketing and other social science research, a sample whose selection is not random but rather involves the judgment (and possible bias) of the researcher. The three major types of nonprobability samples are the CONVENIENCE SAMPLE, the JUDGMENT SAMPLE, and the QUOTA SAMPLE. Nonprobability samples are sometimes preferred by market researchers, particularly when certain special expertise is an important characteristic of the sample group. However, the results of research using nonprobability samples contain many unknowns, and must be regarded with caution when used to draw conclusions about the total POPULATION. See also SAMPLE.

nonprobability sampling A method of selecting a sample for marketing and other social science research in which the judgment (and possible bias) of the researcher enters into the selection process. The three major types of nonprobability samples are the CONVENIENCE SAMPLE, the JUDGMENT SAMPLE, and the QUOTA SAMPLE. Nonprobability sampling is sometimes preferred by market researchers over probability sampling, particularly when certain special expertise is an important characteristic of the sample group. This sampling method may also be desirable when there are budget or time constraints. However, the results of research using nonprobability samples contain many unknowns, and must be regarded with caution when used to draw conclusions about the total POPULATION. See also SAMPLE.

nonproduct A product or service prepared for a specific segment of the market, only to find that the need for the product, or the segment itself, did not actually exist. If the item or service is offered, it generally fails.

nonprofit advertising ADVERTISING used by nonprofit organizations to increase donations, promote sales of used goods in their retail stores, or gain volunteer support for their efforts.

nonprofit corporation An incorporated institution whose owners have limited liability and that exists to provide a social service rather than to make a profit.

nonprofit marketing Marketing conducted by organizations operating on a not-for-profit basis. Such marketing is almost always concerned with services and ideas rather than with physical products and may include a wide variety of political, social, and religious activities. Also called *nonbusiness marketing* and *not-for-profit marketing*. See also NONBUSINESS ORGANIZATION.

nonprofit organization (NPO) Synonym for NONBUSINESS ORGANIZATION.

nonpromotional store A store that gives little emphasis to price except for rare events such as a semiannual clearance. The accent is on quality, uniqueness, good taste, distinctiveness, service, or convenience. Sometimes called an *institutional store*. Also spelled *non-promotional store*.

nonrecognition brand See BRAND NONRECOGNITION.

nonsalable Of merchandise, not fit to be offered for sale because of its poor condition or some other factor.

nonsampling error A mistake that occurs in any stage of the data collection, recording, and enumerating process, whether accidental or deliberate. This may be a miscalculation, a misinterpretation of a question or response, falsified responses, etc. However, the error is unrelated to the methods used to select the sample itself. These mistakes may occur in either census or sample methods of MARKETING RESEARCH (MR). Compare SAMPLING ERROR.

nonseasonal staples Staple merchandise that is in demand throughout the year, or even for a number of years. Demand for nonseasonal staples is not affected by seasonal variations. For example, hardware, foodstuffs, and toiletries represent nonseasonal staples. Compare SEASONAL STAPLES. See also STAPLE.

nonselling area The space in a store devoted to activities not directly related to the selling of merchandise. For example, loading docks, executive offices, workrooms, stockrooms, dressing rooms, elevators, and escalators are all considered nonselling areas.

nonsigner's clause A common feature of many state RESALE PRICE MAINTENANCE (RPM) laws that grew out of the MILLER-TYDINGS ACT (1937). A nonsigner's clause allowed a manufacturer to impose resale price agreements in a state if even one retailer signed a contract agreeing to resale price maintenance. Also spelled *non-signer's clause.*

nonstore retailing A form of retailing not involving a traditional store building. The retailer (*nonstore retailer*) and the customer transact their business through such means as direct mail, door-to-door sales, vending machines, two-way television, and Internet sales.

nontariff (trade) barrier Any government policy or law, other than a TARIFF, that restricts international trade. Nontariff barriers include content laws, surcharges at border crossings, licensing regulations, performance requirements, government export subsidies, safety and health standards, import quotas, government purchasing rules, packaging and labeling regulations, and size and weight requirements. Not all of these barriers are discriminatory and protectionist, as they may be imposed to protect public health and safety.

non-title-taking agent middleman Synonym for AGENT INTERMEDIARY.

nontraceable common cost Any business expense that cannot be assigned to a particular function (e.g., executive salaries, interest payments).

no-order Merchandise that arrives at a retailer's distribution center without a supporting purchase order.

normal good Any good for which demand increases as income increases. The term does not refer to the quality of the good. Compare GIFFEN GOOD, SUPERIOR GOOD, and INFERIOR GOOD.

normal inflation Inflation at rates of less than 3 percent annually.

normal margin retailer A retail establishment that offers merchandise at prices comparable to those found at other stores at the same market level or in the same TRADING AREA. The normal margin retailer has chosen not to compete by attempting to undersell the competition.

normal price The price to which the market price tends to return after fluctuations up or down.

normal sale A purchase transaction in which both buyer and seller are satisfied and no unforeseen situations arise.

norms Social rules or standards that, although not universally observed, form a basis for day-to-day behavior. Norms influencing consumer behavior and lifestyle are factors the marketer must consider when marketing products or services either in the domestic market or abroad.

North American Free Trade Association (NAFTA) Perhaps the most famous FREE-TRADE AREA, including the United States, Canada, and Mexico. The partnership went into effect in 1993. The participating nations agree to drop trade barriers among themselves, but each is permitted to maintain independent trade relations with countries outside the group. Essential elements of the agreement (known as the *North American Free Trade Agreement,* also abbreviated NAFTA) include: elimination of tariffs on most products crossing the borders of the three countries; elimination of quota requirements on most apparel made from yarn and fabric from any of the three countries; and elimination of duties on yarn made in Mexico and used in items involved in an 807 program (an initiative to encourage manufacturing in selected Caribbean countries). NAFTA also provides advantages to retailers in member countries. For example, relaxed import regulations allow Mexican retailers to purchase more U.S. goods for their stores.

North American Industry Classification System (NAICS) A taxonomy or scheme for classifying establishments by the type of economic activity in which they are engaged. The NAICS replaced the STANDARD INDUSTRIAL CLASSIFICATION (SIC) system in 1997. NAICS was developed jointly by the United States, Canada, and Mexico to provide new comparability in statistics about business activity across North America. Like the SIC, the statistical census is conducted every five years. The NAICS database may be accessed through the U.S. Census Bureau Web site at www.census.gov. See also NORTH AMERICAN PRODUCT CLASSIFICATION SYSTEM (NAPCS).

North American Product Classification System (NAPCS) A classification system for products and services, under development by the United States, Canada, and Mexico. The project was launched in 1999 to develop a comprehensive product classification system complementing the new industrial classification NAICS of 1997. The long-term objective of NAPCS is to develop a market-oriented classification system for products that can be linked to the NAICS industry structure, is consistent across the three participating countries, and promotes improvements in the identification and classification of service products across existing international classification systems. The NAPCS database may be accessed through the U.S. Census Bureau Web site at www.census.gov. See also NORTH AMERICAN INDUSTRY CLASSIFICATION SYSTEM (NAICS).

nose-to-nose selling See BELLY-TO-BELLY SELLING.

note A document, such as a PROMISSORY NOTE, recognized as legal evidence of a debt. The borrower promises to pay a certain amount of money on a specified date to a certain business, individual, or bank (i.e., the lender). See also NOTES PAYABLE.

notes payable In accounting, current liabilities to banks and other lending institutions, payable on a specific date. See also NOTE.

not-for-profit marketing Synonym for NONPROFIT MARKETING.

not-for-profit organization Synonym for NONBUSINESS ORGANIZATION.

notions Small sundry items such as needles and thread, ribbon, buttons, etc., displayed together for sale.

not married but cohabiting The consumer category comprising households, usually dual-income, whose heads are common-law spouses. They are less future-oriented than the NEWLY MARRIED. Clothing and entertainment expenditures are significant, but making joint purchases for the home is less important than self-actualization.

not married but cohabiting note A document, such as a PROMISSORY NOTE, recognized as legal evidence of a debt. The borrower promises to pay a certain amount of money on a specified date to a certain business, individual, or bank (i.e., the lender). See also NOTES PAYABLE.

nouveau niche The marketing trend in which success is based on one's ability to identify and cater to new niches in the marketplace. The trend was identified and the term coined by trendwatching.com at www.trendwatching.com. See also NICHE, NICHE MARKET, and NICHE MARKETING.

nouveau riche An individual whose wealth is newly acquired, especially one regarded as ostentatious or uncultivated.

novelties Small decorative or amusing articles, usually mass-produced.

NP-II See NONPERSONALLY IDENTIFIABLE INFORMATION (NP-II)

NPO See NONBUSINESS ORGANIZATION.

NRF See NATIONAL RETAIL FEDERATION (NRF).

NRMA See NATIONAL RETAIL FEDERATION (NRF).

NSFNet In the development of the INTERNET, NSFNet is the high-speed network backbone developed by the National Science Foundation (NSF) that connected supercomputers for academic research purposes. Originally restricted to academic users, the NSFNet backbone was opened to all users in 1986.

nuclear family The so-called typical family of father, mother, and children living in one dwelling. In recent years, the predominance of the nuclear family has diminished in the United States and Western Europe. See also FAMILY LIFE CYCLE (FLC).

number Synonym for a DESIGN, specifically when referring to a particular item. Many manufacturers, retailers, and catalog merchants actually assign numerical codes to distinguish their various products. Also called a STYLE NUMBER.

number of stock turns See STOCK TURNOVER (ST).

nutritional labeling   The practice of indicating on the packages of food products the nutritional value of the product (in particular, the proportion of the U.S. recommended daily allowances supplied by a specified quantity of the product) and the specific ingredients it contains. See also NUTRITION LABELING AND EDUCATION ACT (NLEA) (1990).

Nutrition Labeling and Education Act (NLEA) (1990)   U.S. federal legislation requiring detailed nutritional information on the labels of most foods regulated by the FOOD AND DRUG ADMINISTRATION (FDA). It also requires that all nutrient content claims (e.g., high fiber, low fat) and health claims be consistent with FDA regulations. The requirements were phased in during 1993 and 1994, with juice and juice drink labeling exempted until 1994. The labels provide distinctive, easy-to-read formats detailing information about the amount per serving of saturated fat, cholesterol, dietary fiber, and other nutrients of health concern to consumers. Nutrient references are expressed as % Daily Values. Claims about the relationship between a nutrient or food and a disease or condition (e.g., calcium and osteoporosis, or fat and cancer) are also included, as are standardized serving sizes (for easier comparisons by the consumer). For juice drinks, the nutritional label must include a declaration of the total percentage of juice in the drinks. The FDA provides detailed information about NUTRITIONAL LABELING on its home page at www.fda.gov.

NYSE (New York Stock Exchange)   See STOCK EXCHANGE.

OBC   See OWNED BY CHINA (OBC).

objection   In sales, a prospect's reason for rejecting the salesperson's offer. See also SALES APPROACH.

objective   A specific, short-range target an organization hopes to achieve en route to fulfilling its MISSION STATEMENT. While the term *objective* is sometimes used interchangeably with the term GOAL, goals are actually the broad, long-range targets of the organization, whereas objectives are the intermediate benchmarks or reference points an organization must reach as it pursues its goals. A retailer's objectives may relate to sales, profit, image, etc., and are periodically reevaluated during the RETAIL AUDIT. Also called an *organizational objective*. See also MANAGEMENT BY OBJECTIVES (MBO).

objective-and-task approach   See OBJECTIVE-TASK METHOD OF PROMOTIONAL BUDGETING.

objective-task method of promotional budgeting   A method of budgeting for promotional expenditures, including advertising, based on preset goals and objectives and on an analysis of the activities necessary to reach them. The method consists of three steps: stating the promotional and communications objectives; developing the strategies and determining the tasks necessary to accomplish them; and estimating the costs associated with implementing these activities. The budget is an aggregate of the costs identified with the performance of the promotional activities. Also known as the *objective and task approach*, *objective and task method*, *objective and task technique*, *objective-task approach*, *objective/task method of promotional budgeting*, *task and investment method* or *building method*. See also PROMOTIONAL BUDGETING.

objective value   The price an item can command relative to other items in the marketplace.

object-of-expenditure costs   See NATURAL CLASSIFICATION OF EXPENSES.

obligee   A person or organization to whom another is obligated (i.e., morally or legally bound), as in a contract. A CREDITOR, for example, may be considered an obligee.

obligor   A person or organization legally obligated (i.e., morally or legally bound) to another, as in a contract. A DEBTOR, for example, may be considered an obligor.

observation   A MARKETING RESEARCH (MR) technique frequently used in retailing in which primary data is collected by watching individuals (e.g., store customers) either directly or with cameras in order to record their shopping behavior and buying habits. Also called the *observational research*.

observational method/research   See OBSERVATION.

obsolescence   1. The phenomenon by which a product or style passes out of use or is discarded as an outmoded type.   2. In fashion, a stage in the FASHION LIFE CYCLE at which a style is no longer viewed with favor and is therefore no longer salable.

obsolete   Of a product or style, no longer in general use because outmoded or discarded.

obsolete material   In retailing, inventory items that have little or no possibility of being used in the near future. Such items include products that have undergone structural design changes or that have been discarded in favor of newer models or versions. See also OBSOLESCENCE.

occupancy expense   Any expenditure relating to the use of property. Occupancy expenses include rent, utilities, heating, lighting, depreciation, upkeep, and the general care of the property. See also LEASING AND RENTING.

Occupational Safety and Health Act (OSH Act) (1970)   U.S. Public Law 91-596, passed December 29, 1970, and amended through January 1, 2004. The legislation, which was implemented in phases beginning in 1970 and 1971, established the OCCUPATIONAL SAFETY AND HEALTH ADMINISTRATION (OSHA). The complete text of the legislation may be found at the OSHA Web site at www.osha.gov.

Occupational Safety and Health Administration (OSHA)   A U.S. federal agency established by the OCCUPATIONAL SAFETY AND HEALTH ACT (OSH ACT) (1970) to oversee employee working conditions. The Secretary of Labor is empowered by the act to set standards for workplace safety, enforce OSHA regulations, and impose penalties (including fines and imprisonment) for violations. OSHA is charged not only with preventing accidents, but also with eliminating work-related diseases such as black lung among coal miners and brown lung among textile workers, and harm from toxic chemicals such as asbestos. OSHA also offers compliance assistance, consultation, and training. The agency maintains a Web site at www.osha.gov.

OCR See OPTICAL CODE READER (OCR) and OPTICAL CHARACTER RECOGNITION (OCR).

OCR-A A set of standardized letter and number characters constituting a monospaced font, developed to meet the standards set by the American National Standards Institute in 1966. OCR-A may be read by the human eye as well as by machines (e.g., wands, scanners, price ticket readers) and was designed for the processing of documents by banks, credit card companies, and similar businesses. In retailing, OCR-A is used on price tags and labels, credit cards, bank checks, etc. It is also used in advertising and display graphics when a modern, technical look is desired. The formal name for the font is *Optical Character Recognition—Font A*. See also OCR-B.

OCR-B A set of standardized letter and number characters constituting a monospaced font developed in 1968 to meet the standards of the European Computer Manufacturers Association. It was intended for use on products that were to be scanned by electronic devices (e.g., wands, scanners, price ticket readers) as well as read by humans. OCR-B was made a world standard in 1973, and is more legible to human eyes than most other OCR fonts. The OCR-B font also has a distinctive technical appearance that makes it popular with graphic designers. The formal name for the font is *Optical Character Recognition—Font B*. See also OCR-A.

oddball pricing The setting of the same price for a variety of goods, regardless of cost, markup, or customary pricing.

odd-cent/odd-ending pricing See ODD-LINE PRICING.

odd-even pricing See ODD-LINE PRICING and EVEN-LINE PRICING.

odd-line pricing The use of retail prices ending in odd numbers (especially five, seven, or nine) to convey the impression of a lower price. For example, a retailer using odd-line pricing would charge $9.99 rather than $10.00 to convey the idea of a bargain. Also known as *odd pricing, odd-value pricing, odd-ending pricing, off-even pricing, odd-cent pricing, psychological pricing*, and *penny pricing*. Compare EVEN-LINE PRICING.

odd lot Synonym for JOB LOT.

odd-number/value pricing See ODD-LINE PRICING.

odd pricing See ODD-LINE PRICING.

odds and ends Miscellaneous leftover merchandise in incomplete assortments of style, color, and sizes. See also BROKEN ASSORTMENTS.

odd-value pricing See ODD-LINE PRICING.

off-brand A trade name or symbol not readily identified by the consumer.

offer response method of research A technique used to test the effectiveness of an advertisement. The customer is required to present proof of having read the ad, such as a COUPON, at the time of purchase.

offer test A test for assessing the effectiveness of pricing strategies and other promotional options. The test may be used to measure responses to differing prices and/or terms of an offer. For example, offer tests have been used to show that a price offer of $9.95 generally results in a greater number of purchases than the same merchandise at $10.00.

off-even pricing See ODD-LINE PRICING.

off-factor The total of a chain discount expressed as a percent. For example, a chain discount of 40% and 10% equals a discount of 46%, which is the off-factor. The ON-FACTOR, which is its complement, is calculated by subtraction from 100%, and is therefore 54% in this example. See also CHAIN DISCOUNT.

offline Not connected to the INTERNET (i.e., not ONLINE). All traditional marketing and retailing efforts (such as BRICKS-AND-MORTAR retail establishments) are offline.

offline-online promotion synergy See PROMOTION SYNERGY.

off-price See OFF-PRICE MERCHANDISE and OFF-PRICE DISCOUNT STORE.

off-price center A SHOPPING CENTER or MALL featuring at least one off-price discounter as a tenant. Such centers feature brand name goods sold at much lower prices than conventional department and specialty stores. See also OUTLET CENTER and VALUE CENTER.

off-price discounter Synonym for OFF-PRICE DISCOUNT STORE.

off-price discount store A DISCOUNT STORE that buys manufacturers' irregulars, seconds, overruns, closeouts, and cancelled orders, as well as returns and end-of-season or closeout merchandise from other retail stores. Many modern discounters also offer first-quality in-season merchandise in addition to last year's styles and irregular merchandise. Some manufacturers make goods especially for off-price stores, thus making good use of extra reams of fabric and slack production time. Off-price discount stores are positioned to compete with department stores, selling department store brands for 20% to 60% below department store prices. Also called an *off-pricer, offpricer, off-price store*, or *off-price discounter*.

off-price merchandise Retail goods, often carrying status or premium labels, offered at lower than regular retail prices. This merchandise, which may be manufacturers' surplus in the form of end-of-season liquidations or other retailers' overstocked merchandise, is in perfect condition. Increasingly, in-season merchandise is being made available to off-price retailers by vendors because these merchants often pay cash and seldom ask for promotional allowances, markdown money, or return privileges. See also OFF-PRICE RETAILING.

off-pricer Synonym for OFF-PRICE DISCOUNT STORE. Also spelled *offpricer*.

off-price retailer Synonym for OFF-PRICE DISCOUNT STORE.

off-price retailing The selling at retail of merchandise, often carrying status or premium labels, at less than regular prices. In contrast to DISCOUNT RETAILING (where the discounter pays the same price for merchandise as everyone else and sells it for less than traditional retailers), off-price retailers buy merchandise at cut-rate prices and pass the savings along to their customers. In addition, expenses are kept low by limiting advertising expenditures, turning stock over quickly, and other cost-cutting techniques. An off-price retail establishment may be an independent organization specializing in off-price merchandise, a FACTORY OUTLET, or a CLOSED-DOOR DISCOUNT HOUSE. See also OFF-PRICE MERCHANDISE.

off-price sourcing The purchase of merchandise at cut-rate prices, particularly for the purpose of passing those savings along to the customer. Both small and larger retailers often utilize salaried buying offices for access to off-price sourcing. See also SALARIED (BUYING) OFFICE.

off-price store Synonym for OFF-PRICE DISCOUNT STORE.

off-retail Of a MARKDOWN (MD), applied to the original retail price.

off-retail (markdown) percentage See MARKDOWN PERCENTAGE.

off-season A slow period, either before or after the regular selling season for a category of merchandise. See also OFF-SEASON PRICING.

off-season pricing A MARKDOWN (MD) given during a slow period to move merchandise. This may occur during a preseason or postseason period. Off-season pricing reaches a different, more PRICE-CONSCIOUS market segment than regular-season customers.

offset deal A COMPENSATION TRANSACTION in which the selling company guarantees to use some products or services from the buying country in the manufacture of the final product. These transactions are particularly common when large government purchases are involved.

offshore production The transfer of some or all of a firm's manufacturing activities to plants in foreign countries. As in the apparel manufacturing industry, this practice is embraced in order to take advantage of lower production costs. See also OUTSOURCING.

off-the-peg British term for READY-TO-WEAR (RTW).

off-the-rack Especially of clothing, ready-made, that is, READY-TO-WEAR (RTW). See also BUYING OFF THE RACK/PEG.

OJT See ON-THE-JOB TRAINING (OJT).

OLAP See ONLINE ANALYTICAL PROCESSING (OLAP).

oldbies People with extensive INTERNET experience who have become sophisticated users of the WORLD WIDE WEB (WWW) and all its resources. Such consumers are increasingly willing to purchase goods and services ONLINE, suggesting that e-tailers and other e-marketers need to improve the quality of their Web sites to better serve this growing class of potential customers. The trend was identified and the term coined by trendwatching.com at www.trendwatching.com. See also E-TAILING and E-MARKETING.

oligopolistic competition The condition that obtains in the marketplace when a relatively small number of large competing firms sell similar or identical products in an extremely price-sensitive environment. Oligopolistic competition exists in such industries as chemicals, petroleum, steel, and automobiles. Also called an *oligopolistic market structure* or, simply, an *oligopoly*.

oligopolistic market structure See OLIGOPOLISTIC COMPETITION.

oligopoly See OLIGOPOLISTIC COMPETITION.

oligopsony A market condition in which there are few buyers and many suppliers, giving the buyers (i.e., the retailers or other marketing intermediaries) a great deal of power.

omnibus cooperative advertising/advertisement A full-page print ad placed by a retailer and bearing the retailer's name, but consisting of mats supplied by various vendors of different products. The retailer bills each vendor a prorated share of the ad's cost. See also COOPERATIVE ADVERTISING.

Omnibus Trade and Competitiveness Act (1988) U.S. federal legislation designed to protect U.S. industry and trade. The act includes the switch to a harmonized system of tariff codes, the reduction of licensing requirements for exports to U.S. allies, and a strengthening of U.S. import restrictions. It gives U.S. presidents the right to negotiate orderly marketing arrangements and set countervailing duties to deal with the problems of trade deficits, protected markets, and dumping. The use of the *orderly marketing arrangement* or VOLUNTARY EXPORT RESTRICTIONS (VERS) has since spread to textiles, clothing, steel, automobiles, shoes, machinery, and consumer electronics. The *Gephart Amendment*, commonly known as *Super 301*, the most controversial provision of the legislation, is designed to protect U.S. commercial interests from foreign attack.

on account 1. Of a purchase or sale, made on an open account (i.e., with credit). 2. Of a payment, made toward the settlement of an open (i.e., credit) account.

on approval See APPROVAL SALE.

on approval offer   See APPROVAL SALE.

on consignment   See CONSIGNMENT.

one-brand name strategy   See INTEGRATED, ONE-BRAND NAME STRATEGY.

one-cent sale   A sales promotion event in which two items of the same classification are sold for the price of one, plus one cent.

one hundred percent location   The best possible site for a particular store (i.e., the site within a major business district that gives the retailer the greatest exposure to the store's target customers).

one hundred percent traffic area   Any area of a store that gets very heavy customer TRAFFIC. These areas are located in front of and around escalators or elevators, at entrances or exits, and near major featured spots like restaurants, atriums, and central meeting areas.

one-item display   The presentation and promotion of a single garment or other single item. For example, a gown designed by a prominent designer, a one-of-a-kind piece of jewelry, or a new automobile may constitute a one-item display.

one-level channel   A CHANNEL OF DISTRIBUTION in which there is only one intermediary, commonly a retailer, between the producer and the consumer.

oneline marketing   Integration of online and offline activities to develop a synergy between the two where the effect of the whole (online plus offline) is greater than the sum of the parts.

one-more-yes close   A CLOSING sales method based on the notion that people are creatures of habit. The SALESPERSON raises a series of questions about the prospect's feeling about the product, posed in such a way as to elicit a positive response. The final question, asking whether the prospect would like to buy the product or service, invites a similarly positive reply.

one-price policy   A PRICE POLICY in which retail prices are fixed and uniform for all customers and not subject to negotiation. The seller sets a price for a particular point in time and buyers can take it or leave it, with no quantity discounts allowed. Also called *fixed price*, *rigid pricing*, or *fixed price policy*. Compare VARIABLE-PRICE POLICY and SINGLE-PRICE POLICY. See also FLAT RATE.

one-price store   A store in which all merchandise of a particular type is sold at the same price. See also SINGLE-PRICE POLICY.

one-shot deal   Merchandise that cannot be reordered, often purchased for a specific promotional event. Also called a *one-shot promotion*.

one-shot promotion   See ONE-SHOT DEAL.

one-stop shopping   A retail outlet that purports to house everything a customer would need under a single roof. HYPER-MARKETS, for example, capitalize on the one-stop concept.

1/10 net 30 (one ten net 30)   In the DATING OF INVOICES (i.e., billing), a term of sale meaning that a 1% discount is given if the invoice is paid within 10 days. Otherwise, the full amount of the payment is due within 30 days.

one-time purchaser   A customer who makes an initial purchase but does not reorder or buy additional quantities of the product or service. Compare REPEAT BUSINESS.

one-to-one marketing   Synonym for DATABASE MARKETING.

on-factor   The difference between 100% and the OFF-FACTOR (i.e., the percentage representing the total of a CHAIN DISCOUNT). For example, a chain discount of 40% and 10% equals a single discount of 46%, which is the off-factor. The on-factor, its complement, is 54% (100% − 46%).

online   Connected to an Internet provider or other connector and entering a network, intranet, extranet, or the INTERNET. A user may go online to send or receive e-mail, surf the WORLD WIDE WEB (WWW), chat in a CHAT ROOM, or participate in a newsgroup discussion. Businesses go online for a variety of reasons, but primarily to promote and sell products.

online analytical processing (OLAP)   Software tools that provide analysis of DATA stored in a DATABASE (DB). OLAP tools enable users to analyze the various dimensions of multidimensional data (e.g., time series and trend analyses). OLAP software is often used in DATA MINING.

online auction   A public sale of merchandise that takes place on the Internet. Online auctions are popular with consumers selling products C2C (consumer-to-consumer). An *exchange manager* such as eBay facilitates the bidding and purchasing process while participants follow the bidding at their leisure from their home computers. These person-to-person auctions offer a venue for the sale of a broad assortment of products. A GENERAL AUCTION accepts items from many product categories while others are product-specific (see PRODUCT-SPECIFIC AUCTION). The classic *forward auction*, where participants bid up a price and the highest bidder wins, is most common, but the *reverse auction*, where the lowest bid wins, are also frequent. Other types of auctions include *pooled*, *private*, *reserve price*, and the DUTCH AUCTION. Auctions are the primary venue for consumers to become online sellers. Some retailers, meanwhile, have experimented with the *house auction* to auction off their clearance products At times, live auctions taking place in real time are broadcast electronically, with remote participants competing electronically with bidders at the auction house site. See also AUCTION.

online automated supply procurement   Synonym for E-PROCUREMENT.

online brainstorming   See BRAINSTORMING.

online couponing   See ELECTRONIC COUPON.

online culture An extension of offline culture that includes conventions and standards regarding the look and feel of Web sites. These conventions govern such features as the use of color, measurements and standards, the inclusion of politics, humor, history, children, animals, flags, acronyms, abbreviations, and even how much text or animation is acceptable on a Web page. Because online culture influences responses to Web sites, it helps determine the effectiveness of e-mail marketing, online promotions, and pricing strategies. Sites can be *culturally neutral* (i.e., avoiding cultural nuances and attempting to appeal across cultures), *culturally local* (i.e., targeting local customers with specific cultural nuances), or *culturally centric* (e.g., biased in favor of U.S. culture).

online exchange An electronic marketplace used by purchasing agents to simplify the ordering process and increase purchasing efficiency. Typically, a purchasing agent submits a REQUEST FOR QUOTES (RFQ) to the online exchange and receives price quotes and specifications from many different vendors. Online exchanges also allow purchasing agents to compare offers quickly, reducing paperwork and time spent on placing large institutional orders.

online interview An interview technique used primarily by executive recruiters for online chats with business executives. The interviews can be simultaneously broadcast to different locations as well as taped for playback. The success of online interviewing depends on having sufficient bandwidth and state-of-the art video online systems. Also called a *video online interview (VOI)*.

online marketing Synonym for E-MARKETING.

online-offline promotion synergy See PROMOTION SYNERGY.

online oxygen A consumer trend recognizing the fact that many consumers not only want online access 24/7, they regard it as an absolute necessity. The trend was identified and the term coined by trendwatching.com at www.trendwatching.com.

online panel A hybrid type of quantitative MARKETING RESEARCH (MR) conducted online. Most online panels are OPT-IN and based on a combination of surveys, collecting information by monitoring chat rooms and online discussions and asking visitors to post open-ended opinions to research questions. Participants are recruited by e-mail or are intercepted when they visit a Web site or click through from a pop-up advertisement. Most panels use a CONVENIENCE SAMPLE, selecting participants because they are available. Demographic and behavioral information is collected for these panel members, allowing a PURPOSIVE SAMPLE (a group of individuals having the characteristics typical of the population being studied) to be drawn. Also called an *e-panel*. See also ONLINE REVIEW.

online review A nonscientific variant of the ONLINE PANEL that can nevertheless offer insight into what consumers are thinking and doing. Consumers provide written opinions of products using a variety of responses from short answers and multiple choice to extended written comments. Participants are generally self-selected. They are asked whether they would recommend a given product (or Web site) to others, how they would rate the product (or Web site) on a scale from one to five, etc. Alternatively, reviews can be extended written reports on product use. Representative comments are typically posted to the Web site.

online service A for-profit business enterprise that gives subscribers access to a variety of data transmitted over telecommunications lines. Online services provide an infrastructure enabling subscribers to communicate with one another through E-MAIL or through FORUM or CHAT ROOM discussions. In addition, the online service can connect users with third-party information providers, including e-tailers. The INTERNET itself is the largest online service, but differs from other online services in that it is not centrally controlled by any one organization and is not operated for profit. Compare BULLETIN BOARD SYSTEM (BBS).

online shopping The act of researching and purchasing products over the INTERNET or other online service. Consumers who prefer to purchase their selections in stores, through catalogs, by telephone, or by fax may nevertheless want to perform research, including product evaluations and price comparisons, on the Internet. Other consumers may prefer to make purchases directly online. Online shopping has a number of advantages over stores, such as greater product assortment, availability of products that cannot be found in stores, and a large number of sellers for comparison shopping. Direct delivery of online purchases can be made to a local address, giving shoppers in remote areas access to products. Online shopping also has a number of disadvantages, however, including security and privacy issues, delivery risk, the inability to touch, feel, smell, or taste the products, and the fact that quality is often difficult to assess. See also E-TAILING, BRICKS-AND-CLICKS, and CLICKS-ONLY.

online showroom An INTERNET marketplace bringing together multiple buyers and sellers where they can collaborate and negotiate without ever leaving their offices, completing complex transactions at a fraction of the cost and time previously needed. In addition, online showrooms provide easy access for international buyers and for buyers in geographical areas without easy access to traditional markets. Such showrooms make money by charging a percentage of the value of each transaction they host. Also called a *virtual showroom*. See also SHOWROOM.

online storefront Synonym for E-TAILER. See also BRICKS-AND-CLICKS and CLICKS-ONLY.

online survey A set of questions (i.e., a SURVEY or QUESTIONNAIRE) designed to collect specific information from Web site visitors, buyers, businesses, institutions, or organizations. These surveys make use of standardized forms, constructed in HTML, since they are simple to administer, code, and analyze. Online surveys have been found to have significantly higher response rates and lower costs than traditional surveys (such as telephone surveys).

on memorandum (buying)   See MEMORANDUM BUYING.

on order   Of merchandise, ordered by the buyer but not yet received by the store. This represents a commitment of the planned purchase figure and affects the OPEN-TO-BUY (OTB). Also known as an *open order,* such unfilled orders are generally charged to the month during which delivery is expected so that the buyer may better control open-to-buy.

on-pack (premium)   A free gift or other item attached to the outside of a package. The premium acts as an incentive to purchase the merchandise offered for sale. The two items may be held together by a band of paper or tape or by plastic film. Also called *banded premium, pack premium,* or *package band.*

on-percentage   The result (i.e., product) of multiplying together the complements of a series of discount percentages.

on sale   1. Of merchandise, offered at a reduced price. See also SALE PRICE. 2. Sometimes, a synonym for FOR SALE (i.e., available for purchase).

on-screen entertainment   A form of DIRECT RESPONSE advertising frequently viewed at a movie theater. On-screen entertainment is the slide show before the movie, featuring advertisements interspersed with trivia and Hollywood gossip. Retailers and other small businesses located near the movie theater are often the featured advertisers.

on the books   Of purchases, made through an OPEN ACCOUNT.

on the floor   Of a BUYER, spending time in the selling department. This provides the buyer with customer and salesperson contact as well as information about what is being requested, what is selling, and what needs to be reordered.

on-the-job training (OJT)   Employee instruction that takes place during regular business hours while the employee is also doing productive work and being paid regular wages. Supervisors guide new employees through real-life work experiences as part of the training.

on-the-water report   A report notifying merchandisers that products are being shipped. Also called a *shipping report.*

on time   On an INSTALLMENT PLAN/CONTRACT/BUYING. Goods purchased on time are paid for by remitting a portion of the price at regular intervals. Newlywed couples, for example, may furnish their homes by buying their furniture "on time." The practice was more prevalent before the hegemony of the credit card.

OOH   See OUT-OF-HOME (OOH) ADVERTISING.

OP   See OVERALL PERFORMANCE (OP).

open account   1. An arrangement under which goods are sold on credit, with the buyer's account being debited but no written evidence given by the seller. The practice of recording such transactions in a ledger gave rise to the popular term, *on the*

books. Also called an *open-book account, open credit,* or an *open-credit account.* This form of credit is most often extended by small neighborhood retail stores to local customers they know well or by vendors to retailers. 2. Any credit account in which there remains a balance to be paid. See also CHARGE ACCOUNT.

open-air center   See TOWN CENTER.

open-air market   Any outdoor market, whether flea market or farmers' market. Such markets sell consumer goods through multiple vendors and generally take place in the same location at regular intervals (such as weekly).

open-air parking   See PARKING.

open assortment   A collection or set of items in which the consumer does not have available all the items usually needed. Compare CLOSED ASSORTMENT.

open-back window   A backless DISPLAY WINDOW providing an unobstructed view of the store's interior to passersby. This allows the entire store to become a display. Also called *see-through window, no-back window,* or *open display.*

open bid   An offer to perform a service or supply goods, submitted to a buyer and announced openly so that all bidders know the prices submitted in the competitive bidding process. Compare SEALED BID.

open-book account   Synonym for OPEN ACCOUNT.

open-book credit   An informal arrangement whereby a purchaser may obtain products before paying for them. Payment terms allow the purchaser to take possession of the goods and pay for them later. For example, the owner of a sportswear store may place an order for swimsuits with the manufacturer, who lets the storekeeper have them on credit. Later, when the store owner begins to sell the suits, the bill is paid to the manufacturer. Many business transactions involving merchandise are financed through open-book credit, sometimes referred to as an OPEN ACCOUNT. Open-book credit is a form of UNSECURED CREDIT.

open charge account   See CHARGE ACCOUNT.

open-code   See OPEN-CODE DATING/LABELING.

open-code dating/labeling   A system for marking food products using a code that is intelligible to customers (i.e., open). The code indicates the last day that the product may be sold in the store. Open codes help customers make judgments regarding the freshness of the merchandise. Also called *open dating, open-code,* and *open-date labeling.* See also PULL DATE.

open credit   See OPEN ACCOUNT.

open credit account   See OPEN ACCOUNT.

open-date labeling   Synonym for OPEN-CODE DATING/LABELING.

open dating   Synonym for OPEN-CODE DATING/LABELING.

open display   See OPEN-BACK WINDOW.

open distribution   Distribution of the same merchandise by a variety of dealers in the same area or region, with no restrictions governing the number of items a dealer sells. Compare EXCLUSIVE DISTRIBUTION, INTENSIVE DISTRIBUTION, and SELECTIVE DISTRIBUTION.

open-end contract   An agreement between suppliers and buyers in which the supplier contracts to meet the buyer's requirements for a specific item during a specified period. The agreement is open-ended because all the terms are left indefinite.

open-end discount store   A DISCOUNT STORE open to the general public with no membership requirement. Compare CLOSED-DOOR DISCOUNT HOUSE.

open front   A store entrance, often used in an interior mall, that has no physical barriers such as doors and windows. This design encourages customers to enter the store, browse, and shop.

opening   1. The public showing of a new line of fashions by producers and designers at the beginning of a particular season.   2. An available position in a retail store or other business.   3. Part of the RECEIVING process in which received merchandise shipped from a vendor is opened and inspected.   4. See STORE OPENING.

opening balance   1. In a credit account, the amount remaining unpaid at the beginning of an accounting period (e.g., a month).   2. In a bank account, the amount on deposit at the beginning of the accounting period.

opening bid price   In classic forward auctions, both online and offline, the price set by the seller. Factors influencing the opening bid price are product state (i.e., new or used), condition of the product (e.g., worn or MINT), original or list price (i.e., price paid by the seller when the item was originally purchased), comparative price (i.e., the price of identical or comparable products), recent sale price (if a comparable item was recently sold at auction), and auction fee (paid by the seller). The practice of using this price is known as *opening bid pricing*.

opening inventory   The value, either cost or retail, of goods on hand at the beginning of an accounting period.

opening physical inventory   See PHYSICAL INVENTORY SYSTEM.

opening price (point)   The lowest level at which merchandise in a particular classification is priced at retail.

open money   That portion of the OPEN-TO-BUY (OTB) a store permits the RESIDENT BUYER to commit without prior approval during a specified period of time.

open order   1. An ORDER placed with a RESIDENT BUYER without any restrictions as to price, vendor, or delivery, a pro-cedure generally used when the goods are needed in a hurry. The resident buyer is given the authority to seek out the merchandise, select the vendor, and negotiate the best possible terms. See also GOOD-TILL-CANCELED ORDER (GTC).   2. A synonym for ON ORDER and STANDING ORDER.

open pricing   The practice of marking merchandise with prices clearly shown in acceptable symbols readable by humans.

open-sell fixture   A floor fixture giving customers access to merchandise and allowing selection without the assistance of a salesperson. Open-sell fixtures result in lower selling costs than closed-sell fixtures, since fewer salespeople are needed to serve customers. Customers are more likely to purchase goods that they can readily test, feel, or try on. Compare CLOSED-SELL FIXTURE.

open shop   A workplace employing both union and nonunion employees, in which the latter pay no dues to the union representing their colleagues.

open stock   Merchandise kept on hand in retail stores and sold either as sets or as separate pieces. Additional or replacement pieces are carried in bulk over a period of several years. This policy is followed most often in the sales of china, glassware, and flatware. Compare CLOSED STOCK.

open-the-kimono   (Slang) The revelation of company plans (e.g., future products) to prospective customers. The goal is to convince the buyer that the company is developing new or superior items and should be preferred over its competitors.

open-to-buy (OTB)   The amount (expressed in dollars or units) that a buyer is permitted to order for a specified period of time. In terms of dollars, a department's open-to-buy would be the total amount budgeted less the value of goods yet to be delivered in the specified period. Open-to-buy is traditionally determined by calculating the difference between planned sales and the combination of inventory already owned and merchandise on order. In short, open-to-buy is the amount the buyer has left to spend for a period, and is reduced each time a purchase is made. The purpose of open-to-buy is to prevent overinvestment in merchandise. See also MERCHANDISE PLAN, BUYING PLAN, and SALES PLAN. OTB is calculated as follows: (a) calculate PLANNED PURCHASES AT RETAIL by combining planned sales, planned EOM, and planned reductions and then subtracting planned BOM; (b) convert this figure to PLANNED PURCHASES AT COST by multiplying it by 100% minus the percent of initial markup; (c) from this figure, subtract the value of merchandise on order.

open-to-buy by classification   The OPEN-TO-BUY (OTB) broken down for each category or classification of merchandise.

open-to-buy report   A document used to calculate the OPEN-TO-BUY (OTB). The report summarizes the existing or projected relationship between inventory and sales and is generally prepared on a weekly basis for the department BUYER. It indicates the amount of merchandise on hand at the beginning of the period, the amount received, the amount sold, markdowns, current inventory, and merchandise on order.

open-to-receive (OTR)   The amount of merchandise that may be received (regardless of what is ON ORDER) during the period if the planned stock is to be achieved. Same as OPEN-TO-SHIP, but from the store's viewpoint.

open-to-reduce   The dollar amount of markdowns that may be taken in a department during a specified period. See also MARKDOWN (MD).

open-to-ship   The amount of merchandise a vendor is permitted to ship to a retail store, regardless of what is ON ORDER, during the specified period if the planned stock is to be achieved. Same as OPEN-TO-RECEIVE (OTR), but from the vendor's viewpoint. Like OPEN-TO-BUY (OTB), open-to-ship defines inventory needs. Merchandise allocators use open-to-ship to determine the type and amount of merchandise to ship to stores from a DISTRIBUTION CENTER (DC). Essentially, open-to-ship is the difference between a store's projected inventory needs and its inventory on hand.

open-to-spend   The remaining money to be spent for the fiscal period, based on actual expense commitments already made by a buyer as compared to the planned expenditures of OPEN-TO-BUY (OTB). This information is periodically summarized in the *open-to-spend report*.

open-to-spend report   See OPEN-TO-SPEND.

open window   Synonym for OPEN-BACK WINDOW.

operating account   Synonym for NOMINAL ACCOUNT.

operating data   Synonym for INTERNAL DATA.

operating division   A functional division of a retail store responsible for such matters as merchandise receiving, store maintenance and housekeeping, security, and certain special services such as restaurants. Also called *store management division* and *store operations division*.

operating expense   Any expenditure incurred in the course of the ordinary activities of the company, such as overhead, salaries, supplies, insurance, etc. In a retail store, these may be divided between the direct expenses (i.e., those paid out for the benefit of a particular department) and the indirect expenses (i.e., those paid out for the benefit of the entire store). Expenses of financing the company are not included, nor are merchandise costs. See also NONOPERATING EXPENSE.

operating income   That portion of the NET PROFIT derived from the normal operations of the business. It is the amount remaining when operating expenses are deducted from gross profit, and indicates in dollars how much merchandise has been sold. In retailing, the operating income is derived from the sale of goods or services and is therefore sometimes used synonymously with SALES or SALES VOLUME.

operating leverage   The distribution of fixed costs over sales. As more products are sold, the fixed costs may be spread over the larger sales volume, thus reducing costs per item.

operating loss   Any loss incurred in the normal operation of a store.

operating margin   The difference between the revenues from sales and the current replacement costs of goods sold. Used as a measure of operating efficiency. Also called *current gross margin* and *current margin*.

operating profit   Synonym for NET PROFIT.

operating profit ratio   The ratio of a store's NET PROFIT (i.e., operating profit) to its NET SALES.

operating ratio   A FINANCIAL RATIO that shows the efficiency of a firm's management. It is calculated by dividing the firm's operating expenses by its net sales (or operating revenue). The smaller the ratio, the greater the organization's ability to generate profits if revenues decrease. The ratio does not take debt repayment or expansion into account.

operating revenue   In accounting, the amount remaining when operating expenses are deducted from the GROSS PROFIT of a store or other business. Compare NONOPERATING REVENUE. See also OPERATING EXPENSE.

operating statement   Synonym for INCOME STATEMENT.

operating stock level   A sufficient quantity of stock, in addition to the reserve stock, to carry the store or department through the buying period.

operating supplies   See SUPPLIES.

operational buying motive   Any consumer buying motive based on how the given product functions (e.g., an automobile may be chosen for purchase on the basis of its performance).

operational data tool   Any of a number of computer-based techniques used by marketers and others to learn more about their own online operations, their competitors, and their customers (both current and prospective). These techniques include databases, data warehouses, cookies, server log files, Web analytics, etc. See also OPT-IN and OPT-OUT (LIST).

operational marketing plan   A detailed step-by-step, month-to-month (or week-to-week or day-to-day) action plan for meeting a firm's marketing goals and performance objectives within a short period of time, usually one year. Operational marketing plans generally contain subplans for product management, pricing, distribution, and customer relationship management.

operational satisfaction   The sense of gratification experienced by the buyer of a product when the product performs properly.

operational sign   A sign relating to the day-to-day business of a store, such as one that lists store hours, return policies, emergency exits, locations of help phones, department locations, or fitting room policies.

operations   Store functions such as maintenance, security, delivery, receiving, customer service, and general housekeeping, frequently grouped together into the store's OPERATIONS DIVISION.

operations budget   A long-range plan for sales and expenses for a specific time period (as much as several years in advance). The operations budget may be regarded as a projected INCOME STATEMENT. Also called a *revenue-and-expense budget.*

operations division   The branch of the retail store responsible for sales support functions such as facilities management, security, customer service, merchandise processing, and warehousing. The head of the division is the VICE PRESIDENT (VP) OF OPERATIONS. See also OPERATIONS.

OPIC   See OVERSEAS PRIVATE INVESTMENT CORPORATION (OPIC).

opinion approach/strategy   A SALES APPROACH in which the SALESPERSON shows the product to the PROSPECT and asks for an opinion. This approach focuses attention on the product and directly involves the prospect in the presentation. Also called an *opinion strategy.*

opinion leader   A respected member of a group who serves as its trendsetter in many aspects of decision making. The opinion leader plays a key role in marketing, since she or he is emulated by a group of followers. Also called an *influential* and a *trendsetter.* See also FASHION INFLUENTIAL.

opinion survey   A SURVEY technique used in MARKETING RESEARCH (MR) to obtain consumer opinions rather than facts.

opportunistic pricing   A strategy in which a company raises the prices for its products or services during a time of shortage in an effort to take advantage of increased consumer demand.

opportunity cost   Any cost incurred by choosing one alternative over another. If marketing alternative A is chosen over alternative B, then the opportunity cost of alternative A is any benefit lost by not pursuing alternative B. Opportunity costs may more accurately be regarded as foregone profits. In retailing, opportunity costs are what the retailer would have earned if shelf space had been allocated to a better-selling manufacturer or brand. See also SCARCITY COST AND OPPORTUNITY COST.

opportunity forecast   An effort to predict future conditions in the MARKETPLACE, especially when regarded from the point of view of potential openings for the development or introduction of new products or the possibility of reducing production costs. Such a forecast may also alert the retailer or other business to changes in the marketing environment that might prove detrimental to the organization, giving it the advantage of preparation.

optical character reader (OCR)   Synonym for OPTICAL CODE READER (OCR).

optical character recognition (OCR)   The capability of a computer and scanning device (such as a wand, a light pen, etc.) to read tickets and price tags encoded in machine-readable fonts such as OCR-A and OCR-B. See also OPTICAL CODE READER (OCR), OCR-A, and OCR-B.

optical character recognition-font A   See OCR-A.

optical character recognition-font B   See OCR-B.

optical code reader (OCR)   A minicomputer used to record, calculate, store, and transmit coded data to the main computer by means of a wand, scanner, or LIGHT PEN. The light pen focuses a beam of light on a bar-coded surface and senses reflections from it. The reader may be stationary and connected to a cathode ray tube (CRT) display device or it may be portable. The portable reader may be battery-operated and contains a light pen and either a keyboard or a scanboard for data input. An optical code reader may also be called an *optical code scanner, optical character reader,* or a *terminal.* See also OCR-A and OCR-B.

optical code scanner   Synonym for OPTICAL CODE READER (OCR).

optical mouse   See MOUSE.

optical scanner   Synonym for OPTICAL CODE READER (OCR).

optical scanning   The reading, by a wand or similar device, of the letters and numbers of a code (sometimes in human-readable form) and the translation of these into computer language. See also OPTICAL CODE READER (OCR).

optical scanning of machine-readable symbols   An information processing technique converting data into an acceptable medium for computer input. The system utilizes reflected light to identify information for use by the computer. The two basic types of symbols used are OPTICAL CHARACTER RECOGNITION (OCR) symbols and the BAR CODE.

optical weight   In VISUAL MERCHANDISING, the weight that an object appears to have as opposed to what it actually weighs. Optical weight also includes how large or important an object appears to be in a display versus how large it is in actual scale. For example, a foam pillow covered with dark fur may appear heavy because of the texture and color of the covering. In reality, however, the pillow is very light. Optical weight is a consideration in maintaining balance in a DISPLAY. Shape, color, and texture contribute to the optical weight of an object and determine its placement in a display. Lighting also affects the optical weight of an object.

optically scannable symbols   See OPTICAL CHARACTER RECOGNITION (OCR) and OPTICAL SCANNING OF MACHINE-READABLE SYMBOLS.

optimal lot size   Synonym for ECONOMIC ORDER QUANTITY (EOQ).

optimum stock level   The right amount of merchandise on hand to satisfy customer needs without being either overstocked or understocked.

opt-in   The mechanism, on many marketers' Web sites, by which the visitor's permission is requested before adding him or her to an e-mail distribution list for future contact. The site contains a specific place where permission is given, sometimes with a single click of the mouse. See also DOUBLE OPT-IN and AFFIRMATIVE CONSENT.

opt-in e-mail   Promotional E-MAIL messages sent only to people who specifically request them. Opt-in e-mail is targeted, often personalized, and carries information about specific topics or promotions that users are interested in learning about. Opt-in emails typically contain newsletters, product information, or special promotional offers.

option account/terms   (Rare) Synonym for REVOLVING CREDIT.

optional (charge) account   (Rare) Synonym for REVOLVING CREDIT.

optional consumption   The purchase of items and services not required for an individual's daily fulfillment and well-being. See also LUXURIES.

optional customer service   Any customer service provided by the retailer beyond the primary and expected services. For example, a children's playroom staffed by attendants is generally considered an optional customer service.

optional product pricing   A PRICING STRATEGY applied to those products, such as automobiles, that are offered to the public with a number of choices (e.g., options). Decisions are made regarding which items are to be included in the price of the core product and which are to be offered as options at additional cost to the buyer. Optional products may be priced to generate a profit or priced to act as enticements to the purchase of the core product.

optional service   See OPTIONAL CUSTOMER SERVICE.

option-credit account   (Rare) Synonym for REVOLVING CREDIT.

opt-out (list)   An opportunity, on a Web site, for visitors to indicate that they do not wish to receive mailings from the site. While some sites automatically capture visitors' e-mail addresses when they enter the site and add them without their permission to an e-mail distribution list, most sites have a place where visitors can choose to opt out.

orange goods   A category in a system of classification based on frequency of replacement. Orange goods are consumer goods, such as clothing, that will eventually wear out and have to be replaced. The frequency of replacement is at the consumer's discretion. Compare RED GOODS and YELLOW GOODS.

order   A request to deliver, sell, receive, or purchase goods or services. Retail buyers order merchandise from vendors and suppliers such as marketing intermediaries and manufacturers. Consumers order merchandise from retailers, e-tailers, and at times directly from the vendor. See also PURCHASE ORDER MANAGEMENT (POM) SYSTEM.

order blank   Synonym for ORDER FORM.

order cancellation   The act of revoking an order previously placed with a vendor. The buyer may be motivated to cancel an order due to an overabundance of merchandise on hand, a downswing in the economy, or a reevaluation of the merchandise on order. Vendors are not required to offer stores the privilege of making such changes. However, large department stores or chains have enough clout based on their size to convince vendors to accept the cancellations.

order checking   Synonym for CHECKING.

order cycle   The activities of the vendor, from order transmittal to delivery. The order cycle consists of four parts: *order transmittal* (what happens to the order from its initiation by the customer to the time it gets to the vendor), *order processing* (what the vendor does from the moment the order is received to the notification of the proper WAREHOUSE to prepare the order for shipping), *order picking* (warehouse activities involved in the preparation of the order for pickup and in placing the shipment into the hands of the carrier); and *order delivery* (the process of pickup and final delivery to the customer). Both the processes and the time they take are considered in the cycle. See also LEAD TIME.

order cycle time   Synonym for LEAD TIME.

order delivery   See ORDER CYCLE.

order entry   The process of entering customer orders into an *order processing system* to fulfill the order. Efficient order entry helps ensure that customers receive their merchandise quickly and as ordered.

order filling   1. From the vendor's vantage point, all the processes involved in the ORDER CYCLE.   2. From the retailer's vantage point, similar processes used to fulfill customers' orders placed electronically, by telephone, or by mail and requesting shipping.

order filling cost   Any cost incurred by a store in the process of storing, packing, shipping, billing, extending and collecting credit, etc.

order follow-up   An organized system of checking on ordered merchandise to ensure its prompt delivery to the store. Buyers arrange the orders by their due date and contact vendors when the due date comes up. The buyer is expected to follow through and protect the best interests of the retailer, making it clear to the vendor that goods received late may not be accepted. Entries about consistently late deliveries from particular vendors are entered into the buyer's RESOURCE DIARY to warn against future purchases.

order form   1. A blank used by buyers to place their official orders with a vendor. It may be previously prepared or printed with information about the product or service offered for sale. The order form becomes an important document, since it contains all details of the business transaction. The back of the form usually contains stipulations concerning the arrangements under which the vendor is held legally responsible when accepting the order from a buyer. These provisions and the information contained on the front of the order form constitute a legal contract when signed by the store's authorized agent (i.e., the buyer) and accepted by the seller. Also called an *order blank* or, in industry slang, *paper*. See also PREPRINTED ORDER FORM.   2. A similar blank or preprinted form used by a consumer to place orders for merchandise selected by catalog and ordered by telephone, mail order, or on the Internet.

order getter   A salesperson who informs the customer about goods or services and persuades the customer to purchase them. The order getter gives advice, suggests alternatives, and recommends additional purchases of related merchandise. A good deal of creative selling is involved. Also called an *order getting salesperson*. Compare ORDER HANDLER and ORDER TAKER.

order getting cost   Any marketing cost incurred in an effort to attain a desired sales volume and mix.

order getting salesperson   Synonym for ORDER GETTER.

order handler   A salesperson who completes the sale of goods already selected by the customer. A supermarket cashier is an order handler. Also called an *order handling salesperson*. Compare ORDER GETTER and ORDER TAKER.

order handling salesperson   Synonym for ORDER HANDLER.

ordering   See ORDER.

ordering cost   Any cost of doing business directly related to the ordering of goods and services. Ordering costs include the operating expenses associated with the order and receiving departments.

order lead time   See LEAD TIME.

orderly change   The principle that management should encourage systematic change in employee positions as the company evolves. This includes promotions as well as job reassignments. Often referred to as the *principle of orderly change* or the *theory of orderly change*.

orderly marketing arrangement   Synonym for VOLUNTARY EXPORT RESTRICTIONS (VERS). See also OMNIBUS TRADE AND COMPETITIVENESS ACT (1988).

order picking   See ORDER CYCLE.

order placement   1. Originally, the ordering process performed by resident buying offices for their client stores.   2. The buyer's act of filling out the order form after determining the desired merchandise assortment and negotiating the terms and conditions of sale. A buyer may order merchandise by telephone, electronically, or in person.

order point   See REORDER POINT (ROP).

order processing   See ORDER CYCLE.

order processing cost   Any cost associated with handling merchandise, processing order forms, generating invoices and shipping bills, maintaining credit records, etc.

order processing system   See ORDER ENTRY.

order register   A store's official record of orders placed with vendors. The order register includes the date of the order, the vendor's name, amount of the order, month the shipment is due, etc.

order size   The quantity of merchandise, parts, and other items to purchase at one time. The appropriate amount depends on the availability of quantity discounts, the resources of the firm, the inventory turnover rate, the cost of processing each order, and the cost of maintaining goods in inventory.

order taker   A salesperson involved in the routine clerical and sales functions of taking customers' orders for goods and services. Most retail salespeople are regarded as *inside order takers,* as most of their customers are already in the store, on the phone, or on the Web site and are inclined to make a purchase. *Outside order takers* include salespeople who call on customers, note the merchandise they need, and turn in the order. Little or no creative SELLING is involved. Compare ORDER GETTER and ORDER HANDLER.

order taking sales personnel   Synonym for ORDER TAKER.

order transmittal   See ORDER CYCLE.

ordinary course of trade   A principle that sets the dutiable value of merchandise at the price at which it would normally sell if customary channels of distribution were observed.

ordinary dating   See REGULAR DATING.

ordinary interest   Interest calculated on a 360-day-a-year basis. Different kinds of lending arrangements make use of different interest conventions. Compare EXACT INTEREST, which is calculated on a 365-day-a-year basis.

ordinary terms   See REGULAR DATING.

organic   In food retailing, organic refers to animals, produce, etc., raised or grown without synthetic fertilizers, feed, pesticides, or drugs.

organizational buying objectives   The outcomes sought by the retail establishment in the buying process. These include the availability of items, the reliability of vendors, consistency of quality, delivery, price, and customer service.

organizational chart   See ORGANIZATION CHART.

organizational climate   The overall atmosphere produced by six measurable dimensions of the workplace environment that have a direct impact on the motivation, behavior, and performance of an organization. These dimensions include: structure (the degree to which jobs are well-defined and employees understand their roles in the organization); standards (the degree to which employees feel pressure to improve their performance, and the pride employees have in doing a good job); responsibility (the degree to which employees feel empowered and encouraged to take risks and try new approaches); recognition (the degree to which employees feel they are rewarded for a job well done and that the organization has an appropriate mix of rewards and criticism); support (employees' feeling of trust and mutual support and a sense of being part of a well-functioning team); and commitment (the degree to which employees share a sense of pride in belonging to the organization and commitment to the organization's goals). These properties of the work environment are perceived by customers and are considered a major factor in influencing customer behavior. Compare ORGANIZATIONAL CULTURE.

organizational consumer   Any member of the category that includes manufacturers, wholesalers and distributors, retailers, government agencies, and nonprofit organizations. They use the products they buy to make other products, maintain the organization's operations, or resell to others.

organizational consumer expectations   The perceived potential of alternative suppliers and brands to satisfy a consumer's explicit and implicit objectives. See also CONSUMER BEHAVIOR and MOTIVE.

organizational consumer's decision process   A view of the consumer decision making process that takes into account consumer expectations, the actual buying process, conflict resolution, and other situational factors. See also CONSUMER RESEARCH and MOTIVE.

organizational culture   A narrowing of the general concept of culture applied to life within an organization (such as a retail store or other business). According to A. M. Pettigrew (1979), it is the system of "publicly and collectively accepted meanings operating for a given group at a given time." Culture includes an amalgam of beliefs, ideology, language, ritual, and myth. To this may be added the environment in which the organization operates (determining what the organization must do in order to succeed), values (which define success in concrete terms for employees and establish standards or achievement within the organization), heroes (people who personify the culture's values and, as such, provide tangible role models for employees to follow), rites and rituals (which show employees the kind of behavior expected of them and provide visible examples of what the organization stands for), and the cultural network (the primary, but informal, means of communication within an organization). Organizational culture may also be seen as a coping mechanism that enables people and groups of people to deal with and minimize anxiety; it lets them know "how we do things around here." As such, organizational culture is inherently conservative, favoring the status quo. Also called *corporate culture*. Compare ORGANIZATIONAL CLIMATE.

organizational integration   See INTEGRATION.

organizational market   The market segment made up of individuals and firms that buy merchandise and services for reasons other than individual consumption (e.g., goods to be used in the manufacture of other goods). Each ORGANIZATIONAL CONSUMER is part of the organizational market. Purchasers in this market engage in large-volume, highly professional, and detail-oriented purchasing efforts. See also INDUSTRIAL PURCHASING.

organizational mission statement   See MISSION STATEMENT.

organizational objective   Synonym for OBJECTIVE.

organizational portfolio analysis   See BOSTON CONSULTING GROUP (BCG) MATRIX.

organizational products   Synonym for INDUSTRIAL GOODS.

organizational structure   The manner in which and degree to which a retail store or other business organization is set up by departments, divisions, regions, etc. The organizational structure, including the lines of reporting and communication, is reflected in the company's ORGANIZATION CHART.

organizational trends   In retail organization, current trends reflecting various dichotomies such as centralization versus decentralization, whether or not to separate the buying activity from the selling activity, decisions about the types of goods offered, and the store's dollar volume (i.e., small retail establishment versus large multiunit organizations).

organization chart   A graphic representation (i.e., a diagram) of the relationships between the various functions, departments, and employees of a business, showing the chain of command (i.e., hierarchy) as well as lines of communication and responsibility in the ORGANIZATIONAL STRUCTURE. Also called *organizational chart* or *table of organization*.

organization man/woman   An individual, especially one employed by a large corporation, who has lost his sense of personal identity by adapting to what the company expects of him in terms of actions, thoughts, and mode of behavior. The gender-neutral term *organization person* is also used. Sometimes called a *company man*.

organization marketing   An effort on the part of nonprofit organizations to sell their objectives and goals and solicit contributions. Included are mutual benefit organizations (unions, fraternal organizations, political parties, etc.), service organizations (charities, schools and colleges, etc.), and government organizations (the military, police and fire departments, etc.).

organization person   See ORGANIZATION MAN.

organized market   Synonym for COMMODITY EXCHANGE.

organizing skills   The techniques used by marketing managers to specify and structure the relationships among marketing personnel within the firm, both formal and informal. See also ALLOCATING SKILLS, MONITORING SKILLS, and INTERACTING SKILLS.

orientation   See EMPLOYEE ORIENTATION.

orientation booklet   See EMPLOYEE ORIENTATION BOOKLET.

original   An item of merchandise actually designed and made by designers and their assistants, in contrast to copies or reproductions. See also DESIGNER MERCHANDISE and HAUTE COUTURE.

original cost   The first price paid to a vendor for merchandise, exclusive of discounts, shipping charges, etc.

original markon   Synonym for INITIAL MARKUP.

original markup   Synonym for INITIAL MARKUP.

original order   The first order received from a specific customer.

original price   1. The first price quoted by a vendor for merchandise, exclusive of discounts, shipping charges, etc.   2. At retail, the first price at which an item will be offered for sale. INITIAL MARKUP is added to cost to establish the original price. Also called the *regular price* or ORIGINAL RETAIL.

original retail   The first price set by the retailer for an item of merchandise, prior to discounts, markdowns, and other reductions. Also called ORIGINAL PRICE or the *regular price*.

OS&D   See OVER, SHORT, AND DAMAGED (OS&D).

OSHA   See OCCUPATIONAL SAFETY AND HEALTH ADMINISTRATION (OSHA).

OSH Act   See OCCUPATIONAL SAFETY AND HEALTH ACT (OSH ACT) (1970).

OTB   See OPEN-TO-BUY (OTB).

OTC drug   See OVER-THE-COUNTER (OTC) DRUG.

other-directed   Of individuals, guided primarily by those around them and holding values, goals, and ideals that stem more from the opinions of others than from their own inner feelings. Other-directed people are often considered conformists by their peers. Also called *outer-directed*. Compare INNER-DIRECTED.

other income   In retailing, INCOME, such as interest and dividend income, not derived from the sale of merchandise.

others-self-concept/others-self-image   The way an individual thinks others perceive him or her. See also IDEAL OTHER and SELF-IMAGE.

OTR   See OPEN-TO-RECEIVE (OTR).

outbound telemarketing   A DIRECT MARKETING technique in which telemarketers seek out customers and prospects by phoning individuals in their homes or offices. The technique is used both to generate leads and to verify them. See also TELE-MARKETING.

outdoor advertising   An advertising medium, such as a BILLBOARD, that depends on being strategically placed to be seen by a maximum number of passersby. Outdoor advertising also includes STREET FURNITURE (such as advertising on public benches), TRANSIT ADVERTISING (such as advertising cards displayed in subway cars, buses, bus shelters, airports, and terminals), and other outdoor and in-mall displays. Outdoor advertising may be matched with other media to extend the reach of an advertising campaign or used on its own to saturate a market and keep the product or service prominently in the mind of the consumer. See also OUT-OF-HOME (OOH) ADVERTISING.

outer belt   See OUTER LOOP.

outer-directed   Synonym for OTHER-DIRECTED.

outer envelope   In DIRECT MAIL, the envelope that includes the package's promotional materials. Another envelope (for use by the customer for payment or response) may be enclosed inside. Compare INNER ENVELOPE.

outer loop   A ring of urban growth formed where a radial artery intersects with other roads. The loop holds a certain amount of retailing potential.

outlay   Synonym for EXPENDITURE.

outlet   See FACTORY OUTLET and RETAIL OUTLET.

outlet center   A strip or enclosed SHOPPING CENTER with a tenant mix composed of factory outlet stores. Although outlet centers originally attracted retailers of moderately priced goods, an increasing number of producers of upscale merchandise now operate outlet stores. Outlet centers provide manufacturers with an opportunity for VERTICAL INTEGRATION. To avoid conflict between manufacturers and their conventional retail channels, outlet centers are often located 50 miles or more from traditional stores. They are destination centers to which customers drive an average of 125 miles and where tour buses are the mainstay of marketing programs. Though manufacturers' outlets represent the majority in an outlet center's tenant mix, off-price retailers are becoming more common in these centers. Consequently, an outlet center may also be considered an OFF-PRICE CENTER or a VALUE CENTER. See also FACTORY OUTLET MALL.

outlet retailing   See FACTORY OUTLET.

outlet store Synonym for FACTORY OUTLET and RETAIL OUTLET. See also FACTORY OUTLET MALL.

out-of-home (OOH) advertising Billboards and transit advertising, commonly referred to as OUTDOOR ADVERTISING.

out-of-home direct response media Advertising signage and displays that reach the consumer in transit. They are placed on bus shelters, bus exteriors, taxi rooftops, kiosks, street furniture, etc., and are used to elicit a DIRECT RESPONSE from potential customers. Such advertisements include phone numbers, e-mail addresses, URLs, and, sometimes, a packet of coupons so that the consumer can get additional information or contact the advertiser to make a purchase. See also OUTDOOR ADVERTISING.

out-of-home (OOH) media See OUT-OF-HOME (OOH) ADVERTISING.

out-of-stock See STOCKOUT.

out-of-stock cost The estimated profits lost as the result of having insufficient quantities of inventory on hand to meet customer demand. Customers and sales are lost through a STOCKOUT. Also called an *out-of-stock loss*.

outparcels Tracts of land on the periphery of a shopping center or other commercial site, often owned by the developer of the property.

outplacement Job-hunting and other assistance that some companies provide to their laid-off workers, most often at the executive level. Such services as résumé-writing courses, use of office space during the job search, and secretarial help are offered. More recently, laid-off middle managers and blue-collar workers have also received some outplacement assistance.

outpost display Merchandise displayed within the store but away from its regular selling department. Informative signs are used to direct customers to the merchandise. Sometimes the merchandise is sold directly from the outpost. For example, merchandise may be displayed and/or sold on escalator landings, at the entrance to the store, or in another department likely to attract the same sort of target customer as the displayed merchandise.

outrigger In visual merchandising, a decorative or functional element mounted to a wall at right angles in order to define, separate, and frame categories of merchandise presented on shelves or display fixtures. The outrigger divides the wall into sections.

outshopper An individual who leaves his or her home town to shop. Traditionally, an outshopper was a person from a small town who went to a larger town or city to shop. Now, however, the term includes urban shoppers who shop at suburban malls.

outshopping 1. The practice of shopping outside one's own community. See also OUTSHOPPER.   2. The frequency of shopping trips made outside a consumer's own trading area during a specified period of time.   3. The proportion of dollars spent by consumers outside their normal trading area. Differences in state and local sales taxes may contribute to outshopping.

outside auditor An independent accounting firm hired by a retailer or other company to check their records and statements and attest to their accuracy, fairness, and conformity to accepted accounting standards. See also EXTERNAL AUDIT.

outside buying organization See SALARIED (BUYING) OFFICE.

outside merchandise source Synonym for VENDOR and RESOURCE.

outside order taker See ORDER TAKER.

outside shop (Slang) An APPAREL CONTRACTOR.

outsizes Sizes larger than the standard, such as 20 to 40 and 16½ to 26½. Also called *special sizes*.

outsourcing The farming out of some of a business's functions to outside companies and, particularly, to offshore subcontractors. For example, a number of American firms have outsourced their customer service telephone and e-mail functions to overseas workers who provide services for much less money than domestic American workers. The ability to outsource these functions depends on modern Internet and telecommunications technologies. Similarly, some companies may outsource certain functions considered not central to their line of business. For example, a bank may outsource its facilities management functions to a company specializing in facilities management. See also CUSTOMER ELIMINATION MANAGEMENT (CEM) and OFFSHORE PRODUCTION.

outstanding Of a debt, unpaid or uncollected.

outstanding order Merchandise on order from a vendor but not yet received by the retailer. See also PARTIAL SHIPMENT.

outstanding transfer list form A form used whenever merchandise is transferred from one store to another (e.g., a branch) to record the number of units transferred, unit cost, total cost, unit retail, and total retail. This record is used to indicate the change of ownership of merchandise. Merchandise may also be transferred from one department to another. See also TRANSFER OF GOODS, TRANSFER-IN, and TRANSFER-OUT.

over See STOCK OVERAGE.

overage Short for STOCK OVERAGE.

overage of merchandise See STOCK OVERAGE.

overall expenses technique A method for determining the COST OF GOODS SOLD by dividing the seller's total expense over time by the number of products sold during that time.

overall family branding   See FAMILY BRAND.

overall performance (OP)   A method of measuring a retailer's performance that combines REVENUE AND SERVICE (RS) with INVENTORY AND PROFITABILITY (IP). The method was developed by Ting-Sheng Lin in 1996 to evaluate the benefit of multiple delivery strategies. Lin found that for a selling period of 10 weeks or less, multiple delivery strategies did not improve overall performance (OP). However, they are useful for the 20-week selling period.

overall store pricing   A pricing policy in which the MARKUP is generally uniform throughout the store. This practice is frequently used by off-price merchandisers. These merchants do not consider the various merchandise classifications they have in their inventory when determining prices, and do not pay attention to the pricing policies of the competition. The goal of overall store pricing is to achieve a specific markup on everything sold by the store and move the merchandise as quickly as possible.

overassorted merchandise   A selection of merchandise that has too much breadth and too little depth. The retailer is limited in the amount of space that can be dedicated to the selection within each line. In general, it is preferable to carry full assortments of a few product lines than sparse assortments of many product lines. Exclusive specialty shops, where uniqueness is a fundamental assortment characteristic, are an exception to this generalization.

overbought   Of a store or department, in a situation in which its BUYER has committed for purchases beyond the planned allotment for the period. Also called *overordered*.

overcarriage   The transportation of goods beyond their intended destination, sometimes as a result of the goods having been refused at their original destination point.

overcut   The production of goods, particularly apparel, in excess of demand.

overdue   Of a payment or delivery, late.

overfull demand   A condition in the marketplace in which demand for a product exceeds the capacity of the suppliers to produce it.

overhead   Those business costs other than direct labor (i.e., the wages of the workers actually making a product or delivering a service) and direct materials (i.e., the actual components incorporated into the product). Overhead includes the wages of support personnel, fringe benefits paid to all workers, handling and shipping expenses, etc. Unlike fixed costs, overhead expenses are directly related to production levels and sales volume. Also called *burden*. Compare FIXED COSTS (FC).

overheating   Evidence of excessive price or monetary activity. Some economists believe overheating will lead to inflation.

overinventoried   Of a department or store, having a BEGINNING OF MONTH (BOM) INVENTORY that significantly outweighs its sales. This results in a high STOCK-TO-SALES RATIO (SSR) and indicates that goals for the store or department were set too high and that too much merchandise was allocated to it. Too much stock remains at the end of the period. Compare UNDER-INVENTORIED.

overkill   Anything in excess of what is suitable. The term may be applied to an advertising campaign, a visual merchandising display, a style of merchandise, etc. The excess may lead to diminishing returns because it repels rather than attracts potential customers.

overlapping environments   Cultural, ecological, economic, political, regulatory, social, and technological spheres in which both a firm and its EXTERNAL COALITIONS operate. These environments require particular attention in the merchandise planning process.

over order   Merchandise ordered by a buyer in excess of demand. Also spelled *overorder*.

overordered   Synonym for OVERBOUGHT.

overproduction   A situation that exists when a manufacturer produces more than can be sold at a profitable price (or, sometimes, at any price). See also OVERRUN.

overring   A cash register error in which a higher price than the actual price of the goods is recorded on the register. Also spelled *over-ring*.

overrun   Production in excess of what was originally scheduled. See also OVERPRODUCTION.

Overseas Private Investment Corporation (OPIC)   An agency formed by the United States government in 1969 to facilitate the participation of private U.S. firms in the development of less-developed countries. OPIC now covers domestic as well as foreign investors. OPIC offers project financing and political risk insurance, covering losses caused by currency inconvertibility, expropriation, and actions such as war and revolution.

overseas sales branch/subsidiary   In DIRECT EXPORT, a subsidiary (or branch) of the exporting firm, located in the host country. This allows the exporter greater exposure and control in the foreign market and also avoids total reliance upon a domestic-based export department employing an independent international marketing intermediary.

over, short, and damaged (OS&D)   In international merchandising, the difference (i.e., discrepancy) between the amount and condition of cargo on hand and that shown on the bill. Compare CLEAN BILL OF LADING.

overstock   Merchandise in stock and on order in excess of planned quantities required to meet consumer demand. See also OVER ORDER and OVERBOUGHT.

overstored   Of an area, having more stores than can operate profitably (i.e., too much retail space per consumer). The result is often cannibalization (i.e., obtaining sales in one store at the expense of another). The heightened competition means that existing stores must work much harder to survive. See also RETAIL SITE LOCATION and TRADING AREA.

over-the-counter (OTC) drug A medicine or other remedy that may be sold without a physician's prescription. Sometimes referred to as *patent medicine* or a *proprietary drug*.

over-the-counter selling/sales 1. The sale of selected merchandise kept in display cases, in drawers, or on shelves. A salesperson is needed to show the stock to the customer and to complete a sale. 2. Selling by a salesperson in a retail store. Over-the-counter selling takes place in most retail stores unless they are self-service operations. The salesperson helps the customer make a decision about a purchase.

overweight consumers A growing demographic segment of the American public whose weight exceeds what is considered normal and healthful. Such consumers are open to the marketing of diet and exercise products and services as well as large-sized clothing. See also PLUS SIZES and BIG AND TALL MEN'S.

owe To be indebted to another and obliged to pay.

own/owned brand See STORE'S OWN BRAND (SOB).

owned by China (OBC) A trend in which Chinese companies are setting up factories and buying companies in the U.S., Europe, and Asia to sell their branded merchandise worldwide. The trend was identified and the term coined by trendwatching.com at www.trendwatching.com.

owned department A store department that is an integral part of the store organization (i.e., not a licensed or LEASED DEPARTMENT).

owned goods service A service, provided by a department of a retail store or an independent shop, that involves repairing, maintaining, or improving products already owned by the customer. Examples of owned goods services include upholstery shops, automobile repair services, alteration of clothing by a tailor, tree trimming, clock and watch repair shops, shoe repair shops, etc. Often these shops or departments also sell auxiliary goods at retail, such as shoe polish, shoelaces, upholstery sprays, automobile ice scrapers, tire inflators, etc.

owner's equity See EQUITY.

ownership Possession of legal title to goods or property with the right to enjoy the benefits derived from any assets accompanying or accruing from such title. Ownership of a retail establishment can be either *public* (i.e., with many owners or shareholders and shares traded on a public STOCK EXCHANGE) or *private* (i.e., without stocks traded on a public stock exchange). The term INDEPENDENT is most often used to refer to a single, privately owned store, although it may also refer to privately held multistore organizations. Other forms of retail ownership include the CHAIN STORE and the CONGLOMERATE. See also PUBLICLY HELD COMPANY and PRIVATELY HELD COMPANY.

ownership flow See CHANNEL FLOW.

ownership franchise A type of franchise operation in which the franchiser maintains a partial ownership in the individual outlets.

ownership group See DEPARTMENT STORE OWNERSHIP GROUP.

ownership structure See OWNERSHIP.

ownership utility The usefulness, value, or consumer satisfaction added to a product or service when it is in the possession of the right person at the right time. Also called *possession utility*.

P   See PETITE.

PAC   See POLITICAL ACTION COMMITTEE (PAC).

pack   1. n. A container or carrying case in which something is stored for convenience and ease of carrying. Often used as a combining form, as in *six-pack*, *snack-pack*, etc.   2. v. To fill a bag or box with items (as occurs at the CHECKOUT COUNTER in a supermarket).   3. v. To put merchandise (particularly food) into cans, boxes, and other containers for preservation or sale. See also PACKAGING.

package   1. A wrapper or container in which a product is stored and sold. In addition to protecting the product, the package provides space for labels, instructions, and other useful information. It may also serve as a powerful vehicle for MARKETING and establishing BRAND identity. See also PACKAGING. 2. Synonym for PROMOTIONAL KIT.

package band   See ON-PACK (PREMIUM) and PACKAGE-BAND PREMIUM.

package-band premium   A gift or other special offer advertised on a strip wrapped around the package of the product being promoted. The gift may be free or offered at a reduced price to purchasers of the product, but is not physically attached to the original product as it is with the ON-PACK (PREMIUM).

package consolidating agency   Synonym for FREIGHT FORWARDER.

package delivery   Synonym for DELIVERY.

packaged environment   A physical entity such as a theme park, stadium, shopping mall, or cultural center that has a highly developed identity calculated to enhance the presentation of goods and services. Entertainment complexes such as Disney World are the most elaborate packaged environments, but the concept is applied on a smaller scale to such facilities as Chicago's Water Tower Place (an enclosed shopping mall).

packaged goods   See PACKAGE GOODS.

packaged staple   See STAPLE.

package engineering   The application of scientific and engineering principles to solve problems of functional design, formation, filling, closing, and/or preparation for the shipment of containers, regardless of the type of product enclosed.

package goods   1. Items sold in a container designed for display and handled by the retailer (e.g., detergents, paper goods, cereals). Also called *packaged goods*. Compare LOOSE GOODS. 2. In some states, alcoholic beverages intended to be consumed off the premises. See also PACKAGE STORE.

package insert   Printed material enclosed with an item of merchandise to explain its proper operation and care. Also called a *package stuffer*.

package store   A retail store selling alcoholic beverages by the bottle, to be consumed off the premises.

package stuffer   Synonym for PACKAGE INSERT.

package wrap   See WRAPPING.

packaging   The wrapper or container in which a product is stored and sold. In addition to its protective function, packaging performs several marketing functions. It provides BRAND identification as well as product identification, helps differentiate the brand from the competition, attracts the customer's attention, etc. Packaging is of particular importance in self-service stores as the manufacturer's only in-store means of communicating with the ultimate consumer. The packaging also carries selling messages and other information the customer needs to make buying decisions. Essentially, the package must provide protection, ease of carrying and handling, convenience, and information. For most consumer products the package, like a promotional DISPLAY, relates the product to the manufacturer's advertising. See also LABELS AND LABELING, CORE PRODUCT, SUPPORT, and PRODUCT POTENTIAL.

packaway   Merchandise bought considerably in advance of the selling season and stored until the appropriate time (e.g., season) for it to be sold. Often used in the plural (i.e., *packaways*).

pack date   The month, day, and year on which a food item was packed, canned, or boxed, etc. It may appear on a package to indicate possible loss of freshness. See also SELL BY (DATE).

packing house   Synonym for FREIGHT FORWARDER.

packing slip/list   A list enumerating the number and kinds of items being shipped and identifying the intended recipient of the shipment. Additional information required for shipping may also be provided. The packing list is generally enclosed with the merchandise in the shipping container, though it may also be affixed to the outside of the carton or other container.

pack premium   See ON-PACK (PREMIUM).

Pac-Man defense   In hostile takeovers and acquisitions, a maneuver in which a company turns around and tries to take over its pursuer. Named after the popular Pac-Man video game. See also ACQUISITION.

page   1. In print media (e.g., books, newspapers, or magazines), a single leaf of a publication.   2. In INTERNET terms, a synonym for WEB PAGE.

page hosting   Synonym for WEB HOSTING.

page impression   1. A single instance of accessing or viewing a specific WEB SITE. The number of page impressions is an important piece of information for the site owner. A page impression is also known as a *hit*.   2. In online advertising, a single opportunity to see an ad. The number of page impressions is the number of times the ad is available for viewing. Since the HOME PAGE (i.e., *front page*) is the entry point to most Web sites and receives the most impressions, most advertisers prefer to purchase space on the home page. Also called *impression* or *page view*. Compare PAGES.

pages   A metric used to gauge the effectiveness of INTERNET advertising. The term refers to the number of pages downloaded from a WEB SITE. Since the visitor may not actually choose to view each page or its ads, the usefulness of the measure is limited. Compare PAGE IMPRESSION.

page view   Synonym for PAGE IMPRESSION.

paid buying office   See SALARIED (BUYING) OFFICE.

paid inclusion service   An arrangement to ensure a site's inclusion in a search engine on the Internet. In exchange for a fee, the search engine owner guarantees that one's Web site is kept in the search engine's database and regularly indexed, ensuring that the visitor always sees the most current listing for the site. Paid inclusion is also used to test titles and descriptions to see which achieve more click throughs. Also called *paid spidering* or *paid indexing*.

paid indexing   Synonym for PAID INCLUSION SERVICE.

paid money   Synonym for CO-OP MONEY.

paid programming   See INFOMERCIAL.

paid spidering   Synonym for PAID INCLUSION SERVICE.

painting the bus   (Slang) The act of changing the superficial appearance of a presentation, proposal, or idea without changing any of its underlying basic elements.

palazzo design   An architectural design style adopted by the earliest department stores and copying the design of Italian palaces, or *palazzos*. Beginning with A.T. Stewart's, an EMPORIUM built in 1846 near City Hall in New York City, these large stores were conceived as COMMERCIAL PALACES. Early department stores replaced the earlier specialty shops that sold only one class of items (such as silks or silver). Sometimes extending the length of an entire city block, these buildings added enormous display windows set between cast-iron columns. The palazzo-style department store buildings increased in number and created entire shopping districts known as LADIES MILE (Broadway between 14th and 23rd Streets) and FASHION ROW (Sixth Avenue between 14th and 23rd Streets). Design features included enormous central light courts, large display windows, and up-to-date innovations such as elevators and escalators.

pallet   A low, portable platform used in the physical distribution (i.e., moving or storage) of goods. See also PALLETIZE.

palletize   To place items of merchandise on low, portable platforms (i.e., pallets) for efficient handling. Goods so arranged are moved as a unit by motorized lift trucks. The practice is known as *palletization*. See also PALLET.

Palm handheld organizer   See PERSONAL DIGITAL ASSISTANT (PDA) and POCKET PC (PPC).

pamphlet   See BROCHURE.

Pan-Asian marketing strategy   See REGIONAL STRATEGY.

p-and-l statement   Short for *profit and loss statement*. See INCOME STATEMENT.

Pan-European marketing strategy   See REGIONAL STRATEGY.

panregional brand   In global marketing, a BRAND whose products are recognized by name and sold outside its home country across a region such as Asia, North America, or the Caribbean. A brand recognized and sold throughout Europe, for example, is known as a *Eurobrand*.

panregional marketing   Integrated, international marketing strategies, such as a Pan-European strategy, that try to address areas larger than a single country in order to take advantage of economies of scale. Compare GLOBAL MARKETING and MULTINATIONAL MARKETING.

pantihose form   A lightweight female form that extends from waist to toes. The toe can be inserted into a toe bracket, permitting the form to stand in an upright position. A pantihose form may also be inverted to rest on its waist with the legs extended upward. May also be used to display stretch tights and pants.

pantry inventory   A study of consumer product usage based on an actual checking and listing of items in the homes of the study group. Also called *pantry check*.

pants form   A male or female form from the waistline down to and including the feet. If the legs are crossed, one leg will be removable to facilitate dressing the form. A pants form may be provided with a foot spike to hold the form in a standing position. Also called a *slacks form*.

panty form   A waist-to-knees form for showing panties, girdles, or bikini bottoms. These forms are about two feet tall and are usually used for counter and ledge displays.

paper   (Slang) 1. A retail installment contract.   2. An ORDER FORM.

paper profit   An apparent gain due to valuing ending inventory at the higher current market value rather than at the lower original cost price. This situation generally arises during a period of rising prices and results in an understatement of the cost of goods sold and an overstated PROFIT. These profits exist on paper, but may not actually be earned when the ending inventory is carried over into the next accounting period.

PAR   See PRODUCTION ACTIVITY REPORT (PAR).

parallel imports   Synonym for GRAY MARKET.

parasalesperson   A sales trainee who performs one or more selling functions but leaves the closing to a more experienced SALESPERSON. See also SUPPORT SALESPERSON.

parasite store   A store that depends on the customer TRAFFIC generated by neighboring stores for its clientele rather than on its own promotional efforts, image, merchandising, or customer service. For example, small specialty clothing stores may locate close to a major department store, hoping to benefit from the department store's traffic. Similarly, a leading bridal salon may be surrounded by tuxedo rental firms, florists, bridal accessories shops, photography studios, travel agencies, etc., hoping to benefit from the bridal salon's traffic by providing related goods and services.

parcel delivery   See DELIVERY.

parcel post (PP)   The division of the U.S. Postal Service that delivers small packages and fourth-class literature. It is used frequently by retailers when sending small packages (i.e., up to 70 lbs. in weight and up to 130 inches in combined length and distance around the thickest part) to customers outside the normal delivery area. Parcel post and other U.S. mail rates (e.g., priority mail and express mail) may be found at the U.S. Postal Service Web site at www.usps.com. See also DELIVERY.

parcel shipment   A small package containing samples of goods or advertising matter.

parent (company/organization)   A company that owns most, if not all, of another company's stock and takes an active part in managing that other company (known as a SUBSIDIARY [COMPANY]). The terms *parent company* and *parent organization* are often used to refer to a CONGLOMERATE. Compare HOLDING COMPANY.

parent store   Synonym for FLAGSHIP STORE/DIVISION.

Pareto Principle   Synonym for EIGHTY-TWENTY (80-20) PRINCIPLE. Named for Italian economist Vilfredo Pareto (1848–1923), who observed that for many phenomena 80 percent of the consequences stem from 20 percent of the causes. Also known as the *law of the vital few* and the *principle of factor sparsity*.

parity price   A price adopted by a retailer that is the same price used by direct competitors for identical or comparable products. See also FOLLOW-THE-LEADER PRICING. A policy of adopting parity prices is called *parity pricing*.

parking   A space where vehicles, particularly automobiles, may be stationed while the customer is shopping. Open-air or decked parking surrounds most regional and superregional shopping centers. Indoor parking may be called a *parking deck* or a GARAGE. Outdoor parking may be called a *parking lot* or, simply, a LOT. Stores located in downtown urban areas, where parking is at a premium, sometimes work out reciprocal arrangements with independent garages to provide customer and/or employee parking. Customers may have their parking tickets validated by the store to avoid paying parking fees. See also SHOPPING CENTER and VALIDATE.

parking deck/garage   See PARKING and GARAGE.

parking lot   See PARKING and LOT.

parlor shipper   See DROP SHIPPER.

part   See FABRICATING PART.

partial compensation   In global marketing, a COMPENSATION TRANSACTION in which the exporter receives a portion of the purchase price in hard currency and the remainder in merchandise. The exporter is unable to convert the merchandise into cash until a buyer can be found, and even then must usually do so at a discount. See also FULL COMPENSATION.

partially integrated global marketing strategy   See GLOBAL MARKETING MIX STRATEGY.

partial payment   A payment that is less than the full amount owed. It is not intended to constitute full payment. It is generally understood that the remaining amount due will be paid at a later date.

partial shipment   An incomplete order shipped to the store by the vendor. The remaining merchandise may be back-ordered and shipped at a later date. See also OUTSTANDING ORDER.

participatory management   A management style designed to involve employees in the firm's decision making process on a regular and systematic basis. Its success depends on managers who are willing to involve others and lead them in productive meetings and group problem-solving sessions and on well-informed, experienced employees.

partner A person having a voluntary but legally binding association with one or more persons in a business enterprise and sharing, along with the other persons, the liability for all debts of the partnership. Also known as a *general partner*. See also ARTICLES OF PARTNERSHIP.

partnership An association of two or more persons engaged in business as co-owners. The legal agreement into which they enter is known as ARTICLES OF PARTNERSHIP. A partnership is sometimes referred to as a *general partnership*.

parts See FABRICATING PART.

part-time employee A worker in a store or other business who does not work a full workweek of 35 to 40 hours. In a retail store, part-time employees are usually hired for additional coverage during peak sales hours of the day or during peak selling periods such as the pre-Christmas rush. Sometimes called a *part-time worker* or a *part-timer*. Compare FULL-TIME EMPLOYEE/WORKER.

part-time worker/part-timer Synonyms for PART-TIME EMPLOYEE.

party-plan selling A personal selling program focusing on home gatherings. The hosts or hostesses invite their friends and neighbors to their homes or offices where a salesperson demonstrates the product or line of products. Each guest is a potential customer and the host or hostess is rewarded with a small gift. Also called a *party plan, party selling, party-plan direct selling, party plan of selling, private party selling*, or a *group plan*. An example of party-plan selling is the Tupperware party. Mary Kay Cosmetics is another marketer employing this form of DIRECT SELLING.

party selling Synonym for PARTY-PLAN SELLING.

pass-along circulation The group of readers who see a newspaper or magazine in addition to the initial subscriber or purchaser, giving the publication a wider circulation (i.e., readership) than what is reflected in the circulation statistics. Also called *pass-along readership*. See also CIRCULATION and PASS-ALONG RATE.

pass-along deal An arrangement between a vendor and a retailer under which the vendor offers the retailer a lowered price (or other similar inducement) with the understanding that this price reduction will be passed along to customers. The goal of the deal is to increase VOLUME and, perhaps, the vendor's MARKET SHARE.

pass-along rate The number of readers who may see a newspaper or magazine in addition to the initial subscriber or purchaser. Also referred to as *readers per copy*. See also PASS-ALONG CIRCULATION.

pass-along readership Synonym for PASS-ALONG CIRCULATION.

passive business relations In online marketing, a Web site that does not actively sell directly to buyers. The site may provide one-way information and even advertise, but it maintains a low level of business activity and does not have even minimum contact with visitors. Compare INTERACTIVE BUSINESS RELATIONS.

passive international Internet marketer An Internet marketer that accepts orders from foreign countries but does not actively seek them. Compare ACTIVE INTERNATIONAL INTERNET MARKETER.

passive pricing A pricing method based on a retailer's DIFFERENTIAL ADVANTAGE (e.g., location or unique product mix) rather than on beating competitors' prices. Passive pricing methods include skimming (i.e., setting a high initial price on a product when there is little competition or when customers are insensitive to price), differential pricing (basing prices on past sales history), and blind item pricing (used when products are rare or not easily found in other stores). Compare AGGRESSIVE PRICING and NEUTRAL PRICING.

password A secret word or alphanumeric combination used by an authorized person to gain access to information, etc. Used frequently on Web sites to gain access to one's personal account information. See also USER ID.

past-due order Merchandise that has not been shipped by the vendor to the retailer by the date specified.

past-due statement A reminder sent to a customer by the store or other creditor when a credit payment has remained unpaid for a specified period. A past-due statement usually includes a request for payment.

paste See FASHION JEWELRY.

paste-up Synonym for MECHANICAL.

past sales record A record of previous or prior sales of merchandise. The retail BUYER takes past sales into consideration when planning the merchandise assortment. Sales records provide valuable information about sales made and lost, returned goods, and customer complaints. Various records can be used to gather past sales information, including unit control records, special promotion records, charge accounts, and files from the adjustment office. The buyer's personal observations on the selling floor may also prove useful. Buyers typically examine the records of the previous year (or of the past two or three years) and use the information as a basis for planning sales in any given season.

patent A government grant of protection to an inventor, conferring exclusive rights to manufacture and sell an invention (or use a new process) for a fixed period of time. In order to be patentable, an invention must generally be novel and useful. In the United States, the U.S. Patent Office issues patents granting the owner the right to exclude others from making, using, or selling the invention for 17 years. See also INFRINGEMENT.

patent infringement   See INFRINGEMENT.

patent medicine   See OVER-THE-COUNTER (OTC) DRUG.

Patent Office   See PATENT.

pathway (floor) plan   A store layout that is particularly well-suited to large, one-level stores. Pathway floor plans engineer traffic from the front of the store to the rear and back again by means of designated walkways. The pathway winds its way through the entire store. Also called a *pathway plan*.

patron   Synonym for CUSTOMER.

patronage (buying) motive   The reason, whether rational or emotional, for which a customer chooses to patronize one establishment rather than another. Also called *patronage demand*.

patronage demand   See PATRONAGE (BUYING) MOTIVE.

patronage discount   See CUMULATIVE QUANTITY DISCOUNT.

patronage dividend   1. Any earnings in excess of the needs of the business that result from sales and are distributed to members of a cooperative store or wholesaler.   2. The payment to a retailer by a wholesaler of a pro rata share of earnings from one or more of the wholesaler's goods. It is used by wholesalers as an incentive to generate GOODWILL and increase sales. Compare PATRONAGE REBATE.

patronage motive   See PATRONAGE (BUYING) MOTIVE.

patronage rebate   A refund by a wholesaler of part of the retailer's original payment for merchandise, given as an expression of appreciation for the retailer's continuing business. The patronage rebate is used by wholesalers as an incentive to generate GOODWILL and increase sales. Often called, simply, a *rebate*. Compare PATRONAGE DIVIDEND.

patronize   To frequent a store or other business, especially as a regular customer.

pattern check run (PCR)   In apparel sourcing, the production of samples to ensure that all aspects of construction and sizing are properly understood and can be properly executed by the contractor.

pay   1. v. To give what is due (e.g., money) for goods received or services rendered.   2. v. Of a project, enterprise, or investment, to be worthwhile or profitable.   3. n. A synonym for WAGES in the form of salary or other remuneration.

pay as you go   A plan that allows the business, customer, or other individual to meet expenses as they arise. An alternative to PAY IN ADVANCE.

payback   The amount of money a new product must earn (calculated as net income before depreciation but after taxes) to recover the initial investment made in its development. See also PAYBACK PERIOD and BREAK-EVEN POINT.

payback period   The estimated time required for the revenues generated by an investment to cover the initial cost of that investment. In new store planning, it is the time it will take the store to generate profits equal to the cost of the site and construction of the facility. See also BREAK-EVEN POINT and PAYBACK.

paybox icon   See HONOR SYSTEM.

payee   A person who receives a sum of money for goods or services transferred to another. This is in contrast to the PAYER, who gives the sum of money in exchange for goods or services.

payer   A person who gives a sum of money in exchange for goods or services received. This is in contrast to the PAYEE, who receives the sum.

pay in advance   A plan that allows the business, customer, or other individual to prepay expenses before they arise or before goods are received or services rendered. An alternative to PAY AS YOU GO.

payment flow   See CHANNEL FLOW.

payment guarantee   A statement made by a retailer or other reseller to the supplier of merchandise that payment will follow upon the completion of obligations (e.g., delivery).

payment option   Any of several alternative methods of paying for goods and services. In retailing, payment options available to the customer may include cash, a store charge account, personal checks, or third-party charges (e.g., Visa and MasterCard). Each of these methods requires separate and special treatment and incurs costs to the retailer.

payoff   (Colloquial) 1. A BRIBE.   2. The climax or culmination of a series of events (i.e., the results of an enterprise that make it worthwhile).

payout planning   A PROMOTIONAL BUDGETING strategy used for the introduction of new products, on the assumption that a new product requires 1.5 to 2 times as much promotional expenditure as an existing product. The promotional budget is determined by looking at the planned revenues for a period of three to five years and setting an expected rate of return to serve as a basis for creating the payout plan. Planners assume that the product will lose money during the first year, almost break even during the second year, and show profits by the third year. Advertising and promotion rates are highest in the first year and decrease during the second and third years.

PayPal   An online payment processing service for business. Options include electronic invoicing, shopping-cart functionality, payment notification, and shipping tools. PayPal allows the user to pay anyone who has an e-mail address, as well as request money and track funds. For example, users may pay for an auction item (e.g., on eBay), split a restaurant bill or rent, pay for online purchases, send money to family or friends, pay bills online, receive payments for auctions, send an invoice to a customer, collect money for a group gift, etc. Similarly, merchants may use PayPal to accept credit card payments online, manage their payments, pay for and track shipping, and automate inventory management.

pay-per-view (PPV) A form of interactive television, usually delivered via cable or satellite hookups, that allows consumers to watch shows of their choice at times predetermined by the producer. Consumers pay a one-time fee for viewing the program, which is often a full-length movie or sporting event. See also VIDEO-ON-DEMAND (VOD).

pay phone A public, coin-operated telephone provided for the convenience of customers. Also called a *pay telephone*, *coin-operated phone*, *public phone*, *public telephone*, or *coin-operated telephone*.

pay station See PAY PHONE.

PBA (perpetual budget account) See REVOLVING CREDIT.

PC See PERSONAL COMPUTER (PC).

PCI See PER-CAPITA INCOME (PCI).

PCR See PATTERN CHECK RUN (PCR).

PD See PHYSICAL DISTRIBUTION (PD).

PDA See PERSONAL DIGITAL ASSISTANT (PDA).

PDR See PUPIL DILATION RESPONSE (PDR).

peak 1. An exceptionally busy period in a business (as in PEAK SEASON). 2. The highest point (as in PEAK INVENTORY).

peak inventory The highest level of stock of the season. Inventory is usually brought to a peak just in time for the selling season .

peak season 1. The time of year in which a particular item or line of merchandise is in greatest demand by customers. This varies from item to item and from line to line. For example, the peak season for air conditioner sales is in the early summer. 2. The time of year when a retail store does the greatest volume of sales, such as the weeks immediately prior to Christmas. Also called *peak selling* or *peak selling season*.

pecuniary Pertaining to, involving, or consisting of money. For example, a financial gain may also be called a pecuniary gain. See also PROFITABLE.

peddler An itinerant hawker, or seller, of goods. Unlike the CANVASSER, who merely writes orders, peddlers carry the merchandise with them. Also called a *street peddler*.

pedestrian mall An open-air downtown area that has undergone extensive renovation and enhancement, including the closing of its streets to vehicular traffic. The area is frequently redesigned to create a parklike ambiance with trees and benches. This is intended to facilitate foot traffic, convey an atmosphere of freedom and safety, and attract customers back to the downtown stores away from suburban shopping centers. The first pedestrian mall was built in Kalamazoo, Michigan, in 1959. Pedestrian malls have met with mixed success and some have been converted back to conventional paved roadways with sidewalks. See also TRANSIT MALL.

pedestrian traffic The number of people who pass by a location on foot. In studying an area for a potential RETAIL SITE LOCATION, pedestrian traffic is monitored by time of day and the age and gender of people in transit. See also TRAFFIC, STREET TRAFFIC, and VEHICULAR TRAFFIC.

peer group A group of individuals of similar age and social background who spend a considerable amount of time together. The peer group tends to be fairly homogeneous and has a great deal of influence on the individual consumer since the group's interests, lifestyle, and aspirations are most like one's own. For example, a group of teenage boys or girls constitute a peer group that significantly influences teenage buying behavior.

peer-to-peer (P2P) computing The sharing of computer resources, data, and information by the direct exchange of data from one computer to another, neither one being a client or server of the other. The Napster music-sharing project is an example of P2P computing.

pegwall system A wall fixture featuring backer panels with a network of holes into which pegs, hooks (i.e., *pegwall hooks*) and other specialty fixtures may be inserted. Compare GRIDWALL SYSTEM and SLATWALL SYSTEM.

penetrated market The total number of persons who are already customers for a product or service. See also MARKET and MARKET SEGMENTATION.

penetration 1. A measure of the performance of a single unit of a business (e.g., one store in a CHAIN STORE SYSTEM [CSS]) by comparing it to the aggregate business (e.g., the sum of all the stores in the chain). For example, a 4% penetration means that the store has generated 4% of the sales of all stores in a chain. The measure may also be applied to a category or CLASSIFICATION of merchandise, in which case a 4% penetration would mean that the merchandise category has generated 4% of the sales of all categories in a department. 2. The practice of setting a low initial price on a product when competition is high. The goal is to generate demand for the product and to encourage repeat purchases. See also PENETRATION PRICING. 3. In advertising, the total number of persons or households that are physically able to be exposed to a medium by the nature of that medium's geographical circulation or broadcast signal.

penetration pricing A PRICING STRATEGY in which a new product is introduced into the marketplace at a lower than usual price (a *penetration price*) in an effort to penetrate the market rapidly and build sales volume by encouraging repeat sales. Penetration pricing is sometimes called *impact pricing*, as the strategy is also calculated to increase consumer awareness of the product. The strategy may be used when customers are sensitive to price, competition is intense, large groups of initial users are sought, or market share growth is desired. After the introductory period, during which losses are expected, prices may be raised or lowered depending on the reaction of customers and competitors.

penetration strategy A method used to introduce a new product or service to the marketplace. A *rapid penetration strategy* involves setting low prices on the product or service and dedicating a large amount of money for promotion. The goal is to get the fastest market penetration and build market share quickly. This method is used where there is a low level of product awareness and the potential market is large. A *slow penetration strategy* involves setting a low initial product price and allocating minimal money for promotion. Market acceptance is anticipated because of the low price, while minimal advertising and promotion help keep costs down. This method is used when the market is large and product awareness is quite high.

penny pricing See ODD-LINE PRICING.

pennysaver An advertising flyer, generally in the shape of a multipage booklet, distributed free of charge to local residents. The ads contained in a pennysaver come primarily, if not exclusively, from local merchants, services, and other businesses. Pennysavers also include classified advertising placed by local residents themselves (e.g., notification of garage sales, help wanted, real estate for sale or rent, pets for adoption or sale). Also called a SHOPPER.

per annum By the year; annually. For example, an executive may earn a salary of a particular dollar amount *per annum*.

per capita gross national product A nation's total GROSS NATIONAL PRODUCT (GNP) divided by its population. This figure, which reveals the gross national product per person, is frequently used to compare two or more economies. Per capita GNP, however, reveals nothing about the way in which the income is distributed among the people.

per capita income (PCI) An economic indicator used to help determine market size. It is a crude indicator of market potential per consumer, particularly when taken together with the GROSS NATIONAL INCOME (GNI).

perceived risk See CONSUMER-PERCEIVED RISK.

perceived value The worth that customers place on merchandise, regardless of its true value. For example, some customers may be willing to pay a premium price for goods with a designer label or upscale brand name. See also PERCEIVED VALUE PRICING.

perceived value pricing A PRICING STRATEGY in which the price of a product or service is based on the buyer's perception of its value rather than on the seller's cost of production. For example, some customers may be willing to pay a premium price for goods with a designer label or upscale brand name. See also PERCEIVED VALUE.

percentage cost markup Synonym for MARKUP.

percentage deviation method of inventory See PERCENTAGE VARIATION METHOD OF INVENTORY.

percentage lease An arrangement under which the amount of rent paid is related to the retailer's gross sales or profits rather than being set at a fixed amount. See also SLIDING SCALE LEASE.

percentage markdown See PERCENT MARKDOWN and MARKDOWN PERCENTAGE.

percentage markup system A retail price-setting system in which items are marked up to a level that, taken for all items together, will produce a specific average markup percentage for the entire store. A *single markup percentage* cannot be applied to every item because different items sell at different rates and generate different selling costs.

percentage-of-completion See COST-TO-COST METHOD OF ACCOUNTING.

percentage of gross profit The ratio that results from dividing the store's profit for the accounting period by the sales for that period. It represents GROSS PROFIT and is expressed as a percentage.

percentage sales increase (or decrease) An aggregate measure used to evaluate the performance of individual stores in a chain by comparing each store's sales to the aggregate performance for the entire chain for a given period (e.g., a year). This is an example of a CONTROL STANDARD or benchmark used to measure performance.

percentage variation method of inventory A method of planning stock levels based on the relationship between average stock and average sales on the one hand, and actual stock and actual sales on the other. According to this theory, the actual stock on hand should deviate from the planned average stock only half as much as the actual sales deviate from the planned average sales. For example, if sales for a particular month are running 50% ahead of expectations, stock should be increased by 25% over the average monthly stock. Also called the *percentage deviation method of inventory*.

percent change in exports A ratio comparing exports in the current year to those in the previous year, expressed as a percentage. The previous year's exports are subtracted from the current year's exports, and the result is divided by the previous year's exports. The quotient is then multiplied by 100 to yield a percentage.

percent change in imports A ratio comparing imports in the current year to those in the previous year, expressed as a percentage. The previous year's imports are subtracted from the current year's imports, and the result is divided by the previous year's imports. The quotient is then multiplied by 100 to yield a percentage.

percent change in sales   A ratio comparing sales in the current selling period to those in the previous selling period, expressed as a percentage. The previous year's sales are subtracted from the current year's sales, and the result is divided by the previous year's sales. The quotient is then multiplied by 100 to yield a percentage.

percent markdown   Markdown dollars expressed as a percent of net sales. This calculation helps the retailer in the end-of-period trend analysis in conjunction with sales volume, turnover, MARKDOWN PERCENTAGE, maintained markup, and current sales trends.

percent of sales approach to promotional budgeting   A method of computing the advertising budget for a store or other business based on a specified percentage of projected sales. Also called the *percentage of sales approach to promotional budgeting, percent of sales method of promotional budgeting, percent of sales method, percentage of sales method,* or *top-to-bottom method of promotional budgeting.* See also PROMOTIONAL BUDGETING.

perception   The process by which an individual becomes aware of elements in the environment through sensory stimuli and interprets those elements in light of personal experience. Perception, therefore, involves not only receiving stimuli, but also evaluating and remembering them. In marketing, the subjective or evaluative component of perception is important in explaining why various consumers react differently to products. Marketers, therefore, attempt to differentiate their otherwise similar products through packaging, advertising, and other marketing tools. See also SELECTIVE PERCEPTION, SUBLIMINAL PERCEPTION, THRESHOLD OF PERCEPTION, and JUST NOTICEABLE DIFFERENCE (JND).

perceptual mapping   A MARKETING RESEARCH (MR) tool in which a number of factors (e.g., product attributes, customer preferences, and particular brands) are plotted on a graph on the basis of computer analysis. Since various factors tend to form clusters, it is possible for marketers to distinguish between various competing brands and spot open niches in the marketplace. See also NICHE MARKETING.

perceptual screen   A mental filtering mechanism employed by persons exposed to a large number of advertising messages. The screen enables consumers to respond selectively to advertising by mentally blocking out uninteresting, annoying, or irrelevant advertising messages.

perfect competition   See PURE COMPETITION.

performance analysis   A method used to compare the actual performance of a RETAIL STRATEGY or MARKETING PLAN with the expectations for the plan. For example, one sales territory may be compared with another, or the sales performance of previous years may be compared with that of the current year.

The intent is to improve operations, identify problems, and correct shortcomings.

performance appraisal   The personnel function of periodically evaluating an employee, particularly to compare the employee's performance with the job description. This is generally a written report and may be accompanied by an annual or semiannual PERFORMANCE REVIEW. An effective performance appraisal starts with the setting of realistic, timed, and measurable goals by the employee and the supervisor. Also called *employee evaluation.*

performance index   A quantitative measure, expressed as a percent, of the relationship between a firm's standards and its actual performance in a particular area, such as dollar sales. In a *sales performance index,* for example, the actual sales are divided by the expected sales (for a particular area, sales representative, or product, etc.), and multiplied by 100.

performance measure   Any aspect of the work on a project that can be evaluated to determine its success or failure. Having a CONTROL STANDARD in place (representing the firm's objectives and goals) makes performance easier to measure, as actual achievement can be measured against those goals and objectives. Also called a *performance measurement.* See also PRODUCTIVITY MEASURES.

performance monitoring research   Research, generally in the form of an INTERVIEW or QUESTIONNAIRE, used to check on the progress of a particular MARKETING PROGRAM and provide the MARKETING MANAGER with the feedback required to evaluate the firm's marketing activities.

performance review   The process of assessing an individual's progress and productivity in a given job, used to help provide job security to those who meet the firm's standards and reward those who surpass them with salary increases, promotions, or other rewards. It also helps the firm to remediate or, as a last resort, fire those individuals who are not living up to their responsibilities. See also JOB EVALUATION and PERFORMANCE APPRAISAL. Also called *employee evaluation.*

performance standard   A specific, measurable criterion by which an employee's job performance may be measured. The performance standard may also be used to communicate the employer's expectations to new employees.

performance test   A standardized test administered to job applicants to ascertain their ability to handle specific aspects of a job.

perimeter wall   The continuum of walls that surround the selling area. The perimeter wall is among the first merchandising spaces viewed by a potential consumer and serves as an invitation for the customer to come into the area to browse. See also DISPLAY and STORE LAYOUT AND DESIGN.

period costs   See FIXED COSTS (FC).

periodic actual count   A system of unit inventory control in which the merchandise on hand is counted on a systematic, regular basis at specified intervals during the season. See also PERIODIC STOCK CONTROL.

periodical   A publication issued under the same title at regular intervals. See also MEDIA.

periodic fill-in of staple stock   See PERIODIC REPLENISHMENT OF STAPLE MERCHANDISE/STOCK.

periodic fill-ins   The reorder of merchandise at predictable intervals. The reorder period is based on the normal sales rate expected during the delivery and reorder periods, the length of the delivery period, the reserve stock on hand, and merchandise already on order. The periodic fill-in of staples is necessary to maintain a well-balanced ASSORTMENT of merchandise. In the home furnishings categories, since much of the merchandise is ordered according to customer specifications, merchandise need not be reordered periodically. See also REORDER.

periodic inventory   A frequent (usually annual or semiannual), systematic physical count of the merchandise on hand to approximate the dollar value of sales. Opening inventory is added to purchases, after which the sum of closing inventory and markdowns is subtracted from this total to determine sales. Periodic inventory is a system of dollar control; the system devised for the count is known as the *periodic inventory system*. Also called a *periodic stock-checking system* and *periodic stock count control*.

periodic inventory method of classification control   A system involving frequent counts of the merchandise on hand within each classification to determine sales data for that particular classification. Compare PERPETUAL INVENTORY METHOD OF CLASSIFICATION CONTROL.

periodic replenishment of staple merchandise/stock   A formula for the replacement of STAPLE merchandise based on the number of units sold during a typical selling period, the time lapse between the arrival of reorders, and a safety (i.e., reserve) stock. The maximum inventory needed for the period (M) is equal to the sum of the reorder period frequency (RP) and the delivery period (DP), times the rate of sale (S), plus the reserve stock (R) needed to avoid stockouts if sales exceed plan. For example, when the reorder period is 2 weeks, the delivery period is 1 week, the rate of sale is 100 units per week, and the reserve stock needed is 40 units: M = 3 weeks (that is, 2 weeks + 1 week) × 100 units + 40 units, or 340 units.

periodic stock-checking system   Synonym for PERIODIC INVENTORY.

periodic stock control   A unit control system in which stock is identified and recorded periodically and sales for the intervening time periods are calculated. See also STOCK CONTROL.

periodic stock count control   Synonym for PERIODIC INVENTORY.

peripheral service   Any additional service offered as a complement to a basic product or service offering. Peripheral services, which add to operating costs, are generally provided to enhance a firm's competitive advantage. For example, a cable television firm may offer free installation as a peripheral service to its basic bundle of products and services.

peripheral site   A store location in the fringe areas of a community or on an access road off the main highway.

peripheral unit control system   See PERPETUAL UNIT CONTROL.

perishability   1. In terms of food products, the rate at which the product's freshness, quality, and salability deteriorate over time.   2. In terms of fashion goods, the rate at which the fashion appeal of a product declines in popularity and salability.

perishability of services   A view of services that likens them to perishable goods. The concept suggests that services, by their very nature, have a limited life span (i.e., services left unperformed cannot be stored and used at some future time).

perishable   Any food product that tends to spoil rapidly, has a short life span, and therefore requires special handling such as refrigeration, freezing, etc. Perishables may be ordered online through a variety of e-tailers, several of whom have been delivering frozen foods to customers since before the advent of the Internet. Also called a *perishable good*.

perishable distinctiveness   The novelty and uniqueness of a product, seen as waning over a period of time (five years is considered a typical cycle). In the beginning, a product may have *exclusive distinctiveness*; it represents a novel style or innovation and experiences little competition. As time passes and competitors enter the market, the product loses its uniqueness. Eventually, as competitors capture a larger share of the market, the product falls into *declining distinctiveness*.

perk   A nonmonetary reward for work done or attached to a position held by the employee. For example, free lunches or the keys to the executive restroom are sometimes given as perks. Short for *perquisite*. Compare INDIRECT COMPENSATION.

permanent markdown   A price reduction for goods that never return to the regular retail price (or any higher price) at a later date. A clearance markdown is always a permanent markdown. See also CLEARANCE MARKDOWN, TEMPORARY MARKDOWN, and PERMANENT MARKDOWN PRICE.

permanent markdown price   A price achieved by a MARKDOWN (MD) that will not be reversed at a future date. It is often a clearance price reflecting a decline in the value of the merchandise based on low salability.

permanent signage   Signs made of durable materials not intended for frequent change (e.g., exterior lighted signs and in-store signs identifying selling areas). Also called *permanent signs*. Compare TEMPORARY SIGNAGE. See also SIGNAGE.

permission   See AFFIRMATIVE CONSENT.

perpetual actual count   A system of unit control of inventory that relies on a continuing physical count of the merchandise on hand.

perpetual budget account (PBA) Synonym for REVOLVING CREDIT.

perpetual control See PERPETUAL UNIT CONTROL.

perpetual inventory (control) A system of dollar inventory control in which daily sales, discounts, and markdowns are continuously deducted from the book inventory. Perpetual inventory provides a picture of the inventory that agrees with the actual stock on hand, provided no shortages have occurred. The movement of goods into and out of stock are continuously recorded. This system is used in the RETAIL METHOD OF ACCOUNTING. Also called *perpetual merchandise control, a perpetual inventory system,* and *perpetual inventory control.* See also DOLLAR INVENTORY CONTROL and BOOK INVENTORY. Compare NONPERPETUAL INVENTORY.

perpetual inventory method of classification control A system used to determine sales data for a particular classification of merchandise by means of a continuous and ongoing physical count of the merchandise on hand within that classification. Compare PERIODIC INVENTORY METHOD OF CLASSIFICATION CONTROL.

perpetual merchandise control See PERPETUAL INVENTORY (CONTROL).

perpetual unit control A system of unit inventory control in which all factors affecting the number of units on hand (e.g., purchase orders, receipts of merchandise, and sales for individual styles) are recorded on a continuing basis as they occur. Also called *perpetual control* and a *perpetual unit control system.*

perpetual visual count A system of unit inventory control that relies on the continuous eyeballing of the merchandise by the retailer and the replacement of items that are low. See also EYEBALL CONTROL and UNIT (INVENTORY) CONTROL.

perquisite See PERK.

personal care item Any of a variety of products intended to help improve grooming and appearance. Included are hair dryers, electric shavers, saunas, etc.

personal communication channel Any method of communication involving two or more individuals communicating directly with each other. Communication may be face-to-face or use telephones, television, mail, computers, etc. See also NONPERSONAL COMMUNICATION CHANNELS.

personal computer (PC) A computer intended for a single user at a workstation. The term was popular in the late 1970s and early 1980s when such computers were first produced. Today, the terms *PC, desktop, laptop,* and *computer* are mostly used instead. Also called a MICROCOMPUTER.

personal consumption expenditure Any purchase made by individuals or households for consumer items. The dollar amount available for personal consumption expenditures is calculated by subtracting savings from DISPOSABLE INCOME. See also DISCRETIONARY EXPENDITURE.

personal digital assistant (PDA) A WIRELESS, interactive, portable electronic device that can be used to access the INTERNET and to organize personal information (such as addresses). A PDA is smaller, cheaper, and less complex than a PERSONAL COMPUTER (PC). Consumers worldwide use PDAs for keeping in touch with family and friends, downloading information, making purchases, trading stocks, and, in some countries, making vending machine purchases. Advertisers also use PDAs to reach potential customers with e-mail advertisements. Also called a *handheld computer, handheld device,* or *handheld wireless device.* See also POCKET PC (PPC).

personal disposable income See DISPOSABLE INCOME.

personal expenditure Synonym for DISCRETIONARY EXPENDITURE.

personal finance company Synonym for FINANCE COMPANY.

personal identification number (PIN) A unique number assigned to an individual allowing him or her access to a computer system by means of an AUTOMATIC TELLER MACHINE (ATM), a POINT-OF-SALE TERMINAL (POST), or similar device, including a computer network.

personal income (PI) According to the U.S. Bureau of the Census, for statistical purposes, income from wages and salaries, self-employment (including losses), Social Security and Supplemental Security, public assistance (except noncash benefits), interest, dividends, rents, royalties, veterans' payments, unemployment compensation, and public and private pensions. Personal income does not include capital gains or losses. For the population as a whole, personal income is the sum of the above payments for everyone in the country. See also BUYING POWER.

personal influence The power of people (particularly certain individuals) to sway the purchasing decisions of others. For this reason, retailers attempt to identify those people who exert influence over others. See also BLUEFINGERS, FASHION INFLUENTIAL, and ADOPTION PROCESS.

personal interview See INTERVIEW.

personality The composite of characteristics that make each individual unique. One's personality consists of one's habitual patterns of behavior, distinctive character traits, personal identity, and individuality. Marketers are interested in linking the consumer's personality to choices made in the marketplace and in gearing their marketing programs to appeal to the personality traits of target customers. See also TARGET MARKET.

personality segmentation See PSYCHOGRAPHIC SEGMENTATION.

personalization Customized one-to-one E-MARKETING. The online storefront operator uses software to learn about customers, their buying behaviors, and their preferences and then uses this data to customize offers to potential customers ONLINE. The information is gathered through COOKIES, the monitoring of chat room messages, sales transactions, and e-mail feedback, and onsite tracking. It is organized into databases and mined to identify consumers with the highest probability of responding to specific marketing offers.

personalizing shopper A retail customer who seeks out and patronizes those retail outlets in which he or she feels most secure. In particular, personalizing shoppers seek out salespeople whom they trust and with whom they can relate. Compare APATHETIC SHOPPER, ECONOMICAL SHOPPER, and ETHICAL SHOPPER. See also PERSONAL TRADE.

personal needs The needs of the individual to achieve personal satisfaction (e.g., self-esteem, accomplishment, enjoyment, and relaxation). Personal needs are unrelated to the opinions and actions of others, except to the extent that those others reinforce and affirm personal needs. See also MASLOW'S HIERARCHY (OF NEEDS) and NEED AWARENESS.

personal organizer 1. A small notebook with sections for personal information such as names and addresses of contacts, appointments, memorandums, etc. 2. A handheld computer that allows individuals to store and search similar information.

personal promotional aid Any of the services that directly affect the selling activity of the retailer or other business that buys them. Personal promotion aids include selling aids and promotional allowances. Compare NONPERSONAL PROMOTION AIDS (i.e., those that directly influence the buying behavior of the consumer, such as DEALER HELPS and consumer inducements). See also SELLING AID and DEALER AID.

personal selling Any sales technique in which a salesperson interacts with an individual customer. It frequently involves face-to-face contact but may also be conducted electronically or by telephone. In wholesale and contact selling, the SALESPERSON initiates the contact by making a call on the customer; in retail selling, the customer initiates the contact by entering a store and approaching the salesperson. Online personal selling takes the form of E-MAIL, INSTANT MESSAGING (IM), or live CHAT and may be accomplished on the Internet, the Web, intranets, or extranets. Also called *direct promotion*.

personal selling service A philosophy of sales that emphasizes knowledgeable sales associates who play major roles in the firm's customer service and sales activities. In the retail sector, sales associates increase sales by turning browsers into shoppers and building long-term relationships with customers. See also PREMIER CUSTOMER SERVICE, CUSTOMER SERVICE, and CUSTOMER RELATIONSHIP MANAGEMENT (CRM).

personal shopper An employee of a retail store whose job it is to select merchandise for customers in response to mail, Internet, or telephone requests and to accompany shoppers in the store to help them select merchandise. A personal shopper generally has good knowledge of the specific customer's preferences for brands, styles, and colors and will coordinate mer-

chandise groupings that are likely to appeal to the customer. Personal shoppers may also call customers when new merchandise that may appeal to them arrives in the store. The office or department from which the personal shopper operates may be known as a *personal shopping bureau* or a *personal shopping service*.

personal shopping bureau/service See PERSONAL SHOPPER.

personal trade An ongoing relationship between a customer and a salesperson in which the same salesperson serves that customer over a long period of time. The salesperson comes to know the customer's preferences and the customer comes to trust the salesperson's advice and judgment. See also PERSONALIZING SHOPPER.

personal trade file Synonym for RESOURCE FILE.

person marketing Activities undertaken to cultivate the attention, interest, and preference of a target market for a person (rather than for goods or services). These activities consist of press conferences, media coverage, public appearances, etc. Both POLITICAL CANDIDATE MARKETING and CELEBRITY MARKETING are forms of person marketing.

personnel The employees of an organization, collectively. See also EMPLOYEE.

personnel department/division See HUMAN RESOURCES DIVISION.

personnel director/manager Synonym for HUMAN RESOURCES MANAGER.

personnel space Those areas of the store reserved for use by the store's employees. For example, locker rooms, break rooms, and employee cafeterias are part of the store's personnel space.

person-to-person auction See ONLINE AUCTION.

persuasion The act of causing someone to do or believe something using strategies of reasoning, urging, or convincing. One of the purposes of ADVERTISING is to persuade customers to try products or services. Persuasion may create PRIMARY DEMAND, that is, demand for an entire product category, or SELECTIVE DEMAND (i.e., *secondary demand*), that is, demand for a certain firm's brand (and for the product category only secondarily).

persuasive impact The level of influence a form of communication has upon consumers. Television is said to have a high degree of persuasive impact because it reaches the consumer through more than one of the senses.

persuasive label In packaging, a label whose chief purpose is to promote the product rather than to inform the consumer.

persuasive pricing A form of PSYCHOLOGICAL PRICING intended to convey a sense of extra value to the consumer. See also ODD-LINE PRICING.

PERT See PROGRAM EVALUATION AND REVIEW TECHNIQUE (PERT).

petite 1. In apparel manufacture and retailing, the size range for women of shorter than average height. Petite apparel is usually sized from 6 to 16. *Junior petite* sizes, for short-waisted women, generally run from size 5 to size 15. 2. The smallest size for pantyhose, bodysuits, and nightgowns. Frequently abbreviated as *P.*

phantom freight The difference between the estimated shipping cost (as quoted by the vendor to the retailer) and the actual shipping cost. This difference is considered an illusion (i.e., phantom).

phantom shopper A vendor's representative who poses as a customer in order to assess methods used by retailers and other resellers when selling the firm's items.

pharmacist An individual licensed to prepare and dispense drugs and medicines. Also called a *druggist.* See also PHARMACY.

pharmacy Traditionally, a retail store where drugs and medicines are prepared and dispensed according to a physician's written prescription. While most pharmacies were small, independent retail establishments until the 1980s, the DRUG STORE CHAIN organization has dominated the classification for the past 25 years. In addition, many non-drug store organizations (such as supermarkets and department stores) have added pharmacy departments. See also DRUG STORE and PHARMACIST.

phony list price A bogus LIST PRICE designed solely to be shown to customers as evidence that the price charged has been discounted from list. Customers who are unduly impressed by the size of the supposed DISCOUNT may end up paying more than the actual MARKET PRICE. This practice is banned by the WHEELER-LEA ACT (1938).

photographer's model See MODEL.

physical distribution (PD) Although the flow of raw materials to the producer may be regarded as a part of physical distribution, the process is more commonly seen as beginning with the completed manufactured product as it enters the appropriate marketing channels and moves through various transportation and storage stages to its final consumption. See also DISTRIBUTION, PHYSICAL DISTRIBUTION FUNCTIONS, and CHANNEL OF DISTRIBUTION.

physical distribution functions Those activities or functions involved in physically transferring goods from the point at which they are produced to the point of their consumption. Physical distribution functions include transportation, warehousing, wholesaling, and retailing. See also PHYSICAL DISTRIBUTION (PD) and DISTRIBUTION.

physical distribution management Logistic activities concerned with the movement of completed products from point of manufacture to the ultimate consumer. The employee whose job it is to supervise and coordinate these activities is known as the *physical distribution manager.*

physical distribution manager See PHYSICAL DISTRIBUTION MANAGEMENT.

physical environment See ENVIRONMENTAL REVIEW.

physical flow See CHANNEL FLOW.

physical goods Synonym for GOODS.

physical inspection system A program for checking the inventory level by either a *periodic actual count* or *eyeball control.*

physical inventory The dollar value at retail of merchandise on hand during inventory-taking. Includes only the stock actually present in the department or store. The physical inventory usually includes the unit count, quantity, and the weight or measure in addition to the dollar value. Some retailers prefer to outsource their physical inventory process. See also PHYSICAL INVENTORY SYSTEM and STOCK COUNT.

physical inventory system A means of deriving net sales for a period of time. The previous physical inventory (i.e., the *opening physical inventory*) is carried over and added to new purchases received from vendors during the period. The ending physical inventory is subtracted from this total. The resulting figure approximates NET SALES. The numbers are approximate because the physical inventory system does not take stock shortages into account. See also PHYSICAL INVENTORY.

physical obsolescence With regard to manufactured products, a broken or worn-out state or condition generally reached through normal wear and tear.

physical risk The CONSUMER-PERCEIVED RISK that a product may injure the user.

physical standard See CONTROL STANDARD.

physiological motive/need See BIOGENIC NEED and MASLOW'S HIERARCHY (OF NEEDS).

physiological profile A series of techniques used in ADVERTISING RESEARCH to overcome the biases associated with voluntary reactions on the part of participants. The physiological profile is thus designed to measure involuntary responses to the ads (such as eye, skin, and brain wave reactions). See also EYE CAMERA, GALVANIC SKIN RESPONSE (GSR), PUPIL DILATION RESPONSE (PDR), and BRAIN WAVE MEASUREMENT.

PI See PERSONAL INCOME (PI).

PIC See PRELIMINARY INSPECTION CERTIFICATE (PIC).

pick-and-pack 1. In warehouse distribution, a method of selecting goods from a warehouse based on what has been ordered by each customer. The selection is then packed and shipped.   2. In the retailing of food, particularly produce, a system in which customers select individual products (e.g., oranges, tomatoes, cucumbers) from merchandise displayed in open bins. The merchandise is then packed at the checkout counter. Also called *pick-and-pay*.

pick-and-pay   Synonym for PICK-AND-PACK.

picketing   Strike activity in which union members carry signs and march in front of the entrances to company premises to try to persuade nonstriking workers to walk off the job and others to cease doing business with the company. Compare SLOW-DOWN and STRIKE.

picking   One of the major functions performed by a retail DISTRIBUTION CENTER (DC), namely, the distribution of put-away goods to stores or customers. Other functions are RECEIVING, CHECKING, MARKING AND TICKETING, PUTAWAY, DISTRIBUTION, SHIPPING, VENDOR RETURN, and TRAFFIC.

pickup   1. Returned merchandise brought from the customer's home back to the store by either the store's own delivery service or an independent parcel delivery company.   2. Merchandise the customer selects in the SELLING AREA but retrieves at a designated place (e.g., the entrance to the store's loading dock).

pictograph   A type of diagram used in presenting business data. It is essentially a variation on the BAR CHART using symbols or pictures instead of bars, each instance of a symbol or picture representing a fixed quantity.

piece goods   Fabrics and accessory items such as lace and other trims, generally sold by the yard. The term is used most frequently in apparel manufacturing and the retailing of products for the home sewer. Also called *yard goods*.

piecework   Work done and paid for by the piece (i.e., the number of items completed), sometimes associated with the apparel manufacturing industry. See also PIECEWORKER.

pieceworker   A worker who gets paid on the basis of the number of items completed rather than the amount of time spent at the workplace. The apparel manufacturing industry, for example, is frequently associated with pieceworkers and PIECEWORK. Also called a JOBBER.

pie chart   A type of diagram used in presenting business data. Essentially, it is a circle divided into proportionately-sized slices labeled as percentages of the whole circle (i.e., 100%). A pie chart is useful for showing relationships rather than for showing precise data.

piecy   See BROKEN ASSORTMENTS.

pier   1. A wide area of masonry separating display windows in a BANK OF WINDOWS.   2. In a store's interior, a thickening or extension outward from a constructed wall. Compare COLUMN, which is free-standing.

piggyback   1. A coordinated transportation agreement in which truck trailers are loaded directly onto railroad freight cars. Through the use of containerized freight, piggyback helps eliminate costly and time-consuming unloading and reloading of the merchandise being shipped. Also known as *trailer-on-flatcar (TOFC)*, *piggyback service*, *piggyback transportation*, or *rail-trailer shipment*. See also CONTAINERIZATION.   2. In broadcast media advertising, a one-minute spot in which two distinct products of one advertiser appear in separate, back-to-back commercials rather than as a part of a single message.

pig in a python   An analogy used in DEMOGRAPHICS to express the impact of a baby boom. The increased birth rate produces a bulge in the population statistics when they are represented graphically. As time passes, the bulge occurs in different age sections of the population, just as a pig swallowed by a python produces a bulge that moves through the snake. See also BABY BOOMERS.

pilferage   The stealing of a store's merchandise or cash in small amounts. When the stealing is done by the store's own employees, it is called *employee pilferage*. See also SHOPLIFTING.

pilfer-proof fixture/case   A FIXTURE, particularly a COUNTER FIXTURE, designed to lock in the merchandise and allow customers to see but not freely touch it. For example, better jewelry and handbags are frequently locked in fixtures that require a salesperson with a key to take the item out of the fixture for the customer.

PIMS   See PROFIT IMPACT OF MARKETING STRATEGIES (PIMS).

PIN   See PERSONAL IDENTIFICATION NUMBER (PIN).

pinochle season   (Slang) In the garment industry, the OFF-SEASON. The reference to the card game is to suggest leisure activity reserved for the slack period.

pin ticket   A price tag attached to the product by means of a pin, staple, or other fastener. A pin ticket may contain additional information such as size, color, and style number for use in STOCK CONTROL.

pinup display/technique   In the VISUAL MERCHANDISING of apparel, a DISPLAY that makes use of an interior panel, wall, or other vertical surface onto which a garment can be pinned, shaped, and dimensionalized. The technique utilizes pads, tissue, and straight pins rather than forms or mannequins. The garment is pinned onto the panel and then the tissue is crumpled and added to fill out the garment where form is needed. Accessories are pinned on at appropriate locations. Also called a *pinup*. A *semi-pinup display* may utilize abstract geometric forms or a traditional hatstand or coat rack, etc., on which to pin the garments.

pioneering advertising   Synonym for PRIMARY DEMAND ADVERTISING.

pioneering stage   See INTRODUCTORY STAGE.

pipe rack   A utilitarian display FIXTURE equipped with wheels and used to display apparel. Pipe racks are made of round tubing and may have a flat wooden base to which the wheels are attached. This form of display utilizes the rack to move merchandise from the receiving area to the sales floor as a DISPLAY unit. See also RACK.

piracy   The counterfeit reproduction of copyrighted material such as books, recorded music, and software. See also COUNTERFEIT PRODUCT.

pitch   A presentation by a salesperson to a prospect in order to obtain an order or new business. Similarly, a SALES PITCH is a strong statement aimed at persuading a potential customer to buy the salesperson's product or service. See also SALES APPROACH.

place   1. n. One of the FOUR PS OF THE MARKETING MIX, the act of reaching the market with one's products through adequate distribution channels.   2. v. To give an order to a supplier.   3. v. To put an advertisement into a suitable vehicle for distribution and promotion.   4. v. In visual merchandising, to arrange an object appropriately in a display, on the rack, or on the shelf.

place-distribution intensity response function   The RESPONSE FUNCTION illustrating the likely results of different degrees of market exposure, ranging from EXCLUSIVE DISTRIBUTION to INTENSIVE DISTRIBUTION. Since sales may level off toward the extreme end of intensive distribution, in which most outlets already carry the product, the response function shows that little increase in sales can be expected from the last few marginal outlets. Also called *distribution intensity response function*.

placement   See PRODUCT PLACEMENT.

place utility   The usefulness, value, or consumer satisfaction derived from products being available where buyers want them, that is, delivered to the right place at the proper time. In E-TAILING and other E-COMMERCE, products may be found on a corporate Web site, an e-tailer's Web site, an online shopping mall, linked to a portal, or on an extranet. Often the same product may be found in multiple Web sites. Web shopping eliminates travel time and expense; the product is always available at the customer's fingertips.

plan   See BUYING PLAN, MERCHANDISE PLAN, or SALES PLAN.

planned average monthly stock   A planning figure arrived at by dividing the planned sales for the season by the expected turnover. The result is an estimate of the average amount of STOCK that should be on hand for each month of the selling season and a reminder/signal to add additional stock as needed. See also INVENTORY.

planned economy/economic system   See ECONOMIC SYSTEM.

planned end of month (EOM) inventory   The retail value of the ending inventory for each period. In merchandising plans, the beginning of month (BOM) inventory for a period (usually a month) must be the value of the end of month (EOM) inventory for the preceding period.

planned expenses   Anticipated expenditures for the store as a whole and for each department, on the basis of which an expense plan is drawn up. Part of the overall planning process, the purpose of EXPENSE PLAN/PLANNING is to make careful and accurate forecasts of expenses so that proper controls can be established to meet them, thus safeguarding the store's profit objective.

planned functional obsolescence   See PLANNED PRODUCT OBSOLESCENCE.

planned gross margin   The GROSS MARGIN projected by the retailer for a future accounting period.

planned markdown   A price reduction anticipated by the store's buyer for a particular selling season. Since the markdown is expected, it is taken into account in sales projections for that season. Planned markdowns are often used to generate store traffic.

planned markup   See INITIAL MARKUP.

planned monthly purchases at retail   See PLANNED PURCHASE.

planned obsolescence   A marketing strategy in which products are deliberately changed to encourage their replacement. Planned obsolescence commonly takes one of two forms: PLANNED PRODUCT OBSOLESCENCE, and PLANNED STYLE OBSOLESCENCE.

planned product obsolescence   Planned obsolescence in which a product is designed to wear out quickly or is in some way functionally improved. Also called *product obsolescence, functional obsolescence, managed obsolescence,* and *planned functional obsolescence.*

planned profit   A store's anticipated PROFIT (i.e., total revenue less all costs and expenses) for a future accounting period.

planned purchase   In the MERCHANDISE PLAN, the sum of the PLANNED SALES for the month plus planned markdowns and planned end of month inventory (EOM) minus beginning of month inventory (BOM). Planned purchases are used to derive OPEN-TO-BUY (OTB). See also PLANNED PURCHASES AT RETAIL and PLANNED PURCHASES AT COST.

planned purchases at cost   Purchases planned at retail prices and then converted to cost value by applying the planned markup percent. PLANNED PURCHASES AT RETAIL must therefore be established first. See also OPEN-TO-BUY (OTB).

planned purchases at retail   A method used to determine the dollar value of merchandise to be brought into stock during a given season or other period so as to ensure that enough stock will be on hand for sales, basic stock, and reductions. The buyer can determine planned purchases by adding together planned sales, planned reductions, and planned stock (stock planned for the end of the month or for the beginning of the next month) and subtracting from this total the planned stock at the beginning of the month. Also called *planned monthly purchases at retail, planned purchases,* and *planned receipts.* See also OPEN-TO-BUY (OTB).

planned receipts   Synonym for PLANNED PURCHASES AT RETAIL.

planned reduction   A RETAIL REDUCTION anticipated by the store for a particular accounting period. This figure is an estimate based on past performance and is taken into account when projecting the store's NET PROFIT for the period. A broader term than planned markdown, planned reductions also include projected discounts to customers and employees and inventory shortages. See also PLANNED MARKDOWN.

planned sales   Projected SALES at retail for a particular accounting period. Planned sales is a useful concept for formulating projections based on previous sales patterns of comparable periods. Also called *plan sales.* See also INVENTORY, SALES PLANNING, and SALES FORECASTING.

planned shopping center   Synonym for SHOPPING CENTER.

planned spontaneity   A consumer trend in which making spontaneous decisions to go somewhere or do something is becoming the norm. The trend was identified and the term coined by trendwatching.com at www.trendwatching.com.

planned stock   The dollar amount of merchandise a retailer intends to have on hand to meet sales expectations and inventory requirements. Planned stock may be calculated for a department, merchandise classification, price line, etc. The four basic methods of planning stock are the BASIC STOCK METHOD OF INVENTORY, the PERCENTAGE VARIATION METHOD OF INVENTORY, the WEEKS OF SUPPLY METHOD, and the STOCK-TO-SALES RATIO (SSR). See also INVENTORY.

planned style obsolescence   Planned obsolescence in which the appearance of a product is changed with the intention of creating dissatisfaction among owners of earlier models. Also called *fashion obsolescence, style obsolescence,* and *psychological obsolescence.*

planner   A BUYER specialization frequently found at the corporate merchandising level, where buying may be split into four specialized functions: buying, planning, distribution, and product development. The planner projects sales and inventories based on an analysis of sales history, current market trends, and the organization's performance objectives. See also PLANNING, ASSISTANT PLANNER, PLANNING MANAGER, and SENIOR PLANNER.

planning   The process of establishing the goals of an organization and projecting the most effective means of accomplishing them. Planning attempts to anticipate the needs of the organization in both the near and distant future, and is there-fore short-range as well as long-range. A SHORT-RANGE PLAN is generally developed for those situations likely to occur monthly, weekly, or daily, and may be covered by procedures, practices, rules, etc. A firm's budget is a common form of short-range plan. A long-range plan, on the other hand, is generally developed for up to several years and involves the long-term goals of the organization, often expressed in a MISSION STATEMENT. The firm's objectives and policies are designed to accommodate long-range planning. See also PLANNER, MARKET PLANNING, MANAGEMENT BY OBJECTIVES (MBO), TACTICAL PLANNING, and STRATEGIC PLANNING.

planning decisions (in unit planning)   See UNIT PLANNING.

planning manager   In a large retail establishment, the executive who works with the divisional merchandise managers and buyers to determine the firm's short- and long-term strategies and create seasonal merchandising plans. The planning manager also partners with other merchandising executives to ensure that the firm's objectives are being met. See also PLANNER.

plan of reorganization (POR)   In CHAPTER 11 proceedings prior to BANKRUPTCY, the plan devised by a debtor organization to regain profitability while retaining its assets. For retail organizations, this plan may include such strategies as terminating the organization's leadership; hiring a new leader with a track record of rescuing ailing retailers; closing unprofitable stores; implementing expense-saving measures; and selling unprofitable units or divisions (and using the cash to reduce debt).

planogram   In retail SPACE MANAGEMENT, a visual model of product arrangements developed by visual merchandisers in concert with buyers and store planners. Planograms are visual models of product arrangements that incorporate an organization's standards for merchandise presentation, product adjacencies, and customer convenience. These detailed scale drawings illustrate precisely where each fixture and piece of merchandise is to be placed in a store. Planograms ensure the consistent arrangement of goods in stores forming part of multiunit organizations. A planogram can represent an entire store, a store section, or a single fixture or wall section (i.e., a *wall planogram*). It can be general, indicating the location of whole categories of merchandise, or specific, indicating the precise location of individual items on fixtures. In some organizations planograms are advisory, in others, conformance to the plan is mandatory. Planograms are periodically reset to reflect seasonal changes, with planograms of fashion goods being reset more often than those of basic goods. Space management software is used to produce color planograms with product images in scaled dimensions that can be electronically transmitted to stores. The planograms are automatically adjusted by store based on sales data scanned at point of sale. Quantities of slow-turning items are reduced (or deleted) from the assortment, while quantities of fast-turning items are increased.

plan purchase   See PLANNED PURCHASE.

plan sales   Synonym for PLANNED SALES. See also INVENTORY and BUYING PLAN.

plastic money   (Slang) A CREDIT CARD.

plateauing   A leveling off, stabilization, or gradual decline in sales, growth, or productivity, etc., so that the accounting period shows little or no change. The period during which this occurs may be referred to as a *plateau*.

platform display   See ISLAND DISPLAY.

platform (fixture)   See RISER.

play money   See CREDIT SLIP.

PLC   See PRODUCT LIFE CYCLE (PLC).

PLU   See PRICE LOOKUP (PLU) TECHNOLOGY.

plug   1. v. To mention a product or service favorably in a media interview, etc.   2. n. A recommendation; a favorable mention of a product or service in a media interview, etc.

plus business   The amount of sale of goods or services that exceeds expectations and projections for the period. Also called *gravy* (Slang). See also PLUS OVER NORMAL (PON).

plus over normal (PON)   PLUS BUSINESS expressed as a percentage of the expected volume of sales for the period. Also called *plus over normal (PON) business*.

plus sizes   Sizes in women's apparel that are at the upper range of the sizes manufactured. Retailers generally include sizes 14 and above in this category. *Women's sizes* are sized for women with heavier figures than the MISSES (SIZES), with even bust sizes ranging from 38 to 50. *Half sizes* are cut for a fully developed figure, short-waisted in the back and larger in the waist and hips. They are usually sized 10½ to 24½. *Queen sizes* are fashions designed for large women; the term is particularly used for pantyhose. Frequently abbreviated 1X, 2X, 3X, etc. Also called *full-figure fashions*.

PM   See PUSH MONEY (PM).

PMSA (primary metropolitan statistical area)   See PRIMARY STATISTICAL AREA (PMSA).

pneumatic tubes   See TUBE SYSTEM.

pocket PC (PPC)   A handheld computer that runs a specific Windows operating system. It has many of the capabilities of desktop PCs and many of its available applications are freeware. Some pocket PCs also include mobile phone features and can be used with other add-ons such as barcode readers and cameras. The device enables users to store and retrieve e-mail messages, contacts, and appointments, play multimedia files and games, exchange text messages, browse the Web, etc. Pocket PC is commonly abbreviated as *PPC*. See also PERSONAL DIGITAL ASSISTANT (PDA).

POE   See PORT OF ENTRY (POE).

POI   See POINT-OF-IMPULSE (POI).

point-of-entrance   The place through which a customer enters a retail store. Generally, this is the first or main level. However, some mall stores have *entry points* on more than one level. A store's points-of-entrance affect TRAFFIC FLOW. Direct entrances from parking lots and garages also enhance and balance store traffic.

point of equal probability   The point between two major shopping areas at which each becomes equally desirable to potential retail customers. It is calculated as the distance in miles between site A and site B, divided by 1 plus the square root of population A divided by population B. Also called the *point of indifference*. See also REILLY'S LAW OF RETAIL GRAVITATION and GRAVITY MODELS.

point of equilibrium   The point at which SUPPLY equals DEMAND.

point-of-impulse (POI)   An updated term for POINT-OF-SALE (POS) or POINT-OF-PURCHASE (POP). The term adds to these the expectation of IMPULSE BUYING (i.e., consumer purchases made without prior planning at the checkout).

point of indifference   See POINT OF EQUAL PROBABILITY.

point of origin   The location at which goods are gathered for shipping. See also FREE ON BOARD (FOB) POINT. Distinguished from COUNTRY OF ORIGIN.

point-of-purchase (POP)   1. The section of a store or department where the sale is consummated (i.e., where the customer pays for and generally receives the merchandise). This is often the location of point-of-purchase displays and other promotions designed to catch the attention of the customer. Also called *point-of-sale (POS)*. See also POINT-OF-PURCHASE (POP) DISPLAY and POINT-OF-IMPULSE (POI).   2. A register-based data collection system used by retailers.

point-of-purchase (POP) advertising   Promotional signs and interior displays located at the POINT-OF-PURCHASE (POP) or alongside displays of merchandise. POP advertising may include counter displays, mobiles, display bins, etc. These are often provided by the vendor. Point-of-purchase (POP) advertising is especially valuable in self-service outlets and for the stimulation of IMPULSE BUYING. Also called *point-of-sale (POS) promotion* and *point-of-sale (POS) advertising*. See also POINT-OF-PURCHASE (POP) DISPLAY and POINT-OF-IMPULSE (POI).

point-of-purchase (POP) display   In retailing, an interior display of merchandise at the register, checkout counter, or other point-of-sale, designed to attract the customer's attention at a place closely associated with purchase decisions to stimulate impulse buying. Display materials are frequently supplied by the vendor. Also called *point-of-purchase (POP) advertising/promotion*, *point-of-sale (POS) advertising*, *point-of-sale (POS) display*, and *vendor display*. See also TRAY PACK, SPACE MISER, and WRAPAROUND.

point-of-purchase (POP) graphic A VENDOR FIXTURE often linked to a national advertising campaign.

point-of-purchase (POP) promotion See POINT-OF-PUR-CHASE (POP) ADVERTISING.

point-of-purchase (POP) signage A VENDOR FIXTURE in the form of a sign, often linked to a national advertising campaign.

point-of-sale (POS) Synonym for POINT-OF-PURCHASE (POP). See also POINT-OF-IMPULSE (POI).

point-of-sale (POS) display See POINT-OF-PURCHASE (POP) DISPLAY.

point-of-sale (POS) markdown A temporary markdown programmed into the cash register. The markdown is recorded when the item is sold at the reduced price. Point-of-sale (POS) markdowns eliminate the need to mark the goods with the reduced price and, subsequently, to remark the goods to the original price when the markdown is cancelled. See also MARK-DOWN CANCELLATION.

point-of-sale (POS) perpetual inventory control system An automated retail system in which the store cash registers are linked to computer processing systems. The automated equipment handles marking, checkout, and the recording of data. Merchandise is ticketed with bar code tags that are read with wand readers at the CHECKOUT COUNTER. The computer accumulates sales transaction information on magnetic tape for daily input into the computer memory bank or storage system. Also called *point-of-sale inventory control system, point-of-sale inventory system,* or, simply, *point-of-sale system.*

point-of-sale (POS) promotion See POINT-OF-PURCHASE (POP) ADVERTISING and POINT-OF-PURCHASE (POP) DISPLAY.

point-of-sale (POS) system See POINT-OF-SALE (POS) PER-PETUAL INVENTORY CONTROL SYSTEM.

point-of-sale terminal (POST) A CASH REGISTER or terminal linked to a computer. The register controls and records all sales (cash, charge, COD, layaway, etc.) where the sale is consummated. The terminal issues sales checks, prints transaction records, and feeds information about each transaction into the computer's database. Also called an *electronic cash register (ECR)* or simply shortened to POINT-OF-SALE (POS) in common usage. The terminal is part of a POINT-OF-SALE (POS) PERPETUAL INVENTORY CONTROL SYSTEM that utilizes the information in the database to plan and control inventory.

point scoring A system of evaluating a credit applicant's creditworthiness. Point values are given to such factors as home ownership, other credit cards, bank accounts, income, length of time at present job, etc. A minimum score is established for the granting of credit. See also STORE CREDIT.

poison pill Any step taken by a company in danger of being acquired that will make the takeover so expensive that the predator gives up. For example, the target company may issue shares to shareholders that could be turned into cash if the takeover is successful. See also ACQUISITION.

Poison Prevention Packaging Act (PPPA) (1970) U.S. federal legislation that requires manufacturers to use safety packaging on products containing substances deemed harmful to children. Specifically, the legislation was enacted to prevent young children from accidentally ingesting hazardous substances ordinarily stored around the house. The law requires toxic, corrosive, or irritative substances to be packaged in such a way that it will be difficult for children under five years of age to open them, yet not too difficult for adults to open. The first product to fall under this law was aspirin, on August 8, 1972, with the law gradually encompassing more and more hazardous substances, including some prescription and over-the-counter medications.

polarity of retail trade The theory that in the future all retailers will fall into two extreme categories. On the one hand will be the high-volume mass merchandisers, and on the other will be high-yield specialty boutiques. Also called *retail polarity.*

policy A plan, course of action, or method of doing business. Policies are developed for the sake of expediency, facility, etc. See also RETAIL POLICY.

policy adjustment A departure from the standard return or adjustment policies of a store to accommodate a customer and retain the customer's goodwill and continued patronage. See also POLICY ALLOWANCE.

policy allowance A reduction in the retail price of merchandise that goes against a store's standard adjustment policies. The price reduction is made to retain the customer's goodwill and continued patronage. See also POLICY ADJUSTMENT.

political action committee (PAC) A group formed under U.S. federal election laws to raise money for candidates. Since campaign laws limit businesses' ability to donate money directly to candidates, businesses routinely funnel contributions to candidates through PACs. Through a PAC, a company can solicit contributions from its employees, then allocate the money to various campaigns. In addition to operating company PACs, many companies also work through TRADE ASSOCIATION PACs.

political candidate marketing A form of PERSON MARKETING in which activities are undertaken to create, maintain, or alter attitudes and/or behavior toward a person seeking elective office. By the latter half of the twentieth century political candidate marketing had become a major industry and area of specialization as office seekers hired an increasing number of advertising professionals to assist in their campaigns. See also CELEBRITY MARKETING.

political risk In INTERNATIONAL MARKETING, the possibility that an unexpected and drastic political change in the host country will negatively impact business operations. Political risks include sudden changes of power such as an unexpected coup d'état or a revolution. Compare REGULATORY CHANGE. See also POLITICAL RISK ASSESSMENT (PRA).

political risk assessment (PRA)   Systems used by companies doing business internationally to analyze and try to anticipate POLITICAL RISK. A company will use PRA in an attempt to avoid making new investments in countries facing impending government instabilities as well as to monitor existing operations and their political environment for future action. PRAs help companies assess the host country's political stability, the host government's commitment to ownership and contractual rights issues, the length of time the government of the host country is expected to remain in power, the possible effects of succession by another government or regime on the host country as well as on the business relationship, and decisions and actions to be taken in light of those effects.

polycentrism   A semidecentralized form of organization found in some multinational marketing firms in which marketing efforts made outside the home country are undertaken by marketing groups located in each foreign (i.e., host country) market.

polygon method/analysis   A method used to determine a store's TRADING AREA by considering natural and man-made phenomena such as parks, bodies of water, uninhabitable land (e.g., swamps and wildlife preserves), etc., as dividing the space into straight-sided geometric shapes (i.e., polygons). The method departs from the notion that customers are dispersed equally in the trading area. Compare RING ANALYSIS.

polygraph   1. A test that simultaneously records blood pressure, pulse rate, respiration, etc., as the subject answers questions, as changes in these bodily signs are assumed to occur when the subject lies. Used in preventing and detecting theft as well as, in some cases, hiring employees.   2. The device used to administer this test. The polygraph is commonly known as a *lie detector*.

POM system   See PURCHASE ORDER MANAGEMENT (POM) SYSTEM.

PON (business)   See PLUS OVER NORMAL (PON).

pool car shipment/service   A mode of rail shipment in which two or more companies combine their goods in order to take advantage of the CARLOAD FREIGHT RATE (CL).

pooled auction   See ONLINE AUCTION.

pooled buying/purchasing   A loosely organized, informal, and voluntary consolidation of orders by several independent merchants all dealing with the same vendor. Also called *informal buying group* and *pooled purchasing*.

pooling   A practice found in producers' cooperatives in which each member's contributions are combined with those of other members and sold in the course of the marketing season at prevailing prices. Members are then paid an average price (less operating expenses). See also PRODUCERS' COOPERATIVE/CO-OP.

poor assortment   Slow-selling merchandise that is rejected by consumers, despite the careful planning of the buyer. This situation may result in a MARKDOWN (MD).

poor presentation   A failure in the way goods are placed, fixtured, faced, folded, hung, sized, or colorized that results in slow selling. Poorly presented merchandise may result in a MARKDOWN (MD).

POP   See POINT-OF-PURCHASE (POP) or POST OFFICE PROTOCOL (POP).

pop culture   See POPULAR CULTURE.

POP3   See POST OFFICE PROTOCOL (POP).

popular culture   The culture that prevails in a modern society among the great majority of its people. The content of popular culture is determined in large part by industries that disseminate cultural material (i.e., film, television, anime, publishing, music, and news media industries) and is the result of continuing interaction between these industries and the people of the society who consume their products. As such, popular culture is constantly changing and is specific to place and time. Items of popular culture typically appeal to a broad spectrum of the public. Popular culture may be considered superficial (since it does not require extensive training, experience, or reflection in order to be appreciated) or it may be regarded as the leading edge of culture (first adopted by the innovators and only later adopted by the laggards of the mainstream). Also called *pop culture*.

popular-price merchandise   Merchandise offered for sale at prices considered acceptable to the mass of consumers. Also called *popular-priced merchandise* or *popularly priced merchandise*. See also PRICE.

popular pricing   See POPULAR-PRICE MERCHANDISE.

population   1. In MARKETING RESEARCH (MR), as in other social science research, the entire group under observation by the researcher and about which conclusions will be drawn. The terms *universe* and *sample set* are frequently used synonymously with population. See also SAMPLE, SAMPLING, and TARGET POPULATION.   2. The inhabitants of a place, whether it be a small town or an entire country.

population density   The number of residents per square mile or kilometer of a particular area. Population density may indicate an opportunity for the retailer if the area is understored. See also MARKET SEGMENTATION BY POPULATION DENSITY.

population (density) segmentation   See MARKET SEGMENTATION BY POPULATION DENSITY.

population survey   Synonym for CENSUS.

pop-under (ad)   A half-screen online advertisement that opens behind the browser (i.e., in the background) on the WORLD WIDE WEB (WWW). These persistent and often irritating ads are launched on entering, exiting, or inputting a command.

A pop-under ad is considered somewhat less intrusive than the POP-UP AD, since it does not completely block the user's view of the browser screen. Consumers and their Internet service providers employ a variety of means to block pop-unders. Also called, simply, a *pop-under*. See also FLAME, POP-UP AD, MOUSE-TRAP, STATIC IMAGE AD, and BANNER AD.

pop-up   See POP-UP RETAIL, POP-UP AD, or POP-UP MENU.

pop-up ad   A large, intrusive online advertisement that opens in front of the browser on the WORLD WIDE WEB (WWW). It is intended to increase Web traffic and capture e-mail addresses. These persistent and often irritating ads, usually generated by JavaScript, are launched upon entering, exiting, or triggering a command. Pop-up ads are difficult to ignore or overlook and are claimed to be more effective than static banner ads, as they have a much higher CLICK RATE. Consumers and their Internet service providers employ a variety of means to block pop-ups. Also called, simply, a *pop-up*. See also FLAME, POP-UNDER (AD), MOUSETRAPPING, STATIC IMAGE AD, and BANNER AD.

pop-up establishment   See POP-UP RETAIL.

pop-up hell   (Slang) Synonym for JAVA TRAP.

pop-up menu   See MENU.

pop-up retail   A trend in which retail outlets intentionally come and go in a short period of time. These temporary retail manifestations range from gallery-like shopping spaces to mobile units bringing inner-city chic to rural areas. A world-wide phenomenon, *pop-up stores* tend to start up unan-nounced, quickly draw in the crowds, and then disappear or change into something else. This adds a fresh feel, exclusivity, and an element of surprise to retail. Such a store is also called a *pop-up establishment*. The trend was identified and the term coined by trendwatching.com at www.trendwatching.com.

pop-up store   See POP-UP RETAIL.

POR   See PLAN OF REORGANIZATION (POR).

portal   An interface or gateway offering links to Web sites that are of general interest (*generic* or *horizontal portals*) or of spe-cial interest to a particular group of users (*niche* or *vertical por-tals*). *Portal revenue* comes primarily from selling onsite advertising space. A portal may also be called a *portal site*.

portal revenue   See PORTAL.

portfolio analysis/management   See BUSINESS PORTFOLIO ANALYSIS.

portfolio of brands   A collection of branded product lines, each targeted to a different market, produced by the same man-ufacturer. The different brands within a portfolio are often intended for distribution through different retail channels. A company's portfolio of brands is sometimes highly diversified; for example, a single company may produce food products, hosiery, innerwear, and umbrellas.

portfolio test   In ADVERTISING RESEARCH, a method in which participants are exposed to a collection of test and control advertisements. *Test ads* are the ads actually being measured for their potential effectiveness against the *control ads*, which have been evaluated extensively over a period of time and provide a basis of comparison. Respondents are asked to recall informa-tion from the ads; those ads for which there is high recall are assumed to be the most effective. See also RECALL TEST.

port of entry (POE)   A port in which CUSTOMS authorities are located, designated as a place for the entry and clearance of ves-sels and goods. In the United States, major ports of entry are New York City, Los Angeles, Oakland, and Miami.

POS   Point-of-sale, synonym for POINT-OF-PURCHASE (POP).

POS inventory control system   See POINT- OF-SALE (POS) PERPETUAL INVENTORY CONTROL SYSTEM.

position advertising   See POSITION MEDIA and POSITIONING ADVERTISING.

positioned retailing   The systematic identification of a store's target market and the development of a specific mer-chandising strategy to meet the needs of that market. See also TARGET MARKET.

positioning   The perception a customer has of a given store or product in relation to others, partly as a result of advertising and promotional activities designed for this purpose. Posi-tioning is closely related to store image. For example, a store may be positioned as an extremely customer-oriented store, a high-end fashion leader, or a place where the customer can expect lower prices. To be successful, a store or product must be uniquely positioned and clearly differentiated from its com-petitors. See also STORE IMAGE, MARKET POSITIONING, and BRAND POSITIONING.

positioning advertising   A form of advertising in which a segment of the market is targeted and the product or service presented in a way that specifically appeals to that segment. Consideration may also be given to the product's position as it relates to competing products in the marketplace. See also TARGET MARKET.

position media   Advertising placed on signs, posters, pro-grams, placemats, directories, and vehicles, etc., so as to be noticed by casual passersby. Also called *position advertising*.

positive conversion   See BOOMERANG.

positive correlation   See CORRELATION.

POS perpetual inventory control system   See POINT- OF-SALE (POS) PERPETUAL INVENTORY CONTROL SYSTEM.

possession utility   See OWNERSHIP UTILITY.

POS system   See POINT-OF-SALE (POS) PERPETUAL INVEN-TORY CONTROL SYSTEM.

post 1. n. In an Internet NEWSGROUP, a submission or contribution to the discussion by a user. The newsgroup itself is a repository for messages posted from many users at different locations. When a user posts to one news server, the message is stored locally; that local server then shares the message with other servers that are connected to it if both carry the newsgroup. Also called a *posting*. 2. v. In accounting, to enter debits and credits from the journals into the ledger.

POST See POINT-OF-SALE TERMINAL (POST).

postadoption behavior The final stage in the consumer adoption process, including such activities as continued evaluation of the product, the use and maintenance of the product, and the decision whether or not to purchase the product again in the future. Also called *postpurchase behavior*.

postage stamp pricing A method of setting uniform delivered prices throughout the national market by charging equal freight cost regardless of the actual distance shipped. In this respect it resembles letter postage. Also called *uniform delivered pricing, uniform geographic pricing,* or *uniform delivered price*.

postaudit An audit in which a day's net sales are examined on the following day.

postdating See ADVANCE DATING.

poster A placard that offers reinforcement to a merchandising theme or acts as an artistic decoration on a wall or in a display.

post exchange (PX) A nonprofit retail store operated by the armed forces at a military post or camp. A PX offers general merchandise for personal use at low prices to military and diplomatic personnel and their families. See also BASE EXCHANGE and GOVERNMENT-OWNED STORE.

posting 1. An accounting process by which debits and credits taken from the journals are entered in the ledger. 2. See POST (def. 1).

Post Office Protocol (POP) An application-layer Internet standard PROTOCOL (i.e., a set of rules governing communication between electronic devices) used to retrieve E-MAIL from a remote server over a TCP/IP connection. Nearly all individual Internet service provider e-mail accounts are accessed via *POP3* (the current version of POP).

postponement Short for the *principle of postponement,* a management theory maintaining that a firm should refrain from changing its products and MARKETING MIX until it becomes absolutely necessary to do so and delay changes in the location of its inventories until immediately prior to their sale. This strategy is intended to reduce the risks involved in the FOUR PS OF THE MARKETING MIX. See also POSTPONEMENT AND SPECULATION.

postponement and speculation Short for the *principle of postponement and speculation,* a management theory that combines the principle of POSTPONEMENT with the principle of SPECULATION. The theory maintains that a speculative inventory will appear at each point in a CHANNEL OF DISTRIBUTION when it costs less to move the products than the net savings that would accrue to both buyer and seller if such a movement of inventory were further postponed.

postpurchase anxiety See COGNITIVE DISSONANCE.

postpurchase behavior See POSTADOPTION BEHAVIOR.

postpurchase customer service Any customer service performed by a retail store only after a purchase has been made. Examples include delivery, wrapping, adjustments, returns, alterations, and installation. Also called *postpurchase service*. Compare PREPURCHASE CUSTOMER SERVICE.

postpurchase dissonance/doubt See COGNITIVE DISSONANCE

postpurchase service See POSTPURCHASE CUSTOMER SERVICE.

postseason The period of time following the regular selling period for a category of merchandise.

posttesting In ADVERTISING RESEARCH, any technique used to evaluate the effectiveness of an advertisement after it has been viewed or heard by consumers. Posttesting techniques include the analysis of sales responses, recall tests, impact tests, and consumer interviewing. See also PRETESTING.

potential customer Synonym for PROSPECT.

power aisle See MAJOR AISLE.

power brand A highly recognizable, high-volume-generating brand.

power center Typically an open-air center with a tenant mix of big box retailers such as category killers, warehouse clubs, off-price discount stores, full-line discounters, and supercenters. The mix is sometimes supplemented by a strip of smaller stores with a food supermarket and/or full-line discounter. The format grew quickly in the 1980s and 1990s in the U.S. Power centers operate on a low cost of occupancy. The centers, which range from 300,000 to 600,000 square feet of gross leasable area, are often located near a SUPERREGIONAL (SHOPPING) CENTER in an effort to feed off its traffic. The trading radius for a power center is 20 to 25 miles.

power distance See HOFSTEDE MEASURES OF CULTURE.

power need One of the three basic motivations comprising the TRIO OF NEEDS. The power need is the desire to control one's environment. See also ACHIEVEMENT NEED and AFFILIATION NEED.

power node An area in which numerous freestanding stores are located, consisting of a grouping of big box retailers (including at least one POWER CENTER) located at or near a major highway intersection. See also BIG BOX RETAILER/STORE.

power retailer   A large retail corporation that dominates the marketplace. Power retailers have definite advantages over small, independently owned retailers, such as broad selection, deep assortment, and low prices. Compare INDEPENDENT.

PP   See PARCEL POST (PP).

PPC   See POCKET PC (PPC).

PPI   See PRODUCER PRICE INDEX (PPI).

PPPA   See PACKAGING AND POISON PREVENTION PACKAGING ACT (PPPA) (1970).

PPV   See PAY-PER-VIEW (PPV).

PR   See PUBLIC RELATIONS (PR).

PRA   See POLITICAL RISK ASSESSMENT (PRA).

praise approach   A SALES APPROACH in which the SALESPERSON uses honest praise or compliments to gain the prospect's attention. The salesperson may praise the prospect's furnishings, attire, reputation, etc. Also called the *compliment approach.*

preapproach   In selling, the preparation involved before the prospect may effectively be contacted. Includes analyzing the prospect prior to the interview, developing a sales strategy, planning the sales presentation, and planning the best way to set up the initial contact (i.e., with or without a prior appointment).

preaudit   1. The systematic evaluation of a vendor's invoices, payrolls, claims, and expected reimbursements before payment is made by the retailer.   2. The verification of sales transactions by the retailer before delivery from a vendor.

preauthorization   Credit approval obtained for a CHARGE-SEND SALE/TRANSACTION before the merchandise is permitted to leave the department.

prebuy   To order merchandise before it becomes available at the retail level. Prebuying is practiced by affluent and high-fashion retail customers who order selected merchandise (particularly apparel) from their retailer well in advance of the selling season. Such customers often become aware of the latest fashions by keeping up with the fashion press and fashion Web sites on the INTERNET. They are willing to pay full retail for exclusive, cutting-edge merchandise, and their selections are often an indicator of fashion trends for the upcoming season. The increased availability of fashion news that results in pre-buying makes these customers feel empowered. Retailers may feel, however, that some of the fashion decision making process has been removed from their control. Distinguished from PREBUYING PROCESS.

prebuying process   Planning, budgeting, shopping the competition, and other relevant activities performed by a retail BUYER before going into the market to purchase merchandise for the store or group of stores. Distinguish from PREBUY.

precious stone   The most expensive of the three categories of natural gemstones. Included are the diamond, ruby, and emerald. Stones are regarded as precious largely on the basis of their hardness, brilliance, and rarity. See also SEMIPRECIOUS STONE and DECORATIVE STONE.

preconscious level of need awareness   See NEED AWARENESS.

precustomer contact   The preparation and training of a retail salesperson prior to dealing with customers on the selling floor. Precustomer contact includes learning the stock of the store or department as well as the store's policies and procedures. Also spelled *pre-customer contact.*

predatory price cutting   See PREDATORY PRICING.

predatory pricing   The setting of prices at a level so low as to drive competitors out of business. Much predatory pricing is illegal under the provisions of the CLAYTON ACT (1914) and SHERMAN ANTITRUST (1890) ACT. Consequently, the practice amounts to illegally selling items at very low MARKUP or even below merchandise cost to eliminate competition. Also called *predatory price cutting, put-out pricing* and *extinction pricing.* Compare UMBRELLA PRICING, its opposite. See also RATE WAR and UNDERSELLING.

preemption of a brand name   In global marketing, the legal local hijacking of a BRAND NAME in a country where the owner of the brand has not yet registered that brand name. If the original owner of the brand name decides to enter that market, it will have to buy back its brand name or sell under another. Preemption is especially easy in countries that do not require that the BRAND be sold in the market after registration. Also called brand name preemption.

preemptive marketing   The advertising of a product or service before it is actually available in the marketplace. Preemptive marketing is an effort to forestall the purchase of a competitor's product.

preemptive pricing   A pricing strategy in which price levels are set so low that potential makers of competitive products are discouraged from entering the marketplace. Also known as *keep-out pricing* and *stay-out pricing.*

preference item   An item of merchandise chosen by a consumer even when similar items are available at lower cost. For example, a consumer may insist on Coca-Cola even when a chain grocery store's cola-type soft drink is readily available and less expensive.

preferred customer   A loyal customer identified by spending over a period of time, typically a year. Customers may earn points for every dollar spent. At the end of the year, the points are converted to bonus certificates that can be used for future purchases. See also LOYALTY PROGRAM.

preferred discount   See TRADE DISCOUNT.

preferred position   The placement of an advertisement in a particular desirable location in a print medium. The advertiser pays a higher price than for an ad placed RUN OF PUBLICATION (ROP).

preferred resource   Synonym for KEY RESOURCE.

preferred selling space   A promotional ALLOWANCE from the regular price, offered by a vendor to a retail buyer in exchange for choice space made available for the sale of the vendor's product. This assures the vendor of increased sales volume. See also STORE LAYOUT AND DESIGN.

preferred trading partner (PTP)   A country that engages in trade freely with other countries once it has been approved by the WORLD TRADE ORGANIZATION (WTO). Formerly referred to as a MOST FAVORED NATION (MFN).

preferred vendor list   A roster of prescreened manufacturers and resources chosen to do business with large retail companies, often serving to shut out smaller vendors. See also KEY RESOURCE.

preliminary inspection certificate (PIC)   In the importing of merchandise, a document that authorizes the shipment of goods when they have passed a final AUDIT at the offshore contractor. The PIC is generally required by the bank or other financial institution to release funds to pay the contractor.

premarking   See VENDOR PREMARKING/PRETICKETING.

premier customer service   A sales philosophy that promotes intensive interaction with customers. Sales associates are empowered to do whatever it takes to satisfy customers and are rewarded for unusual customer service efforts. See also PERSONAL SELLING SERVICE, CUSTOMER SERVICE, and CUSTOMER RELATIONSHIP MANAGEMENT (CRM).

premium   Merchandise employed as a sales promotion device. It may be used as an incentive to encourage customers to make a purchase (in which case it may also be called a *consumer premium*) or to reward salespeople for increased productivity. The essential appeal of premiums is that recipients feel they are getting something for nothing. Premiums include the *free gift* (also called *gift-with-purchase*), the *mail-in premium*, and the *self-liquidating premium* in which the consumer sends both money (to cover shipping and handling, for example) and proof-of-purchase to obtain the special offer. Also called a *premium offer, consumer inducement,* or *premium promotion.*

premium approach   A SALES APPROACH in which a free gift or sample is given to the PROSPECT, who then feels obligated to hear the SALESPERSON's presentation. The gift generally ties in with the product or service being sold. Also called a *gift-giving approach.*

premium center   See REDEMPTION CENTER.

premium jobber   A WHOLESALER dealing in incentive merchandise intended for use as premiums. The premium jobber may provide assistance to the marketer in the form of planning and promotional expertise.

premium money   Synonym for PUSH MONEY (PM).

premium offer   See PREMIUM.

premium pack   A promotional package used by manufacturers as an incentive to consumers. Two or more of the same product are banded together at a special price, or a related premium is attached to or included in the product being promoted. See also ON-PACK (PREMIUM), PRICE PACK, and IN-PACK PREMIUM.

premium pay   A wage rate higher than the usual, paid for special assignments such as overtime hours, holiday work, unusual or hazardous work, etc.

premium pricing   See PRICING ABOVE THE MARKET.

premium promotion   See PREMIUM.

premium redemption center   See REDEMPTION CENTER.

premium representative   1. A manufacturer's representative dealing in incentive merchandise to be used as premiums. The premium representative offers services as well as merchandise, including backup support, incentive expertise, and personal service.   2. Synonym for MANUFACTURER'S AGENT. Often shortened to *premium rep.*

premium store   Synonym for REDEMPTION CENTER.

premium trading card   See TRADING CARD.

preowned   See SECONDHAND.

prepack   A practice, followed by some vendors, of preparing standardized shipments of merchandise ready to ship in advance of need. Each shipment is provided with a standard assortment of sizes, colors, and styles. Also called *case pack.* Compare FLOOR-READY MERCHANDISE (FRM), whose assortments are packed specific to the replenishment needs of individual stores. Also spelled *prepak.* See also CASE-PACK/CASE-PACKED GOODS and PREPACKAGED.

prepackaged   Of merchandise, displayed and sold to the ultimate consumer in the vendor's original container. In food merchandising, it is often the store that does the prepackaging, as in the case of meat sold in transparent plastic trays that have already been weighed and priced. See also PREWRAPPED.

prepacking   See PREPACK and CASE PACK/CASE-PACKED GOODS.

prepaid   1. Of a bill or invoice, paid before shipping, at the time the order is placed, or before due.   2. Shipped under an arrangement in which shipping charges have been paid in advance.

prepak   Alternative spelling of PREPACK.

prepared food   Ready-to-eat food products sold at retail and catering to those who do not have the time for food preparation. The increase in the number of two-worker households has sparked the trend in prepared foods.

prepay   To remunerate (i.e., pay) the seller in advance, before goods and services are received.

prepriced merchandise/product   See VENDOR PREMARKING/ PRETICKETING.

prepricing   See VENDOR PREMARKING/PRETICKETING.

preprint   In advertising, a copy of a print advertisement distributed to customers or resources as a flyer prior to its appearance in a newspaper or magazine. When distributed after publication, it is known as a REPRINT.

preprinted (advertising) insert   See ADVERTORIAL INSERT.

preprinted order form   A vendor's ORDER FORM on which the products carried by the vendor are listed. The preprinted order form includes spaces for entering the quantity desired, unit price, and total price. This type of form may also be prepared by retailers for use by their retail customers, particularly in catalog sales.

prepurchase customer service   Any customer service function that takes place before a purchase is made and may facilitate purchasing. For example, interior and exterior displays, telephone and mail order services, fitting rooms, shopping hours, fashion shows, and demonstrations are all considered prepurchase customer services. Also called, simply, *prepurchase service*. Compare POSTPURCHASE CUSTOMER SERVICE.

preretailing   See RETAILING THE INVOICE.

preretail price   See RETAILING THE INVOICE.

prescreening of lines   A service provided by a RESIDENT BUYER, designed to help the retail BUYER make efficient, informed buying decisions while on a market trip. The resident buyer previews the key lines and makes the information available to the store's buyer. This can be done either through verbal or written communication prior to the BUYING TRIP or during the traditional stop at the RESIDENT BUYING OFFICE facility.

prescription drug   A medicine requiring a doctor's written direction (i.e., prescription) for its preparation and use. Prescription drugs may only be prepared and sold by licensed pharmacists. Also called (infrequently) an *ethical drug*.

preseason   The period of time preceding the regular selling period for a category of merchandise.

preseason sale   A sales promotion aimed at introducing new merchandise (particularly apparel) prior to the regular selling season. A preseason sale helps the retailer to determine the appeal of the new merchandise and project sales for the season.

presentation   1. A demonstration or lecture.   2. A manner or style of putting oneself or one's product forward, generally in order to show it to its best advantage. See also VISUAL MERCHANDISING.   3. See also SALES PRESENTATION.

present value   Synonym for NET PRESENT VALUE.

presold market   Purchasers who exist before a product or service is available in the marketplace. These customers are waiting for the arrival of a new product or service and are anxious to acquire it as soon as it becomes available.

presold merchandise   Merchandise for which consumer demand has been stimulated by vendor advertising. Little or no in-store selling is required to move the merchandise.

press clipping bureau/service   Synonym for CLIPPING BUREAU.

press conference   A gathering for news reporters held by a firm seeking PUBLICITY about an event or happening. Press conferences are intended to create publicity about an event in the media in order to increase consumer awareness and interest.

press kit   A collection of facts, figures, photographs, and other promotional materials assembled into a compact package and distributed to members of the press.

press release   PUBLICITY, in the form of written communication of commercially significant news, distributed to the communications media. A press release may be used to announce a special event, new product, change of management, new store opening, change of store policy, etc. The source of the information and the date of use are specified. Some online business services specialize in press releases. Also called a *news release* or *publicity release*. See also PUBLICITY MATERIAL.

press show   A special presentation of fashions for the press. It is generally presented ahead of the regularly scheduled FASHION SHOW to encourage PUBLICITY for the event. Press shows are limited to larger trade and retail sponsors who seek substantial publicity for their event or institution.

pressured shopper   An individual who is always in a hurry and needs to make an immediate purchase. Because time is limited, pressured shoppers may be irritable, distracted, and indecisive. The pressured shopper often expects the sales associate to solve the purchasing dilemma with little information or time spent evaluating comparative products.

prestige advertising   RETAIL INSTITUTIONAL ADVERTISING designed to establish a retail store's fashion leadership. The ads may introduce a new line of merchandise or feature designer special appearances, etc. Although prestige advertisements may draw customers to the store and to particular products, they are created primarily as part of a long-term effort to build and maintain a fashionable reputation.

prestige brand   See PRESTIGE LINE.

prestige builder   An item of merchandise at the top of the line and the most expensive in price. Prestige builders are meant to add status to the store's image and attract status-conscious customers. Also called *prestige merchandise*. See also PRESTIGE LINE and PRESTIGE ZONE.

prestige goods/merchandise   See PRESTIGE BUILDER and PRESTIGE LINE.

prestige line A line of products with a distinct reputation, influence, and BRAND RECOGNITION, associated in the customer's mind with quality and elegance. For example, a HIGH-END prestige cosmetics line distributed through a department store lends a certain CACHET and an upscale image to the store and its cosmetics department. Customers are often willing to pay higher prices for these prestige products. See also BRAND and PRESTIGE BUILDER.

prestige price zone See PRESTIGE ZONE.

prestige pricing A policy of setting a high price on merchandise in order to attract those customers who are interested in the status of owning expensive and exclusive items. Prestige pricing may also be used to attract those customers who associate high prices with top quality. Also called *symbolic pricing*. See also PRICE-QUALITY ASSOCIATION and PRESTIGE ZONE.

prestige product See PRESTIGE LINE.

prestige zone The range of prices covered by a store's most expensive merchandise. Merchandise in the prestige zone is aimed at the customer who is status-conscious and interested in expensive or exclusive merchandise. Also called the *prestige price zone*. See also PRICE ZONE, PRESTIGE PRICING, and PRESTIGE BUILDER.

prêt-à-porter French for READY-TO-WEAR (RTW). See also PRÊT-À-PORTER SHOW.

prêt-à-porter show An international FASHION SHOW in which designers reveal their PRÊT-À-PORTER lines for international markets and READY-TO-WEAR (RTW) lines for American markets. These collections often reflect the same trends as the HAUTE COUTURE fashion shows, but in more commercial price ranges. The prêt-à-porter shows attract the fashion press who report the trends in industry and consumer publications. The major international shows (e.g., Paris, Milan, and London) attract international buyers who identify the upcoming trends and distribute the styles in retail establishments throughout the world.

preteen market Customers who are preadolescent children between 10 and 13 years of age. See also PRETEENS (def. 2).

preteens 1. Apparel designed and sized especially for preadolescent girls between 10 and 13 years of age. Roughly synonymous with SUBTEENS. 2. Synonym for PRETEEN MARKET, which includes both boys and girls in that age group.

pretesting 1. In ADVERTISING RESEARCH, an attempt to evaluate the effectiveness of an ad before it is used. This is usually accomplished by means of a checklist of points and a consumer jury. 2. In MARKETING RESEARCH (MR), similar techniques used to measure the acceptance of an idea, product, or service and to help establish a selling strategy. A trial run of the product, either identified or blind, may be used. Pretesting may also be used for establishing price, determining the effectiveness of direct mailings, etc. Also called a *product pretest*. See also POSTTESTING.

preticketing See VENDOR PREMARKING/PRETICKETING.

previous balance method A method used by retailers to calculate the portion of the balance in a charge account to be assessed interest charges. Under this method, payments made during the billing period are not subtracted from the outstanding balance before the interest charge is assessed. See also ADJUSTED BALANCE METHOD and AVERAGE DAILY BALANCE METHOD.

previously owned Synonym for SECONDHAND.

prewrapped Of gift items (such as perfumes and other toiletries, chocolates and other candies), made available to the customer already gift-wrapped. A sample of what is inside the package is available on display for examination, but the purchaser receives an already gift-wrapped item. The practice has proven popular during busy gift-giving holidays such as Christmas, Mother's Day, Valentine's Day, Father's Day, etc. See also PREPACKAGED.

price 1. n. The amount of money (or other valuable consideration) for which a product or service is bought or sold. Price determines how much a buyer must give up of something (e.g., money) in order to take possession of a product or avail oneself of a service. As such, it serves to allocate products, determining who can buy, possess, and use them. 2. v. To set such a price competitively for one's goods in the marketplace as one of the FOUR PS OF THE MARKETING MIX. See also PRICE POLICY and PRICING.

price adjustment Any raising or lowering of the retail price of an item. A price adjustment provides the retailer with a mechanism to draw customers into the store as well as to increase profits. Also called a *price change*.

price agreement plan A central buying arrangement in which the BUYER for a chain of stores arranges prices, colors, sizes, styles, and assortments of merchandise as well as the terms of shipping. The manager of the individual store can order from the pre-selected assortment as needed. Also called a *catalog plan*.

price-based shopping goods/product Any product(s) for which consumers perceive little difference in the attributes of alternatives and for which they therefore seek only the lowest price available. See also SHOPPING GOODS.

price bracket Synonym for PRICE ZONE.

price break An advertised reduction in prices (i.e., discount), designed to attract customers to the store.

price ceiling See CEILING PRICE.

price change Synonym for PRICE ADJUSTMENT.

price change form A blank form used for recording any raising or lowering of the retail price of merchandise in stock. Additional markups, markup cancellations, and markdowns (MDs) would all be recorded on price change forms.

price code   A coded symbol appearing on the price tag or pin ticket indicating the cost of the merchandise to store personnel while concealing this information from the retail customer.

price collusion   See COLLUSION.

price comparison   The reduced or sale price compared to the regular or list price, both of which may appear on the price tag or label. The presence of both prices allows consumers to recognize the true value of a purchase. In accordance with FEDERAL TRADE COMMISSION (FTC) rulings, the regular price must be accurate and not artificially raised.

price competition   1. A marketing strategy frequently employed as a means of gaining or maintaining a competitive advantage. Typically, a firm may reduce prices in an effort to attract new customers or as a response to the price reductions of a competitor. Some organizations, such as discount stores, engage in price competition on a permanent basis as a matter of policy. See also PRICING.   2. COMPETITION among firms that seek to differentiate their merchandise based on price alone. Items are considered preferred based on how much less they will cost. Compare NONPRICE COMPETITION.

price-conscious   Of a shopper, sensitive to price differences between retailers and regularly seeking bargains and sales. An advertised reduction in prices will generally attract the price-conscious consumer to the store. See also PRICE-SENSITIVE.

price controls   1. Government-mandated ceilings on the prices a firm may charge for its products. In general, such government interventions are designed to combat INFLATION and slow or reduce increases in the COST OF LIVING. In some countries, it is the norm for government and regulatory agencies to control the prices of products and services. These price controls may be applied to an entire economy or may be applied selectively to specific industries and products. Firms failing to abide by the government regulations and guidelines are generally subject to penalties.   2. In merchandising, a manufacturer's regulation (i.e., control) of the resale price for its goods, preventing the retailer or other reseller from setting prices independently.

price cross-elasticity   Synonym for CROSS-ELASTICITY.

price cutter   See PRICE CUTTING.

price cutting   A selling strategy, usually encountered at the retail level, in which goods or services are offered at prices below those recommended by the vendor, below cost, below cost plus expenses, or at levels recognized by the general public to be lower than regular retail. Discounters (i.e., *price cutters*) use this practice, particularly on national brands, to develop a customer following. See also DISCOUNT STORE.

price dealing   See INTRODUCTORY PRICE.

price decline guarantee   See PRICE GUARANTEE (def. 1).

price-demand curve response function   See PRICE-DEMAND RESPONSE FUNCTION.

price-demand elasticity   See ELASTICITY OF DEMAND.

price-demand response function   The RESPONSE FUNCTION that shows the impact of price level variations on sales and quantity of goods sold. Ultimately, the price-demand response function illustrates that it is not possible to expand total dollar sales indefinitely through price cutting. Also called *price-demand curve response function*, *price-oriented response function*, and *price response function*.

price differential   1. A departure from the usual one-price policy, granted by the vendor to the retailer on the basis of the size of the purchase, the type of customer, or the geographical location of the retail store. Price differentials include quantity discounts, trade discounts, and other reductions in price. See also DISCOUNT.   2. The difference between the base price for goods of a certain size or quality and the base price for similar goods that can be accepted as substitutes even though they differ in quality or size from the original. The price differential may be expressed as a percentage of the base price or as a fixed amount deducted from the base price.

price discretion   The decision making latitude by which a sales representative may change the price of an item for the purposes of making a sale.

price discrimination   The sale of goods by vendors to competing retailers at different prices under similar conditions of sale. If no savings to the seller can be demonstrated, or if the sale tends to create a monopoly or restrain trade, this practice is outlawed by the ROBINSON-PATMAN ACT (1936). See also DISCRIMINATORY PRICING and the CLAYTON ACT (1914).

Price Discrimination Chain Store Act   Popular name for the ROBINSON-PATMAN ACT (1936).

price discrimination laws   See CLAYTON ACT (1914) and ROBINSON-PATMAN ACT (1936).

priced out of the market   See PRICE OUT OF THE MARKET.

price-earnings ratio   The financial ratio that results when the market price per share of a company's common stock is divided by the earnings per share of its common stock for the previous year. The ratio is used as an indicator of a company's financial position at a given moment in time. See also FINANCIAL RATIOS.

price elasticity of demand   See ELASTICITY OF DEMAND.

price elasticity of supply   See ELASTICITY OF SUPPLY.

price ending   The practice of manipulating the final digit of the price to create a desired psychological effect in the mind of the consumer. For example, an original retail price may be set in full or whole dollar prices (e.g., $10.00), markdowns may all end in 99¢ (e.g., $5.99), and promotional merchandise may all end in 90¢ (e.g., $6.90). See also ODD-LINE PRICING and EVEN-LINE PRICING.

price equalization A competitive pricing policy for goods delivered to a customer, composed of the price of the item at the factory plus the shipping cost to the customer. The latter, however, is calculated as though the shipment began at the shipping point of the company's competitor nearest to the company's customer. The policy is designed to build business by taking differences in shipping distances and rates out of the equation, thus equalizing the prices offered by closer and more distant suppliers.

price escalation Increases in ultimate prices due to such factors as transportation and distribution costs, unanticipated middleman expenses, shrinkage, and (in international marketing) tariffs and other special taxes.

price-feature advertising ADVERTISING in which the emphasis is on the reduced price of the merchandise offered for sale rather than on features such as usefulness, quality, availability, etc. Compare MERCHANDISE-FEATURE ADVERTISING.

price file A computer memory bank used with the UNIVERSAL PRODUCT CODE (UPC). It matches the store price to each item and is central to the effectiveness of UPC operations in the store.

price fixing 1. The setting of prices at an agreed-upon level by mutual consent of competitors. It is usually regarded as collusive and illegal. See also RESALE PRICE MAINTENANCE (RPM) and CONSCIOUS PARALLEL ACTION. 2. A similar but often unintentional or unplanned activity in e-commerce, arising out of the constant online monitoring of competitors' price changes. To further complicate matters, open online bidding in exchanges means that price information is shared by participants, some of whom may work together to fix the price. This noncompetitive behavior is, however, nonetheless illegal. See also HORIZONTAL PRICE FIXING. Also called *signaling*.

price floor See FLOOR PRICE.

price floor pricing See FLOOR PRICE.

price gouging The act of marking up retail prices to an unreasonably high level. For example, an unscrupulous retailer might unreasonably raise the prices of the basic necessities of life (e.g., bottled water) during a crisis such as a flood, earthquake, tsunami, etc. Price gouging is generally regarded as extortion or swindling. Also called, simply, *gouging*. See also GOUGE.

price guarantee 1. An incentive offered by a vendor to a reseller (i.e., a wholesaler or a retailer) who buys well in advance of the season and places a large order. The vendor promises to reimburse the retailer for any losses resulting from a decline in the market price of the goods between the date of purchase and the start of the normal selling season. Also called *price decline guarantee*. 2. A promise made by a vendor to a reseller (i.e., a wholesaler or a retailer) to reimburse the difference between the planned selling price and the actual selling price if the reseller is unable to trade the goods as planned and must mark them down. Also called *price protection, price protection rebate*, or *vendor-paid markdown*.

price index A measure used to illustrate changes in the average level of prices. See also CONSUMER PRICE INDEX (CPI).

price-inelastic demand See INELASTICITY OF DEMAND.

price inelasticity See INELASTICITY OF DEMAND.

price inflater Any of a number of possible charges added to the list price of a product, increasing its true selling price. These include dealer preparation charges, handling fees, credit charges, service contracts, etc.

price information asymmetry A situation in which one party to the buyer-seller exchange has more information about price than the other. Buyers (particularly ultimate consumers) are generally at a disadvantage because they lack comparative price information. Online exchanges are expected to offset a portion of this disadvantage by allowing consumers to access more information about products and prices. Compare PRICE INFORMATION SYMMETRY.

price information symmetry A situation in which both buyer and seller have the same information about the price of products being exchanged. Online information available in buyer-seller exchanges allows consumers, previously disadvantaged in the exchange of information, to acquire more information about prices and products than was ever available offline if they have the time, skill, and motivation to do so. Compare PRICE INFORMATION ASYMMETRY.

price leader 1. The company in any industry that, apparently without collusion, is the first to make price changes and, consequently, sets the prices for that industry. Because the price leader is often the largest company in the industry and has the largest market share, smaller companies tend to fall in line. 2. A synonym for LOSS LEADER, particularly in the food retailing industry. Compare PRICE TAKER. See also PRICE LEADERSHIP.

price leadership The tendency in some industries to acknowledge the predominance of one company and adopt that company's prices. See also PRICE LEADER (def. 1).

price level Synonym for PRICE ZONE.

price level discount A discount from list price offered on particular items to avoid reprinting the entire price list. Customers are advised that certain products carry an additional percentage discount from what they see on the price list.

price line See PRICE LINE (INVENTORY) CONTROL and PRICE LINING (METHOD).

price line (inventory) control A form of dollar inventory control based on a single retail price. A department or classification of merchandise may be broken down by particular price lines (e.g., $19.99 for a certain classification of men's shirts). Price line control enables the retailer to ascertain how many of those shirts sold at that price. The information is used as a guide to buying and reordering. See also DOLLAR INVENTORY CONTROL.

price lining (method) 1. A retail PRICING strategy in which merchandise is offered for sale at a limited number of predetermined price points. For example, a store may offer men's shirts at $25, $35, and $45 in an effort to simplify the buying process and present the customer with a manageable number of choices. All men's shirts would, therefore, be sold at one of the three price points. The store's buyer actively seeks out merchandise that can be sold to the consumer at these prices. Price lining is often part of a good-better-best approach to pricing and affords some range of choice to customers at various income levels. Ideally, the prices are set far enough apart to make differences in quality and style readily discernible. 2. The practice of placing several items of varying costs together and selling them at the same price. This is a promotional method frequently used in retailing, particularly to clear merchandise at the end of a season. For example, a store may offer all the bath and beauty products displayed on a particular table or in a particular bin for a uniform $5 sale price. See also PRICE SPACE.

price loco The price for an item of merchandise at the place (i.e., location) where the purchase actually occurs. For example, if promotional discounts are given at the cash register, the price will differ from the price on the price tag.

price lookup (PLU) technology A computerized system file that facilitates adjustments to book inventory due to price changes. PLU involves maintaining a computerized system file of every STOCK KEEPING UNIT (SKU) in inventory and a corresponding retail price. When the SKU is identified at the register by a number or bar code, the system looks up the price and transmits it to the cash register display or monitor while processing the transaction. Prices in the file can readily be changed for PROMOTIONS AND SALES, thus eliminating the need for a physical count of inventory before or after the promotion. Customers may be notified through appropriate signage that the reduction will be taken at the register. PLU permits retailers to increase the frequency of promotions by reducing the stock-handling costs associated with event preparation and recovery. A PLU system also allows improved price control by preventing salespeople from discounting nonpromotional items. See also PRICE VERIFICATION PROCEDURE.

price-maintained line See RESALE PRICE MAINTENANCE (RPM).

price maintenance See RESALE PRICE MAINTENANCE (RPM).

price-minus pricing A method used to determine the price of a planned product or service by first estimating the price at which that product or service might achieve a particular share of the market or goal sales volume, and then proceeding to develop the product or service to be profitable at that price.

price mix A store's strategy of raising and lowering prices in response to COMPETITION.

price negotiation Polite synonym for *bargaining*. See BARGAIN.

price-off deal/discount A price reduction used to induce trial or increased usage of a product. The percentage reduction is generally noted on the product's package. For example, the package may read, "10% off regular price." See also DISCOUNT and PROMOTIONS AND SALES.

price-oriented response function See PRICE-DEMAND RESPONSE FUNCTION.

price out of the market To charge such high prices for goods or services as to be no longer competitive.

price pack Products offered at a reduced price to the consumer, commonly in the form of a banded pack in which two items are offered for the price of one, or two products are sold together (e.g., shaving cream and a razor). See also PREMIUM PACK.

price planning The systematic decision making process behind all aspects of PRICING.

price point The dollar amount at which a product or service is offered for sale, viewed as occupying a specific position on a continuum the seller wishes to cover and hence a specific category in the assortment's PRICE RANGE. The price range of an assortment is defined by its lowest and highest price points. For example, a gift shop may establish three price points as follows: gifts under $10; gifts between $10 and $100; and gifts over $100. A store's price points are important considerations in UNIT PLANNING. See also PRICE LINING and PRICE SPACE.

price policy The guidelines or general framework within which the retailer makes all PRICING decisions. This policy reflects the retailer's position regarding such factors as competing stores, costs, promotional expenditures, etc., and includes those considerations that follow the establishment of a firm's pricing objectives. Also called *pricing decision making policy* or *pricing policy*. See also PRICE and PRICING.

price promotion A practice found at both the wholesale and retail levels in which prices on some items are reduced for a short period to stimulate sales. These promotions may be simple price reductions or they may be in the form of allowances, discounts, free goods, premiums, etc.

price protection (rebate) See PRICE GUARANTEE.

price-quality association The theory that consumers equate high prices with high-quality goods and low prices with low quality goods. See also PRESTIGE PRICING.

price/quality display A grouping of goods by price point or level of quality, used especially when these vary widely over an assortment. For example, to facilitate customer selection, a department store may group handbags as designer, bridge, better, and moderate. Also called a *quality/price display*.

price range The spread between the highest and lowest possible variations in price. While there is no specific correlation between price and quality, better quality merchandise is usually offered at a higher price than inferior quality merchandise. Since a store cannot offer merchandise at all possible price ranges, management must determine particular price lines and suitable quality for the store. Compare PRICE ZONE. See also PRICE POINT.

price reducer Any strategy used to lower the actual selling price of a product. Price reducers include various discounts and allowances, free services, rebates, trading stamps, etc.

price reduction Synonym for MARKDOWN (MD).

price response function See PRICE-DEMAND RESPONSE FUNCTION.

price-sensitive 1. Of an item or service, characterized by a close link between demand and the price at which the item or service is offered. Small changes in price create large changes in demand. See also ELASTICITY OF DEMAND and PRICE SENSITIVITY. 2. Of a consumer, so PRICE-CONSCIOUS that a small change in price will determine the decision to buy or refrain from buying a product.

price sensitivity The tendency of the demand for an item or service to vary based on variations in price. Some items or services are more PRICE-SENSITIVE than others. Retailers and other markets of price-sensitive items often test new prices before implementing them to assess the impact of the price on demand. See also ELASTICITY OF DEMAND.

price setting 1. The PRICING of merchandise or services. Prices are typically set within a range. The CEILING PRICE is the highest price buyers can or are willing to pay for a product, and is also the price set by direct competitors for identical products. The FLOOR PRICE is the lowest price that a business can afford or is willing to accept. It is usually the BREAK-EVEN POINT, but is sometimes below break-even when deliberately set at a *penetration price* level to develop market share quickly in a new market, or when the product is used as a LOSS LEADER designed to attract traffic. See also PRICE. 2. A synonym for RESALE PRICE MAINTENANCE (RPM).

price shading A PRICING policy in which DISCOUNTS are offered by a manufacturer to wholesalers and retailers or by salespeople to the consumer. Price shading is used as a means of increasing DEMAND for the product without changing the list or book price.

price space The gap existing between price points in a product line (i.e., the distance from one price to the next). See also PRICE LINING and PRICE POINT.

price stability A condition in the marketplace in which price competition between firms is kept to a minimum, usually as the result of the PRICE LEADERSHIP provided by one or more large firms in an industry.

price strategy Synonym for PRICING STRATEGY.

price support Artificially maintained price levels at or above market values, often resulting from government action (e.g., subsidies). For example, the government may buy surplus crops in order to give support to agricultural prices.

price tag A tag (i.e., a piece of paper, plastic, etc.) or ticket attached to merchandise, usually by the retailer. In addition to the retail price of the item, the price tag may contain such information as the style number, vendor number, coded date of purchase, coded cost price, size, and other information to be used in INVENTORY. Also known simply as a *tag, ticket,* or *price ticket.* The placing of price information on the merchandise in the form of a label or on a price tag is called *price ticketing.* See also TAG PRICE and VENDOR PREMARKING/PRETICKETING.

price taker A firm that has no market power over price. The market dictates prices for such a firm. Compare PRICE LEADER.

price testing In E-TAILING, the practice of using online pricing processes to try out various prices and determine the optimum selling price. Prices can be tested by offering different prices to different customers in real time and then tracking buyer receptiveness to each price. The tests are run on different segments of buyers and a COOKIE may be used to identify customer characteristics. Product prices can then be set to vary according to preselected variables (e.g., region of the country) and adjusted based on buyer PRICE TOLERANCE. For example, if testing shows that customers are willing to pay the higher price, then the higher price will be charged. If, however, buyers are shown to be PRICE-SENSITIVE, a lower price is set instead.

price ticket See PRICE TAG and VENDOR PREMARKING/PRETICKETING.

price ticketing See PRICE TAG.

price tolerance The capacity of consumers in the marketplace to accept a particular price for an item of merchandise or a service.

price transparency A condition in the marketplace in which prices for competing products are clearly visible and easily obtainable by all interested parties (i.e., buyers, sellers, competitors, and regulators). Transparency highlights price discrepancies. Buyers with this information are better equipped to make more effective purchase decisions based on price. Also called, simply, TRANSPARENCY (def. 4).

price value See COMPANY ANALYSIS.

price variable The part of the MARKETING MIX concerned with establishing product prices. Price is a variable in that it can be altered as conditions warrant. See also FOUR PS OF THE MARKETING MIX.

price verification procedure A process used to ensure that the price on a ticket, or on the shelf, matches what the customer will see on the register at the checkout. See also PRICE LOOKUP (PLU) TECHNOLOGY.

price war A fiercely competitive situation in which competing firms drastically lower their prices in an attempt to undersell each other and attract each other's customers. Price wars sometimes result in one or more participants being forced out of business.

price zone A series of prices or price lines likely to appeal to one group of consumers. Each price zone is designed to appeal to one particular segment of a store's customers. The PROMOTION ZONE represents low-end merchandise sold at low prices; the VOLUME ZONE is the middle price range; and the PRESTIGE ZONE includes the status, high-end merchandise. Also called a *price bracket* or *price level*. Compare PRICE RANGE. See also PRICE LINING and STRATIFYING THE MARKET.

pricing Any of a variety of methods used by retail merchants and other marketers to determine the prices at which to sell their merchandise. These methods include DEMAND-ORIENTED PRICING, the FULL COST APPROACH TO PRICING, the FLEXIBLE APPROACH TO PRICING, FLEXIBLE PRICING, GOING-RATE PRICING, GROSS MARGIN PRICING, and MANUFACTURER'S SUGGESTED RETAIL PRICE (MSRP). Pricing objectives (e.g., profit maximization, volume sales goals, image-driven objectives, and status quo objectives) are set before detailed pricing strategies and techniques are determined. See also PRICE, PRICING OBJECTIVE, PRICE SETTING, and PRICE POLICY.

pricing above the competition See PRICING ABOVE THE MARKET.

pricing above the market A policy of setting prices above those of the competition so as to convey an image of superior product quality or prestige and to differentiate the product in the minds of potential customers. Retailers who wish to convey a high-end, high-fashion image may price goods above the market to appeal to trendsetters and other fashion-conscious clientele. Also called *pricing above the competition* and *premium pricing*. See also MARKET-PLUS PRICE.

pricing at the competitive level See PRICING AT THE MARKET.

pricing at the market A policy of setting prices at approximately the same level as one's competitors, thus minimizing the use of price as a competitive factor. Also called *pricing at the competitive level, market-based pricing,* and *meeting competition*.

pricing below the competition See PRICING BELOW THE MARKET.

pricing below the market A policy of setting prices below those of the competition in an effort to maximize the use of price as a competitive factor. This strategy may also be an alternative to expensive promotional efforts. Pricing below the market conveys a desirable discounter's image to the PRICE-CONSCIOUS consumer. Also called *below-the-market pricing, below-the-market strategy,* or *pricing below (or under) the competition*.

pricing decision making policy See PRICE POLICY.

pricing error An incorrect original price, generally too high, so that the merchandise does not move. A pricing error may be corrected through a MARKDOWN (MD).

pricing objective/goal Any of the various considerations that precede the establishment of price policies. Pricing objectives are the comprehensive goals that the firm expects to achieve in the long run. Included may be the maximization of sales or profits, the achievement of a predetermined return on investment, an increase in market share, the maintenance of a status quo with respect to price competition, etc. See also PRICE POLICY and PRICING STRATEGY.

pricing policy See PRICE POLICY.

pricing strategy 1. In retailing, the long-range planning that uses price as a means of attracting customers to the store. It may be used in conjunction with or as a substitute for a prime location, advertising expenditures, and other promotions. 2. A component of a firm's overall marketing strategy consisting of the establishment of a realistic price framework. The pricing strategy plays a crucial role in determining a company's competitive position in the marketplace. Also called a *price strategy*. See also PRICING.

pricing under the competition Synonym for PRICING BELOW THE MARKET.

primary advertising Synonym for PRIMARY DEMAND ADVERTISING.

primary advertising medium Synonym for PRIMARY MEDIUM.

primary (buying) motive The reason an individual purchases a particular class or type of merchandise, regardless of the particular brand. See also PRIMARY DEMAND.

primary circulation The distribution of a periodical (i.e., newspaper or magazine) that includes not only the buyers of the issue but also members of their immediate families. Also called *primary readership*. See also CIRCULATION.

primary customer service Any customer service function considered basic to a retail operation. These vary from store to store and from region to region, but the following are usually included: maintaining convenient store hours, having sales personnel available, display, wrapping, adjustments, and parking facilities. Also called *basic customer service* and *essential customer service*.

primary data Information collected as the result of original research, surveys, interviews, experiments, etc., to address specific research issues. Compare SECONDARY DATA. See also PRIMARY RESEARCH.

primary demand Consumer demand for a class or type of product rather than for a particular brand (e.g., the demand for jeans in general as opposed to the demand for Levi's jeans in particular). Also called *generic demand*. Compare SELECTIVE DEMAND. See also CONSUMER DEMAND.

primary demand advertising   Advertising whose objective is the development of demand for a product or service without making reference to a specific manufacturer or a particular brand. This form of advertising is used primarily for innovative products in the first stages of the PRODUCT LIFE CYCLE (PLC). Also called *pioneering advertising, primary advertising,* and *primary demand stimulation.*

primary group   Any REFERENCE GROUP to which an individual belongs that exerts a strong influence on the individual's attitudes and behavior. The most significant primary groups for most individuals are the family and the peers with whom they frequently associate. Also called a *primary membership group.* See also MEMBERSHIP GROUP.

primary job assignment   An employee's chief responsibility as specified in the JOB DESCRIPTION.

primary lighting   The allover level of illumination in an area, such as a store or a store's department. It is usually the light that fills the selling floor from overhead light fixtures, but it does not include accent lights, wall washers, and display highlighting lamps (i.e., forms of SECONDARY LIGHTING). Primary lighting also does not include glamour or decorative lighting such as sconces, counter or table lamps, indirect lighting, etc. Also called *general lighting.*

primary listening area   Synonym for PRIMARY SERVICE AREA (PSA).

primary market   1. In the fashion/apparel industry, suppliers of the raw materials needed for production such as textiles, leather, and furs. Primary market producers work 12 to 24 months in advance of the fashion season to project color forecasts, fiber selection, and fabrication processes. See also PRIMARY MARKET FORECAST, SECONDARY MARKET, and TERTIARY MARKET.   2. In food merchandising, the local level at which farm goods are assembled from a number of farmers for processing or distribution. Also known as a *local market.* See also ASSEMBLING.

primary market area   The area or region representing major sales and distribution for particular goods or services. For example, the primary market area for bathing suits would be a warm climate area such as the southern United States.

primary market forecast   FASHION FORECASTING derived from primary market producers (e.g., producers of raw materials such as fabrics). Primary market producers are the earliest market to project upcoming trends. They work 12 to 24 months in advance of the season to project color themes, fiber selection, and fabrication processes. See also PRIMARY MARKET, SECONDARY MARKET FORECAST, and TERTIARY MARKET FORECAST.

primary market segment   The essential target group identified for marketing and advertising communications. For example, the primary market segment for children's apparel may be parents, while the *secondary market segment* may be grandparents. See also SECONDARY MARKET SEGMENT.

primary medium   Any medium, print or broadcast, used to carry the main idea or initial impact of an advertising campaign. For example, television advertising may be used as a primary medium and may be coupled with secondary, backup advertising at the POINT-OF-PURCHASE (POP). Also called a *primary advertising medium.* See also MEDIA, ADVERTISING MEDIA, POINT-OF-PURCHASE (POP) DISPLAY, and SUPPORT MEDIUM.

primary membership group   Synonym for PRIMARY GROUP.

primary motive   See PRIMARY (BUYING) MOTIVE.

primary need   See BIOGENIC NEED.

primary package   The protective container into which a product is initially placed. For example, glass or plastic jars, cans, tubes, etc. are all primary packages. Often this packaging is supplemented by another package (such as a box) for further protection and brand identification.

primary readership   See PRIMARY CIRCULATION.

primary research   The process by which a researcher gathers original information without relying on information gathered or analyzed by others. In retailing and other areas of marketing, primary research is designed to answer a specific marketing question or solve a marketing problem. Qualitative marketing research produces qualitative data from participants' opinions, behavioral intentions, and beliefs. Quantitative primary research generates projectable numerical data. Compare SECONDARY RESEARCH. See also SECONDARY DATA, QUALITATIVE (PRIMARY) RESEARCH, and QUANTITATIVE (PRIMARY) RESEARCH.

primary service   See PRIMARY CUSTOMER SERVICE.

primary service area (PSA)   1. In broadcasting, the geographical area reached by a television or radio station with a high-level signal at all times. Also called a *primary viewing area* or *primary listening area.*   2. Synonym for PRIMARY TRADING AREA.

primary stage   See INTRODUCTORY STAGE.

primary statistical area (PMSA)   Prior to 2000, a metropolitan area closely related to another MSA. Formerly *primary metropolitan statistical area,* hence the abbreviation *PMSA.* See CORE-BASED STATISTICAL AREA (CBSA).

primary supplier   Synonym for KEY RESOURCE.

primary trading area   The geographical area closest to the store within which 50% to 80% of the store's customers reside. Also called the *primary service area (PSA)* or *primary trade area.* See also SECONDARY TRADING AREA and FRINGE TRADING AREA.

primary viewing area   Synonym for PRIMARY SERVICE AREA (PSA).

prime contractor The business awarded the contract on a large and complex project that commonly necessitates subcontracting various parts of the job to other businesses.

prime rate In the United States, the interest rate charged by the Federal Reserve Bank to commercial lending institutions. Changes in the prime rate may affect consumers and businesses in a variety of ways. For example, lower interest rates usually precede a rise in new home construction, which may in turn lead to an increase in furniture and home furnishings sales.

prime resource Synonym for KEY RESOURCE.

prime time The continuous period during which peak audiences are reached by one of the broadcast media. In general, individual stations designate prime time for their own audiences and charge a higher rate for advertising during this period than at other hours. In television, it is usually between 8:00 p.m. and 11:00 p.m. (7:00 p.m. and 10:00 p.m. Central Standard Time); in radio, prime time is generally DRIVE TIME.

prime time television See PRIME TIME.

prime variable The criterion that best enables a retailer to divide a given market into distinct groups (i.e., segments). Prime variables vary from product to product. For example, prime variables in the jewelry market would be income, age, gender, and status. The same variables would not be applicable to the market for milk. See also SEGMENTATION VARIABLE.

prime vendor Synonym for KEY RESOURCE.

principal In law, a person who authorizes another to act in his or her stead. For example, a BROKER or a COMMISSION HOUSE serves this function in the grocery industry.

principal city The largest city in each metropolitan statistical area (MSA). Additional cities qualify if specified requirements are met concerning population size and employment. Titles of metropolitan divisions are typically based on principal city names, but in certain cases consist of county names.

principal resource Synonym for KEY RESOURCE.

principal resource list A tool used by buyers to keep track of and evaluate their vendors. The document lists the retailer's main resources (i.e., vendors) ranked by the total dollar value of purchases made from each of them. The information may be arranged by department or by season of the year. The principal resource list shows the growth or decline of business with each vendor on a seasonal or annual basis, providing buyers with the means to make year-by-year comparisons. Also called, simply, a *resource list*. See also VENDOR ANALYSIS FORM and RESOURCE DIARY.

principle of factor sparsity Synonym for EIGHTY-TWENTY (80-20) PRINCIPLE.

print media See MEDIA.

print server See SERVER.

prior donor file A computerized list of customers who have purchased gifts from a retailer or marketer, such as a gift magazine subscription (that has since expired) or a gift floral bouquet. Prior donors are considered excellent prospects for future gift promotions.

priority order See RUSH ORDER.

prior source A VENDOR from whom the buyer has previously received merchandise. See also KEY RESOURCE.

prior stock Merchandise that has been in INVENTORY for the duration of the previous season, generally in excess of six months. See also PRIOR STOCK REPORT and INVENTORY.

prior stock report A report prepared by the retailer that summarizes quantitative information about all STOCK ON HAND (SOH) remaining from the previous season. See also PRIOR STOCK and INVENTORY.

Privacy Act (1974) U.S. federal legislation designed to protect citizens from the invasion of privacy by the federal government. The law permits individuals, for the first time, to inspect information about themselves contained in federal agency files and to challenge, correct, or amend the material. The act also prohibits agencies and businesses, including retailers, from selling or renting an individual's name or address for mailing list use.

private See PRIVATELY HELD COMPANY.

private auction See ONLINE AUCTION.

private bonded warehouse See CUSTOMS BONDED WAREHOUSE.

private brand A BRAND developed, owned, and controlled by the retailer, distributor, dealer, or other marketing intermediary. This merchandise is generally lower in cost than other brands. The merchant becomes both the producer of record and the marketer so that the manufacturer's only responsibility is to make the merchandise according to the merchant's specifications. Depending on the level of the channel member for whom the brand is named, a private brand may be designated a *distributor brand, dealer brand, house brand, reseller brand, middleman brand, store's own brand (SOB), store brand,* or *private distributor brand*. Also known as a *confined label,* a *private label,* and a *private label brand*. The process of developing and maintaining such a brand is *private branding*.

private brand label A label specifically developed and designed for a private brand or a store's own brand. The label is an important factor in the success of private branding; it may include the store's name, names that conjure up a particular image for the shopper, and/or signatures of celebrities from different walks of life that bring instant recognition to the merchandise. The use of such a label is known as *private brand labeling*.

private buying office A store-owned resident buying office maintained in a MARKET CENTER by a large retail store. Owned and operated by a single retail organization, it allows that organization to maintain a market presence even when its corporate office is located far from a major market. Buyers perform functions similar to those in an ASSOCIATED BUYING OFFICE or INDEPENDENT BUYING OFFICE, but there are no other stores with whom to exchange information. A large retail organization may choose to maintain its own private buying office in a market for economic reasons, particularly if its sales volume would require an extremely high fee to be paid to a SALARIED (BUYING) OFFICE. Also called an *individual buying office* or an *individual resident buying office*.

private carrier   A transportation firm (rail, truck, barge, etc.) engaged in shipping merchandise. Unlike a COMMON CARRIER, a private carrier is owned by the firm for which it performs the shipping function and is thus exempt from certain forms of government regulation. Compare CONTRACT CARRIER.

private company   See PRIVATELY HELD COMPANY.

private corporation   See CLOSELY HELD CORPORATION.

private costs   For purposes of calculating the cost of doing business, those costs actually incurred by a company, i.e., appearing on their financial statements. Compare SOCIAL COSTS.

private distributor brand   See PRIVATE BRAND.

private import wholesaler   An importing firm serving many sizes and types of retail stores that stock foreign products. Private import wholesalers purchase samples of foreign products and offer them to retailers through catalogs and salespeople. Even though the goods procured from this type of foreign resource cost more than they would if a direct foreign contact were used, the private import wholesaler's expertise in a particular merchandise category may prove invaluable. In addition, the wholesaler frequently assumes the risks and financial responsibilities involved in foreign buying. Many small retail firms use private import wholesalers. Also called an *import wholesaler* or *private wholesaler*.

private label (brand)   See PRIVATE BRAND.

private-label buying   See SPECIFICATION BUYING.

private labeling   See PRIVATE BRAND.

privately held company   A company whose stock is not traded on a public stock exchange. A privately held company has fewer owners than a PUBLICLY HELD COMPANY; sometimes, only one. The owners may be a family, or they may be a group of investors within or outside the organization. When a publicly held company is bought by private investors, the organization is said to be *taken private*. Also called a *private company* or, informally, a *private*.

privately held retail organization   See PRIVATELY HELD COMPANY.

private office   See PRIVATE BUYING OFFICE.

private party selling   See PARTY-PLAN SELLING.

private sale   The sale of merchandise at reduced prices to a special group of customers, such as charge customers or preferred customers. The sale is advertised in mailings to those customers, but not to the general public. A private sale may immediately precede a sale of the same merchandise to the general public, with the selected customers getting an early start to purchase the best buys. Also called an *unadvertised sale*.

private warehouse   A storage facility operated by the user. It has the advantage of total user control, important when items needing special treatment (e.g., chemicals and pharmaceuticals) are being stored or when storage volume is large and handling volume is constant. Also called a *company warehouse*. Compare PUBLIC WAREHOUSE and CONTRACT WAREHOUSE.

private wholesaler   See PRIVATE IMPORT WHOLESALER.

privatization   The sale of state-owned enterprises or their assets to individuals or private firms. Rather than investing the money necessary to revamp state-owned enterprises, governments often elect to *privatize* them instead.

prize money   See PUSH MONEY (PM).

prize money allowance   See PUSH MONEY (PM).

PRIZM   The original and most widely used neighborhood target marketing system. PRIZM defines every neighborhood in the United States based on 60 demographically and psychographically distinct neighborhood types called *clusters*. Information used in segmenting a market is based on a combination of geographic and demographic variables. The data defines areas by zip code, census tract, and block. Retailers use PRIZM data to determine new store sites, plan product assortments, and target customer mailings. See also CLUSTER.

proactive selling   A sales effort in which customers are actually pursued by a firm's sales force. Compare REACTIVE SELLING.

probability sampling   In marketing and other social science research, a method of selecting a representative subset of the total POPULATION to study so that each member has a known and equal chance of being selected. There are three basic types of probability samples: the RANDOM SAMPLE, the STRATIFIED (RANDOM) SAMPLE, and the AREA SAMPLE. In each type of probability sample the members of a given group are selected through an objective process without the interference of judgments made by the researcher.

probationary period   The period of time after which a new, provisional employee may be evaluated and considered for a permanent position. See also PROBATIONARY PROCESS and PROBATIONARY PROMOTION.

probationary process   The practice of evaluating a new, provisional employee's job performance over a period of time to determine whether or not the employee will become a permanent staff member. When the same process is applied to an employee who is provisionally promoted, it is known as a PROBATIONARY PROMOTION. See also PROBATIONARY PERIOD.

probationary promotion   The practice of evaluating a provisionally promoted employee over a period of time to determine whether or not the employee is successful in the new position. Also called a *provisional promotion*. See also PROBATIONARY PERIOD and PROBATIONARY PROCESS.

problem analysis   The systematic identification and examination of performance problems preliminary to coming up with solutions and corrections.

problem awareness   The stage in the consumer's decision making process in which it is recognized that the merchandise or service under consideration may solve a problem or fulfill a desire.

problem child   (Slang) A high-growth product that commands a low MARKET SHARE. Such a product is viewed as a problem because it would require a considerable expenditure of additional money to increase market share. The company must choose between building up the product or dropping it. Also called a *question mark* or a *wildcat*.

problem definition   The first stage of marketing or other social science research, in which a clear statement of the problem is elaborated. See also MARKETING RESEARCH (MR).

problem detection study/analysis   Research that focuses on the complaints of customers in order to determine product performance in the marketplace. Products may subsequently be modified or replaced. A similar type of study may also be used in the service industry.

problem-solving approach   A SALES APPROACH aimed at helping the PROSPECT solve either a specific problem known to the SALESPERSON or a common problem assumed to affect the prospect.

procedural screen   In global marketing, one of the barriers or hurdles that must be overcome by a firm seeking to do business with a foreign government. During this stage of negotiations, the firm must follow numerous bureaucratic procedures and properly fill out numerous forms. The firm may need to take special care to discover who is actually in charge and understand exactly what needs to be done. Hiring local consultants who have experience with the process is often recommended. See also ELIGIBILITY SCREEN, LINKAGE SCREEN, COMPETITIVE SCREEN, and INFLUENCE SCREEN.

process departmentalization   In manufacturing, the practice of grouping workers according to the major steps in the process of producing a product. For example, a table-manufacturing company might departmentalize its workers for each phase of manufacturing a table: shaping and sizing the wood; drilling and rough-finishing the pieces; and assembling and finishing the table. Also called *departmentalization by process*. See also FUNCTIONAL DEPARTMENTALIZATION.

processing in transit   See TRANSIT PRIVILEGES.

process materials   Synonym for INDUSTRIAL GOODS.

procurement (function)   See INDUSTRIAL PURCHASING.

produce   In food retailing, fresh fruits and vegetables and the department of the store in which they are sold. This is in contrast to FARM PRODUCTS, which are farm-grown raw materials used in the manufacture of processed goods and which become part of a physical good. The produce category also includes floral products.

produce exchange   A market for perishable agricultural products (e.g., fruits, vegetables, and flowers). See also EXCHANGE.

producer   1. A MANUFACTURER of goods or a provider of services.   2. In broadcast organizations, a producer is a top manager with responsibilities similar to those of a publisher of a print medium. The producer is responsible for raising money, hiring personnel, and generally supervising business matters for a stage, film, television, or radio production.   3. Informally, an individual who is highly successful, particularly in SALES.

producer-controlled brand   A BRAND owned or controlled by a firm that is primarily in the business of manufacturing. Also called *natural brand*.

producer goods   Synonym for INDUSTRIAL GOODS.

producer market   The producer market includes a wide variety of organizations that purchase goods to be incorporated into other goods, goods used to produce other goods, or goods consumed in the day-to-day operations of the organization. The producer market is part of the larger INDUSTRIAL MARKET. See also GOVERNMENT MARKET and INSTITUTIONAL MARKET.

producer outlet   Synonym for MANUFACTURER'S STORE.

producer-owned wholesaler   A wholesale business owned by the producer instead of by an independent businessperson. The two types of producer-owned wholesalers are the MANUFACTURER'S BRANCH OFFICE and the MANUFACTURER'S SALES OFFICE.

Producer Price Index (PPI)   A monthly BUREAU OF LABOR STATISTICS (BLS) report of data on changes over time in the selling prices received by domestic producers of goods and services for their output. Replaces, in the United States and the United Kingdom, the WHOLESALE PRICE INDEX. Compare CONSUMER PRICE INDEX (CPI).

producers' cooperative/co-op   A marketing organization formed by a group of small farmers and involved with the sale of the members' products. It may perform assembly, brokerage, processing, and distribution for members, enabling them to obtain some of the competitive advantages of larger marketing concerns. Also called a *marketing cooperative, producers' cooperative marketing,* or *producers' cooperative marketing association.* See also POOLING.

producers' cooperative marketing (association) See PRODUCERS' COOPERATIVE/CO-OP.

produce stand See FARM STAND.

product 1. Any physical object, service, idea, or activity that fulfills a need for the consuming public, whether it be at the industrial, business, institutional, or retail level. In its broadest sense the term encompasses a cluster of attributes that may include, for example, the social and psychological benefits attached to the product. 2. In a narrower sense, a particular class of such objects, services, ideas, or activities. For example, the product known as a truck may be manufactured in a number of forms (four-wheel drive, flatbed, etc.), and the various forms may be sold under a number of brand names (Chevrolet, GMC, etc.). 3. In the MARKETING MIX, product is the variable that determines how strategies are developed for the other Ps (PRICE, PLACE, and PROMOTION). See also FOUR PS OF THE MARKETING MIX.

product adaptation The modification of products to meet local needs and requirements. For example, goods shipped overseas may sometimes be adapted to special conditions such as different electric current, local air pollution standards, etc.

product adoption process See ADOPTION PROCESS.

product advertising Advertising whose objective is the stimulation of demand for a specific product or service. Product advertising may seek an immediate response on the part of the customer, in which case it is termed DIRECT ADVERTISING or *direct-action advertising.* Conversely, product advertising may seek a response at some time in the future, in which case it is termed INDIRECT ADVERTISING or *indirect-action advertising.* See also RETAIL PRODUCT ADVERTISING and BRAND ADVERTISING.

product analysis 1. In retailing, the research conducted by a BUYER to determine the performance of a purchased item. The aim of the research is to achieve the desired level of quality and the lowest possible price. 2. In advertising, the study of a product to decide which aspects to feature in an ADVERTISING CAMPAIGN.

product approach See EXHIBIT APPROACH.

product assortment See ASSORTMENT.

product attribute Any objective characteristic of a PRODUCT (e.g., color, line, design, materials, and quality of workmanship) or subjective characteristic of a product (e.g., the reputation of the manufacturer and the brand image). Also called a *product characteristic.* Compare PRODUCT DISFEATURE.

product audit The process of identifying weaknesses in marketing, strategy, image, performance, etc., within a product or line of products and recommending improvements. A product audit is sometimes undertaken by a committee called the PRODUCT AUDIT COMMITTEE.

product audit committee A committee of marketing employees whose job it is to point out any weaknesses in the marketing, image, performance, etc., of a product and make recommendations for improvement.

product augmentation A strategy employed in marketing products that have reached the maturity stage in the PRODUCT LIFE CYCLE (PLC). The life of a product may be extended by enhancing the way it is presented (e.g., updated, more attractive packaging), augmenting it with services (e.g., repairs), or periodically changing it superficially, as in the women's ready-to-wear industry. See also MATURITY STAGE.

product breadth See PRODUCT WIDTH and ASSORTMENT BREADTH.

product buyback agreement Synonym for BUYBACK AGREEMENT.

product buying motive The reason an individual purchases a particular product or brand of product instead of alternative products available in the MARKETPLACE. Also called *product motive.*

product category Synonym for CLASSIFICATION.

product characteristic Synonym for PRODUCT ATTRIBUTE.

product class A group of items that are treated as natural substitutes and/or complements for each other by most consumers.

product classification Synonym for CLASSIFICATION. See also PRODUCT LINE DEPARTMENTALIZATION.

product concept A marketing management orientation in which the consumer is seen as primarily concerned with the acquisition of quality goods at reasonable prices. The manufacturer who adopts the product concept emphasizes product improvement and efficiency of production. See also PRODUCTION CONCEPT, MARKETING CONCEPT, and SELLING CONCEPT.

product decay curve Synonym for DECAY CURVE.

product deletion The withdrawal of a product from a company's line of products, generally because it is no longer profitable. Also called *pruning, product pruning,* and *product line pruning.*

product demonstration A SPECIAL EVENT orchestrated to promote new or improved products by illustrating how consumers can use the merchandise. Demonstrations are common in accessory and cosmetic departments of department stores and in warehouse retailing, where product representatives are often set up at stations within the store. See also SALES DEMONSTRATION.

product departmentalization Synonym for PRODUCT LINE DEPARTMENTALIZATION.

product depth   The number of items in each product line offered for sale by a marketing firm. Not to be confused with ASSORTMENT DEPTH, a measure of the quantity of each item available in a retailer's assortment. Also called *product mix depth.*

product design   See DESIGN.

product design simplification   A marketing strategy in which a product's design is simplified in an effort to reduce manufacturing costs and increase profits. Generally, the consumer will perceive no difference in such a redesigned product. See also DESIGN.

product developer   A retail worker charged with generating ideas, designing prototypes, and arranging for the production of exclusive products for the retailer, particularly, but not solely, by overseas manufacturers. The position requires expertise in material specification, textile performance standards, manufacturing procedures, and quality control. The position is a BUYER specialization frequently found at the corporate merchandising level, where buying may be split into four specialized functions: buying, planning, distribution, and product development. This relatively new position is an outgrowth of increased dependence on GLOBAL SOURCING. Product developers often speak the language of the countries in which they do business. See also BUYER and PRODUCT DEVELOPMENT.

product development   1. In the retailer's use of GLOBAL SOURCING, the generation of ideas, design of prototypes, and arrangement for the production of exclusive products for the retail organization. The responsibility for product development often falls to the PRODUCT DEVELOPER, an employee of the retailer.   2. Synonym for NEW PRODUCT DEVELOPMENT.

product differentiation   The unique features of an item of merchandise that give it a competitive edge over other products within the same classification. This may be an actual difference (such as quality), or a difference of image resulting from promotional efforts. Product differentiation may be achieved by recombining the FOUR PS OF THE MARKETING MIX (i.e., product, place, price, and promotion) to meet consumer needs. Also called *product differentiation marketing.* See also BRAND DIFFERENTIATION and DIFFERENTIATION.

product differentiation marketing   See PRODUCT DIFFERENTIATION.

product differentiator   Any difference in a product that helps distinguish it from competitors' products.

product diffusion   Synonym for DIFFUSION PROCESS.

product disfeature   A PRODUCT ATTRIBUTE disliked by the consumer (often its price).

product diversification   See DIVERSIFICATION.

product division of authority   In marketing management, an organizational structure in which LINE ORGANIZATION is set up to correspond to the lines of products being manufactured. This arrangement is most common in large firms making a highly diversified line of products. Compare MARKET DIVISION OF AUTHORITY.

product-driven   A term used to describe a company orientation in which products are developed and produced with little regard for the wants and needs of the customer. See also PRODUCTION CONCEPT.

product duplication   1. The manufacture of identical or very similar products by different companies, either by accident or as a result of one company copying the other.   2. The deliberate production of nearly identical products by a single manufacturer with the intention of using them to compete against one another in the marketplace. For example, a detergent manufacturer may wrap identical products in different packages to command maximum supermarket shelf space.

product fit   The degree to which a product meets the needs of the marketplace.

product franchise   A franchise limited to a specific product line. In automobile and gasoline retailing, for example, product franchises are strategic partnerships between a producer and a retailer to sell a product. The producer provides the retailer with product training and marketing incentives, while the retailer agrees to maintain specified levels of inventory, sales staffing, and promotional activity. Also called a *trade franchise* or an *authorized dealership.*

product image   The perceptions and impressions a customer has regarding a particular product. See also BRAND IMAGE and STORE IMAGE.

product improvement   A program designed to increase the sales of a product by upgrading the item's attributes to attract new customers or encourage existing customers to purchase the product more frequently. Product improvement may involve *quality improvement* (e.g., improving the product's durability or effectiveness), *feature improvement* (e.g., adding new features to improve versatility or convenience), and *style improvement* (e.g., altering the item to enhance its physical or aesthetic appeal). Also called *product modification.*

production   1. Those activities that add value to goods and services (e.g., creation, transportation, and warehousing). Production transforms resources and raw materials into a form that people need or want.   2. Generally, but not always, the same as MANUFACTURING.

production accessories   Synonym for ACCESSORY EQUIPMENT.

production activity report (PAR)   A status report for use by merchandisers, summarizing contractor shop floor production activity.

production-based alliance   In global marketing, a STRATEGIC ALLIANCE based on sharing the construction or production of a product, either through the provision of parts or through developing and producing the product jointly. Production-based alliances have become widespread in the automobile industry in an effort to improve efficiency and reduce research and development costs. See also TECHNOLOGY-BASED ALLIANCE and DISTRIBUTION-BASED ALLIANCE.

production budget   A forecast of the number of units a firm must produce in order to fill expected sales and maintain inventory for a given budget period. The quantitative data used to determine the production budget is derived by adding projected sales to the number of units expected to remain in inventory at the end of the budget period and subtracting the number of units on hand at the beginning of the budget period.

production concept   A marketing management orientation in which the desires of the consumer are seen as secondary to the efficient production of high-quality products that may be sold at competitive prices. The production concept is commonly held in traditional manufacturing organizations, where a good product is believed to be assured success in the marketplace. Such a company is said to be PRODUCT-DRIVEN. Also called a *production orientation*. See also PRODUCT CONCEPT, MARKETING CONCEPT, and SELLING CONCEPT.

production division   In an apparel manufacturing firm, the division responsible for mass-producing merchandise and filling orders placed by retailers. Production in an apparel company includes pattern-making, cutting, bundling, sewing, finishing, and maintaining quality control. Some apparel firms hire outside companies to perform specific manufacturing processes. See also OFFSHORE PRODUCTION.

production era of marketing   A stage in the evolution of marketing (during the Industrial Revolution) characterized by a high level of competition. Manufacturers concentrated their efforts on producing goods and moving them to their customers as efficiently as possible. Little consideration was given to the wants and needs of the consumer, which were simply assumed.

production fit   The degree of compatibility between a new product and the manufacturer's existing production machinery.

production line   Synonym for ASSEMBLY LINE.

production orientation   Synonym for PRODUCTION CONCEPT.

production-oriented diversification   Synonym for CONGRUENT PRODUCTION DIVERSIFICATION.

production-oriented marketing   A form of business orientation, prevalent in the United States until the 1930s, in which the focus was on the demands of mass-production techniques rather than on customer wants and needs. Manufacturers were generally able to sell all they produced and could comfortably limit their marketing efforts to taking orders and shipping goods. For example, Henry Ford focused on ways to produce automobiles more quickly and inexpensively rather than on customer preferences; consequently all the automobiles he pro-

duced were black. Compare SALES-ORIENTED MARKETING, the MARKETING CONCEPT, and COMPETITIVE MARKETING.

production show   The most elaborate and expensive type of FASHION SHOW, replete with theatrical and dramatic elements (e.g., theatrical backdrops and scenery, lighting effects, live or specially produced music, and dancing or specialized choreography). High-end, fashion-forward merchandise, including couture, evening wear, bridal, or ready-to-wear collections are usually the highlights of production shows. Also known as a *spectacular.*

product item   A particular product having enough distinctive attributes to be easily distinguished from other products in a line. For stock keeping purposes, product items are frequently assigned unique identifying numbers. Also called a *product variant.* See also ATTRIBUTE-BASED SHOPPING PRODUCT, PRODUCT ATTRIBUTE, and STOCK KEEPING UNIT (SKU).

productivity   The output of a business or other organization per man-hour expended. Productivity is determined by dividing the workload, or work completed, by the number of hours required to perform the work. In short, productivity is a measure of the number of units of output per unit of input. See also PRODUCTIVITY MEASURES.

productivity-based budget   A budget similar to a fixed-base budget. The difference is that several budgets are prepared, each at a different sales level, to allow for those expenses that vary with sales volume. This flexibility is particularly valuable when sales fluctuations are seasonal. See also FIXED BASE BUDGETING.

productivity measures   PRODUCTIVITY is a measure of the number of units of output per unit of input. Productivity is a measure of performance in that high productivity indicates that output has been maximized with a minimum investment of input. Low productivity can be corrected by increasing output, decreasing input, or both. Measures of productivity are common in the manufacturing sector, where input and output are often quantitatively defined. The concept of productivity is not as easily applied within service industries because of the difficulty in quantitatively defining output and input. Though sales are numerically measured, other outputs (e.g., customer satisfaction) are intangible and difficult to quantify. Nevertheless, retailers apply productivity measures whenever a relationship between input and output can be defined numerically. For example, in retailing, productivity is measured in terms of STOCK TURNOVER (ST), STOCK-TO-SALES RATIO (SSR), and SALES PER SQUARE FOOT. See also PERFORMANCE MEASURE.

product launch   A SPECIAL EVENT designed to set in motion the promotion and sale of a new product or line of products, typically as the climax to many months of preparation and planning. Its goal is to make sure every marketing element (i.e., advertising, press releases, and direct mail pieces) has a cohesive, sustained message that enhances the BRAND EQUITY of the product. Many product launches are conducted at retail stores, but the events are planned in cooperation with the producers, manufacturers, or designers of the product. See also LAUNCH.

product layers A concept that treats each product as a series of multiple layers, each of which adds value and the opportunity for marketers to reach potential buyers. The layers are: the core product (i.e., functional elements, design, benefits offered, needs satisfied, and patent protection); packaging (i.e., brand name, style, quality, product attributes, package, packing, trademark, trade dress, price, and image); support (i.e., delivery, credit, warranty, guarantee, installation, post-sale service, repairs, spare parts, and training); and product potential (i.e., proposed product extensions, modifications, improvements, repositioning, and rebranding). See also the comparable BUNDLE OF BENEFITS CONCEPT.

product liability The legal responsibility of a manufacturer or seller of a product to pay damages to parties injured through the use of the product when it has proven to be defective or unsafely designed. See also STRICT (PRODUCT) LIABILITY.

product licensing See LICENSING.

product life Synonym for SHELF LIFE. See also PRODUCT LIFE CYCLE (PLC).

product life cycle (PLC) A series of stages through which a product or service passes as it evolves in the marketplace. Four stages are readily identifiable: introduction of the product (INTRODUCTORY STAGE); growth of demand (GROWTH STAGE); market maturity (MATURITY STAGE); and the ultimate SATURATION of the market by the product (or its failure to capture a market) and its eventual decline. Also called the *customer acceptance trend,* the *merchandise acceptance curve,* the *merchandise life cycle,* the *merchandising life cycle,* and the *life span of merchandise.* See also ADOPTION PROCESS.

product line 1. In retailing, a group of products closely related by some factor such as physical characteristics, price, end use, etc. Various lines make up what is known as variety, a component of the merchandise assortment. 2. In manufacturing, a group of closely related items produced by the same manufacturer. For example, Nokia cell phones constitute a product line.

product line consistency See LINE CONSISTENCY.

product line departmentalization The organization of a retail store, and the division of jobs in it, around the various types of merchandise and services sold. Also called *departmentalization by product* and *product departmentalization.*

product line extension Synonym for LINE EXTENSION.

product line marketing A strategy in which two or more products are marketed by a firm under a common (and frequently respected) BRAND NAME. Product line marketing enables a company to expand its product lines and develop coordinated advertising campaigns. See also BRAND MARKETING.

product line pricing See FULL LINE PRICING.

product line pruning Synonym for PRODUCT DELETION.

product line strategy A company's overall decision making policy about the number of different goods and services to offer. A FULL LINE STRATEGY involves selling a wide number and variety of products, while a LIMITED LINE STRATEGY focuses on selling a few selected items.

product management Those business activities concerned with the development of new products or brands, their introduction into the marketplace, and their passage through the PRODUCT LIFE CYCLE (PLC). See also PRODUCT MANAGER and PRODUCT MANAGER SYSTEM.

product manager An executive responsible for the planning and development of a particular product or product line. The product manager oversees the development of a competitive strategy, coordinates all aspects of planning, and directs advertising and promotional efforts on behalf of the product. In essence, the product manager is the MARKETING MANAGER for the product. The product manager reports to a GENERAL PRODUCT MANAGER, particularly in larger firms. Sometimes called a *products manager, project manager,* or *program manager.* See also PRODUCT MANAGEMENT and PRODUCT MANAGER SYSTEM.

product manager system A middle management system employed by firms marketing a relatively large number of distinct products. Each product has a manager who is fully involved in the development and marketing of the product from its conception through its commercialization. Such a system is meant to ensure that each product in the marketing mix receives adequate attention. In a BRAND MANAGER SYSTEM, managers are assigned to individual brands rather than products. See also PRODUCT MANAGEMENT and PRODUCT MANAGER.

product market A market in which vendors offer similar products that may be considered substitutes for each other because they are either physically or conceptually similar and hence comparable in satisfying a consumer need. For example, all luxury automobiles would be considered part of the same product market, since they may substitute for each other in satisfying customers' needs for transportation, luxury, and status. Compare GENERIC MARKET.

product-market diversification See DIVERSIFICATION.

product-market erosion Loss of MARKET SHARE for a product or service due to a decrease in DEMAND. Market erosion frequently occurs as new competitive products enter the marketplace.

product-market opportunity matrix A method employed in developing marketing plans in which four alternative strategies for increasing business are set forth: MARKET DEVELOPMENT (increasing sales by expanding into new markets); PRODUCT DEVELOPMENT (creating new products for existing markets); MARKET PENETRATION (increasing sales of current products in existing markets); and DIVERSIFICATION (creating new products for new markets). Also called the *strategic opportunity matrix.*

product mix In marketing, the aggregate of products offered for sale by a firm. The product mix may be measured in breadth (i.e., the number of product lines carried) or in depth (i.e., the assortment of sizes, types, colors, and styles within each product line). The consistency of a company's product mix depends on how the various lines relate to one another in terms of distribution requirements, ultimate end use, etc. The term ASSORTMENT is often used in retailing to denote essentially the same concept.

product mix depth   See ASSORTMENT DEPTH and PRODUCT DEPTH.

product mix diversification   A product marketing strategy in which unrelated product lines are sold to entirely different markets by a single marketer. The strategy is designed to increase profitability and to expand into new markets with new products. See also PRODUCT MIX and DIVERSIFICATION.

product mix width   See PRODUCT WIDTH and ASSORTMENT BREADTH.

product modification   Synonym for PRODUCT IMPROVEMENT.

product motive   See PRODUCT BUYING MOTIVE.

product objective   Any goal set for the characteristics of a product, usually as part of NEW PRODUCT DEVELOPMENT. The product objective, which is based on meeting the needs of customers, may be set forth in a document that specifies the kind of product a company wishes to produce and market, which customer need the company hopes to satisfy, and to whom the company intends to sell the product.

product obsolescence   See PLANNED PRODUCT OBSOLESCENCE.

product-or-exhibit approach   See EXHIBIT APPROACH.

product orientation   1. In the MARKETING CONCEPT, the emphasis placed by some marketers on the product or on the manufacturing process when making marketing decisions and setting objectives. This is in contrast to the CONSUMER ORIENTATION. Compare SALES ORIENTATION and PRODUCTION CONCEPT. 2. In advertising, a focus on promoting goods (i.e., products) rather than on promoting the company. See also PRODUCT ADVERTISING.

product-oriented advertising   Retail advertising that emphasizes the sale of a particular product or product line rather than the store as a whole.

product placement   The use of a branded product instead of an unbranded, generic product as a prop in a movie or television show. Product placement has become a popular means of increasing product or brand publicity. It may be either planned or unexpected. Public relations personnel representing clothing lines, for example, contact set designers and wardrobers to put their clothes on movie and television stars. Beverages, candy bars, and other branded products are often easily identifiable in the movie or television show. See also CRIBTIMONIAL.

product planning   The process leading to the development of new products, including the identification of goals, procedures,

and the nature of the merchandise. MARKETING RESEARCH (MR) figures prominently in the process. Also called *new product planning*. See also NEW PRODUCT PLANNING PROCESS.

product planning committee   A group of executives drawn from various areas of management whose primary responsibility is the evaluation of new product ideas. Although primarily concerned with idea generation and screening, a product planning committee may guide the product further down the line through the developmental stages of marketing. Once this stage has been reached, the committee may be disbanded or continue to meet on a part-time basis. Also called a *new product committee*. See also PRODUCT LIFE CYCLE (PLC) and VENTURE TEAM.

product policy   A general guideline for making product decisions, established by the marketer. The product policy spells out the ways in which the company plans to meet its product objectives.

product portfolio concept   A STRATEGIC MARKETING tool in which a firm views the products it produces as part of a larger product mix and then treats the various product mixes (or divisions within the company) as though they were parts of a stock portfolio. These units are evaluated in terms of profitability and either given support or sold off in the same way that stocks with a poor RETURN ON INVESTMENT (ROI) are sold off. The portfolio approach to MARKETING MANAGEMENT is somewhat limited in that it takes a short-run view of product performance.

product positioning   Synonym for MARKET POSITIONING.

product potential   Those aspects of a product that relate to its future development and capacity for growth in the marketplace. These include proposed product extensions, modifications, improvements, repositioning, and rebranding. See also CORE PRODUCT, PACKAGING, and SUPPORT; all three, along with product potential, are components in the creation of a complete product. See also PRODUCT IMPROVEMENT.

product pretest   See PRETESTING.

product protection   In television advertising, the interval between an advertiser's commercial and the commercial of a competitor. Up to 15 minutes of separation between the two commercials is usually guaranteed by the station.

product pruning   Synonym for PRODUCT DELETION.

product publicity   See PUBLICITY.

product quality   See QUALITY.

product quality response function   The RESPONSE FUNCTION that shows how a product's quality and the features it contains will influence sales. Since, however, additional quality and features will also increase production costs, the profit response function may reach a high point and then decline. The best level for product quality, therefore, will be the high point achieved prior to the decline. Also called a *quality response function.*

product recall   The act of calling for the return of all exemplars of a product found to be defective in some way. The product may be returned to the retailer or the manufacturer for repair or replacement. In the United States, product recalls are listed on the Web sites of the FOOD AND DRUG ADMINISTRATION (FDA) at www.fda.gov and the CONSUMER PRODUCTS SAFETY COMMISSION (CPSC) at www.cpsc.gov. Also called, simply, *recall.*

product reliability   The probability that a product will perform satisfactorily under normal conditions for a specified period of time without failure. See also GUARANTEE, WARRANTY, and RELIABILITY.

product repositioning   See REPOSITIONING.

product rotation   The practice of placing new merchandise beneath or behind older merchandise already on the shelf in order to ensure the sale of the older merchandise first. Also called *rotation of stock* and *rotation of products.*

product screening   A stage in the new product planning process during which product proposals deemed unsuitable are weeded out and dropped from further consideration. See also NEW PRODUCT DEVELOPMENT and PRODUCT PLANNING.

product segmentation   In industrial marketing, the subdivision of a market on the basis of product specifications that meet the requirements of the purchaser.

products manager   Synonym for PRODUCT MANAGER.

product-specific auction   An AUCTION (whether online or offline) that features one kind of product or one class of products. This distinguishes the product-specific auction from a GENERAL AUCTION, in which a wide variety of merchandise is auctioned off. See also ONLINE AUCTION.

product spotter   In VISUAL MERCHANDISING, any eye- or ear-catching device (e.g., a brightly colored spotlight) designed to draw the attention of potential customers to the product. Product spotters are most frequently used to call attention to a new item in the store. See also DISPLAY.

product testing   Synonym for TEST MARKETING.

product value   The sum of all aspects of a product that satisfy the customer's needs, minus any negative aspects of the product. See also VALUE and UTILITY.

product variable   Any aspect of a product that is subject to change (e.g., color, size, price, operating cost, reliability, availability, brand name, packaging). Product variables are MARKETING MIX variables in that they are internal and therefore controllable by the organization. They are unlike variables in the external MARKETING ENVIRONMENT, which are largely out of the control of the firm.

product variant   Synonym for PRODUCT ITEM.

product warranty   See WARRANTY.

product width   The number of product lines offered for sale, without reference to the quantity. Compare ASSORTMENT BREADTH.

professional advertising   1. Advertising by professionals (e.g., lawyers, physicians, dentists) directed at the general public in hopes of building up a client base.   2. Advertising directed to professionals (e.g., lawyers, physicians, dentists) by manufacturers or distributors of products whose success in the marketplace depends on their being accepted and approved by those professionals. The message is directed to the professionals in the hope that they will recommend or specify the particular product. For example, physicians are encouraged to prescribe particular drugs, engineers to specify particular building materials, etc.

professional discount   A reduction from the usual or list price given to customers in a particular field or profession. For example, a hardware store may give a professional discount to builders and contractors who are frequent customers. Professional discounts are used primarily to generate goodwill and ensure repeat business. See also CO-OP MONEY.

professional pricing   A pricing strategy employed by professionals (e.g., lawyers, doctors, architects) in which services are rendered for a flat, predetermined fee rather than calculated on an hourly basis. See also GENTLEMEN'S PRICING.

profile   See AUDIENCE PROFILE and CUSTOMER PROFILE.

profit   In a general sense, the abstract goal of a business or profession. In its marketing context, it is generally taken to mean total revenue less all costs and expenses. Profit is commonly qualified by another term such as gross or net, making the concept more precise. See also EARNINGS, GROSS PROFIT, MARGINAL PROFIT, NET PROFIT, PROJECTED NET PROFIT, PAPER PROFIT, and PLANNED PROFIT.

profitable   Of a product or enterprise, generating a pecuniary (i.e., financial) gain.

profitability   A company's ability to earn a profit (i.e., its ability to generate a PECUNIARY or financial gain), including potential for future profit.

profitability range   The difference between the most PROFITABLE and the least profitable lines of merchandise, calculated on the basis of GROSS PROFIT PER SQUARE FOOT OF SELLING SPACE.

profit and loss statement   Synonym for INCOME STATEMENT.

profit-based pricing objective   Any PRICING OBJECTIVE that orients a store's pricing strategy toward a profit goal. Such objectives include PROFIT MAXIMIZATION, satisfactory profit, RETURN ON INVESTMENT (ROI), and early recovery of cash.

profit booster An item of merchandise bearing an inflated retail price to offset losses from loss leaders. Sometimes called, simply, a *booster*.

profit center Any area of the retail store that contributes to the overall profit of the store (i.e., a selling area). In department stores, profit centers correspond to departments, while in smaller stores they may be based on product lines. Each profit center, or unit, must be sufficiently distinct from other units of the store so that its contribution to profits may be measured. Compare EXPENSE CENTER.

profit-centered service Any store service activity that is merchandised for profit. Profit-centered services may be the principal business of the organization (e.g., dry cleaning) or they may represent part of the business (e.g., a restaurant in a store).

Profit Impact of Marketing Strategies (PIMS) A database of market profiles and business results of major American and European companies that began in 1970. It was developed with the intention of indicating, through empirical evidence, which business strategies lead to success. The study, based on a survey conducted between 1970 and 1983, identified several strategic variables that typically correlate with profitability, the most important of which were market share, product quality, investment intensity, and service quality. PIMS sought to establish a typical profit rate for each type of business, predict future operating results based on current strategies, and determine which strategies are likely to improve future operating results. For each business surveyed, PIMS gathered information on the characteristics of the business environment, the competitive position of the business, the structure of the production process, the method used to allocate the budget, strategic movement, and operating results.

profit margin See GROSS MARGIN.

profit maximization The realization of the highest attainable profit in a business enterprise. Profit maximization is a primary goal when a firm sets a PRICING strategy. See also RETURN ON INVESTMENT (ROI) and MAXIMIZING PROFIT.

profit maximization objective A firm's stated desire to make as much profit as it can. Since this is considered somewhat socially undesirable and not in the public interest, it is more common among small firms operating away from public scrutiny. However, both business and consumers may be seen to benefit from this objective if the increase in profits is viewed as deriving from greater efficiency or better service. The profit maximization objective may be stated as a rapid RETURN ON INVESTMENT (ROI). Also called *charging what the traffic will bear* or *all the traffic will bear*.

profit mix The factors that contribute to a retailer's profit, all of which may be adjusted and altered for a desired profit result. These component factors include price, volume, sales, cost of goods sold, operating expenses, etc.

profit motive The moneymaking impetus driving business enterprises to make the effort required to produce and or sell products or services.

profit-oriented audit An evaluation of a marketing plan in terms of the expenses and revenues generated by that plan. See also MARKETING AUDIT.

profit per square foot of selling space See GROSS PROFIT PER SQUARE FOOT OF SELLING SPACE.

profit response function See RESPONSE FUNCTION.

profit sharing A system of compensation in which employees receive a portion of the profits of the store or other business. This compensation is generally in addition to, and not in lieu of, salary or commission.

profit target analysis A method used to calculate the volume of sales needed to pay for all costs (both fixed and variable) of operation and return a predetermined profit. Similar to a BREAK-EVEN ANALYSIS except that fixed costs include a predetermined desired level of profit. That level of profit represents a TARGET RETURN ON INVESTMENT, often required by the firm's management.

pro forma invoice A preliminary estimated invoice of goods sold. Forwarded by the seller prior to shipment of the goods and advising the buyer of the weight and value of the merchandise. Compare PRO FORMA STATEMENT.

pro forma statement In accounting, a hypothetical financial statement prepared as it would appear if some event (such as an increase in sales) were to occur. Compare PRO FORMA INVOICE.

program evaluation and review technique (PERT) An analytical process in which large projects are broken down into component parts and probability is used to estimate the time needed to complete each part. The technique is similar to CRITICAL PATH METHOD (CPM).

program manager Synonym for PRODUCT MANAGER.

programmed merchandiser A RESOURCE that offers many services to the retailer in addition to a product line. These services are performed in exchange for the retailer's commitment to buy merchandise. PROMOTIONAL ASSISTANCE is one of the services provided by most programmed merchandisers.

programmed merchandising The systematic planning of advance sales and promotional activities to produce predetermined profits. A limited number of carefully selected key resources are involved, with the retailer usually purchasing entire lines of merchandise from these resources for an extended period (generally one year). See also PROGRAMMED MERCHANDISER.

program ratings In the measurement of media audiences, an estimate of audience size (i.e., of the total number of homes reached) expressed as a percentage of the total population. Also called, simply, *ratings*. Ratings are established by an independent research service. A rating of 20, for example, equals 20% of people in the market. The program rating is calculated by dividing the number of households (HH) tuned to a particular show by the total number of households in the area under study. For example, if 10 million U.S. households watch a particular show, and the total number of U.S. households is considered to be 94 million, the national program rating would be 10.6. See also HOUSEHOLD (HH).

prohibited article In shipping, any class of merchandise that will not be handled by the shipper.

projectable A term used to describe MARKETING RESEARCH (MR) (or other research) whose results can be generalized or projected to the POPULATION under study. Such results must be valid, reliable, and based on an appropriate SAMPLE in order to be projectable. See also VALIDITY and RELIABILITY.

project design See RESEARCH DESIGN.

projected net profit The anticipated excess of all the revenues of the business over all costs and expenses incurred to obtain that revenue during the accounting period as reflected in a firm's BUDGET. See also NET PROFIT.

projecting Synonym for FORECASTING.

projection Synonym for FORECAST.

projective technique A methodology used in MARKETING RESEARCH (MR) in which respondents are asked to perform a particular task (e.g., a sentence completion test or word association test) in the belief that they will, in the course of completing the task, reveal certain attitudes that motivate their behavior. See also MOTIVE.

project management A form of organization in which employees from various functional areas are brought together temporarily to work together on a project or accomplish a particular goal. The *project management team* disbands when its task has been accomplished.

project management team See PROJECT MANAGEMENT.

project manager 1. In marketing, a synonym for PRODUCT MANAGER. 2. The individual who heads a PROJECT MANAGEMENT team consisting of employees from various functional areas who are brought together temporarily to work on a project or accomplish a particular goal.

project team See PROJECT MANAGEMENT.

promissory note An unconditional written commitment by a borrower to pay the creditor a fixed sum of money on a specified date in return for immediate credit. There is generally an interest rate charged, indicated on the note itself. See also TRADE CREDIT.

promo (Slang) Short for *promotional message*. See MESSAGE.

promote 1. To help or encourage something to exist or flourish. 2. In retailing, to encourage the sales, acceptance, or

recognition of a product, service, or the store itself. 3. In employee management, to advance an employee in rank, dignity, or position. See also PROMOTION.

promotion 1. The ongoing process of informing the target market of the product. Promotion is one of the FOUR PS OF THE MARKETING MIX. See also INTERNAL PROMOTION, EXTERNAL PROMOTION, and SALES PROMOTION. 2. A single, specific event, activity, or campaign designed to introduce a product or increase customer traffic and sales. See PROMOTIONS AND SALES. 3. In employee management, an advancement of an employee in rank or position within the organization. See also PROMOTE.

promotion-advertising response function The RESPONSE FUNCTION showing the increase in sales that would follow from advertising. Although, through personal selling and other promotional efforts, some sales would occur with absolutely no advertising, sales will increase with additional advertising up to a certain point as demonstrated on the curve. Where sales begin to level off, and perhaps even decline, additional advertising becomes undesirable. Also called *promotional-advertising response function*, *advertising response function*, and *promotional response function*.

promotional advertising ADVERTISING created by a retailer with the intent of generating sales of a specific item or group of items and bringing customers into the store immediately. Promotional advertising is used to announce special sales and the arrival of new or seasonal merchandise as well as to create a market for the regular stock. As such, it may be considered DIRECT ADVERTISING. Regular price advertising, sale price advertising, and clearance sale advertising are all forms of promotional advertising. See also PROMOTIONS AND SALES.

promotional-advertising response function See PROMOTION-ADVERTISING RESPONSE FUNCTION.

promotional allowance A price reduction granted to a buyer (i.e., the retailer or other reseller) by a seller (i.e., the manufacturer, wholesaler, or vendor) of a product or service in compensation for the buyer's special promotional efforts on the part of the product or service. Promotional allowances are usually calculated as a percentage of the final invoice price. Sometimes called a *merchandise allowance* and/or a *promotion allowance*. See also COOPERATIVE ADVERTISING.

promotional assistance Help with promoting a product or service, provided to a retailer by a PROGRAMMED MERCHANDISER.

promotional budgeting The process used by retailers and other marketers to determine how much is to be spent on advertising and other sales promotion efforts. The budgeting process is based on the plans that define the organization's mission, goals, and objectives, and has many variations. For accounting purposes, the amount of money spent on advertising and sales promotion is most often (but not always) considered a current expense. The result of the promotional budgeting process is a *promotional budget*. See also DIMINISHING RETURNS MODEL, S-SHAPED CURVE MODEL, and MEDIA BUYER.

promotional buying The selection and purchase, by the store's buyer, of merchandise particularly geared to the store's upcoming special events and sales promotion activities. Such purchases may fall outside the store's usual product mix.

promotional calendar See SALES PROMOTION CALENDAR.

promotional communication See SALES PROMOTION.

promotional department store A discount store which, due to its size and merchandise mix (both hard and soft lines), approximates a DEPARTMENT STORE. Promotional department stores operate at lower gross margins than traditional department stores because of their relatively low-rent locations, lack of amenities, and minimal service. They are, however, often as profitable as other types of stores in their price class. Also called a *full line discount store*. See also FULL LINE DISCOUNTER.

promotional discount A price reduction contributed by the VENDOR to the retailer in exchange for the promotion of the vendor's goods. See also CO-OP MONEY and CO-OP PROMOTION.

promotional display A visual display that advances or emphasizes a particular concept, trend, or item in order to promote and sell merchandise. For example, a Mother's Day promotional display will tie in with and advance the store's advertising campaign and feature Mother's Day gift ideas.

promotional elasticity of demand The percent change in customer demand for a product or service that results from a percent change in promotional activity when all other factors are constant. See also ELASTICITY OF DEMAND.

promotional fit In product marketing, the degree of compatibility between a new product and the firm's established promotional and advertising programs. Also called, simply, *fit*.

promotional item See PROMOTIONAL MERCHANDISE.

promotional kit A vendor's package of materials presented to the retailer for use in promoting the vendor's goods. A promotional kit may include plans, ideas, and suggestions for displaying and selling the merchandise as well as actual displays, advertising copy, and consumer information literature (e.g., a BROCHURE or FLYER). Also called a *kit*, *package*, or *promotional package*. See also PROMOTIONAL TOOLS and DEALER DISPLAY.

promotional markdown A reduction in retail price for the purpose of stimulating store TRAFFIC. Unlike clearance markdowns, promotional markdowns are regarded as part of the store's strategy calculated to increase sales. Compare CLEARANCE MARKDOWN.

promotional merchandise Goods offered for sale to the consumer at an unusually low price so as to generate volume sales and store traffic. Such an item is generally a SPECIAL PURCHASE from a vendor and may be advertised as such. Also called *promotional stock* or *promotional item*.

promotional merchandise policy A policy adopted by a VENDOR (i.e., a *resource*) in which regular customers (i.e., resellers) are afforded the opportunity to buy the vendor's leftover goods that have not sold well (i.e., DISTRESS MERCHANDISE). These closeouts are made available to the retailer before the goods are disposed of elsewhere. Often, this MARKDOWN (MD) occurs in the midst of the retail selling season and gives the retailer an opportunity to bolster the store's inventory at lower costs. When the retailer then runs a sale, it is more profitable because of this price advantage. See also CLOSEOUT.

promotional message See MESSAGE and ADVERTISING MESSAGE. Often shortened to *promo*.

promotional mix The selected combination of advertising, publicity, sales promotion, customer service, and personal selling used to communicate with, inform, and sell goods to the consumer. The elements may be varied to arrive at the most effective and cost-effective program. A typical large-scale promotion campaign includes many forms of promotion implemented concurrently or sequentially. In Internet marketing, online and offline forms are often designed to work in a complementary and synergistic promotional effort. Also called *promotion blend*, *promotion mix*, *promotion communications mix*, or *marketing communications mix*. See also PROMOTIONS AND SALES, PROMOTION PLANNING, PROMOTION VARIABLE, and PROMOTION SYNERGY.

promotional mix calendar See SALES PROMOTION CALENDAR.

promotional money Synonym for CO-OP MONEY.

promotional objectives Synonym for ADVERTISING OBJECTIVES.

promotional package Synonym for PROMOTIONAL KIT.

promotional planning See PROMOTION PLANNING.

promotional price A reduced PRICE, offered on a temporary basis, to promote particular merchandise or to increase store TRAFFIC. See also PROMOTIONAL PRICING and PROMOTIONS AND SALES.

promotional pricing The practice of setting prices below that which is usual or customary in order to increase sales for a particular product or increase store TRAFFIC. See also SPECIAL EVENT PRICING and PROMOTIONAL PRICE.

promotional program See SALES PROMOTION.

promotional quadrangle See FOUR Ps OF THE MARKETING MIX.

promotional response function See PROMOTION-ADVERTISING RESPONSE FUNCTION.

promotional stock Synonym for PROMOTIONAL MERCHANDISE.

promotional strategy The specific plan used to achieve a marketing objective through promotions. This includes a statement of objectives, budgeting for the promotion, planning the promotional mix, and reviewing and evaluating the outcome. Also called *retail promotional strategy*. See also MARKETING OBJECTIVES.

promotional tools   Signs, posters, sound and video systems, electronic kiosks, and displays used in internal promotion to communicate ideas to customers inside the store (i.e., INTERNAL PROMOTION). Promotional tools also include the use of the broadcast, print, and electronic media to communicate ideas to potential customers to get them into the store (i.e., *external promotion*). See also PROMOTIONAL KIT, INTERNAL PROMOTION, and DISPLAY. Compare EXTERNAL PROMOTION.

promotional variable   Synonym for PROMOTION VARIABLE.

promotion blend   Synonym for PROMOTIONAL MIX.

promotion budget   The money allocated by a firm for advertising and sales promotion. Retailers and other marketers use a variety of methods to determine how much to spend for these activities. See also PROMOTIONAL BUDGETING.

promotion calendar   See SALES PROMOTION CALENDAR.

promotion communications mix   Synonym for PROMOTIONAL MIX.

promotion division   1. The division of a retail store responsible for promoting products and services. This division generally comprises four departments: advertising, fashion, public relations, and visual merchandising. The ADVERTISING DEPARTMENT is responsible for planning and creating ads, placing them in the media, and evaluating their effectiveness. The FASHION DEPARTMENT is involved in developing the fashion image of the company by interpreting general trends to meet the needs of the store's target customer. Salespeople are informed of the trends and trained to sell them by members of the fashion department. Fashion shows and special events are also designed by the fashion department staff. The PUBLIC RELATIONS DEPARTMENT is responsible for developing broad-range policies and programs to create a favorable public opinion of the firm. The VISUAL MERCHANDISING DEPARTMENT is involved in creating window and interior displays, developing signs and visual identity, and selecting merchandise fixtures and showcases. This department is frequently also responsible for store planning, layout, and design. The promotion division is headed by the VICE PRESIDENT (VP) OF SALES PROMOTION.   2. In a manufacturing or fashion design firm, the division that plans and implements a range of services such as direct marketing materials, merchandise catalogs, advertisements, fashion show production, and special events. Many manufacturing firms, however, hire outside agencies to handle promotional activities. See also PUBLICITY DEPARTMENT.

promotion from within   The practice of filling vacant positions by selecting employees from within the company to be advanced into these positions rather than hiring new people from the outside. See also PROMOTE (def. 3) and PROMOTION (def. 2).

promotion mix   Synonym for PROMOTIONAL MIX.

promotion-mix calendar   See SALES PROMOTION CALENDAR.

promotion objectives   Synonym for ADVERTISING OBJECTIVES.

promotion planning   Those activities that lead to the development of a firm's comprehensive promotional plan, including the formulation of objectives, budgeting, and the development of an appropriate PROMOTIONAL MIX.

promotion point of contact   Any of the many and varied encounters through which an audience gains knowledge and forms a perception of a brand, product, service, or business. In addition to the traditional elements of the PROMOTIONAL MIX, promotion points of contact include such nontraditional elements as distinctive package design, the visual appearance of a Web storefront, product guarantees, and product delivery conditions. Promotion points of contact are important instruments for communicating marketing messages, particularly raising awareness, building brands, and driving traffic.

promotion price zone   See PROMOTION ZONE.

promotion program   See SALES PROMOTION.

promotion response function   See PROMOTION-ADVERTISING RESPONSE FUNCTION.

promotions and sales   Those activities of a retail organization designed to increase customer TRAFFIC and sales by communicating information to customers regarding assortments, prices, services, and other sales incentives. PROMOTION, also called sales promotion, includes ADVERTISING, VISUAL MERCHANDISING (display), PUBLIC RELATIONS (PR) (free publicity), special events, and the selling efforts of the store's salespeople. One of the FOUR PS OF THE MARKETING MIX, promotion is essentially the act of informing the TARGET MARKET of the product or service or of the store itself. A SALE is a promotional event designed to increase traffic and move categories of merchandise by offering them at a lower than regular price. In large department stores this is generally handled by a separate division. See also SALES PROMOTION.

promotion segment   See PROMOTION TARGET.

promotion synergy   The result of all elements of the PROMOTIONAL MIX coming together to form a unified whole that is greater than the sum of its parts. In promotion synergy, the various forms of promotion work together in an integrated, coordinated way, communicating the same relevant, consistent, coherent message to the customer. *Synergistic promotion* requires that all promotions deliver the same consistent, integrated message, design, and feel. The impact on the customer is far greater than when promotions deliver uncoordinated, conflicting messages and images. See also SYNERGISM.

promotion target   The audience selected to receive advertising and marketing messages because of their anticipated receptivity to the market offers. The selection of promotion targets helps keep sponsors from wasting their money sending messages to uninterested or inappropriate targets. Also called a *promotion segment*. See also TARGET MARKET.

promotion tools See PROMOTIONAL TOOLS and PROMOTOOLS.

promotion variable Any element in the PROMOTIONAL MIX that may be manipulated or changed to affect the firm's promotional activities. Promotion variables include publicity, advertising, sales promotion, and personal selling. Also called a *promotional variable*.

promotion vice president See VICE PRESIDENT (VP) OF SALES PROMOTION.

promotion zone The range of prices covering low-end merchandise sold at low prices. Promotion zone merchandise is aimed at the customer with limited resources or who is otherwise budget-conscious. Also called the *promotion price zone*. See also PRICE ZONE.

promotools A variety of media used in the promotional mix (e.g., demonstrations, contests, free giveaways, catalogs). See also PROMOTIONAL TOOLS.

proof-of-purchase Evidence that an item or service has been bought by the customer. A CONTINUITY program is one that requests users to retain a collection of proofs-of-purchase over time in order to receive a premium. A proof-of-purchase often takes the form of a portion of the product's packaging, such as a box top or a UPC symbol. See also CONTINUITY PREMIUM, MAIL-IN PREMIUM, and REDEMPTION.

prop 1. In VISUAL MERCHANDISING, any functional structure on which merchandise may be leaned or placed. A *functional prop* is used as a physical support (e.g., a mannequin and/or furniture used to hold merchandise). 2. A decorative element used symbolically in a DISPLAY to create a mood. A *decorative prop* may be a basket, a plant, a flag, a banner, a musical instrument, etc. Furniture, for example, can be used to create the illusion of a room.

proportion In VISUAL MERCHANDISING, the relationship between elements, and between each element and the entire DISPLAY composition, in terms of size, scale, or OPTICAL WEIGHT. For example, a pair of baby shoes placed alongside a giant teddy bear will make the shoes seem even more delicate.

proprietary drug See OVER-THE-COUNTER (OTC) DRUG.

proprietary store A retail store selling essentially the same merchandise as a DRUG STORE, with the exception of prescription drugs.

proprietor A person who owns and operates a business establishment.

proprietorship An unincorporated business. See also SOLE PROPRIETORSHIP.

proprietorship equation See BALANCE SHEET.

proscenia Plural form of PROSCENIUM.

proscenium In a DISPLAY WINDOW, an arch consisting of a top valance (which masks the lighting across the top of the window) and side valances (which separate one window or display grouping from the next and also hide any side-lighting devices). It is analogous to the structural arch, called by the same name, surrounding the curtains in some theaters. The plural form is *proscenia*.

pro shop An outlet for the retail sale of sporting goods, accessories, and sports apparel, usually located at an athletic facility such as a golf course, skating rink, or country club. Some similar establishments, located away from athletic facilities, also call themselves pro shops.

prospect In sales, a potential customer, whether a person or organization. Also called a *sales prospect*. Compare LEAD and QUALIFIED PROSPECT.

prospecting Activities centering on seeking out new customers by looking up and checking out sales leads or stimulating regular customers to buy more products. Prospecting involves a certain amount of selectivity on the part of the salesperson to decide which individuals or organizations to pursue. Prospecting may take one of two forms: CHAIN PROSPECTING (also known as the *endless chain method*) and the CENTERS OF INFLUENCE METHOD. Compare QUALIFYING.

prospect list A list of potential customers for a product or service. Prospects are targeted for promotions in the expectation that they can be reached and will become customers. See also HIT LIST.

prosperity See BUSINESS CYCLE.

prosperity denial Among consumers, unfounded resistance to spending money on minor indulgences even though one's personal wealth and prosperity allow for it. Deep, almost generational convictions remain about exuberant versus responsible behavior. Prosperity denial is found in the avoidance of such small indulgences as drinking gourmet coffee, taking a taxi, purchasing premium seats for a concert, etc. Marketers of such small luxuries are encouraged to work on changing the attitude of those characterized by prosperity denial, making them understand that it is not wrong to treat oneself, at least occasionally. The phenomenon was identified and the term coined by trendwatching.com at www.trendwatching.com.

protection department Synonym for SECURITY.

protection in transit In shipping, the function performed by a product's PACKAGE (i.e., preventing damage to the product). See also PACKAGING.

protectionism Government policy and legislation designed to shield domestic industries from loss due to competition with imported goods by placing restrictions on the foreign producers of such goods. Protectionism takes the form of trade barriers and restrictions, tariffs, quotas, and orderly marketing arrangements (i.e., voluntary export restrictions). See also PROTECTIVE TARIFF and TRADE RESTRICTIONS.

protective tariff   A TARIFF designed to insulate domestic manufacturers or producers from the effects of foreign competition by forcing foreign competitors to raise the price of the imported goods to a competitive level. See also PROTECTIONISM and TRADE RESTRICTIONS.

protocol   In online communications, an agreed-upon format for transmitting data between two devices, specifying how computers talk to each other on a network. The protocol determines the type of error checking to be used, the data compression method (if any), how the sending device will signal that it has finished sending a message, and how the receiving device will indicate that it has received a message. The protocol can be implemented in either hardware or software.

prototype   The original or model on which something is patterned. In manufacturing, it may be the first or experimental working model of the thing to be manufactured, usually on a large scale. The prototype is prepared and tested before large-scale production begins.

provisional   promotion   Synonym   for   PROBATIONARY PROMOTION.

prox dating   See PROXIMO DATING.

proximal area method   The use of geographical information systems (GIS) in RETAIL SITE LOCATION to forecast sales potential for possible new stores. The method works on the assumption that consumers will select the retail store nearest to them. Market analysts forecast sales by analyzing the characteristics of the population residing within the TRADING AREA. The method provides a broad view of the spatial pattern of store locations and trade areas in the region by constructing a *Thiessen polygon* of the trading area.

proximo dating   In the DATING OF INVOICES, an agreement indicating that the cash discount period and the NET PAYMENT PERIOD begin at a specified day in the month following delivery. Similar to END OF MONTH (EOM) DATING except that a date is specified. For example, 3%, 10th proximo, net 60 days, means that the 3% discount may be taken if the bill is paid prior to the 10th day of the month following delivery. A credit period of 60 days from the first of the month following delivery is allowed to those who have not availed themselves of the discount. The full amount must be paid within 60 days of the first of the month following delivery. Also called *prox dating* or *proximo terms*.

proximo terms   See PROXIMO DATING.

proxy   A document authorizing another person to vote on behalf of a SHAREHOLDER in a CORPORATION.

pruning   Synonym for PRODUCT DELETION.

PSA   See PRIMARY SERVICE AREA (PSA) or PUBLIC SERVICE ADVERTISING (PSA).

pseudo sale   A type of TEST MARKETING in which customers indicate their reactions to a product and its marketing strategy, but do not actually spend money or make a purchase.

Ps of the marketing mix   See FOUR PS OF THE MARKETING MIX

psychic distance   The extent to which a foreign market is similar to or different from the home market. Marketers believe that their success in the home market is more easily transferable to markets similar to the one in which they already compete. Consequently, a company deciding to enter foreign markets will tend to enter first those that are psychically closest, or most similar, to its home market. For example, a U.S. firm will most likely select Canada, Australia, or the United Kingdom in which to begin its foreign expansion. The premise behind the selection of similar markets is the desire to minimize RISK in the face of uncertainty. See also MARKET SIMILARITY.

psychic income   Nonmonetary compensation such as job satisfaction, desirable location of employment, etc.

psychogenic need   Any need that stems from the socialization process. Psychogenic needs involve intangibles such as status, acquisitiveness, or the need for love and admiration. They affect the behavior of individuals and groups of individuals, including consumer behavior. Compare BIOGENIC NEED. See also PSYCHOLOGICAL (BUYING) MOTIVE and EGO-BOLSTERING DRIVE.

psychographic market segmentation   See PSYCHOGRAPHIC SEGMENTATION.

psychographics   A research framework in which consumer behavior is explained, at least in part, by the study of such variables as personality, lifestyle, attitudes, and self-concept. The goal of psychographic studies is to predict consumer responses to products, stores, advertising, etc. See also PSYCHOGRAPHIC SEGMENTATION.

psychographic segmentation   The division of a population of potential customers into subgroups based on such sociopsychological determinants as personality, lifestyle, attitudes, and self-concept. Also called *personality segmentation*. See also PSYCHOGRAPHICS.

psychographic segmentation variables   See PSYCHOGRAPHIC SEGMENTATION.

psychological (buying) motive   Any factor affecting a consumer's decision to buy merchandise or services that is rooted in social or psychological needs. Products such as expensive automobiles and jewelry are frequently purchased to satisfy psychological needs. Psychological buying motives essentially derive from the consumer's psychogenic needs. See also PSYCHOGENIC NEED and EGO-BOLSTERING DRIVE.

psychological discounting The use of deceptive prices in the promotion of products or services. The illusion created is that the current selling price is a substantial reduction from a previous price (i.e., the reference price), even though there was never any intention of charging the reference price. Also called *superficial discounting* or *was-is pricing.*

psychological moment The point in a SALES APPROACH or presentation at which the SALESPERSON feels ready to attempt the trial close.

psychological obsolescence See PLANNED STYLE OBSOLESCENCE.

psychological pricing See PERSUASIVE PRICING, ODD-LINE PRICING, and EVEN-LINE PRICING.

psychological product The physical product along with its warranties, services, and psychological overtones (e.g., benefits, satisfaction, emotional appeal, and needs fulfillment). See also PSYCHOLOGICAL SATISFACTION.

psychological risk The CONSUMER-PERCEIVED RISK that a product, if purchased, could somehow be damaging to the consumer's ego.

psychological satisfaction The sense of gratification experienced by the buyer of a product as a result of the product's emotional appeal rather than its operational efficiency. See also PSYCHOLOGICAL PRODUCT.

P2P computing See PEER-TO-PEER (P2P) COMPUTING

PTP See PREFERRED TRADING PARTNER (PTP).

public 1. With reference to a business organization, all persons external to the organization who in some way affect its operations. They may be consumers, middlemen, government agencies, stockholders, or any other segment of the population that affects marketing strategies. 2. Synonym for PUBLICLY HELD COMPANY.

public access Internet terminal See ELECTRONIC KIOSK.

public bonded warehouse See CUSTOMS BONDED WAREHOUSE.

public corporation See CORPORATION and PUBLICLY HELD COMPANY.

Public Health Smoking Act (1970) U.S. federal consumer legislation that banned cigarette advertising on radio and television and required a warning to be printed on all cigarette packaging and print advertisements.

publicist An individual whose job it is to help sell the client or the client's product through good publicity. Publicists may work for a public relations agency or as freelance consultants.

publicity Any free, nonpersonal communication to the public to stimulate interest in and demand for a product, service, individual, or business. This may take the form of a news story or editorial feature carefully planted in the print, electronic, or broadcast media and conveying commercially significant news about the company, person, or product being promoted. Publicity may be used to enhance a store's image. These activities are usually coordinated by the retailer's own PUBLIC RELATIONS DIRECTOR or by a specialist in publicity specially hired for the purpose. See also PROMOTION DIVISION, PUBLIC RELATIONS, MEDIA, and ADVERTISING.

publicity coordinator The individual responsible for all promotional activities surrounding a FASHION SHOW. This person may work in cooperation with the advertising or promotion department. Also called the *publicity and advertising coordinator.*

publicity department A department, generally part of the sales promotion division of a department store, responsible for developing material about the store for public information. This material, often in the form of a PRESS RELEASE, is designed to generate free coverage of store events in the news media. See also PUBLICITY MATERIAL. Also called a *public relations division* or a *public relations department.*

publicity director See PUBLIC RELATIONS DIRECTOR.

publicity material Items such as press releases used to generate free coverage of a store or other business in the MEDIA. Publicity material is planned and written with a specific medium (e.g., print, broadcast) and type of story (e.g., lifestyle news) in mind. Print materials are prepared specifically for a column, department, editorial, or magazine photo layout. Broadcast materials are designed for radio or television as commentary or a news show. See also PRESS RELEASE.

publicity outlet Any mass communication medium used by a firm or agency to communicate with the public about a product, service, idea, or event. The same outlets that are used for ADVERTISING are used for publicity, including print, broadcast, and online media. A publicist or publicity director for a firm sends publicity to the most appropriate outlet to assure the greatest opportunity for publication or broadcast.

publicity plan A company's overall plan for nonpaid, nonpersonal promotional activities. The publicity plan includes objectives, rationale, program evaluation, and the media used.

publicity release Synonym for PRESS RELEASE.

publicity writer The individual responsible for actually composing a PRESS RELEASE or other form of PUBLICITY MATERIAL.

public-key encryption A type of ENCRYPTION used on the Internet. Public-key encryption uses two keys, a public key known to everyone and a private or secret key known only to the recipient of the message. The sender uses the recipient's public key to encrypt the message. The recipient uses the private key to decrypt it. Only the public key can be used to encrypt messages and only the corresponding private key can be used to decrypt them. Also called *asymmetric encryption.*

Compare SYMMETRIC ENCRYPTION, which uses the same key to encrypt and decrypt the message.

publicly held company   A retailer or other business organization that has many owners (i.e., shareholders). A public company's stock is available to the general public and is traded on a public STOCK EXCHANGE such as the New York Stock Exchange (NYSE) or the American Stock Exchange (AMEX). Publicly held companies often evolve from privately held companies that go public with an initial public stock offering (IPO) on a public stock exchange. Also called, simply, a *public*. Compare PRIVATELY HELD COMPANY. See also CORPORATION.

publicly held retail organization   See PUBLICLY HELD COMPANY.

public market   A municipal or community-sponsored market dealing in the wholesale or retail sale of food and related products. Also known as a *municipal market* and a *community market*.

public phone   See PAY PHONE.

public policy environment   The part of the total MARKETING ENVIRONMENT that is directly influenced by the activities of the government. The public policy environment includes the laws regulating trade, the regulations of various administrative agencies, public policy decisions affecting marketing activities, etc.

public relations (PR)   The management function of creating or improving a company's public image through a planned program of activities. Public relations includes evaluating public attitudes, identifying the company's goals with the public interest, and executing a program of communications to enhance GOODWILL or the prestige of the company. Often aimed at the business community at large as well as at the public, these promotional activities often include the support of charitable foundations or social causes. See also PUBLICITY.

public relations advertising   See INSTITUTIONAL ADVERTISING.

public relations department   In a retail firm, the part of the PROMOTION DIVISION responsible for creating a favorable public opinion of the firm. It sends press releases to the media to report community involvement, charitable work, and other activities designed to generate a favorable public image. The head of the public relations department is generally called the PUBLIC RELATIONS DIRECTOR. See also PUBLICITY DEPARTMENT.

public relations director   The individual in a firm who oversees activities designed to create a favorable public opinion of the firm. In large corporations, the public relations director may report to the promotion director but also works very closely with the market research department to understand the public's perception of the firm. A corporate head office may create national publicity pieces while local branches may be responsible for locally publicized events. In smaller companies, a public relations or advertising individual may be responsible for all publicity, public relations, and advertising. Also called a *publicity director*.

public relations division   See PUBLICITY DEPARTMENT.

public relations firm   An outside firm that may be employed to manage public image, relationships with consumers, and any other services related to publicity for its client. The task of the public relations firm is to evaluate the relationship between the client and the relevant constituencies (e.g., stockholders, suppliers, employees, government, labor groups, and the general public). Once the public relations firm has evaluated the appropriate constituencies, it determines how the client's operation impacts the public, develops public relations strategies and approaches, puts these programs into action, and evaluates their effectiveness.

public service advertising (PSA)   ADVERTISING designed to serve the general public on a nonprofit basis. Such advertising is generally meant to inform the public or to encourage or discourage certain behavior (e.g., campaigns against drunk driving). Also called a *public service announcement (PSA)*. Distinguished from INSTITUTIONAL ADVERTISING.

public service announcement (PSA)   See PUBLIC SERVICE ADVERTISING.

public telephone   See PAY PHONE.

public warehouse   An independently owned storage facility serving a variety of users. The public warehouse operator does not own or take title to the goods stored. Users are charged on the basis of cost per unit, and storage arrangements are made on a month-to-month basis. Other services such as receiving, packing, and invoicing may be available at an additional cost. Compare PRIVATE WAREHOUSE and CONTRACT WAREHOUSE.

puff   (Slang) A free promotion of a good or service.

puffery   A slightly exaggerated advertising claim regarding the benefits of a product or service. The use of puffery is intended to put the product or service in the best possible light and make sales. The line between puffery and DECEPTIVE ADVERTISING is sometimes hazy, however, and the practice has come under close scrutiny by the FEDERAL TRADE COMMISSION (FTC). Also called *trade puffery*.

puffing   The practice of using PUFFERY in advertising.

pull   The power of an advertisement or direct mailing to bring customers into the store and produce sales.

pull date   In food retailing, the date on the package that indicates when a product should be removed from the shelves due to loss of freshness. See also OPEN-CODE DATING/LABELING.

pull distribution strategy   Direct appeals to the ultimate consumers, encouraging them to ask their dealers to stock an item. This level of CONSUMER DEMAND is expected to "pull" the merchandise through the channel of distribution from the producer to the ultimate consumer, since retailers are inclined to carry products that they know consumers will ask for upon seeing them advertised. Synonymous with FORCED DISTRIBUTION. Also called *pull strategy, pull-through marketing,* and *pulling strategy.* Compare PUSH DISTRIBUTION STRATEGY.

pull-down menu See MENU. Sometimes spelled *pulldown menu.*

pulling power A store's ability to attract customers, especially when the location is good. See also RETAIL SITE LOCATION.

pulling strategy Synonym for PULL DISTRIBUTION STRATEGY.

pull method of secondary research See SECONDARY METHODS.

pull strategy Synonym for PULL DISTRIBUTION STRATEGY. See also FORCED DISTRIBUTION.

pull-through marketing Synonym for PULL DISTRIBUTION STRATEGY. See also FORCED DISTRIBUTION.

pulse publication Any extremely up-to-date or even real-time report on the WORLD WIDE WEB (WWW), including dedicated Web sites, blogs, foneblogs, etc. Such instant publications provide retailers and other marketers with information on the latest trends around the world and allow them to keep abreast (i.e., take the "pulse") of global trends. The trend was identified and the term coined by trendwatching.com at www.trendwatching.com.

pulsing In the SCHEDULING of advertising, a strategy designed to build customer awareness by increasing advertising at certain times of the year. For example, fragrance and cosmetic lines use a pulsing strategy, advertising throughout the year but increasing their advertising and promotional efforts during holidays such as Christmas, Valentine's Day, and Mother's Day and at the start of a fall or spring fashion season. Compare CONTINUITY and FLIGHTING, two other methods of scheduling advertising.

pupil dilation response (PDR) In ADVERTISING RESEARCH, a method of measuring a participant's PHYSIOLOGICAL PROFILE. PDR measures minute differences in pupil size and is used as a gauge of the amount of information processed in response to a stimulus. Researchers assume that if the participant's pupil dilates on seeing the ad, interest is strong.

purchase 1. v. To buy an item or service, that is, to acquire it by the payment of money or its equivalent. 2. n. Something that is bought. See also PURCHASE PRICE.

purchase act The act of buying a product or service. In the consumer ADOPTION PROCESS, the purchase act follows the evaluation and trial stages of the purchase process.

purchase agent Synonym for PURCHASING AGENT.

purchase allowance A price reduction from the vendor to the retailer when the merchandise ordered does not meet the expectations as identified in the invoice.

purchase behavior See CONSUMER BEHAVIOR.

purchase channel for foreign merchandise Any of a variety of ways a retail firm may add imported goods to its merchandise assortment. Purchase channels for foreign merchandise include private import wholesalers, foreign exporters or selling houses, purchasing agents or commissionaires, and store-owned foreign buying offices. The buyer may also make buying trips to foreign markets and attend import trade fairs. See also BUYING.

purchase contract An agreement between a buyer and a seller that itemizes the products and services in the transaction and the terms of sale and delivery (if applicable). See also CONTRACT.

purchase cycle The usual interval of time between acquisition of a product and its routine replacement. For example, the purchase cycle of health and beauty products may be several months, whereas the purchase cycle of a winter coat may be two or three years. Certain sales promotion techniques encourage the consumer to replace a product before he or she has completely finished the current supply. For example, coupons with an expiration date or a limited time offer are used to accelerate the purchase process.

purchase decision process Synonym for ADOPTION PROCESS.

purchase discount See CASH DISCOUNT.

purchase distribution The percentage of all retail outlets that received shipment of a product since a previous AUDIT, whether or not the product was in stock at the previous or current audits.

purchase history The record of purchases made by a consumer over a period of time. Purchase histories may be used in MARKETING RESEARCH (MR) to determine consumer shopping habits and identify trends.

purchase invoice Synonym for INVOICE.

purchase journal A monthly or semimonthly report prepared by a BUYER, including information about merchandise purchased from vendors, suppliers, and manufacturers for the department for which the buyer is responsible. The purchase journal may be prepared by the department store buyer or the central buyer. For each purchase it records the vendor's name, invoice date, style number, quantity, cost per unit, unit retail cost, receiving apron number, total cost, total retail discounts, and balance paid or owed. The purchase journal is used to compare dollar amounts of merchandise receipts against planned purchase figures; it shows what has been received and what is on order so that the buyer can adjust the inventory turnover to conform to the merchandise budget. Also called a *billing record.*

purchase order A contractual sales agreement in the form of a written document made out by the buyer (i.e., the retailer), authorizing a seller (i.e., the vendor) to deliver goods at a specified price to be paid later. The purchase order becomes a contract upon its acceptance by the vendor. Purchase orders typically specify the items of merchandise, prices, delivery dates, and payment terms. See also PURCHASE ORDER MANAGEMENT (POM) SYSTEM.

purchase order management (POM) system A computerized system designed to prepare and transmit purchase orders electronically. POM systems also track purchase orders by order number, delivery date, vendor, and category of merchandise. See also PURCHASE ORDER.

purchase planning See PLANNED PURCHASE, PLANNED PURCHASES AT RETAIL and PLANNED PURCHASES AT COST.

purchase price The amount of money for which an item or service is actually bought.

purchase-privilege offer See TRADING CARD and SEMI-LIQUIDATOR.

purchaser The individual who actually buys a product or service. The purchaser may be a BUYER at the industrial or retail level or a CUSTOMER at the consumer level.

purchase requisition A request from a department to its purchasing department to acquire (i.e., purchase) particular goods or services required by the department. See also REQUISITION, STORE'S REQUISITION, and RESERVE REQUISITION.

purchase returns and allowances See RETURNS AND ALLOWANCES FROM SUPPLIERS.

purchase-with-purchase (PWP) A special gift or bonus offered to customers at a special price with the purchase of a certain dollar amount of other merchandise. Cosmetic companies use this type of premium extensively. It is similar to a GIFT-WITH-PURCHASE (GWP) except that there is an additional charge for the gift.

purchasing 1. The acquisition of goods and services by the payment of money or its equivalent (i.e., BUYING). 2. See INDUSTRIAL PURCHASING.

purchasing agent 1. A professional buyer employed by a governmental, industrial, or institutional organization to procure equipment and supplies for use in the organization. Also called a *purchase agent.* 2. The individual who represents a foreign RESIDENT BUYING OFFICE under American management. See also COMMISSIONAIRE.

purchasing cooperative/co-op See CONSUMER COOPERATIVE.

purchasing leverage The power advantage that results from being a large buyer, especially the ability to negotiate for lower prices and better deals. This has a direct impact on profitability. Large chains and cooperatives have the ability to negotiate the best possible deals. See also BUYING POWER.

purchasing power Synonym for BUYING POWER.

purchasing-power parity In computing a foreign market's ability to buy, especially in terms of PER-CAPITA INCOME (PCI), a statistic that takes into account national differences in product prices.

pure competition A market condition so rare as to be largely theoretical, in which there are so many sellers and buyers that no one party can control prices; buyers and sellers are familiar with the market and can quickly react to changes in the supply-and-demand situation; the product or commodity being sold is highly substitutable; and there are relatively few barriers to parties entering and leaving the market. In pure competition, no single firm or group of firms in an industry is large enough to influence prices and thereby distort the workings of the FREE MARKET ECONOMY/SYSTEM. Conditions approaching pure competition are sometimes encountered in the trade in agricultural commodities. Also known as *perfect competition* and *free competition.*

Pure Food and Drug Act (1906) See FOOD AND DRUG ACT (1906).

purely competitive market structure See PURE COMPETITION.

pure market-directed economy See FREE MARKET ECONOMY/SYSTEM.

pure monopoly A market condition in which there is a single seller of a given product or service (i.e., there is no COMPETITION). Also called a *monopolistic market structure.*

pure research Research that is scientific in nature and conducted to find new knowledge about a subject rather than new ways of using existing knowledge. For example, textile companies use pure research to create new fibers and finishes. Also called *fundamental research.* Compare APPLIED RESEARCH.

purposive sample In marketing and other social science research, a NONPROBABILITY SAMPLE with the specific characteristics of the POPULATION being studied. For example, a study may require that participants be working mothers, twenty-five to forty-five years old, college-educated, with two children living at home. Drawing a random sample would be meaningless in such a study, since only participants sharing these characteristics are of interest.

pushcart A light, wheeled vehicle or wagon that can be pushed by hand, as by a STREET VENDOR.

push distribution strategy A marketing distribution strategy in which a manufacturer's promotional efforts are directed toward motivating (i.e., "pushing") members of the channel of distribution (e.g., wholesalers, distributors, and retailers) through such devices as advertising allowances and discounts to stock and sell the firm's products. Also called a *push marketing strategy, pushing strategy,* or a *push strategy.* Compare PULL DISTRIBUTION STRATEGY.

pushed content A method of online distribution and sale of content (such as secondary marketing research data) that takes advantage of the Internet's interactivity. For example, research firms send opt-in e-mail or newsletters containing announcements about current research to interested users. Pushed content is designed to motivate the receiver to click through to the Web site and buy the report or establish a business relationship with the research company that may result in a future transaction. Many research newsletters are sent on a monthly or biweekly basis. Other types of e-marketing firms can use the same techniques to push other forms of content for purchase.

pushing strategy Synonym for PUSH DISTRIBUTION STRATEGY.

push marketing strategy Synonym for PUSH DISTRIBUTION STRATEGY.

push method of secondary research See SECONDARY METHODS.

push money (PM) Bonus payments to salespersons as an incentive to vigorously promote the sale of specified products. Push money is paid by a manufacturer to the salespersons employed by wholesalers and retailers and may also take the form of prizes such as appliances and trips. Also called *prize money, premium money, a push money allowance, spiff,* or a *prize money allowance.*

push site In E-MARKETING, a WEB SITE that does not sell directly to buyers. Instead, it provides information that encourages buyers to complete the sale offline by telephone or fax, visit the store, send for a catalog, or contact a member of their traditional sales force. Some businesses use push sites because their products are not appropriate for storefront selling. Others

do so because they want to avoid problems associated with online selling or they do not have the resources or revenue stream to maintain an online storefront.

push strategy Short for PUSH DISTRIBUTION STRATEGY.

put-away The retail DISTRIBUTION CENTER (DC) function of warehousing basic merchandise for future replenishment of stores, or bulk items (such as furniture) for direct shipment to customers.

put-out pricing See PREDATORY PRICING.

PWP See PURCHASE-WITH-PURCHASE (PWP).

PX See POST EXCHANGE (PX).

pyramid (format) display See FLOOR PYRAMID.

pyramiding See PYRAMID SCHEME.

pyramid scheme A fraudulent selling and distribution program in which profits derive from getting paid for recruiting new distributors and the distributors they recruit in turn. The result is a pyramid-like series of layers of distribution, each more populous than the one above. The people at the top of the pyramid make money; most others do not. There are government regulations against certain types of pyramid schemes. Also called *pyramid selling* and *pyramiding.*

pyramid selling See PYRAMID SCHEME.

Q

QR See QUICK RESPONSE (QR).

QSR Short for *quick service restaurant*, a synonym for FAST FOOD RESTAURANT.

Q-system A STOCK CONTROL system that holds the reorder quantity constant and shifts the reorder period. Also called a *reorder system*. See also REORDER.

quad rack Synonym for FOUR-WAY RACK.

qualified lead Synonym for QUALIFIED PROSPECT.

qualified prospect In sales, a potential customer, whether a person or an organization, who not only is known to want, need, or potentially benefit from the product or service being sold, but also has the authority to make the purchase and the financial ability to pay for it. Also called a *qualified lead*. Compare LEAD and PROSPECT.

qualifying The process of determining whether or not a sales prospect is a serious potential customer. The seller determines whether the prospect has the funds needed to purchase the item or service, the authority for making the decision to buy, and a need for the product or service. Compare PROSPECTING.

qualifying dimensions The needs and preferences of the customer that are relevant to a product market and help determine whether an individual or firm is a potential customer for a particular class of products, without determining which brand or specific product type the customer will select. Such factors as sufficient income to purchase the product, suitability of the product to meeting the customer's need, and the ability of the customer to use the product are examples of qualifying dimensions. See also MOTIVE and DETERMINING DIMENSIONS.

qualitative analysis Analysis that is not based on precise measurement and quantitative claims, used primarily in research seeking to understand phenomena in ways that do not lend themselves to measurement. For example, the researcher may seek to observe social behavior without counting instances of a particular behavior. See also QUALITATIVE (PRIMARY) RESEARCH.

qualitative control A merchandising tool that provides information about current status and future planning while ascertaining that the retailer does not waver from its charted course. Qualitative controls measure performance descriptively. For example, a customer satisfaction survey might ask respondents to rate a store's customer service according to their own subjective perceptions. Compare QUANTITATIVE CONTROL.

qualitative data See QUALITATIVE (PRIMARY) RESEARCH and QUALITATIVE ANALYSIS.

qualitative (primary) research In retailing and other marketing activities, original research designed to answer a specific marketing question or solve a marketing problem. Qualitative research aims at the fundamental underlying assumptions that govern individual and group behavior. It utilizes methods such as focus groups, interviews, participant observation, and online chat analysis to gather data about participants' opinions, behaviors, intentions, and beliefs. Such data is called *qualitative data*. Compare QUANTITATIVE (PRIMARY) RESEARCH. See also QUALITATIVE ANALYSIS.

quality A degree of excellence or fineness (e.g., high, low, good, poor, first), often in conformance to a preestablished standard. See also USELESS QUALITY.

quality assurance A company-wide system of practices and procedures to ensure that the company's products satisfy customer needs and expectations. Quality assurance includes QUALITY CONTROL as well as doing the job right the first time, demanding quality components from suppliers, improving worker training, and encouraging workers to take pride in their work. In manufacturing, quality assurance also includes the concept of STATISTICAL PROCESS CONTROL, in which the process of production is monitored through the use of control charts.

quality check A form of merchandise CHECKING done in the receiving department, in which the condition of the arriving merchandise is determined. Compare QUANTITY CHECK.

quality circle A regularly scheduled meeting of a small group of workers (i.e., 5 to 15) who usually work in the same area. The purpose of the meeting is to identify and suggest solutions to problems relating to quality, safety, and production. With management's approval, these suggestions may be implemented. The goal of quality circles and similar problem-solving activities is to improve the final product, increase worker satisfaction, and create a sense of unity among the employees of the company.

quality control   1. An activity that includes the monitoring of products as they are produced in an effort to measure their quality, the comparison of the product to an established standard, and all subsequent efforts to maintain that standard. Also called *quality assurance.*   2. More narrowly, product inspection. 3. The department responsible for quality assurance.

quality creep   In new product development, the constant improvement of a product to the point where it is simply better than it needs to be to satisfy its target customer.

quality improvement   The making of modifications to enhance the durability of a product. See also PRODUCT IMPROVEMENT.

quality market   A segment of the market in which quality is more important than price.

quality-price association   See PRICE-QUALITY ASSOCIATION.

quality/price display   See PRICE/QUALITY DISPLAY.

quality response function   See PRODUCT QUALITY RESPONSE FUNCTION.

quantitative analysis   The use of sophisticated statistical methods to analyze *quantitative data* in order to test hypotheses and demonstrate relationships between variables. See also QUANTITATIVE (PRIMARY) RESEARCH.

quantitative data   See QUANTITATIVE (PRIMARY) RESEARCH and QUANTITATIVE ANALYSIS.

quantitative control   A merchandising tool that provides information about current status and future planning while ascertaining that the retailer remains on course. Quantitative controls measure performance numerically and consistently. For example, the calculation of a 5% increase over last year's sales will yield the same result regardless of who performs the calculation. Consequently, quantitative controls are considered objective. Compare QUALITATIVE CONTROL.

quantitative mathematical models of promotional budgeting   The use of computer simulations and economic forecasting models to set the promotional budget. Techniques involving multiple regression analysis are used to analyze the relationship of variables to the relative contributions of promotional activities. Computer simulations may also be used to correlate awareness levels, purchase frequency, sales, and profitability with alternate television media schedules and other media placements. See also PROMOTIONAL BUDGETING.

quantitative (primary) research   Empirical research generating projectable data by sampling a portion of the population, analyzing the results using statistical methods, and generalizing them to the population at large. Surveys (i.e., questionnaires),

experiments, and observations are popular quantitative research methods. Compare QUALITATIVE (PRIMARY) RESEARCH. See also QUALITATIVE ANALYSIS, SAMPLE, and SAMPLING.

quantity check   A form of merchandise CHECKING done in the receiving department, in which it is verified that the correct amount of merchandise has been received. Compare QUALITY CHECK.

quantity (price) discount   A reduction from list price given to retail buyers purchasing in unusually large quantities from the manufacturer or supplier. The quantity discount may take the form of free units (i.e., additional merchandise) or dollars (i.e., a percentage of the purchase price). Also called *volume bonus.* See also CUMULATIVE QUANTITY DISCOUNT.

quasi-chain   A group of independently owned retail establishments that are affiliated and have a form of central organization. See also VOLUNTARY CHAIN.

queen sizes   Synonym for PLUS SIZES.

query   1. n. A request for information from a customer or prospective customer. For example, charge customers may request information about the status of their charge accounts. Similarly, a prospective customer may request additional information about products or services offered by the retailer. Mail order and Internet customers may submit a query about the status of their orders.   2. v. To make or submit a request for information about something.

question approach   A SALES APPROACH in which the SALESPERSON gives the PROSPECT an interesting fact about the product or service, phrased as a question. This question is intended to stimulate the prospect's participation in the sales presentation.

question mark   (Slang) Synonym for PROBLEM CHILD.

questionnaire   An instrument (usually a printed form but increasingly an online form) used to collect information from respondents in the form of responses to questions. One of four methods is employed: personal interview, telephone interview, mail survey, or (increasingly) an online survey. The data is generally subjected to QUANTITATIVE ANALYSIS. See also SURVEY, STRUCTURED QUESTIONNAIRE, and UNSTRUCTURED QUESTIONNAIRE.

questionnaire method   See QUESTIONNAIRE and SURVEY.

queue   In the United Kingdom, a line of people waiting. See also QUEUING THEORY.

queuing theory   A theory of behavior, generally expressed in mathematical terms, relating to how people behave in waiting lines and how they will be waited upon or otherwise processed. Also called *waiting-line theory.* See also QUEUE.

quick assets   Receivables, cash, and securities that are already liquid (i.e., cash) or are easily and quickly converted into cash.

346 quick markdown pricing

Quick assets are compared to current liabilities to calculate the ACID TEST RATIO. See also ASSET and CURRENT LIABILITY.

quick markdown pricing A PRICING STRATEGY designed to provide high value for the bargain shopper. It is used for fashion and seasonal goods that have several selling periods during the course of a year. While some shoppers shop at the beginning of the selling season, when assortments are more complete, others wait for the markdowns later in the season. At that point, assortments are usually broken, however, so that even though the price may be comparatively low, it may become difficult to find desired companion pieces. Under quick markdown pricing, the price reduction is introduced earlier in the season so that shoppers can take advantage of it before assortments become broken. See also MARKDOWN (MD).

quick ratio Synonym for ACID TEST RATIO.

quick response (QR) An umbrella term for integrated supply chain distribution systems through which orders are replenished rapidly and automatically using a computer linkup. QR depends on a cooperative relationship between retailers and their vendors. See also QUICK RESPONSE (QR) REPLENISHMENT SYSTEM and MERCHANDISE REPLENISHMENT.

quick response (QR) inventory system Synonym for QUICK RESPONSE (QR) REPLENISHMENT SYSTEM.

quick response (QR) operation Synonym for QUICK RESPONSE (QR) REPLENISHMENT SYSTEM.

quick response (QR) replenishment system A cooperative effort between retailers and their vendors to reduce retail inventory while providing a merchandise supply that more closely addresses the buying patterns of consumers. In a QR system a manufacturer or service provider attempts to supply its customers with products or services in the precise quantities required at exactly the right time. Quick response operations are sometimes found in the soft goods industry, where an attempt is made to shorten the LEAD TIME in the pipeline from textile maker to apparel manufacturer to retailer. A QR system's multiple delivery strategies use frequent reestimates of customer preferences based on up-to-date POINT-OF-PURCHASE (POP) data. Production capability and merchandise offered is adjusted to respond to customer demand based on POP information and style testing. Also called *a quick response (QR)*

inventory system. See also VOLUNTARY INTERINDUSTRY COMMERCE STANDARDS ASSOCIATION (VICS) and MERCHANDISE REPLENISHMENT MODEL.

quick service restaurant (QSR) Synonym for FAST FOOD RESTAURANT.

quick trip shopper A customer who visits a retail store for just a few inexpensive items, picked up quickly, without spending additional time shopping.

quota 1. A fixed amount (e.g., a dollar amount or unit figure) used as the sales goal for a salesperson. Also called a SALES QUOTA. 2. A share or maximum amount. An import quota for a particular product represents a fixed limit on the quantity of imports a nation will allow for that product. See also TRADE QUOTA. 3. Any quantitative recommendation, such as the number or percentage of employees to be hired from minority groups under an affirmative action plan.

quota bonus plan A compensation plan for salespeople in which a base salary is paid without regard to productivity, to which a bonus is added whenever a fixed quota of sales is exceeded.

quota rent A way of acquiring the right to import more of a specific classification of goods from a specific country than originally allowed. A firm that would otherwise exceed its quota for that import buys ("rents") another firm's excess quota. The cost of doing so depends on market demand at a particular time.

quota sample A type of NONPROBABILITY SAMPLE in which the interviewers are given specific numbers of subjects to find and interview in each of several categories. Participants are selected on the basis of characteristics thought pertinent to the study. For example, a researcher may be told to find 20 women between 35 and 40 years old, half of whom are employed outside the home and half of whom are homemakers.

quotation An offer to sell products or services at a stated price and under specified conditions.

quoted price The stated PRICE for products or services sold under specified conditions.

racetrack floor plan   See CLOSED LOOP LAYOUT.

racetrack layout   See CLOSED LOOP LAYOUT.

racetrack traffic aisle   See CLOSED LOOP LAYOUT.

rack   A floor stand used as an interior display for holding or storing merchandise. A rack may utilize shelves, hooks, or pockets to hold the merchandise. See also PIPE RACK and THREE-PART RACK.

rack display   See RACK.

rack jobber   A type of MERCHANT WHOLESALER that provides extensive services to the retailer. The rack jobber sells specialized merchandise, especially to supermarkets and other self-service retailers. It sets up and maintains displays of this merchandise, provides the requisite display fixtures, stocks inventory, and marks prices on merchandise displayed in a particular section of a store. The rack jobber is usually paid only for goods sold, a percentage of which goes to the retail outlet. Also called a *service merchandiser*.

rack merchandiser/wholesaler   See RACK JOBBER.

radial site   A store location situated along major traffic arteries between the central business area and the surrounding residential areas.

Radiation Control for Health and Safety Act (RCHSA) (1968)   U.S. federal legislation establishing performance standards for consumer electronics items such as television sets, microwave ovens, etc. The act limits the amount of radiation that may be emitted from such products. Its enforcement is within the purview of the FOOD AND DRUG ADMINISTRATION (FDA).

radiation selling   Basing future sales on an initial sale of a product or service. For example, selling a camera leads to sales of film and film processing services. These future sales are thought of as "radiating" out from the initial sale.

radio button   In the design of Web pages using HTML, one of a series of buttons that allows visitors to select from a number of options with a single click. Radio buttons usually appear as small circles, only one of which can be selected at a time. When one option is selected, the other options are blank: ○○●. Radio buttons are used to let the visitor select one and only one option from a set of alternatives. They may be set to display a default selection.

radio frequency identification (RFID)   1. The use of a RADIO FREQUENCY IDENTIFICATION (RFID) TAG equipped with a RADIO FREQUENCY IDENTIFICATION (RFID) CHIP in shopping, particularly supermarket shopping. The use of the RFID system is intended to help retailers take control of inventory, improve supply-chain efficiency, and identify customer preferences. Information about each customer transaction can be tracked, recorded, and analyzed. A reader at the entrance to a store's loading dock can log the arrival of any RFID-tagged contents. In the aisles, antennas suspended from the ceiling track shoppers and beam information about specials (see also ADVERTISING DISPLAY) to consoles on smart shopping carts (see also CART-TOP COMPUTING). Prices on remote-controlled LCD labels on store shelves (see also SMART SHELVES) rise or fall each night with inventory levels (see also DYNAMIC PRICING). The tags can also activate DVD players to show trailers of films at an electronic kiosk for the benefit of potential DVD customers, generate price stickers for produce (see also VEGGIE VISION), and suggest wines (see also SOMMELIER KIOSK) and recipes. In addition, the tags can be used to scan the contents of a shopping cart and debit the customer's bank account (see also CHECKOUT PASS). The customer may elect to keep personal information anonymous through the use of an optional TAG ANONYMIZER. The use of RFID technology in supermarkets is predicted for the near future. In the meantime, until all products are RFID tagged, barcodes can be used as temporary stand-ins for RFID. RFID, however, remains controversial and several states are considering legislation banning RFID tagged products and/or banning tracking customers as they shop. Part of the controversy revolves around invasion of privacy, since the RFID tag continues to beam information (which can be read by anyone with an RFID reader) after the customer has left the store. The development of ways to deactivate the tags before shoppers leave the store is underway. In the meantime, several states are considering legislation that would require a store to notify customers if a package or product they purchased contain an RFID tag.   2. The same technology, used for security. The tag detects the presence of security devices (which may be hidden in fixtures, mannequins, etc.) by means of radio waves. An alarm is triggered if unpaid merchandise passes the detection checkpoint without having been deactivated. See also ELECTRONIC ARTICLE SURVEILLANCE (EAS).

radio frequency identification (RFID) chip   Electronic circuitry, about the size of a grain of sand, used in a merchandise tag and designed to help retailers take control of the supply chain and identify customer preferences. See also RADIO FREQUENCY IDENTIFICATION (RFID).

radio frequency identification (RFID) reader   See RADIO FREQUENCY IDENTIFICATION (RFID).

radio frequency identification (RFID) tag   A merchandise tag equipped with RADIO FREQUENCY IDENTIFICATION (RFID).

rags   (Slang) Garments made by the APPAREL INDUSTRY.

rag trade/business   (Slang) Synonym for APPAREL INDUSTRY.

raider   See HOSTILE TAKEOVER.

railroad   An economical transportation mode used for long hauls of heavy, bulky commodities. Retailers and their vendors transport goods by rail in conjunction with other transportation modes such as trucks. This allows them to benefit from the economical rail charges as well as the door-to-door services of trucks. See also MOTOR CARRIER.

rail-trailer shipment   Synonym for PIGGYBACK.

rain check   In retailing, a certificate entitling the customer to buy an out-of-stock advertised special at a later date at the same advertised price. Sometimes spelled *raincheck*.

Raincheck Rule   The FEDERAL TRADE COMMISSION (FTC) regulation governing cases of out-of-stock advertised merchandise. The guidelines suggest that retailers issue a raincheck allowing customers to buy the advertised merchandise at a later date at the sale price, offer substitute merchandise of comparable value, or offer a compensation that is at least equal in value to the reduction on the promoted merchandise. Also known as the *Unavailability Rule*. See also RAIN CHECK.

raised floor   A DISPLAY WINDOW floor situated higher than the usual 8–9 inches above street level. The raised floor allows the window dresser to create a dramatic presentation by forcing passersby to look up to it. The elevated position adds prestige and also makes it possible for passersby to see over the heads of window shoppers.

raked floor   An inclined DISPLAY WINDOW floor where the back of the floor is several inches higher than the front, creating a ramp effect. This allows small objects, such as shoes and accessories, to be more easily seen when placed in the back.

R&D   See RESEARCH AND DEVELOPMENT (R&D).

random error   In SAMPLING, a mistake, generally statistical, due to blind chance. A certain amount of random error is present in every SAMPLE. Also called a *statistical random error*.

randomized graphics   See GRAPHICS.

random sample   A representative subset of the total POPULATION in which each member of the population has a known and equal chance of being included in the sample group. The members of the random sample are selected on a random basis, such as every tenth name on a list. Random sampling is one form of PROBABILITY SAMPLING. Compare NONPROBABILITY SAMPLE.

random sampling   In marketing and other social science research, a method of selecting a representative subset of the total POPULATION in which each member of the population has a known and equal chance of being included in the sample group. The members are selected on a predetermined basis, such as by taking every tenth name on a list or using a table of random numbers. Random sampling is one form of PROBABILITY SAMPLING.

random storage   A computer model for optimizing the use of storage space in an automated warehouse system. Automated storage and retrieval systems reduce both aisle space and the labor required to access desired merchandise. See also AUTOMATED WAREHOUSE and AUTOMATED STORAGE AND RETRIEVAL (ASR).

rapid inflation   A general rise in prices severe enough or swift enough to lead to changes in consumer attitudes and behavior.

rapid penetration strategy   See PENETRATION STRATEGY.

rapid return on investment   See PROFIT MAXIMIZATION OBJECTIVE and RETURN ON INVESTMENT (ROI).

ratchet (effect)   An economic condition sometimes accompanying inflation, in which prices continue to advance despite a reduction in demand. The term *ratchet* refers to the toothed wheel equipped with a pawl that allows motion in one direction only.

rate   1. n. The factor used to determine the charge or fare for services rendered. For example, a rate may be the amount charged per ad placed on a Web page. In most instances, rates are posted and many can be negotiated. See also RATE CARD. 2. v. A degree of speed or progress, such as the rate at which items are sold in a department. See also RATE OF SALE.   3. v. To evaluate the worth or quality of a product or service. For example, a SURVEY may ask customers to rate a store's services.

rate card   1. An information sheet provided by a newspaper, magazine, television network, or other advertising medium that indicates the costs, mechanical requirements, and other pertinent information to the buyer of advertising time or space.   2. In online advertising, a table or list giving information about advertising on a Web page or Web site. Rates vary by site and are set by the site owner; many are negotiable. Rate cards for online ads tend to give no guarantee on the number of click throughs, but the ad purchaser can generally determine the number of visitors to the host site and the nature of the target market.

rated concern A company whose credit rating has been investigated and evaluated by a credit clearing house.

rate of response The measure of the number of replies obtained compared to the number of contacts made, interviews conducted, or advertisements run. In the print media, the MEDIA BUYER uses the periodical's circulation information to assess the number of potential customers that can be expected to respond to the advertisement. Also called *response rate*.

rate of return on common-stock equity The financial ratio derived by subtracting preferred stock dividends from net income and dividing the difference by the average common stockholder's equity during the accounting period. The ratio is used as a means of examining the company's performance over the accounting period.

rate of return on stockholders' equity The financial ratio that results from dividing a company's net income by the average stockholder's equity during the accounting period (generally one year). The ratio is a means of evaluating the company's operations for the duration of the accounting period.

rate of return pricing A method of calculating prices based on a fixed, predetermined RETURN ON INVESTMENT (ROI).

rate of sale The number of units sold over a given period of time. For STAPLE stock, the rate of sale is calculated as previous inventory plus new merchandise less merchandise currently on hand. The result will be expressed for a specific period (e.g., 250 units per week sold).

rate of stock turnover Synonym for STOCK TURNOVER RATE.

rate war A particularly aggressive form of competition in which a seller drops its prices below its costs in an attempt to force a competing firm (or firms) out of business. See also PREDATORY PRICING. Also called *price war*.

ratings See PROGRAM RATINGS.

ratio See FINANCIAL RATIOS or MARKDOWN RATIO.

ratio analysis The comparison of two elements from the same year's financial figures. For example, sales might be compared to assets or to income. The result of such a comparison is stated as a percentage or ratio, which can then be compared to the firm's own past ratios or to the current ratios of the competition. Like TREND ANALYSIS, ratio analysis is used as an indicator of how the firm is performing relative to other companies in its industry. Unlike trend analysis, however, ratio analysis focuses on certain key areas of current performance instead of on comparisons over time. Most industries have their own "normal" ratios that act as yardsticks for individual firms. Such norms are generally available in published sources. See also RETAIL HORIZONS.

rational buying motive Any factor affecting a consumer's decision to buy that is based on logic, reason, and careful thought. See also its opposite, EMOTIONAL BUYING MOTIVE/TRIGGER.

rationalized retailing The application of modern methods and standards of efficiency to store management. Rationalized retailing implies highly centralized management control.

ratio of finished goods inventory to the cost of goods sold A ratio calculated by dividing the COST OF GOODS SOLD by the average FINISHED GOODS INVENTORY. The resulting figure represents the number of times the investment in the finished-goods inventory has turned over during the period under consideration. The ratio for the current period is compared to similar ratios for several previous periods as an indication of the stability or trend of sales.

raw materials Materials in their unprocessed NATURAL state (e.g., iron ore), or in a semifinished state (e.g., pig iron), used in the production of other goods. Raw materials may be produced (as in the case of cotton, grain, and livestock), or extracted (as in the case of lumber, ore, or fish).

RCHSA See RADIATION CONTROL FOR HEALTH AND SAFETY ACT (RCHSA) (1968).

RDA See RETAIL DISPLAY ALLOWANCE (RDA).

RDF site summary See RSS.

reach The number of households or individuals that may be said to be viewing or listening to a given station, program, or commercial during a particular time slot. Reach may also be measured for an entire advertising campaign or series of commercials, and is expressed as a percentage of the total audience of unduplicated homes or individuals exposed to an advertising message. Compare COVERAGE, which reports the total potential audience and is therefore always larger than reach. When measured over a period of days, weeks, or months, reach is known as the CUME. Also called *media coverage* and *unduplicated media audience*. See also DUPLICATED MEDIA AUDIENCE.

reach (cumulative) See CUME.

reach plan See TOTAL AUDIENCE PLAN.

reactive selling A sales effort in which customers are allowed to take the initiative in seeking out a vendor. Compare PROACTIVE SELLING.

readability test In ADVERTISING RESEARCH, a test that relies on the forecasting formula developed by Rudolph Flesch to determine the human interest appeal in the ad's material, length of sentences, and familiarity of words. These components are considered and correlated with the educational background of the target audience. For example, the average number of syllables per 100 words is one measure used to assess the readability of copy. Test results are compared to previously established norms for various target audiences. Testing suggests that copy is best understood when sentences are short, words are concrete and well-known, and personal references are made.

reader   1. In print media, one who reads the newspaper, magazine, or book in question and can be expected, by extension, to be exposed to the advertising messages included in that publication. Compare SUBSCRIBER.   2. Short for OPTICAL CODE READER (OCR).

readership (pass-along)   See PASS-ALONG CIRCULATION.

readership (primary)   See PRIMARY CIRCULATION.

readers per copy   See PASS-ALONG RATE.

ready-to-know   Of consumers, expecting any information deemed relevant to their needs and interests to be available instantly, on their own terms. The widespread availability of the INTERNET and the speed of its search engines contribute to this trend in consumer behavior. The trend was identified and the term coined by trendwatching.com at www.trendwatching.com.

ready-to-wear (RTW)   Ready-made clothing mass-produced in factories to standard size measurements so that it may be purchased from racks by consumers. Known as *prêt-à-porter* in French and *off-the-peg* in the United Kingdom. In the United States, RTW is also called *off-the-rack*. See also DESIGNER READY-TO-WEAR.

ready-to-wear forms   A generic term used to include shirt forms, blouse forms, bust forms, swimwear forms, suit forms, etc., used to display ready-to-wear apparel. They may be mounted on flat bases for display on tables or fixtures, or on pedestals for floor display.

real account   Any account that appears on the BALANCE SHEET. For example, the asset account, liability account, equity account, and capital account are all considered real (i.e., permanent) accounts. Consequently, each of these is sometimes called a *balance sheet account*. Compare NOMINAL ACCOUNT.

real estate   The land and any improvements made to it, such as roads and landscaping, together with the buildings on the site. Also called *real property*.

real estate investment trust (REIT)   A financial institution that controls and manages large-scale real estate transactions. An REIT may be involved in the acquisition of land and shopping centers.

real estate manager   The store executive responsible for the land and buildings occupied by a store, a warehouse, or a service facility belonging to a store.

real estate subsidiary   A SUBSIDIARY of a retail organization that exists to own and operate property. Through a real estate subsidiary, a retailer may own an entire shopping center, leasing space to other tenants and controlling the type of store included in the center as well as the hours of business, parking facilities, etc.

real income   Income (of an individual, group, or country) expressed in terms of purchasing power rather than dollars.

Real income is a useful concept when incomes are compared over time and changing price levels must be taken into account. For example, price increases between 1970 and 1980 reduced the value of dollar increases in salaries by about half. See also BUYING POWER and PERSONAL INCOME (PI).

realistic display setting   The depiction of a room, area, or other recognizable locale, either in the DISPLAY WINDOW or inside the store. For example, a realistic display depicting Christmas morning might show a living room populated with mannequins opening presents while dressed in robes and slippers, with a Christmas tree and fireplace to complete the picture. Realistic display settings are intended to provide the customer with an image to which they can easily relate.

realistic mannequin   Formerly, a lifelike human figure resembling a glamorous movie star, made to convey elegance. Today, realistic mannequins are more likely to resemble the average customer. They have become increasingly lifelike over the years and may now be found in a variety of size ranges to portray a wide array of body types, ethnicities, and genders. Hair and facial features are lifelike and expressive.

really simple syndication (RSS)   See RSS.

real property   Synonym for REAL ESTATE.

reason-why approach   See FACTUAL APPROACH.

rebate   1. A reduction in price granted to the buyer of goods (wholesaler, retailer, or ultimate consumer) by the manufacturer or producer for the purpose of encouraging sales. The rebate is generally made as a cash refund sent to the buyer after the transaction has been completed at the regular price. A rebate made to consumers generally requires an original sales receipt and a portion of the packaging (e.g., UPC label) as proof-of-purchase. Rebates to consumers are used in everything from low-end grocery items to high-end appliances and hi-tech equipment. Also known as a *refund offer*, a *money refund offer*, a *cash refund offer*, a *rebate offer*, or a *cash rebate*. 2. Synonym for PATRONAGE REBATE.

rebate offer   See REBATE.

rebranding   See REPOSITIONING.

rebuyer   A person, usually in a large retail organization, responsible for buying additional merchandise after the BUYER has placed the original ORDER. The rebuyer orders merchandise to bring inventories up to their proper level later in the year.

recall   1. v. To bring back from memory, recollect, or remember. Tests are used in advertising research to study consumers' ability to recall, or remember, ads.   2. v. To call back merchandise found to be defective.   3. n. The act of recalling, in either sense. See also RECALL TEST, AIDED RECALL, UNAIDED RECALL, and PRODUCT RECALL.

recall test   A means of measuring the effectiveness of an advertisement by the ability of subjects to remember it. The test subject is given only the name of the brand as a prompt to remember the ad. See also AIDED RECALL, UNAIDED RECALL, SPAN OF RECALL, and PORTFOLIO TEST.

receipt A written or printed statement that merchandise has been received and paid for. The receipt may be produced at the POINT-OF-PURCHASE (POP) by the cash register or computer terminal (in which case it is called a *register receipt*) or it may be handwritten by the salesperson. See also RECEIVE and SALES SLIP.

receipt of goods (ROG) dating In the DATING OF INVOICES, an INVOICE agreement specifying that the cash discount period allowed by the vendor to the retailer does not begin until the goods are actually received by the retailer (i.e., the cash discount period begins when the merchandise reaches the store rather than on the date the shipment was made). For example, if the terms of a shipment invoiced August 15 are 2/10 ROG, and the goods arrive on September 1, a 2% discount may be deducted through September 11. Full payment is due by October 1. Designed to benefit retailers, particularly those located far from their resources, ROG dating is infrequently used.

receipt of goods (ROG) terms See RECEIPT OF GOODS (ROG) DATING.

receivables Bills and payments due to a creditor. Receivables may be amounts owed by customers to a store or amounts owed by stores to a vendor.

receivables turnover The financial ratio that results from dividing the net sales on account (i.e., credit sales) by the average net accounts receivable during the accounting period. The ratio is used as a means of examining the company's operation over the accounting period. See also FINANCIAL RATIOS.

receive To take into one's possession something that is delivered or offered. In retail operations, this function is generally undertaken by the RECEIVING division or department.

receiver In advertising and communications, the recipient of a message.

receiving 1. The process of accepting and taking physical possession of goods delivered to a store or warehouse. Receiving includes the unloading of shipments at the dock. 2. The location or department in a store responsible for accepting, opening, checking, and often marking merchandise delivered to the store. The CHECKING activities include comparing the supplier's invoice and the physical contents of the shipment against the original PURCHASE ORDER, inspecting the incoming shipment for defects, and recording any disagreement. The department handling these processes is generally referred to as the *receiving department*. See also OPENING and MARKING AND TICKETING.

receiving apron Synonym for INVOICE APRON.

receiving book The retailer's record of incoming merchandise shipments. Recorded information includes the number of packages, the names of vendors, dates of arrival, etc. Tradition-ally this information was entered in an actual log book, but modern records are kept in computer terminals.

receiving by invoice The process of CHECKING a shipment of merchandise as it arrives at the store or warehouse against the accompanying INVOICE.

receiving by purchase order The process of CHECKING a shipment of merchandise delivered to a store against the PURCHASE ORDER, a copy of which has remained on file in the store.

receiving department See RECEIVING.

receiving dock Synonym for DOCK.

recency/frequency (RF) A criterion for evaluating a customer or group of customers, based on the number of purchases made and the length of time between purchases (i.e., frequency) as well as the time passed since the last purchase (i.e., recency). The most valued customers have a high degree of recency and frequency. See also RECENCY/FREQUENCY/MONETARY VALUE (RFM).

recency/frequency/monetary value (RFM) A criterion for evaluating a customer or group of customers, based on the number of purchases made, the length of time between purchases (i.e., frequency), the time elapsed since the last purchase (i.e., recency) and the amount of money spent at the store (i.e., monetary value). The most valued customers have a high degree of recency and frequency and spend the most money in the store. See also RECENCY/FREQUENCY (RF).

recent sale price In auctions, both online and offline, the price at which a comparable item sold at another auction in the not-too-distant past. See also OPENING BID PRICE.

receptivity to innovation The extent to which a person or firm is willing to consider and purchase a new item or process.

recessed front A store entrance that is set back to include a space or niche in which customers may get out of the flow of traffic on the sidewalk or mall promenade, examine the store's window displays, and through which they may enter the store. See also DISPLAY WINDOW.

recession See BUSINESS CYCLE.

reciprocal advertising links In E-COMMERCE, free ads swapped between cooperating host sites. Banner ads and links allow visitors to click through to the other site. An advertiser placing an ad on a host's Web site reciprocates by hosting the other marketer's ad on its own site.

reciprocal buying See RECIPROCITY.

reciprocal (sales) lead The name and address of a prospect, provided by another company in exchange for similar information from the recipient.

reciprocity 1. The practice of two companies agreeing to buy each other's products so that each is the other's supplier as well as customer. The practice of reciprocity is subject to scrutiny under existing antitrust laws since it tends to limit competition and restrain trade. *Simple reciprocity* (sometimes called *innocent reciprocity*) in which there is no effort on the part of one firm to dominate another, may degenerate into *coercive reciprocity* if one firm attempts to force a subordinate firm to purchase its products. Also called *reciprocal buying.* 2. In an international trade agreement, such as the GENERAL AGREEMENT ON TARIFFS AND TRADE (GATT), the understanding that if one country lowers its tariffs against another's exports, it should expect the other country to do the same for its own exports. See also TRANSPARENCY and NONDISCRIMINATION, the two other underlying principles embodied in GATT.

recognition survey/test A test of advertisement RECALL in which subjects are usually aided by reproductions of the advertisement with proprietary names obscured. See also AIDED RECALL, UNAIDED RECALL, and RECALL TEST.

recommended retail price See MANUFACTURER'S SUGGESTED RETAIL PRICE (MSRP).

reconstructuring A consumer trend involving the ability to reconstruct any event, online or offline, through the use of ubiquitous recording equipment. Examples include the "Nanny Cam" and the "Drive Cam" as well as the "Sent" box on one's e-mail account. Consumers increasingly expect that events can be reconstructed, though many of them are torn between privacy concerns and the convenience of having access to more and more back-data. The trend was identified and the term coined by trendwatching.com at www.trendwatching.com.

record In DATABASE (DB) design, one complete set of fields, such as all the information about an individual customer. Multiple records of one kind are assembled into a *file* (e.g., a file containing the information about all customers).

recording delay The time lag between the actual buying of merchandise and the appearance of the purchase in the manufacturer's accounting records. Recording delays have an impact on reorders, promotional needs, etc.

recovery See BUSINESS CYCLE.

recreational shopping Less focused shopping in which the customer engages in browsing, cross-shopping, and comparison shopping from store to store. Malls and large department stores are often the favored venues for recreational shopping. Compare VALUE SHOPPING and FASHION SHOPPING.

recruitment The act of attracting, hiring, or engaging the services of new employees.

rectangular layout See GRID LAYOUT.

red See IN THE RED.

redemption The act of returning a PROOF-OF-PURCHASE or COUPON to a retailer or manufacturer to receive either a DISCOUNT on future purchases or a PREMIUM. Firms monitor the

number of redemptions they receive to measure the effectiveness of a promotion. See also REDEMPTION CENTER.

redemption center An outlet operated by a trading stamp company at which consumers may exchange the trading stamps they've collected for merchandise. Sometimes called *redemption store, trading stamp redemption store, premium center, premium store, premium redemption center,* or *trading stamp redemption center.*

redemption coupon See COUPON.

redemption store See REDEMPTION CENTER.

red goods A category in a system of classification based on frequency of replacement. Red goods are food items and other consumer goods that are consumed and replaced at a rapid rate. They also have a low profit margin. Compare ORANGE GOODS and YELLOW GOODS.

rediscount To discount for a second time. Used primarily in finance in relation to short-term negotiable debt instruments that are discounted for a second time after an initial discount from a bank. See also REDISCOUNT RATE.

rediscount rate The interest rate charged by the Federal Reserve Bank for loans to its member banks. See also REDISCOUNT.

red label A shipping label indicating flammable contents.

reduced-price pack A package conspicuously marked with a price lower than regular retail.

reduced rate See ALLOWANCE and DISCOUNT.

reduction (from retail) See RETAIL REDUCTION.

redundancy The existence of many possible paths to a given destination. In terms of the Internet, redundancy ensures that if one part of the network slows down or stops, data packets can be carried by means of other parts.

refer 1. To pass the responsibility for credit authorization to a supervisor or credit manager, usually when a credit customer's account status is in doubt. See also REFER ACCOUNT. 2. To make a REFERRAL. See also CHAIN PROSPECTING.

refer account A charge account that requires credit office approval for further charges. The necessity for approval and clearance arises when the credit limit has been exceeded or payments have been habitually late. See also REFER (def. 1) and FLAGGING AN ACCOUNT.

reference group Those persons from whom an individual derives values, standards, tastes, etc. and on whom the individual models his or her attitudes and behavior; that is, a group that forms a basis of comparison for the individual. A person need not belong to a group nor have direct contact with it for it to serve as a reference group. In fact, certain groups exert a negative influence on nonmembers, who avoid certain kinds of behavior in order to avoid identifying with the group. See also MEMBERSHIP GROUP, DISSOCIATIVE GROUP, PRIMARY GROUP, STATUS, and ASPIRATIONAL GROUP.

reference point   See VALID REFERENCE POINT.

referral   1. In hiring, the name of any of an informed person's acquaintances who might be a potential new employee.   2. In sales, short for a *referral lead*. See CHAIN PROSPECTING.

referral approach   A SALES APPROACH in which the SALESPERSON mentions the name of someone known to the PROSPECT who has suggested that the individual might be interested in the good or service being sold.

referral gift/premium   A gift or other reward offered to a satisfied customer whose recommendation brings in additional prospects and additional sales.

referral lead   See CHAIN PROSPECTING.

referral sample   See SNOWBALL SAMPLE.

refund   Repayment to a customer, upon the return of merchandise, of the money originally spent on the merchandise. A refund may be in the form of a check, cash (i.e., a *cash refund*), or store CREDIT SLIP.

refund check   A statement or document showing that a customer's purchase has been returned.

refund offer   Synonym for REBATE.

refusal-to-deal   A stipulation that a private manufacturer or distributor may refuse to sell to a buyer only if its agreement with its existing customers, dealers, or franchisees has no anticompetitive purpose or motive. The stipulation is an attempt to prevent conspiracy to fix prices and/or restrain trade. It does not, however, prohibit a manufacturer or distributor from restricting its sales to authorized dealers or from providing exclusive territories to dealerships. See also COLGATE DOCTRINE (1919) and RESTRAINT OF TRADE.

refusal-to-sell   The right of a seller to refuse to sell merchandise to another party. For example, a manufacturer may refuse to sell merchandise to a wholesaler or retailer because that party fails to meet specified standards or qualifications.

regiocentrism   A decentralized form of business organization, found in some multinational marketing firms, in which the marketing effort centers on a REGION rather than on an individual country (ETHNOCENTRISM) or the entire world market (GEOCENTRISM). Such regions may comprise countries that are contiguous to each other, share a common language, are at similar levels of economic development, or belong to the same ECONOMIC COMMUNITY.

region   A large, indefinite area or extensive continuous part of the earth. A region may be part of a country, such as the regions of the United States commonly referred to as the

Northeast, Southwest, Southeast, Midwest, and the Pacific Northwest. Other regions consist of a number of countries in close proximity (e.g., regions such as Western Europe, Southeast Asia, the Pacific Rim).

regional   Pertaining to an area of considerable extent (i.e., a region) rather than merely local.

regional advertising   Advertising that allows the retailer or other advertiser to take advantage of widely distributed media within a limited geographical area. Several national magazines offer regional advertising opportunities through regionally distributed editions. A store with outlets only in the northeastern United States, for example, may purchase advertising space in a magazine distributed only to readers in that part of the country.

regional apparel mart   See REGIONAL MART.

regional center   See REGIONAL SHOPPING CENTER.

regional chain   A CHAIN STORE SYSTEM (CSS) whose activities are limited to a particular area or REGION of the country, such as (in the United States) the Northeast, Southwest, Midwest, etc.

regional cooperation group   An association of two or more countries cooperating in one or more joint ventures. Each country contributes to the financing of the project and agrees to buy a percentage of the project's output. See also JOINT VENTURE.

regional department store   A DEPARTMENT STORE whose several branches serve an area larger than a state or metropolitan area but not as large as the entire country.

regional integration agreement   An international trade agreement that involves member countries from specific regions of the world. For example, the NORTH AMERICAN FREE TRADE ASSOCIATION (NAFTA) is one example of a regional integration agreement. It includes Canada, the United States, and Mexico.

regional manager   In a large retailing organization, the individual responsible for overseeing the activities of all the stores in a particular geographical part of the country. A regional manager supervises a group of district managers and usually reports to a vice-president or director of stores at the corporate level, although some retail organizations link stores to the corporate office directly through the regional manager. Sometimes called a *territory manager*. The term is used similarly in other types of sales. See also MULTISTORE RETAILER.

regional mart   A central location where manufacturers, importers, and other resources display their merchandise for store buyers and merchandise managers from within that general area of the country (i.e., REGION). The Chicago Merchandise Mart is an example of a regional mart. Also called *regional merchandise mart* or *regional apparel mart*. See also MERCHANDISE MART.

regional merchandise mart   See REGIONAL MART.

regional service provider (RSP)   A large INTERNET SERVICE PROVIDER (ISP) that connects small, local ISPs to the BACKBONE.

regional shopping center   One of the largest types of shopping center, anchored by two or more full line department stores and complemented by 80 to 150 (or more) smaller retail stores and related businesses. A regional shopping center typically contains between 400,000 and 800,000 square feet of retail space and draws customers from a wide geographical area; it requires 150,000 or more customers to support it. Major tenants occupy large, usually corner or end stores and are called anchor stores. Regional shopping centers are usually located outside a major business district, readily accessibly to vehicular traffic by roads. In recent years, many have had to reinvent themselves in light of competition from superregional shopping centers. In some cases, for example, they have removed department stores as anchors, replacing them with category killers, off-price retailers, and full line discounters to create a more value-oriented shopping experience. Also called a *regional center*. See also SUPERREGIONAL (SHOPPING) CENTER and ANCHOR STORE.

regional store   A branch store distinguished by its considerable distance from the downtown or FLAGSHIP STORE/DIVISION. A regional store is frequently managed autonomously and its BUYING is often done independently from that of the parent. The regional store, however, operates under the name of the *parent store*.

regional strategy   A marketing strategy deployed across a number of countries in close proximity. Regional strategies can help achieve critical mass and economies of scale.

regional wholesaler   See SECTIONAL WHOLESALER.

regional wrap   See CENTRAL WRAP.

register   Short for CASH REGISTER.

register audit   See FLOOR AUDIT.

registered mark/trademark   Synonym for TRADEMARK.

register receipt   See RECEIPT.

register tape   The paper tape on which are recorded all sales transactions performed by a CASH REGISTER.

regression analysis   A statistical modeling method used in the social sciences. When used in GEOGRAPHICAL INFORMATION SYSTEMS (GIS), regression analysis helps retailers forecast the potential sales for new and existing stores by including several variables (such as square footage of the store, inventory turnover, and characteristics of the trading area) in their analysis of a specific site. The use of multiple variables is called *multiple regression*; the method helps retailers pinpoint which of the variables are most likely to impact potential sales.

regression stage   See ECONOMIC EMULATION STAGE.

regrouping activities   Synonym for SORTING PROCESS.

regular   See BOYS' SIZES.

regular (charge) account   Synonym for CHARGE ACCOUNT.

regular dating   In the DATING OF INVOICES, an agreement indicating that the cash discount may be deducted if the INVOICE (i.e., bill) is paid within the discount period. Otherwise, the full payment is due at the end of the period indicated. Both the cash discount period and the NET PAYMENT PERIOD are counted from the date of the invoice, which is usually also the date of shipment. For example, if the stated terms are 1/10 net 30, the discount period is 10 days beginning with the date of invoice (DOI) and the end of the credit period is 30 days from the date of invoice (DOI). Also called *ordinary dating* or *ordinary terms*. The discount given is known as a *terms-of-payment discount*.

regularly unsought goods   Products that consumers need regularly but will not extend themselves to find. For example, gravestones, insurance, and encyclopedias are all regularly unsought goods. This class of goods requires extensive promotion. See also NEW UNSOUGHT GOODS/ITEMS and UNSOUGHT GOODS/PRODUCTS.

regular merchandise allowance   See RETURNS AND ALLOWANCES TO CUSTOMERS.

regular order   An order placed by the BUYER directly with the VENDOR. Regular orders give complete specifications regarding time, quantity, and shipment.

regular price   See ORIGINAL PRICE.

regular price advertisement   In RETAIL PRODUCT ADVERTISING, an advertisement featuring merchandise in the introductory stages of the fashion cycle or seasonal or holiday merchandise. These ads attract the fashion leaders and innovators rather than price-conscious bargain shoppers. Regular price ads generally include information about the sizes, colors, prices, and manufacturers of the merchandise. Consumer appeal is based on the product's characteristics and desirability.

regular retail   See RETAIL PRICE.

regular terms   See REGULAR DATING.

regular wholesaler   See FULL-SERVICE WHOLESALER.

regulation   A law or rule designed to control or direct conduct, particularly as prescribed by a government or government agency. Some governments are more intrusive and restrictive than others, an important consideration in both E-COMMERCE and GLOBAL MARKETING.

regulatory change   In international marketing, any moderate and/or predictable modification in the political and regulatory climates of a nation with which a marketer does business. Regulatory changes include a variety of possible government actions such as a change in tax rates, the introduction of price controls, and the revision of labeling requirements. Such changes, while not drastic, can prove costly to international marketers. Companies faced with regulatory change in their host country may adopt any of a number of strategies. They may, for example, try to alter the government's policies, make strategic moves that bypass the impact of the government's action, adjust their operations to comply with government requirements, or seek strategic alliances to avoid some risks of regulatory change. More drastic and dramatic changes are considered POLITICAL RISK.

regulatory environment   See ENVIRONMENTAL REVIEW.

rehabilitation   1. The renovation, remodeling, and modernization of the physical plant (e.g., a store).   2. In an EMPLOYEE ASSISTANCE PROGRAM (EAP) or medical plan, a program to help the employee with physical, mental, or substance abuse problems. The goal is to return the employee to full productivity.

Reilly's Law of Retail Gravitation   A theory concerning the relative pull of two competing shopping areas on the potential customers residing between them. The theory proposes that customers from the intermediate town lying at or close to the POINT OF EQUAL PROBABILITY will be drawn to each area in direct proportion to the populations of the two shopping areas and in inverse proportion to the squares of the distance between the town and the two shopping areas. Also called *Reilly's Law*, *Reilly's Law of Retail Gravity*, and *Reilly's Law of Retail Trade Movement*. See also GRAVITY MODELS.

reinforcement   In the learning process, the presentation of a reward or the satisfaction of a need following a particular response. The reward, or *reinforcer*, reduces the tension of the original drive and strengthens the relationship between the cue and the response. This results in an increase of that behavior, so that a similar response may be given the next time the drive occurs. Repeated reinforcement may lead to the development of a habit, making the decision making process routine for the individual. For example, an individual experiencing thirst (a drive) may encounter a billboard advertising a particular brand of soft drink (a cue) while driving along the highway. If the individual's response is to purchase that brand of soft drink, and if the beverage satisfies the initial drive, reinforcement will occur. In the future, the individual may find it quicker to satisfy the same need with the same soft drink, and may be said to have developed a liking for the product. If, on the other hand, the beverage fails to satisfy the individual's thirst, the experience is unsatisfactory, and the individual may be said to have developed a dislike for the product. See also REINFORCEMENT ADVERTISING.

reinforcement advertising   Advertising assuring purchasers of a product or service that they have made a wise choice and informing them about how to derive the most satisfaction from it.

reinforcer   See REINFORCEMENT.

reinstatement   1. Restoration of a worker to a former position without loss of benefits or seniority.   2. Restoration of a customer's credit account to good standing and active status after it has been suspended, canceled, or relegated to inactive status.

reintermediation   The addition of intermediaries, channel partners, and distribution centers (i.e., the creation of a CHANNEL OF DISTRIBUTION) by a former direct marketer to better meet customer needs. See also DISINTERMEDIATION, its opposite.

REIT   See REAL ESTATE INVESTMENT TRUST (REIT).

rejection   See BRAND REJECTION.

related items advertisement   In RETAIL PRODUCT ADVERTISING, an ad featuring merchandise that may have been purchased for the store by different buyers. For example, the related items ad could feature apparel from the children's division along with back-to-school supplies, which would have been selected by different buyers.

related items display   See RELATED MERCHANDISE DISPLAY.

related merchandise   Items that complement or otherwise go with the item being purchased by the consumer. These items may be separates, accessories, items meant to be used together, items of the same color, or items that share an idea or theme. Also called *companion goods*.

related merchandise display   A visual presentation or promotion showing items that go together, such as accessories and coordinates. The items in the display are presented together because they are meant to be used together, are the same color, or illustrate a common idea or theme. For example, a DISPLAY WINDOW might show all items from one country. Similarly, a color promotion might have all red clothing in one window and all red housewares in another. The items in a related merchandise display reinforce each other and may lead to multiple sales.

related packaging   The coordination of package design and/or coloring for all products of a particular manufacturer or BRAND to promote customer recognition.

relationship marketing   Synonym for DATABASE MARKETING.

relative advantage   In NEW PRODUCT DEVELOPMENT, the degree to which the product is viewed by potential customers as superior to all the products available for sale in the marketplace.

relative loss   Unrealized profit opportunities and unused capacity resulting from a manufacturer's inability to sell goods to a retailer. Also called the *principle of relative loss*.

relative market share   The portion of the total market held by a firm or product as compared to that of a competitor. See also MARKET SHARE.

relevance marketing   The practice of organizing one's retailing practices and policies around benefits for shoppers. It involves evaluating everything one does as a retailer with reference to how it helps shoppers (e.g., greater convenience, better pricing, a shorter wait, improved service, or a fresher product), and changing the way things are done accordingly. Relevance marketing acknowledges the fact that lower prices are not the only consideration in the shopper's selection of (and loyalty to) a retail store.

relevant market In STRATEGIC PLANNING, the market in which to sell one's goods or services that most closely corresponds to the firm's own purposes. The relevant market offers the firm opportunities to attain its objectives given its available resources. The market selected should be bigger than the firm's current market, allowing for expansion, but not so large that the firm would be unable to become a significant competitor in it. For example, a small manufacturer of children's clothing that distributes its goods locally may have the production and marketing capability to expand to a national market, but worldwide distribution may be considerably beyond its grasp.

reliability In MARKETING RESEARCH (MR), reliability is the accuracy with which data portrays reality, particularly when a SAMPLE group is studied in order to make generalizations about a total population. Reliability ensures that results will be consistent across all administrations of the survey or other instrument. Not to be confused with VALIDITY; a *reliable measure* is not necessarily valid. See also SAMPLING and PRODUCT RELIABILITY.

reliable measure See RELIABILITY.

relief cashier A CASHIER who takes the place of regular floor cashiers on a rotating basis while they take their lunch and breaks.

remaindered See REMAINDERS.

remainder liquidator A discounter that takes merchandise from bankruptcies, receiverships, freight claims, and other distress situations to sell at extremely reduced prices. Remainder liquidators may be found operating in both the traditional BRICKS-AND-MORTAR and ONLINE environments.

remainders Goods that are left over and put on sale at reduced prices. The term is often applied to books that have been marked down, but it may be applied to other types of merchandise as well. An item that has been reduced in this fashion is said to have been *remaindered*.

remarketing A MARKETING STRATEGY aimed at reviving demand for a product that has been in a state of decline. For example, space heaters for use in the home were remarketed as the cost of heating oil increased.

remarking 1. Changing the price of an item by marking the new price directly on the price tag. In general, if the new price is lower than the original, both prices remain visible. If a higher price replaces a lower one, the old price is often covered. The FEDERAL TRADE COMMISSION (FTC) requires that both the old price and the new price be accurate. 2. Replacing tickets on merchandise that have been lost or mutilated or removed due to customer returns. New tickets must contain all of the information found on the original for accurate STOCK CONTROL.

remerchandising A strategy to improve the salability of a product while leaving the product itself unchanged. Changes are made instead to the accompanying services (e.g., standardization of product quality, improvement of product service, and the provision of promotional guarantees). PACKAGING may also be modified in design, cost, and size. BRANDING, the broadening of price points, and an increase in the variety of styles offered may also be used to strengthen the MARKET SHARE of the product.

reminder promotion 1. A sales promotion aimed at encouraging consumers to stock up on certain products prior to price increases. 2. Synonym for INSTITUTIONAL ADVERTISING. Also called *retentive advertising*.

remittance Payment. For example, cash, check or money order sent by mail to cover the cost of merchandise ordered by mail or to pay a balance on a credit account. Electronic bill payment has made remittance by credit card a popular form of payment, particularly for items purchased on the INTERNET.

remittance envelope An envelope supplied by the creditor to facilitate the payment of bills. A remittance envelope is often enclosed with the monthly statement and payment coupon. The envelopes may be preprinted with the creditor's address or contain a transparent window through which the creditor's name and address (printed on the payment coupon) are visible.

remnant A small piece of cloth, ribbon, or other PIECE GOODS remaining at the end of a bolt.

remote delivery A delivery strategy that involves shipping goods from a central WAREHOUSE to customers through area delivery stations located in the suburbs.

remote display A display in which products are featured away from the POINT-OF-PURCHASE (POP). It is the physical presentation of merchandise by a retailer or manufacturer placed in a high-traffic location such as a hotel lobby, exhibit hall, or public transportation terminal. Another type of remote display involves a mall retailer that places a merchandise display in a case at the shopping center entrance, away from the store, to encourage customers to visit the store. The remote display can attract attention and create interest, but the customer must still travel to or otherwise contact the store in which the merchandise is sold.

removal sale A reduction in the price of merchandise by a retailer who is relocating. Often storewide and generally intended to reduce inventories as much as possible before the move, the removal sale provides liquid assets to the retailer and reduces the cost of moving large quantities of merchandise.

rent See LEASING AND RENTING.

rented goods service A customer service firm or department of a retail store engaged in renting products for a fee to customers for their temporary use. The rental of rug shampooing equipment by supermarkets is one such service.

reorder A store's request for additional merchandise from a VENDOR to replenish depleted stocks of previously purchased, fast-moving merchandise. It is, therefore, an order for previously ordered goods. Basic goods are more likely to be reordered than fashion goods (which quickly go out of style). Also called a *replenishment order*.

reorder number   A fast-selling item that retailers continually replenish with additional merchandise from the vendor. See also BEST SELLER, FAST MOVER, HOT ITEM, and FAD.

reorder period   The planned spacing of time between orders of a specific item.

reorder planning   The work of monitoring inventory positions, comparing actual sales against merchandise plans, identifying best-selling styles, colors, and sizes, accurately reestimating customer demand, and incorporating these revised estimates into reorders.

reorder point (ROP)   The preestablished minimum INVENTORY level at which additional orders should be placed for a particular item so as to avoid going into a STOCKOUT position. Also known as *threshold-point ordering*. See also REORDER POINT SYSTEM.

reorder point system   A method of STOCK CONTROL by which orders for additional merchandise are automatically placed when the stock reaches a preestablished minimum.

reorder system   Synonym for Q-SYSTEM. See also REORDER.

reorder unit   The minimum quantity of an item that may be reordered (e.g., a dozen or a gross).

reorder window   In fashion merchandising, the time period during which a style may be reordered (usually between the eleventh and the twenty-eighth days of its having been on the selling floor) with a degree of confidence that enough information has been gathered on sales to justify a reorder and that enough time remains in the life of the style to sell additional items without taking excessive markdowns.

rep   Short for SALES REPRESENTATIVE.

repairs   Expenditures for the upkeep of the existing physical plant. Includes the cost of labor and supplies. Does not include capital expenditures that improve and add to the property value of the establishment.

repair supplies   See SUPPLIES.

repeat business   Sales resulting from a customer's return to the store (or Web site, etc.) to purchase additional goods or services. Compare ONE-TIME PURCHASER.

repeat demand   The demand for items that are frequently requested and purchased more than once. See also REPEAT SALE/PURCHASE.

repeated (special) event   A sales promotion featuring the sale of specially priced merchandise, repeated after its initial success. A repeated event generally requires a reorder of the merchandise to replenish stock. Also called a *repeat event*.

repeating technique   See MIRROR RESPONSE TECHNIQUE.

repeat item   See REPEAT SALE/PURCHASE.

repeat purchasing   Additional purchases of the same item or service from the same supplier over a period of time.

repeat sale/purchase   The purchase of additional quantities of an item previously purchased by the same customer at the same retail store. Such items are known as *repeat items*. See also REPEAT DEMAND and SECOND SALE.

repetition   In VISUAL MERCHANDISING, the reiteration of an idea, motif, color, line, shape, or form in a DISPLAY to make the concept more emphatic, more important, and more dominant.

repetitive manufacturing   A form of HARD MANUFACTURING in which the same process is carried out over and over. Repetitive manufacturing is economical only if similar items are produced at a steady rate. Compare FLEXIBLE MANUFACTURING.

replacement branch   A new BRANCH STORE replacing and substituting for an older unit of the same PARENT (COMPANY/ORGANIZATION). In general, the replacement branch is larger than the original and is located in a REGIONAL SHOPPING CENTER.

replacement cost   See REPLACEMENT PRICE.

replacement potential   The sales potential of merchandise, stated in units or dollars, to customers who will require a replacement within a specified period of time.

replacement price   The current market price of an item that must be reordered. This is an important consideration both in setting the retail price and in making the decision to reorder.

replacement rate   The frequency with which merchandise is bought by consumers to replace or replenish merchandise purchased previously. This is particularly relevant for consumables such as food and household products (e.g., laundry detergent). See also REPURCHASE RATE.

replenishment of staple merchandise/stock   See PERIODIC REPLENISHMENT OF STAPLE MERCHANDISE/STOCK.

replenishment order   See REORDER.

repo   (Slang) Short for REPOSSESSION.

reporting service   A fee-based subscription service that surveys and analyzes specific industry segments. For example, the *Tobe Report* is a heavily illustrated fashion report that serves as a guide for apparel retailers hoping to identify the hottest fashion trends and merchandise resources. See also FORECASTING SERVICE.

repositioned product A product that has changed its features, functions, target markets, or marketing strategy. See also REPOSITIONING.

repositioning A MARKETING STRATEGY designed to increase the consumption of an already existing product by changing its TARGET MARKET. For example, the product may be repositioned to appeal to a larger or faster-growing market segment. Brands, too, may require repositioning (i.e., *rebranding*). Shifting customer preferences or the incursion of a competitor into the brand's original market may leave a company's brand with diminished demand and a smaller MARKET SHARE. In order to capture a new target market and increase sales, a company will select a new group of consumers to whom it gears its advertising and other promotional activities. As with the original selection of a target market, the new target group is selected on the basis of the number of potential customers in the group, their average purchase rate of similar products, the quality and quantity of competitors in the segment, and the pricing structure of the brands in the new segment. Also called *product repositioning* or *rebranding*. See also MARKET POSITIONING, BRAND POSITIONING, REPOSITIONED PRODUCT, and TARGET MARKET.

repossession The act of taking merchandise back from a customer who has failed to complete payments when due. The shorter slang term, *repo*, is often used.

repricing 1. The taking of small markdowns to stimulate buying interest early in the season when most customers are still in the market. Timing is important here, since later in the season only drastic price reductions will attract customers. 2. Repricing is also important when the replacement cost of the merchandise increases. In this case, merchandise on the shelves must be marked up to cover the higher replacement costs. See also REPLACEMENT PRICE.

reprint In advertising, a copy of a print advertisement that has been published in a newspaper or magazine, specially made for distribution to customers or resources as a flyer. When distributed prior to publication, it is known as a PREPRINT.

repurchase rate The frequency of repeat sales of a product (i.e., sales to customers who are buying the product for the second or third time or more). See also REPLACEMENT RATE.

request for quotes (RFQ) In the industrial or institutional purchasing process, a request by a company to vendors, asking them to submit specifications and bids to provide a service or product to the company. The traditionally lengthy and labor-intensive process can be expedited by putting the RFQ on an ONLINE EXCHANGE (i.e., an electronic marketplace).

requisition A written request from one department of a company to its purchasing department to release materials to be used in the production process or other activity on a specific date. See also STORE'S REQUISITION, PURCHASE REQUISITION, and RESERVE REQUISITION.

requisition stock control Synonym for RESERVE SYSTEM OF STOCK CONTROL.

requisition system of stock control Synonym for RESERVE SYSTEM OF STOCK CONTROL.

resale The selling of goods or services that have been bought by the seller in essentially the same form as they are being resold. Most retailers and many marketing intermediaries are engaged in resale. See RESELLER MARKET.

Resale Price An agreement that legalized RESALE PRICE MAINTENANCE (RPM) between manufacturers and retailers in 1931. The legislation has since been modified and generally overturned. See also FAIR TRADE ACTS/LAWS.

resale price maintenance (RPM) 1. A trade practice in which manufacturers or suppliers attempt to control the price at which their products will be sold at subsequent steps of distribution. Producers enforce the sale of their products at prescribed *manufacturer's suggested retail price (MSRP)*. Interstate price maintenance agreements, which were most commonly imposed on retailers, have been terminated by the CONSUMER GOODS PRICING ACT (1975). Also known as *fair trade, vertical price fixing,, price maintenance, price setting,* and *retail price maintenance*. The prices achieved in this manner are called *maintained prices*. See also HORIZONTAL PRICE FIXING and MANUFACTURER'S SUGGESTED RETAIL PRICE (MSRP). 2. Legislation enacted by some states to control the minimum price at which specific products (e.g., milk) may be sold at retail. See also FAIR TRADE ACTS/LAWS.

research See DATA, MARKETING RESEARCH (MR), RESEARCH AND DEVELOPMENT (R&D), and RESEARCH DEPARTMENT.

research and development (R&D) The use of a firm's time, energy, money, and other resources to find new knowledge about products, processes, and services (i.e., research) and apply that knowledge to create new and improved products, processes, and services that meet identifiable needs in the marketplace (i.e., development).

research department The department of an ADVERTISING AGENCY responsible for collecting, analyzing, and interpreting data used to develop promotional activities. This information may be gathered through primary research or from secondary sources. Also called the *research division*, particularly in larger, full service agencies. The department is headed by the *research director*.

research design The formal model or plan for the conduct of a research study. The research design usually states the hypothesis to be tested, the research method to be employed, and the manner in which the collected data is to be analyzed. Also called *project design*.

research director See RESEARCH DEPARTMENT.

research division See RESEARCH DEPARTMENT.

reseller See MARKETING INTERMEDIARY and RESALE.

reseller brand See PRIVATE BRAND.

reseller market Those marketing intermediaries (e.g., wholesalers, distributors, and retailers) who buy finished goods for the purpose of reselling them. Resellers generally do not significantly alter the goods they sell nor incorporate them into other products. Also called *selling intermediaries*.

reserve See RESERVE STOCK.

reserve bank Synonym for CASH REGISTER BANK.

reserve price auction See ONLINE AUCTION.

reserve requisition A written request that merchandise located in a reserve or warehouse area be brought forward to the selling floor.

reserve requisition control Synonym for RESERVE SYSTEM OF STOCK CONTROL.

reserves Short for RESERVE STOCK.

reserve stock A supply of merchandise kept on hand to act as a cushion against the possibility of a STOCKOUT due to unexpectedly high demand or delivery delays. The reserve stock is calculated according to a formula involving rate of sale and lead time. Synonymous with *backup stock, backup merchandise, buffer stock, buffer inventory, coverage, cushion, reserves,* and *safety stock*. See also RESERVE SYSTEM OF STOCK CONTROL.

reserve stock control Synonym for RESERVE SYSTEM OF STOCK CONTROL.

reserve system of stock control A system of UNIT (INVENTORY) CONTROL that focuses on the stock in the reserve stockroom rather than on the selling floor. Records are kept of all goods received from vendors. The reserve stock is determined by subtracting all goods sent to the selling floor (as though they were already sold) and adding new goods received from vendors. An actual count is not performed. Also called *requisition stock control, requisition system of stock control, reserve requisition control,* and *reserve stock control*. See also STOCK CONTROL.

resident buyer A market representative employed in a RESIDENT BUYING OFFICE, which acts in turn as an agent for its clients or member stores. The resident buyer is often a specialist, buying in a particular segment of the market. Resident buyers inform client stores about market conditions such as fashion trends, new resources, hot items, opportunistic buys, and promotional opportunities. Their expertise derives from their market contacts and the information they receive from vendors, member stores, mills, research firms, designers, and the trade media. Once the merchandise has been purchased, the resident buyer, unlike the store buyer, has no further merchandising responsibilities (i.e., the resident buyer does not have to resell the merchandise as does the retailer). Also called *market specialist, market rep,* or *market representative*. See also RESIDENT BUYING OFFICE.

resident buying office An office made up of buyers in national or international market centers who daily shop the market in order to gather information for their clients or member stores and select and buy merchandise for them. The resident buying office serves as a marketing and research consulting firm to its member or client stores, providing market information (e.g., forecasts, consumer behavior studies, information about emerging trends), merchandising guidance, and other services including product development and importing. Some buying offices specialize in certain categories of merchandise or types of stores. The member stores are often similar in terms of merchandise mix, size, and retailing format. A resident buying office may be independent (SALARIED [BUYING] OFFICE or COMMISSION BUYING OFFICE) or company-owned (PRIVATE BUYING OFFICE, ASSOCIATED BUYING OFFICE, or CORPORATE BUYING OFFICE). Frequently referred to simply as a *buying office*. See also INDEPENDENT BUYING OFFICE and COMPANY-OWNED BUYING OFFICE.

resident salesperson A vendor's salesperson, located within the structure of one of the vendor's primary customers. The resident salesperson devotes full attention to the customer's needs.

resort apparel/wear Synonym for CRUISEWEAR.

resource A VENDOR from whom salable and reliable goods are purchased on a recurring basis over an extended period of time. Also called KEY RESOURCE, SOURCE, *merchandise resource, outside merchandise source,* or *merchandise source*.

resource analysis The ongoing evaluation of vendors to determine those from whom the store should continue to buy merchandise. Such factors as product line, reliability, delivery time, etc., are taken into account by means of the RESOURCE DIARY and the RESOURCE FILE. See also VENDOR ANALYSIS FORM.

resource diary A record kept by buyers to use in the evaluation of vendors. The resource diary is traditionally a compact book, usually loose-leaf, that lists the essential features of each VENDOR (e.g., type of merchandise sold, location, contact people, importance to the store, terms of past purchases). It is generally carried by the BUYER on trips to the MARKET. Each vendor's record can be easily examined for any number of purposes. In recent years, electronic devices have replaced the loose-leaf notebook, but the data collected about each vendor remains largely the same. See also RESOURCE FILE, VENDOR ANALYSIS FORM, and PRINCIPAL RESOURCE LIST.

resource file A compilation of facts relating to each VENDOR with whom the store has done business. Facts include the performance of goods, delivery record, condition of goods, etc. Also called a *personal trade file*.

resource list See PRINCIPAL RESOURCE LIST.

resource rating The statistical measurement and evaluation of vendors with whom the store has done business to determine each vendor's contribution to the store's sales volume and profits. See also RESOURCE ANALYSIS.

resources See TANGIBLE RESOURCES and INTANGIBLE RESOURCES. Distinguished from RESOURCE.

response   1. In communications, the reaction on the part of the receiver of a message.   2. In consumer behavior, the individual's reaction to environmental cues.

response function   A mathematical or graphic representation of ways in which a firm's TARGET MARKET is expected to react to changes in particular MARKETING FUNCTIONS. The response function is usually plotted as a curve, showing how sales and profits will vary with different levels of marketing expenditure, changes in price, changes in promotional mix, changes in the level of quality, etc. A response function may be plotted for each of the FOUR PS OF THE MARKETING MIX, or for the MARKETING MIX as a whole. The response functions for each of the four Ps of marketing are the PLACE-DISTRIBUTION INTENSITY RESPONSE FUNCTION, PRICE-DEMAND RESPONSE FUNCTION, PRODUCT QUALITY RESPONSE FUNCTION, and PROMOTION-ADVERTISING RESPONSE FUNCTION.

response rate   See RATE OF RESPONSE.

responsibility   Any aspect of the job to be done by an individual, referred to in the measurement of the individual's performance. The responsibilities of any given job are generally defined in the JOB DESCRIPTION, as is the degree of power or authority associated with that position.

restraint of trade   An act or agreement calculated to limit the free exercise of commercial COMPETITION. Restraint of trade often takes the form of monopolies, attempts by one or more parties to control prices or levels of production, or other limits on free trade to the detriment of the public. There are, however, some exceptions. For example, see COVENANT NOT TO COMPETE.

restricted articles   In shipping, merchandise handled only under specified conditions. Munitions, explosives, fireworks, flares, and compressed air canisters are restricted articles on airplanes. Similarly, certain classes of plants and animals are often considered restricted articles at border crossings.

restrictive lease   A limiting section in a store's lease, particularly employed in shopping centers, that seeks to control the type of merchandise to be carried, discounting, hours and days the store is open, employee parking, etc.

results monitoring   See MONITORING RESULTS.

résumé   An individual's employment history, reflecting the individual's organizational and communication skills as well as his or her education and prior experience. Résumés are used in the employment process to help employers determine which individuals to call in for interviews. A résumé may be *chronological* (i.e., showing past experiences in order, beginning with the individual's current position) or *functional* (i.e., stressing competencies and experiences gained on the job without reference to a timeline).

retail   1. The sale of merchandise in small quantities to the ultimate consumer. See also RETAILING and RETAIL TRADE.   2. Sometimes, short for RETAIL PRICE.

retail accordion theory   A theory that attempts to describe the evolution of retail institutions from general, broad-based outlets with wide assortments to narrow-based institutions carrying specialized assortments, and back to general, broad-based assortments. Also called the *general-specific-general theory*. However, some retailing businesses evolve over a *specific-general-specific cycle*.

retail accounting   See RETAIL METHOD OF ACCOUNTING.

retail advertising   ADVERTISING specifically directed to the ultimate consumer by retailers. It differs from national and trade advertising in several ways: it is trading-area specific; it is directed at distinct target markets; it arouses more immediate reader interest; it has a set of immediate response expectations, particularly that the customer will come in to the store and make a purchase; and price, used to generate the immediate response, is often a key element in the advertisement. Since much retail advertising is targeted by stores to customers in their immediate vicinity, it is often called LOCAL ADVERTISING.

retail assembly line   A conveyor belt system used in retail mail order companies to assemble customer orders. As merchandise is taken from stock, it is put on conveyor belts and moved to a central location for shipping.

retail audit   A periodic, systematic evaluation of a retail organization for the purposes of determining the organization's strengths and weaknesses, examining its objectives, and improving its overall performance. Sometimes called a *retail market audit*.

retail brand   See PRIVATE BRAND.

retail buyer   See BUYER.

retail calendar   A planning calendar used by retailers that divides the year into four thirteen-week quarters. Each week and month begins with a Sunday and ends with a Saturday. Also called a *four-five-four (4-5-4) calendar*, since the first and last "months" in each quarter contain four weeks and the middle "month" contains five weeks. A retail calendar begins the year at the end of January or the beginning of February. This standardization enables retailers to plan sales by reference to past sales for equal periods of time. Also called a SCHEDULE.

retail catalog showroom   See CATALOG SHOWROOM.

retail chain   See CHAIN STORE and CHAIN STORE SYSTEM (CSS).

retail conglomerate   Synonym for MERCHANDISING CONGLOMERATE.

retail cooperative/co-op   A voluntary association of independent retailers who jointly own and operate their own wholesale facilities and/or act together as a buying club in order to achieve the economies of large-scale purchasing. The member stores often display a common emblem or logo and carry, in addition to nationally recognized brands, their own distributor brands. Also referred to as *retail cooperative chain, retailer cooperative, retailer-owned cooperative, retailers' cooperative chain, retailing cooperative, cooperative group, cooperative wholesaler, retail store cooperative, affiliated cooperative, semi-integrated organization,* and *retailer-sponsored cooperative.* See also MERCHANDISING GROUP.

retail credit card Synonym for CHARGE CARD.

retail deal A temporary special offering of merchandise at retail, either in the form of a price reduction or as multiple units at a special price.

retail display See DISPLAY.

retail display allowance (RDA) A price reduction given by the manufacturer to the retailer in exchange for a more favorable display of the manufacturer's merchandise in the store or on the shelf.

retail distribution center See DISTRIBUTION CENTER.

retail environment See ENVIRONMENT.

retailer A merchant intermediary (either an individual or a firm) engaged in selling goods or services to the ultimate consumer. The term is sometimes restricted to enterprises that generate at least one half of their total income from such sales. Some manufacturers and wholesalers are now considered retailers because they realize more than 50 percent of their sales at retail. There are eight major classifications of retailers as defined by the NATIONAL RETAIL FEDERATION (NRF). They are: food stores; general merchandise stores; apparel and accessories stores; building materials and gardening supplies stores; furniture and home furnishings stores; automotive dealers and service stations; eating and drinking places; and miscellaneous retailers such as drug stores, gift shops, bookstores, catalog retailers, etc. A retailer may operate in a traditional BRICKS-AND-MORTAR environment or in the electronic, BRICKS-AND-CLICKS, and nonstore (e.g., CLICKS-ONLY) environments. Also called a *store retailer* (particularly the bricks-and-mortar establishments).

retailer brand See PRIVATE BRAND.

retailer cooperative See RETAIL COOPERATIVE/CO-OP.

retailer-owned cooperative See RETAIL COOPERATIVE/CO-OP.

retailers' cooperative chain See RETAIL COOPERATIVE/CO-OP.

retailer-sponsored cooperative See RETAIL COOPERATIVE/CO-OP.

retailer (sponsored) coupon A coupon emanating from a retailer and redeemable only in the issuing store. Retailer coupons are often used to entice customers to the store during busy selling seasons (e.g., between Thanksgiving and Christmas). Catalog retailers and e-tailers use coupons as direct-response media to stimulate buyers who have not made a recent purchase and to generate repeat sales from proven customers. Also called *store coupon* and *store-redeemable coupon.*

retail establishment Synonym for RETAIL STORE.

retail fashion cycle See FASHION LIFE CYCLE.

retail fashion theme calendar See FASHION CALENDAR.

retail format Any of the various instances or methods of selling at retail. Each type of store (e.g., department store, discount department store, outlet center, specialty store, supermarket, superstore) is a retail format, as are catalog retailing, direct marketing, e-tailing, etc.

retail fragmentation The breakdown of traditional delivery systems (i.e., channels of distribution) for various classes of products. For example, the food channel has been eroded and fragmented by mass merchandisers and super-centers that have successfully lured consumers from the traditional supermarket. Conversely, the drug channel has experienced success by positioning itself as a convenience store for one-stop shopping. Time-pressed and cash-strapped consumers see these formats as viable alternatives to grocery stores and supermarkets.

retail franchise A contractual agreement between a franchiser (a manufacturer, wholesaler, or service company) and a retailer that allows the retailer to become a franchisee and conduct a retail business under the established name of the franchiser. The franchisee agrees to follow a specific set of rules.

retail gravitation See REILLY'S LAW OF RETAIL GRAVITATION.

retail holding company A huge conglomerate composed of many individual companies doing business under a variety of names. Retailing may or may not be the primary focus of the retail holding company. See also HOLDING COMPANY.

Retail Horizons An annual NRF study and survey of retailers to define retail trends and industry statistics. Designed to be the definitive source of benchmarking information and in-depth analysis for retailers, the study contains statistically significant data regarding store operations, supply chain management, merchandising, advertising and marketing, customer insight and focus, online sales, information technology, and human resources. Supersedes, at least in part, the MERCHANDISING AND OPERATING RESULTS OF DEPARTMENT AND SPECIALTY STORES (MOR) and the FINANCIAL OPERATING RESULTS OF DEPARTMENT AND SPECIALTY STORES (FOR).

retail hub A center of retail activity where many stores are located. Also called, simply, a *hub.*

retail image Synonym for STORE IMAGE.

retailing The business activity concerned primarily with selling goods and/or services to the ultimate consumer. Retailing includes buying goods from vendors, assembling them in a convenient location, making them available to the consumer, and other related activities. It is the final step in the marketing process. See also RETAIL and RETAIL TRADE.

retailing concept   A retailer's overall idea of the characteristics and needs of its customers, the most appropriate method of maximizing efficiency in the store, and the most effective way to generate sales and realize acceptable profits. See also RETAIL STRATEGY and RETAILING MIX.

retailing cooperative/co-op   See RETAIL COOPERATIVE/CO-OP.

retailing cost   See COSTS.

retailing cycle   Synonym for RETAIL LIFE CYCLE.

retailing function   The act of selling to the ultimate consumer, regardless of who performs it. Although largely performed by conventional retailers, the retailing function may be carried out by producers (as in the case of fruit and vegetables sold at roadside stands, or manufacturers' door-to-door sales of aluminum siding), wholesalers (providing a variety of service and repair functions), or Internet marketers.

Retailing Hall of Fame   An institution founded in 2005 honoring executives who have made significant contributions to the retailing industry. Its stated mission is to "honor the living legends and remembered icons who, by their deeds as company founders, CEOs, presidents, and contributors, personify the many great contributions the retailing industry has made to our way of life."

retailing mix   A retail store's particular combination of controllable variables that give it its distinct image and position in the marketplace. These variables include product assortment, price, advertising and promotion, place (i.e., location), operating policy (i.e., hours of operation), buying, human resources, service, etc. Also called a *retail strategy mix, retailing strategy mix, trade marketing mix,* or *retail store strategy mix.* See also RETAILING CONCEPT and RETAIL STRATEGY.

retailing strategy   Synonym for RETAIL STRATEGY.

retailing strategy mix   Synonym for RETAILING MIX.

retailing the invoice   1. The practice of putting the unit selling price at retail on the vendor's INVOICE as an authorization for the marker to proceed in marking the goods when received. Also called *preretailing.* See also MARKING AND TICKETING.   2. A means of ascertaining the total retail value of goods received from vendors for use in the RETAIL METHOD OF ACCOUNTING.

retail installment credit account   Synonym for REVOLVING CREDIT.

retail institution   Synonym for RETAIL STORE.

retail institutional advertising   INSTITUTIONAL ADVERTISING undertaken by the retail store or organization. The advertisements work to create an image for the firm and show the customer what the firm stands for in terms of fashion merchandising leadership, community social responsibility, and store services.

retail inventory method   See RETAIL METHOD OF INVENTORY.

retail life cycle   A theory that attempts to describe the evolution of a retail store from its inception to its decline. The theory maintains that a retail establishment passes through four identifiable stages: the INNOVATION STAGE, the ACCELERATED DEVELOPMENT STAGE, the MATURITY STAGE, and the DECLINE STAGE. In the innovation stage, the store (or other retail format) is new and must be introduced to customers in the hope that it will attract a following. If the store or concept catches on, it enters a period of rapid growth (i.e., accelerated development) in which other retailers imitate or adopt the store's concept and seek to attract the same target customers. The store itself may experience rapid growth in sales and popularity. As competitors enter the market by using the same or similar strategies, the market eventually approaches SATURATION and, as growth slows, the store enters the maturity stage. Once growth has significantly decreased or even ceased, the store is in the decline stage. This process is comparable to the PRODUCT LIFE CYCLE (PLC). Also called the *retailing cycle.*

retail market   A store's TRADING AREA (i.e., a geographical entity containing potential customers).

retail market audit   See RETAIL AUDIT.

retail marketing   The setting of sales goals on the basis of market potential, with increased attention to the behavior of the consumer. While RETAIL MERCHANDISING has lines and departments in focus (i.e., what is selling), retail marketing is more concerned with who is buying what and the underlying reasons for this behavior.

retail marketing research   The application of the principles of MARKETING RESEARCH (MR) to the formulation of a RETAIL STRATEGY for the sale of goods or services to the ultimate consumer. Information is gathered to facilitate the decision making process as it relates to marketing products and services at the retail level. Also called *retail market research.*

retail merchandise management system (RMM)   A computer system used by retailers to track the performance of merchandise. RMM enables retailers to effect timely reordering of merchandise that is selling well. See also ORDER.

retail merchandising   The principles of merchandising as applied to the sale of goods to the ultimate consumer. Compare RETAIL MARKETING. See also MERCHANDISING and RETAIL MIX.

retail method of accounting   An accounting system in which all percentages relate to the retail price of the goods. For example, if an article purchased for $2 is sold for $4, the margin is $2, which is 50% of the retail price. Compare COST METHOD OF ACCOUNTING.

retail method of inventory (valuation)   A method of computing the ending retail inventory based on the COST-TO-RETAIL RATIO after markup (and markup cancellations) but before markdowns. It is designed to approximate the lower of average cost or market. Also called the *lower cost or market* *approach* to inventory valuation, it reflects an average cost of the items in inventory without considering the loss on any of the items. If markdowns are not considered, the result is the *lower of cost or market method.* For example, consider two items purchased for $5 apiece (for a total of $10) and for which the original sales price was set at $10 each (for a total of $20). One item was subsequently marked down to $2. Assuming no sales for the period, if markdowns are not considered, the result is the lower of cost or market. Using the retail method of inventory, the COST-TO-RETAIL RATIO would be $10 (cost of the two items) divided by $20 (original retail price of the two items) = 50%. The ending inventory at cost would be $12 ($10.00 + $2.00) × .50 (i.e., 50%) = $6. Also called the *retail inventory method* and the *retail method of inventory valuation.* Compare COST METHOD OF INVENTORY.

retail mix The many activities in which retailers engage as they attempt to attract customers to the store and satisfy their needs. The retail mix includes the physical facilities, planning, merchandising, pricing, promoting, distributing, etc. See also RETAIL MERCHANDISING.

retail organization 1. The arrangement and interrelationship of tasks within a store. 2. The interrelationship between the units of a multiunit retail operation (e.g., a parent store and its branches). 3. A company involved in retailing. See also RETAIL STORE.

retail outlet A RETAIL STORE that sells directly to the customer. See also FACTORY OUTLET.

retail personality Synonym for STORE IMAGE.

retail polarity See POLARITY OF RETAIL TRADE.

retail policy In retailing, a plan, course of action, or method of doing business. A retail policy helps to define procedures and objectives for the store's employees and promotes consistency. For example, most retailers have a RETURN POLICY.

retail presentation See LINE PRESENTATION.

retail price The price paid for merchandise by the ultimate CONSUMER. Inherent in the retail price are the costs associated with assembling a selection of products in a variety of fabrications, styles, colors, brands, and prices at a single location. A retail price also covers the cost of amenities, such as attractive facilities, salesperson assistance, and payment options that may include a store charge account, personal checks, or third-party charges (e.g., Visa and MasterCard). The retail price consists, therefore, of the cost of the item to the retailer plus the MARKUP. See also SALES AT RETAIL.

retail price index See CONSUMER PRICE INDEX (CPI).

retail price maintenance See RESALE PRICE MAINTENANCE (RPM).

retail product advertising Advertising for consumer merchandise sponsored by a retailer. Retail stores typically spend most of their advertising budget on the merchandise currently available for sale. Retail advertising may be categorized by the CONDITIONS OF SALE (e.g., regular price, special price, clearance, or Internet/mail order only) or by merchandise category (e.g., single-item, assortment, related items, departmental, or volume advertisements). See also PRODUCT ADVERTISING.

retail promotion A store's advertising, visual merchandising (display), public relations (including publicity), and special events, as well as the selling efforts of the store's salespeople. Stores engage in retail promotion to sell both products and their institutional image to the ultimate consumer. For example, a retail promotion may include a Sunday newspaper advertisement featuring a particular line of products available at the store. In large department stores there is usually a separate division or department for promotion.

retail promotional strategy See PROMOTIONAL STRATEGY.

retail reduction The total of all factors that contribute to the diminished retail value of a store's inventory. These factors include markdowns, employee and other discounts, and stock shortages. Retail reduction is expressed as the difference between the original retail value of the merchandise and net sales. Also called *reduction, reduction from retail, total retail reduction,* or *reductions from retail.* See also MARKDOWN (MD) and PLANNED REDUCTION.

retail sale The sale of merchandise to the ultimate consumer.

retail sales See SALES AT RETAIL.

retail salesperson An employee of a RETAIL STORE who works inside the store assisting customers with their selections and purchases. See also SALESPERSON.

retail saturation See SATURATED AREA and INDEX OF (RETAIL) SATURATION (IRS).

retail security The prevention and detection of merchandise and monetary shortages due to internal and external theft. Retail security measures may include guards, surveillance cameras, and other detection devices in the selling and nonselling areas of the store. See also ELECTRONIC ARTICLE SURVEILLANCE (EAS).

retail selling The process of changing ownership of merchandise from the retailer to the ultimate customer. Retail selling also includes the process of persuading prospective customers to buy specific merchandise by determining the customer's needs and making a sales presentation. See also SELLING.

retail show A FASHION SHOW sponsored by a retailer and directed toward the retail staff and consumer market. Retail shows include the IN-STORE SHOW, the CONSUMER SHOW/FASHION SHOW, the COMMUNITY SHOW, the CHARITY SHOW, and the PRESS SHOW.

retail site location The art and science of selecting the appropriate locale for a store. Factors to be considered include accessibility, nearby stores, demographics and psychographics of potential customers in the surrounding area, degree of urbanization, etc. Retail site location decisions are based on data gathered from government and private research sources, observation, and prior experience. Also called *site location*. See also CORE BASED STATISTICAL AREA (CBSA), GEODEMOGRAPHY, TRADING AREA, and GEOGRAPHICAL INFORMATION SYSTEMS (GIS).

retail space   See SELLING AREA.

retail sponsored cooperative   See RETAIL COOPERATIVE/ CO-OP.

retail store   A business that regularly offers goods for sale to the ultimate consumer. A retail store buys, stores, promotes, and sells merchandise. Also called a *retail establishment, retail institution,* or *retail organization.*

retail store cooperative   See RETAIL COOPERATIVE/CO-OP.

retail store strategy mix   See RETAILING MIX.

retail strategy   The philosophy, objectives, activities, and control mechanisms used by a retailer in an overall plan to attract customers, sell merchandise, and maximize profits. Also called a *retailing strategy*. See also STRATEGY, RETAILING MIX, and RETAILING CONCEPT.

retail strategy mix   Synonym for RETAILING MIX.

retailtainment   In-store entertainment provided by store employees, consisting of product demonstrations and similar activities. These activities are typical of the HYPERMARKET.

retail trade   As defined in the U.S. *Standard Industrial Classification Manual* (major groups 52–29 in that manual), trade that includes establishments engaged in the sale of merchandise for personal or household consumption and in the rendering of services that are incidental to the sale of the merchandise. Retail establishments usually operate at fixed places of business, buy or receive and sell merchandise, engage in activities to attract the general public to buy, and, sometimes, process their products (but such processing is incidental or subordinate to selling). See also RETAIL and RETAILING.

retail trading area   See TRADING AREA.

retail transaction   A sale made to an ultimate consumer. Such sales are retail transactions regardless of how the seller describes itself. For example, a WHOLESALER making sales to the ultimate consumer is engaged in a retail transaction.

retail unit   The quantity of merchandise in a package sold by a retailer to the ultimate consumer.

Retail Virus Control Center   A NATIONAL RETAIL FEDERATION (NRF) clearinghouse for information about computer viruses affecting general merchandise retailing. The Center records and reports viruses affecting retail communications networks and collects and distributes information about products and methods that can be used to ward off or recover from the effects of a virus.

Retail, Wholesale and Department Store Union (RWDSU)   A union of employees in the retail, wholesale, and department stores industries. Founded in 1937 and headquartered in New York City, RWDSU absorbed the *Cigar Makers' International Union of America* in 1974.

retained earnings   That portion of a corporation's net income not distributed to shareholders in the form of dividends. See also CORPORATION.

retenanting   Finding new retail tenants to replace those that have gone out of business or vacated their space at the SHOPPING CENTER or MALL. Retenanting, at its best, is sensitive to changes in trading area demographics.

retention cycle   The period for which an inactive credit customer's record is retained.

retentive advertising   See REMINDER PROMOTION.

retort pouch   A hermetically sealed package for food, consisting of aluminum and plastic laminated layers. It eliminates the need for refrigeration or special care.

retrieval requests   Synonym for CHARGEBACK.

retrofitting   The addition of architectural or construction elements to the original store structure. For example, dividers may be added to a store to break up wall space.

return   See RETURNS or RETURN ON INVESTMENT (ROI).

return activity report   A computerized record of customer returns and exchanges, used by retailers to help limit RETURN FRAUD. See also RETURN EXCHANGE.

Return Exchange   A service organization designed to apprise retailers of possible fraudulent customer returns. The service consists of a database of return activity reports. The organization looks for fraud or abusive behaviors in product returns, based on the frequency of return, the length of time, and the amount of dollars spent.

return fraud   The practice of returning stolen merchandise for cash or store credit. This fraudulent practice has led retailers to restrict the number of returns any customer may make during a given time period, particularly after the Christmas holidays. Return fraud also leads to higher prices as retailers try to cover their losses. The accounts of repeat returners are flagged so that subsequent returns may require the manager's signature. The customer may also be placed on *return probation* or BLACKLISTED and not allowed to return merchandise for a specified period of time. See also RETURN EXCHANGE.

return on assets (ROA)   Synonym for RETURN ON INVESTMENT (ROI).

return on investment (ROI) A measure of the profitability of a business that compares the net profit to the amount of money needed to generate that profit, that is, to operate the business. Also called *return on assets (ROA)*. See also PROFIT MAXIMIZATION OBJECTIVE and TARGET RETURN ON INVESTMENT (ROI).

return on investment (ROI) approach to advertising A method of setting a store's advertising budget by considering advertising as a capital investment rather than a current expense. The profit generated by the advertising is compared to the amount of money needed to advertise. See also PROMOTIONAL BUDGETING.

return on investment price A selling price that will generate a predetermined margin of profit representing a desired RETURN ON INVESTMENT (ROI).

return per square foot The dollar amount of sales contributed by a square foot of selling space within a department. It is calculated by dividing the total sales for a department by the number of square feet of selling space occupied by that department.

return policy The rules governing the return of merchandise by customers in a particular store. The return policy may include or exclude exchange, credit, cash refunds, and adjustments. See also STORE CREDIT and RETURNS AND ALLOWANCES TO CUSTOMERS.

return privilege A SELLING AID provided as a service by a vendor to its client stores. The vendor agrees to take back the merchandise if it is not sold within a specified period of time. In this case, the RISK of markdown is carried by the vendor. Unlike CONSIGNMENT selling, selling with return privilege signifies that the title passes to the store buyer when the goods are shipped. However, the vendor contractually agrees to take back the unsold portion of the stock within a specified time period.

return probation See RETURN FRAUD.

return room A section of the store reserved for the inspection of damaged and unacceptable merchandise before it is returned to the vendor.

returns 1. Purchases the customer brings back to the store because of some dissatisfaction. The customer may exchange the merchandise, receive a cash refund, or accept a credit to a charge account. See also RETURNS AND ALLOWANCES TO CUSTOMERS. 2. Merchandise sent back to the vendor by a retailer because of defects in manufacture, shipment of incorrect merchandise, delivery delay, etc. Also called RETURNS TO VENDOR (RTV). See also RETURNS AND ALLOWANCES FROM SUPPLIERS.

returns and allowances from suppliers The total value of purchased goods shipped back to the vendor (returns) and unplanned reductions in the purchase price (allowances). Each represents a reduction in the cost of the total purchases. Also called *purchase returns and allowances, vendor allowance,* and *allowance from vendor.* See also RETURNS.

returns and allowances to customers The dollar value of goods returned to the store by customers (returns) plus price reductions made to customers (allowances), deducted from gross sales to arrive at net sales. Also called *allowance to customers* and *sales, returns, and allowances.* See also RETURNS.

returns from customers See RETURNS AND ALLOWANCES TO CUSTOMERS.

returns to vendor (RTV) 1. Goods shipped back to a supplier by a store. RTVs may result from errors in filling the order, unacceptable substitutions, late delivery, defective merchandise, or other breaches of contract. RTVs are chargebacks to vendors for merchandise returned for credit. Also called, simply, *returns.* 2. The dollar value of such returns and the resulting unplanned reduction in the cost of the purchase. See RETURNS (def. 1), VENDOR CHARGEBACKS, and RETURNS AND ALLOWANCES FROM SUPPLIERS.

return to stock A transaction authorizing merchandise returned by a customer to be placed back on the selling floor and the item and dollar amount to be added once again to the INVENTORY.

reusable packaging Containers for merchandise, such as canisters, that are of subsequent use to consumers once the original product has been consumed.

revaluation An increase, undertaken by a nation's government, in the value of its currency in relation to other currencies or to gold (i.e., its currency's EXCHANGE RATE). A revaluation is designed to bring a nation's currency more into line with other currencies so as to facilitate international trade. See also DEVALUATION.

revenue 1. The total income derived from the sale of a firm's products or services, together with earnings derived from interest, rents, etc. See also SALES REVENUE and TOTAL REVENUE. 2. The gross intake of a unit of government from such sources as taxes, duties, fines, etc.

revenue-and-expense budget See OPERATIONS BUDGET.

revenue and service (RS) A measure of performance in the apparel retailing industry, introduced by Lin in 1996. The RS factor is influenced primarily by reduced percent of total stockouts. Such reductions in stockouts lead, in turn, to decreases in percent of lost sales and increases in both GROSS MARGIN and TOTAL REVENUE. Reduced stockouts means that more customers are getting the merchandise they want. Revenues increase because of an improved in-stock position. Based on the RS measure, the fewer the stockouts, the higher the revenues. See also STOCKOUT.

revenue center Any area of the store from which particular income or yield can be said to derive.

revenue-oriented audit An evaluation of a MARKETING PLAN in terms of its ability to generate sales of the product. See also MARKETING AUDIT.

revenue tariff   A TARIFF designed to raise money for the importing country rather than one intended to protect domestic industry. Compare PROTECTIVE TARIFF.

reverse auctions   See ONLINE AUCTION.

reverse distribution   Synonym for BACKWARD CHANNEL.

review   Short for MERCHANT REVIEW. See also PERFORMANCE APPRAISAL and PERFORMANCE REVIEW.

review audit   An examination and evaluation of the final results of a MARKETING PLAN. See also MARKETING AUDIT.

review period   The time between a retail buyer's decision to place an order and the actual placement of the order. During this period, the order may be scrutinized by others in the organization. See also BUYING PERIOD.

revision of retail downward   See ADDITIONAL MARKUP CANCELLATION.

revolving charge account   SEE REVOLVING CREDIT.

revolving credit   A regular 30-day charge account that may be paid in full or in monthly installments. If paid in full within 30 days of the date of the statement, there is no finance charge. When installment payments are made, a finance charge, equal to a given percentage of the amount outstanding, is added to the balance at the time of the next billing. The customer may continue to add new purchases to the account until the credit limit is reached. Also called a *flexible charge account, all-purpose revolving account, all-purpose revolving credit, retail installment credit account,* or (less frequently) *option account, option-credit account, option terms, optional account, perpetual budget account (PBA)* or *optional charge account.* See also INSTALLMENT PLAN/CONTRACT/BUYING and CHARGE ACCOUNT.

rewrap   1. v. To enclose merchandise in new or different packaging.   2. n. New packaging, or the provision of new packaging, for merchandise in the event of damage to the original container.

RF   See RECENCY/FREQUENCY (RF).

RFID   See RADIO FREQUENCY IDENTIFICATION (RFID).

RFM   See RECENCY/FREQUENCY/MONETARY VALUE (RFM).

RFQ   See REQUEST FOR QUOTES (RFQ).

rhythm   In VISUAL MERCHANDISING, the self-contained movement or flow from element to element, from background to foreground, and from side to side in a DISPLAY. The rhythm leads the viewer's eye from the dominant object to the subordinate object (or objects) in the display, and from the major presentation of an ensemble down to the arrangement of accessories, etc.

ribbon development   A strip of retail establishments strung out along a major highway, typically containing furniture and appliance stores, fast food restaurants, automobile service establishments, gas stations, etc.

rich site summary (RSS)   See RSS.

rich text format (RTF)   A standard for specifying the formatting of documents. RTF files are actually ASCII files with special commands to indicate formatting information such as fonts and margins. Other document formatting languages include HYPERTEXT MARKUP LANGUAGE (HTML), which is used for documents on the WORLD WIDE WEB, and STANDARD GENERALIZED MARKUP LANGUAGE (SGML).

rider   Synonym for INVOICE APRON.

rifle approach   1. A technique of personal selling that focuses on a few items of greatest interest to a prospective customer, involves the customer in the buying process, and leads persuasively to a rapid buying decision. Also called the *rifle technique.* Compare SHOTGUN APPROACH/TECHNIQUE.   2. A marketing program directed at a highly specific group of target customers.

rigged suit form   Traditionally, a three-dimensional *suit form* that was dressed and pinned to perfection so that there were no wrinkles or creases. The arms usually extended straight down and the shirtsleeve was neatly positioned to peek out. More recently, some suit forms are rigged in a more casual, relaxed manner.

right of rescission   As guaranteed by the CONSUMER CREDIT PROTECTION ACT (1968), the right to cancel a contract without penalty within three business days under certain circumstances. A full refund is made to the customer.

rights of consumers   See CONSUMER BILL OF RIGHTS (1962).

right-to-work laws   State legislation giving employees the explicit right to keep a job without joining a union. Twenty-one states, predominantly in the South and the West, have right-to-work laws in place.

rigid demand   See RIGIDITY OF DEMAND.

rigidity of demand   The degree to which customers are willing or unwilling to accept a substitute for the desired product. The factor on which the customer is unwilling to compromise may be size, color, style, price, materials, brand name, etc. Also called *demand rigidity* or *rigid demand.*

rigid-limit plan   A form of REVOLVING CREDIT in which the customer's credit maximum is determined by the amount of the fixed monthly payment.

rigid pricing   See ONE-PRICE POLICY.

ring analysis   A method of determining a TRADING AREA using an existing or potential retail site as the locus. Analysts study the area using one-, three-, and five-mile radius rings to determine customer potential. Often combined with studies of customer drive-times. Also known as the *concentric circles method*. Compare POLYGON METHOD/ANALYSIS. See also TRADING RADIUS.

ring of perishables   In supermarket retailing, the placement of perishable goods (e.g., produce, dairy products, meats) around the walls of the store.

riser   1. A card or poster in the back of a point-of-purchase display. The riser extends over the merchandise and presents the marketer's message. See also POINT-OF-PURCHASE (POP) DISPLAY.   2. In visual merchandising, a small elevation that raises small items (e.g., toiletries and cosmetics) on a COUNTER or DISPLAY FIXTURE to add interest and catch the customer's eye. Also called a *platform* and/or a *platform fixture*.

risk   The chance of injury, damage, or loss resulting from a given decision or activity. See also COGNITIVE DISSONANCE and DISSONANCE REDUCTION.

risk analysis   In STRATEGIC PLANNING, the identification and evaluation of external threats in the marketplace in terms of their potential impact on the business organization.

risk aversion pricing   A PRICING STRATEGY aimed at the elimination (or at least the reduction) of RISK and uncertainty in the marketing environment through the careful analysis of all available MARKETING INTELLIGENCE. The basis of the strategy is the development of clearly stated price policies aimed at maximizing profits.

risk capital   Synonym for VENTURE CAPITAL.

risk minimization   Synonym for RISK REDUCTION.

risk reduction   The customer's attempt to solve a problem and make a purchase while cutting down on the uncertainties associated with the product or service. Marketers assist in reducing the customer's sense of RISK by providing information about their products and services, explaining the uses and functions of their products and services, and otherwise assisting the customer in making an acceptable choice. Since the customer's sense of risk tends to be greatest when purchasing complex, high-priced goods, marketers of such items are more likely to provide such ancillary services as training, installation, and consultation. In the purchase of home computers, for example, many customers are dealing with a highly complex and high-priced item of which they have little or no prior knowledge or experience. Trained sales personnel, training sessions, support services, warranties, etc. help to reassure the customer by reducing the risk involved in the purchase.

risk taking   A FACILITATING FUNCTION in marketing that includes the handling of uncertainties that are part of the marketing process and exposing oneself and one's firm to the chance of loss or failure.

risk transfer   The passing along of some or all of the MARKETING RISK to another party in the marketing chain. A PRICE GUARANTEE is one form of risk transfer. Insurance against natural disasters is another form of risk transfer. Insurance transfers some marketing risks to the insurance company in return for the payment of an insurance premium.

RMM   See RETAIL MERCHANDISE MANAGEMENT SYSTEM (RMM).

ROA (return on assets)   See RETURN ON INVESTMENT (ROI).

roadblock   A practice used in early broadcast television in which an advertiser would purchase advertising time in such a way that the same commercial would be aired on all three television networks at the same time. Roadblocks were designed to capture consumers who changed channels. Today, cable and television channel proliferation makes a roadblock extremely expensive and difficult or impossible to implement. A similar practice, however, is used in advertising placed on the WORLD WIDE WEB (WWW). See WEB PAGE ROADBLOCK.

road buying   A retail buyer's in-store purchase of goods directly from traveling salespersons. Such purchases are usually made during a buyer's BUYING HOURS.

Robinson-Patman Act (1936)   U.S. federal legislation intended to protect small businesses. The act prohibits vendors from providing extraordinary quantity discounts to large volume retailers, limiting their already considerable buying strength and price advantages. The act forbids a manufacturer engaging in interstate commerce from selling to similar customers at different prices if both sales involve products of the same quality and grade and if the resultant price difference serves to substantially lessen competition or create a monopoly. Certain quantity discounts are allowed, as are different prices for private versus national brands, even if the only difference between them is the label. Popularly known as the *Chain Store Law* and/or the *Price Discrimination Chain Store Act*. The regulations are enforced by the FEDERAL TRADE COMMISSION (FTC). See also CLAYTON ACT (1914).

robot   1. In e-commerce, a program that runs automatically without human intervention. Using artificial intelligence, a robot can react to different situations it may encounter. Two types of widely used Web robots are AGENTS and SPIDERS. Internet robots are frequently called *bots*.   2. A device that responds to sensory input. Robots are widely used in warehouse operations and in manufacturing to perform precision jobs such as welding and riveting. They are also used in situations that would be dangerous for humans, such as cleaning toxic wastes and defusing bombs. The field of computer science and engineering concerned with creating robots is called *robotics*.

robotics   See ROBOT.

ROD   Run of day. Synonym for RUN OF TIME SCHEDULE (ROS).

ROG (dating/terms)   See RECEIPT OF GOODS (ROG) DATING.

ROI   See RETURN ON INVESTMENT (ROI).

role   The set of rights, duties, actions, and activities appropriate to a person who occupies a particular position in a group or in society at large. Also called a *social role*.

role playing   In employee training, an exercise in which individuals participate as actors in order to experience a situation through dramatization.

roll out   To extend the physical distribution or promotion of a product to a wider geographical area than the one previously served. A firm marketing its products regionally, for example, may seek a national market. The firm is then said to have *rolled out* to a national distribution.

rollover menu   See MENU.

ROP   See RUN OF PAPER (ROP) and RUN OF PUBLICATION (ROP).

ROS   See RUN OF TIME SCHEDULE (ROS).

rotated inventory/merchandise control   The practice of inventorying different sections of a department's stock periodically and on an alternating basis. This method serves to help in the collection of stock and sales information necessary for the BUYING process.

rotate stock   See PRODUCT ROTATION.

rotation of products   See PRODUCT ROTATION.

rounder   Synonym for ROUND RACK.

round rack   A floor FIXTURE used to display merchandise. The round rack consists of a circular hang rod, approximately four to six feet above the ground, set on an adjustable upright that is attached to a wide, weighted base. When fully stocked, the round rack can hold approximately 115 inches of shoulder-out merchandise in an area less than five foot square. It is often capable of being turned by the customer for greater convenience and accessibility. A DRAPER is sometimes set on top of the round rack as a means of fully displaying one of the garments from the collection hanging below. Also called, informally, a *rounder*. See also SPLIT ROUNDER, SUPERQUAD, and THREE-PART RACK.

round-the-clock retailing   The practice of keeping a retail store open to customers 24 hours a day.

round trip   See MEMORANDUM BUYING.

round turn   Synonym for STOCK TURNOVER (ST).

router   A device that forwards data packets along networks. A router connects at least two networks, commonly two LANs or WANs or a LAN and its ISP's network. Routers are located at gateways, the places where two or more networks connect.

route selling   The sale of products and/or services to customers on an established delivery schedule. For example, dairy products, dry cleaning, and diaper services are often sold this way.

routine consumer decision making   In consumer behavior, decisions that require little deliberation and planning because of the ordinary, unvarying nature of the purchase. Goods involved are generally low-cost and carry no perceived risk to the consumer. Also called *routinized response behavior*.

routine order taking   See ORDER TAKER.

routine selling   Personal selling that involves contact with the customer prior to the customer's decision to buy, but without requiring a great deal of technical expertise on the part of the SALESPERSON. An instance of this is a *routine sale*.

routing   1. In personal sales, the systematic listing of the salesperson's appointments.   2. In shipping, the selection of the preferred mode of transportation from vendor to store.   3. In retailing, the section of the store's delivery department responsible for checking incoming shipments and directing the merchandise to the appropriate stockroom or selling department.

routing instructions   Directions to the vendor attached to the purchase order by the buyer. These directions specify the shipping instructions and preferred type of transportation.

routinized response behavior   Synonym for ROUTINE CONSUMER DECISION MAKING.

ROW   Run of week. See RUN OF TIME SCHEDULE (ROS).

royalty   1. In FRANCHISING, the payment made by a franchisee to a franchiser.   2. The percentage of price or set dollar amount paid to authors, composers, or other artists for the sale or use of their work.

RPM   See RESALE PRICE MAINTENANCE (RPM).

RS   See REVENUE AND SERVICE (RS).

RSA   An extremely powerful PUBLIC-KEY ENCRYPTION technology that has become the *de facto* standard for industrial-strength encryption, especially for data sent over the Internet. The technology is considered so powerful that the U.S. government has restricted exporting it to foreign countries. RSA stands for Rivest, Shamir, and Adelman, the inventors of the technique.

RSP   See REGIONAL SERVICE PROVIDER (RSP).

RSS   Internet abbreviation meaning, alternatively, *Rich Site Summary* or *Really Simple Syndication*. RSS allows people who publish content online to notify interested parties instantaneously whenever fresh content is available. RSS is both a publication and a syndication channel and works in much the same way that electronic newswire services do. Notification of new content is sent, by means of an RSS FEED, both to people interested in it and to Web sites that aggregate content announcements. RSS feed recipients receive the latest headlines and can click on embedded links to get to the full story if they choose to, avoiding clutter and overload by selecting only those items they wish to pursue further. Feed recipients can sometimes republish all or part of an RSS feed on their own sites, accelerating the spread of the e-tailer's message. RSS is considered a complement to the E-MAIL announcement list in that it does not clutter people's inboxes, is easier to manage for recipients who get a lot of news online, is SPAM-proof, and is easier to manage than an e-mail list.

RSS feed   A special kind of XML file that contains information about an e-tailer's new content (headline, description, excerpt, etc). The recipient must have feed reader software installed to display RSS feeds in a readable file. These feed readers are easily downloadable from the Web.

RTF   See RICH TEXT FORMAT (RTF).

RTV   See RETURNS TO VENDOR (RTV).

RTW   See READY-TO-WEAR (RTW).

rubber-banding   An agreement for cosmetic products that allows the store to return the merchandise to the manufacturer if not sold within a specified period of time.

rub-off   An increase in sales in one department as the result of a promotion in another department.

rule for maximizing profit   See MAXIMIZING PROFIT.

rule of origin   See FABRIC FORWARD.

run   1. v. To cause an ad to appear on a Web site or in another medium. An advertiser pays to run an ad for a specified length of time and is charged accordingly.   2. n. The length of time an ad is scheduled to appear. See also RUN OF TIME SCHEDULE (ROS), RUN OF PUBLICATION (ROP), and RUN OF PAPER (ROP).

runaway inflation   An economic condition in which there are steep increases in prices, perhaps up to 100% at a time.

runner   (Slang) Synonym for BEST SELLER.

running   (Slang) Selling quickly. See also BEST SELLER.

run of day (ROD)   See RUN OF TIME SCHEDULE (ROS).

run of paper (ROP)   An arrangement under which a newspaper advertisement is placed at the publisher's discretion rather than positioned by the advertiser. ROP ads are charged at the ordinary position rate. For other print media, this agreement is referred to as RUN OF PUBLICATION (ROP). Compare PREFERRED POSITION.

run of publication (ROP)   An arrangement under which an advertisement in a print medium (e.g., a magazine) is placed at the publisher's discretion rather than positioned by the advertiser. In newspaper advertising, this is generally referred to as RUN OF PAPER (ROP). Compare PREFERRED POSITION.

run of schedule (ROS)   See RUN OF TIME SCHEDULE (ROS).

run of time schedule (ROS)   An arrangement under which television and radio commercials are scheduled and broadcast at the discretion of the station. Like a BEST TIME AVAILABLE (BTA) plan, the ROS plan may run at any time between 5:00 a.m. and 1:00 a.m. with no guaranteed distribution by day part. Also called *run of schedule (ROS)* and either *run of day (ROD)* or *run of week (ROW)*, whichever is applicable to the specific agreement.

run of week (ROW)   See RUN OF TIME SCHEDULE (ROS).

run-on window   A long DISPLAY WINDOW running 20 or more feet. The only visible divider in the run-on window is the thin metal band that retains the plate glass windows. Compare BANK OF WINDOWS.

run sizes   The number of items manufactured in a given lot.

runway model   See MODEL.

runway show   A presentation of fashion merchandise as a parade with the audience seated at the perimeter of the runway. Haute couture designers and apparel manufacturers use this traditional method almost exclusively to show their lines each season. Also called a *formal runway show*. See also INFORMAL FASHION SHOW.

rush order   An order expedited at great speed by the vendor and the retail distribution center, often to replenish a low assortment of fast-selling merchandise, cover a breaking advertisement, or prepare for the grand opening of a new store. Also called a *priority order*.

RWDSU   See RETAIL, WHOLESALE AND DEPARTMENT STORE UNION (RWDSU).

SA See SEVENTH AVENUE (SA).

sachet marketing A microselling method aimed at new consumers in developing megaeconomies like China, India, the Philippines, Mexico, and Brazil. Products are packaged and marketed in small, affordable portions, sachets, or sizes, so that consumers get to know and like the brand. The manufacturer can still make a good profit from sheer overall volume (i.e., smaller sizes but more buyers). This practice is seen as an alternative to selling bulky goods originally designed for consumers in North America, Western Europe, or Japan. The trend was identified and the term coined by trendwatching.com at www.trendwatching.com.

safety needs The needs of an individual that are concerned with basic protection and physical well-being. Safety needs include health, food, medicine, exercise, etc. See also MASLOW'S HIERARCHY (OF NEEDS).

safety stock Synonym for RESERVE STOCK.

salaried (buying) office An independent RESIDENT BUYING OFFICE that is paid a fee (either as a flat fee or as a percentage of sales, typically ranging from .5 to 1%) on an annual contractual basis by the stores it represents in the MARKET. The fixed fee arrangement is more characteristic of the contracts of smaller stores. Larger stores may contract with salaried buying offices for services such as IMPORT GOODS or OFF-PRICE SOURCING. The salaried buying office, the most common type of resident buying office, is used by store owners and buyers who do not have the time to make frequent market visits or who are located far from the market. Also called a *contract buying office, contract-type buying office, fixed-fee office,* a *fixed-fee buying office,* a *paid buying office,* and an *outside buying organization.*

salary Weekly, monthly, or yearly cash compensation for work. Salaried workers, such as managers and professionals, normally receive no pay for extra hours worked. Compare WAGES (i.e., cash compensation paid to workers based on a calculation of the number of hours worked or the number of units produced), COMMISSION, and STRAIGHT SALARY.

salary plan Synonym for STRAIGHT SALARY.

salary plus commission A compensation system in which one receives a regular salary plus a percentage of one's total sales during a specific period. See also STRAIGHT SALARY, STRAIGHT COMMISSION, and COMMISSION.

sale 1. The exchange of services or property for money or some other valuable consideration. Such merchandise, available for purchase, is said to be FOR SALE or ON SALE. See also TERMS OF SALE. 2. The offering of merchandise at a lower than regular price. See also PROMOTIONS AND SALES.

sale advertising ADVERTISING in which low PRICE is the primary consideration and the building of store TRAFFIC the main objective. See also PROMOTIONS AND SALES.

sale and leaseback See LEASEBACK.

sale merchandise Goods from regular stock that have been reduced in price, or merchandise specially purchased for the purpose of a sale. See also PROMOTIONS AND SALES.

sale price A reduced price offered to consumers to build traffic and move merchandise. Merchandise may be placed ON SALE for a number of reasons (e.g., at the end of a selling season). Distinguished from SELLING PRICE.

sale price advertising A form of PROMOTIONAL ADVERTISING in which merchandise is offered at a sale price or as a special. Consumer appeal is based on the opportunity to save money.

sales 1. Store events featuring merchandise at reduced prices in order to generate traffic and move merchandise. Services may also be offered at reduced prices in this fashion. See also PROMOTIONS AND SALES. 2. The occupation of a SALESPERSON. 3. The gross dollar revenue of an organization before deductions, equal to the total value of opening inventory and subsequent purchases less closing inventory and markdowns. In retailing, the term is sometimes used synonymously with OPERATING INCOME. Also called *total sales.* See also GROSS REVENUE/SALES, SALES AT RETAIL, and NET SALES.

sales administration Synonym for SALES MANAGEMENT.

sales agent Synonym for SELLING AGENT.

sales allowance A lowering of the price of an item when the merchandise delivered is not exactly what was ordered.

sales analysis   The examination of a firm's sales results, generally in terms of territory, product classification, type of customer, cost of sales, order size, or other measurement criterion. The primary objectives of sales analysis are to detect marketing problems before they become acute and to facilitate the MARKETING MANAGEMENT function. See also SALES INVOICE.

sales anchor   A concept or statement used by a sales representative when attempting to overcome customer resistance. The salesperson may continually return to this concept in an attempt to close the sale.

sales and promotions   See PROMOTIONS AND SALES.

sales approach   Contact between a salesperson and a potential customer (i.e., the PROSPECT), particularly the first few minutes of that contact. The sales approach is the stage in the sales presentation that is designed to gain and hold the prospect's attention, and accomplishes the following: (a) the salesperson introducing himself or herself to the prospect; (b) the salesperson selling himself or herself, the product, and the company to the prospect; and (c) the salesperson getting and holding the prospect's attention and interest. During the sales approach, the salesperson draws out the prospect to determine his or her needs. This information will later be used to convince the prospect of the advantages of the salesperson's product or service. There are many different approaches, including the BENEFIT APPROACH (emphasizing the benefit to the prospect of doing business with the salesperson), the CURIOSITY APPROACH (basing the sales presentation on the prospect's curiosity and interest), the DRAMATIC APPROACH (an eye-opening demonstration, often involving the prospect directly), and the FACTUAL APPROACH (using an interesting fact about the product or service to capture the prospect's attention). Also called, simply, the *approach*. See also SELLING PROCESS.

sales aptitude   The ability to achieve success in the sales field, as acknowledged by a sales department and measured by means of interviews and recommendations.

sales associate   See SALESPERSON.

sales at retail   The dollar amount of merchandise sold at its RETAIL PRICE (i.e., not at wholesale). Also called *retail sales*.

sales audit   A complete analysis of the information collected at the points-of-sale in a store for the purpose of establishing accounting controls.

sales-based pricing objective   Any goal that orients a store's PRICING STRATEGY toward high sales volume or the expansion of its share of sales relative to competitors.

sales below cost law   See MINIMUM MARKUP LAW.

sales branch   The local office of a manufacturer that provides services similar to those of a MERCHANT WHOLESALER (i.e., stocking merchandise, filling orders, making deliveries, etc.). The sales branch may also provide space for the local SALES FORCE. See also MANUFACTURER'S BRANCH OFFICE.

sales broker   See BROKER.

sales budget   A budget that sets forth in detail all of a firm's anticipated sales for a given period and makes possible the allocation of the money and materials needed for the firm to achieve these objectives. Commonly, each product offered will require its own sales budget. The sales budget is based on studies of past sales and estimates of future business conditions.

sales by category   See SALES BY CATEGORY REPORT.

sales by category report   A monthly statistical report prepared by a retailer in a CHAIN STORE organization. The report records sales by department, classification, and store, with departmental sales broken out by classification for each store. The calculations may be used to compare the department's sales to sales for the entire classification within the store, to total sales for the individual store, or to the same classification in all stores in the chain. For example, career dresses at one store in the chain may represent 32% of the total dress department sales in that store. They may, at the same time, represent 7% of the total sales for the classification in all stores in the chain. See also SALES REPORT.

sales call   A visit paid to the customer by the SALESPERSON operating in the FIELD. The practice is common in medical sales and INDUSTRIAL PURCHASING, as well as in selling by marketing intermediaries to retailers. See also SALES CALL PATTERN and PERSONAL SELLING.

sales call pattern   The schedule or routine followed by sales personnel in the FIELD when calling on prospective customers. The particular pattern is a function of several factors, including the universe of target customers and their geographical distribution; the frequency of calls required by each customer; the cost-effectiveness of making sales calls; and the selling culture of, and competitive sales environment in, the salesperson's workplace. Also called a *call pattern*. See also SALES CALL and PERSONAL SELLING.

sales check   The form on which a sale is recorded by a salesperson. Also spelled *salescheck*.

sales check control   An INVENTORY system in which information is gathered from sales checks rather than from other sources (e.g., ticket stubs). Compare SALES RECORD CONTROL.

sales clerk   Synonym for SALESPERSON, particularly in retailing.

sales closing   See CLOSING.

sales compensation   Money paid to salespeople. Sales compensation may be in the form of STRAIGHT COMMISSION, STRAIGHT SALARY, or SALARY PLUS COMMISSION. Also called *sales force compensation*.

sales concept   Synonym for SELLING CONCEPT.

sales contest   A manufacturer- or dealer-sponsored competition in which superior sales efforts are rewarded with prizes.

Competitors may be members of the producer's sales force or may be employed by other marketing intermediaries. See also CONTEST.

sales data   Records of INCOME generated by sales of goods or services to customers. In retailing, sales records are usually kept for the entire store, individual departments, and each merchandise classification (for each store and its branches). Sales data assists buyers or managers in determining fast and slow sellers, markdowns, etc. See also SALES DETERMINATION and INVENTORY.

sales-decay constant   See ADVERTISING SALES-RESPONSE AND DECAY MODEL.

sales demonstration   A presentation in which a SALESPERSON shows customers how an item functions and highlights its potential uses. Sales demonstrations may take place in a variety of venues including trade shows (for the benefit of industry clients, marketing intermediaries, etc.) and retail stores (where the audience is the ultimate consumer), where they are particularly common in accessory and cosmetic departments and in warehouse retailing. At times, the in-store DEMONSTRATOR may be employed by a manufacturer rather by than the store. *Demo* is a popular short form of *demonstration*. Also called a *product demonstration* or, simply, a *demonstration*.

sales determination   The calculation of income generated by sales to consumers. The SALES DATA accumulated by the store helps buyers and managers plan for future purchases. Determining sales is an important part of the INVENTORY process.

sales development plan   A SALES PLAN specifically designed to develop new products.

sales discount   See DISCOUNT SALE.

sales division   In an apparel manufacturing firm, the division responsible for selling the line or collection to retail stores. Sales may take place in a showroom, a sales facility located in a major MARKET CENTER, or through personal sales at the retail buyer's office. A member of the sales staff is known as a SALES REPRESENTATIVE or *sales rep*.

sales efficiency   The relationship between sales volume or value and individual and total selling expenses. The lower the expenses required to generate sales, the greater the sales efficiency.

sales era (of marketing)   A stage in the evolution of marketing (following the production era) during which the roles of advertising and the sales force were expanded. No genuine effort was made to determine the consumer's needs before goods were produced. Instead, advertising was used to shape the desires of consumers to fit the attributes of the products already being manufactured. See also SALES-ORIENTED MARKETING.

sales exception reporting   A form of SALES ANALYSIS in which products are reported as slow-selling or fast-selling.

Managers use the resulting *sales exception report* to evaluate the accuracy of the SALES FORECAST.

sales expense budget   A budget showing expenditures allocated to personal selling activities. Included are salaries, commissions, incentives, and expense account charges as well as the cost of managing the sales operation. Such activities as sales meetings are also included.

sales finance company   1. In retailing, a financial institution that takes over a retailer's PAPER at a discount rate. The finance company buys retail installment contracts at somewhat less than their full value and assumes responsibility for collections. 2. An institution that finances inventories, assisting the marketer with the FINANCING FUNCTION. FLOOR PLAN FINANCING is one method used by sales finance companies.

sales force   A term generally applied to a firm's field sales organization (i.e., those salespersons and their immediate supervisors who have direct contact with customers and who perform the function of selling). Also spelled *salesforce*. Also called the *sales staff*.

sales force compensation   See SALES COMPENSATION.

sales force composite   A build-up (i.e., bottom-up) approach to SALES FORECASTING in which members of the firm's SALES FORCE estimate potential sales in their individual territories. This information is added together to form a comprehensive sales forecast for the company.

sales force forecasting survey   See SALES FORCE COMPOSITE.

sales force indoctrination   The initial phase of SALES TRAINING, covering knowledge of the company, its products, policies, and promotional support. Indoctrination may also encompass knowledge of the marketing environment and the competition. Finally, sales force indoctrination covers fundamental selling skills and the principles of time and territory management, where applicable. Also called *sales indoctrination*.

sales force management   Synonym for SALES MANAGEMENT.

sales force planning   Any method used to determine the optimum level and type of sales personnel. The buyer considers such factors as store image, type of clientele, store policies and practices, and type of department when planning the sales force. Other factors to be considered include the fit or match of the sales force with the clientele, the budgeting of full-time and part-time salespeople required, and the potential need for additional sales personnel during busy holiday and/or promotional periods. See also SALES MANAGEMENT.

sales force promotion   An incentive offered by a company to encourage its own SALES FORCE to increase their effectiveness and sales. Such incentives include cash bonus payments, contests, enthusiasm-building sales meetings, etc.

sales forecast   An estimate, based on demand, of the level of sales anticipated for a particular period, expressed either in dollars or in units. See also FORECASTING and SALES FORE-CASTING.

sales forecasting An attempt, on the basis of subjective or statistical methods of research, to predict market response to a product or group of products or to predict the performance of an entire division or company. This predictive effort results in a SALES FORECAST that provides the firm with a reliable guide for planning and efficient production. See also the SUBSTITUTE METHOD OF FORECASTING, SALES PLANNING, FORECASTING, ECONOMIC FORECASTING, TREND EXTENSION, and FASHION FORECASTING.

salesgirl See SALESPERSON.

sales goal The amount that an employer expects a salesperson to sell. Sales goals are typically expressed in quantitative terms of sales volume, sales expense, or number of customers, and are used in the PERFORMANCE APPRAISAL of the sales force. See also SALES INCENTIVE.

sales grabber A SALESPERSON who attempts to wait on more customers than the other salespeople in an effort to gain a disproportionately large share of sales.

sales incentive A prize offered by a manufacturer to the SALES FORCE. Traditionally, the sales incentive is money provided for those salespersons who exceed a preset SALES GOAL. Other incentives may include free trips and other special prizes.

sales indoctrination Synonym for SALES FORCE INDOCTRINATION.

sales invoice A bill or statement representing a sale. Sales invoices may be handwritten, typed, or computer-generated. They are used as a source of SALES ANALYSIS data. See also INVOICE.

sales journal A book in which records of sales are entered, particularly in the precomputer era or in stores that are not yet automated.

saleslady See SALESPERSON.

sales lead See LEAD.

sales letter Correspondence from a marketer to prospective or existing customers, typically providing information about the product or service and urging a quick response from the reader.

salesman See SALESPERSON.

sales management Those supervisory and leadership efforts directed toward the development (i.e., recruitment, selection, and training) and maintenance (i.e., planning supervision, and motivation) of a SALES FORCE. Taken together, these efforts will provide the firm with salespersons able to achieve the dollar volume necessary for the profitable operation of the business. Also called *sales force management*,

supervision of the sales force, and *sales administration.* See also SALES FORCE PLANNING.

sales management (development) training In SALES TRAINING, the stage in which sales personnel are taught to perfect their selling skills and prepare to become sales managers. Sales management development training focuses on acquiring skills in administration, decision making, and leadership.

sales manager 1. In the broadcast media, the employee (e.g., of a television network) who performs the functions of the ADVERTISING SALES MANAGER, selling advertising time to prospective advertisers. 2. In retail stores, a DEPARTMENT MANAGER. The position usually reports to a STORE MERCHANDISE MANAGER and is responsible for an area defined by a department or division. It usually includes both merchandising and operational responsibilities.

salesmanship As defined by retailer John Wanamaker, "the art of so successfully demonstrating the merits of the goods and the service of the house that a permanent customer is made." In short, salesmanship is the art of selling goods and/or services by creating a demand or need for a particular item or service and realizing an actual order.

sales manual A book for sales personnel that describes the product or service to be sold and suggests approaches for selling to a customer. See also SALES APPROACH.

sales mix The combination of the various goods and services accounting for the store's total sales.

sales objective A clear statement of the tasks to be performed by the salespeople in a firm. Sales objectives may be expressed in terms of total sales (in dollars or units), increases over past results, number of sales calls completed, etc. See also SALES QUOTA.

sales office See MANUFACTURER'S SALES OFFICE.

sales orientation Strong emphasis, in a firm's marketing plans, on personal sales and advertising. Compare PRODUCT ORIENTATION and PRODUCTION CONCEPT. See also SELLING CONCEPT.

sales-oriented See SELLING CONCEPT.

sales-oriented marketing In the United States, the marketing orientation of the 1920s. As production capacity increased and business for manufactured goods became more competitive, business leaders realized they would have to persuade people to buy the goods they produced. They began to stimulate demand for their products and spent more on advertising. In addition, they began to develop a trained sales force that could seek out and sell to potential customers throughout the country. Compare PRODUCTION-ORIENTED MARKETING, the MARKETING CONCEPT, and COMPETITIVE MARKETING. See also SALES ERA (OF MARKETING).

sales-oriented objective See SALES QUOTA and SALES OBJECTIVE.

sales-oriented organization   See SELLING CONCEPT.

sales penetration   Synonym for MARKET SHARE.

salespeople   See SALESPERSON.

sales per dollar invested in inventory   The dollar amount generated by the money invested in INVENTORY.

sales performance index   See PERFORMANCE INDEX.

salesperson   1. A broad term that includes a variety of order takers, sales employees at both the wholesale and retail levels, manufacturers' representatives and sales engineers, missionary salespeople, detailers, etc.   2. In a retail store, a person having the responsibility for actually selling merchandise, preparing a sales check, recording the sale, and receiving payment from the customer. The salesperson may also be responsible for keeping merchandise in order and ensuring that stock levels are maintained. Sometimes called a *sales associate, sales clerk, salesman, saleslady,* or *salesgirl.* See also RETAIL SALESPERSON.

salesperson wrap   See CLERK WRAP.

sales per square foot   In retailing, a PERFORMANCE MEASURE used to evaluate the success or failure of the business. Sales per square foot reflects the amount of sales generated relative to the amount of space dedicated to selling the goods. The ratio may be calculated for any time period, but an annual computation is most common. Sales per square foot can be increased by generating more sales, decreasing the square footage dedicated to selling, or both. Generating more sales in less space is the retailer's objective. The figure may be calculated based on all space in the store (including backroom operations) or on the selling space only. See also SALES PRODUCTIVITY METHOD OF SPACE ALLOCATION, SALES PER SQUARE FOOT OF GROSS SPACE, and SALES PER SQUARE FOOT OF SELLING SPACE.

sales per square foot of gross space   The amount of sales, in dollars, generated by an item or line, by a department, or by an entire store, calculated on an annual basis. All square footage in the store is used in making the computation, including nonselling areas. See also SALES PER SQUARE FOOT.

sales per square foot of selling space   The amount of sales, in dollars, generated by an item or line, department, or an entire store, calculated on an annual basis. Only the square footage devoted to actual selling is used in making the computation. See also SALES PER SQUARE FOOT and SALES PER SQUARE FOOT OF GROSS SPACE.

sales pitch   A strong statement by a salesperson, aimed at persuading a potential customer to buy a product or service. See also SALES APPROACH and PITCH.

sales plan   At the retail level, a projection of the sales a buyer expects to achieve, usually for a six-month period. The plan reflects inventory at the beginning of the period, planned purchases, projected markup and markdown percentages, estimated sales, and gross margin. Also called the *six-month merchandising plan.* When expressed in terms of dollars, it is also called a *dollar merchandising plan, dollar merchandise plan,* or DOLLAR PLAN. When expressed in terms of units, also called a UNIT PLAN. Most sales plans span the time from February 1 to July 31 and from August 1 to January 31. See also MERCHANDISE PLAN, BUYING PLAN, and FORECAST-BASED MERCHANDISE PLAN.

sales planning   According to the American Marketing Association, "that part of MARKETING PLANNING work which is concerned with making sales forecasts, devising programs for reaching the sales target, and deriving a sales budget." Sales planning is the first step in the preparation of the MERCHANDISE BUDGET. The first step in planning sales is to refer to department sales records and consider the overall past sales performance of the store or chain store operation as a whole, as well as sales trends for each department in individual branches or units. Factors within the store that may aid or hinder sales activity are taken into account. The buyer then considers outside factors that may affect sales (e.g., economic trends, rates of employment and unemployment, the growth of shopping centers, competitive conditions). After considering the store's sales opportunities as a whole, the buyer next considers how the department or departments will achieve the sales goals based on the store's overall projections. The buyer must consider sales planning according to each classification, price line, size, color, or other subdivision considered to be important. See also PLANNED SALES and SALES FORECASTING.

sales potential   The total amount of goods or services a particular company might reasonably be expected to sell in the marketplace over a specified period of time and to a particular MARKET SEGMENT. At least some of this potential may be as yet latent and unrealized. Sometimes called *company sales potential.* See also SALES POTENTIAL FORECAST, MARKET POTENTIAL, and MARKET SHARE.

sales potential forecast   A prediction of total potential sales for the store for a specific time period. See also SALES POTENTIAL, FORECAST, and FORECASTING.

sales presentation   That stage in the selling process during which the salesperson presents the product, service, or idea, explains its benefits, and attempts to convince the prospect to accept the promises being made and make a purchase. Also called, simply, a *presentation.*

sales productivity method of space allocation   The practice of allocating space to a product category based on the sales (or profits) the product has achieved in the past on a square foot basis. This relationship between sales and space is known as the *sales-productivity ratio.* See also SALES PER SQUARE FOOT.

sales-productivity ratio   See SALES PRODUCTIVITY METHOD OF SPACE ALLOCATION.

sales promotion   Short-term, nonrecurrent efforts to increase buying response on the part of consumers or to intensify sales efforts by the firm's sales force or resellers in the CHANNEL OF DISTRIBUTION. When directed at the sales force, the promotions may take the form of sales contests, bonuses, incentive gifts, prizes, etc. When directed at resellers (i.e., marketing intermediaries and retailers), the effort often takes the form of buying allowances, free goods, cooperative advertising money, push money, sales contests, etc. Sales promotion at the retail level is commonly taken to include advertising, visual merchandising (display), public relations (including publicity), special events, and the selling efforts of the store's sales people. Specific incentives such as coupons, trading stamps, price-off deals, demonstrations, samples, premiums, etc. may also be offered to the ultimate consumer as a stimulus to purchase. Also called *promotional communication, demand creation,* and *demand stimulation.* A firm's planned, structured sales promotion efforts may be called a *sales promotion program, promotion program,* or *promotional program.*

sales promotion agency   A firm that specializes in supplying broad SALES PROMOTION services to its clients. The agency develops and manages sales promotion programs, such as contests, refunds or rebates, premium or incentive offers, sweepstakes, and sampling programs. Although some large full service advertising agencies have created their own sales promotion divisions, many independent sales promotion agencies serve the needs of their clients.

sales promotion calendar   A planning device used to schedule special promotional events and coordinate them with holidays, national observances, seasons, etc. Also called a *promotion calendar, promotion mix calendar, promotional calendar,* or *promotional mix calendar.*

sales promotion manager   The individual within a firm who is responsible for filling the gaps between the sales and advertising managers and handling the firm's diversified SALES PROMOTION activities. In some organizations, the sales promotion manager is responsible to the SALES MANAGER, in others to the MARKETING MANAGER.

sales promotion program   See SALES PROMOTION.

sales prospect   See PROSPECT.

sales quota   A goal or objective in amount to be sold, usually for a specific period of time, set by management as a stimulant to the sales effort. It may apply to individuals, departments, divisions, etc. and may be expressed in terms of dollars or units. Also called a *sales-oriented objective.* See also QUOTA and SALES OBJECTIVE.

sales receipt   See SALES SLIP and RECEIPT.

sales record control   A merchandise information system used in unit control. Sales record control is based on the analysis of sales ticket stubs, sales checks, and other sales records that reflect a change in inventory. Compare SALES CHECK CONTROL.

sales register   Synonym for CASH REGISTER.

sales rep   Short for SALES REPRESENTATIVE.

sales report   A management report that summarizes results of sales performance and the activities of salespersons. Sales reports can detail customer reaction to particular items, services, or company procedures, as well as the efforts of competitors. See also SALES BY CATEGORY REPORT.

sales representative   A SALESPERSON representing a manufacturer in a particular territory. Also called a *sales rep* or, simply, a *rep.*

sales resistance   A customer's unwillingness to make a purchase. The customer typically raises objections and does not succumb to the personal sales effort of the salesperson.

sales-response and decay model   See ADVERTISING SALES-RESPONSE AND DECAY MODEL.

sales-response constant   See ADVERTISING SALES-RESPONSE AND DECAY MODEL.

sales-response model   See ADVERTISING SALES-RESPONSE AND DECAY MODEL.

sales-results test   An effort to measure the impact on sales of a particular advertisement or advertising campaign. See also ADVERTISING SALES-RESPONSE AND DECAY MODEL.

sales retail   The final sales price at retail (i.e., the original RETAIL PRICE less discounts and allowances, shrinkage, and markdowns).

sales, returns, and allowances   See RETURNS AND ALLOWANCES TO CUSTOMERS.

sales revenue   The total income derived from sales for a given period. See also REVENUE.

sales slip   A cash register receipt showing money amounts, tax, and sales total. Before automation, most sales slips did not show details of the transaction. However, most computerized checkouts now produce sales slips that include details of the individual products purchased, the quantity purchased, and the price per item. Also called a *sales receipt.* See also RECEIPT.

sales staff   Synonym for SALES FORCE.

sales supporting services   Those store activities that are provided to support the profitmaking segment of the business (e.g., free alterations or free parking).

sales support staff   Those employees who are not directly involved in selling merchandise but whose activities assist the sales staff directly. For example, members of the sales promotion and publicity department, fashion office staff, and the display or visual merchandising department are all sales support staff.

sales tax   A tax levied by a government on goods and services at the time of their sale, particularly at the retail level. In general, the sales of manufacturers are taxed when the items are considered to be completed goods. The sales of wholesalers are taxed when their goods are sold to retailers and retail sales taxes are collected when consumers purchase the goods or services. Sales taxes affect retail businesses in that they increase the prices customers have to pay for goods and services. While the retailer collects the taxes from the consumer at the time of purchase, the tax money must be turned over to the government. Consequently, retailers incur the administrative costs associated with collecting and forwarding tax money to the government.

sales terms   Synonym for TERMS OF SALE.

sales territory   A geographical area assigned to a SALES-PERSON (or group of salespeople) in the field. The individual or team is responsible for selling the firm's products in the designated area. See also EXCLUSIVE DISTRIBUTION and CLOSED SALES TERRITORY.

sales trainee   A newly hired employee who is learning to sell the employer's goods or services. In general, trainees earn a small salary during their training period. See also SALES TRAINING.

sales training   A company's systematic program of training sales personnel. The objective of such a program is to increase sales and reduce costs by maximizing the effectiveness and efficiency of the SALES FORCE. The company first identifies and analyzes its needs and objectives, allowing priorities to be established and specific programs to be set in motion. The company then determines the type of learning required, the specific training time allowed, and the training methods to be employed. Each of these elements varies considerably from company to company, depending on the nature of the product or service being sold and other related factors. In most companies, training and development includes initial SALES FORCE INDOCTRINATION and training of sales employees (or trainees), advanced training on an ongoing basis, and management development training (for potential sales managers). Trainers may be drawn from sales management, staff training personnel, experienced salespeople, or outside specialists. Training may take place within the firm itself, in the field, or at an outside location (such as a college campus, hotel seminar facility, etc.). See also SALES TRAINEE.

sales trend   An observable pattern of purchasing relating to particular goods and services. Trends may develop over an extended period of time or may appeal to customers for a short period of time (as in a fashion FAD). Buyers endeavor to identify and follow trends in order to better plan their merchandise selections. See also TREND.

sales variance   See SALES VARIANCE ANALYSIS.

sales variance analysis   In COST ACCOUNTING, a method of data analysis in which data on actual sales are compared to the company's SALES OBJECTIVE and the causes of the difference are identified. The analysis of sales variance is important for the study of profit variances. Sales variances may be calculated several different ways so as to show the effect on profit or to show the effect on sales value. The profit or margin method is based on PROFIT and GROSS MARGIN. The value method reveals the effect of various sales efforts on the overall sales value figures.

sales volume   Total sales for a classification during the selling period being evaluated. In retailing, the term is sometimes used synonymously with OPERATING INCOME.

sales volume analysis   A technique employed to evaluate an organization's performance in the MARKETPLACE. Sales volume analysis simply measures the target market's reaction to the firm's offerings by measuring sales. Compare MARKET SHARE ANALYSIS.

sales wave test   A technique employed in TEST MARKETING in which a product is placed in the homes of selected consumers on a trial basis and made available for purchase. Theoretically, repurchase activity on the part of the selected consumers over time will approximate the actual usage that might be expected should the product be introduced into the MARKETPLACE.

sale terms   See TERMS OF SALE.

salon   1. In a retail store (especially a department or specialty store), a specialized shop or area devoted to expensive and exclusive merchandise, particularly apparel. Well-informed staff carry out the sales function on a highly personal and attentive basis. This special treatment is known as *salon selling.* See also SALON DRESSES.   2. A specialized area in a store, or a separate establishment, in which special services are offered. For example, a *beauty shop* is often referred to as a *beauty salon,* whether or not it is located in a department store.

salon de couture   The showroom of a HAUTE COUTURE designer. *Der.* French.

salon dresses   Expensive dresses made by well-known designers and sold in a special room in a department store. Dresses are generally brought out to the customer by the SALESPERSON (rather than displayed on racks) and are sometimes shown on live models. See also SALON.

salon selling   See SALON.

salvage   1. v. To save from shipwreck, fire, or other danger or destruction.   2. n. The act of saving anything from destruction or danger, particularly from a shipwreck.   3. n. The property or goods so saved. See also SALVAGE MERCHANDISE.

salvage merchandise   Merchandise so damaged or shop-worn that it cannot be sold through regular channels at its original price.

sameness syndrome   The tendency of some retailers to offer the same or similar merchandise or services as their competitors. This leads to shoppers reporting boredom and disinterest.

sample   1. A single item used as an example of a much larger lot. For example, apparel manufacturers prepare samples to show buyers in order to generate orders before going into full production. This serves as a prototype for the production model. 2. A trial size portion of a product distributed to consumers so that they can try a product before purchasing it. See TRYVERTISING, TRIAL OFFER, and FREE SAMPLE. 3. In marketing research (and other social scientific and scientific research), a selected representative segment of the POPULATION studied to gain knowledge of the whole. See also TARGET POPULATION.

sample buyer   A customer who buys a product at a special introductory rate or obtains a product SAMPLE at no cost.

sample frame   In SAMPLING, that part of the target POPULATION that is actually studied.

sample maker   In the apparel industry, the skilled employee who makes the prototype samples from which retail buyers select their merchandise.

sample offer/package   See TRIAL OFFER and FREE SAMPLE.

sample room   1. A room, often adjoining the showroom of a manufacturer, in which representative models of the merchandise offered for sale are presented for inspection by the buyer. See also SHOWROOM.   2. In a retail store (particularly in a large retail store), a room in which a manufacturer's samples are put on display. Traveling vendors show their lines by appointment in such sample rooms.

sample selling   A form of personal selling in which the customer picks out a sample of the item (e.g., a shoe) and takes it to a salesperson. The salesperson, in turn, brings out the exact size and color from the reserve stock. Sample selling is common in the shoe industry.

sample set   Synonym for POPULATION.

sample size   1. The number of individuals to be studied as a sample of the total POPULATION in marketing research (and other social sciences research).   2. See TRIAL OFFER and FREE SAMPLE.

sampling   1. In MARKETING RESEARCH (MR) and other social science research, the process of selecting a representative subset of a total POPULATION for obtaining data useful in the study of the whole population. The subset is known as the SAMPLE. Inferences about the characteristics of the population as a whole are drawn from the characteristics of the sample. The total population is known as the UNIVERSE. The study of the characteristics and attitudes of the sample are meant to decrease the time and costs involved in studying the total universe, and may actually be more accurate. All marketing research samples fall into one of two major classes: probability samples and nonprobability samples. Probability samples are those that are selected randomly, so that each member of the total population has an equal and quantifiable chance of being selected. In nonprobability samples, the judgment of the researcher enters into the selection process. See also SAMPLE, TARGET POPULATION, and QUANTITATIVE (PRIMARY) RESEARCH.   2. In sales promotion, the distribution of a

product to a consumer free of charge in an effort to bolster consumer demand. Samples may be placed with channel intermediaries or given directly to end users, as is often done in direct mail marketing. This practice is also often seen in food markets, cosmetic counters in retail stores, and drug stores. For example, a cosmetics salesperson may include free samples of related products with a customer's purchase in hopes of building additional sales in the future.

sampling buying   In INDUSTRIAL PURCHASING, the practice of purchasing a product after examining a portion of the potential shipment for quality. This kind of buying is often used in grain markets.

sampling error   A mistake or error in the MARKETING RESEARCH (MR) sample itself, causing it to be unrepresentative of the universe from which it is drawn. Compare NONSAMPLING ERROR.

sampling plan   The design phase of MARKETING RESEARCH (MR), in which the composition of the SAMPLING UNIT, the SAMPLE SIZE, and the SAMPLING PROCEDURE (probability or nonprobability) are specified.

sampling principle   The concept that if a small number of units (otherwise known as the SAMPLE) are chosen at random from the total POPULATION or *universe* being studied, the sample will tend to have the same characteristics, and in the same proportion, as the universe. This means that the results of the research are *generalizable* (i.e., able to be extended) to the entire population.

sampling procedure   The process used to select the respondents to be studied and interviewed in MARKETING RESEARCH (MR) and other social sciences research. This may be done through PROBABILITY SAMPLING or NONPROBABILITY SAMPLING. See also SAMPLING PLAN and SAMPLE.

sampling unit   The segment of the total POPULATION that is to be sampled in MARKETING RESEARCH (MR) and other social sciences research. See also SAMPLING PLAN and SAMPLE.

S&H   See SHIPPING AND HANDLING (S&H).

San Francisco Fashion Center   A regional MERCHANDISE MART for apparel located in San Francisco, California.

satellite store   1. Sometimes, a BRANCH STORE in a MULTI-UNIT DEPARTMENT STORE organization.   2. In a SHOPPING CENTER, any of the smaller stores clustered around the large ANCHOR STORE or stores.

satisfaction of demand   The degree to which a product or service (or the marketer of that product or service) meets customer needs and desires through product availability, product performance, after-purchase relationships, etc.

satisficing   (Slang) Decision making behavior in which the manager selects an alternative product or service that, while not as good as the original, is good enough (i.e., will yield a satisfactory return to the organization). *Der.* blend of *satisfying* and *sufficing*.

satisfier   Any characteristic of a product that is intrinsically pleasing to the consumer. According to Frederick Herzberg's well-known theory of customer motivation, consumers seek to maximize the number of satisfiers when selecting an item for purchase. Contrast with DISSATISFIER, any characteristic of a product the customer finds displeasing. See also TWO-FACTOR THEORY OF MOTIVATION.

saturated area   A retail trading area in which there are just enough stores to provide goods and services for the population and not so many stores that they cannot make a fair profit. Also called *retail saturation*, *saturated market*, and *saturation*. See also INDEX OF (RETAIL) SATURATION (IRS).

saturated market   See SATURATED AREA and INDEX OF (RETAIL) SATURATION (IRS).

saturation   1. A situation that exists when sales of an item of merchandise fall off dramatically because most consumers likely to be interested in it have already purchased it. Also called *horizontal saturation*. See also PRODUCT LIFE CYCLE (PLC).   2. In advertising, heavier coverage than usual, particularly with radio and TV spots.   3. A situation that exists when there are just enough stores to provide goods and services for the population and not so many stores that they cannot make a fair profit. See also SATURATED AREA and INDEX OF (RETAIL) SATURATION (IRS).

saturation index   See INDEX OF (RETAIL) SATURATION (IRS).

Savile Row   A London street famous for its fine men's tailoring establishments. Savile Row shops cater to wealthy, international customers seeking high-quality conservative attire.

savings and loan association   A bank that offers savings, interest-bearing checking, and loans (particularly mortgages). Customers tend to be individuals and small businesses. Also called a *thrift institution* or *savings bank*.

savings bank   See SAVINGS AND LOAN ASSOCIATION.

SBA   See SMALL BUSINESS ADMINISTRATION (SBA).

SBD   See SECONDARY BUSINESS DISTRICT (SBD).

SBIC   See SMALL BUSINESS INVESTMENT COMPANY (SBIC).

SBP   See SURVEY OF BUYING POWER (SBP).

SBU   See STRATEGIC BUSINESS UNIT (SBU).

scab   Derogatory synonym for STRIKEBREAKER.

scam   A scheme to swindle, cheat, or defraud, particularly when perpetrated on the unsuspecting public.

scam artist   A person perpetrating a fraudulent scheme or swindle on the public.

SCAN (Store Check Authorization Network)   See BANK CHECK FRAUD TASK FORCE.

scan-it-yourself technology (SIY)   A program developed in Europe and most fully realized in the Netherlands, through which customers who register to participate are issued identification cards with magnetic strips for making purchases. Upon entering the store, a customer picks up a portable scanner and uses it to check prices and record selections while shopping. The checkout procedure involves the printing of a receipt and the tendering of a payment. In Australia, scan-it-yourself devices incorporated into shopping carts equipped with plasma screens and product-scanning software were introduced in 2005. The wireless computers allow customers to scan the items they put in their shopping carts, keeping a running tally of the bill as they move through the aisles. The technology, called *U-Scan Shopper*, relies heavily on the honesty of shoppers to scan their products. When customers finish shopping they pay the amount displayed on their shopping cart computer. Checkout attendants spot-check the shopping carts to ensure the contents match with those paid for by the customer. In the United States, *self-check aisles* are becoming increasingly commonplace at supermarkets and large discounters. The *self-check machines* used in these aisles comprise a scanner, a scale, a touch screen, a cash accepter/dispenser, and a credit card reader combined into a single unit.

scanner   See OPTICAL CODE READER (OCR) and OPTICAL SCANNING.

scanner market   The users, current and potential, of optical scanners to gather important information for TEST MARKETING. Scanners are installed in retail stores where the test products are offered for sale, and special arrangements are made to gather all relevant information about both the products and the customers. See also OPTICAL SCANNING.

scanning   See OPTICAL SCANNING.

scarcity cost   The economic concept that whenever resources are limited (i.e., scarce), the decision to use some of those resources means that they will not be available for other uses. See also OPPORTUNITY COST.

scarcity value   An increase in the worth and price of an item due to increased DEMAND and limited SUPPLY. For example, works of art increase in value once the artist has died.

scare purchasing   Unusually heavy buying of specific merchandise, due to hoarding or emergency situations. For example, the purchase of plywood to protect windows in preparation for an impending hurricane far exceeds the purchase of plywood during normal periods. There may be a rush on plywood until all available sources have been depleted.

scenario planning   A disciplined ten-step process for imagining possible futures, applicable to a wide range of business issues. Scenario planning explores the joint impact of various uncertainties, all weighted equally. It attempts to capture the richness and range of possibilities, stimulating decision makers to consider changes they would otherwise ignore.

schedule 1. A systematic plan for the retailer's future operations over a given period. A schedule details the sequence of events and the time allotted for each project or objective. See also RETAIL CALENDAR. 2. Any timetable. See also SCHEDULING (def. 1).

scheduling 1. The organization and distribution of the time needed to carry out a sales effort or other project. 2. In advertising, the process of setting the time(s) for advertisements or commercials to run. The primary objective is to time promotional efforts to coincide with the period when the target audience can best be reached. Three scheduling strategies are generally used by media planners: CONTINUITY (i.e., the steady placement of advertisements over a specified period of time); FLIGHTING (i.e., a much less regular schedule, combining periods of moderate to heavy exposure with a hiatus or lapse prior to restarting the advertising schedule); and PULSING (i.e., a combination of the first two methods.)

scheduling of sales personnel See SCHEDULING.

schlock merchandise Goods that are cheaply made and of inferior quality, both in materials and workmanship. In addition, the term sometimes indicates that the taste level of the merchandise is low or vulgar. Sometimes called, simply, *schlock*. Also spelled *shlock*. *Der.* Yiddish, "curse."

schlock operation A retail store characterized by the sale of shoddy, inferior, and sometimes meretricious (i.e., flashy, vulgar, tasteless) goods.

scientific management A management philosophy popular in the early twentieth century. The program was based on predictable, repeatable, and controllable goals achieved through the application of numbers and formulas.

scientific marketing See ANALYTICAL MARKETING SYSTEM (AMS) and MARKETING SYSTEM.

scientific method A research approach applicable to both the sciences and the social sciences, of which MARKETING RESEARCH (MR) is a part. The scientific method consists of four stages: making an observation; developing a hypothesis or series of hypotheses; predicting an outcome or future; and testing the hypothesis or hypotheses.

SCL See SHIPPING CONTAINER MARKING (SCM).

SCM See SHIPPING CONTAINER MARKING (SCM).

scorched earth policy A firm's negative reaction to a takeover attempt by another firm. Scorched earth is a self-destructive strategy in which a company seeks to discourage a takeover by making itself less attractive. For example, the firm may sell off its most attractive divisions or other assets. See also ACQUISITION.

scorecard credit system A system for the evaluation of credit worthiness. Applicants for retail credit are awarded points for various attributes. Points are totaled to give a final

score used to determine approval or disapproval of the credit application.

S corporation A corporation with no more than 35 shareholders, taxable as a partnership. Also known as a *subchapter S corporation*.

scrambled merchandise A practice by which retailers maintain types of goods not normally found in those types of stores. Clothing sold in a drug store is an example of scrambled merchandise. The practice results in a wider variety of products being represented in the store. See also SCRAMBLED MERCHANDISING and INTERTYPE COMPETITION.

scrambled merchandising In retailing, the practice of offering merchandise for sale that is usually associated with a different kind of store (e.g., the sale of many nonfood items in supermarkets). In scrambled merchandising, the lines added to the merchandise mix will generally be fast sellers that carry a high margin of profit. Also called *mixed merchandising*. See also SCRAMBLED MERCHANDISE.

screening of ideas See SCREENING STAGE.

screening stage In NEW PRODUCT DEVELOPMENT, the stage at which new ideas for products are evaluated to determine which of them may offer opportunities for development by the firm. Also called the *screening of ideas*. See also PRODUCT DEVELOPMENT.

scrip coupon See CREDIT SLIP.

S-curve effect A graphic representation of the decline in sales that follows the withdrawal of advertising support for a product. See also S-SHAPED CURVE MODEL.

SDB See SMALL DISADVANTAGED BUSINESS (SDB).

SD/BL See SIGHT DRAFT/BILL OF LADING (SD/BL).

sealed bid An offer to perform a service or supply goods, submitted to a buyer in a sealed envelope to be opened at a specified future time. Under this system competitive bids are not revealed publicly. Sealed bids are commonly required in government purchasing in an effort to obtain the lowest possible price as required by law. Also known as a *closed bid*. Compare OPEN BID. See also SEALED BID PRICING.

sealed bid pricing A pricing strategy in which a firm, such as a building contractor, sets the prices for its products or services on the basis of what it anticipates its competitors will bid. The competitors' bids are not known, because each bidder submits its proposal within a certain period of time in a manner not visible to its competitors (i.e., sealed). See also SEALED BID.

seamstress Synonym for *dressmaker*, that is, a person whose occupation is DRESSMAKING.

search 1. The process used by customers to gather and interpret information about the goods and services available in the marketplace. The search process helps customers decide whether or not to purchase an item or service and includes the consideration of alternative goods and services. See also SHOPPING GOODS.   2. In INTERNET use, the process of seeking and finding information, generally using a SEARCH ENGINE. The user keys in a term or phrase and the search engine, by means of complex electronic directories, returns a list of specific Web sites that match the query.

search engine   Any of a number of companies that enable the user to find those Web pages on the Internet that can best meet their needs or answer their research question. The user keys in a term or phrase and the search engine, by means of complex electronic directories, returns a list of specific Web sites that match the query. See also WEB SITE.

search engine promotion   The use of SEARCH ENGINES to promote a WEB SITE. See also PAID INCLUSION SERVICE.

search goods   Items of merchandise whose desired qualities (e.g., functionality, appearance, price) are easily determined prior to purchase. The customer actively seeks out products having those qualities. See also EXPERIENCE ITEMS.

search site   A WEB SITE that collects and compares product information for visitors. These sites use intelligent agents, search software, or human monitors to search online stores, collecting price, product, store, and product availability information. Continuous sweeps of the Web are required to capture the most current price and shipping information. Most search sites offer a CLICK THROUGH to each seller's site along with a MERCHANT REVIEW.

season   1. In retailing, a selling period. Commonly there are two seasons in each year, spring (comprising the 26 weeks from February through July) and fall (the 26 weeks from August through January). Also called the *selling season.*   2. In the fashion industry, short for FASHION SEASON.

seasonal dating   See ADVANCE DATING.

seasonal demand   Consumer demand that is directly related to the season of the year or to special holidays such as Thanksgiving and Christmas. For example, ski equipment is in great demand in the winter while swimwear is in great demand in the summer. Selling SEASONAL MERCHANDISE outside its high demand season generally requires special promotions and/or price reductions. Also called *seasonality.*

seasonal department   A section of a department store (or other large store) devoted to merchandise closely related to a particular season of the year (e.g., a Christmas decorating shop).

seasonal discount   A reduction in price offered by a manufacturer to encourage the retailer and/or marketing intermediary to place orders for merchandise ahead of the normal buying period (i.e., in the off-season). Early orders enable manufacturers to even out their production schedules and operate with greater efficiency. Seasonal discounts are most often offered on SEASONAL MERCHANDISE such as skis, swimsuits, air conditioners, lawn mowers, or snow blowers. For example, a manufacturer may offer a seasonal discount of 2% to buyers who place orders for next year's lawn mowers in October. The retailer is thus compensated for the additional warehousing expenses that may be incurred by receiving delivery far in advance of the selling season.

seasonal employee   A person hired during peak selling periods (e.g., Christmas) to temporarily augment the staff.

seasonal fluctuation   Any reasonable and predictable shift in DEMAND (and, consequently, business activity) associated with changes in season. For example, sales of snowplows may be expected to fluctuate throughout the year, with sales increasing in the winter months and decreasing in the summer. Also called *seasonal variation.*

seasonal forecast   A prediction made for a particular future season (such as the fall and spring seasons in apparel). See also FORECAST and FORECASTING. The process of making such predictions is known as *seasonal forecasting.*

seasonal goods/items   See SEASONAL MERCHANDISE.

seasonality   Synonym for SEASONAL DEMAND.

seasonal marketing   The practice of gearing one's product offerings, sales, and promotions to a season, holiday, or event. See also SEASONAL MERCHANDISE.

seasonal merchandise   Goods closely identified with a particular season or holiday (e.g., Christmas decorations, bathing suits, antifreeze, snowblowers). Seasonal merchandise commonly has a short sales life, and extra efforts (such as promotions and price reductions) are generally required to move the merchandise in the OFF-SEASON. A MODEL STOCK PLAN will generally include an assortment of seasonal merchandise. Also called *seasonal goods* or *seasonal items.* See also SEASONAL STAPLES.

seasonal/staple continuum   In apparel merchandising, the full range of items from those that experience no change in demand related to the time of year (i.e., a STAPLE such as underwear) to those for which demand varies seasonally (i.e., SEASONAL MERCHANDISE such as swimsuits). These represent the two extremes of the spectrum. Many items of apparel fall somewhere in between. Compare FASHION/BASIC CONTINUUM.

seasonal staples   Those staple products for which sales vary throughout the year or during specific times of the year in a manner that is predictable. For example, Christmas tree trimmings are considered staples during the Christmas season only. Compare NONSEASONAL STAPLES. See also STAPLE and SEASONAL MERCHANDISE.

seasonal variation   Synonym for SEASONAL FLUCTUATION.

season code/letter   A coded, alphanumeric combination placed on price tags so that the employees (but not customers) can tell when merchandise was received by the store. This information may be used for inventory analysis and for planning markdowns.

second An item of merchandise that has been damaged in manufacture or is otherwise flawed (although still serviceable) and is offered at retail at a greatly reduced price. Often used in the plural (i.e., *seconds*). Distinguished from SECOND-LINE MERCHANDISE/GOODS. See also THIRD. Compare IRREGULAR.

secondary aisle A narrow aisle that interconnects major aisles, often carrying customer TRAFFIC through selling areas. A secondary aisle is not as clearly defined as a MAJOR AISLE. A line of fixtures is sometimes used to define a secondary aisle.

secondary boycott A BOYCOTT of companies doing business with the target of the original boycott. For example, employees boycotting a manufacturer may also boycott the bank financing that manufacturer's operations. The employees encourage the public to boycott the firms as well.

secondary business district (SBD) An unplanned urban shopping area often containing one or more supermarkets, a variety store, a small department store, and a variety of small service stores. Secondary business districts, which characteristically sprout up in outlying areas of cities as populations migrate to the urban perimeters, are often found at the intersection of two main streets. SBDs are traditionally important locations for independently owned specialty stores and service retailers. Also called a *secondary shopping district* or a *subshopping district*.

secondary data Information previously collected by others and made available for research. Secondary data may be internal to the organization (e.g., company files) or external (e.g., data collected by such agencies as the U.S. Bureau of the Census or private sector marketing firms). Also called *secondary information*. Research based on secondary data is called SECONDARY RESEARCH. Compare PRIMARY DATA.

secondary demand See SELECTIVE DEMAND.

secondary information Synonym for SECONDARY DATA.

secondary lighting Supplemental lighting fixtures used to create shadows and highlights on the selling floor and provide extra light where necessary. Secondary lighting may be in the form of chandeliers, wall sconces, track lights, hidden lights that wash a wall with light or color, etc. Also called *accent lighting*. Compare PRIMARY LIGHTING.

secondary market In the fashion/apparel industry, the designers, manufacturers, and the channel of distribution between the *primary market* (i.e., the producers of the raw materials) and the *tertiary market* (i.e., the retailers). Manufacturers are responsible for creating fashions using the forecasted colors and fabrics developed by the primary market. They produce items 6 to 12 months in advance of the selling season and present the designed goods to retail buyers several months in advance of expected delivery. See also SECONDARY MARKET FORECAST, TERTIARY MARKET, and PRIMARY MARKET.

secondary market forecast FASHION FORECASTING made by the *secondary market* (i.e., designers, manufacturers, and members of the channel of distribution). Manufacturers create fashions using the forecasted colors and fabrics delivered by the PRIMARY MARKET and produce items 6 to 12 months in advance of the selling season. They present the designed goods to retail buyers 4 to 6 months in advance of expected delivery. Fashion shows and the fashion press play major roles in disseminating fashion/apparel trends at the SECONDARY MARKET level. See also PRIMARY MARKET FORECAST and TERTIARY MARKET FORECAST.

secondary marketing research MARKETING RESEARCH (MR) based on SECONDARY DATA, both internal and external. A great deal of secondary data is available via the INTERNET. Since much secondary marketing research involves previously published studies, care must be taken to avoid copyright infringement. See also SECONDARY RESEARCH.

secondary market segment An auxiliary target group with potential value to the message sponsor. For example, while the *primary market segment* for children's apparel may be parents, the secondary market segment may be grandparents. See also PRIMARY MARKET SEGMENT.

secondary medium See SUPPORT MEDIUM.

secondary membership group See MEMBERSHIP GROUP.

secondary methods Research procedures used by researchers working with SECONDARY DATA. In the *pull method of secondary research*, the researcher identifies useful secondary sources, contacts the source of the data or accesses it online, and evaluates the contents for applicability. In the *push method of secondary research*, research companies use opt-in e-mails or newsletters to announce the availability of current data to potential clients. Pushed content is designed to motivate the researcher to click through and purchase the report or establish a relationship with the research company that may result in a future purchase.

secondary needs Among the basic motivations that cause individual consumers to make purchase decisions, those resulting from the particular culture or environment in which the individual lives rather than from basic physiological factors such as thirst, hunger, and the need for shelter. Secondary needs would include, therefore, the need for status, self-advancement, individual fulfillment, and other culturally determined factors. See also MASLOW'S HIERARCHY (OF NEEDS) and PRIMARY NEEDS.

secondary research Research conducted using existing in-house or external research reported by others. Secondary research uses published studies conducted by others, or reports and data generated internally for other purposes. If the secondary research compares the results of large numbers of other studies, it is called METARESEARCH. Compare PRIMARY RESEARCH. See also SECONDARY DATA and SECONDARY MARKETING RESEARCH.

secondary shopping district See SECONDARY BUSINESS DISTRICT (SBD).

secondary source   Any government agency, private company, professional group, or organization that collects a broad array of data available for secondary research. The U.S. government, for example, is the largest data collector in the world and hosts a vast number of Web pages containing both free and fee-based information for researchers.

secondary trading area   For a retail store, the zone outside the PRIMARY TRADING AREA from which customers are attracted but with increasing difficulty due to their distance from the store. The secondary trading area contains 20 to 25 percent of a store's potential customers. Also called the *secondary trade area*. See also FRINGE TRADING AREA.

second.coming   A prediction that there will be a resurgence of hundreds of failed dotcom ideas and concepts that disappeared during the INTERNET crash in 2000. These second-chance ideas will enter a new, much more attractive arena in which there are many more avid Internet users and e-tail shoppers. Pronounced *second dot coming*. The trend was identified and the term coined by trendwatching.com at www.trendwatching.com. See also E-TAILING.

second dot coming   See SECOND.COMING.

secondhand   Used merchandise offered for sale at prices generally far less than when the products were new. Secondhand merchandise (e.g., apparel and household effects) is often available for purchase in a THRIFT SHOP or on eBay. The sale of used cars is also a lucrative secondhand business. Also called *previously owned* or *used*.

second-level domain   For online marketers, the most important part of the DOMAIN NAME, since it functions like a brand name in representing the firm to Internet users. The second-level domain should represent the organization as well as possible, be as short as possible while remaining distinctive, and convey the name or purpose of the firm. For example, in www.fairchildpub.com, the URL of the publisher of this dictionary, fairchildpub is the second-level domain.

second-line merchandise/goods   A manufacturer's line of goods sold at a lower price than the regular line. Second-line goods may be of lower quality, but they are not seconds (i.e., they are not defective). A manufacturer may sell second-line merchandise through its FACTORY OUTLET. Distinguished from SECOND.

second markdown   See ADDITIONAL MARKDOWN.

seconds   See SECOND.

second sale   An additional sale made to a returning customer. Second sales are achieved by building on customer satisfaction with the initial purchase. See also REPEAT ITEM.

second shift   Those persons working afternoons and evenings.

sectional wholesaler   A WHOLESALE operation that limits its activities to a fixed and relatively small number of geographic areas or states. Also called a *regional wholesaler*. Compare LOCAL WHOLESALER and NATIONAL WHOLESALER.

section manager   In a department store, a supervisor who has the responsibility for the efficient running of a specific part of the store, usually several related or adjacent departments.

secular trend   A pattern of growth or decline in a particular business, industry, or economy that occurs over a long period of time (e.g., 20 to 30 years). Secular trends may result from changes in population, availability of capital for investment, advances in technology and production methods, changes in consumer behavior, etc. Also called a *long-term trend*.

secured account   Any credit account in which collateral is held by the party extending the credit. See also SECURED LOAN and STORE CREDIT.

secured distribution   A form of field WAREHOUSING in which carload lots are shipped to a distributor's premises. By means of a special arrangement with a BONDED WAREHOUSE, the shipment is released as the distributor needs the merchandise.

secured loan   A loan backed by some specific valuable item or items, known as collateral, which may be seized by the lender should the borrower fail to repay the loan. The three main types of collateral are accounts receivable, inventories, and other property. See also UNSECURED LOAN and SECURED ACCOUNT.

secure electronic transmission protocol (SET)   In ELECTRONIC RETAILING, software that protects transactions between buyers and sellers. Developed by Visa and MasterCard, SET helps to reduce RISK to both retailers and customers.

Secure HTTP (S-HTTP)   A protocol for transmitting individual data messages securely over the WORLD WIDE WEB (WWW). See also SSL.

Secure/MIME   See S/MIME.

Secure Sockets Layer (SSL)   See SSL.

securities   Stocks, bonds, and similar investments in a company. When such investments are available to be turned quickly into cash, they are called *marketable securities*.

security   1. The department charged with the responsibility for protecting the store against losses from pilferage, shoplifting, robbery, and other crimes against persons and property. Some stores hire outside security firms to perform this function. Also called the *protection department, security department, store security,* or *security division*. See also LOSS PREVENTION (LP). 2. See SECURITIES. 3. See JOB SECURITY.

security agreement   A written contract between a buyer and a seller stipulating that the seller retains an interest in the goods.

security department/division   See SECURITY.

see-hear-buy The ability to buy everything one sees or hears, instantaneously and wherever one is, on the INTERNET. The trend was identified and the term coined by trendwatching.com at www.trendwatching.com.

see-through window See OPEN-BACK WINDOW.

segment 1. n. A relatively homogeneous group of consumers or enterprises with similar characteristics and buying behaviors. 2. v. To separate or divide a large group or population into smaller groups.

segmentation See MARKET SEGMENTATION.

segmentation adoption process variables The stages of awareness, interest, evaluation, trial, and adoption experienced by each consumer in the course of becoming a regular purchaser of a product, used as a basis for subdividing a population of potential consumers. These stages are known as the ADOPTION PROCESS. For a new or unconventional product or service (such as home banking by computer) they offer a key to segmentation, helping the retailer or other marketer focus on particular target markets.

segmentation descriptors The individual categories defining each subdivision (i.e., segment) of a potential market. For example, if the segments are established according to a demographic characteristic such as race, the descriptors would be Caucasian, African American, Asian, etc.

segmentation pricing A strategy in which prices are set at different levels for different segments of the population. This legal form of PRICE DISCRIMINATION is commonly found in the airline industry, where different classes of service are provided for different segments of the traveling public, and in other industries where costs do not decline greatly when consumption or use declines. See also MARKET SEGMENTATION.

segmentation strategy Synonym for DIFFERENTIATION.

segmentation variability analysis (SVA) A technique developed by Lawrence G. Golden and Donald A. Zimmerman for the identification and selection of prime variables in any given situation. All possible segmentation variables are listed and analyzed with regard to the importance placed on them by the consumers in a particular market. The technique also takes into account the relative ease with which a variable may be further subdivided to show distinct buying patterns, whether or not a strong sales approach can be planned around the variable, and related factors.

segmentation variable Any factor that can be used to divide the mass of consumers into smaller groups for the purposes of marketing. For example, age, income, education, and lifestyle are all segmentation variables. See also PRIME VARIABLE.

segmented format corporate chain See CORPORATE CHAIN.

segmented merchandising The offering of goods for sale that have been carefully chosen to appeal to certain age groups, persons with similar social and economic backgrounds, etc. See also MARKET SEGMENTATION.

segmenter A marketing firm that employs either the SINGLE TARGET MARKET APPROACH or the MULTIPLE TARGET MARKET APPROACH when developing a marketing strategy.

selection criterion Synonym for SELECTION FACTOR.

selection factor Any quality inherent in merchandise that helps determine the customer's buying behavior (i.e., helps the customer decide whether or not to purchase the merchandise). For example, the color or wool content of a sweater may serve as a selection factor. Also called *selection criterion*.

selective advertising Synonym for COMPETITIVE ADVERTISING.

selective buying motive Any influence or incentive that contributes to a customer's buying behavior by encouraging or discouraging a choice of products or services.

selective demand The market demand for a particular brand of merchandise as opposed to the demand for the total class of products. For example, the demand for Levi's jeans as opposed to the demand for jeans in general. Also called *secondary demand*. Compare PRIMARY DEMAND.

selective distortion See SELECTIVE PERCEPTION.

selective distribution A MARKETING STRATEGY standing between EXCLUSIVE DISTRIBUTION on the one hand and INTENSIVE DISTRIBUTION on the other. Manufacturers engaging in selective distribution restrict the number of marketing intermediaries and retailers who resell their products in a particular area in order to better control both the degree of exposure and the cost of distributing the product. Also called *selective selling* and *limited distribution*. Compare OPEN DISTRIBUTION.

selective exposure See SELECTIVE PERCEPTION.

selective perception The ability of individuals to filter out certain sensory data (i.e., stimuli) while retaining others. Marketers have learned that consumers tend to notice only a portion of the stimuli to which they are exposed (i.e., *selective exposure*), to interpret selectively the information they do receive (i.e., *selective distortion*), and remember only those perceptions that seem relevant to their own lives or current needs (i.e., *selective retention*). Consumers are also more likely to perceive stimuli they anticipate and those that show a major change in price, quality, or design. Marketers have devised various methods of overcoming selective perception, such as increasing the frequency with which advertising messages are repeated, creating unusual and attention-grabbing ads, varying the format of the ads run for any given product, etc. Some marketers have also experimented with the use of SUBLIMINAL PERCEPTION to reach consumers below the level of their conscious perception. See also JUST NOTICEABLE DIFFERENCE (JND), PERCEPTION, and THRESHOLD OF PERCEPTION.

selective retention See SELECTIVE PERCEPTION.

selective selling Synonym for SELECTIVE DISTRIBUTION.

selective stocking The decision making process that is used to determine how much merchandise to stock at each DISTRIBUTION CENTER (DC). The cost of maintaining inventory in stock is balanced against the desire to provide optimum service.

self-actualization The result of becoming all that one is capable of being. When they have reached this level, people feel secure and do not have the need to state their accomplishments through possessions. See also MASLOW'S HIERARCHY (OF NEEDS) and MOTIVE.

self-actualization needs See SELF-ACTUALIZATION and MASLOW'S HIERARCHY (OF NEEDS).

self-check/self-checkout aisle See SCAN-IT-YOURSELF TECHNOLOGY (SIY).

self-check/self-checkout machine See SCAN-IT-YOURSELF TECHNOLOGY (SIY).

self-concept Synonym for SELF-IMAGE.

self-concept theory The idea that two factors influencing one's purchasing behavior are how one perceives oneself and how one wishes to be perceived by others. See also MASLOW'S HIERARCHY (OF NEEDS) and MOTIVE.

self-image The mental picture an individual has of himself or herself and imagines others to have of him or her. Self-image, also called *self-concept*, includes characteristics, traits, possessions, role, behavior, etc., but the emphasis is on the way these things are perceived rather than on the things themselves. An individual's IDEAL SELF, or *ideal self-image*, is the person the individual would like to be, or the end to which the individual is striving. An individual's OTHERS-SELF-CONCEPT is the way the individual thinks others perceive him or her. The problem for the marketer is to determine which concept of self will prompt the purchase of the product or service and how best to appeal to that concept. See also MOTIVE.

self-liquidating display An interior store display provided by the manufacturer or vendor. The cost of the display is passed on to the retailer.

self-liquidating premium/offer A consumer premium in which an item is offered for sale in conjunction with the purchase of another product. The consumer generally sends in both a proof-of-purchase and a cash payment (sometimes described as shipping and handling fees). The promotion is self-liquidating in that the sale price is usually the premium's cost to the firm running the promotion. Also called a *self-liquidator*. See also SEMILIQUIDATOR.

self-liquidator See SELF-LIQUIDATING PREMIUM/OFFER.

self-owned store See SOLE PROPRIETORSHIP.

self-selection A form of retail selling in which the customer is required to find the actual item wanted and take it to the salesperson in the department to complete the sale. Salespeople do not generally assist with the selection process. Cash registers or point-of-sale terminals (POSTs) are usually scattered around the selling floor rather than concentrated at the store's exits as they are in self-service stores. Also called *self-selection selling*. See also SIMPLIFIED SELLING. Compare SELF-SERVICE RETAILING.

self-selection selling See SELF-SELECTION.

self-service A form of retail selling in which merchandise is displayed so that customers can make their selections without the aid of a salesperson. Customers roam about looking for what they want to buy and depend on labels or cartons for product information. The customers then take their selections to a checkout point, usually near the exit of the store, where a cashier completes the transaction. For large items, customers are sometimes expected to rip a ticket off the box or display and take it to a checkout; the customers pay for the product and it is brought to them either inside the store or outside at a loading dock. See also SELF-SERVICE RETAILING.

self-service establishment See SELF-SERVICE RETAILING.

self-service retailing A retail operation in which merchandise is displayed so customers can make their selections without the aid of a salesperson. Customers take their selections to a checkout station, usually located at the store's exit, and pay a CASHIER. Self-service is common in discount and supermarket operations. See also SIMPLIFIED SELLING and SELF-SERVICE.

self-service store See SELF-SERVICE RETAILING and SELF-SERVICE.

sell-and-lease agreement See LEASEBACK.

sell by (date) The month, day, and year by which it is recommended that a food item should be sold. The date is marked on the package as a warning to customers by indicating a possible loss of freshness. See also DISPLAY UNTIL (DATE).

seller beware See CAVEAT VENDITOR/VENDOR.

seller concentration A measure of the number of sellers in a single industry. The greater the number of sellers, the less likely it is that any one firm can dominate the industry and influence price.

seller's lien A seller's right to hold back part of a shipment until the buyer has paid for the goods. See also LIEN.

sellers' market A situation in which the demand for merchandise exceeds the supply. Also called a *tight market*.

seller's surplus The difference between the PRICE a seller actually receives and the lowest price that he or she would accept.

sell-in A manufacturing firm's efforts to convince a retailer to carry and distribute its merchandise.

selling 1. In the most general sense, the offering of goods or services for sale. 2. In retailing, the process of changing ownership of merchandise from the retailer to the ultimate customer. 3. In a more restricted sense, a marketing function whose object is to arouse demand for a product or service on the part of potential customers. This may be a creative endeavor that includes advertising and other forms of promotion, or it may be more mundane (e.g., order taking). CREATIVE SELLING often involves persuading the prospective customer to buy specific merchandise by determining the customer's needs, making a sales presentation, and closing the sale. Also called the *selling function*. See also RETAIL SELLING and ORDER TAKER.

selling against the brand The practice of maintaining artificially high prices on certain categories of merchandise in an effort to increase sales on some other merchandise.

selling agent An AGENT INTERMEDIARY (i.e., middleman) who sells all the products of his client manufacturer under a contractual agreement, but does not take title to the merchandise. The selling agent may also provide the client with market information for the extensive territory covered. Unlike the MANUFACTURER'S AGENT, the selling agent has considerable authority with regard to prices, credit, delivery dates, and other terms of sale and is virtually in charge of the selling activities of the firm. Also called a *sales agent*.

selling aid Any of the benefits and services offered by the merchandise resource to the retailer. Selling aids include demonstrators, finance and credit, return privileges, exclusive distribution, markdown insurance, and memorandum buying. See also PERSONAL PROMOTIONAL AID, NONPERSONAL PROMOTION AID, DEALER HELPS, and DEALER AID.

selling area The total amount of floor space devoted to selling activities, including aisles, fitting rooms, and adjacent stockrooms. Also called *retail space*. See also SELLING FLOOR.

selling calendar A month-by-month plan, often laid out in the form of a calendar, showing coming promotions and other events in a store.

selling concept A MARKETING MANAGEMENT orientation in which persistent personal selling coupled with an aggressive advertising campaign is seen as the most effective way to build sales. Organizations influenced by the selling concept view high sales levels as equivalent to high profits and believe that customer demand can be generated for nearly any product if sufficient effort is expended. Such organizations are said to be *sales-oriented*. Also called the *sales concept*. See also PRODUCT CONCEPT, PRODUCTION CONCEPT, and MARKETING CONCEPT.

selling cost See SELLING EXPENSES.

selling days The actual number of days in a specified period that a store is open for business. Often used in such phrases as "Only 25 selling days left until Christmas." See also RETAIL CALENDAR.

selling equipment Synonym for FIXTURE.

selling error Merchandise that is inadequately displayed or sold to the customer. A MARKDOWN (MD) is generally necessary to correct the error and move the merchandise.

selling expense budget See SALES EXPENSE BUDGET.

selling expenses Any costs incurred through the actual selling process, as well as expenses associated with advertising and promotion. Selling expenses include the wages or salaries of salespeople, advertising, supplies, insurance for the sales operation, depreciation of the store and other sales equipment, and all miscellaneous sales department expenses (e.g., utilities and maintenance). Selling expenses are one of the two subclassifications of operating expenses (the other being GENERAL EXPENSES).

selling floor That part of the store that is devoted to selling activities. It is where merchandise is displayed and customers pass or stop and shop. The maximization of selling floor space is an important store layout consideration since the value of space within a store is predicated on the number of customers that pass through or by the space. See also SELLING AREA.

selling formula approach A sales method that assumes that all customers are alike or at least will respond in a predictable way to a set sales presentation. The method is frequently applied in TELEMARKETING.

selling function Synonym for SELLING.

selling house Synonym for FOREIGN EXPORTER.

selling intermediary See RESELLER MARKET.

selling price The price actually paid for an item at retail. Distinguished from SALE PRICE. Also called the *transaction price*.

selling process A series of steps taken by a salesperson engaged in selling activities. These include PROSPECTING, the PREAPPROACH, the APPROACH, the SALES PRESENTATION, and, finally, the CLOSING. Follow-up activities are sometimes included as part of the selling process. See also SALES APPROACH.

selling season See SEASON.

selling short 1. In retailing, the practice of selling merchandise at a lower-than-desired price in order to move the merchandise and turn a profit. Also called *short selling* or a *short sale*. 2. In stock market transactions, the act of selling stock one doesn't own (i.e., stock borrowed from a broker) in the hope of buying it back again later at a lower price. When the stock is returned to the broker, the investor keeps the difference between the purchase price and the selling price. Also called *short selling*.

selling up See TRADING UP (def. 2).

sell-off Synonym for SELL-THROUGH.

sell out 1. In merchandising, to dispose of the entire stock of a product. 2. To betray a person, organization, principle, or cause, usually for financial profit or other benefit.

sell-through   The amount of merchandise sold over a specified period of time, sometimes expressed as a percentage of the total amount on hand. Also called *sell-off*. See also BEST SELLER and TWELVE-WEEK SELL-THROUGH.

semantic differential scale   A tool used by marketing researchers to determine and measure consumer attitudes. The scale consists of pairs of opposite words separated by a line divided into seven parts. Respondents check the space that most nearly describes their attitude. A check in the fourth (i.e., center) space indicates a neutral attitude and a check in the extreme position on either side indicates a strongly held view pro or con. After the test is completed, a researcher connects the checks to get a composite picture of the attitudes indicated. Also used in other social sciences.

semiabstract mannequin   A figure that is even more stylized than the semirealistic model. For example, facial features may be simply painted on or suggested. Hair is generally painted on. Body proportions remain lifelike.

semidirect expense   Any cost that is not directly chargeable to a store department (as direct expenses would be) but can be associated with that department. For example, the department's use of the store delivery system is considered a semidirect expense.

semi-integrated organization   See RETAIL COOPERATIVE/CO-OP.

semijobber   A MERCHANT WHOLESALER that is vertically integrated, that is, selling at both the wholesale and retail levels of the CHANNEL OF DISTRIBUTION. This practice is known as *semijobbing*. Also called a *split function wholesaler*.

semiliquidator   A premium offer paid for in part by the consumer. Also called a *purchase-privilege offer* and a *semi-self-liquidator*. Compare SELF-LIQUIDATING PREMIUM/OFFER.

semimanufactured goods   Products that have required manufacturing (e.g., plate glass, insulation, textile fabrics) but will be incorporated into another product (e.g., an automobile, a house, apparel).

semi-pinup display   See PINUP DISPLAY/TECHNIQUE.

semiprecious stone   The largest of the GEMSTONE categories. Stones are regarded as semiprecious on the basis of hardness, brilliance, abundance, and current fashion. The amethyst, garnet, and opal are examples of semiprecious stones. See also PRECIOUS STONE and DECORATIVE STONE.

semipromotional store   A category into which many department stores fall. The semipromotional store tries to maintain a quality image while meeting price competition with limited promotions.

semirealistic display setting   In VISUAL MERCHANDISING, the suggestion of a realistic setting to which the customer can easily relate. The display gives just enough of the essence of the scene to make it recognizable to the viewer. Also called a *vignette display setting*.

semirealistic mannequin   A figure that is proportioned and sculpted like a realistic mannequin but with makeup and hair that is more decorative and stylized than natural.

semi-self-liquidator   See SEMILIQUIDATOR.

sender   In communications, the party transmitting (i.e., initiating) the message. Also known as the *source* or the *communicator*.

send transaction   A sale at retail that is to be delivered (i.e., sent) to the customer.

senior allocation analyst   The individual in a large retail organization responsible for handling a large volume of merchandise allocation and for training and supervising retail allocation analysts. The senior allocation analyst ensures that work flow within the department is evenly balanced and sees to it that timely decisions are made. See also ALLOCATION ANALYST.

senior discount   A price reduction offered to individuals of retirement age. For example, a pharmacy may offer a 10% discount to senior citizens on a particular day of the week, often a day that is usually slow. Similarly, movie theaters may make tickets to particular showings available to senior citizens at a reduced rate. In both examples, the senior discount is used to generate additional traffic and build GOODWILL.

senior market   The category to which older individuals, particularly retirees, belong. Such consumers are interested in items such as canes, large-size women's apparel, golf equipment, and greeting cards designed for retirees.

senior planner   A store executive responsible for projecting sales and inventories based on an analysis of sales history, current market trends, and the organization's performance objectives. Many organizations use the title to indicate seniority or level of responsibility. See also PLANNER and PLANNING.

Sensormatic system   An electronic gate system designed to reduce or eliminate shoplifting. Sensormatic is widely used in specialty and department stores in North America. Anti-shoplifting tags are applied to the merchandise, frequently at the point of manufacture, and are detected by the Sensormatic system if not removed by a cashier. See also SOURCE TAGGING.

sensory appeal   Selling efforts that appeal to the senses (i.e., sight, hearing, touch, taste, or smell) and are calculated to influence consumer behavior. For example, a scented insert promoting a perfume (smell) or a beautiful woman promoting automobiles (sight).

separate store organization   A decentralized form of branch store organization in which each branch is treated as a separate entity with separate buying responsibilities.

serial display   A series or bank of display windows that are related to one another in terms of similar merchandise or general theme. Many large department stores use serial displays at Christmas to tell a holiday story.

serial number   A number assigned to an individual product item, usually by the manufacturer, for purposes of identification. In consumer electronics, each computer, printer, scanner, telephone, television, etc. has a unique serial number, often used to register the product for a service contract.

series (trade) discount   See CHAIN DISCOUNT.

serious shopper   An individual who wants or needs a specific item and will not be influenced by alternatives. A serious shopper who leaves a store without making a purchase is more likely to return in the future if the sales associate has been honest in explaining that the store does not have what the customer wants at the moment and has suggested an acceptable alternative.

serpent in the garden   (Slang) A display placed near the entrance to a store. The purpose of the display is to attract customers' immediate attention, bring them into the store, and induce them to seek out the advertised product.

served market   See TARGET MARKET.

server   A computer or device on a network that manages the resources of the network. There are several types of servers. Often they are dedicated to performing specific server tasks. For example, a *file server* is a computer and a storage device dedicated to storing files. A *print server* is a computer that manages one or more printers. A *network server* is a computer that manages network traffic. A *database server* is a computer system that processes database queries. A *chat server* enables a large number of users to exchange information in real-time discussions. *Audio/video servers* enable Web sites to broadcast streaming multimedia content.

server log   See SERVER LOG FILE.

server log file   In INTERNET usage, a plain-text file that gathers WEB SITE traffic data. Most Web servers record every request they receive. These files are not readily readable by human beings but must be read by programs that decipher the code. The data characteristically include the user's name or machine identification number, the Web file or place requested, whether or not the request was successfully filled, the size of the file transferred, the browser used, the date and time when the request was logged, and whether a proxy server was used. Server logs are, therefore, traffic counters that record TRAFFIC on a Web site (i.e., hits). They cannot distinguish between a unique visit and a repeat visit, and do not record any traffic from files that are cached (i.e., stored). They are, however, useful for tracking what users do while they are on a Web site and can be used to compare site visit trends over time. Also called, simply, a *server log*.

service   1. The provision of accommodation and activities required by consumers, such as maintenance or repair (e.g., free alterations). See also STORE SERVICES.   2. The provider of such a service, particularly a company organized to provide that service or group of services (e.g., an air conditioner repair service or a shoe repair service). See also SERVICE BUSINESS. 3. An ENTERPRISE PRODUCT that is a performance (e.g., equipment repairs and maintenance, training, and other activities that contribute to production and operations).

service advertising   A form of INSTITUTIONAL ADVERTISING in which STORE SERVICES such as delivery, parking, etc., are emphasized.

service approach   A SALES APPROACH technique in which the salesperson promises to relieve the prospect of some work or responsibility through the product or service being sold.

service area   A part of a store not directly involved in the selling function, but used by customers. For example, elevators, escalators, and restrooms are service areas.

service building   A building providing a retail organization with space for such activities as alterations, repairs, equipment maintenance, etc.

service business   A business organization that sells services rather than tangible products. A floor waxing business, a shoe repair business, and a cleaning service are all service businesses. Also called a *service provider*. See also SERVICE, SERVICE INDUSTRIES, and STORE SERVICES.

service center   That part of a store devoted to such activities as watch repair, small appliance repair, etc.

service desk   See CUSTOMER SERVICE DESK.

service industries   Businesses that provide intangible products or perform useful labor on behalf of another. The industries included in the service sector include the wholesale and retail trade, finance and insurance, transportation, utilities, consulting, etc. They are distinguished from goods-producing businesses that produce tangible products in the manufacturing sector. See also SERVICE BUSINESS.

service mark   A word, symbol, sign, design, or slogan identifying a particular service. For example, the scales of justice may be used to identify a law firm; a striped pole signifies a barber shop.

service marketing   Those activities that facilitate the sale or delivery of a service. Included are services offered for profit by private concerns, those provided by government agencies, and those furnished by nonprofit organizations. Also called *services marketing*. See also SERVICE POSITIONING.

service merchandiser   See RACK JOBBER.

service mix   The range of customer services offered by a store. These vary considerably, depending on the type of retail format. See also STORE SERVICES.

service positioning   A MARKET POSITIONING strategy in which a service (such as car rental) rather than a tangible product is established in the MARKETPLACE. See also SERVICE MARKETING.

service provider Synonym for SERVICE BUSINESS.

service provider's agent An AGENT INTERMEDIARY (i.e., middleman) who represents a service provider in what is usually an exclusive territory. The service provider's agent may sell the services of a number of noncompeting clients simultaneously. Service provider's agents have limited control over prices and terms of sale. See also MANUFACTURER'S AGENT.

service provider's branch office A form of service provider wholesaling. It includes facilities for warehousing goods, as well as for selling them.

service provider's sales office A service provider wholesale operation located close to the market. No inventory is carried there.

service provider wholesaler A SERVICE PROVIDER that assumes the duties commonly performed by a WHOLESALER or other MARKETING INTERMEDIARY within the CHANNEL OF DISTRIBUTION.

service provider wholesaling A situation in which the SERVICE PROVIDER undertakes all of the WHOLESALING function itself, frequently through sales offices or branch offices. See also SERVICE PROVIDER WHOLESALER.

service retailing The sale, to the ultimate consumer, of services (e.g., car rental, dry cleaning) rather than tangible products.

service retailing organization A retail organization (e.g., a car rental agency) that sells services rather than tangible products to the ultimate consumer.

services See SERVICE and STORE SERVICES.

service salesperson A salesperson concerned with such matters as delivery and installation and whose responsibilities generally begin after the sale has been consummated.

services concept See BUNDLE OF SERVICES CONCEPT.

service selling A form of personal selling in which the buyer already knows what he or she wants. The salesperson is little more than an order taker. See also SALES APPROACH.

service shopper A retail store employee responsible for shopping other stores in order to report on the service features of the competition. The service shopper reports back on such features as the quality of sales personnel, cash and charge systems, delivery, and adjustments. Compare COMPARISON SHOPPER.

services marketing See SERVICE MARKETING.

service wholesaler See WHOLESALER.

SERVQUAL One of the most popular and widely used assessment tools of service quality, developed in the 1980s and 1990s as the result of multi-industry surveys. The developers of the SERVQUAL instrument, Valerie A. Zeithaml, A. Parasuraman, and Leonard L. Berry, identified a set of five dimensions consistently ranked by customers as the most important for service quality. These five dimensions are tangibles (i.e., the appearance of the physical facilities, equipment, personnel, and communication materials such as signs and brochures); reliability (i.e., the ability to perform the service dependably and accurately); responsiveness (i.e., the willingness to help customers and provide prompt service); assurance (i.e., the knowledge and courtesy of employees and their ability to convey confidence and inspire trust); and empathy (i.e., the caring, individualized attention provided to customers).

Sesame Street Generation The generation of U.S. consumers born between 1965 and 1976. They are so called because they grew up with much stronger media influences, beginning in early childhood, than previous generations. See also GENERATION X.

SET See SECURE ELECTRONIC TRANSMISSION PROTOCOL (SET).

setting display See THEME/SETTING DISPLAY.

settlement discount See CASH DISCOUNT.

Seventh Avenue (SA) A street in New York City that runs down the middle of the traditional GARMENT CENTER. The term *Seventh Avenue* has come to be synonymous with the American READY-TO-WEAR (RTW) industry. See also SEVENTH ON SIXTH.

Seventh on Sixth A major New York City designer READY-TO-WEAR (RTW) show held at Bryant Park and usually timed to immediately follow the European PRÊT-À-PORTER shows. However, American designers are increasingly showing their lines in New York two weeks prior to the Seventh on Sixth show in order to strengthen their image as trendsetters. See also SEVENTH AVENUE (SA).

SGML See STANDARD GENERALIZED MARKUP LANGUAGE (SGML).

shadow box A box that can be used to display small items inside or outside a retail store. It is usually a small, framed, elevated box with tiny shelves, and the items displayed are usually luxury items. The purpose of the shadow box is to bring the merchandise nearer to the shopper's eye level for closer scrutiny. When shadow boxes are located on the store's exterior walls, they are often located on side streets or on either side of the entrance to the store. If the store has a foyer or area of separation between the street doors and the doors into the selling floor, shadow box display cases may be used to brighten up the area. As interior features, shadow boxes may be worked into the design of the selling floor. See also SHADOW BOX WINDOW.

shadow box window A small closed-back window used to display small yet relatively expensive items such as fine jewelry, cameras, cosmetics, books, or shoes.

shakeout A decline in the number of retail stores or other businesses, due to consolidation, poor economic conditions, lack of customer interest, etc. Weaker businesses are eliminated, particularly in times of intense competition.

shallow assortment A measure or description of the quantity of each item available in the assortment of goods offered to the customer. An assortment containing only small quantities of an item is said to be *shallow*.

shaping In learning theory, a process in which rewards or reinforcements are employed in an effort to form (or shape) an individual's behavior patterns. The concept is often applied to advertising and promotion. See also CONSUMER BEHAVIOR and CONSUMER RESEARCH.

share Short for AUDIENCE SHARE.

shared business The part of a retailer's business that is generated by the proximity of neighboring stores. See also BUSINESS ASSOCIATED STORES.

shared services Services that may be used by two or more marketers at the same time, such as common carriers, a combined sales force, and public warehousing. These services may be provided by one of the cooperating firms or by a third party.

shareholder One who owns at least some portion of a CORPORATION, generally by purchasing STOCK in that corporation. Also called a *stockholder*. See also EQUITY.

shareholders' equity See EQUITY.

share of audience See AUDIENCE SHARE.

share of the market See MARKET SHARE.

shareowners' equity See EQUITY.

shark repellent Any measure a company takes to fend off a would-be acquirer (i.e., shark). Typical tactics include changing the firm's bylaws to make it more difficult for the would-be acquirer to take control of the firm (e.g., requiring a 75% approval of the shareholders). See also ACQUISITION.

shelf exposure The number of rows of shelf space a product commands, particularly in a supermarket or similar retail format. Also called *shelf space*. See also SLOTTING ALLOWANCE.

shelf life The number of days that a product, particularly a food product, can be held before it begins to deteriorate. Loss of flavor, taste, and color reduce the salability of the item. See also STOCK ROTATION.

shelf miser See SPACE MISER.

shelf space See SHELF EXPOSURE.

shelf stable simple meal (SSSM) Food items such as soup, macaroni and cheese, tuna, pasta sauce, and dry pasta that are considered quick meal staples. These items are generally sold in the center store area and appeal to the busy consumer seeking quick forms of nutritious meals.

shelf stock Merchandise that is available to customers who select what they want from display shelves. Compare FLOOR STOCK and FORWARD STOCK.

shelf talker 1. A printed advertisement hung from the shelf in a retail store, particularly as found in a supermarket or variety store. 2. A small sign or label affixed to the front of a shelf.

shell form A half-round, lightweight, partial torso form, similar to a bra form, blouse form, or sweater form. The front is fully sculpted, but the back is scooped out and hollow.

Sherman Act (1890) See SHERMAN ANTITRUST ACT (1890).

Sherman Antitrust Act (1890) Federal U.S. legislation intended to limit the growth of monopolies that result in the unlawful RESTRAINT OF TRADE. There are two main provisions: (a) all contracts in restraint of trade are illegal; and (b) all attempts to monopolize any part of trade among the several states is a misdemeanor. The Sherman Act is the basis for all U.S. antitrust activity, its major contribution being to turn restraint of trade and monopolization into offenses against the Federal Government. The CLAYTON ACT (1914) and the CELLER-KEFAUVER ANTIMERGER ACT (1950) updated and amended the Sherman Act.

shifting loyal A consumer who switches his or her loyalty from one brand to another. Compare BRAND INSISTENCE.

shill bidder In online auctions, an individual posing as a legitimate bidder in order to decoy others into participating. Groups of shill bidders engage in CROSS-BIDDING, by which they work together to drive up auction prices. They also post highly positive comments about the seller to encourage bidders to trust the seller and enter the auction.

ship date The date a BILL OF LADING (B/L) is signed and the goods are physically in transit.

shipment 1. The transport and delivery of items by a carrier. 2. The total assortment of items transported as a unit. 3. Merchandise sent to a manufacturer to be processed. 4. Merchandise sent from the manufacturer to a wholesaler or retailer in the CHANNEL OF DISTRIBUTION. See also SHIPPING.

shipper container marking (SCM) See SHIPPING CONTAINER MARKING (SCM).

shippers' cooperative A voluntary organization of shippers who pool their shipments in order to benefit from lower freight rates and economies of scale. Owned by the shippers themselves, the organization runs on a not-for-profit basis to benefit its member firms. Shipping cooperatives are particularly useful with regard to foreign freight forwarding.

shipping 1. The retail DISTRIBUTION CENTER (DC) function of routing merchandise to stores. 2. The delivery of goods to the ultimate consumer. See also DELIVERY and SHIPMENT.   3. The delivery of goods to other members in the CHANNEL OF DISTRIBUTION.

shipping and handling (S&H)   The cost of order fulfillment and product delivery. S&H pricing methods vary, the most common being the graduated scale, adding a fixed amount calibrated to the purchase price of the order. Other firms offer a flat shipping rate. Still others offer a variety of shipping methods (e.g., ground, second-day air), each priced differently.

shipping container label (SCL)   See SHIPPING CONTAINER MARKING (SCM).

shipping container marking (SCM)   The identification of the contents of shipping cartons by bar codes that are scanned into a retailer's inventory upon receipt of the shipment at the DISTRIBUTION CENTER (DC). The cartons are then sent directly to stores without further distribution and processing. Used in ELECTRONIC DATA INTERCHANGE (EDI), SCM speeds up the flow of merchandise while reducing processing expenses. The bar code sticker attached to the carton is called a *shipping container label (SCL)*.

shipping date   The delivery date or dates specified in orders placed against OPEN-TO-BUY (OTB). Since orders are placed against OTB for a specific period, the timely arrival of merchandise ensures that inventory levels are appropriate to planned sales. Most purchase orders, therefore, specify two dates to define the delivery parameters: a *do not ship before* date (to make sure that merchandise does not arrive too early) and a *do not ship after* date (to make sure that merchandise does not arrive too late). Both early and late deliveries can be devastating to the sales plan.

shipping order   Instructions from shippers to carriers for forwarding all goods. It is usually a duplicate copy of the BILL OF LADING (B/L).

shipping permit   An authorization to accept and forward goods despite the presence of an embargo.

shipping report   Synonym for ON-THE-WATER REPORT.

shirt form   The male version of the bust form or blouse form.

shlock   Alternative spelling of SCHLOCK. See SCHLOCK MERCHANDISE.

shock approach   A SALES APPROACH in which the SALESPERSON uses a mild form of shock to gain the interest of the PROSPECT. For example, an insurance salesperson may use the possibility of the death of a spouse as a shock to stimulate a prospect's interest in life insurance.

shoe   An external foot covering for the human foot, usually leather or synthetic. Shoes usually include a heavy sole, which makes contact with the ground, and a softer upper. See also FOOTWEAR.

shoe and foot form   A display form in the shape of a foot, used to display footwear. Also called a *foot form* or *shoe form*.

shooting oneself in the foot   (Slang) Synonym for MARKETCIDE.

shop   1. v. To examine goods or services with the intention of making a purchase or for the purpose of making comparisons with other goods and services. See also SHOPPING.   2. n. A small retail establishment, or a clearly defined area in a larger establishment, in which related goods are sold. Also spelled SHOPPE.   3. n. Informally, any place of business, including a retail store. See also SHOP LAYOUT.

shop a line   See SHOPPING A LINE.

shop-at-home retailing   The practice of selling merchandise or services in the customer's home at the customer's invitation (e.g., carpet and furniture cleaning). See also CUSTOM SELLING.

shopbot   A piece of computer software that searches online stores for a specific product. Searchers can use a shopbot to compare prices and check availability.

shopkeeper   Synonym for STOREKEEPER. See also MERCHANT and RETAILER.

shop layout   In a department store, a clearly defined area in which related merchandise is displayed as though it were in a small shop or BOUTIQUE.

shoplifter   A thief, either professional or amateur, who steals merchandise from stores while posing as a customer.

shoplifting   The act of stealing merchandise in a retail store by a person posing as a customer. Shoplifting is one of several forms of retail crime classified as external theft. See also PILFERAGE.

shop merchandising   The creation of special areas (or shops) within a retail establishment to cater to customers' special needs and interests. For example, a store may contain a golf shop or a tennis shop. See also BOUTIQUE.

shop.org   A division of the NATIONAL RETAIL FEDERATION (NRF) for online retailers. Devoted to making the best possible use of INTERNET and multichannel retailing, it serves as a forum for executives of online retail establishments to share information, insights, and experiences. It also conducts workshops, provides statistical information and research studies, holds teleconferences and an annual members' summit, and publishes a weekly e-mail newsletter. The association maintains a retailer-only listserv with ongoing discussions about online retailing. Headquartered in Washington, D.C., shop.org maintains a Web site at www.shop.org.

shoppe   An old-fashioned spelling of SHOP, used in the names of certain types of small stores to denote an old-time quaintness (e.g., an ice cream shoppe).

shopper   1. An individual engaged in a search for goods and services.   2. A retail BUYER who purchases merchandise on behalf of another person or a business.   3. A locally distributed newspaper containing retail advertisements (also called a PENNYSAVER).

shoppertainment   The combination of retail shopping with a variety of forms of entertainment. See also SHOPPERTAINMENT COMPLEX/CENTER.

shoppertainment complex/center   A large center combining retail shopping with a variety of forms of entertainment. Shoppertainment complexes are designed to amuse customers, encourage longer stays, present new activities, and generate traffic and retail sales. For example, some Las Vegas casinos have become shoppertainment centers by adding retailers.

shopping   1. The act of visiting stores and shops, perusing mail order catalogs, television shopping networks, and Internet Web sites, etc., to purchase or examine goods.   2. The act of searching for the right product or service at the best possible price. This use of the term implies expending the time to make comparisons before making a purchase. See also WINDOW SHOPPING and COMPARISON SHOPPING.

shopping a line   The practice of inspecting a vendor's entire line of merchandise with the intention of buying some or all of it. See also BUYER and BUYING.

shopping bag   A paper or plastic bag with handles, used to carry purchases. Retailers frequently provide distinctive shopping bags that help to identify the store to their customers. In Japan, where shopping bags are used many times before finally being discarded, the bags serve as a moving advertisement as well as an essential fashion accessory and status symbol, much more so than they do in the United States. See also WRAPPING.

shopping basket   In E-TAILING, a piece of software that lets customers make selections on the site, compiles the order while they continue shopping, and completes the order of all products selected. An icon shaped like a SHOPPING CART is often used to denote the shopping basket.

shopping basket abandonment   In E-TAILING, the occurrence of customers leaving their SHOPPING BASKET before the sale is completed. E-tailers are concerned about the high rate of shopping basket abandonment, since as many as 65 percent of consumers leave their baskets before the sale is completed. Possible causes for shopping center abandonment are sticker shock, technical problems at checkout, complex forms to complete, out-of-stock merchandise not announced until point of payment, computers crashing, the site not accepting the consumer's credit card, or last-minute decisions not to buy.

shopping bot   One of several available intelligent programs designed to assist consumers in product identification and comparison over the WORLD WIDE WEB (WWW). Shopping bots are designed to search preprogrammed locations online for specific products. In B2C transactions, they report back to the consumer with a list of best buys, allowing consumers to comparison shop a number of competing sites for the best price

and availability without having to visit each and every possible site. Live HYPERLINKS connect the consumer directly to the site of the selected e-tailer. Shopping bots are also used in B2B transactions, facilitating the purchase of office supplies, software, and other business necessities. Like shopping bots used in B2C transactions, these B2B shopping bots allow buyers and purchasing agents to watch the activities of potential suppliers, compare prices, and check availability. Shopping bots derive their revenue partly from banner ads and partly from fees paid by e-tailers to whom customers are directed. Also spelled *shoppingbot*.

shopping cart   1. In traditional BRICKS-AND-MORTAR retailing, a small vehicle pushed by hand and provided by a retail store for a customer's use. Shopping carts allow customers to collect their purchases and bring them conveniently to the checkout area. Particularly useful for shopping in a large store, they are provided by many supermarkets and discount stores. See also SCAN-IT-YOURSELF TECHNOLOGY (SIY).   2. In online E-TAILING, a piece of software that allows the online shopper to select, record, and review (either keeping or discarding) multiple purchases for which they will pay at the end of their shopping visit. Sometimes called a *trolley* (e.g., in Australia).

shopping center   As defined by the International Council of Shopping Centers (ICSC), "a group of retail stores and other commercial establishments planned, developed, owned, and managed as a single property. Commercial tenants are generally clustered around one or more of the large anchor stores." Shopping centers, in response to automobility, generally include extensive parking facilities and are located near convenient access roads to ensure adequate customer traffic. Early shopping centers were not covered by a central roof as are contemporary shopping malls. Also called a *planned shopping center*.

shopping goods   Merchandise the consumer will exert considerable effort to find in an attempt to compare price, quality, and style. The consumer will also characteristically do research on the product, visit several retail stores, and discuss the item with knowledgeable family members and friends prior to making a purchase decision. Shopping goods tend to be high-priced merchandise and the decision to buy is premeditated, time-consuming, and thoughtful. See also CONSUMER GOODS, SEARCH, and PRICE-BASED SHOPPING GOODS/PRODUCT. Compare SUBSTITUTE GOODS.

shopping goods store   A store whose breadth of assortment allows the customer to compare prices, styles, and quality. Most large department stores, discount stores, and supermarkets may be regarded as shopping goods stores. Also called a *shopping store*.

shopping items   See SHOPPING GOODS.

shopping mall   See MALL.

shopping mall intercept   A type of INTERVIEW in which respondents are approached (i.e., intercepted) and asked a series of questions by researchers as they pass a particular spot in a shopping MALL.

shopping motivation   Any reason a customer has for patronizing a particular store.

shopping plaza   See MALL.

shopping products   Synonym for SHOPPING GOODS.

shopping radius   See TRADING AREA.

shopping report   See SHOPPING SERVICE (def. 2).

shopping service   1. An in-store department that assists customers in selecting merchandise for purchase.   2. Professional shoppers hired by large retailers to pose as customers for the purpose of evaluating the store's sales staff. The results of the investigation are submitted to the store in a *shopping report*. Distinguished from COMPARISON SHOPPING.

shopping store   Synonym for SHOPPING GOODS STORE.

shop-within-a-shop   See BOUTIQUE.

shopworn   Of merchandise, soiled or damaged from handling and no longer able to be sold as new. Slow-moving goods, in particular, tend to become shopworn because of exposure or customer handling. Shopworn goods tie up valuable space and inventory dollars. Also spelled *shop-worn*.

short   See STOCK SHORTAGE.

shortage   See STOCK SHORTAGE.

shortage advertising   Advertising that is run when a product or service is in short supply because of an interruption in production, unusually strong demand, etc. The sponsor, instead of simply promoting the product or service, attempts to educate the public or influence it in some other way.

short delivery   A shipment of merchandise that contains less than the amount ordered and indicated on the invoice. See also SHORT MERCHANDISE.

short haul   The process of delivering goods locally to the customer by truck. Short-haul trucking uses smaller trucks than does its counterpart, LINE HAUL.

short hour   Synonym for SHORT-HOUR PART-TIMER.

short-hour part-timer   An employee paid at an hourly rate and working less than a full-time schedule. Such employees are typically used during peak periods of store activity. Also called, simply, a *short hour*.

short line distributor   See SPECIALTY MERCHANDISE WHOLESALER.

short merchandise   Goods not shipped with an order. They may be back ordered for later shipment by the vendor or they may be missing due to a shipping error. See also SHORT DELIVERY, SHORT-SHIP, and BACK ORDER.

short-range plan   A plan developed for those situations likely to occur monthly, weekly, or daily. These situations may be covered by procedures, practices, rules, etc. In general, a short-range plan covers a period shorter than a year, is developed by lower-level managers, and is narrower in scope than a LONG-RANGE PLAN. A firm's budget is a common form of a short-range plan. Also called a *short-term plan*. See also PLANNING and TACTICAL PLANNING.

short-range planning   See SHORT-RANGE PLAN and TACTICAL PLANNING.

short sale   See SELLING SHORT.

short selling   Synonym for SELLING SHORT.

short-ship   To send a retailer an incomplete order. When unable to provide the colors, styles, or sizes ordered by the retailer, a vendor may short-ship. Some vendors substitute other styles, colors, or sizes for out-of-stock items, while others complete the order as specified at a later date. The deficient order is called a *short shipment* or a *short shipping order*. Also spelled *shortship*. See also BACK ORDER and SHORT MERCHANDISE.

short shipment   See SHORT DELIVERY, SHORT MERCHANDISE, and SHORT-SHIP.

short-shipping order   See SHORT-SHIP.

short-term debt   A debt that must be repaid within one year. Short-term debt includes TRADE CREDIT from suppliers, loans from commercial banks or other short-term lending institutions, and the sale of commercial paper to outside investors or other businesses. See also OPEN-BOOK CREDIT and PROMISSORY NOTE.

short-term liability   See LIABILITY.

short-term plan   Synonym for SHORT-RANGE PLAN.

short-term planning   Synonym for TACTICAL PLANNING.

short-term transaction   In the BALANCE OF PAYMENTS between one country and all of its trading partners, a transaction that matures in one year or less. Compare LONG-TERM TRANSACTION.

short-time employee   A person hired to work full-time but for a short period (e.g., during the Christmas season).

shotgun approach/technique   A personal sales technique that attempts to cover a wide variety of products in a haphazard, irregular way in hopes of interesting a potential customer in making a purchase. The technique is generally regarded as inefficient and ineffective as compared to the RIFLE APPROACH.

showcase   1. A closed-sell fixture consisting of a glass cabinet in which merchandise may be viewed but, unless removed by a SALESPERSON, not handled. The showcase fixture is used primarily for presenting high-ticket or fragile goods such as jewelry, cosmetics, and fragrances. Showcases are often used to enclose groupings of similar merchandise. Sometimes called a *showcase fixture*. Sometimes spelled *show case*.   2. Also used as a synonym for COUNTER.   3. To exhibit an item of merchandise or store service in such a way as to highlight its availability and desirability.

showcase fixture   See SHOWCASE.

showing   Synonym for FASHION SHOW.

showroom   Facilities maintained by manufacturers, suppliers, etc., for the purpose of displaying merchandise to buyers. Sometimes spelled *show room*. See also ONLINE SHOWROOM, SAMPLE ROOM, SOUK, and MAJOR SHOWROOM BUILDING.

showroom model   See MODEL.

shrinkage   The difference between BOOK INVENTORY and actual PHYSICAL INVENTORY. Also called *stock shrinkage*. See also INVISIBLE SHRINKAGE, STOCK SHORTAGE, and VISIBLE SHRINKAGE.

S-HTTP   See SECURE HTTP.

shurfer   (Slang) A SURFER (i.e., visitor) on the INTERNET who chooses to shop.

SIC   See STANDARD INDUSTRIAL CLASSIFICATION (SIC).

sideline store   A store run by an organization whose primary activity is other than retailing.

sidewalk sale   A promotional event in which the retailer literally takes selected goods outside the store and sells them at lower than regular price from the sidewalk or mall promenade in front of the store. Merchandise is presented on racks, in bins, or on tables, usually at final prices. The purpose of taking the goods to the sidewalk or mall promenade is to move older, discontinued, and discounted merchandise by attracting the attention of passersby. The sidewalk sale is used extensively in apparel retailing (particularly by small specialty shops), by supermarkets, and by retailers of seasonal merchandise. See also TENT SALE.

side wall   One of the three solid walls helping to form a typical DISPLAY WINDOW. The fourth wall is the WINDOW WALL.

sig cut   Synonym for LOGO.

sight draft/bill of lading (SD/BL)   A form of CASH ON DELIVERY (COD) selling in which the vendor, upon shipping the merchandise to the buyer, sends the draft to the buyer's bank. The buyer, before taking possession of the merchandise, must pay the bank the amount of the invoice. See also CASH DATING.

sign   An inscribed board, placard, etc., bearing a warning, advertisement, or other information and displayed for public view. A sign may be used as a component of a store's image that facilitates shopping by identifying merchandise. The most common uses of temporary and in-store signs are for the identification of brand (e.g., Carter's), category or item (e.g., layette), shop-within-a-shop (e.g., DKNY), characteristics or features of merchandise (e.g., 100% cotton), price (e.g., 25% off ticketed price), promotion (e.g., January White Sale), policy (e.g., all sales are final), and service (e.g., free delivery). See also SIGNAGE, PERMANENT SIGNAGE, and TEMPORARY SIGNAGE.

signage   The signs, posters, symbols, and other graphic forms used to communicate with the customer both inside and outside the store. PERMANENT SIGNAGE is made of durable materials not intended for frequent change (e.g., exterior lighted signs and in-store signs identifying selling areas). TEMPORARY SIGNAGE is made of disposable material, such as paper or card stock, and is intended for frequent change (e.g., in-store signage on fixtures that reinforce advertising, stimulate impulse purchases, and call attention to promotional events and prices). Fact tags, banners, and reprints of newspaper advertising are some of the forms of temporary in-store signage. Also called *signing*. See also SIGN, PERMANENT SIGNAGE, and TEMPORARY SIGNAGE.

signal   In COMMUNICATION, the actual transmission of the message from the encoder (i.e., sender) to the decoder (i.e., recipient). The strength of the message is contingent upon a number of factors such as the frequency with which the signal is transmitted, the skill with which it is designed, the media by which it is transmitted, its ability to compete with all other signals for the decoder's attention, and the degree to which a common pool of experience (or frame of reference) is shared by the decoder and the encoder.

signaling   See PRICE FIXING.

signature brand   See DESIGNER BRAND.

signature cut   Synonym for LOGO.

signature fixture   A one-of-a-kind store furnishing unit (i.e., FIXTURE) that is characteristically positioned at the entrance to a store or a department within a store. The unusual, unique design of the signature fixture is created to attract attention. The signature fixture's design should also reflect the brand image of the store, both in fabrication and style. See also FIXTURE.

signature line   See DESIGNER MERCHANDISE.

signature plate   The logo, emblem, trademark, symbol, or distinctive print that immediately identifies a store to the public. In print advertising, the signature plate is usually placed near the top or bottom of the advertisement. The address of the store, location of branch stores, and the store's slogan are often included alongside the store name. Also called a NAMEPLATE.

signature store   See MANUFACTURER-SPONSORED SPECIALTY STORE.

signing   Synonym for SIGNAGE.

silent partner One who is a legal part of a firm but whose identity is generally not known to the public at large. The silent partner invests financial resources in the firm and shares in its profits and losses, but generally remains aloof from the decision making process.

silent salesperson 1. A synonym for PACKAGING, used to indicate the importance of the marketing aspect of the container. 2. A synonym for MANNEQUIN.

silhouette The overall shape or contour of an item of apparel. It is the basic ingredient that changes, even if slightly, with each new season. For example, the new silhouette of the season may have a longer or shorter skirt length, a looser or tighter torso, or wider or narrower lapels.

simple random sample A sample chosen entirely by chance, in which the possibility of inclusion is equal for each member of the POPULATION.

simple random sampling The basic SAMPLING technique by which a group of subjects (i.e., a SAMPLE) is selected for study from a larger group (i.e., a POPULATION). Each individual is chosen entirely by chance and each member of the population has an equal chance of being included in the sample. Every possible sample of a given size (n) has the same chance of selection.

simple reciprocity See RECIPROCITY.

simplified lifestyle The practice of seeking a more basic, less complicated existence. Customers opting for a simplified lifestyle tend to prefer natural fabrics, organic fruits and vegetables, herbal medicines, and ecology-friendly products. Some psychologists call this mindset *ecopsychology*.

simplified selling A streamlined sales approach in which customers are left more or less on their own in the store, receiving only minimal assistance from sales personnel. Simplified selling is manifested in retailing in two main forms: SELF-SELECTION (in which the customer has access to the merchandise, makes a selection, and takes it to a SALESPERSON for the final sales process) and SELF-SERVICE RETAILING (in which the customer selects merchandise and takes it to a checkout station where it is paid for, as in a supermarket). SCAN-IT-YOURSELF TECHNOLOGY (SIY) is taking simplified selling to the next level.

simulated shopping environment A VIRTUAL REALITY representation of a shelf in a retail store, used in MARKETING RESEARCH (MR). Graphics and three-dimensional modeling are used to create an actual shelf fixture stocked with both the marketer's and its competitors' products. The simulation allows retailers to study customer behavior in a controlled environment. See also VIRTUAL STORE.

simulated test market In MARKETING RESEARCH (MR), a means of determining consumer response to a product by involving them in a situation in which they pretend to purchase the item. The participants do their pretend shopping in a controlled environment. See also SIMULATION.

simulation 1. A decision making technique used in marketing, in which complex conditions in the MARKETPLACE are examined and analyzed by means of a model. The model is commonly created by means of a computer, and the resulting simulation takes the place of the real world in problem-solving activities. The *simulation model* allows researchers to experiment with a variety of possible scenarios and examine the projected results of alternative maneuvers and adjustments. 2. A QUALITATIVE (PRIMARY) RESEARCH method in which participants imitate or enact product trial and use as an alternative to the expensive and time-consuming TEST MARKETING of new products. See also SIMULATED TEST MARKET.

simulation model See SIMULATION.

simulcast 1. An interactive television system that transmits digital information in conjunction with an actual broadcast. Simulcast viewers control the programming by punching in choices on a keypad. Examples include finding additional information during a documentary. 2. A program broadcast simultaneously on radio and television, on more than one station, in several languages, etc. 3. A closed-circuit television broadcast of an event (such as a horse race) while the event is taking place in real time at a remote location.

single delivery The shipment of 100% of a given merchandise ASSORTMENT based on an INITIAL ORDER.

single discount equivalent A discount taken all at once rather than in the form of a CHAIN DISCOUNT.

single heads of households The category that comprises divorced or unmarried adults, often with low *discretionary income*, particularly if divorced. Child support and/or alimony payments may reduce the single head of household's standard of living. Also called a *single parent*, if children are present.

single item advertisement In RETAIL PRODUCT ADVERTISING, an advertisement that focuses on one piece of merchandise. This type of advertising is generally reserved for seasonal trends, products from well-known designers and manufacturers, or best sellers. Single item advertisements often feature color, price, size, and trend information in the advertising copy. The artwork may range from a simple line sketch to a full-color photograph. See also MERCHANDISE ORIENTATION.

single item pricing See UNIT PRICING.

single line retailer See SINGLE LINE STORE.

single line store A retail store that carries only one line of merchandise (or, at most, a very narrow range of merchandise) but has great depth of assortment within that particular line. A typical shoe store exemplifies a single line store. See also LIMITED LINE STORE.

single line wholesaler See GENERAL LINE WHOLESALER.

single, living at home The category of consumers made up of adults who are divorced or have never been married, who live at home with their parents. Their *discretionary income* ranges from low to high. Those who were never married may have a high discretionary income and use it to purchase big-ticket items such as good cars, computers, and expensive clothing.

single market approach   See SINGLE TARGET MARKET APPROACH.

single markup percentage   A theoretical markup percentage applied equally to every item in the store. A single markup percentage cannot, in most instances, actually be applied to every item in the store because different items sell at different rates and generate different selling costs. It is more likely, therefore, that a percentage markup system will be used instead. See also PERCENTAGE MARKUP SYSTEM.

single parent   See SINGLE HEADS OF HOUSEHOLDS.

single price card   In radio advertising, a rate card on which radio stations generally publish their advertising rates. The single price card reflects a single price for each of the day parts, time periods, and days of the week. This is the simplest and most direct method of pricing advertising. Compare GRID CARD.

single price policy   A pricing policy in which all merchandise of a particular type is sold at the same price. A retail establishment following this formula is known as a ONE-PRICE STORE. Distinguished from ONE-PRICE POLICY.

single product strategy   A manufacturing strategy in which a decision is made to produce only one product, or one product with a limited number of options.

single target market approach   A method of MARKET SEGMENTATION in which one homogeneous group is selected as the target market and one MARKETING MIX is used to market the product. Also called a *single market approach*. See also UNDIFFERENTIATED MARKETING.

single variable segmentation   The least complex form of MARKET SEGMENTATION, in which only a single criterion (e.g., age) is used to divide (i.e., segment) the population.

sin tax   Synonym for EXCISE tax.

sister store concept   See EQUAL STORE OPERATION/ORGANIZATION.

site   See WEB SITE or RETAIL SITE LOCATION.

site atmospherics   See WEB SITE ATMOSPHERICS.

site construction   See WEB SITE CONSTRUCTION.

site content   See WEB SITE CONTENT.

site design   See WEB SITE DESIGN.

site flow (aesthetics)   See WEB SITE FLOW (AESTHETICS).

site launch   See WEB SITE LAUNCH.

site location   See RETAIL SITE LOCATION.

site management   See WEB SITE MANAGEMENT.

site map   In Web page design, a road map or interactive overview of the pages in the site, showing their organization. A site map should be used for sites with 20 or more pages. See also MENU.

site redesign   See WEB SITE REDESIGN.

situational management   A flexible management style that adapts general principles of management to the specific objectives and actual needs of one's own business. Also called *contingency leadership*.

situation analysis   A form of business research and analysis used to determine the position of a firm at the present time and to forecast where the present course of action will take the firm in the future. Researchers use situation analysis to ascertain the strengths and weaknesses of a specific company, business plan, or proposed strategy. See also S.W.O.T. ANALYSIS.

six-month merchandise/merchandising plan   See MERCHANDISE PLAN and SALES PLAN.

six Os   In the development of a MARKETING PLAN, the six fundamental elements of organizing and understanding customer buying behavior (all of which begin with the letter O): origins of purchase (Who buys this product?); objects of purchase (What do they need? What do they buy?); occasions of purchase (When do they buy it?); outlets of purchase (Where do they buy it?); objectives of purchase (Why do they buy it?); and operations of purchase (How do they buy it?). See also FOUR OS.

six-pack   Six identical items packaged and sold together as a unit. Beer and soft drinks are often sold in six-packs. A six-pack of bottled beer or soda may take the form of six bottles packaged together in a cardboard basket with a carrying handle. Six-packs of canned beverages, on the other hand, are frequently bound together by a plastic webbing. The six-pack format is so popular that special insulated coolers are sold to hold them and keep the cans chilled.

SIY   See SCAN-IT-YOURSELF TECHNOLOGY (SIY).

size   The spatial dimensions, proportions, etc. of anything, such as a product. Since sized merchandise seldom sells in equal quantities, buyers need to be careful to plan assortments according to the sizes in greatest demand at their particular store. In apparel retailing, an end-of-season clearance rack with a disproportionate number of items in one size range may indicate an overabundance of one size and lost sales to customers seeking other sizes. Suppliers often recommend size distributions based on historical sales records. Shoe manufacturers, for example, pack individual shoe styles in a case lot called a *size run* that includes specific size assortments. See also NATIONAL SIZING SURVEY, ASSORTMENT, and SIZE DISPLAY.

size discrepancy   Unexpected fit problems in which the size on the label does not match the fit of the garment. For example, a pair of jeans may be tighter or shorter than suggested by the size label, or a shirt's collar may be too loose or the sleeves too long. Size discrepancy is often due to size variation between countries. In recent years, however, buyers have begun to supply foreign resources with specific sizes and measurements. Also called *discrepancy of size*.

size display   Sized merchandise arranged in order so as to facilitate customer selection. Sized merchandise is typically presented from small to large, left to right, top to bottom, or front to back. Sizing is often used to present broken assortments such as markdowns. See also SIZE.

size lining   Merchandise, primarily apparel, grouped together in the store by size rather than by lifestyle or price.

size run   See SIZE.

size-up   See SIZING UP.

SizeUSA   See NATIONAL SIZING SURVEY.

sizing up   A retail INVENTORY process frequently used in the retail shoe industry. A count is made of all sizes and styles sold for the purpose of reordering. Also called a *size-up*.

skimming   A pricing policy in which new products are introduced into the marketplace at a relatively high price with the intention of selling as much as possible before competition drives the price down. Skimming is commonly used to set prices when customers are insensitive to price, there is little competition, customers know little about the costs of producing and marketing the new product, and the product is targeted to a small market segment (i.e., the more affluent consumer). Skimming has the advantages of providing high margins and a prestige image. For example, consumer electronics are often introduced at high prices which are eventually adjusted downward due to competition. The product consequently evolves from one that was relatively exclusive to one that is available to most consumers at a variety of price points. Also known as *market skimming pricing, skim pricing, skim-the-cream pricing, step pricing, price skimming,* and *creaming.* The resultant prices are called the *skimming price,* the *market skimming price,* or the *skim-the-cream price.*

skim pricing   See SKIMMING.

skim-the-cream price/pricing   See SKIMMING.

Skinnerian psychology   See BEHAVIORAL ENGINEERING.

skip   (Slang) A charge account customer who moves without leaving a forwarding address, presumably to avoid paying a bill.

skip loss   The financial loss to a retailer due to customers who move without paying their charge account bill and do not leave a forwarding address.

skip marking   A price marking system in which each item is not individually marked.

SKU   See STOCK KEEPING UNIT (SKU).

slack filling   The use of deceptively oversized packages to make a product appear more than it is. This is an unlawful practice regulated by the FEDERAL TRADE COMMISSION (FTC).

slacks form   See PANTS FORM.

slatwall system   A wall system of horizontal backer panels with evenly spaced slots that accept brackets and display accessories with special slatwall fittings. A piece of display hardware designed for the system is a *slatwall fixture.* Compare PEGWALL SYSTEM and GRIDWALL SYSTEM.

sleeper   (Slang) An item that sold in much larger quantities than originally anticipated.

sleepwear   Apparel used for sleeping or preparing for going to bed. Included are pajamas, nightgowns, robes, design gowns, nightshirts, and related apparel merchandise.

slice-of-life format   A form of advertising (mainly television) in which a small segment of a lifelike experience is dramatized in order to spotlight a product. Typically, in the course of the commercial a problem is stated and a solution is found in which the product plays a leading role.

sliding scale   A mechanism for setting prices at higher or lower rates depending on predetermined criteria such as volume of activity, usage over time, or the ability to pay. For example, a day care center may charge parents different rates on a sliding scale based on their ability to pay or eligibility for government subsidies. Similarly, a utility may charge high-volume customers less per unit than they charge low-volume customers in order to attract high-volume business. See also SLIDING SCALE LEASE.

sliding scale lease   An arrangement in which there is a provision for increased rent as the lessee's gross sales increase. See also PERCENTAGE LEASE.

sliding scale tariff   A customs tariff in which rates of duty vary according to the price of the imported goods. In general, lower-priced merchandise carries a lower duty than higher-priced goods.

slim   See BOYS' SIZES.

slippage   1. Lost time. 2. Failure to redeem a coupon, request a rebate, or send in for a premium when purchasing a product eligible for one of these promotional activities.

slotting allowance   A type of SALES PROMOTION aimed at distributors. A slotting allowance is a payment made to retailers in return for their agreeing to take a new product. The allowance helps compensate retailers for the time and effort expended in finding a space for the new product on their shelves. See also SHELF EXPOSURE.

slowdown   A decrease in worker productivity, used as a tactic to pressure management into labor negotiations. Workers continue to do their jobs, but at a snail's pace. Compare STRIKE and PICKETING.

slow mover   Synonym for SLOW SELLER.

slow penetration strategy   See PENETRATION STRATEGY.

slow sales   See SLOW SELLER.

slow seller   An item of merchandise that sells more slowly than anticipated. Some of the more common problems leading to slow sales are unseasonable weather, poor assortment, poor presentation, and late delivery. Clearance markdowns are frequently employed to move slow sellers. Also called *slow mover* or *slow-selling merchandise.*

slow-selling merchandise   Synonym for SLOW SELLER.

SMA (standard metropolitan area)   See METROPOLITAN STATISTICAL AREA (MSA).

small business   According to the SMALL BUSINESS ACT (1953), a concern "that is independently owned and operated and not dominant in its operational area." Its number of employees and annual income fit criteria set for a small business in the United States by the SMALL BUSINESS ADMINISTRATION (SBA) and state law. The definition varies from industry to industry to reflect industry differences. Many small businesses are home-based; others are small retailers, services, manufacturers, distributors, and professionals or others working out of offices, factories, stores, or similar facilities.

Small Business Act (1953)   U.S. federal legislation authorizing the creation of the SMALL BUSINESS ADMINISTRATION (SBA) to encourage and foster the development of American small businesses. See also SMALL BUSINESS.

Small Business Administration (SBA)   The U.S. federal agency responsible for advocating for small businesses and for facilitating a business environment conducive to the success of American SMALL BUSINESS. The SBA, created by the SMALL BUSINESS ACT (1953), sets size standards for eligibility in its programs, based on number of employees and/or annual receipts. The SBA provides financial assistance such as loan programs, surety guarantees, and investment opportunities and contracting assistance programs, including government contracting. The SBA also administers a SMALL DISADVANTAGED BUSINESS (SDB) program for minority business development programs and a network of Women's Business Centers (WBC) that provide assistance and/or training in finance, management, marketing, procurement, the INTERNET, etc. See also SMALL BUSINESS INVESTMENT COMPANY (SBIC) and MINORITY ENTERPRISE SMALL BUSINESS INVESTMENT COMPANY (MESBIC).

small business investment company (SBIC)   A federally licensed, shareholder-owned investment company that provides equity capital to small businesses. Acting through the SMALL BUSINESS ADMINISTRATION (SBA), these companies borrow money at reduced rates to put into new ventures. SBICs are similar in operation to a VENTURE CAPITALIST firm, although they tend to make smaller investments and are willing to consider less glamorous businesses. See also MINORITY ENTERPRISE SMALL BUSINESS INVESTMENT COMPANY (MESBIC).

Small Disadvantaged Business (SDB)   The minority business development program of the SMALL BUSINESS ADMINISTRATION (SBA). The SDB is designed to help small minority businesses grow and prosper by providing a wide range of services (e.g., support for government contractors, access to capital, management and technical assistance, export assistance). The SBA certifies SDBs to make them eligible for special bidding benefits. Information about SDB programs may be found at the SBA Web site at www.sba.gov.

small indulgences   A lifestyle trend in which individuals purchase small items that make them feel happy and offer them a momentary break from the stresses of daily life. Typical purchases in this category include sweets, lingerie, scented soaps or candles, and flavored coffees.

small order   An order of a small number of items. The order may be so small that the transaction may not produce a profit. See also SMALL ORDER PROBLEM.

small order problem   Orders for merchandise that are so small as to yield no profit. See also SMALL ORDER.

small shop/store   Synonym for an INDEPENDENT.

small store person   An individual who is familiar with the requirements of operating a small retail store.

smart card   A small electronic device resembling a credit card that contains electronic memory and possibly an embedded integrated circuit (IC). A smart card containing an IC is sometimes called an *integrated circuit card (ICC).* Smart cards are used for a variety of purposes including storing a patient's medical records, storing DIGITAL CASH, and generating network IDs. Smart cards work with a *smart card reader,* a small device into which one inserts the smart card to pull information from it or to add data to it.

smart card reader   See SMART CARD.

smart shelves   In RADIO FREQUENCY IDENTIFICATION (RFID), computerized shelving that can refresh inventory data in real time by readers embedded in the shelves. The information is conveyed to everyone in the CHANNEL OF DISTRIBUTION, including retailers, distributors, and manufacturers, so that the proper amount of inventory can be maintained.

smiley (face)   See EMOTICON.

S/MIME   Short for *Secure/MIME,* a version of the MIME protocol that supports encryption of messages. S/MIME is based on RSA public-key encryption technology and enables people to send secure E-MAIL messages to one another even if they are using different e-mail clients.

SMM   See STRATEGIC PLANNING MODEL (SPM).

smorgasbord plan   A method of SALES COMPENSATION in which the employee may choose from various combinations of salary, commissions, bonuses, and other fringe benefits, depending on personal preferences and needs. See also CAFETERIA BENEFIT PLAN.

SMSA (Standard Metropolitan Statistical Area)   See METROPOLITAN STATISTICAL AREA (MSA).

snack pack   Packaging for a small serving of a food product, suitable for a between-meal snack or for dessert in a box lunch. Multiple snack-packs are often sold together in large plastic or cellophane bags.

snail mail   (Slang) Regular mail delivered by the postal system. The reference to a snail is intended to evoke the slow pace of regular mail as opposed to instantaneous E-MAIL.

snapper   (Slang) An added incentive used to encourage the purchase of a heavily promoted item or service.

snob appeal   Any quality of a product or service that helps target it to those who believe themselves to have superior tastes and behave condescendingly toward those with different tastes. Compare SNOB IMPACT.

snob impact   The decline in demand for an item because too many other people use it or have it. Customers preferring exclusivity lose interest when the general public adopts a product. Compare SNOB APPEAL. See also ADOPTION PROCESS.

snobmoddities   Mundane commodities that have been turned into chic, popular luxury items or goods, offering consumers a variety of options for what were once nearly invisible parts of daily life. Gourmet salt is an example. Bread, water, and chocolate are other commodities that have become snobmoddities. The trend was identified and the term coined by trendwatching.com at www.trendwatching.com.

snowballing method   A method of developing media advertising schedules in which the climax of a campaign is regarded as the most significant and thus allocated the largest share of the budget. Also known as the *crescendo method*. See also PROMOTIONAL BUDGETING.

snowball sample   A form of NONPROBABILITY SAMPLE in which the research is done in waves. The first stage of the research uncovers other organizations or individuals who may be sampled in a second wave. Also called a *referral sample*.

SOB   See STORE'S OWN BRAND (SOB).

social channel   A personal communications channel consisting of neighbors, friends, family members, and associates talking to potential customers. Also known as *word-of-mouth influence*. See also WORD-OF-MOUTH (WOM) COMMUNICATION.

social class   A relatively distinct and homogeneous division of a society, composed of individuals who share similar values, interests, financial resources, and behavioral characteristics.

Social classes show distinct product and brand preferences and differ in the type and amount of media exposure they receive. The *upper upper class* comprises the *social elite*, who generally have inherited wealth and whose families have been prominent in American society. The *lower upper class* includes persons who have earned exceptional wealth or income through their own business or professional ability. These individuals generally come originally from the middle classes. The *upper middle class* comprises individuals who are primarily concerned with career and who, although they possess neither great wealth nor elevated family status, are highly motivated to better themselves and their children. They tend to be professionals, independent business owners, or corporate managers. *Lower middle class* individuals are primarily white-collar workers, such as office workers and owners of small businesses, gray-collar workers, such as uniformed civil servants, and higher-level blue-collar workers, such as plumbers, electricians, and factory foremen. The *upper lower class* tends to be the largest social class and includes most of the blue-collar working class of skilled and semi-skilled factory workers. Finally, the *lower lower class* is composed of those individuals within the society that are poorly educated, unskilled laborers. They are often unemployed and may require public assistance just to survive. See also MARKET SEGMENTATION and MASS CLASS.

social costs   For purposes of calculating the cost of doing business, those costs incurred by society in the form of damage to the environment, increases in illness, etc. Social costs are viewed in much the same way as PRIVATE COSTS in determining the total costs of doing business, but they are not included on a company's financial statements.

social elite   See SOCIAL CLASS.

socialism   An ECONOMIC SYSTEM in which there is public ownership and operation of key industries considered vital to the common welfare (e.g., transportation, utilities, medicine, communications). The government owns all the facilities and determines what will be produced and how it will be distributed. This is generally combined with private ownership and operation of other industries, so that businesses and individuals are allowed to benefit from their own efforts and market forces are allowed to play a role. Compare CAPITALISM.

socialization   See CONSUMER SOCIALIZATION.

social marketing   The application of marketing strategies, concepts, and techniques to the promotion of social ideas or programs. The effort may be designed to propagate a particular idea (e.g., that freedom and democracy are synonymous), to encourage a particular form of behavior (e.g., voting in an election), or to support a particular nonprofit organization (e.g., the League of Women Voters). See also SOCIETAL MARKETING CONCEPT.

social needs   See MASLOW'S HIERARCHY (OF NEEDS).

social profit   Any benefit that accrues from the operation of nonprofit organizations (e.g., health care, police protection, education, child care).

social responsibility   The obligation, on the part of business, to operate in the public interest. This includes a duty to protect the environment, the rights and safety of the consumer, and the firm's own workers. It also includes the ethical responsibility to deal fairly in the business community and to assist and hire underrepresented groups of workers. Also called *corporate social responsibility.*

social risk   The CONSUMER-PERCEIVED RISK that a product, if purchased, might cause embarrassment to the consumer.

social role   See ROLE.

Social Security   See FEDERAL INSURANCE CONTRIBUTIONS ACT (FICA) (1935).

Social Security Act (1935)   See FEDERAL INSURANCE CONTRIBUTIONS ACT (FICA) (1935).

social trend   Any shift in consumer values as evidenced by the changing social and cultural environment. Retailers and other marketers try to keep abreast of social trends in order to understand customer attitudes to their products. For example, if a social trend is running against a particular kind of product, the marketer may need to increase its advertising budget in order to educate consumers about the product's benefits. Marketers may also need to modify their products in keeping with changing tastes.

societal forces   In the marketing context, societal forces are social pressures and influences that affect the operation of the MARKETPLACE. Societal forces include changes in DEMOGRAPHICS, alteration in LIFESTYLE, modification of expectations, etc.

societal marketing concept   A MARKETING MANAGEMENT orientation in which the interests of society at large are taken into consideration when new products and/or services are planned. Primary among these concepts are the conservation of resources and the preservation of the environment. Societal marketing may be adopted as a strategy for either of two reasons or a combination of both: a company may feel that socially responsible behavior attracts customers and forestalls government regulation; or a company may act responsibly for the simple reason that it is the proper thing to do. See also MARKETING CONCEPT and SOCIAL MARKETING.

sociocultural environment   See ENVIRONMENTAL REVIEW.

socioeconomic segmentation   A method of market segmentation based on such variables as age, income, occupation, education, gender, marital status, social class, stage in the FAMILY LIFE CYCLE (FLC), etc. Several of these will characteristically be used in combination to help identify potential buyers of specific brands or products. The same socioeconomic variables may be used to identify and describe radio, television, Internet, and print media audiences. This correlation enables marketers to use socioeconomic segmentation to find appropriate advertising media for their products and reach a target segment effectively.

sociological consumer behavior   The use of social psychology and sociology to better understand consumer buying behavior. Of particular interest are differences arising from one's SOCIAL CLASS, family interactions, and participation in a MEMBERSHIP GROUP or REFERENCE GROUP.

sock form   See STOCKING (LEG) FORM.

sodium vapor lamp   See HIGH-INTENSITY DISCHARGE (HID) LIGHTING.

SOE   See STATE-OWNED ENTERPRISE (SOE).

soffit   The underside of a beam, ledge, arch, vault, ceiling, cornice, or box reaching down from a store's ceiling to its top shelves or usable wall space. A soffit may be used to hold signs, or to mask nondecorative, functional lighting fixtures that serve to illuminate merchandise displayed on store walls. See also STORE LIGHTING PLAN.

soft-core loyal   A consumer who is loyal to two or three brands. See also SHIFTING LOYAL and BRAND INSISTENCE.

soft goods   1. In global marketing, heavily discounted merchandise that may prove difficult to sell. See also TRIANGULAR COMPENSATION.   2. Merchandise made from textile fabrics, such as apparel, piece goods, towels, sheets, etc. Also called *soft lines* or *softlines.* Sometimes known by the older term *dry goods.*

soft lines   Synonym for SOFT GOODS.

soft manufacturing   Synonym for FLEXIBLE MANUFACTURING. Compare HARD MANUFACTURING.

soft-sculpted figure   A life-size doll made of jerseylike fabric with little or no facial details. The figure's skeleton is made of a bendable wire armature that can be shaped or positioned. The armature is embedded in a soft, spongy foam filler that holds its shape inside the jersey outer layer. The figures are abstract and, with the proper lighting, can be made to blend into the background, drawing attention to the merchandise rather than the body wearing it.

soft sell   See HUMOROUS SELL.

SOH   See STOCK ON HAND (SOH).

sole agent   Synonym for MANUFACTURER'S AGENT.

sole proprietorship   A business owned by a single person, although it may have many employees. Sole proprietorships have a number of advantages, such as the ease of formulation and dissolution, control and freedom, secrecy of operations, and tax advantages. On the other hand, a number of disadvantages are also associated with sole proprietorships. These include a limited potential for big profits, restricted financial resources, a reliance on the owner for all managerial skills, and unlimited liability. The persistence of a sole proprietorship is also contingent upon the owner's continuing interest or life span. Also called a *self-owned store.* See also PROPRIETORSHIP.

sole survivor I The category made up of widows and widowers. Many sole survivors are female. In this stage, they are actively employed, present oriented, and have a good income. The employed sole survivor is in the market for clothing, vacations, and leisure pursuits.

sole survivor II The category made up of widows and widowers who have retired. They are present-oriented and tend to rely on long-time shopping habits. Health care products and medicines may dominate spending. Some reside in nursing homes or with adult children.

sommelier kiosk In RADIO FREQUENCY IDENTIFICATION (RFID), an electronic stall or booth that can inform customers about the vintage, region, and varieties of selection for wines. The kiosk is also able to generate food suggestion ideas to accompany the wine. The customer need only wave the bottle of wine in the direction of the RFID reader in the kiosk. See also ELECTRONIC KIOSK.

sorting 1. The separation of merchandise into groups according to specified rules, such as grade, quality, size, etc. Compare GRADING. 2. Short for SORTING PROCESS.

sorting activities See SORTING PROCESS.

sorting out See ALLOCATION.

sorting process The combined processes of ASSEMBLING, ALLOCATION, GRADING, and ASSORTING in the CHANNEL OF DISTRIBUTION. The sorting process serves to bring homogeneous groups of products together for economical handling and shipping early in the distribution process and, later, to break the inventories down into increasingly smaller quantities on their way to the ultimate consumer. At the retail level, sorting involves distributing a wide variety of merchandise into relatively homogeneous groups called assortments. Also called *regrouping activities* or *sorting activities*. Both DISCREPANCY OF QUANTITY and DISCREPANCY OF ASSORTMENT may be overcome by proper application of the sorting process.

sorting theory A theory of buying behavior in which consumers are seen as problem solvers engaged in collecting an assortment of goods and services for themselves and their families. The collection process is seen to begin with a cluster or conglomeration of all goods and services available. After going through a variety of sorting and decision making processes, the consumer ends with an assortment of goods and services.

souk A showroom shared by a number of small manufacturers, where retailer buyers may shop for what is often trend-setting merchandise. *Der.* Arabic, MARKETPLACE.

source 1. In retailing, a synonym for a VENDOR or a RESOURCE. See also PRIOR SOURCE. 2. In communications, a synonym for SENDER.

source effect In the marketing communication process, the impact of a sender's reputation on the credibility of the message. Sources of information (i.e., individuals, publications,

networks, etc.) that have a high degree of prestige will convey a message with a high degree of credibility.

source marking See VENDOR PREMARKING/PRETICKETING.

source tag See SOURCE TAGGING.

source tagging Tags and labels, whether antitheft devices or price tags, provided by the manufacturer to the retailer by special arrangement. Source tagging leads to greater efficiency by reducing the time it takes for the retailer to get merchandise onto the selling floor. Some retailers make source tagging a requirement of their vendors. See also SENSORMATIC SYSTEM, FLOOR-READY MERCHANDISE (FRM) and VENDOR PREMARKING/PRETICKETING.

sourcing In the development of a line of apparel (i.e., styles, sizes, and colors), the process of determining the most cost-efficient vendor of materials, production, or finished goods at the specified quality and service level offering delivery within a specified time frame. Retail merchandisers may be directly responsible for sourcing or work closely with manufacturers who are responsible for sourcing. Sourcing takes two basic forms: FULL PRODUCT SOURCING (FPS) and CUT, MAKE, TRIM (CMT) SOURCING. See also GLOBAL SOURCING.

souvenir Usually a small and relatively inexpensive article purchased, given, or kept as a reminder of a place visited (such as a vacation spot), an occasion (such as a wedding), etc. See also SOUVENIR SHOP and SOUVENIR STAND.

souvenir shop A small store dealing in small and relatively inexpensive articles purchased, given, or kept as a reminder of a place visited (such as a vacation spot), an occasion (such as a wedding), etc. A souvenir shop, like a SOUVENIR STAND, is often found at vacation spots, entertainment venues, and famous places (such as historical landmarks and monuments).

souvenir stand A small kiosk, stall, booth, or pushcart where souvenirs are sold. A souvenir stand, like a SOUVENIR SHOP, is often found at vacation spots, entertainment venues, and famous places (such as historical landmarks and monuments, etc.). See also SOUVENIR.

space allocation In a retail store, the assignment of specific areas for specific uses. Space is allocated first between selling and nonselling areas. Each line of merchandise is then allotted specific amounts of selling area, often on the basis of its gross profitability per square foot. Also called *allocation of space*. See also SALES PRODUCTIVITY METHOD OF SPACE ALLOCATION and STORE LAYOUT AND DESIGN.

space management The strategic arrangement of products to maximize sales with a minimum investment of space and fixtures. Space management involves the development of a visual model of product arrangements called a PLANOGRAM. Electronic space management software is used to build predictive models of optimum inventory levels and assortments based on the wholesale cost, retail price, and turnover of each product in an assortment. Space management software also produces color planograms with product images in scaled dimensions that can be electronically transmitted to stores. The planograms are automatically adjusted by store based on sales data scanned at point-of-sale. Quantities of slow-turning items are reduced (or deleted) from the assortment, while quantities of fast-turning items are increased.

space miser A POINT-OF-PURCHASE (POP) DISPLAY that carries a promotional message and is created to hold items that can be readily removed. A space miser is frequently placed on the shelf where the item is available for sale. Also called a *shelf miser*.

space productivity index An advanced tool used to help retailers determine the optimum amount of space for a product or product category. The index compares the proportion of a store's gross margin achieved by a specific category of merchandise to the proportion of selling space used for that merchandise. For example, a ratio of 1.0 indicates that the amount of square footage allocated to a department or merchandise category is in direct proportion to the contribution to gross margin it generates. A ratio below 1.0 indicates that the merchandise is not selling well and the space allocated to it should possibly be decreased. A ratio over 1.0 means that the merchandise category is selling better than average. This may indicate that the department should be enlarged. See also SALES PRODUCTIVITY METHOD OF SPACE ALLOCATION.

space-sales ratio method A geographical information system (GIS) used to determine a store's potential trading area. Market analysts estimate the size of the trading area based on past experience and subjective judgment. This trading area is visualized as a circle around the store, with the radius of the circle conceived as the distance consumers are expected to travel to patronize the store. The analyst then combines data on the total population residing in the trading area with information on per capita sales to gauge potential sales for the store's retail category. Finally, the analyst estimates the sales potential for a particular store based on the assumption that the store's market share will equal its share of the total retail space in the area. For example, if a department store has 20 percent of the total department store selling space in the trading area, 20 percent of the potential department store sales in the area will be allocated to it.

spam Electronic junk mail (JUNK E-MAIL) or junk newsgroup postings. Spam may also be defined as any unsolicited e-mail. Real spam is e-mail advertising for a product or service, sent to a mailing list or newsgroup. See also CAN-SPAM ACT (2004), OPT-OUT (LIST), OPT-IN, and UNSOLICITED COMMERCIAL E-MAIL (UCE).

spam cascade Synonym for JAVA TRAP.

span of control A MANAGEMENT theory concerning the number of people that one supervisor will be able to deal with effectively. The concept is based both on personal limits and the demands of various supervisory assignments. According to the theory, the span of control varies inversely with the level of difficulty of the supervisory task. Also referred to as the *span of*

supervision, span of management, theory of span of control, and *principle of span of control*.

span of management Synonym for SPAN OF CONTROL.

span of recall In consumer behavior research, the number of brands a test participant can remember when asked to do so. See also EVOKED SET and RECALL TEST.

span of supervision Synonym for SPAN OF CONTROL.

spatial analysis The overlay of two or more types of data to define more accurately the drawing power of a specific retail site. New information is derived from old or incomplete information. GEOGRAPHICAL INFORMATION SYSTEMS (GIS) may be used to perform this type of analysis. See also RETAIL SITE LOCATION.

special A temporary reduction in the price of regularly stocked goods. Compare SPECIAL PURCHASE.

special event An activity held inside or outside the store to increase the flow of customers or enhance the store's image. Special events include visits by celebrities, parades or fireworks displays sponsored by the store, fashion shows, exhibits, demonstrations, etc. Special events are a traffic-generating promotional strategy often used by department stores and other retailers. See also SPECIAL EVENT PRICING and SPECIAL EVENT ADVERTISING.

special event advertising Retail ADVERTISING to promote a SPECIAL EVENT held at the store or under the store's sponsorship.

special event pricing A form of PROMOTIONAL PRICING in which a sale is advertised in connection with some event, such as a holiday. The objective of special event pricing is to bring inventories into line with demand or to raise cash. See also SPECIAL EVENT.

special events calendar A calendar maintained by the promotion department or the fashion department that lists guest appearances, product demonstrations, vendor promotions, and other special activities. Plans a year in advance are not uncommon.

special events director The individual responsible for the development and staging of store activities such as fashion shows, demonstrations, celebrity visits, etc.

specialization A MANAGEMENT theory that expresses a relationship between the variety of work assigned to an employee and the quality of the decision making process. The theory maintains that reducing the variety of responsibilities assigned to each employee will improve the quality of decision making within the organization. For example, in centralized retail organizations, specialization results in buyers devoting themselves entirely to buying, without the added responsibilities of merchandising and operational functions.

specialized superstore Synonym for CATEGORY KILLER.

special line retailer Synonym for SPECIALTY STORE.

special merchandise Synonym for SPECIAL PURCHASE.

special occasion theme A recurring idea or motif that may be used throughout a store or one of its departments. The special occasion theme emphasizes clothing and other items related to an unusual or traditional event. For example, a store may combine all of the elements required for a wedding to create a wedding theme. Other popular special occasions include baby showers, back-to-school, and holidays. See also THEME.

special order An order from a retailer for certain merchandise not regularly carried in stock, submitted to a VENDOR to fill the needs of a specific individual customer. The special order might consist of a size not usually stocked, a different color of an item than that in inventory, or an item that is currently unavailable. Some retailers wait until enough special orders have accumulated to satisfy the vendor's minimum order requirements. However, this delay in filling the order can lead to customer frustration. Also called *special order buying*.

special order buying See SPECIAL ORDER.

special price advertising In RETAIL PRODUCT ADVERTISING, advertisements that promote merchandise offered as a special purchase at a reduced price. The intent of the advertisement is to build store traffic and sales. The special price is generally the result of the retailer having negotiated a less than normal price with the manufacturer or vendor and passing the savings along to the customer. The merchandise offered may be manufacturer's OVERSTOCK or DISTRESS MERCHANDISE and is sometimes out of season. In other cases it be preseason items that the manufacturer wishes to test in the marketplace prior to the regular buying season.

special project team Synonym for VENTURE TEAM.

special purchase Merchandise bought by a retailer at a lower than regular price. Low price (as opposed to stylishness and quality) is the main attraction of special purchase merchandise, which may be used as a promotional lure to increase store traffic. Also called *special merchandise*. Compare SPECIAL. See also PROMOTIONS AND SALES.

special sizes Synonym for OUTSIZES.

specialty advertising See ADVERTISING SPECIALTIES.

specialty advertising counselor See SPECIALTY DISTRIBUTOR.

specialty chain A retailing firm operating a chain of small stores, frequently located in shopping centers or high-traffic urban shopping areas. Specialty chains are characterized by little advertising (the SHOPPING CENTER in its entirety and the anchor stores are the magnets that draw customers), an emphasis on high markup merchandise (e.g., women's apparel), limited assortments, high turnover rates, and few STORE SERVICES (e.g., delivery service). Some specialty chains do, however, issue their own store credit cards. Specialty chains are particularly adept at precisely targeting a market segment and quickly reacting to shoppers' desires. See also CHAIN STORE SYSTEM (CSS).

specialty department store Synonym for DEPARTMENTALIZED SPECIALTY STORE.

specialty discounter Synonym for CATEGORY KILLER.

specialty discount store A store (often a unit in a CHAIN STORE SYSTEM [CSS]) that carries a single product category (e.g., women's clothing) and sells that merchandise at below regular retail prices. See also CATEGORY KILLER.

specialty distributor A wholesale firm that provides a variety of advertising novelties, generally imprinted with the name and often the logo of the retailer or other marketer. The specialty distributor also assists in advertising campaigns employing these items, which are generally distributed as giveaways or free gifts to customers. See also ADVERTISING SPECIALTIES. Also called *advertising specialty distributor* and *specialty advertising counselor*.

specialty goods/items Merchandise (e.g., athletic shoes) well known to the consumer because of its brand identification, high quality, or other specific characteristic. Brand and retailer preferences are strong and customers are unlikely to accept substitutes. Buying specialty goods involves DESTINATION SHOPPING, since shoppers will go out of their way to purchase them. Possession of the particular item is often more important than the price. Also called *specialty products* or *specialty merchandise*. See also SPECIALTY SERVICES and CONSUMER GOODS.

specialty line marketing research firm A MARKETING RESEARCH FIRM that provides specialized research services (e.g., field interviewing services) to other marketing research firms and to the marketing research departments of clients.

specialty (line) retailer Synonym for SPECIALTY STORE.

specialty line wholesaler See SPECIALTY MERCHANDISE WHOLESALER.

specialty merchandise Synonym for SPECIALTY GOODS/ITEMS.

specialty merchandise wholesaler A full service MERCHANT WHOLESALER organization that concentrates its efforts on a relatively narrow range of products and has an extensive assortment within that range. Also called a *limited line wholesaler*, *specialty wholesaler*, *specialty line wholesaler*, or *short line distributor*.

specialty products Synonym for SPECIALTY GOODS/ITEMS.

specialty salesperson A nonretail salesperson who specializes in the sale of a single product or a few products of one or more manufacturers.

specialty selling The sale of products or services in a person's home or workplace (e.g., the selling of insurance, encyclopedias, and vacuum cleaners). See also DOOR-TO-DOOR RETAILING.

specialty services   Services well-known to the consumer because of their brand identification, high quality, or other specific characteristics. Customers have strong brand preferences and are unlikely to accept substitute service providers. See also SPECIALTY GOODS/ITEMS.

specialty shop   See BOUTIQUE and SPECIALTY STORE.

specialty shopping center   A SHOPPING CENTER generally made up of stores that appeal to a specific clientele (e.g., Asian foods and other imported specialties). Merchandise is often high quality and high-priced, although some specialty shopping centers emphasize price and offer goods at a discount. See also SPECIALTY STRIP SHOPPING CENTER.

specialty store   A retail enterprise carrying a product mix narrower than a DEPARTMENT STORE and broader than a SINGLE LINE STORE. The specialty store has a clearly defined market segment as its target (i.e., buyers who seek a wide variety of unique merchandise). Specialty stores generally offer wide assortments within their product lines, trained salespeople, credit, delivery services, and other amenities. Also called a *specialty retailer, specialty shop, special line retailer,* or *specialty line retailer.*

specialty strip shopping center   A group of stores in the straight line configuration of the common strip shopping center, but with a tenant mix narrowly defined around a particular product classification (e.g., restaurants and food related establishments). These shopping centers are often located near a major MALL and tend to attract affluent customers. See also STRIP CENTER.

specialty wholesaler   See SPECIALTY MERCHANDISE WHOLESALER.

specification buying   Rather than shopping the market for goods already produced, the retail organization (often a large chain store) may submit definite criteria to the manufacturer detailing how goods are to be made. The manufacturer then produces the goods to the retailer's requirements (i.e., specifications). Specification buying includes both requests for minor changes to an existing product and specifications for manufacture from raw materials to final product. Also known as *contract buying* and *private label buying.* See also MADE TO SPECIFICATION and SPECIFICATIONS.

specifications   Exact descriptions of goods. Specifications are commonly used when purchasing is carried on by bidding. See also SPECIFICATION BUYING and MADE TO SPECIFICATION.

specific-general-specific cycle   See RETAIL ACCORDION (THEORY).

specific identification   A method of valuing INVENTORY and determining the cost of goods sold. The actual cost of specific items in inventory is assigned both to those items of inventory that are on hand and to those that have already been sold.

spectacular   Synonym for PRODUCTION SHOW.

speculation   Short for *principle of speculation,* a MANAGEMENT theory maintaining that a firm should take the earliest possible advantage of changing the form of its products and of moving its products to market. This strategy is intended to reduce the costs of production and marketing. It stands in marked contrast to the principle of POSTPONEMENT. Also called the *speculation principle.* See also POSTPONEMENT AND SPECULATION.

speculation and postponement   See POSTPONEMENT AND SPECULATION.

speculation principle   See SPECULATION.

speculative buying   The purchase of merchandise on the basis of an expected rise or fall in wholesale prices. The buyer purchases the merchandise when prices appear lowest; the expectation is that a future price increase will lead to increased profits.

speculative risk   RISK that involves the chance of both profit and loss. For example, businesses generally accept the possibility of losing money in order to make money.

speculative purchasing   See SPECULATIVE BUYING.

speculator   An investor who seeks large capital gains through relatively risky investments. See also RISK.

spend   To pay out or otherwise dispose of money or other resources. See also SPENDING PATTERNS.

spending patterns   In CONSUMER BEHAVIOR, discernable trends in consumer purchases and the underlying motives for those purchases. Retailers and other marketers expect that by studying what causes consumers to buy particular goods and services they will be able to determine which products are needed in the MARKETPLACE, which are obsolete, and how best to present those goods to the consumer. DEMOGRAPHICS and PSYCHOGRAPHICS are frequently studied in relation to spending patterns.

spider   In E-COMMERCE, a program that automatically fetches Web pages, which it feeds to a search engine. A SHOPPING BOT, for example, may troll the Web for sites carrying products requested by the user for purposes of electronic COMPARISON SHOPPING. The term "spider" is used to extend the metaphor suggested by "Web." Also called a *webcrawler.*

spiff   (Slang) Synonym for PUSH MONEY (PM).

spim   Spam (i.e., electronic junk mail or junk newsgroup postings) that pops up in the instant messaging window. The advertisement seems to be a message from a friend or acquaintance. Spim messages often contain viruses spread through the use of e-mail address books.

spin   (Slang) The repair of the damaged image of a product line or service. Also used in politics to denote the repair of a damaged political image. A spin is intended to influence opinion in a certain direction.

split function wholesaler   See SEMIJOBBER.

split item   Merchandise that a firm both produces itself and purchases from other manufacturers.

split order   A large order separated into smaller units that are sold over a period of time. Since a very large order could take a long time to sell and consequently be subject to substantial price fluctuations during that time, it is split in order to prevent this fluctuation from negatively impacting the retailer's MERCHANDISE PLAN. Distinguished from SPLIT SHIPMENT.

split rounder   A DISPLAY fixture for apparel, made up of two circular hang-rods, one elevated above the other, for greater 360-degree visibility. See also ROUND RACK.

split run   In print ADVERTISING, a method by which regional advertisers receive a reduced rate. The publisher divides the periodical's national circulation into smaller, regional sections and merchants may pay only for advertising in the geographic area in which they are most interested. This rate is lower than that charged for advertising nationally.

split shipment   A partial shipment of goods from a vendor or supplier to a retailer, the remainder being back ordered until available and shipped at a later date. See also ORDER. Distinguished from SPLIT ORDER. See also SHORT-SHIP.

split ticket   A price tag that is perforated so that, at the time of sale, a portion (i.e., the stub) can be removed for inventory control purposes. See also STUB and STUB CONTROL.

spoilage   1. Loss of merchandise through damage or defect. 2. The defective or damaged merchandise itself.   3. Specifically, in food retailing, products that have gone bad or exceeded their expiration date.

sponsor   1. In broadcast advertising, a person, business firm, or organization that supports the cost of a radio or television program by buying time for advertising or promotion during the broadcast. See also COMMERCIAL (def. 2).   2. An individual who vouches for, is responsible for, or supports a person or thing. See also SPONSOR METHOD.

sponsor method   A training plan in which new employees are assigned to veteran employees who act as their mentors (i.e., sponsors), helping them to adjust to their new jobs. See also EMPLOYEE ORIENTATION.

sponsorship   1. A Web page ad, usually the size of a small button banner ad, placed adjacent to content related to the sponsor's product. The tie-in between company and Web content is obvious. The sponsored content is offered without charge to site owners with related content and may run on several similar Web sites simultaneously. Site owners benefit by hosting sponsored content in two ways: it encourages visitors to stay on the site longer to read the content; and advertising space on the page can be sold by the site owner. See also WEBCAST AD.   2. The arrangement whereby such an ad is purchased and run. Sponsorships are also used for games and interactive tools such as currency, size, and mortgage calculators.   3. Protection, support, or aegis. See also SPONSOR and SPONSOR METHOD.

spoofing   On the Internet, the illegal use of someone else's identity for an electronic purchase.

sportswear   Originally, clothing designed for particular sports activities such as tennis, golf, ice skating, etc. In the early part of the twentieth century, the term began to include clothing worn for leisure time and for participation in spectator sports. More recently, the term *sportswear* is used for casual wear and even for work clothing in some businesses. Clothing worn for active sports, on the other hand, is now designated as ACTIVEWEAR.

spot check   The inspection, usually in the RECEIVING department, of a small sample of an incoming shipment of merchandise.

spot display   Items displayed in a store aisle, particularly in a discount store or supermarket, complete with an attention-getting device to attract customers.

spotlight   A form of INCANDESCENT LIGHT used in retail stores. They are high voltage with very concentrated beams and are often used to focus attention on a particular item or display. Spotlights can be used as the primary light source, but are usually used as SECONDARY LIGHTING. See also STORE LIGHTING PLAN.

spot price   The number of dollars to be paid for a foreign currency as quoted the same day the currency is purchased or sold. See also FORWARD PRICE and UNCOVERED POSITION.

spot shipment   A shipment of goods by rail that includes instructions for the actual placing (i.e., *spotting*) of the freight car on a siding at the consignee's facility.

spotting   See SPOT SHIPMENT.

spread   1. The difference between a BID and the ASKING PRICE of an item.   2. In retailing, the difference between two prices. 3. In print MEDIA, two facing pages, as of a magazine or newspaper.   4. In print ADVERTISING, an extensive display treatment of a topic in a magazine or newspaper. The ADVERTISEMENT covers one or more pages.

square foot   An area one foot long by one foot wide. See also SQUARE FOOTAGE and SALES PER SQUARE FOOT.

square footage   The area of a store, department, or section of the store expressed in square feet. As a measure of productivity, square footage represents the capital outlay for constructing the retail space and the operational expenses associated with renting, heating, lighting, cleaning, and staffing it. In addition to selling area, square footage often includes stockrooms, fitting rooms, service areas, and adjacent sales. See also SALES PER SQUARE FOOT.

SRA See STATE RETAIL ASSOCIATION (SRA).

SRDS Media Solutions An information service that helps connect media buyers and sellers. SRDS maintains a comprehensive database of media rates and market information. Media buyers use SRDS to select the best advertising options, identify the audiences reached by specific media, and determine how much their ads will cost.

SRO method A CLOSING approach in which the prospect is told that if the sale is not concluded immediately, the item may no longer be available in the future. Considered an unethical practice. The term is borrowed from theater ticket sales, where SRO, meaning standing room only, denotes a hit show with extremely limited availability.

S-shaped curve model A visual representation of how sales are affected by an increase in dollars spent on advertising. The model is based on the belief that initial outlays of the advertising budget have little or no impact on consumers in the early stages of sales. After a certain level of promotional expenditure, advertising efforts begin to have an impact on consumers. Thus, as additional money is spent on promotion and advertising, sales will increase. But this incremental gain continues only up to the point at which the law of DIMINISHING RETURNS takes effect, suggesting that additional expenditures will have little or no impact on sales. Compare DIMINISHING RETURNS MODEL. See also S-CURVE EFFECT and PROMOTIONAL BUDGETING. Compare ADVERTISING SALES-RESPONSE AND DECAY MODEL.

SSL Short for *secure sockets layer (SSL),* a protocol for transmitting private documents via the Internet. SSL works by using a private key to encrypt data transferred over the SSL connection. SSL creates a secure connection between a client and a server over which any amount of data can be sent securely. See also SECURE HTTP (S-HTTP).

SSR See STOCK-TO-SALES RATIO (SSR).

SSSM See SHELF STABLE SIMPLE MEAL (SSSM).

ST See STOCK TURNOVER (ST).

stabilizing price A PRICE maintained at the same level throughout the maturity stage of the PRODUCT LIFE CYCLE (PLC). The goal of setting and charging a stabilizing price is to avoid price wars with competitors. Also called the *status quo price.* See also STATUS QUO PRICING.

stacker A freight handler who loads a vehicle.

staff executive Synonym for STAFF MANAGER.

staff function Any position in a firm considered to be operating in a support capacity not directly related to the organization's main mission. In retailing, for example, staff functions include the legal department and the human resources department. Compare LINE FUNCTION.

staff manager An executive in a firm's staff organization (i.e., that part of the firm responsible for providing line managers with special services and support activities). Also called a *staff executive.* See also LINE MANAGER and STAFF FUNCTION.

stagflation An economic condition characterized by inflation (i.e., rising prices) on the one hand and stagnation (i.e., little or no economic growth) on the other. Stagflation is often accompanied by high levels of unemployment.

staggered markdown policy A price reduction policy in which markdowns are taken in stages.

stagnation An economic condition characterized by little or no growth and, generally, high levels of unemployment.

stake In CHANNEL OF DISTRIBUTION relationships, the dependency of one channel member on another for its success or survival. This dependency can vary by degree. For example, if a channel member sells 75 percent of its products to a single customer within the channel, it has a high stake in its relationship to that customer.

stakeholder An individual or group of individuals to whom a business has a responsibility. These include managers, owners, employees, consumers, and society at large. Each of these groups has an interest in seeing the business succeed.

stand A small kiosk, stall, booth, or pushcart where articles are displayed for sale (e.g., a fruit stand).

stand-alone Internet service provider (ISP) An INTERNET SERVICE PROVIDER (ISP) that is not also an online service. Many standalone ISPs also provide a broad range of INTERNET services in addition to the WORLD WIDE WEB (WWW) and E-MAIL.

stand-alone PC A PERSONAL COMPUTER (PC) not permanently connected to either a LOCAL-AREA NETWORK (LAN) or a WIDE-AREA NETWORK (WAN). A single PC connected to the INTERNET via modem is still considered a stand-alone PC.

stand-alone personal computer See STAND-ALONE PC.

standard classification of merchandise A taxonomy, or classification scheme, in which a store's merchandise and merchandise operations are broken down into merchandise groups sufficiently specific in character to permit meaningful analysis of such matters as dollar sales, inventory, sales trends, etc. For example, 1000 is the code for Adult Female Apparel. This is further subdivided into other areas such as 1600 for Sportswear Tops. Each of these subclassifications may be further subdivided. For example, within code 1600 (Sportswear Tops),1614 represents Sweaters. While the coding system is not universally accepted, the taxonomy has had a significant impact on the way retailers arrange INVENTORY data and maintain inventory counts. It was developed by the *National Retail Merchants Association (NRMA),* now called the NATIONAL RETAIL FEDERATION (NRF). Also called the *standard merchandise classification.*

Standard Container Acts (1916 & 1928)   U.S. federal legislation that established the standard sizes for baskets and containers used to market produce (i.e., fruits and vegetables).

Standard Generalized Markup Language (SGML)   A system specifying the rules for tagging elements of a document. SGML is used to manage large documents that are subject to frequent revisions and need to be printed in different formats.

Standard Industrial Classification (SIC)   A former taxonomy or scheme for classifying establishments by the type of economic activity in which they were engaged. It allowed for meaningful analysis, comparison, and industry studies. In 1997, the SIC was replaced by the NORTH AMERICAN INDUSTRY CLASSIFICATION SYSTEM (NAICS). Like the SIC, the NAICS classifies establishments by their primary type of activity.

standardization   1. The process of insuring that the basic qualities of a product are consistent with previously established criteria. Standardization permits marketing campaigns to extend across national boundaries; in short, it is the transfer of all elements of the MARKETING MIX from one country to another. When cultural, economic, or legal differences make *complete standardization* untenable, marketers may utilize a *modified standardization* approach in which one or more elements of the marketing mix are changed. For example, an identical product may be marketed worldwide, but the advertising campaigns for the product may vary from culture to culture, or different consumers may be targeted in different countries. See also STANDARDIZE.   2. In international trade, the establishment of uniform operational, environmental, and monetary systems across several countries in an effort to promote an integrated economy and facilitate trade.

standardize   To make a product or service conform to an established or uniform size, weight, quality level, etc. Some products may be standardized in conformity to specifications recognized on an industry-wide basis. See also GRADING and STANDARDIZATION.

standard merchandise classification   See STANDARD CLASSIFICATION OF MERCHANDISE.

standard metropolitan (statistical) area (SMA)   (Obsolete) See METROPOLITAN STATISTICAL AREA (MSA).

standard package   The quantity of an item usually shipped in a single carton.

Standard Rate and Data Service (SRDS)   See SRDS MEDIA SOLUTIONS.

standard volume   The expected sales over a given business cycle, based on past performance.

standby cost   See FIXED COST.

standing order   An order for merchandise in which previously agreed-upon amounts are automatically shipped by the vendor over a predetermined period of time. Also called an OPEN ORDER.

standing room only (SRO) method   See SRO METHOD.

staple   An item of merchandise, offered at retail, that consumers buy on a regular basis (e.g., sugar, flour, basic clothing such as underwear, gas and oil). There is active demand for staple merchandise at all times, and retailers always keep such items on hand. They are goods with YEAR-ROUND DEMAND, as opposed to seasonal goods that are only in demand at certain times of the year. Staples are readily available in many different locations and are often disposable and inexpensive. They require minimal cost comparison or purchase effort on the part of the consumer. There are packaged staples (such as toilet tissue, paper towels, coffee, and milk) and nonpackaged staples (such as gasoline and apples). Also called *staple goods, staple items, staple stock,* and *staple merchandise.* Compare BASIC STOCK, which is not associated with either seasonal or year-round demand.

staple stock list   See BREAD-AND-BUTTER ASSORTMENT/GOODS.

star   In the valuation of a company's product line, the product seen as having a high growth rate and substantial MARKET SHARE. Stars require considerable cash to finance their continued growth.

starbucking   The practice of spotting a promising new local business and then quickly copying the concept in other cities, countries, or continents before their founders do. The trend was identified and the term coined by trendwatching.com at www.trendwatching.com.

starting markup   See INITIAL MARKUP.

startling statement approach   A SALES APPROACH in which a surprising assertion about the prospect's known needs or problems is used to attract attention to the sales presentation.

start-up (company)   A new business venture in which all the necessary resources must be assembled and organized from scratch.

starving the stock   Having insufficient inventory to meet demand.

state bank   See COMMERCIAL BANK.

state-bonded warehouse   A PUBLIC WAREHOUSE under state government licensing and supervision. Merchandise is stored there without payment of duties or taxes until it is withdrawn from the warehouse.

statement   1. An itemized listing of charges for goods and services, sent to a credit card customer approximately monthly and meant as a request for payment. The statement often includes a detachable portion for the customer to return with payment. A similar itemized account sent by a vendor or retailer is generally called an INVOICE. Both terms are also known as a BILL.   2. An itemized listing of charges for an accounting period, sent by a vendor to a continuing customer. The statement shows charges for goods and services shipped, payments received, and outstanding balance. It serves as a reminder and check for the customer's own records. This type of statement is not meant as a request for payment.   3. See FASHION STATEMENT.

statement insert   Synonym for BILL ENCLOSURE.

statement of assets and liabilities   See BALANCE SHEET.

statement of cash flows   A financial statement that summarizes the receipts and disbursals of cash in the three areas of operations, investments, and financing.

statement of financial position   Synonym for BALANCE SHEET.

statement of profit and loss   Synonym for INCOME STATEMENT.

statement of purpose   Synonym for MISSION STATEMENT.

statement stuffer   Synonym for BILL ENCLOSURE.

state-owned enterprise (SOE)   A business enterprise owned and operated by a government. SOEs, frequently found in developing countries, have a certain competitive advantage over firms in the private sector, as well as some disadvantages. For example, SOEs frequently receive priority access to scarce financing, are protected from bankruptcy, and are given monopolistic positions in their home markets. However, they may also be asked to sell their goods to the home market at below-market prices to help develop the local economy, and the company's profits may be used to subsidize the general economy.

state retail association (SRA)   A local, statewide U.S. trade organization of retailers. The NATIONAL RETAIL FEDERATION (NRF) includes 50 such state retail associations.

static image ad   A form of POP-UP AD that remains in a fixed position in a window of an ad-supported program. Static image ads do not distract the user in the same way as a traditional pop-up ad. See also FLAME, POP-UNDER (AD), MOUSETRAP, and BANNER AD.

static inventory problem   The tendency of some items purchased for a particular selling season to lose value or fail to sell as the season reaches its end. This may be due to changes in the market, overstock, or competition.

statistical bank   See ANALYTICAL MARKETING SYSTEM (AMS).

statistical demand analysis   A form of statistical sales forecasting based on mathematical formulas. Statistical demand analysis takes into account a number of factors such as the cost of the merchandise, the nature of the store's customers, etc., in order to project future demand for a product or class of products and, by extension, future sales.

statistical map   A type of diagram used to present geographic business data. It consists of an outline map on which both locations and quantities can be shown through variations in color, texture, or shading or by a concentration of dots. It is useful for showing general relationships rather than precise data.

statistical process control   In manufacturing, the monitoring of the production process using control charts. This allows management to determine whether production is proceeding as planned or the quality of performance is backsliding. See also QUALITY ASSURANCE.

statistical random error   Synonym for RANDOM ERROR.

status   A condition, rank, or standing, especially high rank or standing. Status may derive from family of birth, education, nature of employment, place of residence, etc. The use or purchase of certain goods and services may also bestow a measure of status on the individual. These vary within reference groups, but may include such items as luxury automobiles, particular wristwatches, fur coats, jewelry, etc. See also REFERENCE GROUP and STATUS SYMBOL.

status-conscious   Aware of and concerned about one's own standing or rank in the community, organization, or other social group. Consumers who are highly status-conscious may rely on particular products to improve their own self-image as well their image within that social group. See also STATUS, STATUS SYMBOL, and REFERENCE GROUP.

status float   The influence of fashion on different levels of the social spectrum, taking into account the contradictions that seem to appear between social groups with regard to dress and dress code. The wearing of dreadlocks by members of the general population who are not Rastafarians may be considered an example of the *status float phenomenon* in popular culture. See also DIFFUSION PROCESS.

status quo objective   See STATUS QUO PRICING.

status quo pricing   A strategy in which prices are maintained at the level charged in the maturity stage of the PRODUCT LIFE CYCLE (PLC). This practice tends to avoid price wars with competitors and seeks to maintain the company's current market share. Also called *avoiding competition* and the *status quo objective*. See also STABILIZING PRICE.

status symbol   A possession, practice, membership, etc., that tends to bestow social standing or prestige. Status symbols include mannerisms, style of dress, home size and neighborhood, possessions (such as expensive automobiles or wristwatches), and memberships (such as country club memberships). Different products have different values as status symbols. This symbolic quality adds a social and psychological element to the utilitarian virtues of the product or service. The value of a status symbol also varies between different social groups. See also STATUS and STATUS-CONSCIOUS.

statutory copyright COPYRIGHT as created and defined by law.

stay-out pricing See PREEMPTIVE PRICING.

stealth marketing See VIRAL MARKETING.

step format display A display that begins at a low point on one side and climbs incrementally and diagonally to a higher point.

step pricing See SKIMMING.

step-up Synonym for UPGRADING.

sticker An item of merchandise that has not been purchased after a reasonable length of time and is seen as occupying valuable shelf space that might better be used for other purposes. See also DEAD STOCK.

stickiness In E-MARKETING, the number of total page impressions per month divided by the number of unique visitors per month. Stickiness, once considered an indicator of attractiveness to Web advertisers for the purpose of rate setting, has fallen into disuse in recent years. See also PAGE IMPRESSION.

stimulus Any aspect of the environment that provokes feelings or incites activity on the part of an individual. For example, advertising is a stimulus that may provoke a desire or incite a purchase. See also STIMULUS-RESPONSE MODEL and STIMULUS-RESPONSE THEORY OF LEARNING.

stimulus-response model A technique used in the study of CONSUMER BEHAVIOR, in which people are seen to respond to a STIMULUS in a predictable way, but no attempt is made to explain why they do so. Researchers using this model seek to establish relationships between consumer characteristics (e.g., DEMOGRAPHICS), stimuli (e.g., products), and responses (e.g., consumer buying behavior). For example, researchers may seek to predict how consumers with high school education will respond to a new diet soft drink. They use the stimulus-response model to establish a correlation between educational level, the diet soft drink, and consumer beverage buying behavior. See also BEHAVIORISM.

stimulus-response theory of learning In ADVERTISING, a theory according to which a STIMULUS (in the form of an advertising message) must be repeated often enough to produce the desired response (i.e., the purchase of the product or service).

STK See STOCK KEEPING UNIT (SKU).

stock 1. In a retail store, all the merchandise on hand. See also PLANNED STOCK, INVENTORY, MERCHANDISE INVENTORY, and SIZING UP. 2. Shares of ownership in a CORPORATION.

stock ahead To maintain a sufficient quantity of an item in INVENTORY to cover an anticipated increase in DEMAND.

stock alteration An alteration made to goods in inventory (i.e., not yet sold), as distinct from those made to goods sold to customers.

stock balance See BALANCED ASSORTMENT.

stock bin control A form of inventory control in which the relative emptiness of bins or shelves is used as a trigger mechanism for reordering merchandise.

stock book Traditionally, a book, maintained at the department level by the BUYER, in which were entered additions to stock in the form of merchandise received from vendors, and deductions from merchandise representing sales to customers. In the modern store, this function is computerized. See also BUYER'S BLACK BOOK.

stock clerk A store employee responsible for receiving and marking merchandise as it arrives, moving it to the selling floor, maintaining inventory records, and performing other duties such as keeping the BUYER informed as to the status of the RESERVE STOCK.

stock condition The amount of merchandise on hand in the store.

stock control The activity of regulating INVENTORY levels so that stock on hand is properly balanced between market demand on the one hand and production capacity on the other. Also called *inventory control*. See also Q-SYSTEM, PERIODIC STOCK CONTROL, INVENTORY, and RESERVE SYSTEM OF STOCK CONTROL.

stock control method See STOCK CONTROL and INVENTORY.

stock count A periodic inventory in which each item is counted and recorded, generally by unit price within a classification.

stock cover The ratio of current average weekly sales to current stock. The ratio provides information on the quantity remaining in stock before new items need to be ordered. See also ORDER.

stock depth The amount of merchandise kept on hand to meet projected sales volume. Also called *stock support*. See also ASSORTMENT DEPTH.

stock exchange An organization whose members meet on a trading floor to buy and sell securities (i.e., stocks and bonds) for their customers. Stock exchanges bring buyers and sellers together and organize all the information about the prices at which investors are currently willing to buy and sell particular stocks. A number of stock exchanges exist in the United States, including the two national exchanges in New York City: the *New York Stock Exchange (NYSE)* and the *American Stock Exchange (AMEX)*. The *NASDAQ* stock exchange conducts transactions entirely electronically, with no traditional physical floor trading. There are also a number of regional stock exchanges, such as the *Midwest Stock Exchange* in Chicago. Stock exchanges exist in all major cities of the world, including

London, Paris, Hamburg, Tokyo, and Toronto. The world's oldest stock exchange, founded in 1611 when the Dutch East India Company sold its shares to the public, is in Amsterdam.

stockholder Synonym for SHAREHOLDER.

stocking (leg) form A form in the shape of a leg, used to display hosiery, including socks, knee-highs, and pantyhose. A stocking form has a hollow top into which the top of the hose can be inserted. The form may be thigh-high, knee-high, or calf-high, depending on the merchandise to be displayed. Stocking forms may be flat, half-round, or fully round and may be used right side up or upside down. Also called a *leg form* or *hosiery form*.

stock keeping In a retail store, the task of keeping merchandise on the floor and in reserve neat, clean, and accessible.

stock keeping unit (SKU) In inventory control and identification systems, the smallest unit (e.g., a case) for which sales and stock records are kept. Stock keeping units, the individual inventory control numbers, are indicated by bar codes that distinguish one product from another. They are considered an indication of ASSORTMENT VARIETY. Also abbreviated *STK*. See also STOCK CONTROL.

stockless purchasing A method of purchasing in which responsibility for maintaining stock lies with the vendor. The vendor ships ordered items to the customer on a just-in-time basis, cutting back on the customer's need to warehouse the materials. Institutions such as hospitals and universities frequently maintain stockless purchasing contracts with vendors for basic supplies. See also SYSTEMS SELLING.

stock level The amount of INVENTORY carried by a retailer.

stock on hand (SOH) The amount of merchandise actually in inventory at a particular time. Traditionally, the retailer's orders for basic and staple goods are assembled from a manufacturer's stock on hand. See also PRIOR STOCK REPORT.

stockout A situation in which stock of a particular item is completely exhausted before new stock has arrived. A stockout generally arises when insufficient quantity was ordered to meet customer demand. Also called *out-of-stock*. See also MINIMUM STOCK.

stock overage A condition that exists when the actual merchandise on hand, as determined by physical inventory, is greater than the amount indicated in the stock records. Also called *overage of merchandise*, *merchandise overage*, *overage*, or, simply, *over*. Compare STOCK SHORTAGE.

stock plan/planning See BUYING PLAN, MERCHANDISE PLAN, and SALES PLAN.

stockroom Space off the selling floor in which reserve stocks of merchandise are stored for future display and sale. See also ADJACENT STOCKROOM.

stock rotation The practice of putting new, incoming products behind older merchandise of the same kind so that the older products are sold first and INVENTORY remains fresh. See also SHELF LIFE.

stock-sales ratio (SSR) See STOCK-TO-SALES RATIO (SSR).

stock-sales ratio method See STOCK-TO-SALES RATIO (SSR).

stock shortage Unrecorded SHRINKAGE in the store's merchandise represented by the difference between book inventory and actual physical inventory. Also called *merchandise shortage*, *stock shrinkage*, or, simply, *shortage*. Compare STOCK OVERAGE.

stock shrinkage See SHRINKAGE and STOCK SHORTAGE.

stock spotting In WAREHOUSING, a practice by which manufactured goods or other commodities are warehoused near the customer rather than at the point of production in an effort to reduce delivery time and transportation costs.

stock support Synonym for STOCK DEPTH.

stock-to-sales method A method of planning inventory levels based on planned sales for a given month. The ratio of stock to sales of the same month in the previous year is used as a guide for the plan in the current year. See also STOCK-TO-SALES RATIO (SSR).

stock-to-sales ratio (SSR) A formula expressing the relationship between current retail stock and sales; it is used to determine the proper amount of stock to be kept in inventory. Beginning-of-month (BOM) or sometimes end-of-month (EOM) inventory is divided by projected sales for that month in order to calculate how fast the BOM stock will be sold. For example, if the stock for a classification of merchandise on November 1 is worth $50,000 at retail, and sales for November are $25,000, the stock-to-sales ratio is 2. SSR is also used in planning for specific merchandise items. For example, a store may calculate that it needs 25 shirts to sell one, given the variety of sizes, styles, and sleeve lengths included in the classification. In retailing, the stock-to-sales ratio (SSR) is one of several PRODUCTIVITY MEASURES. Also called *stock-sales ratio (SSR)*. See also STOCK TURNOVER (ST) and STOCK-TO-SALES METHOD.

stock-to-sales ratio report A monthly report prepared by retailers. The report includes the END-OF-MONTH (EOM) inventory and sales for each store or department as well as the resulting STOCK-TO-SALES RATIO (SSR). The report may also include each store's MARKET SHARE. In chain operations, the report will also include monthly sales for the category by store and for the total chain, with percentage comparisons to the previous year.

stock turnover (ST) 1. The number of times average inventory on hand was sold during a selling period. In this sense, it is synonymous with *stock turnover rate*. Also called a *turn* or a *round turn*. In retailing, stock turnover (ST) is used as one of several PRODUCTIVITY MEASURES. 2. A financial ratio commonly calculated for one year. Stock turnover can be calculated in three ways. To calculate on the basis of retail selling price, the dollar value of net sales is divided by the dollar value of average stock at retail price. To calculate on the basis of cost of stock, the cost of goods sold is divided by the average cost of stock. To calculate on the basis of units in stock, the number of units sold is divided by the average number of units in stock. Also called *inventory turnover, merchandise turnover, number of stock turn,* or, simply, TURNOVER.

stock turnover rate   The number of times the average inventory has been sold and replaced in a given period. Also called the *rate of stock turnover.* See also STOCK TURNOVER (ST).

stock turn (rate)   See STOCK TURNOVER (ST).

stop and hold   The record status of an inactive customer. It is used when merchandise is undeliverable or when services must be discontinued. Also called *suspend.*

storage   An intermediate stage in the distribution chain, usually accomplished in warehouses. Storage involves holding goods until demand meets supply. Storage activities include receiving, sorting, assembling, and shipping. They may be accomplished at the manufacturer-production level, or later in the CHANNEL OF DISTRIBUTION by wholesalers or retailers. The department in which the materials are held is known as the *storage department.*

storage fixture   A store furnishing unit used to hold fill-in or backroom inventory.

storage warehouse   See WAREHOUSE.

store   1. n. A business establishment, generally retail, that regularly offers products and services for sale to the ultimate consumer (i.e., to customers who will use the product or service themselves, not resell it). Stores commonly buy, store, and promote the merchandise they sell. Some wholesale businesses give the outward appearance of being retail stores but, in fact, restrict their customers to members of the trade. See also entries for specific types of stores (e.g., DEPARTMENT STORE, SPECIALTY STORE). 2. n. A supply or stock of something, such as items of merchandise. 3. v. To supply or stock with something (such as merchandise or supplies) or to accumulate something (such as merchandise or supplies) and hold it in reserve for future use.

store audit   A data collection method employed in retailing to track the performance of particular brands or products in a specific time frame. Also called a *trade audit.*

store brand   See STORE'S OWN BRAND (SOB).

store card   See CHARGE CARD.

Store Check Authorization Network (SCAN)   See BANK CHECK FRAUD TASK FORCE.

store cluster   A small group of stores, generally with off-street parking, serving a neighborhood.

store count distribution   A measure of the success of a product's distribution based on the number of stores in

which it is carried. For example, a product sold in 90 percent of all grocery stores would have a 90 percent store count distribution.

store coupon   See RETAILER (SPONSORED) COUPON.

store credit   A sum of money due to a customer for returned merchandise, defective merchandise, or other overpayment. Some stores prefer to issue a store credit to the customer rather than issue a *cash refund,* since the credit must be used in the issuing establishment.

store credit record analysis   A means of determining the extent of a store's TRADING AREA. The store's credit records are examined to determine the trading area being served by the store. The addresses of the credit customers provide some indication of the extent of the trading area.

store credit slip   See CREDIT SLIP.

store design   See STORE LAYOUT AND DESIGN.

store division   See DIVISION.

store door delivery   Synonym for DROP SHIPMENT.

store equipment   Cash registers, trucks, elevators, and all other implements used for a specific purpose or activity inside and outside the store.

store fixture   See FIXTURE.

storefront   1. The exterior face of a store (i.e., the façade, windows, entrances, etc.). Also called a *façade.* 2. Short for *online storefront.* See E-TAILER.

store generative power   A measure of a store's ability to attract customers. The stronger the store's generative power, the greater the distance customers will travel to shop there. See also TRADING AREA.

store identity   Synonym for STORE IMAGE.

store image   The store as perceived by the customer. Factors that contribute to store image are location, price ranges, merchandise, architecture, ambiance, advertising, salespeople, etc. Retailers strive to achieve the desired image for their business through advertising and other promotional activities. For example, a store's image may be value-oriented, fashion-forward, and prestigious. A store's image may also be negative (although never intentionally), as in stodgy, overpriced, or boring. Stores also strive to update their images when necessitated by such factors as shifts in customer lifestyles, competition, and company goals. Also called the *retail image, retail personality, store personality,* or *store identity.* See also POSITIONING, BRAND IMAGE, and PRODUCT IMAGE.

store induction   The informal orientation of a new retail employee to the particular store in which he or she will be working. Usually performed by the store manager, the store induction highlights the general nature of the new employee's work, the department, and the job title. A store induction also involves familiarizing the new employee with the store's selling and nonselling departments and personnel spaces. It may also include an introduction to the employee's coworkers and department manager. See also COMPANY INDUCTION, EMPLOYEE ORIENTATION, and JOB INDUCTION.

storekeeper   An individual who owns or operates a STORE. Also called a *shopkeeper*. See also MERCHANT and RETAILER.

store layout and design   In retail stores, the interior arrangement of departments and of merchandise within departments, as well as space allocation for aisles, counters, fixtures, etc.

store lighting plan   The general, overall design of the illumination of the retail space as well as the accent lighting (i.e., the highlighters that point out what is new, unique, or special). See also PRIMARY LIGHTING and SECONDARY LIGHTING.

store line   See BUYING LINE.

store load   The percentage added by retailers to the landed cost of imported merchandise in order to compensate for lost markdown and advertising money usually received from domestic manufacturers. Store load varies from store to store and from classification to classification of merchandise, but usually ranges from 5% to 20%. For example, a $10.00 landed item with a 20% store load (i.e., $2.00) and a 60% markup (i.e., $7.20) carries a store price of $19.20.

store management division   Synonym for OPERATING DIVISION.

store manager   An executive responsible for the profitable operation of the store. The store manager spends a significant amount of time on the selling floor and is thus able to supply his superiors with detailed information on the operation of the store. In addition to having broad merchandising responsibilities, the store manager develops staff, contributes to the store's public relations efforts, and supervises the maintenance of the store. Also called a *general manager*.

store merchandise manager   In retail stores, an executive reporting to the GENERAL MANAGER and responsible for specific merchandise divisions. Also called a *divisional sales manager* and *assistant store manager of merchandising*. See also MERCHANDISE MANAGER.

store money   See CREDIT SLIP.

store opening   A celebration marking the beginning of business for a new retail store or a new branch of a retail store system. The merchant may have the store stocked and ready for sales, or show the space where a future store will be located. The store opening is often marked by special events, advertising, and special sales to help build customer traffic. Large chains may plan several store openings at once across the country and have special store savings at every location. Sometimes called, simply, an *opening*.

store operations division   Synonym for OPERATING DIVISION.

store-owned brand   See STORE'S OWN BRAND (SOB).

store-owned buying office   See COMPANY-OWNED BUYING OFFICE.

store-owned delivery service   A system owned and operated by the individual retailer for delivering merchandise to the consumers who have purchased it. For small retailers, a panel truck, minivan, or station wagon may suffice. Some large retailers have well-organized systems including a fleet of trucks bearing the store name. See also DELIVERY.

store-owned foreign buying office   See COMPANY-OWNED BUYING OFFICE, ASSOCIATED BUYING OFFICE, and FOREIGN BUYING OFFICE.

store-owned office   See COMPANY-OWNED BUYING OFFICE.

store ownership group   Short for DEPARTMENT STORE OWNERSHIP GROUP. See also DEPARTMENT STORE.

store personality   Synonym for STORE IMAGE.

store policy   See POLICY and RETAIL POLICY.

store records   A retailer's internal sources of information, particularly past sales and inventory data. Analysis of store records is essential for buyers who attempt to bring planned merchandise purchases in line with customer demand.

store redeemable coupon   See RETAILER (SPONSORED) COUPON.

store retailer   Synonym for RETAILER, with particular reference to BRICKS-AND-MORTAR establishments.

store saturation   See SATURATION, SATURATED AREA, and INDEX OF (RETAIL) SATURATION (IRS).

store security   See SECURITY.

stores director   Synonym for DIRECTOR OF STORES.

store services   Tangible or intangible tasks or activities provided by a retail establishment to attract customers and make their shopping experience easier, more pleasant, and more convenient. Some store services, such as layaway plans, personal shopper services, delivery, etc., may be free or carry a charge. Typical store services include convenient hours, parking, checkout facilities, courteous sales associates, customer information, merchandise selection assistance, fitting rooms, alterations, packing/wrapping, methods of payment, delivery service, merchandise return, and other amenities (e.g., comfortable waiting areas and child care). Also called *nonmerchandise services*. See also SUPPORT.

store's lighting plan   See STORE LIGHTING PLAN.

store's own brand (SOB)   A PRIVATE BRAND controlled by a retailer who is both the producer of record and the marketer of the goods. The anonymous manufacturer's only obligation is to make the merchandise according to the retailer's specifications. Also called *store brand, store-owned brand, store's owned brand, owned brand,* and *private label,* SOB products originated in the United States as a lower-priced alternative to branded products, but this is no longer the primary attraction. According to *ACNielsen's 2003 Private Label Study,* price sensitivity remains a driving influence for SOBs, and blue-collar and lower-income households continue to rank prominently among the biggest buyers of store brands. However, the demographic is broad-based, especially in terms of families with children and in rural areas. The study showed that the distribution of spending on private label merchandise has shifted considerably toward small and/or childless households and affluent customers. See also PRIVATE BRAND.

store's owned brand   See STORE'S OWN BRAND (SOB).

store's requisition   A form used to secure materials that are held in normal stock. The form goes directly to the *storage department,* from which materials are then supplied for use. See also REQUISITION, PURCHASE REQUISITION, STORAGE, and RESERVE REQUISITION.

store traffic   See TRAFFIC.

storewide event   Promotions involving all (or nearly all) areas of the store and virtually all categories of merchandise. An *anniversary sale* or a *summer clearance* are examples.

storewide theme   A recurring idea used broadly throughout the entire store, including all apparel and home furnishing departments (e.g., a camping theme). Virtually every department may contribute some article to the extensive THEME.

store-within-a-store   Synonym for BOUTIQUE.

storing   See STORAGE.

storyboard   A graphic presentation comprising advertising layout and script that describes a planned television COMMERCIAL. The process of creating the presentation is called *storyboarding.* See also WEB STORYBOARDING.

storyboarding   See STORYBOARD and WEB STORYBOARDING.

storyline format   A form of advertising in which a scenario that features the product (or in some way relates the history of the product to a present-day useful purpose) unfolds to the viewer in the form of a dramatization or vignette.

straight commission   A method of compensating salespeople in which the salesperson receives, as sole compensation, a fixed percentage on his or her total sales. There is no regular base salary. See also COMMISSION. Compare STRAIGHT SALARY and SALARY PLUS COMMISSION.

straight extension strategy   A strategy employed in international trade in which a company exports the same products that it manufactures for the domestic market, with no attempt to alter them to meet the requirements of foreign markets.

straight-front window   A storefront featuring windows that are parallel to the road or sidewalk. It may be a single window or several windows (i.e., a bank of windows). The entrance to the store may be on one side or between two windows. Often used by large, downtown retailers, straight-front windows are often closed-back windows and lend themselves to elaborate displays.

straight lease   The simplest form of lease agreement, in which the retailer pays a fixed rent over the entire life of the lease without regard to the amount of business done in the store.

straight rebuy   In industrial buying, a situation in which the buyer reorders a product that needs no modification. It is generally a routine transaction. Straight rebuys are often repeated on numerous occasions. Also called the *straight rebuy purchase process.* See also MODIFIED REBUY and NEW TASK BUYING/PURCHASING.

straight salary   A method of compensation in which an individual is paid a fixed amount at regular intervals, independent of productivity considerations. Also called a *salary plan.* Compare STRAIGHT COMMISSION and SALARY PLUS COMMISSION.

straight traffic flow   The movement of customers within a retail store in more or less straight lines due to use of a grid pattern in laying out counters and displays.

strategic alliance   In global marketing, a relationship between two or more global firms in which each partner supplies a particular, usually complementary, resource. Strategic alliances may take several forms, including the TECHNOLOGY-BASED ALLIANCE and the PRODUCTION-BASED ALLIANCE.

strategic business unit (SBU)   A division, line of products, or individual product within a large business organization. Strategic business units are parts of the business that are strong enough to stand by themselves in the marketplace; they are generally treated as separate profit centers by the organization. One or more products, brands, divisions, or market segments may be combined to form a single SBU, particularly if they share the same distribution system. Each SBU has its own mission, its own set of competitors, and its own strategic plan. The term was first used at General Electric.

strategic competence   The ability to focus on the long-term (i.e., strategic) requirements needed to be successful in the global marketplace.

strategic leader   A local SUBSIDIARY of an international company, responsible for developing a new range of products to be used by the entire company. The strategic leader is usually located in a market of strategic importance. Compare IMPLEMENTER and CONTRIBUTOR, two other models of the subsidiary's relationship to the parent.

strategic marketing   A marketing posture in which an effort is made to increase a company's customer orientation by evaluating the relationship and forging a stronger link between MARKETING functions and STRATEGIC PLANNING functions. Generally, MARKETING RESEARCH (MR) and NEW PRODUCT DEVELOPMENT are given a larger share of the organization's budget. See also STRATEGIC MARKETING PLAN.

strategic marketing plan   A formal written document specifying the actions to be taken to enable a firm to satisfy customer needs so that it may reach its ultimate goals. A strategic marketing plan generally sets out the activities to be conducted over a longer period of time than does the annual MARKETING PLAN, often three to five years or more. The strategic marketing plan provides a vision for what marketing can accomplish during that period. However, it lacks the details, or action steps, of the OPERATIONAL MARKETING PLAN. See also WEB MARKETING PLAN.

strategic marketing planning   See STRATEGIC PLANNING and STRATEGIC MARKETING PLAN.

strategic opportunity matrix   Synonym for PRODUCT-MARKET OPPORTUNITY MATRIX.

strategic partnering   In CHANNEL OF DISTRIBUTION relationships, the sharing of information on sales, orders, and inventory levels by retailers and vendors. Such sharing and cooperation is designed to eliminate duplication of effort, speed the distribution process, and improve profitability for all parties.

strategic plan   A long-term plan covering a period of three, five, or sometimes ten years. See also STRATEGIC PLANNING and TACTIC.

strategic planning   Long-range business planning in which the organization's capabilities, resources, goals, and abilities are matched against existing or projected opportunities in the marketplace. Strategic plans are typically established for periods of two to five years, though longer spans are sometimes used. Top managers are usually responsible for strategic planning. The mission statement, statement of tactical objectives, and operational objectives are all key components of the long-range strategic plan. Sometimes called *long-range planning*, *long-term planning*, or *company planning*. See also STRATEGIC MARKETING, MARKETING PROGRAM, and PLANNING. Compare TACTICAL PLANNING.

strategic planning gap   The difference between the present position of a store in the MARKETPLACE and its desired future position. STRATEGIC PLANNING activities aim at closing the gap.

strategic planning model (SMM)   A planning technique developed in the late 1980s by Hewlett-Packard to generate and test alternative business strategies. SMM uses several marketing research methodologies, including choice modeling, cluster analysis, and needs segmentation. These methods may be applied to consumer market analysis as well as to strategic issues in more complex international markets.

strategic window   In planning, that particular period of time during which a firm's competencies best match the requirements of the MARKETPLACE, giving the marketer an excellent opportunity to improve its business. For example, a strategic window opens when a manufacturer's ability to produce items in demand by the public corresponds to increasing sales of that product. Similarly, a retailer's strategic window opens when the firm's ability to secure items in demand by the public is matched by increasing sales of that product. As the opportunity afforded by the strategic window may be of limited duration, the firm is under pressure to seize the opportunity in a timely manner. See also STRATEGIC MARKETING, MARKETING PROGRAM, and STRATEGIC PLANNING.

strategy   In a marketing context, strategy refers to the long-range plan of action calculated to achieve the objectives of the organization. See also RETAIL STRATEGY.

stratified (random) sample   A RANDOM SAMPLE selected in a two-stage process of PROBABILITY SAMPLING. The units of a POPULATION are first divided into groups according to a common characteristic or attribute relevant to the study (e.g., age, gender, or educational level). Particular members of each group are then randomly selected for study. Researchers often choose *stratified random sampling* over other methods when the total population to be investigated is composed of several heterogeneous subgroups. See also STRATIFIED SAMPLING.

stratified sample   See STRATIFIED (RANDOM) SAMPLE.

stratified sampling   A two-stage method of PROBABILITY SAMPLING in which the units of a POPULATION are first divided into groups according to a common characteristic or attribute relevant to the study (such as age, gender, or educational level). A predetermined number of members of each group are than randomly selected for study. Researchers often choose stratified sampling over other methods when the total population to be investigated is composed of several heterogeneous subgroups.

stratifying the market   The practice of determining, given various price levels for an item or service, the number of consumers who may purchase it at each level. See also PRICE ZONE and PRICING.

streaming   A technique for transferring data so that it can be processed as a steady and continuous stream. Streaming is particularly valuable in downloading large multimedia files (such as music or graphic images) quickly. With streaming, the client browser or plug-in can start displaying the data before the entire file has been transmitted. Data must arrive quickly enough for the presentation to appear smooth and uninterrupted. A BUFFER stores the excess data if it is received more quickly than required.

street furniture   Public benches and other resting places that display advertising messages as a form of OUTDOOR ADVERTISING.

street peddler   See PEDDLER and STREET VENDOR.

street traffic   The number of customers or prospective customers who pass by the store. See also TRAFFIC, PEDESTRIAN TRAFFIC, and VEHICULAR TRAFFIC.

street vendor   A seller of goods who operates in a nonstore environment. Street vendors typically sell their wares outdoors, operating from a stand, PUSHCART, or table on the sidewalk. Street vendors typically sell fruit, apparel, accessories, etc., to passersby. Some retail stores, facing competition from street vendors operating right outside their premises, take issue with the street vendors and try to have them removed. See also PEDDLER.

strengths, weaknesses, opportunities, and threats   See S.W.O.T. ANALYSIS.

stress interview   See INTERVIEW.

strict (product) liability   A concept that extends the scope of PRODUCT LIABILITY to include even indirect involvement in loss, injury, or death regardless of apparent or actual fault. In strict product liability, businesses are responsible for damages or injuries resulting from the use of their products, whether or not the companies are proven to have been negligent. Also called *strict liability*.

strike   A temporary work stoppage aimed at forcing management to accept union demands. Compare SLOWDOWN and PICKETING.

strikebreaker   An employee who crosses a picket line to get to work during a STRIKE. Also called by the derogatory term *scab*.

string street   A street having a large number of stores side by side, generally with curbside parking in front. String streets are located away from central business districts and contain thriving clusters of retail shops in or near residential neighborhoods. They frequently become centers for innovative specialty retailing. Intermingled with national chains, string streets often become destination points for local residents and workers as well as tourists. Examples of successful string streets are Rodeo Drive in Beverly Hills, California, and Spring Street in the SoHo neighborhood of New York City.

strip center   According to the International Council of Shopping Centers (ICSC), an attached row of stores or service outlets managed as a coherent retail entity. A strip center is not enclosed and climate-controlled. It is, therefore, a shopping center, and not really a mall, although it is frequently called a *strip mall*. See also STRIP SHOPPING CENTER.

striping   The utilization of a vertical display of merchandise to highlight the retailer's deep merchandise assortments. Most effective in stores with high ceilings, striping is used to show the vast assortment available, to warehouse stock, to maximize store productivity, and to create visual excitement. The inaccessibility of some of the merchandise to customers is not considered an important consideration.

strip mall   See STRIP SHOPPING CENTER and STRIP CENTER.

stripped-down price   A product's base price, that is, the price for the product without all or most of the amenities a consumer might want. For example, a car may be advertised at a particularly low price, but once at the showroom, the customer discovers that the car offered at the low price lacks many of the amenities most consumers desire in a new car. All of those amenities are available (e.g., air conditioning, CD player, power windows), but at an additional charge that significantly impacts the expected, advertised price.

strip shopping center   A shopping center configuration in which the stores are arranged in a straight line along a street or highway. The line of stores is usually set back enough to allow for a covered pedestrian walkway and for automobile parking between the street and the row of shops. Also called a *strip mall*. See also NEIGHBORHOOD SHOPPING CENTER and SPECIALTY STRIP SHOPPING CENTER. See also STRIP CENTER.

strivers   That portion of the global population of consumers (23 percent according to the *Roger Starch Worldwide* study) who consider material things extremely important. Strivers value wealth, status, ambition, and power. They tend to be middle-aged males from developed or developing nations such as Japan and the Philippines. Newspapers are their primary information source. See also VALS SEGMENTATION.

strong inflation   An economic condition in which the rate of general price increase has risen to 10 percent or more.

strong market   A market situation in which DEMAND exceeds SUPPLY.

structural approach to attitude   See COGNITIVE COMPONENT, CONATIVE COMPONENT, and AFFECTIVE COMPONENT.

structured questionnaire   A QUESTIONNAIRE in which all the questions are precisely sequenced to elicit a particular type of response. The interviewer adheres to the formula and does not depart from the wording and arrangement of the questions. The questions are arranged in a logical order with difficult or personal questions reserved for the end of the interview so that the participant does not become defensive. Compare UNSTRUCTURED QUESTIONNAIRE.

strugglers   See VALS SEGMENTATION.

stub   That part of a price tag removed by the salesperson at the time of sale and retained for inventory control purposes. See also STUB CONTROL and SPLIT TICKET.

stub control   An inventory control system based on those portions of the price tag removed at time of sale. See also STUB.

student discount   A price reduction offered to students, particularly to those attending schools located near the retail store. For example, a bookstore, coffee shop, or art supply store may offer a 10 percent discount to students attending a nearby college. The student discount is used to generate additional traffic and build GOODWILL.

stuff   (Slang) To sell goods that are not genuine or that have been stolen. See also COUNTERFEIT PRODUCT and PIRACY.

stuffer   Synonym for BILL ENCLOSURE.

style   1. The quality that distinguishes an object from all others of its kind.   2. In the apparel industry, a particular design (e.g., *I'm afraid we're out of that style at the moment*). 3. A particular, distinctive mode of acting or behaving; especially, an individual's characteristic tastes, attitudes, and mode of behavior. According to John Fairchild of *Women's Wear Daily,* style is "an expression of individualism mixed with charisma."   4. An elegant, fashionable, or luxurious mode of living (i.e., *to live in style*).   5. The prevailing mode of dress, art, architecture, etc. (e.g., *the Baroque style*).   6. A synonym for FASHION.

style display   A retail display presenting merchandise by style for customer convenience and visual impact. Goods often grouped by style include men's dress shirts (e.g., long-sleeve and short-sleeve or button-down and plain collars) women's hats (e.g., narrow brim and wide brim), and silk scarves (e.g., square and oblong). Vendor styles are also grouped together at times.

style improvement   The alteration of a product to enhance its physical or aesthetic appeal. See also PRODUCT IMPROVEMENT.

style modification   The changing of a product (mainly in terms of appearance) in an effort to create a new image for it or differentiate it from other brands.

style number   A coded number assigned by an apparel manufacturer to a specific garment style. The number, often consisting of four digits, indicates the season and/or year for the style and other style information. In this way the manufacturer keeps track of the style throughout the development, marketing, and production phases. See also NUMBER.

style obsolescence   See PLANNED STYLE OBSOLESCENCE.

style-out (technique)   A technique used in fashion merchandising in which potential best-selling styles are identified on the basis of high initial sales. The specific product characteristics that attract customers are identified by separating the fast-moving products from the slow-moving ones and then studying the former to uncover the common features that may explain their greater sales. See also BEST SELLER.

style piracy   See PIRACY and KNOCKOFF.

style sheet   A list of products prepared for CUSTOMS in order to establish duty rates and quota classifications. In the importation of apparel, for example, the merchandiser is required to describe the construction and fabric of the garment.

style show   See FASHION SHOW.

style status report   A weekly report of the distribution of specific style numbers among stores. The report includes the TWELVE-WEEK SELL-THROUGH (i.e., the number of units sold in the past 12 weeks divided by the number of units received in that period) as well as the rate-of-sale information by store and chain.

stylist   An independent individual who works as a contractor for a corporate art director. The stylist purchases props and prepares home fashion products or fashion apparel for advertising or graphic photo shoots. Also called an *independent stylist.*

subchapter S corporation   See S CORPORATION.

subclassification   Any of the groups of merchandise within a CLASSIFICATION that are defined more narrowly and specifically. For example, shoes may be divided into fashion, rugged, casual, dress, sneakers, heavy-duty, comfort, work boots, etc., each of which would be a subclassification.

subcontractor   A manufacturer who produces goods for another manufacturer, a common practice in the apparel industry. See also CONTRACT MANUFACTURING.

subculture   A clearly distinguishable subgroup existing within a larger surrounding CULTURE. Subcultures may be based on such factors as age or race or upon a form of distinctive behavior. In a marketing context, subcultures may be used as a basis for MARKET SEGMENTATION.

subjective price   A consumer's perception of the PRICE of an item or service. The consumer may perceive the price to be high, low, or fair.

subliminal perception   The level at which individuals receive sensory stimuli without being aware of having picked up any messages. Marketers have experimented with subliminal perception by hiding messages in print ads, magazines, and TV commercials. Fear of the brainwashing implications of subliminal perception have made its practice controversial, and even illegal in certain areas. Wilson Bryan Key's book *Subliminal Seduction* (1974) alerted the public to the dangers of the practice. See also JUST NOTICEABLE DIFFERENCE (JND), PERCEPTION, and THRESHOLD OF PERCEPTION.

subliminal seduction   See SUBLIMINAL PERCEPTION.

suboptimization   A condition in an organization in which at least one component, division, or department is operating at a level lower than its very best.

subscriber   One who receives media (e.g., a print or electronic periodical, cable television service, or satellite radio transmissions) on a regular basis in exchange for a sum paid in advance. The *subscription* usually runs for a defined period of time, after which it may be renewed. Compare READER.

subscription   See SUBSCRIBER.

subshopping district   See SECONDARY BUSINESS DISTRICT (SBD).

subsidiary   A separate company that is a part of a larger business organization. The larger company controls the smaller company but does not necessarily wholly own it. When the larger company completely owns the subsidiary, it is called a WHOLLY OWNED SUBSIDIARY. See also SUBSIDIARY CORPORATION and FOREIGN SUBSIDIARY.

subsidiary corporation   A corporation whose stock is owned entirely or almost entirely by another corporation. The owning corporation is known as the PARENT (COMPANY/ ORGANIZATION).

subsidiary ledger   A LEDGER that contains the details related to a given GENERAL LEDGER.

subsidy   Direct financial aid furnished by a government to a commercial enterprise or business, an individual, or another government. In international trade, some countries prefer to subsidize domestic producers so that their prices will be substantially lower than import prices. This tactic is often employed to help build up an infant industry until it is strong enough to stand on its own. The greatest amount of subsidy money, however, goes to agricultural subsidies paid to farmers (e.g., corn supports in the United States and rice supports in Japan).

substandard   Defective or flawed in some way. In retailing, substandard goods are referred to as *seconds*. See SECOND.

substantiation   The act of providing proof of a claim. The submission of data in support of an advertising claim (e.g., 9 out of 10 doctors prefer our product) would be substantiation; the data would support (i.e., *substantiate*) the claim. Claims that cannot be supported by such data are considered *unsubstantiated*.

substitute goods   Products that can easily be replaced by other, similar goods either in production or in consumption (e.g., synthetic fibers for natural fibers or strawberries for raspberries). The greater the number of acceptable substitutes available, the greater the elasticity of demand. Soft drinks, for example, have many substitutes and will thus have an elastic DEMAND CURVE, in contrast to a product such as salt that has few or no acceptable substitutes and therefore tends to have an inelastic demand curve. An increase in the price of one of the substitute goods encourages increased purchases of the other. Also called *substitutes*. Compare SHOPPING GOODS.

substitute method of forecasting   In FORECASTING sales of new products, a method used to predict the upper limit on potential sales of that product. Researchers examine and analyze the sales of existing products that may be displaced by the new one. The resultant figures must then be modified to include customer preferences at various price points and the availability of other substitutes in the marketplace. The substitute method may be used in both the consumer and the industrial markets. See also SALES FORECASTING.

substitutes   See SUBSTITUTE GOODS.

substitution   An item shipped by a vendor to a retailer in place of the merchandise actually ordered.

substitution law   An economic theory holding that if one product or service can be a replacement for another, the prices of the two must be close to each other. Also called the *law of substitution*.

subteens   An identifiable segment of a store's customers whose members are girls from about 9 or 10 years of age to about age 13. Also called PRETEENS.

suburb   An area lying immediately outside a city or town, especially a small residential community. Residents of a suburb often work in the city or town to which they are adjacent. The area composed of such districts is called *the suburbs* or *suburbia*.

suggested price/pricing   See MANUFACTURER'S SUGGESTED RETAIL PRICE (MSRP) and LIST PRICE.

suggested resale/retail price   See MANUFACTURER'S SUGGESTED RETAIL PRICE (MSRP) and LIST PRICE.

suggestion selling   A sales technique in which the SALESPERSON recommends related merchandise to the customer, encouraging additional purchases. For example, the salesperson might suggest shoes and accessories to complement a dress selected by the customer. Also called *suggestive selling*.

suggestive selling   See SUGGESTION SELLING.

suggest pricing   See MANUFACTURER'S SUGGESTED RETAIL PRICE (MSRP).

suit form   See COAT FORM.

summer clearance (sale)   A major promotion at the end of the traditional selling season. A summer clearance sale is designed to empty the store of all remaining summer merchandise in preparation for the new fall lines. Particularly applicable to clothing sales.

Sunday hours   See SUNDAY OPENING.

Sunday opening   The provision of shopping opportunities seven days a week by opening the store or shopping center on Sunday. This practice began as a response to consumer demand and in opposition to BLUE LAWS. The increased participation of women in the workforce has intensified the need for seven-day shopping to accommodate family work schedules.

sundries   Small, inexpensive, miscellaneous items often sold in variety stores, supermarkets, or vending machines.

sunk costs   Costs, generally developmental, that have been incurred and are unrecoverable.

superagency   A large advertising agency equipped to provide services such as direct mail, coupons and other promotions, publicity releases, and public relations activities as well as traditional advertising functions. See also INTEGRATED MARKETING.

supercenter   A combined SUPERMARKET and FULL LINE DISCOUNTER, actually a scaled-down version of a HYPERMARKET. Supercenters combine the advantage of frequency of food store shopping with the higher profit margins of the full line discounter. They epitomize the concept of one-stop shopping and are the fastest growing discount-store format. Also known as a *combination store*. Sometimes spelled *super center*.

supercomputer   Large, fast, and expensive computers capable of performing as many as a billion arithmetic operations per second. They have been used mainly in research and engineering to solve scientific problems involving billions of calculations. A new generation of supercomputers, however, promises to be more affordable and more readily available to business.

superette   A grocery store in which much of the merchandise is arranged for self-service, but in which counter service is still available. Superettes stand between supermarkets and mom-and-pop stores or convenience stores in terms of size and merchandise carried. See also SUPERMARKET, BANTAM STORE, and MOM-AND-POP STORE/OUTLET.

superficial discounting   See PSYCHOLOGICAL DISCOUNTING.

superior goods   Products and services for which demand increases as incomes rise (e.g., luxury cats, caviar, fur coats). Also called *normal goods*. See also LUXURY GOODS.

supermarket   A large retail store specializing in groceries, produce, meat, dairy products, and a wide variety of nonfood items. Supermarkets operate on a self-service basis with customers paying at a central CHECKOUT COUNTER. These stores are characterized by high unit volume, low unit prices, and a broad assortment of merchandise. They operate on very low profit margins. Many sell generic and private label brands in addition to national brands. Also called a *conventional supermarket* or *traditional supermarket*. See also SUPERETTE and SUPERSTORE.

supermarket loyalty card   See LOYALTY CARD.

superquad   A four-armed store fixture designed to hold basic items that have been purchased in depth. Superquads allow for the display of items with different sleeve or hem lengths and work extremely well when featuring coordinate groupings composed of pants, skirts, blouse, sweaters, or jackets. The superquad is also useful for showing broken or unrelated assortments and can be used for displaying a collection of clearance merchandise. See also DRAPER, FOUR-WAY FIXTURE/DISPLAY/RACK, SPLIT ROUNDER, ROUND RACK, and THREE-PART RACK.

superregional (shopping) center   A shopping center consisting of three or more anchor stores and as many as 350 specialty and service retailers. The superregional shopping center has almost three times the gross leasable area of the typical regional shopping center (i.e., in excess of 800,000 square feet of retail space) and may include hotels, office buildings, and recreation centers. Food courts are typical features of superregional shopping centers, and many also include movie theaters. Superregional centers often serve a population of over a million potential customers and draw shoppers from a 25-mile radius. Compare REGIONAL SHOPPING CENTER.

superstitial   A pre-cached INTERSTITIAL (i.e., rich media ad) that is less intrusive than the traditional interstitial. The superstitial does not block the site visitor's progress and access to site content as the superstitial invisibly downloads into the visitor's browser's temporary memory whenever the modem goes idle. When the commercial is fully downloaded, intact, and ready to play, the superstitial begins playing as the site visitor moves to a new Web page. The new page loads behind the superstitial. While loading in the background is less annoying to visitors than interstitials, privacy issues have been raised by the practice.

superstore   A large retail establishment combining many of the features of the SUPERMARKET with those of the DISCOUNT STORE. Superstores may have 150,000 square feet of floor space and carry food and nonfood general merchandise in a ratio of approximately 70% to 30%. These stores carry three to four times the number of products found in the conventional supermarket, out of which the superstore evolved. Superstores are geared to meet all the routine needs of the customer in one stop. Consequently, they have a much broader profit base than smaller supermarkets and permeate the retail scene, especially in heavily populated urban and suburban areas. The term also applies to the CATEGORY KILLER, even though these stores do not usually carry food, and the DISCOUNT STORE. Also called a MEGASTORE.

superstore retailing   See SUPERSTORE.

Super 301   See OMNIBUS TRADE AND COMPETITIVENESS ACT (1988).

supervision of the salesforce   Synonym for SALES MANAGEMENT.

supervisory management   The bottom level of an organization's management hierarchy. These are the managers who oversee the day-to-day work of operating employees and who put into action the plans developed at higher management levels. Included are the supervisor, foreman, department head, and office manager.

super warehouse (outlet/store)   A store at least twice the size of the typical supermarket, operating on a high-volume, low-overhead basis. The super warehouse is a hybrid, being partly a no-frills warehouse outlet but at the same time stocking much of the merchandise found in a traditional supermarket. Goods are often displayed in cartons, and customers are expected to pack and carry their own groceries. See also WAREHOUSE STORE.

supplier   1. In advertising and promotions, an individual who assists clients and advertising departments or agencies in preparing promotional materials. Suppliers include photographers, graphic designers, audio and/or video production personnel, typesetters, printers, etc.   2. Synonym for VENDOR.

supplier/distribution intermediary contract   A written agreement between suppliers (i.e., vendors) and marketing intermediaries. Such contracts focus on price policies, conditions of sale, territorial rights, the services/responsibility mix, contract length, and conditions of termination.

supplies   Business or industrial goods treated as expense items and not incorporated into a finished product. Most supplies fit into one of three categories: *maintenance supplies* such as cleaning materials and paint; *repair supplies* such as glass and pipe; and *operating supplies* such as paper and fuel. The three categories are sometimes known as *MRO items* (for *maintenance, repair,* and *operating*).

supply   The quantities of goods or services that producers are willing and able to provide at a particular point in time and at various prices. See also LAW OF SUPPLY, DEMAND, and POINT OF EQUILIBRIUM.

supply and demand   Countervailing market forces that, taken together, drive the FREE MARKET ECONOMY. Sellers will supply more of a product when they can sell it at a higher price, and buyers will buy more of a product when they can buy it at a lower price. As consumer demand for a product increases, suppliers will increase their prices. As consumer demand decreases, suppliers will be forced to lower their prices in order to move their remaining merchandise. Often referred to as the *law of supply and demand*. See also MARKET ECONOMY, FREE ENTERPRISE, and MARKET PRICE.

supply chain   Synonym for CHANNEL OF DISTRIBUTION.

supply chain lean practice   See LEAN PRACTICE.

supply channel   The chain of suppliers of raw materials, supplies, and parts necessary for production. The supply channel also includes the equipment and materials needed to maintain and operate the enterprise. See also CHANNEL OF DISTRIBUTION.

supply cooperative   A cooperative organization selling SUPPLIES to members at less than open-market prices.

supply curve   A chart or schedule, generally represented as a graph, depicting the relationship between the quantity of goods entering the market and the price being offered for the goods. High prices commonly draw more goods into the market, causing the supply curve to slant upward. The chart or graph in numerical form is called a *supply schedule*.

supply house   See INDUSTRIAL DISTRIBUTOR.

supply (law of)   See LAW OF SUPPLY.

supply price   The lowest price needed to produce a specified output, and therefore the lowest price a seller can accept for the act of supplying a given quantity of a commodity.

SVA   See SEGMENTATION VARIABILITY ANALYSIS (SVA).

supply schedule   A table of data used in graphing the SUPPLY CURVE.

support   Those aspects of a product that involve its DELIVERY, CREDIT, WARRANTY, GUARANTEE, installation, post-sale service, repairs, spare parts, and any training required for its use. See also CORE PRODUCT, PACKAGING, and PRODUCT POTENTIAL, all of which are components in the creation of a complete product. See also SUPPORTIVE SERVICE.

support consumable   Any expense item used in running a business. Support consumables include inexpensive items used to support the business (e.g., rubber bands, paper, file folders, janitorial services). Industrial buyers shop for these supplies and services and make the buying decisions for the firm.

supporting activities   See SUPPORTIVE SERVICE.

supporting salesperson   See SUPPORT SALESPERSON and SUPPORTIVE SERVICE.

supportive service   In marketing, any auxiliary benefit or service that makes the product more attractive to the customer. Supportive services contribute to the firm's overall marketing effort. For example, the extension of credit is a supportive service that facilitates the selling process. Warranties, guarantees, installation, and initial free service contracts are also supportive services that may encourage customers to select one product over another. Also called *support service* and *supporting activities*.

support medium   Any secondary communications medium used in an ADVERTISING CAMPAIGN as a backup for the PRIMARY MEDIUM. For example, if the primary medium is a series of television commercials, OUTDOOR ADVERTISING and POINT-OF-PURCHASE (POP) ADVERTISING may be used as support media to reinforce the sales message. Also called the *secondary medium*. See also MEDIA and ADVERTISING MEDIA.

support salesperson   A salesperson generally not directly involved in order getting, but more concerned instead with the technical details of the product being offered for sale. The DETAILER, the TECHNICAL SALESPERSON, and the PARASALESPERSON are all employed in a support role. Also called a *supporting salesperson*.

support service   See SUPPORTIVE SERVICE.

suprafirm   A form of retail organization in which a large firm develops a relationship with a number of small stores (e.g., in a COOPERATIVE or VOLUNTARY CHAIN, FRANCHISE system, SHOPPING CENTER) in order to bring the smaller stores the advantages of larger numbers. In return, the smaller stores give up some of their autonomy.

surety bond   A three-party contract that protects companies against losses incurred through the nonperformance of a contract. One party (often an insurance company) agrees to be responsible to a second party for the obligations of a third party.

surfer   On the Internet, an individual who moves from site to site seeking topics of interest. See also SHURFER.

surfing   1. The practice of moving around from site to site on the INTERNET, seeking information but not necessarily doing a focused search or using a search engine. Surfing has become, for many Internet users, a recreational activity in and of itself. Also called *Internet surfing* and *Web surfing*. 2. The practice of flipping from channel to channel on television, enabled by a remote control. Channel surfers are sometimes in search of something interesting to watch and sometimes trying to avoid commercials. Also called *channel surfing*.

surf the Net/Web   To move from site to site on the Internet, seeking topics of interest.

surplus   Anything remaining or left over above what is used or needed.

surplus merchandise   Goods, often clothing and equipment from the armed forces, that has been declared SURPLUS by the U.S. government and sold for ultimate resale in the civilian market. See also SURPLUS STORE.

surplus store   A store that sells, along with other goods of nongovernment origin, merchandise that has been declared SURPLUS (i.e., excess, no longer needed) by an agency of the U.S. government. Typical merchandise includes clothing and equipment no longer of use to the armed forces. Often called an *army/navy store*. See also SURPLUS MERCHANDISE.

survey   A method of MARKETING RESEARCH (MR) in which facts and opinions are obtained directly from consumers through a questionnaire, consumer panel, or series of interviews. A survey consists of a set of questions designed to collect specific information from buyers, businesses, institutions, organizations, or visitors to online sites. Also called a *marketing survey* or the *survey method*. There are various types of surveys including the FACTUAL SURVEY, the OPINION SURVEY, and the INTERPRETIVE SURVEY. See also QUESTIONNAIRE and ONLINE SURVEY.

survey approach   A SALES APPROACH in which the SALESPERSON asks the PROSPECT a number of surveylike questions. This approach is designed to ascertain the prospect's familiarity with a particular product or service. Questions may range from the simple and straightforward to the specific and technical. The method serves to qualify prospects as well as to lead into the sales presentation.

survey method   See SURVEY and SURVEY APPROACH.

Survey of Buying Power (SBP)   An annual compilation of statistical data designed to help marketers and retailers analyze U.S. markets. Data for the current year as well as five-year projections are included for every state, core-based statistical area (CBSA), county, major city, and designated market area (DMA) in the United States. The survey includes information about population, effective buying income, retail sales, and buying power.

suscipient business   That portion of a retailer's business that relies on customers who are in the vicinity of the store for purposes other than shopping. A retailer located in a sports arena, for example, would have suscipient business.

suspend   Synonym for STOP AND HOLD.

SVA   See SEGMENTATION VARIABILITY ANALYSIS (SVA).

swap   To EXCHANGE or BARTER.

swap market   A meeting place where people gather to exchange goods, generally personal or household articles that they no longer need. Early swap markets did not involve the exchange of money, but soon evolved into more conventional retail operations like the flea market. See also SWAP SHOP.

swap shop   An ONLINE site for swapping or bartering merchandise. BARTER in a swap shop can take at least two forms, DIRECT BARTER and NETWORK POOL BARTER. In direct barter, items are traded one for one. In network pool barter, members do not trade directly but work through BARTER DOLLARS (trade credits or tokens) credited to their accounts and used to make a purchase. Most sites offer free memberships and some have small transaction fees for products traded. Also spelled *swapshop*. See also SWAP, BARTER, EXCHANGE, and SWAP MARKET.

swarm sighting   The tendency of large numbers of ordinary citizens, reporting to a central entity (usually a Web site), to track and trace virtually everything. Individuals use e-mail, cell phones, digital camera phones, text messaging, etc. to instantaneously track people and objects around town or around the world. The trend was identified and the term coined by trendwatching.com at www.trendwatching.com.

sweater form   See BUST FORM.

sweatshop   A manufacturing establishment, particularly in the garment industry, that employs workers under unfair and unsanitary conditions. Globalization is seen as contributing to the growth of sweatshops both domestically and abroad, as the drive to compete and cut costs becomes overwhelming.

sweepstakes   A sales promotion device in which the participant competes for prizes by simply entering his or her name. At some future date the winners are determined by drawing names at random from among all those entered. A sweepstakes requires no skill of the participant and has no fixed, predictable odds. Compare GAME and CONTEST.

swell allowance   A price reduction given on the invoice cost to provide for the loss of value of an item due to damage in shipping.

swimsuit   See SWIMWEAR.

swimwear   Apparel designed for recreational bathing (i.e., swimming and wading). The individual garments are called *swimsuits*.

swimwear form   See INNERWEAR FORM.

swing area   A key area in a store, used for rotating displays or small temporary departments. For example, the swing area may feature Christmas decorations in the fall and winter and SWIMWEAR in the spring and summer. Swing areas are used to capture attention and guide customers to other key areas of the store.

swing shop   In a department store, an area where trendsetting merchandise is featured. It takes its name from the idea that the area can quickly swing from one look to another as fashions change.

switcher   Short for BRAND SWITCHER.

switching customers   The practice of bringing in a sales specialist to close a sale when the salesperson who began the transaction cannot.

switch selling   Synonym for BAIT AND SWITCH.

switch trade, switch trader   See TRIANGULAR COMPENSATION.

S.W.O.T. analysis   A business research method used to evaluate a company's strengths, weaknesses, and opportunities, as well as the threats (both internal and external) to which it is vulnerable. S.W.O.T. analysis involves surveying the environment in which the retailer or other organization operates and identifying the opportunities and threats that the company faces. It is used to determine the future direction the company should take, or, often, its WEB READINESS. The name is derived from the initial letters of the factors or variables studied (i.e., strengths, weaknesses, opportunities, and threats). See also SITUATION ANALYSIS.

symbiotic marketing   A marketing strategy in which two or more firms enter into a venture jointly (e.g., the marketing of

European automobiles in the United States through established dealerships for American cars).

symbolic pricing   See PRESTIGE PRICING.

symmetrical balance   In the layout of a selling floor or visual merchandising display, the positioning of items on either side of a center line so that they are equally weighted optically. Also called *formal balance*. Compare ASYMMETRICAL BALANCE. See also BALANCE (def. 2).

symmetric encryption   A form of ENCRYPTION used on the INTERNET, in which the same key is used to encrypt and decrypt the message. Compare PUBLIC-KEY ENCRYPTION, which uses one key to encrypt a message and another to decrypt it.

sympvertising   A trend in which consumer advertising is infused with a pinch of sympathy for the tougher times consumers are facing. This strategy is useful when catering to those less than fabulously rich. The trend was identified and the term coined by trendwatching.com at www.trendwatching.com.

syndicated buying office   A CORPORATE BUYING OFFICE owned and operated by a MERCHANDISING CONGLOMERATE. The syndicated buying office may be responsible for product development, imports, and domestic market coverage for a number of operating divisions of the parent conglomerate. At times, the buyers at the divisional level may select merchandise from the suppliers selected by the buying office.

syndicated service research firm   A MARKETING RESEARCH FIRM/COMPANY that gathers consumer and trade information on a regular basis and sells the data to clients for a fee. An example would be the reports on television audiences prepared by the ACNielsen Co.

syndicate office   See SYNDICATED BUYING OFFICE.

synergism   In the context of a marketing system, the cooperative interaction of the various parts of the system so that its total effect is greater than the sum of the effects of the individual parts. See also PROMOTION SYNERGY.

synergistic promotion   See PROMOTION SYNERGY.

synergy   See PROMOTION SYNERGY and SYNERGISM.

systems approach   1. A concept in which the various components of the MARKETING ENVIRONMENT are viewed as interrelated and interdependent. Together, they make up a rational system. Also called *systems theory*.   2. The systems approach also refers to a form of company organization in which the firm's various functions are integrated to facilitate the marketing effort. The interrelationships and interdependence of the many components of the firm's marketing activities are treated as a single, rational system.

systems buying The purchase of a multifaceted product or service, such as a telecommunications system. Instead of having to coordinate the efforts of multiple vendors, firms participating in systems buying purchase the entire system from a single contractor, who takes full responsibility for assembling subcontractors to provide the complete package. See also SYSTEMS SELLING.

systems contracting Synonym for SYSTEMS SELLING.

systems selling 1. In retailing, the merchandising of a group of related items as a package rather than as single items (e.g., a matching tie and handkerchief). 2. A form of selling found primarily in industrial markets, in which products, supplies, and services are sold in combination in an effort to meet the needs of the customer on a continuing basis. For example, one firm may sell a materials handling system that includes both transporters and an array of packaging materials used for shipping. Another systems seller may assemble all subcontractors required to complete a project for the purchaser. In essence, systems selling involves selling a complete solution to a problem or need rather than one or more of the component parts. Also called, in this sense, *systems contracting*. See also TEAM SELLING and SYSTEMS BUYING.

systems theory See SYSTEMS APPROACH.

table   A grid used to display relationships between sets of data. Tables are frequently used to present data when there is a lot of precise numerical information to organize and convey.

table of organization   Synonym for ORGANIZATION CHART.

tabletop merchandise   Glassware, china, flatware, and textile products, such as tablecloths and napkins, used for serving food and home entertaining.

T-account   In accounting, a method of expressing the effect of certain transactions in the form of a T (i.e., a horizontal crossbar combined with a vertical line separating debits on the left from credits on the right).

tactic   A specific, generally short-term course of action taken to execute a STRATEGIC PLAN. See also TACTICAL PLANNING.

tactical planning   Short-term business planning, particularly when focused on the implementation of the organization's long-term strategic goals. Tactical plans cover one year or less and the kinds of situations that are likely to come up monthly, weekly, or daily. Middle managers and supervisors are more involved in planning over the short term than they are in STRATEGIC PLANNING. Tactical plans tend to be specific, characteristically including procedures, practices, rules, and a budget for accomplishing the short-term goal. Sometimes called *short-range planning* or *short-term planning*. See also PLANNING and SHORT-RANGE PLAN.

tactical price change   A strategic MARKUP or MARKDOWN (MD) that falls within a retail PRICE ZONE defined at one end by a retail price with a standard markup and at the other end by a retail price with an inflated markup.

Taft-Hartley Act   See LABOR-MANAGEMENT RELATIONS ACT (LMRA) (1947).

tag   Short for PRICE TAG.

tag anonymizer   In RADIO FREQUENCY IDENTIFICATION (RFID), an ELECTRONIC KIOSK that allows customers to delete product information and personal data from the store's records after checkout, allowing their choices to remain anonymous.

tagging   See SOURCE TAGGING.

tag price   The price for an item of merchandise that is actually listed on the product's PRICE TAG.

tag switcher   A customer who changes (i.e. switches) price tags from less expensive merchandise to more expensive merchandise and then attempts to complete the sales transaction, paying the lower price. Also called a *ticket switcher*.

tailor   1. n. An individual who makes clothing, mends clothing, or does alterations. The tailor shop may be situated in the retail store or it may be an independent establishment. Compare DRESSMAKING.   2. v. To fit and fashion clothing for a particular individual, as opposed to READY-TO-WEAR (RTW).

tailor-made   Of a garment, made specifically for one individual customer by a tailor. The customer's measurements are taken and several fittings are generally necessary. See also CUSTOM-MADE and MADE-TO-MEASURE.

take   (Slang) The proceeds in the retailer's cash register at the close of the business day.

take-and-pay contract   An agreement to purchase a specified quantity of merchandise provided it is delivered by the contracted time. The term may be used similarly for the purchase of services.

take home pay   See DISPOSABLE INCOME.

taken private   See PRIVATELY HELD COMPANY.

takeover   See ACQUISITION.

take private   See PRIVATELY HELD COMPANY.

take stock   To prepare an INVENTORY of items on hand.

take transaction   Synonym for CARRYOUT.

take-with (transaction)   Synonym for CARRYOUT.

taking inventory   The procedure of counting all inventory on hand at a time set aside for this purpose. See also INVENTORY and TAKE STOCK.

tall organization   Synonym for CENTRALIZED ORGANIZATION.

tally   See TALLY CARD.

tally card   A form on which a salesperson records each transaction. The form is sometimes printed on a *tally envelope* into which the *tally* (i.e., the next day's starting amount of money) may be placed.

tally envelope   See TALLY CARD.

Talmadge-Aiken Agreement   See MEAT INSPECTION ACT (1906).

talon   A special coupon appended to a receipt, usually at the bottom (e.g., a voucher stub). The consumer may detach the coupon to use sometime in the future.

tame cat distributor   (Slang) A WHOLESALER owned and controlled by a manufacturer.

TAMS   See TAXONOMY OF THE APPAREL MERCHANDISING SYSTEM (TAMS).

tandem management   In large retail organizations, the sharing of top management functions by two individuals. Generally, one will be the Chairman/woman of the Board and the other the President. The individual designated CHIEF EXECUTIVE OFFICER (CEO) is "first among equals" in the event of a disagreement between the two. See also BOARD OF DIRECTORS.

tangible asset   A real thing possessed by a firm, such as a building, merchandise, cash, etc. See also ASSET and TANGIBLE RESOURCES.

tangible product   See PRODUCT.

tangible resources   A firm's physical plant and equipment, cash reserves, raw materials, etc. See also TANGIBLE ASSET.

tape plan   A promotional strategy characteristically run by supermarkets and drug store chains. Premiums are offered in return for cash register receipts totaling a specific dollar amount of purchases accumulated over a specified period of time. For example, a supermarket may offer a free turkey at Thanksgiving or Christmas for customers who have spent a certain dollar amount in the weeks leading up to those holidays. With the advent of the POINT-OF-SALE TERMINAL (POST), the store's own computer can keep track of the customer's expenditures. Consequently, the collection and presentation of actual register tapes is generally no longer necessary. Also called a *cash register tape redemption plan*.

tare (weight)   1. The weight of the wrapping or packaging containing goods.   2. A deduction from the gross weight of an item to allow for the weight of the packaging.

target   1. The individual or group to whom a sales or advertising message is addressed. See also ADVERTISING TARGET.   2. A portion of the total market identified as the primary customer group for a retail store, product, or service. See also TARGET MARKET.

target audience   See ADVERTISING TARGET.

target customer   See TARGET MARKET.

targeting of global competitors   In global competition, the identification of actual and potential global competitors and the selection of an overall posture (e.g., stack, avoidance, cooperation, acquisition) toward them.

target market   The particular subdivision or segment of a total potential market selected by a company as the object of its marketing efforts. Choice of a target market is usually based on some common characteristic possessed by the market segment (e.g., gender, education level, income level, native language, age, marital status, family size). Also known as a *market target, customer base, ideal customer, target customer,* or *served market.* See also MARKET SEGMENT, PROMOTION TARGET, POSITIONING ADVERTISING, and POSITIONED RETAILING.

target marketing   See TARGET MARKET and MARKET TARGETING.

target market segment   See MARKET SEGMENT.

target markup   Synonym for MARKON.

target population   In SAMPLING, that part of the population at large from which a SAMPLE is selected. See also SAMPLE, SAMPLING, and POPULATION.

target positioning   Synonym for MARKET POSITIONING.

target (profit) pricing   A PRICING STRATEGY in which the selling price of a product is determined by adding a sum to the fixed cost of the product to achieve a predetermined profit margin or RETURN ON INVESTMENT (ROI). Also called *target return pricing.* See also GROSS MARGIN.

target rating points (TRPs)   In media planning and measurement, the number of people in the primary target audience to be reached by the media buy. See also GROSS RATING POINTS (GRPS).

target return on investment   The income goal to be achieved by pricing, representing a predetermined percentage of the firm's investment. Also called the *targeted return on investment.* See also RETURN ON INVESTMENT (ROI) and PROFIT TARGET ANALYSIS.

target return pricing   See TARGET (PROFIT) PRICING.

target segment   See MARKET SEGMENT.

tariff   1. A tax levied against imported products. The actual amount of the tax is referred to as the DUTY or CUSTOMS DUTY. There are two forms of tariff: the REVENUE TARIFF, designed to raise money, and the PROTECTIVE TARIFF, designed to protect domestic producers or manufacturers by raising the price of imported goods to a competitive level and thereby possibly excluding foreign competitors. See also IMPORT TARIFF and EXPORT TARIFF. 2. The rates charged by shippers (e.g., rail, truck, air freight, barge) for their services. More specifically, under the INTERSTATE COMMERCE ACT (1887) and the Civil Aeronautics Act (1938), tariffs are those schedules containing all interstate rates, charges, and regulations for shipping between different points. Once published, such tariffs have the force of law as long as they are in effect.

task and investment method of promotional budgeting   See OBJECTIVE-TASK METHOD OF PROMOTIONAL BUDGETING.

task force   1. In NEW PRODUCT DEVELOPMENT, a group of individuals drawn from a number of functional departments within the firm. The task force is responsible for seeing that the development of the new product is given coordinated and sufficient support. Members of a task force generally perform these duties in addition to their regular duties.   2. More generally, a similar group of individuals drawn from a number of departments within a firm to accomplish a particular goal. Members are selected on the basis of their expertise, interest, and experience. Unlike committees, task forces are generally disbanded after the goal has been accomplished.

task method of promotional budgeting   See OBJECTIVE-TASK METHOD OF PROMOTIONAL BUDGETING.

taste   An individual's sense of what is good or appropriate, particularly in relation to aesthetic qualities (e.g., appeal, harmony, and beauty) and social acceptability. See also TASTE LEVEL.

taste level   With regard to retail merchandise, the subjective level of individual preference that includes a sense of quality, beauty, and appropriateness. See also TASTE.

tax-free shopping week   A week set aside by some state and local governments during which no sales tax is collected on purchases of clothing and footwear (usually up to a certain maximum amount, such as $100). The practice is meant to generate sales for retailers and provide relief for consumers. New York and Connecticut are two states that have experimented with tax-free shopping weeks.

taxonomy of the apparel merchandising system (TAMS)   A classification scheme, developed by G.I. Kunz, for LINE PLANNING, LINE DEVELOPMENT, and LINE PRESENTATION in the apparel industry. TAMS provides a framework for examining merchandising activities in that industry.

Tax Reform Act (1986)   U.S. federal legislation that eliminated deductions for sales tax and interest payments from the income tax returns of individuals. The legislation also closed many former tax loopholes for corporations.

TC²   See NATIONAL SIZING SURVEY.

TCP/IP   Transmission Control Protocol/Internet Protocol, standards for data packet transmission on the Internet. See also DATA LINK CONTROL (DLC) and PROTOCOL.

TE   See TECHNOLOGY AND ENTERTAINMENT (TE).

team selling   A sales technique in which several salespeople work together to present the product or service. The technique is used primarily in the sale of highly technical or complex products or services requiring the combined expertise of several individuals. See also SYSTEMS SELLING.

tearoom modeling   An INFORMAL FASHION SHOW that takes place in a restaurant on a regularly scheduled day. Models walk from table to table showing the merchandise to interested dining guests. Models are discouraged from interacting with the guests unless they are specifically asked about the merchandise. See also FASHION SHOW.

tear sheet   In retail advertising, a page from a magazine or newspaper submitted by the publisher to the advertiser as evidence of the ad having been run in the publication. Also spelled *tearsheet*.

teaser   See FIN.

teaser advertising   ADVERTISING meant to arouse curiosity on the part of the reader or viewer rather than to impart specific information.

teaser campaign/plan   See CAMPAIGN PLAN.

technical base   Synonym for TECHNOLOGICAL BASE.

technical package   In apparel SOURCING, the product specifications that accompany and supplement the GARMENT PURCHASE AGREEMENT (GPA). The technical package details construction, measurement, patterns, and markers.

technical salesperson   An individual salesperson whose principal duties are those of the technical consultant. Technical salespeople, who often possess special knowledge and skills, are commonly called upon to provide assistance to purchasers of complex equipment such as computers. Also called a *technical specialist*. See also SUPPORT SALESPERSON.

technical specialist   Synonym for TECHNICAL SALESPERSON.

technological base   The skills and equipment available in a given society, country, or culture. Also called a *technical base*. See also TECHNOLOGICAL ENVIRONMENT.

technological environment   The manner in which technical skills and equipment are converted into output in the particular economy in which a marketer conducts business. These skills and equipment form the economy's TECHNOLOGICAL BASE. RESEARCH AND DEVELOPMENT (R&D), an important component of technological advancement, leads to breakthroughs that affect the way businesses produce and market their goods. In recent years, these technological improvements have involved greater use of computer technology. As new developments occur, a marketer's use of (or failure to use) each technological improvement can affect the competitive position of the firm. See also ECONOMIC ENVIRONMENT.

technological forces Those technical developments in a society that influence the way people live and what they desire, and hence, in turn, affect the activities of marketers who supply these wants and needs. See also TECHNOLOGICAL ENVIRONMENT.

technological obsolescence PLANNED OBSOLESCENCE based upon new technological advances that render the older product either less useful than new models or virtually useless. For example, innovations and structural changes in personal computers (such as types of floppy drives or memory chips) tend to render older models technologically obsolete, particularly when compared to faster models with additional memory, enhanced functionality, and greater connectivity.

technology and entertainment (TE) A product category that includes interactive video and computer games as well as simulations. The games and simulations may be delivered in electronic form on media (such as DVDs) or via the INTERNET.

technology-based alliance In global marketing, a STRATEGIC ALLIANCE based on the exploitation of complementary technologies, access to markets, and the need to reduce the time it takes to bring a technological INNOVATION to market. Technology-based alliances have become widespread in the biotechnology and information industries. See also PRODUCTION-BASED ALLIANCE and DISTRIBUTION-BASED ALLIANCE.

technotot Synonym for CYBERBOOMER.

teen board A group of teenagers working with a retail store in a volunteer advisory capacity, with particular attention to matters of fashion. See also COLLEGE BOARD and FASHION BOARD.

teleconference 1. n. A business meeting, conference, or educational activity conducted among participants in different locations via telecommunications equipment such as telephones or two-way interactive televisions. 2. v. To participate in this type of long-distance meeting. See also VIDEOCONFERENCE and WEB CONFERENCE.

telemarketing A term commonly employed to describe two distinct forms of marketing: (a) the sale of products and services via telephone (at both the industrial and the consumer levels) and (b) the sale of products and services via an interactive system or two-way television (i.e., electronic in-home or in-office systems that employ cable television, telephone lines, data banks, etc.). Also, though rarely, called *teleselling*. Telemarketing conducted exclusively by telephone is also called TELEPHONE MARKETING or TELEPHONE RETAILING. See also ELECTRONIC DIRECT MARKETING and OUTBOUND TELEMARKETING.

telephone agency A firm engaged in making or receiving TELEMARKETING calls for another organization or individual.

telephone interview An INTERVIEW conducted over the telephone.

telephone marketing TELEMARKETING conducted by telephone. Customers may be individuals, institutions, or other firms. Also called *telephone sales* or *telephone selling*. See also TELEPHONE RETAILING.

telephone retailing Selling by telephone at the retail level (i.e., to the ultimate consumer). It may involve making telephone calls to canvass potential customers or solicit purchases. Alternatively, customers may be encouraged by other advertising (e.g. print, radio, or television) to call the retailer themselves to place an order. Also called *telephone sales* or *telephone selling*. See also TELEMARKETING, TELEPHONE MARKETING, and TELESHOPPING.

telephone sales/selling Synonym for TELEPHONE MARKETING and TELEPHONE RETAILING.

telephone sales department (TSD) The department in a retail store charged with the responsibility for all sales generated by telephone, whether in the form of solicitation or as a response to advertising. See also TELEPHONE RETAILING.

teleselling Rarely used synonym for TELEMARKETING.

teleshopping The use of the telephone by customers to order merchandise or services they have seen in print advertising, heard about on the radio, or seen on television. Teleshopping is frequently facilitated through the use of toll-free numbers for inbound calls. See also TELEPHONE MARKETING and TELEPHONE RETAILING.

television monitor See MONITOR.

television retailing See TELEMARKETING and INTERACTIVE TELEVISION (ITV).

television shopping channel A type of nonstore, electronic retailing in which a company describes and demonstrates products on television and provides an opportunity for consumers to place an order. Cable shopping networks have grown dramatically since the 1980s and represent competition for traditional retailers. Also called *direct response retailing*. See also HOME SHOPPING NETWORK.

Telnet A transfer service that allows users to connect directly to other computer systems on the INTERNET and access stored files.

temp 1. n. (Informal) A temporary employee, hired to fill in at busy times or to substitute for absent permanent employees. Also called a *temporary employee* or a *temporary worker*. Collectively, such employees are known as *temporary personnel*. 2. v. To work as a temporary employee.

template page A Web page that serves as a model for the consistent use of text, graphics, and layout. Web page developers maintain consistency on a site by using the template to duplicate the basic elements of each page.

temporary employee/personnel See TEMP.

temporary markdown A reduction in price given on a short-term basis. Promotional markdowns are temporary markdowns since the promotional goods are marked back up to regular price after the promotional event has ended. To ensure the credibility of a promotional event, promoted merchandise is not offered at promotional markdown prices during nonpromotional periods. Compare PERMANENT MARKDOWN.

temporary signage   Signs made of disposable materials, such as paper or card stock, and intended for frequent change. The most common forms of temporary signage include in-store signage on fixtures. Temporary in-store signs are important sales promotion vehicles that reinforce advertising, stimulate impulse purchases, and enhance customer convenience by calling attention to promotional events and prices. Fact tags, banners, and reprints of newspaper ads are among the various forms of temporary in-store signage. The most common uses of temporary and in-store signs are for the identification of brand (e.g., Carter's), category or item (e.g., layette), shop-within-a-shop (e.g., DKNY), characteristics or features of merchandise (e.g., 100% cotton), price (e.g., 25% off ticketed price), promotion (e.g., January White Sale), policy (e.g., all sales are final), and service (e.g., free delivery). Compare PERMANENT SIGNAGE.

temporary worker   See TEMP.

tenant mix   See BALANCED TENANCY.

tentative trade/trading area   In RETAIL SITE LOCATION, the territory immediately surrounding the site from which the store might reasonably expect to attract customers. It is just outside the expected TRADING AREA.

tent sale   A promotional event in which the retailer takes selected goods outside the store and sells them at reduced prices from a tent acquired for that purpose. Used extensively in automobile sales, tent sales are also used by supermarkets and retailers of seasonal merchandise such as outdoor furniture. The purpose of the event is to call attention to the selected merchandise (which is often heavily discounted) by attracting passersby. See also SIDEWALK SALE.

term   1. The time an individual or firm has to make installment or credit payments as specified in a loan or contract. 2. The duration of an agreement. See also TERMS OF SALE.

terminal   See OPTICAL CODE READER (OCR).

terms file   A record maintained by retailers of the TERMS OF SALE imposed by each vendor with whom they are doing business.

terms of credit   See CREDIT TERMS.

terms of occupancy   Matters specified in a leasing agreement such as sale price or terms of the lease, responsibility for repair, renovation, and maintenance, local ordinances, taxation, etc.

terms-of-payment discount   See REGULAR DATING.

terms of purchase   Synonym for TERMS OF SALE.

terms of sale   The conditions governing a sale as set forth by the seller. The terms of sale include the amount of the discount (if any), the payment period, the date of delivery, the point of transfer of title from the seller to the buyer, the allocation of transportation costs, and any other specific obligations and conditions. Also called *sale terms*, *sales terms*, and *terms of purchase*. See also CREDIT TERMS.

terms of trade   In INTERNATIONAL TRADE, the quantity of items that must be surrendered for one unit of goods obtained by a group or nation that is a party to a transaction.

territorial departmentalization   Synonym for TERRITORY DEPARTMENTALIZATION.

territorial franchise   See FRANCHISE (def. 2).

territorial potential   The total possible (i.e., potential) demand for a product or service within a particular geographic area (i.e., territory).

territory departmentalization   The practice of, or the structure that results from, arranging a retail organization or other business into departments according to geographic location. This type of departmentalization is commonly used when an organization is spread over a wide geographic area and differences among areas are important enough to merit special attention. For example, in a U.S. retail organization with territory departmentalization, the East Coast, West Coast, and Midwestern regions of the United States might each correspond to a department, with another for foreign branches. Territory departmentalization allows the large organization to be more responsive to local customs, styles, product preferences, etc. It also expedites local promotions and allows the organization to take advantage of local economies (e.g., low price for raw materials). In addition, territorial departmentalization provides a training ground for the company's future top-level managers. Also called *departmentalization by territory* and *territorial departmentalization*.

territory manager   Synonym for REGIONAL MANAGER.

territory screening   Synonym for CANVASSING.

territory-structured sales force   The result of structuring an organization in such a way that each salesperson is assigned an exclusive geographic area. This provides sales personnel with a clear knowledge of their responsibilities and increases their chances of developing closer relationships with prospects, customers, local businesspeople, etc. It also saves on travel costs. See also SALES FORCE.

tertiary market   In the fashion/apparel industry, the retailers, responsible for communicating trends to consumers. These trends are developed previously by the primary market (i.e., the producers of raw materials such as fabrics) and secondary market (i.e., designers, manufacturers and distributors). Based on information about their customers, retailers forecast which items will be best sellers for their stores in the upcoming season. Each retailer interprets trends in a slightly different way to match the brand position of its organization. See also TERTIARY MARKET FORECAST, PRIMARY MARKET, and SECONDARY MARKET.

tertiary market forecast FASHION FORECASTING at the tertiary (i.e., retail) market level. Retailers are responsible for communicating to consumers the trends developed by primary and secondary producers. Based on information about their customers, retailers forecast what the best-selling items will be for their stores in the upcoming season. Buyers for retail stores view fashions four to six months in advance of delivery. Those whose primary customers are fashion innovators will expect very early delivery of goods, before the selling season starts, and will make their forecasts based on expected sales. Those purchasing goods for the fashion majority, on the other hand, will buy closer to the selling season and make forecasts based on tested trends from the fashion innovators. See also TERTIARY MARKET, PRIMARY MARKET FORECAST, and SECONDARY MARKET FORECAST.

tertiary trade/trading area See FRINGE TRADING AREA.

test 1. v. To carry out any trial or experiment designed to gather information. For example, an advertiser may test a series of advertisements by presenting them first to a focus group. A retailer may test a product by placing a small sample order on display and ascertaining customer reaction before ordering a larger quantity from the vendor. 2. n. Any such trial or experiment. See also TEST MARKET and TEST MARKETING.

test ad In a PORTFOLIO TEST, any of the ads actually being pretested and measured for their potential effectiveness. Compare CONTROL AD.

testimonial A statement (either paid or unpaid, solicited or unsolicited) endorsing the use of a product or service. The testimonial is intended to encourage others to purchase. The spokesperson may be a celebrity (to encourage emulation) or an average person (to encourage identification). See also CELEBRITY TESTIMONIAL.

test market A limited geographic area (i.e., a region, a city, or even a single store) used to gauge consumer acceptance of a new product, an established product introduced in a new way (e.g., different packaging, a new price), or an advertising campaign. A test market must have demographic, socioeconomic, and psychographic profiles similar to those of the desired target population. See also TEST MARKETING and TEST PROMOTION.

test marketing A MARKETING RESEARCH (MR) technique in which a new product or service is introduced in a limited, carefully selected geographic area (i.e., a TEST MARKET) in an effort to predict its performance in the marketplace. Test marketing also provides management with the opportunity to correct production problems before a total market commitment has been made. Also called *market testing* and *product testing*. See also PSEUDO SALE and TEST PROMOTION.

test promotion At the retail store level, any advertising, personal selling, or sales promotion activity intended to determine customer reaction to new products and established products presented in a new way. See also TEST MARKET and TEST MARKETING.

Texas Meat and Poultry Inspection Act (1969) See MEAT INSPECTION ACT (1906).

Textile Fiber Products Identification Act (TFPIA) (1960) U.S. federal legislation that requires fiber content to be identified on all apparel. Sellers of natural and synthetic yarns and fabrics (other than wool) and household items made of these must attach labels to the goods listing the fibers by generic name and indicating the percentage by weight of each. The name of the manufacturer and the country of origin must also be identified. Also called the *Textile Fiber Identification Act* or the *Textile Products Identification Act*. See also LABELS AND LABELING.

text messaging The practice of sending short, typed communications to a device such as a cellular phone, PDA, or pager. The term is used for messages that are no more than a few hundred characters in length, exchanged between two or more mobile devices.

text-only browser An Internet BROWSER that reads only words and ignores graphics or other multimedia-rich elements. When developing product pages, e-tailers and other Internet marketers who consider the needs of potential customers with text-only browsers do well to include text descriptions of products where appropriate.

text-only option The ability to view a Web page without the use of a graphical browser. E-tailers and other Internet marketers can make this option available for potential customers who do not have graphical browsers, people with visual disabilities using digital readers, and those who want to speed downloads.

TFPIA See TEXTILE FIBER PRODUCTS IDENTIFICATION ACT (TFPIA) (1960).

theme In the fashion/apparel industry, a theme is a recurring idea seen in color, silhouette, fabric, and other design components. Themes may be based on style, economics, history, politics, weather, science, humor, or some other aspect of society and are used at all levels of the industry. Sales promotion products are selected around a theme. Manufacturers also use themes to create a feeling about merchandise presented to buyers. When organizing a line, designers coordinate groups of styles so that the styles reflect a theme. These themes are promotional tools used to create moods and prepare consumers for what they will see in the marketplace. A retailer may elect to use a STOREWIDE THEME, a COLOR THEME, a FABRIC THEME, a LIFESTYLE THEME, or a SPECIAL OCCASION THEME.

theme advertisement In RETAIL PRODUCT ADVERTISING, coordinated advertisements featuring groups of products from individual departments, divisions, or the entire store. The items selected express a particular theme or motif, such as fashion trends, season (e.g., back-to-school, Christmas, or

Easter), special and annual events (e.g., a White Sale or an Anniversary Sale), or an international promotion (e.g., British Designer Week).

theme display   See THEME/SETTING DISPLAY.

theme/festival center   See FESTIVAL MARKETPLACE.

theme/setting display   A retail display in which the products to be sold are presented in an environment having a particular theme or subject orientation.

theme shopping center   See FESTIVAL MARKETPLACE.

Theory X   A management style based on the assumption that employees do not really want to work and that the primary motivation for work is money; the average employee, according to the theory, must be forced, controlled, directed, or threatened with punishment in order to be motivated to expend enough effort to achieve the organization's objectives. Consequently, this view of management holds that the average person prefers to be directed, wishes to avoid responsibility, has relatively little ambition, and wants security. Theory X addresses the lower level needs of individuals, that is their physiological and safety needs, as defined in MASLOW'S HIERARCHY (OF NEEDS). Compare THEORY Y and THEORY Z. Theories X and Y were described by psychologist Douglas McGregor in 1960.

Theory Y   A management style, described by Douglas McGregor in 1960, that incorporates multidimensional communication, problem solving, and empowerment in all parts of the organization. McGregor proposed that managers address the higher-level needs of their employees as defined in MASLOW'S HIERARCHY (OF NEEDS). In Theory Y, he suggests that (a) the average person does not dislike work; (b) external control and threat of punishment are not the only ways to motivate people to meet the organization's goals; (c) the level of a person's commitment to the organization's objectives depends on the rewards for achieving them; (d) the average person learns not only to accept responsibility for work but also to seek it; and (e) people are capable of using imagination, cleverness, and creativity to solve problems that arise within an organization. Compare THEORY X, also by McGregor, and THEORY Z.

Theory Z   A human relations-based management style developed by William Ouchi on the analogy of, and in contrast to, McGregor's THEORY X and THEORY Y. Theory Z assumes that the best management involves workers at all levels and treats employees as if they were a family in which everyone works harmoniously toward the same goal. It addresses the lower-, middle-, and higher-level needs delineated in MASLOW'S HIERARCHY (OF NEEDS). Theory Z is often called *Japanese management* because it refers to techniques used at American companies that have adopted a Japanese approach to business (in which everyone participates in decision making and duties are rotated to avoid boredom, extreme specialization, and rigidity). See also TOTAL QUALITY MANAGEMENT (TQM).

Thiessen polygon   See PROXIMAL AREA METHOD.

thin wallet   See DIGITAL WALLET.

third   An item of merchandise of decidedly poor quality, lower in grade than a SECOND. Often used in the plural (e.g., *thirds*).

third party plan   A retail credit plan offered and administered by a bank or other credit-extending organization and accepted by a store. See also CONSUMER CREDIT.

thirds   See THIRD.

third world distribution   (Slang) Among manufacturers, such nontraditional retail institutions as discounters, promotional department stores, and off-price merchants.

thirteen-month merchandising calendar   An annual calendar divided into equal "months" of four weeks each, used in planning retail seasons. Compare RETAIL CALENDAR.

thirteenth month   The selling period between Christmas and New Year's Day.

thirty-day charge   Synonym for CHARGE ACCOUNT.

thirty-three   (Slang) A potential customer who resists making a purchase from one salesperson and is consequently turned over to another.

three Bs   See BETTER BUSINESS BUREAU (BBB).

three-click rule   In Web design, the rule of thumb that a visitor should be able to reach his or her destination page in only three clicks. The rule is often used as a measure of design efficiency.

three Cs of credit   Character, capacity, and capital as used to determine whether or not an individual is an acceptable credit risk. Character is considered an indication of the individual's determination to pay. Capacity is the measure of the ability to pay. Capital is the individual's financial resources or net worth. See also CONSUMER CREDIT.

three-level channel   A CHANNEL OF DISTRIBUTION in which there are three levels of marketing intermediaries between the manufacturer/producer and the ultimate consumer. For example, there may be an agent or broker, a wholesaler or distributor, and a retailer acting as intermediaries. See also MARKETING INTERMEDIARY.

three-part rack   A round RACK comprising three separate but equal arcs. The height of each arc is usually separately adjustable. Three-part racks are effective for displaying separates, coordinates, or assorted colors and styles of a particular item. Also called a *trilevel round rack* (also spelled *tri-level round rack*).

three-quarter form   A three-dimensional representation of the top portion of the human body, extending to the knees or just below the knees. It usually has a head. The three-quarter form can be used to display a wide variety of apparel. An adjustable metal rod (located beneath the form or in the butt) and a weighted base enables the form to be lowered or raised to meet a variety of display needs.

threshold expenditure level The minimum dollar expenditure required for a firm to be in a market and obtain sales. After this minimum level, small increases in expenditures may lead to large increases in sales, up to the point at which additional expenditures lead to fewer and finally no sales increases, with an actual decline in profits. See also DIMINISHING RETURNS.

threshold of perception The point at which individuals no longer consciously sense stimuli. This is an important consideration for advertising and marketing. See also PERCEPTION, SELECTIVE PERCEPTION, SUBLIMINAL PERCEPTION, and JUST NOTICEABLE DIFFERENCE (JND).

threshold point ordering See REORDER POINT (ROP).

thrift institution See SAVINGS AND LOAN ASSOCIATION.

thrift shop A store offering used, SECONDHAND merchandise to cost-conscious consumers at prices far below the price for new merchandise. Some thrift shops are operated by charitable organizations, such as hospitals, as fundraisers. Merchandise is generally donated by consumers.

thrillboard A company message, offline or online, that actually means something to the customer and motivates the customer to want to buy the product or service immediately. Examples of thrillboards include Krispy Kreme's Hot Light sign (indicating that fresh doughnuts are available right at that moment) and Amazon.com's gold treasure chest (suggesting that tantalizing, limited-time deals are waiting inside it). Thrillboards combine excitement, the prospect of instant gratification, and an appeal to the desire to be in the know. The trend was identified and the term coined by trendwatching.com at www.trendwatching.com. See also BILLBOARD.

throughput The movement of merchandise through marketing intermediaries on to the ultimate consumer. See also CHANNEL OF DISTRIBUTION.

throughput agreement An arrangement to put a stated amount of merchandise through a production facility (such as a factory) in an agreed period of time. If production is not completed during the stated period of time, the manufacturer must still pay for the availability of the facility. For example, an agreement to ship a specified amount of crude oil through a particular pipeline during a specified period of time would be a throughput agreement.

throwaway Synonym for FLYER.

throwout (Slang) The paper receipt produced by a CASH REGISTER.

thrust area A prime location in a store, used for the display of featured items such as new, high-margin, or seasonal merchandise.

thumbnail 1. A brief or concise review, biographical sketch, synopsis, etc. 2. In Web design, a scaled-down visual image that can be clicked to display a larger graphic. Also called a *thumbnail image*.

thumbnail image See THUMBNAIL (def. 2).

ticket See PRICE TAG and JOB TICKET.

ticketing See MARKING AND TICKETING.

ticket switcher Synonym for TAG SWITCHER.

tickler file/system A record, generally in the form of a file, organized in such a way (generally, chronologically) that it will bring needed information to one's attention at an appropriate time in the future.

tie-in See MAGAZINE PROMOTIONAL TIE-IN.

tie-in agreement In consumer service retailing, an agreement in which the retailer sells a service (e.g., furniture or carpet cleaning) under its own name and handles the billing, while a different party, the vendor of the service, actually performs the work.

tie-in products/sales Products sold together as a package either literally (e.g., a razor and shaving cream) or as a deal (e.g., cosmetic products sold so that the purchase of one is contingent on the purchase of another). Some tie-in arrangements have been found to be in RESTRAINT OF TRADE and thus illegal.

tie-in promotion In retailing, in-store displays and sales approaches that relate directly to an active advertising or promotional media campaign. The goal of the tie-in promotion is to create immediate sales, particularly when introducing new merchandise, and a variety of approaches are used simultaneously to achieve that goal. Tie-in promotions have also been used successfully by manufacturers and not-for-profit institutions to call attention to new products, new lines of products, or fund-raising efforts. See also CROSS-PROMOTION and MAGAZINE PROMOTIONAL TIE-IN.

tie-in purchase A retail purchase in which two products are sold together as a package. For example, a razor may be either sold with a package of blades or given away with the purchase of the blades. See also TIE-IN PRODUCTS/SALES.

tie-in sales See TIE-IN PRODUCTS/SALES.

tier table (fixture) A shelved store fixture used primarily to hold and display folded apparel. Though commonly known as a *gap table*, because the fixture was popularized by the Gap, the term "table" is a misnomer. The fixture consists of a freestanding stack of open shelving in which folded apparel is generally displayed according to size and color. Customers may select the desired item from the appropriate tier.

tight market Synonym for SELLERS' MARKET.

till The cash drawer in a CASH REGISTER.

time budgeting of purchases A store's purchase of small numbers of items from a vendor over short periods of time. This practice assures that the average price paid by the store for each product will approximate the true average for the period. However, the practice also tends to increase the total cost of purchasing the items.

timeline A plan that includes dated deadlines by which specific tasks are to be accomplished in the completion of a larger project.

time order An order that becomes a LIMITED ORDER (i.e., with price restrictions) at a specified date .

time payment See INSTALLMENT PLAN/CONTRACT/BUYING.

time rate of demand The quantity of an item (at a given price) that can be absorbed by the market over a specified period of time.

time series Historical records of past economic and/or sales behavior, used in TIME SERIES ANALYSIS to predict future trends. For example, a time series may show the sales of a particular product in a particular country over the past 15 years, so that the rate of growth or decline in this market may be analyzed and predictions made about future sales. A LEADING SERIES is a related time series that shows a change occurring in the same direction as the one in the main series under study but consistently preceding it. The leading series is watched particularly closely as an indicator of future trends. See also TIME SERIES ANALYSIS.

time series analysis A sales forecasting technique in which the analysis is based on the performance of the firm, product, or service over past time. An effort is made to discover patterns of activity that can be used to forecast sales volume in the future. Also called *time-series forecasting* and *trend projection*. See also TIME SERIES and MOVING AVERAGE.

time series comparison A comparison of income statement components of two or more time periods, used as a measure of change in performance. See also COMPONENT PERCENTAGE.

time series forecasting See TIME SERIES ANALYSIS.

times interest earned The financial ratio that results from dividing a company's income before interest charges (and sometimes before income tax) by the interest charges. The ratio is used to summarize the operations of the company during a specified accounting period. See also FINANCIAL RATIOS.

time utility The usefulness, value, or consumer satisfaction added to a product when it is available at the precise time a customer wants it. In E-TAILING and other E-COMMERCE, products can be made available 24 hours a day, 7 days a week, 365 days of the year.

time value See COMPANY ANALYSIS.

tinge (Slang) A salesperson who sells undesirable merchandise in order to earn bonus payments.

title/ownership flow See CHANNEL FLOW.

Title VII of the Federal Civil Rights Act (1964) See CIVIL RIGHTS ACT (1964).

TL See TRUCKLOAD (TL).

toddlers Garment sizes worn by children ranging in age from 18 months to about three years. The range includes sizes 1T through 4T (T stands for toddlers). Also called *toddler sizes*.

TOFC (trailer-on-flatcar) See PIGGYBACK.

token order 1. A small order placed to sample a product and assess its quality. 2. A small order placed to appease a bothersome salesperson.

toll-free (telephone) number See EIGHT HUNDRED NUMBER (800 NUMBER).

T.O. man See CLOSER.

ton-mile In shipping, the movement of one ton of goods one mile, and/or the charge for doing so.

tonnage 1. (Slang) Merchandise purchased in large quantities by retail buyers. The merchandise generates a high volume of retail sales. 2. In shipping, the capacity of a merchant vessel (i.e., a ship or boat) expressed in units of weight or volume. 3. A duty paid by ships or boats at a given rate per ton of cargo or freight.

toolbar A series of selectable buttons in a GRAPHICAL USER INTERFACE (GUI) that allow the user to easily select desktop, application, or Web browser functions. Toolbars are typically displayed as either horizontal rows or vertical columns around the edges of the GUI.

top-down approach to promotional budgeting Overall PROMOTIONAL BUDGETING for the entire retail firm or manufacturer established at the highest senior executive level. The money is then allocated to the various departments or divisions. A top-down budget approach is dependent on the experience and knowledge of the top management, and for this reason is also called a *judgmental approach*. The top-down methods include ALL-YOU-CAN AFFORD APPROACH, ARBITRARY APPROACH, COMPETITIVE PARITY, PERCENT OF SALES APPROACH TO PROMOTIONAL BUDGETING, and RETURN ON INVESTMENT (ROI) APPROACH TO ADVERTISING. Compare BOTTOM-UP APPROACH TO PROMOTIONAL BUDGETING.

top-down plan A plan directed, controlled, and conducted by top management. A top-down plan may allocate money to each department in keeping with decisions made at the upper management levels of the organization. Similarly, the sales objective for the entire organization may be determined by upper management and then broken down by division and department. Most organizations combine top-down and bottom-up planning, recognizing that planning requires input at every managerial level. Compare BOTTOM-UP PLAN and INTERACTIVE PLAN.

top-down planning　See TOP-DOWN PLAN.

top-level domain (TLD)　The two- or three-letter code at the end of a domain name, designating the type of organization or the location outside the United States. The following are some examples of top-level domains: .com (commercial organizations, businesses); .net (used by organizations supporting the Internet and by some businesses); .edu (educational institutions—four-year colleges and universities only); .org (nonprofit organizations); .gov (U.S. government agencies—nonmilitary); .mil (U.S. government military organizations); .int (international organizations); .uk, .ca, etc. (country codes). See also SECOND-LEVEL DOMAIN.

top-of-counter fixture　A store furnishing unit placed on top of a counter-height fixture to display goods such as carded earrings.

top out　The peak period of DEMAND for a product or service, after which demand declines either slowly or rapidly.

top stock　Merchandise displayed on top of a COUNTER in an open display.

top-to-bottom method of promotional budgeting　See PERCENT OF SALES APPROACH TO PROMOTIONAL BUDGETING.

torso form　A three-dimensional representation of the top portion of the human body, from the shoulders to the knees or just below the knees.

total area　In a retail store, the SELLING AREA and NON-SELLING AREA added together.

total audience plan　In radio advertising, a package plan in which a rate is given for a combination of different time periods and the station determines the distribution of announcements to be run in each period. This strategy uses a broad combination of day parts to give the advertiser an increased opportunity to reach more potential customers. Also known as a *guaranteed audience plan* and a *reach plan*.

total cost　The sum of a firm's fixed and variable expenses.

total cost approach　In the management of physical distribution, a planning tool that attempts to take into account possible variations in transportation, inventory, and order-processing costs by showing the hypothetical results of alternative strategies. The technique considers all distribution costs in total and emphasizes trading off certain types of costs for others until the lowest possible cost is determined. In order to accomplish this, planners identify all possible transportation, warehousing, inventory control, and order entry and processing costs, so as to view the total picture rather than attempt piecemeal reductions. Also called *total cost concept*.

total cost concept　See TOTAL COST APPROACH.

total cost of goods/merchandise sold　See COST OF GOODS SOLD.

total loss　Items that have been so badly damaged that they are not considered worth repairing, such as a car damaged in a head-on collision or merchandise partly destroyed by fire). See also LOSS.

total markdown ratio　See MARKDOWN RATIO.

total market approach　Synonym for UNDIFFERENTIATED MARKETING.

total merchandise cost　See COST OF GOODS SOLD.

total merchandise handled　The sum of the value of opening inventory, additional purchases, and applicable transportation charges, expressed as a dollar amount and calculated at cost prices.

total physical distribution concept　A management strategy in which all DISTRIBUTION functions in an organization are fully integrated, generally by making the distribution department the equal of the marketing and production departments. The objective is to minimize distribution costs while maintaining adequate customer service. See also PHYSICAL DISTRIBUTION (PD).

total product concept　A marketing concept in which all the services and benefits that may accompany a product are considered as a package with the product itself. For example, a new automobile brings with it transportation, but also a warranty, a sense of pride, and other benefits. Sometimes referred to as the GENERIC PRODUCT because consumers are seen as shopping not just for products but for a *cluster of benefits* that includes the product itself.

total quality management (TQM)　A management system that encourages teamwork and a sense of employee ownership of the production, distribution, or retailing process. The goal of TQM is to increase customer satisfaction by delivering high-quality products. These products are produced and distributed by employees who buy into the organization's goals and objectives through participatory management. TQM incorporates the concepts of product quality, process control, quality assurance, and quality improvement. Since many of the TQM concepts originated with the work of W. Edwards Deming, the American statistician who guided the Japanese industrial recovery after World War II, TQM took hold in Japan long before it became popular in the United States. See also THEORY Z.

total receipts　Synonym for TOTAL REVENUE.

total rent　The sum of all the various payments a retailer must make to lease a store, particularly in a planned shopping center. In addition to the monthly fee for the site itself (i.e., rent), the prospective tenant must consider fees for the maintenance of common areas, dues to the center's merchants' association, and minimum lease guarantees.

total retail reduction   See RETAIL REDUCTION.

total revenue   The total amount of money taken in by a store during a given period of time. Total revenue is equal to the price per unit of merchandise times the number of units sold. Also called *total receipts*.

total sales   See SALES.

total systems competition   In retailing, the most sophisticated and complete form of competition, in which the organization owns and/or controls sources of manufactured goods, storage/distribution systems, and a highly developed network of retail outlets. The organization can effectively bring all its resources to bear on any competitive situation. See also VERTICAL MARKETING SYSTEM (VMS).

total variable costs   Costs that change directly with the store's output (e.g., fuel, labor). See also VARIABLE COST.

total vertical integration   See VERTICAL INTEGRATION.

to the trade only   An expression used by wholesalers, vendors, dealers, etc., to indicate that they do not sell at retail to the ultimate consumer.

town center   A new open-air shopping center (or a renovation of an old one) suggesting a retail urban village and consisting of buildings with nostalgic architectural features or theme designs. Some older malls have been converted to town centers. Town centers tend to develop in towns and suburbs peripheral to cities. Historically, they have been important as locations for independent specialty stores and service retailers. In recent years, however, chain store retailers have shown interest in opening stores in town centers. Also called an *open-air center*.

Toy Safety Act (1984)   U.S. federal legislation that granted power to the government to recall dangerous toys from the marketplace.

TPM   See TRADE PROMOTIONS MANAGEMENT (TPM).

TQM   See TOTAL QUALITY MANAGEMENT (TQM).

traceable common costs   Those expenses in a business that can be assigned to a particular activity despite not being immediately apparent. For example, the costs related to production space in a plant may be determined by calculating the proportion of square footage given over to that activity and subtracting that proportion from the plant's known total costs.

tracer   A person in the shipping and/or receiving department whose function is to check into lost or delayed shipments from vendors and trace lost or delayed deliveries to customers.

tracking   1. A system for analyzing the cause and extent of markdowns in order to ensure more profitable BUYING in the future.   2. In e-mail marketing, a means of checking the effectiveness of an e-mail campaign. When e-mail messages are dis-

tributed, an identifier code number is placed in the e-mail. When receivers click through on the link contained in the e-mail, the code number tracks and reports back that they have reached the site from the distributed e-mail.

track lighting   Display lighting that consists of moveable units mounted on vertical or horizontal tracks. See also STORE LIGHTING PLAN.

trade   1. n. Transactions, collectively, involving the exchange of goods or services for profit between legal entities (e.g., international trade).   2. v. To buy, sell, or exchange commodities (e.g., trading on the stock exchange).   3. n. A purchase or sale made in a business deal or transaction (e.g., a fair trade).   4. n. One's occupation, particularly in skilled manual or mechanical work or a craft (e.g., the clothing trade).   5. n. The people engaged in a particular line of work or industry (e.g., the building trades).   6. n. A field of business activity (e.g., the retail trade).   7. n. The customers, or a category of customers, of a business activity (e.g., the carriage trade).

trade acceptance   A draft drawn and accepted by an individual or a corporation, usually the buyer of goods in a transaction. A statement that the acceptor's obligation arises out of the purchase of the goods often appears on the face of the draft.

Trade Act (1974)   U.S. federal legislation containing one of the government's most effective weapons in fighting trade practices that are unfair or that are disadvantageous to the United States. Section 301 of the Trade Act of 1974 allows the president to deny foreign companies access to the United States if their government has curbed American exports. Under this law, the federal government initiates cases against foreign countries for such infringements as limiting competition, restricting U.S. companies operating abroad, controlling a variety of products, or failing to provide patent and copyright protection.

trade advertising   ADVERTISING by the producers of products or the providers of services, directed to customers other than the ultimate consumer (i.e., wholesalers, distributors, marketing intermediaries, retailers, etc.). The objective is to widen the distribution of the product or service. Such an advertisement is generally placed in a TRADE PAPER or other specialized business-to-business (B2B) medium geared to industry professionals.

trade alliance   A partnership between member countries, such as the NORTH AMERICAN FREE TRADE ASSOCIATION (NAFTA), that promotes trade among member nations. See also FREE-TRADE AREA.

trade allowance   An incentive in the form of a price reduction provided by a manufacturer to retailers and other channel intermediaries to stock, display, or promote the manufacturer's goods.

trade area   See TRADING AREA.

trade association   A nonprofit voluntary organization of businesses having common interests. A trade association typically sponsors research, promotes educational programs, attempts to form public opinion, and lobbies the government to influence the passage of relevant legislation. Sometimes called, simply, an *association*.

trade audit See STORE AUDIT.

trade balance Synonym for BALANCE OF TRADE.

trade card See TRADING CARD.

trade channel Synonym for CHANNEL OF DISTRIBUTION.

trade credit Credit offered by manufacturers and wholesalers to their customers (e.g., retailers or other marketing intermediaries) on a short-term basis. Trade credit is a widespread source of short-term financing for business. Two of the most common forms of trade credit are the OPEN-BOOK CREDIT and the PROMISSORY NOTE.

trade deal See DEAL.

trade deficit A condition in international trade in which the value of a country's imports exceeds the value of its exports. Compare TRADE SURPLUS.

trade discount A discount offered by manufacturers to wholesalers, marketing intermediaries, and (sometimes) retailers to compensate them for undertaking the performance of some marketing function; hence often called a *functional discount*. A trade discount is independent of quantity discounts and is applicable regardless of when payment is made. Trade discounts may be quoted as a series of discounts. For example, an item costing $1,000 (list price) may be offered with discounts of 40% and 10% (not the same as 50%). Each discount is computed on the amount that remains after the preceding discount has been taken. Also called a *preferred discount* or a *trade position discount*. See also CHAIN DISCOUNT.

trade down See TRADING DOWN.

trade dress The legally registered image of a product, used in its marketing and consisting of nonfunctional design elements, packaging, colors, shapes, and symbols.(e.g., the distinctive Coca-Cola bottle). Trade dress is protected in the United States under the LANHAM TRADEMARK ACT (1947).

trade embargo See EMBARGO.

trade exhibit A vendor's wares shown at a TRADE SHOW.

trade fair Synonym for TRADE SHOW.

trade franchise See PRODUCT FRANCHISE.

trade in To surrender an old product as partial payment for a new one (such as an automobile). The book value of the old product (called a *trade-in*) counts as credit toward the price of the new product. An additional payment is required to make up for the depreciation of the item traded in. See also TRADE-IN ALLOWANCE.

trade-in allowance A price reduction granted by a seller to a customer in the form of a credit for traded-in equipment (e.g., automobiles, major appliances). The list price is unaffected, but the buyer pays less as a result of the allowance. See also TRADE IN.

trade industry In INDUSTRIAL MARKETING, any of the industries made up of organizations like wholesalers and retailers who, for the most part, purchase for resale to others or for use in conducting their business. See also CHANNEL OF DISTRIBUTION.

trademark A word, symbol, sign, or design (or any combination of these elements) identifying a particular product or service. Certain trademarks are registered with the U.S. Patent and Trademark Office and are thus afforded added protection from infringement by competitors. Some controversy surrounds the use of trademarks as generic terms for a family of products, regardless of manufacturer. For example, the Xerox Corporation insists that while *a Xerox photocopy* is correct usage for a copy made on a machine manufactured by Xerox, *to xerox* (verb) or *a xerox* (common noun) are unacceptable generic uses that threaten the validity of the trademark. Nevertheless, trademarks and trade names have traditionally entered the language in this way. For example, paper tissues are often called *kleenex* and refrigerators are often called *frigidaires*, regardless of the actual manufacturers of the products. Also called a *mark*, a *registered mark* or a *registered trademark*. See also LANHAM TRADEMARK ACT (1947).

Trademark Act (1947) See LANHAM TRADEMARK ACT (1947).

trademark franchise A franchise arrangement with a franchiser that has a widely recognized trade name and highly standardized method of operation. Included are motel chains, car rental firms, fast food restaurants, etc.

trademark infringement See INFRINGEMENT.

trade marketing mix Synonym for RETAILING MIX.

trade mart Synonym for MERCHANDISE MART.

trade name A name used to designate a particular business organization (i.e., the firm together with its reputation and accrued GOODWILL), a service, or a particular class of goods. Trade names may or may not be exclusive. The term *trade name* is not applied to individual products that often carry the firm's TRADEMARK. Sometimes known as the *commercial name*. See also BRAND.

tradeoff analysis See CONJOINT MEASUREMENT/ANALYSIS.

trade pact An agreement between participating countries to encourage trade among member nations. See also ECONOMIC COMMUNITY.

trade paper A publication, usually in the form of a newspaper, for persons associated with a particular line, trade, industry, or profession.

trade position discount   See TRADE DISCOUNT.

trade premium   An incentive (e.g., a vacation, a prize, free merchandise) from a manufacturer to a retailer or wholesaler who achieves a specific level of sales of the manufacturer's merchandise. See also TRADE SALES PROMOTION.

trade price   A manufacturer's or wholesaler's special price to a retailer. Also called the *trade rate*.

trade promotion   1. Sales promotion efforts directed by a manufacturer toward retailers and wholesalers, offering incentives (e.g., gifts, price-off discounts, trips, merchandise) to those who agree to carry, or increase their inventory of, the manufacturer's merchandise. 2. A sales promotion in which both the retailer and manufacturer cooperate. COOPERATIVE ADVERTISING is one form of trade promotion. Also included are displays, demonstrations, and exhibitions.

trade promotions management (TPM)   Computer software that enables manufacturers to analyze and increase the profitability of their promotional activities. It allows manufacturers to increase their sales volume and profitability by selecting the optimal format for their promotional activity, including discount levels, price relativities, ad and display vehicles, and combinations of channels and customers. It also aids in understanding and managing the interaction between promoted products and non-promoted products (e.g., cannibalization and pull-through effects); improving support levels from retailers; increasing sales by improving in-store compliance with negotiated trade promotion programs; reducing costs of promotional administration; and improving financial control to reduce promotional overspending.

trade puffery   See PUFFERY.

trade quota   In international trade, a specific limit on the amount of goods that may be imported into a country. Quota restrictions are generally quite specific as to category, fabrication, and country of origin. See also QUOTA.

trader   1. Anyone involved in trade or commerce (i.e., a businessperson). See also MERCHANT.   2. A member of a STOCK EXCHANGE or COMMODITY EXCHANGE.   3. A speculator in stocks or commodities.

trade rate   See TRADE PRICE.

trade reference   An individual or firm to which a seller is referred for credit data on a potential customer.

trade restrictions   Restraints placed on the buying and selling activities of foreign producers who produce the same goods as domestic manufacturers. The goal of trade restrictions is to protect domestic industries from harm they might suffer from free trade and imports that exceed their ability to compete. Government policies designed to restrict trade include quotas and tariffs and regulations controlling the quantity, quality, and price points of the imported goods. See also PROTECTIONISM and PROTECTIVE TARIFF.

trade salesperson   A manufacturer's, dealer's, or vendor's salesperson whose primary responsibility is promotional (i.e., helping retailers or wholesalers promote the manufacturer's products by setting up displays, stocking shelves, providing demonstrations, etc.). Although they write orders, trade salespeople are, for the most part, concerned with maintaining good relations with established customers. This practice is known as *trade selling*.

trade sales promotion   A manufacturer's short-term, nonrecurrent promotional effort whose objective is an increased buying response from wholesalers and retailers. These efforts commonly take the form of buying allowances, free merchandise, cooperative advertising money, push money, sales contests, etc.

trade sanctions   Penalties imposed on one country by another in an attempt to curb trade practices perceived as unfair. The government of the sanctioning country may impose tariffs or ban the importation of products from the offending country. The WORLD TRADE ORGANIZATION (WTO) mediates trade disputes and approves trade sanctions. Trade sanctions can drive up retail prices considerably, placing products out of reach for many consumers.

trade selling   The functions performed by the TRADE SALESPERSON.

trade show   A gathering of manufacturers or wholesalers in a particular industry (e.g., housewares, food, electronics, apparel) for the purpose of exhibiting their wares. Trade shows are an excellent resource for discovering trends. Commonly held in exhibition centers or hotels, they give buyers at the retail level an opportunity to see many lines of merchandise in one place and to form an opinion as to what is available in the market. Also called a *trade fair*.

tradesman/tradeswoman   See TRADESPERSON.

trade specialty house   An industrial distributor that serves a specific type of customer. The trade specialty house carries a full line of items required by the business or industrial customer (e.g., barbershop supplies, shoe repair supplies).

tradesperson   An individual engaged in trade (i.e., a merchant, shopkeeper, storekeeper, etc.).

trade style   The unique way in which a store displays its name in print advertisements and on letterheads, etc. See also LOGO and TRADEMARK.

trade surplus   A condition in international trade in which the value of a country's exports exceeds the value of its imports. Compare TRADE DEFICIT.

trade union   A labor union of workers engaged in related skilled crafts, as distinguished from general workers or a union including all workers in an industry regardless of their particular activity. Also called a *craft union*. See also LABOR UNION.

trade up See TRADING UP.

trading across A practice in which a firm (e.g., a store), in an effort to broaden its customer base or to reposition itself in the marketplace, alters its marketing strategy in a way calculated to appeal to a new market segment. In trading across, the firm is seeking to attract a customer on the same economic level as the original segment, but whose lifestyle, demographics, or psychographics are somewhat different. Compare TRADING DOWN and TRADING UP.

trading area 1. In a general sense, the geographic zone containing the people who are likely to purchase a given firm's goods or services. 2. Specifically in retailing, the area from which a store or shopping center attracts most of its customers. Also known as a *retail trading area, trade area,* or *shopping radius.* See also CORE-BASED STATISTICAL AREA (CBSA), RETAIL SITE LOCATION, GEODEMOGRAPHY, and GEOGRAPHICAL INFORMATION SYSTEMS (GIS).

trading area overlap An area from which more than one store in the same retail organization is drawing customers.

trading area overlay A transparent plastic sheet on which is plotted each store's trading area. The sheet is placed over a city map. This method is used (primarily by chain retailers having more than one outlet in a city) to determine areas from which the chain is not drawing customers. The technique shows where a new store may profitably be located.

trading away See BAIT AND SWITCH.

trading bloc A major geographic trading area such as Europe, North America, South America, or the Pacific Rim countries in Asia.

trading card A card given to customers that may eventually be redeemed for a free gift, such as a coffee or frozen yogurt. Customers may collect their gift after having made the required number of purchases as recorded by hole-punching or ink-stamping their trading cards. Sometimes called *trade card, purchase-privilege offer,* or *premium trading card.*

trading company A company organized to do business in foreign countries (or, for example, in Japan where they operate within the country) and involved in all aspects of buying, accumulating, transporting, distributing, and selling goods. See also DOMESTIC-BASED EXPORT AGENT and INDIRECT EXPORT.

trading down A practice in which a firm (typically a store), in an effort to broaden its customer base or reposition itself in the marketplace, alters its marketing strategy by reducing prices, lowering the quality of its products, and promoting itself in a way calculated to appeal to customers on a lower socioeconomic level. Compare TRADING ACROSS and TRADING UP.

trading radius A store's TRADING AREA as determined by the RING ANALYSIS method. It is determined by using an existing or potential retail site as the locus to determine customer poten-tial within one-, three-, and five-mile radius rings. See also RING ANALYSIS.

trading stamp redemption center/store See REDEMPTION CENTER.

trading stamps Printed stamps given to customers by retailers as a CONTINUITY PREMIUM for shopping in the store. Each stamp is worth a small percentage of the total amount paid for purchases. Stamps are pasted into books and redeemed for merchandise or for their value in cash. Trading stamps, a popular form of continuity premium in the mid-twentieth century (e.g., S&H Green Stamps), are regarded as a form of NONPRICE COMPETITION.

trading up 1. A strategy in which a firm (frequently a store) alters its marketing strategy to attract customers of a higher socioeconomic level, generally by offering goods of higher quality for sale at higher prices than before and by promoting itself in a manner calculated to attract more affluent customers. Compare TRADING ACROSS and TRADING DOWN. See also UPGRADING and UPSCALING. 2. The practice, by a salesperson, of encouraging a customer to buy more expensive merchandise. Also called *selling up.* See also UPSELL.

traditional See TRADITIONAL MERCHANDISE and CLASSIC MERCHANDISE.

traditional break-even analysis See BREAK-EVEN ANALYSIS.

traditional channel system See CONVENTIONAL CHANNEL.

traditional department store See DEPARTMENT STORE.

traditional merchandise Products that change little from year to year, particularly in terms of style. Such merchandise is considered MAINSTREAM because it is so widely accepted. See also CLASSIC MERCHANDISE.

traditional supermarket See SUPERMARKET .

traffic 1. In retail stores, the number of customers or prospective customers who either pass by (i.e., STREET TRAFFIC) or enter the store or any of its departments. Also called *store traffic.* See also PEDESTRIAN TRAFFIC and VEHICULAR TRAFFIC. 2. In E-TAILING and other Internet marketing ventures, the number of visitors to a site. Internet traffic may be generated by registering with search engines, joining Web rings and gift communities, adding reciprocal links, and using e-mail permission marketing. 3. In a slightly more general sense, the collective customer presence in a store. The movement of this traffic is related to and affected by STORE LAYOUT AND DESIGN. 4. In a retail DISTRIBUTION CENTER (DC), the coordination of inbound delivery from suppliers and outbound shipment to stores.

traffic appliances Portable home appliances such as toasters, blenders, irons, microwave ovens, etc.

traffic building merchandise 1. Items that consistently sell well and help to generate store TRAFFIC. Also called *traffic* *items.* 2. A synonym for GIVEAWAY (i.e., a free item given out by a store to help generate traffic).

traffic count   1. In retail stores, the process of counting customers as they pass a predetermined point in the store.   2. In RETAIL SITE LOCATION studies, either pedestrian or vehicular traffic counted as a determining factor in locating a new store.

traffic department   1. In a retail organization, the department responsible for monitoring incoming shipments, filing claims with carriers, determining routes and shippers for outgoing merchandise, adjusting claims with customers, and handling other similar situations.   2. In large advertising agencies where there are many clients and types of projects, the department responsible for organizing all phases of production and ensuring that deadlines are met. The traffic department may be part of the creative services, media, or account management divisions.

traffic flow   The entry of customers or prospective customers into a store or department and their movement within and through it. The store's layout and design is generally structured to encourage a particular pattern of movement. Consequently, traffic flow is closely related to the type of floor plan, aisle width, lighting, merchandise, and fixture placement as well as other intangible factors known as *traffic flow variables. Traffic flow engineering* refers to the methods used to draw customers efficiently through the store.

traffic flow engineering   See TRAFFIC FLOW.

traffic flow variables   See TRAFFIC FLOW.

traffic items   Synonym for TRAFFIC BUILDING MERCHANDISE.

traffic management   1. In a narrow industrial sense, the purchase of transportation services for the purpose of shipping goods. This includes such functions as the determination of freight charges, the application of tariff regulations, freight consolidation, etc.   2. In a broader marketing sense, the transportation and warehousing of goods in the CHANNEL OF DISTRIBUTION. Also called *transportation management.* See also TRAFFIC MANAGER.

traffic manager   At the retail store level, the executive responsible for the movement of goods to and from the store. This includes, on the one hand, supervision of the store's trucks and delivery system and, on the other, all matters pertaining to the receipt of goods, claims against carriers, etc. Efficiency of movement and cost reduction are primary goals of traffic managers. See also TRAFFIC MANAGEMENT.

trailer-on-flatcar (TOFC)   See PIGGYBACK.

transaction   An individual reciprocal act of giving and receiving involving either money or barter. A transaction nearly always involves the transfer of ownership of some product, or the transfer of the use of some service, from one party to another. See also EXCHANGE.

transactional flow   Synonym for CHANNEL FLOW.

transactional (marketing) function   Any marketing function that involves the transfer of ownership of either goods or services between parties. Transactional marketing functions include buying, selling, risk assumption, and related tasks. They overlap somewhat with facilitating functions. Also called a *transactional function.* See also MARKETING FUNCTIONS and FACILITATING MARKETING FUNCTION.

transactional Web site   Synonym for TRANSACTION WEB SITE.

transaction authority markup language (XAML)   A vendor-neutral standard used to coordinate and process complex online business transactions. Based on XML, XAML uses a set of XML message formats and interaction models to provide business-level transactions that span multiple parties across the Internet.

transaction price   See SELLING PRICE.

transaction risk   In INTERNATIONAL MARKETING, the possibility that there may be a change in the exchange rates of the countries involved between the invoicing date and the settlement date of the transaction.

transactions per square foot   The number of transactions per square foot of selling space in a retail store, computed by dividing the number of sales transactions by the number of square feet of selling space.

transaction Web site   A highly interactive Web site where products are sold. Compare INTERACTIVE WEB SITE, where customers can look at but not purchase products online, and INFORMATION WEB SITE, which provides information without allowing for interactions or selling. Also called a *transactional Web site.* See also WEB STOREFRONT.

transfer   Synonym for DECAL/DECALOMANIA.

transfer book   A book or ledger used to record merchandise that has been transferred from one department to another. Included in each record are the number of units transferred, unit cost, total cost, unit retail, and total retail. In computerized establishments, the information may be recorded in computer databases instead of physical books. See also OUTSTANDING TRANSFER LIST FORM.

transfer cost   Any expenditure incurred when a department accepts items supplied by other departments. See also TRANSFER-IN and TRANSFER-OUT.

transfer impact   A feature of a product or service that encourages consumers to shift (i.e., transfer) their allegiance from an old product or service to the new one.

transfer-in   Merchandise being moved into a department or branch from another part of the same retail organization. See also TRANSFER-OUT and TRANSFER OF GOODS.

transfer of goods   The movement of merchandise in or out of a store or department. When merchandise is transferred from one store to another (e.g., a branch), an OUTSTANDING TRANSFER LIST FORM is used to record the number of units transferred, unit cost, total cost, unit retail, and total retail. This record is used to indicate the change of ownership of merchandise. Merchandise may also be transferred from one department to another. See also TRANSFER-IN, TRANSFER-OUT, and TRANSFER BOOK.

transfer of title   The point in a TRANSACTION at which ownership of the goods passes from seller to buyer.

transfer-out   Merchandise being moved out of a department or branch to another part of the same retail organization. See also TRANSFER-IN and TRANSFER OF GOODS.

transfer price   An intracompany charge made for goods transferred from one division to another or for goods shipped to foreign subsidiaries. See also INTERNATIONAL TRANSFER PRICE.

transfers   Merchandise being moved from department to department, or branch to branch, within a single retail organization. See also TRANSFER OF GOODS, TRANSFER-IN, and TRANSFER-OUT.

transit advertising   OUTDOOR ADVERTISING in the form of car cards, posters, etc., used both inside and outside vehicles of public transportation (buses, trains, taxicabs, etc.) and in their stations (including airports). Transit advertising includes airport displays, bus displays (interior and exterior), mobile displays, subway and rail displays (exterior graphics, interior posters, and traincards), taxi displays (tops, trunk and interior displays and exterior wraps), truckside displays (sides, tails, and headers), and vehicle wraps (cars, vans, and SUVs). Like outdoor advertising generally, transit advertising relies on the volume of foot or vehicular traffic to reach consumers.

transitional customer   A retail customer who bridges the gap between the traditional customer (one who has a practical, utilitarian approach to clothing) and the contemporary customer (one who is more fashion-conscious).

transition merchandise   Merchandise used to bridge two seasons. For example, cotton dresses in dark colors may be used to bridge winter and spring.

transit mall   A PEDESTRIAN MALL closed to traffic except public transportation. Examples of transit malls include the Nicollet Mall in Minneapolis, Minnesota, and the State Street Mall in Chicago, Illinois.

transit privileges   In transportation, the opportunity offered to a shipper by a shipping company (usually a railroad) to unload goods in transit in order to process them and then to reload the processed goods without incurring additional charges. The goods then continue on their way to their destination. An example would be wheat, unloaded in transit in order to be milled into flour and then reloaded. Also known as *processing in transit* or *milling in transit*.

transit time   1. The period between the time a vendor ships merchandise and the time the merchandise is received by the retailer.   2. The period during which a carrier (e.g., a railroad, trucker) has possession of a shipment.

transloading   A practice in rail shipping in which lots of goods of less than a carload each are combined into one carload and shipped to a point nearest the majority of a firm's customers. At that point the various lots are unloaded and reloaded onto freight cars headed for the specific destination of each lot. This practice allows shippers of relatively small lots of goods to take advantage of the railroad's carload rates for at least part of the trip. Also called the *transloading privilege*. See also CARLOAD FREIGHT RATE (CL) and LESS-THAN-CARLOAD LOT (LCL).

Transmission Control Protocol/Internet Protocol (TCP/IP)   See TCP/IP.

transnational company   Synonym for MULTINATIONAL CORPORATION (MNC).

transparency   1. In contractual relations, a policy that all information and transactions be open to scrutiny.   2. In global marketing treaties (such as GATT), a policy that all participating nations make any trade restrictions overt. See also NONDISCRIMINATION and RECIPROCITY, the other two principles underlying the GATT   3. Synonym for DECAL/DECALOMANIA.   4. Synonym for PRICE TRANSPARENCY.

transportation   A part of the PHYSICAL DISTRIBUTION (PD) function concerned with the movement of goods from the point of manufacture to the consumption point. Modes of transportation include ground (trucks and railroads), air, water (ships), and pipelines (for such commodities as gasoline and natural gas).

transportation cost   Any expense involved in shipping merchandise from a vendor to a retailer.

transportation management   Synonym for TRAFFIC MANAGEMENT.

transportation service company   A marketing specialist that handles the shipments of small and moderate-sized packages. Government-sponsored parcel post, private parcel post, and express services are all considered transportation service companies.

transshipping   A trade practice in which authorized dealers of merchandise sell their overstock to discounters, often to the dismay of the manufacturer, who wants to maintain the original retail price.

transumer   A consumer in transit at an airport. The trend was reported by trendwatching.com at www.trendwatching.com. See also TRANSUMERISM.

transumerism   Finding new ways to market goods and services to consumers in transit at airports, bus terminals, train stations, etc. The trend includes the ability of these traveling consumers to shop electronically while waiting in various depots. The trend was identified and the term coined by trendwatching.com at www.trendwatching.com. See also TRANSIT MALL.

traveling export sales representative   Synonym for EXPORT SALES REPRESENTATIVE.

traveling salesperson   A firm's traveling representative who covers a particular region or territory soliciting orders for the firm's products. Also called a *commercial traveler* or *traveling sales representative.*

traveling sales representative   Synonym for TRAVELING SALESPERSON.

tray pack   A POINT-OF-PURCHASE (POP) display where the top of the case of goods can be opened and folded back. The case then becomes a display container that is readily placed on a shelf or counter in the store. See also POINT-OF-PURCHASE (POP) DISPLAY.

treasure hunter   Synonym for TREASURE HUNT SHOPPER.

treasure hunt shopper   A customer who, regardless of income level, is entertained by the experience of looking for bargains.

trend   A prevailing tendency or direction. In fashion, a trend is that which is currently popular and moving toward wide acceptability in the marketplace. See also FASHION TREND.

trend analysis   The process of comparing financial data from year to year in order to detect changes. Trend analysis points up shifts in the nature of the business over time and may also be used to compare the company with others in its industry or with the economy as a whole. Most large public companies provide data for trend analysis in their annual reports. Also called *end-of-period trend analysis.* Compare RATIO ANALYSIS. See also DURING-THE-PERIOD TREND ANALYSIS.

trend extension   A method used to forecast sales for existing products. Since such products have a record of previous sales data, market forecasters simply project past sales performance into the future. See also FORECASTING, ECONOMIC FORECASTING, SALES FORECASTING, and FASHION FORECASTING.

trend merchandising   A strategy in which new merchandise is presented in the store in such a way as to capitalize on developing directions and tendencies perceived by the merchandising staff.

trend projection   Synonym for TIME SERIES ANALYSIS.

trendsetter   See OPINION LEADER.

trend shop   A merchandising area set apart by special flooring, walls, or ceiling treatments. At a mall store, the trend shop may be at the retailer's entrance, set apart by a carpeted sales floor. In a traditional downtown department store, it may be an area close to an escalator or elevator. This space is converted into a theme shop based on whatever merchandise promotions or seasonal events are going on. Also known as a *highlight shop.*

trial   1. The process of trying and testing a new product (e.g., a clinical trial for new pharmaceutical products).   2. A consumer's first use of a product or service. This is a critical point in the ADOPTION PROCESS, as it determines the subsequent acceptance or rejection of the product by the consumer.

trial-and-error pricing   The practice of setting the initial price for a new product or service experimentally and provisionally. In stores with more than one location, the product may be priced differently at each of the various locations. An assessment of customer response to each of the prices is then made and a more permanent price is established.

trial balance   a method of checking double entry bookkeeping in which all debits and all credits are added to ensure that they cancel one another out. A balance indicates that the debits and credits are in balance (i.e., equal), but does not guarantee their correctness.

trial buyer   A first-time purchaser of an item (or service) who is allowed to examine, use, or test it for a short period of time before deciding to buy it or not. See also TRIAL OFFER.

trial offer   A special arrangement allowing a first-time purchaser to examine, use, or test an item for a short period of time, often free or at a reduced rate, before deciding to buy or decline it. Such offers are often made with a small quantity of the product, called a *trial size.* Also called *free examination offer* or *free trial offer.* See also FREE SAMPLE and TRIAL BUYER.

trial sampling   In sales promotion, the encouraging of product trial by the consumer through the giving of free samples. See also TRIAL OFFER.

trial size   See TRIAL OFFER and FREE SAMPLE.

triangular compensation   In global marketing, a COMPENSATION TRANSACTION in which three countries are involved. The exporter delivers HARD GOODS (i.e., salable merchandise) to an importer. As payment, the importer transfers SOFT GOODS (i.e., heavily discounted merchandise that may prove more difficult to resell) to a specialist firm or *switch trader.* The switch trader then reimburses the exporter for the merchandise received and arranges to resell it. Also known as *switch trade.*

trickle-across theory   See HORIZONTAL FLOW THEORY.

trickle-down theory   See DOWNWARD FLOW THEORY.

trilevel round rack   Synonym for THREE-PART RACK.

trio of needs   Three of the basic motivations that cause individual consumers to make purchase decisions. These are the needs for power, affiliation, and achievement. The *achievement need* is the drive for personal accomplishment; the *affiliation need* is the drive to belong to a particular group; the *power need* is the drive to control one's environment. The trio of needs are sometimes considered to be independent of the five levels of need identified by Maslow, although a case can be made for including them in MASLOW'S HIERARCHY (OF NEEDS).

tripartite view (of attitude)   A theory of attitude research that views attitude as the result of a combination of three components: affect, cognition, and conation. See also AFFECTIVE COMPONENT, COGNITIVE COMPONENT, and CONATIVE COMPONENT.

triple net   Originally, the terms of a retail lease that enumerated the retailer's responsibility to pay for insurance, utilities, and internal upkeep. More recently, other items may be included and the three responsibilities may be somewhat different. Triple net charges may now include COMMON AREA MAINTENANCE (CAM), promotional funds, taxes, insurance, and utilities.

Trojan Horse   A computer program that, like the Trojan Horse of mythology, may appear to be useful or beneficial but is actually harmful: it will damage the user's computer once installed or run. Users on the receiving end of a Trojan Horse are usually tricked into opening it because they believe they are receiving legitimate software or files from a legitimate source. While the terms *Trojan Horse*, WORM, and VIRUS are often used interchangeably, they are not the same.

trolley   In the United Kingdom, Australia, and some other places, a SHOPPING CART.

troubleshoot   1. To resolve disputes and impasses in a business, international affairs, etc.   2. To discover and eliminate the cause of trouble in equipment (such as computers). One who performs either of these activities is known as a *troubleshooter*.

TRPs   See TARGET RATING POINTS (TRPS).

truck distributor   See TRUCK WHOLESALER.

trucker   Synonym for MOTOR CARRIER.

truck freight   A method for transporting goods over land. As an alternative to railroad freight, truck deliveries are increasingly the method of choice for the domestic transportation of retail goods. Larger trucks and specialized vehicles have proven effective in handling all types of merchandise. While relatively expensive, truck freight serves extensive areas, allows for flexibility in shipment scheduling, provides speedy local delivery, and has the potential for handling a large variety of products. The two major categories of truck transportation are LINE HAUL and SHORT HAUL.

truck jobber   See TRUCK WHOLESALER.

truckload (TL)   A full truck's worth of goods, for which motor carriers charge a lower shipping rate than for partial loads. Sometimes spelled *truck load*.

truck wholesaler   A limited service wholesaler that operates from a truck. Truck wholesalers sell and deliver merchandise and collect payments. They carry a limited line of goods (e.g., bread or dairy products) and generally service retail outlets, industrial facilities, or institutions. Also called a *merchandise distributor*, *merchandise deliverer*, *truck jobber*, *truck distributor*, *wagon distributor*, or *wagon jobber* (deriving from the earlier use of wagons rather than trucks).

true customization   See CUSTOMIZATION.

trunk form   See BODY TRUNK.

trunk show   All or part of a manufacturer's line, brought to a store, hotel, exhibition space, etc., and shown to the public. A manufacturer or designer ships the line to the retail store in trunks or sales representative's cases. The shows are advertised in advance and orders are written for future shipment, either through the store or directly to customers' homes.

trust receipt   Written acknowledgment (i.e., a receipt) used by a dealer to obtain merchandise that has been financed by a lending institution. The dealer signs the receipt as an obligation to repay the lender. The dealer may or may not take title to the goods in the course of the transaction.

truth in advertising   The obligation of a firm or store to truthfully explain the attributes or benefits of the products or services they advertise. The FEDERAL TRADE COMMISSION (FTC) can take disciplinary action against retailers or other firms whose advertisements are deemed to be untruthful, deceptive, unsubstantiated, or misleading.

Truth in Advertising Act   See FEDERAL TRADE COMMISSION (FTC) and FEDERAL TRADE COMMISSION ACT (FTCA) (1914).

Truth-in-Lending Act (1968)   See CONSUMER CREDIT PROTECTION ACT (1968).

Truth-in-Packaging Act (1966)   Alternative name for the FAIR PACKAGING AND LABELING ACT (1966).

tryvertising   A new breed of PRODUCT PLACEMENT in the real world, integrating goods and services into daily life in a relevant way so that consumers can make up their minds based on their experience, not the marketer's advertising messages. The trend is seen as a response to experienced consumers' indifference to commercials, ads, banners, and other advertising that is forced upon them. Obvious examples include the distribution of free samples. More subtle instances of tryvertising include the placement of single servings of products in hotel rooms, shampoo and fragrance samples in magazines, and various items on Web sites devoted to free products. See also TRIAL OFFER and FREE SAMPLE. The trend was identified and the term coined by trendwatching.com at www.trendwatching.com.

TSD   See TELEPHONE SELLING DEPARTMENT (TSD).

T-stand   Synonym for TWO-WAY FIXTURE/DISPLAY.

tube system   An old-fashioned communication system still found in some retail stores. A series of *pneumatic tubes* transport cylinders containing sales checks and cash to a central cashier's office. When cashiers have made change or authorized a credit purchase, the carrier is returned through the tube system to the counter where the transaction originated. The system is similar to that used in some closed-stack libraries to request books to be retrieved from the stacks.

turn   Synonymous with STOCK TURNOVER (ST).

turnaround   The path taken by a freight carrier (i.e., a driver) in which the driver loads or unloads cargo and returns to the point of origin.

turnaround time   The time that elapses between an action and the response to that action. For example, the time that passes between the placement of an order with a vendor and the receipt of that order by the retailer.

turnkey   Of a contractual agreement, being one in which an organization agrees to provide full services or a complete product to a customer. See also TURNKEY OPERATION.

turnkey operation   1. A business, typically one being offered for sale, that is completely ready to begin operation, so that all the buyer needs to do is "turn the key" and enter. For example, a franchiser may provide a franchisee with a planned retail store or service operation that is ready to begin business, for which the franchisee pays the franchiser a flat fee and an ongoing percentage of sales. See also FRANCHISING. 2. By analogy, any arrangement providing full services or a complete product to a customer; specifically, a business arrangement involving a buyer, a prime contractor, a number of subcontractors, and a product, in which the prime contractor brings all the subcontractors together, manufactures the product, and finally delivers it to the buyer in complete readiness.

turnover   The number of times AVERAGE RETAIL STOCK is sold during a given period. In retailing, turnover is one of several PRODUCTIVITY MEASURES. Synonym for STOCK TURNOVER (ST).

turnover man   See CLOSER.

turnover of plant and equipment   The financial ratio resulting from dividing a firm's net sales during an accounting period by the average dollar value of its land, buildings, and equipment (i.e., its fixed assets) during the same period. The ratio is used to measure how efficiently a firm's fixed assets are being utilized. See also FINANCIAL RATIOS and FIXED ASSET.

turnover report   A report used by chain stores to assess the performance of individual stores within the chain as well as the chain itself. The report includes: the current year's sales as well as those for last year; the average inventory by store and chain; and the percentage of change (compared to last year) for each. Turnover for the current year and last year is calculated by store and for the whole chain. Retailers assess sales and turnover performance by comparing an individual store's record to that of the entire chain. Turnover issues can be traced to sales and average inventory by means of the turnover report. See also STOCK TURNOVER (ST).

tuxedo   See FORMAL ATTIRE.

T-wall   In a store's interior, a two-sided wall or partition that extends from the back or perimeter wall out into the aisle. The flat end of the T-wall can be converted into display space. A panel used to cover the end of the unit makes the top stroke of the letter T and the merchandising wall forms the upright of the letter T. See also DISPLAY and STORE LAYOUT AND DESIGN.

twelve-week sell-through   The number of units sold in the past 12 weeks divided by the number of units received in that period. See also STYLE STATUS REPORT.

twig (store)   A small branch store that carries a selection of its parent store's merchandise, generally targeting a specific group of customers. For example, a large specialty store may open a *twig* in a university town. The twig store carries merchandise from the main store's university shop specifically selected to appeal to college students.

twin pack   A retail package containing two of the same products bound together in the same wrapper or container. The twin pack is generally sold at a lower price than the items would cost if purchased separately.

twinsumer   A fellow consumer who shares one's tastes, opinions, patterns of consumption, etc. In a trend related to the growing number of consumer purchase decisions determined by word-of-mouth, peer-to-peer, and other (largely online) recommendations, consumers looking for the best merchandise connect with their twinsumers, or "taste twins", online. The trend was identified and the term coined by trendwatching.com at www.trendwatching.com. *Der.* twin + consumer.

two-factor theory of motivation   A theory of consumer motivation developed by Frederick Herzberg. Herzberg postulated that consumers seek to maximize *satisfiers* (i.e., characteristics of a product that are intrinsically satisfying) and minimize *dissatisfiers* (i.e., characteristics of a product that are not pleasing). According to this theory of motivation, marketers must be aware of the dissatisfiers that may keep their product from selling.

twofer   (Slang) Short for TWO-FOR-ONE SALE.

two-for-one sale   An offer of two units of merchandise for the regular price of one. The seller makes this offer to consumers to encourage sampling and increase unit sales. Popularly called a *twofe*r in retail slang.

two-level channel   A channel of distribution in which there are two levels between the manufacturer/producer and the ultimate consumer. For example, there may be a wholesaler or distributor and a retailer acting as marketing intermediaries.

two-step flow model   A theory of mass communication holding that both mass media and opinion leaders influence audience behavior. In this two-step process, information is seen to flow from the mass media to the opinion leaders, who then influence the general population. The MULTISTEP FLOW MODEL has largely superseded the two-step model. See also HYPODERMIC NEEDLE MODEL.

two-way fixture/display   A two-armed FEATURE FIXTURE, often made of chrome. Goods are hung so that their most visually appealing side faces the customer. Two-way fixtures are frequently used to feature small quantities of trend merchandise, test merchandise, COORDINATES, and separates that are being presented as coordinated outfits. Also called a *T-stand*. See also ENSEMBLE DISPLAY.

tying agreement/contract   An agreement in which a manufacturer requires a dealer or marketing intermediary to purchase certain goods in order to purchase certain other goods, or in which the manufacturer requires that the dealer not sell competing goods. In return, the dealer may be granted exclusive rights to sales of the manufacturer's products in a specified territory.

tying clause   See TYING AGREEMENT/CONTRACT.

𝒰

über premium   All products and services that are truly out of reach of the vast majority of consumers. The restrictions are not merely financial; they include not being invited or not being informed. The term refers to a trend toward exclusivity. The trend was identified and the term coined by trend-watching.com at www.trendwatching.com.

UCC   See UNIFORM COMMERCIAL CODE (UCC) and/or UNIFORM CODE COUNCIL (UCC).

UCCnet   A not-for-profit subsidiary of the UNIFORM CODE COUNCIL (UCC), the global standards organization, created to provide its stakeholders with information on standards. For example, UCCnet provides data to users of the GLOBAL DATA SYNCHRONIZATION NETWORK (GDSN). UCCnet was founded in 1999 to address the costly problems of inaccurate supply chain data.

UCE   See UNSOLICITED COMMERCIAL E-MAIL (UCE).

ultimate consumer   See for CONSUMER.

umbrella brand   See FAMILY BRAND.

umbrella liability insurance   See UMBRELLA POLICY.

umbrella mark   See FAMILY BRAND.

umbrella policy   An insurance policy that provides retailers and other businesses with coverage beyond that provided by other parts of a liability policy. Business umbrella liability insurance provides supplementary coverage for costs associated with lawsuits, legal fees, and settlements. It can also cover bodily injury and personal property claims. Also called *umbrella liability insurance.*

umbrella pricing   A PRICING STRATEGY in which a large firm maintains the prices of its products at a level higher than necessary in an effort to protect smaller competitors from ruinous competition. Umbrella pricing is the opposite of PREDATORY PRICING.

unadvertised sale   See PRIVATE SALE.

unaided recall   A consumer's ability to remember an advertisement without help, subjected to an *unaided recall test* as a means of determining the ad's effectiveness. Participants are asked to identify advertisements they have recently seen or heard but are given no stimuli to aid their memory (i.e., they are not shown the actual ads and are not given any other hints or clues). Compare AIDED RECALL.

Unavailability Rule   See RAINCHECK RULE.

unbilled revenue   Earnings, during a given period, from the sale of goods and services that have not yet been billed to the customers who purchased them.

unbranded merchandise/product   See GENERIC BRAND and GENERIC PRODUCT.

unbundling price/pricing   A price, set of prices, or pricing policy allowing customers (usually at retail) to choose certain products or services separately rather than purchasing the full ensemble of products or services. Prices are separated out (i.e., *unbundled*) for individual elements of the package. Also called *unbundling, unbundled pricing,* or *unbundled price.* Compare BUNDLED PRICING.

uncertainty avoidance   See HOFSTEDE MEASURES OF CULTURE.

unchanging list price   A LIST PRICE (i.e., the retail price suggested and sometimes advertised by the manufacturer) that remains the same for an extended time, despite the fact that both markups and discounts may affect the actual selling price of the goods.

unconscious level of need awareness   See NEED AWARENESS.

uncontrollable factors   Those elements in the marketing environment that are out of the control of the retailer or other business organization (e.g., shifts in the economy, government regulations, international politics).

uncovered position   In GLOBAL MARKETING, a price quoted in a foreign currency that is left until the due date and paid at whatever SPOT PRICE prevails at that time. This practice exposes the company to risk associated with fluctuating exchange rates. See also FORWARD PRICE.

undercharge   To unintentionally charge a customer less than the proper or fair price for goods or services.

undercover marketing See VIRAL MARKETING.

undergarment An item of apparel worn next to the skin, beneath the visible outer garments. The category includes such items as corsets and girdles, bras, panties, slips, camisoles, teddies, undershirts, boxer shorts, briefs, etc. Also called *underwear*.

underground economy Economic activity that is not reported and, consequently, not calculated in a country's GROSS NATIONAL PRODUCT (GNP). Examples of underground economic activities include illegal drug sales, prostitution, illegal gambling, and other crimes as well as any purchases or payments made, or services performed, UNDER THE TABLE.

underinventoried Of a department or store, having its BEGINNING OF MONTH (BOM) INVENTORY significantly outweighed by sales. This results in a low STOCK-TO-SALES RATIO (SSR) and indicates that goals for the store or department were set too low and that merchandise was, therefore, inadequately allocated. The assumption is that additional stock would have generated additional sales. Compare OVERINVENTORIED.

underordering The ordering of insufficient merchandise to meet consumer demand.

underpackaging The use of inadequate packaging materials for the level of protection needed for a given product. Underpackaging may result in damaged merchandise.

underring A cash register error in which a price lower than the actual price of goods is recorded on the register. Also spelled *under-ring*.

underselling The practice of selling merchandise at a price lower than that listed by a competitor. Some discounters vow not to be *undersold* by their competitors. See also RATE WAR and PREDATORY PRICING.

underselling store Synonym for DISCOUNT STORE.

undersold See UNDERSELLING.

understored area A retail trading area in which there are too few stores selling a specific product or service to meet the needs of the population.

under the table Of a purchase or payment, made off the record (and hence without the collection of tax). See also UNDERGROUND ECONOMY.

underwear See UNDERGARMENT.

underwriter An insurance company employee who decides which risks to insure, for how much, and for what premiums (i.e., payments). See also RISK.

undifferentiated marketing A marketing strategy in which one or more products are offered for sale to the total market (i.e., no attempt is made to address individual market segments). Undifferentiated marketing, which is usually applied to staple products (e.g., gasoline, sugar, salt), focuses on those characteristics that are common to large numbers of customers. It is a simpler and cheaper strategy to execute than DIFFERENTIATED MARKETING. Also called the *total market approach* or *market aggregation*. Essentially the same as the WHOLE MARKET APPROACH/METHOD. See also CUSTOMIZED MARKETING and MARKET SEGMENTATION.

undifferentiated product A product or service that is not marketed on the basis of what makes it different, unique, superior, or preferable to the competitors' product. Consumers may have difficulty selecting an undifferentiated product or service over similar ones offered by the competition. Compare DIFFERENTIATED PRODUCT.

undiscounted Merchandise sold at the full price without discounts or allowances. Undiscounted goods are often staple items with little price elasticity.

unduplicated media audience Synonym for REACH. Compare DUPLICATED MEDIA AUDIENCE.

uneven exchange A transaction in which the customer returns a purchase and exchanges it for merchandise of a different value.

unfair competition Any dishonest and unethical activity growing out of competitive rivalry and designed to damage or inhibit other businesses.

unfair practices See UNFAIR TRADE PRACTICES.

unfair sales acts Synonym for UNFAIR TRADE PRACTICES ACTS.

unfair trade practices In INTERNATIONAL TRADE, discriminatory activities in which goods are either excessively subsidized, dumped, or otherwise illegitimate (e.g., counterfeit).

unfair trade practices acts U.S. state laws intended to discourage PREDATORY PRICING by wholesalers and retailers. In general, the acts prohibit the reselling of goods for less than their purchase price (except in the case of legitimate clearance sale merchandise) and, in addition, may require a minimum markup of, for example, 6%. In some states, these laws apply to all products. In others, they apply only to certain categories of products (e.g., alcoholic beverages, groceries). Also known as *unfair trade acts, unfair sales acts,* and *minimum markup laws*. See also MINIMUM MARKUP LAW, SHERMAN ANTITRUST ACT (1890), FEDERAL TRADE COMMISSION ACT (FTCA) (1914), and the WHEELER-LEA ACT (1938).

unified format corporate chain See CORPORATE CHAIN.

uniform Any special clothing required for wear by members of the armed forces, police and fire departments, educational institutions (e.g., a private school), particular occupations (e.g., nursing), a sports team, a particular business organization, etc.

Uniform Code Council (UCC)   A membership organization with a global system of commerce used by more than one million companies doing business in more than 140 countries across 23 industries. The Uniform Code Council (UCC) began in 1971 as a domestic, single-industry mandate to administer the UPC bar codes. Member companies now rely on the standards and services of the Council for the effective management and control of their supply chains. The Council serves as the secretariat to the VOLUNTARY INDUSTRY COMMERCE STANDARDS ASSOCIATION (VICS).

Uniform Commercial Code (UCC)   A set of statutory laws (adopted in its entirety by 49 states between 1953 and 1969 and partially adopted by the state of Louisiana), designed to standardize and facilitate commercial transactions for firms doing business in more than one state. The Uniform Commercial Code covers sales, contracts, warranties, the physical transfer of goods, financing, bills of lading provided by transport carriers to shippers, etc. The courts of the state in which an alleged offense has occurred decide any disputes that arise concerning matters covered by the UCC. The National Council of Commissioners on Uniform State Laws and the American Law Institute jointly developed the UCC.

uniform cross-channel pricing   The use of the same price for a product across all channels in which it is sold. For example, BRICKS-AND-CLICKS retailers may use the same price for in-store, catalog, and Internet sales of their merchandise. Price transparency has forced many companies to adopt a uniform cross-channel pricing policy. Compare VARIABLE CHANNEL PRICING.

uniform delivered price/pricing   See POSTAGE STAMP PRICING.

uniform geographic pricing   See POSTAGE STAMP PRICING.

uniform (percentage) markup   A PRICING system in which an attempt is made to apply a single MARKUP PERCENT/PERCENTAGE to all goods offered for sale. If nearly all merchandise in a store or department is of one kind, a uniform percentage markup may be possible. However, if (as in a supermarket) various classifications generate widely varying selling costs, then a uniform markup cannot generate a reasonable profit.

uniform pricing code (UPC)   See UNIVERSAL PRODUCT CODE (UPC).

uniform pricing strategy   In global marketing, the use of a standardized pricing policy on a global scale. This requires that a company charge the same price everywhere and translate that price into a base currency. See also MODIFIED UNIFORM PRICING.

Uniform Product Code (UPC)   See UNIVERSAL PRODUCT CODE (UPC).

Uniform Product Code Council (UPCC)   An organization of manufacturers, processors, retailers, and wholesalers of products sold through high-volume checkstands. The goal of this organization is to develop a UNIVERSAL PRODUCT CODE (UPC) system for assigning a unique identification number to every product sold in the United States.

uniform resource locator (URL)   A unique designation for each Internet site that serves as its address on the Internet. The URL includes the PROTOCOL type (e.g., hypertext transfer protocol or HTTP), the HOST NAME, and the DOMAIN NAME. Some URLs also include the names of particular directories or files and the markup language used (e.g., HTML).

union   See LABOR UNION.

union shop   A workplace in which the employer may hire new employees who are not union members, but only for a probationary period. At the end of the probationary period, the new employees must join the union.

unique product code (UPC)   See UNIVERSAL PRODUCT CODE (UPC).

unique selling proposition (USP)   In advertising, a competitively and convincingly made promise positioning the product clearly in the minds of consumers. The unique selling proposition characterizes hard-hitting campaigns based on the incomparable (i.e., unique) properties of a product as verified by research. It was the brainchild of Rosser Reeves, co-founder of the Ted Bates advertising agency, who explained the concept in his 1961 book, *Reality in Advertising*.

unique visitor   A single individual visiting a Web site. Unique visitors are identified by cookies or IP numbers. A single visitor viewing the site multiple times is, thereby, only counted once. Compare VISITORS (TO A WEB SITE).

unitary demand   See UNITARY ELASTICITY.

unitary elasticity   A market situation in which a 1% decrease in price produces exactly a 1% increase in demand. Also called *unitary demand*.

unitary falloff   A percentage decrease in sales volume (i.e., number of units) equal to the percentage increase in the price of a good or service.

unit billing   A list of all purchases made by a customer, prepared on a single billing statement. See also BILLING.

unit contribution   See CONTRIBUTION.

unit contribution margin   The excess of the sales price of one unit of merchandise over its variable costs. See also VARIABLE COST.

unit (inventory) control   A stock inventory system based on individual items of merchandise rather than dollar value. Under a unit inventory control system, a record is kept of the physical stock on hand, amounts on order, and the amounts sold in an effort to determine proper inventory levels and balanced assortments. Also called *unit control*.

unitizing The consolidation of a number of boxes or packages into one load, frequently stacked on a pallet, to facilitate movement. In short, to *unitize* is to make a single unit out of several items.

unit open-to-buy See OPEN-TO-BUY (OTB).

unit plan The SALES PLAN expressed in terms of units. The unit plan determines the quantity of goods that can be made available during the selling period, traditionally the result of dividing the dollar allocation by the average merchandise price. See also UNIT PLANNING.

unit planning The process by which the MERCHANDISE MANAGER and the BUYER determine where to place the greatest emphasis in the store's ASSORTMENT. Since no one store can carry all merchandise categories, decisions about which merchandise assortments to carry are not left to chance but are based on a number of factors, including the type of retail institution, past sales records, determination of consumer preferences, type of goods currently offered, and the possible elimination of some merchandise lines to accommodate new ones. Also called *assortment planning*. See also UNIT PLAN.

unit pricing The practice of setting the price for merchandise (groceries, meats, eggs, baked goods, etc.) relative to a common denominator (e.g., price per pound, price per quart, price per dozen). The label displaying unit pricing may also display the price for the package as a whole (i.e., DUAL PRICING). The practice is intended to facilitate comparison shopping by the consumer. Also called *single item pricing*.

unit sales Sales for the accounting period expressed in terms of the number of units sold rather than monetary (i.e., dollar) terms. Compare DOLLAR SALES.

unit store 1. A retail business comprising a single place of business (i.e., store). 2. An individual store that is part of a chain. See also CHAIN STORE and CHAIN STORE SYSTEM (CSS).

unit train Trains that carry a single type of cargo (e.g., bulk grain) nonstop between two points.

unity of command A management theory maintaining that each individual employee should report to only one immediate supervisor. Also called the *principle of unity of command* or the *theory of unity of command*.

universal bar code See UNIVERSAL PRODUCT CODE (UPC).

universal functions of marketing See MARKETING FUNCTIONS.

universal marketing functions See for MARKETING FUNCTIONS.

Universal Product Code (UPC) Information identifying a product, encoded in a set of alternating black stripes and white spaces (i.e., a bar code) that can be read electronically. Universal product codes are currently found on most items. The encoded data includes identifying information about vendors, departments, classifications, style numbers, etc. When the

Europeans adopted their 13-digit bar code system in 1977, they patterned it after the 12-digit American system but added a thirteenth digit to allow more space for identifying products and countries. In January 2005, the United States and Canada switched to the 13-digit EUROPEAN ARTICLE NUMBERING CODE to facilitate globalization. Also called the *uniform product code (UPC)*, *unique product code (UPC)*, *zebra code*, and *uniform pricing code (UPC)*.

universal resource locator (URL) See UNIFORM RESOURCE LOCATOR (URL).

universal vendor marking (UVM) A voluntary marking system in which the manufacturer attaches an identifying tag or label to its products. The tag or label contains such information as size, color, style, price, etc. Data is presented in OCR-A, which is readable by the human eye as well as by wands and other scanners. See also UNIVERSAL PRODUCT CODE (UPC).

universe Synonym for POPULATION.

unloading 1. Selling merchandise at a relatively low price or through the use of premiums and other special offers in order to sell as much remaining merchandise as possible. 2. A synonym for DUMPING.

unpaid balance In credit card accounts or cash loans, the difference between the amount of the credit purchase or loan and the amount already repaid. The remaining unpaid balance is the amount that must still be paid; the interest charge is applied to this balance.

unplanned business district A group of retail establishments that have grown up together without benefit of formal planning. A CENTRAL BUSINESS DISTRICT (CBD) is generally an example of an unplanned business district.

unprotected consumers Those groups of consumers who are relatively unable to defend their rights in the marketplace and for whom sufficient protective legislation has not been written. Children, the elderly, the poor, and the infirm are regarded as unprotected consumers. See also CONSUMER ADVOCATE, CONSUMER LAWS/LEGISLATION, and CONSUMERISM.

unsecured credit Credit extended without collateral being required by the lender. See also OPEN-BOOK CREDIT.

unsecured loan A loan that requires no COLLATERAL. The lender relies on the strength of the general credit record and earning power of the borrower. Compare SECURED LOAN.

unselfish display A form of ALTRUISTIC DISPLAY that features items not sold by the store (e.g., promotional materials for charitable organizations or community events).

unselling Synonym for COUNTERMARKETING.

unsolicited commercial e-mail (UCE) Advertising messages sent to consumers via e-mail without the consumers' permission to do so. See also SPAM, JUNK E-MAIL, OPT-IN, and OPT-OUT (LIST).

unsought goods/products   Merchandise that customers do not know about, feel is not a good value, or believe they do not need, and hence do not seek out. Occasionally, customers must search for these products out of necessity (e.g., funeral caskets). See also NEW UNSOUGHT GOODS/ITEMS and REGULARLY UNSOUGHT GOODS.

unstructured questionnaire   A QUESTIONNAIRE in which the number of questions is limited and the interviewer is allowed to vary their wording and sequence. The interviewer is also given some latitude in probing the subject for more information. Compare STRUCTURED QUESTIONNAIRE.

unstuffing   In CONTAINERIZATION, the act of unloading cargo from a container.

unsubstantiated   See SUBSTANTIATION.

unsystematic freight equalization   FREIGHT ABSORPTION (PRICING) that meets competitors' locational discounts and delivered prices so as to retain market share. It is considered an unfair pricing practice if used with predatory intent.

unwholesome demand state   A market situation in which efforts are made to discourage the use of a product or service, particularly harmful items such as cigarettes or alcohol. Advertising and other messages are used to decrease the consuming public's use of the product.

UPC   See UNIVERSAL PRODUCT CODE (UPC).

UPCC   See UNIFORM PRODUCT CODE COUNCIL (UPCC).

updated classics   Synonym for UPDATED FASHIONS.

updated fashions   Apparel items derived from a classic style (e.g., a blazer) and brought into currency with a more contemporary appearance by revising lines, colors, fabrics, etc. The styles are new, but not as FASHION-FORWARD as AVANT-GARDE styles would be. Also called *updated classics*.

upfront   In E-TAILING, what the visitor to the Web site sees and experiences. The INTERFACE is where upfront and BACK-END interact.

upgrading   In retailing, the addition of higher quality merchandise to assortments, with a concomitant elevation of price points. Also called a *step-up*. See also UPSCALING and TRADING UP.

upload   To transfer software or data from a computer (such as a personal or client computer) to a larger computer (such as a server or mainframe). Compare DOWNLOAD.

upload/download status test   A standard used by courts to determine jurisdiction in international INTERNET cases. The country in which the site's server is located is typically held to have jurisdiction. By this standard, a nation clearly has jurisdiction over what its citizens upload and download from servers and ISPs within its borders. However, countries sometimes prosecute their own citizens for crimes, such as the distribution of pornographic materials, resulting from accessing foreign Web sites.

upload status test   See UPLOAD/DOWNLOAD STATUS TEST.

upper class   See SOCIAL CLASS.

upper lower class   See SOCIAL CLASS.

upper middle class   See SOCIAL CLASS.

upper upper class   See SOCIAL CLASS.

upscale   1. Of people, at the upper end of a social or economic class. See also SOCIAL CLASS.   2. Of stores, merchandise, neighborhoods, etc., targeted for that segment of the market. See also HIGH-END.

upscaling   The internal changes in a retailing organization that lead to upward movement in the store's level of fashion sophistication and price. The objective is to attract the upscale customer, commonly viewed as being well educated, sophisticated, and affluent. See also UPGRADING and TRADING UP.

upsell   To successfully encourage a customer to purchase a better quality, more expensive item than he or she originally intended. See also TRADING UP.

upstairs store   All of the store that is, literally, above the basement level, including the main or street floor. The term was formerly used to distinguish the more expensive main shopping area from the bargain basement.

upstream value   In a SUPPLY CHANNEL, value added to a product at the beginning of the production and distribution process. Supply channel members add value by bringing raw materials, supplies, and parts directly into production and by furnishing the equipment and materials necessary to maintain and operate the enterprise. Compare DOWNSTREAM VALUE.

upward flow theory   A theory of fashion adoption in which young, lower-income individuals are seen as the innovators of new styles. Fashion then spreads upward through the various social classes. However, the next group to adopt the fashion may be members of the confident, secure upper class. The new fashion is then likely to spread widely throughout the population. Also known as *bottom-up fashion* and the *bottom-up theory*.

upwardly mobile   Of individuals and families, striving for a higher socioeconomic position. Many products are targeted to upwardly mobile people. See also SOCIAL CLASS.

urban core   See CENTRAL BUSINESS DISTRICT (CBD) and DOWNTOWN BUSINESS/SHOPPING DISTRICT.

urbanization   The process by which a locality takes on the characteristics of a city. See also MARKET SEGMENTATION BY DEGREE OF URBANIZATION.

urban specialty center　See FESTIVAL MARKETPLACE.

urgent consignment　Merchandise, such as perishable goods, that requires expeditious clearance by customs officials.

URL　See UNIFORM RESOURCE LOCATOR (URL).

usable site　A Web site that is easy for visitors to use, is suitably constructed for its purpose, and that employs appropriate technology. See also USABILITY TESTING.

usability testing　In Web design, the process by which testers actually use and report on site functions to ensure that a site is usable and that all features work as planned. See also USABLE SITE.

usage rate segmentation　A method of subdividing a population of potential customers based on the rate at which consumers buy and use specific products. Usage rate segmentation typically divides the market into heavy, light, and non-users. Data is gathered by research firms, usually through the use of a selected group of consumers who record daily purchases in a diary. The data is then analyzed by product category and the terms "heavy," "light," and "non-user" are defined for that category. See also DIARY STUDY/METHOD.

U-Scan Shopper　Australian version of SCAN-IT-YOURSELF TECHNOLOGY (SIY).

U.S. Customs and Border Protection (CBP)　See U.S. CUSTOMS SERVICE.

U.S. Customs Service　In the United States, the agency responsible for the establishment of duty rates and quota classifications. Originally established in 1789, the agency is now called U.S. Customs and Border Protection (CBP) and is part of the U.S. Department of Homeland Security. The agency is responsible for assessing and collecting customs duties, excise taxes, fees, and penalties due on imported merchandise. It is also responsible for interdicting and seizing contraband (including narcotics and illegal drugs), detecting and apprehending persons engaged in fraudulent practices to evade Customs, protecting American business and labor and intellectual property rights by enforcing quota provisions, and enforcing import and export restrictions and prohibitions, including the export of critical technology, etc. See also CUSTOMS BONDED WAREHOUSE.

use by (date)　A label or stamp on a food package indicating that the contents must not be eaten after the specified date. The food is considered unsafe for consumption and a health risk after the specified date. The advisory is intended to protect consumers from buying or consuming food that is potentially hazardous and to motivate resellers to remove the merchandise from their shelves. Compare BEST BEFORE (DATE).

used　Synonym for SECONDHAND.

useless quality　Quality, dependability, or performance standards that are superior to those demanded, required, or expected by the consuming public.

Usenet　A worldwide system of computerized discussion groups. Usenet is completely decentralized and not all Usenet computers are on the Internet. Each of the 10,000+ discussion areas is called a NEWSGROUP. Usenet communication is facilitated by NETWORK NEWS TRANSPORT PROTOCOL (NNTP). See also GOOGLE.

Usenet newsgroup　See NEWSGROUP.

user　Anyone who requires the services of a system or product and who employs that service or product. The term is frequently used with specific reference to a *computer user*.

user call　A CALLBACK made by a sales representative to a customer who has already purchased merchandise.

user expectation　A sales forecast based on a consumer survey or other form of consumer research. The forecast indicates the number of anticipated potential users of a product or service.

user group　An organization formed for the exchange of information and services among computer users. User groups frequently form around the use of particular hardware or software applications.

user ID　A code or screen name used by a visitor to a Web site to establish membership or registration status. Often used in conjunction with a PASSWORD. Also called *user identification*.

user population　The composite group of individuals who actually utilize a particular service, product, or program. The term frequently refers, specifically, to the total group of individuals who utilize the WORLD WIDE WEB (WWW) for their shopping and information needs. A user population is, consequently, the online version of an AUDIENCE.

use tax　A tax levied on goods purchased outside the taxing authority's jurisdiction and brought into it after purchase. Use taxes are typically imposed by state or local tax laws designed to discourage the purchase of products not subject to a sales tax; they are taxes on consuming, storing, or using a product for which no sales tax has been paid. Consumers, rather than vendors, are responsible for paying the use tax on transactions that would be subject to sales tax if the purchases were made in the state or local jurisdiction. While many states have had use taxes on the books for many years, they have been largely ignored. The recent rise of Internet, TV, and catalog sales has encouraged states to begin to enforce use laws.

USP　See UNIQUE SELLING PROPOSITION (USP).

utility　The characteristics of a product or service that make it capable of satisfying a customer's need or want. Utility may be regarded as VALUE. For example, in E-MARKETING, intermediaries add utility by smoothing out discrepancies between supply and demand. See also PRODUCT VALUE.

Uuencode　An encoding scheme for email attachments. See ATTACHMENT.

UVM　See UNIVERSAL VENDOR MARKING (UVM).

valet fixture   A freestanding unit, similar to a COSTUMER, used on a floor, ledge, or counter to display apparel. The valet fixture has a heavier and wider adjustable hanger along with a slacks bar, which makes it useful for displaying men's clothing. A valet fixture may also include a shoe platform attached to the same vertical rod on which all the other pieces are assembled. See also DRAPER.

valid   See VALIDITY.

validate   To substantiate or confirm. In retailing, this generally refers to having one's parking receipt or stub stamped by the store. When presented to the local parking facility with which the store has a reciprocal relationship, the stamped ticket allows the customer to avoid paying the parking fee. See also PARKING and GARAGE.

validity   In MARKETING RESEARCH (MR) and other quantitative inquiries (i.e., surveys), the test of whether or not the research actually measures the phenomena it is intended to measure. A *valid measure* shows differences that are true differences, and nothing else. The researcher must take into account whether or not the data was obtained from an informed source and whether the problem under study has been answered with the collected data. Compare RELIABILITY.

valid measure   See VALIDITY.

valid reference point   When projecting future sales based on past sales, the time periods and business units must be truly comparable, sound, just, and verifiable (i.e., valid). The comparable period, or *reference point*, is deemed valid when it is measuring the same time period (e.g., the weeks before Christmas or the first week of school) as that used in prior years. For example, the number of actual shopping days between Thanksgiving and Christmas must be taken into account when comparing one year's selling season to another.

valorization   The maintenance of the VALUE or PRICE of a commodity or other product, especially through the use of government subsidies.

VALS segmentation   A method of psychographic segmentation that uses eight values and lifestyle descriptors to describe how people perceive their lives and use their financial resources. The classifications include: *actualizer* (the consumer who possesses the most resources, is open to new ideas and products, but is leery of advertising); *fulfilled* (the consumer who is not interested in status, cares about education, and purchases goods for the home); *achiever* (the consumer who is drawn to top-quality merchandise and reads business and self-improvement publications); *experiencer* (the fashion-conscious consumer who tends to be an impulse buyer and listens to rock music); *believer* (the ethnocentric consumer who is resistant to change and frequently watches TV); *striver* (the consumer concerned with personal image who uses credit extensively and does more TV watching than reading); *maker* (the consumer who purchases value-oriented basic merchandise, listens to the radio, and is not interested in luxury goods); and *struggler* (the consumer who uses coupons and follows sales, reads tabloids, and believes advertising messages). Also called, simply, *VALS*.

valuation   The act of appraisal used to place a value on a product or service.

valuation account   Synonym for CONTRA ACCOUNT.

valuation of inventory   See INVENTORY VALUATION.

value   1. The inherent worth possessed by a product or service, generally expressed in terms of its price (i.e., in monetary terms), as credit, or as other goods and services. See also UTILITY, PRODUCT VALUE, SCARCITY VALUE, and VALUES.   2. Popularly, a good buy (i.e., something obtained for a relatively small expenditure of money, given its worth). See also MARKET VALUE.

value added   The increase in the worth of a product as the result of the processes it passes through in the CHANNEL OF DISTRIBUTION. See also VALUE-ADDED TAX (VAT).

value added by marketing   The increase in the worth of a product or service as the result of the marketing processes it passes through in the CHANNEL OF DISTRIBUTION. It may be computed as the value of sales, less the cost of goods sold, less the cost of supplies, energy, and all other activities involved in the marketing of the product.

value-added reseller (VAR)   A reseller that purchases goods from a producer and adds value through assembly, modification, and/or customization of the basic product. See also MARKETING INTERMEDIARY.

value-added tax (VAT)   An EXCISE tax levied on the increased worth of goods at each level of the CHANNEL OF DISTRIBUTION. The VAT is represented by the difference between the cost of goods at the beginning of one stage in the process (i.e., the cost of goods and services used in production) and the sales price of the end products. A retailer, for example, would be taxed on the difference between the wholesale price of goods and their retail price. While not yet adopted in the United States, VATs are the main type of tax on the sales of goods and services in Europe. See also VALUE ADDED.

value analysis   An effort made by the purchasers of products, parts, and materials to examine the quality level of their acquisitions and reduce COSTS to the lowest possible level.

value center   A cross between a POWER CENTER and a FACTORY OUTLET MALL, featuring discounters, warehouse clubs, category killers, off-price discount stores, and manufacturer's or factory outlet stores as tenants. Very often targeted to a tourist market, these centers need a concentration of about 1.5 million customers to be successful. Also called *value-oriented center*.

value determination   See DATE FOR VALUE DETERMINATION.

value in use   The worth of goods to the individual who uses them. See also UTILITY.

value judgment   The result of a consumer's comparison of two or more alternative items or services and the attempt to choose between them.

value megamall   A large hybrid MALL containing elements of power, value, and outlet centers with the addition of entertainment components (e.g., movie theaters and restaurants). Value megamalls range in size from one to two million square feet. National specialty chains and designer outlets may coexist with category killers, off-price stores, discounters, food, and entertainment retailers. See also MEGAMALL.

value-oriented center   See VALUE CENTER.

value-oriented store   A store that focuses on the customer seeking good quality plus reasonable prices. Discounters, warehouse clubs, category killers, off-price discount stores, and manufacturer's or factory outlet stores may be considered value-oriented stores.

value pricing   1. A pricing policy for merchandise in which the retailer provides the best quality for the lowest price as viewed by the customer. Value pricing dominated the strategies of retailers in the 1990s. 2. A pricing policy for services in which the price of the service is based on the consumer's perception of the value of the service. The price is therefore largely based on what the market will bear without much regard for the actual costs.

values   1. Those broad standards and ideals shared by the members of a society or subgroup of that society, reflecting its moral order. Values strongly affect consumer behavior and lifestyle, and are hence factors that the marketer must take into consideration.   2. Popularly, good buys (i.e., items of worth for a relatively small expenditure of money). See also VALUE.

values and lifestyles (VALS)   See VALS SEGMENTATION.

value shopping   Focused shopping in which the customer is looking for a particular item of merchandise and seeking the best possible quality for the least possible price. The customer generally seeks out a particular DESTINATION STORE for such purchases. Value shopping is often compared to RECREATIONAL SHOPPING and FASHION SHOPPING.

van container   A standard trailer used to carry cargo.

VAR   See VALUE-ADDED RESELLER (VAR).

variability in service quality   The differences in the level of service experienced from one purchase to another. Inconsistencies in service may be due to a number of factors including the difficulty of diagnosing a problem, the inability of the customer to verbalize the problem, etc.

variable budget   A budget that separates fixed costs from variable costs. The fixed costs remain unchanged. The variable costs are allowed to fluctuate on a predetermined basis.

variable channel pricing   A model for setting prices in which different prices are charged for the same merchandise in the various channels in which a product is sold. For example, the in-store, catalog, and Internet prices may each be different. Compare UNIFORM CROSS-CHANNEL PRICING.

variable cost   Any cost that fluctuates directly with output levels, sales volume, or other factors such as transportation and delivery costs. See also TOTAL VARIABLE COSTS.

variable costing system   A method for determining the cost of goods in which every cost must be classified as either variable or fixed. Variable costs fluctuate in direct proportion to changes in output. Fixed costs remain constant regardless of changes in output. Under variable costing, only costs that vary directly with production volume are charged to products in the course of their manufacture. Also called a *direct costing system*. See also ABSORPTION COSTING SYSTEM.

variable expense   See VARIABLE COST.

variable leader pricing   A type of LEADER PRICING commonly found in the supermarket industry, in which the leader items are frequently changed, often on a weekly basis. See also LOSS LEADER.

variable location retailer   A street peddler or wagon distributor who, being mobile, may set up shop at different locations on different days or at different times.

variable markup policy   A model for PRICING in which different categories of goods and services receive different markup percentages. The model recognizes that some items require greater personal selling efforts, customer service, alterations, and end-of-season markdowns than do others.

variable presentation   A model for setting retail prices that takes into consideration such factors as customer services, salespersons' expertise, store image, assortment, variety, competition, and customer satisfaction. Retailers use the model to arrive at a price that the customer anticipates and is prepared to pay. Also called a *variable sales presentation*. See also PRICING.

variable price policy   A PRICE POLICY in which retail prices are not fixed. The retailer may reduce the price in order to make a sale, or the customer may try to negotiate more favorable terms. A *variable price* is used primarily when the customer realizes that the list price is merely the starting point in reaching a final price, as in the case of automobiles sold by dealerships. In addition, price reductions may be given for quantity purchases. For example, there may be one unit price for quantities of 10 items or less and a lower unit price for larger quantities. Also called *variable pricing* or *varying pricing*. See also FLEXIBLE PRICING and NEGOTIATED PRICE. Compare ONE- PRICE POLICY.

variable sales presentation   Synonym for VARIABLE PRESENTATION.

variable slot location system   In WAREHOUSING, the use of computers to keep track of the location of stored merchandise. Merchandise may be placed wherever there is room for it rather than in a particular location assigned to its category.

variety   In retailing, the number of lines of merchandise (i.e., the different kinds of products) carried in a store or a department. Variety is one of the elements of the ASSORTMENT PLAN.

variety display   See ASSORTMENT DISPLAY.

variety-prone   Of a BRAND SWITCHER, motivated by the desire to try something different. This trait shows up in the snack food industry, for example, where consumers may opt for a new cookie or other taste treat just for the sake of change. See also VARIETY-SEEKING BEHAVIOR.

variety-seeking behavior   The type of shopping behavior exhibited by a VARIETY-PRONE customer (a type of BRAND SWITCHER). The behavior is indicative of a desire to try something new or different.

variety store   The original *five and ten, five and dime*, or *dime store*, now stocking a wide range of product classifications but in a limited number of assortments and at relatively low prices. The format dates back to the nineteenth century, when merchants such as Sebastian S. Kresge and Frank W. Woolworth opened stores that sold goods at five and ten cents retail. While now close to extinction due to competition from full line discounters, variety stores remained a dominant retailing format for many decades. They thrived in downtown shopping areas as well as early suburban shopping centers. The five-and-dime era came to an end in 1997 when F. W. Woolworth announced the closing of its remaining Woolworth's stores.

varying price policy   See VARIABLE PRICE POLICY.

VAT   See VALUE-ADDED TAX (VAT).

Veblen goods   Goods purchased for the purpose of CONSPICUOUS CONSUMPTION. The reference is to Thorstein Veblen (American economist, 1857–1929), best known for his work, *The Theory of the Leisure Class*, in which he theorizes that some consumers at the upper reaches of the economic order purchase certain goods simply for the purposes of status and display. Veblen goods, therefore, are those for which the buyer has no intrinsic need. The demand for these goods, contrary to what is commonly the rule, often increases as the price increases, as purchasers tend to identify high price with quality and desirability.

vegetable stand   See FARM STAND.

veggie vision   In RADIO FREQUENCY IDENTIFICATION (RFID), the use of self-service scales with built-in digicams (i.e., digital cameras) that identify produce by size, shape, and color and then print price labels. Eventually, veggie vision scales will generate an RFID tag for all items.

vehicular traffic   Traffic patterns, congestion times, and road conditions, particularly as studied in conjunction with RETAIL SITE LOCATION. Vehicular traffic information is particularly important for establishments located in areas where there is no public transit or little pedestrian traffic. See also TRAFFIC, STREET TRAFFIC, and PEDESTRIAN TRAFFIC.

vend   To engage in selling merchandise, particularly as one's occupation, and particularly at a level other than retail.

vendee   The customer or purchaser of items of merchandise, especially at a level other than retail.

vending machine   A coin-operated machine generally used for selling small items of merchandise such as candy, soft drinks, and SUNDRIES.

vending machine operator   A merchant who sells products on a nonpersonal basis through coin-operated machines, usually on the premises of other businesses. Also called a *merchandise vending machine operator*.

vending machine retailing   See AUTOMATIC VENDING.

vendor   An individual or business (manufacturer, importer, jobber, agent, wholesaler, etc.) who sells goods to other businesses for RESALE. Commonly known as a *supplier* and, in the retail trade, a RESOURCE. Also called an *outside merchandise source, merchandise source,* or *merchandise resource*.

vendor advertisement   An advertisement featuring merchandise from a single manufacturer or designer. If the ad features a variety of different products through the use of the vendor name, the ad becomes a variation of an ASSORTMENT ADVERTISEMENT.

vendor aid　Synonym for DEALER AID.

vendor allowance　See RETURNS AND ALLOWANCES FROM SUPPLIERS.

vendor analysis　An examination of how well a particular supplier performs. Included in the analysis are matters of price (Are they competitive? Are their terms reasonable?), matters of reliability (Is the merchandise of consistently high quality? Are deliveries on time?), and resale considerations (How much can the merchandise be marked up? What percentage will have to be marked down?). Essentially the same as RESOURCE ANALYSIS. See also VENDOR ANALYSIS FORM.

vendor analysis form　A computer-generated report used by a retail buyer. The report shows the gross margin for each style of each vendor. The information generated comes from data stored in the computer and is used to help the buyer evaluate vendors. See also VENDOR ANALYSIS, RESOURCE DIARY, RESOURCE ANALYSIS, and PRINCIPAL RESOURCE LIST.

vendor catalog　A book or pamphlet (i.e., a CATALOG) that includes merchandise offered for sale by a VENDOR, prepared for the use of the retail BUYER. The catalog often includes pictures or line lists to facilitate the buyer's selection process. Each item is given a style number that indicates to the manufacturer the particular season, silhouette, fabric, etc.

vendor characteristics　Factors considered in the selection of a resource (i.e., a VENDOR). Vendor characteristics include merchandise offered, the VENDOR DISTRIBUTION POLICY, PROMOTIONAL MERCHANDISE POLICY, advertising allowances, shipping and inventory maintenance, VENDOR COOPERATION, competitive pricing, and adherence to purchase order specifications.

vendor chargebacks　Goods returned to the vendor, accompanied by an adjusted invoice. See also RETURNS TO VENDOR (RTV).

vendor co-op　An agreement by a VENDOR to share with a store the expense of ADVERTISING or of hosting a special event. The manufacturer indicates the maximum dollar expenditure allowed or the specified percentage of the costs for which it will pay. Co-op advertising dollars may also be obtained from trade associations or (in the case of apparel) textile manufacturers. A typical co-op ad split is 50-50, with the vendor and the store each paying half of the expenses. In special cases, such as the opening of a new store or the introduction of a new vendor line, the manufacturer may contribute a greater percentage. See also COOPERATIVE ADVERTISING and PROMOTIONAL ALLOWANCE.

vendor cooperation　In selecting a vendor, the set of factors that amount to ways in which the vendor helps the buyer. Vendor cooperation includes the truthfulness of the sales representative's presentation, a willingness to provide promotional assistance, the presentation of special events, the provision of VISUAL MERCHANDISING materials, training in the use of certain products, and merchandise ticketing services.

vendor coupon　See MANUFACTURER COUPON.

vendor display　See DEALER DISPLAY, POINT-OF-PURCHASE (POP) DISPLAY, and VENDOR FIXTURE.

vendor distribution policy　A policy, adopted by some vendors (particularly in the apparel industry) that restricts certain parts of the collection to certain retailers. This endows the retailers with some degree of exclusivity without breaking the law. Other merchants may still carry the vendor's brand, but not the exact merchandise carried by the competition.

vendor event　A RETAIL PROMOTION featuring a single supplier, with the advertising expense shared by that supplier. See also VENDOR WEEK and CO-OP MONEY.

vendor fair　An opportunity for new suppliers (i.e., vendors) to sell their merchandise to a retail conglomerate's buyers. The vendor fair, which is run like an open house, is particularly directed at vendors whose merchandise fits the organization's merchandising objectives but who are not yet part of the retail organization's VENDOR MATRIX.

vendor fixture　A FIXTURE supplied by a manufacturer to retailers, specifically designed to display the manufacturer's products. Manufacturers provide these fixtures in order to control how their products are presented in hopes of strengthening their brand image. Also called a *vendor-supplied fixture* or a *vendor-provided fixture*. See also VENDOR SHOP and FIXTURING.

vendor helps　See DEALER HELPS.

vendor-managed inventory (VMI)　Technology that utilizes scanners at the retail level to gather information for manufacturers about the sales of their products in stores, catalogs, and on the Internet. VMI technology allows manufacturers to replenish retailers' inventories continuously, thus actively involving the vendor in making replenishment decisions for the retailer.

vendor matrix　A list of preferred vendors selected by a retail conglomerate. Inclusion depends on the product line's compatibility with the organization's merchandising objectives, favorable price negotiations, and various forms of vendor support in exchange for the retailer's commitment to space and established inventory levels. Some conglomerates limit their buyers to conducting business only with matrix vendors. This practice has streamlined vendor structures and reduced the number of vendors with whom the conglomerates conduct business by as much as 50 percent. However, use of a matrix also leads to large retailers dealing only with large suppliers, limiting business opportunities for small suppliers. Another possible criticism of the vendor matrix is that it reduces the buying function to an order filling function by limiting a buyer's autonomy. To negate these criticisms, some retailers host a periodic VENDOR FAIR to give vendors outside the matrix the opportunity to sell to the organization's buyers. The use of a vendor matrix in the buying process is called *matrix buying*.

vendor money   Synonym for CO-OP MONEY.

vendor paid markdown   Synonym for PRICE GUARANTEE.

vendor partnership   A collaboration between a supplier (i.e., a vendor) and a retailer that goes beyond the traditional interactions and results in greater channel efficiency and better service to consumers. These partnerships often involve strategies for moving goods through the CHANNEL OF DISTRIBUTION more rapidly and efficiently. The net results are often reduced distribution costs, better inventory control, increased sales, and improved gross margin and GMROI. Vendor partnership interactions include, for example, the provision of FLOOR-READY MERCHANDISE (FRM), MARKDOWN ALLOWANCE, promotional support, and ELECTRONIC DATA INTERCHANGE (EDI).

vendor premarking/preticketing   The procedure by which the manufacturer attaches price tags and labels to merchandise in accordance with the retailer's specifications prior to shipping. Merchandise so marked is referred to as *prepriced product* or *prepriced merchandise*. Also called *manufacturer's marking*, *manufacturer's preticketing*, *manufacturer's premarking*, *manufacturer's ticketing*, *prepricing*, and *source marking*.

vendor-provided fixture   Synonym for VENDOR FIXTURE. See also FIXTURING.

vendor relationship   The mutual respect, trust, and cooperation that ideally exist between the buyer and the seller. This, however, is not always the case, and retailers (particularly smaller retailers) may rely on a few key vendors to protect themselves from being edged out by larger competitors.

vendor reliability   The ability of the vendor to meet the conditions of its contract with the store.

vendor return   In a retail DISTRIBUTION CENTER (DC), the function of processing returns of damaged or slow-selling goods to suppliers for credit. See also RETURNS TO VENDOR (RTV).

vendor sales report   A weekly sales report prepared by a retailer. The report is arranged by major vendors for each department within the store or stores. The report includes this year's and last year's sales by vendor, the percentage change from last year's sales to this year's sales, and sales penetration by vendor. The report includes week-to-date, month-to-date, season-to-date, and year-to-date figures.

vendor shop   Fixtures, signage, graphics, and décor elements provided by manufacturers to retailers to create an entire shop-within-a-shop for their brand within the store. The fixtures are designed as modules that can be extended, contracted, added onto, or rearranged to suit the spatial requirements. The vendor shop is often a miniature of the brand name or designer's freestanding store, located within a major department or specialty store. Here the vendor tries to recreate, in the limited space, the essence of the retail image presented in the freestanding store. Manufacturers provide the vendor shop in order to control how their products are presented and to strengthen their brand image. Retailers welcome the vendor shops as a way of benefiting from the national or worldwide advertising campaigns and special promotions sponsored by the brand name or designer. The right mix of vendor shops adds stature to the store's own fashion image. See also VENDOR FIXTURE.

vendor-supplied fixture   Synonym for VENDOR FIXTURE. See also FIXTURING.

vendor week   A SPECIAL EVENT that features a particular vendor (e.g., Levi's). The event may be store-specific (i.e., at one store) or involve several competing retailers. During the week, in-store events are held at the participating stores to increase sales of the vendor's merchandise. Events may include fashion shows, celebrity appearances, musical performances, etc. See also VENDOR EVENT and CATEGORY WEEK.

venture capital   Funds invested or available for investment in a new business enterprise. Also called *risk capital*. See also VENTURE CAPITALIST.

venture capitalism   See VENTURE CAPITALIST.

venture capitalist   An investment specialist who raises capital to fund new businesses in exchange for a portion of their ownership. Venture capitalists typically fund those businesses that seem likely to evolve into public corporations. The investment funds available to venture capital firms come from corporations, wealthy individuals, pension funds, and other pools of capital, such as university endowments. See also START-UP (COMPANY), SMALL BUSINESS INVESTMENT COMPANY (SBIC), and MINORITY ENTERPRISE SMALL BUSINESS INVESTMENT COMPANY (MESBIC).

venture team   A group of specialists within a firm, brought together for the specific purpose of planning and developing a new product and introducing it into the marketplace. Venture teams are usually disbanded when their assignments have been completed. Also called a *special project team*. See also PRODUCT PLANNING COMMITTEE.

venue   A location where special events (such as fashion shows) or entertainments take place.

VER   See VOLUNTARY EXPORT RESTRICTION (VERS).

vertical advertising   See VERTICAL COOPERATIVE ADVERTISING.

vertical channel conflict   Dissonance between channel members at different levels in the distribution chain (e.g., between producers and wholesalers or between wholesalers and retailers). Also called *vertical conflict*. Compare HORIZONTAL CHANNEL CONFLICT. See also CHANNEL CONFLICT.

vertical channel integration   See VERTICAL INTEGRATION.

vertical conflict   See VERTICAL CHANNEL CONFLICT.

vertical cooperative advertising   A strategy in which advertising costs are shared by a seller and a reseller (commonly a manufacturer and a retailer) involving more than one level of the market. Ads are run at the local level by the retailer and part of the cost is reimbursed by the manufacturer upon receipt of verification (generally in the form of a TEAR SHEET) that the ads were actually run. Also called *vertical advertising*. See also COOPERATIVE ADVERTISING and VENDOR CO-OP. Compare HORIZONTAL COOPERATIVE ADVERTISING.

vertical fashion trend   See DOWNWARD FLOW THEORY.

vertical industrial market   A narrow market for industrial goods, in which nearly every organization is a potential customer.

vertical integration   The ownership, achieved by merger or internal expansion, of the marketing channel intermediaries connecting the manufacturer/producer with the consumer. Vertical integration may be accomplished through FORWARD INTEGRATION (the manufacturer owns its own distribution network and retail outlets) or through BACKWARD INTEGRATION (in which the retailer controls the sources of supply). Also called *channel integration*, *vertical channel integration*, *corporate distribution system*, and *total vertical integration*. See also DUAL DISTRIBUTION and INTEGRATED RETAILING.

vertically integrated channel   A CHANNEL OF DISTRIBUTION in which marketing intermediaries at various levels are owned or controlled by a single management. See also VERTICAL INTEGRATION.

vertical mall   Generally found in downtown areas, the vertical mall is a SHOPPING CENTER occupying the lower floors of a high-rise, multiuse building, the upper floors of which may be devoted to offices and/or residential space. The renovation of downtown areas, the scarcity of land, and the concentration of customers in urban areas have contributed to the development of vertical malls such as Trump Tower and the Time Warner Building in New York City. Also called *vertical shopping center*.

vertical marketing system (VMS)   A large, centrally managed, industrial organization in which two or more levels of the market (i.e., manufacturing, wholesaling, or retailing) are controlled by a dominant member of the channel. The system may be organized in one of three ways: as an ADMINISTERED VERTICAL MARKETING SYSTEM, CORPORATE VERTICAL MARKETING SYSTEM, or CONTRACTUAL VERTICAL MARKETING SYSTEM. Vertical marketing systems aim at operating economies resulting from greater size, increased efficiency achieved through closer control, economies achieved through the elimination of duplicated activities, and increased bargaining power resulting from large-scale operations. See also TOTAL SYSTEMS COMPETITION.

vertical merger   A MERGER that involves companies in different phases of the same business. For example, a manufacturer of children's toys may merge with a retailer of children's toys. The aim of a vertical merger is often to guarantee access to supplies or to markets.

vertical portal   See PORTAL.

vertical price fixing   See RESALE PRICE MAINTENANCE (RPM).

vertical price maintenance   See RESALE PRICE MAINTENANCE (RPM).

vertical shopping center   See VERTICAL MALL.

very profitable item (VPI)   Merchandise that a retailer believes to be easy to sell to consumers.

very small aperture terminal (VSAT)   A satellite communication system linked to a computer network without using telephone lines. VSAT allows retailers and other businesses to communicate crucial information faster and more accurately, giving participants a competitive advantage.

vest pocket supermarket   Synonym for BANTAM STORE.

vice president (VP) of finance   In a traditional retail organization (such as a department store), the executive responsible for accounts payable, accounts receivable, inventory control, customer charge accounts, merchandise information systems, and finance. May also be called the CORPORATE CONTROLLER. See also FINANCIAL CONTROL DIVISION.

vice president (VP) of human resources   In a traditional retail organization (such as a department store), the executive responsible for hiring, maintaining, and training store personnel. See also HUMAN RESOURCES DIVISION.

vice president (VP) of marketing   Synonym for MARKETING MANAGER.

vice president (VP) of merchandising   In a traditional retail organization (such as a department store), the executive who oversees divisional merchandise managers (DMMs), buyers, and assistant buyers. May also be called the GENERAL MERCHANDISE MANAGER (GMM). See also MERCHANDISING DIVISION.

vice president (VP) of operations   In a traditional retail organization (such as a department store), the executive to whom the warehouse and store managers, department sales managers, and salespeople report. See also OPERATIONS DIVISION.

vice president (VP) of sales promotion   In a traditional retail organization (such as a department store), the executive in charge of advertising, public relations, and VISUAL MERCHANDISING. Also called a *promotion vice president*. See also PROMOTION DIVISION.

VICS   See VOLUNTARY INTERINDUSTRY COMMERCE STANDARDS ASSOCIATION (VICS).

VICS EDI (Retail Users Group)   See VOLUNTARY INTERINDUSTRY COMMERCE STANDARD (VICS EDI).

video catalog   A catalog produced on videocassettes used in NONSTORE RETAILING. Cassettes are sent to consumers to introduce new merchandise, demonstrate product features, and explain product uses. The use of video catalogs in the consumer market is largely confined to consumers of specialty, upscale products since the expense of mass mailings of video catalogs is prohibitive. Some marketers send the videocassettes only to potential customers who have actually requested them (e.g., in response to an advertisement).

videoconference   A conference conducted by means of television equipment, so that participants at different locations can interact. Business meetings, educational sessions, etc., may be conducted in this way. See also TELECONFERENCE and WEB CONFERENCE.

video datacasting   A technology that uses television airwaves to send INTERNET data, combining the best aspects of Internet technology and television. Using an Internet connection and a TV tuner card, viewers can receive data from broadcast television or satellite broadcasts on their computer screens. The technology is expected to enable people to participate in true INTERACTIVE RETAILING in the near future.

video-on-demand (VOD)   A type of interactive television viewing, usually via cable or satellite, in which viewers can control what and when they watch. See also PAY-PER-VIEW (PPV).

video online interview (VOI)   See ONLINE INTERVIEW.

video production show   A FASHION SHOW specifically produced to be videotaped and distributed to sales representatives or retailers. Common uses of videotaped fashion shows include POINT-OF-PURCHASE (POP) (used as sales promotion tools on the sales floor), instructional (for in-store training of sales personnel, illustrating fashion trends and special features of the product), and documentary videos (focusing on the designer or the behind-the-scenes activities of the manufacturer). Also called a *videotaped fashion show.*

video shopping services   Technology that allows retailers to present information, receive orders, and process customer transactions electronically. Video shopping services include merchandise catalogs on videodiscs and videocassettes, and in-store and in-home ordering systems.

videotaped fashion show   See VIDEO PRODUCTION SHOW.

view   Short for PAGE VIEW.

vignette display setting   See SEMIREALISTIC DISPLAY SETTING.

viral marketing   Word-of-mouth advertising that is spread through Internet chat rooms as well as in person. The marketing message or gossip is started by the marketers' employees who are paid to pose as regular participants in the chat. Most often they pose as young people who are savvy and "in the know." Marketers talk up the advantages of the product and describe how pleased they are that they have purchased it themselves. Other chat participants are relied upon to carry the message to their friends and acquaintances without ever realizing they have seen an advertisement. These messages are pri-

marily aimed at the youth market (i.e., teens and young adult consumers). The message spreads "like a virus," hence the term *viral.* Discussion boards, listservs, and other areas on the Internet can be used to build positive buzz about a brand. In essence, each recipient of the message becomes a potential new marketer for the product or service, helping to spread the word. The goal of viral marketing is to distribute one's message as widely as possible at minimal expense. See also GUERILLA MARKETING. Also called *undercover marketing* and *stealth marketing.*

virtual   Existing on, or by means of, computers (e.g., VIRTUAL REALITY or virtual discussions on the INTERNET).

virtual group   Synonym for CYBER GROUP.

virtual hosting   See WEB HOSTING.

virtual reality   A realistic simulation of an environment by a computer system. Virtual reality uses interactive software and hardware and includes three-dimensional graphics. See also VIRTUAL STORE.

virtual showroom   Synonym for ONLINE SHOWROOM.

virtual store   A representation of a retail store in VIRTUAL REALITY. Graphics and three-dimensional modeling are used to create the look and feel of a retail store on a computer screen, allowing retailers to study customer behavior in a controlled environment. See also SIMULATED SHOPPING ENVIRONMENT.

virus   A computer program designed to penetrate and infect a host computer or network. Often launched from infected e-mail, viruses range from mere nuisances to dangerous security problems that can crash a hard drive or steal data. Severe viruses can severely damage the user's hardware, software, or files. Also called a *computer virus.* While the terms TROJAN HORSE, WORM, and *virus* are often used interchangeably, they are not the same.

visibility   In retail site location, the ability of a location to be seen by either pedestrian or vehicular traffic.

visible inventory control   See EYEBALL CONTROL.

visible shrinkage   Stock shortages due to breakage or wear and tear on merchandise. This type of SHRINKAGE is accounted for as it takes place. Compare INVISIBLE SHRINKAGE (shrinkage discovered only through physical inventory).

visible supply   Stock in a DISTRIBUTION CENTER (DC) that is available to the retailer when needed. Compare INVISIBLE SUPPLY.

visitors (to a Web site)   One measure of a Web site's advertising effectiveness, equal to the total number of people who visit a Web site during a specified period. If an individual visits multiple times, each time is counted. Consequently, this is a duplicative measure. Compare UNIQUE VISITOR.

visual (inventory) control See EYEBALL CONTROL.

visual merchandising A strategy frequently used in retailing for the in-store presentation of merchandise so that it will be shown to its greatest advantage. Visual merchandising, which includes traditional DISPLAY techniques, increasingly involves planning store layout, décor, and activities that appeal to other senses, such as music. Effective visual merchandising makes it easier for the shopper to locate and self-select the desired merchandise and to accessorize and coordinate related items. It also provides information on sizes, colors, prices, etc. In these ways it takes some of the stress out of shopping, saves the shopper time, and makes the shopping experience more comfortable, convenient, and customer-friendly. The object of these efforts is to increase the sale of merchandise. Also called *display merchandising*.

visual merchandising calendar A tool developed to organize visual presentations for the manufacturing or retail business. For example, manufacturers will put together displays in their showrooms prior to the start of a market week. Retail stores present merchandise as window displays, interior displays, or special theme shops. Visual merchandising in the retail environment is frequently based on the FASHION THEME CALENDAR.

visual merchandising department In a retail organization, the part of the PROMOTION DIVISION involved in creating window and interior displays, developing signs and visual identity, and selecting merchandise fixtures and showcases. The department is also responsible for store planning, layout, and design. The head of the visual merchandising department is generally called the *director of visual merchandising*. See also DISPLAY, VISUAL MERCHANDISING, and STORE LAYOUT AND DESIGN.

visual merchandising director See VISUAL MERCHANDISING DEPARTMENT.

visual system of stock control See EYEBALL CONTROL.

VMI See VENDOR-MANAGED INVENTORY (VMI).

VMS See VERTICAL MARKETING SYSTEM (VMS).

VOD See VIDEO-ON-DEMAND (VOD).

VOI See ONLINE INTERVIEW.

void An incorrectly written sales slip or incorrect register transaction that has been invalidated and corrected. Slips are retained for audit.

volume The total value of a store's retail sales for a given period, usually a year, expressed in dollars.

volume advertisement In RETAIL PRODUCT ADVERTISING, an advertisement created for best-selling products. These tend to be classically styled items that remain popular for many years (e.g., wool pullover sweaters or polo shirts). Volume ads emphasize price and/or quality and immediate availability.

Typically, the products featured in the volume advertisement are offered in a wide range of sizes and colors.

volume bonus A reward, in the form of a QUANTITY (PRICE) DISCOUNT, offered for the purchase of large quantities of merchandise. See also ROBINSON-PATMAN ACT (1936).

volume discount A price reduction for large quantity or multiple purchases. Synonymous with *bulk discount*.

volume error The difference between actual demand and planned volume. For example, the retailer may underestimate demand and order too few of what turns out to be a very popular item. On the other hand, the retailer may order too many of an item that turns out to be a slow seller. The error can be reduced by reestimating customer demand after evaluating POS feedback.

volume fashion Synonym for MASS FASHION.

volume merchandise allowance A manufacturer's price reduction offered to a wholesaler or retailer for purchasing larger quantities of goods.

volume per SKU for the assortment (VSA) The average number of units available for sale per STOCK KEEPING UNIT (SKU). VSA allows retailers to quantify their assortments as to their diversity and focus (i.e., ASSORTMENT DIVERSITY). The general rule of thumb is that the more diverse the assortment, the less focused it is and the lower its financial productivity. Instead of ascribing the relative values of assortment width and assortment depth, the retailer can use the VSA to assign a numeric value to the assortment. The smaller the VSA, the more diverse the assortment. The larger the VSA, the more focused the assortment. VSA is calculated by dividing the number of units (ASSORTMENT VOLUME) by the total number of SKUs in the same assortment. For example, an assortment of 100 units with 50 SKUs has a VSA of 2, meaning it is more diverse; an assortment of 100 units with 5 SKUs has a VSA of 20, meaning it is more focused. See also ASSORTMENT DIVERSITY INDEX (ADI).

volume per SKU for the initial delivery (VSID) The number of units allocated, on average, for each STOCK KEEPING UNIT (SKU) in the initial delivery.

volume price zone Synonym for VOLUME ZONE.

volume purchasing Buying in large quantities.

volume seller Any item or class of items that sells in large quantities.

volume zone The range of prices covering middle-priced merchandise, aimed at customers who are moderately budget-conscious but tend to buy a lot of merchandise if they find it affordable. Also called the *volume price zone*. See also PRICE ZONE.

voluntary bankruptcy See BANKRUPTCY.

voluntary chain A voluntary association of independent retailers that is sponsored by a WHOLESALER. The member stores buy all or most of their merchandise from the sponsoring wholesaler, who in turn provides certain management services such as accounting systems, direction regarding display, standardized merchandise packages, central data processing, etc. Members of voluntary chains often display common identifying names or logos. Also known as a *voluntary cooperative, voluntary group, voluntary wholesale group, wholesaler-sponsored cooperative,* or *wholesaler-sponsored voluntary.* See also QUASI-CHAIN.

voluntary cooperative See VOLUNTARY CHAIN.

voluntary export restrictions (VERs) An agreement between countries to share markets by limiting foreign export sales. These arrangements frequently have a set duration and provide for some annual increase in foreign sales to the domestic market. Also called an *orderly marketing arrangement.*

voluntary group Synonym for VOLUNTARY CHAIN.

Voluntary Interindustry Commerce Standard (VICS EDI) A voluntary interindustry commerce standard used by the general merchandise retail industry for computer operations. VICS EDI is used by thousands of companies, including department and specialty retail stores, mass merchandisers, and their suppliers. The standards now support the following business functions: product development/merchandising; ordering; logistics; financial; business support; and import. See also ELECTRONIC DATA INTERCHANGE (EDI).

Voluntary Interindustry Commerce Standards Association (VICS) An association dedicated to improving the efficiency and effectiveness of the entire CHANNEL OF DISTRIBUTION. In 1991, VICS pioneered the implementation of cross-industry standard QUICK RESPONSE (QR) REPLENISHMENT SYSTEM that simplified the flow of products and information in the retail industry for both retailers and suppliers.

voluntary response See PHYSIOLOGICAL PROFILE.

voluntary simplicity A consumer lifestyle based on ecological awareness. These consumers seek material simplicity and durability, strive for self-reliance, and purchase more inexpensive products.

voluntary wholesale group See VOLUNTARY CHAIN.

voluntary wholesaler See VOLUNTARY CHAIN.

voucher See CREDIT SLIP.

VP Abbreviation for vice president.

VPI See VERY PROFITABLE ITEM (VPI).

VSA See VOLUME PER SKU FOR THE ASSORTMENT (VSA).

VSAT See VERY SMALL APERTURE TERMINAL (VSAT).

VSID See VOLUME PER SKU FOR THE INITIAL DELIVERY (VSID).

wage-price spiral See INFLATION.

wages Cash compensation to an employee based on a calculation of the number of hours worked or the number of items the employee has produced. Most blue-collar and some white-collar workers are remunerated in the form of wages. Wages produce a direct incentive to the worker; the more hours worked or the more pieces completed, the higher the worker's pay. Compare SALARY, which denotes a weekly, monthly, or yearly cash compensation for work. Sometimes called PAY.

Wagner Act See NATIONAL LABOR RELATIONS ACT (1935).

wagon distributor/jobber See TRUCK WHOLESALER.

wagon retailer A marketing intermediary engaged in selling anything for a profit.

waiting-line theory See QUEUING THEORY.

walk 1. n. (Slang) A customer who leaves the store (i.e., walks out) without making a purchase. Also called a *walk-out*. 2. v. (Slang) To be stolen (e.g., "If it's not bolted down, it will walk"). 3. v. (Slang) To go on strike (e.g., "The unionized employees decided to walk").

walk-by A shopper who passes by a store without entering. Compare WALK-IN.

walk-in A shopper who comes into the store to shop. VISUAL MERCHANDISING, particularly store windows, arouses the shopper's curiosity so that he or she enters the store on the spur of the moment and wanders through it. Compare WALK-BY.

walk-in shopper A customer who lacks the transportation necessary to get to a downtown area, a mall, or a shopping center and, consequently, shops at the most convenient local stores (literally, those to which the customer can walk).

walk-out 1. Synonym for WALK (def. 1). 2. A labor strike.

wall display An interior presentation made up of posters and/or actual merchandise hung from the walls of the store. Wall displays are used to attract the customer's attention and to promote the sale of particular merchandise. Also called a *wall setup* or a *wall presentation*.

wall divider An architectural or decorative design element used to separate a long wall into shorter, clearly defined sections. Dividers may be permanent, like architectural columns, semipermanent, like paints and textured wall coverings, or nonpermanent. A nonpermanent wall divider, such as an OUTRIGGER or a detachable panel for displaying coordinated outfits, may be repositioned as merchandise categories expand or contract. The materials used for wall dividers can help shape the store's ATMOSPHERICS and enhance its physical image. Also called, simply, a *divider*.

wall planogram See PLANOGRAM.

wall presentation See WALL DISPLAY.

wall setup See WALL DISPLAY.

wall system A system of full-height perimeter partitions and high partitions placed between departments. See also WALL DISPLAY.

wall system face-out A wall unit DISPLAY in which garments are arranged facing outward so that the customer sees the entire front of the item head on. See also WALL DISPLAY.

WAN See WIDE-AREA NETWORK (WAN).

wand Synonym for LIGHT PEN.

want See WANTS.

want book A book in which salespeople record the items requested by shoppers but not in stock or not carried by the store. This information is communicated to the BUYER as input for merchandise planning. Some retailers now create computer databases instead of using actual books.

wants In the study of CONSUMER BEHAVIOR, NEEDS that have been learned over the consumer's lifetime. For example, everyone experiences thirst, a need for a beverage, but some consumers have learned to want a particular brand of soft drink. See also MOTIVE.

want slip   Written notations given by salespersons to buyers, indicating items requested by customers but not in stock or not carried by the store. Some retailers compile this information into a WANT BOOK. Others enter the information into computer databases. These customer inquiries and sales staff suggestions provide input into merchandise planning.

WAP   See WIRELESS APPLICATION PROTOCOL (WAP).

warehouse   A commercial establishment in which large quantities of goods may be stored. Also called a *storage warehouse*. See also WAREHOUSING.

warehouse and requisition plan   A form of retail buying in which the CENTRAL BUYER selects merchandise in the market for a group of stores and has the initial stock for each store shipped to the store directly. The remainder of the merchandise is shipped to a central WAREHOUSE to which the store managers must send requisitions to meet customer demands.

warehouse club   A large, bare-bones retail store that sells a broad assortment of merchandise to small businesses as well as to families and individuals. Customers are required to enroll and pay a membership fee before shopping. See also CLUB PLAN SELLING. Also known as a *membership club* or *membership warehouse club*. Merchandise sold at warehouse clubs is often in the form of large, institutionally sized CLUB PACKS.

warehouse control system   A system of inventory control in which the store informs its warehouse of all sales so that the warehouse can adjust inventory records to reflect the change. The warehouse can, at any time, inform the store as to how much merchandise is available.

warehouse discounter   Synonym for WAREHOUSE STORE.

warehouse receipt   A written acknowledgment issued by a PUBLIC WAREHOUSE to the depositor of goods. This receipt may, in turn, be used by the depositor as collateral for obtaining loans, since the goods in the warehouse will not be released until the receipt has been surrendered. See also FIELD WAREHOUSER.

warehouse retailing   A form of mass merchandising carried out in facilities lacking traditional amenities. A *warehouse retailer* offers few customer services, pays low rent, and operates out of an isolated building reminiscent of a warehouse. Merchandise (especially food, appliances, and furniture) is sold at prices below regular retail in these facilities. See also SUPER WAREHOUSE (OUTLET/STORE), WAREHOUSE STORE, WAREHOUSE CLUB, and BOX STORE.

warehouse showroom   A DISCOUNT STORE that operates with low overhead and high turnover. The showroom, which features selections of the merchandise stored in the warehouse, is open to the public. Customers pay cash and, for the most part, must transport the merchandise themselves.

warehouse stock   Backup merchandise housed in a WAREHOUSE. Some of the merchandise will be moved into the store for sale on the floor. Other merchandise will be sold from the store, but shipped directly to consumers' homes or offices from the warehouse.

warehouse store   A no-frills retail operation where merchandise is stacked high on pallets, on wood or metal racks, or in open cartons. The objective is to cut presentation and storage costs so that the merchandise may be offered at the lowest possible cost. Also called a *warehouse discounter* or *box store*. See also SUPER WAREHOUSE (OUTLET/STORE).

warehousing   The storage of merchandise in facilities specially designed for that purpose. The merchandise is physically stored and held in anticipation of sales and transfers within the CHANNEL OF DISTRIBUTION. See also WAREHOUSE and MATERIALS HANDLING.

wares   Old-fashioned term for items of merchandise that are offered for sale.

warranty   A GUARANTEE given by the manufacturer of a product as to the product's quality and performance, with a statement relating the conditions under which the product will be replaced or repaired should it prove defective. A warranty may be verbalized (either orally or in writing), in which case it is an EXPRESSED WARRANTY, or it may be understood implicitly (i.e., there is a general understanding that the product is safe and in proper operating condition), in which case it is an IMPLIED WARRANTY. The law recognizes both. Also called a *product warranty*. See also MAGNUSON-MOSS WARRANTY ACT (1975) and PRODUCT RELIABILITY.

wash and wear   See DURABLE PRESS.

wash sale   (Slang) An illegal sale in which the seller becomes the purchaser of what he or she sells. The purpose of a wash sale is to create activity in the items or to establish a market price.

was-is pricing   See PSYCHOLOGICAL DISCOUNTING.

wastage   The deterioration of property as the result of wear or use.

waste circulation   In advertising, the number of persons reached by an ad campaign who are not potential customers for the product or service. Several factors may cause waste circulation, such as the unavailability of the product or service in the reached area. See also CIRCULATION.

wasting assets   Synonym for nonrenewable NATURAL RESOURCES.

water carrier   Any ship, freighter, barge, etc., used to transport goods. A slow but economical mode of transportation used by retailers primarily to import goods directly from foreign sources.

waterproof   Of clothing, not penetrable by water. Waterproof garments are usually of rubber, plastic, or heavily coated fabric.

waybill   Synonym for BILL OF LADING (B/L).

wayfinding   The process by which customers find their way around the store and locate the merchandise they seek. See also WAYFINDING TOOL/STRATEGY.

wayfinding tool/strategy   Any tool, device, or strategy that enables customers to find their way through a store, including signs positioned in highly visible areas (on walls or hanging from the ceiling) and lifestyle graphics indicating both product category and trend direction.

weakest link   The part of a product that wears out first. See also WEAKEST LINK THEORY.

weakest link theory   The theory that no part of a product should be so durable as to greatly outlast the part that wears out fastest (the *weakest link*), as the product will generally be discarded at that point.

weak market   A market situation characterized by low demand and high availability (i.e., supply). More of a product is available in the marketplace than there are buyers wanting to buy it.

wearout   The tendency of consumer response to a SALES PROMOTION to diminish over time (i.e., wear out).

weather   Atmospheric conditions seen as a cause of slow sales of merchandise, possibly resulting in a MARKDOWN (MD). Unseasonable weather affects the sale of seasonal goods such as boots, wool sweaters, patio furniture, shorts, etc.

Web   Short for WORLD WIDE WEB (WWW).

Web address   See UNIFORM RESOURCE LOCATOR (URL).

Web advertising clutter   See CLUTTER.

Web advertising metrics   The ensemble of methods used to measure online advertising. These include COST PER THOUSAND (CPM), PAGE IMPRESSION (each single opportunity to see an ad), CONVERSION RATE (proportion of audience members who respond to an ad and become customers), and CLICK THROUGH (each instance of a visitor clicking on a banner ad so as to activate the hypertext link and be linked to the advertiser's site).

Web analysis/analytics   The process of, and technology involved in, collecting, organizing, and analyzing the huge amount of data needed to plan, track, and evaluate marketing applications of E-TAILING and other forms of E-COMMERCE. Professionals trained in Web analytics, including the required software, analyze results and evaluate changes in channel strategy.

Web beacon   A single-pixel electronic GIF image placed on a Web page by a third-party media and research company. Used in conjunction with COOKIES, Web beacons greatly increase the number of Web sites where data can be collected. Web beacons, also called *bugs*, collect Non-Personally Identifiable Information (NP-II) such as a user's cookie number, the time and date when a page was viewed, and a description of the page where the Web beacon is placed. They also give the e-marketer the ability to track cookies on more than one site, since the beacons record visits resulting from links from the original site to other Web sites. The information is sent to the third party. See also NETWORK ADVERTISING INITIATIVE (NAI).

Web browser   See BROWSER.

Web budget   Short for WEB MARKETING BUDGET.

Web bug   See WEB BEACON.

Webb-Pomerene Export Trade Act (1918)   U.S. legislation to encourage domestic companies to do business abroad. The act allows U.S. companies to cooperate in developing export markets without running afoul of the antitrust laws that limit joint activities in the United States. See also the EXPORT TRADING COMPANIES ACT (1982).

Webcast   An audio, video, or audio-video streaming broadcast on the WORLD WIDE WEB (WWW). Some Webcasts are live, others are rebroadcasts, many are archived, and a large number consist of streaming audio from traditional radio stations.

Webcast ad   Advertising sold on the WORLD WIDE WEB (WWW) by a WEBCASTER. Revenue is generated by selling in-stream ads that appear within the streamed content and gateway ads that appear on the page carrying the link to the Webcast. Most Webcasters sell a combination of forms of advertising, including the SPONSORSHIP, the IN-STREAM AD, and the GATEWAY AD.

Webcaster   A broadcaster who utilizes the WORLD WIDE WEB (WWW) instead of or in addition to the airwaves (as in traditional radio and television broadcasting) to transmit audio, video, or audio-video streaming broadcasts.

Webcasting   The broadcasting of news, entertainment, etc., using the INTERNET, especially the WORLD WIDE WEB (WWW). See also WEBCAST.

Web conference   A conference conducted by means of computer equipment on the INTERNET, so that participants at different locations can communicate and interact. Business meetings, educational sessions, etc. may be conducted using this method. See also TELECONFERENCE and VIDEOCONFERENCE.

Webcrawler   Synonym for SPIDER.

Weber's Law   See JUST NOTICEABLE DIFFERENCE (JND).

Web exchange   A business, such as eBay, that acts as a manager for others' buying and selling activities. A Web exchange facilitates auctions and other commercial activities for consumers as well as for other businesses. A B2B WEB EXCHANGE uses its software and management expertise to bring business, industrial, government, or nonprofit buyers and sellers together to negotiate sales, schedule payments, arrange deliveries, and provide after-sale service.

Web host   See HOST and WEB HOSTING.

Web hosting   The business of being a HOST on the Web, that is, providing the equipment and services required to maintain files for one or more Web sites and provide fast Internet connection to those sites. Most hosting is shared (i.e., the Web sites of multiple companies are on the same server) in order to cut costs. *Virtual hosting* means that services will be transparent, so that each site has its own DOMAIN NAME and E-MAIL addresses. *Dedicated hosting* means that the hosting company provides all the equipment and assumes all the technical support for the WEB SITE. Also called *Web site hosting*, *page hosting*, or (simply) *hosting*.

Web host name   See HOST NAME.

Weblog   See BLOG.

Web marketing budget   A blueprint for allocating funds to various Web marketing activities. It is a detailed plan that identifies priority spending areas and shows how marketing will be conducted to achieve its performance goals. A Web marketing budget may be part of the overall marketing budget or a separate entity. Also called the *Web budget*.

Web marketing plan   In e-tailing, a MARKETING PLAN whose methodology has been transferred to the electronic marketing environment. The Web marketing plan may be freestanding, particularly for CLICKS-ONLY retailers that market exclusively on the Web, or integrated into a traditional marketing plan that may or may not include other Internet vehicles such as e-mail. It consists of a detailed set of instructions for the conduct of marketing on the business's WEB SITE over a specified period of time. It includes an OPERATIONAL MARKETING PLAN specifying the steps that will be taken in order to help the e-tail firm achieve its marketing goals in keeping with its mission statement and business plan goals. If the firm is a BRICKS-AND-CLICKS marketer, the Web marketing plan also specifies how the two aspects will work together. The Web marketing plan includes company and market analysis, marketing mix analysis, an action plan, financials, and controls and feedback mechanisms. See also WEB READINESS.

Webmaster   An individual responsible for the execution of the design of a WEB SITE and for regular technical maintenance of the site. See also WEB SITE PROJECT DIRECTOR.

Web page   A HYPERTEXT document on the WORLD WIDE WEB (WWW) that can include text, graphics, sound, etc. Sometimes used synonymously with WEB SITE or HOME PAGE.

Web page roadblock   A practice in which one advertiser purchases all available space on a page, or a site owner serves house ads only. This practice emulates the advertising ROADBLOCK set up on early network television channels to capture viewers who avoided ads by changing channels.

Web readiness   A firm's ability to operate successfully in an ONLINE environment. Web readiness is examined from management, cost, and human resources perspectives. S.W.O.T. ANALYSIS is often used to determine a firm's readiness to engage in E-TAILING or other E-MARKETING activities. See also WEB MARKETING PLAN.

Webscape   See WEB SITE ATMOSPHERICS.

Web site   A location on the WORLD WIDE WEB (WWW). Each Web site contains a home page, which is the first screen that visitors see when they enter the site. The site may also contain additional documents and files, each of which is called a *Web page*. Each site is owned and managed by an individual, company, or organization. See also TRANSACTION WEB SITE and INFORMATION WEB SITE.

Web site atmospherics   Design elements, comparable to the ATMOSPHERICS of a physical store, used throughout the various pages of a site to establish a mood and consistent image. A site can be thought of visually as a landscape on the Web, or a *Webscape*. Consistency is achieved by adopting a page model and replicating it for each page in the site. This template specifies primary, secondary, and complementary colors; font type and size; graphics; navigation bars, buttons, marks, and icons; and other elements standardized across the site. Also called *site atmospherics*.

Web site construction   The technical processes that make a WEB SITE accessible and functional as planned. Web site construction for the e-tailer includes service center operations, order processing, and CUSTOMER RELATIONSHIP MANAGEMENT (CRM). See also BACKEND CONSTRUCTION. Also called *site construction*.

Web site content   The substance of a WEB SITE, including information about products, special features, market offers, and services that customers want to access and the e-tailer needs to provide. In short, content is what visitors seek at a site. Online content refers to both verbal and textual elements, such as newspaper stories, product descriptions, magazine articles, dictionaries, travel schedules, etc., and to nonverbal elements, such as images, graphics, interactive devices, etc.

Web site design   The way a WEB SITE looks and feels (i.e., its structure and organization and visual and aural appeal). Web site design includes layout, the integration of text, colors, and images, use and positioning of graphics, and other elements. Also called *site design*.

Web site flow (aesthetics)   The aspect of WEB SITE DESIGN that enables visitors to navigate the space easily because of its familiarity and flow. *Web site flow* is comparable to the flow of traffic in BRICKS-AND-MORTAR stores. When customers are so familiar with the store layout and the location of frequently purchased products, they can navigate the space easily without conscious effort. Also called *site flow aesthetics*.

Web site hosting   See WEB HOSTING.

Web site launch   The act of putting one's WEB SITE up on the WORLD WIDE WEB (WWW). After the initial launch, sites need to be maintained, kept up, and redesigned on a regular basis. Also called *site launch*.

Web site management   The ongoing maintenance and refreshment of a WEB SITE so that the information it provides is always up to date. For an E-TAILER, Web site management includes keeping the prices and merchandise offerings current as well as keeping up with the latest developments in Web site design. External links must also be checked constantly to make sure they are still active. Also called *site management*.

Web site project director   The individual in an online E-TAILING or other E-MARKETING firm responsible for making sure the WEB SITE serves the needs of its customers. The Web site project director works with brand managers, graphic and interface designers, information system architects, programmers, usability experts, and others to create and maintain the site. See also WEBMASTER.

Web site redesign   The ongoing revision of a WEB SITE to make sure that it is appropriately linked, is presented in an organized way, and utilizes the latest features and programs to facilitate Internet shopping. Customer feedback, focus group results, and server log files that track site use can indicate when redesign is required. In addition, Web site redesign may be triggered by the Web activity of competitors. Also called *site redesign*.

Web storefront   A highly visible TRANSACTION WEB SITE through which e-tailers and other electronic merchants can sell products directly. Web storefronts may be CLICKS-ONLY or BRICKS-AND-CLICKS.

Web storyboarding   A process that identifies what will be contained on Web pages, in terms of text, graphics, and interactive features, and how the pages will be linked. A similar process is used in television advertising; see STORYBOARD.

Web surfing   See SURFING.

WebTV   A technology representing the convergence of television, computers, and the INTERNET. A black box sitting on a television set lets the viewer surf the Internet and check e-mail. The consumer purchases the box and pays a monthly Internet access fee.

weed out   To identify slow-moving merchandise and remove it from stock.

weekly percent sell   An indicator used by some retailers to determine weeks of supply. The weekly percent sell is the percent of stock on hand that will sell in one week at the current rate of sale. The higher the percentage, the faster the inventory will turn. See also WEEKS OF SUPPLY METHOD.

weeks of supply method   A method for planning inventory for fast-selling merchandise that has to be planned for shorter periods of time than the usual month. The method is based on the idea that the amount of inventory required to support planned sales for a week is driven by the number of weeks that the inventory will last based on a projected turnover. Weeks of supply is calculated by dividing 52 (the number of weeks in a year) by the projected turnover. For example, if the desired turnover is 6.0, then weeks of supply is $52 \div 6 = 8.7$, meaning that in order to achieve an annual turnover of 6.0, a buyer must have sufficient inventory on hand throughout the year to support 8.7 weeks of sales. See also DAYS OF SUPPLY.

week's supply method   A method of retail inventory planning based on the amount of stock expected to be sold in one week. Turnover is regarded as uniform so that inventory levels may be planned in one-week multiples. Week's supply is calculated by dividing 52, the number of weeks in a year, by the desired STOCK TURNOVER (ST).

weighted average   1. An average that takes into account the proportional relevance of each component, rather than treating each component equally. The more important elements of the equation are given additional weight by being multiplied by a preset number.   2. In retailing, a periodic INVENTORY cost flow assumption whereby the cost of goods sold and the ending inventory are determined to be a weighted average cost (i.e., a cost given weight or importance above that of other factors in the equation) of all merchandise available for sale during the period.

wellness trend   See BEING ALIVE.

wet goods   Liquid merchandise.

Wheeler-Lea Act (1938)   An amendment to the FEDERAL TRADE COMMISSION ACT (FTCA) (1914) authorizing the FEDERAL TRADE COMMISSION (FTC) to protect consumers in general as well as competitors. It outlaws unfair methods of competition and unfair and deceptive acts and practices. It also deals with truth in advertising, and declared illegal the false advertising of foods, drugs, cosmetics, and therapeutic devices. Also known as the *Wheeler-Lea Amendment (1938)*. See also PHONY LIST PRICE.

wheel of retailing theory/concept   A theory propounded by Malcolm P. McNair (Harvard Business School, 1958), viewing retail institutional change according to a cycle of stages. Retail innovators begin the growth cycle as low-status, low-margin, low-price operators. A period follows during which facilities become more elaborate, costs increase, and higher margins are required to survive. Eventually, the innovators come to resemble the conventional retailers they hoped to replace, and the cycle begins again with the next low-margin innovator. The complete cycle is envisioned as one turn of the wheel. Also called, simply, the *wheel of retailing*.

white-collar worker   See SOCIAL CLASS.

white goods   1. Appliances of substantial size and cost, such as refrigerators, freezers, washing machines, and stoves. The name is derived from the white enamel finish commonly used. See also MAJOR APPLIANCES (MAJAPS). Compare BROWN

GOODS.   2. Sheets, pillowcases, and linens, etc. These items are so named because of the early tradition of manufacturing them only in white. Under a different classification system based on frequency of replacement, these are called YELLOW GOODS because they are generally replaced only after many years of service. Compare RED GOODS and ORANGE GOODS.

white knight   In hostile acquisitions and takeovers, a corporation that rescues another in a takeover fight. The knight rescues the embattled firm by agreeing to acquire it on better terms than the pursuer would provide. For example, the white knight may offer a higher purchase price for the company's stock and assurances that executives will not be forced to use their GOLDEN PARACHUTE. See also ACQUISITION.

white mail   Customer correspondence received in the customer's own envelope rather than the remittance envelope provided by the retailer. White mail often includes customer inquiries, complaints, or changes of address.

white sale   A special promotion featuring sheets, pillowcases, towels, and similar WHITE GOODS. January is the traditional time for white sales. Also called a *linen sale*.

white space   In advertising layout, the portion of an advertisement that is not used for text or illustrations. In general, the more white space in an advertisement, the more upscale the store. Discount stores, seeking to maximize the utility of their more limited advertising expenditure, are likely to use little white space in their ads.

whole market approach/method   A marketing method geared to the entire range of potential customers, neither recognizing nor attempting to appeal to the differences between various segments of the market. Essentially the same as UNDIFFERENTIATED MARKETING. Compare MARKET SEGMENTATION.

wholesale   The sale of goods to retailers, other wholesalers, and business, institutional, or industrial users. See also WHOLESALING and WHOLESALER.

wholesale club   See CLOSED-DOOR DISCOUNT HOUSE.

wholesale cooperative   A full service merchant WHOLESALER owned by member firms to economize distribution functions and offer broad member support. The wholesale cooperative may be owned by retailers or producers. Also called *wholesaler cooperative*.

wholesale merchant   See FULL SERVICE WHOLESALER.

wholesale presentation   See LINE PRESENTATION.

wholesale price   The price charged by a manufacturer, vendor, or other resource for its merchandise.

Wholesale Price Index   A percentage used to compare wholesale prices for goods in one period with those in a base or standard period. Now largely replaced in the United States and the United Kingdom by the PRODUCER PRICE INDEX (PPI). Compare CONSUMER PRICE INDEX (CPI).

wholesaler   A term applied to a category of WHOLESALING MIDDLEMAN primarily engaged in buying merchandise from a producer and selling it to an industrial user, institutional user, or retailer, but seldom to the ultimate consumer. The wholesaler ordinarily takes title to and possession of the goods sold. Wholesalers fall into two broad categories: the full function or FULL SERVICE WHOLESALER who performs a number of functions including assembly, warehousing, breaking bulk, selling, delivery, credit extension, etc., and the limited function or LIMITED SERVICE WHOLESALER who performs fewer service functions. Wholesalers are sometimes called *merchant wholesalers, service wholesalers, jobbers,* or *distributors*.

wholesaler merchant   See FULL SERVICE WHOLESALER.

wholesaler-sponsored cooperative   Synonym for VOLUNTARY CHAIN.

wholesaler-sponsored (retail) franchise   See FRANCHISING.

wholesale-sponsored cooperative   See VOLUNTARY CHAIN.

wholesaler-sponsored voluntary   Synonym for VOLUNTARY CHAIN.

wholesaler's salesperson   A sales representative of a wholesale firm who calls on retailers (and sometimes manufacturers) who are the wholesaler's customers.

wholesale transaction   Any nonretail sale. Wholesale transactions include sales by manufacturers to marketing intermediaries and retailers, sales by manufacturers to other manufacturers, sales from farmers to processors, government sales, etc.

wholesaling   The sale of goods to retailers, other wholesalers, and business, institutional, or industrial users for the purpose of resale, use in performing the organization's basic functions, or incorporation into another product. The most important function of wholesaling is breaking bulk (i.e., providing buyers with manageable lots of merchandise that the wholesaler has bought in large quantities). See also WHOLESALER.

wholesaling intermediary   Any firm that engages primarily in WHOLESALING activities. See also WHOLESALER.

wholesaling middleman   A term generally applied to a number of marketing intermediaries including a WHOLESALER, AGENT, BROKER, MANUFACTURER'S BRANCH OFFICE, MANUFACTURER'S SALES OFFICE, and certain cooperative organizations. A wholesaling middleman is also known as a *marketing middleman, merchant intermediary,* and *merchant middleman*.

Wholesome Meat Act (1967)   U.S. federal legislation enacted to protect the consumer by strengthening the standards of slaughterhouse and red meat inspection. See also MEAT INSPECTION ACT (1906).

wholly owned subsidiary   1. A separate firm, owned and completely controlled by a PARENT (COMPANY/ORGANIZATION). 2. In international marketing, a type of JOINT VENTURE in which the operations in the host country are fully owned by a foreign parent firm.

wide-area network (WAN)   A system of local-area computer networks that connects them to each other and to similar networks over any distance via telephone lines and radio waves. See also LOCAL-AREA NETWORK (LAN) and COMPUTER NETWORK.

width   See PRODUCT WIDTH and ASSORTMENT BREADTH.

width of assortment   See ASSORTMENT BREADTH.

wildcat   (Slang) Synonym for PROBLEM CHILD.

will call   A term applied to merchandise for which the customer has paid in full and which will be picked up at some future time. The term is sometimes used as a synonym for LAYAWAY.

window display   Store merchandise attractively arranged in a store's DISPLAY WINDOW to attract the attention of passersby. Window displays reflect the style and quality of the store's merchandise. The goal of a window display is to attract potential customers into the store.

windowless window   Used primarily in enclosed shopping malls, windowless windows are open store entrances. The wide openings at the front of the store are intended to increase customer traffic and make shopping easier. However, security is sometimes a risk, since the open format also makes shoplifting easier.

window shopping   1. In a BRICKS-AND-MORTAR environment, consumer activities that involve looking at merchandise but not necessarily making purchases. Consumers may literally browse a store's exterior windows or browse within the store itself to see what is available, get a feeling for current styles, engage in COMPARISON SHOPPING, plan future purchases, etc. Also called *browsing*. 2. In the E-TAILING environment, the act of browsing an e-tailer's WEB SITE without making a purchase. Online consumers may use the information they gather about a store and its products to guide their offline purchases in the physical store (i.e., in a BRICKS-AND-CLICKS environment). Alternatively, consumers may use that information to engage in COMPARISON SHOPPING, possibly resulting in a purchase from a competitor's Web site or physical store. See also SHOPBOT.

window store   A store that attracts customers primarily by means of its window displays rather than through other forms of advertising. See also WINDOW DISPLAY.

window wall   The fourth wall of a DISPLAY WINDOW, typically made of glass. See also SIDE WALL.

win-win situation   (Slang) A state of affairs in which both the purchaser and the seller are pleased with their completed transaction.

wireless   Of telecommunication technology, using radio waves, infrared waves, and microwaves (instead of cables or wires) to carry a signal. Wireless devices include pagers, cell phones, portable PCs, computer networks, location devices, satellite systems, and handheld digital assistants (i.e., PDAs). Wireless technology enables users to move around while using a given device. See also WIRELESS ACCESS, NONCABLED POINT-OF-SALE, and PERSONAL DIGITAL ASSISTANT (PDA).

wireless access   Connection to the Internet by means of portable computers, desktop computers, small-screen devices and cell phones with WIRELESS APPLICATION PROTOCOL (WAP) capability to connect to the Internet without telephone connections or other cables. Also called *wireless Net access*. See also WIRELESS and PERSONAL DIGITAL ASSISTANT (PDA).

wireless advertising   Synonym for MOBILE AD.

Wireless Application Protocol (WAP)   A secure specification that allows users to access information instantly via handheld wireless devices such as cell phones, pagers, two-way radios, etc.

wireless handheld computer/device   See PERSONAL DIGITAL ASSISTANT (PDA).

wireless Net access   See WIRELESS ACCESS.

wireless point-of-sale   Synonym for NONCABLED POINT-OF-SALE.

withdrawal   In CONSIGNMENT sales, an item bought out of a consignment. The CONSIGNEE (i.e., reseller or agent) reports on and pays for these items on a periodic schedule.

without recourse   Of an agreement between a purchaser and a seller, stipulating that the purchaser accepts all risks in the transaction and gives up all rights to file a claim against the seller. Compare WITH RECOURSE. See also RISK.

with-pack premium   A free gift or other item packed inside or on the outside of another product.

with recourse   Of an agreement between a purchaser and a seller, giving the purchaser the right to file a claim against the seller for sustained damages if the seller is unable to meet the obligations of the contract. Compare WITHOUT RECOURSE. See also RISK.

wobbler   (Slang) A sign constructed on a spring assembly that allows it to jiggle to attract customer attention. Wobblers are frequently found in grocery and drug stores. Compare AISLE INTERRUPTER and DANGLER.

WOM communication   See WORD-OF-MOUTH (WOM) COMMUNICATION.

women's sizes   Synonym for PLUS SIZES.

Wool Products Labeling Act (1939; 1941)   U.S. federal legislation requiring products containing wool to carry a label indicating the fiber content. The law further stipulated that the label must specify whether the wool was wool, new wool, or virgin wool (all of which have never been used before) or recycled wool (wool that had been returned to the fibrous state). Contents of various types of wool constituting more than 5 percent of the total content must also be stated on the garment's label by percentage.

word-of-mouth (WOM) communication   Personal communication via the spoken word. Although not strictly speaking a form of advertising, it can be crucially important to the success or failure of certain business endeavors, as, for example, the success of a motion picture. In the age of online communication, CHAT and VIRAL MARKETING supplement in-person, face-to-face communication. Also called *word-of-mouth marketing* and *buzz marketing*. See also SOCIAL CHANNEL and MARKETING COMMUNICATION.

word-of-mouth influence   See SOCIAL CHANNEL and WORD-OF-MOUTH (WOM) COMMUNICATION.

word-of-mouth marketing   See WORD-OF-MOUTH (WOM) COMMUNICATION.

Workers' Compensation Insurance   Insurance that partially replaces lost income, medical costs, and rehabilitation expenses for employees injured on the job. It also provides death benefits to the survivors of any employee killed on the job. Workers' Compensation Insurance is required by law throughout the United States, though its administration varies somewhat from state to state. Workers Compensation laws include some that are designed to protect employers and fellow workers by limiting the amount an injured employee can recover from an employer and by eliminating the liability of co-workers in most accidents. State Workers' Compensation statutes establish this framework for most employment. Federal statutes are limited to federal employees or those workers employed in some significant aspect of interstate commerce. Familiarly called *Workers' Comp*.

working capital   The money being used, at any given time, to run a business. Working capital represents the excess of current assets over current liabilities. See also CURRENT ASSET and CURRENT LIABILITY.

working hypothesis   See HYPOTHESIS.

workload   The amount of work that a machine, employee, or group of employees is expected to perform.

workload analysis   1. A method used to assign members of a sales force by dividing the total WORKLOAD in hours by the number of selling hours available from each salesperson.   2. The practice of estimating the sales activities needed to fulfill the potential of a sales territory.   3. A similar analysis used to determine the appropriate workload for a machine, employee, or group of employees (i.e., other than the sales force).

workroom   In a retail store, a part of the NONSELLING AREA devoted to such support services as apparel alterations, drapery fabrication, etc. See also WORKROOM CHARGES.

workroom charges   The price placed on services performed in the workrooms of retail stores (e.g., alterations of apparel). See also STORE SERVICES and WORKROOM.

world corporation organization   A form of decentralized organizational structure applicable to certain multinational firms. In a world corporation organization, the entire world is viewed as the firm's area of operation and no single national market draws greater attention than its size merits. Markets, techniques, ideas, personnel, processes, and products are drawn from the entire area of operation. Divisions for each of the national territories operate side by side as equals rather than as part of a hierarchical scheme. See also MULTINATIONAL CORPORATION (MNC) and GLOBAL CORPORATION.

World Trade Organization (WTO)   A globally oriented international organization concerned with establishing and monitoring the rules of trade between nations in the global economy. WTO is the successor to the GENERAL AGREEMENT ON TARIFFS AND TRADE (GATT). WTO agreements, negotiated and signed by the majority of the world's trading nations and ratified in their legislatures, form the basis for the organization's work. Located in Geneva, Switzerland and founded in 1995/1996, the WTO includes 146 countries. It administers trade agreements, handles trade disputes, monitors national trade policies, provides technical assistance and training for developing countries, and fosters cooperation with other international organizations. The WTO also grants PREFERRED TRADING PARTNER (PTP) status, regulates trade, and settles disputes among members (considered the major advantage that WTO offers over GATT). WTO maintains a Web site at www.wto.org.

World Wide Web (WWW)   One of many services that operates on the Internet matrix, and perhaps the best known. It is the hypermedia sector of Internet services, where most e-commerce and Internet marketing occur and electronic mail can be exchanged via Web mail. HYPERTEXT TRANSFER PROTOCOL (HTTP) governs functions on the World Wide Web. Known informally as the *Web*, *WWW*, and *W3*. See also WEB SITE.

worm   A program (or algorithm) that replicates itself over a computer network and usually performs malicious actions, such as using up the computer's resources and possibly shutting the system down. A worm is similar to a virus by its design, and is considered to be a subclass of viruses. Worms spread from computer to computer, but unlike a virus, the worm has the ability to travel without any help from a person, taking advantage of file or information transport features on the user's system. The biggest danger of a worm is its ability to send out hundreds or thousands of copies of itself, create a devastating effect, consuming memory, and causing Web and network servers as well as individual computers to stop responding. While the terms TROJAN HORSE, worm, and VIRUS are often used interchangeably, they are not the same.

worth-debt ratio   Synonym for EQUITY RATIO.

wrap   To enclose an item of merchandise in something wound or folded about it, such as a covering of paper or similar materials (e.g., to wrap a customer's purchase). See also WRAPPING.

wraparound   A decorative banner draped around an in-store merchandise display. See also POINT-OF-PURCHASE (POP) DISPLAY.

wrapper   1. A person whose job it is to WRAP the merchandise in a retail store. See also WRAPPING.   2. A sheet of flexible material (e.g., paper, foil) or lamination used to cover a product for storage, sale, or shipment.

wrapping   1. The covering in which an item of merchandise is enclosed.   2. The enclosing of merchandise in a box, bag, or paper at the customer's request or as a routine function of the store. It may serve either a utilitarian or a decorative function. Wrapping includes gift wrapping, wrapping for the purpose of mailing, and the wrapping of carryout merchandise. The material used is often distinctive and helps to identify the store. Also called *package wrap*.

wrap-up   (Slang) Among salespeople, a customer who buys readily. The sale is closed without much expenditure of effort on the part of the salesperson.

write-up   1. The documentation of the making of a sale (e.g., the preparation of the sales slip).   2. A written review or account (e.g., the fashion show received an excellent write-up in today's newspaper).

writing (an order)   The act of recording and sending an order for merchandise to the vendor, a task usually performed by the BUYER. See also BUYING.

W3   See WORLD WIDE WEB (WWW).

WTO   See WORLD TRADE ORGANIZATION (WTO).

WWW   See WORLD WIDE WEB (WWW).

XYZ

XAML See TRANSACTION AUTHORITY MARKUP LANGUAGE (XAML).

xed-out (Slang) Discontinued, particularly in reference to merchandise.

XL A size designation, such as that appearing on a label, indicating that the item is either extra large or extra long.

XML See EXTENSIBLE MARKUP LANGUAGE (XML).

x-out (Slang) An item or line of discontinued merchandise.

XS A size designation, such as that appearing on a label, indicating that the item is extra small.

XXL A size designation, such as that appearing on a label, indicating that the item is doubly extra large.

Yankee peddler An itinerant merchant popular in the early United States until after the Civil War. The original Yankee peddlers were based in New England and are considered the forerunner of the modern-day TRAVELING SALESPERSON.

yard goods Fabric sold by the yard at retail stores for home sewing. Synonym for PIECE GOODS.

yearly order See BLANKET ORDER.

year-round demand DEMAND for goods or services that spans all seasons.

year-round goods STAPLE goods for which demand spans all seasons.

yellow dog contract An agreement that forces workers to promise, as a condition of employment, not to join or remain in a union.

yellow goods A category in a system of classification based on frequency of replacement. Yellow goods are household items, especially linens, that are generally replaced only after many years of service. These goods are also sometimes called WHITE GOODS simply because of their traditional color. Compare RED GOODS and ORANGE GOODS.

Yellow Pages Originally a print publication (printed on yellow stock) that provided paid classified advertising space for participating businesses. Listings included the addresses and telephone numbers of the businesses, which were alphabetized by name within their category. Arrangement was by type of business, product, or service, and the publisher was frequently the local telephone company. As such, the Yellow Pages served as a classified counterpart to the alphabetically arranged white pages, aiding consumers and other businesses in seeking particular products and services. While the print publications continue to exist (and continue to be provided to consumers by both telephone companies and other publishers), several online, interactively searchable versions currently exist on the INTERNET. See also DISPLAY ADVERTISING, CLASSIFIED ADVERTISING, and YELLOW PAGES ADVERTISING.

Yellow Pages advertising Directional advertising provided in both print and online YELLOW PAGES. Potential customers go to local print directories when they are actively seeking information and are ready to purchase. The same is true online, where the CLICK RATE is almost five times higher than for banner ads.

yes, but technique A sales approach designed to deal with objections made by the prospective customer. The SALESPERSON first sympathizes with the prospect and then attempts to demonstrate how the prospect's point of view is inadequate. Also called the *agree and counterattack technique* and the *agreeing and neutralizing technique*.

young and single The category comprising individuals who have never married and who are living independently at the early stages of their careers. Discretionary income is moderate for this group. They tend to purchase new cars, furniture, small appliances geared to a first apartment, and career clothing, as well as entertainment and electronic goods.

young contemporary customer A category of retail customers with a strong interest in clothing, but who are not really fashion pacesetters. These young people are extremely peer-conscious and, although they may be FASHION-FORWARD, they are not trendsetters. See also ADOPTION PROCESS.

young juniors Synonym for YOUNG TEENS.

young menswear   Synonym for YOUTHS.

young teens   The size range between GIRLS' SIZES and JUNIOR SIZES, including sizes 5/6 to 15/16. Also called *young juniors*.

youth market   The segment of the population aged 14 to 24.

youths   A size range of apparel for teenage boys or young men, usually ranging from 14 to 18 or 20. Also called *young menswear*.

yuppies   (Informal) Young, relatively affluent, upwardly mobile professionals who work in fields such as law and business.

ZBB   See ZERO-BASE BUDGETING.

zebra code   Synonym for UNIVERSAL PRODUCT CODE (UPC).

zero-base budgeting (ZBB)   A method of determining the budget for a store or other business that requires each department or sales area to justify each item on its expense budget. Past history is not considered justification for any expenditure.

zero-level channel   See DIRECT SELLING.

zone delivered pricing   See ZONE PRICING.

zone pricing   A system used by manufacturers in which a market is divided into geographic areas (i.e., zones) and all customers within each area are quoted uniform prices regardless of individual transportation charges. Each customer is charged the base price for the merchandise plus the standard freight rate for that zone. This price is called the *zone price* or the *zoning price*. Also called *zone delivered pricing*.

zoning price   See ZONE PRICING.

zoom box   See BOX.

Bibliography

Abercrombie, Nicholas, Stephen Hill, and Bryan S. Turner. *The Penguin Dictionary of Sociology*. 2nd ed. London: Penguin Books, 1984.

About.com. "Retail Glossary and Dictionary." http://retailindustry.about.com (accessed November 18, 2007).

American Marketing Association. "Dictionary of Marketing Terms." http://www.MarketingPower.com (accessed November 18, 2007).

Ayto, John, and John Simpson, eds. *The Oxford Dictionary of Modern Slang*. Oxford: Oxford University Press, 1992.

Bell, Judith, and Kate Ternus. *Silent Selling: Best Practices and Effective Strategies in Visual Merchandising*. 2nd ed. New York: Fairchild Publications, 2002.

Bohlinger, Maryanne Smith. *Merchandise Buying*. 5th ed. New York: Fairchild Publications, 2001.

Browse Legal Topics. "Browse Legal Definitions." http://www.legal-definitions.com (accessed December 2, 2007).

Calasibetta, Charlotte Mankey, and Phyllis Tortora. *The Fairchild Dictionary of Fashion*. 3rd ed. New York: Fairchild Publications, 2003.

Catalano, Frank, and Bud Smith. *Internet Marketing for Dummies*. Foster City, CA: IDG Books Worldwide, 2001.

Clodfelter, Richard. *Retail Buying: From Basics to Fashion*. 2nd ed. New York: Fairchild Publications, 2003.

Corstjens, Judith, and Marcel Corstjens. *Store Wars: The Battle for Mindspace and Shelfspace*. Chichester, England: John Wiley & Sons, 1995.

Deal, Terrence E., and Allan A. Kennedy. *Corporate Cultures: The Rites and Rituals of Corporate Life*. Reading, MA: Addison-Wesley, 1982.

Diamond, Jay, and Gerald Pintel. *Retail Buying*. 6th ed. Upper Saddle River, NJ: Prentice Hall, 2001.

Donnellan, John. *Merchandise Buying and Management*. 2nd ed. New York: Fairchild Publications, 2002.

"Echo Boomers." *60 Minutes* [TV]. Reported by Steve Kroft. Aired October 3, 2004. 14 minutes. Clip #601470. Available at www.createspace.com/Store.

The Economist. "Economics A–Z: A Glossary of Economics-Related Terms." http://www.economist.com/research (accessed November 18, 2007).

Enzer, Matisse. "Glossary of Internet Terms." http://www.matisse.net/files/glossary.html (accessed December 2, 2007).

Fact Index. "Reference for Business." http://www.fact-index.com (accessed November 18, 2007).

Fiore, Frank. *E-Marketing Strategies*. Indianapolis, IN: Que, 2001.

Free Advice. "Kanban." http://business-law.freadvice.com (accessed December 2, 2007).

The Free Dictionary. http://encyclopedia.thefreedictionary.com (accessed November 18, 2007).

Gillespie, Kate, Jean-Pierre Jeannet, and H. David Hennessey. *Global Marketing: An Interactive Approach*. Boston: Houghton Mifflin, 2004.

Guthrie, Karen M., and Cynthia W. Pierce. *Perry's Department Store*. 2nd ed. New York: Fairchild Publications, 2003.

Harborview Injury Prevention and Research Center. "Consumer Safety." http://depts.washington.edu/hiprc (accessed December 2, 2007).

Highlight Investments Group. "Trading Glossary." http://www.trading-glossary.com (accessed November 18, 2007).

Hussey, Roger. *Oxford Dictionary of Accounting*. New ed. Oxford: Oxford University Press, 1999.

"InvestorWords" (online investment glossary). http://www.investorwords.com (accessed December 2, 2007).

IT Toolbox Wireless Knowledge Base. "Browse by Wireless Topic." http://wireless.ittoolbox.com (accessed December 2, 2007).

Kerlinger, Fred N. *Foundations of Behavioral Research*. 3rd ed. Fort Worth, TX: Holt, Rinehart & Winston, 1986.

Kieso, Donald E., and Jerry J. Weygandt. *Intermediate Accounting*. 9th ed. New York: John Wiley & Sons, 1998.

Kinnard, Shannon. *Marketing with E-mail*. 3rd ed. Gulf Breeze, FL: Maximum Press, 2002.

Kotler, Philip, and Gary Armstrong. *Principles of Marketing*. 9th ed. New York: Prentice Hall, 2001.

Kunz, Grace I. *Merchandising: Theory, Principles, and Practice*. New York: Fairchild Publications, 1998.

Littlejohn, Stephen W. *Theories of Human Communication*. 3rd ed. Belmont, CA: Wadsworth Publishing, 1989.

MarketingProfs. "Marketing Topics"& "Research" (Reports and surveys on the latest practices in marketing). http://www.marketingprofs.com (accessed December 2, 2007).

McHugh, Josh. "Attention Shoppers." *Wired*, July 2004, 151–155.

Monash University Department of Business & Economics. "Marketing Dictionary." http://www.buseco.monash.edu.au/depts/mkt/dictionary/ (accessed November 18, 2007).

Murphy, Patrick E., and William A. Staples. "A Modernized Family Life Cycle." *Journal of Consumer Research* 6 (1979): 12–23.

National Retail Federation: The Voice of Retail Worldwide. "About NRF." http://www.nrf.com (accessed December 2, 2007).

Ostrow, Rona. "Library Culture in the Electronic Age: A Case Study of Organizational Change." Ph.D. diss., Rutgers, the State University of New Jersey, 1998.

Ostrow, Rona, and Sweetman R. Smith. *The Dictionary of Marketing*. New York: Fairchild Publications, 1988.

———. *The Dictionary of Retailing*. New York: Fairchild Publications, 1985.

Oxford University Press. *A Dictionary of Business*. 3rd ed. Oxford: Oxford University Press, 2003.

Partridge, Eric. *A Dictionary of Slang and Unconventional English*. Edited by Paul Beale. London: Routledge, 2002.

PC Magazine. "Encyclopedia: Over 20,000 IT Terms." http://www.pcmag.com/encyclopedia (accessed November 18, 2007).

Pegler, Martin M. *Visual Merchandising and Display*. 4th ed. New York: Fairchild Publications, 2001.

Pettigrew, Andrew M. "On Studying Organizational Cultures." *Administrative Science Quarterly* 24 (1979): 570–581.

Poloian, Lynda Gamans. *Retailing Principles: A Global Outlook*. New York: Fairchild Publications, 2003.

Rabolt, Nancy J., and Judy K. Miler. *Concepts and Cases in Retail and Merchandise Management*. New York: Fairchild Publications, 1997.

Rachman, David J., Michael H. Mescon, Courtland L. Bovée, and John V. Thill. *Business Today*. 6th ed. New York: McGraw Hill, 1990.

Retailwire: The Power of Collective Thinking. http://www.retailwire.com (accessed December 2, 2007).

Rosenberg, Jerry M. *Dictionary of Retailing and Merchandising*. New York: John Wiley & Sons, 1995.

Schein, Edgar H. "What Is Culture?" In *Reframing Organizational Culture*, edited by P. J. Frost, L. F. Moore, M. R. Louis, C. C. Lundberg, & J. Martin, 243–253. Newbury Park, CA: Sage Publications, 1991.

Siegel, Carolyn. *Internet Marketing: Foundations and Applications*. Boston: Houghton Mifflin, 2004.

Spears, Richard. A. *NTC'S Dictionary of American Slang and Colloquial Expressions*. 3rd ed. Lincolnwood, IL: NTC Publishing Group, 2000.

Springwise.com: Your Daily Fix of Entrepreneurial Ideas. http://www.springwise.com (accessed December 2, 2007).

Sternquist, Brenda. *International Retailing*. New York: Fairchild Publications, 1998.

Swanson, Kristen K., and Judith C. Everett. *Promotion in the Merchandising Environment*. New York: Fairchild Publications, 2000.

Tepper, Bette K. *Mathematics for Retail Buying*. 5th ed., rev. New York: Fairchild Publications, 2002.

Trendwatching.com. "Monthly Trend Briefing." http://www.trendwatching.com (accessed November 18, 2007).

Trice, Harrison Miller, and Janice M. Beyer. *The Cultures of Work Organizations*. Englewood Cliffs, NJ: Prentice Hall, 1993.

U.S. Census Bureau. "The American Factfinder." http://www.census.gov (accessed November 18, 2007).

University of Texas at Austin. "Dictionary of Advertising Terminology." http://advertising.utexas.edu/research/terms (accessed November 18, 2007).

Webopedia (Online Dictionary and Search Engine). http://www.webopedia.com (accessed November 18, 2007).

Wikipedia: The Free Encyclopedia. http://www.wikipedia.org (accessed November 18, 2007).

Williams, John C., and John A. Torella. *A Guide to Retail Success*. New York: Fairchild Publications, 1997.

Zeithaml, Valarie, A. A. Parasurman, and Leonard L. Berry. *Delivering Quality Service: Balancing Customer Perceptions and Expectations*. New York: Free Press, 1990.